I0820358

"I have sometimes wondered what my last request will be before I die. My mind always gives the same answer: 'Please, read me the opening line of the Heidelberg Catechism.' In those final minutes I want to hear, 'That I am not my own, but belong—body and soul, in life and in death—to my faithful Savior, Jesus Christ.' The Heidelberg Catechism should be preached from the pulpit, taught in the classroom, and recited at the dinner table. I do not exaggerate when I say it is that important. But what we also need is a master historian and wise theologian to come alongside us. Who better than R. Scott Clark? Do not be fooled. This commentary is no mere regurgitation of the catechism but a historical theology and systematic theology in one! With great care, Clark brings his whole career in Reformed theology to bear on each Lord's Day, so that under each rock we discover a jewel. Best of all, he pushes against the cold winds of modernism and plants the flag of Reformed theology deep in the soil of classical Christian orthodoxy. May Clark's commentary serve as a ready guide for every church and family looking to Christ as their only comfort."

—**MATTHEW BARRETT,** professor of Christian theology, Midwestern Baptist Theological Seminary; editor-in-chief of *Credo Magazine*; author of *Simply Trinity: The Unmanipulated Father, Son, and Spirit*

"R. Scott Clark has reflected longer and more deeply on the Heidelberg Catechism—and Reformed confessionalism in general—than most if not all our contemporary voices on this matter. This classic statement of Reformed faith has so clearly shaped his life and ministry in all his prolific output. What a blessing that the church now has this digest of his decades in mining this wonderful confession. Thoroughly grounded in history, profoundly insightful in theology, and consistently aimed at pastoral payoff, Clark's commentary on the Heidelberg is a generation-defining exploration into one of the Reformation's most enduring explanations of the Christian faith."

—**HARRISON PERKINS,** pastor, Oakland Hills Community Church (OPC); senior research fellow, Craig Center for the Study of the Westminster Standards, Westminster Theological Seminary; author of *Reformed Covenant Theology: A Systematic Introduction*

"On the scaffolding of the Heidelberg Catechism, Clark has constructed in this volume an exposition of the Reformed confession and proclamation of the Christian faith that serves not only its adherents but also other Christians as a lively probing of the biblical message and its significance for today. The text of the Catechism serves as an effective grounding for addressing the potential impact of God's Word in Scripture on twenty-first–century Christians and its use for their witness in the world and their defense of the faith against its critics. Clark's scholarly exploration of the Reformed tradition flows into a narrative that speaks to clergy and laity alike about the proclamation and practice of the faith in our current context. Clark guides readers into biblical answers to the questions posed by the catechism and aids readers in carrying out the homiletical, instructional, pastoral, and evangelistic tasks of the church of today. The book will serve all who wish to travel the path of Reformed confessors in bringing the gospel of Christ to our contemporaries."

—**ROBERT KOLB,** professor of systematic theology emeritus,
Concordia Seminary, Saint Louis, MO

"R. Scott Clark has studied the Heidelberg Catechism for decades and has blessed the church by documenting his labors in this monumental study of one of the Reformed church's greatest testimonies to the gospel. Clark informs each chapter with historical detail, scriptural evidence, and theological richness. Readers will want to use this book throughout the year on each Lord's Day and repeatedly return to it as a reliable reference and resource. We should thank Professor Clark for giving the church this labor of love."

—**J. V. FESKO,** The Harriett Barbour Professor of Systematic
and Historical Theology, Reformed Theological Seminary, Jackson, MI

"Books that discuss the Reformed standards are legion; books that are truly remarkable in doing so are few. One of them is R. Scott Clark's commentary on the Heidelberg Catechism. This is a full banquet with all the courses: robust history and doctrine, rich piety and pastoral care, served with profound insight at every turn. Clark shows us why Christians have treasured, memorized, studied, and preached this catechism for centuries. His is an extraordinary treatment of an unsurpassed summary of Reformation Christianity—not only for the past but for the present and future too. Thoroughly recommended."

—**ZACHARY PURVIS,** professor of church history and theology,
Edinburgh Theological Seminary

"R. Scott Clark's *The Heidelberg Catechism: A Historical, Theological, and Pastoral Commentary* is a massive and masterful exposition of one of the Reformed tradition's most beloved confessional documents. With clarity and depth, Clark unpacks the catechism's historical roots, theological richness, and enduring pastoral relevance. This book is an invaluable resource for pastors, teachers, seminarians, and church members seeking a deeper understanding of the Reformed faith."

—**LIGON DUNCAN,** chancellor and John E. Richards Professor of Systematic
and Historical Theology, Reformed Theological Seminary, Jackson, MI

"R. Scott Clark has written a commentary on the Heidelberg Catechism of extraordinary value. Drawing on his profound knowledge of the work of Zacharias Ursinus, the principal author of the catechism, Clark has set the catechism in its immediate historical and theological context while at the same time showing the relevance of the catechism for both perennial and contemporary theological issues. This thoughtful and learned study will help readers to see with deepened understanding the biblical fidelity, true character, and spiritual vitality of Reformed Christianity."

—**W. ROBERT GODFREY,** professor emeritus of church history,
Westminster Seminary California

THE
Heidelberg Catechism

R. SCOTT CLARK

THE Heidelberg Catechism

A HISTORICAL, THEOLOGICAL & PASTORAL COMMENTARY

The Heidelberg Catechism: A Historical, Theological, and Pastoral Commentary

Lexham Academic, an imprint of Lexham Press
1313 Commercial St., Bellingham, WA 98225
LexhamPress.com

Print ISBN 9781683598206
Digital ISBN 9781683598213
Library of Congress Control Number 2025933256

Lexham Editorial: Todd Hains, Claire Brubaker, Ethan McCarthy, John Barach, Mandi Newell
Cover Design: Joshua Hunt
Typesetting: ProjectLuz.com

25 26 27 28 29 30 31 / IN / 12 11 10 9 8 7 6 5 4 3 2 1

This book is dedicated to the memory of the Rev. Mr. Norman Hoeflinger (1925–1996), a mentor, friend, colleague, and role model, and to the Rev. Dr. Warren Embree, who patiently introduced me to the riches of Reformed theology, piety, and practice.

CONTENTS

III. The Third Part of the Catechism

Acknowledgments

I am grateful to those who have helped to make this volume possible: to the readers who first read and commented on this material in a series of articles, to Harrison Perkins for his invaluable help, to Kwan Chen for his corrections, to the many students in the Reformed Confessions course who read the drafts of the typescript, and to the catechism classes and congregations in Kansas City, Missouri; Oceanside, California; Escondido, California; and elsewhere who have endured lectures or catechism sermons. Above all, however, I am grateful to my wife and partner, Barbara, for her unfailing patience and grace while I absented myself from household duties in order to bring this project to completion.

English Bible translations, unless otherwise indicated, are mine. All quotations from the Hebrew Old Testament are taken from the *Biblia Hebraica Stuttgartensia*. Quotations from the Greek New Testament are taken from NA^{28}.

Abbreviations

ANF	*The Ante-Nicene Fathers: Translations of the Writings of the Fathers Down to A.D. 325*. Edited by Alexander Roberts and James Donaldson. 10 vols. 1885–1887
BAGD	Bauer, Walter, William F. Arndt, F. Wilbur Gingrich, and Frederick W. Danker. *Greek-English Lexicon of the New Testament and Other Early Christian Literature*. 2nd ed. Chicago: University of Chicago Press, 1979
BC	Belgic Confession
CCC	*Catechism of the Catholic Church*
CO	*Ioannis Calvini Opera quae supersunt omnia*. 59 vols. Corpus Reformatorum 29–88. Edited by G. Baum, E. Cunitz, and E. Reuss. Berlin: C. A. Schwetschke, 1863–1900
ESV	English Standard Version
HC	Heidelberg Catechism
LW	*Luther's Works*. 82 vols. planned. St. Louis: Concordia; Philadelphia: Fortress, 1955–1986; 2009–
LXX	Septuagint
NA^{28}	*Novum Testamentum Graece*, Nestle-Aland, 28th ed.
NPNF	*A Select Library of Nicene and Post-Nicene Fathers of the Christian Church*. Edited by Philip Schaff and Henry Wace. 28 vols. in 2 series. 1886–1889. Reprint, Peabody, MA: Hendrickson, 1994
ODCC	*The Oxford Dictionary of the Christian Church*. Edited by Frank L. Cross and Elizabeth A. Livingstone. 3rd ed. rev. Oxford: Oxford University Press, 2005
OED	*Oxford English Dictionary*

PG	Patrologia cursus completus. Series Graeca. 161 vols. Edited by J.-P. Migne. Paris, 1857–1866
PL	Patrologia cursus completus. Series Latina. 221 vols. Edited by J.-P. Migne. Paris: Migne, 1844–1864
ST	Thomas Aquinas, *Summa theologica*
WA	*D. Martin Luthers Werke, Kritische Gesamtausgabe.* 73 vols. Weimar: Hermann Böhlaus Nachfolger, 1883–2009
WCF	Westminster Confession of Faith
WLC	Westminster Larger Catechism
WSC	Westminster Shorter Catechism

A Prayer before Hearing the Word

Heavenly Father, eternal and merciful God: we acknowledge and confess before your divine majesty that we are poor miserable sinners, conceived and born in sin and corruption, prone to all evil, and unfit for any good. By our sinful life, we have continually transgressed your holy commandments, provoked your wrath against us, and incurred your just judgment unto eternal death. But, O Lord, we repent in sorrow that we have thus offended you, we condemn ourselves and our iniquities, and we implore you mercifully to help us in our wretchedness and sorrow. Have mercy on us, therefore, O most gracious God and Father, and pardon all our sins, only for the sake of the righteousness of your dear Son, Jesus Christ our Lord.

And grant to us hereafter the grace of your Holy Spirit, that he may teach us heartily to know our unrighteousness and make us to so abhor ourselves that sin may be slain in us, and that we may arise in the newness of life and in this way produce the fruits of holiness and righteousness with which, for Christ's sake alone, you are well pleased.

Grant also that we may rightly understand your holy word, that we may learn to withdraw our confidence entirely from all creatures and to put all our trust in you only. May our old man, with all his sins, be daily crucified more and more that we may present ourselves as living sacrifices to the honor of your holy name, the edification of your church, through Jesus Christ, our only Savior, who taught us to pray: Our Father in heaven, hallowed be your name, your kingdom come, your will be done on earth as in heaven. Give us today our daily bread. Forgive us our debts, as we forgive our debtors. Lead us not into temptation, but deliver us from the evil one. Amen.[1]

1. This prayer is modified from the Palatinate Liturgy of 1563 and 1585 as published in Baird, *Presbyterian Liturgies*, 226–27.

Introduction: What Is a Catechism?

A catechism is a book of question and answers. It comes from the Greek noun *catechesis* (κατήχησις), which originally meant "oral instruction."[1] Our English noun *catechism* also comes from Greek (κατηχισμός) via Latin (*catechismus*). The earliest Christian fathers developed the *rule of faith* (*regula fidei*), which is found in the writings of Ignatius, Irenaeus, and Tertullian in the second and third centuries, and which grew into the Apostles' Creed.[2] That formed and informed early Christian instruction, including the *Didache*, a very early (ca. AD 50–110) summary of Christian moral instruction and church order, which in the fourth century Athanasius recommended as a source of catechesis.[3] Augustine uses the noun *catechismos* in his treatise on *Faith and Works* and wrote an entire work on this topic, *Catechizing the Uninstructed*.[4] So a catechism is a way of teaching. It

1. "The term 'Catechesis' in its widest sense includes instruction by word of mouth on any subject sacred or profane, but is especially applied to Christian teaching, whether of an elementary kind appropriate to new converts, or, as in the famous Catechetical School of Alexandria, extending to the higher interpretation of Holy Scripture, and the exposition of Christian philosophy" (Gifford, "Catechetical Lectures of S. Cyril," xi).

2. See the discussion under *HC* 23.

3. "The earliest known example of a Catechetical work is the 'Teaching of the Twelve Apostles,' which Athanasius names among the 'books not included in the Canon, but appointed by the Fathers to be read by those who are just recently coming to us, and wish to be instructed in the word of godliness (κατηχεῖσθαι τὸν τῆς εὐσεβείας λόγον)'" (Gifford, "Catechetical Lectures of S. Cyril," xii). He cites Athanasius's *Thirty-Ninth Festal Letter*.

4. "His brevitier commemoratis evangelista—non enim totos catechismos inserere debuit—satis significavit pertinere ad eum, a quo baptizandus catechizatur, docere et monere de moribus" (Augustine, *De fide et operibus* 13.19, p. 59). For an English translation, see Augustine, *On Faith and Works*, 27. Lombardo adds, "Tertullian was the first Latin writer to use *catechizare* in the meaning of 'to instruct orally' in the Christian faith. Cf. *De cor. mil.* 9. *Quem Petrus catechizat*. The word *catechismus* (instruction) is first found in Augustine, *On Faith and Works*. See also Augustine, *Catechizing the Uninstructed*.

is an ancient mode of teaching, and those in the Reformation traditions used it to teach the Christian faith to God's people to great effect in the sixteenth and seventeenth centuries.

The primary function of a catechism is to help God's people understand his word by explaining the Christian faith. Traditionally, Christian catechesis has been organized around three texts: the Apostles' Creed, the Ten Commandments, and the Lord's Prayer.[5] The Heidelberg Catechism follows this classic pattern. The Heidelberg Catechism (1563) was intended to explain the Scriptures and the ecumenical Christian faith as understood in the Reformed churches to those who were unsure of what the Reformed churches believed and how the Reformed faith related to what they had learned before, namely, Roman Catholicism and Lutheranism.

THE VALUE OF THE HEIDELBERG CATECHISM

Like the Palatinate Christians in the sixteenth century, we live in a religiously confused time.[6] Like them, we are no longer sure what we believe and why. That much is evident from the bewildering array of evangelical options available. Not only were they confused, but they faced the same temptations we do, to confuse the law ("do this and live") with the gospel ("Christ has done for sinners"). They were tempted to present themselves to God partly on the basis of grace and cooperation with grace. Like us, they struggled with assurance ("Have I done enough? Does God really approve of me?"). Like us, they wondered how they ought to live in light of what Christ has done and what God has revealed in his word.

If relevance is defined by truth, our need, and felicity of expression, then the catechism is more relevant now than ever. It has been a long time since Christians were so confused about theology, piety, and practice. In our time, Reformed churches have probably drifted further from their moorings than at any time since the sixteenth century. Many congregants know a great many things, but experience suggests that too many

5. "In the Middle Ages prescriptions for catechizing the faithful were frequently issued, e.g. at the Council of Lambeth (1281), and books were produced containing explanations of the Pater Noster and the Creed, lists of mortal sins, etc., arranged preferably in groups of seven" (*ODCC*, s.v. "catechism").

6. The Palatinate is a historical region in Germany. It was one of seven electoral districts in the Holy Roman Empire.

of us cannot articulate the rudiments of the doctrine of the Trinity, or the doctrine of justification, or the nature of the Lord's Supper, and yet these are doctrines and matters of piety and practice that Scripture and the church deem essential to the Christian faith and life. The enduring contribution of the Heidelberg Catechism to the Reformed churches and to the broader Christian church is to harvest from and synthesize into one catechism some of the finest Reformation-era catechesis into one document and to preserve, in a memorable way, the achievement of the Reformation.

The Heidelberg Catechism is perhaps all the more valuable because of the circumstances in which it was written and the way it was written. We might say that the catechism's sponsor (Frederick III), its primary author (Zacharias Ursinus), and its revision committee (Caspar Olevianus, Thomas Erastus, and others), as well as the place where they wrote and revised it, were in a sort of vise grip. The Palatinate was the only Reformed electorate (district) in the Holy Roman Empire. They were surrounded by Lutherans and Roman Catholics. The prince, the pastors, and theologians were under immense pressure and suspicion, even the possibility of invasion. Further, from 1556–1563, the official religion of the Palatinate changed three times. When Prince Frederick II died in 1556, the Palatinate was nominally Roman Catholic and officially subject to the papacy. Under his successor, Otto Henry (1502–1559), the Palatinate became officially Lutheran. Upon his death, in 1559, the Palatinate became Reformed under Frederick III. The people were understandably confused. Thus Ursinus and his colleagues had to compose a document that would communicate clearly and pastorally where they agreed with what the people had been taught before Frederick's accession and where they were changing the theology, piety, and practice of the electorate. They had to choose their words carefully, lest they create more confusion and even provoke an invasion, and the thing they wanted to communicate most of all was the gospel of free acceptance with God, by divine favor alone, through faith alone, in Christ alone, and the new life that flows from that free justification, in union and communion with Christ. So the catechism was developed carefully, prayerfully, and collaboratively. They presented the catechism to the watching world as the confession of the Palatinate church.

In a world in which Christians are bombarded with competing messages about what the Christian faith is, the Heidelberg Catechism is much needed. It is theologically sound, well-written, well grounded in Scripture, pastoral, and accessible in its tone and language. It begins and ends with the comfort of the Christian life. It articulates the biblical and Reformation gospel as clearly as any ecclesiastical document in the Reformation period, and there is a surprising depth of teaching on the sacraments and the Christian life.

It used to be the practice of the Reformation churches to require young people not only to memorize Scripture but also to memorize the Heidelberg Catechism. As late as a couple of generations back, there were believers who memorized the catechism in both German and English. More than one Reformed pastor has sat at the beside of older saints who were preparing to see their Savior and heard them recite the first question and answer of the catechism:

> What is your only comfort in life and in death?
>
> That I, with body and soul, both in life and in death, am not my own, but belong to my faithful Savior Jesus Christ, who with his precious blood has fully satisfied for all my sins, and redeemed me from all the power of the devil; and so preserves me, that without the will of my Father in heaven not a hair can fall from my head; indeed, that all things must work together for my salvation. Wherefore, by his Holy Spirit, he also assures me of eternal life, and makes me heartily willing and ready from now on to live for Him.

This is a profound expression of the firm foundation that sustains Christians in every season of life.

THE PRINCIPALS BEHIND THE CATECHISM

Considering its principals, the Heidelberg Catechism was an unlikely document. In the years before moving to Heidelberg, the primary seat of government in the Palatinate, Zacharias Ursinus (1534–1583) was a student under Philip Melanchthon (1497–1560), Martin Luther's most important student and his successor in Wittenberg. Melanchthon was also the author (and reviser) of the Augsburg Confession (1530 and 1540). After his death,

Ursinus resolved some long-standing theological questions, associated with the Reformed, and was invited by Frederick III to join the faculty in the university.[7]

In the year before arriving in Heidelberg, the other contributor to the catechism, Caspar Olevianus (1536–1587), was in his hometown, Trier, preaching the Reformation message, which had landed him jail before the Elector, Frederick III, returned to town to discover it in an uproar caused by evangelical preaching. The Elector bailed him out of jail and brought the young theologian to Heidelberg to help advance the Reformation there.[8]

Frederick III (1515–1576), prince of the house of Simmern, commissioned the Heidelberg Catechism. Under the principle of the Peace of Augsburg (1555), *cuius regio, eius religio* ("whose the region, his the religion"), he set about to bring religious clarity to the Palatinate.[9] In 1562, when he commissioned the Palatinate catechism, the confession of the gospel by the magisterial Protestant churches was clear enough, but the picture on the ground was not so clear.[10] Further, as mentioned above, the Palatinate church had been through much religious and political tumult. In 1543 the Palatinate was nominally Roman Catholic but with a substantial Lutheran presence by permission of the Elector.[11] By 1556, it was Lutheran, and seven years after that, it became confessionally Reformed. The Palatinate churches needed a clear, unambiguous articulation of what Scripture teaches concerning the most important questions of the

7. For more on Ursinus, see Visser, *Zacharias Ursinus the Reluctant Reformer*; Good, *Heidelberg Catechism in Its Newest Light*, 242–54; Smedley, "Covenant Theology of Zacharias Ursinus"; Bierma, "Ursinus and the Theological Landscape."

8. For more on Olevianus's life, see Clark, *Caspar Olevian*, 9–38. Mühling ("Caspar Olevian Und Die Einführung," 25) notes that Count Valentin von Erbach (1517–1563) served as intermediary in bringing Olevianus to the Palatinate.

9. According to Klooster ("Heidelberg Catechism," 22), Ludwig V (1578–1544) tolerated Reformation preaching in the Upper Palatinate but not in Heidelberg.

10. The expression "magisterial" refers to the Lutheran and Reformed churches which were imposed by and cooperated with the civil magistrate, as distinct from the various radical groups, e.g., the Anabaptists.

11. Under Frederick II, Protestant preaching spread in the Palatinate. Martin Bucer had been Frederick's chaplain in 1521, and Frederick consulted with Melanchthon in 1545 and asked him to visit the Palatinate. That year, during the Christmas Mass, the congregation of Holy Spirit Church broke out into a Protestant hymn. Seeing the popular support for the Reformation, Frederick threw his support to Protestants. Between 1545 and 1555, he reformed the Augustinian monastery into the Collegium Sapientiae and instituted a new order of worship. By 1556 he was providing asylum to evangelicals (Klooster, "Heidelberg Catechism," 46, 58, 52).

Christian faith and life. Nothing is more important than the question of how we are right with God, and nothing is clearer in the catechism than the confession of the good news of free acceptance by God in Christ.

Frederick von Simmern might seem an unlikely candidate to advance the Reformed Reformation in the Palatinate.[12] Frederick was born into an impoverished branch of one of the historic houses of Germany, the Wittelsbach, and his was Count Palatine John II of the Palatinate-Simmern (1492–1557). Frederick was well educated at home and abroad. He lived for a time with Charles V and fought with the emperor's army against the Ottoman Empire. He was raised Roman Catholic but married a devout Lutheran woman and through her influence became an evangelical, which led to alienation from his family and further poverty. His Protestant convictions were tested and developed in the period between their marriage and his accession to the electorate in 1559. Charles's attempt to crush the Protestant (Schmalkadic) princes in 1546 and the armed Diet of Augsburg and the interim following (1548) suggested to Frederick that his Protestant convictions would not make life easier. His conscience would not allow him to submit to the Augsburg Interim (which Calvin had called the "Adultero-Interim" because of its compromises with Roman Catholicism), and so he returned to Simmern for eight uncomfortable years.[13]

When the electoral seat fell to him, his own family was religiously divided: some devoutly (*gnesio,* or "genuine") Lutheran and some confessionally Reformed. His eldest son and heir died in a boating accident in France, which is how Frederick became aware of Olevianus. The latter was present for the accident and failed in his attempt to save the young prince. The next son, Ludwig VI (1539–1583), was raised Lutheran and, upon succeeding his father in 1576, ejected most of the Reformed pastors and theologians from the Palatinate and instituted confessional Lutheranism, only to be succeeded by his son Frederick IV (1574–1610), who reinstituted Reformed theology, piety, and practice under the influence of Johann Casmir (1543–1592), Frederick III's younger son.

For his part Frederick III professed not to be a "Calvinist" (an expression created by Lutheran critics of the Reformed) and never to have read

12. For more on the life of Frederick III, see Chadwick, "Making of a Reforming Prince," 44–69.

13. Calvin, *Adultero-German Interim,* 190–238.

Calvin.[14] Whether this claim was true is open to debate, but it illustrates his tense relations with the other electorates in the empire. Nevertheless, almost from the moment he became Elector Palatinate in 1559, he came under scrutiny by the other electors because of his religion. For his entire reign Heidelberg was under threat of potential invasion by Lutheran and Roman Catholic electors because the Reformed confession had no official status under the Peace of Augsburg. The tensions created by the *Pax Augustana* were not relieved until 1648, and then only after the brutal and destructive Thirty Years' War. German-Reformed historian J. I. Good argued a century ago that Frederick's theological turning point occurred in 1561 but that his theological development continued through 1566 as he became more conscious of his growing Reformed convictions.[15]

Frederick III had good reason to be concerned about the state of the Reformed confession in Europe. Three years after the abdication of Charles V in 1559, Ferdinand I (1503–1564) became Holy Roman Emperor until his death eight years later. Philip II (1527–1598) acceded to the throne in Spain and began a violent suppression of the Reformed there, resulting in the martyrdom of thousands of Reformed Christians. The reign of "Bloody Mary" Tudor in England drove English Reformed Christians to Geneva, Frankfurt, and Heidelberg. The outbreak of the French Wars of Religion (1562–1563), which continued intermittently and ended with the St. Bartholomew's Day Massacre (1572), in which perhaps thirty thousand Huguenots[16] were martyred, combined to justify his sense that the Reformed were a persecuted people. It also pressed on him the need to articulate the Reformed confession in a way that would demonstrate the common ground that existed between the Reformed and the Lutherans, as well as the basis for the Reformed dissent from the Lutheran theology on Christology, the sacraments, and worship.

Frederick inherited a religiously confused electorate.[17] Otto Heinrich (1502–1559), influenced by Philipp Melanchthon (1497–1560), had collected representatives from a variety of Protestant traditions: confessional

14. Clark, *Caspar Olevian*, 22.

15. Good, *Heidelberg Catechism in Its Newest Light*, 159–60.

16. *Huguenot* refers principally to French Reformed Christians in the sixteenth and seventeenth centuries.

17. He spoke of it in a letter of March 1563. See Thelemann, *Aid to the Heidelberg Catechism*, n454.

Lutheran (e.g., Tilemann Heshusius [1527–1588]), Calvinist (e.g., Pierre Boquin [1518–1582]), and Zwinglian (e.g., Wilhelm Klebitz [ca. 1533–1568]). There was theological tension and confusion within the university and the church when Frederick arrived. These tensions forced him to study and come to his own conclusions. As he did, he called confessionally Reformed theologians to the university as well as to the church and commissioned the catechism in 1562.[18]

SOURCES AND AUTHORSHIP

According to Lyle D. Bierma, "parts or all of some 90 of the *HC*'s 129 questions and answers can be traced to the text of" Ursinus's Shorter Catechism (*Catechismus Minor*), written in preparation for drafting the Heidelberg Catechism. He notes that there are "linguistic parallels" to the Larger Catechism (*Summa theologiae*) also.[19] Dutch scholar Maurits Gooszen (1890) and German scholar August Lang (1907) pioneered the source criticism of the *HC*.[20] Good summarizes their work by noting "four main sources" of the *HC*: (1) the Strasbourg catechisms by Wolfgang Capito, Martin Bucer, and Matthäus Zell; (2) the Zürich catechisms of Leo Jud and Heinrich Bullinger; (3) Calvin's catechisms (1537, 1541; the 1559 *Institutes* is also a likely influence); and (4) Johannes à Lasko's (Jan Łaski) Emden catechisms and Marten Micronius's catechetical works.[21] Bierma notes that more recent scholarship sees some dependence on Theodore Beza's *Confession of Faith*, Johannes Brenz's catechism, Melanchthon, and Luther's Small and Large Catechisms.[22]

18. Klooster, "Heidelberg Catechism," 9, 32.

19. Bierma et al., *Introduction*, 75, 138–40. Both catechisms are translated into English and published on pages 141–223.

20. Gooszen, *De Heidelbergsche Catechismus*; Lang, *Der Heidelberger Katechismus*.

21. Good, *Heidelberg Catechism*, 42. See Capito, *Kinder Bericht Und Fragstuck*; Bucer, *Catechismus ecclesiae et scholae argentoratensis*; Zell, *Frag Vnnd Antwort*. Jud, *Catechismus*; Bullinger, *Catechesis de praecipuis capitibus religionis christianae*; à Lasko, *De Catechismus*; Faulenbach and Becker, *Reformierte Bekenntnisschriften* 1, 3; Micron, *Ein Kort Unterricht Voor*; Micron, *Short and Faythful Instruction*; Micron, *Der Kleyne Catechismus*. On the influence of the *Institutes*, see, e.g., Klooster, *Our Only Comfort*, 220–21.

22. Bierma et al., *Introduction, 75–76. See* Beza, *Confession de la Foi Chrestienne*; Beza, *Confessio christianae fidei*; Beza, *Christian Faith*. For a brief survey (based on Lang and Gooszen) of several of these documents, see Warfield, *Works of Benjamin Warfield*, 6:389–91.

Frederick III deliberately and successfully obscured the exact authorship of the catechism. From 1644, with the publication of Hendrik Alting's *History of the Palatinate Church*, until 1961 and the publication of the work of Walter Hollweg on this question, the catechism was thought to be the work of Olevianus and Ursinus.[23] Holweg raised serious questions about the traditional story of the joint authorship of the catechism. There is, however, no unambiguous evidence that Olevianus produced any document preparatory to the *HC*. Nevertheless, Bierma criticizes some of Hollweg's methods and conclusions and argues that there remain reasons to think that Olevianus played "more than a minor role" in the production of the catechism.[24] We should regard Ursinus as the most likely major author and the authorized commentator, but given the strong, intentional parallels between Olevianus's 1567 catechism, *Vester Grund* (*Firm Foundation*), and his comments to Bullinger, it seems prudent to read that work as a sort of explanation of Lord's Days 5–24 of the *HC*. We should also bear in mind, however, that the catechism was presented to a committee including superintendents, theology faculty from the university, the "chief ministers" in the churches, and the Elector's personal theologian, Thomas Erastus (1524–1583).[25] The committee seems to have participated in the preparation of the catechism and in its production.[26]

STRUCTURE

The 129 questions and answers of the catechism are organized in three parts:

---

23. Alting, *Historia Ecclesiae Palatinae*. See Bierma's discussion in Olevian, *Firm Foundation*, xv–xvi; Holweg, *Neue Untersuchungen Zur Geschichte*, 124–52; Klooster, "Primacy of Ursinus," 51–72; Bierma et al., *Introduction*, 61.

24. Bierma et al., *Introduction*, 67. In "Ursinus and the Theological Landscape," 9–10, Bierma seems to agree substantially with Hollweg's conclusions.

25. Gunnoe (*Thomas Erastus*, 128) writes, "On balance, the evidence for ascribing a leading role to Erastus in the composition of the catechism, or at a bare minimum, the portion of the catechism dealing with the Lord's Supper, is quite strong." The evidence he adduces for this claim, however, is unpersuasive.

26. Bierma et al., *Introduction*, 53–57. Mühling ("Caspar Olevian Und Die Einführung," 26), ascribes to Olevianus a major role in its promulgation. Bierma ("Ursinus and the Theological Landscape," 11) describes Ursinus as the catechism's "leading homiletician, commentator, and apologist." He observes that Ursinus not only gave the lectures on the catechism but produced three treatises defending it.

- law (2–11)
- gospel (12–85)
- sanctification (86–129)

Ursinus explains, "Hence, the catechism in its primary and most general sense, may be divided as the doctrine of the church, into the law and gospel."[27] He continues by explaining that the catechism "consists of three parts. The first treats of the misery of man, the second of his deliverance from this misery, and the third of gratitude."[28]

The first question sets the tone for the rest of the catechism by centering the Christian's hope and confidence outside the Christian's self, in Christ and in his work for us. The rest of the catechism should be familiar to anyone who knows the basics of Protestant theology. It is a Reformed catechism. It takes distinctly Reformed views on Christology, the sacraments, and worship, but those from outside the Reformed tradition will find much with which to resonate. There is a clear distinction between law and gospel, spiritual union and communion with Christ through faith, the third use of the law (*tertius usus legis*) as the norm of the Christian life, and an affirmation of the unique authority of Holy Scripture. On the Supper, the reader will find that the catechism clearly wants us to understand that the believer is eating nothing less than the true body and blood of Christ. How this happens is left to the mysterious operation of the Spirit, but that it happens is not to be questioned.

Repeatedly, the framers of the catechism sought to articulate the gospel unambiguously. The bad news is that, in Adam, all have sinned and have died. The good news is that Christ rendered perfect obedience to the law for us, and that righteousness and merit is imputed to all who believe so that it is as if they had done all that Christ did for them.[29] Olevianus writes, "The obedience of the death of Christ is the thing itself that is imputed to us as righteousness. For it satisfies for our sins, and there is nothing lacking in this obedience. As Christ said, 'It is finished' [John 19:30], and

27. Ursinus, *Commentary*, 13.

28. Ursinus, *Commentary*, 14.

29. *HC* 21, 60; *Canons of Dort* 2, 8–9, in United Reformed Churches in North America, *Liturgical Forms and Prayers*, 268.

the apostle in Romans 5[:19] contrasts the obedience of Christ with our disobedience."[30]

According to the catechism, our righteousness is *extra nos* ("outside us"), but, following Calvin, Christ cannot remain outside us if we are to benefit from his work.[31] The Spirit raises us to life, works faith (knowledge, assent, and trust) in us, and through it unites us to Christ; it is in this union that we live the Christian life, dying to sin and being renewed inwardly by the Spirit.[32] The catechism is realistic about the nature of the Christian life on this side of glory. In its focus on the gospel, Christ, and a word-and-sacrament piety, it breathes Luther's *theologia crucis* ("theology of the cross").

It is the great need of the confessional Reformed community to recover the Reformed confession.[33] The verb "to recover" signals that something has been lost and needs to be sought and found. That something has been lost seems fairly evident. We have lost important elements of Reformed theology (e.g., the Creator/creature distinction), piety (e.g., the preaching of the gospel and sacraments as the objective means of grace), and practice (e.g., the regulative principle of worship). The two chief reasons for these losses are the quest for illegitimate religious certainty and the quest for illegitimate religious experience. The alternative to these quests is confessional Reformed theology, piety, and practice.[34]

TEXTUAL HISTORY

The first draft of the catechism was complete by 1562. It was revised by a synod in Heidelberg in January 1563 and published on January 19, 1563.[35] There the ministers subscribed it, that is, they wrote their names underneath it as a sign of their affirmation of its doctrine. The first edition had

30. Olevianus, *Exposition*, 103.

31. Calvin, *Institutes* 3.1.1. Unless otherwise indicated, references to the *Institutes* refer to the 1559 Battles edition.

32. *HC* 76, 88–90.

33. By "confessional Reformed community" I mean (1) the sideline Reformed and Presbyterian denominations and federations in the North American Presbyterian and Reformed Council, and (2) the borderline denominations, that is, those moving either toward the confessions or moving away from them. On these categories, see Clark, *Recovering the Reformed Confession*, 1–2.

34. Clark, *Recovering the Reformed Confession*, 39–69, 71–116.

35. Bierma et al., *Introduction*, 104.

some peculiarities. The questions and answers were not numbered. They were numbered in a subsequent edition.[36] The second edition added the first draft of *HC* 80 in response to the Council of Trent (which adopted canons and decrees on the Mass in 1562).[37] In the third edition, *HC* 80 was expanded.[38] That edition was translated into Latin in March 1563, which became the version used in schools and by churches and schools across Europe and the British Isles.[39] It was a Latin translation that was adopted by the Synod of Dort (1619). In the fourth edition, the division into fifty-two Lord's Days was introduced. This edition was incorporated into the church order (*Kirchenornung*) and the liturgy of the churches in the Palatinate.[40] The catechism has been translated into English, Greek, Hebrew, Japanese, Korean, Spanish, and many other languages, and millions of Christians have used it to confess the faith since its publication.

By order of the Elector, scriptural prooftexts were added in the third edition in March 1563.[41] Over the centuries, different denominations have appealed to different prooftexts, so I have omitted them on the theory that, in many instances, the catechism is quoting or paraphrasing Scripture and thus its relationship to Scripture is evident. Further, in the nature of a catechism or confession, the churches are summarizing doctrine drawn and synthesized from a range of passages so that supplying prooftexts is in that way invidious. Because the list cannot be comprehensive, any list is artificial and even potentially misleading.

THE HEART OF THE CATECHISM

When we think of the Reformation, we think of the recovery of the good news of free acceptance by God for Christ's sake alone. That perception

36. The first edition was lost from about the turn of the eighteenth century until 1760, when a copy was discovered by a Dutch historian. It was obscure until another copy was discovered by Albrecht Wolters (1822–1878) and published in 1864. See Lang, *Der Heidelberger Katechismus*; Klooster, "Heidelberg Catechism," 181–85.

37. Bierma et al., *Introduction*, 104. See the discussion under *HC* 80.

38. Bierma et al., *Introduction*, 105.

39. Klooster, "Heidelberg Catechism," 187.

40. Klooster, "Heidelberg Catechism," 188–92.

41. Klooster, "Heidelberg Catechism," 186–87; Mühling, "Caspar Olevian Und Die Einführung," 28.

of the Reformation is certainly correct. What is less well known is that almost as soon as the gospel was recovered, it was attacked:

- In the 1520s the Anabaptists rejected the Protestant gospel on the ground that it would lead to careless living.
- In 1547, Rome decreed that anyone who confessed justification by grace alone, through faith alone, was eternally condemned.
- In 1549, nominally Lutheran theologian Andreas Osiander (1498–1552) was teaching that we are accepted by God on the basis of the indwelling Christ within us.
- In the early 1550s a Lutheran theologian, Georg Major (1502–1574), was teaching that good works were necessary for salvation.[42]
- In 1563, the year of publication of the catechism, leading Lutheran theologian Johann George Karg (1512–1576) was denying that all of Jesus's obedience (active and passive) was for us and is imputed to us on the ground that Jesus had to qualify himself to become a Savior. This denial of the imputation of the active obedience of Christ opened the way for some to later say that Christ makes it possible for us to be saved, but we must do our part.[43]

Thus the Heidelberg Catechism was produced in a controversial and turbulent context. The Reformation achievements, the recovery of the doctrine of justification by God's free acceptance alone (*sola gratia*), through trust, resting, receiving alone (*sola fide*), and the principle of Scripture as the sole magisterial authority (*sola Scriptura*) were all under attack at the very moment the Reformed Church was being established in the Palatinate. The catechism was written to preserve the gospel of justification and salvation by grace alone (*sola gratia*), through faith alone (*sola*

42. Hodge, *Systematic Theology*, 3:239–40.

43. Clark, "Do This and Live," 230–37; Turretin, *Institutes of Elenctic Theology*, 14.13.2.

fide), on basis of the imputation of the finished work of Christ alone in a time when that gospel was being questioned.

HOMILETICAL USE

Reformed churches have a long history of preaching a catechism sermon of some kind in the second service.[44] There are essentially three ways to preach a catechism sermon:

1. Topically: Using the catechism as a guide, the sermon has three points drawn from Scripture. This might be done under each Lord's Day, so that each question-and-answer forms a point, or from a particular question-and-answer.

2. From a single Scripture text, which calls attention to one or more topics raised by a catechism question or Lord's Day.[45]

3. From the catechism itself.

One can find examples of each of these in the Reformed tradition. The intent behind catechetical sermons is that the minister should explain to the congregation, from Scripture, what the church confesses God's word to teach. The primary framers of the catechism were themselves preachers, and the catechism question presents an attractive and useful place to begin the sermon. Because the answers are typically clearly organized in distinct points, the inherent structure of the catechism and of its questions and answers facilitate clear, simple sermon outlines.

CATECHETICAL USE

The most obvious purpose of the catechism is to instruct covenant children and new members, and to function in the Christian education program of the church and in Christian schools (from grammar school through seminary).

---

44. For more on the history of the second service, see Clark, *Recovering the Reformed Confession*, 293–342. Barrs ("Theory and Practice," 233) says that catechism preaching was practiced in "almost every centre of the Reformation."

45. For an example of this approach, see Ames, *Sketch of the Christian's Catechism.*

In his explanation of the necessity and use of catechesis, Ursinus appeals to Deuteronomy 11:19 ("you shall teach them to your sons").[46] Deuteronomy 29:29 says, "The revealed things belong to us and to our sons forever." This is what it means to bring up covenant children in the "nurture and admonition of the Lord" (Eph 6:4). The faith taught in Scripture is intended to be transmitted to covenant households. Reformation churches catechized their children, and the Heidelberg Catechism was intended to be memorized by children. Each phrase is carefully constructed. Each clause and every answer has an intentional rhythm. The catechism repeats essential vocabulary and phrases throughout so that when they occur later, it is no longer new material to be mastered but familiar material to be inserted into a new context.

Tragically, under the influence of some unhappy and unfruitful theories of education that have come to dominate modern education, the practice of memorization has waned and even become unfamiliar. Parents, pastors, and elders have come to assume that it can no longer be done or that we have outgrown memorization as a remnant of a forgotten past. Such assumptions are entirely and demonstrably untrue. Children are just as apt to memorize today as they were in 1563. It is the adults who have failed them by refusing to capitalize on the nature pattern of learning, or in some cases by asking them to learn more verbose translations of the catechism, which effectively ruined the economy so useful for memorization.

Dorothy Sayers (1893–1957) wonderfully summarizes this pattern of learning in her popular 1947 lecture, "The Lost Tools of Learning."[47] She identifies three stages of child development: parrot, pert, and poet. Briefly, in the parrot stage (beginning about age four or five) children delight to memorize without demanding to understand what they are learning. In these years, children ought to memorize Scripture and the catechism. Parents, elders, and pastors do well to spend these years wisely helping children learn *what*, according to the Reformed churches, the Scriptures teach. When the "pert" years begin, in early adolescence, children begin to analyze what they have memorized. In this period, parents, pastors, and elders must be prepared to explain well to children *why* the Reformed

46. Ursinus, *Commentary*, 14.

47. Sayers, "Lost Tools of Learning," 107–36.

churches confess what they do. This is the ideal time to defend the faith to children. Finally, as they mature, young people reach the "poet" stage, in which they want to know *how* to speak about what they believe and why.[48]

A WORD ABOUT TRANSLATION

The first English translation of the catechism appeared in London in 1572 under the title *The catechism, or manner to teach children and others the Christian faith: Used in all the landes and dominions that under the mighty Prince Fredericke, the Palsgrave of the Rhene.*[49] The English translation of the catechism used in this work is modified from the Tercentenary translation published by the Reformed Church in the United States in 1863.[50] That translation follows the third German edition (1863) closely, capturing the meter, phrasing, repetition, economy, and vocabulary. The principal changes made in this work were the removal of archaic pronouns. This work also looks to the Latin translation of the catechism for guidance since the Latin text had official status in the Palatinate schools and in the Reformed churches, as it was adopted by the Synod of Dort (1619).[51] That Ursinus lectured on the Latin text, and that it was used not only in the schools in the Palatinate but by Reformed churches outside Germany and adopted by the churches at Dort, makes the Latin translation something of a contemporaneous commentary on the catechism.

48. For more on this approach to Christian education, see Clark, "Classical Christian Catechesis," 107–19.

49. Bierma et al., *Introduction*, 116.

50. Schaff, *Creeds of Christendom*, 3:307–55. The German text in Roman typeface is in Müller, *Die Bekenntnisschriften*, 682–719.

51. Niemeyer, *Collectio Confessionum*, 428–61.

I

The First Part of the Catechism

QUESTION 1

What is your only comfort in life and in death?

QUESTION 2

How many things are necessary for you to know, that in this comfort you may live and die blessedly?

Lord's Day 1

QUESTION 1

What is your only comfort in life and in death?

That I, with body and soul, both in life and in death, am not my own, but belong to my faithful Savior Jesus Christ, who with his precious blood has fully satisfied for all my sins, and redeemed me from all the power of the devil; and so preserves me, that without the will of my Father in heaven not a hair can fall from my head; indeed, that all things must work together for my salvation. Wherefore, by his Holy Spirit, he also assures me of eternal life, and makes me heartily willing and ready from now on to live for Him.[1]

Our alphabet begins with *A*, but the alphabet of the catechism begins with *C* for comfort (*Trost*)—though not quite in the way we are used to using the word.[2] It does not signify *comfort* as in "comfort food," something that makes one feel better temporarily but that may not be of any real help. The Latin translation of the catechism asks, "What is your only *consolation* in life and in death?" That helps us get a little closer to what the catechism means by "comfort," which refers to the bedrock truth that one knows with heart and mind to be true, that will sustain one when everything else one knows in this life becomes unreliable. Friendships fail. Marriages collapse. Jobs end. The gospel promise, that by grace alone (*sola gratia*), through faith alone (*sola fide*), the believer is Christ's and that Christ is the believer's, is immutable. This is a certainty, a hope, a confidence in which the Christian can and must rest.

1. "Was ist bein einiger Trost im Leben und in Sterben? Dass ich mit Leib und Seele, beides im Leben und im Sterben, nicht mein, sondern meines getreuen Heilandes Jesu Christi eigen bin, der mit seinem theuren Blute für alle meine Sünden vollkommen bezahlet, und mich aus aller Gewalt des Teufels erlöset hat; und also bewahret, dass ohne den Willen meines Vaters im Himmel kein Haar von meinem Haupte kann fallen, ja auch mir alles zu meiner Seligkeit dienen muss. Darum er mich auch durch seinen heiligen Geist des ewigen Lebens versichert, und ihm forthin zu leben von Herzen willig und bereit macht" (Schaff, *Creeds of Christendom*, 3:307–8). "Quae est unica tua consolatio in vita et in morte? Quod animo pariter et corpore, sive vivam sive moriar, non meus, sed fidissimi Domini et servatoris mei Iesu Christi sum proprius, qui precioso sanguine suo, pro omnibus peccatis meis plenissime satisfaciens, me ab omni potestate Diaboli liberavit, meque ita conservat, ut sine voluntate patris mei coelestis, ne pilus quidem de meo capite possit cadere: imo vero etiam omnia saluti meae servire oporteat: Quocirca me quoque suo Spiritu de vita aeterna certum facit, utque ipsi deinceps vivam promptum ac paratum reddit" (Niemeyer, *Collectio Confessionum*, 430).

2. Klooster, *Our Only Comfort*, 1:33.

In the late modern period, it has become customary for people to take solace in narcotics, entertainment, and even in things that people *know* to be false, that people *know* to be imaginary. Such is the influence of subjectivism. Genuine comfort, however, cannot be found in fables (1 Tim 1:4; 4:7; 2 Tim 4:4; Titus 1:14; 2 Pet 1:16). It is found only in the truth, what actually is. All who trust in Christ know with head, heart, and whole soul that as we live this life and leave it, we do so in the arms of the one who loved us and gave himself for us.

In our heart of hearts we know that we are going to die, but we do not like to admit it. It is a mark of our post-Christian age that this culture is obsessed with youth and superficial beauty. Death was once familiar but no longer. Few today die at home. Today we die in antiseptic hospital rooms, then are boxed up, delivered to the funeral home, and, in many cases, never seen again.

It was not so in the sixteenth century. Death was a routine part of life. Life expectancy was rather shorter than it is today.[3] By the middle of the sixteenth century, a European nobleman who was not killed in battle might expect to live into his mid- to late fifties. Ursinus died aged forty-eight. Olevianus died aged fifty. There were no antibiotics. Basic matters of hygiene and health—for example, physicians washing their hands between patients—were unknown. Infant mortality was much higher than it is today.[4]

Indeed, in 1563 the plague came through Heidelberg. By October 1563 the university had closed, the court had fled to Mosbach, and even some of the pastors (except for Olevianus and Ursinus) had fled.[5] In response, one of the pastors or theologians, possibly Ursinus, wrote a tract, *A Pious Meditation upon Death,* which was published anonymously in 1564.[6] His treatise was a defense of the legitimacy of funerals (a controversial question among the Reformed in the sixteenth and seventeenth centuries) as a useful way to be reminded of the inevitability of death.[7] The author

---

3. Cummins, "Lifespans of the European Elite," 406–39.

4. See the discussion under *HC* 58.

5. Clark, *Caspar Olevian*, 20; Gunnoe, *Thomas Erastus and the Palatinate*, 137.

6. It is included in his 1612 *Opera*. See Ursinus, "Godly Meditation upon Death," 247–70. On the questions surrounding the authorship of the treatise, see 248n4.

7. E.g., in art. 65 of the Church Order of the Synod of Dort (1618–1619), the churches agreed, "Where funeral sermons are not held, they shall not be introduced; and where they already have

writes, "Just as there is nothing more uncertain than the hour of death, so there is nothing at all more certain than death itself."[8]

So, for the catechism to ask about our comfort in "in life and in death" was a good and necessary question and remains so now. It is hard enough when friends and loved ones disappoint us, but eventually even our body will disappoint us. When all else fails, on what will we depend? All our works are tainted. Never in our life have our motives been completely pure. Our obedience is not perfect, so it is not trustworthy.

At the heart of the catechism and at the center of the comfort we confess is this phrase, "has fully satisfied for all my sins." Ursinus writes that the "substance of this comfort consists in this: that we are ingrafted into Christ by faith, that through him we are reconciled to, and beloved of God, that thus he may care for and save us eternally."[9] In contrast, Rome taught (and teaches) that Christ died to make salvation possible for those who do their part by cooperating with grace. The Reformed way of speaking about salvation is to say that Jesus accomplished salvation for us and applies it freely to us by his Spirit. According to Rome, in baptism, the Spirit begins the process of sanctification and eventual justification. In the Roman scheme, our duty is to cooperate with grace toward eventual, final justification. When we sin, according to Rome, we are obligated to do penance. The Roman Catechism says:

> The whole power of the sacrament of Penance consists in restoring us to God's grace and joining us with him in an intimate friendship." Reconciliation with God is thus the purpose and effect of this sacrament. For those who receive the sacrament of Penance with contrite heart and religious disposition, reconciliation "is usually followed by peace and serenity of conscience with strong spiritual consolation." Indeed the sacrament of Reconciliation with God brings about a true "spiritual resurrection," restoration of the

---

been accepted, diligence shall be exercised to do away with them by the most appropriate means." See Ridder, *Church Orders*, 554.

8. Ursinus, "Godly Meditation upon Death," 253.

9. Ursinus, *Commentary*, 17.

> dignity and blessings of the life of the children of God, of which the most precious is friendship with God.[10]

Rome recognizes that few are capable of doing penance perfectly. The next section of the Roman catechism turns to the very same doctrine that began to stir the beginnings of the Reformation: indulgences, an instrument instituted by Rome to remove "temporal" (in this life and purgatory) punishments.[11] To obtain an indulgence, one must draw from the "treasury of merit." One may obtain an indulgence, for example, by traveling to Rome in a jubilee year. Rome confesses:

> We also call these spiritual goods of the communion of saints the Church's treasury, which is "not the sum total of the material goods which have accumulated during the course of the centuries. On the contrary the "treasury of the Church" is the infinite value, which can never be exhausted, which Christ's merits have before God. They were offered so that the whole of mankind could be set free from sin and attain communion with the Father. In Christ, the Redeemer himself, the satisfactions and merits of his Redemption exist and find their efficacy.[12]

According to Rome, Christ's merits (and those of the saints) compose a treasury from which one draws and in which one participates by trusting and obeying (cooperating with grace, that is, fulfilling assigned acts of penance).[13] This is an anticipation of the final judgment.[14] Christ is said to have satisfied, but it is always conditional. He is satisfied "if I ..." Acts of penance have the virtue (power) of reconciling us with God, ourselves, and others.

It is not so in the *HC*. According to the Protestant view, Jesus propitiated God's wrath and expiated our sins. He satisfied for "all my sins." He reconciled God to me and all believers. Rome says, "It is begun." Jesus says, "It is finished" (John 19:30). He redeemed his people from all the power of the devil. God is not propitiated, reconciled, nor are we believers

---

10. CCC §1468.
11. CCC §1478.
12. CCC §1476.
13. CCC §1477.
14. CCC §1470.

redeemed in any way by anything the Spirit does *within* us, nor by anything we do in cooperation with grace. It is done *for* us. Luther speaks for us when he writes, "Therefore read these words 'me' and 'for me' with great emphasis, and accustom yourself to accepting this 'me' with a sure faith and applying it to yourself. Do not doubt that you belong to the number of those who speak this 'me.'"[15]

The sole instrument (*BC* 22) is this: "If only I accept such benefit with a believing heart" (*HC* 60). The whole Reformation may be said to turn on the difference between two prepositions. When it comes to being right before God, the Roman Catholic preposition is *in* us, and the Protestant preposition is *for* us.

One doctrine that distinguishes the Reformed confession from its competitors and its derivatives (for example, Arminianism, federal vision theology) is that we confess the doctrine of the preservation and perseverance of the saints.[16] That is the force of the clause "and so preserves me." Scripture teaches, "I give them eternal life, and they shall never perish; no one can snatch them out of my hand" (John 10:28). That is a categorical, unconditional promise to the elect. Jesus did not make that promise lightly. There is someone who would, were it possible, snatch Christ's people from his hand. He was trying to snatch them when he confronted Jesus in the desert. He tried to snatch them by tempting Jesus in the same way he tempted the first Adam by offering power and influence. The first Adam made what Olevianus calls a "false interpretation of the covenant of creation."[17] The last Adam obeyed God's law without wavering. The adversary tried to snatch Jesus's people when Jesus was at his weakest, when our Savior was tempted to doubt. He tried to snatch them as the soldiers mocked Jesus, but our Savior kept his promise. He had all his people firmly in hand, and he never let them go. He took us with him, as it were, when he went into the tomb, when he emerged from the tomb,

15. *WA* 40.1:290; *LW* 26:179.

16. On Arminianism from an Arminian perspective, see Stanglin and McCall, *Jacob Arminius*; from a Reformed perspective, see Godfrey, *Saving the Reformation*, 10–19, 25–31, 185–227. Federal vision theology teaches that, in baptism, all the benefits of Christ—election, justification, union with Christ, adoption, and sanctification—are given provisionally and retained finally by cooperation with grace. See Clark, "Baptism and the Benefits," 3–19; Waters, *Federal Vision and Covenant Theology*; Clark, *Covenant, Justification, and Pastoral Ministry*.

17. Olevianus, *De substantia*, 2:27.

and when he ascended to the Father's right hand in power. Our preservation and perseverance are as certain as Jesus's ascension.

Question 2

How many things are necessary for you to know, that in this comfort you may live and die blessedly?

Three things: First, the greatness of my sin and misery. Second, how I am redeemed from all my sins and misery. Third, how I am to be thankful to God for such redemption.[18]

There can be no doubt that this question organizes the catechism and how we are to understand the essential structure of the Christian faith as confessed by the Reformed churches. Ursinus says this question "contains the statement and division of the whole catechism and at the same time accords with the division of the Scriptures into the Law and Gospel, and with the differences of these parts, as they have already been explained."[19]

THE GREATNESS OF OUR SIN AND MISERY

We cannot understand our need for a Savior until we learn the greatness of our sin and misery (*Sünde und Elend*). The medieval church and the Roman Catholic Church tended to explain the nature of our need rather differently from the way the Reformed understand it. According the Reformed, our fundamental problem is legal, with moral consequences. The medieval and Roman accounts, however, present the human problem essentially as a lack of being. Implied in the Roman scheme is the false

18. "Wie viele Stüde sind dir nöthig zu wissen, dass du in diefem Trofte feliglich leben und fterben mögest? Drei Stücke: Erstlich, wie gross meine Sünde und Elend seien. Zum Andern, wie ich von allen meinen Sünden und Elend erlöset werde. Und zum Dritten, wie ich Gott für solche Erlösung soll dankbar sein" (Schaff, *Creeds of the Churches*, 3:308). "Quot sunt tibi scitu necessaria ut ista consolatione fruens, beate vivas et moriaris? Tria. Primum, quanta sit peccati mei et miseriae meae magnitudo. Secundum, quo pacto ab omni peccato et miseria liberer. Tertium, quam gratiam Deo pro ea liberatione debeam" (Niemeyer, *Collectio Confessionum*, 430).

19. Ursinus, *Commentary*, 20.

notion that the human problem is finitude, which must be remedied by participating in the divine being.[20]

When the *HC* asks, "How many things are necessary for you to know, that in this comfort, you may live and die blessedly?" the answer is not, "We were created finite." The first answer is, "The greatness of our sin and misery." The Roman Catholic understanding downplays the difference between our existence before and after the fall. Rome confesses that the result of the fall means "human nature is weakened in its powers, subject to ignorance, suffering, and the domination of death; and inclined to sin" (concupiscence).[21]

The tendency in both the East and the West, before the Reformation, was to downplay the effects of the fall. The Western church always affirmed unequivocally the fact of the fall and rejected Pelagianism as a heresy.[22] We sin because we are sinners, and we became sinners in Adam's fall. Formally, the Western church agreed thus far with Augustine. Most of the church, however, practically denied Augustine's conclusions about the extent of the effect of the fall. Most of the Western church, almost from the time of Augustine's death, tended to say that we are sinful, but we are not so sinful that we cannot cooperate with grace. The East was more open to Pelagianism.[23] In medieval theology, it was a given that God begins the process of salvation and that our cooperation with grace is of the essence of condign merit, which was essential to justification. According to most medieval theologians, that sanctity is Spirit-wrought makes it condign, but that it involves our cooperation makes it meritorious.[24] Most medieval theologians were either semi-Pelagian or semi-Augustinian, depending on the degree to which they thought we are corrupted by sin. Most of the medieval church transformed sin from depravity to deprivation, that is, the absence of grace or divinity. There were exceptions. Throughout the

20. *ST* 1a2ae 112.1 (resp. to obj.). Some advocates of federal vision theology have adopted an analogous view (see Clark, "Do This and Live," 241–65). See the discussion of federal vision under *HC* 1.

21. *CCC* §418.

22. The Council of Ephesus (AD 431) condemns Coelestius, Pelagius's disciple, in canon 4. "If any of the clergy should fall away, and publicly or privately presume to maintain the doctrines of Nestorius or Celestius, it is declared just by the holy Synod that these also should be deposed" ("The Canons of the Two Hundred Holy and Blessed Fathers Who Met at Ephesus" [*NPNF* 2/14:229]).

23. McGuckin, *Path of Christianity*, 443.

24. E.g., Bernard, *On Grace and Free Choice*.

entire history of the medieval church (one thousand years), there were genuine Augustinians. For example, Gottschalk of Orbais (ca. AD 808–867) stood up for a genuinely Augustinian view of sin and grace. In the late medieval period there was a sort of renaissance of Augustine's doctrines of sin and grace. That neo-Augustinian movement was one of the developments that made the Reformation possible.[25]

The "semi" approach (of whatever sort) to sin and grace, however, remained the dominant view into the sixteenth century. That is why the Reformation was so remarkable. The Reformation not only turned back to Augustine's view of sin and divine sovereignty, but it transformed them in significant ways. Still, almost as soon as the Reformation reintroduced the Augustinian views of sin and grace (*mutatis mutandis*), versions of the old "semi" and even versions of the old Pelagian errors reared their heads. The Anabaptists rejected the Protestant doctrine of salvation in favor of the pre-Reformation views. Of course, Rome rejected the renewed Augustinian views, and even some Protestants were uneasy about the confessional Protestant doctrines, mainly because they all feared that if justification was said to be completely free, then sinners would have no incentive to be good. About thirty years after the Heidelberg Catechism was published, Jacob Arminius (1560–1609) began raising serious questions that helped create a movement that brought back the old view of "grace and cooperation with grace."

In order to appreciate the greatness of our sin and misery, we must have a sense of the exaltation of our position and the glory of the potential blessedness that lie before us. The tree of life symbolized the blessedness promised to us before the fall. Herman Witsius (1636–1708) describes that tree as a sacrament.[26] By analogy, we might call the tree of the knowledge of good and evil a sacrament of death: "The day you eat thereof you shall surely die" (Gen 2:17). These are legal words and categories. Adam was in a legal relation to his God. They were friends, but that friendship was premised on Adam's righteousness, and as soon as God's law was violated, that righteousness was forfeit and the friendship between God

---

25. Oberman, *Forerunners of the Reformation.*

26. Witsius, *Economy of the Covenants*, 1:81.

and humanity was dissolved. That friendship became righteous warfare by God against us and our sin.

It is no small thing, then, that Paul calls Christ the "Last Adam" (1 Cor 15:45). It is one thing for the first Adam, and all we with him, to face a trial and to fail. It is another thing for the last Adam to face that trial, for all who believe, bearing the weight of our sin and knowing the consequences of his obedience. For the first Adam, a successful probation would have led to eternal life and blessedness. For the last Adam, a successful probation meant suffering and death, and only then did he experience the blessedness promised to the obedient (Rom 5:12–21).

Thus, it is important to notice how clear the catechism is when it says that one of the things we need to know is the "greatness of my sin and misery." According to the Reformed confession, we are not a little sinful. Rather, we are dead in sins and trespasses (Eph 2:1–4; Rom 1:1–3:31). According to the catechism, our natural inclination after the fall is to hate God and neighbor. Our natural inclination is to seek our own interests, to defy God by setting up idols, serving those idols by murder, by theft, by covetousness, by lust, by rejection of authority of all kinds. That we do not act out those impulses is due to the goodness of God's providence whereby he restrains us from doing all that we might.

The English noun *misery* is probably derived from the Latin verb *misereo*, "to pity." The Latin adjective *miser* means "wretched." In this phrase "sin and misery" are not synonyms. Rather, in our translation, the noun *misery* (Latin, *miseria*) refers to the consequences of sin. Sin is lawbreaking (1 John 3:4). Lawbreaking has objective and subjective consequences. It should not be a surprise. God promised: "The day you eat thereof you shall surely die" (Gen 2:17). That is what happened. Where, as his image-bearers, we should have entered into a state of objective and subjective blessedness, we actually entered into a state of misery. It is objective because the noun *misery* describes our state. Apart from grace, regardless of our experience at any given moment, our state is miserable, wretched. Subjectively, *wretched* also describes our experience. When we are young, by and large, the body is our servant. It does what we want it to do, when we want, the way we want. Increasingly, however, as we age, we become servants of our bodies. We experience misery in countless other ways. Paul understands this objective and subjective state of misery: "O wretched man that I am!" (Rom 7:24). He connects his state of misery to the "law at work in the members of my body, waging war against the law of my mind and making me a prisoner of the law of sin at work within my members" (Rom 7:23). This is the confession of one who is in touch with reality.

Unless and until we are graciously allowed to see ourselves and our state as they really are, grace holds no interest for us. The catechism was written not just to those who profess the Christian faith but to those who actually believe it. The writers of the catechism had to assume, for the purposes of writing the catechism, that the hearers and readers of the catechism were united to Christ by true faith (*HC* 21).

Remember the question: "How many things are necessary for you to know that in this comfort you may live and die blessedly?" It is not possible for sinners to live blessedly in a conditional covenant wherein righteousness is contingent on their performance of the terms of the covenant. It is impossible because of our sin and misery. Because of sin, we are not even willing to keep the terms of the covenant.

That is why we have a perfectly obedient and wholly trustworthy Savior who performed all the conditions of the covenant of works as the substitute for his people.[27] That is why, in the doctrine of salvation, faith is not "trusting and obeying" but "a certain knowledge and a hearty trust" (*HC* 21). The catechism characterizes faith this way because works and grace are two distinct principles (1 Cor 11:5). The *HC* does not confuse them, and it premises our assurance on Jesus's fulfillment of the covenant of works for us.

27. From the late sixteenth century, most Reformed theologians came to speak *theologically* of three covenants. The prefall covenant of works was between God and Adam, whereby Adam, as the sinless, righteous, and holy representative of the human race, was given a test and the ability to meet the terms of the test and thereby to enter into blessed communion with God. The covenant of grace is the promise that God made to Adam and Eve after the fall, in which he promised to send his Son to defeat Satan and secure our salvation even at the cost of his own life. This covenant was said to be progressively revealed and worked out through the history of salvation, through a series of administrations of the covenant of grace. Behind these two covenants was said to be the pretemporal, eternal covenant of redemption between the Father and the Son, in which the Father gave a people to the Son, and he promised to meet the terms of the covenant on their behalf, to act as their representative, and to secure their redemption. For a brief overview of the history of Reformed covenant theology, see Clark, "Christ and Covenant," 403–28.

REDEEMED FROM ALL MY SINS AND MISERY

The second thing that a believer must know is that "I am redeemed from all my sins and misery." We do not confess that "believers might be redeemed, if they cooperate with grace." We do not confess that "believers are redeemed, but they could lose their redemption." We do not confess that "Jesus made it possible for believers to be redeemed, if they do their part." All these alternatives to the theology and language of the catechism destroy assurance because each of them subtly changes two of the terms of the second thing that believers must know.

First, the alternatives each redefine the noun *believers*. According to the catechism, if one is a believer, then one is united to Christ by grace alone, through faith alone. God the Spirit creates that union, and it is irrevocable. True faith is nothing but a certain knowledge and a hearty trust that Christ has kept the law for me, has died for me, was raised for me, that his righteousness has been credited to me, and that he lives and intercedes for me. True faith necessarily produces sanctity, but sanctity is not the ground or instrument of our salvation.

When the Heidelberg pastors confessed, "I am redeemed from all my sins and misery," they rejected the entire medieval religion of "grace and cooperation of grace." Thereby they rejected the religion of uncertainty and purgatory in favor of pure grace (divine approval). The catechism does not make righteousness merely possible or contingent on cooperation by sinners. Rather, it begins with a true righteousness accomplished for us (*pro nobis*) and outside us (*extra nos*) so that sinners, though they remain intrinsically sinful, can nevertheless know that they are truly righteous before God on the basis of Christ's perfect righteousness imputed to believers.[28]

Some have attempted to resurrect the "grace and cooperation" scheme. The Arminians tried it in the late sixteenth and early seventeenth centuries—they were soundly rejected by the Synod of Dort. Richard Baxter (1615–1691) renewed later it in the seventeenth century.[29] The neonomians

28. The Latin text of the *HC* uses the expression *pro nobis* repeatedly (*HC* 14, 31, 49, 67, 70, 75; in Niemeyer, *Collectio Confessionum*, 432, 437, 440, 444–46).

29. E.g., Baxter, *Aphorismes of Justification*, 280–303.

taught it during the Marrow controversy in the eighteenth century, and the federal visionists teach it today.[30]

The basis of one's assurance is neither the degree to which one has cooperated with grace nor a mystical, extracanonical revelation that one is elect. The basis of assurance is the promise of Christ: "Whoever believes in him shall never perish" (John 3:16). Reformed theology does not ask believers to ask, "Am I elect?" Reformed theology asks believers to ask, "Do I believe?"

SUBSTITUTIONARY ATONEMENT

The second thing every believer must know to live and die blessedly is that believers are redeemed. All who know the greatness of their sin and misery and trust that the promise of the gospel is true are redeemed. Our redemption is anchored in the substitutionary obedience and atonement accomplished for us by Christ. Substitutionary atonement has been under assault for rather a long time. Liberals describe the doctrine of the substitutionary atonement as "slaughterhouse theology."[31] Before the rise of higher criticism, seventeenth-century rationalists, following Hugo Grotius (1583–1645), denied that the atonement was substitutionary. More recently, Steve Chalke, a leader in the emerging church movement, says,

> The fact is that the cross is not a form of cosmic child abuse—a vengeful Father, punishing his Son for an offence he has not even committed [as the doctrine of penal substitution makes it out to be]. Understandably, both people inside and outside of the Church have found this twisted version of events morally dubious and a huge barrier to faith. Deeper than that, however, is that such a concept stands in total contradiction to the statement "God is love." If the cross is a personal act of violence perpetrated by God towards humankind but borne by his Son, then it makes a mockery

30. Clark, "How We Got Here," 15–16; Horton, "Which Covenant Theology?," 216–27; Clark, "Do This and Live," 241–42.

31. Reid, *She Changes Everything*, 16.

> of Jesus' own teaching to love your enemies and to refuse to repay evil with evil.[32]

Those who are advocating this approach to the atonement are not simply attacking one "theory" of the atonement (as did liberals at the time of the 1924 Auburn Affirmation) but, as Don Carson says, are attacking the very foundation of the gospel itself.[33]

Scripture uses more than one metaphor for describing the nature and purpose of Christ's death and, in reaction to the liberal rejection of the doctrine of (penal) substitutionary atonement, fundamentalists and conservatives have focused almost entirely on this one metaphor or image. Some critics simply do not expand the range of metaphors or images by which we may describe the nature and intent of Christ's work. There is a widespread rejection of the assumptions that lie behind the biblical doctrine of the atonement. It is assumed today that the *only* category of analysis that we may use today to describe divine-human relations is the relational category. There is a widespread rejection of legal (forensic) or commercial (e.g., accounting) categories of analysis. The rejection of these ways of speaking and thinking lies behind the current discomfort with the confessional Protestant doctrine of justification. It lies behind the current move to recast the Protestant doctrine of justification as a matter solely of union with Christ or even *theosis* (divinization).[34]

---

32. Chalke and Mann, *Lost Message of Jesus*, 182–83. See Johnson and Gleason, *Reforming or Conforming?*

33. Carson, *Becoming Conversant*, 186–87.

34. "By *theosis* the Orthodox mean the process of acquiring godly characteristics, gaining immortality and incorruptibility, and experiencing communion with God. As a result, deification corresponds somewhat to concepts which evangelicals describe using the terms sanctification, eternal life, and fellowship or relationship with God" (Fairbairn, "Salvation as *Theosis*," 42). Rome, however, does think of *theosis* in ontological terms. In a "General Audience" on June 10, 2009, concerning pantheistic medieval theologian John Scotus Erigena (ca. 810–877), Benedict XVI said, "John Scotus, here too using terminology dear to the Christian tradition of the Greek language, called this experience for which we strive 'theosis,' or divinization, with such daring affirmations that he might be suspected of heterodox pantheism. Yet, even today one cannot but be strongly moved by texts such as the following in which with recourse to the ancient metaphor of the smelting of iron he writes: 'just as all red-hot iron is liquified to the point that it seems nothing but fire and yet the substances remain distinct from one another, so it must be accepted that after the end of this world all nature, both the corporeal and the incorporeal, will show forth God alone and yet remain integral so that God can in a certain way be comprehended while remaining in-comprehensible and that the creature itself may be transformed, with ineffable wonder, and reunited with God' (V, PL 122, col. 451 B)." "General Audience"; *CCC* §§398, 1589, 1997.

Nevertheless, the Bible teaches unequivocally that Christ has redeemed us, that is, that he has purchased us (e.g., 1 Cor 6:20, "You were bought with a price"). Before Anselm (1033–1109), some held that God had to pay a ransom to the devil, as if God were in debt to the Evil One. Anselm helped to recover the biblical doctrine that the debt was not God's but ours.[35] God made us in righteousness with the ability to obey him. When we sinned against God, we incurred a debt to the righteousness of God, which Anselm characterizes as God's honor, that had to be satisfied. Since it was humans who sinned, it had to be humans who satisfied God's justice.

We confess that God has redeemed believers, that is, that he bought us and delivered us from slavery to death and sin. We are owned by another, namely, our Redeemer Jesus Christ. Thus, another key assumption behind the doctrine of the atonement is a denial of human autonomy relative to God (1 Cor 6:19–20; 7:22).

A THANKFUL RESPONSE

The third thing that one must know "that in this comfort you may live and die blessedly" is "how I am to be thankful to God for such redemption." For the Reformed churches, the Christian life is a grateful, fruitful life lived in union with Christ, out of gratitude for the grace of God to sinners in Christ. We live the Christian life in hard times and good times in an objective state of blessedness.

Thankfulness is a major theme for the apostle Paul. As part of his law-preaching prosecution of human sinfulness in Romans 1:21, Paul uses the expressions "glorify God" (ἐδόξασαν) and "give thanks" (ηὐχαρίστησαν) as synonyms. To give thanks is to glorify God. In this case he uses them as part of the first use of the law. It is a fundamental human obligation, as image-bearers, to acknowledge God as our Creator and to glorify him as such. As fallen people, in whom the image has been defaced, we refuse to acknowledge God. In Romans 6:16, Paul says that we are necessarily slaves either to God or to sin. If we sin, we are slaves to sin and death. Verse 17: "But thanks [χάρις] be to God, you who were slaves of sin have become have obedient from the heart." The noun for "thanks" here is the same noun used for "grace." In other words, there is an integral relation

35. Anselm, *Cur deus homo*.

between thanks and grace. Only those who have received the grace, that is, undeserved favor, of God are those who are thankful. When Paul says, "thanks be to God," he is reflecting a basic Christian impulse. We might describe his doctrine of the Christian life as a doctrine of thanks:

"Thanks [χάρις] be to God through Jesus Christ our Lord!" (Rom 7:25). Even though we continue to struggle with sin, "there is now therefore no condemnation for those who are in Christ Jesus" (Rom 8:1). "Thanks [χάρις] be to God who gives us the victory through our Lord Jesus Christ" (1 Cor 15:57). "Thanks [χάρις] be to God who, in Christ, always leads us in triumphal procession" (2 Cor 2:14). "Thanks [χάρις] be to God for his inexpressible gift!" (2 Cor 9:15).

For Paul, thankfulness is not a light matter. It is a powerful motive for the Christian life. It is a recognition of what God in Christ has done for us, what the Spirit is doing within us, and who we are now in Christ. "How can we who died to sin still live in it?" We cannot. With Christ helping us, we will not.

There is, however, a tradition of rejecting thankfulness as the source of the Christian life.[36] The first part of the answer is the medieval setting in which the catechism was written. The essential structure of the medieval approach to the Christian life was twofold: grace and guilt. This approach was not confined to the Middle Ages. It is the religion of all moralists. In response to the Reformation, Rome argued that thankfulness did not provide sufficient motivation for godliness. That is why Rome teaches that one is justified because and to the degree one is sanctified. When the catechism says, "How I am to be thankful to God for such redemption," it is a rich definition of thankfulness. The catechism goes on to elaborate on the ground, power, and structure of thankfulness, but it always assumes the Pauline doctrine of union with Christ wrought by the Spirit whenever it speaks of the Christian life being motivated by gratitude.

The Reformed doctrine of salvation does not make sanctification a second blessing. Rather, it is the natural, organic result of salvation. This is how the Scriptures themselves speak about the Christian life. This is why our Lord himself uses the metaphor of fruit (Matt 3:8; 7:17–19), as does

---

36. E.g., Piper, *Purifying Power of Living*, 31–49. Piper not only misconstrues what Scripture and Reformation mean by gratitude, but he offers in its place an idiosyncratic, Edwardsean recasting of the doctrine of faith.

the apostle Paul (Rom 7:4; Gal 5:22–23; Phil 1:11; Col 1:10; see also Heb 12:11; 13:15), to describe the Christian life. *BC* 24 speaks at some length about sanctity as the fruit, that is, the logically and morally necessary result of salvation.[37] When the catechism says, "How we are to be thankful for such redemption," it is focusing on the existential, personal motive for the Christian life. The catechism will turn to our union with Christ later on.

37. Dennison, *Reformed Confessions*, 2:438.

QUESTION 3

From where do you know your misery?

QUESTION 4

What does the Law of God require of us?

QUESTION 5

Can you keep all this perfectly?

Lord's Day 2

Question 3

From where do you know your misery?

From the Law of God.[1]

When a physician gives a prognosis of death, that is bad news. When a physician says that a patient is cancer-free, that is good news. These are two different announcements. The law is a tutor (παιδαγωγὸς; Gal 3:24) that teaches us our sin and misery. In the first part of Romans (1:18–3:20), Paul is preaching the law, in its pedagogical use, to teach the Roman congregation (and all of us) the greatness of their sin and misery (and ours) outside Christ. His intent is to drive them (and us) to Christ for salvation. The law condemns all, whether Jew (under the law) or gentile (outside the law). The natural law is the substance of the moral law, and it condemns all who are outside Christ and his righteousness imputed and received through faith alone.

In Romans 3:19 Paul says this very thing: "Now we know that whatever the law says it speaks to those who are in the law [ἐν τῷ νόμῳ], so that every mouth may be shut, and the whole world may be indicted before God." Why? "Because by works of the law no man will be justified in his sight, because through the law comes knowledge of sin" (3:20). This is the pedagogical use of the law. In this use Paul calls the law a "schoolmaster" or a "pedagogue." In our day teachers are not ordinarily allowed to strike students, but in the ancient world educational corporal punishment was expected. In Paul's scheme here, no believer is still under the law as a pedagogue.

HC 115 reasserts the pedagogical use of the law when it says that God so strictly enjoins the moral law on us "that we may learn more and more to know our sinful nature, and so the more earnestly to seek forgiveness of sins and righteousness in Christ." This was the Protestant pattern. In his 1531 commentary on Galatians, Luther writes,

> The other use of the Law is the theological or spiritual one, which serves to increase transgressions. This is the primary purpose of

1. "Woher erkennest du dein Elend? Aus dem Gesetz Gottes" (Schaff, *Creeds of the Churches*, 3:308). "Unde tuam miseriam cognoscis? Ex Lege Dei" (Niemeyer, *Collectio Confessionum*, 430).

> the Law of Moses, that through it sin might grow and be multiplied, especially in the conscience. Paul discusses this magnificently in Rom. 7. Therefore the true function and the chief and proper use of the Law is to reveal to man his sin, blindness, misery, wickedness, ignorance, hate and contempt of God, death, hell, judgment, and the well-deserved wrath of God. Yet this use of the Law is completely unknown to the hypocrites, the sophists in the universities, and to all men who go along in the presumption of the righteousness of the Law or of their own righteousness. To curb and crush this monster and raging beast, that is, the presumption of religion, God is obliged, on Mt. Sinai, to give a new Law with such pomp and with such an awesome spectacle that the entire people is crushed with fear. For since the reason becomes haughty with this human presumption of righteousness and imagines that on account of this it is pleasing to God, therefore God has to send some Hercules, namely, the Law, to attack, subdue, and destroy this monster with full force. Therefore the Law is intent only on this beast, not on any other.[2]

Calvin agrees with Luther on this.

> But a question arises, what was the instruction or education of this schoolmaster? First, the law, by displaying the justice of God, convinced them that in themselves they were unrighteous; for in the commandments of God, as in a mirror, they might see how far they were distant from true righteousness. They were thus reminded that righteousness must be sought in some other quarter. The promises of the law served the same purpose, and might lead to such reflections as these: "If you cannot obtain life by works but by fulfilling the law, some new and different method must be sought. Your weakness will never allow you to ascend so high; nay, though you desire and strive ever so much, you will fall far short of the object." The threatenings, on the other hand, pressed and entreated them to seek refuge from the wrath and curse of God, and gave them no rest till they were constrained to seek the grace of Christ.[3]

---

2. *LW* 26:309–10.

3. Calvin, *Galatians, Ephesians, Philippians and Colossians*, 108–9.

The catechism appeals to the pedagogical use of the law and answers the question, "From where do you know the greatness of your sin and misery?" by turning to the law and not to the gospel because, to a significant degree, this distinction was at the heart of the Reformation breakthrough. The confessional Protestants (Lutheran and Reformed) were united in their conviction that there are two grammatical moods throughout Scripture: law and gospel. The Protestant recovery of the law/gospel distinction was essential to the Reformation. For a millennium before the Reformation, the church was agreed that there is only one sort of word in Scripture: law. The church distinguished between the old (Moses) law and the new (Christ) law. The only difference between the old and new law was the degree of grace available to aid believers in their obedience to the law.[4]

The Protestants rejected this scheme. They read the Bible as containing two kinds of words throughout: law and gospel. According to the Protestants, the law says, "Do this and live" (Luke 10:28). It requires perfect obedience and righteousness (Deut 27:26; Gal 3:10). The law is utterly unforgiving. The gospel, on the other hand, is a different kind of word. The gospel promises what will be done and declares what has been done for Christ's people. The gospel says, "The seed of the woman will crush the serpent" (Gen 3:15). The gospel says, "I will give you rest" (Matt 11:28). It says, "For God so loved the world ..." (John 3:16).

This distinction is the only way to understand this answer of the catechism. It does not say that the *gospel* teaches us our misery because that is neither the function nor the nature of the gospel. The English word *gospel* is an Old English word meaning "good news."[5] The New Testament Greek word is εὐαγγέλιον, which came over into Latin as *evangelium*. They all mean the same thing.

Unfortunately, partly in reaction to some trends in modern evangelical theology and piety and partly because contemporary Reformed Christians have lost track of their own tradition, in the twentieth century some claimed law and gospel was a Lutheran distinction and not

---

4. For more on this, see Clark, "Law and Gospel," 307–20; Clark, "Letter and Spirit," 331–63.

5. *OED Online*, s.v. "Gospel."

Reformed doctrine.[6] The notion that only Lutherans hold the law/gospel distinction would surprise the many Reformed theologians and ministers who have taught it. For example, Ursinus taught this distinction explicitly in his *Summa theologiae*, written before the *HC*.

> Q.36 What distinguishes law and gospel?
> A. The law contains a covenant of nature begun by God with men in creation, that is, it is a natural sign to men, and it requires of us perfect obedience toward God. It promises eternal life to those keeping it, and threatens eternal punishment to those not keeping it. In fact, the gospel contains a covenant of grace, that is, one known not at all under nature. This covenant declares to us fulfillment of its righteousness in Christ, which the law requires, and our restoration through Christ's Spirit. To those who believe in him, it freely promises eternal life for Christ's sake.[7]

Commenting on *HC* 92, he writes of the importance of having a "proper understanding of the law and the gospel." He writes that the law "promises eternal life and all good things upon the condition of our own and perfect righteousness, and of obedience in us," but the "gospel promises the same blessings upon the condition that we exercise faith in Christ, by which we embrace the obedience which another, even Christ, has performed in our behalf; or the gospel teaches that we are justified freely by faith in Christ."[8]

Calvin's successor in Geneva, Theodore Beza (1534–1605), says: "We divide this Word into two principal parts or kinds: the one is called the 'Law,' the other the 'Gospel.' For all the rest can be gathered under the one or other of these two headings. ... Ignorance of this distinction between Law and Gospel is one of the principal sources of the abuses which corrupted and still corrupt Christianity."[9] In his 1579 commentary on Romans, Olevianus writes that in order to understand Romans, one

6. Clark, "Do This and Live," 350–52; Clark, "Law and Gospel," 307–11.

7. Ursinus, *Larger Catechism*, Q. 36, in Bierma et al., *Introduction*, 168–69.

8. Bierma et al., *Introduction*, 497.

9. Beza, *Christian Faith*, 40.

must understand two things: the gospel of justification *sola gratia, sola fide,* and "the distinction between law and gospel."[10]

We could easily multiply such quotations, but these passages speak for the Reformed tradition. When we understand the distinction between law and gospel, we may understand more clearly why we confess that it is the law, not the gospel, that teaches us our misery.[11]

Question 4

What does the Law of God require of us?

Christ teaches us in summary, in Matthew 22: "You shall love the Lord your God with all your heart and with all your soul, and with all your mind, and with all your strength. This is the first and great commandment. And the second is like it, you shall love your neighbor as yourself. On these two commandments hang all the law and the prophets."[12]

We should note that the catechism does not ask, "What does the law of God give us?" nor does it ask, "What does the law of God do for us?" but rather, "What does the law of God require?"[13] Ursinus writes, "Christ speaks of the doctrine of the law, and not of the promises of the gospel, which is evident from the question of the Pharisee, who asked him which was the greatest commandment, and not, which was the principal

10. "Hoc ut intelligatur cogitandum est discrimen legis et Evangelii" (Olevianus, *Romanos Notae,* 2–3).

11. See the discussion under *HC* 92.

12. "Was ersordert denn das göttliche Gesetz von uns? Diess lehret uns Christus in einer Summa, Matthäi. am 22: Du sollst lieben Gott, deinen Herrn, von ganzem Herzen, von ganzer Seele, von ganzem Gemüth und allen Kräften: diess ist das vornehmste und grösste Gebot. Das audere aber ist dem gleich: Du sollst deinen Nächsten lieben als dich selbst.—In diesen zweien Geboten hanget das ganze Gesetz und die Propheten" (Schaff, *Creeds of the Churches,* 3:308–9). "Quid a nobis postulat Dei? Id docet nos Christus summatim Matthaei 22: Diliges Dominum Deum tuum, ex toto corde tuo, ex tota anima tua, ex tota cogitatione tua, et ex omnibus viribus tuis. Istud est primum et maximum mandatum. Secundum autem simile est huic: Diliges proximum tuum sicut teipsum. Ab istis duobus mandatis tota lex et Prophetae pendent" (Niemeyer, *Collectio Confessionum,* 431).

13. German: *erfordert* (Müller, *Die Bekenntnisschriften,* 683); Latin: *postulat* (Niemeyer, *Collectio Confessionum,* 431).

promise in the law."[14] There is no ambiguity in the catechism's use of the verb "to require" in German, Latin, or English. The use of this verb is significant. It signals again how the Reformed churches viewed the law in its pedagogical use. Indeed, even if we think of the law in its third or normative use, it still never gives what it demands even as it guides the Christian life. The law reflects the divine nature. God is what he is (Exod 3:14). He is immutably holy and righteous (Isa 6:3). He never changes (Mal 3:6–7). His holiness and justice never change. His demand for utter justice and holiness is relentless, as it ought to be.

There has always been a temptation to downplay the demands of the law. Ironically, the downplaying of the demands of the law does not always come from the antinomians, that is, those who deny the abiding validity of the moral law. Rather, it comes just as often from those who want Christians to obey the law. The move to soften the demands of the law or to ignore them altogether usually comes in recognition (implicit or explicit) of our inability to keep the law perfectly. Rather than do what Christians ought to do—seek a perfect law keeper—moralists, whether Roman or Protestant, who want us to be justified by being sanctified, take the sting out of the law by implying that the law does not really mean what it seems to say: "Cursed is everyone who does not continue to do everything written in the book of the law" (Deut 27:26; Gal 3:10). The law says, "Do this and live" (Luke 10:28).

Jesus accused the Pharisees of exactly this error. They had their own "fence around the law," the "tradition of the elders" (Matt 15:2–6) and the "tradition of men" (Mark 7:8), whereby they replaced God's holy law with their own traditions and excused themselves from actually having to obey God's law as it stands. After they lowered the bar of righteousness, they could plot the murder of Jesus while posing as righteous men. Thus Jesus called them "whitewashed tombs" (Matt 23:27).

The medieval church did this in a variety of ways. On one hand, it portrayed God as a righteous and fearsome judge. On the other hand, however, it sent the signal that God does not really demand perfection.

14. Ursinus, *Commentary*, 26.

This was the effect of the doctrine of congruent merit by which God was said to impute merit to one's best efforts.[15]

In truth, there is no such thing as congruent merit. God's righteousness demands utter moral and legal perfection. The Reformed churches have always recognized that the law is truly simple: love God with all our faculties and our neighbor as ourselves. This is what God called us to do in the garden: love God utterly and love one another. After we failed to keep this law, God restated it in a much more elaborate, historically conditioned, temporary form for the Israelite national covenant. The moral law, however, remained constant: love God and neighbor. This is the sum of the law expressed under the new covenant by our Lord himself. It can be expressed in the "Ten Words" (the Decalogue) or in just a few words from Matthew 22.

Further, the law does not give us what it demands. The Synod of Dort (3/4.5) explains:

> In the same light are we to consider the law of the Decalogue, delivered by God to His peculiar people, the Jews, by the hands of Moses. For though it reveals the greatness of sin, and more and more convinces man thereof, yet, as it neither points out a remedy nor imparts strength to extricate him from his misery, but, being weak through the flesh, leaves the transgressor under the curse, and man cannot by this law obtain saving grace.[16]

Even though the law is cast in terms of love, it requires total fidelity and obedience. There is a logical order: love God, then neighbor. The latter is like the former. The latter flows from the former. Without love of neighbor, love of God cannot exist (Jas 2:1–13). All we image-bearers in all places and times owe this love to God and neighbor as a matter of natural obligation. This expression of law also entails a certain view of human beings. We are image-bearers created with faculties (heart, mind—"soul and strength" were cumulative).[17] We are intellective and affective creatures. All our thoughts and everything we love must reflect

15. Thus, it was medieval Franciscans and not the Reformation theologians who taught what Roman critics have called a "fictive" doctrine of justification. See the discussion under *HC* 60.

16. Dennison, *Reformed Confessions*, 4:136.

17. Ursinus, *Commentary*, 24.

love of God. As God's image-bearers, we owe total devotion of these faculties to God and then to neighbor. There are no exceptions. This sobering realization should give us pause before we speak glibly about love of God and neighbor.

QUESTION 5

Can you keep all this perfectly?

No, for I am prone by nature to hate God and my neighbor.[18]

This is the Reformed doctrine of the corruption brought about by the fall. In the history of Christianity, not everyone has shared the catechism's view of the consequences of the fall. There are three views about how sinful we are:

1. Pelagianism says that we are not sinners until we sin, that Adam set a bad example for us that we can choose not to follow.
2. Semi-Pelagianism says that we sinned in Adam, but we are not so sinful that we cannot cooperate freely with grace even before we are in a state of grace.
3. Augustinianism (and the view of the Reformation) says that we sinned in Adam and the consequences were, as God said they would be, deadly. We are unable to do anything toward redemption.

The effects of the fall are so profound that we are not even able to cooperate with grace. This is our understanding of Romans 1:18–3:21; 1 John 1:8, 10; and Ephesians 2:1–3. "The wages of sin is death" (Rom 6:23). The fall inflicted a mortal wound. In contrast, in his *Sentences* Peter Lombard

18. "Kannst du diess Alles vollkommen halten? Nein: denn ich bin von Natur geneigt, Gott und meinen Nächsten zu hassen" (Schaff, *Creeds of the Churches*, 3:309). "Num haec omnia perfecte servare potes?Minime: natura enim propensus sum ad odium Dei et proximi" (Niemeyer, *Collectio Confessionum*, 431).

(ca. 1100–1160) appeals to the parable of good Samaritan (Luke 10:30–37), in which we are wounded, "half dead" (ESV) but not utterly unable.[19]

The Augustinian and Reformed (and confessional Protestant generally) account of the effect of the fall not only distinguishes us from some of the fathers and from much of the medieval church (both East and West), but also from much of evangelicalism since the eighteenth century. Pelagianism is false on its face, and the ecumenical church—ancient, medieval, and Protestant—has condemned it as heresy.[20] Both the denial of the fall and the downplaying of its effects are contrary to the truth.

At the Synod of Dort (3/4.3), the Reformed churches of Europe and the British Isles reaffirmed the Augustinian consensus: "Therefore all men are conceived in sin, and are by nature children of wrath, incapable of saving good, prone to evil, dead in sin, and in bondage thereto; and without the regenerating grace of the Holy Spirit, they are neither able nor willing to return to God, to reform the depravity of their nature, or to dispose themselves to reformation."[21] This is not to say that all humans are as wicked as they can be.[22]

19. Lombard, *Sentences* 2.35.4.

20. See the discussion under *HC* 2.

21. Dennison, *Reformed Confessions*, 4:135.

22. See the discussion under *HC* 8.

Question 6
Did God create man thus wicked and corrupt?

Question 7
From where then comes this depraved nature of man?

Question 8
But are we so depraved, that we are wholly incapable of any good and prone to all evil?

Lord's Day 3

Question 6

Did God create man thus wicked and corrupt?

By no means, rather God created man good and after his own image, that is, in righteousness and true holiness, that he might rightly know God his Creator, heartily love him, and live with him in eternal blessedness, to praise and glorify him.[1]

The Reformed churches are known for teaching that God controls all that happens. When we think about salvation, this doctrine of divine sovereignty is a great comfort. It means that we did not save ourselves, and our salvation is in the safe and good hands of our all-powerful and gracious Father. When it comes to accounting for sin and evil, the doctrine of divine sovereignty is more difficult, especially for those whose theology begins and ends with divine sovereignty.

To be sure, the problems of sin and evil are no less severe for those who deny divine sovereignty. The notion that God voluntarily withdraws his control or only occasionally exercises control over history faces great biblical-theological problems. Scripture presents God as constantly in control. He spoke creation into existence (Gen 1:1–3; John 1:1–3). He flooded "the world that then was" (Gen 7:11–24; 2 Pet 3:6). He hardened Pharaoh's heart (Exod 9:16; Rom 9:16–17). Divine control over all things is the essential premise of the entire book of Job. The reality of God's sovereign control over all things caused Paul to exclaim, "What therefore will we say? Is there injustice with God? May it never be!" (Rom 9:14), and "You will say to me, 'Why then does he blame us? For who resists his will,'" to which Paul replies, "O man, who are you to talk back to God?" (Rom 9:19–20). Paul offers this apologetic because of the apparent problem.

1. "Hat denn Gott den Menschen also böse und verkehrt erxschaffen? Nein: sondern Gott hat den Menschen gut und nach seinem Ehenbild erschaffen, das ist, in wahrhaftiger Gerechtigkeit und Heiligkeit; auf dass er Gott seinen Schöpfer recht erkenne, und von Herzen liebe, und in ewiger Seligkeit mit ihm lebe, Ihn zu loben und zu preisen" (Schaff, *Creeds of the Churches*, 3:309). "Num ergo Deus hominem ita pravum et perversum condidit? Nequaquam: Imo vero bonum et ad imaginem sui condidit eum, hoc est, vera iustitia et sanctitate praeditum, ut Deum creatorem suum recte cognosceret, ex animo diligeret, cum eo beatus in aeternum viveret, idque ad eum laudandum et celebrandum" (Niemeyer, *Collectio Confessionum*, 431).

That does not mean that there is nothing to say. First, it does not advance our understanding of Scripture, nor is it faithful to ecumenical Christianity, to attempt to shade the Christian confession, "I believe in God the Father *almighty*" (*Credo in Deum Patrem omnipotentem*).[2] Second, we should do as Paul and recognize our intellectual, moral, and metaphysical limitations. Third, we can mitigate and more clearly understand the problem by doing as the Scriptures and the catechism do, by looking at the nature of the creation and fall itself.

Contrary to the assumption that some make about Reformed theology, the Reformed churches approach the problem of sin and evil not by looking first at eternity and the divine decree but rather by looking at history. The mainstream of confessional Reformed theology has appealed to the decree as a source of explanation *a posteriori*, that is, after the fact. In the catechism we do not start with the divine decree and deduce a system of theology from it.[3]

When the Reformed churches turn to history to begin to explain or mitigate the problem of sin and evil, we are following Scripture. God created everything and everyone *good* (Gen 1:25). We say that God made humans "in righteousness and true holiness." This affirmation is important. By contrast, Aquinas taught that humanity, by nature, could not attain eternal blessedness because of its finitude.[4] We say, however, that Adam, *before the fall*, was capable of attaining eternal blessedness. Before the Reformation it was widely assumed that there was a sort of scale of being (think of a ladder) at the top of which was God and at the bottom of which was creation.[5] It was thought that what creation needed was perfection, that is, to

2. Schaff, *Creeds of the Churches*, 2:45.

3. Contra the "central dogma" interpretation of the history of Reformed theology of Alexander Schweizer (1808–1888) in *Die Glaubenslehre*. The "mediating theologians" followed this approach through the nineteenth century, and they in turn dominated the way the history of Reformed theology was told through the first half of the twentieth century (Muller, *Post-Reformation Reformed Dogmatics*, 1:124–32). On this movement, see Purvis, *Theology in the University*.

4. *ST* 1a, 95. art. 1, art. 3.

5. Aquinas was deeply influenced by Pseudo-Dionysius (ca. 500), who synthesized Neoplatonism with Christianity. "The aim of all Dionysius' works is the union of the whole created order with God, which union is the final stage of a threefold process of purification, illumination, and perfection or union: a triad which has been vastly influential in the Christian mystical tradition."

move up the scale of being toward God. In this scheme, the fundamental human problem is not sin but finitude. Sin was regarded as a symptom of a more fundamental problem, a lack of being or a lack of divinity.

This doctrine continues to be the magisterial teaching of the Roman Catholic Church, which teaches that humans and God both participate in being.[6] This way of thinking also influences many evangelicals of the revivalist traditions. Their piety and theology revolve around the quest to deny or overcome their humanity. One sees this in the fundamentalist rules that say, in effect, "do not touch" and "do not taste" (Col 2:21). The influence of this scale-of-being idea reflects itself in a false dichotomy, where what is immaterial is good, and what is material is thought to be either evil or worthy of suspicion. The old Roman Catholic and the modern fundamentalist view of sex as inherently sinful reflects such a dichotomy. Such a dichotomy feeds the modern evangelical neglect of the visible, institutional church. Much of that neglect or denial is grounded in the view that God does not operate through human, created things such as sermons, water, bread, and wine. One sees this tendency in the Roman doctrine of transubstantiation. The elements cannot remain mere elements. The essence of the elements of Communion must be transformed into divinity.

Even more fundamental to this whole discussion is the question of the relation of nature to grace. There is much confusion surrounding this topic. There are four basic views:

1. Thomas and the Reformed say that grace perfects nature.[7] For example, J. H. Alsted, the *Synopsis Purioris*, and Johannes Scharp all use the very same language that Thomas uses.[8]

---

6. *CCC* §34.

7. *ST* 1a 1.8, repl. obj. 2. "Cum igitur gratia non tollat naturam, sed perficiat." "Gratia peficit naturam" (*ST* 1a.62.5, resp. dic.).

8. The Thomistic dictum *gratia perficit naturam* does not appear frequently in classic Reformed texts, but similar expressions do occur. E.g., Alsted writes, "gratia non distruit naturam sed eam perfecit" ("Grace does not destroy nature but perfects it"; Alsted, *Methodus Sacrosanctae Theologiae*, 1.1.2). The *Synopsis purioris* (11.11) says, "Divina enim providentia non corrumpit naturam, sed perficit; non tollit" ("For the divine providence does not destroy nature but perfects it"; te Velde, van den Belt, and van Asselt, *Synopsis Purioris Theologiae*, 1:268). Alsted's point, made also by Owen (*Works* 2:413) and others, is that nature and grace agree, that, e.g., belief in the Trinity is reasonable (not against reason) even though the truth is, as Owen says, "above reason," which was not exactly what Thomas intended by the language. Thanks to Michael Lynch for sending these references. I have also found the expression ("gratia non tollit naturam sed perficit") in Scharp (*Cursus Theologicus*, 292), where

They are arguing against the Anabaptist notion that grace "destroys" (*distruit* and *corrumpit*) nature. They are arguing for the essential goodness of nature as created. The Reformed associate corruption not with nature per se but with the fall and the subsequent corruption of nature. Thus they have tended to teach that, in salvation, grace *renews* human nature in the image of Christ.[9]

2. The Anabaptists (and many modern evangelicals) say that grace obliterates nature. This view regards nature as inherently evil. It expects grace utterly to replace creation altogether.

3. Pantheists equate grace with nature. In this scheme there is no distinction whatever between nature and grace.

4. Pelagians and semi-Pelagians conflate nature and grace by reducing grace to natural endowments.

The Reformed view is that, in redemption, grace renews fallen human nature.[10] There is no question whether humans are fallen and sinful. We have already seen under this under *HC* 3–4.

Humans sinned and are redeemed and renewed by grace. Humanity, however, remains humanity even in the states of grace and glory. We confess that God made us not only good, that is, without defect or lack of being, but also righteous and holy.[11] Strictly defined, the adjective *righteous* speaks to our conformity with the law. To say that God created us *holy* means that God created us without moral stain or corruption. Holiness is the antithesis of the corruption that results from sin. It is the opposite

---

he defends the abiding validity of the moral law. Like other Reformed writers, as part of his defense of second causes, he defends the category of creation (nature) against the "Catabatist" notion that grace destroys nature (e.g., 191, 210). Tuckney (*Praelectiones Theologicae*, Q. 18, p. 467) argues against the Roman doctrine of the *donum superadditum*.

9. The question of *exactly* what Thomas intended by his language is a matter of debate. Perkins, *Righteous by Design*, chap. 3, is an important contribution to this discussion.

10. E.g., Ursinus, *Commentary*, 42, 82, 93, 227; Olevianus, *De substantia* 1.1.2; 2.65; Olevianus, *Romanos Notae*, 168; Bavinck, *Reformed Dogmatics*, 4:23.

11. Ursinus, *Commentary*, 27–28.

of defilement and impurity. It also refers to being eligible to stand before God in worship.

Our first parents had a right to be in the garden. They were worthy of their estate. Further, they not only met the terms of justice, but Adam, as the first human and the federal head of all humanity, was the priest, the prophet, and the king of God's garden. He was to rule creation (symbolized by the act of naming the animals), he was to speak God's word to all creatures, especially to those who would oppose God and his kingdom, and he was to serve as the legal representative of humanity before God and to keep his holy garden clean from all potential impurity.

Since God created him in righteousness and true holiness, he had the potential to fulfill these duties.[12] Nothing about being human before the fall necessitated the fall. We say that, prior to the fall, nature (Adam as our federal head) *was* capable of the supernatural. We also confess this understanding of Scripture over against those who speculatively propose to replace the biblical and historic Reformed doctrine of merit with "maturity."[13] By proposing that Adam needed to mature, rather than to obey the "commandment of life,"[14] they imply that God created Adam deficient. Scripture never portrays his probationary condition as immaturity. We confess that Adam had the potential to love God with all his faculties and his neighbor (Eve and us) as himself. In *BC* 14, we confess that he was "capable in all things to will agreeably to the will of God."[15] He did, for some period of time, obey the law. We confess that he "willfully subjected himself to sin and consequently to death and the curse, giving ear to the words of the devil. For the commandment of life, which he had received, he transgressed." It is clear that he was not "under grace" (Rom 6:14, 15), as if he were a sinner in need of divine favor, but a righteous federal head of humanity under law.[16]

12. Ursinus, *Commentary*, 608. See the discussion under *HC* 7.

13. Clark, "Do This and Live," 243n64.

14. *BC* 14, in United Reformed Churches in North America, *Liturgical Forms and Prayers*, 166–68.

15. Dennison, *Reformed Confessions*, 2:432.

16. The Reformed, including the *BC*, generally followed Augustine against the Pelagians when he distinguished the kind of grace shown to Adam *before* the fall from that shown to him *after* the fall (Augustine, *Treatise on Rebuke and Grace*). See the discussion under *HC* 7.

The Reformed churches also confess that God created Adam with a purpose in view. The second half of this answer has not received the sort of attention that it needs. It begins with a purpose clause, "that …" or "in order that …" In other words, the Reformed churches teach that God created Adam in his holy and righteous state for a purpose: "that he might rightly know God his Creator, heartily love him and live with him in eternal blessedness, to praise and glorify him."

Centuries before the *HC* was written, the patristic and medieval church had taught that Adam was in a probationary state before the fall. Augustine (354–430) writes, "For the first covenant, which was made with the first man, is just this: 'In the day ye eat thereof, ye shall surely die.'"[17] The Vulgate rendering of Hosea 6:7 both reflects and influenced the pre-Reformation covenant theology: "For they, like Adam, transgressed the covenant there they prevaricated against me."[18] Augustine's discussion of "prevarication" confirms the influence of Hosea 6:7. The Reformation theologians and churches inherited the doctrine that Adam might have obeyed the covenant and entered into a state of final blessedness, and it appears here in the catechism (and again in catechism 9). Richard Muller explains the immediate background:

> Had Zacharias Ursinus, for example, used a vernacular Bible either during his studies in Wittenberg or during his time in the Rhenish Palatinate, he would most surely have examined Luther's version (1522–1534; revised, 1539–1541), in which Hosea 6:7 was rendered, "*Aber sie übertreten den Bund, wie Adam; darin verachten sie mich.*" Protestant vernacular Bibles of the first half of the sixteenth century echoed the Vulgate and Luther, retaining the reference to Adam and rendering *berith* not as a "pact" or "testament," but as a "covenant" or *foedus*, a shift of significance for the federal theology. Thus, Coverdale (1535)—evidencing, as in many other places, his reliance on Luther: "But even like as Adam dyd, so have they broken my covenaunt, and set me at naught." The Zürich Bible of 1524–1529 (in which the prophetic books were independent of Luther's German)

17. Augustine, *City of God* 16.27.

18. "Ipsi autem sicut Adam transgressi sunt pactum ibi praevaricati sunt in me" (*Biblia Vulgata*).

offers, "*Sy aber habend minen pundt gebrochen wie der Adam und mich übersehen.*"[19]

We know that Ursinus was thinking in these terms as he was preparing his draft of the catechism since in his Larger Catechism 10 he asks, "What does the divine law teach?" and answers, "It teaches the kind of covenant that God established with mankind in creation, howe he managed in keeping it."[20] Again, in Larger Catechism 36 he explicitly identifies the moral law with the prelapsarian covenant:

> Q. What is the difference between the law and the gospel?
> A. The law contains a covenant of nature begun by God with men in creation, that is, it is a natural sign to men, and it requires of us perfect obedience toward God. It promises eternal life to those keeping it, and threatens eternal punishment to those not keeping it. In fact, the gospel contains a covenant of grace, that is, one known not at all under nature. This covenant declares to us fulfillment of its righteousness in Christ, which the law requires, and our restoration through Christ's Spirit. To those who believe in him, it freely promises eternal life for Christ's sake.[21]

For Ursinus, the law is a covenant of works, and the gospel a covenant of grace. The correlation could not be clearer.[22]

---

19. Muller, *Post-Reformation Reformed Dogmatics*, 2:436.

20. Bierma et al., *Introduction*, 164. "10.) Quid docet lex divina? Quale in creatione foedus cum homine Deus iniverit; quo pacto se homo in eo servando gesserit" (Zacharias Ursinus, *Catechesis: summa theologiae*, in Reuter, *D. Zachariae Ursini*, 1:10).

21. Bierma et al., *Introduction*, 168–69. "Quod est discrimen Legis et Evangelii? Lex continet foedus naturale, in creatione a Deo cum hominibus initum, hoc est, natura hominibus nota est; et requirit a nobis perfectam obedientiam erga Deum, et praestantibus eam, promittit vitam aeternam, non praestantibus minatur aeternas poenas. Evangelium vero continet foedus gratiae, hoc est, minime natura notum existens: ostendit nobis ejus justitiae, quam Lex requirit, impletionem in Christo, et restitutionem in nobis per Christi Spiritum; et promittit vitam aeternam gratis propter Christum, his qui in eum credunt" (Reuter, *D. Zachariae Ursini*, 1:14).

22. Smedley, "Covenant Theology of Zacharias Ursinus," 196–230. In 1999 Lyle Bierma suggested that Ursinus matured beyond his initial interest in the covenant of works ("Law and Grace," 101). Smedley replies, however, that Ursinus continued to teach the covenant of works implicitly in his account of the nature of the law, its conditionality and demands, and in his continued use of the distinction between law and gospel. Further, he notes that as part of his exposition of *HC* 114, Ursinus appeals to the distinction between a legal covenant and a gracious covenant in terms that mirror the language in Larger Catechism 10 and 36 (Ursinus, *Commentary*, 609 [resp. obj. 4]; Clark, "Do This and Live," 257n95). Cf. Bierma, "Ursinus and the Theological Landscape," 18.

Olevianus also understood the prelapsarian probation in representative (federal), legal, covenantal terms. In his 1578 commentary on Galatians he writes:

> This obedience of the Son was superior to all the justice of the Law. For Adam also, if he willed, could have remained in the righteousness of the Law. And to the degree that the curse was owed for every sin of the elect, to the same degree he had to fulfill all righteousness without any complaint, not even all the Angels were able to do this. Therefore, this obedience of the Son was not only regarding the righteousness of the Law, such as Adam received in creation, and such as the Law required of him, but also it exceeded the righteousness of all the Angels.[23]

In his most important exposition of covenant theology, *De substantia* (1585), he makes the covenantal aspect of the probation explicit: "At the beginning of the human race that old serpent led humanity away from the word of the law, and thus from the covenant of creation by a false interpretation. ... The summary of this law shining forth in the image of God was that he love the Lord his God with all his heart ... and as a testimony of this love refrain from eating from the one tree."[24] These passages from Ursinus and Olevianus are valuable for the interpretation of the catechism because they illustrate the conceptual framework within which the theology of the catechism was formed. Remember that Ursinus was principal author of the catechism, and Olevianus was a contributor and a likely editor. It was published in the midst of a turning point in the history of Reformed theology: the Reformed articulation of the prelapsarian covenant of nature (*foedus naturale*) or, later, the "covenant of works" (*foedus operum*).[25]

That doctrine held that Adam was under a temporary legal test. If he passed, he, and we with him, would enter into eternal blessedness and glory. This is the background of the catechism's language "and live with

23. Olevianus, *Galatas Notae*, 57.

24. Olevianus, *De substantia*, 2.27; see 2.5 regarding the *foedus naturale* (natural covenant) of *naturalis obligatio*, *lex naturae*, the "law of creation" (*ius creationis*) written partly *in mentibus* and partly in Scripture; 2.8 regarding the *legale foedus* (legal covenant); and 2.13.

25. Clark, "Christ and Covenant," 408–16.

him in eternal blessedness." God did not create Adam in eternal blessedness. God created Adam under the law. It is clear from the narrative in Genesis 2:16–17: "And Yahweh Elohim commanded the man, saying, 'You may surely eat from every tree of the garden but of the tree of the knowledge of good and evil you shall not eat, because in the day that you eat thereof you shall die the death.'"

Implied in the phrases "you shall not eat" and "in the day you eat thereof" is a test. That this was a test appears in 3:1. The Evil One came to tempt the first Adam (just as he later came to tempt the last Adam—and we know certainly that probation was temporary). He questioned the truth of God's word. He suggested that God feared his creature. Would Adam obey God? Would he exercise his offices as prophet, priest, and king? Would he crush his head in the name of Yahweh? Of course, we know the answer, and so did the framers of the catechism.

One of the great tragedies of the fall is the corruption of the image of God (*imago Dei*) in humanity. In short, the image means that God created us "in true righteousness and holiness" (Eph 4:24). This is the language of *HC* 6. Ursinus explains briefly the Christian doctrine of humanity as the divine image-bearer.[26] He defines the image of God in humanity as "a mind rightly knowing the nature, will, and works of God; a will freely obeying God; and a correspondence of all the inclinations, desires, and actions, with the divine will; in a word, it is the spiritual and immortal nature of the soul, and the purity and integrity of the whole man; a perfect blessedness and joy, together with the dignity and majesty of man, in which he excels and rules over all other creatures." Here we are thinking about the image as it is per se, without considering the effect of the fall. Ursinus lists five aspects of the human person comprehended by the image:

1. the "spiritual and immortal substance of the soul together with the power of knowing and willing";
2. our natural knowledge of God, his works, and his will;
3. righteous and holy inclinations and choices;

26. Ursinus, *Commentary*, 30.

4. blessedness, glory, and delight in God without corruption; and
5. dominion over creation.

"In all these respects, our rational nature resembles, in some degree, the Creator; just as the image resemble the archetype; yet we can never be equal with God."[27]

Of course, the fall corrupted the image, and insofar as the fall brought death and condemnation, the image may be said to have been lost.[28] This is the language Ursinus uses. Nevertheless, there are "some remains and sparks of the image of God still left in man, after his fall, and which even yet continue in those who are unregenerated."[29] Humans are still body and soul, we still have free choice—not relative to God but relative to creatures—we are still able to study the arts and sciences, we retain some remnants of the moral virtues, we are still able to enjoy "temporal blessings," and we still exercise some dominion over creation.[30]

The effects of the fall on the image are nonetheless profound. After the fall, by nature, we are no longer truly righteous and holy. We are just the opposite. Our natural understanding of God and his works, relative to our salvation, is sufficient only to condemn us. Where we were originally friends with God with the potential to enter into eternal blessedness, now, by nature, we are God's enemies and rightly subject to condemnation. Where there was order there is now "a dreadful disorder and depravity of the inclinations and motions of the heart and will, from which all actual sin proceeds."[31] These truths require the church to face fearlessly the reality of sin within and outside the church. We address it in our liturgy when we read the law, confess our sins, and declare the forgiveness of sins in Christ alone, through faith alone, by grace alone. It means that we must face these realities in the counseling room, without being surprised or shocked that God's people sin. It means that we are as realistic as Paul is in Romans 7 when he describes the experience of the Christian's struggle

27. Ursinus, *Commentary*, 30.
28. Ursinus, *Commentary*, 31.
29. Ursinus, *Commentary*, 31.
30. Ursinus, *Commentary*, 31–32.
31. Ursinus, *Commentary*, 32.

with sin, and perhaps most of all, it means we must address sin plainly, graciously, but firmly from the pulpit. We ought to avoid therapeutic language and categories in favor of categories that God's word gives us, and we ought to wield those categories that we might proclaim wrath on the impenitent, deliverance to the grieving, hope to the hopeless, and peace to the penitent, believing sinner.

QUESTION 7

From where then comes this depraved nature of man?

From the fall and disobedience of our first parents, Adam and Eve, in paradise, whereby our nature became so corrupt that we are all conceived and born in sin.[32]

Here we affirm that God made us good but that, despite that goodness and righteousness, we voluntarily willed to sin. There is no flattening out the mystery of sin. The fall was disobedience, the transgression of the divine law (1 John 3:4), not a fall from grace.

Here we should qualify Ursinus's account of how the fall happened. He raises an important objection: "He who withdraws, in the time of temptation, that grace, without which it is not possible to prevent a fall, is the cause of the fall. But God withdrew, from man, his grace, in the trial through which he was called to pass, so that man could not but fall. Therefore, God was the cause of the fall of man."[33] The objection essentially blames God for the fall for withdrawing his preserving grace. Ursinus argues that premise would be true if God were obligated not to withdraw his grace and were Adam desirous of it and had Adam not rejected it.[34] He argues that God is not the cause of sin (which is the real

32. "Woher kommt denn solche verderbte Art des Menschen? Aus dem Fall und Ungehorsam unserer ersten Eltern, Adam und Eva, im Paradies, da unfere Natur also vergiftet worden, dass wir Alle in Sünden empfangen und geboren werden" (Schaff, *Creeds of the Churches*, 3:309–10). "Unde igitur existit haec naturae humanae pravitas? Ex lapsu et inobedientia primorum parentum Adami et Evae. Hinc natura nostra ita est depravata, ut omnes in peccatis concipiamur et nascamur" (Niemeyer, *Collectio Confessionum*, 431).

33. Ursinus, *Commentary*, 34–35.

34. Ursinus, *Commentary*, 25.

apologetic question here) because he withheld grace at the time of temptation. Humanity alone, he argues, is responsible for its free choice to sin.

Did Ursinus teach effectively a doctrine of superadded grace (*donum superadditum*) before the fall, and how might he have come to speak thus? The question is what Thomas actually taught. Louis Berkhof summarizes the medieval view of superadded grace thus:

> The harmony thus established is called *justitia*—natural righteousness. But even so there remained in man a natural tendency of the lower appetites and passions to rebel against the authority of the higher powers of reason and conscience. This tendency, called concupiscence, is not itself sin, but becomes sin when it is consented to by the will and passes into voluntary action. In order to enable man to hold his lower nature in check, God added to the *dona naturalia* certain *dona supernaturalia*. These included the *donum superadditum* of original righteousness (the supernatural likeness to God), which was added as a foreign gift to the original constitution of man, either immediately at the time of creation, or at some later point as a reward for the proper use of the natural powers. These supernatural gifts, including the *donum superadditum* of original righteousness, were lost by sin, but their loss did not disrupt the essential nature of man.[35]

Harrison Perkins, however, argues that, for Aquinas, the *donum superadditum*, "although distinct from human nature, was given as part of our original constitution."[36] Thus, it was effectively a *donum concreatum*, which, Todd Smedley argues, is what Ursinus was teaching.[37] That is, God created Adam with original righteousness (it was not an addition to nature). Effectively, the problem is that God did not providentially prevent the fall, which Ursinus describes in terms of grace rather than providence.[38]

The catechism, however, does not speak of grace this way, and pedagogically the church is better served by speaking the way Scottish

35. Berkhof, *Systematic Theology*, 208.

36. Perkins, *Righteous by Design*, 3.

37. Smedley, "Covenant Theology of Zacharias Ursinus," 224n84.

38. Ursinus is repeating an ancient anti-Pelagian argument. See Augustine, "Treatise on Rebuke and Grace," 484.

Reformed theologian Robert Rollock (ca. 1555–1599) does: "Therefore the ground of the covenant of works was not Christ, nor the grace of God in Christ, but the nature of man in the first creation holy and perfect, endued also with the knowledge of the law."[39] The grace of which Ursinus writes is not saving grace. In a state of righteousness and true holiness, Adam was not in need of saving grace. Like Rollock, we should be careful to observe that what we say about the first Adam has implications for what we say about the last Adam. We should not give the impression that he was in a covenant of grace. To blur the distinction between the covenant of works and the covenant of grace, or to place our Mediator Jesus in a covenant of grace, as if he were a mere believer or example for us, is verging on Pelagianism.

The law that Adam was to obey entailed, in the single symbolic command, obedience to the moral law to love with all his faculties his Creator and his neighbor as himself. When he chose to disobey, he chose to love himself, to make himself equal with God, to abuse his name, to violate the law of rest and worship—instead of sustaining the probation and entering into the rest symbolized by the creational rest, he chose to create his own rest and worship the Evil One, to lie, to steal, and covet what was not his.[40]

In the modern period, of course, we have had great trouble with the very idea of sin.[41] Frequently the idea of sin has been denied *a priori*. It is often assumed that sin cannot exist. Moderns believe in progress above all and human perfectibility. These are two of the great religious heresies of the age. Further, even within conservative Christian and Reformed circles, some suggest that we can think of relationships without considering legal or forensic categories. Some suggest that to think of God relating to humans on the basis of law, even before the fall, is inappropriate. Yet it is difficult to think of any relationship that is not predicated on law. Few relationships are as intimate as family, but even that most tender bond is premised on the law. One may love family, but if one has no legal relationship to them, they are not family. Biological and adopted children

39. Rollock, "Treatise of God's Effectual Calling," 35. See the discussion under *HC* 6.

40. Ursinus, *Commentary*, 33–34.

41. E.g., Menninger, *Whatever Became of Sin?*

are recognized by law. Marriage is recognized and governed by law. If the legal relationship is violated, then the familial relationship is violated.

So it was with Adam as the federal head of humanity, as he represented us to God. His filial relation to God was premised on his legal righteousness. When he violated that law, he also violated a relationship. Hence the catechism says, "whereby our nature became so corrupt." The idea that humans are, by nature, corrupt is heresy to modernity. One of the planks of modern religion is the essential goodness of humanity. That humans are not really very sinful was a fundamental doctrine of the Second Great Awakening and continues to undergird the theology of theological heirs of Charles Finney (1792–1875).

Pelagius (fl. ca. AD 410) notoriously denied original sin. There were others after him, whom we call semi-Pelagians, who affirmed the existence of original sin but who denied Augustine's doctrine and Paul's doctrine of total depravity. Most of the medieval church was semi-Pelagian. Most of the medieval church held that we are sinful, that we are in need of grace, but we are not so sinful that we cannot do our part to cooperate with grace. A number of medieval theologians criticized semi-Pelagianism beginning as early as the ninth century. By the fourteenth century criticism of semi-Pelagianism was widespread. There were a number of notable strongly Augustinian theologians in the late medieval church.[42]

In the Reformation, Luther rejected semi-Pelagianism in his lectures on the Psalms (1513–1515) and on Romans (1515–1516). Luther read Augustine's lectures on the Psalter and realized that Augustine's account of the theology of the Psalms was much closer to the biblical text than what he learned in university. As he worked through Romans, he was confirmed in his view that, by virtue of the fall, we are not only sinful but dead in sin and completely unable to cooperate with grace. This became Calvin's doctrine and the doctrine of the Reformed churches as reflected in the catechism. The Remonstrants (i.e., the Arminians), however, rejected the strict Pauline, Augustinian, and Reformed doctrine of original sin. They adopted something closer to the medieval, semi-Pelagian position. We

42. E.g., Thomas Bradwardine (1295–1349), Gregory of Rimini (d. 1358), John Wycliffe (ca. 1330–1384), and Johann von Staupitz (1460–1524).

see how the Reformed churches understood the Remonstrant approach to sin in Canons of Dort 3/4, rejection of errors paragraph 4:

> We reject the errors of those who teach: That the unregenerate man is not really nor utterly dead in sin, nor destitute of all powers unto spiritual good, but that he can yet hunger and thirst after righteousness and life, and offer the sacrifice of a contrite and broken spirit, which is pleasing to God. For these things are contrary to the express testimony of Scripture: "you who were dead in your trespasses and sins" (Eph 2:1, 5). And: "every intent of the thoughts of his heart was only evil continually" (Gen 6:5; 8:21). Moreover, to hunger and thirst for deliverance from misery and for life, and to offer unto God the sacrifice of a broken spirit, is peculiar to the regenerate and those that are called blessed (Ps 51:17; Mt 5:6).[43]

The Pauline doctrine and the doctrine of the Reformed churches, however, is not semi-Pelagian. We do not merely confess that, by virtue of the fall, we are sinful. We confess that we are corrupt in all our faculties such that we are "dead in sins and trespasses." Relative to salvation, we are utterly helpless. Unlike those medieval theologians and the Arminians who held that God gives a sort of prevenient grace that gives all the opportunity to be saved if we do our part, we confess no such view of grace and human ability.

Partly because of our doctrine of sin, we confess that saving grace is the free, unconditional favor of God, merited for sinners by Christ, toward those who cannot do anything toward their own awakening from spiritual death to life (regeneration) and who cannot even cooperate sufficiently with grace toward salvation. Since we have been raised with Christ (Col 2:12; 3:1), since we have been united to Christ by grace alone, through faith alone, we are being graciously conformed to Christ in sanctification. This will be addressed under the third part of the catechism.

Paul, quoting Psalm 14:1, says that, after the fall, there is not a single human who is righteous, not one (Rom 3:10). We have all sinned in Adam. Further, we all have our own actual sins. Every one of our faculties is corrupted. Paul says that the wages of sin is death. Our first instinct after the

43. Dennison, *Reformed Confessions*, 4:141.

fall is to murder (e.g., Cain), and when we build civilizations (e.g., Gen 6) they become uncivilized. Utopian dreams deny the nature and consequences of sin. Of course there will be wars and rumors of wars (Luke 21:9). After the fall, human beings are inherently wicked. The modern dogma of human progress, however, has blinded us to the reality of sin.

QUESTION 8

But are we so depraved, that we are wholly incapable of any good and prone to all evil?

Yes, unless we are born again by the Spirit of God.[44]

Large-scale evil is easy to see. Subterranean evil, if you will, is harder to see but just as bad: suburban sex parties, cheating on taxes, and stealing from the boss. It is everywhere because we are everywhere, and wherever we are, there sin is also. Pelagianism is the dominant modern religion. It tells us that we are basically good. There is real human goodness, but it is *civil* goodness, and that is a dim reflection of our original, created goodness. Because of the fall, however, that goodness is of no spiritual value. It is always corrupted. It is always at some level self-serving and does not meet the standard of God's righteousness.

The modern religion of basic human goodness not only is a lie but also assumes that we are not fallen with Adam. It rejects the very notion of a federal solidarity with Adam as unjust and federal solidarity with Christ as superfluous. Modern evangelical Christianity, as distinct from confessional Reformed theology, piety, and practice, is the child of modernity.[45] We might call it semimodern. Most evangelicals know that we are sinful, but they do not think that we are so sinful that we cannot cooperate with grace unto salvation. This idea has even infiltrated into the Reformed

44. "Sind wir aber dermassen verderbt, dass wir ganz und gar untüchtig find zu einigem Guten und geneigt zu allem Bösen? Ja: es sei denn, dass wir durch den Geist Gottes wiedergeboren werden" (Schaff *Creeds of the Churches*, 3:310). "An vero adeo corrupti sumus, ut ad bene agendum prorsus non simus idonei, et ad omne proclives? Certe: nisi per Spiritum sanctum regeneremur" (Niemeyer, *Collectio Confessionum*, 431).

45. Clark, "'Magic and Noise,'" 74–91.

churches at different times in the garb of Arminianism and now in federal vision theology. This is a basic premise of all "grace and cooperation with grace" schemes. Anyone who says that we must or can cooperate with grace toward justification denies the nature and effects of sin.

- Genesis 6:5: "Yahweh saw that the wickedness of man was great in the earth, and that every intention of the thoughts of his heart was only evil continually."
- Psalm 5:9: "Their throat is an open grave" (ESV).
- Psalm 143:2: "Enter not into judgment with your servant, for no one living is righteous before you" (ESV).
- Romans 1:18: "For the wrath of God is revealed from heaven against all ungodliness and unrighteousness of men, who by their unrighteousness suppress the truth" (ESV).
- Romans 1:21: "For although they knew God, they did not honor him as God or give thanks to him, but they became futile in their thinking, and their foolish hearts were darkened" (ESV).
- Romans 3:9–18: "For we have already charged that all, both Jews and Greeks, are under sin, as it is written:

  'None is righteous, no, not one;
  no one understands;
  no one seeks for God.
  All have turned aside; together they have become worthless;
  no one does good,
  not even one.'
  'Their throat is an open grave;
  they use their tongues to deceive.'
  'The venom of asps is under their lips.'
  'Their mouth is full of curses and bitterness.'
  'Their feet are swift to shed blood;
  in their paths are ruin and misery,

> and the way of peace they have not known.'
> 'There is no fear of God before their eyes.'" (ESV)

It is not as if Scripture is describing only mass murderers and despots. It is characterizing every one of Adam's children. Until one recognizes oneself in these verses, Jesus and his righteousness for sinners and the grace of God to sinners mean nothing. That is why the catechism is completely realistic about what sort of people we have become after the fall. We need to recapture that realism without falling into despair or cynicism, which is a denial of grace and redemption. The catechism preaches the law because it wants to drive us to Christ and his gospel, but the gospel is for sinners. God redeems sinners.

The catechism says "born again." Of course, it is referring to Jesus's dialogue with the Pharisee Nicodemus (John 3:1–21). The latter came to Christ late one night to ask him some important questions. He came at night because he could not come by day. He could not afford to be seen treating Jesus with respect or asking him serious questions. Remember that the Pharisees were the masters of the law. They had their own fence around the law to keep God's people from breaking any of the commandments of the Torah. They were known for their knowledge of and outward obedience to the law, or at least their outward obedience to their interpretation of the law.

Nicodemus understood that Jesus had real power and authority. This troubled him because his paradigm told him that, if anyone should have such things in this world, it should be the Pharisees, but they did not. He knew that they had power and influence with people but not with God. Jesus, however, had divine power and authority.

Jesus replied, "Amen, amen, I say to you, except one is born again he cannot see the kingdom of God" (John 3:3). This was not what Nicodemus expected. He expected some sort of method. He expected some rule. He expected something he could do.

Jesus said, in effect, "You cannot do anything about your spiritual condition." That is the point of saying "born again." In fact, if we read the word "again" the way it is usually used in John's writings, it is even better understood to mean "from above." It could well be that Jesus meant to imply two things at the same time. We must be born again, and that birth is "from above."

Paul says that we are dead in sins and trespasses (Eph 2:1–4). Jesus says the same thing by using the metaphor of birth. From an observational perspective, we mark the beginning of life at birth. To say "born again" or "born from above" is to say, "You are not really born, you are dead, oblivious. You lack the principle of life." Nicodemus did not understand—he was not born again, nor from above. Jesus was preaching the law. This was why he speaks below of "bearing witness." This is not an informal expression. He is invoking the legal standard of courtroom testimony. As a Pharisee, who had memorized the Torah, Nicodemus should have understood immediately what Jesus was doing, that the Lord was prosecuting Nicodemus for his sin and unbelief. He is teaching Nicodemus about his fundamental need.

The Lord said, "Amen, Amen, I say to you, unless one is born of water and the Spirit, he cannot enter the kingdom of God. That which is born of the flesh is flesh, and that which is born of the Spirit is spirit. Do not be amazed because I said to you, 'You must be born again.' The wind blows where it will, and you hear its sound, but you do not know where it comes from or where it goes. So it is with everyone who is born of the Spirit" (John 3:5–8). Nicodemus said to him, "How can these things be?" Nicodemus had physical, biological life, but he did not have spiritual life, because only God the Holy Spirit gives life and, as yet, the Spirit had not given life to him. The Spirit who hovered over the face of the deep is the Spirit who gives life to sinners. It is not we who must do anything to "be born again." It is the Spirit of God who must do. He must give life. He must regenerate.

John does not say explicitly that Nicodemus was born again, but it is certainly suggested. Those associated with the care of Jesus's body were those who loved him. The rest of the Pharisees were nowhere to be seen, but Nicodemus was there. Perhaps it was because the Spirit had done his mysterious work?

The fall destroyed the freedom of the human will (*de libero arbitrio*) to choose the good. It is an essentially modern fiction, of course, that humans can will the contrary to God.[46] Nevertheless, we the Reformed agree with Bernard of Clairvaux and Aquinas that humans do make free

---

46. Ursinus, *Commentary*, 58–59.

choices insofar as they choose according to their nature without external coercion.[47] Ursinus writes,

> The term freedom, or liberty, sometimes signifies a relation, power or right, be it the ordering or disposing of a person or thing, made by the will of a certain person, or by nature, for the purpose of acting with one's own choice, or from fear according to just laws, or the order which is in harmony with the nature of man; for the purpose of enjoying those benefits which are fit and proper for us, without any prohibition and restraint; and for the purpose of being relieved from enduring the wants and burdens which are not peculiar to our nature.[48]

With Ursinus (and Luther and Calvin), however, we differ fundamentally on whether sinners can cooperate with grace and accumulate merit (condign or congruent) and the like. Whatever free choices we make are comprehended within the providence of God, with which he acts by concursus to establish his providence.[49]

Relative to spiritual and saving good, Luther spoke for all the magisterial Protestants when he declared at the Heidelberg Disputation (thesis 13) in 1518, "'Free will' after the fall, is nothing but a word, and as long as it is 'doing what is within it' it is committing deadly sin."[50] The Reformed stood with Luther on the bondage of the will (sometimes against the Lutheran orthodox as, e.g., at the Colloquy of Montbeilard, 1580).[51]

Ursinus's account of the degrees of the freedom of the will was essentially Bernard's. There is one degree of freedom before the fall, another after, still another in the state of grace, and finally complete freedom of the will in glory.[52]

This is the appropriate place to discuss briefly the distinction between common and special grace and the restraining mercies of the Lord. The Reformed theologians in the classical period distinguished between *gratia*

---

47. McGinn, *On Grace and Free Choice*; *ST* 1a-2ae 6.1, 4.

48. Ursinus, *Commentary*, 57; McGinn, *On Grace and Free Choice*, 61.

49. Olevian, *Firm Foundation*, 24.

50. *LW* 31:39.

51. See *LW* 33 for an English translation.

52. Ursinus, *Commentary*, 62–63.

communis (common grace) and *gratia particularis* (special grace).[53] In the Second Helvetic Confession (1566), the Swiss Reformed churches confessed, "Wherefore there is some intelligence [*intelligentia ... non est nulla*] of earthly things in fallen man. For, out of his mercy, God left behind [*reliquit*] natural ability, though far distant from what it was before the fall. He commanded us to develop our natural ability while he adds gifts and progress [*profectum*] and it is manifest that we accomplish nothing in the arts without his blessing."[54] William Perkins (1558–1602) argues that there is a "twofold" grace at work in the world, "renewing and restraining." The latter is "that which bridles and restrains the corruption of men's hearts from breaking forth into outward actions, for the common good, that societies may be preserved and one man may live orderly with another."[55] This distinction found expression at the Synod of Dort under the third/fourth heads of doctrine.[56]

53. Berkhof, *Systematic Theology*, 434; Bavinck, *Reformed Dogmatics*, 1:319–20.

54. Translation mine; see Müller, *Die Bekenntnisschriften*, 180; Kuiper, *Calvin on Common Grace*.

55. Perkins, *Cases of Conscience*, 113 [spelling modernized].

56. Dennison, *Reformed Confessions*, 4:135–36.

Question 9

Does not God then do injustice to man by requiring of him in his Law that which he cannot perform?

Question 10

Will God suffer such disobedience and apostasy to go unpunished?

Question 11

Is then God not also merciful?

Lord's Day 4

QUESTION 9

Does not God then do injustice to man by requiring of him in his Law that which he cannot perform?

No, for God so made man that he could perform it, but man, through the instigation of the devil, by willful disobedience deprived himself and all his posterity of those divine gifts.[1]

Scripture teaches that God created us good. We need to repeat this truth because it has been denied so widely and often that one suspects that most Christians, whether evangelical, Roman, or Orthodox, do not really believe that God created us good. Rome teaches and many evangelicals believe that we were in some way defective from the beginning and that the fall happened because we were defective. Of course, Scripture says the opposite: "And Elohim saw that it was good" (Gen 1:31).[2]

Is God unrighteous for demanding of fallen humans, who cannot now perform it, the same obedience that he demanded of them before the fall, when they could actually do it? The answer is no.[3] God is just in his demand of sinners that they obey because he created them with the ability to obey. That they cannot now obey is not God's fault. He has not changed. His law has not changed. His righteousness has not changed. Indeed, in the nature of things, it cannot change, God being who and what he is. There is nothing wrong with God's standard. As Ursinus explains, "If man, by his own fault and free will, cast away this ability with which he was endowed, and brought himself into a state in which he can no longer render full obedience to the divine law, God has not for this reason lost his right to exact the obedience which man is in duty bound to render him."[4]

1. "Thut denn Gott dem Menschen nicht Unrecht, dass er in seinem Gesetz von ihm fordert, was er nicht thun kann? Nein: denn Gott hat den Menschen also erschaffen, dass er es Konnte thun. Der Mensch aber hat sich und alle seine Nachkommen, aus Anstiftung des Teufels, durch muthwilligen Ungehorsam derselbigen Gaben beraubet" (Schaff, *Creeds of the Churches*, 3:310). "An non igitur Deus homini iniuriam facit, qui ab eo in lege sua flagitat, quae praestare non queat? Minime. Nam Deus hominem talem condiderat, ut ea praestare posset: verum homo, impulsore Diabolo, sua ipsius contumacia, se et omnem posteritatem divinis illis donis orbavit" (Niemeyer, *Collectio Confessionum*, 431–32).

2. *CCC* §299 affirms the essential goodness of creation, but as is often the case, what Rome affirms with one hand, she takes away with the other (e.g., her understanding of nature and grace).

3. Ursinus, *Commentary*, 66.

4. Ursinus, *Commentary*, 66.

Part of the problem is that we do not understand the word *righteous* any longer. It means "just, without legal flaw, in perfect accordance with the divine law." Of course, as fallen and corrupt sinners, we think that *we* should be the standard of righteousness. We demand of God that he change his standard to conform to us. The main difficulty is that God is having none of it. Our sin is not, as it were, his problem. It is our problem. He does not have to conform to our changing standards and expectation; we must conform to his immutable, perfect, holy, and righteous law. Its demand is relentless: "Perform." "Do." "Obey." "Love God and neighbor flawlessly and perpetually or die." "The day you eat thereof you shall surely die" (Gen 2:17). "Cursed is everyone who does not continue to do everything written in the book of the law" (Deut 27:26). "Holy, Holy, Holy is the Lord of Hosts" (Isa 6:3).

One corollary to these facts is that the catechism assumes and clearly implies that before the fall we were under the law. The catechism clearly says that God made us so that we could obey it. We did not obey it, but we could and, presumably for an indeterminate period of time, we did obey it. Only after the fall, when we had sinned, may we be said to be under grace.

It is difficult to get modern people to imagine that we were once good but are now by nature bad. It is exceedingly difficult to get late moderns to imagine that we are all by nature under a just and relentless law. The late modern person assumes that there is no universal law that could possibly bind all persons, in all times, without exception. It is of the essence of late modernity to imagine that we are our own lawgivers. This recognition helps us to understand in part why many are so resistant to the notion of a probationary, prelapsarian covenant. Opposition to this covenant is often couched in terms of an answer to critics of the covenant of works. Barthians reject the covenant of works on several grounds, chief among them the *a priori* conviction that there could not have been any such arrangement between God and humanity. Others, influenced by Barth, reject the covenant of works because they want to begin with grace and not law. They do this as a response to the criticism that to begin with the covenant of works is "legalistic." It is true that the prelapsarian covenant of works is a legal covenant. We were under God's holy law. We had to keep it. Our status, our life, and our entrance into eschatological glory were contingent on lawkeeping. The future of the human race was conditioned on our lawkeeping. If we kept the law, God would approve of us. If we failed to keep the law, God would disapprove of us, and that is a bad thing. That is not to say, however, that the covenant of works was *legalistic*. This criticism assumes Barth's denial of the covenant of works, his rejection of the distinction between law and gospel, and his confusion of the pre- and postlapsarian covenants.[5]

It is difficult to see how one can coherently resist a prelapsarian covenant of works but accept *other* strictly legal arrangements. If we run a red light and get pulled over, we cannot complain. We broke the law. Is it legalistic for the officer to write a ticket? We know we did it, and we know we are guilty. Theft is still wrong. Is a shopkeeper legalistic for prosecuting a thief? New employees are routinely put on probation for a time. Reflections of the covenant of works are all around us because they reflect the creational order.

The sinless have nothing to fear from the law (1 Tim 1:9).[6] The law is their friend and does not accuse them. It is the sinner and the sinful who should fear the law. Adam, before the fall, was neither a sinner nor sinful. Jesus, born of a virgin, was neither a sinner nor sinful. They were righteous and able to keep the law. Jesus, the second Adam, *did* keep the law. He was under a covenant of works for us.

Bear in mind our definition of "sin": "any want of conformity unto or transgression of the law of God."[7] That is significant. The Roman Catholic Church defines the fall as a fall from grace. We do not. We confess that the fall was a violation of the law. The fall was not the fault of the law. The law is good, holy, and just (Rom 7:12). God made us to keep the law. We must keep it, and it demands reparations from those who do not keep it.

In this light, we can see why it is so wonderful to speak of a covenant of grace. That covenant announces that someone else has kept the law for us (*pro nobis*), has satisfied its demands, has paid the penalty for our lawbreaking for us as our substitute. This is the good news: Christ the lawkeeper and penalty payer has come. This is what it means for Paul to call him the "last Adam" (1 Cor 15:45). He is the head of all who believe

---

5. Clark, "Letter and Spirit," 350–51; Barth, *Church Dogmatics*, vol. 4.1, *The Doctrine of God*, 58–66.

6. Ames, *Sketch of the Christian's Catechism*, 28–29.

7. *WSC* 14 (Dennison, *Reformed Confessions*, 4:355).

(Rom 5:12–21). By his one act of obedience, we who believe, who are united to Christ by grace alone, through faith alone, are made right again with God for all time.

If we begin with a covenant of grace, however pious it may sound, we actually do a great disservice to Adam and to Christ. We diminish Christ's work for us. If we say Christ was under a covenant of grace, we deny his obedience for us. Grace by definition means that Christ did not really fulfill the terms of justice. How is that not blasphemy? To suggest that Adam was under grace would be to deny his intrinsic, perfect righteousness and holiness.

Just as the last Adam was under law for us, so the first Adam, and we in him, were under law. Only against this background can we understand and appreciate what it means to speak of grace. If the first covenant was gracious and we are under such a covenant, then grace is no longer grace, and law is no longer law, and the good news is no longer the good news. One understands the impulse to make the faith attractive, but giving up the covenant of works is too high a price to pay. As Cornelius Plantinga says about the doctrine of the Trinity, it is attached to the gears and pulleys of the Christian faith.[8]

Question 10

Will God suffer such disobedience and apostasy to go unpunished?

By no means, but He is terribly displeased with our inborn as well as our actual sins, and will punish them in just judgment in time and eternity, as he has declared: "Cursed is every one that continues not in all things which are written in the book of the Law to do them."[9]

8. Plantinga, "Threeness/Oneness Problem," 37–53.

9. "Will Gott solchen Ungehorsam und Abfall ungestraft lassen hingehen? Mit nichten: sondern Er zürnet schreklich, beides über angeborne und wirkliche Sünden, und will sie aus gerechtem Urtheil zeitlich und ewig strafen, wie Er gesprochen hat: Verflucht sei jedermann, der nicht bleibet in allem dem, das geschrieben stehet im Buch des Gesetzes, dass er's thue" (Schaff, *Creeds of the Churches*, 3:310). "Num Deus hanc contumaciam et defectionem hominis dimittit impunitam? Imo vero horrendis modis irascitur, tum ob innata nobis peccata, tum ob ea, quae ipsi committimus, eaque iustissimo iusdicio praesentibus et aeternis suppliciis punit, quemadmodum ipse pronunciat: Maledictus

The first thing the Evil One did was to raise doubts about this very question, "Has God really said?" (Gen 3:1). Is the law really abiding, eternal, and immutable, or is the law situationally determined? The Adversary offered to Adam an alternate explanation of reality, a story that included the fulfillment of innate human potential for deification and a story that implied that God is not really just—and in fact suggested that God was positively unjust for seeking to suppress that innate potential divinity by means of the law.

To reinforce his law and to signal how he regards disobedience, the Lord instituted the strongest possible punishment for disobedience: "The day you eat thereof, you shall surely die" (Gen 2:17). Looking back, of course, it all seems so clear. It is sure that no humans, no image-bearers, died before the fall. It was Pelagius and his followers who taught that Adam would have died even without the fall.[10] Thus, the idea of human mortality must have been strange to Adam, whose office before the face of God was to dispatch the Liar (and father of lies) immediately. He did not. As it turned out, that was only one of a complex of sins (Jas 1:13–15).

It is no small thing that God instituted the death penalty for sin. The apostle Paul understood the consequences and reflects on it when he says, "The wages of sin is death" (Rom 6:23). The moment Adam chose to enter into covenant with Satan, he died spiritually. Now God was no longer his friend (Jas 2:23; 4:4).[11] When God the Son came looking for Adam, it was not in friendship but in judgment, and Adam knew it. Ridiculously, he attempted to hide himself from the omniscient ruler of the universe.[12] This first futile postlapsarian act is immediate and *prima facie* evidence of the effect of the fall on the human intellect. The moment he sinned, he began to decay. Instead of passing the test and entering into glory and life, he failed the test and entered into condemnation and corruption.

Tragically, when he did so, he did not act as a private person. Adam had a public, official role to perform as the representative of all humanity.

---

omnis qui non permanet in omnibus quae scripta sunt in libro legis, ut ea faciat" (Niemeyer, *Collectio Confessionum*, 432).

10. Warfield, *Two Studies in the History*, 12.

11. On covenant and friendship, see Cocceius, *Doctrine of the Covenant*, 21–24, 28.

12. *BC* 17, 23 (Dennison, *Reformed Confessions*, 4:434, 437).

He was created good (Col 3:10), in the image of his Creator. He was, as Augustine said, "able to sin, able not to sin" (*posse peccare, posse non peccare*).[13]

Whatever Adam did, he would do for all of us, and thus, what he did, we did. Adam was not alone in the garden. There is another, literal, sense in which he was not alone. Besides his wife, there was another creature in the garden: the Evil One. According to the Genesis narrative, as the catechism summarizes it, he instigated sin. He tried or tempted Adam. It was the image-bearer's vocation to resist the tempter and to conquer him, to slay him out of devotion to the Lord. The curse for breaking the covenant of works was death. The Evil One was manifestly a liar and the father of sin (John 8:44). He was intent on seducing Eve, and through her Adam, into breaking the covenant (1 Tim 2:13–14). He proposed an alternative to the commandment of life: a covenant of equality with God. Whereas the Lord had promised glorification on condition of obedience to God, the Evil one promised deification on condition of obedience to himself. Adam had a clear, unequivocal choice. He chose equality with God, and with that choice, he also chose death.

The sin he committed was the original sin. When he sinned, he became a sinner. Since, however, we are all Adam's children, it is not that we become sinners when we sin (that was the error of Pelagius). Rather, we sin because, in Adam, we are all sinners (Rom 5:12–21). We all have inborn sin. As a consequence of that inborn sin, we all commit actual sin. Scripture reflects on this relationship in Psalm 51:5: "Behold, I was brought forth in iniquity, and in sin did my mother conceive me" (ESV). David confesses his sin, but he also confesses his sinfulness. When he says that he was conceived in sin, he is not reflecting on the act of procreation but rather on the results of the fall. Adam's children are all sinful from the beginning of our existence. This is the teaching of Romans 5:12. Through Adam's sin, "death spread to all men, because all sinned."

Outside Christ, we face temporal and eternal punishment. Paul is explicit about the devastating effects and the overwhelming evidence of sin. Some would explain away sin by appealing to evolutionary biology, but that is just a convenient dodge, a way of making sin seem normal, a way to

13. B. B. Warfield, "Introductory Essay on Augustin and the Pelagian Controversy" (*NPNF* 1/5:485).

relieve ourselves of responsibility for our choices and their consequences. Sin is abnormal. That is why we experience the sting of death. The pain and grief associated with death are no mere evolutionary response. The scriptural explanation does, however, account for human experience. We grieve because death was the consequence of sin. This is why Hebrews 9:27 relates our death and the coming judgment to the death of Christ.

The death that followed sin is a curse. It is repeated in the history of redemption. Deuteronomy 27:26 says, "Cursed be anyone who does not confirm the words of this law by doing them.' And all the people shall say, 'Amen'" (ESV). The very curse of Genesis 2:17 is repeated and reaffirmed in the context of the Israelite national covenant. Not that Israel's justification before God or even her salvation from sin and death is conditioned on works, but the Sinaitic law restates the law given to Adam. It served to remind Israel corporately of the righteousness of God's law, of the greatness of their sin and misery, and the need for a substitute lawkeeper. This is just how the apostle Paul understands this passage in Galatians 3:10. He quotes this same passage and adds, "Now it is evident that no one is justified before God by the law, for 'The righteous shall live by faith'" (Gal 3:11 ESV).

Whether in the first covenant, in the Mosaic covenant, or now, the wages of sin is death. The law is the standard of righteousness. It is extrinsic, objective, and unyielding. It does not care about our feelings. The penalty is equally relentless. That is why the gospel must be equally objective and extrinsic and why Paul says that "the righteous shall live by faith" (Rom 3:28). Faith is, as we confess in *BC* 22, *the* "instrument" by which we come in possession of the righteousness that has satisfied the law of God.[14]

One of the more difficult doctrines for the modern mind to accept is the doctrine of divine punishment. The modernist creed has three or four points, one of which is universalism, the doctrine that all are saved. It is axiomatic for moderns that God may not distinguish between human beings. It is true that God is no respecter of persons (Acts 10:34), meaning that God does not favor the rich over the poor, that he does not favor ethnic groups as such, and so on. The modernist creed, however, holds much more than that. It teaches that God cannot distinguish or treat one

14. Schaff, *Creeds of the Churches*, 3:408.

human being differently from another. Since this is axiomatic, it is a nearly universal assumption among contemporary evangelicals and especially among liberal Christians.

A closely related corollary to the modern rejection of any idea of reprobation is the modern rejection of the doctrine of hell and punishment. Moderns routinely announce that it is impossible to believe in a God who would send people to hell. Of course, they do not accept the essential premise of the doctrine of hell and punishment: that God alone is righteous and that fallen human beings deserve to be punished. Some have argued that the very idea of a hell of eternal punishment is a sub-biblical notion, pagan in origin, that gradually found acceptance in Christian theology. Thus, the argument goes, to reject the doctrine of hell is an act of reformation. In its place they propose the doctrine of annihilation.

There is considerable biblical evidence, however, for the doctrine of eternal punishment (hell). Our Lord's teaching (Matt 5:22) that whoever says "You fool" will "be liable to the Gehenna of Fire" (γέενναν τοῦ πυρός) hardly makes sense if "Gehenna" refers to annihilation. The same is true of Matthew 5:30. The contrast is between losing a body part temporarily and eternal punishment (εἰς γέενναν). The parallel in Mark 9:43 makes this clear with the addition of the expression "unquenchable fire" (τὸ πῦρ τὸ ἄσβεστον). The force of the "judgment of hell" (κρίσεως τῆς γεέννης; Matt 23:33) is not that conscious existence shall end but that it shall continue endlessly. The adjective "unquenchable" loses its force if annihilation is in view. The background for this imagery is Isaiah 66:24, "And they shall go out and look on the dead bodies of the men who have rebelled against me. For their worm shall not die, their fire shall not be quenched, and they shall be an abhorrence to all flesh" (ESV). Second Peter 2:4 says that, when the angels sinned, they were "with chains of gloom" (σειραῖς ζόφου), they were "cast into Tartarus" (Τάρταρος), where they are being "kept for judgment" (κρίσιν τηρουμένους). Aeschylus, Hesiod, and Homer use *Tartarus* to refer to "the nether world."[15]

The premodern church, by contrast, had relatively less difficulty with this doctrine because they accepted the doctrines of divine righteousness

15. Liddell, Scott, and Jones, *Greek-English Lexicon*, s.v. "Tartarus." Gehenna, of course, was likely a reference to a valley south of Jerusalem notorious as a pagan sacrificial site. See Myers, *Eerdmans Bible Dictionary*, 478.

and human sinfulness. Ursinus defines hell quite simply: "It is the terrifying awareness of divine wrath and judgment and the perpetual torment of soul and body."[16] In the modern period, after the Enlightenment, the proportions of people who accepted and rejected these doctrines were reversed. There were probably always some who rejected the doctrines of sin, hell, and punishment. That number certainly grew during the Renaissance, and a series of theologically deviant movements in the sixteenth century fueled it. All those who reject the doctrines of sin, punishment, and hell have one thing in common: rationalism. Whatever Scripture *seems* to say, the rationalist *knows* that it could not possibly be so because the rationalist knows what justice can be even before coming to Scripture. In contrast, the Christian begins with divine revelation. As the Enlightenment rationalism began to infiltrate into the church, some openly articulated the rationalist ground for rejecting reprobation, punishment, and hell. Liberals accepted that rationalist account but tried to reshape Christianity along more "Enlightened" lines without saying openly what they were doing.[17]

We should not assume, however, that our premodern forefathers had an easy time with the doctrines of reprobation, punishment, and hell. In his commentary on this question, Ursinus hits two chords: (1) he regards the reality of punishment and hell as an "evil," and (2) he affirms them anyway because he (and we with him) understands them to be biblical truths (not mere medieval fancies) and theological consequences of our doctrine of the righteousness and holiness of God and our doctrine of sin.[18] The difference between Ursinus and moderns is that he regarded Scripture as the final authority for faith and life, whereas moderns assume that we are the *principium cognoscendi* ("the beginning of knowing") and the final authority. He believed in sin. By and large, except when discussing corporate entities, moderns do not. He believed in fixed law and righteousness. Moderns do not. He feared God. Moderns do not. They will not have a god they must fear.

16. Ursinus, "*Summa theologiae*," 28; Bierma et al., *Introduction*, 167.

17. Machen, *Christianity and Liberalism*.

18. Ursinus, *Commentary*, 68–69.

Eternal punishment is one thing, but what about temporal punishment? Does God punish sin and sinners in this life? Yes and no. One of the great laments of the psalms is, "Why do the wicked prosper?" Psalm 73 says that the "arrogant" and the "wicked ... have no pangs until death; their bodies are fat and sleek. They are not in trouble as others are; they are not stricken like the rest of mankind" (Ps 73:3b–5 ESV). If the law says, "Do this and live," and "Sin and die," then it would seem that justice requires that those who are wicked in this life should suffer proportionately and that those who are righteous in the life should prosper accordingly. Experience, history, and Scripture all testify to the contrary, however. Indeed, as the psalmist (Asaph) observes, sometimes the corollary seems to be turned on its head. Sometimes the wicked are inordinately prosperous! "Their eyes swell out through fatness" (v. 7 ESV). The dissonance between what is and what should can be so great, in this world, as to make people say, "How can God know? Is there knowledge in the Most High?" (v. 11 ESV). Asaph wrestled with this question almost to despair. He testifies: "But when I thought how to understand this, it seemed to me a wearisome task" (v. 16a ESV). He was almost to despair, but not quite. It was a "wearisome task" until he "went into the sanctuary of God," where he "discerned their end" (v. 17b ESV).

The unbelieving (both inside and outside the covenant community) think that all is well. Indeed, sometimes God does prosper them materially. The mistake we make is how we evaluate blessing and curse. That is what Asaph discovered in the sanctuary. He discovered the true nature of blessing and curse after the fall and relative to God. What seems to the unregenerate, and sometimes to us in our unreflective moments, "blessing" is not really that at all. All that prosperity is really a sort of judgment. Asaph says that God has actually "set them in slippery places" (v. 18 ESV). Everything we reckon as a sign of divine blessing can be "destroyed in a moment, swept away utterly by terrors!" Ask Job. Ask those who were taken away in the captivity. Ask those who were in Palestine when Antiochus invaded (168/67 BC) or when Titus arrived (AD 70).

The problem is not that God is unjust but that we are "brutish and ignorant" (Ps 73:22 ESV). Unbelievers and hypocrites (in and out of the congregation) may have much in this life, but God guides his people in this life with his counsel, and in the next he receives them "to glory" (v. 24).

When we put the question of God's justice in its eschatological perspective, we can say with Asaph, "Whom have I in heaven but you? And there is nothing on earth that I desire besides you. My flesh and my heart may fail, but God is the strength of my heart and my portion forever. For behold, those who are far from you shall perish; you put an end to everyone who is unfaithful to you. But for me it is good to be near God; I have made the Lord God my refuge, that I may tell of all your works" (vv. 25–28 ESV).

Under the typological (old) covenant, under Moses and David, there was a general sort of correlation of earthly prosperity in the land and national, outward, obedience. When they were disobedient, eventually, the national, typological church was taken into captivity. All of that was nothing more than a giant sermon illustration pointing to the coming of the truly and completely obedient Son (Heb 3:5–6), the true Israel of God (Matt 2:15). God graciously granted to Asaph (and to others, we trust) insight into the true nature of things, beyond the typological national covenant.

The reality is that those who are not completely righteous are in jeopardy of eternal punishment (not annihilation), but they also suffer temporal punishment. Ursinus addresses this very issue in his lecture on this question. The catechism says that all sins are punished, but it seems that the wicked prosper; therefore, how can we say that all sins are punished? He replies:

> They will at length be punished: yea they are even in this life punished, 1. In the conscience, by whose stings the wicked are tortured. 2. Also, in those things which they use with the greatest eagerness and delight; and the less they know, and acknowledge themselves to be punished, so much the heavier it is. 3. They are also often afflicted with other grievous punishments. And yet their punishment will be still more dreadful in the life to come, where it will be everlasting death.[19]

The temporal punishments the wicked suffer are only the beginning of what is to come. Even though it "consists of several parts," these are two stages of what Ursinus calls "one punishment." "Present punishment is but the beginning of everlasting punishment." (As an aside, he makes this point in response to the argument that it would be unjust for God to

19. Ursinus, *Commentary*, 68.

punish sin twice. His answer is that God does not punish sin twice! This is interesting because this is one of the traditional objections to the doctrine of the imputation of active obedience.)

What about the sufferings of the righteous, that is, of those to whom God has imputed Christ's righteousness? If their sins have been punished in Christ's active suffering on their behalf, why does God continue to punish them? Ursinus helps us here again. The "afflictions" believers suffer in this life are not to be regarded as punishments for sin, quid pro quo, but as "the chastisement of a father, sent for the purpose of humbling them. Hence it becomes necessary for us."[20] Of course, this is exactly what Hebrews 12:4–7 says.

In the meantime, because we are not national Israel, because we are not charged with the literal destruction of God's enemies, we ought not to long for it. We ought to pray that God would show the same mercy to them that he has shown to us who believe, who also, by virtue of the fall and of our sin, deserve nothing but temporal and eternal punishment.

Question 11

Is then God not also merciful?

God is indeed merciful, but he is likewise just; his justice therefore requires that sin that is committed against the most high majesty of God, be also punished with extreme, that is, with everlasting punishment both of body and soul.[21]

When faced with the question of divine wrath, the catechism has the same response we do: My, that seems harsh. What about mercy? It is odd how sinners, who so often sit in judgment over God and humanity,

20. Ursinus, *Commentary*, 68.

21. "Ist denn Gott nicht auch barmherzig? Gott ist wohl barmherzig, Er ist aber auch gerecht. Derhalben erfordert seine Gerechtigkeit, dass die Sünde, welche wider die allerhöchste Majestät Gottes begangen ist, auch mit der höchsten, das ist, der ewigen Strafe, an Leib und Seele gestraft werde" (Schaff, *Creeds of the Churches*, 3:311). "An non igitur Deus etiam est misericors? Est ille quidem misericors, verum ita ut etiam sit iustus. qua propter postulat eius iustitia, quod adversus summam Dei maiestatem commissum est, id quoque ut summis, hoc est, sempiternis cum animi tum corporis suppliciis luatur" (Niemeyer, *Collectio Confessionum*, 432).

suddenly become interested in mercy when faced with relentless justice. As Ursinus reminds us, "God is exceedingly merciful in such a way, that he is also exceedingly just. Hence he will exercise his mercy in such a manner as not to do any violence to his justice."[22]

To answer the question, the catechism turns to the divine attributes. This is an important move in two ways. First, it says something about how Reformed theology works and how we understand Scripture. God has a nature. There are things that are true of God in perpetuity. We can say true things about God that were true a million years ago, that are true today, and that will be true forever. Unlike the god of the Enlightenment movements (who is either wholly hidden from us or wholly identified with the world) and unlike the god of late modernity (who is the creation of our subjectivity; he/she/it is what we perceive, wish, hope him/her/it to be), the God of Scripture simply is. The god of open theism might be, if we will cooperate. The god of process theism is becoming. The god of late modernity is contingent. In contrast to the Reformed faith, which denies that God has "parts or passions,"[23] the god of late modernity suffers and changes. The god of late modernity is complex, that is, has parts. It is never fully realized and always contingent. He/she/it needs us. The god of late modernity is more like Woody Allen than it is like the Yahweh of Holy Scripture.

The Reformed faith is neither Enlightened (rationalist or empiricist) nor late modern (subjectivist). The Reformed faith seeks to be biblical, and Scripture does reveal God to be merciful to sinners. He reveals himself as "showing mercy to a thousand generations" (Exod 20:6). Scripture says his name (i.e., who he is) is "compassionate, gracious, slow to anger" (Exod 34:6–7). God does relent from his judgments and justice, but that relenting, that restraint of wrath, that not giving to the unjust what they deserve, is premised on the satisfaction of justice. Where that is not present, mercy is not possible. However it may seem to us, mercy is not arbitrary, because the divine justice is not arbitrary, nor is it grounded in something extrinsic to God. This is the great mistake of all rationalist

22. Ursinus, *Commentary*, 69.

23. This is the language of WCF 2.1. See Westminster Assembly, *Humble Advice of the Assembly*, 7. The English noun *passion* is derived from the Latin *patior*, "to suffer." It does not mean that God is utterly without feeling but that he does not become less than he is. He is immutable.

theologies. They want to try to save God from the charge of being arbitrary by showing how some standard outside God can justify his acts. That seems satisfactory until we realize that if God must give account to some standard of justice that binds him and us, then that standard must itself be God. The cost of rescuing God from the charge of being arbitrary is to lose God himself.

The standard to which God answers is himself, his own nature. He never acts contrary to it, and he always acts according to it. It is true that we do not know God's justice exhaustively, because we do not know God exhaustively. We only know him as he reveals himself to us. We can correlate what he does with what he has revealed to us, but when our correlation fails, we must submit to God and to his word. We can and may never stand in judgment over God because such an attempt presumes that we know more about God than he knows about himself. Just to say these words shows how foolish such thinking is.

God is his divine attributes. He is just and he is merciful. His justice is merciful and his mercy is just. They meet perfectly in him. Yes, God is merciful, but he is equally just. Scripture says, "I am a jealous God" (Exod 20:5). "He does not leave the guilty unpunished" (Exod 34:7). In other words, God's definition of justice is himself. We may live in a subjectivist time, but God does not care. He did not submit to the demands of the Enlightenment that he justify himself, and he will not submit to the demands of the post-Enlightenment that he justify himself. Rather, we must be justified by him. God is "just and the justifier of the one who has faith in Jesus" (Rom 3:26 ESV).

God is merciful, but his justice must be satisfied. Outside that satisfaction there is no mercy. He has provided that satisfaction of his justice. Christ Jesus satisfied the justice of God. He did righteousness. He loved God and neighbor. He walked humbly with his God (Mic 6:8). We did not. He obeyed for us. His obedience is imputed to all who trust in him and in his finished work for sinners.

"God is not mocked" (Gal 6:7). If one will not trust in Jesus the satisfier of God's justice, then one must satisfy the justice of God oneself. Is it unjust? Did God sin? Did God rebel? Was it God or we who cursed our neighbor this morning? Was it God or we who committed adultery (with eyes and heart)? Was it God or we who stole from the cash register? Was it God or we who coveted our neighbor's new car? God gave us life; he gave us breath. Despite our sin and rebellion, he has provided for us generously—and how do we thank him, by nature, as sinners? By demanding that he do more, that he meet our corrupted standards.

We are quick to dispense with the justice of God because it does not fit our paradigm. "It is all good," we say. Indeed, it is not. We are not all good. God is good (Mark 10:18), and we are not, and therein lies the problem. "All is well" is what they said as the rain began to fall "in the world that then was" (2 Pet 3:6). They mocked Noah, right up to the time that they could swim no longer as the water began to cause the ark to float. Truth be told they, like we, probably shook their fists at God to the last, cursing him for not meeting their standard of justice even as he was in the act of holding them to his.

We confess that there is an everlasting punishment for sin. This is historic Christian teaching firmly grounded in Scripture.[24] It is not, as some have suggested, a medieval invention, but in view of a shift among some British and American evangelicals since the late twentieth century, it needs to be restated and defended briefly.[25] The modern controversy revolves around whether those outside Christ endure a conscious, eternal punishment or whether they are annihilated. Proponents of annihilationism argue that when our Lord says "destruction" (ἀπώλειαν) in Matthew 7:13, or when Paul uses it in Romans 9:22 and 2 Thessalonians 1:9, it means literally that. The orthodox response is to observe when our Lord speaks of a "Gehenna of fire" (γέενναν τοῦ πυρός) in Matthew 5:22 and 18:9, it assumes an endless punishment. When our Lord in Matthew 10:28 says "destroy" (ἀπολέσαι), it is a figure of speech. Christ qualifies what he means by "Gehenna" (Mark 9:43) when he adds, "unto the unquenchable fire" (εἰς τὸ πῦρ τὸ ἄσβεστον). Second Peter 2:4 assumes a conscious, eternal punishment since those awaiting final judgment are kept in "chains of gloomy darkness" (ESV). There is no indication that those awaiting judgment are annihilated. Then, of course, there is the parable of the rich man (*Dives*) and Lazarus (Luke 16:19–30). The assumption of the parable is that the rich man is conscious and suffering. He is in hell.

24. Peterson, *Hell on Trial*.

25. E.g., Wenham, *Easter Enigma*; Edwards and Stott, *Evangelical Essentials*.

He wants mitigation, but Jesus refuses him. Further, when he begs leave to warn his family about the reality of hell, Jesus refuses on the ground that the law and the gospel are sufficiently clear in the Hebrew Scriptures.

This question touches our understanding of the substitutionary work of Christ for his people. We confess that he suffered the pains and tortures of hell for us. Annihilation significantly weakens that doctrine since the intent of our Lord's active suffering on our behalf was to bear, in our place, the eternal punishment that we deserve. The doctrine of annihilation does not account for our Lord's suffering on our behalf.

II

The Second Part of the Catechism

Question 12

Since then by the righteous judgment of God we deserve temporal and eternal punishment, how may we escape this punishment and be again received into favor?

Question 13

Can we ourselves make this satisfaction?

Question 14

Can any mere creature make satisfaction for us?

Question 15

What kind of a mediator and redeemer then must we seek?

Lord's Day 5

QUESTION 12

Since then by the righteous judgment of God we deserve temporal and eternal punishment, how may we escape this punishment and be again received into favor?

God wills that his justice be satisfied; therefore we must make full satisfaction to the same, either by ourselves or by another.[1]

The catechism begins the second section with the conviction that God's righteousness and eternal punishment[2] create the necessity of perfect obedience to the satisfy the righteous law of God. This is where Ursinus began his lecture on this question: "The law binds all, either to obedience, or if this is not rendered, to punishment; and the performance or payment of either is perfect righteousness, which God approves of in whomsoever it is found."[3] In his (1567) *Firm Foundation,* Olevianus begins with the very same assumptions: "God is just and requires that we either keep the law with a perfect love of God and neighbor or be eternally punished."[4]

God always acts according to his nature, and thus he cannot be said to be arbitrary, especially if we understand that God's understanding of his justice transcends our ability to comprehend it.[5] That is a great difference between the Triune God of Holy Scripture revealed in Christ Jesus and Allah. The God of Islam really is capricious. He may forgive, or he may not. No one can know. Allah cannot really be known. He is utterly hidden. Indeed, he is not even really personal. The alleged identity of

1. "Dieweil wir denn nach dem gerechten Urtheil Gottes zeitliche und ewige Strafe verdienet haben: wie möchten wir dieser Strafe entgehen, und wiederum zu Gnaden kommen? Gott will, dass seiner Gerechtigkeit genug geschehe; detzwegen müssen wir derselben entweder durch uns selbst, oder durch einen Andern vollkommene Bezahlung thun" (Schaff, *Creeds of the Churches,* 3:311). "Quoniam igitur iusto Dei iudicio, temporalibus et aeternis poenis obnoxii sumus: estne reliqua ulla ratio aut via, qua his poenis liberemur et Deo reconciliemur? Vult Deus iustitiae sua satisfieri: quocirca necesse est, vel per nos, vel per alium satisfaciamus" (Niemeyer, *Collectio Confessionum,* 432).

2. See the discussion under *HC* 11.

3. Ursinus, *Commentary,* 77.

4. Olevian, *Firm Foundation,* 3.

5. Junius, *Treatise on True Theology;* Clark, *Recovering the Reformed Confession,* 119–51.

Yahweh and Allah is a great myth of liberalism and universalism. Such a claim is an insult both to Christianity and to Islam.[6]

The God of Scripture is, in himself (*in se*), hidden from us, but he also reveals himself to us, and what he reveals to us is true. There is a great divide between the Creator and the creature. We cannot know things as God knows them, and we cannot know God as he knows himself, but we can know God truly because he has come to us and made himself known. He has revealed himself in creation and in redemption and chiefly in his Son, the Word: Jesus the Messiah.

We can correlate God's promises to his saving acts in redemptive history. We can and must count him faithful to fulfill his law and his promises. He threatens judgment for sin. He threatens death for sin, and he fulfills that curse (Gen 2:17; Exod 20:5). The whole history of the Israelite holy war against Canaan is the history of God's righteous judgment on unbelief and sin. He says: "I will not acquit the guilty" (Exod 23:7). Every human being is personally obligated to produce perfect righteousness before God (Exod 34:7; Ezek 18:4, 20; 2 Thess 1:8–10; Gal 3:10). Unlike Allah, the God of Abraham, Isaac, and Jacob, the God and Father of our Lord Jesus Christ, is not arbitrary. He cannot contradict himself. He cannot be what he is not. He cannot do what is contrary to his nature, and his nature is just. The universal testimony of Scripture is that God's righteousness must be satisfied.

Scripture also testifies, however, that God is gracious and merciful. He is merciful in that he does not give to all sinners what they deserve—hell—but he is gracious in that he gives to sinners what they cannot earn—his

6. The *Qur'an* says, "People of the Book, do not go to excess in your religion, and do not say anything about God except the truth: the Messiah, Jesus, son of Mary, was nothing more than a messenger of God. His word directed to Mary, and a spirit from him. So believe in God and His messengers and do not speak of 'Trinity'—stop [this], it is better for—God is only one God, He is far above having a son, everything in the heavens and the earth belongs to Him and He is the one to trust. The Messiah would never disdain to be a servant of God, nor would the angels who are close to him. He will gather before him all those who disdain His worship and are arrogant: To those who believe and do good works he will give due rewards and more of his bounty; to those who are disdainful and arrogant he will give an agonizing torment, and they will find no one besides God to protect or help them" (4.171–75). It also says, "Those who say, 'God is the Messiah, the son of Mary,' have defied God. … Those people who say that God is the third of three are defying [the truth]: there is only one God. If they do not stop what they are saying, a painful punishment will afflict those of them who persist. … The Messiah, son of Mary, was only a messenger" (5.72, 73, 75; Haleem, *Qur'an*, 106, 121).

favor—and out of his favor (earned for us by Christ), he himself supplies the righteousness required by his justice.

This is the difference between biblical religion and all other religions: only the God of Scripture promises to save his people by fulfilling the obligations of his law for them. All other faiths set up systems whereby we must do for ourselves or, as in the case of rabbinic and Roman Catholic moralism, God is said to have given grace so that we can do so ourselves in cooperation with grace. In the biblical faith, however, God meets the terms of his righteousness for us. Grace and righteousness meet in Christ. For us he became both righteous lawkeeper (last Adam; 1 Cor 15:45) and the mediator of gracious, free salvation *sola fide* to and for all those for whom he came, whom the Father gave to him from all eternity (John 17:6).

The catechism says "God wills ..." Our classic theologians spoke of God's *beneplacitum* or his "good pleasure."[7] Sinners cannot stand before a righteous and holy God. Not only does his nature make it so that only the righteous can stand before God, but also the divine will. God wills according to his nature, but the introduction of the reference to the divine will is very important. God is king, and his will is sovereign. This a great lesson for our age.

The modern age made the human will the arbiter of all things. In late modernity, following Friedrich Nietzsche (1844–1900), we have reduced life to a struggle of the will. Modernity has consistently attempted to make God come to heel, as if it were possible, to make his will subservient to ours. This is an ancient impulse. It is the program of hell, of course, repackaged for every age. The scriptural testimony is overwhelming. God willed and spoke creation into being (Gen 1:3, 6, 9, 11, 14, 20, 24, 26). God knows what he wills and wills what he knows. From the beginning humans have been obligated, by virtue of their mere humanity, their finitude, to submit to the divine will.

The turn to the divine will here is significant because it says something else about our understanding of Scripture. If God's will is free, it is free. It is unconditioned by anything outside himself. This "unconditionedness"

7. Muller, *Post-Reformation Reformed Dogmatics*, 3:457–59.

or freedom is behind grace.[8] He is not obligated to save any of us. He does so because he freely wills to do so. This idea of the freedom of the divine will is essential to the catechism's definition of grace. The medieval doctrine was that grace is a substance (either created or uncreated) with which we are infused, with which we must cooperate, unto eventual justification.[9] The Protestants redefined grace as free divine favor, merited for us by Christ. It is not a substance but a divine attitude. This moves salvation away from the problem of being and into the legal and moral sphere.

Before the fall, we were in a state of favor or divine approval. By virtue of sin, we could no longer be in God's favor. In order to be restored to a state of divine approval, the divine justice needed to be satisfied. Again, this way of speaking reminds us that for Reformed theology there is no dichotomy between legal relations and personal relations. The latter is premised on the former. Sin destroyed our legal standing with God. The law must be fulfilled and the penalty paid in order to restore us to favor.

Who must do it? The catechism, following Paul in Romans 2:13, teaches that it is the "doers of the law who will be justified." The promise of the law is as relentless as the demand of the law. Of course, by virtue of sin we are incapable of performing what the law requires, but that does not disable the promise and demand of the law. Should there be a human being who was not disabled by sin, he could meet the terms of the law and satisfy it is demands and receive its promised rewards. There will be more about this under the following questions, but we note that Olevianus characterized the one who would satisfy for us as our "Mediator" and our "Surety."[10] A mediator is one who stands between two parties (Gal 3:20; 1 Tim 2:5; Heb 9:15). A surety (ἔγγυος; Heb 7:22) is one who guarantees something (e.g., payment of debt) on behalf of another.

Another problem is whether what is done by one human can be transferred to another. There have always been skeptics when it comes to

8. On this see Martin Luther, *Bondage of the Will* (*LW* 33); Calvin, *Bondage and Liberation of the Will.*

9. E.g., Bonaventure, *Breviloquium* 5.1.5; 5.2.4; 5.3.5 (pp. 183, 187, 191). See Horton, *Justification,* 1:103–24.

10. Olevian, *Firm Foundation*, 3.

imputation, and our age is no exception. Some pastors flatly deny the necessity of imputation.[11]

Of course, the catechism does not share such skepticism. It teaches the doctrine of imputation explicitly. Neither does the apostle Paul share this skepticism. Adam's sin was imputed to all humans (Ps 32:2; Luke 22:37). When Aaron put his hands on the scapegoat, confessed Israel's sins over it, he put his hands on the head of the goat. That was a ritual imputation of their sins. When the goat was sent out of the camp and into the wilderness, Israel's sins were ritually taken away (Lev 16:21). That was a graphic illustration of imputation. In the same way, the righteousness of Christ the Lamb of God, who was sacrificed for his elect, outside the city (Heb 13:11–13), has been imputed to believers (Rom 5:12–21).

> For what does the Scripture say? "Abraham believed God, and it was imputed [ἐλογίσθη] to him as righteousness." Now to the one who works, his wages are not imputed [ἐλογίσθη] as a gift but as his due. And to the one who does not work but believes in him who justifies the ungodly, his faith is imputed [ἐλογίσθη] as righteousness, just as David also speaks of the blessing of the one to whom God imputes [ἐλογίσθη] righteousness apart from works. (Rom 4:3–6 ESV modified)

Paul is quoting and interpreting Genesis 15:6. Imputation is essential to his explanation. Because we are sinners by nature, our righteousness, the ground of our right standing before God, is necessarily outside us. The only way Abraham could stand righteous before God was by imputation, to which we shall return later in the catechism (e.g., *HC* 60). On this question Ursinus writes, "This, now, is the substance of what has been said: Man, being fallen, could hope for no deliverance from sin and death, before he heard the joyful promise that the seed of the woman should bruise the head of the serpent."[12] Salvation came because God willed it. He was under no absolute necessity, but he because willed it freely, there is now a sort of consequent necessity (Ezek 18:23). This is because he saves

11. Clark, "Do This and Live," 229–65.

12. Ursinus, *Commentary*, 79. See 81, where he gives four reasons why God, having willed to redeem, could do so in no other way than by the incarnation, obedience, and death of Christ.

his people to praise of his glorious grace (Eph 1:6), because Christ did not die in vain (John 6:38–39), because God "is more inclined to mercy than to wrath."[13] So, the good news is that this joyful promise was given and fulfilled, and it is this reality into which we enter now in the middle (gospel) part of the catechism.

QUESTION 13

Can we ourselves make this satisfaction?

By no means, on the contrary, we daily increase our guilt.[14]

Only Christianity accounts for sin. All sub-Christian and non-Christian religions ultimately deny either the effect of sin or its reality. Christian heresies deny the power of sin and the federal-legal relations between Adam and us. Non-Christian religions tend to deny sin altogether. A thoroughgoing (Pauline-Augustinian) doctrine of sin tends to vitiate a religion of works-righteousness. The compromise between the biblical and Christian doctrine of sin (that sin is lawlessness and necessarily produces death) and nonbiblical views of sin has come to be known as semi-Pelganianism. Speaking anachronistically, several leading rabbis of the first century were semi-Pelagian. They believed in salvation by grace and cooperation with grace. This doctrine of salvation became the dominant soteriology in the medieval church, and the Remonstrants and the neonomians returned to this error in the seventeenth century. It is to this same sort of semi-Pelagianism that the moralists of our day (i.e., the New Perspective on Paul and federal vision theology) would lead us.

Against the errors of Pelagianism and semi-Pelagianism the catechism says, "On the contrary, we daily increase our guilt." Where most of the medieval church and the Council of Trent had it that we sinners could, if we would, increase our merit before God by grace and cooperation with

13. Ursinus, *Commentary*, 81.

14. "Können wir aber durch uns selbst Bezahlung thun? Mit nichten: sondern wir machen auch die Schuld noch täglich grösser" (Schaff, *Creeds of the Churches*, 3:311). "Possumusne ipsi per nos satisfacere? Nulla ex parte: quin etiam debitum in singulos dies augemus" (Nieymeyer, *Collectio Confessionum*, 432).

grace,[15] we confess that, were it up to our doing, our cooperating, our accumulation of intrinsic merit, would be impossible. The only merit that is of any use is the merit of another, a merit extrinsic to us. As sinners, all we can do is to daily increase our guilt and liability before God. Apart from the unmerited favor of God imputing Christ's perfect righteousness to us, we would be utterly lost.

From the biblical view of sin and its consequences, we must not only reject the obvious error of Pelagianism but also semi-Pelagianism in all its forms because it makes grace a mere palliative. In semi-Pelagianism, salvation ultimately depends on our cooperation. In the Reformed faith, grace is really grace because sin is really sin.

Here the Reformed churches distinguish themselves from the view of Huldrych Zwingli (1484–1531), who did not "accept an original guilt in infants,"[16] because he distinguished between original sin and original guilt. He developed this distinction in controversy with the Anabaptists in May 1525. He argued that infants were born with original sin but without original guilt.[17] He argued that they did not become guilty until they sinned voluntarily.[18] Neither the *BC* nor the catechism makes any such distinction. Olevianus writes that Christ "fully paid for my original sin and whatever part is still left in me."[19] The premise of such language is that original sin *is* original guilt. Ursinus likewise identifies original sin and guilt.[20]

QUESTION 14

Can any mere creature make satisfaction for us?

None, for first, God will not punish any other creature for the sin that man committed; and further, no mere creature can sustain the burden of God's eternal wrath against sin and redeem others from it.[21]

15. Council of Trent, session 6, 1547. See Schroeder, *Canons and Decrees*, 42–46.

16. So Bromiley, "Introduction," 126.

17. Stephens, *Theology of Huldrych Zwingli*, 149–53.

18. For this he was attacked as a Pelagian by Luther in 1526 (Stephens, *Theology of Huldrych Zwingli*, 150).

19. Olevian, *Firm Foundation*, 118.

20. Ursinus, *Commentary*, 44–45.

21. "Kann aber irgend eine blosse Creature für uns bezahlen? Nein: denn erstlich will Gott an keiner audern Creatur strafen, was der Mensch verschuldet hat. Zum andern, so kann auch keine

Much of the history of Israel is a history of blood. Moses shed Egyptian blood to save the life of an Israelite slave (Exod 2:12). Yahweh delivered Israel out of the house of slavery through bloodshed. Joshua and the judges shed Canaanite blood as they conquered the promised land. David was a man of blood as he assumed and defended his throne (1 Chr 28:3). The entire Old Testament cultic (religious) system was bloody. Indeed, the quantity of animal blood shed by priests in the service of Yahweh was so great that it has become a scandal to modern sensibilities.

Grasping something of that bloody history of redemption is essential for understanding the death of our Lord Jesus the Messiah. The reason there was so much bloodshed under the Old Testament is not, as the gnostics alleged, that there was a venal and cruel Old Testament god from whom we have been delivered in the New Testament. After all, the old covenant prophets themselves reminded us that God does not "eat the flesh of bulls" or "drink the blood of goats" (Ps 50:13; Isa 1:11). For this reason Hebrews 10:4 reminds us that "it is impossible for the blood of bulls and goats to take away sins."

The reason for all the Old Testament bloodshed was to make a two-sided point, and the first side of that point was and is that the Creator God, the God of Abraham, the God of Isaac, and the God of Jacob, the God who is, the God who is Father, Son, and Holy Spirit, is absolutely righteous, and his justice must be satisfied. The second side of the point is that the sacrifice of animals is of itself futile toward that end.

One thing conferred significance to the sacrifice of animals under the typological administrations of the covenant of grace (i.e., those epochs of redemptive history from after the fall until the inauguration of the new covenant): the obedience and death of Jesus the Messiah as the lamb of God. Every single animal sacrifice, beginning with the slaughter of an animal and the covering of our first parents, Adam and Eve, in bloody animal skins, anticipated and was given significance only by the reality that would one day appear. Every time some sinful priest slaughtered some

---

blosse Creatur die Last des ewigen Zornes Gottes wider die Sünde ertragen, und andere davon erlösen" (Schaff, *Creeds of the Churches*, 3:311–12). "Postestne ulla creaturum in coelo vel in terra, quae tantum creatura sit, pro nobis satisfacere? Nulla: Nam principio non vult Deus, quod homo peccavit, id in ulla alia creatura plectere. Deinde, nec potest quidem, quod nihil nisi creatura sit, iram Dei adversus peccatum sustinere, et alios ab ea liberare" (Niemeyer, *Collectio Confessionum*, 432–33).

animal in the Jewish temple, its meaning was fundamentally not what the priest or the people invested in it. Its meaning, its utility, its power was only in the typological connection it had to the final, eschatological (i.e., that which is from heaven) historical sacrifice of Christ.

All this is to say that there are two schools of thought relative to the typological sacrifices that we should reject. First, we should reject the liberal notion that what made the sacrifices significant was the personal, subjective meaning invested in them by those who offered them or by those for whom they were offered. In other words, we should reject the Schleiermachian notion that what made them significant was the way they helped people subjectively realize a great sense of divine dependence.[22] However interesting it might be to speculate about the subjective meaning the act of sacrifice might have had for the people or the priests, it is basically irrelevant for understanding them. We only know two things about those who participated in the typological administrations: they believed and somehow looked forward to the incarnation and entered into the new covenant by faith (Heb 11), or they did not believe and, in that case, the sacrifices were useless.

A second school of thought regarding the sacrificial system that we should reject is that notion that somehow the sacrificial system was the reality to which redemptive history will one day return. It turns the biblical self-understanding on its head to think that Jesus's self-sacrifice was only provisional and temporary or that that one day God will restore the typological temple system. One of the great burdens of the book of Hebrews is that the entire typological system existed for one purpose: to point to the reality, to point to Christ and to his sacrifice as temple, priest, and lamb. We must understand Jesus's life and death in the light of the typological system, but the spiritual, theological, and historical meaning of the typological system is derived from its relation to Christ and his once-for-all sacrifice.

A third error to be avoided is the notion that the covenant of grace was merely *revealed* but not actually in operation under the Old Testament (and old covenant) types and shadows. Rather, we should think that the

22. This is a reference to the followers, including the "mediating theologians," influenced by Friedrich Schleiermacher (1768–1834). On this movement, see Purvis, *Theology in the University*.

believers under the types and shadows, from Adam until Malachi, participated in the covenant of grace and that the covenant of grace was, to borrow a phrase, in, with, and under the types and shadows.

So far we have seen that the efficacy of divine institution of typological animal sacrifices, prior to the incarnation of God the Son, was dependent on the coming fulfillment of those sacrifices in Christ. The point of working through the meaning of the sacrificial system is to deal with the problem presented by the fact that it was not lambs and goats who sinned against God. It was human beings, image-bearers, who violated the covenant of works. The consequence of sin was death, but it was not humans who were slaughtered in the Jewish temple. In those offerings God was anticipating the final, once-for-all sacrifice made by God the Son incarnate and the culmination of the once-for-all punishment of sin.

God was not obligated to save any. When we consider the absolute divine power (*potentia absoluta*), God might have passed by or reprobated all humans fallen in Adam, and he would have been just in doing so. Nevertheless, God in his mercy (not giving the punishment due) and grace (showing favor that is not due) willed to redeem a people for himself. Because he willed to redeem a people for himself and because it was humans (not lambs and goats) who sinned, the divine justice requires that the same class of beings who committed the sin should make payment for that sin.

Though it was humans who sinned and it is they who owe payment and positive righteousness (i.e., obedience to the law), they do have something in common with lambs and goats: they are all mere creatures. There is an ontological, categorical difference between the being humans have and the being God has. To begin, God simply is (Exod 3:14). We cannot say that of humans. God was, is, and shall be (Heb 13:8). He is not contingent. He is simple (Deut 6:4), immutable (Mal 3:6–7; Num 23:19), impassible, eternal, infinite (Ps 90:2), and immense (1 Kgs 8:26–27). None of those attributes is true of any creature. No purely finite, temporal, passible, mutable, complex, and local creature could satisfy the divine wrath and, after the fall, accomplish positive righteousness.[23]

23. On the categorical distinction, see Clark, *Recovering the Reformed Confession*, 121–34.

All this is to begin to answer the great question posed by Anselm of Canterbury (1033–1109): *Cur deus homo* ("Why the God-Man?")[24] The catechism itself asks who is able to make "satisfaction for us."[25] The short answer is that, having willed to redeem his elect, God could do so only in a way that is consonant with his justice. We know something about God's justice from revelation. There are rough but true analogies to divine justice in nature, and clearer indications of it in the typological revelation, for example, "eye for an eye" (Lev 24:19-21). It is common to hear people mock "eye for an eye." In fact, God wills that his justice be satisfied. There is every indication in the typological revelation that God is completely intolerant of disobedience. Liberals can mock the "slaughterhouse theology" of the Old Testament and of the historic Christian, substitutionary doctrine of the atonement, but we may in turn call them Marcionites and gnostics. They may like to think of themselves as having advanced beyond bloodshed and atonement, but God has not, and there will come a time when they will wish with all they are that they had not been more clever than God.

Certainly Jesus was not above teaching the necessity of substitutionary atonement. In John 15:13 he expressly says that he came to "lay down" (θῇ) his life "on behalf of" (ὑπὲρ) his friends. The grammar and logic of the passage teaches that Jesus intentionally came as a substitute in place of his people. There are other aspects to the doctrine of the atonement, but none of them may displace the substitutionary aspect of the atonement.

24. Klooster (*Our Only Comfort*, 2:1154–67) has a lengthy discussion of the relationship between Anselm's *Cur deus homo*, scholasticism, and *HC* 12–19. He concludes by proposing a rearrangement of the catechism. This work has no sympathy either with the perceived problems associated with scholasticism—the catechism was taught *in schola*—or with Anselmian influence on the catechism. *Pace* van't Spijker, "Theology of the Heidelberg Catechism," 105–7, the structure of Anselm's argument influenced the framers, but they modified Anselm's terms.

25. "Pro nobis satisfacere?" (Niemeyer, *Collectio Confessionum*, 432).

QUESTION 15

What kind of a mediator and redeemer then must we seek?

One who is a true and righteous man, and yet more powerful than all creatures, that is, one who is also true God.[26]

One of the more puzzling and overlooked features of the Barthian, neoevangelical, and federal visionist denial of the doctrine of the prelapsarian legal covenant is that it tends to deny, or at least downplay, the righteousness of God. It retells the entire story of Scripture by changing the plot. Denying the covenant of works (*foedus operum*), or the covenant of nature (*foedus naturae*), or the covenant of law (*foedus legis*), or the commandment of life (*mandatum vitae*),[27] tends to make God seem arbitrary. To be sure, the God of Scripture is absolutely free to act according to his nature. We creatures are not authorized to determine in advance what God may or may not do except to say that he cannot deny himself and he cannot lie. He cannot be what he is not. Within those parameters there are a great number of things that God might do that we cannot predict. God's ways are not our ways. His thoughts are not our thoughts (Isa 55:8–9). These are scriptural data. To deny, however, that God is arbitrary is hardly to deny his freedom or, as some say, to put God in a box.

The Reformed churches do not think of God as arbitrary because we think of him as he has revealed himself in his word. Of course, he has not revealed himself exhaustively. We understand from Scripture (e.g., Deut 29:29) that he has revealed himself sufficiently to allow us to speak about him truly. We cannot explain all that he has done or will do in his providence, but we do know him truly, and we can correlate what he has done in redemptive history with what he said about himself in his canonical word.

26. "Was müssen wir denn für einen Mittler und Erlöser suchen? Einen solchen, der ein wahrer und gerechter Mensch, und doch stärker denn alle Creaturen, das ist, zugleich wahrer Gott sei (Schaff, *Creeds of the Churches*, 3.312); Qualis ergo querendus est mediator et liberator? Qui verus quidem homo sit, ac perfecte iustus, et tamen omnibus creaturis potentior, hoc est, qui simul etiam sit verus Deus" (Niemeyer, *Collectio Confessionum*, 433).

27. Müller, *Die Bekenntnisschriften*, 238.

According to the Reformed reading of Scripture, the God of the Bible entered into a covenant relation with humanity in creation, before the fall. This covenant relation was bounded by a law: love God with all your faculties and love your neighbor as yourself.[28] It was expressed in terms of trees. Adam was free to eat from any tree, even the tree of life, but he was forbidden to eat from the tree of the knowledge of good and evil (Gen 2:15–17). This was a commandment, a law. It seems undeniable that Adam was in a legal relationship with God. The law gave to Adam and Eve permission to "eat from any tree" and a restriction: "except for this one." There was implied blessedness for obedience, and this blessedness was symbolized by the tree of life. The curse of lawbreaking was explicitly revealed: "The day you eat thereof, you shall surely die" (Gen 2:17). What was required of Adam was legal righteousness.

Of course, Adam himself presents another great problem for modernity. We confess that Adam was an historical figure. We confess that because the Bible teaches it. The temptation of modernity has been to place ourselves in judgment over the narrative of Scripture and to say, in effect, "We know *a priori* that the Adam figure of the creation narrative must be a mythic way of expressing a spiritual truth." The Bible, however, does not tell us *fables* for the purposes of teaching moral and spiritual truths. Scripture does use *parables,* but in that case we understand that these are made-up stories told for a specific purpose. The creation narrative has a theology, a structure, and marks of literary skill and interest, but it does not evidently have the marks of a parable.

The modern temptation to treat the creation narrative as *saga* or myth is a Faustian bargain. History tells us that modernists have not been satisfied with any halfway covenants. Starting with Adam, the critics have ridden roughshod through the history of redemption, as it were, with an eraser doing away with very existence of the exodus, the flood (local or universal), and all forms of supernatural religion.

Just as the very idea of an historical Adam offends modern sensibilities, so too the idea of legal relation to God at the outset of human existence also offends the late modern turn to relational categories in place of legal categories.[29] The modern creed has a few basic tenets: the universal father-

28. See the discussion under *HC* 6, 9.

29. See the discussion under *HC* 2.

hood of God, the universal brotherhood of humanity, and human progress. Implicit in the biblical story of a law-giving God and a lawbreaking federal representative man is distinction. There is no reconciling the "law" story of the first man with the "grace" story of all people. If the first man was the legal representative of all humans, and we, in him, broke that original law, then it cannot be that God now universally accepts all humans. Indeed, according to Scripture the exact opposite is true. All humans are, in Adam, universally condemned by God (Rom 3:23).

Thus, to accept the biblical story as we have it is to place ourselves at odds with the whole sweep and spirit of modernism. For this reason, we should be skeptical of anyone who, with the reasoning of being more biblical, invites us to reject the reading of the Adam narrative as the story of a law-giving God and a lawbreaking man. The siren song of the biblicist is seductive, but historically this approach has led to the rejection of the biblical faith. This was the appeal of the Socinian movements in the seventeenth century.[30] They proposed to reform the faith, but on the basis of the autonomy and sovereignty of reason and at the expense of the doctrine of the Trinity, the deity of Christ, and the atonement. Indeed, all the heretics—the anthropomorphites, Marcionites, Montanists, Sabellians, Arians, and Pelagians—quoted Scripture. The Anabaptists and the Socinians said that they were more biblical than the Reformation churches.

It is not a matter of *whether* we are reading the Scriptures, closely, carefully, in historical context, in canonical (redemptive-historical) context, paying attention to the grammar, and comparing one passage with another. It is a question of *where* we are doing so, and with what church, and to what end, and with what confession? This is not to counsel skepticism. Reformation according to the word does happen, and it must happen. This is simply an argument to challenge an assumption that late moderns (particularly individualist, autonomous, egalitarian Americans) seem to accept uncritically, that the isolated interpreter is somehow to be privileged over the historic Reformed confessional reading of Scripture. The confessionalist reading of Scripture is much less indebted to or enslaved by the culture and assumptions of late modernity than autonomous biblicists bent on reshaping Reformed theology in their own image.

---

30. Clark, *Recovering the Reformed Confession*, 19–27. On Socinianism see Morse, *History of Unitarianism*; Mortimer, *Reason and Religion*.

Question 16
Why must he be a true and righteous man?

Question 17
Why must he also be true God?

Question 18
But who now is that Mediator, who in one person is true God and also a true and righteous man?

Question 19
From where do you know this?

Lord's Day 6

QUESTION 16

Why must he be a true and righteous man?

Because the justice of God requires that the same human nature which has sinned should make satisfaction for sin, but one who is himself a sinner, cannot satisfy for others.[1]

There are two very important words here: *justice* and *nature*. These two words have become quite foreign to late moderns. There is a great deal of talk about justice, but we typically conceive of it in relativistic terms. Justice is reckoned to be a human convention. Under the influence of deconstructionism, the radically subjective turn of much philosophy and most of the culture, many of us no longer believe in such things as a divinely constituted standard of right and wrong. Western culture has come to suspect that it is a merely human convention or perhaps even a conspiracy. In the late modern period, when the "hermeneutics of suspicion" reigns, everything is thought to be a mere convention or agreement.[2] The idea of nature has suffered a similar fate for similar reasons.

The deconstruction of justice and nature should not surprise us. Unbelief is bound to swing between rationalism (the autonomy of the human intellect relative to all other authorities) and empiricism (the autonomy of human sense experience relative to all other authorities) with interludes of subjectivism (e.g., Romanticism in the nineteenth century and deconstructionism today).

Christians, however, are bound to believe in such things as justice and nature because we confess that "in the beginning God created the heavens and the earth" (Gen 1:1). For Scripture, and consequently for the Reformed faith, God simply is. He is not a convention. He is not a product of the intellect or a mere deduction from human sense experience. We may see

1. "Warum muss Er ein Wahrer und gerechter Mensch sein? Darum, weil die Gerechtigkeit Gottes ersordert, dass die menschliche Natur, die gesündiget hat, für die Sünde bezahle, aber Einer, der selbst ein Sünder wäre, nicht könnte sür Andere bezahlen" (Schaff, *Creeds of the Churches*, 3:312). "Cur necesse est, cum verum hominem, et quidem perfecte iustum esse? Quia iustitia Dei postulat, ut eadem natura humana, quae peccavit, ipsa pro peccato depndat: qui vero ipse peccator esset, pro aliis depndere non posset" (Niemeyer, *Collectio Confessionum*, 433).

2. This phrase was coined by Paul Ricoeur (1913–2005) but has been used in a variety of ways. See Scott-Baumann, *Ricoeur and the Hermeneutics*.

from nature and conscience that he is and that he has issued a universal moral law, but God is not the result of human rationalism or empiricism or subjectivism. God is who he is (Exod 3:14). He will be what he will be. He has a nature. He has attributes, of which justice is one.

Because God has a nature and because we are his image-bearers, we also have a nature. There is such a thing as human nature. We need not choose sides in the debate over nature versus nurture. We affirm that there is such a thing as human nature, in which we all share, but we also affirm that the fall profoundly marred and corrupted it. It has not been utterly wiped out. Its vestiges remain and are renewed by grace alone, in Christ alone. God the Creator has assigned a nature to us. It is a given. It is a limit. We cannot escape it, and we are morally obligated to it.

We have the same nature as Adam. We are related to him covenantally, legally, and naturally. We were "in him" legally and naturally (Rom 5:12–21). When he fell, we fell. His actions had fatal spiritual consequences for all of us. Thus, on this topic Olevianus writes, "Moreover, the justice of God, who said, 'I will not justify the wicked' (Exod. 23:7), demanded that He not establish a covenant and friendship with the wicked and unrighteous unless the just (namely, Christ) die for the unjust (1 Pet. 3:18)."[3]

We share this common humanity not only with Adam but also with Christ. He has the same nature as we. He is not merely like us (though he is that). Rather, he is one with us. His humanity shares our finitude (Luke 2:52). He was tempted as we are tempted (Heb 4:15). He tired (Luke 8:23). He wept (John 11:35). He ate (Luke 24:43). He was in the womb of the virgin (Matt 1:18). He was "true man."[4] He took his humanity, by the wonderful operation of God the Spirit, "from the Virgin Mary."[5] He suffered. He died. These are all things that happen to real humans, with real, true flesh and blood. This is the consistent message of Hebrews:

> Since therefore the children share in flesh and blood, he himself likewise partook of the same things, that through death he might destroy the one who has the power of death, that is, the devil, and

3. Olevian, *Firm Foundation*, 6.

4. The Latin text of *HC* 16 uses *verum hominem* (Niemeyer, *Collectio Confessionum*, 433). The Definition of Chalcedon says ἄνθρωπον ἀληθῶς (Schaff, *Creeds of the Churches*, 2:62).

5. "Ex Mariae virgine," Apostles' Creed, in Schaff, *Creeds of the Churches*, 2:45.

> deliver all those who through fear of death were subject to lifelong slavery. For surely it is not angels that he helps, but he helps the offspring of Abraham. Therefore he had to be made like his brothers in every respect, so that he might become a merciful and faithful high priest in the service of God, to make propitiation for the sins of the people. For because he himself has suffered when tempted, he is able to help those who are being tempted. (Heb 2:14–18 ESV)

One of the great errors of the medieval church was that it lost sight of Christ's true humanity and erected for itself a pantheon of intercessors in place of Christ via the cult of saints and of the Virgin Mary. As the *BC* (26) reminds us:

> Therefore it was only through diffidence that this practice of dishonoring instead of honoring the saints was introduced; doing that which they never have done nor required, but have, on the contrary, steadfastly rejected, according to their bounden duty, as appears by their writings. Neither must we plead here our unworthiness; for the meaning is not that we should offer our prayers to God on account of our own worthiness, but only on account of the excellence and worthiness of our Lord Jesus Christ, whose righteousness is become ours by faith.[6]

God the Son took on our humanity (not something *like* humanity, as the gnostics and docetists say) for a purpose: to satisfy the divine justice. Just as fixed as the divine nature is, so fixed is the divine justice, the divine standard of right and wrong. This is an immutable standard of righteousness.

There are conventions. Everything we think is not an eternal verity. Stop signs could be green. That stop signs are red is a convention. That fact does not mean that everything is a convention. "You shall not commit murder" (Exod 20:13) is not a mere convention. Some things are contrary to the nature of things. Might God have willed things to be different? He might not have instituted gravity, but since he himself has a nature, because his moral laws reflect that nature, we cannot say the same thing about

6. Schaff, *Creeds of the Churches*, 3:415.

justice and righteousness. These things have a permanence, grounded in the divine nature, which we know via his voluntary self-disclosure.

Few things rankle the modern mind more than the idea that God's justice must be satisfied. Modern, autonomous people do not want to submit their sovereign selves to *El Shaddai,* to *Yahweh Sabaoth* of the Hebrew Scriptures, nor to the "God and Father of our Lord Jesus Christ" (2 Cor 1:3), and certainly not to any God who demands satisfaction by a bloody death of a representative substitute. Autonomous modern people notwithstanding, Scripture unashamedly portrays the God of the Bible not only as just but as angry with sin and sinners "every day" (Ps 7:11). God saves the "upright" or the just (Ps 11:7). That is the consistent testimony of Scripture. The psalmists claim time and again to have been righteous, to have fulfilled the will of the Lord, and on that basis more or less insist that God recognize this fact and deliver them from enemies (Pss 18:21, 23; 73:13; 119:56). This pattern of revelation is grounded in the original condition of humanity. God created and constituted us righteous and holy and able to obey. God gave us a law that we could obey. We freely chose to disobey, due to no fault of God or his creation. Thus the fall is a great mystery.

In the fall, our state or condition changed profoundly, but God's righteous demand for complete obedience did not. Further, God's law having been violated, not only did the demand for conformity continue, but now there is a requirement for satisfaction. The modern mind is outraged at a God who demands damages, but one may be sure that in a property dispute that offended them, modernists would not hesitate to demand satisfaction. Exodus 29 lays out in detail the requirements of Yahweh for the sin offering. The bull is ritually slaughtered outside the camp (v. 14). An entire ram is to be burned on the altar of Yahweh. Verse 18 says, "It is a burnt offering to Yahweh. It is a pleasing aroma, a food offering to Yahweh." The God of the Hebrews, the God of the Bible, is "pleased," or even worse (to modern people) "soothed," that is, propitiated by a bloody, fiery offering.

This is the religious system to which Jesus subscribed, whom modernists would reduce to a mere teacher. Modernists object to the blood in the temple. Jesus objected to the money changers (Matt 21:12–13). Jesus never objected to the bloody temple sacrifices because each time a Jew brought an offering, he was testifying to the nature of divine justice and to the need for a perfect sacrifice to bring the entire sacrificial system to a close (Heb 8:1–9:28). Every time a priest's razor-sharp knife slit the throat of an innocent lamb, Jesus's mission to be, as the Baptizer said, "the Lamb of God" (John 1:29) was illustrated and vindicated.

God has a nature. His nature is righteous. Once offended, the divine justice must be satisfied by a perfect, spotless offering (Ps 7:11; Lev 1:1–13; Dan 9:14; Rom 2:13). The consistent and crystal-clear teaching of the Old Testament prophets and Hebrews 8–10 is that the entire sacrificial system was incapable of providing that satisfaction. God was not pleased with the typological sacrifices and offerings. He demanded love, not sacrifice (Hos 6:6). Jesus was that love, not the squishy sort of love favored by modernists but real, bloody, divine-human love for sinners, willing to take their place. "In this is love, not that we have loved God but that he loved us and sent his Son to be the propitiation for our sins" (1 John 4:10 ESV). Modernists are gnostics. They will not have propitiating love (Rom 3:25; 1 John 2:2). They want an ethereal love that is no love at all because they worship a god that is not God at all, who has no justice. They are rebels who yell for justice, but when true justice is presented to them, they turn their heads like children who turn away from healthy food in favor of candy.

Jesus is our kinsman-redeemer (Matt 1:21). He was born perfectly righteous. He obeyed and suffered not for himself but for us. Ursinus explains,

> It behooved him to be a perfectly righteous man, one that was wholly free from the least stain of original and actual sin, that he might deservedly be our Saviour, and that his sacrifice might avail, not for himself, but for us: for if he himself had been a sinner, he would have had to satisfy for his own sins. "My righteous servant shall justify many." "Who did no sin, neither was guile found in his mouth." "Christ also hath once suffered for sin, the just for the unjust, that he might bring us to God." (Is. 53:11. 1 Pet. 2:22; 3:18.)[7]

This doctrine distinguishes Christianity from all other world religions. As Olevianus noted in 1567, "Only the Christian religion and faith is the true faith; all others are false. For only Christians recognize God as one

7. Ursinus, *Commentary*, 86.

true God, who is perfectly just and perfectly merciful and thus the true God." In the active, substitutionary suffering and death of Christ, we see his justice in the punishment of sin. In that same "one act of righteousness" (Rom 5:18), he manifested his grace and mercy since "absolutely nothing but out of sheer mercy gave us the Son for our payment, without any merit on our part, while we were yet sinners.[8]

QUESTION 17

Why must he also be true God?[9]

That by the power of his deity he might bear in his humanity the burden of God's wrath, and so obtain for and restore to us righteousness and life.[10]

The subtext of Satan's offer in the garden was power (Gen 3:1–5). The covenant of nature ("commandment of life"; *BC* 14)[11] offered glorified, everlasting, consummated fellowship with God on condition of absolute submission and obedience to God. Adam had to trust God's promise, and he had to obey. The general faith that God called Adam to exercise was not like the special, saving faith that God has given us after the fall *sola gratia*. Confusing these two things is one of the great errors of all forms of moralism in that it conflates Adam's duty to trust the promise of life made to him with the faith believers after the fall have in Christ the Mediator and substitute, the last Adam (1 Cor 15:45). By confusing these two kinds of faith, the moralists become Pelagians by seeking to put us after the fall in the same state as we were before the fall.

---

8. Olevian, *Firm Foundation*, 7.

9. "Warum muss Er zugleich wahrer Gott sein? Dass er aus Kraft seiner Gottheit die Last des Zornes Gottes an seiner Menschheit ertragen, und uns die Gerechtigkeit und das Leben erwerben und wieder geben möchte" (Schaff, *Creeds of the Churches*, 3:312). "Quare oportet eum simul etiam vere Deum esse? Ut potentia suae divinitatis, onus irae divinae carne sua sustinere, nobisque amissam iustitiam et vitam reparare ac restitutere possit" (Niemeyer, *Collectio Confessionum*, 433).

10. "Ut potentia suae divinitatis, onus irae divinae carne sua sustinere, nobisque amissam iustitiam et vitam reparare ac restitutere possit" (Niemeyer, *Collectio Confessionum*, 433). The Latin text says Christ sustained the burden of God's wrath in his "flesh," whereas the German text says *seiner Menschheyt* ("his humanity"; Müller, *Die Bekenntnisschriften*, 686).

11. "Commandment de vie" (Schaff, *Creeds of the Churches*, 3:398).

Glorified union and communion with the Triune God is a kind of power. It is conferred, derived power, but it is real power. The Evil One knew that, and thus he offered to us an alternative power without submission to God. It was a false, competing, alternative covenant of works. In his covenant we were required to trust and obey him. In this way, a covenant of works was unavoidable. In this case, the devil's offer was not actually life. The offer was ostensibly knowledge, but it was actually darkness. He offered an alternative source of power that led not to life but to death.

Thus, it is significant that we confess that "by the power of his deity" he, Jesus, God the Son, "might bear in his humanity the burden of God's eternal wrath." Power was offered, and power is required. In the beginning only God had the real authority and real power to confer eternal life. The Evil One is a liar. That is one of the more remarkable aspects of the fall: the Evil One is and has always been nothing more than a creature. A powerful and dangerous creature to be avoided and ultimately defeated, but a creature nonetheless. No *mere* creature ever had authority or the ability to offer or confer eternal life. Only God has that power and only God has that authority.

It is a great proof, then, of Christ's deity that he repeatedly offered eternal life on his *own* authority and on the authority of his Father and in his own name, through faith in himself (John 3:15, 36; 4:14, 5:24; 6:40, 47, 54; 10:28). We should not be surprised that it infuriated the rabbis. It seemed like impossible arrogance, but it was not arrogance. It was a revelation of his divinity. Once again, the Word of God came to humanity and offered eternal fellowship with God on the basis of obedience. Here in the incarnation was a wonderful reenactment of the garden drama all over again. God the Son came to us and once again offered eternal life, union, and communion with God. This time the condition of the offer was not "do this and live" (Luke 10:28; Lev 18:5) but "whosoever believes in me shall never perish" (John 3:16). The basis remains the obedience of Adam, but this time it is the obedience of the last Adam (1 Cor 15:45). The instrument is trust in in him who would obey for us and who had in himself the power of an indestructible life (Heb 7:16). This Adam refused the temptation of the Evil One. This Adam is once again the Mediator of a covenant—not a covenant of works but a covenant of grace. The offer of eternal blessedness and the accomplishment of its terms belongs to God incarnate.

Before glory, however, there is death and the business of obtaining righteousness and life for us. The same Son who in the garden offered to us consummated glory and life now had to "obtain" (*erwerben*) or earn for us righteousness and life.[12] Life of the sort under discussion here always had to be "earned" and restored. Adam had to obey, he had to submit, in order to receive consummated life. This is a great difference before the fall and after. Before the fall God created us "in righteousness and true holiness." After the fall, however, we had to earn and renew righteousness.

We should not miss the implied force of the expression "for us" (Rom 5:18; 8:32; Gal 3:13; Eph 5:2; 1 Thess 5:10; 1 John 3:16). It refers to the elect, to whom the Spirit gives new life and true faith. The intent of the incarnation is not addressed in detail in the catechism, but there are clues, and the phrase "for us" is one of those clues. We see this in *HC* 31, 37, 42, and 45. That prepositional phrase communicates a great deal about the original intent of the framers of the catechism and indicates how we ought to understand it today. Truly, in the second head of doctrine the Synod of Dort was not changing Reformed doctrine but elaborating on what we already confessed. Olevianus reminds us that the doctrine of the Mediator and Redeemer is a gospel of salvation:

> Because it contains promises of salvation, it is called the gospel of salvation, a word of salvation, and a power of God unto salvation (Rom. 1[:16]). Of course the law leads us by the hand, as it were, to this doctrine. For after we are convicted of our unrighteousness and smitten with the awareness of eternal death, the law teaches us not to seek salvation in ourselves but to accept by faith the salvation offered us outside of ourselves in the gospel. St. Paul speaks of this in Rom. 10[:4]: "The end of the law is Christ for righteousness to every believer." Also, "The law was our tutor to bring us to Christ" (Gal. 3[:24]).[13]

12. The Latin text (see above) says, "that he might restore and renew to us lost righteousness and life." On the imputation of active obedience, see Clark, "Do This and Live," 229–65.

13. Olevian, *Firm Foundation*, 8.

We look to Christ for salvation. Like the first Adam, the last Adam had to trust his Father, but, like the first Adam, the faith he exercised was not the saving faith that we sinners exercise. The faith he exercised was that his Father's promise was good, that he would reward his obedient Son with life. It was a general faith (*fides generalis*), as distinct from the special faith (*fides specialis*), which is the gift of the Spirit to the elect. Francis Turretin (1623–1687) explains:

> VI. Faith, therefore, is ascribed to Christ, not inasmuch as it is a fiducial apprehension of the mercy of God. In this sense, it belongs to sinners only; nor is it ascribed in respect of mode of knowledge, as much as it is opposed to the obscurity of an enigma (inasmuch as it is opposed to sight [*eidei,* 2 Cor 5:7], which cannot be done without imperfection, from which Christ is free). Rather it is ascribed to Christ as to substance of knowledge and assent to a thing known (i.e., to the doctrine revealed of God) and as to trust, which rests in the goodness of God providing all things necessary for us.[14]

Faith when attributed to Christ means one thing. When attributed to fallen sinners in salvation, faith means something different. J. Gresham Machen found a confusion of the two in modern theological liberalism:

> In the first place, it will be said, are we not failing to do justice to the true humanity of Jesus, which is affirmed by the creeds of the Church as well as by the modern theologians? When we say that Jesus could not illustrate Christian faith any more than God can be religious, are we not denying to Jesus that religious experience which is a necessary element in true humanity? Must not Jesus, if He be true man, have been more than the object of religious faith; must He not have had a religion of His own? The answer is not far to seek. Certainly Jesus had a religion of His own; His prayer was real prayer, His faith was real religious faith. His relation to His heavenly Father was not merely that of a child to a father; it was that of a man to his God. Certainly Jesus had a religion; without it His humanity would indeed have been but incomplete. Without

14. Turretin, *Institutes of Elenctic Theology*, 13.12.6 (2:348); Murray, *Collected Writings*, 2:241–63.

> doubt Jesus had a religion; the fact is of the utmost importance. But it is equally important to observe that that religion which Jesus had was not Christianity. Christianity is a way of getting rid of sin, and Jesus was without sin. His religion was a religion of Paradise, not a religion of sinful humanity. It was a religion to which we may perhaps in some sort attain in heaven, when the process of our purification is complete (though even then the memory of redemption will never leave us); but certainly it is not a religion with which we can begin. The religion of Jesus was a religion of untroubled sonship; Christianity is a religion of the attainment of sonship by the redeeming work of Christ.[15]

The empty tomb and the ascension of Christ are all the evidence we need that our Father's promise was good. The obedience he rendered to his Father was not, as the moralists would have it, for himself, to qualify himself. He was born qualified. Rather, as Paul says, he was born of a woman, under the law, for us, not for himself (Gal 4:4).

The faith we exercise is also that the Father will reward us with life if we meet the condition of the covenant, but the difference between the law and gospel is that the law demands that we meet the terms of the covenant personally. The gospel announces that Christ has done it for his people. The Mediator makes all the difference, but some want us to take our eyes off the Mediator or want to make him just another believer, a mere example. True faith trusts Jesus our Mediator, who obeyed for us.

Jesus, the last Adam, is the life-giving Spirit (1 Cor 15:45). God raised him from the dead. He has life in himself to give. He earned the right to give to us life. He has the authority, and he has the power. He had to taste death for us. He did, but he also tasted life, on the third day.

He who accomplished all this is true man. Already in the New Testament, the church faced one of its greatest and deadliest heresies: the denial of Jesus's humanity. The Greeks had room for men becoming gods and human-like behavior among the gods, but they had no room for a God-Man. Many of them had a great deal of trouble with the goodness of creation. They were deeply suspicious of the physical, material world.

---

15. Machen, *Christianity and Liberalism*, 78–79; Hodge, *Systematic Theology*, 3:96; Berkhof, *Systematic Theology*, 506.

Many of them tended to regard it as inherently corrupt and corrupting merely because of its materiality. The idea of God becoming man was therefore impossible, because it would mean that God had become corrupt. They associated the purity of a god or the gods with their immateriality. This sort of dualism in being between the good immaterial (spiritual) world and the evil material world probably lay behind some of the difficulties in the Colossian congregation that Paul addressed. Certainly the congregations in Asia Minor (central Turkey) to which the apostle John wrote were troubled by this sort of false dualism (1 John 1:1–3; 4:2–3). For John it is "anti-Christ" to deny that Jesus is true God and true man.

Throughout postapostolic Christian history, the church has continually been troubled by this great heresy. The apologists of the second century (100–200) address this error in various forms, sometimes lumped under the heading of "gnosticism." In the high Middle Ages, the Albigensians denied or downplayed Jesus's humanity. Many sixteenth-century Anabaptists taught a theory that Christ had a "celestial" humanity, thereby denying the true consubstantiality (i.e., sharing our human substance) between us and Christ.[16]

One of the more heated conflicts between the confessional Reformed and Lutheran theologians and churches was the question of the nature of Jesus's humanity. There was a Lutheran doctrine of the *genus maiestaticum*, that is, that Jesus's humanity belonged to a class of one.[17] They affirmed that he was true human but that the communication of the divinity with the humanity was such that his humanity was also quite distinct from ours. Thus, Lutherans affirmed that Christ could know, in his humanity, what God knew the way he alone knew it (*theologia archetypa*), whereas the Reformed affirmed more clearly that his true humanity was consubstantial with us such that even in his humanity he knew only what humans could

16. *BC* 18 (Dennison, *Reformed Confessions*, 3:434). This Christology was confessed by Menno Simon, Dirk Philips, Melchior Hoffmann, and Caspar Schwenkfeld. See Beachy, *Concept of Grace*, 14n32, 79–86. *The Concept of Cologne* (1591), an Anabaptist confession in the tradition of Menno, seems to reflect this Christology in art. 2 (Pelikan and Hotchkiss, *Creeds and Confessions of Faith*, 751). See Dietrich Philips, *The Church of God* (1560), in Williams, *Spiritual and Anabaptist Writers*, 236–37; Calvin, *Treatises against the Anabaptists*, 106–18; Balke, *Calvin and the Anabaptist Radicals*, 301–3. See the discussion under *HC* 35.

17. Clark, *Caspar Olevian*, 107–27.

know (*theologia ectypa*).[18] To the Reformed it seemed that the Lutheran Christology verged on confusing the human and the divine natures, and, of course, the Lutherans accused the Reformed of dividing the two natures.[19] We, however, hold and teach the Christology of Chalcedon (AD 451):

> to be acknowledged in two natures, inconfusedly, unchangeably, indivisibly, inseparably; the distinction of natures being by no means taken away by the union, but rather the property of each nature being preserved, and concurring in one Person and one Subsistence, not parted or divided into two persons, but one and the same Son, and only begotten, God the Word, the Lord Jesus Christ.[20]

With these categories in mind the *HC* says what it does about the Son bearing in his humanity the wrath of God against sin. We need a substitute, and he must be like us in every respect, sin excepted (Heb 2:14–18; 4:15). This is why we speak of "consubstantiality." He must be one of us. He cannot merely appear to be like us. Why not? Because it was one of us, created in righteousness and true holiness, who sinned, who violated God's law and incurred the greatest penalty.

According to Scripture, as understood and confessed in the ancient church and by the Reformed churches, the justice of God is such that it must punish disobedience. This is the nature of justice even in our world. Scripture testifies repeatedly to the existence and righteousness of God's judgment. The strongest evidence for it is that Jesus taught it (e.g., Matt 5:22), and more than that, he submitted himself to it. He was our Mediator and substitute. He came in our place. He came, was incarnate, was born, obeyed, died, and was raised for us (Rom 5:8). That prepositional phrase "for us" says it all. Only a substitute does something for us, in our place.

Jesus came as our consubstantial substitute, and he mediates for us now with God.[21] Paul says that there is "one mediator between God and man, the man Christ Jesus" (1 Tim 2:5). One of the major themes of the

18. For more on this distinction, see Clark, *Recovering the Reformed Confession*, 123–51.

19. Olevianus discusses and refutes the Lutheran Christology at length in *Firm Foundation*, 58–63.

20. Schaff, *Creeds of the Churches*, 2:63.

21. The Definition of Chalcedon says, καὶ ὁμοούσιον τὸν αὐτὸν ἡμῖν κατὰ τὴν ἀνθρωπότητα ("And consubstantial with us according to the humanity"; Schaff, *Creeds of the Churches*, 2:62).

book of Hebrews is Jesus's office and work as our Mediator before the throne of God. This is why we pray in Jesus's name. He stands before the Father for us as the representative righteous man for all of his people. He can do so because he bore in his humanity the wrath of God against sin.

QUESTION 18

But who now is that Mediator, who in one person is true God and also a true and righteous man?

Our Lord Jesus Christ, who is freely given unto us for complete redemption and righteousness.[22]

Even before the end the apostolic era (90s AD), the New Testament church faced a serious challenge from a group of people who professed faith in Jesus but denied the reality of his humanity. They said that Jesus only *seemed* (from the Greek verb δοκέω, "to seem") to be human. This was the docetic Christology, and thus we call them docetists. The ancient church councils declared this heresy against the ecumenical Christian faith. The apostle John's language in 2 John 7 reflects this problem: "For many deceivers have gone out into the world, those who do not confess the coming of Jesus Christ in the flesh. Such a one is the deceiver and the antichrist" (ESV). This heresy, the denial that Jesus is truly human, caused a schism in the church. We see it in 1 John 2:18–19: "Children, it is the last hour, and as you have heard that antichrist is coming, so now many antichrists have come. Therefore we know that it is the last hour. They went out from us, but they were not of us; for if they had been of us, they would have continued with us. But they went out, that it might become plain that they all are not of us" (ESV). According to John, this heresy has far-reaching implications. "Who is the liar but he who denies

22. "Wer ist aber derselbe Mittler, der zugleich wahrer Gott und ein wahrer gerechter Mensch ist? Unser Herr Jesus Christus, der uns zur vollkommenen Erlösung und Gerechtigkeit geschenkt ist" (Schaff, *Creeds of the Churches*, 3:312–13). "Quis autem est ille Mediator, qui simul est vere Deus ac verus ac perfecte iustus homo? Dominus noster Iesus Christus, qui factus est nobis sapientia a Deo, iustitia, sanctificatio et redemptio" (Niemeyer, *Collectio Confessionum*, 433).

that Jesus is the Christ? This is the antichrist, he who denies the Father and the Son" (1 John 2:22 ESV).

Jesus's consubstantial humanity means that our humanity, in the person of Christ as our representative, is present in the holy of holies (Heb 9:11–28). His true humanity, therefore, is essential to his office as mediator. An attack on Jesus's humanity is an attack his office as Mediator. In other words, ecumenical Christian truth and our salvation hang together. The "antichrists" also argued that "Jesus is not from God." Thus, John says, they have the "spirit of the antichrist" (1 John 4:3).

The patristic church battled various forms of the denial of Jesus's humanity. Some of them simply asserted a dualism of being, one inferior and one superior, that existed on a continuum or a ladder. Spirit was said to be at the top of the ladder, and matter (creation) at the bottom. These dualists denied that Jesus's humanity was real. They knew *a priori* that it could not be real.

In the second century, some built on this dualism to assert that not only did Jesus only seem human, but what humans need is salvation from lack of being via secret knowledge to which, they claimed, they alone had access. These were gnostics. They divided humanity into three groups: (1) those who had this knowledge, (2) ordinary Christians, and (3) those who had no idea about a transcendent truth. The gnostics taught an increasingly complex hierarchy of being. They regarded Yahweh as the "god" of the Old Testament and an inferior deity. They knew *a priori* that Yahweh could not be *the* God. They regarded matter as evil, something to be overcome.

This sort of rationalism (setting reason as an authority outside God's word and above God's word) has troubled the church not only from without but also from within. Some within the church also had have trouble confessing that Jesus is true God and true man. Some of them knew *a priori* that God's oneness was such that Jesus was only an *attribute* of the Father (dynamic monarchianism) or that God manifested himself in three distinct modes of being (modalist monarchianism). These monarchians usually also taught that Jesus was a godly man who was adopted into the deity. Hence this view is known as adoptionism.

There were others who taught that Jesus had not two natures and one person but two persons. Nestorius (ca. 361–ca. 451) and his followers were accused of this heresy. Their opponents, the Eutychians, taught that Jesus had only one nature. The Mediator cannot be two persons. He must be one person with two natures. In 1530, in the Augsburg Confession, the Protestants confessed:

> Likewise they teach that the Word, that is, the Son of God, took upon himself human nature in the womb of the blessed Virgin Mary so that there might be two natures, divine and human, inseparably conjoined in the unity of one person, one Christ, truly God and truly a human, being "born of the Virgin Mary," who truly "suffered, was crucified, died, and was buried" that he might reconcile the Father to us and be a sacrifice not only for original guilt but also for all actual sins of human beings. (art. 3)[23]

In the *BC 19* (1561), the Reformed churches confess:

> We believe that by this conception the person of the Son is inseparably united and connected with the human nature; so that there are not two Sons of God, nor two persons, but two natures united in one single person; yet each nature retains its own distinctive properties. As, then, the divine nature has always remained uncreated, without beginning of days or end of life, filling heaven and earth, so also has the human nature not lost its properties but remained a creature, having beginning of days, being a finite nature, and retaining all the properties of a real body. And though he has by his resurrection given immortality to the same, nevertheless he has not changed the reality of his human nature; forasmuch as our salvation and resurrection also depend on the reality of his body.

In the years between the Augsburg and the Belgic confessions, a significant fissure had developed between the way the Reformed and the Lutherans explained the "one person, two natures" formula. The question is explained in the *Epitome* of the *Formula of Concord* (1580): "The chief question was whether on the basis of the personal union of the divine and human natures—and likewise the characteristics of each—are intimately linked with each other within the person of Christ, in reality (that is, in

23. Kolb and Wengert, *Book of Concord*, 39.

fact and in truth), and to what extent they are intimately linked?" (art. 8).[24] The Lutherans characterized the Reformed with the epithet "sacramentarian," referring to the etymology of the Latin noun *sacramentum* as a military oath, which Zwingli had emphasized in his dispute with Luther in the 1520s through 1531. They accused the sacramentarians of asserting that the personal union of the divine and human natures was such that "neither nature in reality (that is, in fact and in truth) shares with the other what is unique to that nature." Thus, they complained, in the Reformed view, the two natures had only "the name in common."[25]

The Reformed and the Lutherans defined "personal union" differently. In effect, according to the Lutherans, if the Reformed disagreed with the Lutherans, they denied a real union. They deemed the Reformed version of the personal union to be mere nominalism. For the Lutherans, what could be said of the divinity could also be said of the humanity. What could be said of the person could be said of either nature. The Reformed, in contrast, wanted to preserve *both* the personal union of the two natures *and* the distinctions between them. Thus, following the Definition of Chalcedon, which says, "the distinction of natures being by no means taken away by the union, but rather the property of each nature being preserved, and concurring in one Person and one Subsistence, not parted or divided into two persons,"[26] *HC* 48 says:

> Since his human nature is not present wherever his deity is, are not then these two natures in Christ separated from one another?
>
> Not at all; for, since the deity is incomprehensible and everywhere present, it must follow that the same is not limited with the human nature he assumed and yet remains personally united to it.

The Reformed were concerned that the Lutheran approach to the communication of properties (*communicatio idiomatum*) placed in jeopardy the Chalcedonian formula, "consubstantial with the Father according to the deity, and consubstantial with us according to the humanity;

24. Kolb and Wengert, *Book of Concord*, 509.

25. Kolb and Wengert, *Book of Concord*, 509. For more on the christological controversy between the Reformed and the Lutherans in this period, see, Clark, *Caspar Olevian*, 104–36.

26. Schaff, *Creeds of the Churches*, 2:63.

in all things like unto us, without sin."[27] That consubstantiality with our humanity means that just as we are locally present, so too, in his human nature, Christ is locally present at the right of the Father. Ubiquity is a property of the divine nature, not his human nature.

The nature of the personal union or the communion of the two natures is a mystery. This is why Chalcedon employs adverbs it does: "*inconfusedly, unchangeably, indivisibly, inseparably.*"[28] According to Chalcedon, each nature remains what it was. The personal union does not change the nature substantially, yet there is one subsistence, not two, one person, not two. According to the catechism, the formula "one person, two natures" (as defined by Chalcedon) is no mere theory. It is essential to our salvation. It was humanity who sinned, but only God can save.

When the catechism says "mediator," it means federal representative. The same human nature that sinned had to perform righteousness, but only God the Son could, as the catechism says, sustain the burden of God's wrath and redeem us from it. We do not have two Mediators, two federal heads, two representatives, but one.

Our assurance rests in the reality of God the Son incarnate and in the obedience he performed for us, which has been imputed to us. As the *BC* reminds us, our hope of the resurrection rests in the consubstantiality of our humanity with his.

When we are at odds with another person, sometimes things come to such a state that the only solution is a go-between, someone whom both parties trust. Such is true for relations between God and humans. We often look for ways to relate to God. We build statues; we pick people living and dead as a representative for us with God. The Israelites wanted a mediator between themselves and the Lord at Sinai. When the Lord thundered from the darkness and gloom of Sinai, the Israelites recognized

27. *ὁμοούσιον τῷ πατρὶ κατὰ τὴν θεότητα, καὶ ὁμοούσιον2 τὸν αὐτὸν ἡμῖν κατὰ τὴν ἀνθρωπότητα* (Schaff, *Creeds of the Churches*, 2:62). As to why Chalcedon says both "indivisibly" *and* "inseparably," that language is also found in the letters of Leo I (d. AD 461), whose *Tome* (*Letter* 28) of AD 449 became the basis for the Definition of Chalcedon. He writes, "Hence both natures abiding in possession of their own properties such unity is the result of the union that whatever of Godhead is there is inseparable from the manhood: and whatever of manhood, is indivisible from the Godhead" (Leo the Great, *Sermons* [*NPNF* 2/12a:141]). Inseparability refers to the humanity to the deity, and indivisibility to the relation deity to the humanity.

28. Schaff, *Creeds of the Churches*, 63. Italics original. *ἀσυγχύτως, ἀτρέπτως, ἀδιαιρέτως, ἀχωρίστως* (62).

that Yahweh had revealed his glory and majesty, and they were justly terrified. "If we hear the voice of the LORD our God any more, we shall die" (Deut 5:25 ESV). In their place, they sent Moses to go to God, to "hear all that the LORD our God will say, and speak to us all that the LORD our God will speak to you, and we will hear and do it" (Deut 5:27 ESV). Moses was a holy man, but he was just a man. He died. He was buried and he remained in his tomb (Jude 9). He was a temporary mediator. He anticipated another mediator. That Mediator is the God-Man Christ Jesus (1 Tim 2:5; Heb 12:24).

QUESTION 19

From where do you know this?

From the holy gospel, which God himself revealed first in paradise, afterwards proclaimed by the holy patriarchs and prophets, and foreshadowed by the sacrifices and other ceremonies of the law; and finally fulfilled by his well-beloved Son.[29]

One of the many wonders about the good news is that someone *has* told us where to find it. We do not need to go rooting about in all the wrong places, looking for the wrong thing. What we need is salvation from the wrath of God, acceptance with God, true righteousness, and renewal in the image of Christ. The gospel announces that Jesus Christ has accomplished all these things for all of his people.

The first thing to notice here is how the Reformed churches specify the place where we learn about salvation: "from the holy gospel." This part of the answer is intentionally parallel to question 3: "From where do you know your misery? From the Law of God." Since in question 3 the churches confess that we learn about our sin and misery from the law, and in *HC* 19 we learn about our salvation from the gospel, we are making a

29. "Woher weisst du das? Aus dem heiligen Evangelio, welches Gott selbst anfänglich im paradies hat geoffenbaret, in der Folge durch die heiligen Erzväter und Propheten lassen verkündigen, und durch die Opfer und andere Ceremonien des Gesetzes vorgebildet, endlich aber durch seinen eingeliebten Sohn erfüllet" (Schaff, *Creeds of the Churches*, 3:313). "Unde id scis? Ex Evangelio, quod Deus primum in paradis patefecit, ac deinceps per patriarchs et prophetas propagavit: sacrificiis filium suum unigenitum complevit" (Niemeyer, *Collectio Confessionum*, 433–34).

distinction that was basic to the Reformation.[30] Martin Luther helped us recover a hermeneutical, theological distinction between law and gospel. This is the sense in which these two words are used here. Law, in *HC* 3, refers to that aspect of God's word that demands perfect obedience and righteousness, killing sinners. Gospel, in *HC* 19, refers to that life-giving aspect of God's word wherein he promises righteousness and salvation freely to all who trust in Christ alone for their righteousness before God.

Protestants established this distinction as fundamental to their understanding of God's word by 1521. By the time the catechism was published, all the magisterial Protestants, Reformed and Lutheran, universally accepted it.[31] Ursinus explains:

> Hence, the catechism in its primary and most general sense, may be divided as the doctrine of the church, into the law and gospel. It does not differ from the doctrine of the church as it respects the subject and matter of which it treats, but only in the form and manner in which these things are presented, just as strong meat designed for adults, to which the doctrine of the church may be compared, does not differ in essence from the milk and meat prepared for children, to which the catechism is compared by Paul in the passage already referred to. These two parts are termed, by the great mass of men, the Decalogue and the Apostles' creed; because the Decalogue comprehends the substance of the law, and the Apostles' creed that of the gospel. Another distinction made by this same class of persons is that of the doctrine of faith and works, or the doctrine of those things which are to be believed and those which are to be done.[32]

He was aware that people had analyzed the catechism in different ways, but each of them, he writes, could all be resolved to the fundamental, hermeneutical, theological distinction between law and gospel. The catechism, he writes, "consists of three parts. The first treats of the misery of man, the second of his deliverance from this misery, and the third of

30. See the discussion under *HC* 3. See also Clark, "Letter and Spirit," 331–63; Clark, "Law and Gospel."

31. Clark, "Letter and Spirit" and "Law and Gospel," provide references.

32. Ursinus, *Commentary*, 13.

gratitude, which division does not, in reality, differ from the above, because all the parts which are there specified are embraced in these three general heads."[33] When, in *HC* 3, the catechism says "law," it refers to the moral law in its pedagogical use. The metaphor of the pedagogue comes from Galatians 3:24, where Paul says, "Thus, the law became our pedagogue [παιδαγωγὸς] unto Christ." A pedagogue in the ancient world was not the friendly figure we might remember from school. Paul's image is of a severe teacher who beats his pupils when they err. So, in its pedagogical use, the law teaches us the greatness of our sin and misery. The third part of the catechism also refers to the law, in its third use, as the norm for the new life. Prayer fits in the third part as the most suitable expression of gratitude (*HC* 116). The second part of the catechism is the gospel as summarized by the Apostles' Creed and exhibited in the sacraments.

In his 1567 catechism, which we may fairly use as a commentary on the *HC*, Olevianus is just as clear about the necessity of distinguishing between law and gospel:

> 10 Q. What is the difference between the law and the gospel?
> A. The law is a doctrine that God has implanted in human nature and has repeated and renewed in His commandments. In it He holds before us, as if in a manuscript, what it is we are and are not to do, namely, obey Him perfectly both inwardly and outwardly. He also promises eternal life on the condition that I keep the law perfectly my whole life long. On the other hand, He threatens eternal damnation if I do not keep every provision of the law my whole life long but violate it in one or more of its parts.[34]

The good news, however, is a completely different message to sinners. Whereas we know the law both in nature and in Scripture, we know the gospel *only* in Scripture, and in it

> God does not demand but rather offers and gives us the righteousness that the law requires. This righteousness is the perfect obedience of the suffering and death of Jesus Christ, through which all sin and damnation, made manifest by the law, is pardoned and

33. Ursinus, *Commentary*, 14.

34. Olevian, *Firm Foundation*, 9.

> washed away (Rom. 5; Gal. 3). Furthermore, God does not give us forgiveness of sins in the gospel on the condition that we keep the law. Rather, even though we never have kept it nor will ever be able to keep it perfectly, He still has forgiven our sins and given us eternal life as an unmerited gift through faith in Jesus Christ. [35]

Luther would have found this language entirely familiar. Both law and gospel offer eternal life, but they do so on different conditions or through different instruments. The law demands personal obedience, and the benefits of the gospel are offered freely to those who believe.

The gospel has always been present after the fall. It was first revealed to Adam and Eve in the garden and progressively unfolded through the history of salvation (*historia salutis*) in the patriarchs and in the prophets, symbolically represented in the entire sacrificial system. Finally our Lord himself fulfilled it in his incarnation, obedience, death, and resurrection.

Biblical theology, that is, the study of the history of redemption, is not new.[36] Since the *Epistle of Barnabas* (ca. 120s AD), the *Epistle to Diognetus* (ca. 150s), and Irenaeus's *Against Heresies* (170s AD), the church has always read the Scriptures with a consciousness that the story was unfolding in types and shadows and finally fulfilled in Christ. Augustine says, "In the Old Testament the new is concealed and in the New Testament, the old is revealed."[37] The Reformers learned a version of this way of reading Scripture and continued to read Scripture this way.[38] Indeed, their sense of the progressive revelation of Scripture caused them to reject the medieval move of reinstituting the Levitical system in the Roman Catholic doctrines of transubstantiation and eucharistic sacrifice. The medieval church (and the Roman Catholic Church following it) took the church back to types and shadows. The Reformation was a return to fulfillment and to the freedom of the new covenant. It was also Reformers' understanding of the

35. Olevian, *Firm Foundation*, 10.

36. Fesko, "On the Antiquity," 443–77; Vos, "Idea of Biblical Theology," 4–24; Clark, "Christ and Covenant," 403–28.

37. Augustine, *Concerning the Catechizing of the Uninstructed* 4.8, in *St. Augustin: On the Holy Trinity*, 287.

38. Clark, *Caspar Olevian*, 11.

substantial continuity of the covenant of grace (in various administrations) that caused them to reject the Anabaptist account of redemptive history.[39]

When the gospel came in fulfillment of the types and shadows, it was not new. It had been revealed in types and shadows since the moment our Lord promised a suffering, head-crushing Savior (Gen 3:15). What is new in the new covenant is the reality, the end of types and shadows, but the substance of the gospel has been present since the garden.

When we look for salvation, it is essential that we look in the right place, in the gospel about Jesus the Savior. The gospel is that salvation finds and keeps us. To be sure, there is more to biblical theology than simply types and antitypes—there is the wonderful interplay between heaven and earth, a vertical dimension that adds layers to the horizontal and historical—but that is a rudimentary part of biblical theology, and it is a starting point.[40]

It is important to notice that, when the catechism turns to the gospel, when it begins to characterize the gospel, it does so in terms that would have been entirely familiar to the apostolic fathers in the second century, Augustine in the fifth century, Gottschalk of Orbais in the ninth century, and the Protestants in the sixteenth century and their heirs in the seventeenth and eighteenth centuries. It characterizes the gospel, in the first instance relative to the history of redemption, the progress of revelation, and the fulfillment of types, shadows, and promises in Christ. To be sure, the catechism is *also* perfectly comfortable in characterizing the gospel in terms of the Apostles' Creed (*HC* 22), which is both historical and more topically theological in nature. The creeds contain propositions about Jesus's life, death, and resurrection, but they relate them to us in historical sequence, so there is no necessary tension between historical acts and doctrinal truths.

According to Ursinus, the Mediator (Christ) is the "subject of the gospel, which teaches who and what kind of a Mediator he is." Indeed,

---

39. The explanation of baptism in *BC* 34 is profoundly redemptive historical (e.g., "who is our Red Sea"), and so is the critique of the Anabaptist denial of infant baptism in *BC* 34 and *HC* 74 (United Reformed Churches in North America, *Liturgical Forms and Prayers*, 191–92). See Clark, "House of Cards?," 74–81.

40. For more on this, see Vos, *Pauline Eschatology*; Vos, *Biblical Theology*.

Christ himself is the "author of the gospel," and the gospel is a part of the covenant.[41]

From the earliest days of the postapostolic church, through the medieval church, and into the Reformation and post-Reformation periods, Christians read the history of redemption not as centered on national Israel but on Jesus, the Israel of God. The idea that Scripture is centered on national Israel is a relatively new idea, about 150 years old. It is very popular in our age, but it simply does not account for Scripture, nor does it account for the way that Scripture interprets itself. Jesus says explicitly that all the Scriptures are about him (Luke 24:25–27; John 8:56; 2 Cor 1:20). Paul says: "For Christ is the end [τέλος] of the law for righteousness to everyone who believes" (Rom 10:4). By "end" he does not mean "stopping point." Rather, he means "purpose or fulfillment or intent." This is how the book of Hebrews would have us read Scripture. For example, Hebrews 3:5–6 argues that as important and faithful (πιστὸς) as Moses was, he was ultimately only a servant (θεράπων) "in God's house." His function was to serve as a "testimony" (μαρτύριον) to Christ, who is the "Son over the house" (υἱὸς ἐπὶ τὸν οἶκον). Of course, this is the unifying theme of Hebrews 11. The whole cloud of witnesses to whom the author appeals were trusting in Christ, who is at the top of Mount Zion, to whom the whole history of redemption points (Heb 12:18–24).

41. Ursinus, *Commentary*, 101.

Question 20
Are all men then saved by Christ as they perished in Adam?

Question 21
What is true faith?

Question 22
What then is necessary for a Christian to believe?

Question 23
What are these articles?

Lord's Day 7

QUESTION 20

Are all men then saved by Christ as they perished in Adam?

No, only those who by true faith are ingrafted into him and receive all his benefits.[1]

Considered as Creator, God is Father to all humans. James says, "Every good gift and every perfect gift is from above, coming down from the Father of lights, with whom there is no variation or shadow due to change" (Jas 1:17 ESV). Our Lord says that his Father "makes his sun rise on the evil and on the good, and sends rain on the just and on the unjust" (Matt 5:45). He actively sustains all that is, such that the apostle Paul said to the pagans at the Areopagus:

> The God who made the world and everything in it, being Lord of heaven and earth ... he himself gives to all mankind life and breath and everything. And he made from one man every nation of mankind to live on all the face of the earth, having determined allotted periods and the boundaries of their dwelling place, that they should seek God, and perhaps feel their way toward him and find him. Yet he is actually not far from each one of us, for
>
> "In him we live and move and have our being";
> as even some of your own poets have said,
> "For we are indeed his offspring."
> Being then God's offspring ... (Acts 17:24–29 ESV)

The natural knowledge of God is so universal that Paul was able to quote two pagan poets to make his point. Nevertheless, this is not what is usually intended when people say that God is the Father of all. What they usually mean is that God universally accepts humans in grace. This

1. "Werden denn alle Menschen wiederum durch Christum selig, wie sie durch Adam sind verloren worden? Nein: sondern allein diejenigen, die durch wahren Glauben ihm werden einverleibt, und alle seine Wohlthaten annehmen" (Schaff, *Creeds of the Churches*, 3:313). "Num igitur omnibus hominibus qui in Adam perierant, per Christum salus redditur? Non omnibus, verum iis tantum, qui vera fide ipsi inseruntur, eiusque beneficia amplectuntur" (Niemeyer, *Collectio Confessionum*, 434).

view, however, errs by confusing God's general providence with his particular salvation.

We confess that only believers are saved. Our Lord says, "I am the way, the truth, and the life. No one comes to the Father except through me" (John 14:6). In Matthew he says: "Enter by the narrow gate. For the gate is wide and the way is easy that leads to destruction, and those who enter by it are many. For the gate is narrow and the way is hard that leads to life, and those who find it are few" (Matt 7:13–14 ESV). Jesus is the door to the sheepfold (John 10:1). According to Jesus, there is no other way to God than through Jesus. The clearly intended inference is that all the other ways that others posit are false. There is only one Savior, Jesus. There is only one Mediator, Jesus (1 Tim 2:5).

The good news is that those "who believed in his name, he gave the right to become children of God, who were born, not of blood nor of the will of the flesh nor of the will of man, but of God" (John 1:12–13 ESV). The Christian faith is *both* exclusive *and* saving. Salvation from the wrath to come does exist, and it is through faith. This is why Hebrews 4:2–3 says, "For the gospel has come to us just as to them, but the word of hearing did not profit them, because they were not united by faith with those who listened. For those who believed entered that rest." True faith is the only instrument by which we embrace Christ and his benefits, and it is only those with true faith who are saved.[2]

Faith in Jesus is a gift from God (Eph 2:8–10). Our Lord says, "It is not possible for one to come to me to me except the Father who sent me draws him. And I will raise him up on the last day" (John 6:44). Jesus calls his people out of darkness and into light. He gives new life and with it true faith, and through faith he gives free justification with God, union and communion with Christ, salvation, adoption, and eternal life. Ursinus writes, "Salvation through Christ is not bestowed upon all who perished in Adam; but only on those who, by a true faith, are ingrafted into Christ, and receive all his benefits." He adds that the reason not all are saved is not any "insufficiency of merit and grace in him." The atonement was sufficient for the sins of the whole world, but the *intent* of the atonement was particular. Yet, the responsibility for condemnation belongs to those

2. Ursinus, *Commentary*, 112.

who do not believe "because men reject the benefits of Christ offered in the gospel, and so perish by their own fault, and not because of any insufficiency in the merits of Christ." Ursinus alludes to the underlying issue here when he writes, in response to an objection, "But the reason why all men do not believe, nor apply these benefits to themselves, is a higher, and deeper question—one which does not properly belong to this place."[3] He is referring, of course, to the doctrine of election and reprobation, which had long been taught in the church by Augustine, the ninth-century Augustinians, Aquinas, the late medieval neo-Augustinians, and the magisterial Protestant Reformers.[4] The catechism itself clarifies some of these matters, as does Ursinus's lecture on *HC* 21. We may be confident that we are meant to understand *HC* 20–21 in light of the doctrine of unconditional election since Ursinus appeals to it through his lectures.[5]

In time, the Remonstrants challenged this Reformed doctrine. In the 1610 Articles of the Remonstrance (art. 1), they confess that God elects those whom God foresees will believe and cooperate with grace to the end, that "Christ died for all men and for every man, so that he has obtained for them all, by his death ... the forgiveness of sins."[6] The Synod of Dort,

3. Ursinus, *Commentary*, 106–7.

4. Clark, "Election and Predestination," 90–122.

5. Bierma writes of the "near silence" of the catechism on predestination. He theorizes that the authors "intentionally steered clear" of it in order to facilitate doctrinal harmony (*Theology of the Heidelberg Catechism*, 49–50). There are two difficulties with this explanation: the catechism does not avoid predestination but rather treats it as Calvin did in book three of the *Institutes*, as an *a posteriori* explanation of who does and does not come to faith. Further, both Luther and Melanchthon, with whom Ursinus studied for several years, taught predestination. On Luther, see *Bondage of the Will*; on Luther and Melanchthon, see Clark, "Election and Predestination," 93–94; on Melanchthon, see Clark, *Caspar Olevian*, 172–73. Ursinus invokes the doctrine of unconditional election under *HC* 6–7, 9, 18–19, 21, 25–27, 29, 33, 40, 51–54 (where he discusses predestination at length), 56–58, 60, 64, 68, 74, 86, 90–91, 94, 96, 98, 100, 103–4, 115–16, and 123. Olevianus teaches the doctrine of double predestination throughout his works (Clark, *Caspar Olevian*, 170–77). See also his 1579 commentary on Romans and his 1585 treatise on covenant theology, *De substantia*; *Firm Foundation*, 30, 37, 54, 65, 90, 110; *Exposition*, 10, 12, 13, 32–33, 47, 60, 69, 71, 112, 129, *et passim*.

6. Schaff, *Creeds of the Churches*, 3:545–46. The question of hypothetical universalism was not yet before the Reformed churches when the catechism was adopted. In Canons of Dort 2.3, the churches affirm the universal *sufficiency* of the atonement and Canons of Dort, rejection of errors 2.3 effectively precludes hypothetical universalism (United Reformed Churches in North America, *Liturgical Forms and Prayers*, 267, 269). There were at least two delegates to the Synod of Dort who were toying with alternative language concerning the atonement. In his 1627 *Dissertation on the Death of Christ*, John Davenant (1572–1641) argues for a kind of hypothetical universalism. He apparently held some version of this view while he was a delegate to Dort. His colleague Samuel Ward (1572–1543) also held some version of this position. After Dort, Moïses Amyraut (1596–1644) and Josué La Place

representing the Reformed churches across Europe and the British Isles, rejected this revision of the faith in the first and second heads of doctrine in Canons of Dort.[7]

The last thing under this question to be addressed is the doctrine of mystical union.[8] The sense of "engrafted" in the answer of *HC* 20 is that grace alone unites us to Christ, through faith alone. The teaching of the catechism and of its major authors and editors is clear.[9] *HC* 32 asks, "But why are you called a Christian?" The answer is, "Because *by faith* I am a member of Christ and thus a partaker of his anointing."[10] Faith is the instrument of our Spirit-wrought union with Christ. Both the German (*die durch wahren Glauben*) and Latin texts (*per fidem*) are clear that faith is the instrument through which we are united to Christ.[11] The Holy Spirit gives new life and true faith (*HC* 65). We need not set the Spirit against faith. The Spirit is the moving cause, and faith is the instrument. Thus we confess in *BC* 22, "We do not mean that faith itself justifies us, for it is the instrument with which we embrace Christ our Righteousness." Rather, Christ's

---

(1596–1665) taught, according to B. B. Warfield, "that election succeeds, in the order of thought, not merely the decree of the fall but that of redemption as well, taking the term redemption here in the narrower sense of the impetration of redemption by Christ. They thus suppose that in His electing decree God conceived man not merely as fallen but as already redeemed. This involves a modified doctrine of the atonement from which the party has received the name of Hypothetical Universalism, holding as it does that Christ died to make satisfaction for the sins of all men without exception if—if, that is, they believe: but that, foreseeing that none would believe, God elected some to be granted faith through the effectual operation of the Holy Spirit" (*Calvin and Calvinism*, 364–65). The Swiss Reformed Churches rejected the doctrine of hypothetical universalism in the Helvetic Consensus Formula (1675; Dennison, *Reformed Confessions*, 5:516–30), as did orthodox Reformed theologians such as Francis Turretin (*Institutes of Elenctic Theology*, 4.14.7) and John Owen (*The Death of Death in the Death of Christ* in *Works*, 10:139–479). Warfield's judgment, "This modification [hypothetical universalism] also received the condemnation of the contemporary Reformed world" (*Calvin and Calvinism*, 363), is correct. For Davenant's remarks on Dort, see Milton, *British Delegation and the Synod*, 218–22. On Hales's relation to Reformed orthodoxy, see Godfrey, "John Hales' Good-Night," 165–80; Milton, "Distorting Mirror."

7. United Reformed Churches in North America, *Liturgical Forms and Prayers*, 259–70.

8. See the discussion under *HC* 32.

9. *Pace* Klooster (*Our Only Comfort*, 1:198–205), who argues that the catechism teaches that faith is the product, not the instrument, of our ingrafting. His conclusion is befuddling because he quotes but ignores not only the plain sense of *HC* 20 but also *HC* 32, as well as the language of Olevianus and Ursinus.

10. Emphasis added. This is a literal rendering of the German.

11. Müller, *Die Bekenntnisschriften*, 691; Niemeyer, *Collectio Confessionum*, 437.

righteousness imputed is the ground of our justification. Nevertheless, "faith is the instrument that keeps us in communion with him."[12]

The question in *HC* 65 says that faith is the instrument of our mystical union with Christ: "Since, then, we are made partakers of Christ and all his benefits *by faith alone* ..." (*Dieweil denn allein der Glaube uns Christi* ...). The Latin text is equally clear. "Since, therefore, faith alone makes us sharers in Christ and all his benefits ..." [13] The answer makes explicit the link between the prevenient work of the Spirit, since "the Holy Spirit works [faith] in our hearts."[14] The Latin text says that the "Holy Spirit kindles faith in our hearts."[15] *HC* 80 synthesizes the work of the Spirit through faith when we confess "by the Holy Spirit we are ingrafted into Christ."[16] It is difficult to imagine how the catechism could be clearer about the instrument of our mystical union with Christ.

We should be confident that the catechism is teaching us that faith is the instrument through which the Spirit works union with Christ since it is what Ursinus wrote, in his *Summa theologiae*, in preparation for the *HC*. In his definition of faith he says, "[Faith] ... having been awakened in the hearts of the elect by the Holy Spirit, makes us living members of Christ."[17] Olevianus published the same view in his 1567 *Exposition of the Apostles Creed*: "since He effectually confederates us to Himself through faith by the power of His Spirit so that He might rule in us."[18] Here again, we see that it is the Spirit (*virtute sui Spiritus*) who unites us to Christ, but he operates through the instrument (*per fidem*) of faith.

---

12. This translation is based on the French text in Schaff, *Creeds of the Churches*, 409.

13. Schaff, *Creeds of the Churches*, 3:328. "Quoniam igitur sola fides nos Christi atque omnium eius beneciorum participes facit" (Niemeyer, *Collectio Confessionum*, 444).

14. "Der Heilige Geist wirket" (Schaff, *Creeds of the Churches*, 3:328).

15. "A Spiritu Sancto, qui eam per praedicationem Evangelii in cordibus nostris accendit" (Niemeyer, *Collectio Confessionum*, 444).

16. "Wir durch den Heiligen Geist Christo werden eingeleibet" (Schaff, *Creeds of the Churches*, 3:335). "Nos per Spiritum sanctum inseri Christo" (Niemeyer, *Collectio Confessionum*, 448).

17. Larger Catechism 38, in Bierma et al., *Introduction*, 169.

18. Olevianus, *Exposition*, 16. "Per fidem virtute sui Spiritus efficaciter se nobis confoederet" (*Expositio symboli apostolici*, 15).

QUESTION 21

What is true faith?

True faith is not only a sure knowledge whereby I hold for truth all that God has revealed to us in his Word; but also a hearty trust, which the Holy Spirit works in me by the gospel, that not only to others, but to me also, forgiveness of sins, everlasting righteousness and salvation are freely given by God, merely of grace, only for the sake of Christ's merits.[19]

We receive Christ and his benefits by faith alone, but what is faith? That is how the Latin text puts the question: "What is faith?"[20] The answer is that faith has three aspects: knowledge, assent, and trust. Our English translation follows the German text, which implies all three, but the Latin text makes them explicit: "It is not only *knowledge*, by which I firmly *assent* to everything which God has given to us in his Word, but also a certain *trust* ignited in my heart by the Holy Spirit through the Gospel."

KNOWLEDGE

"Blind faith" is an oxymoron. True faith knows whom and what it trusts. It is not faith to say, "O Lord, if you exist ..." That is superstition. True faith has a known object, has content. Faith has a reason to believe God because he has revealed himself. Everyone can see that he is (Rom 1:19–20). Everyone knows his law (Rom 2:14–15). There are particularities in faith. Thus Paul writes:

> That is why it depends on faith, in order that the promise may rest on grace and be guaranteed to all his offspring—not only to

19. "Was ist wahrer Glaube? Es ist nicht allein eine gewisse Erkenntniss, dadurch ich Alles für wahr halte, was uns Gott in seinem Worte hat geoffenbaret, sondern auch ein herzliches Vertrauen, welches der heilige Geist durch's Evangelium in mir wirket, dass nicht allein Andern, sondern auch mir Vergebung der Sünden, ewige Gerechtigkeit und Seligkeit von Gott geschenket sei, aus lauter Gnaden, allein um des Verdienstes Christi willen" (Schaff, *Creeds of the Churches*, 3:313). "Quid est fides? Est non tantum notitia, qua firmiter assentior omnibus, quae Deus nobis in verbo suo patefecit, sed etiam certa fiducia, a Spiritu sancto per Evangelium in corde meo accensa, in qua in Deo acquiesco, certo satuiens, non solum aliis, sed mihi quoque remissionem peccatorum, aeternam iustitiam et vitam donatam esse idque gratis, ex Dei misericordia, propter unius Christi meritum" (Niemeyer, *Collectio Confessionum*, 434).

20. Olevianus, *Exposition*, 16–17.

> the adherent of the law but also to the one who shares the faith of Abraham, who is the father of us all, as it is written, "I have made you the father of many nations"—in the presence of the God in whom he believed, who gives life to the dead and calls into existence the things that do not exist. In hope he believed against hope, that he should become the father of many nations, as he had been told, "So shall your offspring be." (Rom 4:16–18 ESV)

Because humans are finite, there are limits to what we can know. Further, after the fall, we are afflicted and limited by sin. Our intellects are clouded by ignorance and confusion. Our senses, though generally reliable—God created the world to be known and created us to know it—sometimes betray us. We certainly do not know things the way God knows them.[21] Nevertheless, God is greater than our limits and our sins. He spits into the dust, makes clay, and gives sight to blind men (John 9:6). God does so by the grace of his sovereign Spirit, who hovered over the face of the waters (Gen 1:2), who, at Pentecost, began to untangle Babel (Acts 2:6), who is the "Lord and giver of life."[22] The same Lord who revealed his law and his gospel enables us, by his Spirit, to know him and his truth with sufficient certainty.

ASSENT

The second aspect of faith is the "the concurrence of the will."[23] Our noun is derived from the Latin noun *assensus*, which has the same sense of approval, agreement, or approbation. Assent depends on knowledge. Like knowledge, it has an object, an extramental reference. It agrees with or to something outside itself. It is not ascent or climbing up a ladder, as it were, into the divine intellect. That was a journey on which a large number of medieval theologians and mystics embarked. It is a journey on which contemporary mystics and rationalists are engaged. The desire to know what God knows, the way he knows it is the quest for illegitimate religious certainty.[24] It is an ancient desire, going all the way back to the garden.

21. Clark, *Recovering the Reformed Confession*, 134–51.

22. Schaff, *Creeds of the Churches*, 2:57.

23. *OED*, s.v. "assent."

24. Clark, *Recovering the Reformed Confession*, 39–70.

Mysticism is just as seductive as rationalism, and it is very much the spirit of our age. In the nineteenth century, when—in Europe, at least—confidence in the power of almighty reason to solve all problems was already beginning to show cracks, the Romantic movement turned to the power of religious experience to explain Christianity. The lines between theological liberalism and evangelical pietism began to blur. Behind those movements were the Anabaptist mystics in the early sixteenth century, and behind them a long line of medieval mystics who sought union with the being of God through contemplation and abandonment of this world.

We live in an ostensibly post-Enlightenment age, but only partly. We have shifted the center of authority from the intellect to affections. Thus, where the Enlightenment movements made claims about objective truth on rationalist and empiricist presuppositions, subjectivists begin with subjective experience and make claims about what is true subjectively. Underneath that subjectivism is the same Enlightenment bedrock conviction of human autonomy.

The Christian faith, however, requires us to give assent to facts, to realities, to truths that exist apart from our experience of them. Our experience does not make the resurrection a fact. The tomb was empty before the disciples and the women got to it, before they experienced it with their senses. Jesus did not rise in their hearts or in their feelings. He rose in objective reality, and he will return in the same way.

Assent implies personal knowledge. It is not mere theory about hypotheticals or possibilities. It is not implicit faith about things that other people claim to know or claim to have experienced. This sort of credulity is a problem for both Roman Catholics and neo-Pentecostalists. True faith rests in God as he has revealed himself, in Christ the Word of God incarnate, and in Holy Scripture, the inspired, infallible word of God written. When we give assent to the Christian faith, we are giving assent to concrete claims and propositions in Holy Scripture about Scripture itself, God, humanity, Christ, salvation, church, and last things.

Through rationalism and mysticism, many have sought to ascend to God instead of being content to assent to him and to his truth. Paul says:

> But the righteousness based on faith says, "Do not say in your heart, 'Who will ascend into heaven?'" (that is, to bring Christ

> down) "or 'Who will descend into the abyss?'" (that is, to bring Christ up from the dead). But what does it say? "The word is near you, in your mouth and in your heart" (that is, the word of faith that we proclaim); because, if you confess with your mouth that Jesus is Lord and believe in your heart that God raised him from the dead, you will be saved. (Rom 10:6–9 ESV)

When we assent to the faith, we are not going up to God, but rather we are agreeing that he has come to us in Christ, that he has revealed himself to us in his word, and that his word is truth.

TRUST

There is a third aspect to the Reformed definition of faith: trust. James characterizes this aspect of true faith as entailing a degree of certainty. "But let him ask in faith, with no doubting, for the one who doubts is like a wave of the sea that is driven and tossed by the wind" (Jas 1:6 ESV). This aspect of faith is the *crux* of the disagreement between Rome and the Reformation over the nature of faith in the act of justification. In session 7 of the Council of Trent (January 13, 1547), Rome declared that when Paul writes that we are "justified by faith and freely," it means, "Faith is the beginning of salvation (*initium salutis*). It is the foundation (*fundamentum*) and root (*radix*) of salvation 'without which it is impossible to please God.'"[25] According to Rome, faith is necessary but not sufficient for acceptance with God. Of course, we have not arrived at Rome's definition of faith. So far, for the moment, we are assuming that Rome means by faith what we mean by faith. So, the first thing to understand is that, even were we to assume the same definition, faith according to Rome has a different function in justification than it has for confessional Protestants.

These different functions are in part because Rome and the Reformation have two different understandings of the nature of justification. According to Rome, justification is not an event. It is a process that begins with grace but that requires us to prepare ourselves and to cooperate with grace unto justification.[26] Therefore, faith can only be the

25. "Cum vero Apostolus dicit, iustificari hominem 'per fidem' [can. 9], 'et gratis' [Rom 8, 22, 24]" (Denzinger, *Enchiridion Symbolorum*, 288, §801).

26. Decretum de iustificatione, cap. 5–6 (Denzinger, *Enchiridion Symbolorum*, 286–87).

beginning. For Rome, justification is not a once-for-all, forensic declaration on the basis of Christ's righteousness and merits imputed, but rather it is God's recognition of what is true of the Christian intrinsically, inherently. In other words, according to Rome, one is only as justified as one is sanctified. Faith is the beginning of justification because it is an essential part in the process of sanctification/justification, which began at baptism.

This brings us to the Roman definition of faith. Aquinas taught that faith is that which is formed by love (*fides formata caritate*), that "charity is the form of faith."[27] In this definition he subtly changes Paul's teaching about faith "working by love" (Gal 5:6), whereby he was teaching that true faith gives evidence of its existence by manifesting itself in acts of charity.[28] This was exactly what James teaches in James 2:14.[29] By turning "working by love" into "formed by love," Thomas turned a fruit into that which makes faith what it is. In other words, Thomas turned faith, in justification, from the empty hand that receives what Christ has done into the part of the ground of justification—remember, for Rome, justification is progressive sanctification. Thus, ordinarily, according to Rome, no one is ever actually justified in this life because no one is ever perfected in this life.

These notions of progressive justification/sanctification and faith formed by love (i.e., that Spirit-wrought sanctity and cooperation with grace make faith what it is) are reflected in Trent's exposition of justification. When Rome speaks of "a translation, from that state wherein man is born a child of the first Adam, to the state of grace," she is not speaking about God's declaration about and to the sinner but of a process of gradual transformation of the sinner by grace and cooperation with grace.[30] This much is made clear when Rome teaches: "The beginning of that justification must proceed from the predisposing grace of God through Jesus Christ, that is, from His vocation, whereby, without any merits on their part, they are called; that they who by sin had been cut off from God, may be disposed through His quickening and helping grace to convert

27. *ST* 2a2ae 4.1., resp. obj. 3; Godfrey, "Faith Formed by Love," 267–84.

28. One sees this conflation and confusion in "Faith," in *ODCC*. This conflation is groundless. Even the in Vulgate the difference between *per caritatem operatur* and *fides formata* is quite clear.

29. Venema, *Children at the Lord's Table*, 76–78.

30. Schroeder, *Canons and Decrees*, 31; Denzinger, *Enchiridion Symbolorum*, 285, §796.

themselves to their own justification by freely assenting to and cooperating with that grace."[31]

We might be forgiven for thinking that this was the language of the Remonstrants. We can see why the Synod of Dort was so vociferous in its rejection of the Remonstrant errors. For Rome, once we are regenerated in baptism, we are engaged in a pilgrimage, the outcome of which is uncertain. God acts first—that is why grace is said to be prevenient—but notice the nature of the grace. It is "exciting" (*excitantem*) and "helping" (*adjuvantem*) but not definitive.[32] We must still do our part, which, according to Rome, we are able to do because, though sin is harmful, sin is not deadly. We say with Paul that, by nature, we are "dead in sins and trespasses" (Eph 2:1). Like the Remonstrants, Rome says that we are wounded but able, grace helping us, to do our part. This is also why the confessional Reformed churches resist errors such as federal vision theology, because once they have invoked the category of covenant, they teach exactly what Rome and the Remonstrants teach.

Rome's synergism in justification is quite clear when she speaks of "converting one's self unto his justification" (*convertendum se ad suam ipso rum justiftcationem*).[33] Rome teaches that justification is by grace and cooperation with grace. Thus, Calvin writes on Galatians 5:6 that when we are discussing justification, we must not talk about love or works, but rather we must adhere resolutely to the "exclusive particle."[34] That particle is the *sola* in *sola gratia* and *sola fide*. Rome teaches grace and faith, but she denies grace *alone* and faith *alone* in their respective offices.

Rome is entirely unembarrassed by her doctrine of preparation. Grace, according to Rome, creates in us a disposition (*habitus*). By the grace of faith we are, according to Rome, *disposed* unto justification, but we are not justified. We must do our part. We must capitalize on the grace whereby we have been roused and excited to do our part, that is, convert ourselves;

31. Trent, session 6, chapter 5, in Schroeder, *Canons and Decrees*, 31–32; Denzinger, *Enchiridion Symbolorum*, 286.

32. Denzinger, *Enchiridion Symbolorum*, 286, §797.

33. Denzinger, *Enchiridion Symbolorum*, 286, §797.

34. "Ergo quum versaris in causa iustificationis, cave ullum charitatis vel operum mentionem admittas, sed mordcus retine particulam exclusivam." Calvin, *Epistolas ad Galatas, ad Ephesios, ad Philippenses, ad Colossenses*, 120.11–13.

we must begin to prepare ourselves for further grace because it is to those who do their part whom God gives grace.[35] Thus, the "justification of the impious" means not that God actually justifies those who are in themselves intrinsically impious or unjust, but rather it means that God justifies those who are not completely, intrinsically just but who have "this disposition or preparation" for justification.[36] By definition, according to Rome, justification is "not remission of sins merely (*sola peccatorum remissio*), but also the sanctification and renewal of the inward man."[37] That sanctification is an act of the human will.[38] That is why, for Rome, justification must be said to be "increased" (*incremento*; cap. X). That is why, according to Rome, grace can be lost.[39] We must cooperate with grace. Faith is necessary, but it is not sufficient. Our cooperation is equally necessary.

With this background in view, it is easy to see why Rome declares, "If any one says, that justifying faith is nothing else but confidence (*fiduciam*) in the divine mercy which remits sins for Christ's sake; or, that this confidence alone (*fiduciam solam*) is that whereby we are justified; let him be anathema."[40]

According to the Council of Trent, anyone who teaches that sinners are declared righteous before God only (*sola*) on the basis of Christ's righteousness for us imputed to us, and that sinners receive Christ and his righteousness only (*sola*) through faith resting on and receiving Christ, is eternally condemned. According to Rome, anyone who claims to know with certainty that he is now justified is presumptuous and arrogant because, apart from a supernatural work of grace (a second blessing), no one can know that he is justified because, ordinarily, no one is actually justified before God before perfection (complete sanctification).

In contrast, in *HC* 21, "a heartfelt trust" (*herzliches Vertrauen*) is of the essence of true faith.[41] The contrast with Rome is explicit in the Latin

35. Denzinger, *Enchiridion Symbolorum*, 286–87, §798.

36. "Hanc dispositionem, seu præparationem" (Denzinger, *Enchiridion Symbolorum*, 287, §799).

37. "Sanctificatio et renovatio interioris hominis" (Denzinger, *Enchiridion Symbolorum*, 287, §799).

38. "Per voluntariam susceptionem gratiæ et donorum" (Denzinger, *Enchiridion Symbolorum*, 287, §799).

39. Decretum de justificatione, cap. 14 (Denzinger, *Enchiridion Symbolorum*, 292–93, §807).

40. Denzinger, *Enchiridion Symbolorum*, 296, §822.

41. Müller, *Die Bekenntnisschriften*, 687.

text, which affirms that faith is a "certain trust" (*certa fiducia*).[42] This word *fiducia* ("trust, confidence") is the very word used by Trent in 1547, which she condemned. According to Trent, it is presumption to say, "I am justified." How did she arrive at this conclusion? In the Vulgate *fiducia* is often used to mean "confidence" or "trust" (e.g., Deut 28:52; Pss 21:10/22:9 in English; 70:5/71:5). It also means "boldness" (Acts 4:29, 31; 9:27) and finally "confidence" (Heb 3:6; 10:19; Eph 3:12; 1 Tim 3:13), but there are passages (e.g., Job 8:14; 18:14) where the sense is closer to "presumption" or "misplaced trust." That is the sense in which Rome tends to use *fiducia*.

The Reformed confess that it is not presumption or arrogance to say that we are certain that we are justified, because we do not share Rome's definition of justification as a process (progressive sanctification), nor do we share its definition of faith as sanctification unto justification. In the act of justification, faith is knowledge, assent, and confidence in God's promises, in Christ. That is why the Palatinate theologians were so pointed about the nature of faith. That is why they chose the words *certa fidicua*. They wanted to be crystal clear that we have a rock-solid confidence because its ground is not our sanctification in this life. Its ground is Christ's perfect righteousness for us (*pro nobis*) imputed to us as if we ourselves had done it (*HC* 60).

Because Christ's righteousness is the ground, our justification is not a legal fiction. When Roman Catholic critics make this charge, they show that they do not understand Scripture or the Reformed confession. Indeed, it is Roman Catholics who are presumptuous, who intend to stand before God on the basis of a legal fiction: their intentions and efforts.

We have confidence because the object of our trust is Christ. He is worthy of confidence, even of boasting. That is what Scripture says. Paul says in Ephesians 3:12 that we have "boldness and access with confidence." That is why we draw near to the throne of grace with confidence, because we have free access to it, through Christ's body, on the basis of his finished work (Heb 4:16). We have confidence (*fiducia*) to enter the holy places through Christ's blood shed for us, not in a eucharistic sacrifice but in the once-for-all death of Christ (Heb 10:19). Our heart does not condemn us, because Christ is for us, and therefore we have confidence (*fiducia*)

42. Niemeyer, *Collectio Confessionum*, 434.

before God (1 John 3:21). This is why we pray with confidence (*fiducia*; 1 John 5:14). The gospel is plain enough in the Vulgate that even Rome should be able to see it, but she cannot because she will not. So, there are thee aspects to faith: knowledge, assent, and trust. A proper definition of faith cannot omit any of the three.

There are those who have a purely historical faith or a temporary faith.[43] There were unbelievers who knew that Jesus had been raised from the dead, but they did not believe (Matt 28:13–14; 13:1–30). They knew the facts of redemption and may even have assented to their truth, at least for a time, but they lacked a hearty trust in Christ. This is because true faith is a gift that involves the intellect and the will, but it is not their product. Faith is a supernatural act by God the Holy Spirit, who makes dead bones live (Ezek 37:4), who raises the spiritually dead to live and who grants to them faith and through it union with Christ and all his benefits.

Faith also knows, assents, and trusts in God's word. We say, "whereby I hold for truth all that God has revealed to us in His Word." When we say "hold for truth" (the Latin text says, "firmly assent to everything that God has revealed in his Word"), we confess that we receive God's word as he presents it. Unlike modernists, the Reformed churches do not stand in judgment over Scripture. It stands in judgment over us. It presents itself as true, and that is how the church has always received it. In *BC* 7, we confess Scripture to be the "infallible rule" for Christian faith and practice.[44] Ursinus writes that a Christian "believes that every thing which the Scriptures contain is true, and from God."[45] In the nineteenth and twentieth centuries, Reformed theologians began to use the words *inerrant* and *inerrancy* in light of the relentless attacks on the reliability of Scripture by modernists, and we were right to do so.[46] We were defending the historic Christian view of Scripture.

Insofar as faith looks to Christ, it is objective. In *HC* 21, however, we confess that Christ and his benefits are not only for others "but for

43. Ursinus, *Commentary*, 109–10.

44. Schaff, *Creeds of the Churches*, 3:388.

45. Ursinus, *Commentary*, 111.

46. E.g., Hodge and Warfield, *Inspiration*; Warfield, *Revelation and Inspiration*; Stonehouse and Wooley, *Infallible Word*.

me also." Here the catechism is surely echoing Luther's 1535 *Lectures on Galatians*, where he says:

> Therefore read these words "me" and "for me" with great emphasis, and accustom yourself to accepting this "me" with a sure faith and applying it to yourself. Do not doubt that you belong to the number of those who speak this "me." Christ did not love only Peter and Paul and give Himself for them, but the same grace belongs and comes to us as to them; therefore we are included in this "me." For just as we cannot deny that we are all sinners, and just as we are obliged to say that through his sin Adam destroyed us and made us enemies of God who are liable to God's wrath and judgment and worthy of eternal death—for all terrified hearts feel and confess this, in fact, more than is proper—so we cannot deny that Christ died for our sins in order that we might be justified. For He did not die to make the righteous righteous; He died to make sinners into righteous men, the friends and sons of God, and heirs of all heavenly gifts.[47]

True faith gives assurance because it begins with and rests in Christ and his promises. Just as believers know the greatness of their sin and misery out of the law of God (*HC* 2–3), so too they know the glory of the gospel, that Christ and all his benefits have been freely given by grace and received through faith alone.

Behind the existential realities of the Christian experience lie deep, reassuring truths. Under question 20, we touched briefly on the question of who comes to faith and why. In his lecture on this question Ursinus answers this question unequivocally:

> Justifying faith is peculiar to all the elect, and to them alone: for it is given to all the elect, and only to them, including even infants, as it respects an inclination to faith. "No man can come to me except the Father draw him." "It is given unto you to know the mystery of the kingdom of heaven: but to them it is not given." "As many as were ordained unto eternal life believed." "Whom he did predestinate,

47. *LW* 26:179.

> them he also called, justified and glorified." "Faith is the gift of God." "But they have not all obeyed the gospel; for Esaias saith, Lord who hath believed," &c., "for all men have not faith?" (John 6:44. Matt. 13:11. Acts 13:48. Rom. 8:30; 10:16. Eph. 2:8. 2 Thes. 3:2.)[48]

This means that believers believe only because God has loved them, elected them unconditionally, in Christ, from all eternity. These truths undergird the doctrine of salvation throughout the catechism.[49]

The catechism briefly lists some of Christ's benefits given to believers through faith alone: forgiveness of sins, everlasting righteousness (both aspects of justification), and salvation. In contrast to those who juxtapose justification and salvation, teaching that justification is by grace alone through faith alone, but final salvation is through faith and works, this idea is completely without support in the *HC*. According to the Reformed churches, both justification and salvation (justification, sanctification, and glorification) are freely given.[50] The Latin text says, "freely, out of the mercy of God."[51]

The last clause is as important today as it was when it was first published and confessed by the Reformed churches: "only on account of the merit of Christ."[52] The Reformed churches are very clear on three things about merit: (1) we believe in merit, (2) we confess that Christ's (condign) merits are imputed to believers as the ground of their justification and salvation, and (3) we deny that believers have any merit, condign or congruent.

That *des Verdienstes* was translated with *meritum* is significant. It placed the Reformed confession in the broader stream of Christian theology, which had long taught a doctrine of merit. It rejected the medieval and Roman doctrine that Christians can accrue condign merit. Aquinas defined condign merit (*meritum de condigno*) as having two aspects: a good work has condign merit because it proceeds from the "divine motion" (*ex vi*

48. Ursinus, *Commentary*, 113.

49. On the preaching of the gospel as the means by which the Holy Spirit brings new life and true faith, see the discussion under *HC* 20, 65.

50. "Aus lauter Gnaden" (Schaff, *Creeds of the Churches*, 3:313).

51. "Gratis, ex Dei misericordia" (Niemeyer, *Collectio Confessionum*, 434).

52. "Allein um des Verdienstes Christi willen" (Schaff, *Creeds of the Churches*, 3:313). "Propter unius Christi meritum" (Niemeyer, *Collectio Confessionum*, 434).

motionis divinae) and from "free choice" (*ex libero arbitrio*).[53] That which has condign merit has intrinsic worth before God. Congruent merit is covenantal merit, whereby God is said to have promised to accept as worthy best efforts. Gabriel Biel notoriously formulates this view: "To those who do what is in themselves, God denies not grace."[54] Aquinas also taught that, insofar as a work is ours (by the exercise of free choice), we may also say that it has congruent merit.[55] The Roman Catholic Church today affirms the doctrine of congruent merit on the basis of the "immeasurable inequality" between God and humanity and that God has "freely chosen to associate man with the work of his grace."[56] In the Roman scheme, God acts first, then we cooperate with grace, thereby accumulating merit.

In *HC* 21 and 84, the Reformed churches explicitly confess that Christ merited for his elect all his benefits. We confess that Christ's condign merit is imputed to us and is the legal basis of our righteousness with God and our salvation from the wrath to come. In *HC* 60, 63, and 86, we explicitly deny that believers have any congruent or condign merit apart from the condign merit Christ imputed. These denials were never intended to be taken as a blanket rejection or denial of merit categorically but only as a rejection and denial of the medieval and Roman doctrine that believers can accumulate condign merit by cooperation with grace or congruent merit by divine covenant.[57] The catechism in its original languages and earlier translations made the Reformed doctrine quite clear, but by omitting the traditional vocabulary of the church, some modern English-language editions have created confusion on this issue.[58]

53. *ST* 1a2ae 114.6, resp. dic.

54. Oberman, "*Facientibus Quod in Se*," 119–41; Oberman, *Harvest of Medieval Theology*, 135–39; Oberman, *Reformation*, 103–4.

55. See the discussion of free choice under *HC* 2. "Secundum quod procedit ex libero arbitrio, inquantum voluntarie aliquid facimus: et ex hac parte est meritum congrui; quia congruum est."

56. CCC §§ 2007, 2008.

57. Witsius reflected the mainstream of Reformed orthodoxy in the classical period when he wrote that Christ condignly merited his reward by fulfilling the covenant of works (*Economy of the Covenants*, 2.3.33 [1.62]).

58. The 1975 edition published by the Christian Reformed Church in North America does not use the word *merit* even though it clearly appears in the German and Latin texts. The absence of this term from this widely used translation has created the impression among some laity and ministers, who are not aware of the older English translations or of the original text, that the Reformed churches do not teach a doctrine of merit (e.g., Klooster, *Our Only Comfort*, 1:192; 2:738, 751, 874,

The Reformed doctrine of salvation *sola gratia, sola fide,* on the ground of the merit of Christ imputed, has not fared well in some parts of the Reformed world since the 1970s. There has been a concerted movement to revise Reformed theology by omitting the doctrine of the covenant of nature (or works or the commandment of life) and with it the doctrine of Christ's merits imputed. In its place the federal vision theology has proposed a version of Biel's doctrine of congruent merit whereby the good works of believers are accepted toward final justification.[59]

Question 22

What then is necessary for a Christian to believe?

All that is promised us in the gospel, which the articles of our catholic, undoubted Christian faith teach us in summary.[60]

Christians often ask, "What must one believe to be saved?" The modern evangelical tendency is toward minimalism in doctrine and practice. In some circles, it is enough to say that one came forward at a rally, prayed a prayer, and signed a card (or clicked yes on a website). The Reformed churches, however, confess a different answer to this question.

The catechism begins with the law and the gospel, the bad news about sin and the good news for sinners, about Christ's incarnation, death, resurrection, and ascension for us, but there is more. The gospel as we understand it is summarized not just in those events but in "the articles of our catholic, undoubted Christian faith." When we say "catholic," of course, we make no reference to the Roman Catholic Church. It is a Greek word (καθολικός) that means "general" or "universal." It has the same sense as

889). Thankfully, the 2018 edition of the catechism published by the United Reformed Churches in North America has corrected this error.

59. Horton, "Which Covenant Theology?," 197–227.

60. "Was ist aber einem Christen nöthig zu glauben? Alles, was uns im Evangelio verheissen wird, welches uns die Artikel unseres allgemeinen ungezweiselten christlichen Glaubens in einer Summa lehren" (Schaff, *Creeds of the Churches*, 314). "Quaenam sunt illa, quae necesse est hominem Christianum credere? Omnia, quae nobis in Evangelio promittuntur, quorum summa in Symbolo Apostolico, seu in capitibus catholicae et indubitatae omnium Christianorum fidei, breviter comprehenditur" (Niemeyer, *Collectio Confessionum*, 434).

"ecumenical" (οἰκουμενικός), which is also a Greek word for "universal." "It is called catholic, because it is the faith of all Christians."[61]

The articles to which this answer refers are the twelve articles of the Apostles' Creed, which are in three sections, organized by the Holy Trinity:

FATHER

1. I believe in God the Father, almighty, maker of heaven and earth

SON

2. And in Jesus Christ, his only begotten Son, our Lord
3. Who was conceived by the Holy Spirit, born of the virgin Mary
4. Suffered under Pontius Pilate, crucified, dead and buried; He descended into hell
5. The third day He rose from the dead
6. He ascended into heaven, and sits at the right hand of God the Father almighty
7. Thence He shall come to judge the living and the dead

HOLY SPIRIT

8. I believe in the Holy Spirit
9. The Holy Catholic Church, the communion of saints
10. The forgiveness of sins
11. The resurrection of the body
12. And the life everlasting.

---

61. Ursinus, *Commentary*, 117.

The gospel section of the catechism explains the twelve articles of the faith. This does not mean that there is not a narrow sense of gospel (as sketched above), but it does mean that when we answer the question of what we must believe, we do not stop at the narrow sense. We include in it the doctrine of the Trinity, a doctrine of God, a doctrine of creation and providence, of sin, of Christ, of salvation, of the church, sacraments, and last things.

Our doctrine of God is intimately connected to our understanding of humanity, salvation, church, and worship. The Reformed faith, however, is biblical and catholic, that is, we believe what the Scriptures teach about God, humanity, Christ, salvation, and so on as understood by the church in all times and places. We do not ask Christians to believe everything possible. We ask them to believe all that is *necessary*. There are limits to what may be set as a condition of salvation. There is a hierarchy of beliefs. They are not all equally ultimate or necessary. There are fundamentalist groups that require adherents to believe things that are not taught explicitly in Scripture, are not a good and necessary consequence of Scripture, and that the Reformed churches do not confess—for example, adherence to certain Bible translations, to a six-day, twenty-hour creation, or to theonomy—as marks of Reformed orthodoxy.[62] Against all such the Reformed churches assert the biblical and Reformation doctrine *sola Scriptura*, "the Holy Scriptures fully contain the will of God, and that whatsoever man ought to believe unto salvation, is sufficiently taught therein. For since the whole manner of worship which God requires of us is written in them at large, it is unlawful for any one, though an Apostle, to teach otherwise than we are now taught in the Holy Scriptures."[63] "Human traditions, the ordinances of popes, and the decrees of councils, are therefore excluded from being the object of faith, for faith cannot rely upon anything but the Word of God as an immoveable foundation."[64] We also assert the sufficiency of the faith revealed in Scripture, summarized in the creed, and

62. Clark, *Recovering the Reformed Confession*, 32–69.

63. *BC* 7 (Schaff, *Creeds of the Churches*, 3:389); Clark, *Recovering the Reformed Confession*, 39–69.

64. Ursinus, *Commentary*, 116.

confessed by the churches against those (e.g., neo-Pentecostalists) who would add to the word of God.[65]

The Reformed churches are Trinitarian. This puts us at odds not only with non-Christian Jews, who reject the Trinity, but also with those evangelicals who seek some theological détente with Mormonism or Islam, which denies the catholic (universal) Christian doctrine of the Trinity.[66]

We believe in divine providence, that God the same God who spoke creation into existence by the power of his Word (John 1:1–3) is actively upholding and governing all things. We reject deism, the doctrine that God is not actively upholding and governing all things. We reject pantheism, the doctrine that everything is God. We reject panentheism, the doctrine that everything is in God. Nature and Scripture reveal the God who is. The God of Scripture has no unrealized potential, that is, God is always all he can be. He is not becoming. There is no process or change in God.[67]

We believe the universal Christian doctrine of the two natures of Christ as summarized in the Nicene-Constantinopolitan Creed (381), in the Definition of Chalcedon (451), and the Athanasian Creed (fifth century AD).[68] He is true God and true man. He remains one person with two distinct, united, inseparable, unconfused natures. What is true of his natures is true of his person, but the distinct properties of each nature are unchanged.[69]

We are not gnostics. We believe that God created humanity good, righteous, and holy, able to fulfill his law and enter into eternal blessedness through obedience to that law (commandment of life, covenant of works). Our first parents, Adam and Eve, disobeyed, and Adam, as the legal representative of all humanity, died spiritually, and physical death entered the creation. All humans were implicated in Adam's fall into sin, death, and guilt. We are all born in sin and death.

---

65. Clark, *Recovering the Reformed Confession*, 71–111.

66. E.g., Pinnock, *Most Moved Mover*, 34–35; Mouw, *Talking with Mormons*.

67. Ursinus, *Commentary*, 123, 126, 150–51; Muller, *Post-Reformation Reformed Dogmatics*, 3:312–20; Berkhof, *Systematic Theology*, 59; Muller, "Incarnation, Immutability," 22–40; Horton, *Christian Faith*, 235–42.

68. Burn, *Introduction to the Creeds*, 145–49.

69. See the discussion under *HC* 16.

There is salvation by a covenant of grace alone (*sola gratia*), through faith alone (*sola fide*), in Christ alone. Just as God, in the garden, offered to Adam eternal blessedness on condition of obedience, so now he has promised eternal life and blessedness to his elect on the basis of the obedience of the last Adam, Jesus. His Spirit grants life to those for whom he obeyed, suffered, was crucified, died, was buried, was raised, and for whom he now intercedes. The Spirit gives the grace of faith to those to whom he has given life, and through faith he grants us free acceptance with God, salvation, union with the risen Christ, and adoption as sons. We believe heartily in a personal communion with the risen Christ, but the Christ to whom we are united, with whom we commune, is the Christ of Scripture and history. He is neither a figment of our imagination nor the creature of our experience.

We are not saved alone, nor to be alone. The Triune God administers his salvation in his visible church.[70] Where the gospel is preached purely, where the sacraments are administered purely, and where there is discipline, there is a true church. In those assemblies is where the Spirit is at work bringing the elect to faith and where believers are growing in sanctity as a consequence of God's grace and fellowship with one another. In those visible covenant assemblies are believers, those who are yet to believe, and those who profess faith but who do not believe. There has always been a universal church, composed in all times and places of believers, since the beginning of the world, and there shall always be this body, united by true faith, in the visible assembly. In the visible church is where all believers are ordinarily found. Believers are those who have been given new life and true faith.[71] By grace alone God justifies and saves believers through faith alone, in Christ.

In that communion of saints God uses visible signs of his promises. To those who believe, these sacraments testify that what they signify is really true for the believer. Christians follow in the footsteps of Abraham and Moses by initiating their children into the visible covenant community in baptism and, upon profession of faith, communing with him at the

70. *BC* 28–29 (United Reformed Churches in North America, *Liturgical Forms and Prayers*, 184–87).

71. See the discussion under *HC* 21.

Lord's Table. These signs and seals tell the truth, and the Spirit uses them to strengthen our faith and to help us grow in Christlikeness.

Sin corrupted creation, especially human nature, and brought death, but that is not the end of the story. Just as there is forgiveness of sins in Christ, so too he has, by his bodily resurrection, begun to reverse the effects of the fall. His bodily resurrection is a promise that, when Christ returns, believers too will be raised from the dead. As we wait for the final day, we do so with the confidence that Jesus ascended bodily, that he, in his true humanity, is at the right hand of our Father praying for us.

The new life that believers have by grace alone is a down payment of the eternal life that is to come in the new heavens and new earth. We live in union with Christ, in communion with the believers, patiently waiting, serving him by fulfilling our earthly vocations, as citizens of his twofold kingdom (eternal and temporal).[72]

The Christian faith has objective content that we must believe. That content is more extensive than many might like to think, but we must appropriate all that content personally by faith or it remains only theoretical. The Spirit works through the proclamation of this gospel to produce new life, true faith, justification, and sanctification. Those to whom he has given new life he has also given a new identity shaped by the catholic, Christian faith. The biblical faith, the catholic faith, is an integral, coherent whole. It is not a patchwork, but neither is it an endless garment.

Question 23

What are these articles?

I believe in God the Father, almighty, maker of heaven and earth.

And in Jesus Christ, his only begotten Son, our Lord; who was conceived by the Holy Spirit, born of the virgin Mary, suffered under Pontius Pilate, was crucified, dead and buried; he descended into hell; the third day he rose from the dead; he ascended into

72. Calvin gave us the categories "duplex esse in homine regimen" in *Institutes* 3.19.15 (Barth, *Joannis Calvini Opera Selecta*, 4:294.5).

heaven, and sits at the right hand of God the Father almighty, thence he shall come to judge the living and the dead.

I believe in the Holy Spirit, a holy catholic church, the communion of saints, the forgiveness of sins, the resurrection of the body, and the life everlasting.[73]

On most Lord's Days, in the second service, the congregation recites the Apostles' Creed. Confessing the faith is an ancient, biblical practice. The church has been reciting creedal formulae since the Israelites first said the *Shema* (Deut 6:4): "Hear O Israel, Yahweh Our God, Yahweh is one," and the apostolic church recited 1 Timothy 3:16:

Confessedly great is the mystery of piety. He was:

Manifested in the flesh,
Vindicated by the Spirit,
Seen by angels,
Preached among the gentiles,
Believed on in the world,
Taken up in glory.

The Apostles' Creed, of course, was not written by the apostles themselves.[74] It developed gradually out of the rule of faith (*regula fidei*) artic-

73. Schaff, *Creeds of the Churches*, 2:45. "Wie lauten dieselben? Ich glaube in Gott Vater, den Allmächtigen, Schöpser Himmels und der Erden. Und in Jesum Christum, seinen eingebornen Sohn, unsern Herrn; der empfangen ist von dem heiligen Geiste, geboren aus Maria der Jungfran; gelitten unter Pontio Pilato, gekreuziget, gestorden und begraben; abgestiegen zu der Hölle; am dritten Tage weider auferstanden von den Todten; aufgefahren gen Himmel; sitzet zu der Rechten Gottes, des allmächtigen Vaters; von dannen Er kommen wird zu richten die Lebendigen und die Todten. Ich glaube in den heiligen Geist; eine heilige, allgemeine christliche Kirche; die Gemeinschaft der Heiligen; Vergebung der Sünden; Auferstehung des Fleisches, und ein ewiges Leben" (Schaff, *Creeds of the Churches*, 3:314). "Quod est illud Symbolum? Credo in Deum Patrem omnipotentem, creatorem coeli et terrae: Et in Iesum Christum, Filium eius unigenitum Dominum nostrum, qui conceptus est de Spiritu sancto, natus ex Maria virgine, passus sub Pontio Pilato, crucifixus, mortuus et sepultus: Descendit ad inferna, tertia die resurrexit a mortuis,ascendit ad coelos, sedet at dexteram Dei Patris omnipotentis, inde venturus est ad iudicatuum vivos et mortuos: Credo in Spiritum sanctum. Credo sanctam Ecclesiam, Catholicam, sanctorum communionem, remissionem peccatorum, carnis resurrectionem, et vitam aeternam" (Niemeyer, *Collectio Confessionum*, 434–35).

74. Ursinus, *Commentary*, 117; Olevianus, *Exposition*, 9; Clark, *Caspar Olevian*, 85–91. There was a pre-Renaissance tradition, traceable to Rufinus (Schaff, *Creeds of the Churches*, 1:22), that held that

ulated by Ignatius of Antioch very early in the second century AD, by Christian apologist Aristides circa AD 125, by Irenaeus in *Against Heresies* (170s AD), and by Tertullian in the early third century.[75] By the middle of the fourth century the creed had reached its essentially mature form.[76]

There are variations in the way the creed is published and recited. One variation is in the way the creed appears in the "Received Form" (*Forma Recepta*) in Latin, the way it appears in translations of the catechism made from the German text of the Heidelberg Catechism, and the way it appears in English translations made from (or influenced by) the Latin text of the catechism. Concerning the Holy Spirit, in the third edition (1563), the catechism says: "*Ich glaube in den heiligen Geist; eine heilige, allgemeine christliche Kirche.*"[77] So, the 2013 edition published by the Reformed Church in the United States says, "I believe in the Holy Spirit, the holy Catholic church."[78] The English translation that appears in the 1959 Christian Reformed Church *Psalter-Hymnal*, however, begins the third part of the creed "I believe in the Holy Spirit" and then repeats the verb "to believe" before the next article: "I believe in a Holy catholic Church."[79]

The source of the variation is the Latin text, which reads "*Credo in Spiritum Sanctum; Credo Sanctam Ecclesiam catholicam.*"[80] The Received Form of the Latin text reads: "*Credo in Spiritum Sanctum; sanctam ecclesiam catholicam.*"[81] Indeed, there is no major version of the Creed that repeats the verb *credo* ("I believe") before "*sanctam ecclesiam catholicam*" ("a holy

---

each of the apostles wrote an article. Nevertheless, the framers certainly believed the doctrine of the creed to be apostolic (Ursinus, *Commentary*, 118).

75. Schaff (*Creeds of the Churches*, 2:11–12) points to Ignatius, *To the Trallians* 9:1–2 (see Holmes, *Apostolic Fathers*, 221). On Aristides, see *ANF* 9:263–79; Kruger, *Christianity at the Crossroads*. For the rule in Irenaeus, see Irenaeus, *Against Heresies* 3.4.2; Tertullian, "On the Veiling of Virgins" (*ANF* 4:27). The Reformed churches adapted the phrase to refer to Scripture as the "rule of faith." Genevan Confession (1536/37), art. 1; Second Helvetic Confession (1566) chap. 2; = Irish Articles of Religion (1615) 1; WCF 1.2 (Dennison, *Reformed Confessions*, 1:395; 2:812; 4:89; Westminster Assembly, *Humble Advice of the Assembly*, 4).

76. Schaff, *Creeds of the Churches*, 2:45–55.

77. Schaff, *Creeds of the Churches*, 3:314.

78. Reformed Church in the United States, *Heidelberg Catechism: 450th Anniversary Edition*, 34. The 2018 edition of the catechism published by the United Reformed Churches in North America in United Reformed Churches in North America, *Liturgical Forms and Prayers*, 148, follows the *forma recepta* of the creed.

79. Christian Reformed Church, *Psalter Hymnal: Centennial Edition*, 67.

80. Niemeyer, *Collectio Confessionum*, 435.

81. Schaff, *Creeds of the Churches*, 3:45.

catholic church"). There is a version of the creed before 341 that has "*Credo in Spiritum sanctum, sanctum ecclesiam,*" which omits both *catholicam* and *credo,* and there are versions from circa AD 350 and circa AD 390 (Italy) that omit the second *credo,* but none that repeat the *credo.* None of the major Greek forms of the creed repeat πιστεύω ("I believe").[82] In both the Reuter (1612) edition of Ursinus's *Corpus doctrinae* (*Body of Doctrine*) and in the 1634 edition of the *Corpus doctrinae, credo* is repeated before the ninth article of the creed.[83] Olevianus, however, does not repeat *credo* before the ninth article in his 1576 *Exposito.*[84] I will address the ninth article of the creed under *HC* 54.

82. Schaff, *Creeds of the Churches,* 3:45–55.

83. Reuter, *D. Zachariae Ursini,* 1:110 (note the printer's error: the page is marked 101 rather than 110); Ursinus, *Corpus doctrinae,* 118. The editions published in the 1580s did not give the text of the creed.

84. Olevianus, *Expositio,* 14; Olevianus, *Exposition,* 17.

Question 24

How are these Articles divided?

Question 25

Since there is but one Divine Being, why do you speak of three persons: Father, Son and Holy Spirit?

Lord's Day 8

Question 24

How are these Articles divided?

Into three parts: the first is of God the Father and our creation; the second of God the Son and our redemption; the third, of God the Holy Spirit and our sanctification.[1]

From the middle of the nineteenth century until the near the end of the twentieth century, the dominant way to understand Reformed theology was to reduce it to a single doctrine: predestination. Scholarship on the history of Reformed theology, led by Richard Muller, Willem van Asselt, and others, has changed significantly since 1978.[2] That scholarship notwithstanding, many continue to think of Reformed theology as organized around the doctrine of predestination. *HC* 24 is *prima facie* evidence that caricature was never true. We have established that there are three parts of the Heidelberg Catechism. This is clear in *HC* 2. Believers must know three things: the greatness of our sin and misery (law), how we are redeemed from all our sins and misery (gospel), and how we are to be thankful for such redemption (sanctification). Now, the catechism adds a correlate structure. The teaching of the Christian faith is organized according to the Trinity:[3]

1. "Wie werden diese Artikel abgetheilt? In drei Theile: Der erste ist von Gott dem Vater und unserer Erschaffung. Der andere von Gott dem Sohne und unserer Erlösung. Der dritte von Gott dem heiligen Geiste und unserer Heiligung" (Schaff, *Creeds of the Churches*, 3:315). "In quot partes distribuitur hoc Symbolum? In tres partes. Prima est de aeterno Patre, et nostri creatione. Altera est de Filio et nostri redemtione. Tertia est de Spiritu sancto, et nostri sanctificatione" (Niemeyer, *Collectio Confessionum*, 435).

2. Muller, Post-*Reformation Reformed Dogmatics*; Ballor, Sytsma, and Zuidema, *Church and School*; Trueman and Clark, *Protestant Scholasticism*.

3. In *Firm Foundation*, 14 (Q. 16), Olevianus divides the articles of the creed into three parts. Nine years later, in his *Exposition*, however, he saw four: "There are four main parts to the creed. The first contains what we believe about God the Father, who out of sheer mercy chose us in Christ before the foundation of the world (Eph. 1[:4]). What is set forth in this first part of the creed, therefore, is, as it were, the first fountain of the covenant or reconciliation, as well as what we ought to believe about the creation of all things. ... The fourth part is about the people with whom God makes this covenant, that is, the church. This section contains the effects of all the preceding parts and the fruit of our faith, both that which we enjoy in this life and that which we shall experience in eternity, when we are fully joined in body and soul to Christ our Head" (*Exposition*, 18).

1. The Father as Creator and Sustainer
2. The Son as Redeemer
3. The Spirit as Sanctifier

To be sure, the *ad extra* acts of God, that is, with respect to creation and redemption, are acts of the all the persons of the Trinity.[4] Nevertheless, we are entitled to think of the Father as Creator and Sustainer, the Son as Redeemer, and the Spirit as Sanctifier without saying or thinking that the other Trinitarian persons are absent in those works.[5]

The Christian faith is a Trinitarian faith, and the doctrine of the Trinity has always been at the heart of Reformed theology.[6] That doctrine is as fundamental as any of our doctrines, and it has a unique role in that it also structures the way we think about and explain the faith. For example, Christology is also a catholic (universal) doctrine, clearly confessed in the most ancient ecumenical creeds, but it does not structure the way we teach the faith in the way that the doctrine of the Trinity does. The Apostles' Creed and Nicene-Constantinopolitan Creed (381) are Trinitarian in structure. The Athanasian Creed is bipartite: Trinity and Christology. The Definition of Chalcedon (451) is focused on Christology.

The doctrine of the Trinity is essential to the Christian faith and fundamental. That is why the Athanasian Creed twice says, "Whosoever will be saved, before all things it is necessary that he hold the catholic faith."[7] The first half of the Athanasian Creed summarizes the doctrine of the Trinity. According to the catholic (universal) Christian faith, "He therefore that will be saved must thus think of the Trinity." So, when we teach the faith, we teach the catholic, Trinitarian faith. When we engage other religions (e.g., Islam, Judaism, and Mormonism), the Trinity is essential to that faith we are defending. If it is marginalized in our confrontation with them, then we are defending something other than Christianity. The God of the Christian faith is one in three persons.

4. Ursinus, *Commentary*, 119.
5. Ursinus, *Commentary*, 120.
6. Clark, *Caspar Olevian*, 74–103.
7. Schaff, *Creeds of the Churches*, 2:66–70.

Clearly, in the mainline (liberal) Presbyterian and Reformed churches (and increasingly in the borderline churches), the doctrine of the fatherhood of God ("I believe in God the Father almighty") has become something of an embarrassment and hard to square with egalitarianism.

The confession of the Reformed churches, however, is a catholic, that is, universal confession. It has a doctrine of creation (which is less interested in the length of the creation days than in the Creator/creature distinction), redemption, and sanctification. It is not idiosyncratic. It is not novel. Strangely, that is what makes it stand out today: its enduring Trinitarian character. The early church would understand our catechism much more than they would understand the quest for an immediate encounter with God. In a sense, all that we have done thus far in the catechism is prologue. Now we have come to the exposition of the faith proper: The Father is God, the Son is God, and the Holy Spirit is God. There are not three Gods but one (and, *contra* some revisions, not one person but three). Each of them has a distinct (but not absolutely so) role in the outworking of creation, redemption, and glorification. Our faith is not lopsided. It is just catholic Christian teaching as construed by the Reformation in light of our renewed appreciation for Scripture and the history of redemption (covenant theology).

Question 25

Since there is but one Divine Being, why do you speak of three persons: Father, Son and Holy Spirit?

Because God has so revealed Himself in his Word, that these three distinct persons are the one, true, eternal God.[8]

The biblical, catholic, Christian doctrine of the Trinity is startlingly brief: God is one in three persons. Yet, the moment we pronounce

8. "Dieweil nur ein einig Göttlich Wesen ist, warum nennest du drei, den Vater, Sohn und heiligen Geist? Darum, weil sich Gott also in seinem Wort geoffenbaret hat, dass diese drei unterschiedlichen Personen der einige wahrhaftige ewige Gott sind" (Schaff, *Creeds of the Churches*, 3:315). "Cum una sit tantum essentia divina: our cur tres istos nominas, Patrem, Filium et Spirtum sanctum? Quia Deus ita se in suo verbo patefectit, quod tres hae distinctae personae sint unus ille, verus et aeternus Deus" (Niemeyer, *Collectio Confessionum*, 435).

that little formula, we have stepped off the shore and into deep waters. To those outside the faith, our claim that God is one in three persons seems contradictory. Because of the apologetic problems it presents, there has always been pressure to modify this formula. The Arians wanted to flatten out the mystery by making the Son (and later the Spirit) not of the same essence as the Father. Thus at Nicaea and Constantinople the church confessed that the Son is "of the same substance" (ὁμοούσιος) with the Father, and the Spirit is "with the Father and the Son worshipped and glorified."[9]

Subordinationists and adoptionists also tried to subordinate the being of the Son to the Father. There have been tritheists who have proposed that God is three in essence. In our time social Trinitarianism holds that we should no longer speak of God's being or essence but only of a social relationship.[10] Recently, some have proposed the formula: God is three persons and one person.[11]

Nevertheless, with the church ecumenical, the Reformed churches confess that God is one in essence or being in three persons. It is instructive that the catechism asks, "Why do you speak of three persons?" One of the principal functions of a confession or catechism is to establish ecclesiastical baselines and boundaries for Christian rhetoric about certain issues. This is not to say that we may use only ecclesiastically sanctioned language. The framers of the catechism themselves did not observe such a rule. They explored concepts and taught things that they did not include explicitly in the catechism, but when we come to the doctrine of the Holy Trinity, we have arrived at the core of the Christian faith, to a shared possession. Reformed Christians are catholic (ecumenical) in our doctrine of the Trinity. We confess the same doctrine that was confessed at Nicaea (AD 325), at Constantinople (AD 381), at Ephesus (AD 431), at Chalcedon (AD 451), in the Apostles' Creed, and in the Athanasian Creed. We accept the Western revision adopted at Toledo (AD 589), so we are Western in our understanding of the double procession of the Spirit

9. Schaff, *Creeds of the Churches*, 2:57.

10. Leftow, "Anti Social Trinitarianism"; Coakley, "Persons in the 'Social' Doctrine."

11. E.g., Van Til, *Introduction to Systematic Theology*, 229–32; Frame, *Doctrine of God*, 703–5; Tipton, "Function of Perichoresis," 289–306. Certainly the neither the *HC* nor the *BC* speaks this way, nor do the classic Reformed theologians speak this way. At best, this formula uses the word *person* in two distinct senses at the same time and is confusing. At worst, it is a contradiction of the word of God as summarized in the ecumenical creeds and confessed by the churches.

("proceeds from the Father and the Son"; *filioque*). This puts us at odds with the Eastern churches post–AD 589, but we receive the ecumenical creeds and understanding of the Trinity.[12]

Thus, when contemporary writers inveigh against the language of being or essence in the doctrine of God, they are not only criticizing the private writings of other philosophers and theologians but the catholic, churchly, universally received rhetoric of the church adopted as a way of articulating the relationship between the divine unity and the divine persons. Scripture itself uses the language of being. "Being then God's offspring, we ought not to think that the divine being [θεῖον εἶναι] is like gold or silver or stone, an image formed by the art and imagination of man" (Acts 17:29 ESV).

We may speak of the divine being. In this case, "divine being" stands for God, but we cannot speak of God without saying that he is. At the same time, we do not say that he "has being," as if God and his creatures share an essence. Fundamental to the biblical revelation of God is that, in the beginning, he was and we were not. He is in a way that we are not and can never be. We could not possibly share in his being, as if there were no distinction between God and creatures or as if humans had the potential to become God. There is no continuum between God and creatures. Sanctification and glorification are not deification. Second Peter 1:4 says that, in sanctification, we become "partakers of the divine nature" (θείας κοινωνοὶ), but in context Peter was not intending to erase or even blur the distinction between Creator and creature but to explain the ground of the development of Christian virtue. Calvin's explanation is sound:

> But the word nature is not here essence but quality. The Manicheans formerly dreamt that we are a part of God, and that, after having run the race of life we shall at length revert to our original. There are also at this day fanatics who imagine that we thus pass over into the nature of God, so that his swallows up our nature. Thus they explain what Paul says, that God will be all in all and in the same sense they take this passage. But such a delirium as this never entered the minds of the holy Apostles; they only intended to say

12. Olevianus, *Exposition*, 23; Ursinus, *Commentary*, 136.

> that when divested of all the vices of the flesh, we shall be partakers of divine and blessed immortality and glory, so as to be as it were one with God as far as our capacities will allow.[13]

We cannot confuse the creature with the Creator without placing ourselves at odds with Scripture, with the catholic creeds, and Reformed confessions.

Neither can we modify the fundamental assertion that God is one. Deuteronomy 6:4 says, "Hear O Israel, Yahweh our God, Yahweh is one." He is not three. He is one. Again, the Nicene-Constantinoplitan Creed says, "We believe in one God."[14] We do not believe in a plurality of Gods. The biblical faith is monotheistic. Thus, the catechism says God is "only" one.

Unity is predicated of the divine nature, but plurality is predicated of the divine persons. We should not confuse the two. God is one, but he is so in three persons. It is the apparent tension between the two predicates (one and three) that creates the tension the catechism must address. Since we say that God is only one divine essence, why then do we also say that God is three persons?[15] The *apparent* tension is between the divine unity and the three persons. God is personal, but by that we mean to say that God is tripersonal or multipersonal. When our theologians speak of God being "personal," it never entered their imaginations that anyone would interpret that adjective to mean "unipersonal." We may not abstract "personal" from the biblical, historic, and confessional understanding that it signals multipersonal, as, for example, in the Hebrew and Aramaic Scriptures, where the Trinity is suggested but not revealed explicitly, or tripersonal, as God is finally revealed in the New Testament Scriptures (on this see *BC* 8–9).[16] We baptize in the name of the Father, the Son, and the Holy Spirit. Not three gods but one God in three persons. Here the precision and clarity of the Athanasian Creed is exceptionally helpful.[17]

---

13. Calvin, *Commentary on the Catholic Epistles*, 371.

14. Schaff, *Creeds of the Churches*, 2:57.

15. We should not worry that the question in the Latin text uses *nominas* (as if the distinction between the persons were only apparent and not real), since the answer uses *personae*. The distinction between the persons, according to the catechism, is not an illusion. We are not modalists.

16. Schaff, *Creeds of the Churches*, 3:389–91.

17. Schaff, *Creeds of the Churches*, 2:66–67.

Why do we speak this way? Because it is the way God reveals himself in Holy Scripture. The Father, the Son, and the Holy Spirit were present in creation. They were present at Jesus's baptism. They were present at Pentecost. God has made himself known as one God, in three distinct, consubstantial, coeternal persons. He has not made himself known as three gods (because he is one). He has not made himself known as one person, because he is three persons.

Each of the persons has his distinct properties. Only the Father is unbegotten. Only the Son is eternally of the Father. Only the Spirit proceeds eternally from the Father and the Son. Those distinctions are real, however difficult they may be for us to grasp. That is why the catechism says "three distinct persons" and "one true and eternal God." We do not need to dissolve the mystery by redefining the divine being as a relationship, and we do not need to further complicate the doctrine by redefining "personal." The Triune God is the God who is, who made himself known in his word as Father, Son, and Holy Spirit.

Question 26

What do you believe when you say: "I believe in God the Father, almighty, maker of heaven and earth"?

Lord's Day 9

Question 26

What do you believe when you say: "I believe in God the Father, almighty, maker of heaven and earth"?

That the eternal Father of our Lord Jesus Christ, who of nothing made heaven and earth with all that is in them, who likewise upholds and governs the same by His eternal counsel and providence, is for the sake of Christ, His Son, my God and my Father, in whom I so trust, as to have no doubt that He will provide me with all things necessary for body and soul; and further, that whatever evil he sends upon me in this vale of tears, he will turn to my good; for he is able to do it, being almighty God, and willing also, being a faithful Father.[1]

One of the most basic impulses of the Enlightenment and post-Enlightenment West has been to get rid of the God of Scripture and to replace him with the god of deism and later the gods of subjectivism. In Christian antiquity, God was said to be, and we were thought to be becoming.[2] In modernity we are, and God is said to be becoming. The God of Scripture, however, simply is. Genesis begins with God without explanation: "In the beginning Elohim created the heavens and the earth" (Gen 1:1). The word knows nothing about a world without God, but it does know of an existence in which there is God and nothing else. In

1. "Was glaubest du, wenn du sprichst: Ich glaube in Gott Vater, den Allmächtigen, Schöpfer Himmels und der Erben? Dass der ewige Vater unsers Herrn Jesu Christi, der Himmel und Erde, sammt allem, was darinnen ist, aus nichts erschaffen, auch dieselbigen noch durch seinen ewigen Rath und Fürsehung erhält und regieret, um seines Sohnes Christi willen mein Gott und mein Vater sei, auf welchen ich also vertraue, dass ich nicht zweifle, Er werde mich mit aller Nothdurft Leibes und der Seele versorgen, auch alles Übel, so Er mir in diesem Jammerthal zuschidet, mir zu gut wenden, dieweil Er's thun tann, als ein allmächtiger Gott, und auch thun will, als ein getreuer vater" (Schaff, *Creeds of the Churches*, 315–16). "Quid credis cum dicis: Credo in Deum Patrem, omipotentem, creatorem coeli et terrae? Credo aeternam Patrem Domini nostri Iesu Christi, qui coelum et terram, cum omnibus, quae in iis sunt, ex nihilo creavit, quique eadem aeterno suo consilio et providentia sustentat ac gubernat: propter Christum Deum meum et patrem meum esse: itaque sic ei confido, sic in eo acquiesco, ut no dubitem, quin provisurus sit omnibus, tum animo, tum corpori meo necessariis. Quin etiam, quae mihi mala in hac aerumnosa vita imittit, ea in meum salutem sit conversurus, eum et facere id possit, ut omnipotens Deus, et facere id velit, ut benignus Pater" (Niemeyer, *Collectio Confessionum*, 435).

2. Calvin's colleague Pierre Viret (1511–1571) is said to have coined the term "deism" (Champion, "Deism," 438).

other words, according to Scripture, God is, and we exist solely at the good pleasure and decree of almighty God. Modernity claimed, however, that God was the result of our consciousness. These two conceptions are irreconcilable. The prevailing modern conception of God and humanity is essentially pagan. In this respect, we have much in common with Moses and the original setting of Genesis, which was given to God's people as they were surrounded by pagans.

In light of that background, the language of *HC* 26 is bracing. Remember, the second part of the catechism is an account of the faith structured by the Apostles' Creed, whence the language of the question is derived. This is the ancient Christian assertion: God is almighty (omnipotent). Any god that is not almighty is not the God of the Bible, the creed, or the catechism.

When we think of God the Father, we must think of him first as the Father of our Lord Jesus Christ. He is our Father by virtue of creation, but we are thinking of him, in this instance, as our Father in grace and salvation. In that case he is our Father by adoption. Not that we adopted him but that, in Christ, he adopted us (Rom 8:15; Gal 4:5; Eph 1:5). He is "Yahweh, Yahweh, God, merciful and gracious, long-suffering, and abounding in goodness and truth" (Exod 34:6–7).[3]

The God whose children we are is the God who spoke creation into being from nothing (*ex nihilo*). One of the great struggles the early church faced was the pagan notion that something else is coeternal with God. The biblical and Christian conviction is that God is the Creator of all that is. The tendency of modernity has been to identify God with creation or to banish him to the attic, as it were. Again, the Christian doctrine of God confesses the antithesis. The God who made all that is sustains all that is. He is not absent, nor is he utterly identified with his creation. He upholds what he made. He is intimately involved with his creation. His continual and sustaining care for his creation is such that, should he withdraw from the world, it would cease to be. To any reasonable person, there is order in creation. That order is evidence of God's detailed and wonderful care for his creation.

3. Olevianus, *Exposition*, 23.

The sustaining wisdom that God exercises in his world is eternal. The world is not a machine, and God is not surprised by the choices made by his creatures. Yes, we do make uncoerced choices, but God has known those choices as eternally and instantly present. Contrary to those forms of paganism that say that it is our free choices that give meaning to an otherwise meaningless universe, Christians should understand that the free choices we make are comprehended in his decree, and it is his good and wise decree that gives our choices meaning—because he chooses to execute his will through our choices.

Modernity has sought to be rid of the God of Abraham, Isaac, and Jacob, the God and Father of our Lord Jesus Christ, but Christian theism still haunts the neopagan West. Even the most irreligious of our late modern age lapse into the language of faith and hope for the future. Few are willing to settle for the bleakness of an utterly chaotic and meaningless existence. We should give thanks that there is no need to trade in the Christian doctrine of the active, sovereign providence of God for the mess of modern stew.[4]

There is a sense in which God is Father to everyone by virtue of creation. He makes the sun to shine on the just and the unjust (Matt 5:45) but, in *HC* 26, we confess the fatherhood of God in a very specific sense. God is our Father for the sake of his Son Jesus, our Father. We are elect "in Christ" (Eph 1:3; 2:7). "In love [the Father] predestined us for adoption to himself as sons through Jesus Christ, according to the purpose of his will" (Eph 1:5 ESV). In Christ "we have also obtained an inheritance, having been destined according to the purpose of him who accomplishes all things according to his counsel and will" (Eph 1:11). This is why we say "my God" and "my Father." "To believe in God the Father, therefore, is to believe in that God who is the Father of our Lord Jesus Christ; and to believe that he is also my Father, and as such has a fatherly affection toward me, for and on account of Christ, in whom he has adopted me as his son. In a word, it is to believe: 1. That he is the Father of our Lord Jesus Christ. 2. That he is a Father to me for Christ's sake."[5] By his grace alone (*sola gratia*), through the gift of new life and faith alone (*sola fide*), we are

4. E.g., Olevian, *Firm Foundation*, 22–23.

5. Ursinus, *Commentary*, 140.

united to Christ and, in him, sons (Rom 8:14, 23; Gal 3:26; 4:5–6). He is not just "a Father" or "some Father" but "our Father" and "my Father" (Matt 6:9; Rom 1:7). He is more intimate to us than our own earthly fathers (Heb 12:9). Of course, when we say that, when Scripture speaks of our earthly fathers, the assumption is that our fathers love us and spend their lives for us. Generally that is true, but we understand that human relations are broken, and sometimes painfully so. Even if our own fathers have sometimes disappointed us, our heavenly Father will never disappoint us. He is always perfectly good, even if his ways are above our ways.

When we were children, we never doubted that our father would provide. That is just the way it is. When he told us to jump, when he promised that he would catch us, even if we were afraid we never doubted his love, his intention, and his strength. Of course he would catch us. If that was true of our earthly father, how much more true is it of our heavenly Father? He never sleeps. He never tires. He always provides. He always sustains us and provides everything we need.

We live in an age where it can be difficult to tell the difference between needs and desires. What we need are clothing, shelter, food, and the basics. We need to love God and our neighbor, to fulfill our vocation in this world. Our heavenly Father will provide these things. Indeed, ordinarily he provides much more than these things. When we consider the Lord's remarkable provision, we are moved to thanks and praise. How many times has the Lord met our needs when we were not sure when or how it would happen? That is the mercy and kindness of a Father to his sons, in Christ.

Even the hard providences that come in this life are not matters of random chance. They too come from the same heavenly Father who has provided for us so richly. The hard things—death, suffering, grief—are, of course, more difficult to accept. Just as we tend to accept God's gifts to us thoughtlessly, so too we are tempted to lash out at our Father just as thoughtlessly for the hard things. Our shortsighted response is natural for fallen people, but it is no less sinful. Our Father does not make mistakes. We are not the measure of all things. God is. We, by his grace, are being renewed in the image of Christ, but he is the standard of goodness. That is a hard truth, but it is a truth. When we are tempted to shake our fists at God our Father, it is because we are measuring him by our own standards. He did not do what we wanted, what we asked, but the truth is that he always does what is right and for good reasons, even if he does not explain himself to us.

"Why?" is not a question to which we will likely have an answer. Of course, we can point to the general effects of sin. This is a fallen world, and with the fall comes sin, suffering, death, and grief. This is not the counsel of stoicism or indifference. We should pay attention to our own choices. We do not know God's providence ahead of time, and we should not seek to know it (Deut 29:29). That is not our business. Our choices are our business, but even those are comprehended within God's perfect, wise, good, and sovereign decree of providence.

We do not know why God sends hard providences, but we do know who and what he is to us: our gentle heavenly Father who so loved us sinners that he sent his only and eternally begotten Son to be born of a woman, to obey in our place, to die as our righteous substitute, to be raised, to ascend, and to be our heavenly high priest before the Father. Whatever grief we have in this life, we must measure it against that love, against that cross.

We should also bear in mind the way the Lord speaks to the problem of hard providences in Job 38:4, "Where were you when I laid the foundation of the earth? Tell me, if you have understanding" (ESV).

Question 27

What do you understand by the providence of God?

Question 28

What does it profit us to know that God created, and by his providence upholds all things?

Lord's Day 10

Question 27

What do you understand by the providence of God?

The almighty, everywhere present power of God, whereby, as it were by his hand, he upholds heaven and earth with all creatures, and so governs them that herbs and grass, rain and drought, fruitful and barren years, meat and drink, health and sickness, riches and poverty, indeed, all things come not by chance, but by his Fatherly hand.[1]

From the moment Adam sought to grasp equality with God (Phil 2:6–8), from the moment he mysteriously rebelled against God's sovereignty and hiddenness and transcendence ("You shall be as God," Gen 3:5), from the moment he ceased to love and adore the Triune God, since that moment submission to the sovereign providence of God has been problematic. On its face, the situation is quite plain. "In the beginning God ..." The Triune God was self-existent (*a se*), simple, spiritual, holy, righteous, good, eternal, immutable, impassible.[2] At that point, as it were, we were not. God was, and nothing else was. There was no coeternal matter. There was just the Triune God in eternal, splendorous communion with himself.

Creation only came into being when that sovereign, Triune God spoke (*ex nihilo*). All creatures are the product of his powerful, sovereign, creative word. There never was when God was not. Given that there was when we were not and that we exist solely at the will and good pleasure of the sovereign, self-existent God, how can there be any real discussion about whether God is utterly sovereign over all things? Nevertheless, because in Adam we all are now fallen and corrupted in intellect, will, and

1. "Was verstehst du unter der Fürsehung Gottes? Die allmächtige und gegenwärtige Kraft Gottes, durch welche Er Himmel und Erde, sammt allen Creaturen, gleich als mit seiner Hand noch erhält, und also regieret, dass Laub und Gras, Regen und Dürre, fruchtbare und unfruchtbare Jahre, Effen und Trinken, Gesundheit und Krankheit, Reichthum und Armuth, und alles nicht von ohngefähr, sondern von seiner väterlichen Hand uns zukomme" (Schaff, *Creeds of the Churches*, 3:316). "Quid est providentia Dei? Omipotes et ubique praesens Dei vis, qua coelum et terram, cum omnibus creaturis, tanquam manu sustinet ac gubernat: ut quae terra nascuntur, pluvia item et siccitas, fertilitas et sterilitas, cibus et potus, nona et adversa valetudo, divitiae et paupertas, omnia denique non temere aut fortuito, sed patero eius consilio et voluntate contingant" (Niemeyer, *Collectio Confessionum*, 436).

2. Olevianus, *Exposition*, 23–24.

affections, we continue to challenge God's sovereign rule over all things. We raise our fist at his judgments. Some question whether he really is sovereign over all things or suggest that the fact of our existence limits him—as if he crippled himself when he made us, as if by virtue of making dust and then by breathing life into dust he limited his omnipotence. Where in Scripture does God reveal himself clearly, unequivocally to have so limited himself? It certainly was not when he declared to Pharaoh, "For this very reason I raised you up?" (Exod 9:16; Rom 9:16), or when he said, "Shall the clay say to the Potter ..." (Rom 9:20). The God of Holy Scripture not only speaks all things into existence but continues to sustain and sovereignly govern them such that he relinquishes none of his power or rights over his creatures.

We are creatures, and God is Creator and sustainer, and that is how things have always been and how they shall ever be. The Latin text of the catechism says *omnipotens*. It means "almighty." We recognize it as the root of omnipotent, all-powerful. God cannot be both omnipotent and not omnipotent. By definition creatures cannot limit God's omnipotence. This not a Reformed idiosyncrasy. This is the language of the ecumenical faith: "We believe in God the Father almighty, maker of heaven and earth."[3] With all believers in all times and places, we confess that God is all-powerful.

Adam foolishly, fatally asserted human autonomy before God, and death was the consequence. God is sovereign, and he freely promised to send the last Adam (Rom 5:12–21; 1 Cor 15:45), who did perform the obedience that the first Adam could have performed but did not. Jesus, the last Adam, being in very nature omnipotent God, did not consider equality with God something to be grasped, but rather he poured himself out in utter obedience to his heavenly Father and in so doing merited righteousness and life for all his people, whom the Father gave to him before eternity (Phil 2:5–11; John 17:2–5).

The Reformed churches are not deist in their conception of God's activity in the world.[4] Quite the contrary, the Triune God is quite active in the world. All three persons were active in creation, and they are equally

3. Schaff, *Creeds of the Churches*, 2:57.

4. Traditionally called Epicureanism (Ursinus, *Commentary*, 147).

active in inaugurating a new creation in Christ. The Father elects, in Christ, and the Spirit sovereignly applies salvation to the elect. Believers, however, are not canonical actors. We are not prophets or apostles. Those offices ended with the close of the canon of Holy Scripture. Pentecost, like the crossing of the Red Sea and the bodily resurrection of our Lord, was a signal event in the history of redemption not to be repeated.

The apostle Paul, in his speech to the Athenian philosophers at the Areopagus, reminds them:

> The God who made the world and everything in it, being Lord of heaven and earth, does not live in temples made by man, nor is he served by human hands, as though he needed anything, since he himself gives to all mankind life and breath and everything. And he made from one man every nation of mankind to live on all the face of the earth, having determined allotted periods and the boundaries of their dwelling place, that they should seek God, and perhaps feel their way toward him and find him. Yet he is actually not far from each one of us, for
>
> "In him we live and move and have our being";
> as even some of your own poets have said,
> "For we are indeed his offspring."
>
> Being then God's offspring, we ought not to think that the divine being is like gold or silver or stone, an image formed by the art and imagination of man. The times of ignorance God overlooked, but now he commands all people everywhere to repent, because he has fixed a day on which he will judge the world in righteousness by a man whom he has appointed; and of this he has given assurance to all by raising him from the dead. (Acts 17:24–31 ESV)

Paul quotes the pagan poet Aratus to remind the pagans that even they know that God is not far away.[5] Notice how easily Paul speaks of God's active providence and sustaining work in the universe. He gives life and

5. *Phainomena* 5 (late fourth to mid-third century BC). See Martin, "Poetry in the NT," 899; Mair and Mair, *Hymns and Epigrams*.

breath to all humans. He made all humanity out of Adam and Eve. He allots boundaries.

Hebrews 1:3 says that Jesus is "bearing" or "upholding" (φέρων) all things by the power of his word. This is the same Word of God incarnate (John 1:1–3), through whom all things came into being and without whom nothing came into being that has been created, who is actively sustaining all things. When the apostles preached the law and the gospel (the whole counsel of God), they taught unbelievers that there is a sharp distinction, a categorical distinction to be made, between God and his creatures. For proof that God is and is active in the world, they appealed not to the miraculous signs and wonders that the Spirit did through them but to the fact of God's continual witness to his active work in the world in giving to all (just and unjust; Matt 5:45) "rains from heaven and fruitful seasons, satisfying your hearts with food and gladness" (Acts 14:17 ESV).

All we have comes from the hand of our Triune God. In his general providence, he sends gifts even to rebels who do nothing but curse and deny him.[6] Believers, by contrast, recognize these gifts for what they are: tokens of his goodness and mercy. The desire for the extraordinary that marked the Anabaptists in the early sixteenth century and neo-Pentecostalism today is a quest for the miraculous that overlooks the ordinary means instituted by God.[7] That desire for the supernatural is not a paradigm that the Reformed churches should seek to satisfy and not a paradigm to which we should conform. The question is not whether God is active in the world but whether we are willing to accept the witness to himself that he has given.

In *HC* 27, we speak of the "almighty, everywhere present power of God, whereby, as it were by His hand, He upholds heaven and earth with all creatures." When we speak of God's "hand," we are, of course, speaking figuratively.[8] We use both literal (nonfigurative) and figurative language about God, and we expect reasonable people to be able to tell the difference. To be perfectly clear, however, we add the qualifier "as it were" to

6. Ursinus, *Commentary*, 155–56.

7. On God's relations to second causes as means, see Ursinus, *Commentary*, 162.

8. Clark, *Recovering the Reformed Confession*, 130–32.

signal just when we are speaking figuratively. God does not literally, actually have a bodily hand.

First Samuel 5:11 speaks of "the hand of God" as a way of describing God's punishment of the Philistines for attempting to keep the ark of the covenant. Scripture here does not intend us to think that God actually has a hand. It is a figure of speech. Second Chronicles 30:12 says, "The hand of God was also on Judah to give them one heart to do what the king and the princes commanded by the word of Yahweh" (ESV modified). In this case Scripture uses a figure of speech to account for God's gracious work in the people to enable them to be courageous. According to Ecclesiastes 2:24, everything under the sun comes "from the hand of God," and this truth keeps life from being meaningless.

> There is nothing better for a person than that he should eat and drink and find enjoyment in his toil. This also, I saw, is from the hand of God, for apart from him who can eat or who can have enjoyment? For to the one who pleases him God has given wisdom and knowledge and joy, but to the sinner he has given the business of gathering and collecting, only to give to one who pleases God. This also is vanity and a striving after wind. (Eccl 2:24–26 ESV)

It is in view of God's sovereign providence that Peter exhorts Christians in 1 Peter 5:6 to submit "to the hand of God," which in this instance means to trust the Lord with all our anxieties and to remember that the Lord who redeemed us also cares for us in our daily needs. Peter warns us to resist the temptation to take things into our own hands because the devil roams about "like a roaring lion seeking someone to devour" (1 Pet 5:8). Notice how Peter juxtaposes figurative language about God (i.e., his hand) with figurative language about the Evil One as a lion. He is not actually a lion, but his relentless attempts to destroy Christians are aptly described with the simile. Just as one would never turn one's back on a lion, so one should never turn one's back on the Evil One.

That Scripture uses figures of speech is a reminder of the broader truth that when we discuss the doctrine of providence, we are talking about God. All biblical, orthodox, catholic, and Reformed theologians recognize that all our language about God, though true, is limited.[9] We do not know God or anything as he knows himself or anything else. Calvin speaks of God's "accommodation" to us. Calvin says, "Who has so little intellect who does not to understand that God, in a certain sense, speaks baby-talk [*balbutire*] with us as nurses do with infants?"[10]

QUESTION 28

What does it profit us to know that God created, and by his providence upholds all things?

That we may be patient in adversity, thankful in prosperity, and for what is future have good confidence in our faithful God and Father, that no creature shall separate us from his love, since all creatures are so in his hand, that without his will they cannot so much as move.[11]

In our postmodern world, the pagan language of chance and the Hindu and Buddhist language of karma has become very widely used.[12] The belief that the world is run by chance seems to be making a comeback, and it is not uncommon to find fortune tellers in cities large and small. The same people who, instead of chanting an incantation and scattering magic powder on the hood of their car, turn the key in the ignition to their

9. Clark, *Recovering the Reformed Confession*, 130–31.

10. Calvin, *Institutes* 1.13.1. "Quis enim vel parum ingeniosus non intelligit Deum ita nobiscum, ceu nutrices solent cum infantibus, quodammodo balbutire?" (Barth, *Joannis Calvini Opera Selecta*, 3:109.13–15).

11. "Was für Nutzen bekommen wir aus der Erkenntniss der Schöpfung und Fürsehung Gottes? Dass wir in aller Widerwärtigkteit geduldig, in Glückfeligkeit dankbar, und auf's Zukünftige guter Zuversicht zu unserm getreuen Gott und Vater sein sollen, dass uns keine Creatur von seiner Liebe scheiden wird, dieweil alle Creaturen also in seiner Hand sind, dass sie sich ohne seinen Willen auch nicht regen noch bewegen können" (Schaff, *Creeds of the Churches*, 3:316). "Quid nobis prodest haec cognitio creationis et providentiae divinae? Ut in adversis patientes, in secundis grati simus, in futurum vero optimum in Deo fidissimo Patre spem repositam habeamus, certo scientes, ihil esse, quod nos ab eius amore abstrahat, quandoquidem omnes creaturae ita sunt in eius potestate, ut sine eius arbitrio, no modo nihil agere sed ne moveri quidem possint" (Niemeyer, *Collectio Confessionum*, 436).

12. "Basil the Great has truly said that 'fortune' and 'chance' are pagan terms, with whose significance the minds of the godly ought not to be occupied" (Calvin, *Institutes* 1.16.8, quoting Basil the Great, *Homilies on the Psalms*, on Ps 32:4).

car when they want it to start; or who, when they want food, put it in the oven rather than dancing around it—they ask another mere mortal to try to peer into the future.

At heart, we all want to be God, and if we know the future, then we have just a little bit more control over things—or at least we think we do. That is what Saul thought when he consulted with the witch at Endor (1 Sam 28). For the same reason, the king of Denmark appointed to his court Melchior Hoffmann (ca. 1495–1543), a lay preacher who claimed to receive direct revelations from the Lord, because he wanted to know the future. Popes and kings consulted with Joachim of Fiore (1135–1202) because they thought he could give them an advantage over their rivals. We also see the turn to chance in the growth of gambling in the North America. Once the preserve of Atlantic City and Las Vegas, now casinos are seemingly everywhere. Our governments advertise gambling as a way of raising revenues.

Against the turn to chance and neopaganism of all sorts, we confess that is no such thing as chance. There is only God's fatherly hand. There is only his providence. That is why the Palatinate form for the celebration of Holy Communion lists gambling among gross sins that disqualify one from the Lord's Table.[13] Under this heading, the first distinction Olevianus makes is between divine providence and "bad luck": "A faithful servant of God should be absolutely convinced inside that all things happen by God's decree and not by chance or by good or bad luck. Therefore, in all things one should fasten the eyes of one's heart directly upon God, with whom he has a covenant, and look upon Him as the original source and cause of everything."[14] To be sure, there a material difference between playing cards for fun with friends and toying with providence or laziness. Some argue that gambling is no different from investing in the stock market. There is, however, a genuine difference between taking a reasonable risk to make an investment in an enterprise that will benefit others through goods and services, and gambling, the essence of which is high risk with

13. Gibson and Earngey, *Reformation Worship*, 619.

14. Olevian, *Firm Foundation*, 24. Calvin (*Institutes* 1.16.9) reminds us that all contingencies, as we experience things, are comprehended in God's good providence.

no labor—were there not considerable risk, we would not consider gambling to be entertainment.

The doctrine of providence tells us that whatever grows, whatever we receive, however things go for us, whatever we eat, whatever the state of our health and wealth (or lack thereof)—it all comes from the all-wise, all-good, all-knowing, all-compassionate, providing hand of God. Whatever God wants us to know about the future—which, judging by Holy Scripture, is not much—is contained in Holy Scripture. This is one facet of the doctrine *sola Scriptura*. The Lord's will revealed in Scripture is that we attend to our vocations in this world (Eph 4:28), love our neighbors (Matt 22:39), honor the king (1 Pet 2:17), and serve and love the Triune God in Christ above all (Matt 22:37; Mic 6:8).

Dame Fortune is a pagan myth. Random chance is a pagan myth. Things do not just happen, even if it might seem that way to us. Getting to grips with the doctrine of providence is central to our piety. Ursinus reminds us,

> From these things it appears that the whole truth of religion, and the very foundation of piety would be overthrown if the providence of God, as it has been defined and explained, be not maintained: Because, 1. We would not be patient in adversity if we did not know that these things are sent upon us from God our Father. 2. We would not be grateful for the benefits which we receive if we did not know that they are given to us from above. 3. We would not have a good and certain hope in relation to future things if we were not fully persuaded that the will of God, in regard to our salvation, and that of all his people, is unchangeable.[15]

We are not the final arbiter of the meaning of life. We barely know our own minds and hearts, let alone God's or the future. We are mere creatures. God spoke into nothing and made all that is, and he will bring everything to a glorious conclusion. In the interim, between the ascension and Christ's bodily return, we work for him out of gratitude for his mercy and grace to miserable sinners.

---

15. Ursinus, *Commentary*, 164.

Question 29

Why is the Son of God called *Jesus*, that is, Savior?

Question 30

Do those also believe in the only Savior Jesus, who seek their salvation and welfare from saints, from themselves, or anywhere else?

Lord's Day 11

Question 29

Why is the Son of God called *Jesus*, that is, Savior?

Because He saves us from our sins, and because salvation is not to be sought or found in any other.[1]

Jesus is an intentionally troublesome figure. He said, "I am the way and the truth and the life. No one comes to the Father except through me" (John 14:6). His claim caused outrage then, and it continues to do so today. Through the history of the Christian faith people have struggled with this truth and have sought a way around it.[2] Origen was perhaps the first Christian universalist.[3] Francis Turretin mentions several more early modern examples of universalism. He mentions a Dutch Anabaptist group, the followers of David Joris (ca. 1501–1556), sometimes referred to as the "Davidists";[4] libertines (those who deny any fixed moral law); Socinians (rationalist biblicists who denied the Trinity, the atonement, and the deity of Christ); and some Remonstrants who denied the proposition "no one can be saved who is not placed in Christ by true faith." Jacob Arminius (1560–1609), in his *Apology*, and his successor, Simon Episcopius (1583–1643), who spoke for the Remonstrants at Dort, admitted "Gentiles and others to salvation, holding that by a right use of the light of nature, the

1. "Warum wird der Sohn Gottes Jesus, das ist, Seligmacher, genannt? Darum, weil er uns selig macht von unsern Sünden, und weil bei keinem Andern einige Seligkeit zu suchen noch zu sinden ist" (Schaff, *Creeds of the Churches*, 3:317). "Quare Filius Dei appellatur Iesus, hoc est, Salvator? Quia nos salvat ab omnibus peccatis nostris: nec ulla salus aliunde peti debet, nec alibi reperiri potest" (Niemeyer, *Collectio Confessionum*, 436).

2. McClymond, *Devil's Redemption*, is the best modern treatment of this topic.

3. McClymond, *Devil's Redemption*, 1:272–73, 317–20.

4. This is a reference to the sixteenth-century group known as Davidists or Davidians. They were followers of David Joris or Joriszoon (modernized, David Georgeson; ca. 1501–1556). Born in Basel, he emigrated to the Netherlands, where he became attracted to the Reformation. He came to see himself as a prophet and the bringer of judgment. He claimed visions and gathered followers (Davidists). They were chiliasts, i.e., they were looking forward to the coming millennium on the earth. Frightened, the authorities cracked down on the Davidists, but Joris escaped their net. Joris's followers came to imagine that he had power to make himself invisible, perhaps an inference from their Christology. In the mid-1540s, he fled to Basel with wealth accumulated from his followers and renamed and rebranded himself as an aristocrat persecuted for the gospel. There he lived in a castle and wrote mystical treatises and in defense of radicals of all sorts, including Miguel Servetus. His true identity was not discovered until after his death, and he continued to have followers through the end of the sixteenth century.

light of grace can be obtained and by grace admission to glory."[5] Some Roman Catholics have taught the same.[6] Michael McClymond argues that Jürgen Moltmann was a universalist.[7] In modernity it has become a liberal commonplace that, of course, salvation is available to all apart from true faith in Christ. Anyone who denies universalism in public is likely to be denounced as a bigot.

Nevertheless, the apostolic message was as clear about this as Jesus's own declaration: "And there is salvation in no one else, for there is no other name under heaven given among men by which we must be saved" (Acts 4:12 ESV). In Scripture the "the name" is a powerful expression. In Genesis 4:26, people began to call on "the name of Yahweh." This passage is widely understood to refer to formal, organized worship of the God revealed in nature and Scripture, who had spoken creation into existence and who had promised a Redeemer to come through the line of the woman. To call on his name is to call on him. Thus, God's name is blessed (Dan 2:20). This is why the third commandment (Exod 20:7) forbids us from using the name of Yahweh, which I take to mean any vain reference to him, that is, carelessly and certainly in any false oath.[8] Scripture says: "Then Moses said to Elohim, 'If I come to the people of Israel and say to them, *The God of your fathers has sent me to you,* and they ask me, *What is his name?* what shall I say?' Elohim said to Moses, 'I am that I am.' And Elohim said, 'Say this to the people of Israel, *I Am has sent me to you*'" (Exod 3:13–14). Moses wanted to know God's name. He was asking, "Who are you to us?" and "How do you intend to relate to us?" and "What sort of God are you?" In contrast to the Egyptian gods, he is the sort of God who simply is. He is not becoming.

Following Scripture, *HC* 29 connects our doctrine of God and his name to our doctrine of Christ. Matthew 1:21 says, "You shall call his name

---

5. Turretin, *Institutes of Elenctic Theology*, 1.4.1; van Asselt, *Introduction to Reformed Scholasticism*, 137–38. Arminius taught the universal salvation of infants in his *Apology against 31 Theological Articles* (*Works*, 2:13–14) and arguably opens the door for a universal salvation outside Christ in art. 15 (*Works*, 2:14–16).

6. McClymond, *Devil's Redemption*, 2:868–935. He characterizes Hans Urs von Balthasar, Henri de Lubac, and Teilhard de Chardin as universalists. He describes Karl Rahner as an "inclusivist" rather than as a universalist strictly speaking, since Rahner required a consent of the will for salvation.

7. McClymond, *Devil's Redemption*, 2:817–30.

8. *HC* 99.

Jesus ['Ιησοῦν], for he shall save his people from their sins."[9] The name Jesus means "Yahweh saves." This is as important for us as it was when the catechism was written. In the sixteenth-century context, the church had been tempted to turn its eyes to a plurality of potential intercessors, mediators, and saviors.[10] Popular medieval piety was devoted to the saints and the blessed Virgin Mary. People widely regarded Jesus principally as a king and judge. So, the Reformers had a job before them to convince Christians that though Jesus is king and a judge, for those who believe, he is a Savior. Thus, the first truth to which Ursinus points us is to Christ's office as Mediator and Savior.[11]

For the medieval church, as for many Christians today, it was tempting to think that Jesus had made salvation possible for those who did their part. In that scheme, Jesus was not so much a savior as a facilitator. In such a scheme he is reduced to a cosmic doorman, who allows us to enter the presence of God but who leaves it to us to stay in. This is the fundamental weakness of the New Perspective(s) on Paul and the federal vision movement—which are not new at all; they are as old as the rabbis, the semi-Pelagians, many medieval theologians, and the Remonstrants.

The biblical picture is to the contrary. Jesus is not a facilitator. He is a Savior. He actually, successfully accomplished what he set out to do: save his people, those whom the Father gave to him, for whom he voluntarily came (John 10:1–18; 17:1–4). He laid down his life for his sheep. All those for whom he intentionally laid down his life, for whom he took it up again, those he saved. In the *HC* (18, 30) and in *BC* 22, the Reformed churches repeatedly confess that Jesus is a complete Savior. Any scheme that suspends our salvation on our cooperation with grace or obedience makes him but "half a Savior" (*BC* 22).[12] Thus, Olevianus explains, "Either Jesus is not a perfect Savior, or those who in full trust accept this Jesus must have in Him all they need for their salvation. Therefore, as often as I hear the name Jesus, I shall remember the full salvation that is promised to me and all believers in the name Jesus."[13]

9. Olevian, *Firm Foundation*, 35.

10. *BC* 26 reflects directly on the rise of the cult of saints (Schaff, *Creeds of the Churches*, 3:414–16).

11. Ursinus, *Commentary*, 164–66.

12. Schaff, *Creeds of the Churches*, 3:408.

13. Olevian, *Firm Foundation*, 35.

Here it is useful to note that the catechism speaks of salvation as something that is accomplished by Christ and applied by the Spirit. This is not the way many evangelical Christians speak today. Well-meaning people ask, "When were you saved?" Truly, however, we should think that we were saved when our obedient substitute, Christ, laid down his life. It was finished—not inaugurated (John 19:30). It was accomplished. It was applied to us in our own lives and experience, and it will continue to be applied by the Spirit until Christ comes again, but all his people have been saved, are being saved, and shall be saved. He shall save his people. That is his name. That is who he is to us: our Savior.

In modernity, of course, the very idea of salvation is problematic. For those who begin with Enlightenment assumptions, it is unthinkable that humans need saving from divine wrath. The gods of the Enlightenment and post-Enlightenment movements that swept across Europe, Britain, and eventually North America in the eighteenth and nineteenth centuries were benevolent, distant deities. The modernist theologians did away with judgment and with it the necessity of salvation. For example, in the social gospel movement of the early twentieth century, led by Walter Rauschenbusch (1861–1918), salvation became a metaphor for cultural, economic, and civic improvement.[14] Gradually, in the twentieth century people began to look to government for salvation from earthly ills. In the late modern period, salvation was transformed into therapeutic categories, chief among them self-esteem. In such a context, what sense is it to talk of salvation—from what? To what?

Holy Scripture begs to differ. John the Baptizer, the last of the old covenant prophets, summarizes the message of all the prophets on this score:

> But when he saw many of the Pharisees and Sadducees coming to his baptism, he said to them, "You brood of vipers! Who warned you to flee from the wrath to come? Bear fruit in keeping with repentance. And do not presume to say to yourselves, 'We have Abraham as our father,' for I tell you, God is able from these stones to raise up children for Abraham. Even now the axe is laid to the

14. Evans, *Kingdom Is Always but Coming.*

> root of the trees. Every tree therefore that does not bear good fruit is cut down and thrown into the fire." (Matt 3:7–10 ESV)

The apostle Paul taught the same doctrine. There is a coming judgment, and for those who are not utterly righteous there is "wrath to come." "For they themselves report concerning us the kind of reception we had among you, and how you turned to God from idols to serve the living and true God, and to wait for his Son from heaven, whom he raised from the dead, Jesus who delivers us from the wrath to come" (1 Thess 1:9–10 ESV). And again to the Thessalonian congregation:

> This is evidence of the righteous judgment of God, that you may be considered worthy of the kingdom of God, for which you are also suffering—since indeed God considers it just to repay with affliction those who afflict you, and to grant relief to you who are afflicted as well as to us, when the Lord Jesus is revealed from heaven with his mighty angels in flaming fire, inflicting vengeance on those who do not know God and on those who do not obey the gospel of our Lord Jesus. They will suffer the punishment of eternal destruction, away from the presence of the Lord and from the glory of his might, when he comes on that day to be glorified in his saints, and to be marveled at among all who have believed, because our testimony to you was believed. (2 Thess 1:5–10 ESV)

The apostle John puts that same teaching in symbolic form, but it is clear enough:

> Then I saw an angel standing in the sun, and with a loud voice he called to all the birds that fly directly overhead, "Come, gather for the great supper of God, to eat the flesh of kings, the flesh of captains, the flesh of mighty men, the flesh of horses and their riders, and the flesh of all men, both free and slave, both small and great." And I saw the beast and the kings of the earth with their armies gathered to make war against him who was sitting on the horse and against his army. And the beast was captured, and with it the false prophet who in its presence had done the signs by which he deceived those who had received the mark of the beast and those who worshiped its image. These two were thrown alive into the lake

> of fire that burns with sulfur. And the rest were slain by the sword that came from the mouth of him who was sitting on the horse, and all the birds were gorged with their flesh. (Rev 19:17–21 ESV)

There is a coming judgment. There is divine wrath, that is, as Louis Berkhof puts it,

> retributive justice, which relates to the infliction of penalties. It is an expression of the divine wrath. While in a sinless world there would be no place for its exercise, it necessarily holds a very prominent place in a world full of sin. On the whole the Bible stresses the reward of the righteous more than the punishment of the wicked; but even the latter is sufficiently prominent. Rom. 1:32; 2:9; 12:19; 2 Thess. 1:8, and many other passages. It should be noted that, while man does not merit the reward which he receives, he does merit the punishment which is meted out to him. Divine justice is originally and necessarily obliged to punish evil, but not to reward good, Luke 17:10; 1 Cor. 4:7; Job 41:11. Many deny the strict punitive justice of God and claim that God punishes the sinner to reform him, or to deter others from sin; but these positions are not tenable. The primary purpose of the punishment of sin is the maintenance of right and justice. Of course, it may incidentally serve, and may even, secondarily, be intended, to reform the sinner and to deter others from sin.[15]

These passages are more than sufficient to demonstrate the falsity of the ancient gnostic claim that there is a "New Testament" Christianity wherein God is "love" and without wrath, righteousness, or judgment. That is not Christianity. That is gnosticism, a religion of cosmic ladders, secret knowledge, and salvation not from wrath but from finitude. In other words, it is the very lie that the Evil One first told in the garden: "You shall be like Elohim" (Gen 3:5).

We labor over this issue because, to the modern mind, the notion that humans need salvation is ignorant. It only seems so on the assumption that there is no God who is, who has revealed himself, who has become incarnate in Jesus the Messiah, and who in Christ is returning to judge

15. Berkhof, *Systematic Theology*, 75–76.

the living and the dead. Not only is the doctrine of a coming judgment manifestly biblical, but it is also the universal doctrine of the church.

The Nicene-Constantinopolitan Creed (AD 381) says: "Thence he shall come again, with glory, to judge the quick and the dead."[16] The Apostles' Creed says: "Thence he shall come to judge the quick and the dead."[17] That is why we speak of salvation. There is a coming judgment of the living and the dead. It is not rude to warn people that a sinkhole has developed in the road ahead. Judgment is coming, and the all-holy God shall execute it (Rev 4:8)—God, before whom no unrighteous person shall stand. Jesus is the way to safety. He is the only way through the coming flood of judgment (2 Pet 2:5), and we enter that ark of deliverance by God's free-to-us favor, through faith alone. All those who have been given new life, who are united to Christ through faith, are saved by God's mercy and grace.

Question 30

Do those also believe in the only Savior Jesus, who seek their salvation and welfare from saints, from themselves, or anywhere else?

No, although they make their boast of him, yet in deeds they deny the only Savior Jesus, for either Jesus is not a complete Savior, or they who by true faith receive this Savior, must have in Him all that is necessary to their salvation.[18]

16. Schaff, *Creeds of the Churches*, 2:57.

17. Schaff, *Creeds of the Churches*, 2:45.

18. "Glauben denn die auch an den einigen Seligmacher Jesum, die ihre Seligkeit und Heil bei Heiligen, bei sich selbst, oder anderswo suchen? Nein: sondern sie verläugnen mit der That den einigen Seligmacher und Heiland Jesum, ob sie sich sein gleich rühmen Denn entweder Jesus nicht ein vollkommener Heiland sein kann, oder die diesen Heiland mit wahrem Glauben annehmen, müssen alles in Jhm haben, das zu ihrer Seligkeit vonnöthen ist" (Schaff, *Creeds of the Churches*, 3:317). "Creduntne igitur illi in uicum Servatorem Iesum, qui a sanctis, aut a se, aut aliunde felicitatem aut alutem quaerunt? Non: Etsi enim verbo quidem eo Servatore gloriantur, re ipsa tamen abnegant unicum Servatorem Iesum. Necesse est enim, aut Iesum non esse perfectum Servatorem, aut qui eum Servatorem fide amplectuntur vera, eos omia in ipso possidere, quae ad alutem requiruntur" (Niemeyer, *Collectio Confessionum*, 436).

Since the garden humans have faced the temptation to listen to an authority claiming to compete with God's authority. Since the beginning voices have questioned, "Has God really said?" Since the beginning voices have raised doubts about whether there is really one way to God. This is one of the great messages of the book of Hebrews. Jewish Christians in the mid-60s AD were tempted to turn away from Jesus and back to Moses. Thus, it is no surprise that, gradually through the history of the church, after the close of the apostolic age, some Christians gradually began to look for other mediators.

The late patristic church began to turn memorial feasts, held in honor of believers who had been martyred for the faith, into something more. Through the medieval period, people came to consider Jesus more remote and solely in regard to his royal office (as distinct from his priestly office). The medieval church accumulated a great number of saints' days and imposed a church calendar in which it assigned each day a saint, and Christians began to seek help and intercession from Christians who had been declared by the church to have special standing (i.e., saints). Eventually this came to include the Virgin Mary. It should be noted, however, that much of what the Roman Catholic Church today confesses about the blessed Virgin was unknown to the patristic church, controversial among orthodox Christians in the medieval church, and indeed was promulgated as dogma only in the sixteenth, nineteenth, and twentieth centuries.[19]

In Roman Catholic usage, a saint is a "holy one" who lived "in union with God through the grace of Christ and receives the reward of eternal

19. The evidence for any developed Mariology is absent from the earliest Christian fathers, e.g., the Apostolic Fathers and the apologists. William Perkins discusses this topic very intelligently in *Problem of Forged Catholicism*, 397–99 (*Works*, 7:397–99), where he observes, "It was the common opinion until Lombard's time ... that the virgin Mary was conceived in original sin." He cited specific places in Augustine, Ambrose, Chrysostom, Eusebius, Bede, Anselm, and Bernard, among others. Bernard, who was devoted to the blessed Virgin Mary, nevertheless opposed the introduction of a feast day for her. Perkins argues that it was Scotus who first proposed the doctrine of the immaculate conception of the blessed Virgin Mary. For documentary evidence of the late ecclesiastical adoption of the Marian dogma, see Schroeder, *Canons and Decrees*, in session 5 (1546), where Rome merely asserts the immaculate conception of the blessed Virgin Mary. See Denzinger, *Enchiridion Symbolorum*, §792; the *CCC* appeals to *Lumen Gentium* 56 (1964) in support of alleged immaculate conception (*CCC* §490nn132–33), which dogma itself was not proclaimed until 1854 by Pius IX, in *Ineffabilis Deus* (see Denzinger, *Enchiridion Symbolorum*, §1641). The assumption of the blessed Virgin Mary was only proclaimed in 1950. See below for more on this.

life."[20] When saints are named by the bishop of Rome, it is the culmination of a usually lengthy process of canonization, or the "solemn declaration by the Pope that a deceased member of the faithful may be proposed as a model and intercessor to the Christian faithful and venerated as a saint on the basis of the fact that the person lived a life of heroic virtue or remained faithful to God through martyrdom."[21] The Roman Catholic Church defines "*intercession*" as a "a form of prayer or petition on behalf of others."[22] According to Roman Catholic dogma, Christ is our "unique" intercessor, but he is not our only intercessor. According to Rome, deceased Christians have the ability to hear and answer prayers. Alleged evidence of such intercession is a necessary part of the process of canonization of a saint. According to Rome, the Blessed Virgin is "sometimes called a Mediatrix in virtue of a her cooperation in the saving mission of Christ."[23] So, under the ninth article of the creed, "'the communion of the saints" (*communio sanctorum*), the Roman Catholic Church confesses, "being more closely united to Christ, those who dwell in heaven fix the whole Church more firmly in holiness ... [the saints] do not cease to intercede with the Father for us, as they proffer the merits which they acquired on earth through the one mediator between God and men, Christ Jesus. ... So by their fraternal concern is our weakness greatly helped.'"[24] Mary, whom Pius XII declared *ex cathedra* in 1950 to have been "assumed" bodily to the right hand of Christ, is said by Rome to be rightly "invoked in the Church under the titles of Advocate, Helper, Benefactress, and Mediatrix."[25]

The fundamental spiritual and theological problem is that Christians began to lose sight of the fact that Christ *alone* is our Mediator, the God-Man, who was tempted in every respect as we are yet without sin (Heb 4:15).[26] He alone has power and authority to help the helpless; he alone has the right to stand before the Father on our behalf, to make our prayers known, to represent us before the Father. In the Reformation, Protestants

---

20. CCC, s.v. "Saint" (898).
21. CCC, s.v. "Canonization" (869).
22. CCC, s.v. "Intercession"(884).
23. CCC, s.v. "Mediator/Mediatrix" (887–88).
24. CCC, §956, quoting *Lumen Gentium* 49.
25. "Munificentissimus Deus" (1950); CCC §§966, 969. See the discussion under *HC* 35.
26. See the related discussion under *HC* 29.

and particularly the Reformed repudiated all competitors to Jesus as Mediator.[27] The Reformation restored biblical and ancient Christian doctrine and practice by returning to Jesus alone (*solus Christus*) as the only Mediator between God and humanity. The apostle Paul says: "For there is one God, and there is one mediator between God and men, the man Christ Jesus" (1 Tim 2:5 ESV). This unequivocal declaration is flatly contrary to the Roman dogma that the blessed virgin is a *mediatrix*. She is not. She is blessed not because she hears our prayers (she does not; death confers glorification but neither omniscience or omnipresence) but because the Lord blessed her by allowing her to become, in the language of Definition of Chalcedon (AD 451), the Godbearer (ἐκ Μαρίας τῆς παρθένου τῆς θεοτόκου).[28] By the supernatural operation of the Holy Spirit, our Lord Jesus took his humanity from the Virgin Mary. In the Apostles' Creed, Christians confess that Christ was "conceived by the Holy Spirit, born of the virgin Mary."[29]

Scripture says nothing to lead us to seek to communicate with Mary after her death. To that point, Scripture says nothing that would lead us to think that she went to be with the Lord without dying. We do well to honor her faith and piety and particularly to remember why she is blessed, which turns the focus back where it belongs: on our Lord Jesus—but it is quite improper to regard her as anything more than a mere Christian, who, like all other Christians, was utterly dependent on God's grace and on the imputation of the perfect obedience and death of the Son of God for acceptance with God. In *BC* 26, the Reformed churches confess that she would be horrified to know that millions of Christians are calling out

27. The Augsburg Confession art. 21 says: "Touching the worship of saints, [the Protestants] teach that the memory of saints may be set before us, that we may follow their faith and good works according to our calling; as the Emperor may follow David's example in making war to drive away the Turks from his country; for either of them is a king. But the Scripture teacheth not to invocate saints, or to ask help of saints, because it propoundeth unto us one Christ the Mediator, Propitiatory, High-Priest, and Intercessor. This Christ is to be invocated, and he hath promised that he will hear our prayers, and liketh this worship especially, to wit, that he be invocated in all afflictions. 'If any man sin, we have an advocate with God, Jesus Christ the righteous' (1 John 2:1)" (Schaff, *Creeds of the Churches*, 3:26).

28. Schaff, *Creeds of the Churches*, 2:62. The Roman abuse of this truth is no cause to abandon it.

29. "Qui conceptus est de Spiritu sancto, natus ex Maria virgine" (Schaff, *Creeds of the Churches*, 2:45).

to her for help and intercession instead of calling out to her Son, whom she and we know to be the only Mediator between God and humanity.[30]

Hebrews 7:25 says that Jesus alone is "able to save to the uttermost those who draw near to God through him" (ESV) because he alone is our substitute and our representative before God. Mary did not obey and die for us. The saints do not love us more than Jesus. The government is on Christ's shoulders, not the shoulders of saints (Isa 9:6). This is Paul's argument to the Corinthians: "Is Christ divided? Was Paul crucified for you? Or were you baptized in the name of Paul?" (1 Cor 1:13 ESV). The expected answer is no. Thus, as Hebrews says, Jesus, not saints, "always lives to make intercession" for us (Heb 7:25).

Roman Catholics and others who seek their salvation or welfare in anyone other than Jesus are guilty of idolatry. Matthew 1:21 says, "For *he* will save his people." It does not say that he will make salvation possible with the intercession of the Virgin Mary or saints. The logic is inescapable. Either Jesus is *the* Savior or he is not. The Roman Catholic dogma of the intercession by the saints reduces Jesus to but half a Savior. We do not boast in anyone except in the righteousness of Christ credited to us (1 Cor 1:31; 2 Cor 10:17). Inasmuch as calling on saints for help and intercession offers something to God other than what Christ accomplished once for all, it is a form of the works-righteousness that Paul condemns in Galatians 5:4. Rather, it is by grace alone, through faith alone, in Christ the only Mediator (1 Tim 2:5; Heb 9:15; 12:24) that sinners are reconciled with God (Col 1:20). We received the free favor of God from him, not from saints (John 1:16). We do not boast in or stand on or rest in our personal sanctity or in that of any mere human, including the saints. We rest *only* in the unique, perfect, condign merits and perfect righteousness of Christ.[31]

30. Schaff, *Creeds of the Churches*, 3:414.

31. This language is virtually identical to the language used in *BC* 26; Ursinus, *Commentary*, 168–69.

Question 31

Why is he called *Christ,* that is anointed?

Question 32

But why are you called a Christian?

Lord's Day 12

QUESTION 31

Why is he called *Christ*, that is anointed?

Because he is ordained of God the Father and anointed with the Holy Spirit to be our chief Prophet and teacher, who has fully revealed to us the secret counsel and will of God concerning our redemption; and our only high Priest, who by the one sacrifice of his body, has redeemed us, and ever lives to make intercession for us with the Father; and our eternal King, who governs us by his Word and Spirit and defends and preserves us in the redemption earned for us.[1]

Jesus is the Christ, and his believers are Christians. That is a profound truth. Christians are often tempted to try to do the work that only Jesus can do. Too often we are not content to be, to bend C. S. Lewis's phrase, mere Christians. This can happen in a variety of ways. Sometimes people want to try to do more than simply tell others the good news. They want to try to do the work of the Spirit in bringing others to Christ. Whenever we try to present ourselves to God on the basis of what we have done (our performance, our cooperation with grace), we deny the finished work of Christ.

As the Reformed churches understand Scripture, however, there is only one Savior. The rest of us are the saved or those who need to be saved. We have been considering our need for salvation under the previous questions. In order to help us understand how Christ is our Savior,

1. "Warum ist Er Christus, das ist, ein Gesalbter, genannt? Weil Er von Gott dem Vater verordnet und mit dem heiligen Geiste gesalbet ist zu unserm obersten Propheten und Lehrer, der uns den heimlichen Rath und Willen Gottes von unserer Erlösung vollkommen offenbaret; und zu unserm einigen Hohenpriefter, der uns mit dem einigen Opfer seines Leibes erlöset hat, und immerbar mit seiner Fürbitte vor dem Vater vertritt; und zu unserm emigen König, der uns mit seinem Wort und Geist regieret, und bei der erworbenen Erlösung schützet und erhält" (Schaff, *Creeds of the Churches*, 3:317–18). "Quare appellatur Christus, hoc est, unctus? Quod a Patre ordinatus, et Spiritu Sancto unctus sit summus Propheta ac Doctor, qui nobis arcanum consilium et omnem voluntatem Patris, de redemtione nostri patefecit; et summus Pontifex, qui nos unico sacrificio sui corporis redemit, assidueque pro nobis apud Patrem intercedit: et Rex, qui nos suo verbo et Spiritu gubernat, et partam nobis alutem tuetur ac coservat" (Niemeyer, *Collectio Confessionum*, 437).

the catechism turns to Christ's threefold office (*triplex munus*): prophet, priest, and king.[2] These are truly essential offices. Calvin writes:

> Therefore, in order that faith may find a firm basis for salvation in Christ, and thus rest in him, this principle must be laid down: the office enjoined upon Christ by the Father consists of three parts. For he was given to be prophet, king, and priest. Yet it would be of little value to know these names without understanding their purpose and use. The papists use these names, too, but coldly and rather ineffectually, since they do not know what each of these titles contains.[3]

Jesus Christ is God the Son incarnate. He took on our flesh, of the Virgin Mary, to be our substitute and our Redeemer. He fulfilled his mission, that is, his being sent, in three offices. Scripture calls him Christ (χριστός) because he is anointed.[4] Peter identifies the office of the anointed one with the office of Son: "You are the Christ, the Son of the living God" (Matt 16:16). The imagery, of course, alludes to David's anointing: "Then Samuel took the horn of oil and anointed him in the midst of his brothers. And the Spirit of Yahweh rushed upon David from that day forward" (1 Sam 16:13).

Jesus was not anointed by a prophet, even as one as great as Samuel. He was anointed by his heavenly Father with an anointing of which David's was a mere shadow (Matt 3:16; Isa 61:1–3; Heb 1:9). Jesus, the God-Man, was anointed with the Holy Spirit to fulfill his offices for us. To say that he was anointed is to say that he was empowered by the Spirit for us. He was so enabled, so blessed by the unique presence of the Spirit and the endowments belonging to his divine nature, that he was utterly uniquely qualified to save his people.

The temptation to blur the line between Christ and his Christian is perennial and powerful. It comes of downplaying the effect of the fall (depravity) and the uniqueness of Jesus's person (his two natures) and his all-sufficient, once-for-all work for us. His three offices ground us in these

2. Ursinus, *Commentary*, 169–70.

3. Calvin, *Institutes* 2.15.1.

4. Olevian, *Firm Foundation*, 36–37.

basics, which helps us to avoid this temptation. In his prophetic office we have the uniqueness and finality of his word (*sola Scriptura*); in his priestly office we have the uniqueness of his grace and salvation received *sola gratia, sola fide*; and in his kingly office, we have his unique sovereign rule over all things, expressed generally in providence and specially in the embassy of his eternal kingdom in the church and her ministry.

Each of Christ's three offices, of course, is rooted in the history of redemption. God instituted each of these offices among his people to serve as a type (an illustration) or a foreshadowing of the ultimate reality to come in the incarnation of God the Son in Jesus the Messiah. The apostle John teaches us to read Scripture this way when he writes, "For the law was given through Moses; grace and truth came through Jesus Christ. No one has ever seen God; the only God, who is at the Father's side, he has made him known" (John 1:17–18 ESV).

According to Hebrews 11:23–28 (among other places), Moses was a Christian who lived under a typological (time of illustrations) administration of the covenant of grace. He was not the Savior, and he knew it. He was looking forward to the Savior to come. He knew Christ by faith just like Abraham, who saw Jesus's day coming and believed (John 8:56). Moses, as it were, worked for Jesus. This is a very important principle that many Christians have not understood and consequently inverted. Frequently well-meaning believers have turned things around so that Jesus works for Moses. One sees this in forms of dispensationalism that anticipate a restoration of the temple and sacrifices. That is exactly contrary to the repeated teaching of Hebrews that Jesus is the final, once-for-all sacrifice (Heb 7:27; 9:12, 26; 10:10). Jesus said, "It is finished" (John 19:30), not, "The sacrificial system is done for now, but it will return when the temple is rebuilt." Rather, Jesus said that he *was* the temple and he was going to raise it again in three days, by which he meant his body (John 2:19–21). The Roman Catholic Church has made the same mistake by effectively reinstituting the sacerdotal (priestly) sacrificial system. That ethical system seeks to reinstitute the Mosaic civil code, which we confess to have expired with the death of Christ.[5]

5. WCF 19.4, in Westminster Assembly, *Humble Advice of the Assembly*, 33.

One of the more important ways that Moses worked for Jesus was in his office as prophet, the first of Christ's three offices.[6] In Deuteronomy 18:15–20 the Lord characterizes the office of prophet:

> Yahweh your God will raise up for you a prophet like me from among you, from your brothers—it is to him you shall listen—just as you desired of Yahweh your God at Horeb on the day of the assembly, when you said, "Let me not hear again the voice of Yahweh my God or see this great fire any more, lest I die." And Yahweh said to me, "They are right in what they have spoken. I will raise up for them a prophet like you from among their brothers. And I will put my words in his mouth, and he shall speak to them all that I command him. And whoever will not listen to my words that he shall speak in my name, I myself will require it of him. But the prophet who presumes to speak a word in my name that I have not commanded him to speak, or who speaks in the name of other gods, that same prophet shall die." And if you say in your heart, "How may we know the word that Yahweh has not spoken?"—when a prophet speaks in the name of Yahweh, if the word does not come to pass or come true, that is a word that Yahweh has not spoken; the prophet has spoken it presumptuously. You need not be afraid of him. (ESV modified)

Moses was to serve as the baseline of the office of prophet. The Lord set up tests by which Israel could empirically verify that one really was a prophet. A prophet would be like Moses, raised up by God. He would have God's word in his mouth, he would speak God's word to his people. Even though he was human, he would have divine authority on the basis of the divine word (*sola Scriptura*). Anyone who presumed to speak an authoritative word that was not from God or who spoke in the name of an alien God (other than Yahweh) was not a prophet and, under the Mosaic-Israelite system temporarily instituted by God, must die (Deut 13:1–5). Anyone who claimed to be a prophet had to meet these tests, and in the course of redemptive history the Lord raised up a succession of prophets *like* Moses. Indeed, when God explained the prophetic office to Miriam

6. Ursinus, *Commentary*, 172–74.

and Aaron, he contrasted Moses with the coming prophets: "And he said, 'Hear my words: If there is a prophet among you, I Yahweh make myself known to him in a vision; I speak with him in a dream. Not so with my servant Moses. He is faithful in all my house. With him I speak mouth to mouth, clearly, and not in riddles, and he beholds the form of Yahweh. Why then were you not afraid to speak against my servant Moses?'" (Num 12:6–8 ESV modified; cf. Deut 34:10).

God gave the old covenant prophets visions. God took them up into heaven. Like Samuel, the succeeding prophets received direct revelation from the Lord (1 Sam 3:20). They all received their commission from God. According to Isaiah 6:1–3, God gave Isaiah a vision of heaven. Isaiah came to God's people as a representative of the heavenly court, as an ambassador from another kingdom to mediate God's word to his people.

The last of those old covenant prophets was John the Baptist. He announced that another was coming after him (Matt 3:11), of whom he, John, was merely the forerunner. That one, whose sandals John said he was unfit to tie, was Jesus (Matt 11:7–12). Jesus described himself as a prophet (Matt 13:57). When he made his triumphal entry into Jerusalem, the people hailed him as a prophet (Matt 21:11, 45). The man who was born blind called him a prophet (John 9:17).

Jesus more than fulfilled all the tests of Deuteronomy 18. In his entire ministry he only spoke God's word, which is why he was arrested and murdered. Israel treated him as she had all the other prophets (Matt 5:12). He announced God's word and his kingdom (Mark 1:15). He spoke with divine authority (Matt 7:29) because he not only had God's word in his mouth, but he *was* God's Word (John 1:1–3) incarnate.

Jesus is the Savior because he is *the* prophet, *the* Word. He is God's authoritative, definitive self-disclosure. The apostles had authority because they ministered the Word, Christ and his revelation. He spoke to Adam and Eve in the garden. He promised a Redeemer. He thundered from Sinai (Heb 12:24), and he promised a prophet, priest, and king to come. This is why we seek salvation in no other one, why we seek no further revelation.

The second aspect of Jesus's threefold office we need to consider is his office and work as our priest.[7] The first time the word *priest* appears

7. Ursinus, *Commentary*, 174–75.

in Scripture, it is in connection to that mysterious figure Melchizedek. Genesis 14:18 records, "And Melchizedek king of Salem brought out bread and wine. (He was priest of God Most High)" (ESV). Abraham recognized Melchizedek's two offices (king and priest) by receiving his blessing and by giving him a tenth of everything (Gen 14:20). A king is a ruler, but a priest is an intercessor. Abraham was right to recognize Melchizedek as a priest "of God Most High." In Scripture, Melchizedek becomes the paradigm for an eternal priesthood. Yahweh says to Adon[8]:

> Yahweh has sworn
> and will not change his mind,
> "You are a priest forever
> after the order of Melchizedek." (Ps 110:4)

For the reader of Scripture who is aware of the extensive teaching about the Aaronic priesthood (e.g., Exod 31:8; 40:11–15; Leviticus) that *Yahweh* should confer on *Adon* a Melchizedekian priesthood, rather than an Aaronic priesthood, might be a surprise. Still, we learn from Aaron what a priest is and does. He receives sacrificial offerings (Lev 1:5–9). He diagnoses ceremonial uncleanness and applies the appropriate stipulations (e.g., Lev 13:1–4). He ministers at the tabernacle, that is, the place of meeting with God (Num 3:5–8). He is responsible for the ritual purity and holiness of the congregation (Num 25:6–9; Lev 5; 13). He makes atonement for the sins of the people (Lev 4). He represents God's people in the most holy place in the temple. The pastor to the Hebrew Christians reminds them (and us):

> For every high priest chosen from among men is appointed to act on behalf of men in relation to God, to offer gifts and sacrifices for sins. He can deal gently with the ignorant and wayward, since he himself is beset with weakness. Because of this he is obligated to offer sacrifice for his own sins just as he does for those of the people. And no one takes this honor for himself, but only when called by God, just as Aaron was. (Heb 5:1–4 ESV)

8. There are two divine figures in Psalm 110, Yahweh and Adon. In the New Testament we learn that Adon is God the Son.

It was essential that a priest be like those whom he represents: "Therefore he had to be made like his brothers in every respect, so that he might become a merciful and faithful high priest in the service of God, to make propitiation for the sins of the people. For because he himself has suffered when tempted, he is able to help those who are being tempted" (Heb 2:17–18 ESV). According to Hebrews 5:6, quoting Psalm 110:4, Jesus is our high priest, but his was not an Aaronic priesthood, because all the Aaronic priests died and were replaced by a successor. Jesus has an eternal priesthood. He has no successor. Like Melchizedek, his coming and going were mysterious. Like Melchizedek, he was also a king. When Yahweh said to Adon, "You are a priest forever," he was not speaking about David, who is dead and buried (Acts 2:29). He was not even speaking about Melchizedek, who was only a man. Rather, in Psalm 110 we are given a window into a pretemporal, eternal covenant between God the Father and God the Son, two distinct persons.[9] In that pretemporal, eternal covenant, God the Father gave to the Son a people to redeem and represent, and the Son accepted that people and pledged to conquer their enemies, to redeem them, and to represent them eternally. Melchizedek was a mysterious figure worthy of honor, but he was not God the Son in eternal communion with the Father. That was someone else.

David was anointed, but he was not *the* anointed. It was not David to whom God made that promise. By contrast, Jesus was killed and buried, but he did not remain dead or in the grave. On the third day, when the women came early in the morning (Luke 24:22), they found his grave empty. The angel who was present asked them why they were looking for the living among the dead. His grave clothes were folded neatly (John 20:7). Death was not able to keep him because he had the power of an indestructible life (Heb 7:16). Jesus is *the* anointed one, the Messiah.

The Messiah is a priest who has "passed through the heavens" (Heb 4:14) yet who is able to sympathize with our weaknesses. He has been "tempted in every respect as we are, yet without sin" (4:15). Hebrews says this because our priest is true human and true God. He has two natures,

9. For more on the *pactum salutis*, see VanDrunen and Clark, "Covenant before the Covenants," 167–96; Fesko, *Covenant of Redemption*; Fesko, *Trinity and the Covenant*.

undivided, unconfused in one person.[10] Jesus is greater than David and Solomon (Luke 11:31).

Indeed, Jesus is not just a priest, he is our "high priest, holy, innocent, unstained, separated from sinners, and exalted above the heavens" (Heb 7:26 ESV). He is a royal priest, seated at the right hand of the Father (Heb 8:1), serving not the copy but in the true holy of holies in the real, eternal, heavenly temple (vv. 2–5). The Aaronic priesthood was intentionally temporary, but not so Jesus's priesthood. By his intercession and ministry, he has secured redemption (Heb 9; 10:10). He is not only the priest, but he is *the* eternal, once-for-all sacrifice (Heb 9:12; 10:11, 20). His body was the temple curtain. In other words, the tabernacle, the temple with all its appointments, the Aaronic priesthood, even the Melchizedekian priesthood, all pointed to Jesus. He is the reality, and they were the shadows, the illustrations.

Jesus's sacrifice was the "one sacrifice of his body," not the repeated, shadowy sacrifice. The temple has done its work. Even were a third temple to be built, it would have *no spiritual virtue*. This is why it is sad and foolish for Christians to invest money in breeding heifers and in sewing uniforms for a reestablished priesthood. The temple has been already been rebuilt in the resurrection of our Lord's true human body (John 2:19). The Lamb of God will not be sitting on a throne in Jerusalem watching men sacrifice lambs, as if *the* Lamb of God had not already died once for all on the cross to take away the sin of the world (John 1:29, 36; Acts 8:32; 1 Cor 5:7; 1 Pet 1:19; Rev 5:6–13; *et passim*).

This is why the Reformed churches are so adamantly opposed to the medieval and Roman reinstitution of the priesthood and the memorial, propitiatory resacrifice of the transubstantiated Eucharist. Because God is one in three persons, Christ's humanity need not be brought down out of heaven from the right hand and the elements transformed. Rather, he *is* the bread. Paul condemns this very impulse (Rom 10:6–7). Remember, Jesus's body was true humanity, not divine. His *person* is divine, but his humanity does not become divine any more than his divinity becomes human. To confuse the two is the Eutychian heresy, just as to separate

10. Definition of Chalcedon (AD 451); Schaff, *Creeds of the Churches*, 2:62.

the two natures is the Nestorian heresy. With the church catholic, we condemn both heresies.

To seek a reinstitution of the priesthood, whether in a putative rebuilt temple in Jerusalem or in a Roman cathedral, is to deny the once-for-all, finished work of Christ, and it is to seek to make ourselves into little saviors rather than being content with being the saved. Christians ought to rejoice and rest in the finished work of Christ *for us* and his ongoing, eternal, perfect intercession *for us* before the Father (Heb 7:25). His righteousness is sufficient. It is perfect. In Christ our head, our representative, our substitute, our High Priest, believers are irrevocably, immutably acceptable to God. He is the Savior. He has saved us. He is saving us, and he shall save us to the uttermost. We are only the saved, but by his grace we are that.

The third of the three offices is the office of king.[11] Americans have a little difficulty with the office of king. In the eighteenth century we rebelled against King George III, and we have not had much direct experience with them since. Scripture, however, takes for granted that we know what a king is. They appear without explanation or comment in Genesis 14. As we saw last time, one of the most significant kings in Scripture was also a priest, Melchizedek. Scripture portrays him as greater than Abraham, and it is to him that Abraham gives a tithe (a tenth). As a priest-king, he blessed Abraham. In the narrative Abraham submits to him as a greater king. We know, of course, from Psalm 110:4 and from Hebrews 7 that Melchizedek, king of Salem, was a type, a foreshadowing of a greater king, Jesus.

The Lord appointed judges over Israel, but the people were not satisfied (1 Sam 8:5), and they asked for a king "to judge us like all the nations." The Lord instructed Samuel to listen to the people and to appoint a king because they had rejected his divine kingship. He warned them about how life under Israelite kings would be:

> These will be the ways of the king who will reign over you: he will take your sons and appoint them to his chariots and to be his horsemen and to run before his chariots. And he will appoint for himself commanders of thousands and commanders of fifties, and

11. Ursinus, *Commentary*, 176–78.

> some to plow his ground and to reap his harvest, and to make his implements of war and the equipment of his chariots. He will take your daughters to be perfumers and cooks and bakers. He will take the best of your fields and vineyards and olive orchards and give them to his servants. He will take the tenth of your grain and of your vineyards and give it to his officers and to his servants. He will take your male servants and female servants and the best of your young men and your donkeys, and put them to his work. He will take the tenth of your flocks, and you shall be his slaves. And in that day you will cry out because of your king, whom you have chosen for yourselves, but the LORD will not answer you in that day. (1 Sam 8:11–18 ESV)

In effect, Samuel says, you will wish that you had not chosen a king. The Israelites again refused to listen to Samuel and demanded a king so that they would be like the other nations and so that he would go fight their battles for them (vv. 20–22). They got their wish. Samuel anointed Saul's head with oil (1 Sam 10:1), and he was temporarily gifted with extraordinary powers for the purpose of fulfilling his new office, but in time it became clear that he was not *the* anointed one. He died in shame and humiliation, but not for the salvation of his people. The king to come came from the line of King David and became the paradigm by which Israelite kings were to be measured. Unlike Saul, though a wretched sinner and a "man of blood" (1 Chr 28:3) whose sins disqualified him from being the one to build God's temple, nevertheless David was a man after God's own heart (1 Kgs 11:4; Acts 13:22). In material terms, Solomon was perhaps Israel's greatest king. The kingdom was at its greatest under his rule, and his wisdom and skill were famous across the ancient world (1 Kgs 10:1).

Jesus's royal office is to be understood against its Old Testament background. He came to Israel as a king, but of a different sort. He came preaching the kingdom of God (Mark 1:15) and the kingdom of heaven (Matt 3:2). Like King David, he came to Israel on a donkey (1 Sam 16:20) in fulfillment of the prophecy of Zechariah 9:9:

> Rejoice greatly, O daughter of Zion!
> Shout aloud, O daughter of Jerusalem!

> Behold, your king is coming to you;
>   righteous and having salvation is he,
> humble and mounted on a donkey,
>   on a colt, the foal of a donkey.

Our Lord Jesus entered Jerusalem in triumph, but not to shed the blood of others. He entered in order to defeat sin and death by the shedding of his own blood. This sort of conquest, this sort of kingdom, was such a reversal of expectations that it was impossible for the Israelites to see it. This was what the Lord had been promising all along. The son of the woman would crush the head of the serpent, but only at the cost of his own life, as the serpent would strike his heel.

Like the rest of us, national Israel liked the head-crushing bit but did not care for the humiliation and shame entailed in heel striking. So, given the choice by the ruling secular authority between a criminal named Bar-Abbas and "Jesus who is called Christ" (Matt 27:17), they cried out for Bar-Abbas (Matt 27:20). The soldiers mocked him as if he were a deluded, *faux* king. His death looked to all the world, even to his disciples and family, as the tragic end of great possibilities—until Sunday morning, the inauguration of the new creation (2 Cor 5:17) and the inauguration of the concomitant new creation Sabbath. When his body was not to be found in the tomb, where they had laid it cold and dead, they began to experience the kingdom of God in power. His risen body could be touched (John 20:27) but was not to be held, as if it were not going to ascend bodily to rule over all things with a rod of iron (Ps 2:9). He is the Shepherd-King, who protects and rules his people as Mediator, by his word and Spirit, in his church (Matt 16:18). He rules all of creation as the anointed Son in his sovereign providence.

Against those who suggest that Jesus is not yet ruling, we confess that Jesus is ruling now. This is the express teaching of the apostle Peter in Acts 2:30–33:

> Being therefore a prophet, and knowing that God had sworn with an oath to him that he would set one of his descendants on his throne, he foresaw and spoke about the resurrection of the Christ, that he was not abandoned to Hades, nor did his flesh see corruption. This Jesus God raised up, and of that we all are witnesses.

> Being therefore exalted at the right hand of God, and having received from the Father the promise of the Holy Spirit, he has poured out this that you yourselves are seeing and hearing. (ESV)

Jesus does not have to wait until the rebuilding of the Jerusalem temple to begin ruling. He is ruling now. David is not the fulfillment of Psalm 110; Jesus is. In Acts 4:25–30, quoting Psalm 2:1–2, the Holy Spirit says that Jesus, not David, is now fulfilling Psalm 2. Those who are waiting for Jesus to begin reigning need to adjust their conception of what his reign and kingdom are. Whatever transpires is his sovereign good pleasure. When Paul wrote Romans 13, the dissolute pagan Roman emperor Nero was about twenty years old, and he was on his throne as Christ's servant, even though he never acknowledged him as king and even though he persecuted the Christians. This was Paul's theology of the King in his preaching in Acts 13. When God raised Jesus the Messiah, the King, from the dead, he fulfilled the promise of Psalm 2:7, "You are my Son, Today have I begotten you." This is the language of royal enthronement, of accession. God the Son is the eternally begotten Son of God, but in the resurrection Jesus assumed his royal throne in glory. He is the fulfillment of Psalm 16. He did not see corruption.

Because they knew and understood him to be king, the early Christians were known for speaking of King Jesus (Acts 17:7). Of course, Pilate had queried Jesus already about his kingly office. That is why Jesus told him that he could have legions of angels descend on Jerusalem, but that was not why he came. That is not the nature of his kingdom. He rules his twofold kingdom (*duplex regimen*) sovereignly but in distinct ways.[12] Through his embassy and his ambassadors or ministers, he rules his spiritual kingdom with spiritual keys. In his general providence he rules everything else and holds the entire world accountable to his moral law revealed in creation and in the conscience (Rom 1:18–2:14). The Christian's whole life is under his lordship, and one day every knee will bow and every tongue confess that Jesus is Lord (Phil 2:10).

Finally, we must remember that our King is also our Savior. We must not repeat the error of the medieval church by thinking of him solely or exclusively in his royal office to the exclusion of the other two. This is

12. Calvin, *Institutes* 3.19.15.

how they came to seek other mediators and other saviors. There is no other Savior, and no one loves us or is more ready and willing to hear us than King Jesus, who obeyed and died in our place and who was raised for our justification.

The doctrine of Christ's kingship and kingdom should bring comfort to those who "who believe and trust in Christ and are baptized into His name" because, through faith alone, they "know that in this life they are in the Kingdom of Christ and not in the Kingdom or dominion of the Devil. They have been redeemed from the power of the Devil. They have been redeemed from the power of the Devil and inserted into the Kingdom of Christ [Col. 1:13], and they are united with Christ their King in such a way that they are members of His body."[13] This certainty gives us peace and confidence before the Lord because we have a heartfelt trust "which is the internal anointing of the Holy Spirit," and we have the "physical sign of the covenant, holy baptism," which testifies to us that just as surely as we believe, so certainly do we belong to the sovereign King.[14]

QUESTION 32

But why are you called a Christian?

Because by faith I am a member of Christ and thus a partaker of his anointing, in order that I also may confess his name, present myself a living sacrifice of thankfulness to Him, and that with a free conscience I may fight against sin and the devil in this life, and hereafter in eternity reign with him over all creatures.[15]

---

13. Olevian, *Firm Foundation*, 37–38.

14. Olevian, *Firm Foundation*, 37–38.

15. "Warum wirst aber du ein Christ genannt? Weil ich durch den Glauben ein Glied Christi, und also seiner Salbung theilhaftig bin, auf dass auch ich seinen Namen bekenne, mich Jhm zu einem lebendigen Dankopfer darstelle, und mit freiem Gewissen in diesem Leben wider die Sünde und Teufel streite, und hernach in Ewigkeit mit Jhm über alle Creaturen herrsche" (Schaff, *Creeds of the Churches*, 3:318). "Cur vero tu Christianus appellaris? Quod per fidem membrem sum Iesu Christi, et unctiois ipsius particeps, ut et nomen eius confitear, meque sistam ipsi vivam gratuidinis hostiam, et in hac vita, contra peccatum et Satanam, libera et bona conscientia pugnem, et postea aeternum cum Christo regnum in omnes creaturas teneam" (Niemeyer, *Collectio Confessionum*, 437).

The catechism connects Christ's threefold office to the Christian. *HC* 31 and 32 are premised on a basic distinction between the Savior (Jesus) and the saved (Christians). Jesus is God the Son incarnate, true God and true man. He obeyed as our substitute, and all of his perfect, actively suffering obedience is imputed to all those who believe (Rom 4:3; 5:12–21). That is the ground of our justification and salvation. We receive justification and salvation freely (*sola gratia*) through faith alone (*sola fide*), resting and trusting in Christ alone. True faith results in sanctification, good works, and fruit of the Spirit (Gal 5), but it is Christ's righteous obedience *for us* and not the Spirit's work *in us* that makes true faith powerful. Faith is formed by Christ, not by love or Spirit-wrought sanctity.

Nevertheless, Christ, by his word and Spirit, does work in us. He grants us new life (regeneration), and he sanctifies us. Sanctification is what Olevianus calls "the second benefit" of the covenant of grace.[16] Sanctification and the good works that flow from it are not a second blessing. In that scheme there are two kinds of believers, those who have had "the blessing" (e.g., tongues, prophecy, sanctification) and those that have not. Such thinking was a feature of the gnostic heresy of the second century, and it continues to appear in the Wesleyan holiness movements, neo-Pentecostalism, and the charismatic movements in modern evangelicalism. There is no such thing, however, as believers who have the first benefit of the covenant of grace but not the second. A second benefit is a *necessary consequence* of the first (justification). Distinguishing justification and sanctification does not make the second less important or nonessential, but if we do not distinguish them, we will lose the gospel of free grace and as Christians come to think of our standing with God as contingent on the degree of our sanctity. This was one of the great errors of the medieval church, and the Roman Catholic Church continues to affirm it. Confessional Protestants, however, reject this notion as unbiblical and contrary to the nature of the gospel. As Luther, Calvin, and many others say, should we attempt to base our standing with God on our sanctity, our assurance, our confidence, and our comfort (*HC* 1) will be shipwrecked. None of these outcomes is necessary, however, as long as we mind certain basics:

---

16. Clark, *Caspar Olevian*, 181–209.

It is sinners, not the sinless, who need salvation. Jesus said that repeatedly. "And when Jesus heard it, he said to them, 'Those who are well have no need of a physician, but those who are sick. I came not to call the righteous, but sinners'" (Mark 2:17 ESV). Paul says that, indeed, Jesus has actually saved his sinful people: "The saying is trustworthy and deserving of full acceptance, that Christ Jesus came into the world to save sinners, of whom I am the foremost" (1 Tim 1:15 ESV). Salvation was accomplished in history, once for all his sheep. The Holy Spirit sovereignly and freely applies it, through the preaching of the gospel and the use of the sacraments (Rom 10:10–14; *HC* 65). So, we were saved at Calvary, but we come into possession of salvation when the Holy Spirit makes us alive, grants us faith, and through that faith unites us to Christ. So Jesus is the Christ, the Messiah, the Anointed One, and by his Spirit, by his free favor alone, through faith alone, we are united to him and become, as Luther said, his Christians.[17]

Notice how the catechism speaks about union with Christ. It is very straightforward. It speaks here about what Reformed theologians call mystical union with Christ, that is, that union worked by the Spirit through faith.[18] On this Ursinus says, "To be a member of Christ is to be engrafted into him, and to be united to him by the same Holy Spirit dwelling in him and in us, and by this Spirit to be made a possessor of such righteousness and life as is in Christ: and to be made acceptable to God on account of the righteousness of Christ imputed unto us by faith, in as much as this righteousness is imperfect in this life."[19] In distinction from some of the more confusing approaches to union proposed in the last few decades, the mainstream Reformed approach, reflected in the catechism, is not difficult.

There are two other aspects of the doctrine of union with Christ that we might discuss, but the catechism here focuses on the third, so that is where this discussion will stay. We are called Christians because "by faith I am a member of Christ." We have already considered at length the teaching of *HC* 20–21 on the nature of true faith. We confess that faith is not something we generate. It is a free, unconditional gift of the sovereign

17. *LW* 27:241.

18. See the discussion under *HC* 20.

19. Ursinus, *Commentary*, 177–78.

Holy Spirit. He does not give us new life and faith because he foresees anything in us, nor did he merely establish conditions and elect whomever might meet those conditions. Rather, election is of grace (Eph 1:1–14; Rom 9:6–13). If the gifts of new life and faith were conditioned on anything foreseen in us, then they would not be gifts, and salvation would not be by grace (Rom 11:6). We need new life in order to believe because by nature, in Adam, we are dead in sins and trespasses (Eph 2:1–4). "But God," Paul says, when were dead, made us alive by his Spirit.

Faith is the gift of grace (Eph 2:8–10), and through it we are made members of Christ. To say "member" is a metaphor. Sometimes, when Paul uses this expression, it refers literally to Christ's physical body. Sometimes, however, it refers metaphorically to the church and to believers who make up "the body of Christ" (1 Cor 12:12). This is the sense in which the catechism uses the word "member" here. As members of Christ, it is as if, when he was anointed by the Spirit, we too were anointed. Remember, God does not anoint us to save but because he has saved us (and is saving us). We are participating, by grace, in what is true originally of Christ. He is *the* anointed, *the* Messiah, and we share in that anointing by his grace.

Christ has three offices, so his Christians have been redeemed by his grace to reflect those three offices: prophet, priest, and king. By virtue of our Spirit-wrought union with Christ, through faith, we too are prophets, priests, and kings, but just as Christ is the Savior and we the saved, we must distinguish clearly between the way he possesses and fulfills those offices and the way we do. God the Son is the prototype for the biblical offices as they were revealed progressively in the history of redemption. When he became incarnate of the Virgin, he not only fulfilled the types and shadows from the history of redemption but manifested in the flesh the full reality of those offices on which the types and shadows were based. Put simply, the types and shadows work, as it were, for Jesus, not the reverse. So, he is the original; we are his image-bearers. We partake in his offices, but they are *his* offices. We reflect them as servants to whom gifts have been given. As servants, we administer his belongings, on his behalf and on behalf of his kingdom.

We use four verbs to capture our fulfillment of the three offices: *confess*, *present*, *fight*, and *reign*. Our prophetic office is to confess his name. As prophet, Jesus reveals God and his salvation to us. We are not revealers.

We are recipients of revelation. This is has been a difficult distinction for people to accept. At least since the Montanists in the third century, Christians have been tempted to dislocate Scripture as the sole, unique authoritative revelation from God. The Montanists wanted ongoing revelation. Ultimately the medieval church replied to such approaches by saying, in effect, "We have continuing revelation in the teaching magisterium" (councils and popes). In the 1520s the Anabaptists claimed to receive continuing revelation and accused the Reformed of being "ministers of the dead letter."[20] Since 1801 (e.g., the Cane Ridge Revival) and particularly since the early twentieth century (e.g., Topeka and Azuza Street), American evangelicals have regularly claimed to have renewed apostolic gifts and revelation. In contrast, the Reformed are content with Holy Scripture as God's inspired, inerrant, infallible word.

Simply repeating what God's word said is evidently not very interesting to many who profess to hold the Christian faith. Confessing God's word, however, is a holy privilege. When we confess the faith in our confession, our catechism, and the Canons of Dort, we are fulfilling our prophetic duty.[21] When Christians talk about the church's "prophetic role," we do not often hear and read about the duty to confess. Often the prophetic role is invoked when Christians seek a change in the law or policy, but there are a small number of instances when the church as Christ's institutional representative might speak to the state. WCF 31.4 says: "Synods and councils are to handle, or conclude nothing, but that which is ecclesiastical: and are not to intermeddle with civil affairs which concern the commonwealth, unless by way of humble petition in cases extraordinary; or, by way of advice, for satisfaction of conscience, if they be thereunto required by the civil magistrate."[22] This way of thinking about the questions that the church as institution should address was not original to the Westminster divines. They inherited a view that had long existed among the Reformed and some medieval thinkers. Ecclesiastical assemblies have taken to speaking to all manner of social questions on which faithful believers, who confess the same faith, may well legitimately differ.

20. This was the rhetoric of Thomas Müntzer. See Matheson, *Collected Works of Thomas Müntzer*, 372–79.

21. So Ursinus, *Commentary*, 179.

22. Westminster Assembly, *Humble Advice of the Assembly*, 54.

When ecclesiastical assemblies pronounce on social issues, they are not likely to find much opposition from the powers of this age. When they perform their *actual* prophetic duty, resistance is much more likely. So it has been since Christianity first came into contact with the pagan world in the first century. We certainly know how pagans thought of the Christians in the second century. They wanted them to conform and to recite civil-religious formulas (e.g., "Caesar is Lord") to show their conformity. Many Christians refused out of fidelity to Christ the Lord, and they fulfilled their office as prophets by confessing that Jesus is Lord and Savior, that he was righteous, that he was unjustly arrested, tortured, and crucified, and that he was raised from the dead on the third day. That brought genuine resistance from the powers of this age, including arrest, torture, and martyrdom.[23]

Confessing to one's neighbor that all humans are born in sin, spiritually dead, and totally dependent on God's free, sovereign grace for salvation is rather more likely to demonstrate the antithesis between belief and unbelief than many other things we are tempted to say as churches and believers. Christ is our chief prophet and teacher. His Spirit has given to us his word in Holy Scripture. The church has confessed an understanding of that word. Christians are prophets, and we honor our King when we confess his word to a watching world.

We are also priests. Since the Reformation was, in part, a rejection of the medieval renewal of priestcraft in the institution of a memorial, propitiatory sacrifice in the Mass, it might seem like an odd thing for a Reformed Christian, for a Protestant, to assert that we are priests, but it is not.[24] Scripture clearly and repeatedly teaches that we are priests. The question is not *whether* we shall make sacrifices but *what* we offer and *why*. "You yourselves like living stones are being built up as a spiritual house, to be a holy priesthood, to offer spiritual sacrifices acceptable to God through Jesus Christ" (1 Pet 2:5 ESV; see also v. 9). As priests, we do make offerings. Paul writes of the offering made

23. E.g., *Martyrdom of Polycarp* 6.1–15.2.

24. This happened via the institution of transubstantiation at the Fourth Lateran Council in 1215, at the Second Council of Lyons in 1274, and the Council of Florence in 1439.

by the Philippians in support of his ministry: "I have received full payment, and more. I am well supplied, having received from Epaphroditus the gifts you sent, a fragrant offering, a sacrifice acceptable and pleasing to God" (Phil 4:18 ESV).

Just as Jesus is *the* Christ, *the* anointed, *the* Messiah, he is *the* High Priest. Melchizedek pointed to Christ (Heb 5:10). Aaron pointed to Christ (Heb 7:11–14). H*is* priesthood makes their priesthood significant.[25] In other words, when Aaron and his successors made offerings, it was not they or their sacrifices that gave significance to Christ's offering of himself. Rather, it was as they looked forward to his priestly work that theirs had significance. Only to the degree that their work partook in and anticipated his was it of any benefit to believing Israelites. The blood of bulls and goats does nothing. The blood of Christ alone is satisfactory for our sins.

Olevianus explains the chief benefit of Christ's priesthood:

> that by the one sacrifice of Christ, which retains its efficacy forever, my sins are wiped away—not only until death but forever. God will remember them no more. He also appears forever in heaven before the face of the Father with the very body and soul in which my sins were fully punished and my salvation was obtained. Thus I may be assured that every hour and moment the Father has before His eyes the guarantee of the once-for-all, eternally valid sacrifice of Christ. I may also be assured that He does not demand any payment for my sin, which in the full severity of His divine justice He has punished in His Son, who presents Himself before the Father on my behalf and prays for me. The justice of God in no way allows that the debt paid by Christ be required again of my body and soul; the guarantee that the eternal payment of that debt has been made is the body and soul of the eternal Son of God appearing before the face of the Father.[26]

Our priesthood adds *nothing* to Christ's. He has not inaugurated a new daily, ritual, memorial, propitiatory offering. His suffering obedience and sacrificial death completed all such priestly work. Jesus, not we, went

25. Vos, *Teaching of the Epistle*, 56, 91–116.

26. Olevian, *Firm Foundation*, 41.

outside the city to make his holy offering for us who are legally sinful, morally corrupt, and ritually unclean: "So Jesus also suffered outside the gate in order to sanctify the people through his own blood. Therefore let us go to him outside the camp and bear the reproach he endured. For here we have no lasting city, but we seek the city that is to come" (Heb 13:12–14 ESV). The pattern in Scripture is to say that Jesus has done his work *for us;* therefore, let us respond appropriately, in union with him, in light of his work. That is why our priesthood is *figurative*. We have become priests by virtue of our union with Christ *the* priest. The offering we make is only because of his once-for-all offering of himself.

Nevertheless, we are called priests, and Holy Scripture says that we make offerings. Paul says, "I appeal to you therefore, brothers, by the mercies of God, to present your bodies as a living sacrifice, holy and acceptable to God, which is your spiritual worship" (Rom 12:1 ESV). The writer to the Hebrews exhorts us, in light of all that Christ has done for us, to gather in congregation: "Through him then let us continually offer up a sacrifice of praise to God, that is, the fruit of lips that acknowledge his name" (Heb 13:15 ESV).

Unlike the Levitical priests, who went daily to the temple, in Christ we are now his temple by faith, by virtue of his grace and the Spirit-wrought union (1 Cor 3:16–17; 6:19). As Christians, we offer praise and ourselves to his worship. We are not turning away God's wrath. That work has been done. The temple has been destroyed, and it was raised on the third day, and by our union with Christ *the* Temple, we are his temple (1 Cor 3:16–17; 6:19; 2 Cor 6:16; Eph 2:21). We are the temple over which the Glory Spirit hovers (1 Pet 4:14) as we await his glorious, visible return.[27]

We should not think that our service in this life has no significance. It does. We are priests, anointed by Christ for his worship. When we gather together, we do so as the temple, as priests, and as sacrifices, accepted only for the sake of Christ's righteousness imputed and, in him, a sweet-smelling offering with which he is pleased.[28]

It is essential not to blur the line between Christ and Christian, but liberals and moralists do this when they make Jesus *primarily* an example

27. Ursinus, *Commentary*, 256–66.

28. Ursinus, *Commentary*, 179.

to be followed rather than a Savior of sinners to be trusted.[29] We seek, by grace alone, through faith alone, to imitate Christ as appropriate. For example, unlike those misguided folk in the Philippines who literally crucify themselves each Easter, we do not imitate Christ thus. We are called in Scripture to imitate him *figuratively* by crucifying the old nature. We are imitating Christ but we do so recognizing the difference between Christ and Christian.[30]

Liberals also seek to make Jesus the first Christian by questing after his religious experience. This was Friedrich Schleiermacher's (1768–1834) program. Each locus of theology in his *Christliche Glaubenslehre* (1821–1822) is not an account of the doctrine of the objective Christian faith but a different way of talking about the Christian's subjective quest to imitate Christ's experience. As Schleiermacher was the child of pietist parents, Enlightenment rationalism rocked his faith in university. As a consequence, he repudiated the naive pietism of his parents in favor of what he called a "mature pietism" in which he divorced their quest for illegitimate religious experience from the Christ of history and the historic Christian faith. He replaced their desire to experience the risen Christ immediately with a quest to recover Jesus's religious experience.[31]

The theology of Norman Shepherd, one of the godfathers of the federal vision movement, illustrates one way in which nomists seek to make Jesus into the first Christian and thus blur the line between Christ and

29. On this see Machen, *Christianity and Liberalism*, 81–83, 87. Historically, theological liberals and moralists have been closely related. The same rationalism that gives birth to moralism tends to lead to liberalism. Richard Baxter is a great example. He was a rationalist-moralist who rejected the Protestant doctrine of justification, e.g., in his *Aphorisms of Justification*, and whose congregation became unitarian, which is the religious-institutional embodiment of rationalism. The Remonstrants rejected the Reformation doctrine of salvation and within a generation their leaders became unitarians. See Allison, *Rise of Moralism*; Trueman, "Small Step toward Rationalism."

30. Thus, in the Reformed confession, Jesus's human nature can be said to be at the right hand of the Father, and yet it is also true that believers eat his "proper and natural" (*BC* 35) body and blood in Communion. He is truly present in Communion, but not literally, and yet we are really, truly fed by his actual body and blood. How this can be is a mystery, but we trust God's word and the power of the Holy Spirit. We need not therefore be tempted by the doctrine of transubstantiation, whereby the elements are said (by Rome) to become Christ's body and blood, or by the Lutheran doctrine that his body is physically "in," "with," and "under" the elements. For the confessional Lutheran doctrine see *Solid Declaration*, article VII, in Kolb and Wengert, *Book of Concord*, 592–615.

31. On this quest see Clark, *Recovering the Reformed Confession*, 71–116.

Christian.[32] He does this in a variety of ways but particularly in his teaching that Jesus had faith and works and we should have the same faith and works, as if they were essentially the same thing. This is a form of Pelagianism. In Christian doctrine, in contrast to Shepherd's teaching, Jesus trusted his Father and obeyed not for himself but *for us*. He did not believe for us in the sense that we do not have to believe. Rather, we must believe (which faith is God's gift of grace; Eph 2:8–10), but he did trust his Father when he confronted the Evil One in the desert. As the last man, the last Adam (1 Cor 15:45), he obeyed his Father in our place, and his obedience is credited to us as the ground of our justification. That is why justification is God's free gift to sinners, by grace alone, through faith alone. Because he rejected these basic distinctions, Shepherd made a hash not only of covenant theology but also of the doctrine of justification, including the definition of faith and the imputation of the active obedience of Christ. So, it is most important for us to understand the relationship between Christ and the Christian since on both sides of this road lie genuine dangers.

Our third office is that of king. In contrast to the way that Christ's dominion and lordship are often discussed today (usually with the first reference to the broader culture), we confess that the first way in which believers exercise their ruling office is by fighting against sin. As Ursinus says, "The kingly office of Christians, is" first to "oppose and overcome, through faith, the devil, the world, and all enemies," and second, after we have subdued sin finally in death, to enter into glory.[33] In other words, where the religio-social movements have tended to focus the question of the believer's dominion first of all *outside* the believer, the catechism wants us to begin with our own sins. This was Jesus's teaching about specks and logs: "Why do you see the speck that is in your brother's eye, but do not notice the log that is in your own eye? Or how can you say to your brother, 'Let me take the speck out of your eye,' when there is the log in your own eye? You hypocrite, first take the log out of your own eye, and then you will see clearly to take the speck out of your brother's eye"

32. Waters, "Theology of Norman Shepherd," 207–31; Venema, "Call of Grace," 245; Clark, "How We Got Here," 17–19; VanDrunen, "Where We Are," 48–52; Jones, "Justification by Faith Alone," 291–92; Clark, "Do This and Live," 239n39.

33. Ursinus, *Commentary*, 179.

(Matt 7:3–5 ESV). Certainly believers must engage the world about us from a Christian interpretation of reality, but we do so with a consciousness of our own sins and with an awareness that we stand before God by grace that Christ earned for us, on the basis of his righteousness imputed to us. We stand for a fixed moral law revealed in nature, every human conscience, and Holy Scripture (Rom 1:18–2:14), and we should seek to apply that to every area of life *as appropriate*. No postcanonical nation, however, is a new Israel, and no elected official is King David. In God's general providence, we have much to learn from nonbelievers about the civil life we share together. Christians do well to make sure that our congregations are hospitable and warm to seekers and believers from every tribe, tongue, and nation. We should follow the catechism, *contra* some revisionist movements.[34]

The catechism follows Paul in applying the Christian's office of ruler to the fight with sin and the devil. Here we could look at the second half of virtually all of his epistles. We could study Romans 6:5–11 and Colossians 2:11–12 about how we have died with Christ that we might put to death sin and the old man. The relative silence of the New Testament about "taking back" Asia Minor or any other geopolitical entity should be instructive. When the New Testament speaks of the kingdom of God, it is virtually impossible to discern a social program. Here we can learn from the framers of the catechism, who on this topic wrote nothing about transforming cultural institutions but rather about our struggle with sin and our subordinate kingship over other creatures.[35] For Olevianus and Ursinus, the transformation of this world awaits the new heavens and the new earth.[36]

What we see in Scripture and in the catechism is that the kingdom of heaven is first of all eschatological, that is, it is heavenly. It entered history in typology (e.g., in the tabernacle and temple and in the destruction of the Canaanites), but it entered history definitively with the advent of King Jesus, who came preaching the kingdom of God. His rule was inaugurated in

34. *Pace* Klooster (*Our Only Comfort*, 1:375), who writes, "What the catechism says of a Christian's kingly office is true but inadequate." Belcher (*Prophet, Priest, and King*, 176–77) simply assumes that the revisionist view is that of the catechism. The author is grateful to Jennifer Kuiper for her help with these references.

35. E.g., Ursinus, *Commentary*, 180.

36. Ursinus, *Commentary*, 180; Olevian, *Firm Foundation*, 39; Olevianus, *Exposition*, 9–15.

power when he was crucified as if he were a common criminal. This is paradigmatic for the kingdom of God on the earth until Christ returns. To the watching world, whether Pilate, second-century Romans, or neo-pagans today, Christ's seems to be a foolish kingdom with foolish keys, but it is Christ's kingdom, and he will consummate it when he returns—not a moment before. Then, at the judgment, we will reign openly, visibly, literally with him. In the interregnum we wait, obey, and serve him faithfully by his grace.

Question 33

Why is He called God's "only begotten Son," since we also are the children of God?

Question 34

Why do you call him "our Lord"?

Lord's Day 13

QUESTION 33

Why is He called God's "only begotten Son," since we also are the children of God?

Because Christ alone is the eternal, natural Son of God; but we are children of God by adoption, through grace, for his sake.[1]

One of the most basic doctrines of the New Testament is that Jesus is God the Son and the Son of God. In Matthew 4:3 we read, "The tempter came and said to him, 'If you are the Son of God, command these stones to become loaves of bread'" (ESV). In verse 6 he again challenges our Lord's claim to be the Son of God: "If you are the Son of God, throw yourself down" (ESV). The demons recognized Jesus as the Son of God: "What have you to do with us, O Son of God? Have you come here to torment us before the time?" (Matt 8:29 ESV). The disciples recognized his divinity: "And those in the boat worshiped him, saying, 'Truly you are the Son of God'" (Matt 14:33 ESV). He was convicted by the Jewish authorities for claiming to be the Son of God (Matt 26:65). He was mocked on the cross by one of the thieves for his claim (Matt 27:40–43; Luke 23:40–43). The Roman centurion recognized him as God's Son: "Truly this was the Son of God!" (Matt 27:54).

As it distinguishes between the Savior and the saved, the catechism distinguishes between two types of sonship: natural and adopted. Jesus Christ is God the Son incarnate (John 1:1–3, 14–18). Believers are God's sons by adoption (Gal 4:5; Eph 1:5; Rom 8:15).[2] Through history, however, the church has struggled mightily to get this right. One of the earliest controversies we faced was the question of how to speak about God as one in three persons. The other was the question of Christ's two natures. In the question of Jesus's sonship they converge. The great enemy to the biblical, catholic, and Reformed doctrines of both the Trinity and

1. "Warum heisst Er Gottes eingeborner Sohn, so doch wir auch Gottes Kinder sind? Darum, weil Christus allein der ewige natürliche Sohn Gottes ist, wir aber um seinetwillen aus Gnaden zu Kindern Gottes angenommen sind" (Schaff, *Creeds of the Churches*, 3:318). "Quam ob causam Christus vocatur Filius Dei unigenitus, cum os quoque simus filii Dei? Quia solus Christus est coaeternus, et naturalis aeterni Patris Filius: nos autem propter eum, ex gratia, a Patre adoptati summus" (Niemeyer, *Collectio Confessionum*, 437).

2. Ursinus, *Commentary*, 180.

Christology is rationalism, and closely related to that is biblicism. In this context "rationalism" refers to the subordination of Scripture and inferences from Scripture to human reason or to the human intellect. It is the denial of mystery, and mystery is at the heart of the biblical and Christian doctrines of the Trinity and Christology.

Scripture teaches and we confess that Jesus is true man and true God. The natures are inseparable but distinct. We confess that God the Son always was (more on this below). There never was when the Son was not. He always was, and he always was the Son, and yet he was coequal, coeternal, consubstantial with the Father and the Spirit.[3] He did not become the Son, but he did become incarnate. He was not adopted. It is not as if the Father looked, as it were, at humans, after the birth of Jesus, and decided, "I will make that one my son." Not at all. The blessed Virgin Mary carried in her womb God the Son. That is why we say in the Definition of Chalcedon (AD 451) that she was *Theotokos* (θεοτόκος), "God-bearer," and yet, in the mystery of the incarnation, the deity did not become less than it was, nor did the humanity become more than it was. Christ has two, distinct, inseparable natures: true God and true man.[4]

Any doctrine of Christ that confuses the two natures (Eutychianism) or that makes them into two persons (Nestorianism) is heresy. It denies fundamental, biblical, catholic truth and is to be heartily rejected by all Christians. According to our understanding of the teaching of Scripture, God the Son has always been the Son. He has been the Son from eternity. There has been considerable debate, however, over how we should express this truth. At least since the Nicene-Constantinoplitan Creed (AD 381), we have often spoken of the Son as "eternally begotten."

This seems to be the implication of John 1:1–3, 14. In the prologue to John's Gospel we read: "In the beginning was the Word and the Word was with God and the Word was God. This one was in the beginning with God. All things were created through him and nothing was created without him." According to John, God the Son is the *Logos* (λόγος), the eternal, preexistent Son. Of course, "beginning" is a reference to Genesis 1:1–3. "In

3. See the discussion under *HC* 17–18.

4. ὁμοούσιον τῷ πατρὶ κατὰ τὴν θεότητα, καὶ ὁμοούσιον τὸν αὐτὸν ἡμῖν κατὰ τὴν ἀνθρωπότητα (Schaff, *Creeds of the Churches*, 2:62).

the beginning *Elohim* ..." John is saying that Elohim is tripersonal and that the Second Person, through whom all things came into being, is the consubstantial, Second Person of the Trinity, the Word. Just as Elohim *is,* the Word is, God the Son is. Elohim is not becoming. Elohim is not adopted, and neither is the Word. When we read, in Genesis 1, "And *Elohim* said," we are to think of the Word—not that the Word was an expression of the Father (dynamic monarchianism) but that creation was executed through the God the Son, the Word, and by the one God in three persons.

The eternal relation between the Father and the Son is clarified in John 1:18, "the only begotten God [μονογενὴς θεὸς], who is at the side of the Father, he has revealed him." There is a personal distinction between the Father and the Son. Both are God, but the Father is unbegotten. The Son is eternally begotten. Some copies of this passage say "only begotten Son," but that was probably an attempt by copyists to smooth out what seemed to them a great difficulty. What does it mean to say "only begotten God"? Indeed. It is a great mystery but a glorious truth. Our God is Father, Son, and Holy Spirit, and they have a relationship to one another that transcends our ability to explain. Any God we could explain comprehensively would be an idol.

The church at Constantinople (381) confessed that God the Son was "begotten of the Father from eternity."[5] At Constantinople we also added the language of the Spirit "proceeding" from the Father (and at Third Council of Toledo, Spain, in 589, the West added the expression "and the Son" [*filioque*] to indicate that the Spirit proceeds from the Father *and the Son*). Athanasius (AD 296–373) inferred that just as the Spirit is eternally and actively proceeding, so the Son is actively and eternally begotten of the Father. Kevin Giles explains:

> Athanasius held that the eternal begetting of the Son and its counterpart, the eternal procession of the Spirit, spoke of two necessary "acts of divine self-differentiation *ad intra* (within the life of God in eternity)." These acts produce nothing exterior to God. Augustine added to this insight by clearly distinguishing between what takes place in eternity and what takes place in history. He

5. τὸν ἐκ τοῦ Πατρὸς γεννηθέντα πρὸ πάντων τῶν αἰώνων (Schaff, *Creeds of the Churches*, 2:57).

> thus differentiated between the "mission" (sending) of the Son and the Spirit for the works of creation and redemption, divine acts *ad extra* (acts of God "outside" of the divine life, in space and time), and the eternal begetting of the Son and procession of the Spirit in eternity *ad intra* (within the life of God).[6]

The Son has always been the Son and always begotten. That begetting never started, and it has never stopped.

This way of thinking of speaking influenced the Definition of Chalcedon (AD 451), in which we say, "begotten according to the deity from eternity of the Father," and it is in light of this expression that we understand the use of "only begotten" (μονογενῆ) in the definition.[7]

In the Athanasian Creed we confess: "The Son is of the Father alone, neither made, nor created but begotten."[8] In other words, we are not Arians. We are not subordinationists. The Son has a unique relation to the Father, and that relation is eternal. The Son is not merely *like* the Father, though he is the image of the Father. He is, as we confess in the Athanasian Creed, "God of the substance of the Father, begotten before the worlds. … Equal to the Father as touching His Godhead." The Reformed churches confess that the Son was eternally begotten. In *BC* 10 we say:

> We believe that Jesus Christ, according to his divine nature, is the only begotten Son of God, begotten from eternity, not made nor created (for then he would be a creature), but co-essential and co-eternal with the Father, the express image of his person, and the brightness of his glory, equal unto him in all things. Who is the Son of God, not only from the time that he assumed our nature, but from all eternity.[9]

This language and way of thinking is similar to *HC* 33. God the Son is the *natural* Son, that is, according to his divine nature. He is the eternal Son. The principal authors and editors of the catechism wrote frequently

6. Giles, *Eternal Generation of the Son*, 20.
7. πρὸ αἰώνων μὲν ἐκ τοῦ πατρὸς γεννηθέντα κατὰ τὴν θεότητα (Schaff, *Creeds of the Churches*, 2:62).
8. "Filius a Patre solo est: non factus, nec creatus: sed genitus" (Schaff, *Creeds of the Churches*, 2:67).
9. Schaff, *Creeds of the Churches*, 3:394.

that the Son was "begotten from eternity" (*genitus ab aeterno*).[10] We can be confident that the catechism means to teach that the Son was eternally begotten since its principal author and authorized commentator, Zacharias Ursinus, says (on *HC* 25): "So in like manner the eternal Father hath by eternal generation communicated to the Son his essence, but not his person—that is, he begot not the Father, but the Son; neither is the Father the Son, or the Son the Father, although each is very God."[11] As Olevianus explains in his *Exposition*, the doctrine of the eternal generation of the Son is a strong source of comfort for the believer since "Christ is and is called the only begotten Son of God because He alone is the eternal Son of the eternal Father, begotten of the substance of the Father from eternity, and therefore true God," and since we are united to him by the Spirit, *sola gratia, sola fide,* believers are "children of God not by nature but by adoption and grace, grace by which God thought us worthy of being adopted in Christ as His children." Therefore, being called "children of God" is no empty title. Because of Christ's power and divinity we have, "by His grace, a real "communion (κοινωνίαν) with Him."[12]

EXCURSUS: THE DOCTRINE OF THE ETERNAL GENERATION OF THE SON

Ursinus addressed this question in his lecture on *HC* 25. In light of the contemporary confusion over this doctrine, it seems useful to address this at some length.[13]

§

In the summer of 1570, the Reformation in Heidelberg faced a crisis. Several Zwinglians, who had sided with Erastus against the Calvinist order in the Palatinate, were perceived by their Calvinist opponents to

10. E.g., Olevianus, *Expositio*, 45; Olevianus, *Philippenses Et Colossenses Notae*, 23, 91; Olevianus, *De substantia*, 1.2.1, 4; 1.3.1, 17; Ursinus, *Summa*, 45 (in Bierma et al., *Introduction*, 170); Reuter, *D. Zachariae Ursini*, 1:119–31, 180, 181; Clark, "God the Son."

11. Ursinus, *Commentary*, 131.

12. Olevianus, *Exposition*, 26.

13. This excursus first appeared in print as Clark, "God the Son."

be arguing for something that looked like Arianism.[14] This was a crisis because the Lutheran electors were already suspicious of Frederick III (1515–1576) because of his Calvinism. As such, he denied the Lutheran version of the communication of properties (*communicatio idiomatum*), the ubiquity of Christ's humanity, and the Lutheran view of the Supper. The Lutherans had already summoned him to the Colloquy of Maulbronn in 1564 to answer for his Reformed convictions, and had he failed to satisfy them, he faced a possible invasion. Thus, both the political *and* the theological stakes were high in the discovery of any heresy against the ecumenical faith in Heidelberg. One of the heretics, Adam Neuser (ca. 1530–1576), escaped arrest and fled to Turkey, but the controversy with the anti-Trinitiarians continued until December 23, 1572, when, despite the judgment of the civil judges that he should receive only corporal and not capital punishment, Frederick III bowed to pressure from the theologians, including Caspar Olevianus (1536–1587), and ordered that capital punishment be applied to Johann Sylvan.

That heresy against the ecumenical faith should be a capital crime was hardly unusual in premodern Christendom, nor was it unusual to see theologians demanding the state to enforce religious orthodoxy. This episode illustrates the intensity with which the Heidelberg Calvinists held to the ancient, ecumenical Trinitarian faith, including the doctrine of the eternal generation of the Son.[15]

Olevianus is typically understood only as a figure relative to the development of Reformed covenant theology or in light of his contribution to the *HC*. That is a truncated view of the nature of Reformed covenant theology of Olevianus's contribution to it. For Olevianus, catholic orthodoxy, including the eternal generation of the Son, was an element of the substance of the covenant of grace.

Peter the Lombard (ca. 1100–1160) wrote the most influential theological textbook in the medieval period. Lecturing on his *Sentences* (ca. 1158) was a necessary step in becoming an accredited theologian in the university. His appropriation and synthesis of the Christian tradition influenced

14. For a brief discussion of the controversy and a survey of some of the literature, see Clark, *Caspar Olevian*, 75–77; Merkle, *Defending the Trinity*.

15. When Kevin Giles subtitles his defense of eternal generation "maintaining orthodoxy in Trinitarian theology," he echoes that tradition (Giles, *Eternal Generation of the Son*).

Western theology for four hundred years after it first appeared. Though we are not always aware of it, Christians continue to rely on Peter's formulations. So it is instructive to note that, for him, to teach the doctrine of God (book 1) was to teach the doctrine of the Trinity, and to teach doctrine of the Trinity was to teach the doctrine of the eternal generation of the Son.

As Peter the Lombard understood the history of Christian teaching, the doctrine of eternal generation was a basic part of Christian orthodoxy. Beginning in distinction 4, he treats as axiomatic for Christians to say, "We know, and it is true beyond doubt, that God the Father begot the Son."[16] He quotes the Nicene-Constantinopolitan Creed, "Light of light, true God of true God," which he takes to be the ecumenical confession of the eternal generation of the Son. He carries on this discussion through distinction 5, citing along the way Augustine, *On the Trinity*; Fulgentius of Ruspe, *On Faith*; Hilary, *On the Trinity*; and Ambrose, *On Faith*, as well as John Chrysostom and Origen.[17]

Thus, when Calvin explains the doctrine of the Trinity, in *Institutes* 1.13, he speaks first to the unity and simplicity of God (1.13.1), then to the subsistence of the Father, Son, and Holy Spirit (1.13.2–6). His third topic under heading of the Trinity is the deity of the Son and the Spirit (1.13.7). It would be "absurd" to imagine that the "Word of God" (*verbum Dei*) refers to anything temporary.[18] Rather, that *verbum* is the eternal wisdom of God that resides with God.[19] Thus it was the Spirit of Christ who spoke through the Old Testament prophets (1 Pet 1:10–12).[20] "Because Christ was not yet manifested [under the Old Testament], it is necessary to understand that the Word was begotten of the Father before from eternity."[21] Later in the *Institutes*, he reasserts the doctrine of the eternal generation (*ab aeterna genitura*) of the Son against Michael Servetus (ca. 1509/11–1553)

16. Lombard, *Sentences* 1.4.1.

17. On the history of the doctrine of the eternal generation of the Son, see Giles, *Eternal Generation of the Son*.

18. Barth, *Joannis Calvini Opera Selecta*, 3:117.1. On the development of the doctrine of eternal generation within Reformed theology from Calvin through the period of high Reformed orthodoxy, see Ellis, *Calvin, Classical Trinitarianism*.

19. Barth, *Joannis Calvini Opera Selecta*, 3:117.5.

20. Barth, *Joannis Calvini Opera Selecta*, 3:117.8–9.

21. "Necesse est Sermonem intelligere ante secula ex Patre genitum" (Barth, *Joannis Calvini Opera Selecta*, 3:117.10–11).

and Nestorius's error of making Christ a composition of human and divine elements.[22]

In his lectures on *HC* 25, Olevianus's colleague Ursinus taught explicitly the doctrine of the eternal generation of the Son. "Therefore the order of the existing of the persons is this: the Father is the first person and the source of divinity of the Son and of the Spirit. Because to him deity is communicated by no one but from himself he communicates deity to the Son and to the Holy Spirit. The Son is the second person [of the Trinity] because deity is communicated to him from the Father through eternal generation."[23] Ursinus appealed to the *datum* of the Son's eternal generation throughout his lectures, for example, in his defense of the deity of the Son under *HC* 33 in response to those who, by confusing the creature with the Creator, denied the Son's eternal deity. The objection says: "Whatever has a beginning is not eternal. The Son has a beginning. Therefore he is not that eternal Jehovah, who is the Father."

Ursinus responds, "He is not eternal who has a beginning of essence and of time. But the Son is not said to have a beginning of essence and of time but only of person and order. For he has one and eternal essence with the Father, not of time, but by eternal generation."[24] One finds the same sorts of arguments in early Reformed orthodox theologians such as Thomas Cartwright (1535–1603), Franciscus Junius (1545–1602), and William Perkins (1558–1602).[25]

22. Calvin, *Institutes* 2.14.5; Barth, *Joannis Calvini Opera Selecta*, 3:465.14. There is debate in the secondary literature about how to understand Calvin's doctrine of eternal generation. E.g., Warfield, *Calvin and Calvinism*, 245–51; Ellis, *Calvin, Classical Trinitarianism*, 39–63, 169–73; Van Dixhoorn, "Post-Reformation Trinitarian Perspectives," 180–207.

23. "Ordo itaque personarum in existendo hic est. *Pater* est prima persona, et quasi fons divinitatis filii et Spiritus sancti: quia deitas ei a nullo est communicta, sed ipse deitatem communicat filio et Spiritui sancto. *Filius* secunda persona: quia deitas ei a patre communicatur per aeternam generationem" (Ursinus, *Corpus doctrinae*, 130).

24. "2. Habens principium non est aeternus. Filius habet principium. Ergo non est aeternus ille Iehoua, qui est pater. *Respond. ad maiorem*. Aeternus non est, habens principium essentiae et temporis. Filius autem dicitur habere principium non essentiae et temporis, sed solummodo personae, et ordinis. Habet enim unam et aeternall essentiam cum patre, non temporali, sed aeterna genratione" (Ursinus, *Corpus doctrinae*, 200).

25. Cartwright, *Christian Religion*, 11–12, 137; Junius, *Defensio Catholicae Doctrinae*, 11, 13, 15, 17; Perkins, *Golden Chain*, in *Works*, 6:21, 48.

THE COVENANTAL CONNECTION

Reformed covenant theology inherited its most basic structures from the patristic reaction to the gnostics and the Marcionites. Barnabas (ca. AD 120), Justin (ca. AD 150), and Irenaeus (ca. AD 170) all made substantially identical arguments in favor of the unity of salvation between the Old and New Testaments. By 1524 Huldrych Zwingli (1484–1531) was employing similar and even more explicit arguments in favor of the unity of the covenant of grace against the Anabaptists, in whom he discerned a similar atomizing tendency. His successor as *Antistes* in Zürich, Heinrich Bullinger (1504–1575), in his 1534 treatise *On the Testament or Covenant of God,* elaborates on Zwingli's arguments for the unity of the covenant of grace against the Anabaptists.[26] In the work of Ursinus and Olevianus, Reformed covenant theology reached a turning point. Arguably, Ursinus was the first to use explicitly the language of the covenant of nature (*foedus naturale*), in his 1562 *Summa theologiae* (Q. 36). The covenant of nature shortly came to be known as the covenant of works.[27]

As Ursinus mainly worked out his covenant theology in the context of his lectures on the *HC,* Olevianus developed his covenant theology mainly in the context of his three commentaries on the Apostles' Creed, *Firm Foundation* (1567), the *Exposition of the Apostles' Creed* (1576), and *On the Substance of the Covenant of Grace between God and the Elect* (1585).[28]

ETERNAL GENERATION IS PART OF OUR *FIRM FOUNDATION*

Olevianus's first major exposition of covenant theology was in the form of an expanded catechism published, in German, as *Vester Grund* (*Firm Foundation*) in 1567. In this work, aimed at the laity, he writes, "[Christians] forget that it is easy, not difficult, to find a firm foundation if they just take hold of the articles of our old, true, undoubted Christian faith."[29] Published in the wake of the final edition of the *HC, Firm Foundation* echoes the

26. Bullinger, *De testamento,* translated as *Brief Exposition,* 99–138.

27. Ursinus, *Summa theologiae,* 14. For more on the history of covenant theology, see Clark, "Christ and Covenant," 403–28.

28. *Vester Grund* is translated as Olevianus, *Firm Foundation. Expositio symboli apostolici* is translated as Olevianus, *Exposition.*

29. Olevian, *Firm Foundation,* xli.

catechism and serves as an commentary on large sections of it. The articles to which he refers are those things necessary for a Christian to believe, that is, "all that is promised us in the Gospel, which the articles of our catholic, undoubted Christian faith teach us in sum.[30]" Note that, in the *HC*, the articles of the Apostles' Creed are *gospel*, not law, and form the middle of the catechism.

Olevianus follows the ancient Christian tradition of turning to the eternal generation of the Son in his exposition of the doctrine of the Trinity. In question 21 of *Firm Foundation* he appeals to the traditional prooftexts in defense of the traditional formula, one divine being in three distinct persons, which he links to Christian baptism. In question 22, as proof of the deity of the Son, he affirms that the "Son is true, essential God precisely because He is the Son of God, who from eternity was generated from the divine essence of the Father (John 1[:2], Rom. 9[:5], Heb. 1[:3]). John 17[:5]: 'Father, glorify me with the glory which I had with you before the foundation of the world.' See Romans 1 and Jeremiah 33."[31] Under his exposition of the first article of the creed, "I believe in God the Father" (question 27), he explains that we call God Father for two reasons, first "in view of His Son Christ, who is the eternal, essential wisdom of the Father, who was begotten of Him from eternity (Prov. 8[:23]), and who after taking upon Himself a human nature, was revealed as the Son of God (Rom. 1[:4]; Luke 1[:35])."[32]

After explaining the threefold office of Christ for us (prophet, priest, and king), he turns to his anointing as Messiah and the distinction between our adoption as sons and Christ's relation to the Father:

> 63 Q. Since then we are all children of God, why does Scripture call Christ His only begotten Son?
> A. So that a distinction is made between Christ and all believers. For Christ is and is called the only begotten Son of God because *He alone is the eternal and natural Son of the Father*, begotten from eternity of the substance of the Father and therefore true God, in whom we should believe. *We, however,* are called and actually are

30. Schaff, *Creeds of the Churches*, 3:314.

31. Olevian, *Firm Foundation*, 18.

32. Olevian, *Firm Foundation*, 21.

> children of God not by nature but *by grace: God has adopted us as His children* by incorporating us into His Son through faith and the working of the Holy Spirit and by making us now His true and living members—we who otherwise were by nature children of wrath (Eph. 2[:3]).[33]

Christian certainty about salvation and adoption into God's grace is grounded in the Son's natural, eternal, generation. Olevianus repeats this same point in this 1576 *Exposition of the Apostles' Creed.*[34]

ETERNAL GENERATION IS OF THE SUBSTANCE OF THE COVENANT OF GRACE

Perhaps Olevianus's most interesting use of the doctrine of eternal generation occurs in his most extended exploration of covenant theology, *On the Substance of the Covenant of Grace between God and the Elect* (1585). The work is in two parts: (1) the substance of the covenant of grace, structured by the twelve articles of the Apostles' Creed, and (2) the external administration of the substance of the covenant of grace in the visible church.

He begins with a brief exposition of Jeremiah 31:31–33, which, with Barnabas, Justin, Irenaeus, and the first-generation Reformers, he understood as a contrast between Moses and Christ. The new covenant is a promise of the gospel, the substance of the covenant of grace.[35] Each of the articles of the faith is to be explained relative to the covenant of grace. God is the author of the covenant of grace.[36] Humanity is considered as the recipient of the covenant of grace.[37]

Even under the new covenant, however, not all who participate in the external administration receive the substance, which has to be outwardly administered in the visible church.[38] Only the elect, however, receive the substance of the covenant, "for to all the elect and to them alone, this part, the remission of sins, renewal in the image of God, and the knowledge of

33. Olevian, *Firm Foundation,* 46. Emphasis original, signaling allusions to the *HC.*

34. Olevianus, *Exposition,* 62.

35. Olevianus, *De substantia,* 1.1.1, 1.1.2.

36. Olevianus, *De substantia,* 1.1.3.

37. Olevianus, *De substantia,* 1.1.3.

38. Olevianus, *De substantia,* 1.1.2.

God itself is promised."[39] As noted, however, the substance of the covenant must be administered. The promise of the covenant of grace, in Genesis 17, says, "This is my covenant in your flesh. Certainly the substance of that covenant was not in their flesh."[40] After all, not all the hearts of the Israelites and their children were circumcised, which is the substance of the promise of the covenant of grace, which is offered freely in the external administration of the covenant. Almost unexpectedly, Olevianus pivots back to the substance of the covenant of grace, in which he quite pointedly includes the doctrine of the eternal generation of the Son:

> Therefore, the covenant of grace, if you see its essence, is a promise and oath unto God, a gift by God, never to be angry with us (Isa 54) and our adoption unto sons of God, and heirs of eternal life in Jesus Christ, *the eternal and only begotten Son of God,* the seed of Abraham who is Christ. And [it is a promise and oath] to all men, who, by faith, who are given freely to be engrafted to this seed, and in whom they are freely justified and glorified without condition or any stipulation of knowledge *bonae ex ipsorum*: in order that his gracious goodness might be celebrated by us in this life and life eternal (Hos 2; Isa 54; Gen 22; Heb chapters 1, 6; Gal 3:15–18, 22, 26, 29).[41]

One of the grounds of the reliability of the covenant of grace was Olevianus's Trinitarian doctrine of God: "The God who promises is Father, Son and Holy Spirit setting up that covenant of adoption in the person of the Mediator or the *Logos* incarnate."[42] In other words, the substance of the covenant of grace rests in the nature of God and particularly

39. "Nam iis omnibus et solis utraque illa pars promittitur, peccatorum remissio et instauratio ad Dei imaginem" (Olevianus, *De substantia,* 1.1.2).

40. Olevianus, *De substantia,* 1.1.2.

41. "Foedus itaque gratuitum, si essentiam eius spectes, est promissa et iurata à Deo donatio suimet in Deum nunquam nobis irascentem Isai. 54. Et assumtio nostri in filios Dei et haeredes vitae aeternae in Iesu Christo aeterno et unigenito Dei Filio, facta semini Abrahae qui est Christus, et omnibus qui fide gratis donati huic semini inseruntur, et in eo gratis iustificantur et glorificantur citra conditionem aut stipulationem ullius cogitationis bonae ex ipsorum viribus: ut pro gratuita sua bonitate ab iis celebretur in hac et aeterna vita, Hos. 2. Isai. 54. Genes. 22. Heb. 1. & 6. Gal. 3. V. 15. 16. 17. 18. 22. 26. 29" (Olevianus, *De substantia,* 1.1.2).

42. "Deus promittens est Pater, Filius, et Spiritus Sanctus erigens foedus hoc adoptionis in persona Mediatoris seu λόγῳ incarnato" (Olevianus, *De substantia,* 1.1.3).

in the nature of God the Son, the Mediator of the covenant. He qualified the Son as the "eternal and only begotten Son." By grace alone, believers are adopted sons of God, in the eternally generated Son of God. In the next section Olevianus makes that connection explicit, again focusing on the eternal generation of the Son. "God is a spiritual essence, eternal, infinite, omnipresent, intelligent, true, good, pure, omnipotent, most free, just, merciful. The eternal Father, who begat from eternity, from his substance, the Son, his representation of his being. And the Son was begotten from the Father from eternity. And the Holy Spirit proceeds from eternity from the Father and the Son."[43] The Son is a reliable Mediator and Redeemer and worthy himself to be the substance of the covenant given to all the elect because he is consubstantial, from eternity, with the Father. In Christ, the Father elects, and in the Holy Spirit he applies the work of Christ to the elect in the external administration of the covenant of grace.

In his discussion of the nature and need of humanity after the fall, Olevianus contrasts the natural state of the Son with the corruption of human nature in the fall. He for whom it was not robbery to be considered equal to God "for he was from eternity begotten of the substance of the Father, and there also equal in all things, which we confess according to the writing of the Athanasian Creed," nevertheless poured himself out for us.[44]

One of the contributions Olevianus made to Reformed covenant theology, which has not always been appreciated, was his development of what came to be known as the "covenant of redemption" (*pactum salutis*), the pretemporal covenant between the Father and the Son, which David VanDrunen and I call "the covenant before the covenants."[45] In *De substantia* 1.2, he turns to that pretemporal covenant as another ground of the Christian's confidence, and the eternal generation of the Son again appears as an element of the substance of the covenant of grace.

43. "Deus est essentia spiritualis, aeterna, infinita, omnipraesens, intelligens, verax, bona, pura, omnipotens, liberrima, iusta, misericors: Pater aeternus, qui Filium characterem suae hypostaseos ab aeterno genuit è sua substantia: et Filius ab aeterno à Patre genitus: et Spiritus sanctus ab aeterno procedens à Patre et Filio" (Olevianus, *De substantia,* 1.1.4).

44. "Erat enim ab aeterno è substantia Patris genitus, eoque et aequalis in omnibus, ut antea secundum scripturas ex symbolo Athanasii confessi sumus" (Olevianus, *De substantia,* 1.1.8).

45. VanDrunen and Clark, "Covenant before the Covenants," 167–96.

The covenant of redemption contains a solemn promise (*sponsio*) that the Son would be our surety (*fideiussio*), and to fulfill it the Mediator had to be the "only begotten Son of God" constituted as our head and eternal Lord, in our flesh. On account of our adoption, because of the Father's infinite love for us, had also to be begotten from eternity.[46]

He hits this same note again under the third article of the creed, "conceived by the Holy Spirit, born of the Virgin Mary." In order that the gracious covenant of our adoption might be "most firm" God the Son, "begotten of the Father from eternity," had to become incarnate, in the womb of the Virgin, by the work of the Spirit.[47]

CONCLUSION

If Giles is correct, American evangelical and Reformed theologians since Charles Hodge (1797–1878) have doubted or rejected the doctrine of the eternal generation of the Son.[48] The number and influence of contemporary evangelical theologians who have rejected the doctrine of the eternal generation of the Son is impressive.[49]

For Olevianus, however, the doctrine was neither disposable nor the product of a nebulous Greek philosophy, but a biblical and ecumenical truth confessed in the Athanasian Creed, which he recites early in *De substantia* to drive home the catholicity of the doctrine. It was also, therefore, of the essence of the covenant of grace, because it grounds the redemption of the elect and their inclusion in the covenant of grace in the very nature of God the Son and in his eternal consubstantiality with the Father and with us in his incarnation.

46. Olevianus, *De substantia*, 1.2.4.
47. Olevianus, *De substantia*, 1.3.1.
48. Giles, *Eternal Generation of the Son*, 30–31.
49. Giles, *Eternal Generation of the Son*, 30–37; Barrett, *Simply Trinity*, 213–60.

Question 34

Why do you call him "our Lord"?

Because, not with gold or silver, but with his precious blood, he has redeemed and purchased us, body and soul, from sin and from all the power of the devil, to be his own.[50]

Christ's dominion and lordship is certainly beyond question for those who read Scripture with the historic Christian church, with the Protestant Reformation, and with the Reformed churches and confessions. Christ is Lord. We do not have to make him Lord, though we agree that all believers ought to recognize that fact and adjust their faith and life accordingly. With the early Christian fathers and the Protestant Reformers, the Reformed believe that believers, having been justified and saved by grace alone, through faith alone, in Christ alone must as a consequence commit themselves to a life of sanctity, to a life of mortification (dying to sin) and vivification (living to Christ).[51]

Those who defend Christ's dominion and lordship typically appeal to his sovereignty over all things in creation and providence.[52] There is no question that he is Lord of creation and providence. He spoke everything into being by the power of his word (Gen 1:1–3; John 1:1–3). His voice breaks the cedars of Lebanon (Ps 29:5). The wind and the sea obey him (Mark 4:41). We have already considered the providence of God under *HC* 26–28. When the catechism, however, asks the question "Why do you call Him 'our Lord'?" it does not appeal to creation and providence but to grace and salvation.[53] Olevianus explains:

50. "Warum nennest du Ihn unsern Herrn? Weil Er uns mit Leib und Seele von der Sünde und aus aller Gewalt des Teufels nicht mit Gold oder Silber, sondern mit seinem theuren Blut ihm zum Eigenthum erlöset und erkaufet hat" (Schaff, *Creeds of the Churches*, 3:318). "Qua de causa appellas eum Dominum nostrum? Quia corpus et animam nostram a peccatis, non auro, nec argento, sed pretioso suo sanguine redimens, et ab omni potestate Diaboli liberans nos sibi proprios vidicavit" (Niemeyer, *Collectio Confessionum*, 437).

51. E.g., Polycarp, *To the Philippians* 4.1–8.2.

52. Ursinus, *Commentary*, 203.

53. Ursinus, *Commentary*, 203.

> In order that His covenant partners or believers, in genuine trust, might completely surrender themselves with quiet and tranquil hearts to such a faithful Lord, for He cares for them. He has set us free from the power of darkness not with gold or silver but with His own precious blood, has acquired us to be His very own, and has not only acquired us once for all but as a faithful Lord will also forever protect and keep us with that acquired grace. Furthermore, by calling Him Lord they are also admonished that they are not their own but have been bought with a great price, so that they should glorify God in their bodies and souls, which are God's. They are also admonished that all covenant partners or believers should gladly let themselves be ruled by such a Lord, namely, by the Word and Spirit of Him who was ordained by the Father to bring us under His rule and lordship and to be the head of all holy angels and believing people (1 Cor. 6; 1 Pet. 5; Eph. 5; Col. 1).[54]

The reader may recognize in this quotation and in *HC* 34 a quotation of 1 Peter 1:18–19: "Knowing that you were ransomed from the futile ways inherited from your forefathers, not with perishable things such as silver or gold, but with the precious blood of Christ, like that of a lamb without blemish or spot" (ESV). This is not the early medieval ransom theory, the doctrine that all the fallen belong to the devil by right. By virtue of the fall, however, we all did become children of darkness by nature. In the parable of the sower, the weeds represent "the sons of the evil one" (Matt 13:38). The risen Christ commissioned Paul "to open their eyes, so that they may turn from darkness to light and from the power of Satan to God, that they may receive forgiveness of sins and a place among those who are sanctified by faith in me" (Acts 26:18 ESV). According to Hebrews 2:14, the devil has the power of death. God is sovereign over all, and nothing transpires outside his providence, and yet the Evil One is a reality, and salvation is a real deliverance from the devil's power.

The catechism is addressing those who profess faith in Christ, who, if they believe, have been redeemed, who have a "superior covenant" and

54. Olevian, *Firm Foundation*, 47–48.

are possessors of the "substance of the covenant of grace."[55] One of the ideas behind *redemption* is not far from the notion behind the verb Peter uses in 1 Peter 1:18, "ransomed." They both involve a purchase. Both are forms of deliverance. The apostle Paul uses this same sort of language in 1 Corinthians 6:20, "for you were bought with a price. So glorify God in your body" (ESV), 1 Corinthians 7:23, "you were bought with a price; do not become slaves of men," and Titus 2:14, "who gave himself for us to redeem us from all lawlessness and to purify for himself a people for his own possession who are zealous for good works" (ESV). In Colossians 1:14 he connects the idea of redemption with the forgiveness of sins: "in whom we have redemption, the forgiveness of sins."

Scripture generally assumes the propriety of property ownership. The owner of the vineyard can dispose of his property as he will: "Am I not allowed to do what I choose with what belongs to me?" (Matt 20:15 ESV). According to Paul, those whom God has purchased with the blood of Christ belong to him. They are not free agents.

He has complete say over us because he has purchased us, as Peter says, not with precious things but with the most precious thing, the most valuable thing: his own life. The one who laid down his life for us, to pay the penalty that we owed, was God the Son incarnate. For that reason believers belong to the Lord to whom the Lord said, "Sit at my right hand" (Ps 110:1; see Matt 22:43). He is, as Psalm 110 says (and as our Lord quotes in Matt 22:41–46), putting his enemies under his feet. Peter proclaimed at Pentecost, "Let all the house of Israel therefore know for certain that God has made him both Lord and Christ, this Jesus whom you crucified" (Acts 2:36 ESV). He is, by his Spirit, making us willing servants of the King. According to Psalm 110, as it is interpreted in the New Testament, Christ is not becoming Lord. His dominion and lordship is not contingent on our recognition of him. He *is* Lord. He is sovereign, and he is the Savior.

Peter similarly reflects on redemption and lordship in 1 Peter 2:9 when he says to believers, "You are a chosen race, a royal priesthood, a holy nation, a people for his own possession, that you may proclaim the excellencies of him who called you out of darkness into his marvelous light" (ESV). As the redeemed, believers owe thankful obedience to him who

55. Olevian, *Firm Foundation*, 47; Olevianus, *De substantia*, 1.1.2; Clark, *Caspar Olevian*, 102.

redeemed them not at a distance but by going through the Red Sea judgment for them so that we who believe might, as it were, walk through on dry ground (Exod 14:16).[56]

56. See *BC* 34, where we confess that Christ "is our Red Sea" (Schaff, *Creeds of the Churches*, 3:426).

Question 35

What is the meaning of "conceived by the Holy Spirit, born of the Virgin Mary"?

Question 36

What benefit do you receive from the holy conception and birth of Christ?

Lord's Day 14

QUESTION 35

What is the meaning of "conceived by the Holy Spirit, born of the Virgin Mary"?

That the eternal Son of God, who is and continues true and eternal God, took upon himself the very nature of man, of the flesh and blood of the Virgin Mary, by the operation of the Holy Spirit; so that he might also be the true seed of David, like his brothers in all things, sin excepted.[1]

The ecumenical Christian doctrine is that the humanity in which God the Son became incarnate was mysteriously conceived by the Holy Spirit, in the womb of the blessed Virgin Mary. This happened in fulfillment of the prophecy given by the Spirit through the prophet Isaiah: "Therefore the Lord himself will give you a sign. Behold, the virgin shall conceive and bear a son, and shall call his name Immanuel" (Isa 7:14 ESV).[2]

The doctrine of the virgin birth of Christ is a most ancient and ecumenical Christian doctrine. Ignatius of Antioch affirms it.[3] As J. Gresham Machen noted in 1930, Irenaeus affirms it in his articulation of the rule of faith.[4]

1. "Was heisst, dass Er empfangen ist von dem heiligen Geist, geboren aus Maria der Jungfrau? Dass der ewige Sohn Gottes, der wahrer und ewiger Gott ist und bleibet, wahre wenschliche Natur aus dem Fleisch und Blut der Jungfrau Maria, durch Wirkung des heiligen Geistes, an sich genommen hat, auf dass Er auch der wahre Same Davids sei, seinen Brüdern in allem gleich, ausgenommen die Sünde" (Schaff, *Creeds of the Churches*, 3:319). "Quid credis cum dicis: Conceptus est per Spiritum Sanctum, natus ex Maria Virgine? Quod ipse Filius Dei, qui est, et permanet verus ac aeternus Deus, naturam vere humnam ex carne et sanguine virginis Mariae, operatione Spiritus Sancti assumpsit, ut simul sit verum semen Davidis, fratribus suis per ominia similis excepto peccato" (Niemeyer, *Collectio Confessionum*, 438).

2. Notoriously, in 1952 the RSV translated the Hebrew noun for virgin (עַלְמָה) as "young woman." The NEB followed suit in 1970, and the NRSV did it again in 1989, but the overwhelming majority of English translations use "virgin." The LXX uses the noun παρθένος, which the New Testament authors also use. The rationalist critics rule out "virgin" *a priori*, but the inspired NT authors (e.g., Matt 1:23; Luke 1:27) understand Isa 7:14 to say that Mary was a virgin, i.e., a young woman who had never had sexual relations with a man, when God the Son took on a true human nature in her womb. On this doctrine, see Machen, *Virgin Birth of Christ*.

3. γεγεννημένον ἀληθῶς ἐκ παρθένου (Ignatius, *To the Smyrnaeans* 1:1, in Holmes, *Apostolic Fathers*, 249).

4. Machen, *Virgin Birth*, 3–43.

On the one hand, Mary was truly blessed. God graciously ordained that she should bear in her womb God the Son, that she would be what the Definition of Chalcedon (451) calls the God-bearer (θεοτόκος). The New Testament treats her with respect and reserve. She is mentioned, of course, in conjunction with Joseph (Matt 1:18), the conception narrative (Luke 1:27–32), the *Magnificat* (Luke 1:46–55), the nativity (Luke 2:15–20), and presentation (Luke 2:22–33). Thereafter she does not appear often in the Gospels, and only once outside the Gospels (Acts 1:14), and never as an object of prayer or adoration. When she was mentioned in the second century, it was with respect but not as an object of reverence or prayer. The veneration of the blessed Virgin was a high medieval development and not without controversy. By the time of the Reformation, however, the Virgin, along with the saints, had to a significant degree supplanted Christ as an intercessor with God.[5] Where Paul had written that "there is one mediator between God and man, the man Christ Jesus" (1 Tim 2:5), the Roman Catholic Church had substituted the Virgin and exchanged a *mediatrix* for the mediator, which has become Roman dogma in the modern period.

Nevertheless, the sixteenth-century Reformed did not react to the elevation of the Virgin in the way that we have done since. It was widely held by the sixteenth-century Reformed that Mary remained "ever virgin." Zwingli taught this, as did Heinrich Bullinger,[6] in the Second Helvetic Confession: "We also believe and teach that the eternal Son of God was made the Son of man, from the seed of Abraham and David, not from the coitus of a man, which the Ebionites said, but was conceived most

5. She would not be elevated to *mediatrix* until much later. See the discussion under *HC* 30.

6. "1. *Fidei Ratio* (1531), art. 5: V. And I believe that this humanity was conceived of the virgin, made pregnant by the Holy Spirit, and was brought forth by preserving her perpetual virginity that He, who from eternity was born Lord and God from a father without mother, might be born into the world as deliverer and healer of souls from a virgin mother, in order that a holy and spotless offering might be made to Him unto whom all altars, loaded with animals, smoked to no purpose, and men might repent of sacrificing beasts and turn to the offering of their hearts, when they would see that God had prepared and offered to Himself a victim in the form of His own Son." Zwingli, *Latin Works of Huldreich Zwingli*, 2:244–45.

purely by the Holy Spirit and born of the ever virgin Mary" (*ex Maria semper virgine*).[7]

Calvin was aware of the Jerome's position, as well as that of Helvidius (ca. fourth century AD), who, against Jerome, had inferred that Mary must have had children with Joseph. He himself took an agnostic position: "No just and well-grounded inference can be drawn from these words of the Evangelist, as to what took place after the birth of Christ."[8] *BC* 18, however, refers to Mary as "the blessed Virgin Mary."[9] *HC* 35 says nothing about the perpetual virginity of Mary.[10]

One of the reasons the Reformed have historically had a high, if reserved, view of Mary is our understanding of Scripture and the teaching of the catholic creeds that our Lord Jesus, by the mysterious operation of Holy Spirit, took his humanity from her. The Definition of Chalcedon captures this teaching when it uses the phrase "of Mary the Virgin, the Godbearer, according to the humanity."[11] A half century earlier, at Constantinople (AD 381), Christians confessed that the Son took on humanity "from the Holy Spirit and the Virgin Mary."[12] The purpose of this language was never to exalt Mary but to exalt Christ and to recognize the glorious truth that he is true man and true God. His humanity was not an illusion. Christ's humanity made the gospel foolishness to Greeks, and his deity was a stumbling block to the Jews (1 Cor 1:23).[13] That is why the incarnation and the cross was a stumbling block and a scandal. Under the influence of a general spirit-matter dichotomy, which saw true reality as that which is spiritual and which made them suspicious of the

7. Author's translation; see Müller, *Die Bekenntnisschriften*, 183.23–28. Zürich asserted the perpetual virginity of Mary as early as 1524 in *Responsio ad hugonem episc. de idolis et missa*, in Zwingli, *Opera D. Huldrychi Zwinglii*, 217.

8. Calvin, *Commentary on a Harmony*, 1:107.

9. Schaff, *Creeds of the Churches*, 3:403. On the development of the title ἀειπάρθενος ("Ever-Virgin"), see Kelly, *Early Christian Doctrines*, 494–95, who observes that there were orthodox in the period who taught that our Lord had siblings from Mary and Joseph.

10. That phrase does not occur in Ursinus's lectures on the catechism or in Olevianus's works. By the late sixteenth and early seventeenth centuries, when it occurred in Reformed writers, it was most often in a polemical (anti–Roman Catholic) context.

11. ἐκ Μαρίας τῆς παρθένου τῆς θεοτόκου κατὰ τὴν ἀνθρωπότητα (Schaff, *Creeds of the Churches*, 2:62).

12. ἐκ Πνεύματος Ἁγίου καὶ Μαρίας τῆς παρθένου (Schaff, *Creeds of the Churches*, 2:57).

13. The author is grateful to S. M. Baugh for his help with this passage.

material, physical world, some early Christians struggled mightily with the truth that Jesus has a true human nature. The apostle John was already facing that error when he wrote to the churches in Asia Minor (1 John 4:2; 2 John 7). That struggle intensified in the second century as a gnostic heresy attacked Christ's humanity as an illusion and offered "salvation" from bodily existence through secret knowledge and a magical, hierarchical world. Challenges to Jesus's humanity came from other quarters too. The Eutychians taught that his deity transformed his humanity into something else. Doubts about Christ's true humanity persisted through the medieval church among the Albigensians (and related movements) and even among the Anabaptists, who taught that Jesus was incarnate with a "celestial flesh."[14]

Thus, the preposition "from" is more important than it might seem. Jesus's humanity was and remains a true, genuine, real humanity consubstantial with ours. His humanity is not merely *like* ours, nor does it merely overlap with ours. It is ours. That is why the apostle Paul is at pains to say that he is our mediator and that he is true man (1 Tim 2:5). He is the God-Man, but he is still a true man. This is a major burden of the Epistle to the Hebrews. Jesus did not come for angels, nor was he an angel (Heb 2:16). He came for the sons of Abraham. The author writes:

> Since therefore the children share in flesh and blood, he himself likewise partook of the same things, that through death he might destroy the one who has the power of death, that is, the devil, and deliver all those who through fear of death were subject to lifelong slavery. For surely it is not angels that he helps, but he helps the offspring of Abraham. Therefore he had to be made like his brothers in every respect, so that he might become a merciful and faithful high priest in the service of God, to make propitiation for the sins of the people. For because he himself has suffered when tempted, he is able to help those who are being tempted. (Heb 2:14–18 ESV)

Our assurance is grounded in the truth that our representative, our substitute, our federal head Jesus is like us in every respect (sin excepted;

14. This Christology was confessed by Menno Simons, Dirk Philips, Melchior Hoffmann, and Caspar Schwenkfeld. See Clark, "House of Cards?," 74n19.

Heb 4:15), and it is as if when he made propitiation, we too made propitiation (i.e., turned away God's wrath; Gal 2:19–20). This is why there are no more sacrifices, not even memorial sacrifices. His was the once-for-all sacrifice to turn away God's wrath. He is the Lamb, the Mediator, the sacrifice, the priest, and the temple. "It is finished" (John 19:30).

Only we sinned, and only God could save us. Having willed to save us, he could do so only by becoming incarnate, and he did so "of the Virgin Mary." The doctrine of the virgin conception of Christ was much disputed by theological liberals at the end of the nineteenth century.[15] That Christ was born of a virgin is the teaching of Scripture. It is the fulfillment of Isaiah 7:14, "Behold, the virgin shall conceive and bear a son, and shall call his name Immanuel" (ESV). Matthew 1:23 expressly says that the Holy Spirit overshadowed the Virgin Mary and thus fulfilled the prophecy of Isaiah (see also Luke 1:31). "It behooved the Messiah to be born of the Virgin according to the predictions of the prophets, that he might be a High Priest without sin, and the type or figure of our spiritual regeneration, which is not of the will of flesh, but of God."[16] Conceived and born sinless, "in the fullness of time ... born of a woman" (Gal 4:4), he alone is the fulfillment of the promise made in Genesis 3:15. As Olevianus writes, the

> basis and foundation of the royal priesthood of Christ, and thus of the eternal covenant between God and humanity, is contained in this article of the person of Christ. These two natures, divine and human, belong to His substance and being and are thus bound together in such a way that they form an essential, actual Christ while still retaining their distinctive attributes. This is, in God's decree, the beginning and cornerstone of our salvation.[17]

His humanity was and remains as real as ours. He really was in Mary's womb. He had an umbilical cord. The conception was miraculous, but his birth was truly human. His humanity, like ours, was frail. He wept (John 11:35). He ate (Luke 24:43). He suffered. When they beat him, it

15. Machen, *Virgin Birth of Christ*.

16. Ursinus, *Commentary*, 206; Olevian, *Firm Foundation*, 49; Olevianus, *Exposition*, 65–73.

17. Olevian, *Firm Foundation*, 50–51.

hurt. When they nailed him to the cross, it hurt. When he struggled for breath on the cross, it hurt. He died a true, human death. It was a real, cold, lifeless body that they buried in the tomb, and it was that very, true body that was raised on the morning of the third day (Luke 24:39–40).

This strong emphasis in the Scriptures, the catholic creeds, and the Reformed confessions should make us cautious about speculating about the nature of his postresurrection humanity. Why should we suppose that he dematerialized in order to enter a room (John 20:19)? That comes perilously close to the very Anabaptist error denounced by our confessions.[18] On this question Calvin writes:

> "And while the doors were shut." This circumstance was expressly added, because it contains a manifest proof of the Divine power of Christ; but this is utterly at variance with the meaning of the Evangelist. We ought, therefore, to believe that Christ did not enter without a miracle, in order to give a demonstration of his Divinity, by which he might stimulate the attention of his disciples; and yet I am far from admitting the truth of what the Papists assert, that the body of Christ passed through the shut doors. Their reason for maintaining this is, for the purpose of proving not only that the glorious body of Christ resembled a spirit, but that it was infinite, and could not be confined to any one place. But the words convey no such meaning; for the Evangelist does not say that he entered through the shut doors, but that he suddenly stood in the midst of his disciples, though the doors had been shut, and had not been opened to him by the hand of man. We know that Peter (Acts 12:10) went out of a prison which was locked; and must we, therefore, say that he passed through the midst of the iron and of the planks? Away, then, with that childish trifling, which contains nothing solid, and brings along with it many absurdities! Let us be satisfied with knowing that Christ intended, by a remarkable miracle, to confirm his disciples in their belief of his resurrection.[19]

18. I.e., the Anabaptist doctrine of the "celestial flesh" of Christ condemned in *BC* 18 (Schaff, *Creeds of the Churches*, 3:403). See the discussion under *HC* 17.

19. Calvin, *Commentary on the Gospel according to John*, 2:264.

He was and continues to be true God and true man. His humanity has been raised and glorified, and it is true that we do not know all that entails, but we do know that whatever it entails it does not include any disruption of his shared humanity with his redeemed people, on which so much rests.

Question 36

What benefit do you receive from the holy conception and birth of Christ?

That he is our mediator, and with his innocence and perfect holiness covers, in the sight of God, my sin, wherein I was conceived.[20]

When two social equals are at odds with each other, the best thing to do is for one to approach the other to seek resolution and restoration. When, however, they do not have equal status, restoration becomes more complicated. When we change the scenario to an all-holy, righteous God and a sinful human creature, the problem is infinitely greater because God's righteous anger against sin is infinite and eternal, and we, collectively, are the guilty party. Our sin in Adam and our own actual sins deserve nothing less than eternal condemnation. God made us "in righteousness and true holiness" (*HC* 6) so that we could obey his law.[21] We had the natural ability to obey God. We confess, in *BC* 14, that we were created "capable in all things to will agreeably to the will of God."[22] Mysteriously, tragically, and fatally, we chose to disobey God, to make a false covenant with Satan rather than to obey God, to keep covenant with him by obeying "the commandment of life" (*BC* 14). Had Adam obeyed,

20. "Was für Nutzen bekommst du aus der heiligen Empfängniss und Geburt Christi? Dass Er unser Mittler ist, und mit seiner Unschuld und vollkommenen Heiligkeit meine Sünde, darin ich bin empfangen, vor Gottes Angesicht bedecket" (Schaff, *Creeds of the Churches*, 3:319). "Quem fructum percipis ex sancta conceptione et nativiatate Christi? Quod is noster sit Mediator, et sua innocentia, ac perfecta sanctitate, mea peccata, in quibus conceptus sum, tegat, ne in conspectum Dei veniant" (Niemeyer, *Collectio Confessionum*, 438).

21. See the discussion under *HC* 6, 9.

22. Schaff, *Creeds of the Churches*, 3:398.

he would have passed the probation and entered into eternal fellowship with our God (*HC* 6).

Because Adam sinned, we are all born dead in sins and trespasses (Ps 51:5; Eph 2:1–4). By nature we are "children of wrath" (Eph 2:3), idolaters (Gal 4:8), at war with God, given to all manner of wickedness (Gal 5:19–21). God is justly angry with us. Only because of God's mercy and grace do we not experience the full effects of the fall constantly and immediately. Christians, those who believe and profess the Christian faith, who are trusting in, resting on, and leaning on Christ and his finished work for sinners, have a Mediator, a substitute, a go-between of the most extraordinary sort. If we have trouble at work, we might ask a friend to go talk to our boss on our behalf, but in this case, God the Son, who is true God of true God, consubstantial with the Father and the Holy Spirit (and yet personally distinct from both), took on our nature, a true human nature, and has become our Mediator.[23] We did not go to God to seek a mediator. He took it on himself. That is free favor toward judgment-deserving sinners.

Jesus Christ is true God and true man, and he took his true humanity from the Virgin, by the miraculous operation of the Holy Spirit.[24] Christians rejoice in the holy conception and birth of Christ. We believe and accept the miracle on the evidence of Holy Scripture. "The Holy Spirit will come upon you, and the power of the Most High will overshadow you; therefore the child to be born will be called holy—the Son of God" (Luke 1:35 ESV). God the Spirit is the Spirit of holiness. He is pure. By his work the human nature that the Son took on himself, in Mary's womb, was utterly holy. It far exceeded all the Levitical requirements for holiness because it was no type or foreshadowing of the Holy One of Israel to come. Jesus Christ *is* the Holy One of Israel (Isa 41:14). He is our Redeemer.

Jesus did not come merely because we are human. Our problem has never been mere finitude. God the Son would not have become incarnate if we had not fallen. Rather, he came for humans who are made in his image, who voluntarily became sinners and morally corrupt before God's law and subject to his wrath. This is why we confess that all that Jesus did, he did

23. Nicene-Constantinopolitan Creed (AD 381), in Schaff, *Creeds of the Churches*, 2:57. See the discussion under *HC* 17; see Ursinus, *Commentary*, 208–9.

24. See the discussion under *HC* 35.

so not for himself but for us (Rom 5:8; Gal 3:13; Titus 2:14; 1 John 3:16). *Contra* those who deny the imputation of Christ's active obedience on the ground that he had to qualify himself in order that his suffering (passive) obedience might be imputed to us, Scripture says no such thing. This is a rationalist theory grounded in an interpretation of Anselm's argument in *Cur deus homo* (1098).[25] Christ did not have to qualify himself. He was born qualified. Thus Paul says, he was "born of a woman, under the law" (Gal 4:4). He was born "like his brothers" (Heb 2:16–17) to be our propitiation. He came with a true human nature to help fallen humans, who were unable and unwilling to help themselves. This is why he had to be made like us in every respect, sin excepted (Heb 4:15). This is why the early church, beginning in the apostolic period, had to contend so vigorously for both of Christ's true natures: divine and human (1 John 4:2). The Jews could not believe that God would take on flesh, and the Greeks could not believe that God would be a true man (1 Cor 1:23). Jesus confounded both groups and everyone else.

An earthly mediator is important, but "there is one Mediator between God and man, the man Christ Jesus" (1 Tim 2:5). His holiness, purity, and righteousness was and is for me and for my sins and for you and yours, if you believe. He is our substitute, our representative, our holy Mediator. He alone (not the blessed Virgin and not the saints) is our substitute. Only his righteousness and merit imputed to us justifies and saves.[26]

25. Cap. 9, in Schmitt, *S. Anselmi*, 2:61.8–32. See Clark, "Do This and Live," 229–65.

26. Olevianus, *Exposition*, 68–70.

QUESTION 37

What do you understand by the word "suffered"?

QUESTION 38

Why did he suffer "under Pontius Pilate" as judge?

QUESTION 39

Is there anything more in his having been crucified than if he had suffered some other death?

Lord's Day 15

QUESTION 37

What do you understand by the word "suffered"?

That all the time he lived on earth, but especially at the end of his life, he bore, in body and soul, the wrath of God against the sin of the whole human race; in order that by His passion, as the only atoning sacrifice, he might redeem our body and soul from everlasting damnation, and obtain for us the grace of God, righteousness and eternal life.[1]

When Olevianus came to this article, he saw two aspects: Christ's fulfillment of prophecy and his active, substitutionary, obedient suffering for us.[2] Isaiah foreshadowed the suffering of our Lord Jesus when he wrote, "His appearance was so marred, beyond human semblance, and his form beyond that of the children of mankind" (Isa 52:14 ESV). The prophecy foretold that the Messiah would be "numbered among the transgressors" (53:12), that he would be "despised and rejected" (53:3), that he would be rejected by people and smitten by God, crushed for our iniquities, that he would bear our griefs and be led like a silent lamb to the slaughter (53:3–10). This is a characterization of Christ's entire life. We know that the Holy Spirit inspired Isaiah to point forward to Jesus because the same Philip interpreted this passage in Isaiah for us. The Ethiopian eunuch asked, "About whom does the prophet speak, himself or another?" Philip, says Luke, "told the Ethiopian the gospel about Jesus" (Acts 8:34–35). Olevianus notes that, in Luke 18:31–33, our Lord Jesus knew that he had to go to Jerusalem to fulfill this prophecy, that he was the suffering servant. After his resurrection, he explained on the road to

1. "Was derftehft du unter dem Wörtlein: Gelitten? Dass Er an Leib und Seele die ganze Zeit seines Lebens auf Erden, fonderlich aber am Ende desselben, den Zorn Gottes wider die Sünde des ganzen menschlichen Geschlechts getragen hat, auf dass Er mit seinem Leiden, als mit dem einigen Sühnopfer, unsern Leib und Seele von der ewigen Verdammniss erlösete, und uns Gottes Gnade, Gerechtigkeit und ewiges Leben erwürbe" (Schaff, *Creeds of the Churches*, 3:319). "Quid credis cum dicis: Passus est? Eum toto quidem vitae suae tempore, quo in terris egit, praecipue vero in eius extremo, iram Dei adversus peccatum universi generis humani, corpore et anima sustinuisse: ut sua passione, tanquam unico sacrificio propitiatorio, corpus et animam nostram ab aeterna damnatione liberaret, et nobis gratiam Dei, iustitiam ac vitam aeternam acquireret" (Niemeyer, *Collectio Confessionum*, 438).

2. Olevianus, *Exposition*, 74–76; Olevian, *Firm Foundation*, 64–66.

Emmaus that the Messiah had to suffer all these things (Luke 24:25–27). Stephen said that Herod and Pilate were merely fulfilling the foreordained purpose of God (Acts 4:27–28). The Shiloh of Genesis 49:10 prophecy was "completely fulfilled when the scepter transferred from Judah, and when Pilate, in the name of Caesar, executed judgment."[3]

Jesus was born innocent, sinless, and righteous. His humanity was conceived by the miraculous work of the Holy Spirit, in the womb of the Virgin. When Jesus was an infant, Herod, the governor, sought to murder him (Matt 2:13). He was homeless: "The birds have nests," he said, "and foxes have holes but the Son of Man has nowhere to lay his head" (Matt 8:20). He was utterly righteous and true in all that he said and did, and yet the authorities unjustly sought not only to silence him but to murder him (John 5:18; 7:1, 19, 25; 8:37, 40). Eventually he allowed himself to be arrested. He was tried in a mockery of judicial procedure. He was stripped and beaten. He was humiliated. Finally, when they had exhausted their rage against the Righteous One, they made him carry his own cross up Golgotha until he could carry it no farther. Then they crucified him, and even as they did they mocked him. The concluding chapters of the Gospels record the heart-rending scenes. The apostle Peter, who witnessed much of this, summarized the suffering at the end of his life: "He committed no sin, neither was deceit found in his mouth. When he was reviled, he did not revile in return; when he suffered, he did not threaten, but continued entrusting himself to him who judges justly" (1 Pet 2:22–23 ESV). What the Holy Spirit gave to Isaiah in types and shadows (Isa 53:10–12), our Lord fulfilled in his body. He poured out his soul to death. He bore the sins of many.

This leads us directly to the second aspect, Christ's substitutionary, obedient suffering for us. Olevianus explains:

> The other aspect of the life of Christ that faith looks at and appropriates is the submissive, obedient humiliation that Christ the Lord in our person showed the Father throughout His whole life. For although our salvation is due above all to the obedience Christ showed in His death, the rest of His life is not excluded: throughout His whole life He took on the form of a servant. The Apostle

3. Olevianus, *Exposition*, 74–75.

> Paul includes the entire submissive humiliation of the Son from beginning to end when he says in Philippians 2[:8], "He humbled himself and became obedient to the Father to the point of death, even the death of the cross."[4]

Notice that, as in *HC* 37 itself, there is no implication that Christ had to qualify himself to be a Savior. His entire life was for us and credited to us. This is the clear teaching of *HC* 60, but it is anticipated here.[5] We do not confess that there were stages in Christ's life, for example, a period of active obedience (for himself) and a period of suffering (passive) obedience at the end of his life. All his obedient life was substitutionary, for us (*pro nobis*), and imputed to us who believe. Ursinus taught the same thing: "His whole life was one continued scene of suffering and privation."[6] Thus, when we say "obtained," we mean "earned." Anyone who denies that Jesus earned our acceptance with God denies the gospel of our Lord Jesus. Anyone who says or implies that Jesus was accepted by grace denies the gospel.[7]

This is the doctrine of, as the Epistle to Diognetus puts it, the "sweet exchange" (γλυκείας ἀνταλλαγῆς).[8] As Peter says, "He himself bore our sins in his body on the tree, that we might die to sin and live to righteousness. By his wounds you have been healed" (1 Pet 2:24 ESV). His wounds are our healing. He was our substitute. He is our righteousness. That which we earned, suffering and death, the wrath of God against sin, was given to him. To those who believe, what he earned, righteousness, is given. That is why the apostle John describes him as "the propitiation for our sins, and not for ours only but also for the sins of the whole world" (1 John 2:2 ESV).

Believers are redeemed people, bought with the life and death of our Lord Jesus. It is not that we will be redeemed or that we might be redeemed. Believers *are* redeemed presently, and nothing or no one has the power to change that reality. We have been bought with a great price: the life and death of Christ.

---

4. Olevian, *Firm Foundation*, 64.

5. On Anselm's doctrine that Christ owed obedience for himself, see the discussion under *HC* 36; Clark, *Caspar Olevian*, 168–69.

6. Ursinus, *Commentary*, 212.

7. Clark, "Do This and Live," 229–65.

8. Epistle to Diognetus 9.5, in Holmes, *Apostolic Fathers*, 711.

In *HC* 37, we affirm, as Ursinus explains, that Christ suffered the wrath of God as our substitute in his person. When Acts 20:28 says that God purchased (περιεποιήσατο) the church "with his blood," this is said, as Ursinus notes, "according to the communication of properties" (*communicatio idiomatum*). It is a *synecdoche*, a figure of speech in which one part is made to represent the whole. "God, that is, that person which is God and man, purchased the church with his blood, which he shed in respect to his humanity. By this communication of properties, we attribute to the whole person, what is peculiar to one nature."[9]

Against Rome, we confess only one penal, atoning sacrifice. The Roman doctrine of the continuing, memorial, propitiatory sacrifice is irreconcilable with that great truth. Rome confesses: "As a sacrifice the Eucharist is also offered in reparation for the sins of the living and the dead to obtain spiritual or temporal benefits from God."[10] This doctrine is a denial of the "once for all" (ἐφάπαξ) sacrifice of Christ (Heb 7:27; 9:26; 10:10).[11]

The doctrine of the penal, substitutionary atonement should not be juxtaposed with the doctrine of *Christus Victor*, which "emphasizes the triumph of Christ over the evil powers of the world, through which he rescues his people and establishes a new relationship between God and the world."[12] They are complementary truths. He conquered death through his suffering and death as our sin-bearing substitute.[13]

In article 21 of the *BC*, the Reformed churches confess that Christ "presented himself in our name before his Father, to appease his wrath with full satisfaction by offering himself on the tree of the cross and pouring out his precious blood for the cleansing of our sins, as the prophets had predicted."[14] The language and intent of the church was to say to *believers*

9. Ursinus, *Commentary*, 215. Olevianus writes, "quae in natura humana patitur" ("who suffered in his human nature"), in *Romanos Notae*, 187.

10. *CCC* §414.

11. In *CCC* §612, Rome confesses: "Christ's death is the unique and definitive sacrifice," but she does not affirm that his death is the once-for-all sacrifice.

12. Kolb, "Christus Victor"; *pace* Aulén, *Christus Victor*. See also Clark, "Atonement"; Horton, *Justification*, 2:235–47.

13. See Ignatius, *To the Romans* 6.1 (τὸν ὑπὲρ ἡμῶν ἀποθανόντα; Holmes, *Apostolic Fathers*, 231); Cyril of Jerusalem, *Gospel according to St John*, 2:623–24. On Augustine, see Godfrey, "Tensions within International Calvinism," 72–74; Rainbow, *Will of God and the Cross*, 9–22; Prosper, *Defense of St. Augustine*, 16. See *ST* 3a 49.

14. *BC* 21, in United Reformed Churches in North America, *Liturgical Forms and Prayers*, 174.

that God's intent was to accomplish the salvation of all of the elect, those whom God "in his eternal decree and unchangeable counsel, he has elected and chosen in Jesus Christ our Lord by his pure goodness, without any consideration of their works."[15] The teaching of the Reformed churches on the atonement is most clearly confessed in the second head of doctrine of the Canons of Dort, which were written to respond to the teaching of Jacob Arminius and the objections (1610) of the Remonstrants.[16] The Remonstrants had sought to revise the Reformed confession and to capitalize on the language of *HC* 37, but the synod responded by affirming, "This death of God's Son is the only and entirely complete sacrifice and satisfaction for sins," and "It is of infinite value and worth, more than sufficient to atone for the sins of the whole world."[17]

It is true that *HC* 37 speaks of Christ's death relative to the whole world or human race. This is because Christ's death is sufficient for every human who ever lived. The question, however, is what God *intended* by the atonement. When we read *HC* 37 in light of its broader context, in light of the other writings of its principal authors and framers and in light of the rest of the catechism, it is clear that *HC* 37 does *not* teach a universal atonement. Ursinus addresses this question directly. He poses the objection: "If Christ made satisfaction for all, then all ought to be saved. But all are not saved. Therefore, he did not make a perfect satisfaction."[18] The premise of the question is that Christ's death is efficacious, not hypothetical. In his response to the objection, he does not question the assumption but goes instead to the *intent* behind the atonement, which is of the essence of the later Reformed response to the Remonstrants:

> Christ satisfied for all, as it respects the sufficiency of the satisfaction which he made, but not as it respects the application thereof; for he fulfilled the law in a two-fold respect. First, by his own righteousness; and secondly, by making satisfaction for our sins,

15. *BC* 16, in United Reformed Churches in North America, *Liturgical Forms and Prayers*, 170; first head of doctrine, *Canons of Dort*, in United Reformed Churches in North America, *Liturgical Forms and Prayers*, 259–67.

16. United Reformed Churches in North America, *Liturgical Forms and Prayers*, 267–70.

17. *Canons of Dort* 2.3, in United Reformed Churches in North America, *Liturgical Forms and Prayers*, 267; see also rejection of errors 2.1, p. 269.

18. Ursinus, *Commentary*, 215.

> each of which is most perfect. But the satisfaction is made ours by an application, which is also two-fold; the former of which is made by God, when he justifies us on account of the merit of his Son, and brings it to pass that we cease from sin; the latter is accomplished by us through faith. For we apply unto ourselves, the merit of Christ, when by a true faith, we are fully persuaded that God for the sake of the satisfaction of his Son, remits unto us our sins. Without this application, the satisfaction of Christ is of no benefit to us.[19]

He distinguishes between the *sufficiency* of the atonement and its *efficiency* or its intent and application. The Spirit creates new life in us and with it true faith, and through true faith we lay hold of Christ, who died for the elect.

Olevianus consistently casts the entirety of salvation in covenantal terms. When he explains these same articles, using the same language as the catechism, it is always in the context of the covenant of grace between God and the elect. He consistently quotes or paraphrases the Abrahamic promise from Genesis 17:7. For example, in his 1579 commentary on Romans, on 5:8, "For God commends his love toward us, because while we were yet sinners, Christ died for us," he writes, "The efficacy of his benefits do not remain in Christ, but are communicated to us."[20] The whole discussion is conducted in the first-person plural, "we" and "for us." For Olevianus, as for Ursinus (and *HC* 37), Christ accomplished redemption "for us," that is, for the elect.

The catechism was written before John Davenant (1572–1641) and Moises Amyraut (1596–1644) theorized about hypothetical universalism, in which Christ was said to have "died to make satisfaction for the sins of all men without exception if—if, that is, they believe: but that, foreseeing that none would believe, God elected some to be granted faith through the effectual operation of the Holy Spirit."[21] The doctrine of hypothetical

19. Ursinus, *Commentary*, 215.

20. "Efficaciam huius beneficii non in Christo manere, sed nobis communicari" (Olevianus, *Romanos Notae*, 187). He quotes Beza, *Novum domini*.

21. Warfield, *Calvin and Calvinism*, 364–65. See also the discussion of these issues under *HC* 20. Roger Nicole writes, "John Davenant (1570–1641) held views on the extent of the atonement which resemble Amyraut's (cf. his *Dissertationes Duae: Prima de Morte Christi* ..., Cambridge, 1650;

universalism has a widespread purchase among evangelicals in our time. We should be careful not to read back into the *HC* the doctrine of hypothetical universalism. Further, when the Remonstrants sought to revise our doctrine of the atonement, it was resisted by all the Reformed churches at the Synod of Dort, who did not understand *HC* 37 to imply a universal atonement. The "promiscuous" (*promiscue*; 3/4.5), "indiscriminate" (*indiscriminatim*; 3/4.5), and "serious" (*serio*; 3/4.8) offer of the gospel is universal, but the atonement is not.[22] The intent of the atonement was not merely to make salvation available to those who do not resist (Lutheranism), or to those who cooperate with grace (Arminianism), but to accomplish it and to apply it efficaciously to the elect.[23] Thus the synod held that Christ died that he might "efficaciously redeem" (2.8; *efficaciter redimeret*) the elect.

QUESTION 38

Why did he suffer "under Pontius Pilate" as judge?

That he, being innocent, might be condemned by the temporal judge, and thereby deliver us from the severe judgment of God, to which we were exposed.[24]

When we read the Gospel accounts, we may be tempted to disconnect them from the historical context in which the life of Christ occurred. One of the several functions of this article of the Apostles' Creed, "suffered under Pontius Pilate," is to reconnect the Gospel accounts of the life of Christ to their surrounding context. Pilate was, according to an inscription in Caesarea, prefect (governor) of Judea (*Praefectus Iudaeae*).[25]

Eng. trans. by J. Allport in the 2d vol. of Davenant's *Exposition of … Colossians*, London, 1831, 1832)" (Nicole, *Standing Forth*, 328).

22. Schaff, *Creeds of the Churches*, 3:565–66.

23. Rejection of errors, under the second head of doctrine (United Reformed Churches in North America, *Liturgical Forms and Prayers*, 269–70).

24. "Warum hat Er unter dem Richter Pontio Pilato gelitren? Auf dass Er unschuldig unter dem meltlichen Richter verdammet würde, und uns damit von dem strengen Urtheil Gottes, das über uns ergehen sollte, erledigte" (Schaff, *Creeds of the Churches*, 3:320). "Quid causae fuit, cur sub iudice Pilato pateretur? Ut innocens coram iudice politico damnatus, nos a severo Dei iudicio, quod omnes manebat, eximeret" (Niemeyer, *Collectio Confessionum*, 438).

25. Sherwin-White, "Pilate, Pontius," 867.

Tacitus (ca. 115) mentions him in connection with the death of Christ.[26] As prefect, Pilate was ruthless. He confiscated the temple treasury to build an aqueduct (the Romans were great plumbers and road builders). Luke 13:1 records that he "mixed the blood of Galileans" with their sacrifices. His violence eventually offended even Roman sensibilities, such that he was recalled to Rome in AD 36 to answer for his attack against the Samaritans. What happened to him after that is a matter of legend and speculation. Eusebius says he committed suicide.[27] There was another suggestion that he was beheaded, but that seems unlikely. Both of these assume that the Romans came to see that the Christians were treated unjustly and responded accordingly. We may properly doubt that. What would have offended them was Pilate's transgression of Roman law and procedure. There is a late second-century letter purporting to be by Pilate to the Emperor Claudius, but its authenticity is rightly doubted. It was almost certainly fabricated by a well-meaning but misguided Christian in an attempt to show that even Pilate came to his senses and realized that the Christians were correct.[28] Remarkably, certainly because of the legend of his conversion to Christianity, Pilate is remembered with a feast day in both the Ethiopian and Greek Orthodox traditions.

In Scripture, Pilate appears as ruthless and calculating as extrabiblical sources say he was. Luke 23:3–5 records our Lord's trial before Pilate: "And Pilate asked him, 'Are you the King of the Jews?' And he answered him, 'You have said so.' Then Pilate said to the chief priests and the crowds, 'I find no guilt in this man.' But they were urgent, saying, 'He stirs up the

---

26. Myers, *Eerdmans Bible Dictionary*, s.v. "Pilate, Pontius." Tacitus (*Annals* 15.44) writes: "But all human efforts, all the lavish gifts of the emperor, and the propitiations of the gods, did not banish the sinister belief that the conflagration was the result of an order. Consequently, to get rid of the report, Nero fastened the guilt and inflicted the most exquisite tortures on a class hated for their abominations, called Christians by the populace. Christus, from whom the name had its origin, suffered the extreme penalty during the reign of Tiberius at the hands of one of our procurators, Pontius Pilatus, and a most mischievous superstition, thus checked for the moment, again broke out not only in Judaea, the first source of the evil, but even in Rome, where all things hideous and shameful from every part of the world find their centre and become popular. Accordingly, an arrest was first made of all who pleaded guilty; then, upon their information, an immense multitude was convicted, not so much of the crime of firing the city, as of hatred against mankind. Mockery of every sort was added to their deaths. Covered with the skins of beasts, they were torn by dogs and perished, or were nailed to crosses, or were doomed to the flames and burnt, to serve as a nightly illumination, when daylight had expired."

27. Eusebius, *Ecclesiastical History* 2.7.

28. Elliott, *Apocryphal New Testament*, 205.

people, teaching throughout all Judea, from Galilee even to this place'" (ESV). Discovering that Jesus was a Galilean, Pilate then sent him to Herod for disposition. After our Lord was brutally punished and shamefully mocked, Herod sent Jesus back to Pilate. Strangely, according to Luke, Pilate and Herod became friends during this episode (Luke 23:12). "Pilate then called together the chief priests and the rulers and the people, and said to them, 'You brought me this man as one who was misleading the people. And after examining him before you, behold, I did not find this man guilty of any of your charges against him. Neither did Herod, for he sent him back to us. Look, nothing deserving death has been done by him. I will therefore punish and release him'" (Luke 23:13–16 ESV). To this point Pilate followed typical Roman custom and procedure, but John 18:33–19:16 makes it clear that Pilate was a cynic ("What is truth?"), that he himself did not believe Jesus to be guilty of any crime and that he nevertheless turned Jesus over to the crowd, that he did not send away the Jewish authorities. By right he ought to have said, "Caesar fears no mobs"; that he capitulated to the mob supports the image we have of Pilate as a vicious, self-seeking climber. His disappearance into the shadows of history is more fitting than the more romantic ends proposed by legend. All that we know from secular history and Scripture more than justifies the confession of the Reformed churches in *HC* 38.

Jesus was legally innocent under both God's law and Roman civil law. He posed no threat to Pilate, Herod, or the empire. His kingdom, as he told Pilate, was not of this world. Had it been, he would never have permitted himself to be so humiliated. He could have wiped out Pilate, Herod, and Caesar in a moment, and one day he shall. At that day, Pilate, Herod, and all the Caesars of this world will bow their knees and confess that Jesus, not Caesar, is Lord (Phil 2:10; Rev 21:24).

The question remains why our Lord permitted this. Indeed, "permitted" may not be strong enough a word. When it was time, our Lord virtually orchestrated the events leading up to his arrest and persecution. Our Lord was no mere victim of a series of gross injustices. He took on true human nature and suffered obediently all his life in order to redeem his people from divine judgment. Paul says, "Christ redeemed us from the curse of the law by becoming a curse for us"(Gal 3:13). That phrase "for us" is most important. Jesus had no need to suffer and die for himself. He "suffered once for sins, the righteous for the unrighteous, that he might bring us to God" (1 Pet 3:18 ESV). As true man, he belonged to a category of one, insofar as he was "conceived by the Holy Spirit and born of the virgin Mary." Inasmuch as he was the holy, righteous, federal head of a people, we can say that he was a member of a class of two: the first Adam and the last (Rom 5:12–21; 1 Cor 15:45).

Our Lord Jesus was innocent of all civil crimes just as he was innocent of all spiritual crimes. His civil innocence, to which even Pilate testified, was another confirmation that our Savior, our substitute, our Mediator, was truly a spotless lamb. Olevianus says Christ had to be condemned by an earthly judge so that we would know that he really bore all our sins as our substitute:

> He was being tried before God, laden with your and my sin and that of the whole world, so that He might take the judgment of our damnation and punishment upon Himself. We should have been brought before the judgment seat of God and received the sentence of damnation, but Christ took our damnation upon Himself. For that reason He had to be brought to trial as if He were each of us, and He had to be sentenced and condemned to death by God Himself through Pilate the judge, who of course had something quite different in mind.[29]

His trial before Pilate was more than a civil trial. We say that "thereby" he delivered all his people, all the elect, all who have believed, believe now, and shall believe until he returns, from God's wrath. That was his purpose. That was his intent.[30]

This doctrine, that God has wrath against sin and sinners, is a hard one to receive in our age. Modernity rejected the biblical narrative of our creation in the image of God, the probation (test), and our fall as a "saga" (as Karl Barth puts it).[31] It is a deeply held conviction in the modern period that humans are essentially good—not just by creation but at birth. Thus, the biblical, Pauline, and Augustinian notion that humans are, by virtue of

29. Olevian, *Firm Foundation*, 65.

30. Olevian, *Firm Foundation*, 64–67; Ursinus, *Commentary*, 217–18.

31. Barth, *Church Dogmatics* III/1:81.

their union with Adam, dead in sins and trespasses (Eph 2:1–4) is deeply offensive. Since we tend to consider ourselves naturally innocent, we do not reckon with the reality that every single human being is, as we say, "exposed" to divine judgment. Nevertheless, we are. Deuteronomy 27:26 and Galatians 3:10 say to Israelites and to everyone, "Cursed is everyone who does not continue to do everything which is written in the book of the law." Paul says in Romans 3:13 that all humans are born corrupt. Our throats are an open grave. Our hearts are corrupt. We exchanged the glory of God for idolatry (Rom 1:23). We have all turned to disobedience and death. Jesus said, "Why do you call me good? There is no one good but God alone" (Mark 10:18). Indeed. Our Savior Jesus is true man and true God, and he was good. He was good for us sinners.

QUESTION 39

Is there anything more in his having been crucified than if he had suffered some other death?

Yes, for thereby I am assured that he took upon himself the curse which lay upon me; because the death of the cross was accursed of God.[32]

It was not many decades ago that wearing a cross as a fashion statement would have been considered to be in bad taste. Today, however, it is not uncommon to see people who make no profession of faith, who seem to have no awareness of the historical or religious significance of the cross, wearing a one as a fashion statement. When the early Christians thought of the cross, it was anything but a fashion statement. We think of the cross as a Roman implement of torture, and that it was. As with many other things in Roman culture, the Romans did not invent it. They

32. "Ist es etwas mehr, dass Er ist gekreuziget worden, denn so Er eines andern Tobes gestorben wäre? Ja: denn dadurch bin ich gewiss, dass Er die Vermaledeiung, die auf mir lag, auf sich geladen habe, dieweil der Tod des Kreuzes von Gott verflucht war" (Schaff, *Creeds of Christendom*, 3:320). "Est vero quiddam amplius, quod affixus sit cruci, quam si alio genere mortis affectus esset? Sane amplius: Ex hac enim re sum certus, eum maledictionem, quae mihi incumbebat, in se recpisse: nam mors crucis a Deo erat maledicta" (Niemeyer, *Collectio Confessionum*, 438–39).

merely perfected it. Crucifixion is first attested among the Persians,[33] perhaps derived from the Assyrian practice of impalement. The Greeks later employed it, especially Alexander the Great, and the Carthaginians, from whom the Romans adapted the practice as a punishment for slaves and noncitizens, and occasionally for citizens guilty of treason.[34]

In the Old Testament the impaling and public exhibition of a corpse was a sign of accursedness: "And if a man has committed a crime punishable by death and he is put to death, and you hang him on a tree, his body shall not remain all night on the tree, but you shall bury him the same day, for a hanged man is cursed by God. You shall not defile your land that Yahweh your God is giving you for an inheritance" (Deut 21:22–23). The Seleucids introduced what we know as crucifixion into Palestine. Antiochus Epiphanes IV (ruled 175–164 BC) crucified rebellious Jews (1 Macc 1:44–50).[35] The Romans crucified thirty-six hundred Jews circa AD 66. The most famous crucifixion in all history, of course, is that of one person, the God-Man, Jesus Christ. The intent behind the civil-political and military use of the cross was to evoke terror and cause a conquered people to submit. It was a bloody, painful, and visible signal: this is what we do to those who get out of line.

Naturally, to the Jews the cross was a hated symbol of Roman oppression. The Romans regarded anyone who was crucified as disgusting. They valued outward conformity as a sign of civilization and even humanity. To resist the empire and the emperor, to be judged a criminal by the empire, was a scandal. The Romans assumed that anyone who was crucified probably had it coming to them. In the first century, the Roman cross was the perfect sign of revulsion and rejection by God and society.

The writer to the Hebrews reflects the shame associated with the cross and connects it to Old Testament priestly practice: "For the bodies of those animals whose blood is brought into the holy places by the high priest as a sacrifice for sin are burned outside the camp. So Jesus also suffered outside the gate in order to sanctify the people through his own blood. Therefore let us go to him outside the camp and bear the reproach

---

33. Herodotus, *Historiae* 1.128.2; 3.132.2, 159.1.

34. Myers, *Eerdmans Bible Dictionary*, sv. "cross," 246.

35. Myers, "Cross," 246.

he endured" (Heb 13:11–13 ESV). So it is appropriate that our catechism considers the cross.

Jesus did not merely die. He died an accursed death. We know that he was neither the first nor the last Jew to be crucified, but he was the only man who bore the wrath of God against sin. He, not national Israel, nor the Jews, was the suffering servant of Isaiah. He was the substitute. He was (and is) the Mediator. This is the consistent testimony of Scripture (1 Tim 2:5; Heb 9:15; 12:24; Gal 3:20). Olevianus explains,

> This happened *because* we owed God an accursed death for our sins, and *death by crucifixion was accursed* not only by humans but also by God Himself. As He said in Deuteronomy 21[:23], "Cursed be everyone who hangs on a tree." Hence it was necessary that Christ our surety suffer this very death, so that by His satisfaction He might redeem us from the curse of God. As St. Paul teaches in Galatians 3[:13–14], "Christ took our curse upon Himself by being accursed for us when He was hanged on the tree, that the blessing promised to Abraham might come upon us." Therefore, from the death of the cross, the sign of God's curse, we clearly and unmistakably see that the burden of God's curse that should have lain on us was laid on Christ. This is something we could not have been certain about if Christ had died normally or *had suffered a different kind of death.*[36]

Christ redeemed us from the curse of the law by becoming a curse for us—for it is written, "Cursed is everyone who is hanged on a tree"—so that in Christ Jesus the blessing of Abraham might come to the gentiles, so that we might receive the promised Spirit through faith (Deut 21:23; Gal 3:13–14).

His death fulfilled the Old Testament curses. Because he was innocent, his death shocked even the conscience of battle-hardened soldiers who had seen it all. The Roman centurion who witnessed it testified, "Truly this man was the Son of God!" (Mark 15:39). Thus, ironically, the message about a crucified Messiah, a humiliation to the Jews, disgusting

---

36. Olevian, *Firm Foundation*, 66. Emphasis original.

to the Romans, and foolishness to the Greeks, is to us who believe "the power of God" (1 Cor 1:18).

The early Christians embraced the cross as a symbol of their salvation. They did not brandish it in gold or silver, however. They used it surreptitiously. Among other things, copyists added it to early copies of New Testament texts.

> Some of the oldest manuscripts of the Greek New Testament contain what are likely the earliest evidences of cruciform symbolism. Called a "staurogram" (from the Greek word *σταυρός*, stauros, "cross") the symbol combines the Greek tau (T) and rho (P)—two of the letters in Greek words meaning "cross" or "crucify"—to represent the figure of a man hanging on a cross. The staurogram appears in seven verses in John 19 in a second-century papyrus (P66). There are also three instances in Luke (P75, third century) and one in Matthew (P45, early third century). The words in which the staurogram appear are treated as *nomina sacra*, or "sacred names."[37]

When in our Christian experience we are tempted to think that God has turned his back on us, we should think of that cross, because it was there that God really did turn his back on sin and, in that moment, executed justice against all our sins past, present, and future. He did so not that we might continue sinning but that we might be set free from the power of sin, that we might die to self and sin and live to Christ. Our Father, who is our Father for Christ's sake, may withdraw the sense of his presence for a season, but he never turns his back on his children. That work is finished. Thus, a right understanding begins with seeing what the cross signifies. It does not say to us that Jesus began a process that we must complete. It does not say that Jesus has made it possible for us to be saved but that on that horrible cross he *accomplished* our salvation. It is ours, by grace alone, to believe, to trust that all that Jesus did on the cross for us. As we remember the centrality of the cross, then, we are rightly oriented to take the next step in the Christian pilgrimage.

---

37. Barry et al., *Lexham Bible Dictionary*, s.v. "cross."

Question 40
Why was it necessary for Christ to suffer death?

Question 41
Why was he buried?

Question 42
Since then Christ died for us, why must we also die?

Question 43
What further benefit do we receive from the sacrifice and death of Christ on the cross?

Question 44
Why is it added: “he descended into hell”?

Lord's Day 16

Question 40

Why was it necessary for Christ to suffer death?

Because the justice and truth of God required, that satisfaction for our sins could be made in no other way than by the death of the Son of God.[1]

From a purely human point of view, from a historical point of view, from an intellectual point of view, there have been few historical figures as compelling and important as Jesus of Nazareth. Many regard him as a sort of Jewish Socrates, a provocative and important teacher, a moral philosopher. In that light, one might well ask why he had to die. After all, if we consider all the good Socrates might have done had he lived longer, his death seems tragic.

Certainly, Jesus's death was tragic and horrible. To put the question this way, however, is to miss some very important truths about Jesus. He was indeed a teacher, but that was but one of his offices.[2] He has three offices: prophet, priest, and king. In his prophetic office, he not only spoke God's word, after the pattern of Moses (Deut 18), but he *is* the Word. "In the beginning was the Word and the Word was with God and the Word was God" (John 1:1). As king, he came announcing the inauguration of "the Kingdom of God" (Mark 1:15), which he also called "the kingdom of heaven" (Matt 3:2). Third, and definitive for answering the question before us, Jesus holds the office of priest. According to the Mosaic law, the function of a priest is to offer sacrifices for the sins of the people (Lev 1–7). Those sacrifices were to be a substitute for the people. He was to be the mediator between God and his people. All those Levitical sacrifices, offered daily in the temple, were a picture of a priest to come. According to the book of Hebrews, Jesus is that priest (Heb 2:17; 3:1; 4:14–15; 5:5–6; 6:20; 7:3, 11, 15, 21; 8:1–3; 9:11; 10:21). He is our Mediator. He is our

1. "Warum hat Christus den Tod müssen leiden? Darum, weil wegen der Gerechtigkeit und Wahrheit Gottes nicht anders für unsere Sünden möchte bezahlet werden, denn durch den Tod des Sohnes Gottes" (Schaff, *Creeds of Christendom*, 3:320). "Cur necesse fuit, ut Christus ad mortem usque se demitteret? Propterea quod iustitiae et veritati Dei nullo alio pacto pro nostris peccatis potuit satisfierei, quam ipsa morte filii Dei" (Niemeyer, *Collectio Confessionum*, 439).

2. See the discussion under *HC* 31.

representative. His priesthood is greater than that of the Levites. His has no beginning and no end. Melchizedek (Gen 14:18) was a type, an illustration, and a foreshadowing of Jesus our great High Priest. But he was more than a priest; he was also the sacrifice. Unlike the Levitical priests, he did not have to make sacrifices for himself. He came to make a sacrifice for us, to be the propitiation for our sins (Rom 6:23), that is, to be the offering that turned away God's wrath from his people, and to be the basis on which God is justly favorable toward his people.

Those who view Jesus merely as a teacher (a reduced sort of prophet) cannot account for his death except as a tragedy. Christians, however, confess that it was much more than a tragedy. We say that it was a satisfaction owed to the justice of God because of our sin. The very notion of justice is something with which our age has some difficulty. Some think that justice is arbitrary. To be sure, there is a much injustice in the world, and it may be that much injustice shall never be made right in this life. Nevertheless, we do all have some notion of justice or righteousness. In the sentence above I used the phrase "made right" with the expectation that the reader would understand it. Lawyers use the striking expression "to make whole" as a justification for a lawsuit seeking to recover damages. We do sometimes see genuine acts of justice, even when that justice is delayed. Law enforcement pursue cold cases for years until they find a murderer. So, we do see approximations of justice such that we know what it is.

Of course, the Scriptures clearly teach what justice is. Our Lord made what the *HC* framers call a "covenant of nature" (*foedus naturale*) and what the *BC* calls a "commandment of life" (14) conditioned on obedience to his law, which is essentially identical to what Ursinus and Olevianus call the "covenant of nature" and that later writers call the covenant of works.[3] God said that we might eat from any of the trees in the garden but one. The day we ate from that tree, "You shall surely die" (Gen 2:17). We ate, and true to his word, the Lord exacted the promised punishment. That is the nature of justice. We see it too under Noah:

3. Schaff, *Creeds of Christendom*, 3:398. See the discussion under *HC* 3.

> And for your lifeblood I will require a reckoning: from every beast I will require it and from man. From his fellow man I will require a reckoning for the life of man.
>
> "Whoever sheds the blood of man,
> by man shall his blood be shed,
> for God made man in his own image." (Gen 9:5–6 ESV)

Justice is built into the nature of creation before the fall and after. It is reflected in the laws of Moses: "Whoever takes a human life shall surely be put to death. Whoever takes an animal's life shall make it good, life for life. If anyone injures his neighbor, as he has done it shall be done to him, fracture for fracture, eye for eye, tooth for tooth; whatever injury he has given a person shall be given to him" (Lev 24:17–20 ESV).

To be sure, the exact application of justice may vary through the history of redemption. The same principle has different applications. Under Moses the Israelites were commanded to reflect justice by animal sacrifices and by prosecuting a holy war against the Canaanites (e.g., Exod 23:23–33; Deut 20:1–21:14). Those requirements have been abrogated and have expired. The creational law, however, given under Noah (before Moses, before the "old covenant," strictly defined) is permanent. This is one reason why the death penalty is not temporary, like the animal sacrifices and holy war. It is a part of natural justice. Justice is not arbitrary because it is grounded not only in the nature of creation, but more fundamentally and importantly, it is grounded in the nature of God. He is justice. As Louis Berkhof explains, "The fundamental idea of righteousness is that of strict adherence to the law." There is no law above God, but "there is certainly a law in the very nature of God, and this is the highest possible standard, by which all other laws are judged." God reveals his intrinsic righteousness in his dealings with his creatures.[4]

Justice is righteousness. God is right. All that he does is right. Whatever he does is right, even if it is difficult for us to understand. Of course, in the nature of things, God being what he is—almighty, transcendent, holy (morally pure, good, without stain)—is in himself beyond our full understanding. We are not only finite (and thus inherently limited as creatures)

4. Berkhof, *Systematic Theology*, 74–75.

but sinful, and thus we are corrupted in our understanding, in our affections (what we love), and in our wills. When we sinned, we broke God's holy law. God could not merely overlook it any more than a human court could overlook a murder. We would not want a human court to overlook a heinous crime. What we did, in violating God's law, was a heinous crime punishable by death. We knew the terms of the covenant before we broke it. We acted voluntarily, without compulsion, and in that sense freely. There was nothing in us that made us liable to sin. God did not create us with any propensity to sin. God created us created good, holy, and righteous. Our sin is indeed a great mystery.

We all know intuitively, naturally, that there is justice (even if sin keeps us from seeing it clearly) that must be satisfied. Sometimes in the debate over the death penalty, people will criticize the principle of *lex talonis* (the law of punishment) as something beyond which we have evolved right up to the point where their loved one is killed. We know that justice must be satisfied, and the greatest crime, ours, required the greatest satisfaction. Jesus's death was not arbitrary. It was necessary.

We should not think that justice was something merely found before Christ, as if there were a vengeful Old Testament (in the broad sense) God and a friendly New Testament God. That was (and is) the great Marcionite heresy. No figure in redemptive history had a more acute sense of divine justice than Jesus of Nazareth: "Woe to you, scribes and Pharisees, hypocrites! For you tithe mint and dill and cumin, and have neglected the weightier matters of the law: justice and mercy and faithfulness. These you ought to have done, without neglecting the others" (Matt 23:23 ESV).

He explicitly promised that there would be a final justice: "And will not God give justice to his elect, who cry to him day and night? Will he delay long over them? I tell you, he will give justice to them speedily" (Luke 18:7–8 ESV). He promised explicitly that there would be a final, perfectly just judgment (e.g., Luke 10:14). This is the same Jesus who turned over tables in the temple as a manifestation of divine justice. Scripture says, "Hear O Israel, the Yahweh our God, Yahweh is One" (Deut 6:4; Mark 12:29). The same justice that was brought to bear on Adam and us in the garden, on the "world that then was" (2 Pet 3:6) under Noah, among the Israelites and the surrounding nations under Moses, David, and the prophets, will be exacted manifold at the judgment, and John says that the clock is ticking. Judgment has come into the world (John 3:19).

The bad news is that every human being owes satisfaction to God's justice for all their sins both original and actual. Those who choose to stand before God without Christ shall have to make satisfaction by themselves. Believers, however, have much for which to give thanks. Just as we broke the "commandment of life" and brought death, the obedient death of our Lord Jesus is the only way by which our sins are forgiven.[5] We have a substitute, Jesus the sinless one, the Holy One of Israel (Isa 41:14), our Mediator, who satisfied God's righteousness for us. We stand before God as if we have done all that Jesus did for us.

QUESTION 41

Why was he buried?

To show thereby that he was really dead.[6]

Scripture says:

> Now there was a man named Joseph, from the Jewish town of Arimathea. He was a member of the council, a good and righteous man, who had not consented to their decision and action; and he was looking for the kingdom of God. This man went to Pilate and asked for the body of Jesus. Then he took it down and wrapped it in a linen shroud and laid him in a tomb cut in stone, where no one had ever yet been laid. It was the day of Preparation, and the Sabbath was beginning. The women who had come with him from Galilee followed and saw the tomb and how his body was laid.

5. The Latin text of the catechism's answer says *nullo alio pacto* (Niemeyer, *Collectio Confessionum*, 439), which is an idiomatic Latin way of saying "by no other way." Nevertheless, in the context in which the Latin translators used this expression, it might bear more meaning than simply "way." I am grateful to Harrison Perkins for pointing this out to me.

6. "Warum ist Er begraben worden? Damit zu bezeugen, dass Er wahrhaftig gestorben sei" (Schaff, *Creeds of Christendom*, 3:320). "Quare etiam sepultus est? Ut eo testatum faceret, se vere mortuum esse" (Niemeyer, *Collectio Confessionum*, 439).

> Then they returned and prepared spices and ointments. (Luke 23:50–56 ESV)

> And Joseph took the body and wrapped it in a clean linen shroud and laid it in his own new tomb, which he had cut in the rock. And he rolled a great stone to the entrance of the tomb and went away. Mary Magdalene and the other Mary were there, sitting opposite the tomb. (Matt 27:59–61 ESV)

> Nicodemus also, who earlier had come to Jesus by night, came bringing a mixture of myrrh and aloes, about seventy-five pounds in weight. So they took the body of Jesus and bound it in linen cloths with the spices, as is the burial custom of the Jews. (John 19:39–40 ESV)

The clear, repeated testimony of Scripture is that Jesus truly died (Rom 5:6, 8; 6:8; 8:34; 14:15; 1 Cor 8:11; 15:3; 2 Cor 5:14; Gal 2:21; 1 Thess 4:14). Nevertheless, even before the end of the apostolic era (ca. AD 100), one of the most pernicious and persistent heresies, which flourishes today, was that Jesus's human nature was not genuine, that it was only apparent.[7] Since the time of Plato (ca. 420s BC–ca. 328 BC) at least, there were philosophical influences among the Greeks that doubted the reality of the physical world. Plato himself in his *Republic* tells the allegory of the cave, the clear message of which is that one's sense experience of the physical world is not to be trusted (514a–520a). This physical world is illusory. That way of thinking was transmitted to the hellenized world, in which the early church came into being. Thus, some were prepared to accept that Jesus was God (or a god), but others had great difficulty with the notion that he was true God and true man.

Struggles over the true humanity of our Lord lie behind one of the earliest confessional statements, preserved for us in 1 Timothy 3:16, "manifested in the flesh." The apostle Peter reminds his readers in Asia Minor that Jesus was "put to death in the flesh" (1 Pet 3:18) and "suffered in the flesh" (4:1). According to the apostle John, one of the marks of antichrist is to deny that Jesus is God in the flesh: "Beloved, do not believe every spirit, but test the spirits to see whether they are from God, for many false

7. This heresy is called docetism, from the Greek verb δοχειν, "to seem" or "to appear."

prophets have gone out into the world. By this you know the Spirit of God: every spirit that confesses that Jesus Christ has come in the flesh is from God, and every spirit that does not confess Jesus is not from God. This is the spirit of the antichrist, which you heard was coming and now is in the world already" (1 John 4:1–3 ESV). Indeed, the first thing the apostle wrote to the congregations was an affirmation of the true humanity of Christ: "That which was from the beginning, which we have heard, which we have seen with our eyes, which we looked upon and have touched with our hands, concerning the word of life—the life was made manifest, and we have seen it, and testify to it and proclaim to you the eternal life, which was with the Father and was made manifest to us" (1 John 1:1–2 ESV).

Though the apostles and the church catholic (universal), including the Reformed churches, soundly rejected the docetic heresy, it has not disappeared. According to Irenaeus, the gnostic teacher Basilides (ca. AD 120–140) denied that Jesus had actually died. "Wherefore he did not himself suffer death, but Simon, a certain man of Cyrene, being compelled, bore the cross in his stead; so that this latter being transfigured by him, that he might be thought to be Jesus, was crucified, through ignorance and error, while Jesus himself received the form of Simon, and, standing by, laughed at them."[8] The Qur'an denies that Jesus was crucified and that he died (*Surah* 4.157–58). It claims that it was Simon the Cyrene who was crucified, thus hollowing the Muslim claim to honor Jesus as one of God's prophets. Jesus himself prophesied his death and burial: "But he answered them, 'An evil and adulterous generation seeks for a sign, but no sign will be given to it except the sign of the prophet Jonah. For just as Jonah was three days and three nights in the belly of the great fish, so will the Son of Man be three days and three nights in the heart of the earth'" (Matt 12:39–40 ESV). According to Scripture. Jesus fulfilled prophecy. To deny Jesus's crucifixion, death, and resurrection denies a central biblical and Christian truth, that Jesus really died, that it was not an appearance (the "swoon theory"). When they took him down from the cross, there was no respiration, no pulse. They wrapped his body. They prepared it for burial and placed it in the tomb before the beginning of the Jewish Sabbath. His cold, lifeless body lay in the tomb, which was covered with a large stone,

8. Irenaeus, *Against Heresies* 124.4 (*ANF* 1:349).

marked with a seal, and guarded by elite troops whose lives were in jeopardy should anyone steal the body (Matt 27:65–66).

Because Jesus died and was buried, we know that the wrath of God against the sins of all his people was fully exhausted.[9] Believers need not fear judgment because Christ our substitute, our Mediator, has endured it for us. We may also live as those who have been crucified with him, who have died to sin that we might live a new life in union with Christ.

Jesus was not first person in the history of salvation to be buried. The patriarchs (Abraham, Isaac, and Jacob) were buried. Scripture is at pains to note their burial. "Isaac and Ishmael his sons buried him in the cave of Machpelah, in the field of Ephron the son of Zohar the Hittite, east of Mamre, the field that Abraham purchased from the Hittites. There Abraham was buried, with Sarah his wife" (Gen 25:9–10 ESV).

Why the emphasis on their burial? There are at least a couple of things at stake here. First, Abraham was buried in Canaan, in the promised land, so the future inheritance by the Israelites is foreshadowed. Even more significant, his burial pointed to his expectation of a heavenly home. Canaan was not ultimately about Canaan. It was a picture of heaven. Scripture says, "For he was looking forward to the city that has foundations, whose designer and builder is God" (Heb 11:10 ESV).

> These all died in faith, not having received the things promised, but having seen them and greeted them from afar, and having acknowledged that they were strangers and exiles on the earth. For people who speak thus make it clear that they are seeking a homeland. If they had been thinking of that land from which they had gone out, they would have had opportunity to return. But as it is, they desire a better country, that is, a heavenly one. Therefore God is not ashamed to be called their God, for he has prepared for them a city. (Heb 11:13–16 ESV)

Christian burial, whether Abraham's or ours, is an act of faith, looking forward to something beyond. Our Lord Jesus was buried to show that he was dead, but he was also buried in hope, in expectation of his resurrection.

---

9. Olevian, *Firm Foundation*, 69.

What about cremation? This is an inherently difficult question because it touches a very personal and private decision: what to do with the remains of a loved one or what one wants to be done with one's own remains. It is also difficult because these are challenging decisions often made in a very emotional time.

Nevertheless, there are biblical patterns and doctrines from which we can learn and apply to this situation. There is a consistent biblical pattern of burial of human remains. Perhaps the most outstanding Old Testament example is Abraham's quest to bury Sarah (Gen 23:19) as a sojourner in a foreign land. Other significant examples could be cited (e.g., Jacob, Joseph, and others). This is clearly the biblical pattern, carrying right through the care given to the deceased body of our Lord himself.

According to the apostle Paul, the biblical pattern was not grounded in sentiment but in a conviction: the resurrection. In 1 Corinthians 15:35–49 the apostle Paul uses an agrarian metaphor to explain the hope of the resurrection. According to Paul, our bodies are like seeds planted in hope, in the expectation of a glorious harvest: the resurrection body, that is, a glorified human body.

The act of cremation is at odds with the act of planting a body in the soil. For one thing, the imagery is not the same at all. Burial is done with regard to the body's status as part of the image of God. We do not just have a body. We are body and soul. That is who we are as image-bearers.[10]

In modernity, we have been taught to regard the body as a machine, and in our disposable age we know what to do with broken-down machines: we throw them away. But however much we may think we know about the body, it is not just a machine. We are persons made in the divine image. Our bodies are part of our personhood. That is why it is wrong, a violation of creational law, to murder (Gen 9:1–6). To attack the body is to attack the image of God. Thus, burial is not just a cultural custom. It is an act of faith. Indeed, WSC 37 rightly says that even in death our "bodies being still united to Christ, do rest in their graves until the resurrection."[11] When there is a choice between burial and cremation, the latter is not

10. I am grateful to my friend and colleague Steve Baugh for making this point to me.

11. Westminster Assembly, *Humble Advice of the Assembly*, 11.

just a convenience or an economy; it is a message about the body and the nature of our humanity and our status as image-bearers.

To be sure, there may be times when burial is simply impossible. In those cases, we must act like sojourners and make do, but just because some are forced by circumstances to a difficult and unhappy choice does not make that choice desirable or preferable. As we contemplate the last thing that will likely happen to our bodies, let us at least give some serious thought to the message we are sending about the body and its relation to the image and to human dignity rooted in the image of God. If cremation is unavoidable, we can at least arrange some clear testimony to the hope of the resurrection. If, however, cremation is just one option among many, then we must ask, are we, as much as lies within us, testifying to our hope of the bodily resurrection, or are we unintentionally sending another message? There is no question whether God can and shall reconstitute bodies at the resurrection; the question is, what message are we sending by our acts?

That Christ was buried for us is a source of Christian comfort. Ursinus writes Christ was buried "that we might not be terrified in view of the grave, but might know that he has sanctified our graves by his own burial, so that they are no longer graves to us, but chambers and resting places in which we may quietly and peacefully repose until we are again raised to life."[12]

Question 42

Since then Christ died for us, why must we also die?

Our death is not a satisfaction for our sin, but only a dying to sin and an entering into eternal life.[13]

Until the return of Christ, we all must die. One might ask, why? After all, has not Christ conquered death in his own death? Indeed, he has. Scripture says, "And one of the elders said to me, 'Weep no more;

12. Ursinus, *Commentary*, 225.

13. "Weil denn Christus für uns gestorben ist, wie kommt's, dass wir auch sterben müssen? Unser Tob ist nicht eine Bezahlung für unsere Sünde, sondern nur eine Absterbung der Sünden, und Eingang zum ewigen Leben" (Schaff, *Creeds of Christendom*, 3:320–21). "At cum Christus pro nobis

behold, the Lion of the tribe of Judah, the Root of David, has conquered, so that he can open the scroll and its seven seals'" (Rev 5:5 ESV). Paul celebrates that reality:

> But in fact Christ has been raised from the dead, the firstfruits of those who have fallen asleep. For as by a man came death, by a man has come also the resurrection of the dead. For as in Adam all die, so also in Christ shall all be made alive. But each in his own order: Christ the firstfruits, then at his coming those who belong to Christ. Then comes the end, when he delivers the kingdom to God the Father after destroying every rule and every authority and power. For he must reign until he has put all his enemies under his feet. The last enemy to be destroyed is death. (1 Cor 15:20–26 ESV)

Nevertheless, the resurrection of Christ was not the end of all things but the *beginning* of the end of all things. In his resurrection he inaugurated a new order, a new creation (2 Cor 5:17). The consummation of the new order is not yet. This is still the time for planting seeds in the ground (1 Cor 15:42). A principle is at work, but it is not yet fully realized. This is why Hebrews 9:27 says, "It is appointed for man once to die and then the judgment."

In contrast to New Age gurus, the Christian Science movement (i.e., the Church of Christ Scientist), theosophy, and gnostics of every sort, we affirm that death is real and not an illusion. Against the Platonists, we affirm that God created our bodies good (Gen 1:31). Created matter is not intrinsically evil or deficient. God's affirmation of its created goodness refutes all the pagan attempts to blame God for the corruption that is. He did not introduce it; we did. God is sovereign and superintends all things. His providence includes all things, yet he is it not the author of sin, death, and corruption. First, this is so because there is no sin, death, or corruption in him. Second, he did not sin. Third, he is righteous in all that he does. Fourth, Genesis says that we made a free, uncoerced choice. Fifth, Scripture always holds *us* liable for sin and death, and never God.

Death was the promised judgment and the sentence passed on sin: "The day you eat thereof you shall surely die" (Gen 2:17). Christ's death,

---

mortem oppetierit, cur nobis quoque moriendum est? Mors nostra non est pro peccatis nostris satisfactio, sed peccati abolitio, et transitus in vitam aeternam" (Niemeyer, *Collectio Confessionum*, 439).

however, has changed the meaning of our death. For everyone who is united to Christ by his Holy Spirit, by grace alone, through faith alone, our death cannot be a payment or a satisfaction to God's righteous judgment. Because Christ has satisfied God's righteous judgment, "there is therefore now no condemnation for those who are in Christ Jesus" (Rom 8:1).

Our death is not an act of justification but a part of our sanctification, a final step in our conformity to Christ and an entrance into our glorification (Rom 8:17, 30).[14] Christ has paid for our sins, and his perfect righteousness is imputed to believers so, "as far as it respects the guilt thereof, is taken away, but not as it respects the matter of sin which is not yet entirely abolished, but remains in us, to be removed gradually, that we may be required to exercise repentance, and be fervent in prayer, until, in the life to come, we be perfectly freed from all the remains of sin."[15] In that light it is appropriate to note that the Latin text of the catechism says that our death is not a satisfaction for sin but "the abrogation of sin" in our lives, and so it is.[16]

In this life, until we die, we struggle with sin. We have won the war, but our life is a series of battles to be fought against sin by grace alone, through faith alone, with the Spirit's help. Through these struggles he is bringing us into conformity to Christ. Through them, we come to see more clearly our utter dependence on Christ for his imputed righteousness and on the Spirit for his gracious work in us. Through them, we come to see more clearly what we, if left to ourselves, are and how righteous Christ is. Through them, however, we are also being given a love for his law, in true righteousness, in conformity to Christ.

At death the struggle with sin ends. As we journey toward glory we need not despise the remaining struggle. Though death is death, it is also life. There is no need to rush toward it, albeit some reason to respect it—it is the last enemy. Yet there is no need to fear it. Christ has gone through it for us, and we, by his grace, shall follow him (Heb 2:10; 12:2). His death is for us and our sin, and our death, in him, is to sin and a joining to him in his glory.

14. Olevian, *Firm Foundation*, 68–69.

15. Ursinus, *Commentary*, 226.

16. *Sed abolitio peccati* (Niemeyer, *Collectio Confessionum*, 439). Thanks to Harrison Perkins for calling my attention to this.

QUESTION 43

What further benefit do we receive from the sacrifice and death of Christ on the cross?

That thereby our old man is crucified, slain and buried with him, that so the evil lusts of the flesh may no more reign in us, but that we may offer ourselves unto him a sacrifice of thanksgiving.[17]

When Scripture illustrates the nature of the Christian life and sanctification, it uses two images: death and life. The natural covenant ("commandment of life"; *BC* 14),[18] made with Adam as the federal representative of all humanity, had in view everlasting life and blessedness with God. There was, however, a threatened curse: "The day you eat thereof you shall surely die" (Gen 2:17). Mysteriously, inexplicably, Adam chose death rather than life. He chose to enter into what Olevianus calls "a covenant of Satan."[19] After the fall, God came to him and promised a curse on the serpent and a Savior to fallen humanity:

> Because you have done this,
> cursed are you above all livestock
> and above all beasts of the field;
> on your belly you shall go,
> and dust you shall eat
> all the days of your life.
> I will put enmity between you and the woman,
> and between your offspring and her offspring;
> he shall bruise your head,
> and you shall bruise his heel. (Gen 3:14–15)

17. "Was bekommen wir mehr für Nutzen aus dem Opfer und Tod Christi am Kreuz? Dass durch seine Kraft unser alter Mensch mit Jhm gekreuziget, getödtet und begraben wird, auf dass die bösen Lüste des Fleisches nicht mehr in uns regieren, sondern dass wir uns selbst Jhm zur Danksagung aufopfern" (Schaff, *Creeds of Christendom*, 3:321). "Quid praeterea capimus commodi ex sacrificio et morte Christi? Quod virtute eius mortis vetus noster homo, una eum eo crucifigitur, interimitur, ac sepelitur, ne pravae cupiditates et desideria carnis posthac in nobis regnent, sed nos ipsos ei hostiam gratitudinis offeramus" (Niemeyer, *Collectio Confessionum*, 439).

18. See the discussion under *HC* 6.

19. *Foedus Satanae* (Olevianus, *De substantia* 2.8).

The Evil One was doomed. The eternal life promised originally in the tree of life, offered in the covenant of works, was to come, but the salvation to be brought by the seed of the woman would be costly. The serpent must strike his heel even as the seed of the woman triumphs over the serpent. After the fall, life comes through death. So it is with the Christian life. We live in Christ, but our Christian life begins with our identification with Christ's death.

In *HC* 43, we anticipate the teaching of the third part of the catechism (e.g., *HC* 88–90) and one of the great outcomes of his death: the sanctification of the believer. Not only should believers have confidence that God has freely accepted (justified) believers for Christ's sake alone and has saved us, is saving us, and shall save us by his favor alone (*sola gratia*), through faith alone (*sola fide*),[20] but by virtue of our union with Christ, we will also be conformed to the image of Christ (sanctified) and glorified.[21] This is just how Paul talks about our new life in Christ.

> For if we have been united with him in a death like his, we shall certainly be united with him in a resurrection like his. We know that our old self was crucified with him in order that the body of sin might be brought to nothing, so that we would no longer be enslaved to sin. For one who has died has been set free from sin. Now if we have died with Christ, we believe that we will also live with him. We know that Christ, being raised from the dead, will never die again; death no longer has dominion over him. For the death he died he died to sin, once for all, but the life he lives he lives to God. So you also must consider yourselves dead to sin and alive to God in Christ Jesus. (Rom 6:5–11 ESV)

Our renewal into the image of Christ happens only by God's grace, through a Spirit-wrought union with Christ, and that union happens only through faith, which is God's gift to his people (Eph 2:8–10). Those who

---

20. Ursinus, *Commentary*, 227.

21. Ursinus (e.g., *Commentary*, 227) and Olevianus regularly use the word "regeneration" in this context to mean "sanctification" or renewal into the image of Christ (Clark, *Caspar Olevian*, 184–89). After the conflict with the Remonstrants, Reformed theologians tended to reserve "regeneration" for the divinely-wrought spiritual awakening from death to life. Nevertheless, it continued to be used to refer to sanctification too.

have been united to Christ by the Spirit, through faith alone, "shall be united with him in a resurrection life like his," as Paul says (Rom 6:5). In other words, the Christian life is a dying to self and sin and living to Christ, but the outcome is a glorious resurrection—not because we have been good but because God is gracious and graciously at work in us. We are raised to glorification, which is the consummation of the good work that God began in us when he gave us new life and true faith (Phil 1:6). Christ's death puts to death the reigning power of sin (Rom 6:14). Believers have been delivered from its perpetual control.

This truth does not mean that we personally experience the full realization of this truth, but there is in us, by the Spirit, a principle of new life. Before we were united to Christ we were, spiritually speaking, dead people walking, zombies. Now, in Christ, the chains of death have been broken. By God's grace, by virtue of our union with Christ, we can resist sin (Jas 4:7; Rom 8:9). We can flee temptation (1 Cor 10:13). Zombies do not know they are zombies. Now, having been given new life, having been united to Christ, we are able to see what we were. We are able to see a real difference.

In Colossians Paul makes the same argument. He says, "In him also you were circumcised with a circumcision made without hands, by putting off the body of the flesh, by the circumcision of Christ, having been buried with him in baptism, in which you were also raised with him through faith in the powerful working of God, who raised him from the dead" (Col 2:11–12 ESV). We are "in Christ" by God's free favor, through faith alone, by the work of the Spirit. By virtue of that union, we "were circumcised," not physically but spiritually. The act of circumcision was about cutting away uncleanness. It was also a ritual death. Then Paul turns to baptism to illustrate the same truth. It too is a ritual death and the putting off of uncleanness (Heb 10:22; Titus 3:5). Circumcision and baptism are outward identifications with Christ. Circumcision looked forward to the death of Christ as he was cut off, as it were, for us.

As we meditate on Christ's death for us, we must always remember that, by virtue of our union with him, we also died with him. Because that is so, sin has been put to death in us and we are free, the Spirit helping us, to put to death the old man and to be made alive by the Spirit in the new man. In this life, our sanctification is always only inchoate, that is, it is always and only a small beginning, but it is a beginning.[22] We may now, in Paul's words, by God's mercies, offer ourselves to God as a "living sacrifice, holy and acceptable to God, which is your spiritual worship" (Rom 12:1 ESV).

Question 44

Why is it added: "he descended into hell"?

That in my greatest temptations I may be assured that Christ my lord, by his inexpressible anguish, pains and terrors, which he suffered in his soul on the cross and before, has redeemed me from the anguish and torment of hell.[23]

This part of the fifth article of the creed generates questions among the faithful. Some traditions hold that in this article Christians are confessing that our Lord, after his death, went to the place of the dead.[24] The Reformed churches, however, have understood it figuratively to refer to Christ's suffering. So Calvin and the *HC* interpret this clause.[25]

The *descendit* ("he descended") does not appear in Ignatius's summary of the faith, or in Irenaeus's rule of faith, or Tertullian's, or Lucian of

---

22. Olevianus writes of two parts of the "obedience of faith," the second of which is "sanctification or inchoate obedience" ("Altera pars est sanctificatio, sive inchoata obedientia"; *Romanos Notae*, 7).

23. "Warum folget: Abgestiegen zu der Hölle? Dass ich in meinen höchsten Anfechtungen versichert sei, mein Herr Christus habe mich durch seine unaussprechliche Augst, Schmerzen und Schrecken, die Er auch an seiner Seele am Kreuz und zuvor erlitten, von der höllischen Angst und Pein erlöset" (Schaff, *Creeds of Christendom*, 3:321). "Cur additur: Descendit ad inferna? Ut in summis doloribus et gravissimis tentationibus, me consolatione hac sustentem, quod Dominus meus Iesus Christus inenarrabilibus animi sui anguistiis, cruciatibus et terroribus, in quos cum antea, tum maxime in cruce pendens, fuerat demersus, me ab anguistiis et cruciatibus inferni liberaverit" (Niemeyer, *Collectio Confessionum*, 439).

24. *Formula of Concord*, art. 9, in Kolb and Wengert, *Book of Concord*, 514–15. See Scaer, "He Did Descend to Hell," 91–99. Rome confesses, "The crucified one sojourned in the realm of the dead prior to his resurrection" (*CCC* §632); art. 3 of the Anglican Articles (1571) affirms, "As Christ died for us, and was buried, so also is it to be believed, that He went down into Hell" (Schaff, *Creeds of Christendom*, 3:488; spelling modernized).

25. Calvin, *Institutes* 2.16.8–11.

Antioch's.[26] In Epiphanius, we see no reference to the descent of Christ.[27] In the Old Roman form of the creed (ca. AD 341), it does not appear.[28] Indeed, it did not appear until AD 390, in Rufinus's version of the creed.[29] It appears that, early on, *descendit* was used interchangeably with *sepultus* ("buried") and had the same meaning as late as the fourth century.[30] Thus, "he descended" was another way of saying, "he was buried."[31] Rufinus (AD 390) has *descendit in inferna*. The form used in the received text did not appear until AD 650 in the Sacramentarium Gallicanum.[32] By AD 750, however, the received form of the creed included both "he was buried" and "he descended into hell."[33] Thus, by that time, *descendit* was no longer being used to mean "buried," but rather it was used temporally and sequentially to mean "he went to the place of the dead" (in the reading *descendit ad inferos*).[34]

Olevianus flatly rejects the Roman Catholic doctrine of the *limbus patrum*, that is, the Roman doctrine that Old Testament believers, between death and the resurrection, are on the "fringes" (hence *limbus*) of hell.[35] As he notes, one root of this error of the Roman error of the *limbus* is another error, that the Old Testament believers did not already have full salvation *sola gratia, sola fide* because, as the doctrine went, Christ had not yet died. Scripture nowhere teaches the existence of a *limbus*.[36] Further, Psalm 32:1

---

26. Ignatius, *To the Traillians* 9:1–2; Irenaeus, *Against Heresies* 1.10.1; 3.4.1–2; 4.33.7; Tertullian, *De virginitate 1;* Lucian of Antioch, *Epistle de synodis arimini.*

27. Schaff, *Creeds of Christendom*, 2:33–38.

28. Schaff, *Creeds of Christendom*, 2:47.

29. Schaff, *Creeds of Christendom*, 2:49.

30. As late as the late fourth and early fifth centuries, some versions used *sepultus*, and others used *descendit*. Rufinus explained ca. 410: "§18. They who have handed down the Creed to us have with much forethought specified the time when these things were done—'under Pontius Pilate,'—lest in any respect the tradition should falter, as though vague and uncertain. But it should be known that the clause, 'He descended into Hell,' is not added in the Creed of the Roman Church, neither is it in that of the Oriental Churches. It seems to be implied, however, when it is said that 'He was buried'" (*Commentary on the Apostles' Creed, NPNF* 2/3:550).

31. Olevianus, *Exposition*, 87.

32. Schaff, *Creeds of Christendom*, 3:54.

33. Schaff, *Creeds of Christendom*, 3:54.

34. There is a link between chiliasm (belief in a literal thousand-year reign of Christ on the earth) and the Christian adoption of the doctrine of a "subterranean intermediate state." See Hill, *Regnum Caelorum*, 245–48.

35. Olevianus, *Exposition*, 86–87; CCC §§634–35. On the alleged *limbus infantum*, see Turretin, *Institues of Elenctic Theology*, 12.11; Berkhof, *Systematic Theology*, 687–88.

36. Ursinus, *Commentary*, 229.

implies not only that David's sins were forgiven but that he knew he had forgiveness of sins "through trust in the sacrifice of Christ."[37] Our Lord taught us that Abraham is already in heaven (Matt 8:11).

On the cross our Lord said, "Today you shall be with me in paradise" (Luke 23:43).[38] Further, 1 Peter 3:18–20 leads us away from thinking that Christ went, after his death, to the place of the dead:

> Because Christ also suffered for sins once, the just in place of the unjust, in order that, after being put to death in the flesh and being made alive in the Spirit, he might bring us to God. In whom Christ went and proclaimed to the spirits in prison, who, once upon a time, were disobedient, when the patience of God waited, in the days of Noah, when the ark was being constructed, in which a few, that is, eight souls, were saved through the water.

Peter's intent is to remind believers to conduct themselves as those whom Christ has redeemed. The basis for the exhortation is that Christ suffered not as a sinner or a lawbreaker but as the righteous one, as the substitute. As Peter says, "the just in place of the unjust." He did so "in the flesh," but he was raised from the dead by the Holy Spirit. Peter is not teaching that Jesus was made alive by the Holy Spirit in his bodily resurrection. The first phrase in 1 Peter 3:19, "in whom," refers back to the Holy Spirit: "*in whom* he went" (ἐν ᾧ). Jesus went in the Holy Spirit, not in his soul or bodily. Where did he go "in the Spirit"? To the souls who were in prison. Where and when were these souls in prison? In the days of Noah.[39]

Peter's point here, which he also makes in 2 Peter 2:5, is that our time is just like Noah's. He is drawing on the analogy that Jesus had made between our time and Noah's, "as it was in the days of Noah" (Luke 17:26). Just as Jesus, by the Spirit, was preaching to the world through Noah, so too he is preaching now to the world through the apostle Peter and the other ministers. The prison to which Peter refers is metaphorical. There is no hint of a subterranean intermediate state or of a *limbus*. The entire scene that Peter gives us takes place in the days of Noah. "Prison" is a figurative way to refer to those who were facing impending judgment. Just as

---

37. Olevianus, *Exposition*, 87.

38. Ursinus, *Commentary*, 229.

39. Ursinus, *Commentary*, 230.

the world was disobedient and faced a cataclysmic judgment, so too our world faces an even greater and final judgment.

We may be sure of the parallel since, in the subsequent verses, Peter argues that baptism is a witness to this reality. Just as Noah and the others were saved in the midst of (not by) the floodwaters of judgment, so we, in our baptism, have been identified with Jesus's passage through those waters, as it were, on the cross. We who believe should be confident that he has endured it all and in that confidence live as those who have been redeemed. There is nothing in this passage about Jesus going to the place of the dead or to the dead ones. That notion arose because of the influence of pagan ideas that were adopted by Christians and synthesized with Christian doctrine.

Some have advocated that, since we do not believe that Christ went to the place of the dead, we should remove that clause from the creed. Others have defended retaining it.[40] The Reformed retain the clause but have understood it to refer to Christ's sufferings. The original sense was merely "buried." Certainly, the truth we confess is vital: Jesus did certainly endure the "anguish, pains and terrors" of hell before his crucifixion and on the cross. He did so not for any macabre reason but as a satisfaction of God's justice.[41]

One aspect of Christ's suffering on the cross is that he was forsaken by God for us, which raises the question of how that could be. Olevianus answers:

> Christ is truly God and truly human. He had to be forsaken by God for a time in His human nature in such a way that His divine nature did not show forth its power; it "rested," as the ancients put it. This was so that what God had said through the prophets might be fulfilled: "God was pleased to bruise him with weakness, that he give his soul as an offering for sin" [Isa. 53:10]. Therefore, Christ was forsaken by God for a time in order that we might be reconciled with God and never be forsaken by Him (Heb. 5:7).[42]

---

40. Olevianus, *Exposition*, 88–91; Ursinus, *Commentary*, 230–32; Hyde, *In Defense of the Descent*.

41. See the discussion under *HC* 40.

42. Olevian, *Firm Foundation*, 71.

The answer lies in the mystery of the two natures in the one person of Christ, who was forsaken for us *in his human nature*. God the Son could never be and was never separated from the Father and the Spirit, nor was he separated from humanity, even on the cross and in the tomb, even though in death we must say that his body and soul were temporarily separated.[43] Here, of course, we have entered into great mysteries.

Christ's active suffering is a part of the ground of our assurance. When we are tempted, we ought to think of Jesus's suffering. The assumption seems to be that we do not always resist temptation, which of course resonates with Christian experience (Rom 7:7–25; *HC* 60, 114–15). As we struggle with sin, however, it is of the greatest value to remember and to meditate on Christ's sufferings, because even as we struggle we are also tempted to think that God no longer loves us, and that lie leads only to more sin. In *HC* 44, we confess that Christ suffered hell on the cross *for us* so that in our temptations (*Anfechtungen*) we must rest in the assurance that Christ has quenched the fires of hell for us.[44]

Jesus did not endure what he did, which we are not able to articulate or understand fully, so that we might be lost or continue in sin (Rom 6:1). He did not suffer and die to make it possible that we might be saved but to accomplish salvation for those who, of themselves, even with the help of grace, are helpless. If our salvation depends even the littlest on our cooperation, then to the degree our cooperation is imperfect, to that degree we are unsaved. Jesus did it all. That is why we say "redeemed." We have been saved. We are being saved now, and we shall be saved. We have been purchased. This is the basic truth of *HC* 1: "What is your only comfort in life and in death?" We say, "That I, with body and soul, both in life and in death, am not my own" (1 Cor 6:20; 7:23; Luke 1:68; Gal

43. Olevianus explicitly denied the doctrine of "soul sleep" and taught Christ's "soul did not rest in the grave, nor did it go about on the earth. Rather, as soon as it separated from its body, it traveled to that place where the souls of believers who are severed from their bodies live in joy and happiness, namely, Paradise (Luke 23[:43])" (*Firm Foundation*, 73–74).

44. In his preface to his German works, Luther writes, "Thirdly, there is *tentatio*, *Anfechtung*. This is the touchstone which teaches you not only to know and understand, but also to experience how right, how true, how sweet, how lovely, how mighty, how comforting God's Word is, wisdom beyond all wisdom" (*LW* 34:286–87). The German noun *Anfechtungen* includes more than temptation (*tentatio*) to sin. It includes anxiety, fear, doubt, depression, and even terror. It was an important category in Luther's work, and his use almost certainly lies behind its use here. See Scaer, "Concept of *Anfechtung*," 15–30; Janz, "To Hell (and Back)," 41–55; Oberman, *Luther*, 175–79.

3:13). We have been purchased body and soul by our Lord Jesus, who suffered in our place, as our substitute, our representative, and the suffering Savior (Isa 53:10). He is our Mediator. He stands before the Father now perfectly righteous, with the scars on his hands and back, and those most eloquent marks say it all.

As we struggle against sin, as we seek to die to self and to live to Christ, as we seek, by God's grace alone, through faith alone, in union with Christ, to be conformed to his image, we do so with the confidence that all that justice required for our sins has been paid. No outstanding debt remains. Hell has no claim on us. When we are tempted that we have transgressed beyond the limits of grace, we ought to remember our suffering Savior. The believer's salvation is not lost. It is as certain as the empty tomb and the scars on the true, glorified humanity of our Lord Jesus.

QUESTION 45

What benefit do we receive from the "resurrection" of Christ?

Lord's Day 17

QUESTION 45

What benefit do we receive from the "resurrection" of Christ?

First, by his resurrection he has overcome death, that he might make us partakers of the righteousness which he has earned for us by his death. Secondly, by his power we are also now raised up to a new life. Thirdly, the resurrection of Christ is to us a sure pledge of our blessed resurrection.[1]

There are benefits to living in modernity. We may doubt whether the benefits we experience are *due* to modernity, but it is true that in the modern period we captured electricity, improved medicine, and set loose the digital revolution. The technological developments of the modern period have given rise to a kind of arrogance and fueled the notion that we live in a closed world. In *HC* 45, however, we are confronted with a truth that challenges such assumptions. The last part of the fifth article of the creed claims that Jesus of Nazareth was dead and was made alive by the operation of the Holy Spirit. Scripture says that his body was placed in a tomb hewn out of stone and that the tomb was closed by means of a great stone (Luke 23:53). Matthew writes: "And Joseph took the body and wrapped it in a clean linen shroud and laid it in his own new tomb, which he had cut in the rock. And he rolled a great stone to the entrance of the tomb and went away. Mary Magdalene and the other Mary were there, sitting opposite the tomb" (Matt 27:59–61 ESV).

Not only was he dead, laid in a tomb that was blocked with a stone, but Pilate ordered that the tomb be sealed, thus making it a capital crime against Caesar to tamper with it, and the tomb was guarded by highly trained soldiers whose very lives were at stake should his body be stolen

1. "Was nützet uns die Anferstehung Christi? Erstlich hat Er durch seine Auferstehung den Tod überwunden, dass Er uns der Gerechtigkeit, die Er uns durch seinen Tod erworben hat, könnte theilhaftig machen. Zum andern werden auch wir jetzt durch seine Kraft erwecket zu einem neuen Leben. Zum britten ist uns die Auferstehung Christi ein gewisses Pfand unferer feligen Auferstehung" (Schaff, *Creeds of Christendom,* 3:321–22); "Quid nobis prodest resurrectio Christi? Primum sua resurrectione mortem devicit, ut nos posset eius iustitiae, quam nobis sua morte pepererat, participes facere. Deinde, nos iam quoque eius potentia ad novam vitam excitamur. Postremo, resurrectio capitis nostri Christi, nobis gloriosae resurrectionis nostrae pignus est" (Niemeyer, *Collectio Confessionum,* 439–40).

(Matt 27:65–66). After Jesus was raised (to which we will return), some of the guards, knowing their great jeopardy,

> went into the city and told the chief priests all that had taken place. And when they had assembled with the elders and taken counsel, they gave a sufficient sum of money to the soldiers and said, "Tell people, 'His disciples came by night and stole him away while we were asleep.' And if this comes to the governor's ears, we will satisfy him and keep you out of trouble." So they took the money and did as they were directed. And this story has been spread among the Jews to this day. (Matt 28:11–15 ESV)

Conspiracy theories are notoriously unreliable, but in this case, under the inspiration of the Spirit, Matthew reports a cover-up of Jesus's resurrection. The authorities lied about what actually happened to Jesus's body.

That Jesus was raised from the dead is the cornerstone of the Christian faith. Indeed, the apostle Paul says that if Christ has not has not been raised from the dead, "we are, of all people, most to be pitied," because our entire faith rests on this historical claim (1 Cor 15:19). The resurrection in view, about which the Jewish authorities lied, which Paul proclaimed to be the essential to the Christian religion, was an objective fact, not a subjective experience. The Scriptures will permit none of this. They know nothing of a subjective reality that is true for you but not for me.

> But on the first day of the week, at early dawn, they went to the tomb, taking the spices they had prepared. And they found the stone rolled away from the tomb, but when they went in they did not find the body of the Lord Jesus. While they were perplexed about this, behold, two men stood by them in dazzling apparel. And as they were frightened and bowed their faces to the ground, the men said to them, "Why do you seek the living among the dead? He is not here, but has risen. Remember how he told you, while he was still in Galilee, that the Son of Man must be delivered into the hands of sinful men and be crucified and on the third day rise." (Luke 24:1–7 ESV)

The tomb to which the women and disciples went was not a metaphor. It was an empty tomb, the reality of which they experienced with their senses. Scripture assumes the validity and general reliability of human sense experience. It is within that framework that we must understand the biblical claims about the historical, literal reality of Jesus's bodily resurrection. The Gospels and Acts record numerous pieces of evidence that Jesus was in fact raised bodily from the dead. "Mary Magdalene and the other Mary went to see the tomb" (Matt 28:1), and Joanna (Luke 24:10) found the empty tomb on Sunday morning. As they ran to tell the disciples, they met Jesus, who greeted them (Matt 28:9). The eleven disciples saw him (Matt 28:17). Paul adds, "He appeared to Cephas, then to the twelve. Then he appeared to more than five hundred brothers at one time, most of whom are still alive, though some have fallen asleep. Then he appeared to James, then to all the apostles. Last of all, as to one untimely born, he appeared also to me. For I am the least of the apostles" (1 Cor 15:5–9 ESV). The entire Christian faith rests on the objective reality of the resurrection. That reality has objective consequences for believers. Our catechism calls these consequences *benefits*.

The first benefit is that Christ has overcome death. The Latin text of the catechism says that Jesus has "subdued" (*devicit*) death.[2] The nature of human existence has been changed. To the moment when the women found the resurrected Christ, humans had been in bondage to death. The promised sanction of the covenant of works was, "The day you eat thereof you shall surely die" (Gen 2:17). We sinned and died. Believers thereafter planted bodies in the ground, as it were, in anticipation of the resurrection, but it was a hope that was only realized on that Sunday morning. Only in that quiet, confusing moment were the hopes of all the believers hitherto vindicated and validated. Jesus overturned the curse of death that we brought on ourselves. Death took him as a victim, but death could not keep him.[3] It is to this victory that Paul refers when asks rhetorically, "Death, where is your sting?" (1 Cor 15:55).

Jesus's resurrection was his vindication. It demonstrated that he was actually, legally, morally, spiritually, inherently, perfectly righteous. He did not die to pay for his sins because he had none. He obeyed and died as our substitute, as payment for our sins. By his resurrection his righteousness

2. Olevian, *Firm Foundation*, 73.

3. Olevianus, *Exposition*, 93.

was confirmed. This is what Paul means in 1 Timothy 3:16 when he says "vindicated by the Spirit." The Spirit was operating in Jesus's resurrection, in which he, Jesus, was vindicated. In his vindication, the demonstration of his righteousness is our justification.[4] "But the words 'it was counted to him' were not written for his sake alone, but for ours also. It will be counted to us who believe in him who raised from the dead Jesus our Lord, who was delivered up for our trespasses and raised for our justification" (Rom 4:23–25).

Believers—those who, by God's free favor, through faith alone, by the Spirit are united to Christ—are as justified as Jesus is vindicated. His righteousness is now ours. It is as if believers have done all that Jesus did, and all that he did is credited to us (*HC* 60). This is how Paul interprets Genesis 15:6, "Abraham believed God and it was credited to him for righteousness." The "it" there does not refer to Abraham's faith—an unworthy ground of justification—but to Jesus the Righteous One, the object of Abraham's faith (John 8:56). Our faith does nothing but unite us to Christ, who has done all *for us*. Notice, too, that Jesus is said to have "earned" (*erworben*) righteousness for us.[5] This is the language of commerce and law. This is tied to our doctrine that Jesus is the last Adam, who obeyed and died as our substitute (Rom 5:12–21). He was raised to be our Mediator.[6]

Here is an essential distinction between the Savior and the saved. Jesus earned our righteousness by his obedience. We receive it through faith alone (*sola fide*) in Jesus and his righteousness. We are beneficiaries of what Christ has done for us, and all those benefits are signaled by his bodily resurrection.

It is one thing to consider the accomplishment of our justification, that is, our righteous status before God and our salvation, but how do we benefit from it? Calvin addresses this problem well:

> We must now examine this question. How do we receive those benefits which the Father bestowed on his only-begotten Son—not for Christ's own private use, but that he might enrich poor and needy

4. Olevian, *Firm Foundation*, 72; Olevianus, *Exposition*, 94; Ursinus, *Commentary*, 237.
5. Ursinus (*Commentary*, 238–39) stresses Christ's condign merit earned for us.
6. Ursinus, *Commentary*, 235–36.

> men? First, we must understand that as long as Christ remains outside of us, and we are separated from him, all that he has suffered and done for the salvation of the human race remains useless and of no value for us. Therefore, to share with us what he has received from the Father, he had to become ours and to dwell within us.[7]

It is the Spirit who unites us to Christ. The instrument of that Spirit-worked union with Christ is faith. The Spirit works through the Word to give us new life, raising us from death to life by his sovereign power.[8] Those to whom he gives new life, he gives faith, and through that faith we receive Christ and his benefits. The whole complex is God's gift. Paul says, "But what does it say? 'The word is near you, in your mouth and in your heart' (that is, the word of faith that we proclaim); because, if you confess with your mouth that Jesus is Lord and believe in your heart that God raised him from the dead, you will be saved. For with the heart one believes and is justified, and with the mouth one confesses and is saved" (Rom 10:8–10 ESV). This is why our catechism speaks of Christ's benefits, that is, those good things that Christ has earned for us and freely gives to us.

The second benefit we receive from all that Jesus did for us is our new life. Christ Jesus confronted Nicodemus with the stark reality of our desperate need for new life: "Truly, truly, I say to you, unless one is born again he cannot see the kingdom of God" (John 3:3 ESV).[9] Embedded in that phrase "born again" (γεννηθῇ ἄνωθεν) is the idea that we must also be born "from above." The word "again" may also be translated "from above." The phrase is inherently ambiguous by intent. We must be born again, but it only happens from above. Only the Spirit brings new life, as Jesus says in his discourse with Nicodemus. The same power by which God raised Jesus's body from the dead is operating in bringing dead sinners to new life: "For as the Father raises the dead and gives them life, so also the Son gives life to whom he will" (John 5:21 ESV).

Notice how Jesus moves from bodily resurrection to "new life." Paul says, "Just as Christ was raised from the dead by the glory of the Father,

7. Calvin, *Institutes* 3.1.1.

8. Calvin, *Exposition*, 96–97.

9. Olevian, *Firm Foundation*, 73.

we too might walk in newness of life" (Rom 6:4 ESV). By virtue of our new life and our union with Christ, we are "a new creation" (2 Cor 5:17). We were "dead in sins and trespasses" (Eph 2:1), and now, by God's marvelous favor earned for us by Christ and freely bestowed on us, we have been "made alive together with Christ" (Eph 2:5). Paul repeatedly associates our new life (regeneration) with Christ's resurrection. That is how he is able to say, "If then you have been raised with Christ, seek the things that are above, where Christ is, seated at the right hand of God" (Col 3:1 ESV). By God's free, sovereign grace, we have been given new life, we have been raised. We are united to Christ, by the Spirit, through faith, and we are seated with him. Those are objective facts, but they make all the subjective difference in the world.

Here we are also addressing the topic of eschatology, or last things and the end times. There is some distinction between last things and end times. The latter refers to a specific set of events in the future. Last things, however, is more inclusive. It includes things that have already happened, that are now, and that shall be. In that sense, "eschatology" refers to heaven and the study of the relations between the final state of things and history. The apostle John speaks about eschatology this way. When he writes, "The law came through Moses but grace and truth came through Jesus Christ" (John 1:17), he is teaching us an eschatology, a way of thinking and speaking about the relationship between heaven and earth. What Moses brought, to the degree it was distinctly Mosaic, was temporary, provisional. It had built-in obsolescence. It was never meant to be permanent. To be sure, some of what came through Moses was intended to be permanent. Because it is grounded in God's nature and revealed in nature, the moral law given at Sinai is permanent. Indeed, all the narratives and laws are God's word, and they always have something to teach us, but the judicial and ceremonial laws were never intended to be permanently binding on us. They had a specific function that was fulfilled in Christ. Thus, our Lord explained, "Truly, truly, I say to you, it was not Moses who gave you the bread from heaven, but my Father gives you the true bread from heaven" (John 6:32 ESV). Notice how Jesus identified the "true bread" with that which is from heaven. As Geerhardus Vos (1862–1949) explained in 1927, *true* and *truth* in John do not always refer to true as distinct from false but sometimes to heavenly as distinct from provisional.[10]

Eschatology also speaks to those events that are associated with the end of all things. Nothing is more essential to the end times than the resurrection of Christ and our resurrection. With Jesus's death and resurrection, the end was inaugurated. Jesus said, "Now is the judgment of this world; now will the ruler of this world be cast out" (John 12:31 ESV). Thus, Hebrews 1:2 calls our time "these last days" (ἐσχάτου τῶν ἡμερῶν τούτων). James 5:3 says that believers have "stored up treasure in the last days." First Peter 1:20 says that Jesus was revealed "in the last times" (ἐπ' ἐσχάτου τῶν χρόνων). According to 2 Peter 3:3, the scoffing he was seeing already in the early 60s AD was an indication that we live in "the last days." In 1 John 2:18 it is said already to be "the last hour" (ἐσχάτη ὥρα). Nevertheless, according to 1 Peter 1:5, there is still an end to be realized. We might call this an inaugurated or semirealized eschatology.[11]

The third benefit of Christ's resurrection is that it promises that we too shall also be bodily, literally raised at the last day.[12] Scripture is marvelously clear about this. Our Lord repeatedly affirmed the bodily resurrection. When the Sadducees tried to trap him on the nature of postresurrection existence, he denied the false premise of the question while affirming the bodily resurrection (Matt 22:22–33). He raised Lazarus by the power of his word (John 11:43). It became a well-known fact that Lazarus had been raised from the dead (John 12:9). There were bodily resurrections at the moment of Christ's death:

> And behold, the curtain of the temple was torn in two, from top to bottom. And the earth shook, and the rocks were split. The tombs also were opened. And many bodies of the saints who had fallen asleep were raised, and coming out of the tombs after his resurrection they went into the holy city and appeared to many. When the centurion and those who were with him, keeping watch over Jesus,

10. Vos, "'True' and 'Truth.'"

11. Historic amillennialism should be distinguished sharply from the error of Hymenaeus et al. (1 Tim 1:20; 2 Tim 2:17), who taught that Jesus had already returned. This is the heresy (i.e., the contradiction of the ecumenical creeds) of full preterism.

12. Olevian, *Firm Foundation*, 73; Ursinus, *Commentary*, 239–40.

> saw the earthquake and what took place, they were filled with awe and said, "Truly this was the Son of God!" (Matt 27:51–54 ESV)

These were hints of what is to come. There is an entire chapter of Scripture devoted to the reality of our future bodily resurrection. Christ's resurrection was the "firstfruits" (1 Cor 15:20) of the future resurrection. When Christ returns bodily, visibly, audibly (not secretly), the dead in Christ shall rise (1 Thess 4:16), and then those who are alive will be taken up to meet our returning King as he descends. The angel promised that Jesus would return as he was seen rising (Acts 1:11). After the resurrection, the Son will deliver the consummated kingdom to his Father (1 Cor 15:23).

We must affirm that our bodies that are buried are the same bodies in which we shall be raised. They change, but it is not the sort of change that is sometimes imagined. They are sown perishable and raised "Spiritual" (1 Cor 15:42). The *S* in "spiritual" should be capitalized. The word does not mean "immaterial" but "conformed to the Holy Spirit" or conformed to the realm of the Holy Spirit. This is the very state of existence of which Jesus spoke when he distinguished between that which is true or heavenly and that which is provisional or temporary. Our bodies will be human, finite, and glorified. We will be as we were intended to be had we passed the covenant of works. We will be as our Lord Jesus is. We know that after the resurrection one of the women grabbed him, Thomas touched him (John 20:27–28), and he ate (Luke 24:43). His humanity is real, not apparent—that is, we do not become docetists about his humanity because of the resurrection. "Spiritual" refers to the putting on of immortality (1 Cor 15:53). We will be raised. It is as certain as Jesus's resurrection. It is as certain as the empty tomb.

Question 46
How do you understand the words: “he ascended into heaven”?

Question 47
Is Christ then not with us even unto the end of the world, as he has promised?

Question 48
Since his human nature is not present wherever his deity is, are not then these two natures in Christ separated from one another?

Question 49
What benefit do we receive from Christ’s ascension into heaven?

Lord's Day 18

Question 46

How do you understand the words: "he ascended into heaven"?

That Christ, in the sight of his disciples, was taken up from the earth into heaven; and continues there in our behalf until he shall come again to judge the living and the dead.[1]

Being separated from a family member, dear friend, or a mentor is never easy. Whether through death, relocation, or some other reason, when we suffer such a loss, the grief is genuine. The disciples experienced that grief in stages. When Mary realized that the fellow with whom she was speaking was our Lord himself, she cried "*Rabboni!*" (teacher) and took hold of his feet (Matt 28:9). To this Jesus said, "Do not cling to me, for I have not yet ascended to the Father; but go to my brothers and say to them, 'I am ascending to my Father and your Father, to my God and your God'" (John 20:17–18 ESV).

The joy of discovering Jesus's resurrection was quickly muted by our Lord's announcement of his coming ascension and separation from them. After our Lord had taught his disciples about their vocation to give testimony about Jesus, about his obedient suffering, his death, and his resurrection, he ascended bodily right before their eyes. Scripture says: "And when he had said these things, as they were looking on, he was lifted up, and a cloud took him out of their sight. And while they were gazing into heaven as he went, behold, two men stood by them in white robes, and said, 'Men of Galilee, why do you stand looking into heaven? This Jesus, who was taken up from you into heaven, will come in the same way as you saw him go into heaven'" (Acts 1:9–11 ESV). Our Lord Jesus is one person with two distinct, inseparable natures.[2] Each of those natures retains its natural properties. His humanity did not become divinity (deity), and

1. "Wie verftechst du [diess], dass Er ist gen Himmel gefahren? Dass Christus vor den Augen seiner Jünger ist von der Erde aufgehoben gen Himmel, und uns zu gut daselbst ist, bis dass Er wiederkommt zu richten die Lebendigen und die Todten" (Schaff, *Creeds of Christendom*, 3:322). "Quomodo intelligis illud: Ascendit ad coelos? Quod aspicientibus discipulis, Christus de terra in coelum sublatus est, atque etiamnum nostra causa ibidem est, et erit, donec redeat ad iudicandum vivos et mortuos" (Niemeyer, *Collectio Confessionum*, 440).

2. See the discussion under *HC* 17.

his deity (Godhead) did not become humanity. That is the catholic faith confessed by all Christians in all times and places, as summarized by the Definition of Chalcedon (451). Those two natures are united in one person "inconfusedly, unchangeably, indivisibly, inseparably; the distinction of natures being by no means taken away by the union, but rather the property of each nature being preserved, and concurring in one Person and one Subsistence, not parted or divided into two persons, but one and the same Son, and only begotten, God the Word, the Lord Jesus Christ."[3] Thus, Jesus's ascension before the eyes of the disciples was no parlor trick or illusion. Their senses were reporting the truth. His body actually ascended before them until he disappeared from sight. His body was in one local place and then, after a bit, in another local place. There was a genuine separation. The disciples were puzzled, perplexed, and surely grieved by this turn of events. A great victory, the resurrection, suddenly must have seemed like a great loss. This is why the two white-robed "men" attending our Lord's ascension remonstrated with them, "Why do you stand looking into heaven?"

Why did Jesus go away from his disciples? To what benefit? After Jesus's resurrection, the disciples were thinking that it must be the time to "restore the kingdom to Israel" (Acts 1:6). They were still thinking in the wrong categories. They did not understand the nature of the kingdom of God. With Christ's death, the period of redemptive history in which God's saving work was largely confined to a national people came to a close. Now, Christ's people are no longer confined to a single nation, under a single earthly king, in a single location. Now, the advent of the kingdom is to be announced to all the nations (v. 7), but only after the Holy Spirit has been poured out at Pentecost.

Jesus had to leave them bodily in order to apply to the elect the redemption he had accomplished by his suffering obedience and death. Now his office is to act as our Mediator before the Father. Hebrews says: "Therefore he is the mediator of a new covenant, so that those who are called may receive the promised eternal inheritance" (Heb 9:15 ESV). Whereas the old covenant saints under Moses, the mediator of the old covenant, had come to a mountain of fire, smoke, and terror, in the new

3. Schaff, *Creeds of Christendom*, 2:63.

covenant we have come to a mountain that no human or animal can touch. We have come to Zion, the heavenly Jerusalem, rejoicing angels, "the assembly of the firstborn who are enrolled in heaven," to Jesus the Mediator of the new and better covenant (Heb 12:23). He is our perfect, Melchizedekian high priest who has the power of an indestructible life (Heb 7:16). We have an intercessor before God, which makes all the difference for believers: "Who shall bring any charge against God's elect? It is God who justifies. Who is to condemn? Christ Jesus is the one who died—more than that, who was raised—who is at the right hand of God, who indeed is interceding for us" (Rom 8:33–34 ESV).

Jesus must be absent from us now in order to represent us before the Father. It is this same Jesus, the angels announced, who will return. Just as the disciples saw him ascend, so we will all see him return bodily. How it is possible for people at different points on the globe see a single event at the same time is difficult to say. How was the Lord able to part the Red Sea (or the Sea of Reeds) and drown the Egyptians in it? How was the Noachian flood able to destroy the world that then was (2 Pet 3:6)? How was God able to speak creation into existence by the power of his word? That is why we speak of supernatural or miraculous acts. God is capable of doing such things. If we understood all that he did, he would not be God, and we would not be his creatures. We must be content to wait and see.

Because he is ascended, he has poured out his Holy Spirit on all his people. With his ascension come a number of blessings. Charles Hodge summarizes these blessings in four points:

1. In the first place He came from heaven. Heaven was his home. It was the appropriate sphere of his existence. His presence makes heaven, and therefore until this earth is purified from all evil, and has undergone its great process of regeneration, so as to become a new heavens and a new earth, this world is not suited for the Redeemer's abode in his state of exaltation.

2. It was necessary that as our High Priest He should, after offering Himself as a sacrifice, pass through the heavens, to appear before God in our behalf. An essential part, and that a permanent one, of his priestly office was to be exercised in

heaven. He there makes constant intercession for his people. As He died for our sins, He rose for our justification. All this was typified under the old dispensation. The victim was slain without in the court of the temple; the high priest bore the blood with much incense within the veil and sprinkled it on the Mercy Seat. What the high priest did in the earthly temple, it was necessary for the High Priest of our profession to do in the temple made without hands, eternal in the heavens. This is set forth with all clearness in the Epistle to the Hebrews.

3. It was expedient, our Lord said, that He should go away; "for if I go not away, the Comforter will not come unto you; but if I depart, I will send him unto you." (John 16:7.) It was necessary that redemption should not only be acquired but applied. Men if left to themselves would have remained in their sins, and Christ had died in vain. The great blessing which the prophets predicted as characteristic of the Messianic period, was the effusion of the Holy Spirit. To secure that blessing for the Church his ascension was necessary. He was exalted to give repentance and the remission of sins; to gather his people from all nations and during all ages until the work was accomplished. His throne in the heavens was the proper place whence the work of saving men, through the merits of his death, was to be carried on.

4. Again our Lord told his sorrowing disciples, "I go to prepare a place for you. And if I go and prepare a place for you, I will come again and receive you unto myself; that where I am, there ye may be also." (John 14:2, 3) His ascension, therefore, was necessary for the completion of His work.[4]

Our Lord Jesus is separated from us bodily, but he is as near to us as the Spirit and the word. "But what does it say? 'The word is near you,

4. Hodge, *Systematic Theology*, 2:634–35.

in your mouth and in your heart' (that is, the word of faith that we proclaim)" (Rom 10:8 ESV).

Just a few years before *HC* was drafted, the gnesio-Lutheran theologians had declared their doctrine of the "majestic genus" (*genus maiestaticum*).[5] This doctrine held that, as a result of the incarnation, Christ's humanity was transformed by personal union with his deity. They charged the Reformed with Nestorianism (i.e., turning the two natures into two persons) and blaspheming Christ's majesty. According to Lutheran theologian Johannes Brenz (1499–1570), the Logos cannot be said, after the incarnation, ever to have worked beyond Christ's humanity. Jacob Andrae (1528–1590) argued that Christ's humanity was, with his deity, omnipresent and immense, even when Christ was *in utero* in the Virgin Mary. This, of course, was a version of the Lutheran doctrine of the ubiquity of Christ's humanity.[6]

As a pastoral matter, to the degree the presence of Christ with his people had been cast in terms of the ubiquity of Christ's humanity and that Christ must necessarily be bodily in, with, or under the elements of the Lord's Supper, the Reformed had to explain and persuade the Christians in the Palatinate that Christ is with us by the power of his Holy Spirit and that he does truly feed us with his body and blood, but he does so by the mysterious operation of the Spirit, through faith. So, Olevianus, Ursinus, and the rest of the Reformed had to reiterate the Chalcedonian distinction between the two natures. Olevianus taught that Christ's deity, being omnipresent, was always in heaven, at the right hand of the Father.[7] When Christ ascended bodily, it was the fulfillment of Psalm 110:1.[8] Now, as the Christ, the incarnate Savior, he had acceded to his royal throne to begin building his spiritual kingdom. "For in Him both God and man are one person: both are the one Jesus Christ, who is omnipresent insofar as He is God, but only in heaven insofar as He is human. This is the

---

5. The adjective *gnesio* means "genuine," from the Greek adjective γνήσιος. It was used to distinguish the allegedly legitimate heirs of Luther from others. On the relationship between the Reformed and Luther, see Clark, "'Subtle Sacramentarian' or Son?," 35–60. On the *genus maiestaticum* and Olevianus's response, see Clark, *Caspar Olevian*, 107–31.

6. Ursinus, *Commentary*, 245. Under *HC* 46 Ursinus uses the term *ubiquitarii* (Reuter, *D. Zachariae Ursini*, 1:184).

7. Olevianus, *Exposition*, 101.

8. Olevianus, *Exposition*, 100; Ursinus, *Commentary*, 243–44.

confession of the Christian Church, according to the simple understanding of the Articles of the Christian Faith."[9] According to Olevianus, the doctrine of the ubiquity of Christ's humanity is a contradiction of the creed. We might add that it reduces the ascension, the first clause of the sixth article of the creed, to a figure of speech.

We confess, however, that Jesus truly comes to us in the preached gospel and in the gospel made visible in the sacraments. We are truly united to him by his Holy Spirit, and he is returning. The separation we experience now is not permanent. Even so, come, Lord Jesus (Rev 22:20).

Question 47

Is Christ then not with us even unto the end of the world, as he has promised?

Christ is true man and true God. According to his human nature he is now not on earth, but according to his deity, majesty, grace, and Spirit, he is at no time absent from us.[10]

As we emphasize the reality of Jesus's bodily ascension, we must make sure that we do not create the impression that Christians are orphans. We are not. Nevertheless, there are certain mysterious truths of the Christian faith that believing, catholic Christians must affirm first because God's word teaches them and secondarily because all believers everywhere, in all times and places, affirm them.[11] Among the more central truths of the faith is the incarnation of God the Son. Jesus Christ is true God and true man, one person with two distinct, unconfused,

9. Olevian, *Firm Foundation*, 76.

10. "Ist denn Christus nicht bei uns bis an's Eude der Welt, wie Er uns derheissen hat? Christus ist wahrer Mensch und wahrer Gott: nach seiner menschlichen Natur ist Er jesst nicht auf Erden, aber nach seiner Gottheit, Majestät, Gnade und Geift weicht Er nimmer von uns" (Schaff, *Creeds of Christendom*, 3:322). "An ergo Christus non est nobiscum usque ad finem mundi, quemadmodum promisit?Christus est verus Deus, et verus homo; itaque secundum naturam humanam, iam non est in terra: at secundum divinitatem suam, maiestatem, gratiam et spiritum, nullo unquam tempore a nobis abest" (Niemeyer, *Collectio Confessionum*, 440).

11. This is the language of the Athanasian Creed: "Whosoever will be saved, before all things it is necessary that he hold the catholic faith; Which faith except every one do keep whole and undefiled, without doubt he shall perish everlastingly" (Schaff, *Creeds of Christendom*, 2:66).

inseparable natures.[12] This is biblical, universal Christology. The ascension of Christ seems create a problem relative to his promise to be with us always. Matthew says:

> Now the eleven disciples went to Galilee, to the mountain to which Jesus had directed them. And when they saw him they worshiped him, but some doubted. And Jesus came and said to them, "All authority in heaven and on earth has been given to me. Go therefore and make disciples of all nations, baptizing them in the name of the Father and of the Son and of the Holy Spirit, teaching them to observe all that I have commanded you. And behold, I am with you always, to the end of the age." (Matt 28:16–20 ESV)

How can it be that Jesus is both away from us and with us at the same time? Christ has two distinct, inseparable natures united in one person. What is true of his natures is true of his person, by virtue of the personal (hypostatic) union of the two natures.[13] It is true that Christ is away from us. Jesus did say, "Do not cling to me, for I have not yet ascended to the Father" (John 20:17 ESV). The subject of the verb is Jesus. When the woman poured the expensive perfume on Jesus's feet, some complained. Jesus replied, "Why do you trouble the woman? For she has done a beautiful thing to me. For you always have the poor with you, but you will not always have me" (Matt 26:10–11 ESV). He testified that he was going to the Father (John 16:28; 17:11). He said, "A little while, and you will see me no longer" (John 16:17).

He also said, "I will be with you always." He said, ""I will not leave you as orphans" (John 14:18 ESV). This is why we never confess that Jesus is "part God and part man." Jesus is not a composition. As we say in the Athanasian Creed, the properties of his deity and the properties of his humanity are unchanged in the incarnation. His deity does not become human, and his humanity does not become deified. Jesus is away from us and is with us *simultaneously*.

---

12. These are the qualifiers used in the Definition of Chalcedon (AD 451; Schaff, *Creeds of Christendom*, 2:62).

13. Ursinus, *Commentary*, 247.

How is it possible? It is so because he is present with us, as we say, by his deity, his majesty, his unconditional favor (grace), and his Holy Spirit. He has kept his word. He has fulfilled his promise. He is with us. He will be with us. No one can dissolve the bond, the union, between Christ and his people. No one is closer to us than Jesus. No one is more present with us all, everywhere, in all times and places than Jesus. Remember, God the Son was working to save his people before his incarnation. He was with his people in the garden and after. He was delivering Noah and the rest of the visible church through the flood. He delivered Israel through the Red Sea. He was with them in the wilderness (1 Cor 10:1–5). In the new covenant, however, we are particularly blessed. He promised:

> I will ask the Father, and he will give you another Helper, to be with you forever, even the Spirit of truth, whom the world cannot receive, because it neither sees him nor knows him. You know him, for he dwells with you and will be in you.
>
> I will not leave you as orphans; I will come to you. Yet a little while and the world will see me no more, but you will see me. Because I live, you also will live. In that day you will know that I am in my Father, and you in me, and I in you. (John 14:16–20 ESV)

We are not orphans because God is not one person. He is three persons: God the Holy Spirit is with us, and through the word and sacraments, he communicates Christ to us. It was that same Spirit of whom Jesus said, "When the Spirit of truth comes, he will guide you into all the truth, for he will not speak on his own authority, but whatever he hears he will speak, and he will declare to you the things that are to come. He will glorify me, for he will take what is mine and declare it to you. All that the Father has is mine; therefore I said that he will take what is mine and declare it to you" (John 16:13–15 ESV). The Holy Spirit is the Spirit of truth. Just as Jesus spoke on his Father's authority, so the Spirit spoke on Jesus's authority. Jesus conquered death. He ascended "far above the heavens" (Eph 4:10). He poured out his Holy Spirit and has given "some to be apostles, some prophets, some evangelists, some pastors and teachers, toward the equipping of the saints, unto the work of ministry, for building up the body of Christ" (Eph 4:11–12).

The two natures and one person of Christ are a great mystery. We cannot say *how,* but we must say *that* Christ is as near to us as the word. When we hear his word, we hear him. When we see the water, the bread, and the wine, we are seeing him and his promises to us. He is with us always and will return bodily, so we shall always be with the Lord.

Christ is not divided. By the power of the Spirit, through faith, by virtue of our union with Christ, we always have the whole Christ. Olevianus explains:

> The person was not divided when the tiny body of the child was limited to the virgin's womb and yet heaven and earth could not contain His divinity. In the same way, the two natures are not separated just because the body of Christ is in heaven and His divinity is both in its body and beyond it in heaven and on earth. For since the divinity is not limited and is present everywhere, it is evident that Christ's divinity is surely beyond the bounds of the humanity He has taken on, but at the same time this single and whole divinity is in and remains personally united to His humanity (Col. 2[:9]).[14]

The Reformed answer to the Lutheran doctrine of the ubiquity of Christ's humanity is what the Lutherans called the *extra Calvinisticum* or the "Calvinistic beyond."[15] The Son operated in the humanity and beyond (*extra*) it. He did not cease to be the *Logos* of the prologue of John, by whom all things were made and who actively sustains all things.

Jesus has not abandoned us. Our hope is not misplaced. The Holy Spirit, the word, and the sacraments are a down payment (Eph 1:13–14), sign, and a seal to believers that our confidence is justified.[16]

---

14. Olevian, *Firm Foundation*, 76–77.

15. On this see Willis, *Calvin's Catholic Christology*, who shows that the view, which the Lutherans attributed to Calvin, was actually widely held long before Calvin. The Latin text of *HC* 48 uses the adverb *extra* in this sense. See the discussion under *HC* 48–49; McGinnis, *Son of God*; Drake, *Flesh of the Word*.

16. Olevian, *Firm Foundation*, 79.

QUESTION 48

Since his human nature is not present wherever his deity is, are not then these two natures in Christ separated from one another?

Not at all; for since the deity is incomprehensible and everywhere present, it must follow that the same is not limited with the human nature he assumed, and yet remains personally united to it.[17]

Early in postapostolic Christian history, confused Christians and heretics sought either to conflate the two natures of Christ, with the result that Christ was made to have only one nature (the monophysite heresy), or to separate the two natures so that Christ was made to be essentially two persons (Nestorianism). Eutyches (ca. 378–454) reacted to Nestorius (ca. 351–ca. 451) by concluding in effect that there was more than a *union* of two natures in one person. He taught that, after the incarnation, there was only one nature (hence "monophysite," μόνος, "one," + φύσις, "nature"). He was condemned, then acquitted briefly by Leo I, who reconsidered and condemned him in his famous Tome. The Council of Chalcedon condemned Eutyches in AD 451, declaring that Christ is one person, "perfect in deity" (τέλειον τὸν αὐτὸν ἐν θεότητι) and "perfect in humanity" (τέλειον τὸν αὐτὸν ἐν ἀνθρωπότητι). He is one person in two natures, inconfusedly (ἀσυγχύτως), indivisibly (ἀτρέπτως), and inseparably (ἀδιαιρέτως).[18]

The Definition of Chalcedon also affirms "the distinction of natures being by no means taken away by the union" and the "the property of each nature being preserved, and concurring in one Person and one Subsistence."[19] These were all aimed at the Eutychian or monophysite

17. "Werden aber auf diese Weise die zwei Naturen in Christo nicht von einander getrennt, so die Menschheit nicht überall ist, da die Gottheit ist? Mit nichten: denn weil die Gottheit unbegreiflich und allenthalben gegenwärtig ist, so muss folgen, dass sie wohl ausserhalb ihrer angenommenen Menschheit, und dennoch nichts desto weniger auch in derselben ist, und persönlich mit ihr vereiniget bleibt" (Schaff, *Creeds of Christendom*, 3:322). "An vero isto pacto duae naturae in Christo, non divelluntur, si non sit natura humana, ubicunque est divina? Minime: Nam cum divinitatis comprehendi non queat, et omni loco praesens sit, necessario consequitur, esse eam quidem extra naturam humanam, quam assumsit, sed nihilo minus tamen esse in eadem, eique personaliter unitam permanere" (Niemeyer, *Collectio Confessionum*, 440).

18. Schaff, *Creeds of Christendom*, 2:62.

19. Schaff, *Creeds of Christendom*, 2:62.

error. Jesus is one person with two natures, but his humanity does not become deity or even deified even though it is resurrected and glorified. Further, his deity does not become humanity. Eutychianism, however, leads to the notion that Jesus's humanity (not his person) is omnipresent or ubiquitous. Again, there is no question among Christians whether Jesus is omnipresent, but what is in doubt is that we may speak of his true, consubstantial (ὁμοούσιον) humanity as if it possessed the properties of the deity.[20] Neither the Scriptures nor the ecumenical creeds speak of the humanity as if the properties of the deity are communicated to it.

The other heresy to be avoided is Nestorianism, named for Nestorius, an Antiochene monk who became archbishop of Constantinople over the objections of the locals.[21] He was accused of doing more than just distinguishing the two natures of Christ. He was accused of separating them and thereby, were it possible, creating two persons. Scholars now dispute whether Nestorius actually taught this, but it is certain that he used infelicitous language at best.[22] Cyril of Alexandria, whom Gerald Bray calls an "unscrupulous" man, had asked Nestorius whether Mary was the God-bearer (θεοτόκος), that is, whether she bore in her womb God the Son incarnate.[23] Nestorius affirmed but was uncomfortable with this language, preferring *Christokos*, "Christ bearer." He and others thought that θεοτόκος smelled of adoptionism. Some were also using it to foster an unhealthy devotion to the Virgin Mary. His reluctance gave Cyril an opportunity to charge him with error, and a council was held in Rome (430), at which Celestine, the bishop of Rome, condemned him. He was sentenced at the Council of Ephesus (431). Most of Nestorius's writings were destroyed, but one of his later works, written after his banishment, suggests that he actually agreed with the orthodox against Eutychianism. He preferred to speak of a "conjunction" (συνάφεια) of the two natures and wills rather than a "union" (ἕνωσις).[24] The latter became the language of orthodoxy and is much to be preferred over Nestorius's language. In Reformation polemics, the Reformed refusal to affirm the omnipresence of Christ's

20. See the discussion under *HC* 17, 47.

21. See the discussion under *HC* 18.

22. Kelly, *Early Christian Doctrines*, 316. Pelikan (*Christian Tradition*, 1:251–68) surveys the issues.

23. Bray, *Creeds, Councils, and Christ*, 155.

24. *ODCC*, s.v. "Nestorian."

humanity was wrongly attacked by the gnesio-Lutherans as Nestorian. The Reformed, however, heartily and sincerely affirm the Chalcedonian *formulae*.

These controversies lie in the background of *HC* 48. As shown in the discussion under *HC* 47, the *extra* work of the Son is not peculiar to Reformed theology. The Son not only was the agent of creation (John 1:1–3) but walked with Adam in the garden, appeared as the "angel of the Lord" (e.g., Gen 16:7–14), and was with the Israelites in the desert:

> For I do not want you to be unaware, brothers, that our fathers were all under the cloud, and all passed through the sea, and all were baptized into Moses in the cloud and in the sea, and all ate the same spiritual food, and all drank the same spiritual drink. For they drank from the spiritual Rock that followed them, and the Rock was Christ. Nevertheless, with most of them God was not pleased, for they were overthrown in the wilderness. (1 Cor 10:1–5 ESV)

When Paul says, "the Rock was Christ," he wants the Corinthians to know that God the Son, who was with his people under the types and shadows, is he who became incarnate. The New Testament writers consistently teach that it was God the Son who was saving his people under the Old Testament. Jude 5 says, "Now I want to remind you, although you once fully knew it, that Jesus, who saved a people out of the land of Egypt, afterward destroyed those who did not believe" (ESV). In other words, God the Son has always operated beyond the humanity. He worked in creation, providence, and salvation before the incarnation and continued to do so in the incarnation. He says, "Heaven is my throne" (Isa 66:1; Acts 7:49). He says, "Am I a God at hand, declares Yahweh, and not a God far away? Can a man hide himself in secret places so that I cannot see him? declares Yahweh. Do I not fill heaven and earth? declares Yahweh" (Jer 23:23–24).

God the Son is ubiquitous, immense, filling everything with all of himself always. Those attributes are proper to God. His humanity, retaining its properties, is local. That is why the Bible describes his ascension as a local phenomenon. The disciples (Acts 1:9–11) saw him ascend. When Stephen looked into heaven, he saw the true, glorified, local humanity of Jesus (Acts 7:56). When Jesus manifested himself to Paul (Acts 9:3–6) and to John (Rev 1–3), he manifested his humanity as true, glorified humanity. If his human nature is not truly local, then it is not consubstantial with us. Hebrews says he is "like us" (ὁμοιωθῆναι) in "every respect" (sin excepted; Heb 2:17; 4:15). Hebrews clearly wants us to think that Christ's humanity is in one place, at one time, as we are. If we say anything else, we verge on docetism, the heresy that says he only appeared but was not actually truly human. When Paul wants to express Christ's omnipresence, he appeals to Christ's deity, not to his humanity: "For in him the whole fullness of deity dwells bodily, and you have been filled in him" (Col 2:9–10 ESV). We have been filled "in Christ," in his person, but the reference is to his deity, which dwells bodily. Paul does not say to the Colossians that his humanity fills them. Jesus said to the disciples that he was glad that he was not present bodily when Lazarus died (John 11:15). Even after his resurrection, as we saw earlier, the angel said, "He is not here" (Matt 28:6). Thus, the Reformed reject the Lutheran doctrine that Christ belongs to the *genus maiestaticum*, so that his humanity may be said to possess properties that no other human person has.[25]

The two natures were united in the tomb, even as his true, rational human soul was temporarily separated him his body in death.[26] The two natures were united in the resurrection and ascension. The incarnation is a great mystery, of course, but we can say what we should say, and we should always say that Christ is one person, not a composition, in whom two distinct natures are indivisibly, inseparably united. The incarnation is for our salvation and for the glory of God.

QUESTION 49

What benefit do we receive from Christ's ascension into heaven?

First, that he is our advocate in the presence of his Father in heaven. Secondly, that we have our flesh in heaven as a sure pledge, that he as the head, will also take us, his members, up to himself. Thirdly,

25. See the discussion of these issues under *HC* 47.

26. "Rational soul" is the language of the Definition of Chalcedon (Schaff, *Creeds of Christendom*, 2:62).

that he sends us his Spirit as an earnest, by whose power we seek those things which are above, where Christ sits at the right hand of God, and not things on earth.[27]

When Jesus ascended in the sight of his disciples, there were horses, chariots, and ships. Messages took days, weeks, and months to arrive, if they arrived. If a messenger was robbed, killed, or died, then of course the message would never get through, and the sending and receiving parties might never know. A trip from one town to another, too, might take days, weeks, or months. Travel was expensive and dangerous. If one reads about Paul's journeys in Acts, one gets a clear sense of how hazardous it could be.

Thus, the confusion and sense of separation experienced by the disciples was understandable. Jesus was visibly, physically going to a place they could not really even imagine. Why did he not stay with them? What good was it for him to leave? Christians still struggle with this question. To ease the sense of separation, well-intended but misguided Christians have written hymns about walking with Jesus and talking with him now. Frequently Christians talk about Jesus "living in my heart" in the same way people now say that departed family members have not really left us since they are "in our hearts." The danger of speaking figuratively about Jesus walking with us or living in our hearts is that it turns the reality of Jesus's ascension into a figure of speech or a matter of subjective experience.

HC 49 gives us three reasons why it is good for us that Jesus ascended to be with the Father. Having someone else act in one's place can be truly wonderful. In case of legal trouble, is it not wonderful to have a lawyer, recognized by the court, appearing in one's place? That is a mundane

27. "Was nützet uns die Himmelsahrt Christi? Erstlich, dass Er im Himmel vor dem Angesicht seines Vaters unser Fürsprecher ist. Zum andern, dass wir unser Fleisch im Himmel zu einem sichern Pfand haben, dass Er, als das Haupt, uns, seine Glieder, auch zu sich werde hinauf nehmen. Zum dritten, dass Er uns seinen Geist zum Gegenpfand herab sendet, durch welches Kraft wir suchen, was droben ist, da Christus ist, fitzend zur Rechten Gottes, und nicht, das auf Erden ist" (Schaff, *Creeds of Christendom*, 3:323). "Quem fructum nobis adfert ascensio Christi in coelum? Primum quod in coelo apud patrem pro nobis intercedit. Deinde quod carnem nostram in coelo habemus, ut in eo tanquam certo pignore confirmemur, fore, ut ipse qui caput nostrum est, nos sua membra ad se extollat. Tertio, quod nobis suum Spiritum mutui pignoris loco mittit, cuius efficacia non terrena sed superna quaerimus, ubi ipse est ad dextram Dei sedens" (Niemeyer, *Collectio Confessionum*, 440).

analogy of a much greater reality. Jesus is not just any lawyer. He is *the* lawyer. That is what we mean by "advocate." He is much more, however, than a mere lawyer: "My little children, I am writing these things to you so that you may not sin. But if anyone does sin, we have an advocate [παράκλητος] with the Father, Jesus Christ the righteous. He is the propitiation for our sins, and not for ours only but also for the sins of the whole world" (1 John 2:1–2 ESV).[28]

Our representative before the court is the one who satisfied the law for us (*pro nobis*). The effect of his satisfaction is twofold, to expiate (put away) our sins and to propitiate (turn away) God's wrath against us. In other words, it is much better that he appear for us than that we should appear on our own behalf (*pro se*). He has turned away God's wrath for all of his people, in all times and places. God approves of us who believe only because of Jesus's righteousness for us. Thus, Paul says: "Who shall bring any charge against God's elect? It is God who justifies. Who is to condemn? Christ Jesus is the one who died—more than that, who was raised—who is at the right hand of God, who indeed is interceding for us" (Rom 8:33–34 ESV).

Paul adds a twist to the narrative. The advocate is also the coming judge. This is the answer to Romans 2:16. Part of Paul's gospel is that Jesus is the coming judge, but the rest of the story is that those who are united to Christ by the Spirit, through faith alone (*sola fide*), are already judged righteous. We do not fear condemnation, and those who have been declared righteousness will never be declared to be anything else. God will not change his word. So, according to Olevianus, the first benefit of Christ's ascension is our justification.[29]

The second benefit of Christ's ascension is that it serves as a pledge, assurance, or promise that at the last day he will raise from the dead all his people, those whom he loved from all eternity (Eph 1:1–14), whom the Father gave to him (John 17:6), for whom he willingly laid down his life (John 10:15).

The catechism uses two important images to illustrate the nature of the promise inherent in Christ's resurrection: a pledge and a body. In the

28. Olevian, *Firm Foundation*, 78.

29. Olevianus, *Exposition*, 103; Olevian, *Firm Foundation*, 78.

ancient world, as today, there were a couple of reasons to make a down payment, to leave security or a surety: as a promise of a future payment or another personal obligation. In Genesis 38, we see Judah leaving behind personal property as a pledge of future payment.[30] The apostle Paul says, "And it is God who establishes us with you in Christ, and has anointed us, and who has also put his seal on us and given us his Spirit in our hearts as a guarantee" (ἀρραβών; 2 Cor 1:21–22 ESV; see 5:5). The word for "guarantee" may also be translated as "down payment" or "surety" or "security."

Jesus's resurrection is a guarantee of our resurrection. "Let not your hearts be troubled. Believe in God; believe also in me. In my Father's house are many rooms. If it were not so, would I have told you that I go to prepare a place for you? And if I go and prepare a place for you, I will come again and will take you to myself, that where I am you may be also" (John 14:1–3 ESV). The empty tomb and the witnesses to the resurrected Christ testify to us that we too will be raised. His ascension is a promise of our ascension. "But how could Christ have given us a kingdom, if he himself, as the first-begotten, had not first taken possession of it? And in as much as he has ascended and now reigns there, he will translate us, who are citizens of his kingdom, to the same place. 'Where I am, there shall also my servant be.'" "I will receive you unto myself; that where I am there ye may be also'" (John 12:26; 14:3).[31]

We know this because we are united to Christ. Paul says, "For if we have been united with him in a death like his, we shall certainly be united with him in a resurrection like his" (Rom 6:5 ESV). By grace alone, by the Spirit, through faith, we are already "alive together with Christ—by grace you have been saved," and God has "raised us up with him and seated us with him in the heavenly places in Christ Jesus" (Eph 2:5–6 ESV). The Spirit testifies to us through the gospel that what has already been realized in Christ is being realized in us and will be brought to fruition. The classic place is Ephesians 1:13–14: "In him you also, when you heard the word of truth, the gospel of your salvation, and believed in him, were sealed with the promised Holy Spirit, who is the guarantee of our inheritance until we acquire possession of it, to the praise of his glory" (ESV). Note well

30. Hartley, "Pledge," 886; Olevian, *Firm Foundation*, 79.

31. Ursinus, *Commentary*, 252.

that Paul does not say that we will be sealed when we have some sort of postconversion experience. He says that all those who, by God's grace, through faith, are "in Christ" were given new life when they heard the word of truth and "were sealed with the promised Holy Spirit." All believers are sealed. There are not two classes of believers, those who have had a second blessing and those who have not. The roots of the notion that there are two kinds of believers is not in historic Christian teaching but rather in gnosticism. The gnostics distinguished between those who had a special illumination into secret knowledge (hence γνῶσις) and those who were merely Christians, who had not the special blessing, illumination. The Spirit has been given to us as a guarantee, pledge, surety, security of a future good (inheritance). We will come into the full possession of the inheritance earned for us by Christ at the bodily resurrection.

The second image Paul uses is that of headship. Believers are so united to Christ that he is our head and we, believers, are his body. "And he is the head of the body, the church. He is the beginning, the firstborn from the dead, that in everything he might be preeminent" (Col 1:18 ESV). The very notion of firstborn entails that others will follow. Believers are those who will follow him in his resurrection. The tomb becomes, as it were, a womb. When Jesus walked out of the tomb, he inaugurated a new creation (2 Cor 5:17), in which we participate by the work of the Spirit. Paul elaborates on the image a bit later when he warns about those who boast in "angels" and who insist on "asceticism," who go on about "visions" because they are "not holding fast to the Head, from whom the whole body, nourished and knit together through its joints and ligaments, grows with a growth that is from God" (Col 2:19 ESV).

Paul uses the image of the human body to characterize our relationship with Christ. We could not be more closely united to him because the union is by the Holy Spirit, who is consubstantial with the Father the Son and who, by his power, overcomes the distance between us and the risen Christ. Calvin calls the Spirit a "bond" (*vinculum*) between us and Christ.[32] Paul calls Jesus our "head" and us his "body" because we are as connected to Christ as a human head is connected to a human body. We

32. "Huc summa redit, Spiritum sanctum vinculum esse, quo nos sibi efficaciter devincit Christus" (Calvin, *Institutes* 3.1.1; Barth, *Joannis Calvini Opera Selecta,* 4:2.4–6).

are not conscious of the connection; it is just the way things are. No one checks each day to make sure his head is still attached. If he is able to ask whether it is attached, that is evidence that it is attached. So too, we do not ask whether we have become disconnected from Christ. No one who is truly connected to Christ can be severed from him. So, just as he is raised, ascended, and seated at the right hand, so too will we be raised (if we have died before he returns), and so we will always be with the Lord. Without the ascension, the Holy Spirit would not have been poured out. That is why our Lord said that it was necessary for him to go away. That is why the Spirit is the comforter (John 14:26–28). He communicates Christ to us, he strengthens us, he renews us, he sanctifies us and assures us that, despite our sins and doubts, it really is all true.

Question 50

Why is it added: "And sits at the right hand of God"?

Question 51

What does this glory of Christ, our head, profit us?

Question 52

What comfort is it to you, that Christ "shall come to judge the living and the dead"?

Lord's Day 19

QUESTION 50

Why is it added: "And sits at the right hand of God"?

Because Christ ascended into heaven for this end, that he might there appear as the head of his church, by whom the Father governs all things.[1]

It is basic to historic Christian teaching and confession that Jesus is reigning and ruling now. In the sixth article of the Apostles' Creed, all Christians confess, "He ascended into heaven, and sits at the right hand of God the Father Almighty." Our interest just now is in second clause of the sixth article: "and sits at the right hand of God the Father almighty."[2] This is a truly ancient confession. Ignatius of Antioch, writing well before AD 150, confessed, "and sits at his right hand" (*καὶ ἐκάθισεν ἐκ δεξιῶν αὐτοῦ*).[3] In the early third century Tertullian confessed that Christ is "sitting now at the right hand of the Father" (*sedentem nunc ad dexteram Patris*). He used virtually identical language in his summary of the Rule of Faith (*regula fidei*) *Against Praxeas* and in his *Prescription against Heretics*.[4]

Scripture teaches that Christ is presently ruling over all things generally and specially, savingly, over his kingdom in his ascension. It was revealed to David under types and shadows, in the form of a dialogue between two divine figures in Psalm 110. Verses 1–3 are parallel to verses 5–6. Verse 4 is the center of the psalm and has no parallel. Those parallel verses teach Christ's ascension and royal session:

> *Yahweh* says to my *Adon*
> "Sit at my right hand,
> until I make your enemies your footstool."

1. "Warum wird hinzugesetzt, dass Er fitze zur Rechten Gottes? Weil Christus darum gen Himmel gefahren ist, dass Er sich daselbst erzeige als das Haupt seiner christlichen Kirche, durch welches der Vater alles regieret" (Schaff, *Creeds of Christendom*, 3:323). "Cur additur: Sedet ad dextram Dei? Quia Christus ideo in coelum ascendit, ut se ibi caput suae Ecclesiae declaret, per quod Pater omnia gubernat" (Niemeyer, *Collectio Confessionum*, 441).

2. Schaff, *Creeds of Christendom*, 2:45.

3. Schaff, *Creeds of Christendom*, 2:11–12.

4. Schaff, *Creeds of Christendom*, 2:17.

Yahweh sends forth from Zion
 your mighty scepter.
 Rule in the midst of your enemies!

Adon is at your right hand;
 he will shatter kings on the day of his wrath.
He will execute judgment among the nations,
 filling them with corpses;
he will shatter chiefs
 over the wide earth.

We need not guess as to the identity of *Yahweh* and *Adon,* since our Lord Jesus explains it for us:

> Now while the Pharisees were gathered together, Jesus asked them a question, saying, "What do you think about the Christ? Whose son is he?" They said to him, "The son of David." He said to them, "How is it then that David, in the Spirit, calls him Lord, saying,
>
> "'The Lord said to my Lord,
> "Sit at my right hand,
> until I put your enemies under your feet'"?
>
> If then David calls him Lord, how is he his son?" And no one was able to answer him a word, nor from that day did anyone dare to ask him any more questions. (Matt 22:41–46 ESV)

The Pharisees sought to trap Jesus by forcing him to take a position on a disputed issue, but Jesus answered them in an unexpected way, by appealing to and interpreting Psalm 110. Jesus's argument is that David recognized the Messiah as superior to himself and thus called him "my Lord" (κυρίῳ μου). Before Jesus was David's son, which he is in his humanity, he was David's Lord, the one to whom the Father said, "Sit at my right hand." Jesus identifies himself as the *Adon* of Psalm 110.

The apostles continued this interpretation of Psalm 110. Peter preached that Jesus was the fulfillment of Psalm 110:1, that he was the *Adon* of whom David spoke:

> This Jesus God raised up, and of that we all are witnesses. Being therefore exalted at the right hand of God, and having received from the Father the promise of the Holy Spirit, he has poured out this that you yourselves are seeing and hearing. For David did not ascend into the heavens, but he himself says,
>
> "'The Lord said to my Lord,
> Sit at my right hand,
> until I make your enemies your footstool.'"
>
> Let all the house of Israel therefore know for certain that God has made him both Lord and Christ, this Jesus whom you crucified. (Acts 2:32–36 ESV)

In the language of Scripture, to be "at the right hand" (Ps 16:11; Matt 20:21, 23; 26:64) is in this context to be in a position of power and authority.[5] According to Peter, Christ is in that very position of royal authority and power. Pentecost was an illustration of his royal benefits. After his ascension, after "taking captivity captive," he gave good gifts to people (Ps 68:18; Eph 4:7–8). For Peter, to say "made him both Lord and Christ" is to say that Jesus is *Adon* and he is Messiah in royal, ruling power and authority. We see the same doctrine in Acts 5:31, where Peter and apostles affirm that "God exalted" Christ at his "right hand." Peter teaches the same in 1 Peter 3:22, where he writes that Jesus is "at the right hand of God," where "angels, authorities, and powers" have been "subjected" to him. Stephen saw Jesus at the "right hand" of God (Acts 7:55–56). Paul affirms this as part of the ground of our assurance (Rom 8:34; Eph 1:20) and a motive for sanctification (Col 1:20). Arguably the entire book of Hebrews is a commentary on Psalm 110, and throughout it affirms that Jesus is ruling and reigning now (Heb 1:13; 8:1; 10:12; 12:2).[6]

Olevianus explains the doctrinal significance of this article in terms of Christ's kingly office *and* his priestly office:

> The sitting at the right hand of God the Father is the exaltation of Christ in His kingdom and priesthood. That means that He now

5. Ursinus, *Commentary*, 254–55.

6. In *Exposition*, 107–8, Olevianus begins his explanation of this clause of the sixth article of the creed with an appeal to Ps 110.

> administers His kingly and priestly offices not in weakness and destitution, as before, but in manifest heavenly majesty and glory. Therefore, you believe in Christ's sitting at the right hand of God the Father almighty only when you believe that He intercedes for you in heaven in great glory and that He governs His kingdom with great power, so that He hears you, grants you the Spirit of comfort and wisdom, and defends you more effectively than if He were still here on earth in His body and speaking with you.[7]

Whereas the *accomplishment* of our salvation required Christ's humiliation in active, vicarious suffering, the *application* of that work to the elect requires his glorification and exaltation. This is part of Christ's mediatorial work on behalf of his church. "It is peculiar to Christ; because he alone is that almighty person and mediator through whom the Father immediately governs all things, and especially his church, which he defends against all her enemies."[8]

In light of the widespread influence of various forms of dispensationalism, it is important to observe that the notion that Christ is reigning now, over his (twofold) kingdom, is an ancient and even universal Christian doctrine. It is not peculiar to Reformed, nor even to Augustinian, Christians. It is beneficial to observe the ancient roots of this confession since many evangelicals have little or no familiarity with the Apostles' Creed and thus have not had the experience of saying these words on a regular basis. For some dispensationalists, the conception of Christ's millennial reign includes such earthly glory and conquest that, absent those features (e.g., the rebuilt temple and his visible, glorious reign on the earth), they cannot say that he was reigning now. Thus, it is interesting that John Walvoord, under the heading, "The Premillennial Concept of the Present Age," makes no mention of Christ's present reign from heaven. He writes that the premillennial point of view makes "the inter-advent period unique and unpredicted in the Old Testament."[9] In 1996, Stephen J. Nichols argued that "the rejection, postponement, and entirely future fulfillment of the Davidic kingdom is and has been a consistently held

7. Olevianus, *Exposition*, 108; Olevian, *Firm Foundation*, 80.

8. Ursinus, *Commentary*, 255. See the discussion under *HC* 51.

9. Walvoord, *Millennial Kingdom*, 134.

view within 'normative' dispensationalism."[10] He notes that Charles Ryrie's revised version of dispensationalism had four ways of speaking about the kingdom.[11] It is not clear to me how each of these relates to the traditional Christian view that Christ is now seated at the right hand, but perhaps the traditional view is implicit in one or more of them.

The problem inherent in classic and revised dispensationalism is that, in their scheme, the kingdom that Jesus announced seems to be closely associated with an offered, earthly, Davidic kingdom that was rejected. In that case it becomes more difficult to speak of his present reign. Ryrie writes: "Though He never ceases to be King and, of course, is King today as always, Christ is never designated as King of the church. ... Though Christ is a King today, He does not rule as King."[12] J. Dwight Pentecost says essentially the same thing: "The allegation that Christ is seated on the father's throne reigning over a spiritual kingdom, the church, simply does not fulfill the promises of the covenant."[13] In this view, Christ is king, but, in view of the rejection and postponement of the offered, earthly, Davidic kingdom, he seems, according to influential versions of dispensationalism, to be a king in waiting. Indeed, Nichols objects to the absence in progressive dispensationalism of the earthly, Davidic kingdom offered, rejected, and postponed: "Discussions of the offer, rejection, and postponement of the Davidic kingdom are absent in the work of the progressives. Bock argues that Luke-Acts teaches that Christ has already inaugurated His reign of Christ as Davidic king, that His present position of 'being seated on David's throne is linked to being seated at God's right hand,' and that a future consummative stage of the kingdom rule will follow."[14] To the degree his assessment is correct, Reformed Christians ought to welcome such developments among progressive dispensationalism, since this seems to be a move closer to the historic Christian view. Namely, Christ is king now over his church specially and generally and all things in his providence,

10. Nichols, "Dispensational View," 216.

11. "Under this rubric, he distills four concepts: (1) the universal kingdom; (2) the Davidic/Messianic kingdom; (3) the mystery form of the kingdom; and (4) the spiritual kingdom" (Nichols, "Dispensational View," 218).

12. Nichols, "Dispensational View," 224.

13. Nichols, "Dispensational View," 226.

14. Nichols, "Dispensational View," 231.

and the kingdom has always been under the period of types and shadows but may be said to have been announced and inaugurated particularly at the coming of Christ when he said: "The time is fulfilled, and the kingdom of God is at hand; repent and believe in the gospel" (Mark 1:15 ESV).

Jesus did not restrict his announcement as if to say, "Now, understand that I am offering an earthly Davidic kingdom to the Jews." The only way to see that sort of qualification is to know it is there *a priori*. One would have to think that there are two parallel tracks in redemptive history, a plan for a national Jewish kingdom on the earth and something else, a church-mystery. Apart from such an assumption, one could not arrive at such a reading of Jesus's language.

Further, there is no consensus among New Testament scholars that there is in the Gospels any great distinction between the kingdom of heaven and the kingdom of God. There is good evidence to think they are synonymous. The parallel to Mark 1:15 in Matthew 4:17 says, "From that time Jesus began to preach, saying, 'Repent, for the kingdom of heaven is at hand'" (ESV). Both forms of the announcement regard the same entity. That the expressions "kingdom of God" and "kingdom of heaven" are interchangeable teaches us that the kingdom that Jesus inaugurated is principally eschatological but was manifested clearly during his ministry on the earth. According to the early church, the Apostles' Creed, the medieval church—during which the question was not whether Christ is reigning now but through whom and in what order—Jesus reigns now, from heaven, over the earth generally and particularly over his people, the church.

Dispensationalism generally exists outside the Reformed churches, but there is within Reformed churches another, more subtle approach—postmillennialism. Postmillennialism affirms that Jesus is presently reigning, but after future developments (e.g., conversion of the nations, the affirmation by political leaders and governments of Christ as Lord) then he will be *truly* reigning.[15] In contrast to such a view and to any other view that might suggest that Jesus is not truly ruling and reigning now, we should think that Jesus is as much a king now as he will ever be before his bodily

15. Bavinck, *Reformed Dogmatics*, 4:674; Berkhof, *Systematic Theology*, 271; Hoekema, *Bible and the Future*, 177–80; Riddlebarger, *Case for Amillennialism*, 236–39; Venema, *Promise of the Future*, 341–54.

return. The biblical evidence is overwhelming that Jesus is presently seated and reigning in royal power and glory. He testified to his kingship before the high priest:

> And the high priest said to him, "I adjure you by the living God, tell us if you are the Christ, the Son of God." Jesus said to him, "You have said so. But I tell you, from now on you will see the Son of Man seated at the right hand of Power and coming on the clouds of heaven." Then the high priest tore his robes and said, "He has uttered blasphemy. What further witnesses do we need? You have now heard his blasphemy. What is your judgment?" They answered, "He deserves death." Then they spit in his face and struck him. And some slapped him, saying, "Prophesy to us, you Christ! Who is it that struck you?" (Matt 26:63–68 ESV)

The irony was that they really were mocking the King of kings. That he allowed them to abuse him thus was a great demonstration of his forbearance and grace toward sinners. Now is the time of salvation and free acceptance with God. When he returns, that time will have ended.

He testified to his disciples, "I am, and you will see the Son of Man seated at the right hand of Power, and coming with the clouds of heaven" (Mark 14:62 ESV). In the interregnum, "the Son of Man shall be seated at the right hand of the power of God" (Luke 22:69). Paul says that in his resurrection, the Father seated his Son as King, at the right hand,

> according to the working of his great might that he worked in Christ when he raised him from the dead and seated him at his right hand in the heavenly places, far above all rule and authority and power and dominion, and above every name that is named, not only in this age but also in the one to come. And he put all things under his feet and gave him as head over all things to the church, which is his body, the fullness of him who fills all in all. (Eph 1:19–23 ESV)

Paul says that we are also presently seated with him, by his grace alone, through faith alone, by virtue of our union with him: "If then you have been raised with Christ, seek the things that are above, where Christ is, seated at the right hand of God" (Col 3:1 ESV). It is true that we do not experience this royal authority yet, but we will.

Hebrews 8:1 says that not only is Jesus King but he is also a high priest, "one who is seated at the right hand of the throne of the Majesty in heaven" (ESV). He is a Melchizedekian priest-king who earned his place in glory, "who for the joy that was set before him endured the cross, despising the shame, and is seated at the right hand of the throne of God" (Heb 12:2 ESV). In his vision of heaven, the apostle John saw Jesus's present royal reign (Rev 5:1). He is on the throne. He has the scroll (5:7).

To be sure, there is a distinction between the present time, the interregnum, and that period after his return, the judgment, and consummation of all things. We do not see every knee bowing and every tongue confessing that Jesus Christ is Lord (Phil 2:10–11; Rom 14:11). As Hebrews 2:8 says, presently "we do not see everything under subjection to him," but when he returns we will see it. Here is the distinction. Christ is presently sovereign over all things. Nothing happens without his royal decree or permission. Nothing is outside his providence. When the Christians were arrested and martyred in the second century, that happened according to King Jesus's good pleasure. When Christians today suffer for the faith, that happens according to his good pleasure. Psalm 2:4–6 says:

> He who sits in the heavens laughs;
> the Lord [*Adonai*] holds them in derision.
> Then he will speak to them in his wrath,
> and terrify them in his fury, saying,
> "As for me, I have set my King
> on Zion, my holy hill." (ESV)

He rules the nations with a rod of iron, and with that royal scepter he will smash them all in his return. He has no particular national people now. That singular relationship, with national Israel, was intentionally temporary (Gal 3:16–20) and ended with his crucifixion. There are no new national peoples, but he has people in every nation, in every tribe, from every tongue (Rev 5:9). He is Mediator and King of his church particularly; those are his special, covenanted people. In his general, sovereign providence, he rules everything and everyone.[16]

16. The Reformed churches do not confess the doctrine of the mediatorial kingship of Christ, i.e., that Christ rules over nations in the same way he rules over the church. It is better. This view is defended in Symington, *Messiah the Prince*. This view was only one of a variety of views advocated at

Jesus is reigning now. We need to resist the temptation that, because we do not see him presently putting all opposition under his feet, because he has not yet crushed Satan underfoot (Rom 16:20), he is not truly reigning. He is working by his sovereign Holy Spirit, through his ordained means of grace (*media gratiae*) to call his elect to faith and to sanctify those whom he has justified. When that work is done, then his kingdom will be manifest in all its glory. Until then we submit to his rule, we live in his kingdom, we trust his good purposes, and we wait patiently. "Amen. Come, Lord Jesus" (Rev 22:20).

Question 51

What does this glory of Christ, our head, profit us?

First, that by his Holy Spirit he bestows the heavenly gifts upon us, his members; then, that by his power he defends and preserves us against all enemies.[17]

Our Lord Jesus is bodily distant from us. The disciples saw him go.[18] He told them (and us) that he was leaving and that he would return. To leave such that one must return indicates a spatial separation. We have also seen, however, that he is also completely present with us by the power of his deity, by his word and Spirit. He is omnipresent. Jesus is true God and true man. He is *both* with us and away from us.

He is also our presently reigning, sovereign, glorious King. In a purely human kingdom, a distant king, with distant armies, is not of much use. One thinks of the story of Robin Hood, in which as a loyal subject of Richard I (1157–1599; "the Lionheart"), who was away on the Third Crusade, he

---

the Westminster Assembly (see Mckay, "From Popery to Principle," 138–39). E.g., Samuel Rutherford specifically rejected the doctrine of the mediatorial kingship of Christ (140–41).

17. "Was nützet uns diese Herrlichkeit unsers Hauptes Christi? Erftlich, dass Er durch seinen heiligen Geift in uns, seine Glieder, die himmlifchen Gaben ausgeusst; darnach, dass Er uns mit seiner Gewalt wider alle Feinde fchüsset und erhält" (Schaff, *Creeds of Christendom*, 3:323). "Quid nobis prodest haec gloria nostri capitis Christi? Primum, quod per Spiritum sanctum in nos sua membra, coelestia dona effundit. Deinde, quod nos sua potentia contra omnes hostes protegit ac defendit" (Niemeyer, *Collectio Confessionum*, 441).

18. See the discussion under *HC* 46.

and others in Nottinghamshire suffered under the cruel tyranny of his evil brother. It was fine to have a good king, but so long as Richard I was away, he was both unaware of the plight of his people and unable to help.

It is not so in Jesus's kingdom. Even though we are temporarily separated from him, it is not as if he is not with us. After he left, as Paul says, he gave us good gifts. "(He who descended is the one who also ascended far above all the heavens, that he might fill all things.) And he gave the apostles, the prophets, the evangelists, the shepherds and teachers, to equip the saints for the work of ministry, for building up the body of Christ" (Eph 4:10–12 ESV).

The same Jesus who was buried also ascended to heavenly reign and glory. He ascended because he defeated death and, as a conquering king, distributes gifts to his followers. In Ephesians 4:8 Paul paraphrases Psalm 68:18:

> You ascended on high,
> leading a host of captives in your train
> and receiving gifts among men,
> even among the rebellious, that *Yahweh Elohim* may dwell there.

Paul, however, adds an interesting twist. Where Psalm 68 says that the king receives gifts, Paul (writing under the inspiration of the Holy Spirit) says that King Jesus gives gifts. This is just what happened.

Psalm 2 pictures the ascended King Jesus as the sovereign conquering hero:

> Yahweh said to me, "You are my Son;
> today I have begotten you.
> Ask of me, and I will make the nations your inheritance,
> and the ends of the earth your possession.
> You shall break them with a rod of iron
> and dash them in pieces like a potter's vessel." (Ps 2:7–9)

Jesus, the eternally and uniquely begotten Son of God, is the Son, the reigning king, who has been installed in royal power in recognition of his righteousness in fulfilling the covenant of works for us. He is in the process of conquering the nations by his royal word and through the sovereign power of the Holy Spirit (Rom 16:20). What is pictured here as one event is a process that we know to have been inaugurated and that will be consummated at his glorious return. Paul says, "For he must reign until he has put all his enemies under his feet. The last enemy to be destroyed is death" (1 Cor 15:25–26 ESV). The logic of inauguration and consummation is clear. Jesus is putting his enemies under his feet by making them into his people, though death continues to take his victims—but that too will end when Jesus returns.

In his exposition of this article, Olevianus describes four fruits of the priestly aspect of Christ's present intercession for those "who are in covenant with God": (1) we know that covenant of grace is efficacious and permanent; (2) we may pray with confidence of being heard; (3) we are free to offer ourselves and our gifts to God through Christ; (4) his intercession renders our sufferings holy and glorious in the sight of God.[19] Olevianus notes three fruits of Christ's royal session for us: (1) through Christ we rightly know and worship God through Christ—"God hates all forms of worship that are not directed to Christ, in whom alone He wishes to be known, called upon, and glorified";[20] (2) Christ gives his Holy Spirit to his church to edify her and to advance his kingdom; (3) as King, he defends his church against all enemies worldly and spiritual.[21]

When Jesus ascended to the right hand as King, he gave the most wonderful gift, the Holy Spirit, and with the outpouring of the Spirit at Pentecost he gave remarkable gifts: healing; the ability, without study, to speak foreign languages; the ability to interpret foreign languages; the ability to receive and speak direct revelation from God (Acts 2:1–13; 1 Cor 12:1–12, 27–31; 14). To address a widespread concern: Those gifts that were specific to the apostolic age have ceased. Now, in God's grace and providence, we have the completed apostolic rule (canon) of God's word written. The apostles are gone, but the Holy Spirit remains. He still operates mysteriously and powerfully, but not in the way that some Anabaptists and neo-Pentecostalists imagine. The Spirit may still perform wonders through people, but not on command. Most of what is claimed as Pentecostal today is common among world religions and has nothing to

19. Olevianus, *Exposition*, 109–12; Ursinus, *Commentary*, 259.

20. Olevianus, *Exposition*, 113.

21. Olevianus, *Exposition*, 112–15; also Olevian, *Firm Foundation*, 80.

do with the supernatural ability to speak natural languages.[22] Geerhardus Vos argues that, in the New Testament context, the biblical gift of natural languages was "sub-eschatological" and "praemonitions of the world to come."[23] What is today passed off as apostolic ministry in too many places is a sad mockery of the reality experienced by the apostolic church. The belief that the Spirit operates today exactly as he did in the apostolic age rests on the assumption that what happens today is what happened then.

In *HC* 51, we confess that the elect are safely under the reign and power of Christ our King. "I give them eternal life, and they will never perish, and no one will snatch them out of my hand. My Father, who has given them to me, is greater than all, and no one is able to snatch them out of the Father's hand. I and the Father are one" (John 10:28–30 ESV). What he has given to us no one, not Satan, not death, can take from us because that gift, salvation, is promised by the gospel, the royal word of promise. It is sealed with the royal signet, baptism and the holy Supper, and even more by the promised Holy Spirit (Eph 1:13; 4:30).

Question 52

What comfort is it to you, that Christ "shall come to judge the living and the dead"?

That in all my sorrows and persecutions, with uplifted head, I look for the very same one, who before offered himself for me to the judgment of God, and removed all curse from me, to come as judge from heaven, who shall cast all his enemies and mine into everlasting condemnation, but shall take me with all his elect to himself into heavenly joy and glory.[24]

22. Scholars in more than one discipline (e.g., sociology and neurolinguistics) have long observed the phenomenon of *glossolalia* ("tongues") in a variety of contexts, some of them with no connection to Christianity (e.g., Santeria and voodoo). See Goodman, "Phonetic Analysis of Glossolalia," 227–39; Samarin, "Sociolinguistic vs Neurophysiological Explanations," 293–96; Mueller, "Linguistic Analysis of Glossolalia," 186–91.

23. Vos, *Redemptive History and Biblical Interpretation*, 116.

24. "Wes tröstet dich die Wiederkunft Christi, zu richten die Lebendigen und die Todten? Dass ich in aller Trübsal und Verfolgung mit aufgerichtetem Haupt eben des Richters, der sich zuvor dem Gerichte Gottes für mich dargestellt und alle Vermaledeiung von mir hinweggenommen hat, aus dem

The word *gospel* means "good news." The verbal form of the noun "gospel" (εὐαγγέλιόν), which Paul uses in Romans 1:16, in secular Greek "is always used in a context of joy, at least from the point of view of the messenger: 'I bring good words, happy news (*logous agathous pherōn euangelisasthai*) that I want to be the first to announce to you ... they wanted to crown me for the good news (*euangelia*)' (Aristophanes, Eq. 643)."[25] That same idea is present in Isaiah 52:7:

> How beautiful upon the mountains
> are the feet of him who brings good news,
> who publishes peace, who brings good news of happiness,
> who publishes salvation,
> who says to Zion, "Your God reigns." (ESV)

Verse 7 in the LXX of uses a participle of the same word (εὐαγγελιζομένου) for announcement of good news. In Isaiah 52, the announcement is peace, happiness, and salvation. This is the best news.

Sometimes Paul's language in Romans 2:15–16 is interpreted to imply that *gospel* can also mean bad news. It is true that the word *gospel* is used in a broader sense, and that may be the case here, but even if the word *gospel* can be bad news for some, this passage tells us that it is always good news for believers, those who have been given new life by God's Holy Spirit, who have been given the gift of faith (Eph 2:8–10), and who, by the Spirit, through faith, have been united to Christ.

In context, beginning in Romans 1:18, Paul has been explaining the nature and function of God's law. He has been prosecuting the entire human race for its sin and the consequences of sin, namely, corruption and death. Because the law was given before the fall, because it is revealed in nature, because it is imprinted on the conscience of every human (Rom 1:20; 2:12–14), we are all without excuse. We voluntarily, freely,

---

Himmel gewärtig bin, dass Er alle seine und meine Feinde in die ewige Verdammniss werfe, mich aber, sammt allen Auserwählten, zu sich in die himmlische Freude und Herrlichkeit nehme" (Schaff, *Creeds of Christendom*, 3:323–24). "Quid te consolatur reditus Christi ad iudicandum vivos et mortuos? Quod in omnibus miseriis et persecutionibus, erecto capite, eundem illum, qui se prius pro me iudicio dei statuit, et maledictionem omnem a me abstulit, iudicem e eolo exspecto, qui omnes suos et meos hostes, in aeternas poenas abiiciat; me vero cum omnibus electis ad se in coelestia gaudia, et sempiternam gloriam traducat" (Niemeyer, *Collectio Confessionum*, 441).

25. Spicq and Ernest, *Theological Lexicon*, 82–83.

and mysteriously chose to disobey God. We chose to break the covenant of works or commandment of life.[26] We had the ability before the fall to obey the law. We were "created in righteousness and true holiness that we might rightly know God our Creator, heartily love him, and live with him in eternal blessedness."[27] Before the fall, Adam was good. After the fall, that original goodness was corrupted. He, and we all in him (Rom 5:12–21), became bad by nature and therefore subject to the promised judgment: "The day you eat thereof you shall surely die" (Gen 2:17). We became fugitives. We covered ourselves pitifully with fig leaves and lied to our maker (Gen 3:7).[28] Therefore, we should not be surprised when Paul, as he preaches the law to the congregation in Rome and to us now, announces the coming judgment. Our Lord Jesus repeatedly proclaimed the coming judgment:

> You have heard that it was said to those of old, "You shall not murder; and whoever murders will be liable to judgment." But I say to you that everyone who is angry with his brother will be liable to judgment; whoever insults his brother will be liable to the council; and whoever says, "You fool!" will be liable to the hell of fire. (Matt 5:21–22 ESV)

> Truly, I say to you, it will be more bearable on the day of judgment for the land of Sodom and Gomorrah than for that town. (Matt 10:15 ESV)

> But I tell you, it will be more bearable on the day of judgment for Tyre and Sidon than for you. … But I tell you that it will be more tolerable on the day of judgment for the land of Sodom than for you. (Matt 11:22, 24 ESV)

> The men of Nineveh will rise up at the judgment with this generation and condemn it, for they repented at the preaching of Jonah, and behold, something greater than Jonah is here. (Matt 12:41 ESV)

---

26. See the discussion under *HC* 6.

27. *HC* 6.

28. *BC* 23 (Schaff, *Creeds of Christendom*, 3:410).

> ... and come out, those who have done good to the resurrection of life, and those who have done evil to the resurrection of judgment. (John 5:29 ESV)

Paul says,

> He will render to each one according to his works: to those who by patience in well-doing seek for glory and honor and immortality, he will give eternal life; but for those who are self-seeking and do not obey the truth, but obey unrighteousness, there will be wrath and fury. There will be tribulation and distress for every human being who does evil, the Jew first and also the Greek, but glory and honor and peace for everyone who does good, the Jew first and also the Greek. For God shows no partiality.
>
> For all who have sinned without the law will also perish without the law, and all who have sinned under the law will be judged by the law. For it is not the hearers of the law who are righteous before God, but the doers of the law who will be justified. For when Gentiles, who do not have the law, by nature do what the law requires, they are a law to themselves, even though they do not have the law. They show that the work of the law is written on their hearts, while their conscience also bears witness, and their conflicting thoughts accuse or even excuse them on that day. (Rom 2:6–16 ESV)

The final judgment will be universal.[29] It will judge those who had the law of Moses (*Torah*), and it will judge those who had the law of nature, the moral law "written on their hearts." The moral law is the same law in both. The standard is obedience to that law. That is why Paul says it is not hearers who are justified but "doers" (ποιηταὶ) who will be justified.

Nothing in this passage suggests that it is believers, aided by the Spirit, who are the "doers." This passage is not announcing the future acceptance of believers on the basis of their sanctification or good works. It is announcing condemnation for all those who are not perfectly righteous, perfectly conformed to God's holy law. For those who do not believe, that judgment is indeed bad news because they will die in their sins. For those

29. Ursinus, *Commentary*, 260–62.

who believe, however, the judgment is good news because the perfect, condign righteousness of Christ has been imputed to them.

The announcement of judgment on those who have not perfectly obeyed every syllable of God's holy law is not good news for sinners because we have not obeyed, nor will we obey, God's law perfectly, not even with the help of the Holy Spirit. Even the apostle Paul confessed that he did not do what he wanted to do and even as a believer sometimes despaired (Rom 7:14–25). This was Paul's gospel (κατὰ τὸ εὐαγγέλιόν μου) "through Christ Jesus." We may translate Paul thus: "On the day when God judges the secrets of men according to my announcement of Good News through Jesus Christ."[30]

Those who believe in Christ have righteousness by virtue of his obedience for them, which has been credited to them and received through faith alone (*sola fide*)—Paul will go on to explain these truths in Romans 4–6—so that the final judgment is not a source of terror for us. It is a source of terror for those who seek to stand before God on the basis of their own obedience or their own sanctity, or even on the basis partly of Christ's righteousness imputed and partly anything else (e.g., Spirit-wrought sanctity). For those who are in Christ Jesus, that is, united to him by his free favor, by the work of the Spirit, and reckoned righteous in him, the judgment is good news because it announces to the world what has already been announced in the gospel: "And to the one who does not work but believes in him who justifies the ungodly, his faith is counted as righteousness" (Rom 4:5 ESV). God justifies the unrighteous. Paul explains in chapter 5:

> For while we were still weak, at the right time Christ died for the ungodly. For one will scarcely die for a righteous person—though perhaps for a good person one would dare even to die—but God shows his love for us in that while we were still sinners, Christ died for us. Since, therefore, we have now been justified by his blood, much more shall we be saved by him from the wrath of God. For if while we were enemies we were reconciled to God by the death of his Son, much more, now that we are reconciled, shall we be

30. ἐν ἡμέρᾳ ὅτε κρίνει ὁ θεὸς τὰ κρυπτὰ τῶν ἀνθρώπων κατὰ τὸ εὐαγγέλιόν μου διὰ Χριστοῦ Ἰησοῦ..

> saved by his life. More than that, we also rejoice in God through our Lord Jesus Christ, through whom we have now received reconciliation. (Rom 5:6–11 ESV)

Not only did Christ die for the ungodly—*contra* Pelagius, who uses that word as a synonym for "unrighteous"—but even more scandalously, he justifies those who are in themselves intrinsically unrighteous. It is not that they should remain unrighteous, not at all. Of course, the justified have a reverent fear of God (2 Cor 7:1), but there is a difference between *servile* fear and *filial* fear.[31] Christians worship God with reverence and awe, but not servile fear (Heb 12:28). Paul makes clear that, after we are declared righteous for Christ's sake alone, we ought to grow in sanctity and personal righteousness because we have been declared righteous. We know, too, that there are not two stages of justification, initial and final. Rather, believers are as justified now as they will ever be. At the judgment, however, we will be vindicated.[32] It will be declared to the whole world what we are, in Christ. Therefore, the judgment is a *comfort* and good news to those who believe. The one whose return we anticipate is not our judge as much as he is our Savior, our Friend, our Mediator, our substitute. He has borne in his own body the judgment we deserve. The righteousness he accomplished for us in his life and in his death is ours.

The experience of believers and unbelievers in the judgment is the difference between law and gospel: "The righteous and wicked will be judged according to the law and gospel, which means, that they will be declared righteous or wicked at the tribunal of Christ. The acquittal of the righteous will be principally according to the gospel, but will be confirmed by the law. The condemnation of the wicked, on the other hand, will be chiefly by the law, and confirmed by the gospel."[33] Believers should not fear the judgment. "Now is the judgment of this world" (John 12:31). Our Lord Jesus declared this gospel: "Truly, truly, I say to you, whoever hears my word and believes him who sent me has eternal life. He does not come into judgment, but has passed from death to life" (John 5:24 ESV).

31. Ursinus, *Commentary*, 514.

32. See the discussion under *HC* 60.

33. Ursinus, *Commentary*, 263.

There has always been a temptation to turn the judgment into a covenant of works, were it possible, for believers, as if the sentence will be passed on the basis of works and law, not faith and gospel. Ursinus responds to that objection by conceding that God "will render even to the elect according to their works" but that is not because the works are meritorious or instrumental but because they are the "effects of faith," which is to say that believers shall be judged according to their faith, which is the same thing as to be judged according to the gospel. God will vindicate believers "from the fruits of their faith, that it was a true faith which they possessed, and that they are the persons to whom eternal life is due according to the promise."[34]

Olevianus explains:

> He will judge in such a way that He fully frees the godly and adorns them with eternal glory, but on the other hand fully executes the judgment of condemnation upon those who scorn such great long-suffering. He will drown Satan (like Pharaoh) with all his army, but lead His covenant partners, fully freed from all the tyranny of the ungodly, into that true heavenly inheritance—into the Promised Land, as it were.[35]

Believers are not condemned prisoners waiting for the execution of a death sentence. We have been declared righteous. The righteous cannot fear judgment because it has no hold on them.

---

34. Ursinus, *Commentary*, 264.

35. Olevianus, *Exposition*, 118; Olevian, *Firm Foundation*, 83–84.

QUESTION 53

What do you believe concerning the Holy Spirit?

Lord's Day 20

QUESTION 53

What do you believe concerning the Holy Spirit?

First, that he is co-eternal God with the Father and the Son. Secondly, that he is also given unto me, through true faith makes me a partaker of Christ and all his benefits, comforts me and shall abide with me forever.[1]

Scripture has a deep and robust doctrine of the Holy Spirit. He is revealed as hovering over the face of the deep in the acts of creation (Gen 1:2). The Holy Spirit is the Spirit of life (Rom 8:2). He manifested himself in the history of redemption in the glory cloud, the pillar of cloud by day and the pillar of fire by night (Exod 13:21). It was the Holy Spirit who conceived, in the womb of the blessed Virgin, Christ's human nature (Matt 1:18, 20). He anointed Jesus at the beginning of his earthly ministry (Matt 3:16). By the power of the Holy Spirit, Jesus cast out demons and healed the sick (Matt 12:28). Our Lord Jesus was "full of the Holy Spirit" (Luke 4:1) and was led by the same Spirit who led the church through the wilderness for forty days. He communed with the Spirit, who sustained and cooperated with him in his ministry (Luke 4:14, 18; 10:21). Because he is consubstantial with the Father and the Son, blasphemy against the Holy Spirit is called the unforgivable sin (Matt 12:31). Acts describes the acts of the Spirit, in the visible church, operating in special, supernatural ways, in the establishment of the visible church. Thus, insults to the Spirit bring about death (Acts 5:3–5). Our Savior promised that his disciples would be baptized in the Spirit (Acts 1:5, 8), and they were. He empowered them supernaturally to speak known, natural foreign languages supernaturally (Acts 2:4, 7; 1 Cor 12:4–11; 14:10–11), to interpret languages, to prophesy, and to perform apostolic miracles. By his power they healed the lame (Acts 3:7), raised the dead (Acts 9:41), and even put to death the

1. "Was glaubest du vom Heiligen Geiste? Erstlich, dass Er gleich ewiger Gott mit dem Vater und dem Sohne ist. Zum andern, dass Er auch mir gegeben ist, mich durch einen wahren Glauben Christi und aller seiner Wohlthaten theilhaftig macht, mich tröstet und bei mir bleiben wird bis in Ewigkeit" (Schaff, *Creeds of Christendom*, 3:324). "Quid credis de Spiritu Sancto? Primum, quod sit verus et coaeternus Deus, cum aeterno Patre et Filio: deinde, quod mihi quoque datus sit, ut me per veram fidem, Christi et omnium eius beneficiorum participem faciat, me consoletur, et mecum in aeternum maneat" (Niemeyer, *Collectio Confessionum*, 441).

disobedient (Acts 5). The Spirit of the Lord supernaturally transported Philip as he had the Old Testament prophets (Acts 8:39). Saul of Tarsus was given the gift of the Holy Spirit, new life, true faith, and was made an apostle of the Lord Jesus (Acts 9:17–21). That same Holy Spirit inspired and sustained the prophets (2 Pet 1:20–21). It is the Holy Spirit who now hovers over the church (1 Pet 4:12–16). Believers and their children are baptized in the name of the Triune God, including the name of the Holy Spirit (Matt 28:19).

For Paul especially, the person and work of the Spirit was a major emphasis. It is the Spirit who grants us new life and true faith. Believers have been set free from the bondage of the law and sin to walk in "newness of life" (Rom 7:6; 8:2–6). The Holy Spirit is the "Spirit of adoption" (Rom 8:15), by which believers have been made sons and children of God. The Spirit helps us to pray (Rom 8:26–27). The most remarkable thing that the Spirit did, however, which he continues to do even now, is raise those who are dead in Adam and make them alive with Christ. Olevianus writes, "In sum, the Holy Spirit is that bond of union by which Christ abides in us and we in Him. As the branches incorporated into the vine receive their nourishment and life from the vine, so we are incorporated into Christ by the Holy Spirit so that we might have true fellowship with Him and receive eternal life from Him (John 15:1)."[2]

Despite the abundant biblical testimony to the deity and consubstantiality of the Spirit, in the early fourth century the Arians sought to deny that the Son was consubstantial (ὁμοούσιος) with the Father. After Nicaea, by the 350s AD, the battle shifted to the consubstantiality of the Spirit with the Father and the Son. The "Spirit fighters" (*Pneumatomachians*) denied the consubstantiality of the Spirit with the Father and the Son.[3] Athanasius defended the consubstantiality of Spirit *and* the Son.[4] At the Council of Constantinople (AD 381), the ecumenical church confessed: "We believe in the Holy Spirit, the Lord and Giver of Life, proceeding from the Father, who, with the Father and the Son is together worshiped

2. Olevian, *Firm Foundation*, 92.

3. Kelly, *Early Christian Doctrines*, 115–16. This group was also known as the Macedonians or Eunomians (after Eunomius and Aetius). Muller notes that the Socinian John Biddle also denied the personality of the Holy Spirit (Muller, *Post-Reformation Reformed Dogmatics*, 4:334).

4. Kelly, *Early Christian Doctrines*, 258–63.

and glorified."[5] The fundamental confession of the church about the Spirit is aptly expressed in the Athanasian Creed: "But the Father, Son, and Holy Spirit are one deity: equal in glory, coeternal in majesty."[6] The attributes of deity are the Spirit's: uncreatedness (*increatus*), immensity, eternality, omnipotence; therefore "the Father is God, the Son is God, and the Holy Spirit is God."[7] The Spirit is a distinct person of the Trinity, with *personalia*, that is, personal properties that distinguish him from the Father the Son. In the language of the Athanasian Creed: "The Father is neither made, nor created, nor begotten. The Son is of the Father only, neither made nor created but begotten. The Holy Spirit is of the Father and the Son: neither made, nor created, nor begotten, but proceeding."[8]

Since the early sixteenth century, among Bible-believing Christians, the view of the person and work of the Holy Spirit has been greatly affected by a series of enthusiastic movements. These movements, which have roots in parts of the Anabaptist movements in the 1520s, manifested in the Northhampton, Massachusetts, revivals in the 1730s and 1740s and in a more pronounced and radical way at Cane Ridge, Kentucky (1801), and again in Topeka, Kansas (1901), and at Azusa Street (1906) in Los Angeles. To be sure, there were differences between the First and Second Great Awakenings, but one thing that unites all these events is a quest for an immediate experience of the Holy Spirit.[9] Particularly in the nineteenth-century revivals, American evangelical piety was dominated by versions of Anabaptist theology and piety. Two centuries before Northampton, however, Thomas Müntzer (1489–1525) and others like him were advancing the notion that true believers must replicate the

---

5. Καὶ εἰς τὸ ΠΝΕΥΜΑ ΤΟ ΑΓΙΟΝ, τὸ κύριον, (καὶ) τὸ ζωοποιόν, τὸ ἐκ τοῦ πατρὸς ἐκπορευόμενον, τὸ σὺν πατρὶ καὶ ὑιῷ συν προσκυνούμενον καὶ συνδοξαζόμενον (Schaff, *Creeds of Christendom*, 2:57–58). The *filioque* ("and the Son") clause would not become a fixed part of the Nicene-Constantinopolitan Creed, in the Western Church, until the Synod of Toledo (AD 589).

6. "Sed Patris et Filii et Spiritus Sancti una est divinitas: aequalis gloria, coaeterna majestas" (Schaff, *Creeds of Christendom*, 2:66).

7. "Ita dominus Pater: dominus Filius: dominus [et] Spiritus Sanctus" (Schaff, *Creeds of Christendom*, 2:67).

8. "Pater a nullo est factus: nec creatus, nec genitus; Filius a Patre solo est: non factus, nec creatus: sed genitus; Spiritus Sanctus a Patre et Filio: non factus, nec creatus, nec genitus: sed procedens" (Schaff, *Creeds of Christendom*, 2:67–68).

9. Clark, *Recovering the Reformed Confession*, 71–118.

experience of the apostolic church (as reconstructed by Müntzer and others). In this, they were following earlier, primitivist movements.[10]

Because the notion that if only we have enough faith or if only we use the right techniques (or both), we can recapture the original apostolic experience is so widespread, and because the contrast between the Reformed understanding of the person and work of the Spirit is starkly different from that of neo-Pentecostalism in all its forms, it is very difficult for American evangelical Christians to understand or appreciate the Reformed confession of the person and work of the Holy Spirit. Heidelberg and Azusa Street represent two radically different paradigms for understanding the person and work of the Holy Spirit. The Reformed theology, piety, and practice begins with the *sufficiency* of Scripture. Müntzer was explicit in his conviction of the insufficiency of Scripture. In the modern period, the Pentecostal and charismatic movements imply insufficiency of Scripture by their doctrine of continuing extracanonical revelation. The means of grace (*media gratiae*) are essential to Reformed theology and piety but not to the Pentecostal and the Charismatic movements.[11] The union of Reformed theology and these movements is achieved by radically redefining Reformed theology, by reducing it to a single element—divine sovereignty—and by seeking to add to it Pentecostalism or charismatic piety.

In order to understand the Reformed doctrine and piety of the Holy Spirit, that doctrine must be received and judged on its own terms. If we judged it by the standards of Müntzer, Cane Ridge, Azusa Street, or even Safenwil, it will of course fail, but those are false tests. Confessional Reformed Christianity rejects enthusiasm (e.g., Anabaptism, revivalism, and existential encounters with the word). We do, however, accept the teaching of God's holy word and the holy catholic faith.

The transition from the evangelical-charismatic-Pentecostal paradigm to the Reformed confession of the Spirit can be difficult and even painful. The first step is to recognize that Reformed theology and piety and Pentecostal or charismatic theology and piety are two distinct things.

10. See discussion under *HC* 32. For more on this, see Clark, "'Magic and Noise.'"

11. E.g., Ursinus, *Commentary*, 351–53; Clark, *Recovering the Reformed Confession*, 326–37; Clark, *Caspar Olevian*, 190–91.

Second, the reader must understand that Reformed piety is every bit as spiritual (and arguably more so) than the Pentecostal and restorationist attempts to recreate the apostolic experiences. At the same time, Reformed Christians need to stop feeling ashamed that they are not charismatics or Pentecostals. This is especially true for those who have grown up in Reformed congregations and wonder whether they might be missing out on something. They are not.

For one, we should not casually equate modern claims about the work of the Spirit with the apostolic phenomena. The great works of the Spirit in redemptive history were not healing services in which the miracle was contingent on one's faith (or lack thereof). The prophecies given, the revelations received, were not fallible.[12] They were Spirit-inspired, holy, inerrant words from the infallible Holy Spirit. The apostles were not faith healers. When a viper bit the apostle Paul (Acts 28:5), he was unhurt. The apostles had a divinely instituted office, an objective authority, and power by the Spirit that ended when they died. Every attempt to replicate their ministry or to claim a restoration necessarily redescribes ordinary postapostolic experience in biblical terms (pasting over the discontinuities and radical differences) or simply fabricates experiences (e.g., postapostolic speaking in tongues) that is both common to world religions and completely different from what was given to the apostles and the apostolic church.

The Spirit is not merely a power or even the energy of God. He is the Third Person of the Holy Trinity, in whom we believe with our whole heart. Olevianus writes,

> I believe that the Holy Spirit is true and eternal God, and of the same substance with the Father and the Son. Nevertheless, He is a person distinct from both inasmuch as He proceeds from both. Since He is true God, I place my trust in Him as I do in the Father and the Son, and I am confident that He will work out in me, who is devoid of all good, all that He has promised in His Word and on account of which He is sent by the Father and the Son.[13]

---

12. *Pace* Grudem, *Gift of Prophecy*, 71–89. The case of Agabus (Acts 21:10–14) is not obviously a instance of fallible, Spirit-inspired prophecy, nor did it seem so, e.g., to Calvin (*Commentary upon the Acts*, 2:271–73). The claim that the Holy Spirit spoke fallibly then and now is on its face exceeding dubious.

13. Olevianus, *Exposition*, 124.

In Olevianus's affirmation of the person and work of the Spirit, we see the traditional Reformed union of orthodoxy with a genuine, heartfelt piety. Our confession that the Spirit is Lord and giver of life is also a doxology sung in thanks and praise for his grace to sinners.

QUESTION 54

What do you believe concerning the "Holy Catholic Church"?

QUESTION 55

What do you understand by the "communion of saints"?

QUESTION 56

What do you believe concerning the "forgiveness of sins"?

Lord's Day 21

QUESTION 54

What do you believe concerning the "Holy Catholic Church"?

That, out of the whole human race, from the beginning to the end of the world, the Son of God, by His Spirit and Word, gathers, defends and preserves for Himself to everlasting life a chosen communion in the unity of the true faith; and that I am and forever shall remain a living member of the same.[1]

In our late modern era there is much doubt about the visible, institutional church, but Scripture teaches that there has always been a visible church, in all times, drawn out of all people. It is the Christ-confessing covenant community. Under the types and shadows, believers received Christ by faith (John 8:56; Heb 11:1, 13–25). Moses "considered the reproach of Christ greater wealth than the treasures of Egypt" (Heb 11:26). The rock from which they drank was Christ (1 Cor 10:4).[2]

In the Old Testament, the primary Hebrew word for "church" (קהל) refers to the regular, visible, institutional, assembly of God's people (Deut 9:10). Under Moses, that is, under the old covenant (2 Cor 3:4–18), the קהל were those who were assembled and constituted the people of God by the voice of God himself. Just as when at creation God spoke and all things came into being, at Sinai, God spoke and constituted his covenant people out of refugees from Egypt. Whereas the Hebrew Scriptures use קהל to refer to the visible assembly of God's people, the New Testament uses ἐκκλησία. A good example is Deuteronomy 23:2, which uses the phrase בִּקְהַל יְהוָה, which the LXX translates "church of the Lord" (ἐκκλησίαν κυρίου). This is the background for the New Testament teaching about

1. "Was glaubest du von der heiligen allgemeinen Christlichen Kirche? Dass der Sohn Gottes aus dem ganzen menschlichen Geschlechte sich eine auserwählte Gemeine zum ewigen Leben, durch seinen Geist und Wort, in Einigkeit des wahren Glaubens, von Anbeginn der Welt bis an's Ende versammle, schütze und erhalte; und dass ich derfelben ein lebendiges Glied bin, und ewig bleiben werde" (Schaff, *Creeds of Christendom*, 3:324–25). "Quid credis de sancta et catholica Christi Ecclesia? Credo Filium Dei, ab initio mundi ad finem usque, sibi ex universo genere humano coetum ad vitam aeternam electum, per Spiritum suum et verbum, in vera fide consentientem, colligere, tueri, ac servare: meque vivum eius coetus membrum esse, et perpetuo mansurum" (Niemeyer, *Collectio Confessionum*, 441–42).

2. Ursinus, *Commentary*, 288.

the visible church. 'Εκκλεσία occurs over one hundred times in the new covenant Scriptures. Usually it refers to a local identifiable circle of believers. For example: "Great fear seized the whole ἐκκλησία" (Acts 5:11). Paul speaks about the "churches in the province of Asia," "the churches" in Cilicia, Galatia, Asia, Macedonia, and Judea (Acts 15:41; 1 Cor 16:1, 19; Gal 1:2; 2 Cor 8:1; Gal 1:21). These passages refer to local assemblies. We know from our Lord's institution of the keys of the kingdom (Matt 16:18–19) that he instituted a visible covenant community. The keys (i.e., the preaching of the gospel, the administration of the sacraments, the use of church discipline) are given to an organization to be used. In Matthew 18:15–20 Jesus explicitly commissions the visible church to exercise church discipline.[3]

In *BC* 29, the Reformed churches distinguish between the true church, the false church, and sects.[4] In his explanation of *HC* 54, Ursinus uses the distinction between the true and false church: "The church is either true, or false. When we speak of the church, however, as false, we do not use the term in a proper, but in an improper sense; and mean by it every assembly which arrogates unto itself the name of the Christian Church, but which, instead of following it, rather persecutes it."[5] Thus, even to speak of the "false church" is to use the word *church* in a different sense. For the Reformed churches, the true and false churches are distinguished by marks (*marques* or *notae*). This is the language of *BC* 29, and these are the categories Ursinus uses in his lectures.[6] In the *BC*, the marks of the true church are the "pure preaching [*prédication*] of the gospel," the "pure administration of the sacraments," and the use of "church discipline to correct [*corriger*] sins." Ursinus's list is almost identical.[7] He further notes that it is one thing to claim the marks but another to possess them. He was convinced, and Reformed churches remain so today, that the marks

3. The "two or three" of Matt 18:20 is not a charter for small groups. It is an allusion to the "two or three witnesses" of v. 16, which itself is an allusion to Deut 17:6, "On the evidence of two witnesses or of three witnesses the one who is to die shall be put to death; a person shall not be put to death on the evidence of one witness" (ESV).

4. Schaff, *Creeds of Christendom*, 3:419–21.

5. Ursinus, *Commentary*, 286.

6. Schaff, *Creeds of Christendom*, 3:419–20; Ursinus, *Commentary*, 288–89.

7. Ursinus, *Commentary*, 288.

of the true church are objective and empirically verifiable.[8] Whether a congregation has the marks of the true church is discernible.

The church universal is *holy* insofar as it is a "holy congregation" and "an assembly of true Christian believers, expecting all their salvation in Jesus Christ, being washed by his blood, sanctified and sealed by the Holy Spirit."[9] Olevianus explains:

> The church is holy in two ways, by renewal and by imputation (John 13[:10]). By renewal in itself, such holiness has only begun (Rom. 7[:13–25]). Regarding this first kind of holiness, 2 Corinthians 7[:1] says, "Perfecting your sanctification" (see also 1 Thess. 4[:7]). But by imputation the church's holiness is most perfect in Christ, as He says [John 17:19]: "For their sakes I sanctify Myself." In this second kind of holiness, I believe that there is no sin and death in the church, that is, that no blame or punishment is imputed to true members of the church. For those who believe in Christ are not sinners and not liable to death. Rather, they are unconditionally holy and righteous, lords in Christ over sin and death, and those who live forever (Rom. 5:8–9; Heb. 10:14; Col. 2:10; Rom. 8:1; 1 Thess. 5:10).[10]

For Olevianus, the first sort of holiness is what we call progressive sanctification. The second he regards as identical with justification.

Under this question, Ursinus also distinguishes between the church considered as visible institution and as invisible. Considered as visible, it is "an assembly of persons, who embrace and profess the entire and uncorrupted doctrine of the law and gospel, and who use the sacraments according to the appointment of Christ, and profess obedience to the teachings of God's word."[11] Within the visible church, there are both those who have been regenerated by the Holy Spirit and those who have not been regenerated but who nevertheless profess faith and consent outwardly to the teaching and practice of the church.[12] This is the reality that

8. Ursinus, *Commentary*, 289.

9. *BC* 27, translated from the French text in Schaff, *Creeds of Christendom*, 3:417.

10. Olevianus, *Exposition*, 130.

11. Ursinus, *Commentary*, 286–87.

12. Ursinus, *Commentary*, 287.

our Lord foretold, that within the visible church there would be wheat and weeds (Matt 13:29–30). Because the visible church is a mixed assembly, there will be those at the last day who say, "Lord, Lord," but whom the Lord sends away (Matt 7:21–23). Both the adjectives "catholic" and "holy" apply to the true church.[13]

The catholicity or universality of the church is closely related to these questions. Our English word *catholic* comes from the Greek adjective καθολικός, which, centuries before Christian usage, denoted "general" as distinct from "particular."[14] It has no necessary reference to Roman Catholicism. The term *catholic* does not appear in the New Testament, but it does appear in some early Christian writings from the second century. Ignatius of Antioch wrote seven epistles to congregations that had supported him on his way toward his eventual martyrdom in Rome. In his *Epistle to the Smyrnaeans* (8.1), probably from the first quarter of the second century, he may have been the first postapostolic writer to use the adjective *catholic*.

> See that you all follow the *episkopos* [ἐπίσκοπος], even as Jesus Christ does the Father, and the *presbyterion* [πρεσβυτέριον], as you would the apostles; and revere the *diakonous* [διάκονος], as being the institution of God. Let no man do anything connected with the church without the *episkopos*. Let that be deemed a proper thanksgiving, which is either even as, wherever Jesus Christ is, there is the catholic church. It is not lawful without the *episkopos* either to baptize or to celebrate a love-feast; but whatsoever he shall approve, that is also pleasing to God, so that everything that is done may be secure and valid.[15]

From the context it is clear that Ignatius is using the adjective *catholic* to describe the universal church, and that understanding is confirmed by the clause "wherever Jesus Christ is, there is the catholic church." We see a similar usage in the salutation in the *Martyrdom of Polycarp* from late in the second century: "The Church of God which sojourns at Smyrna,

---

13. *BC* 27–29, in Schaff, *Creeds of Christendom*, 416–21; Ursinus, *Commentary*, 289.
14. Arndt et al., *Greek-English Lexicon*, s.v. "καθολικός."
15. Translation modified from Holmes, *Apostolic Fathers*, 255.

to the church of God sojourning in Philomelium, and to all the congregations of the holy and catholic Church [καθολικῆς ἐκκλησίας] in every place: Mercy, peace, and love from God the Father, and our Lord Jesus Christ, be multiplied."[16]

The second-century church had no notion of a Roman Catholic church. The expression "Roman Catholic" found currency among seventeenth-century Protestants. The Roman Catholic Church, however, speaks of the catholic church in communion with and in subjection to the Roman bishop. As a matter of history, we cannot say that the Roman Catholic Church existed in any recognizable way until the episcopacy of Gregory I (AD 590–604). The notion of the supremacy of the Roman bishop over all other pastors, and the Roman church over all other churches, developed gradually, but it certainly was not inherent in the ancient ecumenical (universal) creeds. When we say, "I believe in the holy catholic church," we are not confessing, "I believe whatever the Roman Catholic Church declares to be dogma." The Reformed churches, however, certainly believe the holy and catholic faith taught in Holy Scripture and confessed by true church in all times and places. It is to that faith that the Athanasian Creed refers when it says, "Whosoever will be saved, before all things it is necessary that he hold the catholic faith."[17] It is the universal, Christian faith, the ecumenical faith, not Roman Catholic dogma we affirm and hold to be necessary to salvation. Indeed, there is a great difference between true catholicity and Roman Catholicism. The very expression "Roman Catholicism" is an oxymoron. The Reformation churches of the sixteenth century reclaimed the adjective and returned to its original sense, which is the sense of the word as it appears in the ecumenical (catholic) creeds.

Because the church is a divine (and not a human) institution, because Christ has given to her ministry of the keys of the kingdom, because, by divine ordination, the Spirit of God uses the gospel preached in and by the church to bring the elect to new life and to true faith (Rom 10:14–17), the church has confessed since the mid–third century that outside the true church, there is ordinarily no salvation (*extra ecclesiam nulla salus est*).

---

16. Holmes, *Apostolic Fathers*, 307.

17. Schaff, *Creeds of Christendom*, 2:66.

This is the confession of the Reformed churches (*BC* 28): "and outside of it there is no salvation."[18]

It is under this question that Ursinus addresses the doctrine of predestination.[19] Ursinus gave his lectures well before the Synod of Dort (1618–1619) addressed this topic definitively for the Reformed churches.[20] Nevertheless, we should observe that his extensive treatment of the doctrine in his lectures illustrates that it is the shared conviction of the Reformed churches. When the churches of Europe and the British Isles gathered at Dort to defend them against the Remonstrants, they were not creating novelties but defending a shared, Augustinian, Protestant heritage. This they traced from Scripture through Augustine and the great Augustinian tradition (e.g., Gottschalk of Orbais, Thomas Aquinas, Thomas Bradwardine), and through Luther and all the magisterial Protestants.[21]

It is a biblical doctrine. The Scriptures are replete with explicit and implicit teaching that God has elected, in Christ, a people from all eternity. Deuteronomy 4:24–27 illustrates the nature of unconditional election through the temporary, national election of Israel (Deut 4:34; 7:7–8). Yahweh did not choose Israel because of any qualities inherent or foreseen in her but that he might demonstrate his glory (Exod 9:16; Rom 9:16) through Pharaoh. In Romans 9, Paul appeals to national Israel as an illustration of the way he elects his people, those for whom Christ died.[22] Isaac represents the elect and Esau the reprobate (Rom 9:7–8). Isaac was elect before he had done anything. Election, which concerns those chosen in Christ from all eternity (Eph 1:3–5), is not conditioned on foreseen faith

18. Schaff, *Creeds of Christendom*, 3:418. The Latin text of the Belgic uses language virtually identical to the formula used by Cyprian (*Epistle* 73.21): "extra eam nulla sit salus" (Müller, *Die Bekenntnisschriften*, 243). Cyprian writes, "Quia salus extra ecclesiam non est" (*Opera Omnia*, 3/2:795). For the English translation, see Cyprian of Carthage, *Epistles of Cyprian* (*ANF* 5:384). I am grateful to Harrison Perkins for his help with this reference.

19. Ursinus, *Commentary*, 293–304. This location seems to reflect the pedagogical influence of his longtime teacher and friend, Philip Melanchthon, who, in the later editions of his *Loci communes*, moved his discussion of predestination under the doctrine of the church (Clark, *Caspar Olevian*, 172–73).

20. "The First Main Point of Doctrine: Divine Election and Reprobation," in United Reformed Churches in North America, *Liturgical Forms and Prayers*, 259–67.

21. Clark, *Caspar Olevian*, 170–77; Clark, "Election and Predestination," 90–122.

22. Ursinus, *Commentary*, 294.

or faithfulness.[23] Indeed, in the decree the elect are considered created and fallen (Eph 2:1–4). In the decree of reprobation or passing over, the reprobate are considered created and fallen and are left in that state.[24]

We should also note that for Ursinus, Olevianus, and the Reformed churches at Dort, predestination includes both aspects of the divine decree: election, in Christ, to new life and to true faith, as well as reprobation, the passing over of others in their fallen state. Ursinus's connection between the doctrine of the church and the doctrine of predestination reflects the Reformed conviction that the decrees of election and reprobation are worked out within the visible church.

The divine decree (election and reprobation) lies behind redemptive history (*historia salutis*) and the application of redemption (*ordo salutis*). Ursinus lists eight effects of predestination: the establishment and gathering of the church, the sending of Christ, the effectual call and regeneration of the elect, faith, justification, sanctification, good works, perseverance, and glorification.[25]

The doctrine of predestination should not be a source of doubt but rather a source of comfort. Calvin taught that we do not seek to know our election *a priori*, that is, by asking, "Am I elect?" The answer to that question requires one to climb into heaven and peer into the hidden things of God (Deut 29:29). Rather, "If we have been chosen in him, we shall not find assurance of our election in ourselves; and not even in God the Father, if we conceive him as severed from his Son. Christ, then, is the mirror wherein we must, and without self-deception may, contemplate our own election."[26] Ursinus affirms that approach: We can know whether we are elect. "But of our own election in particular, we not only may, but ought to be certain, the knowledge of which is obtained, *a posteriori*, that is, from our conversion to God, or from true faith and repentance, which are the effects of our election unto eternal life. That we may know and believe that we are certainly chosen of God, we must believe in Christ,

23. Ursinus, *Commentary*, 297–99.

24. Ursinus, *Commentary*, 297–98.

25. Ursinus, *Commentary*, 299. He also lists a parallel set of effects among the reprobate. NB: Ursinus uses "regeneration" in his order of salvation, but by that he meant merely sanctification. The assignment of regeneration to "awakening from death to life" did not occur until after Dort.

26. Calvin, *Institutes* 3.24.5.

and also in eternal life."[27] This was the view confessed at Dort against the Remonstrants.[28] Christians will struggle with doubt and uncertainty, but we look to Christ and to his promises first and then find encouragement in the evidence of his gracious work in us, bringing us to faith and beginning to conform us to Christ in this life.

Finally, a related question should be addressed under *HC* 54, that is, the translation of the ninth article of the Apostles' Creed. Should we say "a holy catholic church" or "the holy catholic church"? The evidence is overwhelmingly on the side of translating the received Latin text of the creed as "the holy catholic church." The eighth and ninth articles are usually translated, "I believe in the Holy Spirit, the holy catholic church." Olevianus raised this question in 1567:

> In the first place, why do you not say, "I believe in the holy catholic church" instead of "I believe in a holy catholic church"?
>
> A. We believe that a church, that is, a community or people of God, is that which has the covenant and promises of God and that we also are members of this community. But we do not believe in the Church or the people of God, for that little word "in" is reserved only for the Creator, not the creation. It is similar to our saying "I believe a resurrection of the body," not "I believe in the resurrection of the body."[29]

He made two points: first, it is an article of faith that the holy catholic or universal church exists. Second, the church itself is not the object of faith.

Most English translations use the definite article, but two influential English translations use the indefinite article: the 1959 *Psalter Hymnal* and the 1984 Canadian Reformed *Book of Praise*.[30] The 2018 translation published by the United Reformed Churches in North America returns to the traditional translation.[31]

---

27. Ursinus, *Commentary*, 301.

28. *Canons of Dort* 1.12–13.

29. Olevian, *Firm Foundation*, 96–97.

30. Christian Reformed Church, *Psalter Hymnal: Centennial Edition*, 36; Canadian Reformed Churches, *Book of Praise*, 482.

31. United Reformed Churches in North America, *Liturgical Forms and Prayers*, 209.

The Latin text says: "Credo in Spiritum Sanctum; sanctam ecclesiam catholicam."[32] Of course, the Latin text has no definite article before either "Holy Spirit" or "holy catholic church," but grammatically and theologically, if we believe "the" Holy Spirit (we do), then on what ground would we proceed to say "a holy catholic church" but then confess "the communion of the saints, the remission of sins"? It seems arbitrary to move between the definite and indefinite that way. One counterargument would be to say that, if the way we speak of the Spirit should control the way we speak of the church, then we should say we believe "in" the church as we believe "in" the Holy Spirit. Both William Perkins (1558–1602) and Herman Witsius (1636–1708) argue against this on the grounds of the distinction between the Creator and the creature.[33] We do not believe "in" the church in the same way we believe "in" the Holy Spirit. We confess "the holy catholic church," but the Holy Spirit is an object of faith. The church is not an object of faith.

Other translations give us some help. The Greek text signals the definite article explicitly (τὸ ΠΝΕΥΜΑ ΤΟ ΑΓΙΟΝ, ἁγίαν καθολικὴν ἐκκλησίαν), and that article controls the subsequent phrases. The German text of the Heidelberg Catechism (1563) is ambiguous. It begins with the definite article (*den Heiligen Geist*) but then uses *eine* before "*heilige, allgemeine Christliche kirche*," which could be translated either "a" or "one." The German text of the catechism, however, is typically translated into English with "the holy catholic church" in recognition of the influence of the definite article before *Heiligen Geist*. The Dutch (*een heilige, algemene, christelijke kerk*) might be ambiguous, but it does not seem to demand an indefinite article any more than the German does. In other words, the choice of an indefinite article by a few English translators seems theological more than grammatical.

Traditionally, when writing in English, Reformed writers use the definite article or are translated into English with the definite article (e.g., Heinrich Bullinger, Caspar Olevianus, Thomas Cartwright, Petrus DeWitte).[34] In addition, the Allen, Beveridge, and Battles translations of

32. Schaff, *Creeds of Christendom*, 2:45.

33. Perkins, *Works*, 5:323–24; Witsius, *Sacred Dissertations*, 2:361–62.

34. Bullinger, *Decades*, 6.1; Olevianus, *Exposition*, 16; Cartwright, *Confutation of the Rhemists*, 321; DeWitte, *Catechizing upon the Heidelbergh Catechisme*, 151.

Calvin's *Institutes* 4.2.1 all use the definite article. Ursinus and Witsius are both translated with the definite article.[35] Archibald Alexander Hodge uses the definite article.[36] Cartwright uses the indefinite in his explanation but not in his quotation of the creed. It is not easy to find Reformed writers using the indefinite article for the church in their rendering of the creed.[37]

It seems that the best English translation of the creed should be "*the* holy catholic church." The argument for the indefinite would appear to rest almost entirely on a possible ambiguity in the German text (and possibly in the Dutch translation) of the catechism, but that is outweighed by the relative clarity of the earlier Latin and Greek texts. Theologically, it seems sounder to say, "I believe the holy catholic church." The church is not a potential but a reality that is manifested in the world. This is what we say in *BC* 27. "We believe and confess one only catholic or universal church" (*une seule Église catholique ou universelle*).[38] The confession twice thereafter says *cette Église* ("this church") in article 27 and *cette sainte assemblée* ("this holy assembly") in article 28. We believe that there is a true church (art. 29) and that the true church is manifested visibly and has marks that are empirically verifiable. We believe that there is a body of believers in all times and places, but it is always manifested as and in the church, if even in small, scattered, persecuted congregations at times.

We should be cautious about revising the received translation and understanding of a catholic, ecumenical creed for reasons that are not clearly understood, expressed, and received widely in the visible church. The use of the indefinite article in the ninth article in English translations does not seem to have a very good pedigree, nor is it well-attested among ecclesiastical documents and Reformed writers.

---

35. Ursinus, *Commentary*, 117; Witsius, *Sacred Dissertations*, 361.

36. Hodge, *Commentary on the Confession*, 22–23.

37. Cartwright, *Confutation of the Rhemists*, 24.

38. Schaff, *Creeds of Christendom*, 3:416–17.

QUESTION 55

What do you understand by the "communion of saints"?

First, that believers, one and all, as members of the Lord Jesus Christ, are partakers with him in all his treasures and gifts; secondly, that each one must feel himself bound to use his gifts readily and cheerfully for the advantage and welfare of other members.[39]

The answer begins with our spiritual union with Christ but turns to our union in Christ with one another.[40] In his exposition of this article of the creed, Olevianus notes that there are two aspects to our communion: internal and external. Regarding the latter, all who profess the faith are part of one communion organized around the ministry of word and sacrament. Those who profess the Christian faith look to the "truth of the prophetic and apostolic teaching" as the "indubitable" mark of the visible church (1 Tim 3:15).[41] The "communion of the saints," however, "also signifies that inward union by which those whom the Lord has forever chosen to be a part of this visible assembly, that is, those who truly believe, are united by the same Spirit with the Father, His Son Jesus Christ, and with each other."[42] Ursinus characterizes the internal aspect of the communion of saints as "an equal participation in all the promises of the gospel" or "the common possession of Christ, and all his benefits; and the bestowment of the gifts which are given to each member for the salvation of the church."[43]

39. "Was verstehest du unter der Gemeinschaft der Heiligen? Erstlich, dass alle und jede Gläubigen als Glieder an dem Herrn Christo und allen seinen Schätzen und Gaben Gemeinschaft haben. Zum andern, dass ein jeder seine Gaben zu Nutz und Heil der andern Glieder willig und mit Freuden anzulegen sich schuldig wissen soll" (Schaff, *Creeds of Christendom*, 3:325). "Quid sibi vult Communio Sanctorum? Primum, quod universi et singuli credentes, Christi et omnium eius bonorum, tamquam ipsius membra communionem habeant. Deinde, quod singuli, quae acceperunt dona, in commune commodum et universorum salutem prompte et alacriter conferre debeant" (Niemeyer, *Collectio Confessionum*, 442).

40. Since 1975, the version of the catechism adopted by the Christian Reformed Church paraphrases the first part of the answer: "First, that believers one and all, as members of this community share in Christ and in all his treasures and gifts ..." (Klooster, *Our Only Comfort*, 2:678). This paraphrase is without warrant in the German or Latin versions.

41. Olevianus, *Exposition*, 132.

42. Olevianus, *Exposition*, 132. Olevianus's language in this section of the *Exposition* mirrors that of *BC* 28 almost word for word.

43. Ursinus, *Commentary*, 304.

Thus, however valuable self-reliance is in civil life or, more broadly, in the secular sphere (and it is highly valued), that same spirit of independence must be severely curbed when it comes to the life of the church or, more broadly, in the sacred sphere.[44] Believers were not redeemed to live their Christian lives in isolation from the broader culture (1 Cor 5:10) or in independence from other believers (Heb 10:25). Christians are redeemed with the intention that they should become part of the visible expression of the church universal, the Christ-confessing covenant community.[45] It is enough to say here that the Scriptures everywhere assume and teach that believers are ordinarily redeemed in community and for community, and that community is called the church. The history of redemption in Scripture is also a church history. Adam and Eve and their children formed not only a civil society but also the church. Sometimes the visible church has been great (a great number crossed the Red Sea) and sometimes almost invisible. Only eight people were in the ark (Gen 7:7; 1 Pet 3:20). Acts describes the apostolic period of the history of the visible church. The Epistles were written to known, visible assemblies, congregations, churches gathered around the ministry of the word and sacraments.

There is no way to understand Paul's language that we are "one body" and "members of one another" (Rom 12:5) apart from a robust doctrine

44. Though oft maligned in the twentieth century, some sort of distinction between sacred and secular is both biblical and unavoidable. The word *secular* is derived from the Latin noun *saeculum*. In non-Christian usage, it refers to a generation. In biblical usage (i.e., in the Latin translations of Scripture), it can signal "forever" (Exod 21:6; Rom 1:25; Gal 1:5). It also refers to a generation (Gen 6:4). It is also used for Jesus, Paul, and James's expression "this age" (Matt 12:32; 1 Cor 1:20; 2:6) and "the world" (Mark 4:19; Jas 4:4), which are negative. A derivative is used in Heb 6:5 to refer to the eternal state. It is also used, however, in 1 Cor 6:3 to refer to "this life" and in 2 Tim 2:4 to daily life, which is common to believers and unbelievers. It is in this last sense that I am using it here. Remember, even in creation, before the fall, there was ordinary time (six days) and a sacred day set aside (the seventh day). As a matter of logic, if everything is holy, then nothing is holy, because nothing is set aside or distinct from anything else. In traditional Reformed usage, the distinction between secular and sacred did not imply that God is sovereign over some things but not others. There is a Christian worldview (defined correctly), but there is also Christian liberty. A proper Christian worldview not only recognizes Christ's sovereignty over all things but also that, in his ordinary providence, believers live in this world with unbelievers and that, as image-bearers, we share much in common with unbelievers even if we interpret the significance of the world quite differently. Nevertheless, God makes the sun to rise and the rain to fall on the just and the unjust (Matt 5:45). It is the same rain. It is the same sun for believers and unbelievers. If we express the antithesis between believers and unbelievers so that the sun and rain become *essentially* different for believers as compared to unbelievers, we run the risk of falling into a sort of gnosticism.

45. See the discussion under *HC* 54.

of the visible, institutional church. Paul did not send those words originally to individuals but to a congregation meeting at one time and in one place, where they were read to the congregation. First Corinthians 11 and 14 describe public worship services held by the congregation. One might make an entire study of Paul's "one another" language in Galatians, Ephesians, and Colossians (Rom 12:10, 16; 14:13; 15:5, 7; 2 Cor 13:11; Eph 4:32). The clear implication in those places is that he was writing to congregations to instruct them about the gospel, grace, and the moral and spiritual consequences of the gospel. How can we "encourage one another" (1 Thess 4:18; 5:11), as Paul exhorts the Thessalonian congregation, unless we are gathered together? To put it briefly: membership matters.

It was against this great backdrop that the early medieval church confessed the "communion of the saints" (*communio sanctorum*). Though it did not appear in the Apostles' Creed until circa AD 550, it was long believed and taught by the postapostolic church.[46] Like the New Testament, many of the earliest documents in the early church were letters to congregations offering guidance and instruction. The fathers did not know about a Christian faith formed or a Christian life lived in isolation from the Christ-confessing covenant community. The *BC* says in article 28:

> We believe, since this holy congregation is an assemblage of those who are saved, and out of it there is no salvation, that no person of whatsoever state or condition he may be, ought to withdraw himself, to live in a separate state from it; but that all men are in duty bound to join and unite themselves with it; maintaining the unity of the Church; submitting themselves to the doctrine and discipline thereof; bowing their necks under the yoke of Jesus Christ; and as mutual members of the same body, serving to the edification of the brethren, according to the talents God has given them. And that this may be better observed, it is the duty of all believers, according to the Word of God, to separate themselves from those who do not belong to the Church, and to join themselves to this congregation, wheresoever God hath established it, even though the magistrates and edicts of princes be against it; yes, though they

46. Schaff, *Creeds of Christendom*, 2:56.

should suffer death or bodily punishment. Therefore all those who separate themselves from the same, or do not join themselves to it, act contrary to the ordinance of God.[47]

When *HC* 55 says "communion of the saints," it is thinking in precisely the same categories as the *BC*. Believers are bound together by the Spirit, into a visible assembly. In that assembly they give up their autonomy, their independence, even as Christ gave up his prerogatives—he might have called down legions of angels, but he did not—for our sakes. Yes, we have liberty chartered in the word of God (*sola Scriptura*). The visible church may not impose as required any ceremony in worship or any doctrine that is not taught explicitly in Scripture or deduced by "good and necessary consequence" (WCF 1.6; *BC* 7, 32) but within that liberty there is order, there is structure, there are offices, and there is a communion divinely instituted and to which we are all obligated.

The noun *saints* has no reference to the attempt by the Roman Catholic Church to establish a minor pantheon but rather refers to believers. This is a biblical way of speaking of believers gathered together. Paul wrote to the "saints" (ἅγιος) gathered in Rome (Rom 1:7). This is part of his typical salutation. As Ursinus notes, we are saints in three respects, by the imputation of Christ's righteousness (justification), by our progressive sanctification, and by our separation from the rest of humanity in gathered, public worship.[48]

QUESTION 56

What do you believe concerning the "forgiveness of sins"?
That God, for the sake of Christ's satisfaction, will no more remember my sins, nor the sinful nature with which I have to struggle all my life long; but graciously gives to me the righteousness of Christ, that I may nevermore come into condemnation.[49]

47. Schaff, *Creeds of Christendom*, 418–19.

48. Ursinus, *Commentary*, 305.

49. "Was glanbest du von der Vergebung der Sünden? Dass Gott um der Genugthuung Christi willen aller meiner Sünden, auch der sündlichen Art, mit der ich mein Leben lang zu streiten habe, nimmermehr gedenken will, sondern mir die Gerechtigkeit Christi aus Gnaden schenket, dass ich in's

It is not always easy for us to forgive others. First, when a wrong has been done, quite apart from its effect on us (and its affect in us), justice itself has been violated. Second, it hurts to be wronged. That hurt fogs the mind through anger and depression so that we cannot see or think clearly. We know from Matthew 18:21–35 that it is often difficult for us to forgive others. That is why Peter asked how often he had to forgive his brother who sinned against him.

If it is difficult for us sinners to forgive other sinners who have offended, how much more the Righteous One? Imagine a legal system in which every transgression were met with immediate and just retribution. Under such a system, our misdemeanors and vices would be immediately exposed and punished. Our murderous thoughts would be met with the just punishment for murder: death. In that system none of us would fare well. Our Lord Jesus said as much he asked the rich young ruler (Luke 18:18–29; Mark 10:17–31), "Why do you call me good? No one is good but God alone." He was saying to the man that, if he intended to relate to God on the basis of strict justice, he was doomed to fail the test. That is why Jesus imposed on him what he knew to be an impossible requirement: to go and sell all he had and give it to the poor. He was not, as Antony of Egypt (ca. AD 251–356) and others thought, establishing a charter for the monastic life, nor was he explaining how we can be accepted by God through faithfulness (or congruent merit).[50] Rather, he was preaching the

---

Gericht nimmermehr soll kommen" (Schaff, *Creeds of Christendom*, 3:325). "Quid credis remissione peccatoris? Deum propter satisfactionem Christi, meorum peccatorum, atquae illius etiam pravitatis, cum qua mihi per omnem vitam pugnandum ets, memoriam omnem deposuissse, et me iustitia Christi gratis donare, ne unquam in iudicium veniam" (Niemeyer, *Collectio Confessionum*, 442). NB: The tercentenary edition of the Heidelberg Catechism ambiguously translates *schenkt* ("gives") with "imparts," which might create the impression that *HC* 56 teaches justification through sanctification. The Latin text clearly says *donare* ("to give"). The 2018 United Reformed Churches in North America's choice of "grants" is better choice in this context. See Schaff, *Creeds of Christendom*, 3:325; United Reformed Churches in North America, *Liturgical Forms and Prayers*, 223.

50. Congruent merit (*meritum de congruo*) was a medieval theory that has reappeared among federal visionists and proponents of the New Perspective(s) on Paul, whereby God is said to have covenanted to grade on a curve, as it were, so that he imputes perfection to us when we do our best. See the discussion under *HC* 21. The Reformation categorically rejected this doctrine in salvation as a complete fiction. The only merit we know from Scripture is condign (*meritum de condigno*), whereby God recognizes Christ's actual, perfect righteousness and credits it to believers for their justification. For a discussion of the Reformed use of *meritum ex pacto* in the covenant of works and to explain the work of Christ for us, see Perkins, "*Meritum Ex Pacto*," 57–87.

law, in its pedagogical use, to teach the rich young ruler the greatness of his sin and misery.

The problem of our sin and God's perfect holiness (Isa 6:3) and righteousness (Ps 7:11) would seem to be insurmountable. Hebrews 12:29 reminds us that our God is a consuming fire. So, is not a small thing for Christians to confess in the Apostles' Creed that we believe in the forgiveness of sins. God is not obligated to forgive. He chooses freely to forgive sinners and to do so without compromising his justice. He has satisfied his righteousness for us that he might be just and "the justifier of the one who has faith in Jesus" (Rom 3:26).

It is also important to remember that we come to this article of the creed under the doctrine of the Holy Spirit and under the doctrine of the church. Though the church has no power or authority to *create* anything (that would be sacerdotalism), it does have authority and a duty to announce the truth and to recognize reality and act accordingly (e.g., in church discipline). The church is a minister, a servant of the word of God. The church, however, is also the place where that truth is ordinarily (in both senses, i.e., by divine ordination and usually) announced and where the benefits of the gospel are received.

When the Reformed churches confess the forgiveness of sins, we begin not with the church but with God. He forgives sins, which is why it was so scandalous for our Lord Jesus to announce, "Your sins are forgiven" (Mark 2:1–12; Matt 9:2). This is why he was falsely accused of blasphemy. He demonstrated that he had (and has) the right, authority, and power to forgive sins. Only God heals paralytics, raises the dead, and forgives sins, and those are the things Jesus did because he is God the Son incarnate.

The ground or legal basis for God's forgiveness of our sins is "Christ's satisfaction." This is shorthand for what we have already discussed under *HC* 37, that Jesus actively suffered all his life and that all his active, righteous suffering is credited to all those who believe. That phrase, "for Christ's sake" (*propter Christum*), is an axis of Reformed theology. Critics of the Reformed confession have sometimes accused it of being legalistic because it is concerned to account for God's law.[51] The assumption of the criticism is that God can ignore his own nature (or perhaps that he has

51. Vos, "Alleged Legalism in Paul's Doctrine," 161–79.

no such thing) and act arbitrarily. He is free, but we also are obligated to account for the way he has revealed himself. He reveals himself as just and a law-giving and law-keeping God. Christ's obedience and death were not arbitrary and, in that sense, cruel. Jesus was treated cruelly and shamefully but subjected himself to that treatment for our sake that we might be accepted for his sake, by God's grace alone (*sola gratia*), through faith alone (*sola fide*), in Christ alone. His righteousness is the legal basis for the forgiveness of our sins.

It is a good thing that Christ was our righteous substitute and remains our righteous Mediator because, even after we are given new life and faith and through faith mystical union with Christ, we remain sinners (*simul iustus et peccator*).[52] Perfectionists and gnostics cannot account for that reality, but one of the most needed and lovely aspects of the catechism is its realism about the Christian life. In his providence, God certainly sees our sins, but with respect to our justification we say that "he no more remembers our sins." This is the language of Scripture (e.g., Ps 25:7, among other places). For God to "remember" our sins would be to place us again under condemnation. Yes, he chastises us as earthly fathers discipline their children. That discipline means our father loves us, not that he has rejected us (hence the evil of the health-and-wealth doctrine).

In Christ, we are not under a covenant of works ("do this and live," Luke 10:28) but under a covenant of grace: Christ has done all that we may live. God has forgiven us. He has settled our account for Christ's sake. Christ achieved perfect righteousness for us (*pro nobis*). That is why he cried, "It is finished" (John 19:30). God has redeemed us, but we are still pilgrims. We still sin and we will for the rest of our earthly lives. God, however, is gracious. Because he has executed his righteous wrath on Christ, he bears with us and works in us by his Spirit. In Christ, he accepts us.

There is nothing in *HC* 56 (or anywhere else in the catechism) about our obedience or our faithfulness *for* justification. The doctrine of the catechism is that the forgiveness of sins and acceptance with God (justification) is not based on our obedience. It is not received through our faithfulness or through our cooperation with grace or through our

52. "*Sic homo Christianus simul iustus et peccator, sanctus, prophanus, inimicus et filius Dei est*" (*WA* 40.1/1:368.27–27).

sanctification. We obey because God has declared us righteous before him for Christ's sake alone. Paul says in Romans 3:28: "For we say that a man is justified by faith apart from works of the law," and in Galatians 2:16: "But we know that a man is not justified from works of the law but only through faith in Jesus Christ, so we also have believed in Christ Jesus, in order to be justified from faith in Christ and not from works of the law, because from works of the law no man will be justified."

By "works of the law" Paul means more than the Mosaic ceremonies and Torah. He is referring to our every attempt either by ourselves or with the help of grace to satisfy God's righteous law for justification. The Galatian heresy lives. In combating antinomianism, the medieval church fell into the error of justification by sanctification. The Reformation returned us to the biblical gospel, but some soon fell again into moralism. Richard Baxter (1615–1691) rejected the Protestant gospel in favor of moralism.[53] The General Assembly of the Church of Scotland attacked the gospel as antinomian when it attacked the *Marrow of Modern Divinity* (1645 and 1649) and the eighteenth-century "Marrow men" (e.g., Thomas Boston and the Erskines) who were in fact heroes for the gospel of grace and the gospel mystery of sanctification.[54]

Remarkably, wonderfully, mysteriously, there is forgiveness for sinners. Christians who are content to rest in Christ and in his finished work find the gospel of forgiveness in Christ's church. Indeed, the "pure preaching of the gospel" (*BC* 29) is one of the marks of the true church. We live together in the communion of the saints as forgiven sinners who, for Christ's sake alone, will never come into condemnation (Ps 146).

---

53. Baxter, *Aphorisms of Justification*, is a categorical rejection of the Reformation doctrine of justification by grace alone, through faith alone, and was interpreted so by John Owen, who refuted him in his treatise *Doctrine of Justification*.

54. Clark, "How We Got Here," 15–16; Ferguson, *Whole Christ*, 34–36, 78–79, 137–38. Contrast Ferguson's careful account of the *Marrow* with that found in Jones, *Antinomianism*, 13–15.

Question 57

What comfort does the "resurrection of the body" afford you?

Question 58

What comfort do you have from the article of "life everlasting"?

Lord's Day 22

Question 57

What comfort does the "resurrection of the body" afford you?

That not only my soul after this life shall be immediately taken up to Christ its head; but also, that this my body, raised by the power of Christ, shall be reunited with my soul, and made like unto the glorious body of Christ.[1]

For all the political and civil benefits the Enlightenment movements brought, these movements also carried certain costs theologically. The Enlightenment movements posed as world-expanding, mind-expanding movements, which promised to free us from the shackles of a benighted, narrow view of the world. Ironically, the Enlightenments did just the opposite. Whether through rationalism (what the human intellect cannot comprehend cannot be true) or through empiricism (what cannot be reproduced in a laboratory cannot be true) or, later, through the Romantic-subjectivist reaction (the world is what I say it is), the world became much smaller than it had been. The rationalists and empiricists banished Christian mystery (e.g., the Christian doctrines of God, Christ, and salvation), and the subjectivists reinterpreted the doctrines as metaphors for human experience. Each of the Enlightenment movements in its own way put human existence in a box. If the Enlightenment movements are right, then perhaps Jean-Paul Sartre or even Friedrich Nietzsche were correct. Either we should learn to value every moment for what it is, despite the absurdity of it all, or we should exercise the will to power.

The Enlightenment movements were proposing substitute religions for Christianity. The god of the Enlightenment and post-Enlightenment

1. "Wes tröstet dich die Auferstehung des Fleisches? Dass nicht allein meine Seele nach diefem Leben alsbald zu Christo, ihrem Haupt, genommen wird, sondern auch, dass diess mein Fleisch, durch die Kraft Christi auferwecket, wieder mit meiner Seele vereiniget, und dem herrlichen Leibe Christi gleichsörmig werden soll" (Schaff, *Creeds of Christendom*, 3:325–26). "Quid te consolatur Resurrectio carnis? Quod non tantum anima mea, postquam e corpore excesserit e vestigo ad Christum suum caput assumetur: verum quod haec quoque caro mea, potentia Christi excitata, rursus animae meae unietur, et glorioso Christi corpori conformabitur" (Niemeyer, *Collectio Confessionum*, 442).

religions is humanity, who became "the measure of all things."[2] Humanity says what heaven is or is not or whether heaven can be. The existentialist cannot even prove absolutely, from a god's-eye point of view, that he exists. The rationalist and the empiricist assumes his existence. The radical subjectivist does not really know or care much about what is objectively true. What matters is what the radical subjectivist experiences affectively. In the end, the radical subjectivist is irrational.

There is an alternative to the crypt of modernity: biblical and catholic Christian eschatology. The Roman authorities lay Jesus's body in the grave fully expecting him to stay put, only to find—much to the dismay of the Roman and the Jewish authorities—that he had rebelled against their expectations. Jesus is that sort of Savior. Few expected that God the Son would take on true humanity, that his humanity would be conceived by God the Spirit in the womb of a virgin, but there he was healing the sick, raising the dead, and walking on water. Paul calls the incarnation a mystery (μυστήριον; Eph 3:3; Rom 16:25; Col 2:2). To the truly rational, the stark reality of Christ's bodily resurrection should be empirical evidence enough. After all, he was seen and touched by the disciples, and later he was seen by five hundred before his ascension (1 Cor 15:6). The Jewish authorities knew him to be raised. The guards were silenced. Conspiracy theories usually fail, but that does not mean that there are no conspiracies to silence the truth (Matt 28:11–15).

According to Paul, there are other mysteries. One of the greatest is the bodily resurrection from the dead.

> I tell you this, brothers: flesh and blood cannot inherit the kingdom of God, nor does the perishable inherit the imperishable. Behold! I tell you a mystery. We shall not all sleep, but we shall all be changed, in a moment, in the twinkling of an eye, at the last trumpet. For the trumpet will sound, and the dead will be raised imperishable, and we shall be changed. For this perishable body must put on the imperishable, and this mortal body must put on immortality. When the perishable puts on the imperishable, and

2. The slogan "Man is the measure of all things" is traced to the Greek Sophist Protagoras (ca. 490–420 BC). Most of what we know about him is drawn from Plato (ca. 428–ca. 348 BC). See Nill, *Morality and Self-Interest*, 4. It certainly became modernist dogma.

> the mortal puts on immortality, then shall come to pass the saying that is written:
>
> "Death is swallowed up in victory."
> "O death, where is your victory?
> O death, where is your sting?"
>
> The sting of death is sin, and the power of sin is the law. But thanks be to God, who gives us the victory through our Lord Jesus Christ. (1 Cor 15:50–57 ESV)

The nature of the resurrection body is challenging but not impossible when we remember the relation between Christ's humanity and ours. We confess that Jesus is "true man and true God."[3] Scripture repeatedly teaches by narrative and explanation that Jesus was and remains true man. Mary and Thomas touched our Lord's human body after the resurrection (John 20:17, 27; Luke 24:39). Our Lord ate fish after the resurrection (Luke 24:42–43). Against those antichrists who denied Christ's true humanity, the apostle John testified:

> That which was from the beginning, which we have heard, which we have seen with our eyes, which we looked upon and have touched with our hands, concerning the word of life—the life was made manifest, and we have seen it, and testify to it and proclaim to you the eternal life, which was with the Father and was made manifest to us—that which we have seen and heard we proclaim also to you, so that you too may have fellowship with us; and indeed our fellowship is with the Father and with his Son Jesus Christ. (1 John 1:1–3 ESV)

Notice how he emphasizes the reality of Christ's true humanity and the general reliability of sense experience. God made the world to be known and made humans to know it. *Contra* the apparently growing gnostic spirit of the age (*Zeitgeist*), Christians say that our sense experience is not an illusion. The ideas that became gnosticism did not coalesce until the second century. Gnosticism was a heresy of Christianity, a reaction to

3. "Deum verum et hominem verum" (Schaff, *Creeds of Christendom*, 2:63).

the orthodox Christian doctrine of the two natures of Christ. The seeds of that movement, however, clearly existed by the 70s, when the apostle John confronted them in Asia Minor.

Just as the Holy Spirit raised Jesus's very real body, so too will the Spirit raise our very real bodies. "If the Spirit of him who raised Jesus from the dead dwells in you, he who raised Christ Jesus from the dead will also give life to your mortal bodies through his Spirit who dwells in you" (Rom 8:11 ESV). Real bodies, because of sin, are mortal. They are not illusions. Mary Baker Eddy (1821–1910) was wrong. Her denial of our humanity (and Christ's) is heresy. The gnostics were wrong. The spirit-matter dualists are wrong. The human body is real now and will really be raised, just as Jesus's body was.

We are complex, that is, we have parts. We are body and soul. Should we die before the Lord Jesus returns bodily—what a shock that will be to the gnostics—then our bodies will go to the grave just as Jesus's body was buried. Our soul, that part of us that can be separated from the body, which is essential to our person, our spirit (the biblical synonym for "soul"), will go immediately to be with the Lord. Our Lord Jesus told the believing thief, "Today you shall be with me in paradise" (Luke 23:43). There is a proper, biblical, Christian body-soul dualism or distinction. Ordinarily soul and body belong together. Their separation is not the natural or desired state of things. Thus, Paul characterizes being present before the Lord without our bodies as being naked.

> For we know that if the tent that is our earthly home is destroyed, we have a building from God, a house not made with hands, eternal in the heavens. For in this tent we groan, longing to put on our heavenly dwelling, if indeed by putting it on we may not be found naked. For while we are still in this tent, we groan, being burdened—not that we would be unclothed, but that we would be further clothed, so that what is mortal may be swallowed up by life. He who has prepared us for this very thing is God, who has given us the Spirit as a guarantee. (2 Cor 5:1–5 ESV)

The Lord, however, promised not to allow us to remain in this intermediate state. Body and soul will be reunited. It is better to be with the Lord than to be absent, but it is best for the Lord Jesus to return. Nevertheless, that decision belongs to him, does it not? So he has given us his Holy Spirit as a promise that things will be made right.

The promise of our bodily resurrection, to which Paul devotes an entire chapter of Scripture (1 Cor 15), is essential to our faith. If the dead be not raised, then our faith is empty because it rests on the resurrection of Christ, and if there is no resurrection, then Christ has not been raised and the object of our confidence is false—but he has been raised. He reigns now and he will return in his glorified humanity, and those of our brothers and sisters who have gone ahead of us will return with him, and we will meet him in the air to escort him as a waiting city escorts a conquering king (1 Thess 4:13–18).[4]

Because he was raised, we know with certainty that we are justified before God and saved from the wrath to come. Olevianus explains, "For if even one of all their sins (which, without exception, Christ took on Himself) had remained, either incompletely punished or completely unpunished, then Christ could not have arisen as our Surety and Guarantor of the covenant."[5]

As our bodies suffer the effects (and affects) of the fall, it is well to remember the empty tomb. It is an objective fact, and on it we may rest our confidence. Death could not hold Jesus, and even though it may take us, it will not hold us. Our Savior is receiving our brothers and sisters from across the world right now, and should he delay (from our point of view) his return, he will receive us, and so we will always be with the Lord (1 Thess 4:17).

Even then, ironically, the rationalists will not fully comprehend his glorious return. The empiricists will have the evidence they claim to want. The existentialists will find meaning, and the nihilists will be sorry they denied the suffering Savior in favor of the *Übermensch*, but it will be too late for all of them.

The bodily resurrection is the consummation of our union with Christ, which the Holy Spirit began in us, through faith, after we were given new life (regenerated). Olevianus says it is "the eternal and blessed life that will be fully revealed in our bodies and souls in the Kingdom of our

4. Olevian, *Firm Foundation*, 102–3; Ursinus, *Commentary*, 309–10.

5. Olevianus, *Exposition*, 94.

heavenly Father." In that state, "we are fully united with our head Jesus Christ, fully born anew in body and soul, and transformed forever into the image of Christ and into His glory (1 John 3[:2]; Phil. 3[:21])."[6] That vivifying process, in our progressive sanctification, is already underway as a fruit of Christ's resurrection.[7]

From Christ's resurrection, we know that we, who are united to him by the Spirit, through faith, will also be raised like him. "Therefore, although we die, we shall rise again to life immortal. This is because the right to life is awarded to us by the raising up of the Son, and because, like branches into a vine, we are engrafted into this risen Christ—both by the external testimony of the gospel and the internal testimony of the Holy Spirit."[8]

One concluding note on the Roman Catholic speculation about purgatory, that place where the dead are said to go to complete their sanctification prior to entering heaven.[9] The roots of this speculation are found in early Christian chiliasts such as Tertullian.[10] As the medieval church came to think of justification as progressive sanctification and the process of cooperating with grace, and as it came to think of our part in salvation to include propitiatory suffering, it was relatively easy to extend that process to a subterranean, conscious place of suffering for incomplete penance in this life.[11] To this theory, Ursinus responds,

> The Scriptures teach, on the contrary, that no fire after death, but that the blood of Christ, purifies our souls in this life from all sin. They also teach that the souls of the faithful, when they die, are not cast into the place of torments, there to be purified by fire, but that they are gathered to Christ in Abraham's bosom, whilst the souls of the wicked are cast into hell, from which there is no way of escape, and where they are now tormented with hellish agonies, being at the same time reserved for the more intolerable torments of that

6. Olevian, *Firm Foundation*, 102.

7. Olevianus, *Exposition*, 96–97.

8. Olevianus, *Exposition*, 99.

9. *CCC* §1472.

10. Hill, *Regnum Caelorum*, 26–28.

11. LeGoff, *Birth of Purgatory*, surveys the rise and development of the idea of purgatory. Though it has ancient roots, it became formal doctrine only in the high and late medieval periods.

> eternal fire which the wrath of God will kindle in the judgment, which Christ will execute at the end of the world.[12]

He cites Jesus's own words in Luke 23:46, "Father, into your hands I commit my spirit," and Stephen's confidence that at his martyrdom he was going immediately to the Lord (Acts 7:56). Scripture says that, at his death, Lazarus was taken immediately to the Lord (Luke 16:22). Paul expected to be with the Lord (2 Cor 5:8). Those who die apart from Christ may expect only judgment, not purgatory (Rom 6:23). Dives (the rich man) was not in purgatory (Luke 16:23).

Question 58

What comfort do you have from the article of "life everlasting"?

That, inasmuch as I now feel in my heart the beginning of eternal joy, I shall after this life possess complete bliss, such as eye has not seen, nor ear heard, neither has entered into the heart of man, therein to praise God forever.[13]

Here we find teaching in the catechism that challenges late modern Christians. When the catechism was written, most people did not expect to live into their eighties, as most Westerners expect today. When the plague swept through Heidelberg in the 1560s, most fled the town because they remembered that about three hundred years prior one-third of Europe had died of the plague in just a few years.[14] There were no flu shots, nor any tuberculosis vaccines. Women frequently died in childbirth, and infant mortality was much higher than we experience in the West

12. Ursinus, *Commentary*, 311.

13. "Wes tröstet dich der Artikel vom ewigen Leben? Dass, nachdem ich jetzt den Anfang der ewigen Freude in meinem Herzen empfinde, ich nach diesem Leben vollkommene Seligkeit besitzen werde, die kein Auge gesehen, kein Ohr gehöret, und in keines Menschen Herz gekommen ist, Gott ewiglich darin zu preisen" (Schaff, *Creeds of Christendom*, 3:326). "Quam consolationem capis ex articulo de vita aeterna? Quod, quoniam in praesentia vitae aeternae initia in meo corde praesentisco, futurm sit, ut post hanc vitam plena perfectaque beatitudine potiar, in qua Deum in aeternum celebrem: quam quidem beatitudinem nec oculus vidit, nec auris audivit, nec ullus homo cogitatione comprehendit" (Niemeyer, *Collectio Confessionum*, 442).

14. Clark, *Caspar Olevian*, 20; Kelly, *Great Mortality*, 11.

today. Death was a constant and visible fact of life in the sixteenth century. People did not die in antiseptic hospital rooms. They died at home. Their bodies were not whisked away and cremated.[15]

So it is no surprise that the catechism turns again to comfort (*tröstet; consolationem*) and to the Christian experience, now, by faith, of the beginning of eternity. Olevianus explains, "I not only confess that such everlasting life exists, I also trust that it is being prepared for and belongs to me. Christ confirms this ownership and initial experience of everlasting life, of which a full enjoyment will follow, when He says, 'Most assuredly, I say to you, he who hears My word and believes in Him who sent Me has everlasting life, and shall not come into judgment, but has passed from death into life' (John 5:24)."[16] We have now a partial experience, a foretaste of this blessedness. Isaiah (64:4), which the catechism quotes, the apostle Paul (1 Cor 2:9), quoting Isaiah, and Revelation 21:22–23 testify to the future "full experience" of the state of complete blessedness.[17]

The focus of the catechism is frankly eschatological. It is not on this life or even the renewal of creation (more about that below). In commenting on this article of the creed a few years after the publication of the catechism, Olevianus wrote that the first function of this language is to point us to God, who "like an ever-flowing fountain ... is the fullness of all good within Himself, so that to be really happy in and through Him, we should desire nothing more than Him." He points to the title of God in Genesis 15:1, *El Shaddai*, which he translates *Deus omnisufficiens* ("God all-sufficient").[18]

From this article we also learn that our "salvation is not experienced fully here on earth."[19] We also learn that we are pilgrims on this earth, that "we should make our way through this world as through a foreign land, always remembering to move on and not become attached in our thoughts to these transient, earthly things, as St. Paul teaches in 2 Corinthians 5[:6–9] and Romans 8[:19–24]."[20]

---

15. See the discussion under *HC* 1.
16. Olevianus, *Exposition*, 139.
17. Olevianus, *Exposition*, 139–40.
18. Olevian, *Firm Foundation*, 105.
19. Olevian, *Firm Foundation*, 106.
20. Olevian, *Firm Foundation*, 106.

By thinking of heaven, we gain patience and overcome the sin of despair. It enables believers to persevere through persecution, poverty, banishment, and troubles for Christ's sake.[21] As we suffer for Christ's sake, we contemplate heaven and

> remember that on the other side of the scale stands the great weight of eternal glory that is being prepared for them, a weight so great that it will make the other burdens light, no matter how heavy they may be for the flesh. "Therefore we do not lose heart," says the apostle in 2 Corinthians 4[:16, 17], "for even though our outward man is perishing, yet the inward man is being renewed day by day. For our affliction, which for a moment is light, is working for us an eternal and all-exceeding weight of glory."[22]

Ursinus reminds us that adjective "everlasting" (*ewigen*) or "eternal" (*aeterna*) signifies a quality of life that transcends our understanding (1 Cor 2:9). Eternal, as applied to God, signifies that which has no beginning or end. As applied to creatures, it signifies a kind of life that has a beginning (because we are creatures) but, because of Christ, has no end. It is "the perfect conformity of man with God, consisting in the true and perfect knowledge and love of God, and in the glory both of the soul and body of man." It includes the eternal and perfect dwelling of God with man.[23]

Eternal life is the free gift of God to sinners justified *sola gratia, sola fide*: "Eternal life is not given on account of our works, whether present, or foreseen; but only out of the free mercy, and love of God toward the human race, and from his desire to manifest his mercy in the salvation of the righteous, through the satisfaction and merits of Christ the mediator, imputed unto us through faith, for this end, that God may be eternally praised by us."[24] Thus, Reformed Christians must resist the move to teach a two-stage doctrine of salvation, wherein justification is said to be *sola fide* but "final salvation" is said to be through works.

---

21. Olevian, *Firm Foundation*, 106.

22. Olevian, *Firm Foundation*, 106; Olevianus, *Exposition*, 140, where Olevianus notes that 1 Pet 1:17 uses "παροικίαν, not κατοικίν," i.e., a temporary sojourn in contrast to a permanent sojourn.

23. Ursinus, *Commentary*, 319–20.

24. Ursinus, *Commentary*, 322.

Olevianus addressed this question directly in 1567:

> 157 Q. Now that we have discussed the various articles and parts of articles of the confession of our Christian faith, I would like to hear from you whether we shall be fully saved through such true faith in Christ?
>
> A. There is only one way to eternal life (as I also said at the beginning of these articles), namely, the crucified Christ accepted through a true faith (1 Cor. 2:2). Since, then, faith (which is a gift of the Holy Spirit) possesses Christ and all His benefits as its own, and Christ is the one freely given us by God to be ours through faith, one of two things must follow: either Christ does not have all that is necessary for our salvation, or, if He does, one who possesses the crucified Christ through a true faith also has everything in Christ that is necessary for salvation.
>
> Through all the Articles of Faith it has been demonstrated that everything necessary for our eternal salvation is in Jesus Christ and that He was not a partial but a complete Jesus, or Savior, who fully accomplished everything necessary for our salvation. Therefore, whoever is grafted into Christ through a true faith has and possesses everything within that is necessary for salvation.[25]

This passage echoes *HC* 30 (see above) and *BC* 22.

From this truth, under *HC* 58 Ursinus also turns to assurance. Salvation, like justification, is *sola gratia, sola fide*.[26] The graciousness (as distinct from a doctrine of *conditional* salvation) produces in believers true assurance: "It is not only possible, but also our duty to assure ourselves of everlasting life; for it is given to all and only to such as believe. And not only so, but to believe in everlasting life is to be fully persuaded that not only shall others be made partakers of it, but that I am also a partaker of it, which we must observe, and hold fast to in opposition to the distrust and uncertainty of the Papists."[27] The Roman Catholic Church, to whom Ursinus refers, at the Council of Trent made our apprehension of heaven conditional on our cooperation with grace, which is always uncertain.

25. Olevian, *Firm Foundation*, 108.

26. Ursinus, *Commentary*, 322.

27. Ursinus, *Commentary*, 323.

Thus the Roman Catholic Church destroyed Christian assurance, as do all two-stage doctrines of salvation.

The doctrine of *HC* 58 is in stark contrast to some contemporary Reformed theology in another way. The catechism here speaks rather differently about the new heavens and the new earth from the way that modern Reformed writers have become accustomed to speaking. For some such movements, there has been a strong notion of continuity between life as we know it now and life in the new heavens and the new earth. One representative writer, Al Wolters, says:

> The new heavens and the new earth the Lord has promised will be a continuation, purified by fire, of the creation we now know. There is no reason to believe that the cultural dimensions of earthly reality (except insofar as they are involved in sin) will be absent from the new, glorified earth that is promised. In fact, John writes that "the kings of the earth will bring their splendor into it. ... The glory and the honor of the nations will be brought into it" (Rev. 21:24, 26). This very likely refers to the cultural treasures of mankind which will be purified by passing through the fires of judgment, like gold in a crucible.[28]

To be sure, there will be continuity between this existence and the new heavens and the new earth. After all, the expression "the new heavens and the new earth," from 2 Peter 3:13, indicates a degree of continuity. Christians will be glorified humans. If we read the biblical language in its immediate context (2 Pet 3:8–13), it is a promise that Christ is coming, that there will be a judgment, there will be a purification of this world. It seems likely that Peter is using a degree of hyperbole to describe the coming judgment and renewal of all things. He is making an analogy with the Noachian flood, in which "the world that then was" was destroyed (vv. 5–7). After the flood, the world continued to exist, but it was purified, in a relative way. It was not utterly destroyed and remade. This is the analogy he uses to describe the coming world, just as our Lord Jesus did when he said, "Just as it was in the days of Noah, so will it be in the days of the Son of Man. They were eating and drinking and marrying and being given in

28. Wolters, *Creation Regained*, 47.

marriage, until the day when Noah entered the ark, and the flood came and destroyed them all" (Luke 17:26–27 ESV).

The judgment will be swift and surprising. So, there is continuity and discontinuity between this present existence and the next. Wolters, however, argues for high degree of continuity between the cultural endeavors of this world and glorified life on the basis of an appeal to Revelation 21. Let us consider the passage in its context:

> And I saw no temple in the city, for its temple is the Lord God the Almighty and the Lamb. And the city has no need of sun or moon to shine on it, for the glory of God gives it light, and its lamp is the Lamb. By its light will the nations walk, and the kings of the earth will bring their glory into it, and its gates will never be shut by day—and there will be no night there. They will bring into it the glory and the honor of the nations. But nothing unclean will ever enter it, nor anyone who does what is detestable or false, but only those who are written in the Lamb's book of life. (Rev 21:22–27 ESV)

Revelation, however, is not a linear road map to the future but rather a cycle of visions intended to explain to believers the nature of the Christian life between the ascension of Christ and his return. It is a deliberately and highly symbolic narrative and of heaven and earth. Whenever we interpret Revelation, we must account for the symbolic, figurative language. This is perhaps the major reason the millennium described in Revelation 20:6 is not to be taken literally. After chapter 3, virtually nothing in Revelation is intended to be taken literally. It is passing strange to interpret the seven historic churches of the prologue figuratively and the millennium literally.[29]

Chapter 21 is a figurative account of the "new heaven and the new earth" (21:1). Immediately in chapter 21, we see that "the first earth had passed away, and the sea was no more" (v. 1 ESV). The narrative begins with discontinuity between this existence and the new. A heavenly Jerusalem descends. All this is figurative language. The throne in verse 5 is, of course, royal imagery, and he who is seated on it declares, "Behold, I am making all things new." That signals discontinuity with our present experience.

29. See Hemer, *Letters to the Seven Churches*; Beale, *Book of Revelation*, 108–51, for a survey of the various approaches, including the progressive recapitulation approach, which finds a series of parallel visions.

The angels are likely actual beings, but the bowls they carry are figurative (v. 9). The heavenly city, its measurements, its jewels, and its glassy and golden streets (vv. 16–21) are meant to be taken figuratively as symbolic.

It is significant for our understanding of the relations between cult (worship) and culture (broadly, ordinary human endeavor) that verse 22 turns to the heavenly temple, which, of course, is not a temple at all but the Lamb. Jesus had promised, "Destroy this temple and in three days I will raise it up" (John 2:19). He was speaking about his resurrection. This is why Christians ought not to be anticipating a rebuilt temple in Jerusalem. The Lord Jesus is the temple. The Jerusalem temple was a shadowy picture of him. He is the holy place where God meets his people. Does this passage really say the things that some infer from it?

> And the city has no need of sun or moon to shine on it, for the glory of God gives it light, and its lamp is the Lamb. By its light will the nations walk, and the kings of the earth will bring their glory into it, and its gates will never be shut by day—and there will be no night there. They will bring into it the glory and the honor of the nations. But nothing unclean will ever enter it, nor anyone who does what is detestable or false, but only those who are written in the Lamb's book of life. (Rev 21:23–27 ESV)

Verse 23 signals strong discontinuity between our present existence and the new heavens and the new earth. The narrative describes a renewal of the creation. As in creation, there is light without sun or moon. There are nations. There are kings. They bring treasures. The imagery is drawn from the exodus and other places in Scripture. It seems difficult, however, to assign it to *cultural* endeavors without being arbitrary. It seems as if one would have to know that *a priori*, before one got to the passage itself. The imagery suggests a comprehensive acknowledgment of Christ as Lord and King of all. To say much more than that seems speculative. The immediate setting is religious. It concerns worship, not cultural endeavors. Of course the two are linked, even as the very words *cult* and *culture* themselves are linked, but they are also distinct. By *cult* (*cultus*) we refer to outward acts of religious devotion such as prayer and praise. By *culture* we refer to ordinary, daily endeavors such as farming, in which crops are cultivated.

The point of verse 27 is that all who are to enter must be cleansed by the blood of the Lamb. That is religious, not cultural, imagery.

In short, when we look at these passages, which reflect directly on the new heavens and the new earth, in context it seems difficult to sustain the strong note of cultural continuity that some sound. Yes, there is continuity between this existence and our glorified existence, but the imagery of Revelation has a strong cultic, religious theme. Temple imagery is prominent through the entire book (e.g., Rev 11; 14; 16; 19–22). When we are given a symbolic glimpse of heaven, what we see is not cultural activity but cultic. Does this mean there will be no cultural activity in the new heavens and the new earth? No, but it means that when Christians make claims about cultural activities in the new heavens and new earth, they are drawing inferences that may or may not be true. They are speculative, that is, they are conclusions drawn from premises but not unequivocally indicated by Scripture itself.

Scripture gives every indication that believers not only desire heaven but see it as their true home, their ultimate destination. Isaiah was not bored by his glimpse into heaven. He was electrified. He was terrified:

> I saw the Lord sitting upon a throne, high and lifted up; and the train of his robe filled the temple. Above him stood the seraphim. Each had six wings: with two he covered his face, and with two he covered his feet, and with two he flew. And one called to another and said:
>
> "Holy, holy, holy is the Lord of hosts;
> the whole earth is full of his glory!"
>
> And the foundations of the thresholds shook at the voice of him who called, and the house was filled with smoke. And I said: "Woe is me! For I am lost; for I am a man of unclean lips, and I dwell in the midst of a people of unclean lips; for my eyes have seen the King, the Lord of hosts!" (Isa 6:1–5 ESV)

True holiness has a way of humbling sinners. This life, as important and good as it is, is not final. It is not ultimate. It is provisional. Our life in the new heavens and the new earth is final.

The Old Testament tabernacle and temple were rough illustrations of heaven. They represented communion with God. Psalm 42:1–4 captures this well:

> As a deer pants for flowing streams,
> so pants my soul for you, O God.
> My soul thirsts for God,
> for the living God.
> When shall I come and appear before God?
> My tears have been my food
> day and night,
> while they say to me all the day long,
> "Where is your God?"
> These things I remember,
> as I pour out my soul:
> how I would go with the throng
> and lead them in procession to the house of God
> with glad shouts and songs of praise,
> a multitude keeping festival. (ESV)

Paul sounds the same note when he says:

> So we do not lose heart. Though our outer self is wasting away, our inner self is being renewed day by day. For this light momentary affliction is preparing for us an eternal weight of glory beyond all comparison, as we look not to the things that are seen but to the things that are unseen. For the things that are seen are transient, but the things that are unseen are eternal.
>
> For we know that if the tent that is our earthly home is destroyed, we have a building from God, a house not made with hands, eternal in the heavens. For in this tent we groan, longing to put on our heavenly dwelling, if indeed by putting it on we may not be found naked. For while we are still in this tent, we groan, being burdened—not that we would be unclothed, but that we would be further clothed, so that what is mortal may be swallowed up by life. He who has prepared us for this very thing is God, who has given us the Spirit as a guarantee.

> So we are always of good courage. We know that while we are at home in the body we are away from the Lord, for we walk by faith, not by sight. Yes, we are of good courage, and we would rather be away from the body and at home with the Lord. So whether we are at home or away, we make it our aim to please him. For we must all appear before the judgment seat of Christ, so that each one may receive what is due for what he has done in the body, whether good or evil. (2 Cor 4:16–5:10 ESV)

Like David, Paul longed to commune with God. He hoped first to be bodily before the Lord, but, if the Lord willed (and he did), he was content to wait for the bodily resurrection. In all events, his desire was to with the Lord. Paul's hierarchy of values was opposite from what ours tends to be. He says that our "citizenship is in heaven" (Phil 3:20), and thus we await Christ's return and the glorification of our bodies so that we may be with him.

Question 59

What does it help you now, that you believe all this?

Question 60

How are you righteous before God?

Question 61

Why do you say that you are righteous by faith only?

Question 62

But why cannot our good works be the whole or part of our righteousness before God?

Lord's Day 23

QUESTION 59

What does it help you now, that you believe all this?

That I am righteous in Christ before God, and an heir of eternal life.[1]

Sandwiched as it is between the doctrine of heaven just before and the great doctrine of justification to come, at first blush *HC* 59 might not seem terribly consequential. Nevertheless, it is most consequential.

What good is it to believe all *what*? This is one of the several summarizing questions that serves to lead us from one subsection to another within the larger tripartite superstructure (guilt, grace, and gratitude) of the catechism. We have been in the gospel section of the catechism since question 5. Before that we learned the greatness of our sin and misery. So "all this" refers to everything we have learned about the human condition before the fall, after the fall, God, Christ, his righteousness for us, his grace to sinners, faith as the instrument of justification and salvation, the Spirit and his ongoing work in his people, and heaven. What good is it to believe all of that? We are justified and saved.

Please notice which verb the catechism used in *HC* 59: *believe* (*glaubest*; *credis*). Note well the sort of verbs that are absent: *doing, obeying, growing, cooperating, keeping*. It is well to remember that salvation is all *sola gratia, sola fide*. The inheritance in view here is not merely justification but *eternal life*, which is to say, glorification, which is the consummation of our sanctification. Olevianus explains: "Through all the Articles of Faith it has been demonstrated that everything necessary for our eternal salvation is in Jesus Christ and that He was not a partial but a complete Jesus, or Savior, who fully accomplished everything necessary for our salvation. Therefore, whoever is grafted into Christ through a true faith has and possesses everything within that is necessary for salvation."[2] The frequency with which the Reformed in this period asserted that not only

1. "Was hilft es dir aber nun, wenn du dietz Alles glaubest? Dass ich in Christo vor Gott gerecht, und ein Erbe des ewigen Lebens bin" (Schaff, *Creeds of Christendom*, 3:326). "At cum haec omnia credis, quid utilitatis inde ad te redit? Quod in Christo iustus sum coram Deo, et haeres vitae aeternae" (Niemeyer, *Collectio Confessionum*, 443).

2. Olevian, *Firm Foundation*, 108.

justification but our whole salvation is entirely found in Christ (and not in us) is a salutary reminder. There is always a temptation to change the doctrine of salvation (soteriology) so as to wedge in human cooperation with grace somewhere and thus to turn the covenant of grace into a covenant of works, if it were possible.

The legal basis for our inheritance is the righteousness of Christ. The instrument of our justification, and thus of our inheritance of eternal life, is faith alone. It is through faith that the Spirit unites us to Christ, and it is in union with Christ, the Son of God incarnate, that we become heirs of the eternal life he earned for us. The unconditional promise of eternal life to believers is meant to be a source of comfort. It is not simply that eternal life exists, but, the believer says, "It is promised and freely given to me. As it has already now begun in me through faith in Christ, it will also be fully revealed in me."[3] To believe that "everlasting life is prepared" for us (because God has promised it) is to believe "that God will keep him constant in true faith until he is brought into life everlasting. Otherwise he could not truthfully say that he believes in life everlasting, that is, that it belongs to him." In short, *HC* 59 is a brief confession of the perseverance of the saints.[4]

Question 60

How are you righteous before God?

Only by true faith in Jesus Christ; that is, although my conscience accuse me, that I have grievously sinned against all the commandments of God, and have never kept any of them, and am still prone always to all evil; yet God without any merit of mine, of mere grace, grants and imputes to me the perfect satisfaction, righteousness, and holiness of Christ, as if I had never committed nor had any sin, and had myself accomplished all the obedience which Christ has fulfilled for me; if only I accept such benefit with a believing heart.[5]

3. Olevian, *Firm Foundation*, 104–5.

4. Olevian, *Firm Foundation*, 107.

5. "Wie bist du gerecht vor Gott? Allein durch wahren Glauben in Jesum Christum: also, dass, ob mich schon mein Gewissen anklagt, dass ich wider alle Gebote Gottes schwerlich gesündiget, und derselben keines je gehalten habe, auch noch immerdar zu allem Bösen geneigt bin, doch Gott

It is symbolic that this question is so near the center of the catechism since this doctrine is at the heart of the Reformed confession of the Christian faith. Calvin calls the doctrine of justification *sola fide* the "principal axis of the faith" (*praecipuus fidei cardo*).[6] Ursinus agrees. In his exposition of *HC* 59–60, which he combines, he uses virtually the same language as Calvin. "The doctrine of justification ... one of the principal heads of the of faith."[7] Olevianus calls justification *sola gratia, sola fide* the first "offered benefit" of Christ.[8] "The primary goal of faith is to look in this Word at the promise of the gospel, the promise that the Father truly presents Himself to us in Christ and through the Holy Spirit graciously justifies those engrafted into Christ," and the "second benefit" is that he "sanctifies us more and more, and preserves us by that same power by which Christ was raised from the dead and had all things subjected to Him."[9] For Olevianus, as for Calvin and Ursinus, justification is always the first benefit from which the other benefits, sanctification and glorification, flow.

As *sola Scriptura* was the formal cause of the Reformation, the material cause was justification *sola gratia, sola fide*. In contrast, the Roman Catholic Church confesses: "If any one says, that by faith alone (*sola fide*) the impious is justified; in such wise as to mean, that nothing else is required to co-operate in order to the obtaining the grace of Justification, and that it is not in any way necessary, that he be prepared and disposed

ohne all mein Verdienst aus lauter Gnaden, mir die vollkommene Genugthuung, Gerechtigkeit und Heiligkeit Christi schenket und zurechnet, als hätte ich nie eine Sünde begangen noch gehabt, und selbst allen den Gehorsam vollbracht, den Christus für mich hat geleistet, wenn ich allein solche Wohlthat mit gläubigem Herzen annehme" (Schaff, *Creeds of Christendom*, 3:326–27). "Quomodo iustus es coram Deo? Sola fide in Iesum Christum, adeo ut licet mea me conscientia accuset, quod aversus omnia mandata Dei graviter peccaverim, nec ullum eorum servaverim, adhaec etiamnum ad omne malum propensus sim, nihlominus tamen, (modo haec beneficia vera animi fiducia amplectar), sine ullo meo merito, ex mera Dei misericordia, mihi perfecta satisfactio, iustitia et sanctitas Christi, imputetur ac donetur; perinde ac si nec ullum ipse peccatum admissem, nec ulla mihi labes inhaereret: imo vero quasi eam obedientiam, quam pro me Christus praestitit, ipse perfecte praestitissem" (Niemeyer, *Collectio Confessionum*, 443).

6. Calvin, *Institutes* 3.2.16. "Hic praecipuus fidei cardo vertitur, ne quas Dominus offert misericordiae promissiones, extra nos tantum veras esse arbitremur, in nobis minime: sed ut potius eas intus complectendo nostras faciamus" (Barth, *Joannis Calvini Opera Selecta*, 4:26.29–32).

7. "Doctrina de iustificatione, quae nunc sequitur, est ex praecipuis fidei nostrae capitibus" (Ursinus, *Corpus doctrinae*, 335; Ursinus, *Commentary*, 324).

8. Olevianus, *Romanos Notae*, 6–7.

9. Olevianus, *Exposition*, 16; Olevian, *Firm Foundation*, 99–102; Clark, *Caspar Olevian*, 137–80.

by the movement of his own will; let him be anathema."[10] The dividing line between Rome and the Reformation is clear. Where Rome confesses that faith is the "beginning of human salvation, the foundation, and the root of all Justification,"[11] the Reformed confess that we are justified by grace alone (*sola gratia*), through faith alone. Rome and the Reformed have two distinct definitions of faith in the doctrine of justification.

According to the high medieval theologians, faith is necessary but not sufficient for acceptance with God. In the *Sentences* Peter Lombard (ca. 1100–1160), whose theological lectures became the basic textbook for Western theology for more than four centuries, taught: "The faith by which one believes, if it is joined to charity, is a virtue, because, as Ambrose says, 'charity is the mother of all virtues'; it informs all of them and without it there is no true virtue. And so faith working *through love* is the virtue by which unseen things are believed."[12] Notice how the Lombard understands and uses Galatians 5:6. Paul's participle ("working"; ἐνεργέω), which for Paul is a *consequence* of faith, has become a virtue and the thing that *informs* faith, the thing that gives shape to it.[13] In his account, love does not function as *evidence* but as that principle that makes faith what it is.[14] Thomas Aquinas (ca. 1224–1274) developed this approach by explaining, "Charity is the form of faith."[15] For Thomas, as for Trent, faith is "formed by love" (*fides formata caritate*).[16] Love—that is, sanctification, obedience, and good works—make faith saving.

10. Schroeder, *Canons and Decrees*, 43; "Si quis dixerit, sola fide impium iustificari, ita ut intelligat, nihil aliud requiri, quo ad iustificationis gratiam consequendam cooperetur, et nulla ex parte necesse esse, eum suae voluntatis motu praeparari atque disponi: anathema sit" (Denzinger, *Enchiridion Symbolorum*, 296.819).

11. Schroeder, *Canons and Decrees*, 34–35.

12. Lombard, *Sentences*, 3.98; Lombard, *Sententiae*, 2.142. Lombard's reference to Ambrose is actually to the *Glossa Ordinaria* on Rom 14:5.

13. *Quae omnes informat* (Lombard, *Sententiae*, 2.142). The transliterated English translation, "informs," is misleading without explanation, as it signals in modern English the sense "to convey information." In Latin the prefix *in-* intensifies *formo* and means "to give form to a thing." Compare Pelikan's account in *Christian Tradition*, 3:155, of Bernard's doctrine of justification, in which the merits given to us in baptism were said to be incentives to sanctification but "not a ground for the divine act of justification, whose basis lay in God and not in man."

14. The Vulgate follows the Greek text: "fides quae per caritatem operatur" (*Biblia Vulgata*).

15. "Caritas est forma fidei" (*ST* 2a2ae 4.1).

16. *ST* 2a2ae 4.1 (*ST* 2a2ae 4.3, "ergo sed contra dilectio caritatis est fidei forma"; 2a2ae 4.4., resp. obj. 1, "unde ipsamet fides informis sit formata"). See Steinmetz, *Luther in Context*, 33–34.

This is not what Paul means at all. Just as James calls for evidence of true faith (Jas 2:14), Paul is teaching that true faith gives *evidence* of its existence by manifesting itself in acts of love (charity). By turning "working by love" into "formed by love," the high medieval theologians turned a fruit of faith into that which makes faith what it is. In other words, Lombard and Thomas turned faith from the empty hand that receives what Christ has done into part of the ground of justification.

Rome followed Thomas here. Thus, ordinarily, according to Rome, no one is ever actually justified in this life because no one is ever perfected in this life. For Rome, grace is "exciting" (*excitantem*) and "helping" (*adjuvantem*) but not definitive.[17] Rome speaks of "converting one's self unto his justification" (*convertendum se ad suam ipsorum iustificationem*).[18] Rome confesses: "If any one says, that justifying faith is nothing else but confidence in the divine mercy which remits sins for Christ's sake; or, that this confidence alone is that whereby we are justified; let him be anathema."[19] Rome officially, intelligently, consciously, and unequivocally rejects the doctrine of justification *sola gratia, sola fide* and eternally condemns all who confess it. Vatican II changed nothing about this rejection and condemnation.[20]

Trent's attack on "confidence" or "trust" makes the issue quite pointed for those who confess the *HC*, since "confidence" (*fiducia*) is of the essence of our definition of faith in *HC* 21.[21] We confess that, by faith alone, resting in, trusting in, leaning on Christ and his finished work, we have the entirety of our justification, and it is through faith alone that we are saved. Good works are necessary as a fruit and evidence of justification and salvation but are no part of the ground or instrument of our salvation.

Rome, however, confesses: "If any one says, that the justice received is not conserved and also increased before God through good works; but

---

17. Denzinger, *Enchiridion Symbolorum*, 286.

18. Denzinger, *Enchiridion Symbolorum*, 286.

19. Council of Trent, session 6, canon 12. "Si quis dixerit, fidem iustificationem nihil aliud esse quam fiduciam divinae misericordiae peccata remittentis propter Christum, vel eam fiduciam solam esse, qua iustificamur: anathema sit" (Denzinger, *Enchiridion Symbolorum*, 296).

20. On whether Vatican II changed Rome's doctrine of justification, Anthony Hoekema wrote in 1989, "There is therefore no evidence of an essential change in Roman Catholic teaching on justification" (*Saved by Grace*, 169).

21. See the discussion under *HC* 21.

that those works are only fruit and signs of justification obtained, but not a cause of its increase; let him be anathema" (session 6, canon 24).[22]

For Rome, justification is progressive. It is initiated by God's prevenient grace but is *retained* and *improved* by our cooperation with grace. The council understood quite clearly what they were rejecting. Indeed, Trent understood more clearly than many ostensible Protestants today what the sixteenth-century Protestants were confessing: that good works are necessary but *only* as fruit and evidence of justification and salvation (including sanctification and glorification) received *sola gratia, sola fide*. By contrast, Rome unashamedly confesses that our good works, which for them are the result of grace and our free cooperation with grace, increase our righteousness before God.

The Reformed understanding of Scripture is that believers are as justified and saved now as we will be at the judgment. There are not two stages of justification, initial and final. Rather, we distinguish between justification and vindication. At the judgment it will be manifest to all that those to whom Christ freely imputed his righteousness, who received that righteousness with true faith, really were justified and saved.

For the Reformed, justification is a once-for-all act; it is definitive. Sanctification is progressive and the necessary consequence of justification. Rome does not distinguish justification and sanctification. They are the same thing. According to Rome, we are only as justified now as we are sanctified, and we are only as sanctified by grace and cooperation with grace.

This remains Roman doctrine. In the 1994 *Catechism of the Catholic Church*, Rome reiterated Tridentine doctrine. It defines justification in two parts, as cleansing from sin and the communication (sharing) of Christ's righteousness.[23] The catechism quotes Trent: "Justification is not only the remission of sins, but also the sanctification and renewal of the interior man."[24] According to Rome, justification "establishes *cooperation between*

22. "Si quis dixerit, iustitiam acceptam non conservari atque etiam non augeri coram Deo per bona opera, sed opera ipsa fructus solummodo et signa esse iustificationis adeptae, non etiam ipsius augendae causam: anathema sit" (Denzinger, *Enchiridion Symbolorum*, 298).

23. CCC §1987.

24. CCC §1989. The quotation is from chapter 7 of the Decree on Justification, session 6 (1547): "quae est non sola peccatorum remissio [can. 11], sed et sanctificatio et renovatio interioris hominis" (Denizinger, *Enchiridion Symbolorum*, 287).

God's grace and man's freedom."[25] In short, according to Rome, justification is the result of grace and our free cooperation with grace, and that cooperation is the *sine qua non* of justification.

The Roman Catholic Church knows *a priori* before it ever gets to Scripture that it cannot teach that justification is a definitive, once-for-all declaration that sinners are declared righteous by God for the sake of the righteousness of Christ earned for us and imputed to us, received through resting, leaning, trusting in Christ alone. The Roman Catholic Church knows *a priori* that God can only recognize as righteous those who are intrinsically, inherently, actually righteous in themselves, and that can only happen by the infusion of the substance of medicinal grace and the cooperation of the free will with that grace unto sufficient sanctification.

The phrase "only by true faith" intentionally evokes *HC* 21. The gospel message is that we are justified and saved, not by anything "wrought in" us or "done by" us, but by grace alone, through faith alone, and that faith is an outward-looking knowledge, assent, and confidence in Christ and his finished work.[26] The Roman Catholic and the Reformed doctrines of salvation are very different.

The question concerns how we are right with God. Righteousness is necessarily a legal category. It is fashionable in some circles to dismiss the question as if it were irrelevant to our age, as if we had matured beyond it, or as if it were a parochial question (e.g., Western as distinct from Eastern).[27] We might like to tell ourselves that justification is passé or parochial, but in truth, in the nature of human existence, the question of righteousness is unavoidable. We will always have laws, and where there are laws there is either righteousness (conformity to the law) or unrighteousness (transgression of the law).[28] Laws are for sinners: "Understanding this, that the law is not laid down for the just but for the lawless and disobedient, for the ungodly and sinners" (1 Tim 1:9 ESV).

---

25. CCC §1993. Italics original.

26. The construction "wrought in … done by" is drawn from WCF 11.1 (Westminster Assembly, *Humble Advice of the Assembly*, 22).

27. E.g., Clendenin, *Eastern Orthodox Christianity*, 123–24. Pelikan discusses the attempt by Melanchthon to build a bridge to the Eastern Orthodox churches and the rejection of the overture by the patriarch of Constantinople in *Christian Tradition*, 2:281–82.

28. WSC 14 (Westminster Assembly, *Humble Advice of the Assembly*, 7).

God created Adam in righteousness and true holiness with the intent that he would know God rightly, love, and, after passing the probation, enter into eternal blessedness with him (*HC* 6). After the fall, we are all under the law (Rom 7:1–6) for righteousness, and the law is good and holy (Rom 7:7–12). The law promises life to all who obey, but because our fall, we are unable to obey (Rom 7:10). In Adam, we are all, by nature, sinners (Rom 5:12–21). As Paul says, after the fall, the law remains good, holy, and righteous, but we do not. The demands of the law do not end simply because we are now, by nature, unable and unwilling to fulfill them perfectly. The law still says: "Cursed is everyone who does not continue to do everything written in the book of the law" (Deut 27:26; Gal 3:10). God's law does not say to lawbreakers, "Good try but not quite. Try again." It says "cursed," which is not a good state in which to be. According to Deuteronomy 28:20, cursedness manifests in frustration. It leads to destruction. Deuteronomy 29:20 says that one who is under a curse is not forgiven, that he is under Yahweh's anger, that is, his holy wrath. It says Yahweh's zeal for his own holiness "will smoke against that man," and his cursedness will result in his name being blotted out from under heaven. Our Lord Jesus said that to be cursed is to be eternally condemned: "Then he will say to those on his left, 'Depart from me, you cursed, into the eternal fire prepared for the devil and his angels'" (Matt 25:41 ESV). When he cursed the fig tree (Mark 11:21), it withered and died. Clearly being accursed is a truly miserable state. Reasonable people would do all they could to avoid it. Tragically, the effects of sin are that we are, by nature, blind to our own state (John 3:18–20; Acts 26:18). Paul says that we are "dead in sins and trespasses" (Eph 2:1–4) and we do not even realize it.

So we need righteousness. Because of our own condition, we can only get this righteousness by faith. We cannot undo what we, in Adam, did. We cannot undo what we have each done individually, actually. We cannot make expiation (payment for sin) or propitiation (the turning away of God's wrath) because whatever we do, we do as sinners. All our affections, our thinking, and our willing are corrupted by sin. Everything we touch is corrupted by sin. To paraphrase Cornelius Van Til, we are like a man of sin, in a sea of sin, trying to climb a ladder of sin. It is futile.[29]

---

29. Van Til, *Defense of the Faith*, 102.

This is why the gospel is such good news. The gospel is that Christ "became a curse" for us who believe: "Christ redeemed us from the curse of the law by becoming a curse for us—for it is written, 'Cursed is everyone who is hanged on a tree'" (Gal 3:13 ESV).

This is why faith is the "sole instrument" of our justification (*BC* 22). This is why we confess in *BC* 24 against all moralists that we are justified "even before we do good works."[30] "For by grace you have been saved through faith. And this is not your own doing; it is the gift of God, not a result of works, so that no one may boast" (Eph 2:8–9 ESV).

According to Scripture, grace is not a medicinal substance with which we cooperate unto justification and salvation; it is by God's favor merited for us by Christ, who was born without sin, who obeyed God's holy, righteous law for us, and who, by his powerful Holy Spirit, raises dead sinners to life, gives them true faith, and through that true faith unites them to Christ. There is no question whether there is cursedness and righteousness.

In order to understand the teaching of the catechism on justification, we must remember that it is explaining to believers how justification happens and what it means for our assurance and for our spiritual life. This is why it turns almost immediately to a highly realistic account of the believer's struggle with sin. The background to this way of thinking and speaking is the Pauline, Augustinian, and Reformed doctrine of humanity (anthropology). Calvin's reading of Romans 7 is echoing in the background of *HC* 60.[31]

Believers continue to struggle with sin. Why bring up this reality under justification? First, because it is the experience of every Christian. It is important to put that experience into its biblical framework lest believers despair and give up. There have been strains of perfectionism (i.e., the doctrine that believers can, if they will, attain to entire sanctification or perfect sanctification in this life) in the church since Pelagius (fl. ca. AD 380–418), but perfectionism has been particularly strong since the Remonstrant movement emerged in 1610 and especially since the rise of Methodism in

30. Schaff, *Creeds of Christendom*, 3:411.

31. Calvin, *Romans*, 243–75; Olevianus, *Romanos Notae*, 264–314; Clark, "Reception of Paul," 297–318; Clark, *Caspar Olevian*, 141–54.

the eighteenth century.[32] It has been so influential that it has affected the way Reformed people talk and think about sanctification.

The *HC* is not perfectionist. We confess "although my conscience accuses me that I have grievously sinned against all the commandments of God, and have never kept any of them, and am still prone always to all evil." The assumption of the catechism is that accusation is essentially accurate. Olevianus reflects on this problem at length in *Firm Foundation*.[33] He distinguishes three accusations of the Evil One against the Christian. The first two have to do with the sufficiency of Christ's righteousness for our justification.[34] The third is that there is an "innate scum" (*Teig*) of sin that sticks to Christians, even though we have been clothed legally in the righteousness of Christ.[35] In this context Olevianus quotes Romans 7:19. Even the apostle Paul confesses an ongoing struggle with sin. The first part of Olevianus's answer is Romans 7:20, the struggle between sin and the new man. He explains, "This struggle should comfort rather than trouble a Christian, for it is a clear indication that one has the Holy Spirit and hence is a child of God. For flesh and blood do not resist sin and self or teach us how to resist. God does that, revealing it and working it out through his Holy Spirit."[36] He appeals to the inherent value of the death of Jesus, whose humanity was conceived by the Holy Spirit and was united to his deity, "that I have no doubt that by giving His pure body in death, Christ fully paid for my original sin and whatever part of it is still left in me."[37] The ground of the Christian's confidence is the "worthiness of that person is such that His humility and obedience surpasses the obedience of every angel and creature. And this obedience or righteousness of Christ is imputed to each believer, so that it becomes His own and he now has much more righteousness in Christ than sin in Himself."[38] For Olevianus, the reality of the legal (forensic) ground of our confidence is essential, but

32. For a Wesleyan account of perfectionism, see Wesley, *Plain Account of Christian Perfection*. For the definitive critique, see Warfield, *Perfectionism*, in *Works, vol.* 2.

33. Olevian, *Firm Foundation*, 117–21.

34. Olevian, *Firm Foundation*, 112–17.

35. Olevian, *Firm Foundation*, 117, Q. 171.

36. Olevian, *Firm Foundation*, 117, Q. 172.

37. Olevian, *Firm Foundation*, 118, Q. 173.

38. Olevian, *Firm Foundation*, 118–19, Q. 174.

he also appeals to our union with Christ: "The cause is the bond of faith and spiritual marriage between Christ and the Church, that is, all believers. This bond and marriage consists of His taking our sin and misery upon Himself and our having everything in common with Him, since we have been engrafted into Him through faith, flesh of His flesh and bone of His bones. Indeed, we are His body."[39]

Our conscience does not lie when it says that believers remain, in themselves, terrible sinners. Luther captures this reality in the slogan *simul iustus et peccator* ("simultaneously just and sinner").[40] Perfectionists want to resolve the tension by way of an overrealized eschatology, but Romans 7 and the *HC* will not permit us to follow. Moralists (Roman Catholic, federal visionist, and others) cannot say *simul iustus et peccator*. For moralists, God may only justify us when we are intrinsically, actually righteous. That means, of course, that moralists must either lie about their sins or lower the bar of justice. Christians need do neither. This truth is an acid test as to whether one is a moralist. When one sins, does one say to oneself, "I am out of favor with God now"? If so, one is a moralist and should repent. Jesus did not die to make it possible for us to be right with God so long as we are sufficiently sanctified. There is no such thing as provisional justification. The gospel is that by God's free favor alone (*sola gratia*), Christ's perfect righteousness (his condign merit) has been imputed to us, and we receive, rest in, and lean on Christ for our righteousness.

Our standing with God does not rise and fall like the stock market according to our actual, gradual sanctification, which itself is a gospel mystery. The Spirit is at work in us, sanctifying us, but we do not know where he comes from nor where he goes. We cannot measure his work, and when we try we do not estimate it correctly. It is ours, by his grace and Spirit, to continue to die to sin and live to Christ. It is ours to trust that his promises are true: "Therefore, since we have been justified by faith, we have peace with God through our Lord Jesus Christ" (Rom 5:1 ESV). Scripture does not say, "Since we have begun to be justified." It says, "We have been justified." Our defense is Paul's "but God":

---

39. Olevian, *Firm Foundation*, 119, Q. 175.

40. Luther writes, "Thus a Christian man is righteous and a sinner at the same time, holy and profane, an enemy of God and a child of God" (*LW* 26:232; *WA* 40.1/1:368.27–28).

> But God shows his love for us in that while we were still sinners, Christ died for us. (Rom 5:8 ESV)
>
> But God chose what is foolish in the world to shame the wise. (1 Cor 1:27 ESV)
>
> But God gave it to Abraham by a promise. (Gal 3:18 ESV)
>
> But God, being rich in mercy, because of the great love with which he loved us ... (Eph 2:4 ESV)

Therefore our consciences continue to testify against us all our lives. Believers say to themselves, "Yes, conscience, that is all very true, but something else is true. God the Son has accomplished all righteousness for me, and that is enough."

The answer to our conscience is not found in our subjective experience. It lies in the objective truth of the gospel, the good news that Christ has accomplished salvation for me, outside me. This is so because our problem, though intimately related to what is within us (sin and death), is ultimately outside us: God's holy justice and wrath. In other words, our greatest problem is not the misery and suffering that sin brings, but rather our greatest problem is the judgment that sin brings.

In the garden God said: "The day you eat of the fruit of the tree of the knowledge of good and evil, you shall surely die" (Gen 2:17). The Hebrew text says literally "to die [the] death" (מוֹת תָּמוּת). It is the same language the serpent used in Genesis 3:4 when he contradicted our Lord: "You shall not surely die [the] death." This and similar expressions (Gen 20:7; 26:11; Exod 19:12; 21:12, 15) occur elsewhere to signal the certainty of punishment. This penalty was not a mere or hypothetical possibility but an inevitability.

In Galatians 3:10, the apostle Paul quotes Deuteronomy 27:26: "Cursed be anyone who does not confirm the words of this law by doing them" (ESV). This is why it is so important that the gospel says to us: "God of mere grace, grants and imputes to me the perfect satisfaction, righteousness, and holiness of Christ." When Ephesians 2:8 says, "For by grace you have been saved through faith," grace signifies divine favor toward sinners merited for us by Christ.

Rome teaches that we are justified because and to the degree that we are sanctified, and we are sanctified (and therefore justified) by the infusion of the (medicinal) grace of "charity poured forth into our hearts."[41] This is premised on a misinterpretation of Romans 5:5, "because God's love has been poured into our hearts through the Holy Spirit who has been given to us" (ESV). It is a misinterpretation because Romans 5:1 says, "Therefore, since we have been justified [Δικαιωθέντες] by faith, we have peace with God through our Lord Jesus Christ" (ESV). The word we translate as "having been justified" is a passive participle signaling something that has been done for us. In contrast, the Roman Catholic view says that justification is sanctification. which is something being presently wrought in us by grace *and* cooperation with grace. Paul teaches that we are justified now. Rome says that we were initially justified in our baptism, but, since we have lost that, our future justification is contingent on our cooperation with grace. There is no way to reconcile the Roman Catholic view with Paul's view. The Roman Catholic view rests on assumptions that Paul did not share, namely that God can only say of us "justified" if we are intrinsically, actually, personally righteous (i.e., fully sanctified). Scripture does not teach this. We know that believers are already justified by faith (ἐκ πίστεως) because we have peace with God.

It is not as if the metaphor of pouring is unimportant. Our Lord Jesus said, "For this is my blood of the covenant, which is poured out for many for the forgiveness of sins" (Matt 26:28 ESV). God the Son did not become incarnate in order to make it possible for us to cooperate sufficiently with grace unto justification but in order to fulfill all righteousness for us. This is why the Protestant Reformers insisted so vigorously on the expression "for us" (*pro nobis*). Further, we believe Paul when he says that the love of God *is* being poured into our hearts, for sanctification.

Where the Roman Catholic doctrine says that we are finally justified because and only to the degree we finally sanctified, Scripture says that the basis of our justification before God is the righteousness Christ accomplished for us, which is credited to us. Paul uses this verb in Romans 5:13: "Sin is not counted [ἐλλογεῖται] where there is no law" (ESV). Paul

41. The Council of Trent, session 6, *Decretum de iustificatione*, cap. VII. Denzinger, *Enchiridion Symbolorum*, 287–88; Schroeder, *Canons and Decrees*, 33–34; CCC §1991.

says to Philemon (v. 18), "Charge [ἐλλόγα] that to my account" (ESV). In Romans 4:7–8 Paul quotes Psalm 32:1–2 (31:1–2 LXX): "Blessed are those whose lawless deeds are forgiven, and whose sins are covered; blessed is the man against whom the Lord will not count [λογίσηται] his sin" (ESV).

Sinners whose sins (lawless deeds) God has forgiven, whose sins God has covered, are blessed. The second clause explains the first. Forgiveness and covering of sins are logically related. Those who sins are not covered are not forgiven. It is not that the sins are not actually present but that they are covered. The next sentence explains the first: the basis of forgiveness is reckoning, counting, or imputing. The verb Paul uses is in the same family as the other verb we have already noticed. The ground of our justification is Christ's righteousness imputed. It is proper to him; it belongs by nature to him. He earned it. He condignly merited it. He deserved it. He was inherently, intrinsically righteous. By nature, all that Christ is and did is alien to us. This is why the Protestants in the sixteenth century spoke of Christ's "alien righteousness" (*iustitia aliena*). In his 1579 commentary on Romans, Olevianus writes, "Whoever would stand before God, it is necessary that he be righteous, either by a proper righteousness, i.e., a righteousness of proper strength, of which sort the law of God itself either written or unwritten, by right of creation requires from us, or an alien righteousness, i.e., of God imputed to the believer."[42] Ursinus vigorously defends the doctrine of the imputation of the "alien righteousness" of Christ.[43] Theodore Beza, following Calvin, adds that though Christ's righteousness is *properly* Christ's, it is ours legally by imputation. Nevertheless, it becomes ours by virtue of our union with Christ.[44] We have already seen this in Olevianus's use of the marriage analogy above.

Only by God's free grace, by his favor, is all that Christ did, all of his righteousness, all of his condign merit, all of his perfect, whole, active, and suffering (passive) obedience, credited or imputed or reckoned to us.

42. "Quicunque coram Deo vult consistere, necesse est ut sit iustus, vel iustitia propria, hoc est iustitia propriarum virium, qualem lex Dei sive ea scripta sit, sive non scripta, iure creationis à nobis requirit: aut iustitia aliena, hoc est Dei, credenti imputata" (Olevianus, *Romanos Notae*, 35).

43. "Ex his, quae de utraque applicatione dicta sunt patet primo: non esse absurdum dicere, nos iustificari iustitia aliena. Non enim iustitia, qua per fidem applicata iusti censemur, est simpliciter aliena sed sit nostra applicatione" (Ursinus, *Corpus doctrinae orthodoxae*, 330–31; Ursinus, *Commentary*, 329).

44. Beza, *Questionum et Responsionum*, 683; Beza, *Little Book of Questions*, Q. 115. See Calvin, *Institutes* 3.1.1.

Thus, when God looks at us, with respect to justification, he does not see our sin. He sees only Christ's perfect righteousness. Not only are all our sins forgiven, but we are made positively righteous before God. It is as if we ourselves had done all that Christ has done for us.

Paul was explaining Genesis 15:6: "Abraham believed God and it was imputed [חָשַׁב] to him for righteousness." He says, "Now to the one who works, his wages are not imputed [λογίζεται] as a gift but as his due. And to the one who does not work but believes in him who justifies the ungodly, his faith is imputed [λογίζεται] as righteousness."

Abraham was not justified because he was sanctified, nor because he cooperated sufficiently with grace. He was justified through faith alone, by which gift he trusted in the Savior Jesus. Abraham is the pattern for new covenant believers because, in the words of Jesus, "Abraham saw my day and rejoiced" (John 8:56). Abraham had true faith. Christ's righteousness for him was imputed to him, and he received that righteousness through faith. Christ's righteousness was imputed to him (Rom 4:9) before he was circumcised, before he even had opportunity to cooperate with grace. His sanctification was a grace that was a *consequence* of the grace of justification, whereby God declared him to be righteous even before he had done good works (*BC* 24; WSC 33). In his explanation of Genesis 15:6, in Galatians 3:7, Paul adds it is those who are "of faith" (in contrast to works) who are Abraham's sons. His circumcision was a seal of the righteousness that had already been imputed to him (Rom 4:11). Paul says that the story of Abraham's justification *sola gratia, sola fide* is recorded for our sakes, so that we will have confidence that we too, who have believed in Christ, are also now already justified. We should be assured that God has credited Christ's perfect, whole obedience to us (Rom 4:22). Because we are now justified on the basis of Christ's imputed righteousness, our sins, with which we struggle all through this life, are not being imputed (λογιζόμενος) to us (2 Cor 5:19).

The English verbs *impute*, *credit*, and *charge* are, of course, commercial terms. These are banking terms. We use credit cards, through which merchants treat us as if we have money that we may or may not actually have. These are also legal terms. When we are declared righteous in court, it is not because there is no sin in us but that our sins are not imputed to us before the law. We are regarded as if we have fulfilled the law and as if we have not transgressed it.

This is not, as the Roman Catholic critics say, a legal fiction. It is not our half-hearted, broken, decrepit "righteousness" (e.g., cooperation with grace) that is being credited to us. That would be a fictive doctrine of justification. Rather, that is the Roman doctrine of congruent merit. We say that Christ's perfect, whole, complete, active, and suffering (passive) righteousness is credited to us. The righteousness that is credited to us is intrinsically worthy. It has condign merit. So we reject the Roman doctrine that believers have, by grace and cooperation with grace, condign merit, and we reject the doctrine of congruent merit in justification (*HC* 60), but we do not reject every notion of merit altogether.

The idea that the Reformed reject every doctrine of merit is contrary to what we confess when we repeatedly contrast our lack of condign or congruent merit with the reality and presence of Christ's condign merit for us. Herman Witsius writes, "But if this righteousness had not been sacred and inviolable, Christ would have been under no necessity to submit to the covenant of the law, in order to merit eternal life for his people. This therefore is evident, that there ought to be a merit of perfect obedience on which a right to eternal life may be founded. Nor is it material whether that perfect obedience be performed by man himself, or by his surety."[45] The basis of our standing with God is not within us, but it is real and it is outside us. It is objective. It is Christ's. He has satisfied God's righteous law and endured his holy and just wrath for us. In justification, when God looks at us, he does not see our sins. He sees only Christ's perfect righteousness for us. That is why believers are not under a covenant of works but a covenant of grace. Christ's real and perfect righteousness does not belong properly to us, and yet we must lay hold of it.

How do we lay hold of Christ's righteousness? How does it become ours? How do we come into possession of that righteousness by which we can stand before God not only forgiven but actively righteous as perfect law keepers? We have already considered *HC* 21 at length, but consider how Paul answers the question:

---

45. Witsius, *Economy*, 1:131.

Yet we know that a person is not justified by works of the law but through faith in Jesus Christ, so we also have believed in Christ Jesus, in order to be justified by faith in Christ and not by works of the law, because by works of the law no one will be justified. (Gal 2:16 ESV)

Now it is evident that no one is justified before God by the law, for "The righteous shall live by faith." But the law is not of faith, rather "The one who does them shall live by them." (Gal 3:11–12 ESV)

For in it the righteousness of God is revealed from faith for faith, as it is written, "The righteous shall live by faith." (Rom 1:17 ESV)

But now the righteousness of God has been manifested apart from the law, although the Law and the Prophets bear witness to it—the righteousness of God through faith in Jesus Christ for all who believe. For there is no distinction: for all have sinned and fall short of the glory of God, and are justified by his grace as a gift, through the redemption that is in Christ Jesus, whom God put forward as a propitiation by his blood, to be received by faith. This was to show God's righteousness, because in his divine forbearance he had passed over former sins. It was to show his righteousness at the present time, so that he might be just and the justifier of the one who has faith in Jesus.

Then what becomes of our boasting? It is excluded. By what kind of law? By a law of works? No, but by the law of faith. For we hold that one is justified by faith apart from works of the law. (Rom 3:21–28 ESV)

And to the one who does not work but believes in him who justifies the ungodly, his faith is counted as righteousness. (Rom 4:5 ESV)

That is why it depends on faith, in order that the promise may rest on grace and be guaranteed to all his offspring—not only to the adherent of the law but also to the one who shares the faith of Abraham, who is the father of us all. (Rom 4:16 ESV)

Therefore, since we have been justified by faith, we have peace with God through our Lord Jesus Christ. (Rom 5:1 ESV)

Notice a theme emerging in these verses. In every case faith is the sole instrument by which we are said to lay hold of Christ's righteousness. That is the significance of the Latin phrase *sola fide*. It is an instrumental phrase. That is why we should not speak of "faith alone" (*sola fides*) but "by faith alone" or "through faith alone." Faith is the sole instrument of our justification. It is the sole means by which we lay hold of what Christ has done. Paul repeatedly and explicitly excludes anything done by us (works) or even anything wrought in us by God's grace (sanctification). Rome agrees that we are justified by grace and faith but omits the "alone." This is why Luther adds *allein* ("alone") to his German translation of Romans 3:28.[46] This is why Calvin insists, in his 1548 commentary on Galatians, "When you turn to the case of justification, beware of admitting any mention of love or works, but hold the exclusive particle tenaciously."[47] *Sola* is that "exclusive particle," of course, to which Calvin held tenaciously.

Sola gratia God grants and imputes to us Christ's righteousness. There is nothing in us, not even that which is worked by grace, that is a cause for his grace. The cause is in himself. Faith is the unique and only instrument by which we apprehend Christ and his righteousness, the only instrument through which we receive what Christ has done for us (*pro nobis*).

Look at those passages closely in their context. In none of them is faith considered to be, in itself, a powerful, Spirit-wrought virtue that sanctifies us unto justification. Scripture teaches repeatedly, clearly, unequivocally that all our works, all our doing, all our obedience is excluded from the ground and the instrument of our justification. That is why we confess in *BC* 24 that we are justified "even before we do good works."[48]

That is why we confess, "if only I accept such benefit with a believing heart." We cannot earn God's favor. Stop trying. Christ has earned God's favor for all his people. Confess your sins and sinfulness, and put your trust in Christ and his finished work. That is why Jesus said, "It is finished" – because it is. Every time we try to earn favor with God and refuse to put our trust solely in Christ and his finished work, we insult

46. In his 1530 *On Translating: An Open Letter,* Luther defends his use of *allein* (*LW* 35:187–98).

47. "Ergo quum versaris in causa iustificationis, cave ullum charitatis vel operum mentionem admittas, sed mordicus retine particulam exclusivam" (Calvin, *Epistolas Ad Galatas, Ad Ephesios, Ad Philippenses, Ad Colossenses,* 120.11–13).

48. Schaff, *Creeds of Christendom,* 3:411.

him by suggesting that Christ's work for us is not sufficient. Scripture has an answer: "It is finished" (John 19:30).

QUESTION 61

Why do you say that you are righteous by faith only?

Not that I am acceptable to God on account of the worthiness of my faith, but because only the satisfaction, righteousness and holiness of Christ is my righteousness before God and I can receive the same and make it my own in no other way than by faith only.[49]

The Reformation was a return to the Scriptures and a challenge to long-held assumptions. The church had always read the word of God, but it had long done so under the control of a set of assumptions, chief among which was that God could only call one righteous if one was, in oneself, properly, inherently righteous. The medieval church gradually developed a scheme whereby a sinner might progressively become righteous by medicinal grace and cooperation with that medicine infused into us by the sacraments.[50] In the medieval and later Roman Catholic program, God was said to recognize as just those who were completely sanctified. The Protestants rejected that scheme as contrary to the biblical teaching that sinners are justified by divine favor alone (*sola gratia*), through faith alone (*sola fide*), which rests and trusts in Christ alone as the

49. "Warum sagst du, dass du allein durch den Glauben gerecht seiest? Nicht dass ich von wegen der Würdigkeit meines Glaubens Gott gefalle, sondern darum, dass allein die Genugthuung, Gerechtigkeit, und Heiligkeit Christi meine Gerechtigkeit vor Gott ist, und ich dieselbe nicht anders, denn allein durch den Glauben annehmen, und mir zueignen kann" (Schaff, *Creeds of Christendom*, 3:327). "Cur sola fide iustum esse affirmas? Non quod dignitate meae fidei Deo placeam, ded quod sola satisfactio, iustitia ac sanctitas Christi, mea iustitia sit coram Deo. Ego vero eam non alia ratione, quam fide amplecti, et mihi applicare queam" (Niemeyer, *Collectio Confessionum*, 443).

50. Clark, "*Iustitia Imputata Christi*," 269–310. Grace was regularly characterized in medieval theology as a medicine with which we cooperate for sanctification, which was said to lead to justification. E.g., Bonaventure, *Breviloquium* 5.2.4–5; 5.3.4–6; Bonaventure, *Soul's Journey Into God*, 120; *ST* 1a2ae 109.7. The "half-dead" man on the side of the road, in the parable of the good Samaritan (Luke 10:30), was a prevailing image in the medieval conception of the effect of the fall, with deep patristic roots. On this see Roukema, "Good Samaritan in Ancient Christianity," 56–74; Abelard, *Commentary on the Epistle*, 245. Bonaventure lists the effects of the fall as "infirmity, ignorance, malice, and concupiscence" (*Breviloquium* 3.5.4).

Righteous One. According to the Protestants, Christ alone is intrinsically, personally, actually righteous. In medieval terms, he alone has condign merit, and his righteousness and merit is imputed to those who believe.

Because the scheme set up by the medieval church and adopted by Rome at the Council of Trent (1545–1563) required our personal sanctification as the precondition to justification, and that by grace and cooperation with grace, Rome had a powerful incentive to multiply the sources of medicinal grace. Thus, between the ninth and thirteenth centuries the number of sacraments grew from the two instituted by our Lord to seven. Since then, Rome has continued to add quasi-sacraments, for example, indulgences. These ecclesiastical creations illustrate the intersection between salvation and worship, between the Reformed doctrines of *sola fide* and *sola Scriptura*. Without them the church is rootless and left to its own devices, to what Paul in Colossians 2:23 calls "will worship" (ἐθελοθρησκίᾳ): "These have indeed an appearance of wisdom in promoting will-worship [ἐθελοθρησκίᾳ] and asceticism and severity to the body, but they are of no value in stopping the indulgence of the flesh." The ESV translates the noun ἐθελοθρησκίᾳ as "self-made religion." That is just right, but the older Reformed theologians call it "will worship" because they want to highlight the difference between worshiping God the way he has commanded and worshiping God the way we think is right.[51] "Will worship" captures the centrality of the human will as opposed to the divine will. Rome is fundamentally committed to what the Reformed churches regard as human-made, church-imposed worship and doctrine. In contrast, we confess that we do in worship only what God has commanded (*BC* 7, 32; *HC* 96–98; WCF 21.1).[52]

What has will worship to do with justification and salvation *sola fide*? Much in every way. Just as God has revealed and appointed the way he is to be worshiped, so he has also appointed the one instrument through which sinners can become righteous. Whereas Rome says that justification is sanctification and that faith is itself a powerful virtue, that is, it is sanctification because it is formed by charity, Scripture teaches no such

51. E.g., Calvin, *Institutes* 4.10.24.

52. United Reformed Churches in North America, *Liturgical Forms and Prayers*, 157–58, 188–89; Westminster Assembly, *Humble Advice of the Assembly*, 37.

thing. Rather, Scripture repeatedly contrasts faith, in the act of justification, as trusting, resting, leaning, receiving Christ and his righteousness. When Paul, in Romans 1:17, quotes Habakkuk 2:4, "The just shall live by faith," he understands faith not as a virtue wrought within us by infused medicine and our free cooperation with that medicine. Rather, he understands it as a divine gift (Eph 2:8) that receives Christ and all that Christ has done for us. That is why just before the quotation he writes, "The righteousness of God is revealed from faith unto faith" (ἐκ πίστεως εἰς πίστιν). Faith is not powerful except insofar as it lays hold of Christ and his righteousness. It is not revealed from faith unto sanctification. It is not revealed from faith unto cooperation with infused medicine. No, it is revealed from faith unto faith because faith—resting, receiving, trusting in Christ—is the only instrument. Nevertheless, Christ, not faith, is powerful. Faith in itself is an empty hand. As Luther says, "*Wir sein Pettler. Hoc est verum.*" "We are beggars. This true."[53] It is against this background that we confess in *HC* 61.

It is not by walking under arches, such as during Rome's Jubilee in 2000, that we are justified and saved. It is only through faith, which looks only to Christ's perfect righteousness, to his satisfaction of God's righteousness for us. There is no other instrument.[54] Baptism does not lay hold of Christ. The Lord's Supper does not lay hold of Christ. They are divinely instituted sacraments that promise justification and salvation to all who believe. They seal those promises to believers, but they are not the instruments by which sinners lay hold of Christ. Good works in this life and in the life to come cannot be the instrument of justification and salvation. They can only be fruit and evidence that we have been justified. Only true faith trusts and lays hold of Christ and all he has done for us.

Not only did Rome challenge the Reformation, but, nearly sixty years after the catechism was published, the Reformed Churches of Europe and the British Isles gathered to defend the Reformation against James Arminius (ca. 1560–1609) and the Remonstrants, who sought to redefine faith. Whereas the medieval theologians and Rome defined faith

---

53. Oberman, "*Wir Sein Pettler*," 91–116.

54. In 1592 Theodore Beza, who taught both Ursinus and Olevianus, defended this conviction at length in "Defense of Justification," 1–124.

as a theological virtue and taught that faith saved because it worked, because it was "formed by love" (*fides formata caritate*), Arminius and the Remonstrants held that we were elected on the basis of foreseen faith (*fides praevisa*).[55] Though he postured as a defender of *sola fide*, Arminius rejected it by making faith rather than Christ's (alien) righteousness the thing imputed to us.[56] The synod recognized these revisions as flatly contrary to the biblical account of faith and its role in salvation.

Thus, though the framers of the catechism intended to reject the Roman doctrine of "faith formed by love" in favor of *sola fide*, whereby it is the object of faith that makes it powerful rather than the sanctification and good works of the believer, the language of the catechism is flatly contrary to the Remonstrant definition of faith. We confess that it is not the worth (*Würdigkeit*) or dignity (*dignitate*) of faith that makes it powerful. Arminius's doctrine of the imputation of faith and the Remonstrant doctrine of foreseen faith both make *faith* into a virtue again and the ground of salvation rather than the empty hand that receives the righteousness of Christ freely given.

In recent years it has become fashionable for some who identify themselves as Reformed to speak of an *initial* justification received *sola fide* and a *final* justification (and salvation) through faith *and* good works.[57] This doctrine vitiates the doctrine of justification *sola fide* in two ways: first by introducing a second stage of justification when Scripture only knows of a single declaration of justification (Rom 3:24, 28; 5:1; 8:30; 10:10). At the judgment the elect will be *vindicated* but will not be justified a second

55. On faith "formed by love," see *ST* 2a2ae 4.1., resp. obj. 3; Godfrey, "Faith Formed by Love," 267–84. On Arminius and foreseen faith, see Arminius, *Works of James Arminius*, 3:485–88; Clark, "Synod of Dort," 9–29; Godfrey, *Saving the Reformation*, 106–8.

56. Stanglin and McCall, *Jacob Arminius*, 168.

57. This scheme is Roman Catholic (*CCC* §2010) but has been adopted and adapted variously by E. P. Sanders, N. T. Wright, Rich Lusk, Richard B. Gaffin Jr., and G. K. Beale, among many. For a survey of Sanders and Wright, see Waters, *Justification and the New Perspectives*. See also Wright, *Justification*, 182–93; Lusk, "Response to 'The Biblical Plan,'" 137; Gaffin, *By Faith Not by Sight*, 95–122; Beale, *New Testament Biblical Theology*, 505–26; cf. Fesko, *Theology of the Westminster Standards*, 392–94, which strongly contests Beale's historical claims regarding a two-stage doctrine of justification. See also VanDrunen, "Where We Are," 27–54; Duguid, "Covenant Nomism and the Exile," 61–62; Horton, "Which Covenant Theology?," 210–11; Venema, *Gospel of Free Acceptance*, 257–85. Vos adds an encouraging note regarding Christians and the future judgment: "The judgement is an event that will make discrimination as to the future rank and enjoyment in the life to come between individual Christians. The differences established may and will be great, but the range covered by them lies within the realm of salvation" (*Pauline Eschatology*, 270).

time, and certainly not on the basis of or through the instrument of works or our obedience.[58] Second, this doctrine introduces a second instrument, obedience. The great point of confessing *sola fide* is to exclude our good works as the ground or instrument of justification. This is why Calvin speaks of the "exclusive particle," that is, the *sola* in *sola fide*. We may be sure that this is the correct understanding of *HC* 61 since Ursinus explains it using this exact language.

> Faith alone is the instrument which apprehends the satisfaction of Christ. Hence it is plain, why the exclusive particle only should be added, as it is in the Catechism, and be maintained against the Papist. It is done, 1. For the purpose of expressing what Paul affirms when he says:" "We are justified freely by his grace, without the deeds of the laws:" And what Christ says: "only believe." (Rom 4:24, 28. Mark 5:36.) 2. That all our own works, and merits, as well as those of others, may be excluded as being the cause of our justification, that faith may be understood correlatively. We are justified *by faith only*, that is, by the merits of Christ alone.[59]

Ursinus has just said that faith has to be the sole instrument because it is in the nature of faith to be such. It is "nothing else than … the apprehension of the merits of Christ."[60] He continues to say, "Faith itself is excluded from that which is received by faith," so faith never becomes meritorious. He invokes the image of the beggar, just has Luther did before him.

QUESTION 62

But why cannot our good works be the whole or part of our righteousness before God?

Because the righteousness that can stand before the judgment-seat of God, must be perfect throughout and wholly conformable to the

58. "Positing two separate verdicts, one in the present and one in the future, inherently diminishes the eschatological "already" of the believer's justification" (Fesko, *Justification*, 322).

59. Ursinus, *Commentary*, 332.

60. Ursinus, *Commentary*, 332.

divine law; but even our best works in this life are all imperfect and defiled with sin.[61]

Because the popular rhetoric in evangelical circles has frequently been that the medieval (or the Roman Catholic) church taught justification by works and the Reformers taught justification by grace, well-meaning but misguided Christians sometimes conclude that so long as in justification we assign everything to grace, all is well. This is a significant mistake. The medieval church, and Roman Catholic Church following that tradition, taught salvation and justification by grace and cooperation with grace. In most cases (as represented by Thomas's account of the sixfold division of grace), supernatural (operating) grace was said to begin the process of sanctification (justification), and supernatural (cooperating) grace was said to facilitate its progressive work within us toward eventual justification.[62] In Bernard of Clairvaux, Thomas Aquinas, and ultimately Trent, however, there is an essential component that we must provide: the exercise of the free choice in cooperation with prevenient and assisting grace.[63] We must cooperate. We must do our part.

The magisterial Reformation theologians and their ecclesiastical communions rejected this scheme, soaked in grace as it was, for a variety of reasons. The medievals regarded grace as a medicinal substance with which we were infused (in the sacraments) and which was said to create in us a disposition (*habitus*) toward sanctification, obedience, virtue, and condign (inherently worthy) merit unto sanctification and eventual justification.[64] They rejected this scheme because it located the ground of

---

61. "Warum können aber unsere guten Werke nicht die Gerechtigkeit vor Gott oder ein Stück derselben sein? Darum, weil die Gerechtigkeit, so vor Gottes Gericht bestehen soll, durchaus vollkommen und dem Gesetz ganz gleichförmig sein muss, aber auch unsere besten Werke in diesem Leben alle unvollkommen und mit Sünden befleckt sind" (Schaff, *Creeds of Christendom*, 3:327). "Cur nostra bona opera non possunt esse iustitia, vel pars aliqua iustitiae coram Deo? Propterea quod oporteat eam iustitam, quae in iudicio Dei consistat, perfecte absolutam esse, et omni ex parte divinae legi congruentem: nostra vero etiam praestantissima quaeque opera, in hac vita sunt imperfecta, atquae adeo peccatis inquinata" (Niemeyer, *Collectio Confessionum*, 443).

62. *ST* 1a2ae 111.1–5.

63. Bernard of Clairvaux, *On Grace and Free Choice*, passim; *ST* 1a2ae 111.2, *resp. dic.*; Schroeder, *Canons and Decrees*, 36, 42–43; CCC §1730, 1742, 1747.

64. See the discussion of medicinal grace under *HC* 62 and on merit under *HC* 63.

justification within us, because it confused justification and sanctification. They found in Scripture that justification is a definitive act, God's declaration that a sinner is just. They rejected the doctrine that justification is a process. They found that the ground of justification is located outside us (*extra nos*), in Christ, and that his righteousness is imputed to us and received through faith alone (*sola fide*). The Protestants concluded that, even though the medieval and Tridentine Roman doctrine talked much of grace, the medieval and Roman doctrine rested on works in two ways: (1) insofar as our cooperation was said to help form inherent righteousness, it made our cooperation part of the *ground* of our justification; (2) insofar as our good works were necessary to form faith, that is, to make faith what it must be, they became part of the instrument of justification. Both of these errors contradict the biblical teaching that salvation and justification are by grace alone (*sola gratia*), through faith alone (*sola fide*), and that works are nothing more or less than the fruit and evidence of salvation and justification.

The medievals commonly admitted that there were two kinds or (in some cases) two aspects of merit. They distinguished first *condign* merit, that merit formed in us by the action of the grace of the Holy Spirit (and cooperation with grace) such that it meets the terms of justice. Thomas Aquinas writes, "Properly speaking a merit is an action on account of which it is just that the agent should be given something."[65]

To the degree that there is a "duty in the giver," and to the degree an act lacks the perfection or inherent, intrinsic justice but insofar as rewarding it is "fitting" (Thomas cites Anselm), an act has *congruent* merit.[66] In the fifteenth century, Gabriel Biel posited that God had made a covenant: "To the one who does what lies within himself, God denies not grace."[67] In either case, however, we were said to be compiling merit (either condign or congruent), and our cooperation with grace (there were different definitions) was of the essence.

---

65. *ST* supplement 14.4, resp. dic.

66. *ST* supplement 14.4, resp. dic.

67. "Facere quod in se est Deus non denegat gratiam." See Oberman, *Harvest of Medieval Theology*, 53, 133–45. Arminius picked up this thread and tried to reintroduce it to Reformed theology. Arminius (*Works*, 2:20, *Apology Against 31 Theological Articles*, art. 17) protested that he did not teach the Franciscan view but then proceeded to affirm the substance of Ockham and Biel's position after denying its caricature.

Just before the catechism was published, the Protestant consensus, reflected in Augsburg Confession article 4, was rocked by a series of controversies, several of which had to do with the place of works in justification. There was worry that teaching justification by unconditional divine favor alone, earned for us by Christ alone, and received *sola fide* would lead to impiety. So some, for example, Georg Major (1502–1574), proposed in the 1550s that good works were necessary for retaining salvation (*ad retinendam salutem*).[68] This provoked a reaction in the opposite direction, tending to antinomianism.[69]

The Protestants rejected the doctrine of congruent merit for justification. They held that Jesus had merited condignly our justification. They rejected any notion that we have either congruent or condign merit. Christ's obedience, we confessed, is perfect. His merit, his obedience, his active and suffering righteousness, is imputed to us. The ground of our acceptance with God as righteous is wholly outside us. We also rejected Major's attempt to wedge works into the doctrine of justification. He had anticipated the "in by grace, stay in by works" formula of the New Perspective on Paul and federal vision theology.

Our cooperation is of no account in our justification, either as its ground or the instrument. Christ's obedience is the ground, and faith is the sole instrument, because our works are defiled and imperfect. After all, Holy Scripture says: "Cursed is everyone who does not continue to everything in the book of the law" (Deut 27:26; Gal 3:10). Christ was born under the law for us (Gal 4:4).

The doctrine of congruent merit says that God grades on a curve. He does not. Uzzah did what lay within him (2 Sam 6:6), and he died. Isaiah 64:6 says that all our works are as filthy rags. There is no intrinsic worth to them. We were born in sin (Ps 51:5). We are dead in sins and trespasses (Eph 2:1–4). Our best works are like dung (Phil 3:8). Grace is not a medicinal substance with which we are infused. That is superstition. It is God's free (to us) favor earned for us by Christ. Yes, the Holy Spirit

68. Clark, "How We Got Here," 13–14; Kolb, "Georg Major as Controversialist," 455–68.

69. E.g., Nikolaus von Amsdorf (1483–1565), who argued that it was harmful to speak of good works. This view is rejected explicitly in the *Epitome of Formula of Concord*, art. 4, neg. thesis 2: "We also reject and condemn the bald expression that "good works are harmful to salvation" (Kolb and Wengert, *Book of Concord*, 499, 36).

works in us. Yes, we are united to Christ, but only as justified sinners, by grace alone, through faith alone. The Spirit works in us, to sanctify us, as a consequence of our free justification. Yes, we do cooperate with grace in sanctification. Yes, we do good works, we obey, as we work out our salvation with fear and trembling (Phil 2:12) because we are justified.

It is not enough to speak of grace. We must define grace as Scripture does. Rome makes much of grace and faith but does not define them as Scripture does. Grace is neither divinity (*gratia increata*) nor a medicinal substance (*gratia creata*) with which we are infused in the sacraments. Faith is not a meritorious, saving virtue wrought in us by grace and cooperation with grace. Neither justification nor salvation is the result of sanctification. Our good works are not instrumental in our salvation, and they have no merit of any kind in justification or sanctification, but Christ's do. He condignly merited our standing before God, and his merits have been freely imputed to us. That is why we should trust and not doubt that we, those who, *sola gratia, sola fide* trust Christ alone for our righteousness with God and salvation, are fully justified now, fully accepted now, and that we will be so received and acknowledged at the last day. Christ is the object of faith. Christ's obedience makes faith powerful.

It is not a mistake that, on this very question, Olevianus speaks not only of *justification* but also of the more comprehensive category of *salvation* as being *sola gratia, sola fide*. He asks "whether we shall be fully *saved* through such true faith in Christ?" He answers that there

> is only one way to eternal life (as I also said at the beginning of these articles), namely, the crucified Christ accepted through a true faith (1 Cor. 2:2). Since, then, faith (which is a gift of the Holy Spirit) possesses Christ and all His benefits as its own, and Christ is the one freely given us by God to be ours through faith, one of two things must follow: either Christ does not have all that is necessary for our *salvation*, or, if He does, one who possesses the crucified Christ through a true faith also has everything in Christ that is necessary for *salvation*. (emphases added)

He continues by explaining that the Articles of Faith (the Apostles' Creed) teach us we have "everything necessary for our eternal salvation in Jesus Christ and that He was not a partial but a complete Jesus, or

Savior, who fully accomplished everything necessary for our salvation. Therefore, whoever is grafted into Christ through a true faith has and possesses everything within that is necessary for salvation."[70]

On this question, Ursinus makes this same point and adds, "Because if our works were even perfect, yet they are still due from us, and so cannot acquit us, or make amends for past delinquences. 'When ye shall have done all those things which are commanded you, say we are unprofitable servants,' &c. Luke 17:10."[71]

70. Caspar Olevian, *Firm Foundation*, 108.

71. Ursinus, *Commentary*, 333.

Question 63

Do our good works merit nothing, even though it is God's will to reward them in this life and in that which is to come?

Question 64

But does not this doctrine make men careless and profane?

Lord's Day 24

QUESTION 63

Do our good works merit nothing, even though it is God's will to reward them in this life and in that which is to come?

The reward comes not of merit, but of grace.[1]

When the medieval church thought about rewards, it thought about merit. Indeed, this is just where Ursinus begins his exposition of this question.[2] The medieval church distinguished between two kinds or aspects of merit. That which we most frequently discuss was called "condign merit" (*meritum de condigno*). Condign merit is intrinsically worthy. The second category was "congruent merit" (*meritum de congruo*). We might call this merit covenantal insofar as the merit is not inherently worthy of recognition, but God has promised or covenanted to recognize it.

For the medieval (and later the Roman Catholic) church, the two were intimately bound up with each other. Thomas addresses the question of "whether a man may merit anything from God."[3] He defines merit briefly as "the effect of cooperating grace."[4] The first objection will seem familiar to many since it is widely held today: "It would seem that a man can merit nothing from God. For no one, it would seem, merits by giving another his due." Indeed, several of the objections to the very existence of merit sound familiar, since they are echoed in contemporary Reformed and evangelical discussions, for example, objection 3: "Whoever merits anything from another makes his debtor. ... Now since God is no one's debtor ... hence no one can merit anything from God." Thomas replies (*sed contra*), "On the contrary, It is written (Jer. 31:16): There is a reward for thy work. Now a reward means something bestowed by reason of merit. Hence it would seem that a man may merit from God."

1. "Berdienen aber unsere guten Werke nichts, so sie doch Gott in diesem und dem zukünstigen Leben will belohnen? Diese Belohnung geschieht nicht aus Verdienst, sondern aus Gnaden" (Schaff, *Creeds of Christendom*, 3:327). "Quomodo bona opera nostra nihil promereantur, cum Deus et in praesenti et in futura vita mercedem pro his se daturum promittat? Merces ea non datur ex merito, sed ex gratia" (Niemeyer, *Collectio Confessionum*, 443).

2. Ursinus, *Commentary*, 334.

3. *ST* 1a2ae 1.114.1.

4. *ST* 1a2ae 111.

For Thomas, rewards are by their nature merited. He explains (*respondeo dicendum*), "Merit and reward refer to the same, for a reward means something given anyone in return for work or toil, as a price for it. Hence, as it is an act of justice to give a just price for anything received from another, so also it is an act of justice to make a return for work or toil." He recognizes that there is disproportionality between God and humanity. "They are infinitely apart," he writes, so the "there can be no justice of absolute equality between man and God, but only of a certain proportion." By casting merit this way, Thomas blurs the distinction between condign and congruent merit. The same act can be said to have condign merit, insofar as it is wrought by cooperating grace and congruent merit insofar as our cooperation is in view.[5]

Nevertheless, he insists that humans can merit eternal life condignly.[6] He anticipates what would become a Protestant objection to humans earning condign merit, that is, "man in grace cannot merit eternal life condignly because 'the sufferings of this time are not worthy (*condignae*) to be compared with the glory to come. …' But of all meritorious works, the sufferings of the saints would seem to be most meritorious. Therefore no works of men are meritorious of eternal life condignly."

He replies that eternal life is granted "in accordance with a judgment of justice." He cites 2 Timothy 4:8 and concludes that humanity merits eternal life condignly. The nature of grace and the movement of the Holy Spirit in us is such that the effect is condignly meritorious. As he says later, insofar as the Spirit produces merit in us, it is condign. Insofar as we are cooperating willingly, an act has congruent merit.[7]

Thomas worked out his view of merit in the context of a strong realism, that is, a very close connection between the relationship between signs and things signified, and against an intellectualist background whereby the human intellect was said to be able to abstract universals (the one), which participate in the divine being, from particulars (the many) and thereby come into contact with the divine intellect.[8] In the centuries that

5. *ST* 1a2ae 1.114.1.

6. *ST* 1a2ae 114.3.

7. *ST* 1a2ae 114.6, resp. dicen.

8. *ST* 1a 12.9, resp. dic.

followed, there was a strong turn among a number of theologians toward emphasizing the divine will over the divine intellect, which sometimes divorced signs from things signified (nominalism). In the early sixteenth century, there was a neo-Thomist movement, but there are serious questions concerning how faithful those who participated were to Thomas. Heiko Oberman and Michael Horton, among others, argue, "Not the Reformation but Trent represents the triumph of nominalism. The Reformers actually stand closer to Aquinas than does Trent."[9]

It was against the older medieval idea that humans accumulate condign merit and the later medieval idea of congruent merit that the Reformed rejected any notion that we sinners can merit justification or salvation from God condignly or congruently. That much is clear from the Reformed confessions. They did not reject the doctrine of merit altogether. Because they were Augustinians (and not Pelagians), they drew the lines between Adam, Christ, and us sinners very carefully. Whereas the Pelagians moved from Adam to us relative to salvation, which is a symptom of Pelagianism, and made Jesus the first believer (as if he were in a covenant of grace) and an example for us to follow in order to be saved, the Augustinians had always connected Adam to us relative to sin and corruption. They drew a line between Christ and us for salvation. They made Christ the Savior more than the example. So, Thomas Bradwardine (ca. 1290–1349) reacted to the Pelagianizing theology of Ockham (ca. 1285–1347) and others by reasserting a strongly Augustinian theology.[10]

This is not to say that the notions of condign and congruent merit could not be put to use in redemptive history. As indicated above, the Reformed repeatedly affirmed that our Lord Jesus condignly merited our justification and our salvation even as they rejected the notion that we could condignly merit them. They, like Thomas and the late medieval Augustinians, rejected utterly the existence of an alleged covenant in which "to the one who does what lies within himself, God denies not grace" (*facere quod in se est Deus non denegat gratiam*).[11] They rejected the underlying anthropology, that is, the collapsing of nature into grace so that God was said to

9. Horton, *Justification*, 1:352.

10. On Bradwardine, see Oberman, *Forerunners of the Reformation*, 151–64; Leff, *Bradwardine and the Pelagians*; Alexander, "'Not by Stars or Skill.'"

11. For more on Biel, see the discussion under *HC* 62.

have endowed humans with antecedent properties with which God was "prepared to cooperate." In short, Biel and others were proposing that God helps those who help themselves. The Protestants, beginning with Luther, Melanchthon, Calvin, and the Reformed churches, rejected that whole scheme as nothing less than a return to Pelagianism. At Heidelberg (1518), Martin Luther said, "The person who believes that he can obtain grace by doing what is in him adds sin to sin so that he becomes doubly guilty."[12] Jesus, they taught and confessed, did not die to make justification and salvation possible or available for those who do their part. Rather, Jesus came as the last Adam to fulfill righteousness, and that righteousness is condignly meritorious and imputed to all who believe.

Thus, when the Reformed churches affirm the existence of rewards and deny that they are merited, they are distinguishing between Christ the meritorious Savior, who merited our justification and salvation, and us sinners, who are saved and justified not by "anything done by us or wrought in us" (WCF 11.1–2) but only for the sake of Christ's condign merits imputed to us and received through faith.[13]

There are heavenly rewards, but they are gifts. They are vastly disproportionate to anything done in us or done by us in the life. To set up some sort of correlation between our sanctity or our obedience and future rewards is to turn the covenant of grace into a covenant of works. The catechism is clear: we are in a covenant of grace. God is pleased *graciously*, that is, freely, unconditionally, to reward our good works. That the reward is by grace breaks the correlation between work and reward. Grace cannot be demanded or required. That which is demanded or required is just payment, and in that case we are back to the covenant of works again.

On rewards Olevianus writes Christ has "branded" us with his Holy Spirit, who "engenders their trust in Christ the Shepherd alone and motivates them to true thankfulness. ... By grace God also rewards our thankfulness, since we are already His children through Christ and He has graciously pardoned our sins. He is like a father who graciously and abundantly bestows gifts upon his child, the heir to all his property, even though the child's obedience has not merited them and such great gifts are beyond

12. Thesis 16 (*LW* 31:40).

13. Bower, *Confession of Faith*, 276–79.

comparison."[14] To speak of our merit relative to rewards is to confuse categories. Believers are the graciously adopted sons of the Father, in Christ (Rom 8:15; Gal 4:5), not employees. As Ursinus observes *contra* Rome, even if our works were perfect, they could never deserve any reward since we owe them to God.[15] To say that our works are meritorious is to deny the nature of faith and grace, and it is, as Ursinus notes, to turn the effect of new life and faith into an instrument or a cause.[16] The only cause of the reward is our Lord's free, fatherly favor toward his children whom he has loved, in Christ, from all eternity.

Finally, Calvin helps us on this question when he explains, "After he has received us into his favor, he receives our works also by a gracious acceptance. It is on this that the reward hinges. There is, therefore, no inconsistency in saying that he rewards good works, provided we understand that mankind, nevertheless, obtain eternal life gratuitously."[17]

QUESTION 64

But does not this doctrine make men careless and profane?

No, for it is impossible that those who are implanted into Christ by true faith, should not bring forth fruits of thankfulness.[18]

The Roman Catholics, Anabaptists, and later the Remonstrants had a shared concern about the Reformation doctrine of salvation *sola gratia, sola fide*: that it would not produce the degree of sanctification and obedience they expected of Christians. Thus, in different ways they either

14. Caspar Olevian, *Firm Foundation*, 85–86.

15. Ursinus, *Commentary*, 335.

16. Ursinus, *Commentary*, 335.

17. Calvin, *Corinthians*, 71–72. As Mike Horton notes, Calvin adds that Paul's expression "God will render to every one according to his works" signals "an order of sequence rather than the cause." As Horton says, "Good works are necessary not *unto justification* but *as a consequence*" (Horton, *Justification*, 2:394; emphasis original).

18. "Macht aber diese Lehre nicht forglose und verruchte Lente? Nein: denn es unmöglich ist, dass die, so Christo durch wahren Glauben sind eingepflanzet, nicht Frucht der Dankbarkeit sollen bringen" (Schaff, *Creeds of Christendom*, 3:328). "An autem haec doctrina non reddit homnes securos et prophanos? Non: neque enim fieri potest, quin ii qui Christo per fidem insiti sunt, fructus proferant gratitudinis" (Niemeyer, *Collectio Confessionum*, 444).

rejected the Reformation doctrine of salvation, as in the case of Rome and the first-generation Anabaptists, or, as in the case of the Remonstrants, sought to revise it without admitting explicitly that they rejected it. This was because none of them accepted the Reformation doctrine that, by the grace of God alone, good trees produce good fruit. John the Baptist implied this negatively when he warned, "Even now the axe is laid to the root of the trees. Every tree therefore that does not bear good fruit is cut down and thrown into the fire" (Matt 3:10 ESV). Our Lord made this explicit: "You will recognize them by their fruits. Are grapes gathered from thornbushes, or figs from thistles? *So, every healthy tree bears good fruit,* but the diseased tree bears bad fruit. A healthy tree cannot bear bad fruit, nor can a diseased tree bear good fruit. Every tree that does not bear good fruit is cut down and thrown into the fire. Thus you will recognize them by their fruits" (Matt 7:16–20 ESV, emphasis added). No sinners are saved (i.e., justified and sanctified) on the basis of the fruits of thankfulness, nor are they saved *through* them but, *sola gratia, sola fide,* by virtue of union with the risen Christ, by the work of the Spirit, they do produce the fruits of thankfulness.

The text of the catechism explicitly grounds this process in the mystery of our union with Christ (*Christo ... insiti sunt*), through faith (*per fidem*). Both the German verb, *eingepflanzet,* and the Latin translation, *insiti sunt,* are well translated with "ingrafted," since both are used in horticultural settings. They fit the biblical imagery and the overarching metaphor of trees and fruit in which the question-and-answer is framed. We should not miss the instrumental function of faith, however. The catechism is speaking of our mystical union with Christ, which is wrought by the Spirit, in those to whom he has given new life, *through faith.*[19]

In this connection we should observe two things: first, the catechism consistently highlights the unique instrumentality of faith (*sola fide*) in salvation, and second, there is a logical (not chronological) order of the application of redemption (*ordo salutis*). Under this question Ursinus first addresses the antinomian argument, that we may be indifferent to sin in this life since we are already finally justified, by replying that, though we

19. For more on the catechism's doctrine of faith, see the discussion under *HC* 21. See also Muller, *Calvin and the Reformed Tradition,* 177–201.

are finally justified already (*contra* any two-stage scheme of justification or salvation), nevertheless "God is always offended at sin, which is the greatest offence of which any one can be guilty." The second reason why Christians ought to be concerned about sin is that sins "deprive us of conformity with God, and bring temporal punishment, even upon the faithful, although they are delivered from such as are eternal."[20]

Ursinus also defends the Protestant doctrine of justification *sola fide* against the Roman Catholic definition of faith (*fides formata caritate*), which teaches that it is our good works that make faith finally justifying.[21] He reminds us of the "exclusive particle" (*sola*) in *sola fide*.[22] We are justified, he writes, on the basis of Christ's "blood and merits," but only as they are "apprehended by faith."[23]

We will be well served by considering his critique of the Roman Catholic doctrine of "faith formed by love" since it is being mooted by some who wish to be considered Reformed. The argument is this:

1. That which is not alone does not justify by itself (major premise).
2. Faith is not alone (minor premise).
3. Conclusion: Therefore it does not justify alone.

Ursinus responds by in essence distinguishing between "is" and "through." It is the case that the faith that justifies is never alone. It is not the case that faith justifies *because* it is not alone or that works thus become instrumental in our justification. To say that because faith is accompanied by works, therefore works are coinstrumental in justification is "what is usually, and correctly, called a fallacy of *composition*; for the exclusive particle *only*, which in the minor is connected with the verb is, is separated from it in the conclusion, and attached to the word *justify*."[24]

It is remarkable that Ursinus responded to a total of thirteen objections to the Protestant doctrine. Several of them are variations on the fallacy

20. Ursinus, *Commentary*, 336.
21. Godfrey, "Faith Formed by Love," 267–84.
22. See the discussion under *HC* 61.
23. Ursinus, *Commentary*, 336.
24. Ursinus, *Commentary*, 337. Italics original.

addressed above, but he also refutes the caricature of the Reformed definition of faith, that it is knowledge alone.[25] Faith is knowledge, *assent*, and *trust*.[26]

On James 2:24, "You see that a person is justified by works and not by faith alone" (ESV), to which the Roman Catholics (and other moralists) appeal in order to deny justification *sola fide*, Ursinus stands on the consensus Protestant view: "The apostle James does not speak of that righteousness by which we are justified before God, or on account of which God regards us as just; but of that righteousness by which we are justified before men by our works."[27] To the objection that good works are necessary for justification, Ursinus replies: "Good works, although they are not required for our justification, are nevertheless necessary to show our gratitude, and the glory of God." To the objection that Phineas (Ps 106:30–31) was justified by his works, Ursinus replies that he was justified in "that God approved of his work; but not that he was justified on account of it: for by the works of the law, no flesh shall be justified in the sight of God." Our works can be no part of our justification since they are all imperfect. Ursinus rejects the objection that our righteousness in this life is only temporary by denying the premise. The righteousness of Christ imputed to us in this life is eternal. The basis of our standing before God now and in eternity is always and only the perfect righteousness of Christ imputed.[28]

Finally, to the objection that the ground of justification must be intrinsic, within the believer (the Roman Catholic doctrine and also that of Andreas Osiander [1498–1552]), Ursinus replies that the righteousness with which we are justified cannot be inherent to us because such a view confuses the creature for the Creator and makes God a nonessential property of the creature.[29]

---

25. Ursinus, *Commentary*, 338.

26. See the discussion of faith under *HC* 21.

27. Ursinus, *Commentary*, 338. See Clark, "Benefits of Christ," 107–34; Clark, "*Iustitia Imputata Christi*," 269–310; Clark, "Do This and Live," 229–66.

28. Ursinus, *Commentary*, 338–39.

29. Ursinus, *Commentary*, 340. For more on the distinction between the Creator and the creature, see Clark, *Recovering the Reformed Confession*, 119–51. Calvin replies at length to Osiander in *Institutes* 3.11.5–12.

Second, the catechism teaches a logical order in the application of redemption. Louis Berkhof was correct to write,

> A great majority of Reformed theologians ... begin the *ordo salutis* with regeneration or with calling, and thus emphasize the fact that the application of the redemptive work of Christ is in its incipiency a work of God. This is followed by a discussion of conversion, in which the work of regeneration penetrates to the conscious life of the sinner, and he turns from self, the world, and Satan, to God. Conversion includes repentance and faith, but because of its great importance the latter is generally treated separately. The discussion of faith naturally leads to that of justification, inasmuch as this is mediated to us by faith. And because justification places man in a new relation to God, which carries with it the gift of the Spirit of adoption, and which obliges man to a new obedience and also enables him to do the will of God from the heart, the work of sanctification next comes into consideration. Finally, the order of salvation is concluded with the doctrine of the perseverance of the saints and their final glorification.[30]

Notice that, in Berkhof's summary of the mainstream of Reformed theology, he has sanctification flowing out of justification. The nexus between the two is the mystical aspect of union with Christ—the other two aspects of union being decretal. These other two aspects are (1) our relation with Christ by virtue of the unconditional decree of election and (2) the federal aspect, that is, our union with him in his obedience and death for us.[31] On this mystical union, Olevianus writes, "The Holy Spirit is that bond of union by which Christ abides in us and we in Him. As the branches incorporated into the vine receive their nourishment and life from the vine, so

30. Berkhof, *Systematic Theology*, 418.

31. On these aspects, see Berkhof, *Systematic Theology*, 447. On the history of doctrine, see Fesko, *Beyond Calvin*. We should dissent from Berkhof's judgment in two respects. He confused the mystical union with the two other aspects (448), and thus was confusing about the role of faith. In the mainstream of Reformed theology, it has been said that it is the called, regenerated, and believing who receive Christ through faith and through that faith are mystically united to him. E.g., WSC 30: "How doth the Spirit applieth to us the Redemption purchased by Christ? The Spirit applieth to us the Redemption purchased by Christ, by working Faith in us, and thereby uniting us to Christ in our Effectual Calling" (*Shorter Catechism*, 9, in Westminster Assembly, *Humble Advice of the Assembly*). See the discussion of union with Christ and gratitude under *HC* 2, 20–21, 65.

we are incorporated into Christ by the Holy Spirit so that we might have true fellowship with Him and receive eternal life from Him (John 15:1)."[32]

The organic, horticultural metaphor highlights the gracious process of the Christian life, whereby good fruit grows, which is just how our confession of faith speaks in article 24: "So then, it is impossible for this holy faith to be unfruitful in a human being, seeing that we do not speak of an empty faith but of what Scripture calls 'faith working through love,' which leads a man to do of himself the works that God has commanded in his Word."[33]

Discomfort with this truth, that progressive sanctification is the ordinary, expected result of grace and union with Christ, is the product of three errors: moralism, rationalism, and antinomianism. These three are united in their often-unspoken conviction that sanctification cannot be a mystery but must be something we can comprehend and explain entirely. Antinomianism, the denial of the third use of the moral law as the norm of the Christian life, and moralism, the doctrine that we are either accepted with God or saved from the wrath to come through sanctification, inherent righteousness, good works, or a combination of them,[34] are both species of rationalism. The moralist sets up a legal scheme to get Christians to be good, whereby either their justification or their salvation is contingent on their obedience to the law, and their sanctification is said to be the product of good works. Typically, in reaction to such nomism, the antinomian, essentially accepting the same view of the law, rejects it.[35] We should reject all three errors.

In order to understand the catechism, we must make the same essential distinction that the catechism itself does, namely, between the law and the gospel or between the covenants of works and grace. Using covenantal categories, we should say that progressive sanctification belongs to the covenant of grace and is the product of the covenant of grace. Before the Reformation, the medieval church had turned the covenant of grace into a covenant of works, whereby the medieval church turned it into a

32. Olevian, *Firm Foundation*, 92.

33. *BC* 24, in United Reformed Churches in North America, *Liturgical Forms and Prayers*, 178.

34. Allison, *Rise of Moralism*.

35. Berkhof, *Systematic Theology*, 615.

process of progressive justification and salvation by grace and cooperation with grace.

In his commentary on Galatians 5:6, William Perkins (1558–1602) expresses well the teaching of the catechism when he writes,

> Faith and love are two hands of our soul. Faith is a hand that lays hold of Christ, and it does (as it were) pull Him and His benefits into our souls. But love is a hand of another kind, for it serves not to receive in, but to give out the good that it has and to communicate itself unto others. Therefore faith cannot justify by love. Lastly, love in order of nature follows justification, and therefore does not justify. For first of all faith lays hold on Christ. Then follows justification. Upon justification follows sanctification, and love is a part of sanctification.[36]

We can hardly miss the most intimate connection between the gospel and sanctification in the catechism. The catechism has been explaining the doctrine of justification *sola gratia, sola fide,* on the basis of the imputation of the righteousness of Christ. It turns naturally to what Walter Marshall (1628–1680) calls "the gospel mystery of sanctification."[37]

In justification Christ acts *for* us (*pro nobis*), but in sanctification he acts *in* us. The prepositions change. Sanctification is the natural, logical, necessary consequence of justification. That is why we confess "it is impossible" that those who, by grace alone, through faith alone, are truly implanted or engrafted into Christ should not produce good fruit. A living tree produces fruit. This is what we confess in *BC* 24: "These works, proceeding from the good root of faith, are good and acceptable to God, since they are all sanctified by his grace. Yet they do not count toward our justification—for by faith in Christ we are justified, even before we do good works. Otherwise they could not be good, any more than the fruit of a tree could be good if the tree is not good in the first place." The function of good works is to give evidence of new life and true faith and to give glory to God. It is not the fruit that makes the tree. That is the Roman Catholic

36. Perkins, *Works,* 2:333. See Calvin, *Institutes* 3.16.1–4, on the motive for sanctification and good works.

37. Marshall, *Gospel Mystery of Sanctification,* 135–36.

doctrine. Rather, it is the tree that makes the fruit, and it is God's grace that makes the tree, as it were. How do we know that the tree is living? It has leaves. It gives fruit. How do we know that a tree is dead? When the season comes, it produces no leaves or no fruit.

Bearing fruit is what living trees do. One does not stand next to citrus trees and hector them, but one does water them, and in the ordinary course of things living trees produce fruit. So it is with the Christian. Scolding or making our future standing with God contingent on being good now is not the way to achieve the desired results. The gospel of free grace does not make Christians careless. If one is or seems careless, we approach that one according to Matthew 18 (there are three marks of the true church). If the person is penitent, then there is fruit. If the person is impenitent, then we provide a reminder of the righteous demands of God's holy law, and of the greatness of the person's sin and misery, and call the person to repentance and faith. Fruitlessness is no fault of the gospel of free grace. It is a sign of the absence of life. The proper response to the absence of life is to preach the message that the Spirit has promised to use to give new life and true faith to the elect: the gospel.

Question 65

Since therefore through faith alone we are made partakers of Christ and all His benefits, from where comes this faith?

Question 66

What are the Sacraments?

Question 67

Are both the Word and the sacraments designed to direct our faith to the sacrifice of Christ on the cross as the only ground of our salvation?

Question 68

How many sacraments has Christ instituted in the New Testament?

Lord's Day 25

QUESTION 65

Since therefore through faith alone we are made partakers of Christ and all His benefits, from where comes this faith?

The Holy Spirit works faith in our hearts by the preaching of the holy gospel, and confirms it by the use of the holy sacraments.[1]

With this Lord's Day, the catechism begins to consider the means of grace (*media gratiae*). Louis Berkhof defines them as "objective channels which Christ has instituted in the Church, and to which He ordinarily binds Himself in the communication of His grace. Of course these may never be dissociated from Christ, nor from the powerful operation of the Holy Spirit, nor from the Church which is the appointed organ for the distribution of the blessings of divine grace."[2] Ursinus writes, "This Question points out the connection which holds between the doctrine of faith and the sacraments."[3] We will come to this connection below.

HC 65 is an excellent example of why it is important to learn both the question and the answer. Catechism questions are not mere placeholders. They often contain important truths. So it is here.

There are three things to be considered: (1) the sovereignty of the Holy Spirit in granting the gifts of new life (regeneration) and faith; (2) the role of faith in our personal, mystical union with Christ; and (3) the Spirit's use of the external means of grace (i.e., the preaching of the gospel and the sacraments) in granting regeneration and faith to the elect.

First, we note the sovereignty of the Holy Spirit in granting new life and true faith. We should note the question. "From where does this faith come?" The answer is: the Holy Spirit. Olevianus explains:

1. "Dieweil denn allein der Glaube uns Christi und aller seiner Wohlthaten theilhaftig macht, woher kommt solcher Glaube? Der Heilige Geist wirket denselben in unsern Herzen durch die Predigt des heiligen Evangeliums, und bestätigt ihn durch den Brauch der heiligen Sacramente" (Schaff, *Creeds of Christendom*, 3:328). "Quoniam igitur sola fides nos Christi atque omnium eius beneficiorum participes facit: unde haec fides proficiscitur? A Spiritu Sancto, qui eam per praedicationem Evangelii in cordibus nostris accendit, et per usum Sacramentorum confirmat" (Niemeyer, *Collectio Confessionum*, 444).

2. Berkhof, *Systematic Theology*, 604–5.

3. Ursinus, *Commentary*, 340.

> For there is no other means whereby we can share in Christ and all His benefits than the Holy Spirit, who incorporates us into Christ. As it says in Romans 8[:9], "Whoever does not have the Spirit of Christ, he is not his." And each of you consider what a miserable pity it would be for someone who is robbed for time and eternity of the fruits of the Holy Spirit mentioned earlier. Thus we can understand how necessary it is for each person to have the Holy Spirit.[4]

Since the *HC* was published almost thirty years before Jacob Arminius (1560–1609) became controversial in the Netherlands, it was not facing the issues as they were framed at Dort. Nevertheless, the notion that the Spirit regenerates the elect from a state of spiritual death to a state of spiritual life did not originate at the Synod of Dort. The synod merely defended what was taught or implied in the catechism and in the *BC*. There is no notion in *HC* 65 of "foreseen faith" (*fides praevisa*), nor is there present anything like the Remonstrant doctrine of prevenient grace, that is, a universal endowment with which God is prepared to cooperate when sinners capitalize on that endowment.[5] Rather, the bestowal of regeneration by the Spirit is entirely unconditional and gracious.

Second, the sole instrument by which we become partakers (*theihaftig macht; participes*) of Christ is faith.[6] The doctrine of salvation *sola fide* is clearly taught in the *HC*.[7] There is no other instrument (*BC* 22) by which we apprehend Christ. The question has in view more than justification since it says "Christ and all his benefits." Both Ursinus (as seen under *HC* 64) and Olevianus are quite clear in their affirmation of *sola fide*. Olevianus writes,

> We can see from the following that this covenant between God and us is a gracious one and does not rest upon any condition of our own worthiness or merit, but exists *through faith alone*. For so far as God is concerned, He, strictly speaking, makes the covenant with us when He seals in our hearts through His Spirit the promise of

4. Olevian, *Firm Foundation*, 92.

5. E.g., as expressed in the fourth article of the 1610 Remonstrance (DeJong, *Crisis in the Reformed Churches*, 208–9).

6. See the discussion of faith under *HC* 20–21, 64.

7. See the discussion of justification *sola fide* under *HC* 21, 56, 60, 64.

> gracious reconciliation offered in the gospel (Titus 3:5–7; 2 Tim. 1:9; Gal. 3:6, 28–29). So far as we are concerned, we receive it *through faith alone* when we are graciously endowed with the Holy Spirit, who brings it about that we want to believe and are able to believe the gracious promise of reconciliation through Christ (Eph. 1; Joel 2; Isa. 59). If you look at the Mediator, our heavenly Father has indeed received from Him the price of reconciliation, and we have satisfaction in Him. For in the same way that the Mediator was graciously sent and given to us, and also imputes to us that merit, the covenant is also gracious. So this whole covenant is purely gracious and exists *through faith alone.*[8]

In one passage Olevianus not only affirms the unconditionality of the covenant of grace but also three times he affirms salvation *sola fide*.

Third is the doctrine of union with Christ, which we have already considered under other questions.[9] There are three aspects to the doctrine of union with Christ. First, believers may be said to have been united to Christ in the divine decree from all eternity (Eph 1:1–6); second, believers were represented federally by Christ (Rom 5:12–21); and third, we are brought into mystical (i.e., Holy Spirit) union with him through faith alone (*sola fide*; Rom 10:17). This would seem to be the view of WSC 30, which asks and answers, "How doth the Spirit apply to us the redemption purchased by Christ? A. The Spirit applieth to us the redemption purchased by Christ, by working faith in us, and thereby uniting us to Christ in our effectual calling."[10] The instrumentality of faith is clearly indicated in the word *thereby*. There is another approach, with roots in the seventeenth century, that holds that we are mystically united to Christ at effectual calling, and that faith and sanctification are the twin products of the union effected in regeneration.[11] John Murray identifies mystical

---

8. Olevianus, *Exposition*, 14. Emphases added.

9. See the discussion under *HC* 20–21, 32, 64.

10. Westminster Assembly, *Humble Advice of the Assembly*, 9. WLC 66–69, 72 provide context to WSC 30.

11. In one place, Herman Witsius teaches that we are mystically united to Christ through regeneration: "III. By a true and a real union, (but which is only passive on their part,) they are united to Christ when his Spirit first takes possession of them, and infuses into them a principle of new life: the beginning of which life can be from nothing else but from union with the Spirit of Christ; who is to the soul, but in a far more excellent manner, in respect of spiritual life, what the soul is to

union with effectual calling and describes mystical union as the comprehensive category under which the entire *ordo salutis* must be understood.[12] Others have proposed that the Reformed *ordo salutis*, that is, the way we understand and speak about the application of redemption, needs "recasting."[13] Some have suggested that the revisionist view was Calvin's view, in contrast to that of the *HC*.[14] If this was so, Ursinus and Olevianus do not seem to have realized that they disagreed with Calvin. There is no such disagreement.[15]

It is clear that the Reformed churches intended to confess and teach that the same faith that is the "sole instrument" (*BC* 22) of our justification is *also* the instrument of our mystical union with Christ. Effectual calling and regeneration are essential. No one comes to faith except those whom God has regenerated and called effectually. Those whom God has regenerated and effectually called are given the gift of faith, which is the instrument of mystical union with Christ.

---

the body in respect of animal and human life. As therefore the union of soul and body is in order of nature prior to the life of man; so also the union of the Spirit of Christ and the soul is prior to the life of a Christian. Further, since faith is an act flowing from the principle of spiritual life, it is plain, that in a sound sense, it may be said, an elect person is truly and really united to Christ before actual faith." He also, however, affirms the view more frequently found among the older Reformed writers: "IV. But the mutual union, (which, on the part of an elect person, is likewise active and operative), whereby the soul draws near to Christ, joins itself to him, applies, and in a becoming and proper manner closes with him without any distraction, is made by faith only. And this is followed in order by the other benefits of the covenant of grace, justification, peace, adoption, sealing, perseverance, &c. Which if they be arranged in that manner and order, I know not whether any controversy concerning this affair can remain among the brethren" (Witsius, *Conciliatory or Irenical Animadversions*, 68–69). The Reformed confessions do not speak as Witsius does in §III. In §IV, he speaks the way the catechism and the confession do. In the seventeenth century, in response to the Remonstrants, some posited that a person might be regenerate and yet not yet believing. The *HC* does not allow such a view. So, we have two different conceptions of regeneration. In the first, the Spirit is said to regenerate, grant faith, and through that faith unite to Christ. In the later conception, the Spirit is said to awaken but not yet necessarily grant faith for a period of time. Under the latter view, union is a two-stage process. However well intended, this move was speculative and has created confusion.

12. E.g., Murray, *Redemption Accomplished and Applied*, 104–5, 205–10. In that tradition, see Rainbow, "Double Grace," 102–5, who juxtaposes what he argues was Calvin's view (the revisionist view) with the teaching of the catechism; Garcia, *Life in Christ*.

13. Letham, *Union with Christ*, 89. This call to recast the Reformed *ordo salutis* is taken up in Evans, *Imputation and Impartation*, 264–65.

14. Gaffin, *Resurrection and Redemption*, 130–41. He writes, "This understanding of present Christian existence as an (eschatological) tension between resurrection realized and yet to be realized is totally foreign to the traditional *ordo salutis*" (138). For more on this discussion, see, e.g., Fesko, *Beyond Calvin*, 17–19 passim; Muller, *Calvin and the Reformed Tradition*, 202–43; Perkins, *Reformed Covenant Theology*, 243–70.

15. Venema, *Accepted and Renewed*; Clark, *Caspar Olevian*.

This question concerns the logical order of benefits (*ordo salutis*).[16] That order is that the effectually called are regenerated, the regenerated come to faith, and those with faith are mystically united to Christ. God's action takes precedence to the human experience. Hence, Geerhardus Vos articulates that the judicial basis in Christ's objective work of acquittal grounds all renovation and change in us.[17] So too, God's act of effectually calling us produces in us the faith that unites us to Christ.

Fourth, the same Holy Spirit who sovereignly and freely creates new life (regeneration) in his elect operates through the means of grace, namely, the preaching of the gospel and the sacraments. This aspect of our confession must be reasserted in our time as it was in the Reformation and post-Reformation periods. When the catechism was being written, the Anabaptists stressed the subjective experience of the Holy Spirit and "the inner light." Many of them were "Spiritualists." Berkhof writes: "The Anabaptists virtually set aside the Word of God as a means of grace, and stressed what they called the internal word, the 'inner light,' and the illumination of the Holy Spirit. To them the external word was but the letter that killeth, while the internal word was spirit and life. External calling meant little or nothing in their scheme."[18]

His summary well describes the views of Thomas Müntzer (1489–1525) and others, for example, the "Men of the Inner Word" or "Spiritualists."[19] The former mocked the magisterial Protestants for their dependence on Scripture. In a notorious 1524 sermon, Müntzer denounced the theologians of Wittenberg, Luther chief among them, as fat and lazy.[20] They fancied themselves keepers of Scripture, but they did not know those "divine secrets" that God reveals to his friends.[21] He mocked the expository preaching of the Scriptures as "babbling" in favor of being "'overshadowed'

16. See the discussion of *ordo salutis* under *HC* 64, 86. In defense of the *ordo salutis*, Vos, *Reformed Dogmatics*, 611–12: "What is further contained in the term *ordo salutis*, 'order of salvation'? That the subjective application of the salvation obtained by Christ not occur at once or arbitrarily. ... There is order and regularity in the application of salvation as well as in every other area of creation."

17. Vos, *Reformed Dogmatics*, 616–17.

18. Berkhof, *Systematic Theology*, 458–59.

19. Williams, *Radical Reformation*, 199.

20. Bornkamm, *Luther in Mid-career*, 160.

21. Müntzer, *Schriften Und Briefe*, 248/7; 245/11; 248/27; 254/12–13; 247/16ff; 255/8–9, in Bornkamm, *Luther in Mid-career*, 160n55.

by the power of the divine Word."[22] In the words of Hans-Jürgen Goertz, for Müntzer "it was not Holy Scripture, but the divine spirit which was the sole reliable authority. Scripture was important to Müntzer because it bore witness to the way of salvation, but it was not itself that way. ... He distinguished sharply between spiritual and creaturely realms: salvation springs from the spirit not Scripture, since Scripture in essence, is creaturely."[23] In contrast to the Protestants, Müntzer claimed to be filled with the Holy Spirit seven times. All the Protestants had were the "icy words of Scripture," stolen from the biblical books.[24] They are false prophets to whom God has not spoken, who deceive God's people and usurp God's words, because "they deny that my spirit speaks to men down the centuries."[25]

Guy de Bres (1522–1567), the author of the *BC*, was one of the Protestants who responded to Müntzer. One of the two major treatises he wrote before drafting the confession of faith was his 1552 work against the Anabaptists, *The Rise, Source, and Foundation of the Anabaptists.*[26] One of his major criticisms of the Anabaptists was of their view of Scripture and specifically of their denial of *sola Scriptura*. He begins his critique by focusing on Müntzer's claim "that ministers and preachers of the gospel were not sent of God, but are ministers of the dead letter."[27] He objects to their claim "that the writing of the Old Testament, and preaching of the eternal word, was not the word of God, but was only the testimony of thereof; and that we must search for the word in the internal part, i.e., in our hearts, where God hath put it, that we need not go far to seek it from without us."[28]

The phenomena de Bres describes and ascribes to Müntzer and other Anabaptists is familiar to most of us from the modern charismatic and Pentecostal movements: claims of continuing revelation, states of ecstasy, being slain in the Spirit, trembling, prophecies, tongues, and

22. Bornkamm, *Luther in Mid-career*, 160.

23. Goertz, *Thomas Müntzer*, 123.

24. Matheson, *Collected Works of Thomas Müntzer*, 372.

25. Matheson, *Collected Works of Thomas Müntzer*, 372.

26. This volume was reprinted in various places in the sixteenth century, e.g., de Bres, *La Racine*. See de Brez, *Rise, Spring and Foundation.*

27. De Brez, *Rise, Spring and Foundation*, 40.

28. De Brez, *Rise, Spring and Foundation*, 34.

claims to have visited heaven. De Bres replies by strenuously defending *sola Scriptura* and condemning Müntzer and others as false prophets, equating him with Muhammad.

The same piety and practice against which de Bres protested later took root in the soil of American evangelicalism in the nineteenth century. Much of what came to be called evangelicalism was just an American renewal of the earlier Anabaptist movements.[29] The Anabaptists anticipated several features of what would come to be known as Pietism, or what I call the quest for illegitimate religious experience.[30] In Pietism, what matters most is the quality of one's subjective religious experience. The focus of Pietism is on the quest for an immediate encounter with the risen Christ. As this quest continues, the means of grace recede farther into the background until they are lost altogether.

Sacerdotalism, the elevation (or denigration) of the means of grace into magic so that they are thought to work automatically (*ex opere operato*), is one overreaction to spiritualism and Pietism. Against such a notion Olevianus objects:

> As Christ did not choose to exercise His omnipotence by coming down from the cross so that they would believe in Him (as they said, "If He is the Son of God, let him come down from the cross, and we will believe him" [Matt. 27:42]), He likewise does not choose to exercise His omnipotence by coming down from heaven into the fingers of thousands of priests so that people will believe in Him there in the priest's fingers. Why? Because as it is an article of the faith that Christ would die on the cross and there fulfill the first part of His priesthood, the sacrifice on the cross, it is also an article of the faith that He ascended from earth into heaven, where He is carrying out the other part of His priesthood, His appearing in heaven for us before the throne of God.[31]

29. Clark, "'Magic and Noise.'"

30. Clark, *Recovering the Reformed Confession*, 71–116; see discussion under *HC* 66.

31. Olevian, *Firm Foundation*, 78. Lyle Bierma notes that Olevianus's colorful expression "coming down from heaven into the fingers of priests" is an allusion to the Roman Catholic doctrine of transubstantiation, when, according to Rome, at the prayer of consecration, the elements are said to be changed into the literal body and blood of Christ (Olevian, *Firm Foundation*, 130n107).

Sacerdotalism is utterly incompatible with the Protestant doctrine of salvation *sola fide*. There is a place between spiritualism and sacerdotalism.

The Holy Spirit uses instruments. He uses the preaching of the Holy Gospel to bring us to new life, and those who have new life believe.[32] He uses means of grace. We should not think that there are regenerate people walking about who do not yet believe. The regenerate believe, and those who believe are those whom the Spirit has sovereignly regenerated. It is not possible that those who are spiritually dead should believe. That, among other things, is what it means to be dead (Eph 2:1–4). Paul says that we are dead in sins and trespasses. The first mistake of Pelagianizing movements is to downplay the spiritual consequences of sin. God said, "The day you eat thereof you shall surely die" (Gen 2:17). He did not say that we would be weakened but still able to "do our part" (covenantal moralism, e.g., the federal vision movement) or to "cooperate with grace" (Rome). No, to be dead is to be inanimate, without the principle of spiritual life.

God, however, by his powerful creative and re-creative Word, operating with and by the Holy Spirit, has the power to speak us to life. This is the picture we get in Genesis 1. God spoke into the void and created all that is. The Holy Spirit was hovering over the face of the deep. Everything that was created came into being, Scripture says, through God the eternally begotten Son, the *Logos* (John 1:1–3). Notice, however, that the Triune God spoke creation into existence. God the Son incarnate operated by this same power when he spoke Lazarus from death to life: "Lazarus, come forth" (John 11:43). By the re-creative power of the gospel, the dead were brought to life. This is just what happens when the Holy Spirit works through the preaching of the message about Jesus's perfect, holy, entire obedience as the substitute for his elect. When the announcement that Jesus obeyed, died, and was raised for our justification is proclaimed, God the Spirit is pleased to use that to bring his elect in the congregation from death to life: "So faith comes from hearing, and hearing through the word of Christ" (Rom 10:17 ESV).

32. On the official preaching of the gospel as the first key of the kingdom, see the discussion under *HC* 84.

The official preaching of the gospel in the churches is not magic. The Spirit works when and where he will (John 3:1–15) but has promised to work through that message in a unique and powerful way. This is one reason why it is so important to get the gospel right and to get it out. The visible, institutional church has a mission from our Lord. The church has been sent (Matt 28:18–20). This is why we preach the gospel freely, promiscuously, seriously to all. "Whosoever will may come," indeed, and it is God the Holy Spirit, working through and with the preaching of the gospel, who determines in any given time whosoever will. He gives new life. He gives faith, and through that faith he creates a living, spiritual union with Christ.[33]

There is, however, a second aspect to the way the Spirit uses means to work in his people. Whereas he uses the preaching of the gospel to bring his people to life and to faith, and through faith into mystical union with Christ, he uses the gospel made visible, the sacraments, to confirm his promises and thereby to strengthen and nourish their faith. The pure preaching of the gospel and the pure administration of the sacraments (*BC* 29) are different administrations of the same gospel.

Federal vision theology says similar things, if for different reasons. According to the federal visionists, baptism works *ex opere* ("by the working or using of it") to create a real union between the baptized and Christ.[34] This union places one in a conditional covenant wherein one is said to be united to Christ, elect, justified, and so on but must fulfill his part of the covenant to retain what has been given in baptism. In federal vision theology, the sacraments become law, as if the message were now: "Do this in order to be accepted or to retain the benefits given."[35] In contrast to federal visionists, the confessional Reformed churches speak of the sacraments as administrations of the gospel through which the Spirit operates freely to strengthen the spiritual life and faith of believers.

Further, we recognize a difference between the sacraments themselves. Baptism is the sign and seal of outward initiation into the visible covenant community, the church. The Spirit does not necessarily create new life

33. On the Reformed doctrine of the free or well-meant offer of the gospel, see Clark, "Janus, the Well-Meant Offer," 149–80; Clark, "Seriously and Promiscuously," 89–104.

34. Clark, "Baptism and the Benefits," 3–19. See also the discussion under *HC* 1–2, 32, 60.

35. Horton, "Which Covenant Theology?," 197–227.

when baptism is administered. Rather, baptism is a sign of what Christ has done for his elect, namely, washing away sins and conferring new life. It seals and promises to those who believe that what is signified in baptism is really true of them. With Luther, believers should say, "I am a baptized person. I belong to Christ."[36] The Lord's Supper is a sign of what Christ has done for the believer—he has saved us—and seal and a promise to believers that just as surely as they taste the bread and wine, so surely has Christ saved them, is at work in them, and is with them. Neither holy baptism nor the Holy Supper creates the realities they signify and seal, but they are gospel sacraments. They are promises of good news to believers. Faith receives what they promise. Faith knows, assents, trusts, and receives all that they promise. The sacraments do not replace faith. They supplement it. They *confirm* or *seal* it the way a registered letter embossed with a government seal confirms a declaration. Take an old diploma out of its frame and you will see signatures and a raised seal stamped into the paper. That seal makes the document authentic. That is what a sacrament is to a believer. The sacraments are an official testimony to the believer that what they signify is really true. In the ancient world, documents were sealed with wax and marked, for example, with the king's signet ring. The impression of the ring in the wax made that document official. We do something similar today with important documents to demonstrate authenticity.

The water of baptism signifies that flood judgment that Christ endured for us. He went through the Red Sea for us. To an unbeliever the sacraments are mere signs of what Christ has accomplished for his people *and* what he has in store for all who will not repent. They promise nothing to unbelievers but destruction. The greater flood of judgment that Christ endured on the cross for his people is waiting for unbelievers if they do not repent and trust in Christ as the only Savior (2 Pet 3:1–7). Unbelievers are Egyptians riding their chariots after the Israelites, and just as the Red Sea swallowed Pharaoh's armies, so it will swallow them.

The Lord has always used means. Paul says: "Our fathers were all under the cloud, and all passed through the sea, and all were baptized into Moses in the cloud and in the sea, and all ate the same spiritual food,

36. *LW* 4:95.

and all drank the same spiritual drink. For they drank from the spiritual Rock that followed them, and the Rock was Christ" (1 Cor 10:1–4 ESV). He adds a caveat: "Nevertheless, with most of them God was not pleased, for they were overthrown in the wilderness" (10:5 ESV). Why was he not pleased with most of them? Because they were idolaters, as he goes on to explain. They did not believe (Jude 5). It is not that they sinned and were overthrown. It is that they did not believe and therefore they sinned impenitently. Their impenitent sin demonstrated their unbelief. Still, those Old Testament sacraments signified and sealed the gospel promises to those who believed. Just as they went through, on dry ground, the Red Sea and the cloud, identified as they were with Moses their (typological) deliverer, so Christ saved them from the final, ultimate Red Sea. Just as they were nourished by the manna in the desert, so too God the Spirit was using the Lord's Supper to strengthen them for the journey to their heavenly city. The Red Sea did not create new life, and the manna did not turn away God's wrath, but they were signs and seals, sacraments of the gospel. So too baptism and the Supper do not create the realities they signify, but they do testify and promise to believers that what the gospel declares is true for them. The Holy Spirit graciously operates through the sacraments to certify to them the truth of the preached gospel and to feed them with the body and blood of Christ.

Question 66

What are the Sacraments?

The sacraments are visible holy signs and seals instituted by God to this end, that by the use thereof he may the more fully declare and seal to us the promise of the gospel: namely, that of free grace, he grants us the forgiveness of sins and everlasting life for the sake of the one sacrifice of Christ accomplished on the cross.[37]

37. "Was sind die Sacramente? Es sind sichtbare heilige Wahrzeichen und Siegel, von Gott bazu eingesetzt, dass er uns durch den Brauch derselben die Verheissung des Evangeliums desto besser zu verstehen gebe und versiegele: nämlich, dass er uns von wegen des einigen Opfers Christi, am Kreuz vollbracht, Vergebung der Sünden und ewiges Leben aus Gnaden schenke" (Schaff, *Creeds of Christendom*, 3:328). "Quid sunt Sacramenta? Sunt Sacra et in oculos incurrentia signa, ac sigilla, ob eam causam a Deo instituta, ut per ea nobis promissionem Evangelii magis declaret et obsignet:

The church has faced two great temptations with respect to the sacraments: to make them more than they are and to make them less than they are. Modern evangelical theology, piety, and practice is an outstanding example of this latter tendency.[38] Rome is the prime example of the former. The Roman Catholic Church defines a sacrament as "powers that come forth" from the church.[39] The Roman Catholic Church confesses, "They confer the grace they signify."[40] They are efficacious because Christ operates "in them."[41] They work "*ex opere operato.*"[42]

According to the Reformed church, by their nature and divine intention and institution, the sacraments are supports for the preaching of the gospel. They are visible and tangible representations and testimonies to the gospel. They are also promises or seals that what the gospel declares is really true for the believing recipient. Through the history of the church, we have tended to make them either more or less than that.

In the medieval sacramental system, the church added five "ecclesiastical sacraments."[43] Increasingly, the church had come to think of grace as a sort of medicinal substance with which sinners could be infused.[44] Given such a view, we can understand why the medieval church (and later Trent) would seek to increase the number of sacraments.

During the medieval period, the church was also developing an unofficial doctrine of salvation by grace and cooperation with grace. It remained unofficial because it was not ratified formally by a council until Trent, in session 6 (January 1547), in reaction to the Reformation. According to Rome, one is justified only insofar as one is sanctified, and one is said to be sanctified by grace and cooperation with grace.

In short, the medieval church (and later Trent) turned the two divinely ordained signs and seals into a kind of magic known as *sacerdotalism*, that

---

quod scilicet non universis tantum , verum etiam singulis credentibus, propter unicum illud Christi sacrificium in cruce peractum, gratis donet remissionem peccatorum, et vitam aeternam" (Neimeyer, *Collectio Confessionum*,444).

38. Clark, "Evangelical Fall," 133–47.

39. *CCC* §1116.

40. *CCC* §1116.

41. *CCC* §1127. The catechism cites Trent 1547.

42. *CCC* §1128. The catechism cites Trent 1547.

43. For more on this, see the discussion under *HC* 68.

44. E.g., *ST* 3a.80.4, ad. 2. See the discussion under *HC* 61.

is, the transformation of the ministry of the church into a priestly religion.[45] The ministers of the new covenant were transformed, were it possible, into "priests of the New Law" according to Rome. This is Roman Catholic doctrine today. "Adhering to the teaching of the Holy Scriptures, to the apostolic traditions, and to the consensus ... of the Fathers," the Roman Catholic Church professes that "the sacraments of the new law were ... all instituted by Jesus Christ our Lord."[46] They are "'powers that come forth' from the Body of Christ, which is ever-living and life-giving, actions of the Holy Spirit at work in his Body, the Church, 'the masterworks of God' in the new and everlasting covenant."[47]

One great problem with the Roman view was identified in the ninth century by Ratramnus, long before the high and late medieval view ever became dogma: if the sacraments necessarily create the realities they signify, or if the sacraments become the reality (e.g., transubstantiation), then by definition the sacrament is no longer a sacrament.[48] He observed that, for the sacrament to remain a sacrament, it requires faith, confidence in the divine promise, through which we receive what the sacrament signifies and promises. Consider this illustration. The title to a vehicle is not a vehicle, but it does tells us about the vehicle, and it certifies that the vehicle is indeed mine. The title is not the vehicle, but no one would say that the title is of no value. So it is with a sacrament.

Nevertheless, in reaction to the medieval and Roman abuse of the sacraments, there has sometimes been an impulse in some quarters to downplay the importance of the sacraments, to make them less than gospel signs and seals, to ignore them, or even effectively to replace them with new rites (e.g., the altar call). This disregard of the divinely ordained means of grace is grounded in Pietism, which has tended to devalue means generally in favor of the immediate encounter with the divine. Pietism as a movement began formally about 1675 and was associated with Philipp Jakob Spener (1635–1705), a Lutheran minister who was influenced by Jean de Labadie (1610–1674) and others. The earlier Pietists were generally orthodox, but

45. The Latin word for priest is *sacerdos*.

46. CCC §1114.

47. CCC §1116.

48. Ursinus, *Commentary*, 406–8.

they tended to have a low doctrine of the visible, institutional church. Pietism was a reaction to perceived spiritual dullness in state-controlled churches. The Pietists worried that the ministers and laity were either not regenerate or insufficiently interested in spiritual matters. The Pietists gave us what we today call "small groups" or "cell groups." In the seventeenth and eighteenth centuries they were called "conventicles." They advocated "little churches within the church" (*ecclesiolae in ecclesia*).[49] The Pietists were engaged in the quest for illegitimate religious experience.[50] They sought a direct, personal, spiritual encounter with the risen Christ apart from the means of grace. The adjective *unmediated* is significant because the visible institutional church is, broadly speaking, a medium or a means, and the preaching of the gospel is the means by which the Spirit brings us to faith, and the sacraments the church administers are means through which the Spirit strengthens our faith and our communion with Christ.[51] This is why the heading of book 4 of Calvin's *Institutes* is "On the External Means unto Salvation."[52]

For those familiar with certain strains of late medieval mysticism, particularly that associated with Bernard of Clairvaux (ca. 1090–1153), and with the spirituality associated with some of the fifteenth- and sixteenth-century humanists, it is clear that Pietism was not utterly novel but a renewal of long-standing trends in the history of the church. Modern American evangelicalism, emerging from the First Great Awakening in the eighteenth century and the consequent Second Great Awakening in the nineteenth century, was deeply influenced by Pietism.[53] As a consequence of the turn to the immediate and the subjective, many American Christians are indifferent about the holy sacraments. Many Americans simply assume a broad Baptistic paradigm in which baptism is the outward sign of one's profession of faith. In this paradigm, the view of holy Communion reduces it to nothing more than an annual memorial of Christ's death, a funeral. For many American Christians, the sacraments hardly function in any

49. Clark, *Recovering the Reformed Confession*, 71–78.

50. Clark, *Recovering the Reformed Confession*, 71–116.

51. See the discussion under *HC* 65.

52. "De externis mediis vel adminiculis, quibus Deus in Christi societatem nos invitat, et in ea retinet" (Barth, *Joannis Calvini Opera Selecta*, 5:1.3–5).

53. Clark, *Recovering the Reformed Confession*, 78–116; Clark, "'Magic and Noise.'"

significant way in their spirituality. For all intents and purposes, their "means of grace" (not that they think in those terms) are the quiet time (devotions) and the small group Bible study.

The Reformed churches should resist both sacerdotalism and Pietism. We understand that the sacraments are holy signs and seals. By *holy* we do not mean to say that they have been imbued with a magical power. We do mean to say that they have been set aside as distinct or for sacred use. In the Reformed liturgy, we do have a prayer of consecration, where the elements are set apart. Nothing happens to the being of the elements (water, bread, and wine). They remain essentially (in their being) what they were before the prayer. But they are designated for a holy use and accompanied with the preached gospel. This is how we speak in *BC* 35:

> Thus, to support the physical and earthly life God has prescribed for us an appropriate earthly and material bread, which is as common to all as life itself also is. But to maintain the spiritual and heavenly life that belongs to believers he has sent a living bread that came down from heaven: namely Jesus Christ, who nourishes and maintains the spiritual life of believers when eaten—that is, when appropriated and received spiritually by faith.[54]

So, we do not parade, worship, or venerate the consecrated elements. They are still bread and wine, but they are not for common use but for sacred use. There is a way to think about the sacraments, a way to regard them that is *between* magic and memory. We see this in Calvin's prayer before the administration of the elements:

> And as our Lord Jesus Christ, not content with having once offered his body and blood upon the cross for the forgiveness of our sins, has also destined them to us as nourishment for eternal life, so grant us of thy goodness, that we may receive this great blessing with true sincerity of heart and ardent desire, and endued with sure faith, enjoy together his body and blood, or rather himself entire, just as he himself, while he is true God and man, is truly the holy bread of heaven that gives us life, that we may no longer live in ourselves,

54. *BC* 35, in United Reformed Churches in North America, *Liturgical Forms and Prayers*, 193.

> and after our own will, which is altogether depraved, but he may live in us, and conduct us to a holy, happy, and ever-during life, thus making us truly part after of the new and eternal covenant, even the covenant of grace; and in feeling fully persuaded that thou art pleased to be for ever a propitious Father to us, by not imputing to us our offenses, and to furnish us, as dear children and heirs, with all things necessary as well for the soul as the body, we may pay thee endless praise and thanks, and render thy name glorious both by words and deeds. Fit us, then, on this day thus to celebrate the happy remembrance of thy Son: grant also that we may exercise ourselves therein, and proclaim the benefits of his death, that thus receiving new increase and strength for faith and every other good work, we may with greater confidence profess ourselves thy children, and glory in thee our Father.[55]

Calvin's prayer is really a prayer of thanks for the benefits we receive from Christ, by grace alone (*sola gratia*), through faith alone (*sola fide*) by the Spirit's work operating through the sacraments on believers. The Supper is a renewal principally of Christ's promises to us and only secondarily of our vows to Christ. Hence we are not sacramentarians, that is, our view of the supper is not determined by the etymology of *sacramentum* as a military oath of allegiance.[56] We recognize that the sacraments are, in the first instance, Christ's gospel promises to those who believe. They are gospel sacraments. Nevertheless, like the preached gospel, they do call for appropriate responses. The first response is to believe. The second response, as Calvin's prayer suggests, is to rejoice, and third that we should "exercise ourselves" in the grace we have received in the gospel, which is signified and sealed to us in the Holy Supper.

The sacraments declare to us the same promises offered and proclaimed to us in the preached gospel. There are not two gospels, the one of preaching and the other of the sacraments. Baptism and the Supper testify to the same good news: God the Son became incarnate of the Virgin Mary, by the mysterious operation of the Holy Spirit. He obeyed in our place.

55. Beveridge and Bonnet, *Selected Works of John Calvin*, 2:105–6.

56. *Sacramentarian* is the pejorative used by the Lutherans of the Zwinglians. E.g., Kolb and Wengert, *Book of Concord*, 503–8.

He was crucified for us. He was raised for our justification. He ascended and is seated at the right hand of God, and he is coming again in glory. To those who believe, the sacraments are tangible gospel promises. They testify to believers our forgiveness and free acceptance with God only on the basis of Christ's righteousness earned for us and freely imputed to us. By faith alone, we really do have all that the holy sacraments signify. We really have been washed. We really are being nourished on the true, proper, and natural body and blood of Christ.[57] The sacraments really are sacred gospel promises to those who believe, and as sacred promises of good news, they should be believed and received with thanksgiving and joy.

QUESTION 67

Are both the Word and the sacraments designed to direct our faith to the sacrifice of Christ on the cross as the only ground of our salvation?

Yes truly, for the Holy Spirit teaches in the gospel and assures us by the holy sacraments, that our whole salvation stands in the one sacrifice of Christ made for us on the cross.[58]

The sacraments are true signs. They tell the truth about who Christ is, what he has done, and what he promises, as we confess in *BC* 33:

> He has added these to the Word of the gospel to represent better to our external senses both what he enables us to understand by his Word and what he does inwardly in our hearts, confirming in us the salvation he imparts to us.

57. *BC* 35, in Schaff, *Creeds of Christendom*, 3:429–30.

58. "Sind denn beide, das Wort und die Sacramente, dahin gerichtet, dass sie unsern Glauben auf das Opfer Jesu Christi am Kreuz, als auf den einigen Grund unserer Seligkeit, weisen? Ja freilich: denn der Heilige Geist lehret im Evangelio, und bestätigt durch die heiligen Sacramente, dass unsere ganze Seligkeit stehe in dem einigen Opfer Christi, für uns am Kreuz geschehen" (Schaff, *Creeds of Christendom*, 3:328–29). "Num utraque igitur, et verbum et Sacramenta eo spectant, ut fidem nostram ad sacrificium Christi in cruce peractum, tanquam ad unicum nostrae salutis fundamentum deducant? Ita est. Nam Spiritus sanctus docet Evangelio, et confirmat Sacramentis, omnem nostram salutem positam esse in unico sacrificio Christi, pro nobis in cruce oblati" (Neimeyer, *Collectio Confessionum*, 444).

> For they are visible signs and seals of something internal and invisible, by means of which God works in us through the power of the Holy Spirit. So they are not empty and hollow signs to fool and deceive us, for their truth is Jesus Christ, without whom they would be nothing.[59]

The sacraments, by divine ordination, seal the truth and reality of God's promises to believers.[60] It is becoming increasingly difficult to tell authentic websites from imposters seeking to collect information for nefarious purposes. How many of us have been fooled by a clever electronic manipulation of a photo?

Words, photos, and videos are all signs.[61] They point to something other than themselves. Now, the question of to what they point is one of the great debates of the late modern age. For most of human history, it was understood that signs—for example, words in a letter or some other document—should be understood in the sense that the author originally intended. Thus, if you send a message to your friend asking them to sell a bicycle on your behalf, the intent is that at the end of the transaction, your friend has traded that bicycle for cash. Were your friend to give away the bicycle for nothing, or were your friend to pay someone on the your behalf to take away the bicycle, those acts would reflect a fundamental misunderstanding of your intent. If your friend were to say, "I am a sovereign reader, and I understood your email to say that I should give away your bicycle because I know that you are a just person, and that is what justice requires," you and your friend would be working at cross-purposes. Nevertheless, the late modern academy has proposed and adopted this very sort of theory of interpretation. The very same authors who want us to acknowledge the reader (and not the author) as sovereign over the text expect us to accept *their* words, in the sense they intend as authors, as they seek to convince us to refuse to grant the same courtesy to other authors. This, of course, is nothing but literary vandalism.[62]

---

59. United Reformed Churches in North America, *Liturgical Forms and Prayers*, 189–90.

60. See the discussion of signs and seals under *HC* 65.

61. See further discussion of the nature of signs under *HC* 69.

62. One of the most important treatments of this question is Augustine's *De doctrina Christiana* 1. See Augustine, *Teaching Christianity*; Embree, "Ethics and Interpretation."

Nevertheless, readers do receive signs (texts, sacraments), and they must interpret them. We may be thankful to our Triune God that he has given us an extensive explanation of the sacraments so that they do not come to us as silent, uninterpreted, brute facts of which we may make what we will. There is a message inherent in the sacraments. Christ instituted them. He spoke words, which he meant us to understand in the sense in which he spoke them. He gave names to the sacraments, and they came to us in the context of a broader narrative about his life, passion, death, resurrection, and ascension. In other words, these signs are inextricably bound up with Christ's own gospel about himself and the significance of his life. We must interpret and receive them in light of that context. We must also receive them in light of the apostolic explanation of them.

Further, the sacraments, as signs and seals of a divinely revealed message (the gospel), are accompanied by the author himself. God the Spirit, who inspired the Gospel writers (Matthew, Mark, Luke, and John) to write and preserve the narratives of the institution of the sacraments, also accompanies and works through the sacraments to communicate to and confirm their truth to believers. This is quite remarkable. Ordinarily, when an author creates a sign, he sends that collection of signs (words, sentences, paragraphs) to the reader in the hope that he has been sufficiently clear and that the reader is of good will and charitable. He cannot personally accompany the words. Thus, writers and readers sometimes go back and forth until they achieve genuine communication. In the case of the sacraments, however, the divine author not only sends them but goes with them to work through them to accomplish genuine communication and communion between the author and the recipient. That is a grace we ought to receive with thanks.

Whereas the late modern tendency is to make all texts and signs about us, about the reader, the sacraments point us to Christ. We are not free to make of them what we will. The recipient does not make the sign or the seal what it is. The author of the sign and seal makes them what they are. The function of the recipient is to acknowledge the author's intent and to receive those signs and seals in faith (knowledge, assent, and confidence) that what they signify is true and what they seal is true "for me" (*pro me*) and "for us" (*pro nobis*) who believe.

People ordinarily use signs (e.g., words) with the assumption that what the author intends to convey is the message the reader intends to receive. If, however, the reader primarily determines the message, then how can the author communicate with the reader? This is the destructive nature of deconstructionism and of the radical subjectivism of our age. It is no wonder that we are suspicious of each other. One might almost get the impression that there are dark spiritual forces in the world seeking to upend the divinely instituted order. Thus, we rightly regard the sacraments as a supernatural, divinely instituted gift and means by which God communicates and seals his favor (grace) to us. Believers can not only know what Christ intends to say to them in the gospel, but they can also be certain that the message is true for them in particular.

This is a great blessing because, even before the onset of late modern subjectivism, skepticism, and deconstructionism, as sinners we already had a propensity to doubt: "Lord, is it really true? How can I know?" Those are important questions. Just as our Lord graciously allowed Thomas (John 20:27) to touch his side, to experience with his senses the wounds to his true humanity, so too he graciously gives us tangible, sensory experiences. With our ears, we hear the gospel preached. With our eyes, we see baptism administered, and we feel the water wash away the outward impurity (Eph 5:26; Titus 3:5). In the Lord's Supper, we feel the bread in our hands, we hold the cup and taste the bread and wine.

The message that our heavenly Father is sending through the sacraments is for the believer. He knows that we doubt; that, like Thomas, we too wonder whether it is really true. He knows that our sins rise up and accuse us, and he knows that we know that, apart from the Christ, his Son, and without the free imputation of his righteousness, we too would be subject to condemnation. The Father loves us so much that he not only gave his only and eternally begotten Son (John 1:1–14; 3:14–16) but gave us truth-telling signs and seals, guarantees to believers, that it is true.

The sacraments testify to and seal to believers that Christ really came, that he did obey, that he was crucified for us, he was raised on the third day, that he is ascended and seated at the right hand of the Father, and that he there intercedes for us. The catechism focuses rightly on his crucifixion as the central act of his lifelong suffering obedience for us.

The catechism was written and published at a time when its recipients were just overcoming the notion that ministers were priests and that the sacraments had a magical power to them, which necessarily created the realities they signified. Many of the original recipients of the catechism had learned that in the Holy Supper, the minister (as a priest) offered a memorial sacrifice that turned away God's wrath. What the Reformed churches wanted people to understand was that Christ died "once for all" (Heb 7:27; 9:12, 26; 10:10; Rom 6:10) for us to pay for our sins and to propitiate (i.e., turn away) God's wrath from believers. Jesus did not initiate new covenant sacrifices or the "priesthood of the new law" (as Rome says) but put an end to the priesthood of the old covenant. He did not die to make salvation possible for those who do their part, but to earn our salvation and to give it freely—for it is by God's free favor you have been saved (Eph 2:8)—so that we might rest in Christ's finished work for us and trust that his Spirit is at work in us as a consequence. This is Paul's teaching in Romans 6:10. By virtue of our federal union with Christ, we too died once for all to sin. By virtue of our mystical union, by grace alone, through faith alone, we receive the benefit of Christ's death. The dominion of sin has been broken. The gospel, signified and sealed by the sacraments, is that God has saved and justified us by his free favor alone, through faith alone, and he will complete the good work he has begun in us (Phil 1:6).

Both those who overestimate and those who underestimate what the sacraments do are confused about how the sacraments relate to the word of God. The sacraments are not the word, but Ursinus observes four ways in which they are like the word: (1) "Both have God for their author," (2) God administers both through the ministers of his church, (3) the Holy Spirit uses both to kindle (*accendendam*) and to strengthen faith, and (4) they both declare the same thing to us: the gospel.[63]

Ursinus distinguishes the word from the sacraments in eight ways: (1) "Words signify and express certain things according to the appointment of men, who use them arbitrarily. The sacraments signify certain things according to the analogy which exists between the signs and the

63. Ursinus, *Commentary*, 351–52. For "kindle," see Ursinus, *Corpus doctrinae*, 367. Olevianus used this same imagery. To "kindle" here is to incite, but below he attributes the *origin* of faith to the Spirit's operation through the word.

things which are signified. We also read, and hear words, whilst we receive signs by feeling, seeing and tasting. Again, words only signify certain things: signs and symbols also confirm."[64] (2) They have distinct objects. The word is preached to all, regenerate and unregenerate alike, but the "sacraments, on the other hand, are dispensed only to those who are members of the church, who profess repentance and faith, and are designed to preserve and strengthen their faith."[65] (3) The Spirit uses the word as the *instrumentum* to *create* (*inchoat*) faith, but he uses the sacraments as the *instrumentum* to *confirm* faith.[66] (4) The word is preached to adults, but the sacrament of initiation (circumcision under the Old Testament, and baptism under the New Testament) belongs to the children of believers. (5) "The word is sufficient and necessary for the salvation of adults; for 'faith cometh by hearing, and hearing by the word of God.' (Rom. 10:17.) The sacraments, however, are not positively and absolutely necessary for all, neither are they in themselves sufficient for salvation independent of the word."[67] (6) The word can be "effectual" without the sacraments, but the sacraments cannot be so without the word.[68] (7) The sacraments confirm the word. (8) Augustine defines a sacrament as a visible word.[69] Insofar as a sacrament is the word, they teach the same thing. Insofar as a sacrament is *visible*, it is distinct.

For Ursinus, the Spirit uses the word and the sacraments to accomplish distinct but closely related things in bringing the elect to new life and true faith. Ursinus does not teach or imply that the Spirit necessarily confers new life and true faith at baptism, but only that, as Olevianus observes,[70] their administration and use is part of how the kingdom of Christ is administered in the world.

64. Ursinus, *Commentary*, 352.

65. Ursinus, *Commentary*, 352.

66. "Verbum est instrumentum Spiritus Sancti, per quod inchoat et confrimrmat in nobis fidem" (Ursinus, *Corpus doctrinae*, 367). The verb *inc[h]o* means "to begin without finishing." Olevianus uses this word regularly regarding our sanctification (Clark, *Caspar Olevian*, 185–86).

67. Ursinus, *Commentary*, 352.

68. Ursinus, *Commentary*, 353.

69. "Sacramentum est verbum visibile" (Ursinus, *Corpus doctrinae*, 368). See Augustine, *In Evangelium Johannis tractatus*, *NPNF* 1/7:344–45. Melanchthon also quotes this formula in his account of the sacraments (Bretschneider, *Corpus Reformatorum*, 24:237).

70. Olevianus, *Exposition*, 10; Olevian, *Firm Foundation*, 37.

Question 68

How many sacraments has Christ instituted in the New Testament?[71]

Two: holy baptism and holy supper.[72]

To Protestants, whether confessional or more broadly evangelical, it may seem obvious that there are only two sacraments, but more than sixty million American Roman Catholics in North America, millions of Roman Catholics across the globe, and those in the various Orthodox communions worldwide affirm that there are seven sacraments. If we begin with Holy Scripture, the only two sacraments that have a dominical origin are baptism (e.g., Matt 28:18–20) and the Lord's Supper (e.g., Luke 22:14–20). Our Lord performed other acts, for example, washing the feet of his disciples (John 13:3–11), but he did not institute footwashing as a ritual or a sacrament, as a sign and seal of the covenant of grace to be observed perpetually until his return. The apostle Paul confirms the sacramental status of baptism (1 Cor 10:2) and the Lord's Supper (1 Cor 10:3–4; Eph 4:3). He nowhere commands or commends any other ritual, sacramental actions. James mentions anointing with oil (Jas 5:14) and does instruct its use, but not as a sacrament. Whereas baptism signifies the death of Christ (and our identity with that death; Rom 6; Col 2:11–12), and the Lord's Supper obviously signifies Christ's death and his nourishment of our souls by the operation of the Holy Spirit, James's exhortation to anoint the sick is no more a sacrament than prayer (Jas 5:13, 15–16), praise (v. 13), or confession of sin (v. 16). These are all good spiritual practices, but not every spiritual practice is a sacrament or a divinely instituted sign and seal of gospel promises.

There is no evidence in the second century AD that the church received from the apostles and practiced any more than the two dominical sacraments (baptism and Communion). The Apostolic Fathers (a collection of

71. The Latin text uses *foedus* as a synonym for "Testament." The *HC* does not contrast a testamentary theology with a federal theology. On federal theology, see Clark, *Caspar Olevian*, 124–31, 190–91.

72. "Wie viel Sacramente hat Christus im Neuen Testament eingesetzt? Zwei: die heilige Taufe und das heilige Abendmahl" (Schaff, *Creeds of Christendom*, 3:329). "Quot Sacramenta instituit Christus in novo foedere? Duo, Baptismum et sacram Coenam" (Niemeyer, *Collectio Confessionum*, 444).

mostly second-century writers gathered together in the nineteenth century and so designated) refer only to baptism and the supper as sacraments. The apologists Justin Martyr (ca. 100–165) and Irenaeus (ca. 130–202) refer only to the two dominical sacraments. Anointing with oil (unction) was performed early on, but it was not regarded as a sacrament in the second century. It began to be performed with more frequency in the fifth century as a "sacramental" (an adjunct to the sacrament). Other sacramentals developed later in the patristic period."[73] They included mixing water with Communion wine, crossing oneself, triple baptismal effusion, feast days, posture, the habit (here meaning special clothing), vestments, incense, blessings, and so on. Gradually, these popular elaborations on the divinely ordained sacraments gained ecclesiastical approval, and in the high medieval period the list of sacraments began to expand. To the two dominical sacraments the high medieval church added confirmation (chrismation), penance, extreme unction (anointing the sick), holy orders, and matrimony. These were described as "sacraments of the new law."[74] As late as the ninth century, when Paschasius Radbertus (ca. 790–ca. 860) and Ratramnus (d. ca. 868) were arguing about the nature of Communion, they agreed that there were only two sacraments.[75] Both were well-read, intelligent writers. It is incredible to think that the universal practice of the church was to receive seven sacraments, and yet they (and all their colleagues, including regional synods, monks, bishops, and others) knew of only two sacraments.

In the twelfth century, Peter Lombard (ca. 1100–1160) mentioned seven sacraments in the *Sentences* (4.13.1), which was imposed as a textbook by the Fourth Lateran Council (1215).[76] Some of the seven were mentioned at the Fourth Lateran Council, but the first assembly in which all seven were mentioned was the Second Council of Lyons (1274) by Eastern Emperor Michael VIII Palaeologus (ca. 1223–1282) in his confession, as part of his submission to the papacy.[77]

73. Marthalier, *New Catholic Encyclopedia*, s.v. "sacramentals."

74. Trent, session 7 (1547), canon 1 (Schroeder, *Canons and Decrees*, 51).

75. See the English translations of Radbertus's and Ratramnus's treatises, both titled *On the Body and Blood of the Lord*, in McCracken, *Early Medieval Theology*.

76. Lombard, *Sentences* 4, dist. 2, in Lombard, *Sentences*, 4.8.

77. Denzinger, *Enchiridion Symbolorum*, 214–17 (§§461–66).

In the same century, Aquinas taught seven sacraments in the *Summa theologica* (1274).[78] That list was formally ratified at the Council of Florence (1439).[79] The five ecclesiastical sacraments were ratified and promulgated unambiguously only in session 7 of the Council of Trent, 1547. Thus, in no way should we imagine that the Reformation rejection of the five ecclesiastical sacraments was the rejection of ancient Christian doctrine and practice. It was in fact a rejection of a relatively recent development.

The history of the corruption of the sacraments reminds us of the importance of being clear about the sole, unique, and final authority of the Scriptures as the canonical word of God (*sola Scriptura*). When the church adhered to this principle, she imposed on God's people only those sacraments that Christ instituted. When she forgot this principle, she corrupted the sacraments by addition. This is also why Calvin speaks of the rule (*regula*) of worship.[80] In the modern period, Reformed people have come to speak of the "regulative principle of worship," according to which rule the church may do in worship (and impose on God's people) only what God has imposed or commanded. This rule is intended to be a check on the creative authority of the church and the restless human desire to invent worship of God.

Confessional Protestants, especially confessional Reformed Christians, should never be tempted to think that they are missing out by observing only the two sacraments instituted by our Lord himself. They are not. What Rome calls additional sources of grace are additional ways of putting Christians under the "new law" (their expression) of cooperation with grace unto eventual acceptance with God. That is not good news. The sacraments that Christ instituted are good news for believers that he has accepted them freely only on account of Christ's obedience for them, which is imputed to them by grace alone (*sola gratia*) and received through faith alone (*sola fide*). Faith and salvation are God's free gifts to his people.

---

78. *ST* 3a.51, resp. dic.

79. Denizinger, *Enchiridion Symbolorum*, 253–59 (§§695–702).

80. E.g., "Deinde ad causam propius accedis, quum demonstras nullam esse nocentiorem animabus pestem, quam perversum Dei cultum. Ad haec, Dei rite colendi eam esse optimam regulam, quae ab ecclesia praescribitur" (*Opera quae supersunt omnia*, 5:388); Calvin, *Reply to Sadoleto* (1539), in Reid, *Calvin: Theological Treatises*, 229. See Clark, "Calvin's Principle of Worship."

Question 69

How is it signified and sealed to you in holy baptism, that you have part in the one sacrifice of Christ on the cross?

Question 70

What is it to be washed with the blood and Spirit of Christ?

Question 71

Where has Christ promised that we are as certainly washed with his blood and Spirit as with the water of baptism?

Lord's Day 26

QUESTION 69

How is it signified and sealed to you in holy baptism, that you have part in the one sacrifice of Christ on the cross?

Thus: that Christ commanded this outward washing with water and joined therewith this promise: that I am washed with his blood and Spirit from the pollution of my soul, that is, from all my sins, as certainly as I am washed outwardly with water, whereby commonly the filthiness of the body is removed.[1]

We see, interpret, and navigate daily life with help of signs almost constantly.[2] Imagine a signless world. Imagine a parent with a small child who needs a place to change a diaper. Just then a true, accurate, clear sign would be most helpful. Poor or improper signs are a bane of life, for example, a sign that suggests the office you want is down this hallway when it is actually down the other. Good, clear signs are indispensable. This book is itself a collection of signs, letters, words, sentences, and paragraphs the reader is decoding.

God created us to interpret signs. In the beginning God instituted two signs: one of life and the other of death. There has been some disagreement within the Reformed tradition as to whether Adam ate from the tree of life prior to the fall, but all agree that we were forbidden to eat from the tree of the knowledge of good and evil.[3] The first tree communicated something about the nature of eternal life and communion, and

1. "Wie wirst du in der heiligen Taufe erinnert und versichert, dass das einige Opfer Christi am Kreuz dir zu gut komme? Also, dass Christus diess äusserliche Wasserbad eingesetzt, und dabei verheissen hat, dass ich so gewiss mit seinem Blut und Geist von der Unreinigkeit meiner Seele, das ist, allen meinen Sünden gewaschen sei, so gewiss ich äusserlich mit dem Wasser, welches die Unsauberkeit des Leibes pflegt hinzunehmen, gewaschen bin" (Schaff, *Creeds of Christendom*, 3:329). "Qua ratione in Baptismo admoneris et confirmaris, te unici illius sacrificii Christi participem esse? Quod Christus externum aquae lavacrum mandavit, addita hac promissione, me non minus certo, ipsius sanguine et Spiritu a sordibus animae, hoc est, ab omnibus meis peccatis lavari: quam aqua extrinsecus ablutus sum, qua sordes corporis expurgari solent" (Niemeyer, *Collectio Confessionum*, 445).

2. For more on signs, see the discussion under *HC* 67.

3. Ursinus himself does not address this question in the *Corpus*, and neither does Olevianus in the *Firm Foundation*, *Exposition*, or *De substantia*. Calvin, commenting on Gen 2:9 (*Commentary on the First Book of Moses*, 117) assumes that Adam ate from the tree of life before the fall, as does Ames, *Sketch of the Christian's Catechism*, 17; Witsius, *Economy*, 1:87; Turretin, *Institutes of Elenctic Theology*, 8.5.3; Heidegger, *Concise Marrow of Christian Theology*, 64–65, Boston, *Human Nature in Its Fourfold State*, 17. In the modern period, Berkhof (*Systematic Theology*, 217) takes this view. By

the second tree communicated death and judgment. God said: "The day you eat thereof, you shall die the death" (Gen 2:17). Adam understood the message communicated by the two signs, and he chose to rebel against the divinely revealed interpretation of the signs in favor of the diabolical suggestion that perhaps the Lord was a liar. "Has God really said?" The Evil One was, of course, the first deconstructionist. He proposed that the relationship between the sign and the thing signified (*res significata*) was arbitrary, that it could be other than what the Lord had said. We chose to believe and trust the lie rather than the truth on the possibility that the Evil One was right, on the possibility that we might be equal with God, and in grasping at equality with God we found what the Lord had threatened: death and destruction. When the Lord came in judgment, the Evil One was nowhere to be found. Rather, it was the Lord who, though fulfilling his promise of judgment, also made a gracious promise of salvation: "The serpent shall strike his heel, and he shall crush his head" (Gen 3:15).

Since the fall, signs have indeed become more complicated—not in and of themselves but because of our sinfulness. It is true that even Holy Scripture, given under the inspiration of the Holy Spirit and preserved by his providence, came through sinful humans and is interpreted by sinners. Ordinarily, however, we compose signs without divine inspiration. Hence the confusion that often surrounds them.

Christ's sacraments are not ordinary signs, even though they are the ordinary means of grace. They are ordinary in the sense that

- They have been ordained by God.
- They are meant to be used often (as distinct from infrequently or rarely).
- The water of baptism remains water, and the bread and wine of Communion remain bread and wine.

They are supernatural signs insofar as God has willed to use them to signify and seal his promises, insofar as the Spirit operates through them.

contrast, Horton (*Christian Faith*, 415) characterizes the tree of life as the "prize awaiting the successful outcome of a trial."

As seals, the sacraments guarantee to believers that what the preached gospel offers generally is really true specifically for believers.[4] It is important not to turn the sacraments into magic (*ex opere operato*), but it is equally essential not to make the sacraments into empty signs.

We begin with baptism because that is the sign and seal of initiation. It is where the Christian life begins insofar as it is when and where we are initiated into the visible covenant community, whether as adult converts or as covenant children, and where our relationship to Christ and his church is formally acknowledged. Our Lord himself instituted the sacrament of baptism in Matthew 28: "And Jesus came and said to them, 'All authority in heaven and on earth has been given to me. Go therefore and make disciples of all nations, baptizing them in the name of the Father and of the Son and of the Holy Spirit, teaching them to observe all that I have commanded you. And behold, I am with you always, to the end of the age'" (Matt 28:18–20 ESV). Ursinus gives three different definitions of baptism, each shorter than the previous.[5] The essence of his definitions is this: a ritual washing with water, whatever the mode, in the name of the Father, Son, and Holy Spirit, which signifies what is true of those who believe, that they have been given new life, that their sins have been washed away, and the mortification of the old man with the making alive of the new.

Baptism is a divinely instituted sign and seal.[6] As mentioned, our Lord did a great number of things that he did not institute for our perpetual use and observance, but he instituted baptism for perpetual use and observance until he returns. It is a sign of the washing away of our sins, and it is a seal of the same.

Notice how the catechism appeals unashamedly to our sense experience. God gave the sacraments to reinforce the preached gospel, to illustrate the preached gospel, to serve as certification to believers that just as certainly as water touches the skin, so surely has Christ made believers clean before God. We are washed by Christ's blood and by his Holy Spirit.

This is how God has always operated in redemptive history and even before the fall in the garden: by speaking, signifying, and sealing his promises to us. Assuming that Adam ate from the tree of life, then whenever

4. See the discussion of seals under *HC* 67.

5. Ursinus, *Commentary*, 357.

6. See the discussion of seals and sealing under *HC* 66.

he tasted that fruit, it was a reminder. It was signified and sealed to him that should he complete the probation that God had put before him and for which God had equipped him so he could to enjoy eternal fellowship with God. Adam had to trust his sense experience and the goodness and trustworthiness of God and his promises.

As sinners, we want to trust everyone but the one whom we should trust. By his grace he has given us new life (Eph 2:1–4). He has made us a new creation (2 Cor 5:17). Baptism *signifies* our identification with his death (Col 2:11–12; Rom 6:1–14), but it does not itself *create* our union with Christ. This distinction is important because federal vision theology has blurred it by teaching that all baptized people are, by virtue of baptism, conditionally elect, regenerated, united to Christ, justified, and adopted so long as they continue to cooperate sufficiently with grace.[7] The teaching of the catechism, as in the *BC* and the Canons of Dort, however, is that there is only one election and it is unconditional, eternal, *sola gratia*.[8] In *BC* 22, we confess that we are justified through "faith alone" and that we remain in communion with Christ through faith alone.[9] In contrast to the federal vision doctrine of two kinds of election (decretal and conditional), at the Synod of Dort the Reformed churches rejected the (Remonstrant) doctrine that there is more than one kind of election.[10] The Reformed confess two ways of being in the one covenant of grace, internally and externally.[11] The Reformed reject the Remonstrant and federal vision doctrine that those who are "baptized into the triune Name are united with Christ in His covenantal life, and so those who fall from that position of grace are indeed falling from grace."[12] The federal visionists deny that the "connection that an apostate had to Christ" was "merely external."[13] The Reformed churches confess the very distinction denied by the federal vision theology, that there is, in the words of Herman Witsius, a

---

7. Clark, "Baptism and the Benefits."

8. See the discussion under *HC* 21, 56–61.

9. Schaff, *Creeds of Christendom,* 3:408.

10. *Canons of Dort* 1.8; United Reformed Churches in North America, *Liturgical Forms and Prayers,* 261.

11. "Joint Federal Vision Profession." See Clark, "Baptism and the Benefits," for documentation.

12. "Joint Federal Vision Profession."

13. "Joint Federal Vision Profession."

"double mode of communion."[14] The catechism itself describes baptism as an "external washing" ("*externum ... lavacrum*"; "*äusserliche Wasserbad*"). In *BC* 29, we distinguish between those who have a merely external relation to the church and those who also have an internal relation to the church and the covenant of grace: "But we speak here not of the company of hypocrites, who are mixed in the Church with the good, yet are not of the Church, though externally in it."[15]

At Pentecost, those who were gathered, who had heard the gospel and seen the power of the Spirit and the power of the risen Christ, said, "What shall we do?" The apostle Peter responded by treating baptism as a sign and a seal and not as the thing itself. He said: "Repent and be baptized every one of you in the name of Jesus Christ for the forgiveness of your sins, and you will receive the gift of the Holy Spirit. For the promise is for you and for your children and for all who are far off, everyone whom the Lord our God calls to himself" (Acts 2:38–39 ESV). For Peter, baptism does not *create* the reality it signifies. Rather, baptism is the *sign* of initiation into the visible new covenant community. John the Baptizer promised this day (Matt 3:11). Water baptism is a sign to all and seal to believers of that reality. It is, as Paul says in Romans 6:3–4 and Colossians 2:11–12, a sign and seal of our identification with Christ. Just as circumcision did not create the reality it signified, so baptism signifies and seals without creating the reality. The Spirit creates the reality through the preaching of the holy gospel, but that does not empty the sacraments of significance.

Throughout his discussion, following the broader Christian tradition, Ursinus links baptism and circumcision.[16] Like circumcision, *contra* the Anabaptists and *pace* the Baptists, baptism is to be administered once "because it is the sign of our reception into the favor and covenant of God, which remains for ever sure and valid in the case of those who repent. He, therefore, that has lost a sense of God's favor by falling into sin, does not need another application of baptism, but repentance for his sins. The same thing is also evident from the fact, that regeneration does not take

14. Witsius, *Hermanni Witsii Exercitationes Sacrae*, 453–54; Clark, "Baptism and the Benefits," 4.

15. Schaff, *Creeds of Christendom*, 3:419.

16. E.g., Ursinus, *Commentary*, 359.

place more than once in the same individual."[17] Baptism is a once-for-all, constant reminder of the good news, and a sign and seal to believers, that *sola gratia, sola fide* we are Christ's and he is ours. There is only one baptism, whether that of John the Baptizer, who looked forward to Christ, or that of the apostles, who baptized retrospectively because there is one covenant of grace in multiple administrations.[18]

The pattern we see in the New Testament is that believers (and their children) are initiated into the church by baptism. Ursinus notes regarding Matthew 28:20,

> The word which is here translated teach, means, according to its proper signification, make disciples, so that it may more properly be translated, go and make disciples, baptizing them, etc. It is thus rendered by John, in the fourth chapter and first verse of his gospel: "The Pharisees had heard, that Jesus made, and baptized more disciples," etc. The same thing is also established by the substitution of baptism in the place of circumcision, which was the sacrament of reception into the Jewish Church.[19]

For the same reason, baptism is the external mark of our initiation into the visible church and thus a prerequisite for Holy Communion. It is our identification with the cross (Matt 20:22).[20] It is a ritual death, as it was for Noah and as it was for the Israelites who went through the Red Sea, who were baptized into Moses.[21]

Christian baptism is also an expression of the catholicity of the church.[22] That one baptism, which unites all believers in all times and in all places, is entailed in the ninth article of the Apostles' Creed, where we say, "the holy catholic church, the communion of the saints."[23] This what Paul implies in Ephesians 4:5, "one Lord, one faith, one baptism."

17. Ursinus, *Commentary*, 359.

18. Ursinus, *Commentary*, 359. This is in distinction from the Council of Trent (session 7, canon 1), which condemns anyone who teaches that the baptism of John had the same power as the baptism of Jesus (Denzinger, *Enchiridion Symbolorum*, 301.857).

19. Ursinus, *Commentary*, 360.

20. Ursinus, *Commentary*, 360.

21. Ursinus, *Commentary*, 360–61.

22. Ursinus, *Commentary*, 361.

23. Ursinus, *Commentary*, 361.

Finally, baptism is a perpetual witness to "free salvation for the sake of Christ's death."[24] Whenever we contemplate our baptism, we are reminded that salvation belongs to the Lord" (Jonah 2:9).

Baptism is, as Olevianus writes, an expression of the reconciliation that God "offers and presents ... in the form of a gracious covenant (2 Cor. 5:18–21; 6:15–18)."[25] Believers should think of baptism as the sign and seal of God's gracious covenant, since after "great hostilities, people are finally pacified in their minds when they have mutually bound themselves by promises and oaths to embrace peace." God also, "in the same way ... out of pure goodness, seeks to quiet our consciences by not hesitating to bind Himself by oath and covenant to us who repent and believe, and to seal this with holy baptism."[26]

Question 70

What is it to be washed with the blood and Spirit of Christ?

It is to have the forgiveness of sins from God through grace, for the sake of Christ's blood, which he shed for us in his sacrifice on the cross; and also, to be renewed by the Holy Spirit and sanctified to be members of Christ, that so we may more and more die unto sin and lead holy and blameless lives.[27]

The previous question addressed *how* the sacrament signifies and seals salvation freely given *sola gratia, sola fide*. This question addresses *what* is signified and sealed, that is, forgiveness and renewal. We see that

24. Ursinus, *Commentary*, 361.

25. Olevianus, *Exposition*, 13.

26. Olevianus, *Exposition*, 14.

27. "Was heisst mit dem Blut und Geist Christi gewaschen sein? Es heisst Vergebung der Sünden von Gott aus Gnaden haben, um des Blutes Christi willen, welches er in seinem Opfer am Kreuz für uns vergossen hat; darnach auch durch den Heiligen Geist erneuert, und zu einem Glied Christi geheiliget sein, dass wir je länger je mehr der Sünde absterben, und in einem gottseligen, unsträflichen Leben wandeln" (Schaff, *Creeds of Christendom*, 3:329–30). "Quid est sanquine et Spiritu Christi ablui? Est accipere a Deo remissionem peccatorum gratis, propter sanguinem Christi, quem is pro nobis in suo sacrificio in cruce profudit. Deinde etiam per Spiritum sanctum renovari, et ipso sanctificante membrum christi fieri, quo magis ac magis peccatis moriamur, et sancte inculpateque vivamus" (Niemeyer, *Collectio Confessionum*, 445).

they are in the closest possible relation without being confused. Uniting definitive justification and progressive sanctification without confusing them is one of the great achievements of the Reformation. Virtually from the moment Luther distinguished them, he nevertheless kept them related as he developed the basics of the Protestant doctrine of salvation from 1513–1521.[28] After he recovered the doctrine of imputation (1517), he taught (1518–1519) a "twofold righteousness" (*duplex iustitia*).[29] The first is what we recognize as the doctrine of free justification (*sola gratia*) on the basis of the imputed righteousness of Christ received through faith alone (*sola fide*). The second is what we call vindication or acknowledgment, which is well expressed in the WLC:

> Q. 90. What shall be done to the righteous at the day of judgment?
> A. At the day of judgment, the righteous, being caught up to Christ in the clouds, shall be set on his right hand, and there openly acknowledged and acquitted, shall join with him in the judging of reprobate angels and men, and shall be received into heaven, where they shall be fully and forever freed from all sin and misery; filled with inconceivable joys, made perfectly holy and happy both in body and soul, in the company of innumerable saints and holy angels, but especially in the immediate vision and fruition of God the Father, of our Lord Jesus Christ, and of the Holy Spirit, to all eternity. And this is the perfect and full communion which the members of the invisible church shall enjoy with Christ in glory, at the resurrection and day of judgment.[30]

Justification is the divine declaration in this life that it is as if we ourselves had done all that Christ has done for us.[31] Vindication is the public acknowledgment of that reality. These are two distinct acts. We see this same distinction in *HC* 52 and especially in *BC* 37, where we confess of believers, "their innocence will be openly recognized by all."[32]

28. See Clark, "*Iustitia Imputata Christi.*"

29. Clark, "Benefits of Christ," 107–34.

30. Orthodox Presbyterian Church, *Confession of Faith and Catechisms*, 227–28.

31. See the discussion under *HC* 60.

32. See the discussion under *HC* 52 and United Reformed Churches in North America, *Liturgical Forms and Prayers*, 199.

Baptism signifies and seals that believers already have, now, the "remission of sins freely on account of the blood of Christ."[33] It is as a consequence of the work of Christ for us (*pro nobis*) that we are being graciously sanctified more and more. Instead of the phrase "double justification," which had a checkered history, Calvin tends to speak of the "twofold grace" (*duplex gratia*) of God.[34] Olevianus speaks of the "double benefit of Christ" (*duplex beneficium Christi*): justification and sanctification.[35] Against the Council of Trent (1545–1563), Calvin writes:

> It is not to be denied, however, that the two things, Justification and Sanctification, are constantly conjoined and cohere; but from this it is erroneously inferred that they are one and the same. For example: — The light of the sun, though never unaccompanied with heat, is not to be considered heat. Where is the man so undiscerning as not to distinguish the one from the other? We acknowledge, then, that as soon as any one is justified, renewal also necessarily follows: and there is no dispute as to whether or not Christ sanctifies all whom he justifies. It were to rend the gospel, and divide Christ himself, to attempt to separate the righteousness which we obtain by faith from repentance.[36]

Through faith alone, in Christ alone, we are justified. Progressive sanctification, as Calvin writes, "necessarily follows." Those whom Christ justifies, he also sanctifies. The two benefits are not to be separated, but they are, as he notes, distinct. Rome, at Trent, made sanctification and justification one thing. Rome confessed that we are justified because and to the degree that we are inherently sanctified, and we are sanctified (and thus justified) by grace and cooperation with grace. With Luther, Calvin and the Reformed and Lutheran churches rejected this doctrine as unbiblical. Christ did not die to make salvation possible for those who would cooperate sufficiently with grace. He obeyed and died to accomplish our redemption, and by his Spirit he sovereignly, freely applies that redemption to us through faith alone.

---

33. "Remissionem peccatorum gratis, propter sanguinem Christi" (Niemeyer, *Collectio Confessionum*, 445).

34. See Venema, *Accepted and Renewed*.

35. Clark, *Caspar Olevian*.

36. Calvin, *Tracts Relating to the Reformation*, 3:115–16.

Calvin's metaphor of sun and light is analogous to that used in *BC* 24: "These works, proceeding from the good root of faith, are good and acceptable to God, since they are all sanctified by his grace. Yet they do not count toward our justification—for by faith in Christ we are justified, even before we do good works. Otherwise they could not be good, any more than the fruit of a tree could be good if the tree is not good in the first place."[37] The sun produces light and heat. A good tree produces good fruit. These are necessary products, but light does not make the sun, nor does fruit make the tree. The sun makes light, and the tree makes fruit.

Baptism testifies to both aspects of the double grace or double benefit: justification and sanctification. The first benefit is justification. It is the justified who are sanctified and not the reverse. Baptism testifies and seals to us believers that God has declared us clean on the basis of Christ's perfect righteousness and condign merit imputed to us. We have come "to Jesus, the mediator of a new covenant, and to the sprinkled blood that speaks a better word than the blood of Abel" (Heb 12:24 ESV). It also testifies and seals to us believers that the Spirit is cleansing us, that is, that the Spirit is progressively, graciously sanctifying us. Christ's sprinkled blood not only justifies but it is unto (toward) actual "sanctification of the Spirit, for obedience to Jesus Christ" (1 Pet 1:2 ESV). As believers who have received, through faith alone, all that is promised us in the gospel and sealed to us in baptism, we give ourselves daily to Christ. This is what it means to take up our cross: we recognize and turn away from our sin (repentance), trust Christ's promises, beg his grace, and in union and communion with him seek to put to death the old man and to be made alive in the new.

QUESTION 71

Where has Christ promised that we are as certainly washed with his blood and Spirit as with the water of baptism?

In the institution of baptism, which says: "Go, therefore, and teach all nations, baptizing them in the name of the Father, and of the Son, and of the Holy Spirit. He who believes and is baptized shall be saved; but he who does not believe shall be damned." This

37. United Reformed Churches in North America, *Liturgical Forms and Prayers*, 178–79.

promise is also repeated, where Scripture calls baptism the washing of regeneration, and the washing away of sins.[38]

If, as the Reformed teach, baptism does not effect what it signifies and seals, then of what value is it?[39] Those who confess the Reformed faith need not be tempted by sacerdotalism, which turns the sacraments into magic, nor should they be tempted to turn them into mere memories. The sacraments are signs and promises.

Because a sacrament is a divinely instituted sign and seal, it is not the thing it signifies and seals (then it would not be a sacrament), but it has the closest possible relation to the thing signified. When our Lord instituted the sacrament of baptism (Matt 28:18–20), he instituted a holy sign and a seal, a visible, outward guarantee to those who believe. Sacerdotalists want us to think that sacraments do what they do without respect to faith, as if faith were a second blessing or as if faith confirmed the sign, which inverts the order of things. Scripture says: "For it is by grace you have been saved, *through faith*" (Eph 2:8). In Ephesians 2:8 the preposition *through* signifies instrumentality. There is an ambiguity in English that requires us to be careful here. We also use the word *through* in a different sense in this discussion. We sometimes say that we were saved *through* the flood and the Red Sea, but in that case we mean something different.[40]

Scripture does not say that baptism is the instrument of salvation any more than the Noachian flood or the Red Sea were the instruments of salvation. Rather, faith is the sole instrument of salvation. God delivered

---

38. "Wo hat Christus verheissen, dass wir so gewiss mit seinem Blut und Geist, als mit dem Taufwasser, gewaschen sind? In der Einsetzung der Taufe, welche also lautet: Gehet hin, und lehret alle Völker, und taufet sie im Namen des Vaters, und des Sohnes, und des Heiligen Geistes: wer da glaubet und getauft wird, der wird selig werden; wer aber nicht glaubet, der wird verdammt werden. Diese Verheissung wird auch wiederholt, da die Schrift die Taufe das Bad der Wiedergeburt und Abwaschung der Sünden nennet" (Schaff, *Creeds of Christendom*, 3:330). "Ubi promisit Christus, se nos tam certo sanguine et Spiritu suo abluturum, quam aqua baptismi abluti sumus? In institutione Baptismi, cuius haec sunt verba: Ite et docete omnes gentes, baptizantes eos in nomine Patris, et Filii, et Spiritus sancti: Qui crediderit et baptizatus fuerit, servabitur: qui non crediderit, condemnabitur. Haec promissio repetitur, cum scriptura Baptismum nominat lavacrum regenerationis, et ablutionem peccatorum" (Niemeyer, *Collectio Confessionum*, 445).

39. See the discussion under *HC* 66.

40. See the discussion of 1 Pet 3:18–20 under *HC* 44 and the discussion of 1 Pet 3:20–22 under *HC* 72. In 1 Pet 3:20, "through" refers to the circumstances (water), not to the instrument of salvation.

us through, that is, out of the flood and the Red Sea. Where the flood and the Red Sea might have killed us, we were instead delivered by God's grace. They symbolize God's saving acts, but they were not the *instruments* of God's saving acts. God did not confer salvation through them. We receive Christ and his benefits by faith alone (*sola fide*). Even faith does not create realities but apprehends them. Baptism testifies to us of the fact that Christ, in his suffering obedience, underwent the flood of God's judgment for us. Baptism testifies and seals to believers that Christ endured the judgment of the Red Sea, as it were, for us. As we say in *BC* 34, Christ "is our Red Sea, through which we must pass."[41] Therefore, though we rightly fear God, we do not fear the coming flood of judgment. Christ endured it for us.

For these reasons we reject the notion that baptism confers new life (baptismal regeneration) or that through it the Spirit necessarily, at the time of administration, operates through it to make the baptized person elect, united to Christ, adopted, and so on. This is the error of the federal vision movement. We confess that there are two ways of relating to the visible covenant community: internally and externally.[42] Everyone who is baptized is admitted visibly into the covenant community. They are participants in the administration of the covenant of grace. Those whom God has freely loved and chosen, in Christ, from all eternity come to faith, and through faith alone receive Christ and all his benefits. So Scripture says: "And now why do you wait? Rise and be baptized and wash away your sins, calling on his name" (Acts 22:16 ESV).

Paul, in recounting how the Lord brought him from spiritual death to spiritual life on the road to Damascus, makes the closest possible connection between baptism and the benefits of Christ. The text says literally, "having risen [ἀναστὰς] be baptized [βάπτισαι] and wash away your sins [ἀπόλουσαι], having called upon [ἐπικαλεσάμενος] his name." There are two participles of circumstance ("rising" and "calling") and two imperatives ("baptize" and "wash"). Did Paul mean to communicate that baptism itself or that the Spirit necessarily through baptism washed away his sins? No. Paul had already been initiated into the visible

41. United Reformed Churches in North America, *Liturgical Forms and Prayers*, 191.

42. See the discussion under *HC* 69.

covenant community (Phil 3:5). He had been circumcised on the eighth day according to the institution of circumcision under Abraham (Gen 17:2). If the sacraments of the covenant of grace necessarily (*ex opere operato*) confer what they signify, then Paul was already regenerated. The only way to avoid that conclusion is to set up an untenable dichotomy between the covenant of grace as it was administered under Abraham and the covenant of grace as it is administered under Christ, but Paul never does that. He does the opposite.

In Romans 4:3–12 the principal burden of his argument is to show the *continuity* between the substance and administration of the covenant of grace between Abraham and the new covenant. Just as Abraham believed and was justified before he was visibly initiated into the covenant community, so he is the father of all the uncircumcised gentiles who believe in Christ. As he was circumcised and yet believed, he is the father of all those Jews who believe in Christ. In other words, Paul makes no radical discontinuity between the covenant of grace as it was under Abraham and as it is under Christ. Paul makes the same argument in Galatians 3–4, where he clearly distinguishes Abraham from Moses. According to Paul (2 Cor 3:7–18), the new covenant is new relative to *Moses*, not Abraham. Jeremiah 31:31–33 says the new covenant will not be like the covenant God made with Israel, when he led them out of Egypt. Jeremiah does not contrast the new covenant with Abraham but with Moses, that is, the old covenant.

In short, Paul, quoted by Luke in Acts 22:16, used sacramental language. He identifies the baptism with the thing signified (*res significata*), but the point of sacramental language is not to make the sign into the thing signified. The intent of sacramental language is not to destroy the sacrament. By analogy of Scripture, we can see even more clearly what Paul means by looking at Titus 3:

> But when the goodness and loving kindness of God our Savior appeared, he saved us, not because of works done by us in righteousness, but according to his own mercy, by the washing of regeneration and renewal of the Holy Spirit, whom he poured out on us richly through Jesus Christ our Savior, so that being justified by his grace we might become heirs according to the hope of eternal life. The saying is trustworthy, and I want you to insist on these

things, so that those who have believed in God may be careful to devote themselves to good works. (Titus 3:4–8 ESV)

Verse 5 should not be quoted without its context. Paul was writing to a pastor. Chapter 3 resumes a thought begun in 2:9. "Bondservants" are to be submissive to rulers and others. Then, in 3:3, Paul begins to set up a contrast between "foolish, disobedient, led astray, slaves to various passions and pleasures, passing our days in malice and envy, hated by others and hating one another" (ESV). By implication, this is true of believers. In verse 4 he points to God's grace, goodness, and faithfulness to his covenant promises to redeem all of his elect. Notice, by the way, that he teaches that God "saved" us by grace and not by (or through) our works. Justification (the narrower category) and salvation (the broader category) are by grace alone (*sola gratia*), through faith alone. Paul uses the metaphor of washing to describe the effect of salvation, the application of Christ's righteousness. Notice too that we have these benefits "not by works done by us in righteousness." By this expression Paul intentionally excludes all of our efforts, all of our obedience, all of our performance or striving.

It is singularly strange that interpreters have through the course of church history sought to restrict Paul's language to refer to obedience to the ceremonial law, thereby making a place for us to contribute to our salvation. Rather, the image here is that of the Red Sea. How did the Israelites contribute to their salvation? They were metaphorically dead and thus helpless. Pharaoh and his armies were nearly upon them and would have destroyed them. It was God, in his marvelous saving power and grace, who parted the waters and "led them by the hand" (Jer 31:32; Ps 77:20) out of Egypt, through the Red Sea, on dry ground. That is why Scripture says, "For it is by God's free favor you have been saved" (Eph 2:8). It is not by favor and our cooperation or performance or doing. We obey only by God's grace and only because we have been saved, not in order that we might be saved if we do enough. To say that is to turn grace into works again.

Paul says believers have been saved "by the washing of regeneration and renewing of the Holy Spirit." Clearly, necessarily, grammatically, logically it is the Holy Spirit who has washed us, who has granted us new life. It is the Spirit who renews. This is the very same teaching as our Lord's in John 3:1–21, in the dialogue with Nicodemus. We must be born again.

Only the Spirit does that. No one who to whom the Holy Spirit has not given new life has been saved or come into possession of Christ and his benefits (e.g., justification and sanctification) since the dead do not believe and salvation is by grace alone, through faith alone and faith is God's free gift. Baptism is a visible representation of what the Spirit does. It is a promise and guarantee to believers that what baptism signifies is true for them, but this passage nowhere says or even implies that regeneration is necessarily granted in baptism. It is the Holy Spirit, not baptismal water, who is poured out upon us, who grants new life and true faith, and through that faith alone God has justified by his free favor (grace). *Believers* are heirs of eternal life. *Believers* devote themselves to good works. Baptism is a wonderful picture of all the benefits that Paul describes in Titus 3:5, but it no more grants them than circumcision granted them under the administration of types and shadows.

Baptism is a powerful testimony and promise to believers that they have been saved and incorporated into the kingdom of God. Olevianus explains:

> This head, Christ, rules His subjects even in this life in such a way that He produces eternal salvation in the hearts of all the elect through the preaching of His holy gospel and the power of His Spirit. He does this by incorporating them into Himself by faith and the testimony of holy baptism, by graciously not imputing their sins to them, by daily purifying them from sin, by living in them and ruling their hearts with His Holy Spirit, and by using as means to that end the preaching of the holy gospel, the administration of the holy sacraments, and Christian discipline.[43]

The means, the keys of the kingdom (Matt 16:19), matter. The witness of baptism to the truth of the gospel is part of the way God incorporates believers into himself. Olevianus further explains that it is those who "believe and trust in Christ and are baptized into His name know that in this life they are in the Kingdom of Christ and not in the Kingdom or dominion of the Devil."[44] Baptism is a source of assurance to believers

43. Olevian, *Firm Foundation*, 37.

44. Olevian, *Firm Foundation*, 37.

because it is a tangible reminder "and a source of great joy and benefit" when a person is certain "that whoever believes in Christ from the heart (which is the internal anointing of the Holy Spirit) and bears the physical sign of the covenant, holy baptism, is under Christ the King and is translated out of the kingdom of darkness into the Kingdom of Christ."[45]

Ursinus writes that baptism in the name of the Father, Son, and Holy Spirit signifies three things. First, "whenever the minister baptizes, it is as if the Father, Son, and Holy Spirit was baptizing. Hence it further follows that these three persons are divine and consubstantial (ὁμοουσία) subsisting (ὑφιστάμενα) of the same deity and one true God in whom we are baptized."[46] Second, baptism signifies that the three persons confirm to us that all the benefits signified by baptism are ours "if we believe."[47] Third, to be baptized is to come under a consequent obligation to give oneself over to the Father, Son, and Holy Spirit, in whose name we have been baptized.[48]

Baptism is the new covenant sign and seal of initiation into the covenant community. It is divinely ordained and therefore should not be neglected. When we are tempted we should remind ourselves that we have been baptized. We have been set apart. The name of the Triune God has been placed on us. We are not our own. Baptism did not create those realities but it is a powerful, tangible sign and seal of all that Christ has done for those who believe.

45. Olevian, *Firm Foundation*, 38.

46. "quando minister baptizat, ac si Deus pater, et filius, et Spiritus sanctus baptizaret. Unde porro liquet, hos tres esse tria ὑφιστάμενα, divina et ὁμοουσία, hoc est, tres personas eiusdem divinitatis, et unum verum" (Ursinus, *Corpus doctrinae*, 377). Benedict Aretius traces the expression "tria ὑφιστάμενα" to Justin Martyr (Aretius, *Short History of Valentinus Gentilis*, 57). This work first appeared in Latin in 1567 as Aretiius, *Valentini Gentilis Iusto Capitis Supplicio*.

47. "Si crediderimus" (Ursinus, *Corpus doctrinae*, 377).

48. Ursinus, *Corpus doctrinae*, 377.

Question 72
Is then the outward washing with water itself the washing away of sins?

Question 73
Why then does the Holy Spirit call baptism the washing of regeneration and the washing away of sins?

Question 74
Are infants also to be baptized?

Lord's Day 27

QUESTION 72

Is then the outward washing with water itself the washing away of sins?

No, for only the blood of Jesus Christ and the Holy Spirit cleanse us from all sin.[1]

Here we need to understand two things: (1) the nature of signs, and (2) the teaching of Scripture as to how we are actually given new life.[2] The Heidelberg theologians engaged their Lutheran counterparts at the Heidelberg Disputation in 1560 and again at Maulbronn in 1564.[3] They were well aware of the tensions between the Reformed and Lutheran approaches to baptism. This language was intended to clarify, for what must have been a confused Palatinate populace, what baptism does and does not do.

According to Rome baptism is the "instrumental cause" of our (initial) justification.[4] According to Roman Catholic doctrine, in baptism, the virtues of faith, hope, and love are infused at the same time (*simul*) in us.[5] Baptism necessarily confers the forgiveness of original sin and new life (regeneration).[6] Rome continues to confess these same dogmas.[7] Indeed, the Roman Catholic dogma of baptismal regeneration and (initial) justification is perhaps clearer today than it was in the sixteenth century.

In 1586, Jakob Andrae (1528–1590), with a team of Lutheran theologians, met at Montbéliard with Theodore Beza (1519–1605) and a team of Reformed scholars, including Abraham Musculus (1534–1591) and Antoine

---

1. "Ist denn das äusserliche Wasserbad die Abwaschung der Sünden selbst? Nein; denn allein das Blut Jesu Christi, und der Heilige Geist reiniget uns von allen Sünden" (Schaff, *Creeds of Christendom*, 3:330). "Estne ergo externus Baptismus aquae, ipsa peccatorum ablutio? Non est: Nam solus sanguis Iesu Christi purgat nos ab omni peccato" (Niemeyer, *Collectio Confessionum*, 445). Note that the Latin text of the answer omits reference to the Holy Spirit. It says only, "It does not for only the blood of Jesus Christ purges us from all sin."

2. See the discussion of signs under *HC* 67.

3. See Clark, *Caspar Olevian*, 104–5n2, for more resources on Maulbronn.

4. Council of Trent, session 6, cap. 7 (Denzinger, *Enchiridion Symbolorum*, 287.799).

5. Council of Trent, session 6, cap. 7 (Denzinger, *Enchiridion Symbolorum*, 288.800).

6. Council of Trent, session 5, "Decretum super peccato originali" (Denzinger, *Enchiridion Symbolorum*, 280.790); session 14, cap. 2 (Denzinger, *Enchiridion Symbolorum*, 313.895).

7. *CCC* §§1215, 1227–28, 1239, 1262–70.

de La Faye (1540–1615), to discuss the differences between the Reformed and the Lutheran churches and confessions.[8] Remarkably, Beza and Andrae used much of the same language about baptism but they meant by it rather different things.[9] Beza distinguished between an *internal* and an *external* relation to Christ. As we have already seen, the catechism speaks of baptism as an *external* sign of internal blessings received through faith, which is given only to the elect and which cannot be lost by the elect. For Lutheran orthodoxy, as represented by Andrae, the sign of baptism necessarily brings what it signifies.[10] Further, for Andrae and others, the blessings given in baptism can be lost because grace is, in the end, resistible.[11]

Thus, the Roman Catholics and the Lutherans agree, to some extent, that baptism necessarily confers what it signifies, namely forgiveness and new life. The Reformed, however, confess that baptism signifies and seals to believers the gift of new life, justification, and the beginning of progressive sanctification, but these benefits are not necessarily conferred in baptism, though they are sealed to those who receive Christ and his benefits by faith alone.

Nevertheless, *contra* those who would empty the sacraments of genuine spiritual power, we should say that because of the sacramental union (metonymy, not identity) between the sign and the thing signified,[12] because of the divine promises attached to the sacraments, and because the Spirit operates through the sacraments to accomplish his purposes, it is wrong to think of them as empty. They cannot be empty because they are instituted by Christ as part of the administration of his covenant of grace. The real question is whether the administration of the covenant of grace is

---

8. See Raitt, *Colloquy of Montbéliard*, for the background and history of the colloquy. See Andreae and Beza, *Lutheranism vs. Calvinism*, 501–80, for a Lutheran presentation of the substance of the debate. On La Faye, see Clark, "Authority of Reason." For the contemporary state of the debate, see Kolb and Trueman, *Between Wittenberg and Geneva*; Kolb and Wengert, *Book of Concord*.

9. Thus, in Luther's catechisms he writes of baptism, "It brings about forgiveness of sins, redeems from death and the devil, and gives eternal life *to all who believe it*" (Kolb and Wengert, *Book of Concord*, 359.5–6; emphasis added). In 1529, Luther confessed that faith is necessary to receive the substance of what baptism offers. In his 1531 commentary on Gal 3:8, however, he affirms that "righteousness and salvation" are given to infants at the moment of baptism (*LW* 26:241–42).

10. Andrae and Beza, *Lutheranism vs. Calvinism*, 568.

11. Andrae and Beza, *Lutheranism vs. Calvinism*, 548–64. See also the *Solid Declaration* in Kolb and Wengert, *Book of Concord*, 557.67–560.83.

12. Ursinus, *Commentary*, 364–65.

significant. Of course it is. Our Lord commanded Abraham to administer the sign and seal of the covenant of grace to believing adults and to their children (Gen 17:1–10). That command alone makes the administration of the covenant of grace significant. Our Lord Jesus instituted baptism as the sign and seal, to believers, of their regeneration, justification, adoption, and sanctification. The visible covenant community is the place where God ordinarily grants saving faith, and baptism is one of the two signs and seals instituted by Christ to confirm the promises of the gospel and to assure of their truth.

Thus, the real issue here is ecclesiology. Christ has a body, the church. The King has given to the visible church the keys of the kingdom (the preaching of the gospel and the administration of discipline) and instruction on how to use the keys.[13] The use of the keys is the outward administration of the covenant of grace. Initiation in the covenant community of believers and their children by baptism is an essential, divinely commanded element of the administration of the covenant of grace in the church.

Second, Scripture clearly and repeatedly assigns the giving of new life and all that follows *not* to the sign and seal of the covenant of grace but to the Holy Spirit. "Baptism, which corresponds to this [ἀντίτυπον], now saves you, not as a removal of dirt from the body but as an appeal to God for a good conscience, through the resurrection of Jesus Christ" (1 Pet 3:21 ESV). Baptism saves, not in the way the Lutherans teach but, as Peter says, "*as an appeal* [ἐπερώτημα] *to God*." The noun Peter uses is unusual, but given the context it seems to be *sacramental* rather than literal language. It is as if to say, "Look here, I believe and I have the seal of the promises."[14]

Peter expressly establishes an analogy between the sign and seal of baptism with regeneration (the granting of new life), but he does not identify them such that baptism *is* the granting of new life. Baptism itself does not save us. Baptism is the antitype of that which saves us, namely, the washing by the Spirit. How do we know this? Read the preceding verse: "because they formerly did not obey, when God's patience waited in the days of Noah, while the ark was being prepared, in which a few, that is, eight persons, were brought safely through water" (1 Pet 3:20 ESV).

13. See the discussions under *HC* 82–83.

14. Hope and Moulton, *Vocabulary of the Greek Testament*, s.v. "ἐπερώτημα."

What is the frame of reference for baptism and washing? It is the flood, which saved no one. It destroyed those who did not believe (there is a judicial aspect of baptism for the reprobate), but God's people were saved out of the judgment by the ark. To what does the ark correspond? Christ. The Noachian baptismal flood was a type of Christ's suffering and death, when he underwent the flood of judgment for us, and it testifies to our outward identity with Christ. To believers it signifies and seals that, just as he suffered the judgment flood for us, as he was drowned in divine wrath, we have died with him, and by his grace he has redeemed us.

In short, the intent of 1 Peter 3:21 is to teach that baptism itself does not necessarily save anyone to whom it is applied. The key here is to notice and understand what a type is: something from the past that points to, illustrates, and corresponds to something in the present. The relationship is between the Noachian flood, baptism, Christ's death for us, and the judgment to come. Jesus uses the flood in a similar way in Matthew 24:39. "The flood came and took them all away." Having established an analogy between the flood and judgment, he applies it to the final judgment. This is why, if we follow his analogy carefully and correctly, we must say that we do not want to be "taken" (in judgment) but we want to left behind, as it were, in salvation.

Paul teaches the same doctrine in Ephesians: "that he might sanctify her, having cleansed her by the washing of water with the word" (Eph 5:26 ESV). It is the word or Christ's Spirit operating through the word that washes and cleanses. Again, holy baptism is a sacrament, a sign and seal of what Christ does for us and in us, but it is not the thing signified. The apostle John assigns our cleansing not to baptism but to the blood of Christ: "But if we walk in the light, as he is in the light, we have fellowship with one another, and the blood of Jesus his Son cleanses us from all sin" (1 John 1:7 ESV).

This is judicial language drawn from the Old Testament. Baptism is a sign and seal to believers that, as the blood of bulls and goats pointed forward to the reality of Christ's final satisfaction of divine justice, so too we are clean. The blood of bulls and goats was sacramental. It did not itself make clean.[15] It was a typological administration of the covenant of

15. Ursinus, *Commentary*, 364–65.

grace that looked forward to Christ's death. Believers who lived under the types and shadows were participating in a real administration of the covenant of grace, and they received real grace, but the blood of animals was always a picture of the reality to come. That is why God repeatedly told the Israelites that he was not pleased with their sacrifices. God demands the reality. Christ is that reality. As a consequence of all he did, he by his Spirit is conforming us to that reality in progressive sanctification. "And such were some of you. But you were washed, you were sanctified, you were justified in the name of the Lord Jesus Christ and by the Spirit of our God" (1 Cor 6:11). It is clear that it is Christ's Spirit who cleanses us. We were ungodly by nature, but now, having been justified *sola gratia, sola fide,* the Spirit is progressively cleansing us, which takes us back to the double benefit of Christ.[16]

Baptism is not magic. It does not place us in a state of grace (acceptance with God) whereby we must cooperate with grace (or at least not resist lest we fall). Rather, baptism signifies that by the same power whereby he rescued Noah out of judgment and the Israelites out of Egypt, he has also finally redeemed us from the judgment to come by the once-for-all obedience and death of Christ, and he is at work in us now, by his grace, to conform us to the image of Christ.

Question 73

Why then does the Holy Spirit call baptism the washing of regeneration and the washing away of sins?

God speaks thus not without great cause, namely, not only to teach us thereby that just as the filthiness of the body is taken away by water, so our sins are taken away by the blood and Spirit of Christ; but much more, that by this divine pledge and token he may assure us, that we are as really washed from our sins spiritually as our bodies are washed with water.[17]

16. See the discussion under *HC* 70.

17. "Warum nennet denn der Heilige Geist die Taufe das Bad der Wiedergeburt und die Abwaschung der Sünden? Gott redet also nicht ohne grosse Ursache: nämlich, nicht allein, dass Er

The catechism is asking and answering why Scripture uses metonymy, that is, a figure of speech in which a word denoting a property or an association is substituted for something else.[18] For example, "referring to the monarchy as 'the crown' or the theatre as 'the stage.'"[19] In this case, regeneration and justification, which are signified and sealed to believers in baptism, are identified as baptism.

The catechism is addressing the language of Titus 3:3. Here is the passage in question:

> For we ourselves were once foolish, disobedient, led astray, slaves to various passions and pleasures, spending our lives in evil and envy, hated by others and hating one another. But when the goodness and loving kindness of God our Savior appeared, he saved us [ἔσωσεν], not out of works done by us in righteousness, but according to his own mercy, by the washing of regeneration [διὰ λουτροῦ παλιγγενεσίας] and renewal [ἀνακαινώσεως] of the Holy Spirit, whom he poured out on us richly through Jesus Christ our Savior, so that having been justified [δικαιωθέντες] by his grace we might become heirs according to the hope of eternal life. (Titus 3:3–7)

Paul is exhorting Titus to godliness, and in order to lay the basis for his exhortation, he contrasts what we were *before* the Spirit applied redemption to us with what we are *now* that Spirit has, by grace alone (*sola gratia*), made us alive and united us to Christ by the Spirit, through faith alone (*sola fide*). We were foolish, disobedient, deceived, and so on. That is the natural state of Adam's children after the fall. When God's goodness and

---

uns damit will lehren, dass, gleichwie die Unsauberkeit des Leibes durch Wasser, also unsere Sünden durch's Blut und Geist Christi hinweg genommen werden; sondern vielmehr, dass Er uns durch diess göttliche Pfand und Wahrzeichen will versichern, dass wir so wahrhaftig von unsern Sünden geistlich gewaschen sind, als wir mit dem leiblichen Wasser gewaschen werden" (Schaff, *Creeds of Christendom*, 3:330–31). "Cur ergo Spiritus sanctus baptismum appellat lavacrum regenerationis et ablutionem peccatorum? Deus non sine gravi causa sic loquitur, videlicet non solum ut nos doceat, quemadmodum sordes corporis aqua purgantur, sic peccata nostra sanguine et Spiritu Christi expiari: verum multo magis, ut nobis hoc divino symbolo ac pignore certum faciat, nos non minus vere a peccatis nostris interna lotione ablui, quam externa et visibili aqua abluti sumus" (Niemeyer, *Collectio Confessionum*, 446).

18. Ursinus, *Commentary*, 365.

19. *OED Online*, s.v. "metonymy."

kindness was manifested, he saved us. That is the next thing to notice. God is the subject of the verb. He did the saving. Paul quickly clarifies the ground and agency of our salvation. He explicitly excludes our works, "done in righteousness," as the ground or instrument and contrasts them with God's mercy, that is, the withholding of judgment.

The agency is the "washing of regeneration." There may be an allusion to baptism here, but the passage does not say or even imply that the Spirit necessarily grants new life with the administration of baptism. We are renewed by "the washing of regeneration," that is, by the actual thing itself, not by baptism. To make it clear Paul adds, "the renewal of the Holy Spirit." Baptism is not that renewal but a sacrament of what the Spirit does for his elect. Clearly there were baptized persons in the New Testament who were not regenerated. For example, Ananias and Sapphira (Acts 5:1–11) were baptized members of the church who received the most extreme sort of church discipline because of their unbelief.[20] Paul denounces Hymenaeus, Alexander, and Philetus by name as those who were part of congregations who had shown themselves to be unbelievers (1 Tim 1:20; 2 Tim 2:17). Jude excoriates those members of the church, false shepherds, as "hidden reefs" at their love feasts, "waterless clouds ... fruitless trees ... wild waves of the sea ... wandering stars, for whom the gloom of utter darkness has been reserved forever" (Jude 12–13 ESV).

The regeneration and renewal Paul describes is not merely initial, nor is it revocable or contingent. He describes new life as the free gift of God. Believers are those whom God has regenerated by his sovereign grace. Regeneration is not the product of our cooperation with God's grace.

Thus, the catechism is concerned to make it clear that baptism itself is not the washing of regeneration. Ursinus explains that there are three reasons why the sign (baptism) is sometimes identified so closely with the thing signified (salvation and justification). Baptism is an illustration of what the Spirit does for those who believe, but he hastens to note that we receive Christ and his benefits through true faith alone. He quotes Mark

20. The conclusion that Ananias and Sapphira were unregenerate seems unavoidable. In the history of redemption, God himself, without mediation, put relatively few (e.g., Nadab, Abihu, and Uzzah, whose sins are analogous to that of Ananias and Sapphira) to death, and those whom he did so kill stand as symbols of unbelief.

16:16, "He who has believed [πιστεύσας] and has been baptized shall be saved but he who has not believed [ἀπιστήσας] shall be condemned."[21] As the second part of the verse makes clear, what is decisive in salvation is not baptism but faith. It is not being unbaptized that excludes one from salvation, but unbelief does exclude. It seems clear that, in Mark 16:16, baptism is an adjunct to faith, especially since it does not reappear in the parallel after the adversative conjunction. Ursinus writes, "Because in the proper use of the sacraments the exhibition and reception of the signs, and things signified, are inseparably connected. And hence the Holy Spirit interchanges the terms, attributing what belongs to the thing signified to the sign, and what belongs to the sign to the thing, to teach us what he gives, and to assure us that he does really give it."[22] Faith is the *sine qua non* for taking possession of Christ and his benefits. Baptism assures believers that what they have received through faith alone, by grace alone, really is true. Olevianus explains the relationship between the sacrament and the benefits thus:

> [Christ] instituted baptism as the seal of this covenant, and He wants us to be baptized no less in His name than in that of the Father and the Holy Spirit, promising salvation to those that believe and are baptized (Matt. 28:19; Mark 16:16; Col. 2:9–11; Acts 8:16; 19:5). But it is a violation of God's will to be baptized in the name of any creature, and it belongs to God alone to make promises and fulfill them. That is why Christ is also the One who baptizes with the Holy Spirit (Matt. 3:11; Acts 2:18, 32).[23]

Believers should take great confidence from their baptism not because of baptism itself but because of what baptism promises to believers: just as water washes the body, so too are we actually clean and righteous before God. *Believers* may say to themselves, "I am a baptized person. I am washed. I belong to Christ."

Baptism is not the instrument of justification or of salvation. *Faith* is the instrument. Scripture does not teach and we do not confess justification

21. We need not accept the longer ending of Mark to grasp Ursinus's point.

22. Ursinus, *Commentary*, 365.

23. Olevianus, *Exposition*, 33.

or salvation through baptism but *sola fide*, through faith alone.[24] After all, if Paul teaches baptismal regeneration in Titus 3, he also teaches baptismal justification, but that would require him to contradict his argument in Galatians 2:20 and 3:2, 5. We live now "through faith" (διὰ πίστεως), and we received the Spirit "from the hearing of faith" (ἐξ ἀκοῆς πίστεως), not by baptism. It is those who are "of faith" (ἐκ πίστεως), not "of baptism" (or circumcision), who are Abraham's children (Gal 3:7–9). We received the Spirit "through faith" (διὰ τῆς πίστεως; Gal 3:14). The promise is "of faith" (ἐκ πίστεως) and is given "to the believers" (πιστεύουσιν), not "of baptism" and "to the baptized" (Gal 3:22). Thus, when Paul says, "For as many of you as were baptized into Christ, have put on Christ" (Gal 3:27), he is speaking of our outward identity with Christ in the same way as he does in Romans 6:3–4. Baptism is the sacramental identification of the Christian with Christ's death just as circumcision was the typological identification with Christ's death (Col 2:11–12).

This is not to demean the significance of baptism but to make clear that baptism, as a sacrament, is just that: a sign and seal of Christ and his benefits. It is not Christ, nor is it his benefits, since in that case it would no longer be a sacrament.

Question 74

Are infants also to be baptized?

Yes, for since they belong to the covenant and people of God as well as their parents, and since redemption from sin through the blood of Christ, and the Holy Spirit who works faith, are promised to them no less than to their parents, they are also by baptism, as the sign of the covenant, to be ingrafted into the Christian church, and distinguished from the children of unbelievers, as was done in the Old Testament by circumcision, in place of which in the New Testament baptism is instituted.[25]

---

24. See the discussion under *HC* 72 on the differences between the Reformed and the Lutherans on the efficacy of baptism. On the federal vision errors on baptism, see Clark, "Baptism and the Benefits."

25. "Soll man auch die jungen Kinder taufen? Ja: denn dieweil sie sowohl als die Alten in den Bund Gottes und seine Gemeine gehören, und ihnen in dem Blut Christi die Erlösung von Sünden

The most likely interpretation of the limited data we have about the earliest postapostolic practice of baptism is that the church widely practiced paedobaptism before the early third century. The direct evidence from the second century is fragmentary but intriguing. Irenaeus says, "For He came to save all through means of Himself—all, I say, who through Him are born again [*renascatur*] to God—infants, and children, and boys, and youths, and old men."[26] What does he mean by *renascatur*? Considering that his objective was to refute the gnostics and not to explain the sacraments, we may never know, but the context does indicate that he believed that infants could be renewed and sanctified.[27] The picture becomes clearer in the early third century inasmuch as both Origen (positively) and Tertullian (negatively) witness to the existing practice of infant baptism. In his commentary on Romans 5:9, Origen (ca. AD 184–ca. 253) writes, "The church received from the apostles the tradition of giving baptism even to infants."[28] He also affirms the practice of infant baptism elsewhere.[29] Tertullian recognizes infant baptism as an existing practice in the same period, even though he comes to advise delaying baptism.[30] His advice is *prima facie* evidence of its existence as a practice.[31] By the middle

und der Heilige Geist, welcher den Glauben wirket, nicht weniger denn den Alten zugesagt wird; so sollen sie auch durch die Taufe, als des Bundes Zeichen, der christlichen Kirche eingeleibt und von der Ungläubigen Kindern unterschieden werden, wie im alten Testament durch die Beschneidung geschehen ist, an welcher Statt im neuen Testament die Taufe ist eingesetzt" (Schaff, *Creeds of Christendom*, 3:331). "Suntne etiam infantes baptizandi? Omnino. Nam cum aeque ac adulti ad foedus et Ecclesiam Dei pertineant: cumque eis per sanguinem Christi, remissio peccatorum, et Spiritus sanctus fidei effector, non minus quam adultis promittatur: per Baptismum Ecclesiae Dei inserendi sunt, et ab infidelium liberis discernendi, itidem ut in Veteri foedere, per circumcisionem fiebat, cui in Novo foedere substitutus et Baptismus" (Niemeyer, *Collectio Confessionum*, 446).

26. "Omnes denim venit per semetipsum salvare: omnes, inquam, qui per eum renascuntur in Deum, infantes, et parvulos, et pueros, et juvenes, et seniores. Ideo per omnem venit aetatem, et infantibus infans facits, sanctifcans, infantes; in parvulis parvulus, sanctificans hand ipsum habentes aetatem, simul et exemplum Ellis pietas effects, et iustitiae, et subjectionis; in juvenilbus juvenis, exemplum juvenibus fiens, et sanctificans Dominio" (Irenaeus, *Adversus haereses* 2.22.4 [*ANF* 1:391]).

27. Jeremias, *Infant Baptism*, 65–66.

28. "Pro hoc et Ecclesia ab apostolis traditionem suscepit, etiam parvulis baptismum dare" (*PG* 14:1047b). See Origen, *Commentary on the Epistle to the Romans*, 367.

29. E.g., his *Homilies on Luke* 14:5 and his homily on Lev 8:3. See Ferguson, *Baptism in the Early Church*, 367–68.

30. Tertullian did not reject infant baptism per se (*On Baptism* 18 [*ANF* 3:678]). Tertullian was not a proto-Baptist. His reason for delaying baptism was his conviction concerning the power of baptism to wash away sin.

31. Also Jeremias, *Infant Baptism*, 55–56, 65–66, 73–86. Aland (*Did the Early Church Baptize Infants?*) disputes Jeremias's conclusions but is never able to explain away the early, clear evidence for infant

of the third century infant baptism (e.g., under Cyprian of Carthage) was widespread, and it was so universal that later Augustine was able to say:

> And this is the firm tradition of the universal Church, in respect of the baptism of infants, who certainly are as yet unable "with the heart to believe unto righteousness, and with the mouth to make confession unto salvation," as the thief could do; nay, who even, by crying and moaning when the mystery is performed upon them, raise their voices in opposition to the mysterious words, and yet no Christian will say that they are baptized to no purpose.[32]

By the time the *HC* was written, the Eastern and Western church had been baptizing infants for no fewer than thirteen hundred years. There was one major variegated movement that had dissented from the Christian consensus that infants of believers should be baptized: the Anabaptists. They rejected the magisterial Protestant consensus that there is one covenant of grace variously administered through the history of redemption, the covenant of grace revealed after the fall, under types and shadows, to Adam (Gen 3:15), to Noah (Gen 6:18), to Abraham (Gen 15:18; 17:1–14), under the Mosaic covenant (e.g., Exod 2:24), under David (1 Chr 16:16), and under the prophets (Mic 7:20).[33] Even though the Particular Baptists disavowed the Anabaptists at important points, for example, "celestial flesh" Christology and involvement in civil life, nevertheless, for the Reformed, the lines between the Anabaptists and the Baptists were blurry, especially on the question of the continuity of the covenant of grace and its consequences for life in the church.[34]

The early Reformed response to the Anabaptists, formulated by Huldrych Zwingli (1484–1531) and Heinrich Bullinger (1504–1575), helped to shape the contours of the Reformed response to the Anabaptists and

---

baptism, e.g., "You are to baptize the little ones first" in *Apostolic Tradition* 21.4 (Behr, *On the Apostolic Tradition*, 110).

32. *NPNF* 4:461.

33. Luther (or, potentially, an early redactor; for the purposes of this argument it does not matter, although this section reads like Luther) took an approach to Abrahamic covenant in Gen 17 that was quite similar to the approach the Reformed had taken (e.g., *LW* 3:114–16).

34. Clark, "House of Cards?," 74–76, 79–80.

to the Baptists.[35] Reformed pastors and teachers are still repeating several of the same arguments that Zwingli lays out in his treatise *On Baptism* (1525) against the Anabaptists.[36] He appeals to the promises made to Abraham and his children.[37] He elaborates on the same arguments in his 1527 *Refutation of the Tricks of the Catabatists.*[38] According to Ulrich Gaebler, Zwingli's principal move was to elaborate on the covenant idea. God renewed with Abraham the covenant he had made with Noah but now, under Abraham, he included children. God makes the same covenant in the New Testament "so as to render them and Israel one people and one church. A single covenant unites the Old and the New Testaments—only a relative difference separates them."[39]

Bullinger, his successor as *Antistes* (principal minister) in Zürich, published a treatise against the Anabaptists in 1534, *On the One and Eternal Testament or Covenant of God*, which articulates the continuity of the covenant of grace.[40] He argues from the promise of God to Abraham (Gen 17:7) to be a God to him and to his seed. [41] He argues, *contra* the Anabaptists (and anticipating a frequent Baptist objection from the seventeenth century forward), that the Abrahamic covenant was essentially a *spiritual* covenant and not an earthly or carnal covenant.[42] The new covenant is the fulfillment of the promises made to Abraham and administered (not merely promised) under the types and shadows.[43] In short, for Bullinger (as for Zwingli and later for Calvin), the new covenant is the new administration of the Abrahamic covenant.

The developments in Zürich are significant for understanding the catechism since both Ursinus and Olevianus studied there with Bullinger.

35. On the history of covenant theology, see Clark, "Christ and Covenant"; Woolsey, *Unity and Continuity*.

36. Zwingli, "Exposition of the Faith," 129–75; Zwingli, *Huldreich Zwinglis Sämtliche Werke*, 4:206–337 (Bretschneider, *Corpus Reforumatum*, 91).

37. Zwingli, *On Baptism*, 138. This section follows Clark, "House of Cards?," 75–78, very closely.

38. Zwingli, *Refutation of the Tricks*; Zwingli, "*Catabaptistarum Strophas Elenchus.*"

39. Gaebler, *Huldrych Zwingli*, 129.

40. Bullinger, *De testamento*, translated as Bullinger, *Brief Exposition*.

41. Bullinger, *De testamento*, 5–10.

42. Bullinger, *De testamento*, 9, 12b. See Calvin's commentary on Gen 17:7 in Calvin, *Commentary on the First Book*, 450.

43. Bullinger, *De testamento*, 21b–24b.

In his *Summa theologiae*, which he prepared as part of the preparation of the catechism, Ursinus asks, "When Moses speaks to the people of Israel does he also address us?" "No less than he did them. First, because God did then for the first time make known the law in the Decalogue, but repeated and clarified for the people of Israel not only what he required of them but also that for which all rational creatures were created. Second, we are the spiritual sons of Abraham and Israel who have been ingrafted into the Christ, who is the natural seed of Abraham."[44] That new covenant believers participate in the new administration of the Abrahamic covenant is basic to Ursinus's understanding of redemptive history. When he explains the Lord's Supper, he appeals to the "covenant of circumcision" to illustrate the nature of sacraments generally.[45] We will consider his lecture on *HC* 74 below.

Olevianus takes the same approach in *De substantia foederis inter deum et electos* (1585). The entire work is a sustained appeal to continuity of the covenant of grace between Abraham and the new covenant. He appeals to or cites Abraham as the paradigm of the covenant of grace no fewer than forty-seven times. The first passage to which he appeals, on the first page of the work, is Jeremiah 31:31–33, which he understands to contrast the Mosaic covenant with the new covenant, which he takes as a renewal of the Abrahamic covenant.[46]

The basis of the entire work is the distinction between the *substance* of the covenant of grace, which Olevianus defines in Abrahamic terms, "I will circumcise your heart and that of your children," quoting Deuteronomy 30 and citing Genesis 17, and the *external* administration of the covenant of grace, that is, its *accidents*.[47]

The same essential commitment to the continuity of the substance of the covenant of grace through redemptive history is evident in *HC* 19 and here in *HC* 74.[48] The ground of infant baptism is the substantial continuity of the Abrahamic covenant. When the catechism says, "They as well as their parents belong to the covenant," it refers to the Abrahamic

44. Ursinus, "*Summa Theologiae*," 1.22; Bierma et al., *Introduction*, 192.

45. Reuter, *D. Zachariae Ursini*, 1:32.

46. Olevianus, *De substantia*, 1–3.

47. Olevianus, *De substantia*, 2–3.

48. See the discussion under *HC* 19.

covenant, in which the children of believers were first explicitly included. In *BC* 34 we confess the same thing: "For that reason we detest the error of the Anabaptists who are not content with a single baptism once received and also condemn the baptism of the children of believers. We believe our children ought to be baptized and sealed with the sign of the covenant, as little children were circumcised in Israel on the basis of the same promises made to our children."[49]

Calvin articulates the same understanding of the essential continuity of the covenant of grace in the *Institutes* and in his treatises against the Anabaptists.[50] Beginning in 1539, he expanded his explanation of baptism to respond to the "ravings" of those "frenetic spirits" who opposed paedobaptism.[51] Baptism and circumcision differ and have similarities.[52] Circumcision is an anagoge of baptism, i.e, it anticipated it.[53] For Calvin, the promise of God (Gen 17:7, 10) that he will be a God to him and to his descendants, is a spiritual promise of eternal life.[54] For Paul to have said to the Ephesians that they were once outside circumcision (Eph 2:11–13) was tantamount to saying that they were "without Christ" (*sine Christo*).[55] Christ is the foundation (*fundamentum*) both of circumcision and of baptism.[56] In short, for Calvin, because circumcision and baptism are administrations of the same covenant of grace, they are distinguished only by their accidents, that is, outward ceremonies.[57]

Baptism is administered to covenant children as something owed to them because under the types and shadows "the Lord did not deign to have them circumcised without making them participants [*participes*]

49. United Reformed Churches in North America, *Liturgical Forms and Prayers*, 192.

50. Calvin, *Treatises against the Anabaptists*, 44–55; Balke, *Calvin and the Anabaptist Radicals*, 217–22.

51. "Phrenetici ... spiritus," "furias" (Calvin, *Institutes* 4.16.1; Barth, *Joannis Calvini Opera Selecta*, 5:303.34, 304.2). The 1536 *Institutes* addresses baptism in 4.11–23. In sections 22 and 23, he only alludes to the Anabaptist denial of infant baptism (Calvin, *Institutes of the Christian Religion*, 100–102; Balke, *Calvin and the Anabaptist Radicals*, 97–98).

52. Calvin, *Institutes* 4.16.3.

53. "Alterum anagoge" (Calvin, *Institutes* 4.16.3; Barth, *Joannis Calvini Opera Selecta*, 5:306.23).

54. Calvin, *Institutes* 4.16.3.

55. Barth, *Joannis Calvini Opera Selecta*, 5:307.9.

56. Barth, *Joannis Calvini Opera Selecta*, 5:307.31–33.

57. Calvin, *Institutes* 4.16.4.

all those things which were signified by circumcision."[58] "If the covenant (*foedus*) still remains firm and steadfast, it applies no less today than to the children of Christians than under the Old Testament it pertained to the infants of the Jews."[59] Of course, his question was rhetorical.

In *De substantia*, Olevianus argues that the promises of the covenant of grace belong to believing parents and to their children. At baptism parents, as an act of faith (*ex fide*), offer their children to God in faith in order that he might make them heirs of redemption. That inheritance is theirs by right of the covenant of grace (*gratuiti foederis iure*). Those children are instructed in the doctrine of faith and repentance so that as adults they might secure the fruit of baptism and glorify God. Olevianus compares those parents who do not baptize their children and raise them in the faith to those parents who offered their children to Moloch.[60] Children who do not submit to the institution and correction of the Lord are contumacious. His entire explanation of infant baptism rests on continuity between the new covenant and the Abrahamic covenant.[61]

Ursinus makes four arguments in defense of infant baptism: (1) Baptism is the first step in discipleship (Matt 28:18–19). We baptize the children of believers because "all the children of those that believe are included in the covenant, and church of God, unless they exclude themselves. They are, therefore, also disciples of Christ, because they are born in the church, or school of Christ; and hence the Holy Spirit teaches them in a manner adapted to their capacity and age."[62] (2) They are qualified. The Abrahamic promise "I will be a God to you and to your children" makes the children of believers qualified for baptism (Gen 17:7). Jesus's invitation to children qualifies the children of believers for baptism (Matt 19:14).[63] The promise of forgiveness of sins and sanctification belongs to believers and to their children, "therefore they ought to be baptized." He quotes Acts 2:39 as proof.[64] If the things signified belong to them, then the sign belongs to them, unless

58. Calvin, *Institutes* 4.16.5; Barth, *Joannis Calvini Opera Selecta*, 5:308.32.

59. Calvin, *Institutes* 4.16.5.

60. Olevianus, *De substantia*, 1.8.31.

61. Olevianus, *De substantia*, 1.8.32.

62. Ursinus, *Commentary*, 366.

63. Ursinus, *Commentary*, 366.

64. Ursinus, *Commentary*, 366.

some condition prevents it. We do not commune children because they cannot yet make profession of faith, but there is no condition preventing the administration of the sign of initiation into the visible church.[65] The sign should apply to covenant children because they are holy (1 Cor 7:14). "The Baptist was sanctified from his mother's womb."[66] (3) Baptism is a "rite of initiation into the church" intended to distinguish the children of Christians from "all the various sects."[67] (4) Baptism "occupies the place of circumcision in the New Testament and has the same use that circumcision had in the Old Testament."[68]

Ursinus addresses the Anabaptists directly and criticizes them for not only depriving the children "of their rights" but also for preventing "the grace of God from being seen in its richness, since God wills that the offspring of the faithful should be included amongst the members of the church, even from the womb."[69] They detract from the grace of the new covenant and narrow it unduly. They weaken in parents and children the sense of gratitude that they should have and the desire to perform their obligations to God. They "wickedly keep back from Christ infants whom he has commanded to be brought to him."[70] For Ursinus, like Olevianus (and Calvin, Bullinger, Zwingli, and others), the denial of infant baptism is not a "trifling error."[71] Rather, it is an "impious dogma."[72] The Anabaptist error is "against the Word of God and the consolation of the church."[73] "Wherefore this and similar follies of the sect of the Anabaptists should be carefully avoided, since they have, without doubt, been hatched by the devil, and are detestable heresies (*haeresibus*) which they have fabricated from various errors and blasphemies."[74]

Ursinus then turns to a number of specific objections by the Anabaptists to infant baptism. Because in some parts of the world (e.g., the United

65. Ursinus, *Commentary*, 367.
66. Ursinus, *Commentary*, 367.
67. Ursinus, *Commentary*, 367.
68. Ursinus, *Commentary*, 367.
69. Ursinus, *Commentary*, 367.
70. Ursinus, *Commentary*, 368.
71. Ursinus, *Commentary*, 368.
72. "Sed impium dogma" (Ursinus, *Corpus doctrinae*, 382).
73. "Verbo Dei et consolationi Ecclesiae adverum" (Ursinus, *Corpus doctrinae*, 382).
74. Ursinus, *Commentary*, 368; Ursinus, *Corpus doctrinae*, 382.

States) among evangelicals these Baptist objections are widely accepted, it is useful to summarize briefly the objections and answers.

> Objection: We may only do in church what is commanded or exemplified in Scripture. The Scriptures do not expressly teach infant baptism.
> Response: The command "Baptize all nations" (Matt 28:19) includes infants. We have examples. The apostolic church baptized whole households (Acts 16:15, 33; 1 Cor 1:16).[75]
>
> Objection: Christ does expressly command that infants be baptized.
> Response: Neither does he expressly say that adults, men, women, citizens, farmers, and other classes be baptized. "He commands that all who are included in the covenant and church of God should be baptized, of whatever age, sex, or rank they may be." The Anabaptists themselves do not exclude women from the Lord's Supper even though there is no express command to commune them.[76]
>
> Objection: Those who are baptized are to be instructed first, but infants cannot be instructed first.
> Response: That is true about adults who were the first to hear but false regarding children born in the church to parents professing faith. Children are received on the basis of the Abrahamic promise: "I will be a God to you etc." (Gen 17:7), since children were included in the covenant before they could make profession.
>
> Objection: When Acts 16 says that whole families were baptized, it is a synecdoche, a figure of speech.
> Response: Scripture does not imply that Luke is using a figure of speech.[77] The objection denies natural reading of the passage unnecessarily.

---

75. Ursinus, *Commentary*, 368; Ursinus, *Corpus doctrinae*, 382–83. See 1 Cor 10:1–4, where Paul says that all the Israelites, including infants, were baptized into Moses. Consider, too, that Jude 5 says that it was *Jesus* who led the Israelites out of Egypt. On the textual variant in Jude 5, Metzger writes, "Critical principles seem to require the adoption of Ἰησοῦς, which admittedly is the best attested reading" (*Textual Commentary*, 657). The NA[28] uses Ἰησοῦς.

76. Ursinus, *Commentary*, 368; Ursinus, *Corpus doctrinae*, 383.

77. Ursinus, *Commentary*, 369; Ursinus, *Corpus doctrinae*, 384.

Objection: The apostle preached the gospel before the household baptisms, which does not apply to infants.
Response: (1) Christ wills that all who belong to him should be baptized. Infants belong to him, therefore they should be baptized. (2) Of course the parents heard the gospel and their children were baptized with them.[78] Acts 11:4 speaks to Cornelius and all his household.[79]

Objection: Baptism is for those who believe. Mark 16:16 requires faith before baptism, which may not be given to the condemned.[80]
Response: (1) Circumcision was given to infants, "who did not believe."[81] (2) The restriction was intended for adults, whose baptism was conditioned on faith. The Anabaptists do not know with certainty which professors of faith *actually* believe.[82] After all, Simon Magus was baptized, and yet he turned out to be a hypocrite.[83] (3) "Faith is required for the use of baptism": actual faith for adults and an "enclitic faith, which is worked in them by the Spirit of God, suffices for infants."[84] Those who lack either actual or enclitic faith, that is, the potential of faith, are not to be baptized.[85]

Objection: If infants may receive baptism, then they should receive the Lord's Supper also.
Response: Baptism is the sign of *initiation* and reception into the church. The Lord's Supper is the sacrament of our abiding in the church.[86]

---

78. We should add to Ursinus's argument that this follows the Abrahamic pattern of circumcising hitherto uncircumcised adults males along with their sons.

79. Ursinus, *Commentary*, 369; Ursinus, *Corpus doctrinae*, 384–85.

80. In the sixteenth century many assumed the validity of the longer ending of Mark.

81. "Quia non credunt" (Ursinus, *Corpus doctrinae*, 385).

82. This argument goes back to Luther's 1528 response to the Anabaptists (*LW* 40:239–42).

83. Ursinus, *Commentary*, 370.

84. "In infantibus sufficit inclinativa, quam in iis operatur Spiritus Dei" (*Corpus doctrinae*, 385). Willard's translation "an inclination to faith" (Ursinus, *Commentary*, 370) is inaccurate. The adjective Ursinus used here refers, in grammar, to small particles that attach to another word.

85. For more on this question, see the excursus on infant faith and presumptive regeneration.

86. Ursinus, *Commentary*, 370.

> Objection: If baptism replaces circumcision, then only males should be baptized, and on the eight day.
> Response: You have confused the circumstances of circumcision with its substance. In the new covenant, the command is general and not encumbered with the typological circumstances.[87]

The confession of the Reformed and Presbyterian churches, their official interpretation of Scripture, is quite clear. We do not baptize the children of believers because we believe that it necessarily confers new life (baptismal regeneration) like the Lutherans, nor because we think it works automatically (*ex opere operato*) like the Roman Catholics. We baptize the children of believers for the same reason that Abraham circumcised the children of believers: because God commanded and attached promises to the outward administration of the covenant of grace.

> "Behold, my covenant is with you, and you shall be the father of a multitude of nations. No longer shall your name be called Abram, but your name shall be Abraham, for I have made you the father of a multitude of nations. I will make you exceedingly fruitful, and I will make you into nations, and kings shall come from you. And I will establish my covenant between me and you and your offspring after you throughout their generations for an everlasting covenant, to be God to you and to your offspring after you. And I will give to you and to your offspring after you the land of your sojournings, all the land of Canaan, for an everlasting possession, and I will be their God."
>
> And God said to Abraham, "As for you, you shall keep my covenant, you and your offspring after you throughout their generations. This is my covenant, which you shall keep, between me and you and your offspring after you: Every male among you shall be circumcised." (Gen 17:4–10 ESV)

Since the second century, Christian theologians and churches have repeatedly argued that, though the Mosaic covenant was temporary and illustrative of future realities, the Abrahamic covenant was permanent

87. Ursinus, *Commentary*, 371.

in a way that the Mosaic (old) covenant was never intended to be.[88] The Reformed inherited this understanding of redemptive history. That distinction between the role that Abraham played in the history of redemption and the special, temporary role that Moses played is often overlooked and especially as it touches the continuity of the covenant of grace and baptism.

God established a covenant of grace with Adam, renewed it with Noah, Abraham, and Moses, and administered it under types (illustrations of future realities) and shadows (anticipations of future realities) throughout redemptive history. Nevertheless, there were differences. The way that God administered the covenant of grace under Moses and David was different because the administration was attached to a temporary national people and to a sacrificial system. Through the prophet Jeremiah (Jer 31:31–33), the Lord promised a new covenant. It is often assumed that the new covenant contrasts to Abraham, but that is not how the New Testament speaks, nor the way Jeremiah speaks. The new covenant contrasts with Moses, not with Abraham, who is repeatedly cast as the father of all believers in the new covenant (e.g., Rom 4:1–12; Gal 3:7–18; 4:21–31; Heb 11:8–12).

The apostle Peter iterated the fundamental continuity of the administration of the covenant of grace when he told the Jewish men, heads of households, at Pentecost: "For the promise is for you and for your children and for all who are far off, everyone whom the Lord our God calls to himself" (Acts 2:39 ESV). This was a restatement of the promise of the covenant of grace made to Abraham and restated in the prophets (e.g., Joel 2:28–32). Peter assumed, and the Christian church assumed until the rise of the Anabaptist movement in the early sixteenth century, as Reformed Christians confess, that there is a distinction between the *substance* of the covenant of grace and its outward *administration*. The question of whether infants are to be baptized is answered by that distinction. Whether one receives the substance of the covenant of grace is ultimately down to God's unconditional, eternal election in Christ. Whether children of believers are to be initiated visibly into the Christ-confessing covenant community is not determined by anything other than the divine command to initiate

88. *Epistle of Barnabas* 6–12; Justin Martyr, *Dialogue with Trypho;* Irenaeus, *Against Heresies* 4.6–9.

children into the covenant community and God's promise to be a God to believers and to their children.

Baptism is no guarantee that all children of believers will come to faith. It was never any such promise. The first person to receive infant initiation into the visible covenant community was Ishmael (Gen 17:25). Esau was initiated into the covenant by circumcision, and we know from Romans 9:13 that he was reprobate. We must not attempt to seek the divine decree behind the promise and the administration. We believe the promise and administer it as God commanded. We trust the Spirit to work out his decree according to his good pleasure. We pray for our covenant children, we catechize them, and we call them to a personal saving faith in Jesus the Savior. Baptism does not confer new life, faith, and salvation on them any more than circumcision conferred it on Ishmael and Esau. Nevertheless, they were initiated. God also saved some of those who were initiated, for example, Isaac. So let us trust the promises and the God who made them and ratified them in the death of his beloved Son.

EXCURSUS: PRESUMPTIVE REGENERATION AND INFANT FAITH

The question of infant faith arose in the 1520s in response to the Anabaptist critiques of infant baptism. Closely related to this theory is the doctrine of presumptive regeneration, which is most closely associated with Abraham Kuyper.[89]

According to Paul Althaus, Luther's "doctrine of baptism is basically nothing else than his doctrine of justification in concrete form."[90] He argues that, in response to the Anabaptists, Luther taught initially that infants were baptized on the basis of their parents' faith or that of their godparents.[91] After 1522 he began to speculate about infant faith. When the Anabaptists replied that infants could not believe, he attacked them as rationalists.[92] The doctrine of infant faith persisted despite the fact that

89. Kuyper, "Calvinism and Confessional Revision" (esp. 387–91).

90. Althaus, *Theology of Martin Luther*, 365.

91. E.g., *LW* 36:73–74.

92. Althaus, *Theology of Martin Luther*, 364–74. See, e.g., Luther's 1528 response to the Anabaptists (*LW* 40:239–42), where he argues against rebaptism on the ground that profession of faith is not faith itself and that we cannot be sure that infants do not believe.

it was essentially a capitulation to the Anabaptist demand that all candidates for baptism be believers.

The Reformed articulated a slightly different version of this view. In his 1558 *Confession of the Christian Faith,* Theodore Beza argues that we do not know whether infants have faith.[93] It is even probable, he argues, that they do not have it, unless God works in them in an extraordinary manner (e.g., as in the case of John the Baptizer).[94] He concedes that, although "they may not have faith with its effects, such as those who are of age, they may have however the seed and germ of it (*tamen fidei semen et germen*); seeing that the Lord has sanctified them the mother's womb (1 Cor 7:14) and distinguished them from the children of unbelievers in virtue of the promise which has been embraced by their parents."[95]

He concedes that not all the children of believers are elect, but we leave that to God. "We generally expect (*praesumimus*) the children of believing parents to be sanctified."[96] This is the expectation even when only one of the parents is a believer (Gen 17:7; 1 Cor 7:14).[97] Beza's doctrine of "the seed or germ of faith" seems quite similar to Ursinus's doctrine of "enclitic faith."

In the *Synopsis of A Purer Theology* (1625), Antonius Walaeus (1573–1639) defends the Reformed against the "certain Ubiquitarians" (Lutherans), who bind the Holy Spirit's regenerative power in baptism to the outward water in such a manner that this power is either inherent in the water itself or at least does not initiate regeneration except in the very act of baptism.[98] Instead, he proposes that infants have "the beginning or seed of regeneration" even before baptism.[99]

Like Beza, Francis Turretin acknowledges that the infants of believers do not necessarily have actual faith.[100] The Anabaptists, however, are

93. Beza, *Confession De Foi*; Beza, *Confessio Christianae Fidei*; Beza, *Christian Faith*, 4.48.

94. Beza, *Confession*, 4.48. Beza does not cite the Baptist as an example, but it fits his argument.

95. Beza, *Confession*, 4.48.

96. "sanctificatos esse quicunque ex fidelibus parentibus" (Beza, *Confession*, 4.48).

97. Beza, *Confession*, 4.48.

98. Te Velde, van den Belt, and van Asselt, *Synopsis Purioris Theologiae*, 4.27. Herman Witsius discusses this passage in "On the Efficacy," 167–68.

99. "regenerationis initium ac semen" (te Velde, van den Belt, and van Asselt, *Synopsis Purioris Theologiae*, 4.27).

100. Turretin, *Institutes of Elenctic Theology*, 19.20.18.

wrong to call the infants of believers "unbelievers" because they cannot yet make a profession of faith.[101] They are capable of "passive regeneration" according to the mysterious work of the Spirit.

In the late nineteenth century, Abraham Kuyper (1837–1920) capitalized on passages such as these and others (e.g., Calvin's doctrine of "seed of faith and repentance") to develop the doctrine of "presumptive regeneration."[102] He argues that Johannes Maccovius (1588–1644) and Gijsbertus Voetius (1589–1676) both taught it. What the passages quoted show is that they carried on Calvin's view, which we have already considered. Kuyper argues forcefully that we must administer baptism on this ground.[103]

Immediately in his argument he has to admit that the Reformed confessions, including the *HC*, say nothing of presumptive regeneration, the seed of faith, or the disposition toward faith among covenant children.[104] Further, Kuyper's appeal to Canons of Dort 1.17, which comforted grieving parents whose covenant children had died in infancy with the promise that since the children of believers are holy "by virtue of the gracious covenant in which they together with their parents are included, believing parents ought not to doubt the election and salvation of their children whom God calls out of this life in infancy,"[105] is somewhat misleading. The canons themselves neither imply nor teach presumptive regeneration. The comfort that synod offered to believing parents (about which we agree) is based entirely on the promise of the covenant, not the spiritual state of the infant.[106]

In 1905, Synod Utrecht in the Gereformeerde Kerken (lit. the "Re-Reformed Churches) in the Netherlands, the progenitors of the Christian Reformed Church in North America and the United Reformed Churches in North America, ruled that (1) we must regard our children as regenerate until they demonstrate that they are not, and (2) we do not baptize on the basis of presumed regeneration but on the basis of the

---

101. Turretin, *Institutes of Elenctic Theology*, 19.20.19.

102. Calvin, *Institutes* 4.16.21; Kuyper, "Calvinism and Confessional Revision," 386–91.

103. Kuyper, "Calvinism and Confessional Revision," 390.

104. Kuyper, "Calvinism and Confessional Revision," 391.

105. Modified from United Reformed Churches in North America, *Liturgical Forms and Prayers*, 263. I translate *pii parentes* as "believing parents" (Schaff, *Creeds of Christendom*, 3:556).

106. Clark, "Baptism and the Benefits," 17–18.

command and promise of God.[107] "Synod is of the opinion that the representation that every elect child is on that account already in fact regenerated even before baptism can be proved neither on Scriptural nor on confessional grounds, seeing that God fulfills his promise sovereignly in His own time, whether before, during, or after baptism. It is hence, imperative to be circumspect in one's utterances on this matter, so as not to desire to be wise beyond that which God has revealed."[108] The synod cautions that we should always exercise the judgment of charity, that is, accepting one's profession of faith until one should "manifest the contrary by their way of life or their doctrine."[109] They remind the churches that the judgment of charity does not imply that all the baptized are necessarily regenerate and remind the churches of the danger of presumption.

The thread in Reformed theology speculating about "a seed of faith" (Calvin), "enclitic faith" (Ursinus), and the like seems gratuitous. We have evidence that some infants were regenerated in the womb (e.g., John the Baptizer) but have no promise that such is universal and nothing in Scripture that leads us to infer that such necessarily happens or that the "seed of faith" is promised. The holiness to which Paul refers in 1 Corinthians 7:14 is better understood in Old Testament ritual categories. The children of believers are ritually clean. They are not outside the covenant, and therefore they are eligible for initiation into the visible covenant community. The heart of our defense of infant baptism is the continuity of the covenant of grace and the Abrahamic promise, which is restated by the apostle Peter (Acts 2:39). We certainly baptize in hope and prayerful expectation that the Lord will bring our covenant children to a personal faith, and we hope and pray that they never know a day when they are not trusting the Lord.

107. Shaver, *Polity of the Churches*, 2.34–37.

108. Shaver, *Polity of the Churches*, 2.37.

109. Shaver, *Polity of the Churches*, 2.37.

QUESTION 75

How is it signified and sealed to you in the holy supper, that you partake of the one sacrifice of Christ on the cross and all his benefits?

QUESTION 76

What does it mean to eat the crucified body and drink the shed blood of Christ?

QUESTION 77

Where has Christ promised, that He will thus feed and nourish believers with his body and blood, as certainly as they eat of this broken bread and drink of this cup?

Lord's Day 28

QUESTION 75

How is it signified and sealed to you in the holy supper, that you partake of the one sacrifice of Christ on the cross and all his benefits?

Thus: that Christ has commanded me and all believers to eat of this broken bread and to drink of this cup in remembrance of him, and has joined to it these promises: First, that his body was offered and broken on the cross for me and his blood shed for me, as certainly as I see with my eyes the bread of the Lord broken for me and the cup communicated to me; and further, that with his crucified body and shed blood he himself feeds and nourishes my soul to everlasting life, as certainly as I receive from the hand of the minister and taste with my mouth the bread and cup of the Lord, which are given me as certain tokens of the body and blood of Christ.[1]

We speak of the new covenant meal as the Lord's Supper because Christ instituted it and because Paul calls it such (1 Cor 11:20).[2] He calls it the "Lord's Table" (1 Cor 10:21). It is also called "the Eucharist" because it is a thanksgiving of praise (1 Cor 11:24).[3] It is the second sac-

1. "Wie wirst du im Heiligen Abendmahl erinnert und versichert, dass du an dem einigen Opfer Christi am Kreuz und allen seinen Gütern Gemeinschast habest? Also, dass Christus mir und allen Gläubigen von diesem gebrochenen Brot zu essen, und von diesem Kelch zu trinken befohlen hat, zu seinem Gedächtniss, und dabei verheissen: Erstlich, dass sein Leib so gewiss für mich am Kreuz geopfert und gebrochen, und sein Blut für mich vergossen sei, so gewiss ich mit Augen sehe, dass das Brot des Herrn mir gebrochen, und der Kelch mir mitgetheilet wird; und zum andern, dass Er selbst meine Seele mit seinem gekreuzigten Leib und vergossenen Blut so gewiss zum ewigen Leben speise und tränke, als ich aus der Hand des Dieners empfange und leiblich geniesse das Brot und den Kelch des Herrn, welche mir als gewisse Wahrzeichen des Leibes und Bluts Christi gegeben werden" (Schaff, *Creeds of Christendom*, 3:332). "Qua ratione in Coena Domini admoneris et confirmaris, te unici illius sacrificii Christi in cruce oblati, atque omnium eius bonorum participem esse? Quod Christus me atque omnes fideles de hoc fracto pane edere, et de poculo distributo bibere iussit, in sui memoriam, addita hac promissione: Primum corpus suum non minus certe pro me in cruce oblatum ac fractum, et sanguinem suum pro me fusum esse: quam oculis cerno, panem Domini mihi frangi, et poculum mihi communicari. Deinde animam meam non minus certo ipsius corpore, quod pro nobis crucifixum, et sanguine qui pro nobis fusus est, ad vitam aeternam ab ipso pasci: quam panem et vinum, Symbola corporis et sanguinis Domini, e manu ministri accepta, ore corporis percipio" (Niemeyer, *Collectio Confessionum*, 446).

2. Ursinus, *Commentary*, 377.

3. εὐχαριστήσας. See Olevianus, *De substantia*, 2.69, for his discussion of the Eucharist as a thanksgiving.

rament instituted by our Lord Jesus. Whereas baptism is the sacrament of initiation, the Supper is the sacrament of renewal. Baptism is intended to be applied once. The Supper is intended to be received frequently.[4]

In the ninth century, Paschasius Radbertus (ca. 790–ca. 860), a Benedictine monk, wrote perhaps the first monograph on the Lord's Supper, *On The Body and Blood of the Lord*,[5] where he first proposes that the substance of the bread and the wine miraculously become the true (i.e., literal) body and blood of Christ. This claim engendered a heated debate. Ratramnus (d. ca. 868) replied, in a work of the same title, by arguing that the bread and wine are only figuratively the body and blood, but the true (i.e., literal) body and blood of Christ are seated at the right hand of the Father and that believers are fed by them by the operation of the Spirit by faith.[6]

Radbertus does not use the term *transubstantiation* but was the first to make this argument. In this way, the ninth century was a turning point in the history and doctrine of the Western church. Nevertheless, the doctrine of transubstantiation did not become dogma in the West until the thirteenth century.[7] When the Protestants rejected the Roman sacramental system, including the doctrine of transubstantiation, they were not rejecting ancient Christian doctrine but a relative novelty. The great problem with Radbertus's understanding of the Lord's Supper was, according to Ratramnus, that he conflated the thing signified (*res significata*) with its sign and seal (sacrament). In this way, though attempting to strengthen our understanding of the sacrament, Radbertus unintentionally destroyed the sacrament logically. If the sign becomes the thing, then it is no longer a sign, and it is of the essence of a sacrament to be a sign and not the thing signified. Radbertus also criticizes Ratramnus's abuse of the distinction

4. Thus Reformed scholastic theologian Petrus van Mastricht (1630–1706) distinguished between baptism as the "sacramentum regenerationis" and the Supper as the "sacramentum nutritionis." See *Theoretico-practico Theologia*, 2:828–45; Clark, "Evangelical Fall," 141, 146n23; Ursinus, *Commentary*, 380–81.

5. *De corpore et sanguine Domini* (831–833; rev. 844). For an English translation, see McCracken, *Early Medieval Theology*, 94–108.

6. See the English translation in McCracken, *Early Medieval Theology*, 118–47.

7. At the Fourth Lateran Council (1215; see Denzinger, *Enchiridion Symbolorum*, §430). The CCC (§1376), however, appeals to Trent, session 13 (1551; see Denzinger, *Enchiridion Symbolorum*, §877). See the discussion under *HC* 68; Ursinus, *Commentary*, 406–8.

between substance and accidents. Radbertus wanted us to think that the substance of the Supper was transformed into something else, namely, the substance of the body and blood of Christ. He also wanted us to think that this was so even though the appearance of the bread and wine remained (the accidents).

This was in effect a docetic argument. It said that our sense experience of the bread and wine was a lie, that the elements only *seemed* to remain, after consecration, bread and wine. Here we also see the enchantment of the physical world. Christian theology was turning toward magic in place of providence and in place of true mystery, since the biblical and Reformed doctrine of the Lord's Supper is thoroughly mysterious. The ordinary, the secular (as distinct from the sacred), was deemed unclean and insufficient for divine purposes. This trend only intensified through the thirteenth century, and only the Reformation stopped and reversed it. The Reformed argued that creation was intrinsically good, if corrupted by the fall, that grace does not *perfect* nature as such (*contra* Rome) but rather *restores* fallen human nature in regeneration, justification, sanctification, and glorification.[8] The secular, they argued (following Luther), is not intrinsically evil or inferior. Instead, again following Luther, they taught a doctrine of vocation and the priesthood of every believer. It is not just monks and priests who have a vocation (a calling) in this world. Every Christian has a vocation from God to love God and neighbor to rest on Christ's good works for us and imputed to us, through faith alone (*sola fide*), by grace alone (*sola gratia*), and to give our good works to our neighbor (who needs them) for God's glory alone (*soli Deo gloria*). The Reformation rescued the categories of common and natural, and the doctrine of the goodness of creation.

We have no promise in Scripture that the bread and wine become anything more than bread and wine. There is no clear teaching in the church, prior to the ninth century, that in Communion the bread and wine become anything other than bread and wine. Even then, Ratramnus hotly and effectively contested Radbertus's revolutionary doctrine. We certainly find no biblical teaching or even any ancient Christian teaching to support the idea that ministers are priests and what they offer is the

8. See the discussion under *HC* 6.

memorial, propitiatory sacrifice of our Lord's body and blood (Trent). We rightly reject this as a blasphemous assault on the finished work of Christ and a desecration of the Holy Supper.[9]

In the Reformation, the magisterial Protestants developed four distinct views on the Lord's Supper: the Lutheran, the Zwinglian, the post-Zwinglian, and the Calvinist. Luther summarizes the Lutheran position in the *Large Catechism* (1528).[10] "The Sacrament of the Altar" is "the true body and blood of the Lord Christ, in and under the bread and wine, which Christians are commanded to eat and drink." It is bread and wine "set within God's Word and bound to it."[11] In 1577, in the *Formula of Concord* (art. 7), the Lutherans elaborated on Luther's words by adding that, in the Supper, "the true body and blood of our Lord Jesus Christ" is "truly and essentially present, distributed with the bread and wine, and received by mouth by all those who avail themselves of the sacrament—whether they are worthy or unworthy, godly or ungodly, believers or unbelievers—to bring believers comfort and life and to bring judgment upon unbelievers."[12] Underlying Lutheran doctrine of the Supper, of course, is the Lutheran understanding of the communication of properties (*communicatio idiomatum*), that what is true of Christ's divine nature may also be said to be true of his humanity. Thus, when Christians confess that Christ, in his humanity, is at the right hand of the Father, it means that his humanity is everywhere, since the right hand is everywhere.[13]

In his 1530 *Fidei Ratio*, submitted to the emperor at the Diet of Augsburg (1530), Huldrych Zwingli (1484–1531) confesses that, in contrast to Rome, "the true body of Christ is present" in the Supper "by the contemplation of faith."[14] All that Christ has done for believers is "present by the contemplation of faith."[15] Against Rome he confesses that to say "the body of Christ in essence, i.e., the natural body itself … is either present in the

9. See the discussion under *HC* 80.

10. Kolb and Wengert, *Book of Concord*, 467.1–476.87.

11. Kolb and Wengert, *Book of Concord*, 467.8–9.

12. Kolb and Wengert, *Book of Concord*, 504.2. This language is phrased as a question in the formula.

13. Kolb and Wengert, *Book of Concord*, 505.10–14. For background, see Clark, *Caspar Olevian*, 104–36.

14. Dennison, *Reformed Confessions*, 1:126.

15. Dennison, *Reformed Confessions*, 1:126.

supper or masticated with our mouth and teeth, as the Papists or some who look back to the fleshpots of Egypt [Lutherans] assert, we deny."[16] He categorically denies that the body can be fed by a spiritual substance, and the soul cannot be fed by a corporeal substance.[17] *The Tetrapolitan Confession* (1530), also submitted to the diet, however, was more conservative concerning the language used by the Lutherans. In chapter 9, it confessed that in the Supper "the faithful are being fed with his body and blood unto eternal life."[18]

In the *First Helvetic Confession* (1536), produced by Heinrich Bullinger (1504–1575), Samuel Grynaeus (1539–1599), and others, speak of the "mystical supper," wherein "the Lord offers His body and His blood, that is, his own self truly to his own."[19] It denies that the body and blood of Christ are "joined naturally to the bread and wine" or "included locally in them, or placed in them by any carnal presence." It confesses that the "true sharing of His body is exhibited ... in the nourishment of eternal life."[20]

In the 1541 *Genevan Catechism*, Calvin teaches that the Supper signifies that our Lord "instituted it to assure us that by the communication of his body and blood, our souls are nourished, in the hope of eternal life."[21] Just as bread nourishes our bodies, his body and blood act "toward our souls" by refreshing them spiritually.[22] Christ gave himself for us on the cross, but the believer "must receive him, in order that we may feel in

16. Dennison, *Reformed Confessions*, 1:126.

17. Dennison, *Reformed Confessions*, 1:129. Zwingli's doctrine of the Supper is contested. The Lutherans denounced him and his followers as "crude sacramentarians" (Kolb and Wengert, *Book of Concord*, 504.3), i.e., they understood the Supper as our oath (*sacramentum*) to God rather than as his gospel to us. W. P. Stephens disputes this view in *Theology of Huldrych Zwingli*, 218–59. See, e.g., Zwingli, "On the Lord's Supper," 185–238; Zwingli, *Exposition of the Faith*, 254–62.

18. Dennison, *Reformed Confessions*, 1:160.

19. Dennison, *Reformed Confessions*, 1:349.

20. Dennison, *Reformed Confessions*, 1:349. The *Consensus Tigurinus* (1549) marked an advance on the *First Helvetic Confession* but was probably a concession for Calvin, since the language to which he agreed is not as high as the language he had used in the 1540 *Short Treatise* or in the Genevan Catechism of 1541. See Dennison, *Reformed Confessions*, 1:537–45; Davis, *This Is My Body*. The *Second Helvetic Confession* (1566), art. 21, approximates Calvin's view. The reader can track Calvin's development on the Supper by comparing his *Short Treatise* (1540) with the 1559 *Institutes* (e.g., 4.17.32–34), and the 1561 *Clear Explanation of Sound Doctrine Concerning the True Partaking of the Flesh and Blood of Christ in the Holy Supper*. The *Short Treatise* and *Clear Explanation* are found in Reid, *Calvin: Theological Treatises*. See Beza, *Clear and Simple Treatise*.

21. Torrance, *School of Faith*, 59, Q. 340.

22. Torrance, *School of Faith*, 60, Q. 341.

ourselves the fruit and the efficacy of His death and passion."[23] It is true that we are united to Christ by the Spirit through faith, but the Supper ratifies Christ's union and communion with us.[24] The Supper is not only a memorial; the things signified are truly given to believers in it. "Thus in accordance with what he promises and represents in the Sacrament, I do not doubt that he makes us partakers of his very substance, in order to unite us with himself in one life."[25] How this happens is an incomprehensible mystery worked by the Holy Spirit himself.[26]

The language Calvin uses is familiar to students of the (1561) *BC* (35).[27] There the Reformed church confesses that Christ ordained the Supper "to nourish and support" those to whom the Spirit has already given new life and whom he has united to the church. As we have seen, there is a twofold life, bodily and spiritual.[28] Christ, "the bread that descended from heaven," nourishes believers when they "apply and receive him by faith, in the Spirit."[29] The bread and wine of Communion signify (*figurer*) the spiritual food and drink.[30] They are a sacrament of his body and blood, which we receive, through faith (the hand and mouth of the soul), "as certainly as we receive and hold this sacrament in our hands."[31] *How* he feeds our souls on his body and blood, by the Holy Spirit, is a mystery "surpassing our understanding."[32] It is "by the Spirit through faith." Lest there be any ambiguity about *what* believers eat and drink in the Supper, the *BC* is quite pointed: it is nothing less than "proper and natural body and the proper blood of Christ."[33] We affirm that the sacraments are "connected with the thing signified," but, against the Lutherans, we deny that

---

23. Torrance, *School of Faith*, 60, Q. 343.

24. Torrance, *School of Faith*, 60–61, QQ. 344–46.

25. Torrance, *School of Faith*, 62, Q. 353.

26. Torrance, *School of Faith*, 62, Q. 355.

27. Schaff, *Creeds of Christendom*, 3:428–31.

28. Schaff, *Creeds of Christendom*, 3:428–29.

29. Schaff, *Creeds of Christendom*, 3:429.

30. Schaff, *Creeds of Christendom*, 3:429.

31. Schaff, *Creeds of Christendom*, 3:429. The clauses "as certainly as I see with my eyes" and "as certainly as I receive from the hand of the minister and taste with my mouth" seem to echo *BC* 35.

32. Schaff, *Creeds of Christendom*, 3:429–30.

33. "Son propre et naturel corps de Christ, et son propre sang est bu" (Schaff, *Creeds of Christendom*, 3:430); "proprium et naturale corpus Christi idique quod bibitur proprium eius sanguinem" (Müller, *Die Bekenntnisschriften*, 247.32–33).

"both are received by all men."[34] Unbelievers receive the sacrament and condemnation, but they do not receive Christ.[35]

It is against this background that we must interpret the catechism's language about Holy Communion. With the broader Christian tradition, we affirm a symbolic aspect and a memorial aspect (Luke 22:19) to the Supper, but the catechism tells us that more is happening. In the *HC*, as in the *BC*, the Reformed churches confess that Communion is also a supper, a meal. There is a mysterious operation occurring in believers by the Spirit in Communion. Thus, we agree with the Lutherans and the Roman Catholics *that* we are being fed by Christ, but we disagree about *how* it happens.

Rome errs by turning the Supper into a propitiatory memorial sacrifice.[36] It is not that, but it *is* a memorial of the once-for-all sacrifice that Christ made for us. When our Lord said, "It is finished" (John 19:30), that was not a signal to begin offering memorial sacrifices. One of the great points of the book of Hebrews, written to Jewish Christians who were tempted to go back to the old covenant system of sacrifices and ceremonies, is that they all pointed to Christ and his "once for all" sacrifice (Heb 9:12; 10:1; cf. Rom 6:10). Against the Lutherans, we deny that Christ's true humanity is ubiquitous.[37] We deny that his humanity is in, with, and under the elements.[38]

Christians need a robust sense of the Supper as a means of grace. Unfortunately, in reaction to Rome, many American Christians have lost something of the mystery of the Supper. They think of it solely in

34. Schaff, *Creeds of Christendom*, 3:430.

35. Schaff, *Creeds of Christendom*, 3:430.

36. See the discussion under *HC* 80.

37. Olevianus denounces the Lutherans as "half-evangelicals, who want to serve both idols and the gospel, both the Devil and God, at the same time" (*Firm Foundation*, 17). He traduces the doctrine of the ubiquity of Christ's humanity as "Satan's fabrication that the body of Christ is ubiquitous in heaven and on earth, and his claim that the cause and origin of this ubiquity is the personal union of the divinity and humanity of Christ, which occurred in the body of the virgin" (*Firm Foundation*, 61). See Clark, *Caspar Olevian*, 107–10.

38. Thus the Lutherans characterize the Reformed as "cunning sacramentarians, the most dangerous kind" since we, they allege, "appear to use our language" and "pretend that they also believe in a true presences of the true, essential, living body and blood of Christ in the Holy Supper, but that this takes place spiritually, through faith" (Kolb and Wengert, *Book of Concord*, 504.5). They do not accept our understanding that it is through the mysterious operation of the *Holy Spirit* that we are fed on Christ's true body and blood.

funereal terms. They see it principally as an opportunity to grieve over their sins and as a time for repentance. To be sure, a preparatory service is most useful, but the funereal aspect of the Supper seems to be the principle reason why many Christians instinctively oppose more frequent Communion.[39] The objection that a more frequent observation of the Supper will decrease its significance rests on the assumption that Communion is principally a funeral rather than a meal and a means of grace.[40] What makes the Supper significant is not sentiment but Christ's presence. This much is clear enough from Ursinus's lecture on this question, where he writes:

> This sacrament, therefore, consists in the rite and the promise annexed to it, or in the signs and things signified. The rite, or signs are the bread which is broken and eaten, and the wine which is poured out, and drunk. The things signified are the broken body, and shed blood of Christ, which are eaten and drunk, or our union with Christ by faith, by which we are made partakers of Christ and all his benefits, so that we derive from him everlasting life, as the branches draw their life from the vine.[41]

According to Ursinus, the Supper is intended to strengthen our faith by confirming it as a "most sure proof of our union, and communion with Christ, who feeds us with his body and blood unto everlasting life." We

39. The United Reformed Churches in North America have forms that account both for less frequent Communion and for weekly Communion (United Reformed Churches in North America, *Liturgical Forms and Prayers*, 37–55). Calvin wished to administer the Supper weekly in Geneva but was prohibited by the city council (*petit conseil*). Calvin confessed that he was "truly pleased with a monthly celebration of the supper" ("Iam vero singulis mensibus coenam celebrari maximo nobis placeret"), but he added, "Nevertheless I undertook to have recorded in the public acts that our custom is corrupt, in order that correction might be easier and more free for future generations" ("Curavi tamen referri in acta publica vitiosum esse morem nostrum, ut posteris facilior esset ac liberior correctio"); Bretschneider, *Corpus Reformatorum*, 38:213; Calvin, *Calvin's Ecclesiastical Advice*, 96. See *Institutes* 4.17.46, where Calvin argues explicitly for the weekly administration of the Supper: "Longe aliter factum oportuit: singulis ad minimum hebdomadibus proponenda erat Christianorum coetui mensa Domini" (Barth, *Joannis Calvini Opera Selecta*, 5:412.18–19; see Clark, "Evangelical Fall," 133–47). Some of the material in this note was taken from Clark, *Recovering the Reformed Confession*, 283n206.

40. This section is taken from Clark, "Evangelical Fall," 133–47.

41. Ursinus, *Commentary*, 378.

are to receive "these signs from the hands of the minister ... as if the Lord himself gave them unto us with his own hand."[42]

Unlike some traditions, the Reformed do not practice private Communion, which for Ursinus is a contradiction in terms.[43] Ursinus seems to envision frequent Communion when he writes, "It is also necessary for us frequently to have our faith confirmed in regard to the perpetuity of the covenant."[44]

So, it is necessary for the Christian life that believers be fed by the crucified body and shed blood of our Lord Jesus. This reality may shock some, but our Lord Jesus shocked his hearers when he said: "Truly, truly, I say to you, unless you eat the flesh of the Son of Man and drink his blood, you have no life in you. Whoever feeds on my flesh and drinks my blood has eternal life, and I will raise him up on the last day. For my flesh is true food, and my blood is true drink. Whoever feeds on my flesh and drinks my blood abides in me, and I in him" (John 6:53–56 ESV). There are two edges to these words. To refuse to eat his flesh is death. To eat his flesh and to drink his blood is true food and drink, true communion, and eternal life. Radbertus and Rome attempted to turn the sacrament into the thing signified (Christ), thus destroying the sacrament. Many American evangelicals have reduced Christ's feast to a funeral. The Reformed churches, however, receive the Supper as sign and seal of the gospel and of the covenant of grace, as a true fellowship with the risen Christ, as a true, mysterious, and wonderful feast. It is not that we have climbed into heaven but that Christ has come down out of heaven, as it were, and taken us to himself. It is he who feeds us and not we ourselves. As surely as we eat bread and wine, as surely as we receive them from the hand of the minister, so sure is Christ's promise that we believers belong to him and he to us.

42. Ursinus, *Commentary*, 379.

43. "A private supper is no communion" (Ursinus, *Commentary*, 379).

44. Ursinus, *Commentary*, 381.

QUESTION 76

What does it mean to eat the crucified body and drink the shed blood of Christ?

It means not only to embrace with a believing heart all the sufferings and death of Christ, and thereby to obtain the forgiveness of sins and life eternal; but moreover also, to be so united more and more to his sacred body by the Holy Spirit, who dwells both in Christ and in us, that, although He is in heaven and we on earth, we are nevertheless flesh of his flesh and bone of His bone, and live and are governed forever by one Spirit, as members of the same body are by one soul.[45]

One of the great tragedies of the debates about the nature of the sacraments is that they force us to look at the sacraments instead of looking at the one they signify and communicate to believers, Christ, and what they promise, the gospel. As a means of grace, the Supper is a real, mysterious communion, by the operation of the Holy Spirit, in the true body and blood of Christ. This is a glorious truth, but in their nature the sacraments are meant to strengthen our union and communion with Christ. This is not the counsel of Pietism and its quest for illegitimate religious experience.[46] To look at Christ is not to marginalize the sacraments. The sacraments want us to look to Christ.

What is it to eat Christ's true crucified body? It is to believe. The catechism is restating Augustine's famous saying, "Do not get thy mouth ready,

45. "Was heisst den gekreuzigten Leib Christi essen und sein vergossenes Blut triuken? Es heisst nicht allein mit gläubigem Herzen das ganze Leiden und Sterben Christi annehmen, und dadurch Verge bung der Sünden und ewiges Leben bekommen, sondern auch daneben durch den Heiligen Geist, der zugleich in Christo und in uns wohnet, also mit seinem gebenedeiten Leibe je mehr und mehr vereiniget werden, dass wir, obgleich Er im Himmel, und wir auf Erden sind, dennoch Fleisch von seinem Fleisch und Bein von seinen Beinen sind, und von Einem Geiste (wie die Glieder unsers Leibes von Einer Seele) ewig leben und regieret werden" (Schaff, *Creeds of Christendom*, 3:332–33). "Quid est crucifixum corpus Christi edere, et fusum eius sanguinem bibere? Est non tantum totam passionem et mortem Christi certa animi fiducia amplecti, ac per id remissionem peccatorum et vitam aeternam adipisci: sed etiam per Spiritum sanctum, qui simul in Christo et in nobis habitat, ita sacrosancto eius corpori magis ac magis uniri, ut quamvis ipse in coelo, nos vero in terra simus, nihilominus tamen caro simus de carne eius et os de ossibus eius: utque omnia corporis membra ab una anima, sic nos uno eodemque Spiritu vivificemur et gubernemur" (Niemeyer, *Collectio Confessionum*, 447).

46. Clark, *Recovering the Reformed Confession*, 39–116.

but thine heart."[47] In 1520, Luther paraphrased this saying famously and influentially in *The Babylonian Captivity of the Church*: "Why make ready teeth and stomach? Believe and you have already eaten."[48] All believers eat Christ by faith, but, *pace* the Lutherans, not all who receive Communion receive Christ. The material cause of the Reformation was *sola fide*. Faith is the *sole* instrument by which we receive Christ, through which we are united to Christ. It is through faith alone that we embrace Christ and his benefits (justification and sanctification). The Spirit operates powerfully through the gospel preached to create new life and true faith.[49] He operates powerfully, mysteriously through the Holy Supper to strengthen that union and communion.

We confess that it is the person of the Holy Spirit who unites us to Christ, who is in heaven. In other words, it is not necessary that the substance of bread be transformed (transubstantiation). It is not necessary that Christ be locally present in, with, and under the elements of the Supper. By virtue of our union with him, through the Holy Spirit, we are with him and he with us. We have the most intimate and wonderful union and communion, and it is progressive, like a marriage (Eph 5:25, 30, 32). A husband and wife gradually become more and more united. So it is with Christ and his bride, the church. We are "flesh of his flesh and bone of his bone." We live by the Spirit. We walk by the Spirit. We are governed by the Holy Spirit operating through the word.

This is sanctification, conformity to Christ, and the Spirit is gradually conforming us to Christ through union and communion with Christ. To be sanctified is to be governed by the Spirit (as distinct from the sinful nature). Our union is so close that it is as if we all are members of the same body, governed by one soul. In other words, we are being sanctified together, not in isolation from each other.

One of the great temptations of in the history of the church has been to withdraw from other Christians in pursuit of sanctity. This was the first stage of Christian monasticism, which failed. It was not long before *eremitic*

---

47. Augustine, *Sermon* 112 (*NPNF* 1/6:448; PL 38:645).

48. *LW* 36:19. Ursinus: our eating "non est corporalis, sed spiritualis" (*Corpus doctrinae*, 397).

49. See the discussion under *HC* 65.

monasticism became *cenobitic* monasticism.[50] The error has been to think that if we can just get away from the sins and corruption of others, we can attain greater sanctity. History tells us that the project has failed, because wherever we go we take our sinful nature and corruption with us. This is one of the gospel mysteries of sanctification, that the Spirit operates in the visible church through the preached gospel to bring us to new life and true faith, and in the work of the Spirit through the gospel made visible in the Supper to sanctify us.[51]

Holy Communion draws believers *together*, in covenant community, because in the Supper we are lifted up, as Calvin explains, to the heavenly table, where as one body we are fed together on Christ's true body and blood by the Spirit, through faith. We leave the Communion table in our shared union with Christ and in our renewed communion with one another.

Ursinus explains that our eating embraces four things: (1) faith in the obedient suffering and death of Christ; (2) the forgiveness of sins (the negative aspect of justification) and "the gift of eternal life through faith (the positive aspect of justification);" (3) our union with Christ, through the Holy Spirit; and (4) "the benefit of vivification through the Spirit."[52]

> Hence to eat the crucified body and to drink the shed blood of Christ is to believe that God receives us into his favor for the sake of Christ's merits, that we obtain the remission of our sins, and reconciliation with God by the same faith, and that the Son of God, who having assumed our nature united it personally with himself, dwells in us, and joins us to himself, and the nature which he assumed, by granting unto us his Spirit, through whom he regenerates us, and restores in us light, righteousness, and eternal life such as belongs to the nature which he took upon himself.[53]

---

50. *Eremitic*, from the Greek ἐρημίτης, "of the desert," and *cenobitic*, from the Greek κοινόβιος, "to live in community."

51. Olevianus, *De substantia*, 2.71.

52. "Beneficium vivificationis per eundem Spiritum"(Ursinus, *Corpus doctrinae*, 397).

53. Ursinus, *Commentary*, 382.

In short, those who in the Supper eat the "crucified body and drink the shed blood of Christ" are those who believe, and they receive, through faith, all that God promises to those who believe in Jesus.

QUESTION 77

Where has Christ promised, that He will thus feed and nourish believers with his body and blood, as certainly as they eat of this broken bread and drink of this cup?

In the institution of the Supper, which says: "The Lord Jesus the same night in which He was betrayed took bread: and when He had given thanks, He broke it, and said, 'Take eat: this is my body, which is broken for you: this do in remembrance of me.' After the same manner also he took the cup, when he had eaten, saying, 'This cup is the new covenant in my blood: this do, as often as you drink it, in remembrance of me. For as often as you eat this bread and drink this cup, you show the Lord's death until he comes.'" And this promise is also repeated by St. Paul, where he says: "The cup of blessing which we bless, is it not the communion of the blood of Christ? The bread which we break, is it not the communion of the body of Christ? For we being many are one bread, and one body: for we are all partakers of that one bread."[54]

54. "Wo hat Christus verheissen, dass Er die Gläubigen so gewiss mit seinem Leib und Blut speise und tränke, als sie von diesem gebrochenen Brot essen, und von diesem Kelch trinken? In der Einsetzung des heiligen Abendmahls, welche also lautet: Unser Herr Jesus, in der Nacht, da Er verrathen ward, nahm Er das Brot, dankete, und brach's, und sprach: 'Nehmet, esset, das ist mein Leib, der für euch gebrochen wird; solches thut zu meinem Gedächtniss.' Desselben gleichen auch den Kelch, nach dem Abendmahl, und sprach: 'Dieser Kelch ist das Neue Testament in meinem Blut; solches thut, so oft ihr's trinket, zu meinem Gedächtniss.' Denn so oft ihr von diesem Brot esset, und von diesem Kelch trinket, sollt ihr des Herrn Tod verkündigen, bis dass Er kommt. Und diese Verheissung wird auch wiederholet durch St. Paulum, da er spricht: Der Kelch der Danksagung, damit wir danksagen, ist er nicht die Gemeinschaft des Bluts Christi? Das Brot, das wir brechen, ist das nicht die Gemeinschaft des Leibes Christi? Denn Ein Brot ist's, so sind wir viele Ein Leib, dieweil wir alle Eines Brots theilhaftig sind?" (Schaff, *Creeds of Christendom*, 3:333–34). "Quo loco promisit Christus, se credentibus tam certo corpus et sanguinem suum sic edendum et bibendum daturum, quam fractum hunc panem edunt, et peculum hoc bibunt? In Institutione Coenae, cuius haec sunt verba: Dominus noster Iesus Christus, ea nocte qua proditus est, accepit panem: et gratiis actis, fregit ac dixit: accipite, (comedite,) hoc est corpus meum, quod pro vobis frangitur: hoc facite in mei recordationem. Itidem et poculum, postquam coenassaent, dicens hoc poculum est novum foedus

Like baptism, the Lord's Supper is an institution of our Lord Jesus Christ (1 Cor 11:23–25).[55] This is in distinction from the five ecclesiastical sacraments, which developed through the medieval period and which were not formally ratified until the thirteenth century.[56]

Thus Scripture norms our theology, piety, and practice of the Lord's Supper. We confess what we do about the promises and realities of the Supper because they are biblical. In Holy Scripture (Matt 26:26–29; Mark 14:22–25; Luke 22:14–23; 1 Cor 11:17–34), the Holy Spirit has preserved for us our Lord's institution of the Holy Supper. We know nothing of a secret, unwritten apostolic tradition because it does not exist. When the early Christian fathers appealed to apostolic tradition, they referred to public teaching and practices handed down in Scripture.[57] That talk of tradition was gradually transformed into an allegedly secret, unwritten tradition.

Today the Roman Catholic Church asks all its adherents to place implicit faith (*fides implicita*) in the Roman Catholic Church, in her officers, in her councils, and in her alleged apostolic traditions.[58] No human is omniscient, and therefore implicit faith is unavoidable, but the question is what the object of implicit faith is. The Reformed church places it in Holy Scripture. Rome asks us to trust *her* implicitly. That certainly is not how the earliest fathers regarded the church. They put their implicit faith

---

per meum sanguinem: Hoc facite, quotiescunque biberitis, in mei recordationem. Quotiescumque enim ederitis panem hunc, et poculum hoc biberitis, mortem Domini annunciate, donec venerit. haec promissio a Paulo repetitur, cum inquit: Poculum gratiarum actionis, pro gratias agimus, nonne communio est sanguinis Christi? Panis, quem frangimus, nonne communio est corporis Christi? Panis, quoniam unus panis, unum corpus multi sumus: Nam omnes unius panis participes sumus" (Niemeyer, *Collectio Confessionum*, 447).

55. Ursinus, *Commentary*, 384.

56. See the discussion under *HC* 68.

57. E.g., the use of ἀποστόλων παράδοσις in *Ad Diognetum* 11.6 (ca. AD 150) in Holmes, *Apostolic Fathers*, 714–15, where the author lists the Law, the Prophets, the Gospels, and then refers to the "tradition of the apostles," which refers to Acts and the New Testament Epistles.

58. Lombard discusses the question of how much the OT believers understood before the incarnation and how much those with disabilities ("the simple") may be expected to know (*Sentences*, book 3, dist. 25). Thomas affirms, "Man is not bound to believe them explicitly, but only implicitly, or to be ready to believe them, in so far as he is prepared to believe whatever is contained in the Divine Scriptures. Then alone is he bound to believe such things explicitly, when it is clear to him that they are contained in the doctrine of faith" (*ST* 2a2ae.2.5, resp. dic.). The International Theological Commission of the Roman Catholic Church, in March 2020, declared, "Implicit faith in itself includes the fundamental predisposition to identify with the faith of the Church and to unite oneself to it." It is to this conception of implicit faith that the Reformed have always objected. See International Theological Commission, "Reciprocity between Faith," §53.

in Scripture. They, as we, understood that the Scripture forms the church. The Scripture is the canon of the church and not the other way around. Thus, we ought to implicitly trust Scripture as God's holy, inerrant word. Popes and councils err, but Holy Scripture does not.[59]

Thus, when we are determining what we ought to believe about the promises of the gospel contained in, represented by, and sealed by the Holy Supper, we go principally to God's inerrant, infallible word. How do we know that Christ has made such wonderful promises to believers in the Supper? We know it from Holy Scripture. The same Holy Spirit who operates through the Supper to strengthen our union and communion with Christ also gave us the Gospel and Epistle records of its institution. That same Spirit operates through the Supper to renew our assurance and to draw us back to Christ and to his promises (and away from ourselves, our doubts, and our fears). The Holy Spirit testifies to and through Scripture that it is true. There is further confirmation in history. The tomb is empty, and Christ is raised. Of those realities we have hundreds of reliable witnesses (Matt 28:1–10; Luke 24:22; 1 Cor 15:6). It is all true, and it is true for us in particular who believe. Just as certainly as we eat and drink, so certainly are the gospel promises for us.

Scripture says "the same night in which he was betrayed" to remind us that it was the last night of Passover, thereby pointedly signaling the end of the types and shadows.[60] Christ was intentionally substituting a new sacramental system in place of Passover and the other feasts (Col 2:17; Heb 8:5; 10:1). Ursinus notes that the bread that Christ took was set apart from common bread.[61] That he took bread and not his body teaches us something about the nature of the sacrament (*pace* the Lutherans): "Therefore, he did not take his body; neither did he take his body with bread, nor in bread, nor under bread but sacramentally. For his body was

59. Luther, "On The Councils and the Church" (1539), in *LW* 41:9–178.

60. Ursinus, *Commentary*, 384.

61. "Interim panis coenae usu differt a pane communi" (Ursinus, *Corpus doctrinae*, 400). See Ursinus, *Commentary*, 384. He also notes, "The use of unleavened bread at the institution was accidental" (*per accidens*; *Corpus doctrinae*, 400), i.e., nonessential. We are not to infer from its use in the institution "that there is any necessity for the use of such bread in the celebration of the Supper" (Ursinus, *Commentary*, 384).

not lying upon the table but it was sitting at the table."[62] The act of blessing and giving thanks is one thing. Christ did not bless and give thanks to give warrant to the "mystery of the magical consecration of the Papists."[63]

There are four liturgical actions relative to the cup: the taking (λαβὼν), the blessing (εὐχαριστήσας), the giving (ἔδωκεν), and the drinking (πίετε). Each of these is deliberate. When Scripture says that Christ broke the bread, it means, as Paul says (1 Cor 10:16), "the bread which we break."[64] The breaking and distributing of the bread signifies the one body and the many members. It further signifies his suffering, and therefore we should retain it.[65] The fraction of the bread (*fratio panis*) is for our comfort, and Scripture expressly teaches it (Luke 22:19; 1 Cor 11:24). Therefore, Ursinus argues, "It is not an indifferent ceremony but because of this mystical significance it is necessary and to be retained," (1) "on account of the example of Christ, who broke the bread"; (2) because he commanded it; (3) because of the example of the apostolic church, which broke the bread; (4) for our consolation, "that we might know that the body of the Lord was as certainly crucified for us as certainly as we see the bread broken for us"; and (5) "That the opinion of transubstantiation might be removed from our souls or that bits of Christ lie in the bread."[66]

---

62. "Non igitur acceptit suum corpus: non accepit corpus cum pane, vel in pane, vel sub pane, nisi sacramentaliter. Nam corpus eius non iacebat in mensa, sed accumbebat mensae" (Ursinus, *Corpus doctrinae*, 400); see Ursinus, *Commentary*, 384.

63. "Mysterium magicae consecreationis pontificae" (Ursinus, *Corpus doctrinae*, 400); see Ursinus, *Commentary*, 384.

64. Ursinus, *Commentary*, 385.

65. Ursinus, *Commentary*, 385.

66. Olevianus teaches the same in *Brevis Admonitio De Re Eucharistica*, 22, and in *De substantia*, 2.91. See Clark, *Caspar Olevian*, 206; Ursinus, *Corpus doctrinae*, 401. "On account of the example of Christ, who broke the bread" translates "propter Christi exemplum, qui panem fregit" (Ursinus, *Corpus doctrinae*, 401). "That we might know that the body of the Lord was as certainly crucified for us as certainly as we see the bread broken for us" translates "ut sciamus, corpus domini tam certo pro nobis crucifixum esse, quam certo videmus panem nobis frangi" (Ursinus, *Corpus doctrinae*, 401). "That the opinion of transubstantiation might be removed from our souls or that bits of Christ lie in the bread" translates "ut eximatur ex animis opinio transubstantionis, vel latentiae corpusculi alicuius in pane" (*Corpus doctrinae*, 401). The Willard translation (Ursinus, *Commentary*, 385) paraphrases this sentence with the term "consubstantiation," but Ursinus does not use that term in his explanation here, though he uses it elsewhere. The heading in the 1634 and 1612 editions uses the term (see Ursinus, *Corpus doctrinae*, 425). Two editions, one published in 1616 in Geneva, and the second in 1651 in Hanover, make it clear that the section, under *HC* 78 on Transubstantiation and Consubstantiation, was actually written by David Pareus. See Pareus, *Corpus Doctrinae* (1616), 494 (marginal note); Pareus, *Corpus Doctrinae* (1651), 437.

The command to "take, eat" is addressed to all believers, from which Ursinus infers, first, that "the Popish mass, in which the Priest gives nothing to be received and eaten by the church, is not the Lord's supper, but a private supper to him that sacrifices, and a mere theatrical (*histrionicum*) performance."[67] Believers are not meant to be spectators but to receive and eat the Supper. The Supper is intended to be corporate and not private.

The much-controverted phrase "This is my body," taken literally, would mean, "the substance of this bread is the substance of my body."[68] To understand the words thus is absurd.[69] Christ was speaking *sacramentally*.[70] The bread *is* his body *sacramentally*. Rome teaches that, at consecration, the bread *becomes* Christ's body. When we say, "This is my body," Ursinus says, "we do not substitute the word signifies, for is, nor do we change the words of Christ, but we retain them as they were uttered by Christ himself."[71] Rather, "This is my body" is a promise added to the sacrament. It teaches us that "the bread in this use *is* the body of Christ, which is exhibited and given to those who partake of it and believe in this promise; or, it is the flesh of Christ which he promised that he would give for the life of the world."[72] This is the eating Christ referred in John 6:53–56. It is by faith, through the mysterious operation of the Spirit, that we apprehend the thing promised and "now present in the sacrament."[73] It is the promise that makes the bread a sacrament. The divine promise to believers is of the essence of the sacrament.[74]

Since most Reformed Communion tables in North America bear the words "Do this in remembrance of me," is it useful to let Ursinus instruct us as to the full sense of those words. They do not consist "merely in meditating upon his history" but include faith, "by which we appropriate to

67. Ursinus, *Commentary*, 385; Ursinus, *Corpus doctrinae*, 401.

68. Ursinus, *Corpus doctrinae*, 402.

69. Ursinus, *Corpus doctrinae*, 402.

70. Ursinus, "sacramentaliter" (*Corpus doctrinae*, 402). Ursinus cites Augustine, *Contra adimantum* 12.3, "Non enim Dominus dubitavit dicere, *Hoc est corpus meum* (Matt XXVI, 26); cum signum daret corporis sui" (PL 42:144). "For it is not doubted that when our Lord said, 'This is my body' he did so with a sign of his body." When the thing signified is attributed to the sign, it is a "sacramental metonymy" (Ursinus, *Commentary*, 386; Ursinus, *Corpus doctrinae*, 403).

71. Ursinus, *Commentary*, 413.

72. Ursinus, *Commentary*, 386. Italics added.

73. Ursinus, *Commentary*, 386.

74. Ursinus, *Commentary*, 386.

ourselves Christ and his merits."[75] "Remembrance of Christ comprehends the remembrance of his benefits, together with faith and the giving of thanks; for Christ by the use of these signs admonishes us of himself and of his benefits, and stirs up and establishes our confidence in him, from which it naturally follows that we also publicly express our gratitude to him."[76] In short, to remember is to trust that all that the Supper offers, Christ and his benefits, is for me and to live accordingly, in union and communion with Christ.

The command that all should drink from the cup (Matt 26:27) is a rebuke to Rome and to all who would deny the cup to the laity.[77] It was the practice of the ancient church and even the early medieval church to commune laity in both elements (bread and wine). With the development of the doctrine of transubstantiation,[78] the grounds were laid to restrict the cup from the laity. Momentum began to build in the twelfth century, but the church did not restrict the cup from the laity finally until the Council of Constance (1415).[79] Thus, the Reformation criticism of the removal of the cup was aimed at a new dogma in the Western church. With the rejection of transubstantiation, and the rejection of authority of the church to revise a dominical institution, the Reformed church restored the cup to the laity in obedience to the clear words and intent of our Lord.

When our Lord called the cup "the new covenant" (καινὴ διαθήκη), he was identifying the substance of the new covenant with the covenant of grace as it existed under the types and shadows of the Old Testament broadly and the old covenant (Moses) more narrowly.[80] Ursinus notes that "new" means "fulfilled." It "consists in our reconciliation with God, and communion with Christ and all his benefits by faith in his sacrifice already offered, without the observance of the ceremonies of the old Passover. The supper is called the new covenant with reference to its signification,

75. Ursinus, *Commentary*, 387.

76. Ursinus, *Commentary*, 387.

77. Ursinus, *Corpus doctrinae*, 403; Ursinus, *Commentary*, 387.

78. See the discussion under *HC* 75.

79. So Schaff, *History of the Christian Church*, 4:569; 5:652; 6:379.

80. Ursinus, *Commentary*, 387–88.

because it is the sign and seal of this covenant, sealing unto us our reconciliation with God, and our union with Christ by faith."[81]

A few brief notes are in order.

1. That Communion is in the blood of Christ points us to his merits *for us* imputed to us, by which we stand righteous before our holy God.[82]

2. Ursinus infers from the phrase "as often as you eat of it" that we should commune frequently (*saepius*).[83] It was Calvin's fervent wish that Communion should be observed weekly in Geneva, but that does not seem to have been the practice in the Palatinate.[84]

3. To show Christ's death until he comes is to believe that he died for you and to profess faith.[85]

4. A Communion of the blood of Christ is a participation in a shared good. By faith alone all believers are united, by the Spirit, to Christ and to one another. Our eating is not corporal, but we are being fed by the true body and blood of Christ.[86]

5. Finally, the matter of intinction has arisen in some quarters of the Presbyterian and Reformed world in recent years. There is no warrant for this practice in Scripture. It is a departure from the Lord's institution and a significant step toward the denial of the cup to the laity. The earliest postapostolic practice was to commune the laity in two kinds. In Matthew 26:27 our Lord says, "Drink" the cup, not "Dip the bread." Like the breaking of the bread, the drinking of the cup is one of the essential liturgical actions in the administration of the Supper.

---

81. Ursinus, *Commentary*, 387–88.

82. Ursinus, *Commentary*, 388.

83. Ursinus, *Corpus doctrinae*, 404.

84. Calvin, *Institutes* 4.14.43. See Clemens, "Foundations of German Reformed Worship," 275–84.

85. Ursinus, *Commentary*, 388.

86. Ursinus, *Commentary*, 388.

Intinction denies or ignores this action. The only dipping that occurred in connection with the Lord's Supper was *before* the Supper, during the Passover, when the bread was dipped in oil. In the institution of the sacrament, however, the bread was not dipped. Though intinction became the practice of the Eastern Church and eventually came to be practiced in the West until the thirteenth century, it has never been the practice of the Reformed churches.[87]

87. Keister, "Intinction," 149–72.

Question 78

Do then the bread and the wine become the real body and blood of Christ?

Question 79

Why then does Christ call the bread his body, and the cup his blood, or the new covenant in his blood, and St. Paul, the communion of the body and the blood of Christ?

Lord's Day 29

QUESTION 78

Do then the bread and the wine become the real body and blood of Christ?

No, but as the water in baptism is not changed into the blood of Christ, nor becomes the washing away of sins itself, being only the divine token and assurance thereof; so also in the Lord's Supper the sacred bread does not become the body of Christ itself, though agreeably to the nature and usage of sacraments it is called the body of Christ.[1]

The Roman Catholic Church teaches that, "by consecration," the elements of the Supper, the bread and the wine, are transformed from bread and wine into the literal body and blood of Christ. The *Catechism of the Catholic Church* (1994) says:

> §1376 The Council of Trent summarizes the Catholic faith by declaring: "Because Christ our Redeemer said that it was truly his body that he was offering under the species of bread, it has always been the conviction of the Church of God, and this holy Council now declares again, that by the consecration of the bread and wine there takes place a change of the whole substance of the

1. "Wird denn aus Brot und Wein der wesentliche Leib und Blut Christi? Nein: sondern wie das Wasser in der Taufe nicht in das Blut Christi verwandelt, oder die Abwaschung der Sünden selbst wird, deren es allein ein göttlich Wahrzeichen und Versicherung ist: also wird auch das heilige Brot im Abendmahl nicht der Leib Christi selbst, wiewohl es, nach Art und Brauch der Sacramente, der Leib Christi genennet wird" (Schaff, *Creeds of Christendom*, 3:334). "Num ergo panis et vinum fiunt ipsum corpus et sanguinis Christi? Nequaquam: verum, ut aquam Baptismi in sanguinem Christi non convertitur, nec est ipsa peccatorum ablutio, sed Symbolum tantum et pignus earum rerum, quae nobis in Baptismo obsignantur: ita nec panis coenae Dominicae, est ipsum corpus Christi: quanquam pro ratione Sacramentorum, et usitata Spiritui Sancto de his loquendi forma, panis Christi corpus appellatur" (Niemeyer, *Collectio Confessionum*, 447–48). There is a source-critical question on *HC* 78. J. I. Good explains, "[Frederick III] left a memorial written in his own hand, in which he expresses approbation of the 78th answer, which was a quotation from the Church Father, Theodoret, and was placed in the catechism so as to show that the sacrament was not merely an allegory or pretense, but that there was a real presence, which, though not a bodily one, was a spiritual one through the Holy Spirit" (*Heidelberg Catechism*, 167). Good notes that *HC* 78 was inserted during the synod that met January 11–17, 1563. It replaced question-and-answer 68 from Ursinus's *catechismus minor*. For the text of that question and answer, see Bierma et al., *Introduction*, 154. Note that the Latin text does not follow the German text by translating *Heilige Brot* into Latin. This move has apparently influenced some modern editions of the catechism, e.g., that published in *Three Forms of Unity*, 94.

> bread into the substance of the body of Christ our Lord and of the whole substance of the wine into the substance of his blood. This change the holy Catholic Church has fittingly and properly called transubstantiation."[2]

The first and most fundamental source cited for this doctrine is declaration of session 13 of the Council of Trent (1551).[3] That council was convened and met intermittently for two decades in order to respond to the Protestant Reformation. It defined the Roman Catholic Church. Until that council concluded, there was still some hope that Rome might repent, that she might embrace the gospel, that the Roman bishop might recognize that he was but one pastor among many. But at Trent, Rome not only embraced the errors of some medieval theologians and councils but codified them and placed the Protestants under an anathema (condemnation) at every key point of disagreement. Despite the fervent wishes of the modern, liberal ecumenical movement, Vatican II (1962–1965) did not revoke those anathemas and, in *Mysterium Fidei* (*The Mystery of the Faith*, 1965) it reaffirmed the Tridentine teaching.[4] The 1994 catechism reaffirmed Tridentine teaching generally and on justification, tradition, and the sacraments.[5] The Roman Catholic Church is a Tridentine communion and not the ancient Christian church.

The key term is *substance*. In the older Christian appropriation (and modification) of Aristotle, the term substance refers to that which makes a thing what it is, that without which it is not (*sine qua non*). Substance is easier to understand if we contrast it with *accidents*. A computer may be silver, black, or white. Its color is accidental to its substance, that is, it does not change what the computer is in its essence. *Accident* here does not refer to an unintentional collision but to a feature that is not essential to it. So, in an electronic device, the color does not make it what it is. Its circuits, chips, and screens make it what it is. They are essential to it. They are of the substance of the device. According to the Roman Catholic doctrine of

---

2. CCC, 347.

3. Denzinger, *Enchiridion Symbolorum*, §877; Schroeder, *Canons and Decrees*, 75.

4. For an example of the case that the condemnations no longer apply, see, e.g., Lehmann, *Justification by Faith*.

5. E.g., CCC §§9, 1989, 75–82, 980. The CCC cites the Council of Trent as an authority 85 times.

the Supper, the substance of the bread is transformed into the substance of the body of Christ, even though the accidents remain unchanged.

Radbertus was the first to postulate this idea, and one of his contemporaries, Ratramnus, criticized it immediately by noting, as the Protestants did in the sixteenth century, that his view (later adopted by the Roman Catholic Church) conflated the sacrament with the thing signified (*res significata*).[6] In so doing, Radbertus unintentionally destroyed the sacrament. Further, Ratramnus objects, Radbertus's view demands that we accept a relation between substance and accidents that is untenable. Implicitly and ironically, Rome's is a docetic view of the sacrament. Rome would have us believe that the elements only *seem* like bread and wine. According to Scripture, our senses are generally reliable. When Scripture says, "Taste and see" (Ps 34:8), or "Look at the birds" (Matt 6:26), it assumes the closest relationship between the accident (e.g., wings and feathers) and the substance of a bird. To use *taste* metaphorically assumes that we know what it is to taste.

Rome, however, asks us to believe that, by the power of consecration, that relationship is broken and though the elements *appear* to be bread and wine, they are not. Ursinus invokes the "analogy of faith" (*analogia fidei*) to help us think through these issues, and it applies here.[7] The expression comes from Romans 12:6, where Paul says, speaking of various gifts in the church, "If prophecy, then according to the analogy of the faith" (ἀναλογίαν τῆς πίστεως). As understood by Calvin, Ursinus, Olevianus, and other classic Reformed writers, it means that whatever one proposes under one head of doctrine must cohere with whatever is said under another head. In this case, the analogy of (the articles of) faith prevents us from affirming, in our doctrine of the Lord's Supper, what our doctrine

6. See the English translations of Radbertus's and Ratramnus's treatises, both titled *On The Body and Blood of the Lord*, in McCracken, *Early Medieval Theology*.

7. Section "III. Genus argumentorum ex analogia articulorum fidei," Ursinus, *Corpus doctrinae*, 413–18; Ursinus, *Commentary*, 396–400. Olevianus also invokes the category of analogy under this heading, although in that case it is "inter testimonium visibile et rem testatam" (*De substantia*, 2.93). Calvin also invokes this category under this heading (*Institutes* 4.17.32). Beza invokes the *analogia fidei* in his critique of transubstantiation and consubstantiation (*Questionum Et Responsionum*, 13; Beza, *Little Book of Questions*, 42–43, Q. 109). The Synod of Dort appealed to the analogy of faith in their conclusion (Schaff, *Creeds of Christendom*, 3:597). See Muller, *Post-Reformation Reformed Dogmatics*, 2:493–96, 501 for a survey of Reformed orthodoxy on this topic.

of Christ rejects, namely that the bread and wine only *appear* to be bread and wine. This is a species of docetism.

That is precisely the same error the gnostics and other dualists asked us to accept. They said that Jesus appeared to be a man, but they knew *a priori* that he could not be true man and true God. His humanity, they argued, was only apparent, hence the label *docetic* (from the Greek verb δοκέω, "to appear or seem"). Scripture does not testify that Jesus only *appeared* to be true man but that he is true man, the Son of Man (e.g., Matt 8:20) who came to seek and save the lost. He is also true God, one person with two natures. The apostle John addresses this heresy directly in 1 John 4:2–3 when he writes, "Every spirit that confesses that Jesus Christ has come in the flesh is from God, and every spirit that does not confess Jesus is not from God. This is the spirit of the antichrist, which you heard was coming and now is in the world already" (ESV).[8] To say that Jesus only appeared to be a true man is contrary to the holy catholic faith. Ignatius of Antioch specifically denounces those who taught that Jesus only appeared to suffer.[9] In *Against Heresies*, Irenaeus vehemently opposes the same error (3.11.3). The ecumenical creeds affirm unambiguously that Christ was incarnate "by the Holy Spirit, *of the virgin Mary*" (*ex Maria virgine*).[10] In the Definition of Chalcedon (AD 451), we confess that Christ is "truly man" (ἄνθρωπον ἀληθῶς).[11] In short, the doctrine of transubstantiation asks us to set aside the way we confess the world to work.

So too, in the Holy Supper, we must reject the gross error of transubstantiation. The Supper is not Christ. It is the gospel made visible. It is a sure, reliable, true sign and seal of the promise of the gospel. Our Lord Jesus did not say, in the institution of the Supper, "This becomes my body." Rather, he said, "This is my body." There is a sacramental union between the sign and the thing signified.

The catechism repeats another of Ratramnus's criticisms of Radbertus's novel view. Why does Rome claim that the substance of the bread has been transformed but does not say the same for baptism? We know that

---

8. He repeats this condemnation in 2 John 7.

9. E.g., δοκεῖν αὐτὸν πεπονθέναι (Ignatius, *To the Smyrnaeans* 2.1).

10. Schaff, *Creeds of Christendom*, 1:45.

11. Schaff, *Creeds of Christendom*, 1:62–63.

the water of baptism is and remains water. Nevertheless, it is a sacrament. If it is not necessary for baptismal water to be transformed, why is it necessary for the bread and wine to be transformed? Of course, it is not necessary, and it does not happen.

Our Lord testified to this sacramental reality when he said, "I will not drink from this fruit of the vine until that day" (Matt 26:29). He spoke these words after he had given thanks, after he had instituted the Supper. If our Lord Jesus could call the sacrament of his body and blood "the fruit of the vine," why should we think that he had transubstantiated it? In 1 Corinthians 11:26–28 the apostle Paul refers to the sacramental elements as "this bread" and "the cup" repeatedly. He identifies them sacramentally with "the body and blood of the Lord." Nowhere does he say explicitly or even implicitly that, by consecration, the elements become other than they were before consecration. In 1 Corinthians 10:1–4 he teaches that the Israelites ate "the same spiritual food" and drank the same "spiritual drink" we do. They ate and drank Christ by faith, by the operation of the mysterious Holy Spirit. God's old covenant people ate manna and water from the rock. Neither the manna nor the rock was transubstantiated.

Most fundamentally, however, Scripture never hints (let alone teaches) that in the institution of the Supper, when Christ said, "This is my body," that his disciples understood him to say, "This bread has now become, by the miracle of transubstantiation, my literal body." He was using, as Ursinus reminds again under this question, a sacramental *metonymy*.[12] A metonymy is substitution of one thing for another. It is a kind of figure of speech. Ursinus correctly calls the phrase in Luke 22:19, "This is my body," a *sacramental* metonymy, an application of a figure of speech to the sacrament. This is why the Reformed regularly use the adverb *sacramentally*.[13] The Supper is Christ's body *sacramentally*, that is, figuratively, but also as a gospel promise from Christ to believers. Because that promise is attached to the visible sign, believers expect to be fed, by the mysterious operation of the Holy Spirit, by nothing less than the true body and blood, "the proper and natural body and the proper blood of Christ."[14]

12. Ursinus, *Commentary*, 389. On the interpretation of the clause "this is my body" (Luke 22:19), see the discussion under *HC* 77.

13. E.g., Ursinus, *Commentary*, 390.

14. *BC* 35 (Schaff, *Creeds of Christendom*, 3:430). See the discussion under *HC* 75.

There is no mystery about *what* we are fed, but there is great mystery as to *how* believers are fed by the Spirit, through faith. Thus, Ursinus quite vigorously but fairly traduces both the Roman Catholic doctrine of transubstantiation and the Lutheran doctrine of "coexistence of the body with the bread."[15] In contrast to both the Lutherans and the Roman Catholics, we "retain the words of Christ simply without any addition, or change, affirming that the bread is the body of Christ, the true and visible body which was offered for us upon the cross."[16]

The analogy of Scripture, where we see what Ursinus calls "sacramental phrases," also requires us to reject the doctrine of transubstantiation.[17] For example, "This is my covenant in your flesh" (Gen 17:10); "the Passover lamb" (2 Chr 30:15); the Sabbath as a "perpetual covenant" (Exod 31:16 ASV); and so on.[18] The blood of Christ "is the New Covenant" (1 Cor 11:25), but so is the cup (Luke 22:20). These are examples of sacramental metonymy, when the sacrament is said figuratively to be the thing itself.

Finally, in the spirit of Ursinus's reply to the Lutherans, which is the last topic he discusses under this question,[19] it is difficult from a Reformed standpoint not to regard the Lutheran rejection of the Reformed doctrine and insistence on the prepositions *in*, *with*, and *under* as a species of rationalism.[20] Their rejection of the Reformed doctrine of the work of the Spirit in feeding believers with the true body and blood seems like rationalism, placing the human intellect over the authority of Scripture by asserting

---

15. "Coexistentia corporis in vel cum pane" (Ursinus, *Corpus doctrinae*, 406). The Willard edition (Ursinus, *Commentary*, 390) imputes to Ursinus the word *consubstantiation*, which Ursinus does not use here.

16. Ursinus, *Commentary*, 390. Ursinus rehearses, at some length, several of the arguments we have already discussed under *HC* 76–77. See his catalogue of patristic quotations (Ursinus, *Commentary*, 404–6). Ursinus's "quotation" of a canon of the Council of Nicaea (AD 325) is actually from an ostensible history of the council attributed to a fifth-century author, Gelasius of Cyzicus. In the sixteenth century, the document was thought to reflect an official of the Council of Nicaea. See Gelasius of Cyzicus, *Συνταγμα Seu Commentarius*, 153–54. This edition was published after Ursinus's death but reflects what he and other authors of the period were reading. His quotation of Cyprian (*Epistle* 62.2) is more accurate (*ANF* 5:359). Roman Catholics read back into the patristic period a theory (transubstantiation) that did not exist in the ancient church.

17. Ursinus, *Commentary*, 400–401.

18. Ursinus, *Commentary*, 401.

19. Ursinus, *Corpus doctrinae*, 425–32; Ursinus, *Commentary*, 409–16.

20. E.g., Mueller, *Christian Dogmatics*, 513.

dogmatically exactly *how* Christ is present when neither Scripture nor the ecumenical faith drives us to any such conclusion. This a great tragedy since the Reformed churches agree with them *that* we are fed by Christ's true body and blood.

Lutheran theologians have historically misconstrued aspects of the Reformed confession regarding this aspect of Communion. E.g., the Formula of Concord (1577) characterizes the Reformed view as teaching "a true presence of the true, essential, living body and blood of Christ in the Holy Supper, but that this takes place spiritually, through faith."[21] This would be quite accurate were "spiritually" capitalized. We see this characterization reflected in the Lutheran dogmatic tradition.[22] The Saxon Visitation Articles' (1592) account of the "Calvinist" position (their epithet for the "cunning sacramentarians," as distinct from the "crude sacramentarians," i.e., the Zwinglians) is less precise and more polemical toward the Reformed on the Supper.[23]

At the same time, the Reformed characterization of the Lutheran view as *consubstantiation* is also inaccurate. Lutheran scholar Robert Kolb explains:

> [Luther's] view is not halfway between a medieval interpretation using Aristotle's concept of substance—transubstantiation—and the symbolic or spiritual interpretations of Zwingli, Karlstadt, and Oecolampadius. Luther instead proceeded from a different set of presuppositions. On the basis of his Ockhamist training, he presumed that God structured his world as he saw fit and was able to place his body and blood in the bread and wine. ... In October [1520] his *Babylonian Captivity of the Church* rejected and deconstructed the use of the Aristotelian concept of substance, setting aside transubstantiation and consubstantiation as well as other medieval aspects of sacramental teaching.[24]

21. *Epitome of the Formula of Concord*, cap. 7 (Kolb and Wengert, *Book of Concord*, 504.4).

22. Mueller, *Christian Dogmatics*, 511. His summary of the Reformed view is inferior to that in the *Epitome*. He paraphrases the Reformed to say, "'The body and blood are absent from the Lord's Supper, but are received spiritually or by faith.'" For more on the Lutheran use of Calvin and the Reformed as bogeymen, see Clark, "Calvin as Negative Boundary Marker."

23. Kolb and Nestingen, *Sources and Contexts*, 259.

24. Kolb and Trueman, *Between Wittenberg and Geneva*, 178. For a different account of Luther's appropriation of Aristotle, see Bagchi, "Sic Et Non," 3–15.

Ursinus, given his years of study in Wittenberg, certainly knew that the Lutherans rejected the term *consubstantiation*, preferring to speak of the "real presence."[25] Indeed, it is likely that during his time in Wittenberg he agreed with the Lutheran doctrine of "in, with, and under."[26] Ursinus is probably incorrect in linking the Lutheran view to Berengar of Tours (ca. 1010–1088), who argued that "the bread and the wine remained in the sacrifice after consecration."[27] Berengar was merely restating Ratramnus's earlier view. In the thirteenth and early fourteenth centuries, John of Paris (ca. 1255–1306) argued, on analogy with hypostatic union, that the substance of the bread, like Christ's humanity, is preserved after consecration. He was willing to speak of the "impanation" of Christ's humanity in the bread.[28] Ursinus's critique that the Lutheran understanding of the words of institution is less than obvious is still true. To say that body of Christ is in, with, and under the bread and wine is hardly equivalent to "This is my body."[29]

Finally, we should close by meditating on what it means to be fed by the body and blood of Christ, by the mysterious operation of the Holy Spirit, through faith:

---

25. On consubstantiation, see Muller, *Dictionary of Latin and Greek Theological Terms*, s.v. "*consubstantiatio*." He defines it as a "doctrine of Christ's sacramental presence in the Eucharist developed in the Middle Ages as an alternative to theory of substantial alteration of the elements either by annihilation or transformation of the substance of the bread and wine. According to the theory of consubstantiation, the body and blood of Christ become substantially present together with the substance of the bread and wine, when the elements are consecrated. The theory is frequently confused with the Lutheran doctrine of real presence. *Consubstantio* indicates the presence of Christ's body according to a unique sacramental mode of presence that is proper to Christ's body as such, and is therefore a local presence. ... The Lutheran view, however, argues a real, but illocal presence of Christ's body and blood that is grounded in the omnipresence of Christ's person, and therefore a supernatural and sacramental, rather than a local, union with the visible elements of the sacrament. *Consubstantio* implies only a presence with and not a union of Christ and the sacramental elements; it was taught as a possibility by Duns Scotus, John of Jandun, and William of Occam." On the background to Luther's doctrine of the Supper, see Osborne, "Faith, Philosophy," 64n6, 76–82. For Ockham's view of the Supper, see Birch, *De Sacramento Altaris*.

26. Klooster, *Our Only Comfort*, 2:844–46.

27. *Pace* Pelikan, *Christian Tradition*, 3:189. Macy argues that Berengar was essentially siding with Ratramnus against Radbertus (*Banquet's Wisdom*, 92–99). See also Macy, *Theologies of the Eucharist*, 35–41; Holopainen, *Dialectical Theology*, 80–107, who comes to a similar conclusion, that Berengar was opposing transubstantiation. Holopainen makes no connection between Berengar and consubstantiation.

28. Pelikan, *Christian Tradition*, 4:57.

29. Ursinus, *Commentary*, 411–15.

> The body of Christ does not nourish us naturally, for it does not produce in us any new qualities, as medicine; but it nourishes and quickens us in a manner different from that which is natural, which requires that we should receive it differently. Now as to the manner in which the body and blood of Christ nourish us, it has, in the first place, a respect to his merit. For the body of Christ was delivered, and his blood shed for us; and it is in view of this that God grants unto us eternal life. Hence Christ's body and blood must quicken us in this manner, as meriting for us eternal life. Secondly, we are quickened and nourished, when we receive by a true faith the merit of the body and blood of Christ; that is, when we believe that we shall have eternal life for the sake of the merit of Christ's body, and blood broken and shed for us. This faith now rests upon Christ as crucified, and not as dwelling in us after a corporal manner. Thirdly, we are quickened by the body and blood of Christ when we are united to him by the same Spirit, who works the same things in us, which he does in Christ; for unless we are ingrafted into Christ, we do not please God, who will receive us into his favor, and grant unto us the remission of our sins, only upon the condition, that we are ingrafted into Christ and united to him by that faith, which the Holy Ghost works in us.[30]

Ursinus's language is substantially identical to that of *BC* (35) when it distinguishes between feeding the body and feeding the soul. Believers are nourished at the Lord's Table, by the true body and blood of Christ, when we receive Christ and his merits for us by faith, when our faith rests on Christ, and when we are united to him by his Holy Spirit. These are the promises of the gospel in the Supper and the blessings sealed to believer when we eat in faith.

30. Ursinus, *Commentary*, 415.

QUESTION 79

Why then does Christ call the bread his body, and the cup his blood, or the new covenant in his blood, and St. Paul, the communion of the body and the blood of Christ?

Christ speaks thus not without great cause, namely, not only to teach us thereby, that just as the bread and wine sustain this temporal life, so also his crucified body and shed blood are the true food and drink of our souls unto life eternal; but much more, by this visible sign and pledge to assure us, that we are as really partakers of his true body and blood by the working of the Holy Spirit, as we receive by the mouth of the body these holy signs in remembrance of him; and that all his sufferings and obedience are as certainly our own, as if we ourselves had suffered and done all in our own person.[31]

In some quarters there is a temptation to treat metaphorical speech as less important than literal speech. That would be a mistake. Metaphors contain and communicate powerful truths. "O Jerusalem, Jerusalem, the city that kills the prophets and stones those who are sent to it! How often would I have gathered your children together as a hen gathers her brood under her wings, and you would not!" (Matt 23:37). Our Lord used a simile,

31. "Warum nennet denn Christus das Brot seinen Leib, und den Kelch sein Blut, oder das Neue Testament in seinem Blute, und St. Paulus die Gemeinschaft des Leibes und Blutes Jesu Christi? Christus redet also nicht ohne grosse Ursache: nämlich, dass Er uns nicht allein damit will lehren, dass, gleich wie Brot und Wein das zeitliche Leben erhalten, also sei auch sein gekreuzigter Leib und vergossen Blut die wahre Speise und Trank unserer Scelen zum ewigen Leben, sondern vielmehr, dass Er uns durch diess sichtbare Zeichen und Pfand will versichern, dass wir so wahrhaftig seines wahren Leibes und Blutes durch Wirkung des Heiligen Geistes theilhaftig werden, als wir diese heiligen Wahrzeichen mit dem leiblichen Mund zu seinem Gebächtniss empfangen, und dass all sein Leiben und Gehorsam so gewiss unser eigen sei, als hätten wir selbst in unserer eigenen Person alles gelitten und genug gethan" (Schaff, *Creeds of Christendom*, 3:334–35). "Cur ergo Christus panem appellat suum corpus, calicem vero suum sanguinem, seu novum foedus per suum sanguinem: Paulus item panem et vinum, communionem corporis et sanguinis Christi? Christus non sine gravi causa sic loquitur: videlicet, non solum ut nos doceat, quemadmodum panis et vinum corporis vitam sustentant: sic etiam crucifixum suum corpus et effusum suum sanguinem, vere esse animae nostrae cibum ac potum, quo ad vitam aeternam nutriatur: Verum multo magis, uț hoc visibili signo ac pignore nobis certum faciat, nos non minus vere, corporis et sanguinis sui, per operationem Spiritus sancti, partcipes esse, quam sacra ista Symbola, in eius memoriam, ore corporis percipimus: Tum etiam, quod eius passio et obedientia, tam certo nostra sit, quam si ipsimet pro nostris peccatis poenas dedissemus, et Deo satisfecissemus" (Niemeyer, *Collectio Confessionum*, 448).

signaled in English with word *as*. From a purely literary perspective, would this passage be as affecting, as informative of our Lord's attitude toward the lost and his sense of mission, had he expressed it more prosaically? Simple imagery is powerful and compelling. That is what well-chosen metaphors do: they communicate important truths powerfully.

The same is true of the discourse around the institution of Lord's Supper. One basic question is this: What is the intent of using a metaphor? The answer is that our Lord, followed by the apostle Paul, speaks metaphorically to great effect. As he sustains us physically by bread and wine, he also sustains us by his body and blood.[32] To insist that the only way one can be fed on the body and blood of Christ is either by transubstantiation or by locating the body and blood in, with, and under the elements is a species of rationalism, to decide what must be the case ahead of time and then insist on it despite the evidence.[33] There is abundant evidence that our Lord intended us to think that, in the Supper, by faith, believers are fed by his true body and blood. This is why is said of the bread, "This *is* my body" (Luke 22:19) and "take, eat" (Matt 26:26). He did not explain *how* the Holy Spirit feeds the believer on the true body and blood of Christ, that is, the "proper and natural body and the proper blood of Christ" (*BC* 35). He only promises that, when we eat in faith, it occurs. There is no evidence in words of our Lord that he intended us to think that the elements are transformed or that his "proper and natural" body is in, with, and under the elements.

We are meant to understand that, in the Supper, by faith, by the mysterious operation of the Holy Spirit, we are "really partakers" of Christ. This is why we should understand and believe in a real communion in the true body and blood of Christ. There is a strong correlation between eating the elements with the mouth and receiving Christ by faith. That is the force of the phrase "just as." When we eat bread, we are not ordinarily in doubt as to whether we have eaten. We experience and remember the sensation of eating, tasting, and swallowing. We have a sensation of being full, of being satisfied. So too it is with the Supper. It does not fill

32. See *BC* 35, in United Reformed Churches in North America, *Liturgical Forms and Prayers*, 193–94.

33. See the discussion under *HC* 78.

our stomachs, but the Spirit does use it to work in us, to communicate Christ to us, to strengthen us, to nourish us spiritually, and to encourage us in faith. According to the promise of the Supper, we are as surely fed by the one as by the other.[34]

Faith is so essential because what the Lord's Supper offers us is the very same Christ, the very same favor (*sola gratia*), the very same benefits offered to us in the preached gospel: "All His sufferings and obedience are as certainly our own, as if we ourselves had suffered and done all in our own person." This is virtually the same language used in *HC* 60. It is the "as if" principle: as if we had ourselves done all that Christ has done for us. When we receive the Supper in faith, we receive a visible, tangible, experience of what is promised in the gospel preached. Each time we eat the Supper in faith, it is a little catechism.

Q: Who receives Christ and his benefits?
A: Those who believe.
Q: Do I believe?
A: Yes.
Q: Are you therefore receiving Christ and his benefits?
A: Yes, through faith alone.
Q: How is this possible?
A: Because Christ promises it in his word.
Q: Who does this?
A: The Holy Spirit.
Q: How does the Spirit do this?
A: It is a mystery.
Q: Why do you believe this mystery?
A: Because Christ promises it.

The Supper is not Christ, but it is a gospel *sacrament* of Christ, a visible, tangible sign and seal. There is a sacramental union between the sign (the bread and wine) and the thing signified: Christ and salvation. For those who believe, it is as if they were one and the same. To those who believe (*sola fide*), to receive the one is to receive the other.

34. Ursinus, *Commentary*, 416.

The relation between the sign (the Supper) and the thing signified (Christ and his benefits) is as close as possible, but the sign is not the thing, or else it would no longer be a sign. Of what value are signs? Much in every way (Rom 3:2). After all, the word of God is a sign that the Spirit uses to accomplish his purposes (Augustine, *Teaching Christianity*, book 2). This gets us back to metaphors. Our Lord compared himself to a hen to help us understand his attitude toward sinners. God sees fit to stoop to us and to use signs, like bread and wine, to help us on our journey. We should receive those signs and all that they communicate (Christ and his benefits) with thanks and joy because what they communicate and the communion that they seal to believers is glorious indeed.

Question 80
What difference is there between the Lord's Supper and the Popish Mass?

Question 81
Who are to come to the table of the Lord?

Question 82
Are they then also to be admitted to this supper who show themselves by their confession and life to be unbelieving and ungodly?

Lord's Day 30

QUESTION 80

What difference is there between the Lord's Supper and the Popish Mass?

The Lord's Supper testifies to us, that we have full forgiveness of all our sins by the one sacrifice of Jesus Christ, which he himself once accomplished on the cross; and that by the Holy Spirit we are ingrafted into Christ, who, with according to his human nature, is now in heaven at the right hand of the Father, and is there to be worshipped. But the Mass teaches, that the living and the dead do not have forgiveness of sins through the one passion of Christ, unless Christ is daily offered for them by the priests, and that Christ is bodily under the form of bread and wine, and is therefore to be adored in them. And thus, at bottom, the Mass is nothing but a denial of the one sacrifice and passion of Jesus Christ, and an accursed idolatry.[1]

In September 1562, the Roman Catholic Church published her "doctrine concerning the sacrifice of the mass" in session 22 of the Council of Trent.[2] In that session, Rome declared that in the institution of the Lord's Supper, Holy Communion, Christ left to his a church "a visible sacrifice,

1. "Was ist für ein Unterschied zwischen dem Abendmahl des Herrn und der päpstlichen Messe? Das Abendmahl bezeuget uns, dass wir vollkommene Vergebung aller unserer Sünden haben durch das einige Opfer Jesu Christi, so Er selbst einmal am Kreuz vollbracht hat; [und dass wir durch den Heiligen Geist Christo werden eingeleibet, der jetzt mit seinem wahren Leib im Himmel zur Rechten des Vaters ist, und daselbst will angebetet werden]. Die Messe aber lehret, dass die Lebendigen und die Todten nicht durch das Leiden Christi Vergebung der Sünden haben, es sei denn, dass Christus noch täglich für sie von den Messpriestern geopfert werde; [und dass Christus leiblich unter der Gestalt Brots und Weins sei, und derhalben darin soll angebetet werden]. Und ist also die Messe im Grunde nichts anders, denn eine Vertäugnung des einigen Opfers und Leidens Jesu Christi [und eine vermaledeite Abgötterei]" (Schaff, *Creeds of Christendom*, 3:335–36). "Quid interest inter Coenam Domini, et Missam Papisticam? Coena Domini nobis testaur, nos perfactam remissionem omnium nostrorum peccatorum habere, propter unicum illud Christi sacrificium, quod ipsemet semel in cruce peregit: tum etiam nos per Spiritum sanctum inseri Christo, qui iam secundum naturam suam humanam tantum in coelis est ad dextram Patris, ibique vult a nobis adorari. In Missa autem negatur, vivos et mortuos habere remissionem peccatorum, propter unicam Christi passionem, nisi etiamnum quotidie Christus pro ipsis a Sacrificulis offeratur: tum etiam docetur, Christum corporaliter sub speciebus Panis et Vini esse ideoque in illis adorandum esse. Atque ita ipsum Missae fundamentum, nihil aliud est, quam abnegatio unici illius sacrificii et passionis Iesu Christi, et execranda idolatria" (Niemeyer, *Collectio Confessionum*, 448).

2. Schroeder, *Canons and Decrees*, 144–59.

such as the nature of man requires, whereby that bloody sacrifice once to be accomplished on the cross might be represented, the memory thereof remain to the end of the world, and its salutary effects applied to the remission of those sins which we daily commit" (cap. 1).[3] He "then made priests of the New Testament, that they might partake, commanding them and their successors in the priesthood by these words to do likewise: 'do this in commemoration of me,' as the Catholic Church has always understood and taught."[4] According to Rome, in the "divine sacrifice" of the Mass, in the transubstantiated elements, Christ is "immolated [killed] in an unbloody manner," and further "the holy council teaches that this is truly propitiatory," that is, it turns away the wrath of God (cap. 2).[5] Thus, according to Rome, when the priest offers the consecrated host (sacrificial victim), that is, Christ, his wrath is turned away. It is a continuation of Christ's sacrifice on the altar of the cross. Rome says the words "once for all" but denies their intent. When Rome says "once for all," she means, "Jesus made a beginning, but we must do our part."

HC 80 did not appear in the first edition of the catechism when it first appeared on January 19, 1563. A shorter version of *HC* 80 did appear in the second edition, probably in March 1563.[6] The question was as we have it now, but the answer read: "The Lord's Supper declares to us that our sins have been completely forgiven through the one sacrifice of Jesus Christ which he himself finished on the cross once for all. But the Mass teaches that the living and the dead do not have their sins forgiven through the suffering of Christ unless Christ is still offered for them daily by the priests. Thus the Mass is basically nothing but an idolatrous denial of the one sacrifice and suffering of Jesus Christ."[7] In the third edition,

3. Schroeder, *Canons and Decrees*, 144–45.

4. Schroeder, *Canons and Decrees*, 145.

5. Schroeder, *Canons and Decrees*, 146.

6. Klooster, *Heidelberg Catechism*, 181. According to de Boer ("Adoration or Idolatry?," 133), the Osterreich Nationalbibliothek, in Vienna, has a copy of the Catechismus oder Christlicher Underricht, which contains a piece of parchment with a handwritten copy of the short version of Q. 80 as it appeared in the second edition.

7. Klooster, *Our Only Comfort*, 2:859. "Diese Frage fehlt in I und tritt erst in II in folgender Fassung auf: Was ist für ein underscheid zwischen dem Abendmal des Herrn und der Paptstlichen Meß? Antwort: Das Abendmal bezenget uns dass wir volkomne vergebunbg aller unser sünden haben, durch das einige opffer Jesu Christi, so er selbst ein mal am creutz volbracht hat, Die Meß aber lehret daß die lebendigen und die todten nit durch das leiden Christi vergebung der süden haben,

published between March and November 1563, twenty-seven words were added to the answer regarding the Lord's Supper: "It also declares to us that the Holy Spirit grafts us into Christ, who with his very body is now in heaven and the right hand of the Father where he wants us to worship him."[8] On the Mass was added the sentence: "It also teaches that Christ is bodily present in the form of bread and wine where Christ is therefore to be worshiped."[9] The final sentence was revised to say: "Thus the Mass is basically nothing but a denial of the one sacrifice and suffering of Jesus Christ and a condemnable idolatry."[10] It is certain that that *HC* 80 was added at the instigation of Olevianus and with the authority of the Elector, Frederick III.[11] It was likely added in response to session 22 (September 1562) of the Council of Trent.[12] We know from a letter Olevianus wrote to Calvin that he had advocated the addition of *HC* 80 in the second (Latin) edition.[13]

Not everyone has received *HC* 80 with equal enthusiasm. Philip Schaff's reservations, articulated in the nineteenth century, are representative of the reservations others have come to hold about *HC* 80:

> The same view of the Romish doctrine of transubstantiation and the sacrifice of the mass was generally entertained by the Reformers, and is set forth as strongly in the Articles of Smalcald and other symbolical books, both Lutheran and Reformed. It must be allowed to remain as a solemn protest against idolatry. But the wisdom of inserting controversial matter into a catechism for the instruction of the youth has been justly doubted. The eightieth

es sei dan, daß Christus noch teglich für sie von den Meßpriestern geopffert werde: Und ist also die Meß im grund ein abgöttische verleugnung deß einigen opffers und leidens Jesu Christi" (Müller, *Die Bekenntnisschriften*, 704.35–40).

8. Klooster, *Our Only Comfort*, 2:859.

9. Klooster, *Our Only Comfort*, 2:860.

10. Klooster, *Our Only Comfort*, 2:860.

11. Bierma et al., *Introduction*, 104.

12. De Boer ("Adoration or Idolatry?," 134), raises questions regarding the timing of the revision of Q. 80 relative to the Council of Trent, but the publication of the decree in September of 1562 gives ample time for Olevianus and the Elector to react.

13. Klooster, *Our Only Comfort*, 2:860; Bretschneider, *Corpus Reformatorum*, 47.683–85. "Mitto ad te, carissime pater, exemplum catechismi latini, et alterum ad D. Bezam: in prima editione germanica, quam ad Scrimigerum miseramus, omissa erat quaestio de discrimine coenae et missae pontificiae. Admonitus a me Princeps voluit in secunda editione germanica et prima editione latina addi" (47.684).

> question disturbs the peaceful harmony of the book, it rewards evil for evil, it countenances intolerance, which is un-Protestant and unevangelical. It provoked much unnecessary hostility, and led even, under the Romish rule of the Elector Charles Philip, in 1719, to the prohibition of the Catechism; but the loud remonstrance of England, Prussia, Holland, and other Protestant states forced the Elector to withdraw the tyrannical decree within a year, under certain conditions, to save appearances.[14]

In various modern editions of the catechism, *HC* 80 appears with a footnote or in brackets with a note explaining that it was the product of a heated debate, and one ecclesiastical committee even suggests that it misrepresents the Roman Catholic doctrine.[15]

The catechism, however, has not misrepresented Rome. Fred Klooster writes, "[*HC* 80] is a true statement of the Mass. The second part of answer 80 correctly states what the Council of Trent maintained. Since that time, changes have occurred in the Roman Catholic Church, but the doctrine of the Mass as adopted by the Council of Trent has never been refuted. In fact, Vatican II (1962–1965) reaffirmed it in its doctrine of the liturgy."[16]

We should disagree with Schaff and with the notion that the catechism is in error here or that it was a mistake to include it. It is not as if years passed between the first and second editions, and the third edition did not change the question materially.

In *HC* 80 the Reformed churches use some pointed language. Moderns have sometimes become queasy about such language, but to corrupt the Supper as Rome did at Trent is to corrupt the gospel. The message of the Roman Catholic doctrine of the Supper is that Christ has opened the way of salvation, that he has made salvation possible, but that those who receive it must do their part.[17] This is represented by the repeated memorial, propitiatory offerings ostensibly made by Roman Catholic priests.

14. Schaff, *Creeds of Christendom*, 1:536. For a reply, see Venema, *Lord's Supper*.

15. Christian Reformed Church, *Lord's Supper*. For the background of this report see Bierma, *Theology of the Heidelberg Catechism*, 123–24.

16. Klooster, *Our Only Comfort*, 2:861.

17. "In brief, the Eucharist is the sum and summary of our faith" (*CCC* §1327). The soteriology of the Roman Catholic Church teaches salvation by grace and cooperation with grace, and that doctrine is visibly summarized in the eucharistic sacrifice.

The gospel, embodied in the Lord's Supper, as the Reformed churches understand it, is that Christ has *accomplished* salvation once for all (Rom 6:10; Heb 9:12), and freely gives it to all who believe. Rome has, were it possible, turned the gospel into law.

By her doctrine of transubstantiation Rome would destroy the sacrament by replacing it with the thing signified. Second, after transubstantiation, Rome turned the sacrament into a sacrifice, a ritual, memorial, propitiatory sacrifice of Christ. Canon 3 of Trent's "Most Holy Sacrifice of the Mass" declares: "If any one says, that the sacrifice of the mass is only a sacrifice of praise and of thanksgiving; or that it is a bare commemoration of the sacrifice consummated on the cross, but not a propitiatory sacrifice; or, that it profits him only who receives; and that it ought not to be offered for the living and the dead for sins, pains, satisfactions, and other necessities; let him be anathema."[18] To say that the Roman, memorial, eucharistic sacrifice is *propitiatory* is to say that it has the effect of turning away the wrath of God.

It is popularly assumed that Vatican II fundamentally changed Rome's doctrine on the Eucharist. This is not true. In her 1994 catechism Rome confesses:

> §1367 The sacrifice of Christ and the sacrifice of the Eucharist are one single sacrifice: "The victim is one and the same: the same now offers through the ministry of priests, who then offered himself on the cross; only the manner of offering is different." "And since in this divine sacrifice which is celebrated in the Mass, the same Christ who offered himself once in a bloody manner on the altar of the cross is contained and is offered in an unbloody manner. … This sacrifice is truly propitiatory."[19]

The Roman catechism cites as an authority for her contemporary doctrine session 22 of the Council of Trent (1562). Rome *still* confesses that, after consecration, the substance of the bread and wine are transformed into the substance of the body and blood of Christ. The priest

18. Schroeder, *Canons and Decrees*, 149; Denzinger, *Enchiridion Symbolorum*, 335.950.

19. CCC, 344.

then resacrifices Christ to the end that, by that memorial, sacrificial act, the wrath of God is turned away.

As both Trent and the *CCC* make clear, Rome says unequivocally that what took place on the cross was not "once for all" but rather only the beginning of a series of sacrifices. Consider the teaching of Hebrews, which speaks directly to the question of the necessity of continuing, propitiatory sacrifices: "For it was indeed fitting that we should have such a high priest, holy, innocent, unstained, separated from sinners, and exalted above the heavens. He has no need, like those high priests, to offer sacrifices daily, first for his own sins and then for those of the people, since he did this once for all [ἐφάπαξ] when he offered up himself" (Heb 7:26–27 ESV). According to the writer to the Hebrews, there was no need for the Jewish Christians to go back to the sacrificial system. Its job was completed at Calvary. We have a perfect high priest, who did not need to offer a sacrifice for himself because he was sinless (Heb 2:17; 4:15). He entered "once for all" (ἐφάπαξ) in the holy place (Heb 9:12). He did not offer himself repeatedly (πολλάκις; Heb 9:25), nor to suffer repeatedly (9:26), but to appear once (ἅπαξ) at the end of the age to put away sin. To be absolutely certain that no one misses the point, Hebrews returns to the finality of Christ's death to say: "We have been sanctified through the once-for-all [ἐφάπαξ] offering of the body of Jesus Christ" (Heb 10:10).

There is no way to square the Roman doctrine of the repeated, memorial, eucharistic sacrifice of Christ in the Mass with the biblical teaching that Jesus's death on the cross was final, "once for all." Christ intentionally put an end to sacrifices and propitiation because he completed the sacrifice and accomplished our propitiation.

So determined was Ursinus to juxtapose the biblical and Reformed doctrine of the Supper with the Roman doctrine, piety, and practice of the Mass that he repudiated the use of even the term *Mass*.[20] In *HC* 30 Ursinus contrasts the Supper as a visible declaration of the good news of free salvation in Christ against the Mass as the opposite, because it teaches that the continued sacrifice by priests is necessary. The Supper teaches that Christ is at the right hand of the Father and eaten by faith through the mysterious operation of the Spirit, whereas the Mass teaches that he is,

20. Ursinus, *Commentary*, 418; Ursinus, *Corpus doctrinae*, 436. See Calvin, *Institutes* 4.18.1–7.

as it were, by transubstantiation, brought down from heaven. The Supper teaches that Christ is to be adored at the right hand of the Father, but the Mass teaches that he is to be adored in the transubstantiated victim.[21]

Against the Lutheran doctrine of the ubiquity of Christ's humanity, Ursinus asked why, if Christ is in the bread, as they say, he should not there be worshiped? Lutheran Tilemann Heshusius (1527–1588) argued that the deity is present in all creatures, but we do not adore it in them.[22] To which Ursinus replied, if, according to the Lutheran theory of the ubiquity of Christ's humanity, it is joined to the deity and is wherever the deity is, then it must be adored in the Eucharist, but the Lutherans will not do this, thus showing the incoherence of their Christology.

The Supper is a gospel sacrament. It speaks of our free justification, grounded in Christ's perfect righteousness for us, received through faith alone and of our consequent union and communion with Christ. It also speaks of the Creator/creature distinction, or the categorical distinction.[23] Rome confuses the creature with the Creator by adoring and venerating the allegedly, ostensibly consecrated host (victim). Again, this is not Protestant hyperbole. This is Rome's own language. The Roman Catechism says:

> §1378 Worship of the Eucharist. In the liturgy of the Mass we express our faith in the real presence of Christ under the species of bread and wine by, among other ways, genuflecting or bowing deeply as a sign of adoration of the Lord. "The Catholic Church has always offered and still offers to the sacrament of the Eucharist the cult of adoration, not only during Mass, but also outside of it, reserving the consecrated hosts with the utmost care, exposing them to the solemn veneration of the faithful, and carrying them in procession."[24]

---

21. Ursinus, *Commentary*, 419; Ursinus, *Corpus doctrinae*, 437–38. Willard (Ursinus, *Commentary*, 420) added the word *consubstantiation* discussion in this section, but it is not present in *Corpus doctrinae*, 439. Ursinus was addressing the Roman Catholic error in this section, not the Lutheran. He turned his attention to the "Ubiquitarians" (Lutherans) in the next section.

22. Ursinus, *Commentary*, 420; Ursinus, *Corpus doctrinae*, 439. The section that follows, against the Roman Catholic doctrine, beginning on p. 421, is incorrectly dated 1669. It should be 1569.

23. Clark, *Recovering the Reformed Confession*, 142–50.

24. CCC §347.

The Reformed reject as specious the distinction between adoration and worship. Adoration and worship (δουλεία and λατρεία) belong only to God.[25] To adore, to venerate, to worship Christ under the species of bread and wine is nothing less than idolatry. God's holy law not only stipulates that we must worship him alone but that we must worship him only as he has commanded.[26] The doctrine of transubstantiation confuses the Creator and the creature, and to worship him there is the very sort of thing that God expressly condemned. The calves at Bethel and Dan (1 Kgs 12:25–33) did not deliver the Israelites out of Egypt. They were not Yahweh, and neither were they authorized representations of Yahweh. Everything that the prophets said about that corruption is also true of the Roman Catholic Mass.

So, the Reformed Churches are quite right to confess that the Mass is *both* an attack on the gospel, by attacking the perfect work of Christ for us, *and* an accursed idolatry by conflating the Creator with the creature (bread and wine) and adoring the creature or adoring the Creator improperly. Everything the catechism says about Rome's doctrine and practice is perfectly true, and we should be ashamed neither of the holy gospel nor of the holy law of God.

QUESTION 81

Who are to come to the table of the Lord?

Those who are displeased with themselves for their sins, yet trust that these are forgiven them, and that their remaining infirmity is covered by the passion and death of Christ; who also desire more and more to strengthen their faith and to amend their life. But the impenitent and hypocrites eat and drink judgment to themselves.[27]

25. On this distinction, see also the discussion under *HC* 96; Ursinus, *Commentary*, 542–48.

26. See the discussion under *HC* 96.

27. "Welche sollen zum Tische des Herrn kommen? Die sich selbst um ihrer Sünden willen missfallen, und doch vertrauen, dass dieselbigen ihnen verziehen, und die übrige Schwachheit mit

Communion or the Lord's Supper is the sacrament (covenant sign and seal) intended for those who have been baptized, who have been instructed in the Christian faith, and who have made a credible profession of faith. Those are the external qualifications. The catechism turns to the internal or spiritual qualifications for the Supper. When the catechism was drafted, adopted, and published, the external qualifications (e.g., memorizing the catechism) were not in question among the confessional Protestants.

The internal, spiritual qualification for the table were important for two reasons: (1) the Supper is for believers and not for hypocrites, and (2) because the Reformed church was the state church in the Palatinate, merely nominal Christianity and the possibility of hypocrites coming to the table was a real problem. There were other practical problems facing the Palatinate Church. When the *HC* was published, the citizens of the electorate were still feeling the effects of the transition to the Reformed confession. One year they were all Roman Catholic, then Lutheran, then, under Frederick III, they were all Reformed, but genuine spiritual, pastoral questions remained. Did they believe? Were they renewed by the Holy Spirit? Did they know personally, genuinely, the greatness of their sin and misery, how they were redeemed from their sins and misery by grace alone, through faith alone, in Christ alone? Were they committed to living lives of grateful obedience, in the grace of God, in union with Christ? Those are the internal, spiritual qualifications for coming to the Holy Supper, which this question sought to address.

It is not enough merely to recite the Apostles' Creed. One must know what it signifies. One must understand it, assent to it, and embrace all that it represents with true faith, which entails knowledge, assent, and trust. Those who truly believe are genuinely sorry for their sins. They acknowledge them before God and struggle against them. This is why the Reformed churches fence the table, meaning that we invite all those

---

dem Leiden und Sterben Christi bedeckt sei, begehren auch je mehr und mehr ihren Glauben zu stärken, und ihr Leben zu bessern. Die Unbussfertigen aber und Heuchler essen und trinken sich selbst das Gericht" (Schaff, *Creeds of Christendom*, 3:336). "Quibus accendendum est ad mensam Domini? Tantum iis, qui vere dolent, se suis peccatis Deum offendisse: confidunt autem sibi ea propter Christum remissa esse: et quas reliquas habent infirmitates, eas passione et morte illus obtectas esse, quique desiderant magis ac magis in fide et integritate vitae proficere. Hypocritae autem, et qui non vere resipiscunt, damnationem sibi edunt et bibunt" (Niemeyer, *Collectio Confessionum*, 448–49).

who are members of the true church (i.e., a congregation with the marks of the true church according to *BC* 29) to come to the table of the Lord. We instruct those who are present but who do not believe or who have not demonstrated true faith by uniting themselves with the true church not to come to the table of the Lord.

Ursinus identifies three conditions for Communion. To come to the table are those who (1) "acknowledge their sins and are truly sorry for them"; (2) "who are trusting that their sins are forgiven through and for Christ's sake"; and (3) "who have genuine disposition toward accomplishing more and more the integrity of faith and life."[28] This is why Paul instructs self-examination before coming to the table (1 Cor 11:28–29). The body to be discerned in Holy Communion is Christ's "proper and natural" (*BC* 35), not the congregation. The Corinthians were profaning the glorified, risen body of Christ (1 Cor 11:30–32), not the members of the congregation. Certainly, there were moral implications of the Supper (e.g., waiting for each other), but the sense of "body" is established in verse 24, "and when he had given thanks, he broke it." The cup in verse 27 is the Communion cup. There is no reason to think that the sense of "body" shifts in verse 29 to mean "members of the congregation."

The spiritual requirements for coming to the table are major reasons why Reformed congregations do not practice paedo-Communion (infant Communion).[29] To commune infants is to collapse the sign of initiation into the sign of renewal. We should baptize the children of believers and initiate them into the visible covenant community, but the Supper has a distinct function.[30] It is not for *initiation* but for *renewal* and *nourishment*.[31] With the exception of adults with diminished capacity, who have given genuine indications of a simple trust in Jesus, the Supper is ordained for those who do understand and who have made a credible profession. The

28. "1. Qui peccata sua agnoscunt, et vere de his dolent: 2. Qui confident ea sibi remissa est, per et propter Christum: 3. Qui habent serium propositum in fide et vitae integritate magis ac magis proficiendi" (Ursinus, *Corpus doctrinae*, 443); Ursinus, *Commentary*, 424. See the discussion of hypocrites under *HC* 82.

29. Venema, *Children at the Lord's Table*; Waters and Duncan, *Children and the Lord's Supper*.

30. See the discussion of infant baptism under *HC* 74.

31. This was the standard Reformed distinction. E.g., Petrus van Mastricht (1630–1706), who distinguished between baptism as the "sacramentum regenerationis" and the Supper as the "sacramentum nutritionis" (*Theoretico-practico Theologia*, 2.828–45).

Spirit does indeed sometimes bring infants to faith (Luke 1:41), but they are not capable of making profession.[32] Olevianus explains that the Supper is intended for those who have already been regenerated.[33] Baptism represents the *beginning* of the Christian life and therefore is available to the children of believers. The Supper, however, may not be received by any except those who are "in covenant" (*in foedere*) inwardly, those who have consciously entered into covenant relations with the Lord.[34] The children of believers are indeed in the covenant of grace, but they are not yet eligible for the sign of covenant renewal. According to Olevianus, the circle of those eligible for Christian baptism is wider than the circle of those eligible for the Supper.[35] Baptism testifies to the divine promise (as does the Supper) and even the expectation of blessing, but the Supper also testifies to and confirms the reality, the "action of grace" within.[36] The Supper is called the Eucharist because it is an act of conscious thanksgiving by Christians.[37]

As to when children should make profession of faith and receive Communion, the key qualifier is "credible." Calvin's earliest church order (1537), proposed to the Genevan city council, required children to be examined before making profession of faith.[38] In the Palatinate, when the catechism was adopted young people were expected to memorize the catechism prior to profession of faith.[39] This was the practice of all the Reformed churches in the British Isles and Europe in the classical period. Ursinus distinguishes between *potential* faith and *actual* faith (*fides actualis*). Those who come to the table must give evidence of an actual faith.[40] Just a little over a decade after the catechism was published, the

32. See the excursus on infant faith and presumptive regeneration. See Ursinus, *Commentary*, 425; Ursinus, *Corpus doctrinae*, 443.

33. Olevianus, *De substantia*, 2.94; see 2.67–68; Clark, *Caspar Olevian*, 204–5.

34. This material is adapted from Clark, *Caspar Olevian*, 205.

35. Olevianus, *De substantia*, 2.68.

36. "Testificandi gratiarum actioni" (Olevianus, *De substantia*, 2.68).

37. Olevianus, *De substantia*, 2.68; see 2.83, 87–88, 91, 93.

38. "Draft Ecclesiastical Ordinances," in Reid, *Calvin: Theological Treatises*, 67.

39. E.g., chapter 3 of the church order of the churches under the cross (1568) required children to memorize the catechism. See de Ridder, "Church Orders," 84.

40. "Infantes nondum sunt capaces coenae, qua nondum fidem habent actua sed tantum inclinatione Hic requiritur fides actualis, initium novae obedientiae propositum pie vivendi" (Ursinus, *Corpus doctrinae*, 443).

Provincial Synod of Dort (1574) required an examination of candidates for Communion as part of the procession of making a profession of faith.[41]

If we adopt Dorothy Sayers's useful paradigm, articulated in her influential essay, "The Lost Tools of Learning," we have a framework for thinking about when children might be expected to profess faith.[42] She distinguishes three stages: the parrot (memorization), the pert (analysis), and poet (transcendence).[43] In their younger years, children naturally delight in repeating what they are told. They have a remarkable facility for memorization. This is when children should memorize Scripture and the catechism. The second stage is that season in which children begin to analyze what they have memorized. They are immature, and so the questions may come out ill-formed, hence "pert." It is important for parents, pastors, and elders to persevere, however, with children because what they are really asking is whether we adults really believe the faith or whether we are going through the motions. The third stage of development is that of the "poet," in which the child begins to realize that there are transcendent realities to which symbols point. It is somewhere in this stage that we might expect a child to make profession of faith, when children are more prepared to speak for themselves, when the faith in which they have been catechized has become not just an inheritance but a personal possession.

Children are not computers, and childhood development occurs at different speeds in different children. Assuming that a child has been well catechized and raised in a reasonably normal Christian way, that is, that the child has been lovingly disciplined and included in public worship and that the family has attended faithfully to the means of grace (preaching of the word and the sacraments as appropriate), parents might ordinarily expect their child to begin to be ready as early as age twelve—perhaps a little earlier or later. Certainly, we should expect covenant children ordinarily to be prepared to profess faith before the elders before high school graduation, and parents should not assume that profession must be postponed as if profession and graduation must go hand in hand.

41. De Ridder, "Church Orders," 162; Monsma, *New Revised Church Order Commentary*, 231–36; Spaan, *Christian Reformed Church Government*, 124–26.

42. Sayers, "Lost Tools of Learning."

43. Clark, "Classical Christian Catechesis."

It is essential that a believer understand the difference between being nourished by ordinary bread and wine and being nourished, by the work of the Holy Spirit, by the true, "proper and natural" body and blood of Christ through faith alone (*BC* 35). It is also essential that the elders and pastor(s) who hear a child's profession be convinced that the profession of faith is genuine and reasonably well-informed because there is some jeopardy attached to the Supper (*HC* 82). God's word says:

> Whoever, therefore, eats the bread or drinks the cup of the Lord in an unworthy manner will be guilty concerning the body and blood of the Lord. Let a person examine himself, then, and so eat of the bread and drink of the cup. For anyone who eats and drinks without discerning the body eats and drinks judgment on himself. That is why many of you are weak and ill, and some have died. But if we judged ourselves truly, we would not be judged. But when we are judged by the Lord, we are disciplined so that we may not be condemned along with the world. (1 Cor 11:27–32 ESV)

Because believers are fed by Christ in a sacred feast, it is a communion, a mysterious, Holy Spirit–enabled fellowship between believers and the risen Christ. It is not for unbelievers. Hypocrites, those who profess faith but who do not believe, put themselves in jeopardy when they come to the table.

A Reformation debate between the Reformed and the Lutherans over the "eating by the impious" (*manducatio impiorum*) is relevant and worth considering briefly here. The Lutherans confess, "Not only those who believe and are worthy, but also those the unworthy and unbelievers receive the true body and blood of Christ, thought they do not receive life and comfort, but rather judgment and damnation, if they do not turn and repent."[44] The Reformed, however, deny that unbelievers receive Christ. In *BC* 35, we confess, "Though the sacraments and the thing signified are joined together, not all receive both of them. The wicked person certainly takes the sacrament, to his condemnation, but does not receive the truth of the sacrament, just as Judas and Simon the Sorcerer both indeed received

44. "Epitome of the Formula of Concord," art. 7, in Kolb and Wengert, *Book of Concord*, 506.16.

the sacrament, but not Christ, who was signified by it."[45] Ursinus responds to the Lutherans in eight points, summarized here:

1. Faith is essential to receiving Christ in the Supper. Faith does not make him present, but we *receive* him only through faith. He is present in the Supper to the unbeliever, but only in judgment. By definition, according to *HC* 76, to eat in the true sense "is to embrace with a believing heart" Christ and his benefits.[46] Our Lord defined eating, in this sense, in terms of believing in John 6:56: "Whoever eats my flesh and drinks my blood abides in me and I in him." This is not true of unbelievers. They do not eat Christ, that is, they do not receive him and are not united to him. The Supper is not magic. It does not *create* faith, but it confirms *faith* that the Spirit creates, through the gospel.

2. We eat Christ by faith alone (*sola fide*).[47] Ursinus adroitly observes that we agree heartily with Luther's *Small Catechism* when he says, "These words, 'for you,' require believing hearts."[48] Therefore unbelievers do not receive Christ.

3. Christ offers (*offert*) his body in the Supper only to those who for whom he died. He did not die for the hypocrites and reprobates (John 17:9; Luke 22:19).[49]

---

45. United Reformed Churches in North America, *Liturgical Forms and Prayers*, 195.

46. Ursinus, *Commentary*, 426; Ursinus, *Corpus doctrinae*, 444. See the discussion under *HC* 76. In principle, Luther agreed. In 1527 he wrote against "the fanatics" (Zwingli et al.): "Thus, all that our body does outwardly and physically, if God's Word is added to it and it is done *through faith*, is in reality and in name done spiritually. Nothing can be so material, fleshly, or outward, but it becomes spiritual when it is done in the Word and in faith. 'Spiritual' is nothing else than what is done in us and by us through the Spirit and faith, whether the object with which we are dealing is physical or spiritual. Thus, 'Spirit consists in the use, not in the object' ['in usu, non in objecto, spiritus est'], be it seeing, hearing, speaking, touching, begetting, bearing, eating, drinking, or anything else" (*LW* 37:92; emphasis added).

47. Ursinus, *Corpus doctrinae*, 444; Ursinus, *Commentary*, 426.

48. "Ut recete dicitur in catech[ismum] Lutheri: Hac verba, pro vobis, requirunt corda credentia" (Ursinus, *Corpus doctrinae*, 445). Luther, *Parvus Catechismus*, 49 is worded slightly differently: "Quia hoc verbum *pro vobis* requirit omnino corda credentia."

49. Ursinus, *Corpus doctrinae*, 445.

4. Because the Spirit of Christ and the body of Christ are never separated and because the body of Christ is a life-giving bread, whoever receives the bread also receives life. Unbelievers may eat the Communion elements, but they have thereby neither Christ's body nor life.

5. Unbelievers eat and drink judgment, not Christ. They are driven from Christ and his benefits. They remain under judgment so long as they do not believe. It is not possible to eat Christ (as defined) and be under judgment.

6. Paul establishes a principle in 1 Corinthians 10:21: it is impossible to commune with Christ *and* demons.

7. To say that unbelievers receive Christ in the Supper is to contradict Matthew 15:26 by giving the children's bread to dogs, that is, unbelievers. It is casting pearls before swine (Matt 7:6).

8. Various fathers taught explicitly that it is impossible for unbelievers to eat Christ at the table.[50]

There are four reasons why we confess that unbelievers eat and drink judgment to themselves:

1. The Supper is sacred, but they profane it, make common the "sacred symbol" by taking it to themselves.[51]

2. Unbelievers profane the covenant of God (*foedus Dei*) by usurping to themselves the sign of the covenant (Heb 10:29).[52] They want to give the appearance of being in covenant with God when in fact they are in covenant with the devil.

3. Unbelievers and hypocrites do not discern Christ's body in the sacrament and so trample his blood under their feet (Heb

50. Ursinus, *Commentary*, 427; Ursinus, *Corpus doctrinae*, 446.

51. "Sacra symbola" (Ursinus, *Corpus doctrinae*, 446).

52. Ursinus, *Corpus doctrinae*, 446.

10:29).[53] Thus do not receive Christ and his benefits offered in the Supper. In so doing they mock God.[54]

4. They condemn themselves by hypocritically professing Christ and approving his teaching but knowingly denying it inwardly.

The Supper is for believers. To borrow from *HC* 98, we not should be wiser than God. We are to observe the Holy Supper in the way that Christ instituted. The great purpose of the Supper is to feed believers with the body and blood of Christ and so more and more unite us with himself and with one another. What fellowship does light have with darkness, or Christ with Belial (2 Cor 6:14–15)? Believers have a sweet, intimate communion, however, with the risen Christ, by the mysterious operation of the Spirit, in which these tangible signs and seals sweetly confirm the gospel promises.

Question 82

Are they then also to be admitted to this supper who show themselves by their confession and life to be unbelieving and ungodly?

No, for thereby the covenant of God is profaned and his wrath provoked against the whole congregation; wherefore the Christian church is bound, according to the order of Christ and his apostles, to exclude such persons by the office of the keys until they amend their life.[55]

53. Ursinus, *Corpus doctrinae*, 446; Ursinus, *Commentary*, 428.

54. Ursinus, *Corpus doctrinae*, 446.

55. "Sollen aber zu diesem Abendmahl auch zugelassen werden, die sich mit ihrem Bekenntniss und Leben als Ungläubige und Gottlose erzeigen? Nein: denn es wird also der Bund Gottes geschmähet, und sein Zorn über die ganze Gemeine gereizet. Derhalben die christliche Kirche schuldig ist, nach der Ordnung Christi und seiner Apostel, solche bis zur Besserung ihres Lebens durch das Amt der Schlüssel auszuschliessen" (Schaff, *Creeds of Christendom*, 3:336–37). "Suntne illi etiam ad hanc Coenam admittendi, qui confessione et vita, ac infideles et impios esse declarant? Nequaquam: Nam eo pacto foedus Dei profanatur, et ira Dei in universum coetum concitatur. Quocirca Ecclesia, ex praescripto Christi et Apostolorum, hos, clavibus regni coelorum utens, a coena arcere debet, quoad resipuerint, et mores mutaverint" (Niemeyer, *Collectio Confessionum*, 449).

HC 81 addressed who ought to come to the table, but here we come to the question of who should be admitted to the Lord's Supper. There are no perfected Christians in this life, so only sinners are admitted to the table. Those, however, who give evidence by their doctrine or life that they are unbelieving are not to be admitted to the Supper.

Fencing the Lord's Table has long been a pastoral challenge in Reformed churches. After all, Calvin's first tenure in Geneva ended in part over his desire to fence the table from certain prominent citizens in Geneva whom he and Guillaume Farel (1489–1565) regarded as scandalous.[56] Today, especially in the West, where Christians do not always distinguish between a democratic republic in civil government and the visible church as an embassy of the kingdom of God, it can be challenging to explain why some professing believers are admitted to the table and others are not.[57]

Nevertheless, the church is not a democracy. She has a King who has instituted keys of that kingdom and entrusted the administration of the keys to the visible church.[58] We have explicit instruction regarding church discipline in Matthew 18:15–20 and 1 Corinthians 5:1–8. The latter case is directly connected to the administration of the Lord's Supper. Paul also addresses the abuse of the Lord's Table in 1 Corinthians 11:17–34. Paul warns against communing unworthily (1 Cor 11:27) and of the importance of spiritual self-examination before communing (1 Cor 11:28–32).

The Reformed churches have long practiced fencing the table. At the provincial Synod of Dort, in 1574, the churches adopted a church order that addressed the fencing of the Lord's Table: "Art. 81. Whoever brings a valid certificate shall be admitted to the Lord's Supper unless it was written a long time ago, in which case one must proceed as if there is no testimony. However, we deem it fitting and are inclined to accept rather than decline those whose piety has been attested either by a written or personal testimony."[59] Though the practice of bringing a certificate may seem foreign to some now, it was the typical practice in the Dutch Reformed Church.

56. Parker, *John Calvin*, 57–66; Gordon, *Calvin*, 71–72.

57. On the influence of democratization on American Christianity, see Hatch, *Democratization of American Christianity*.

58. See the discussion of the keys under *HC* 83–84.

59. De Ridder, "Church Orders," 162.

This practice continues in some places, but whatever we make of it now, it certainly tells us that our forebears took seriously the responsibility to fence the table.[60]

Four years later, the provincial Synod of Dort in 1578 had to address the question of what to do with those who were influenced by the biblicism of the Erasmians and others.

> 35. Whether it is permissible to admit to the Lord's Supper those who do acknowledge the Bible alone as God's Word but will neither answer nor agree to answer the usual questions which are asked of those who go to the Lord's Supper.
> Answer: The churches shall maintain their usual custom of requiring confession of faith. Everyone is bound to give an account of his faith according to the teaching of Peter. It is also not fitting that a usual custom of the congregation should be changed for some particular reason.[61]

The intent of the Reformed churches became clearer by 1581. The language that would be used by the great Synod of Dort was adopted at the national Synod of Middleburg. "43. No one shall be admitted to the Lord's Supper except one who, according to the custom of the church which he joins, has made confession of the Reformed religion, who has testimony of godly behavior, without which those who come from other churches shall not be admitted."[62] The synod required both *objective* evidence of qualification, that is, evidence of membership in a Reformed church and *subjective* evidence, that is, assurance of a degree of piety.[63]

The Synod of Gravenhage in 1586 adopted the language of "confession of the Reformed Religion" and "godly conduct."[64] Thus, the practice of the Reformed churches had been established for forty years by the time the great Synod of Dort met in 1618–1619. The Dort Church Order (1619),

60. Spaan (*Christian Reformed Church Government*, 127) reasserts the necessity of a letter of attestation in 1968. Van Dellen and Monsma (*Church Order Commentary*, 257–58) discuss this in detail.

61. De Ridder, "Church Orders," 228.

62. De Ridder, "Church Orders," 280.

63. We should note that none of the church orders call for evidence of a second blessing as a condition for Communion.

64. Art. 54 in De Ridder, "Church Orders," 358.

article 61, says: "61. Only those shall be admitted to the Lord's supper who, according to the usage of the churches which they join, have made confession of the Reformed religion, together with having testimony of a godly walk, without which also those who come from other churches shall not be admitted."[65] The original Reformed practice then was to guard or fence rather closely. There were fewer Reformed denominations in the late sixteenth and early seventeenth centuries, but they had to address many of the same challenges that we do. There were other traditions in the Netherlands at the same time the Reformed were working out their practice. They were particularly aware of the Anabaptists and other competing groups. They were aware of the problem of people traveling through town, visiting a church, and asking for Communion.

There is another challenge in fencing the table: hypocrites, that is, those who profess the faith but who have not received new life, who do not yet actually believe, who are not actually, by the Holy Spirit, united to Christ.[66] Olevianus addresses the issue directly:

> In this world is the administration of salvation by which Christ the King Himself outwardly, through the gospel and baptism, gathers to Himself and calls to salvation a people or visible church (in which many hypocrites are mixed). To those in this congregation who have always been His elect, He Himself administers and bestows that salvation to which He calls them. He makes the outward call efficacious, granting them the repentance and faith by which they respond to the One calling them.[67]

He explains that just as the Israelites offered their children to Moloch and as outwardly righteous Pharisees rejected Christ, so too there are "hypocrites or reprobates" (*hypocritae seu reprobi*) who participate in "external

65. De Ridder, "Church Orders," 554. The church order of the Christian Reformed Church followed the original art. 61 until the church order was revised in in the 1960s. Compare art. 61 in Stuart and Hoeksema, *Church of the Christian Reformed Church*, 51–52, with the revised art. 60 in Monsma, *New Revised Church Order Commentary*, 239–45. The practice of admitting anyone belonging to an "evangelical church" and making an evangelical profession of faith probably dates to ca. 1972–1973, when a complaint was made against this practice and upheld by a Christian Reformed Synod in 1973. Report 37, received by the Synod of the Christian Reformed Church in 1975, effectively overturned the decision of Synod 1973. See Christian Reformed Church, *Acts of Synod 1975*, 471–83.

66. Ursinus, *Commentary*, 430; Ursinus, *Corpus doctrinae*, 448.

67. Olevianus, *Exposition*, 10.

worship" (*externum cultum*) without actually entering into fellowship with Christ. There are those who participate only in the external administration of the covenant of grace who never receive Christ and his benefits, the substance of the covenant of grace, offered in the administration of the covenant.[68] The sacraments are a genuine offer of grace (*oblatio gratiae*), but Christ will not communicate himself to the reprobate.[69]

Not all sinners are hypocrites. Scripture does not teach that Christians achieve sinless perfection in this life (Rom 7:7–25). We understand, with the prophets and the apostles, that, short of glorification, all believers continue to sin (1 John 1:8–9), but those who are born again, who by grace alone truly believe, embrace Christ, their Savior and their righteousness. They know that they stand before God only on the basis of what Christ has done. The impenitent have yet to honestly reckon with the greatness of their sin and misery. A hypocrite pretends to believe, he wishes to be regarded outwardly as a Christian, but he has not seen himself for what he really is before the perfect bar of God's holy and relentless law. He has not seen Christ for who and what he really is: the only Righteous One, the Holy One of Israel who obeyed and died as the substitute for all of the elect, the only propitiation (turning away of wrath) for God's people. Thus, he has not fled to Christ as his Savior and refuge.

Thus, though we admit penitent, believing sinners, that is, those who are truly believing, who are sorry for their sins, we must fence hypocrites from the Supper because there is jeopardy at the Lord's Table. For example, when they come to the table, hypocrites and the impenitent eat and drink judgment to themselves. Just as baptism signifies God's wrath against sin, in the destruction of the "world that then was" in Noah's day (2 Pet 3:6) and the destruction of Pharaoh's armies in Moses's day (Exod 14:19–30), so too the Supper has two edges. For believers it is a great spiritual feast. For unbelievers it is death. This is why Paul warns the Corinthians that some of them became sick and even died because they abused the Lord's Table (1 Cor 11:28–29). Thus, in *BC* 35, we confess, "Though the sacraments and the thing signified are joined together, not all receive both of them. The wicked person certainly takes the sacrament,

68. Olevianus, *De substantia*, 2.53, 56; Clark, *Caspar Olevian*, 202–3.

69. Olevianus, *De substantia*, 2.52.

to his condemnation, but does not receive the truth of the sacrament, just as Judas and Simon the Sorcerer both indeed received the sacrament, but not Christ, who was signified by it."[70]

We should notice that the catechism says that when hypocrites and the impenitent are permitted to the table, "the covenant of God is profaned." When the catechism says "the covenant," it is referring to the administration of the covenant of grace. God's covenant, "I will be a God to you and to your children" (Gen 17:7), is his gracious promise to redeem all his elect, but that promise, that covenant, must be administered outwardly, and it has consequent obligations. Since God has freely accepted us for Christ's sake alone, there are now responsibilities that entail. We pledge obedience to God's holy moral law in response to his grace. We live in union and communion with the risen Christ as members of his church, the Christ-confessing covenant community. The Supper is the divinely ordained sign and seal of confirmation to us that the promises really are true, but that sign must be administered as a trust to and in the church. To administer it in a way that contradicts our Lord's instruction is to profane, that is, to make common what is holy, what is set apart as belonging to the Lord. This is why Paul, in 1 Corinthians 10:1–4, says that the history of Israel's unbelief and abuse of the sacraments was given to instruct us to avoid the same the sins and consequences.

Ursinus explains that to profane the covenant of grace is to regard as friends of God those who are not.[71] We profane the covenant when we admit to the Supper as members of the covenant of grace those "to whom God promises nothing."[72] Hypocrites also profane it when they take to themselves the signs while being impenitent, and also when ministers "knowingly and willingly administer the signs to such persons as God has excluded from his covenant."[73] This includes both those who deny Christian doctrine and those who live ungodly lives.[74]

We should take Paul's warning in 1 Corinthians 11:30–31 seriously. It seems foolish to test the Lord to see what he might do. Paul's intent is

70. United Reformed Churches in North America, *Liturgical Forms and Prayers*, 195.

71. Ursinus, *Commentary*, 430; Ursinus, *Corpus doctrinae*, 449.

72. Ursinus, *Commentary*, 430.

73. Ursinus, *Commentary*, 430.

74. Ursinus, *Commentary*, 430; Ursinus, *Corpus doctrinae*, 449–50.

clear. We ought not to permit unbelievers, hypocrites, and the impenitent at the Lord's Table. Refusing Communion to such people might have a truly salutary effect in the truest sense. It may be that should the church say to such a person: "We are sorry to say this, but you may not come to the Lord's Table until you recognize your sin, turn from it, and embrace the Lord Jesus in true faith," that the person might be struck in the heart, might realize the gravity of the situation, might do those things for which we pray and hope.

In our radically egalitarian age, in a culture that values autonomy, obeying the clear and repeated teaching of Holy Scripture by fencing the table will not likely be received with favor. It may seem to some as elitist and narrow, even though that is a false judgment of things. It is not elitist to obey him who poured himself out as the suffering servant (Isa 52:13–53:12; Phil 2:5–11). Rather, we must obey God rather than people (Acts 5:29). We must fear God rather than people. We must serve God rather than people, and we must love God first and our neighbor as ourselves. If history is an indication, we are likely going to be criticized no matter what we do, so better to obey our Lord and seek his approval rather than the approval of people.

QUESTION 83

What is the office of the keys?

QUESTION 84

How is the kingdom of heaven opened and shut by the preaching of the holy gospel?

QUESTION 85

How is the kingdom of heaven shut and opened by Christian discipline?

Lord's Day 31

QUESTION 83

What is the office of the keys?

The preaching of the holy gospel and Christian discipline; by these two the kingdom of heaven is opened to believers and shut against unbelievers.[1]

Our Lord gave to the visible church the keys of the kingdom in Matthew 16:18–19: "And I tell you, you are Peter, and on this rock I will build my church, and the gates of hell shall not prevail against it. I will give you the keys of the kingdom of heaven, and whatever you bind on earth shall be bound in heaven, and whatever you loose on earth shall be loosed in heaven" (ESV). Keys lock and unlock. Just as Christ has instituted his visible church (*HC* 54; *BC* 28), so too he has instituted the instruments by which people are admitted and excluded. The Spirit uses the preaching of the good news of Christ's incarnation, righteous obedience, death, resurrection, ascension, and return to open the kingdom to his elect. He uses discipline to chasten his church, to correct erring sheep, and to exclude the impenitent.[2] The power and authority are spiritual, not civil. Nevertheless, the keys, the preaching of the gospel and the use of church discipline, are real.

Individuals compose a kingdom, but it is a corporation with a discernible, authoritative head. It is not a democracy. It has a king and subjects. It has boundaries. In the ancient world, there were walls and gates. An ancient city was an enclosed camp fortified with walls and gates. Those gates had to be opened and closed. Indeed, the noun for "keys" is derived from the Greek verb "to open" (κλείω).

The spirit of modernity is the autonomous individual.[3] That same spirit dominates much of modern evangelical Christianity. The Reformed

1. "Was ist das Amt der Schlüssel? Die Predigt des heiligen Evangeliums, und die christliche Busszucht, durch welche beide Stücke das Himmelreich den Gläubigen aufgeschlossen und den Ungläubigen zugeschlossen wird" (Schaff, *Creeds of Christendom*, 3:337). "Quid sunt claves regni coelorum? Praedicatio evangelii, et Ecclesiastica disciplina: quibus coelum credentibus aperitur: infelibus autem clauditur" (Niemeyer, *Collectio Confessionum*, 449). Ursinus synthesizes the exposition of *HC* 83–85. The exposition resumes under *HC* 85 (Ursinus, *Corpus doctrinae*, 454).

2. "Quid est potestas clavium … ?" (Ursinus, *Corpus doctrinae*, 454).

3. Trueman, *Rise and Triumph*.

church, however, confesses that Christ established an *institutional* church, with offices (ministers, elders, and deacons) and gave to her ministers and elders the authority to exercise the keys. In the civil and secular sphere, individualism may be a virtue. In the sacred, spiritual, or ecclesiastical sphere, the assumption of individual autonomy is disastrous. In the administration of the covenant of grace, Christians are first of all part of a corporation, a body. They are baptized into the visible, institutional church. They are catechized in the church. They receive the means of grace (the preaching of the gospel and the administration of the sacraments) in the church. That administration of the means Christ has instituted is essential to the spiritual growth and vitality of Christians.

To anticipate an objection, as basic as our membership in the corporate covenant community is, it is also true that no one else can believe for another, but we do not have to choose between these truths. It is true that God administers his grace and promises to and through his corporate covenant community (the visible, institutional church), and it is true that one must believe personally in order to receive Christ and his benefits. Ordinarily, that is, by divine ordination and in the ordinary providence of God, it is as a member of the covenant assembly, through the external administration of the covenant of grace, that the elect are given new life and true faith. In scriptural teaching, we are by nature rebels, at odds with God and excluded from his kingdom (Eph 2:1–13). Apart from Christ our righteous substitute and our king, we have no status before God except as condemned before the king. Therefore we very much need God to open the gates to the kingdom of heaven for us.

A second issue is relevant here. Since the late nineteenth century, it has become popular to speak rather broadly about "kingdom work." Certainly believers are citizens of God's twofold kingdom wherever they are and ought to conduct themselves accordingly.[4] That a citizen is doing something does not make that citizen's work kingdom work, at least not in the sense in which the kingdom is in view here. Further, only the visible church is authorized to do this work of advancing Christ's kingdom. There are many organizations and charities doing important work, but they are not the

4. "Duplex esse in homine regimen" (Calvin, *Institutio* 3.19.15; Barth, *Joannis Calvini Opera Selecta*, 3:294.5).

visible, institutional church. They are not charged to preach the gospel, to administer the sacraments, to exercise discipline, and thereby to make disciples. Therefore, when congregations set their priorities, they should remember their centrality and uniqueness in Christ's order and kingdom.

We confess that Christ and his apostles have instituted offices to fulfill that ministry: minister of word and sacrament, and elders.[5] Ministers have the responsibility to use the first key: preaching of the good news that Jesus is God the Son incarnate, that he has obeyed in place of his people, that he died, that he was raised from the dead on the third day, that he has ascended to the right hand of the Father, and that he will return bodily, in glory, to judge the living and the dead. God the Spirit uses that message to bring his people to life (Rom 10:14–16; *HC* 65). To those who do not believe the gospel, it becomes a judgment against them (Rom 2:16). Thus, through the preaching of the gospel, great spiritual works are in operation.

According to Matthew 18:15–22, our Lord Jesus instituted ecclesiastical discipline, for which the elders are chiefly responsible. They have the ruling office in the church. Church discipline is not arbitrary, and its goal is not punitive but restorative. It is to prevent and to address scandal in the church. It is a difficult but necessary work, and the church should do it slowly, graciously, patiently, but firmly. The two great temptations are a rush to judgment out of frustration and a reluctance to do what must be done for the sake of the erring and for the sake of the church.

The Roman Catholic Church invokes Matthew 16:18–19 to justify the papacy.[6] She claims that Peter "holds the first place in the college of the twelve," shares some of his authority to the rest of the Twelve, and gives them their mission.[7] If we consider the passage in its context, however, we have to begin with Peter's confession in verse 16, which is the reason Christ called him "blessed" and gave to him (as a representative of the visible church) the keys. Peter confessed, "You are the Christ, the Son of the Living God."[8] The Father revealed to him that confession (v. 17). It is the Christ-confessing Peter whom Jesus names Πέτρος, the rock (πέτρᾳ)

5. *BC* 30–31, in United Reformed Churches in North America, *Liturgical Forms and Prayers*, 187–88.

6. *CCC* §§551–53.

7. *CCC* §552.

8. σὺ εἶ ὁ χριστὸς ὁ υἱὸς τοῦ θεοῦ τοῦ ζῶντος.

on whom Christ will build his church (v. 18). Obviously, there is a play on words here, but it is Christ, not Peter, who will build the church, against which the gates of Hades will not prevail. The idea of a papacy is utterly absent from our Lord's intent and from Matthew's intent as a narrator and theologian. Thus, we need not be ashamed to say that he gave the keys to Peter the confessor. We may be certain that it is *confessing* Peter who is the rock and to whom Christ gave the keys, because as soon he denied Christ he became "Satan" in verse 23. As Jesus was teaching his disciples about his coming death (Matt 16:21), Peter tried to dissuade him. Jesus responded by denouncing him: "But he turned and said to Peter, 'Get behind me, Satan! You are a hindrance to me. For you are not setting your mind on the things of God, but on the things of man'" (Matt 16:23 ESV). Rome cannot have Peter for a pope unless she will also have him as an antichrist.

Question 84

How is the kingdom of heaven opened and shut by the preaching of the holy gospel?

In this way: that according to the command of Christ, it is proclaimed and openly witnessed to believers, one and all, that as often as they accept with true faith the promise of the Gospel, all their sins are really forgiven them of God for the sake of Christ's merits; and on the contrary, to all unbelievers and hypocrites, that the wrath of God and eternal condemnation abide on them so long as they are not converted. According to this testimony of the Gospel, God will judge men both in this life and in that which is to come.[9]

9. "Wie wird das Himmelreich durch die Predigt des heiligen Evangeliums auf und zugeschlossen? Also, dass nach dem Befehl Christi allen und jeden Gläubigen verkündigt und öffentlich bezeuget wird, dass ihnen, so oft sie die Verheissung des Evangeliums mit wahrem Glauben annehmen, wahrhaftig alle ihre Sünden von Gott, um des Verdienstes Christi willen, vergeben sind; und hinwiederum allen Ungläubigen und Heuchlern, dass der Zorn Gottes und die ewige Verdammniss auf ihnen liegt, so lange sie sich nicht bekehren. Nach welchem Zeugniss des Evangelii Gott beide in diesem und dem zukünftigen Leben urtheilen will" (Schaff, *Creeds of Christendom*, 3:337). "Quo pacto aperitur et clauditur regnum coelorum praedicatione Evangelii? Cum ex mandato Christi credentibus universis et singuilis, publice annunciatur, omnia peccata ipsis divinitus propter meritum Christi condonari, quoties promissionem evangelii vera fide amplectuntur: contra vero omnibus infidelibus

The catechism characterizes the twofold ministry of the church, two of the three marks of the church (*BC* 29), by use of a metaphor "borrowed from stewards, to whom are delivered the keys of the house in which they are stewards."[10] As Ursinus explains, the church is God's house, and the ministers are his administrators (*oeconomi*). Question 84 alludes to Matthew 16:19, "I will give you the keys of the kingdom of heaven, and whatever you bind on earth shall be bound in heaven, and whatever you loose on earth shall be loosed in heaven" (ESV). Ursinus reminds us that we must observe a distinction between the two keys: "In the preaching of the gospel, the first key releases, the second binds."[11]

The preaching of the word was a regular element of apostolic and early Christian worship. We know from the New Testament that preaching was an essential part of Christian worship in the churches of the apostolic era. We infer from the *Didache,* from the very early second century, from the existence of "worthy overseers and ministers of the Lord" (ἐπισκόπους καὶ διακόνους ἀξίους τοῦ κυρίου) that preaching continued to be a regular part of Christian worship.[12] We have an Easter (*pascha*) sermon from Melito of Sardis (ca. AD 130–190), who interpreted passages from Isaiah 52–53 typologically, in light of Christ.[13] The document we know as 2 *Clement* (ca. AD 140), preached by an anonymous presbyter, is perhaps the earliest extant Christian sermon.[14] The sermons of Chrysostom (ca. AD 347–407) are notable for their expository quality and were admired by Calvin for that reason.[15] We know, however, that not all the preaching of the patristic period was expository. Beginning in the late patristic period (e.g., the

et hypocritis denuntiatur, tantisper ipsis iram Dei et aeternam condemnationem incumbere, dum in suis sceleribus perseverant: secundum quod Evangelii testimonium, Deus tam in praesenti, quam in futura vita iudicaturus est" (Niemeyer, *Collectio Confessionum*, 449).

10. Ursinus, *Commentary*, 441; Ursinus, *Corpus doctrinae*, 455. Note that in the *Corpus doctrinae*, the exposition combines questions 83–85.

11. "In praedicatione evangelii claves prius soluunt, deinde ligant" (Ursinus, *Corpus doctrinae*, 455). Regarding church discipline, see the discussion under *HC* 85.

12. *Didache* 15.1, in Holmes, *Apostolic Fathers*, 367.

13. Old, *Reading and Preaching*, 1:285–89.

14. Holmes, *Apostolic Fathers*, 139–65.

15. Old, *Reading and Preaching*, 2:171–96; Kelly, *Golden Mouth*, 94–103, 55–71.

Jerusalem Lectionary),[16] preaching began to dominated by the church calendar. That trajectory continued through the medieval period.[17]

T. H. L. Parker's assessment seems right:

> There is a third style of expository preaching, a style which was practised especially in the fourth and fifth centuries. It consisted of expounding whole books of the Bible, passage by passage. Thus, Chrysostom preached through most of the books of the New Testament and his younger contemporary Augustine expounded the Psalms and the Fourth Gospel. Although in the four or five centuries preceding the Reformation the Bible was far from absent in preaching (we need think only of the Biblical homilies of Anselm, Bernard of Clairvaux, Bonaventure, or Thomas Aquinas), the broad scope of connected series largely dropped out.[18]

Through the course of the medieval period, though expository preaching did happen (mainly in the schools), it was not flourishing.[19] Sermons were not driven by the text read in its canonical context and in its immediate context as much as they were driven by the text's *ecclesiastical* context. The Reformation marked a recovery of expository preaching. As Andrew Pettegree says, the magisterial Protestants "preached incessantly."[20] This was certainly true for Calvin, who more or less preached himself to death.

When the catechism says that it is by the "preaching of the holy gospel" that the kingdom is opened and shut, it reflects the deeply held conviction of the Reformed churches that God has ordained and the Spirit uses the official proclamation of the gospel, in the visible church, to bring his elect to new life and true faith.[21] Thus, Olevianus writes, "Christ is offered to us by the Father in no other way than through the foolishness of preaching, or the promise of the gospel (1 Cor. 2)."[22] In modern evangelical Christianity, however, the line between lay witness and the official

16. Old, *Reading and Preaching*, 2:134–66.

17. E.g., Old, *Reading and Preaching*, 3:143–84.

18. Parker, *Calvin's Preaching*, 80.

19. See Old, *Reading and Preaching*, vol. 5, for a survey of preaching in the medieval church.

20. Pettegree, *Reformation and the Culture*, 10.

21. See the discussion under *HC* 65.

22. Olevian, *Firm Foundation*, 11.

preaching of the gospel has become blurred. The Reformed theologians who composed and edited the catechism, however, and the churches that adopted it, did not blur this line. They certainly expected believers to talk to others about *the faith,* that is, the objective facts of the gospel and about their faith, their own subjective appropriation of Christ and his gospel through faith alone.[23] Nevertheless, they left the preaching of the holy gospel to the church and particularly to the office of minister.[24] As Olevianus explains, when Christ said, "Lo, I am with you always" (Matt 28:20), that was a promise of Christ's presence in the office of preaching.[25]

As inefficient as it may seem to us, God the Spirit has left to the office of preacher the ministry of announcing the good news. Through the act of announcing the incarnation, obedience, righteousness, death, resurrection, ascension, and return of Christ, he has promised to bring all of his elect to new life, to faith, and through faith alone to justification and salvation. "Jesus said to them again, 'Peace be with you. As the Father has sent me, even so I am sending you.' And when he had said this, he breathed on them and said to them, 'Receive the Holy Spirit. If you forgive the sins of any, they are forgiven them; if you withhold forgiveness from any, it is withheld'" (John 20:21–23 ESV).

The pronoun *them* refers to the disciples mentioned in verse 20. The resurrected Christ showed his hands to the disciples. He commissioned them, and to them he gave the authority to "forgive sins" and to withhold forgiveness. The minister is not Christ, whose authority is original and divine. The minister's authority is genuine but derivative. His office is to announce what is true, but when God the Son speaks, he creates realities (Gen 1:3; John 1:3; Mark 4:39). Wonderfully, he has chosen to work, by the Spirit, through the ministry of the word to create new life and true faith.

In Romans 10 the apostle Paul says that it is only through the hearing of the gospel that God's people are brought to faith and saved, and that hearing come through preaching, and preaching comes from being sent:

> How then will they call on him in whom they have not believed? And how are they to believe in him of whom they have never heard? And how are they to hear without someone preaching?

23. See the discussion of lay witness under *HC* 86.

24. See the discussion of the free or well-meant offer of the gospel under *HC* 65.

25. Olevianus, *Exposition*, 58–59.

> And how are they to preach unless they are sent? As it is written, "How beautiful are the feet of those who preach the good news!" But they have not all obeyed the gospel. For Isaiah says, "Lord, who has believed what he has heard from us?" So faith comes from hearing, and hearing through the word of Christ. (Rom 10:14–17 ESV)

There is clear biblical evidence that the officers whom God has called are commissioned to announce the good news everywhere:

> And we are witnesses of all that he did both in the country of the Jews and in Jerusalem. They put him to death by hanging him on a tree, but God raised him on the third day and made him to appear, not to all the people but to us who had been chosen by God as witnesses, who ate and drank with him after he rose from the dead. And he commanded us to preach to the people and to testify that he is the one appointed by God to be judge of the living and the dead. To him all the prophets bear witness that everyone who believes in him receives forgiveness of sins through his name. (Acts 10:39–43 ESV)

Notice Peter's appeal to his status as an authorized messenger: "But to us who had been chosen by God as witnesses." This aspect of the New Testament mission is often overlooked in favor of what is essentially an assumption about what *must* be the case, but we should be careful not to read our modern egalitarian assumptions back into Scripture. Nevertheless, God is calling his people, and he is doing so through the preaching of the gospel. He is sending ministers, and this external call (vocation) is the first key of the kingdom of God. God the Spirit exercises his effective or efficacious call through the public preaching of two words: the law and the gospel. This is how the catechism structures and characterizes the preaching of the holy gospel: "the promise of the gospel" of free justification by grace alone, through faith alone, on the ground of the imputation of Christ's merits. Christ's ministers also announce its contrary: the condemnation of all those who do not believe the gospel.

This twofold gospel is reflected in the Heidelberg liturgy of 1563. There was a declaration of pardon.[26] After the morning sermon, the minister said, "Beloved in the Lord, since we see in God's commandments, as in a

26. Gibson and Earngey, *Reformation Worship*, 611–12.

mirror, how serious and manifold our sins are, for which we deserve temporal and eternal punishment, let us wholeheartedly confess the same to our heavenly Father." The congregation then said a prayer of confession of sins, after which the liturgy charged the minister to "proclaim to the believers the forgiveness of sin ... saying:"

> Now hear the firm comfort of God's grace, which he promises to all believers in the gospel:
>
> Thus says the Lord Christ (in John chapter 3): For God so loved the world that, that he gave his only begotten Son, so that all who believe in him, shall not perish but have eternal life.
>
> As many of you who are displeased with themselves and their sins, and believe that they are completely forgiven through the merit of Jesus Christ alone, and have resolved to die to sin more and more and to serve the Lord in true holiness and righteousness; to them (since they believe in the Son of the living God) I proclaim on account of God's commandment, that they are loosened from all their sins in heaven (as he promises in his holy gospel) by the perfect satisfaction of the holiest suffering and death of our Lord Jesus Christ. Amen.

To those in the congregation who do not believe, however, the minister was to say: "But as many among you, who still take pleasure in their sins and vices or against their conscience persist in sin; to them I proclaim on account of God's commandment, that the wrath and judgement of God remains upon them, that all their sins are retained in heaven, and they may not be dispensed from eternal condemnation until they repent."[27] These two words, law and gospel, are what we understand to be the "whole counsel" of God.[28]

It may seem counterintuitive to us that God the Spirit should choose to use what Paul calls the "foolishness" of preaching (1 Cor 1:25), but that is just what he has done. This is because the kingdom is not brought by

27. Gibson and Earngey, *Reformation Worship*, 612.

28. See the discussion of the distinction between law and gospel under *HC* 3.

our efforts but by the sovereign power of God's Spirit working through the "due use of the ordinary means."[29]

Because of our modern history of revivals, American Christians have been conditioned to neglect the ordained and the ordinary in favor of the unordained and the extraordinary.[30] So, it can be difficult to recalibrate our thinking, but recalibrate we must.[31] Week by week a minister is meant to enter the pulpit and announce these two aspects of the gospel, these two words. He does so with much prayer, fear, and trembling, but with the expectation that God the Spirit is quietly, mysteriously working through the announcement of these words. As we look back over the history of redemption and the history of the church, we can see that it has been so, even if, as we look about us now, it might seem quite hidden. One day it will all be made very clear what the Spirit has been doing.

QUESTION 85

How is the kingdom of heaven shut and opened by Christian discipline?

In this way: that according to the command of Christ, if any under Christian name show themselves unsound either in doctrine or in life, and after several brotherly admonitions do not turn from their errors or evil ways, they are complained of to the church or to its proper officers; and, if they neglect to hear them also, are by them denied the holy sacraments and thereby excluded from the Christian communion, and by God himself from the kingdom of Christ; and if they promise and show real amendment, they are again received as members of Christ and his church.[32]

29. WCF 1.7, in Westminster Assembly, *Humble Advice of the Assembly*, 5.

30. Clark, *Recovering the Reformed Confession*, 74–112.

31. On the ordinary means of grace, see Horton, *Ordinary*; Clark, *Recovering the Reformed Confession*, 71–72, 112–14; Clark, "Evangelical Fall," 133–47.

32. "Wie wird das Himmelreich auf- und zugeschlossen durch die christliche Busszucht? Also, dass nach dem Befehl Christi diejenigen, so unter dem christlichen Namen unchristliche Lehre oder Wandel führen, nachdem sie etlichemal brüderlich vermahnet sind, und von ihren Irrthümern oder Lastern nicht abstehen, der Kirche, oder denen, so von der Kirche dazu verordnet sind, angezeiget, und so sie sich an derselben Vermahnung auch nicht kehren, von ihnen durch Verbietung

With this question the catechism turns to the second of the two keys, church discipline. In our late modern age, it is widely regarded that truth claims and authoritative acts are not genuine but rather a pretense for the exercise of control. In contrast to the spirit of the age, the dominant question of the premodern age, when the catechism was written, was, "What has God said?" and the question of the modern period was, "Has God said?" The question of our age is, "Who is asking?" In the late medieval period the nominalists argued that the relationship between signs and things was arbitrary. Today we live in an age of post-Christian nominalists, who assume there can be no divinely ordained relations between signs (words) and things signified (realities). They assume that the relationship between signs and things signified is purely arbitrary. That we routinely and almost universally use gender (a grammatical category) and sex (a biological category) interchangeably signals how deeply influenced we have become by this notion that there is no fixed reality, no objective truth, no divinely ordered relations between signs and things signified.

Such a setting can make even the idea of church discipline difficult for people to accept because it is easy for late modern Christians to assume that an act of discipline is not an official, churchly recognition of what is, that is, an acknowledgment of God's moral law, of the state of sin (transgression of God's moral law), and the need for repentance. Rather, we can see it as an arbitrary and unjust exercise of authority. To be sure, all church assemblies are composed of sinful, fallible humans, and in this life none reaches sinless perfection. Nevertheless, our Lord gave to the visible church an unambiguous charge to use the keys of the kingdom (Matt 16:19; 18:18–20) and even an outline of how to use the second key, church discipline (Matt 18:15–20). Thus, the Reformed churches confess that the use of church discipline is one of the marks of the true church

---

der heiligen Sacramente aus der christlichen Gemeine, und von Gott selbst aus dem Reiche Christi werden ausgeschlossen; und wiederum als Glieder Christi und der Kirche angenommen, wenn sie wahre Vesserung verheissen und erzeige" (Schaff, *Creeds of Christendom*, 3:337–38). "Quo pacto clauditur et aperitur regnum coelorum per disciplinam Ecclesiasticam? Cum ex mandato Christi, ii qui nomine quidem sunt Christiani, verum doctrina aut vita se ostendunt a Christo alienos, postquam aliquoties fraterne admoniti, ab erroribus aut flagitiis discedere nolunt, Ecclesiae indicantur, aut iis, qui ab Ecclesia ad eam rem sunt constituti, ac si ne horum quidem admonitioni pareant: ab iisdem interdictione Sacramentorum, ex coetu Ecclesiae, et ab ipso Deo, ex regno Christi excluduntur: ac rursum, si emendationem profiteantur, et reipsa declarent, tanquam Christi et Ecclesiae membra recipiuntur" (Niemeyer, *Collectio Confessionum*, 449–50).

(*BC* 29). One of the marks of the "broadening church" is her refusal to discipline heterodoxy and immorality while simultaneously prosecuting the orthodox for being orthodox.[33]

Holy Scripture does not permit Christians to indulge in skepticism about the relationship between God's word and truth, nor about the authority of Scripture, nor about the genuine ministerial authority of the church to recognize reality and exercise the authority the Chief Shepherd has given to her (1 Pet 5:4).[34] Ursinus reminds us that the Holy Spirit works "effectually by his Word" according to the divine promise in John 20:23, "If you forgive the sins of any, they are forgiven them; if you withhold forgiveness from any, it is withheld" (ESV).[35]

The catechism lists essentially two grounds for discipline: wandering from true Christian doctrine or from the Christian life.

> Those who either obstinately deny some article of faith, or show themselves unwilling to repent and to submit themselves to the will of God according to all his commandments, and who do not hesitate to declare their intention to persist in a course of open wickedness,—all such are not to be admitted to the church; and if they have been admitted into the church by baptism, they must, nevertheless, not be permitted to approach the Lord's supper until they renounce their errors and show amendment of life.[36]

Private sins are addressed privately, public sins publicly.[37]

One temptation we always face in the church is to refuse to exercise discipline. This is the path of least resistance. The question is whether there is really an offense, be it doctrinal or moral. There are objective standards for these things. The moral standard is established by God's holy law and explained in the third part of the catechism. We learn our doctrinal standards first in Holy Scripture, summarized mostly briefly

33. The expression "broadening church" comes from Loetscher, *Broadening Church*. Perhaps the most famous case of the persecution of the orthodox by the "broadening church" was the trial of J. Gresham Machen for his support of the Independent Board for Foreign Missions in 1935. On this case see Stonehouse, *J. Gresham Machen*, 469–92; Hart, *Defending the Faith*, 147–57.

34. Ursinus, *Commentary*, 446; Ursinus, *Corpus doctrinae*, 459.

35. Ursinus, *Commentary*, 441.

36. Ursinus, *Commentary*, 447.

37. Ursinus, *Commentary*, 447.

for us in the ecumenical creeds and more fully in the catechism, the confession, and the canons.

Ursinus defends the necessity of church discipline on several grounds. Chief among them:

1. Our Lord and Paul both established and confirmed it (Matt 18:19; 1 Cor 5:1–5);[38]
2. it was the practice of the old covenant church;[39]
3. for the glory of God;[40]
4. to protect against the profanation of the sacrament (1 Cor 11:27);
5. to preserve the safety of the church (1 Cor 11:30);
6. to prevent believers from stumbling;
7. and to distinguish believers from "those who are aliens from the church; as are those who are openly wicked, who are blasphemers, and who have fallen into such errors as Arianism, Mahometanism, etc."[41]

Ordinarily, discipline begins with private admonition. It becomes an ecclesiastical matter only after the first two steps listed by our Lord. If someone offends, you go to him. If he refuses, then you take a brother or two. This is the "two or three witnesses" principle from the Mosaic law (Deut 17:6), affirmed by our Lord (Matt 18:16). Only if he still refuses does a matter go to the visible, institutional church.

This process is important. There are two mistakes to be avoided. First is rushing the process by not following the first two steps. Only if a person shows himself to be impenitent should the matter go to the church, and then the ministers and elders must work together, prayerfully, carefully, to correct the brother. The hope is that a believer recognizes his error or

38. Ursinus, *Commentary*, 442.

39. Ursinus, *Commentary*, 442–43.

40. Ursinus, *Commentary*, 444.

41. Ursinus, *Commentary*, 445.

sin, repents, and can be reconciled (Matt 18:15).[42] That is always the goal of church discipline. When the impenitent person repents, we receive them with joy. It is an answer to much prayer. This is why we leave the ninety-nine sheep (Matt 18:12) and go to great lengths to recover the one. We rejoice because heaven rejoices when they return. We should not be misled by Philip Schaff's translation of *BC* 29. The French and Latin texts say "for correcting vices" (*ad corrigenda viatia*), not "punishing sins."[43]

Exclusion from the Lord's Table is the final step of discipline. We do not, however, follow the Anabaptist practice of the ban.[44] That is, we do not cut off all contact. Rather, we do as Scripture says. We treat the impenitent as they have shown themselves to be, as unbelievers (Matt 18:17). Unbelievers need to hear the law and the gospel. Those who profess Christ but show refusal to acknowledge sin and refusal to repent need especially to realize the greatness of their sin and misery under God's holy law. Perhaps they think that they will repent later, or perhaps they have convinced themselves that God approves of their error or sin. In any event, they need to understand that God's doctrinal and moral standards do not waver. Of course, all this needs to be accompanied with prayer. Only God the Spirit can soften the heart of the unbelieving and stubborn. Further, we certainly do not exclude such a person from public worship, where the law and gospel are preached, where the Spirit works to bring new life and faith. When the table is administered and impenitent persons are excluded, we hope and pray that they will recognize how grave their condition is.

Finally, with Ursinus, we should distinguish between the "power of the keys of the church" and "political power."[45] There is a relatively new body of scholarship that can help us understand Ursinus (and thus the catechism itself) here. In 2010, David VanDrunen pioneered the modern study of the distinction between two kingdoms in Reformed theology in

---

42. Ursinus, *Commentary*, 448–49.

43. Schaff, *Creeds of Christendom*, 3:420. See Müller, *Die Bekenntnisschriften*, 244.23.

44. Leith, *Creeds of the Churches*, 284–85.

45. "Potest clavium Ecclesiae … potestae politica" (Ursinus, *Corpus dotrinae*, 463; Ursinus, *Commentary*, 450).

the sixteenth and seventeenth centuries.[46] Most recently, Jonathan Beeke has advanced our understanding by focusing on the development of the doctrine of the "twofold kingdom" (*duplex regnum*) in Reformed orthodoxy in Leiden (e.g., Franciscus Junius), in Geneva after Calvin (e.g., Francis Turretin), and in Edinburgh (e.g., Johannes Scharpius).[47] Beeke concludes that the Reformed orthodox moved beyond Calvin by more clearly delineating "Christ's twofold kingdom not in terms of scope, but according to the mode whereby Christ rules (i.e., whether considered as *Logos* or *theanthrōpos*)." Nevertheless, he concludes that there is "substantial agreement between the early Reformed and the Reformed orthodox concerning Christ's kingdom and governance."[48]

Ursinus distinguishes between ecclesiastical power and civil power. When he writes, "Ecclesiastical discipline is exercised by the Church. Civil power is exercised by the presiding officer or magistrate," he is making use of the distinction between the two spheres of God's kingdom or between the kingdom of God and the civil polity.[49] In his *Summary of Theology* (*Summa theologiae*), in explaining the threefold office of Christ (prophet, priest, and king) he asks, "What is his Kingdom?" and defines it this way: "It is the Son of God instituting and preserving the ministry of the Gospel and through it converting and giving life to his elect and sanctifying them by the Holy Spirit, defending them against the Devils, raising them to life eternal, and leading them into the sight of the Father, in order that thereafter he may reign openly and not through the ministry."[50] This definition of Christ's kingdom corresponds to the way he explains the catechism, but restricts the kingdom to administration of the covenant of grace in the church and to the eschatological realm.

Thus, he explains, "The [civil] polity judges according to civil and positive laws. The church judges according to divine laws, or the Word

46. VanDrunen, *Natural Law.*

47. Beeke, *Duplex Regnum Christi.*

48. Beeke, *Duplex Regnum Christi,* 219.

49. "Ecclesiastica disciplina exercetur ab Ecclesia: Potestas civilis à praetore vel magistratu" (Ursinus, *Corpus doctrinae,* 463).

50. "(63.) Quid est ejus regnum? Est Filium Dei inde ab initio instituere et conservare ministerium Evangelii, et per illud convertere et vivificare electos et sanctificare eos Spiritu sancto, defendere contra Diabolos, resuscitare ad vitam aeternam, et adducere in conspectum Patris, ut in eis divinitas deinceps regnet palam, et non per ministerium" (Reuter, *D. Zachariae Ursini,* 1.15–16).

of God."[51] God, in his word, has committed the power of the keys to the visible, institutional church. It belongs to her alone to preach the law and the gospel and to make judgments about the spiritual state of the members of the church.[52] The church speaks the word of God to consciences (*ad conscientias*). The civil polity alone wields the sword (*gladius*) and corporal punishment (*poena corporali*).[53] When the contumacious (*contumaces*) reconsider (*retractare*), the church does not execute a penalty, but the civil magistrate does, even when a criminal is repentant.[54] Thus, the church may receive again a penitent adulterer, robber, and thief even as the civil magistrate exercises even the most severe penalty on those same persons.[55]

Like most everyone in the premodern world, Ursinus assumed that the civil magistrate had a right to enforce Christian orthodoxy. Though that notion was nearly universally assumed since the elevation of Theodosius as emperor in AD 379, John Owen was already questioning it in the late seventeenth century.[56] Even so, in his explanation of the catechism, Ursinus follows the pattern Calvin established:

> Therefore, in order that none of us may stumble on that stone, let us first consider that there is a twofold government in man: one aspect is spiritual, whereby the conscience is instructed in piety and in reverencing God; the second is political, whereby man is educated for the duties of humanity and citizenship that must be maintained among men. These are usually called the "spiritual" and the "temporal" jurisdiction (not improper terms) by which is meant that the former sort of government pertains to the life of the soul, while the latter has to do with the concerns of the present life—not only with food and clothing but with laying down laws whereby a man may live his life among other men holily, honorably,

51. "Politia iudicat secundum leges civiles et positivas: Ecclesia secundum leges divinas, seu verbum Dei" (Ursinus, *Corpus doctrinae*, 463).

52. Ursinus, *Corpus doctrinae*, 463; Ursinus, *Commentary*, 450.

53. Ursinus, *Corpus doctrinae*, 463.

54. Ursinus, *Corpus doctrinae*, 463. For Ursinus, the civil magistrate represents only the law or the covenant of nature (*foedus naturae*), but in the church both the law and the gospel are administered. See the discussion under *HC* 15.

55. Ursinus, *Corpus doctrinae*, 463–64.

56. Gribben, *John Owen and English Puritanism*, 101–2. See King, *Emperor Theodosius*; see also the discussion under *HC* 124.

> and temperately. For the former resides in the inner mind, while the latter regulates only outward behavior. The one we may call the spiritual kingdom, the other, the political kingdom. Now these two, as we have divided them, must always be examined separately; and while one is being considered, we must call away and turn aside the mind from thinking about the other. There are in man, so to speak, two worlds, over which different kings and different laws have authority.[57]

Ursinus is making use of Calvin's doctrine of God's "twofold government" (*duplex regimen*) of the world, which makes a clear distinction between the spiritual and the temporal. Within it are two distinct spheres, "the spiritual kingdom" (*regnum spirituale*) and "the political kingdom" (*regnum politicum*).[58] According to Calvin, the political is concerned about *this* life, and it regulates "outward customs" (*externos mores*).[59] The civil magistrate is not concerned about the interior life of the soul. Calvin divides (*partiti*) these two spheres, which, he writes, must *always* be considered separately.

From this we are right to infer that the visible church ought to resist the temptation to ask the civil magistrate to do the disciplinary work of the church or to meddle in church affairs, and the church ought to respect the sphere sovereignty, established by God's providence, of the civil magistrate (e.g., Rom 13:1–7; 1 Pet 2:13–17; 1 Tim 2:2).

This way of distinguishing between the two spheres of God's kingdom, the spiritual and the political, is also expressed in *BC* 36, where, according to Daniel Hyde, the confession

> grounds the civil government in God's goodness, not his grace, in creation, not redemption. God rules over all things, but in two different ways, as the two kingdoms doctrine of the Reformers expressed. This doctrine was that God rules what Calvin called the civil kingdom and what Luther called the kingdom of the left hand as creator and sustainer of temporal, earthly, and provisional matters, while he rules the spiritual kingdom or kingdom of the right

57. Calvin, *Institutes* 3.19.15; Barth, *Joannis Calvini Opera Selecta*, 4:294.4–21.

58. Barth, *Joannis Calvini Opera Selecta*, 4:294.16–17.

59. Barth, *Joannis Calvini Opera Selecta*, 4:294.15.

> hand (Calvin and Luther respectively) as creator, but especially as redeemer of the eschatological kingdom.[60]

Hyde is right to see the distinction between creation (nature) and redemption (grace). It was the Anabaptists, not the Reformed, who confused the two.[61]

---

60. Hyde, *With Heart and Mouth*, 481.

61. See the discussion of nature and grace under *HC* 6.

III

The Third Part of the Catechism

Question 86

Since then we are redeemed from our misery by grace through Christ, without any merit of ours, why should we do good works?

Question 87

Can they then not be saved who do not turn to God from their unthankful, impenitent life?

Lord's Day 32

Question 86

Since then we are redeemed from our misery by grace through Christ, without any merit of ours, why should we do good works?

Because Christ, having redeemed us by his blood, also renews us by his Holy Spirit after his own image, that with our whole life we show ourselves thankful to God for His blessing, and also that he be glorified through us; then also, that we ourselves may be assured of our faith by the fruits thereof; and by our godly walk win also others to Christ.[1]

As noted at the outset, the catechism is in three parts.[2] The evidence from the catechism itself and from Ursinus is conclusive. We must consider the catechism fundamentally organized into guilt, grace, and gratitude. *HC* 86 reflects this organization.

In this section we come to thankfulness or gratitude, which Ursinus calls the "impulsive cause of good works."[3] What is it? Arnold Huijgen writes that gratitude "does not primarily consist in human acts of obedience to God's commandments, although the Heidelberg Catechism stresses that it is impossible for those grafted in through true faith not to produce fruits of gratitude by keeping God's commandments."[4] Primarily, he argues, gratitude is our "receptivity that turns into reciprocity, not what

---

1. "Dieweil wir denn aus unserm Elend, ohne all unser Verdienst, aus Gnaden durch Christum erlöset sind, warum sollen wir gute Werke thun? Darum, dass Christus, nachdem Er uns mit seinem Blut erkauft hat, uns auch durch seinen Heiligen Geist erneuert zu seinem Ebenbild, dass wir mit unserm ganzen Leben uns dankbar gegen Gott für seine Wohlthat erzeigen, und Er durch uns gepriesen werde. Darnach auch, dass wir bei uns selbst unsers Glaubens aus seinen Früchten gewiss seien, und mit unserm gottseligen Wandel unsern Nächsten auch Christo gewinnen" (Schaff, *Creeds of Christendom*, 3:338). "Cum ab omnibus peccatis et miseriis, sine ullo nostro merito, sola Dei misericordia, propter Christum liberati simus, quid est cur bona opera faciamus? Quia postquam nos Christus suo sanguine redemit, renovat nos quoque suo Spiritu ad imaginem sui, ut tantis beneficiis affecti, in omni vita nos erga Deum gratos declaremus, et ipse per nos celebretur. Deinde, ut nos quoque ex fructibus, de sua quisque fide certi simus. Postremo, ut vitae nostrae integritate alios Christo lucrifaciamus" (Niemeyer, *Collectio Confessionum*, 450).

2. See the discussion of the structure of the catechism in the introduction and under *HC* 2.

3. "Quaestio de causis impulsivis bonorum operum" (Ursinus, *Corpus doctrinae*, 478).

4. Huijgen, "Practicing Gratitude," 210.

we give, but what we ask."[5] It is not a "transitional stage" that we overcome in this life but "the lasting result of justification" in which "the believer continuously lives" as both justified and sinner.[6] Olevianus categorically denies that good works "serve to make us right with God" in any way. Rather, they serve three purposes. First, "after we have been freely and graciously justified through the imputation of Christ's righteousness, we show with good works that we are thankful to God the Lord, so that God might be praised through us." Second, "by them as the fruit of faith it is confirmed that we have not a hypocritical but a true faith." Third, "by the example of our good works we win others to Christ and keep those already won from falling away. The longer they are kept close to Christ, the more they are built up."[7]

This is precisely the teaching we find in Ursinus under this question. We do good works not in order to be justified (the Roman Catholic doctrine and the teaching of all moralists). Rather, we do good works out of thankfulness *because* we have been justified.[8]

Some take issue with the very notion of gratitude as the motive for good works, saying it is sub-Christian and a "debtor's ethic."[9] This critique rests on a caricature of the Reformation doctrine of gratitude. Further, the claim that the Scriptures nowhere teach an ethic of gratitude seems to be refuted from Exodus 20:2–17, where the first word that the Lord speaks to his people at Sinai is the gospel: "I am Yahweh your God, who brought you out of the land of Egypt, out of the house of slavery" (Exod 20:2). This is the prologue to the Decalogue.[10] The moral law of God, the norm by which God's redeemed people are to live out of gratitude, follows. Moses has already been teaching thankful obedience to the Lord out of gratitude for his free salvation (e.g., Exod 13:8). The Israelites kept the feast because of what the Lord had done. Moses's instruction in Deuteronomy 4 was

5. Huijgen, "Practicing Gratitude," 210.

6. Huijgen, "Practicing Gratitude," 210.

7. Olevian, *Firm Foundation*, 116–17.

8. Ursinus, *Commentary*, 465; Ursinus, *Corpus doctrinae*, 478–79; Clark, "How We Got Here," 15n27; Baxter, *Aphorisms of Justification*.

9. Piper, "For Freedom"; Piper, "Foundational Passions. Session 1. Part 1." These are elaborations of themes first addressed in Piper, *Purifying Power of Living*.

10. For more on this see the discussion under *HC* 93.

predicated on the Lord's gracious deliverance of his church out of Egypt (Deut 4:40). In Ephesians 5:4 Paul contrasts the sin of coarse talk with gratitude (εὐχαριστία). In Colossians 2:6–7 Paul grounds our Christian obedience in gratitude: "Therefore as you received Christ Jesus the Lord, walk in him, being firmly rooted and established in him and being confirmed in the faith as you were taught, abounding in gratitude" (ἐν εὐχαριστίᾳ). The writer to the Hebrews also appeals plainly to gratitude as a prime motive for Christian obedience: "Therefore let us be grateful [ἔχωμεν χάριν] for receiving a kingdom that cannot be shaken, and thus let us offer to God acceptable worship, with reverence and awe, for our God is a consuming fire" (Heb 12:28–29 ESV). The catechism's use of and appeal to gratitude is thoroughly biblical and in the mainstream of the Reformation doctrine of the Christian life. The rejection of it reveals a misunderstanding of both Scripture and the Reformation relation of good works to salvation. We do good works not in order to be saved but because we have been saved.

The major premise of *HC* 86 is the biblical, Protestant doctrine of salvation *sola gratia, sola fide*, which I have explored and discussed throughout this work. The German text of the answer uses the verb *erkauft*, which is fairly translated "to redeem" or "to purchase." This imagery takes us back to *HC* 1, where we confess that our only comfort in life and in death is that we "belong, body and soul, in life and death" to our faithful Savior Jesus Christ. The language of being bought is Paul's in 1 Corinthians 6:20, "You were bought with a price, therefore honor God with your body," and 7:23, "You were bought with a price; do not become the bondservants of men." The Latin text says *liberati simus* ("we have been liberated") and says, "Since from all our sins and miseries, without any of our merit, only by the mercy of God, on account of Christ we have been liberated, why should we do good works?" The rhetorical effect of the ordering of the phrases is to teach us to discuss good works only *after* reiterating the biblical, Protestant, and Reformed conviction that redemption (salvation) is by grace alone, through faith alone. To make it crystal clear, the catechism rejects any notion that we sinners have merit of any kind, condign or congruent, relative to our standing before God.[11]

11. See the discussion under *HC* 63–64.

The catechism speaks thus because the Reformed had long spoken of the "double grace" (*duplex gratia*) or the "double benefit" (*duplex beneficium*) of Christ.[12] We are justified and sanctified by grace alone, through faith alone in Christ alone. Our new life, our sanctification, that process of being gradually conformed to the image of Christ, is the consequence of our free justification and his gracious salvation of his people.

Luther labeled some "antinomians" in the 1530s. This paragraph from his *First Disputation against the Antinomians* (1537) almost certainly influenced the language of the catechism:

> Human nature has been so corrupted and blinded by the devil's venom in Paradise [Gen. 3:1–6] that it neither comprehends the magnitude of sin nor feels and dreads the punishment of sin, God's wrath, and eternal death. Therefore, it is necessary that the doctrine that reveals and manifests these evils should be preserved in the Church. Now, this doctrine is the Law. On the other hand, when these same evils have been revealed and shown to us by the Law, it is likewise necessary, if we are not to fall into despair, that the other doctrine should be preserved in the Church as well—the one that teaches consolation in the face of the accusation and terrors of the Law, grace in the face of God's wrath, forgiveness of sins and righteousness in the face of sin, and life in the face of death. This doctrine is the Gospel, which teaches that the reason why God through His Word has imprisoned all under sin is so that He may have mercy on all [Rom. 11:32; Gal. 3:22]. It teaches that God most certainly desires to forgive all people their sins, to liberate from death, and to give righteousness and life to all who feel their misery, unrighteousness, and perdition. And He desires to do this freely, without any merit on our part, namely, in such a way that these benefits are imparted to believers on account of Christ.[13]

Luther is explaining the relation between the pedagogical use of the law and the gospel, but this passage illustrates the degree to which the

12. Venema, *Accepted and Renewed*; Clark, *Caspar Olevian*, xviii, 97, 137–209; Clark, "Benefits of Christ."

13. *LW* 73:70.

Reformed were dependent on and influenced by Luther.[14] He also defends what Philip Melanchthon, the Lutheran orthodox, and the Reformed called the third use of the law (*tertius usus legis*): "The Law, therefore, cannot be removed, but it remains—before Christ as unfulfilled and after Christ as to be fulfilled, although the Law is never kept perfectly in this life, even by the justified. For it demands that we love God with our whole heart and our neighbor as ourselves [Luke 10:27; Deut. 6:5; Lev. 19:18]. This will finally be done perfectly in the coming life."[15]

Nevertheless, through the 1540s and 1550s the question persisted among the magisterial Protestants how to relate sanctification and good works to justification. Some argued that we ought not to speak of good works at all, since that tends to lead Christians astray by tempting them to think once again that their good works, done in cooperation with grace, somehow contribute to their standing before God.[16] It is not as if there were no grounds for such a fear. The Leipzig Interim of 1548 omitted the qualifier *sola* from its article on justification.[17] George Major (1502–1574) defended the article by teaching that good works are "necessary for retaining salvation." Melanchthon agreed with him.[18] Major repudiated that formulation in 1570, but the controversy was still roiling Protestantism as the catechism was being drafted.

Remember, the medieval doctrine, out of which the Protestants had come, taught that we are justified because we are sanctified, and we are sanctified by grace and cooperation with grace. There were some, for example Andreas Osiander (1498–1552), who were arguing ingeniously that Christ dwells in us by virtue of our union with him, and God justifies us on the basis of the indwelling Christ.[19] Calvin saw Osiander's move as a fundamental threat to the doctrine of justification, the "chief axis on which our faith revolves," and expanded his discussion of justification

14. Clark, "'Subtle Sacramentarian' or Son?," 35–60.

15. *LW* 73:71.

16. Kolb, *Nikolaus Von Amsdorf*, 123–71.

17. Kolb and Nestingen, *Sources and Contexts*, 184–89; Clark, "How We Got Here," 13–14.

18. Bente, *Historical Introductions*, 112–24; Bretschneider, *Corpus Reformatorum*, 21.421, 775. See Seeburg, *Textbook of the History*, 2:366–74; Kolb, "George Major as Controversialist," 455–68.

19. Clark, "*Iustitia Imputata Christi*," 269, 297–310.

considerably in order to refute him.[20] The catechism sides definitively with Luther and Calvin against Major and Osiander. The third part of the catechism addresses the Christian life, lived in union with Christ, in light of our free justification, through faith alone (*sola fide*). Ursinus writes: "We have learned, from what has been said upon the two former general divisions of the Catechism, that we are redeemed from sin and death, that is, from all the evils of guilt and punishment by no merit of ours, but only by the mere grace of God for the sake of Christ's merits. From this, it follows that we ought to be thankful to God for this great benefit."[21] The third part of the catechism concerns the *fruits* of our justification. Ursinus makes that explicit under his exposition of *HC* 86, when he writes, "We are, nevertheless, bound to render obedience, and perform good works ... because good works are the fruits of our regeneration by the Holy Spirit, which are always connected with our free justification."[22] This is, of course, the very same language of *BC* 24:

> So then, it is impossible for this holy faith to be unfruitful in a human being, seeing that we do not speak of an empty faith but of what Scripture calls "faith working through love," which leads a man to do of himself the works that God has commanded in his Word. These works, proceeding from the good root of faith, are good and acceptable to God, since they are all sanctified by his grace. Yet they do not count toward our justification—for by faith in Christ we are justified, even before we do good works.[23]

Sanctification, that is, gradual, gracious, Spirit-wrought conformity to Christ, and the good works that result from the work of grace in the believer, is the *logically* necessary outcome of the believer's regeneration, justification *sola fide*, and union with Christ. Olevianus writes:

---

20. "Praecipuus fidei cardo vertitur" (Barth, *Joannis Calvini Opera Selecta*, 4:26.29); Calvin, *Institutes* 3.2.16. Compare his discussion of justification in the *Institutes* from 1539–1554 to the dramatically expanded discussion in the 1559 *Institutes* (3.11.5–12; see Calvin, *Opera quae supersunt omnia*, 1:672–80). In the 1559 *Institutes* he spends almost as much space refuting Osiander as he spends in the whole of his earlier discussion of justification.

21. Ursinus, *Commentary*, 464; Ursinus, *Corpus doctrinae*, 477.

22. Ursinus, *Commentary*, 465; Ursinus, *Corpus doctrinae*, 478.

23. United Reformed Churches in North America, *Liturgical Forms and Prayers*, 178.

> I should be zealous to do good works to show that I honor God the Lord and to show that I have a true, not a counterfeit faith. Such faith manifests itself in thankfulness to the Lord for the blessing of the heavenly Father given us by grace as a free gift (Gal. 3) in the blessed seed of Abraham, Jesus Christ. In faith we are also thankful for the inheritance He graciously gives to us as well as to Christ, the natural heir, and for the Kingdom that He has prepared for us in Christ from the foundation of the world—before our birth, without any of our merit.[24]

We live the Christian life, in union with Christ, in a state of favor with God, not seeking his favor by or through our obedience but obeying because we are *already* assured of our full and final acceptance with God. In discussing the Christian's attitude toward the final judgment, Olevianus contrasts the Christian's lack of merit with Christ's merits *for us*. He argues that our inheritance is a matter of *grace,* not works.

> But after I am assured through faith that I am one of Christ's sheep, whom He has redeemed not with gold and silver but with His own blood, I must see to it that I have those marks by which He, through His Spirit, is accustomed to identifying His sheep, namely, fruits worthy of repentance. These are marks like giving food and drink to Christ in His members who are hungry and thirsty, showing hospitality to Christ in strangers, etc. But believers do not depend on these works of gratitude, which is also clear when they say at the judgment, "Lord, when did we see Thee hungry and feed Thee, or thirsty and give Thee drink?" [Matt. 25:37]. Rather, they depend on Christ alone, "who became for them wisdom from God—and righteousness and sanctification and redemption" (1 Cor. 1[:30]).[25]

Sanctification never becomes the ground or instrument of either justification or salvation, but it is the second benefit of Christ, and good works are the fruit of Christ's work *for* us and the Spirit's work *in* us.[26]

24. Olevian, *Firm Foundation,* 85.

25. Olevianus, *Exposition,* 119.

26. On Olevianus's doctrine of sanctification as the second benefit of the covenant of grace, see Clark, *Caspar Olevian,* 181–209.

Here we are speaking of the logical order of salvation (Rom 8:29–30). We are not thinking about time or a temporal or chronological order. Think of it this way: it is the justified, that is, those whom God has declared "righteous," whom the Spirit is graciously and gradually sanctifying. It is the sanctified who do good works. If we reverse the order, then we have become Roman Catholics and turned the good news into bad. Thus, we should reject soundly those who would do away with, as one writer puts it, "*ordo salutis* thinking."[27]

With Luther, Calvin, and all the Reformed churches, we should *also* reject soundly and unreservedly antinomian teaching, any denial of the abiding validity of the moral law of God as summarized in the Decalogue (e.g., Exod 20:2–17) or in the New Testament (e.g., Matt 22:37–40; Rom 13:8–14; Eph 4:17–24), or any teaching that denies the logical necessity of progressive sanctification and consequently grateful obedience to the moral law, in union with Christ, out of gratitude for our salvation. The Spirit *is* gradually conforming believers to Christ's image. Those who have received new life will do good works. Gratitude is not a second blessing any more than oranges are a second blessing on an orange tree (*BC* 24). This is the language of our Lord Jesus in John 15:1–11. Believers "show themselves to be thankful." They manifest their new life by good works. They give evidence of new life and true faith. That is why the two words most often used by the classical Reformed writers and the Reformed confessions in this discussion are *fruit* and *evidence*.

Sanctification has another function in the Christian life: to bolster assurance. This doctrine has also been controversial in some circles. There is a view that says that sanctification can play no role whatsoever in assurance. There is also an approach that says that, in seeking assurance, the first place believers look is to their sanctification. The two clauses in view here are "he be glorified through us" and "we ourselves may be assured of our faith by the fruits thereof." The WSC famously begins by teaching that the "chief end of man" is to "glorify God and enjoy him forever."[28] This notion, however, did not arise in the seventeenth century. It was the

27. E.g., Evans, *Imputation and Impartation*, 264–65. See the discussion of the *ordo salutis* under *HC* 64–65.

28. Westminster Assembly, *Humble Advice of the Assembly*, 1.

common Reformed teaching in the sixteenth century.[29] Adam was created to glorify God and to enjoy him forever.[30] Our Savior, the last Adam, glorified God and now enjoys him forever, and we will, by God's grace, because of Christ's obedience for us, enjoy him forever, and by his grace, with the help of his Spirit, we seek now to glorify him day by day. We do that by obeying him, according to all the teaching of his word and particularly by obeying God's moral law. We will address the role of the law in the Christian life in more detail under *HC* 91.

When, by the grace of God, in union with Christ, with the help of his Spirit, we are obeying him (however imperfectly), that fruit of our free justification and salvation does contribute to our assurance. To be sure, we do not look *first* to our obedience for assurance. In this life, our sanctification is never complete. Therefore, to look at our sanctification as the *primary* ground of assurance must necessarily result in uncertainty. This is not only unbiblical and contrary to our confession but a terrible way to live the Christian life. The ground of our assurance is Christ's obedience and righteousness *for* us, not the Spirit's work *in* us. The ground of our assurance of our salvation and right standing with God is the gospel promise to us, "Whoever believes in him shall not perish but have everlasting life" (John 3:16). The ground of our assurance is objective. It is immutable, established by Christ. It rests on God's immutable, eternal decree and on his immutable, eternal character.

Nevertheless, resting on the fact of Christ's obedience for us and on his promises to us—for example, "it is finished" (John 19:30), "having therefore been justified" (Rom 5:1), "no one can snatch them from my hand" (John 10:28)—we may also look to the work of God's Spirit in us as evidence that we really do believe. We rightly say that we are justified and saved by grace alone (*sola gratia*), through faith alone (*sola fide*), but believers frequently ask the question, "How do I know that I believe?" It is not sufficient to answer that question by simply repeating the exhortation, "Believe!" There are other questions. "Do I know the greatness of

29. E.g., Olevianus, *Romanos Notae*, 130, 131–32, 180–81; Olevianus, *Philippenses et Colossenses*, 180; Olevianus, *De Inventione Dialecticae*, 18; Clark, *Caspar Olevian*, 187; "Ultimus ergo et principalis finis creationis hominis est celebratio Dei. Ideo enim Deus creatuit rationales, angelos et homines, ut ab eis agnitus in aeternum celebretur" (Ursinus, *Corpus doctrinae*, 28); Calvin, *Institutes* 1.5.1; 2.1.3.

30. See the discussion under *HC* 6.

my sin and misery?" and "Do I know the history of salvation?" and "Do I agree that what Scripture says is true?" One who does not yet know oneself to be, by nature, under the wrath of God, who has not sensed the jeopardy in which all of Adam's children exist after the fall, is not ready to flee to Christ as one's only hope and righteousness. Certainly, true faith requires a knowledge of the facts of Christ's saving work and assent to those truths. One must also trust heartily that what Christ did, he did for us (*pro nobis*), for me (*pro me*). This is why it is so important for believers to hear and read over and again God's law and Christ's promises. We must be reminded constantly of what God demands and what Christ has fulfilled for us and promised to us.

Further, it is entirely appropriate and even necessary for the believer to find evidence of faith by observing the evidences, however small they may be, that the Spirit of God has given the believer new life. We begin with the objective, the promises of God represented to us in the preached gospel and in the gospel made visible in the sacraments. We are baptized people, and as such we have been outwardly identified with Christ's death. We have made profession of faith in the church and admitted to Holy Communion, and by the mysterious operation of the Spirit we are being nourished by the body and blood of Christ.[31] We see ourselves for what we are by nature: sinners. We seek our standing before God only in what Christ has done for us. We are grieved by our sins. With Paul we sometimes despair, "Wretched man that I am! Who will deliver me from this body of death?" (Rom 7:24 ESV). That is the cry of the Christian who struggles with and sometimes seems overcome by sin and death. Finally, however, we say: "There is therefore now no condemnation for those who are in Christ Jesus. For the law of the Spirit of life has set you free in Christ Jesus from the law of sin and death. For God has done what the law, weakened by the flesh, could not do. By sending his own Son in the likeness of sinful flesh and for sin, he condemned sin in the flesh, in order that the righteous requirement of the law might be fulfilled in us, who walk not according to the flesh but according to the Spirit" (Rom 8:1–4 ESV). It is because of what Christ has done for us that we can move forward in conformity to Christ. Believers are no

31. See discussion under *HC* 65–79.

longer under the law of sin and death but under the "law of the Spirit of life." Christ has liberated us from condemnation. The same righteous substitute has not only justified but is sanctifying us. Is our sanctification perfect? No, but just as we trust Jesus for our justification and salvation, so we trust him for our sanctification.

The last major point of *HC* 86 is its reference to Christian witness relative to sanctification and good works. This last clause, "and by our godly walk win also others to Christ," is truly important for a variety of reasons. Imagine how Christianity would be viewed were there no scandal caused by clergy sexual abuse of parishioners, if we did not have to account for pederasty among Roman Catholic priests, the Crusades, the Inquisition, or the treatment of Jews in the Middle Ages. Sanctification or its absence has a great effect on the Christian witness to the watching world. Our sanctification or lack thereof has an effect on the plausibility of our testimony to the facts of redemption: the incarnation, Christ's obedience, his death, his resurrection, and his ascension. Now, regardless of our failings, the facts are the facts. Jesus did what he did, and he is returning, and when he does he will settle accounts with the skeptics. Nevertheless, just a very brief review of the history of scandals in the church gives plenty of *prima facie* evidence that keeps us from being cavalier about the corruption of the Christian witness in the world.

The second thing that we should say is that the catechism and the Reformed churches are concerned to reach the lost. Even though the catechism was drafted and adopted in a period when the state imposed the Christian religion on its citizens, in *HC* 86 we find an open recognition that not everyone around us is a believer. This evident concern contradicts the caricature of Reformed indifference to the lost. The assumption behind the caricature is that if God has decreed who is and is not going to come to faith, then Reformed folk must be indifferent. Yes, God is sovereign, but that conviction is hardly distinctive to Reformed theology. The church widely held and taught it for the fifteen hundred years before the Reformation. Augustine taught it, Anselm taught it, and Aquinas taught it, just to name three.[32] These were all major theologians in the Western church. God knows what he has decreed, and we know that he

32. Clark, "Election and Predestination," 90–122.

has decreed, but we do not know whom he has decreed to save and whom he has decreed to reprobate. The church's duty is to make known the law and the gospel and offer salvation freely, seriously, and promiscuously to all who will recognize the greatness of their sin and misery, turn from it, and embrace Christ in true faith.[33]

Evangelism properly is what the minister does in the pulpit when he proclaims the gospel to the world, but each of us as Christians is a witness to the faith (the objective facts) and to our faith, to our personal appropriation of Christ by grace alone, through faith alone.[34] Each of us is ordinarily surrounded by unbelieving friends, relatives, and coworkers. We must pray for them regularly that God the Spirit might do in them what he has done in us who believe: convict them of their need for Christ, grant them new life, and grant them the grace of faith and through it union with Christ. When we pray that way, we should be prepared because God, in his providence, may well give us opportunity to give witness to Christ and to our faith in him.

By God's grace, we do good works that give witness to our faith and to the truth of the Christian faith. When our lives match our profession, opportunities for witness are created. We do not have to choose between a silent witness of good works and a spoken witness to Christ and his truth. We believe in and confess both. They go together. May the Lord give us opportunities to give witness, and may he bless that witness when it is given.

---

33. Canons of Dort 2.5, in United Reformed Churches in North America, *Liturgical Forms and Prayers*, 268; Disputation 30, "On the Calling of People to Salvation," in te Velde, van den Belt, and van Asselt, *Synopsis Purioris Theologiae*, 2.209–27; Wollebius, "Compendium Theologiae Christianae," 115–17. See the discussion under *HC* 65.

34. Clark, "Classical Christian Catechesis," 247–61.

QUESTION 87

Can they then not be saved who do not turn to God from their unthankful, impenitent life?

By no means, for, as the Scripture says, no unchaste person, idolater, adulterer, thief, covetous man, drunkard, slanderer, robber, or the like shall inherit the kingdom of God.[35]

Since the advent of the Second Great Awakening, which shaped American evangelical theology, piety, and practice so profoundly in the nineteenth century, many American Christians have simply assumed that the revivalist paradigm is correct. Many evangelicals have never seen any other approach to salvation and to the Christian life. An important part that approach is the altar call, given at the conclusion of a revival service. The first part of a revival was dominated by the singing of carefully selected, emotionally powerful songs. The second part of the service was the sermon, which was intended to persuade sinners to come forward at its conclusion to pray the "sinner's prayer" at the "anxious bench." Versions of this pattern carried on through the twentieth century, and the basic structure of the revival service still influences the structure of evangelical and even some Presbyterian and Reformed worship services to this day.

Underlying this system for gaining converts is the conviction that once a person has come forward and prayed the sinner's prayer, they are saved no matter what they may later say or do. It is to this doctrine and practice that some refer when they speak of being "once saved, always saved." This approach to conversion and to the Christian life has been roundly criticized as a form of "easy believism" and "cheap grace." Responding to this approach, the "lordship salvation" controversy arose among the dispensationalists.[36]

35. "Können denn die nicht selig werden, die sich von ihrem undankbaren, unbussfertigen Wandel zu Gott nicht bekehren? Keineswegs; denn, wie die Schrift sagt: Kein Unkeuscher, Abgöttischer, Ehebrecher, Dieb, Geiziger, Trunkenbold, Lästerer, Räuber und dergleichen, wird das Reich Gottes erben" (Schaff, *Creeds of Christendom*, 3:339). "Non possunt igitur illi servari, qui ingrati, et in peccatis secure persistentes, a sua pravitate ad Deum non convertuntur? Nullo modo. Nam, ut scriptura testatur, nec impudici, nec idololatrae, nec adulteri, nec fures, nec avari, nec ebriosi, nec convitiatores, nec raptores, haereditatem regni Dei conseqentur" (Niemeyer, *Collectio Confessionum*, 450).

36. MacArthur, *Gospel according to Jesus*; Horton, *Christ the Lord*.

The Reformed confession is neither nomist nor antinomian. We take a quite a different approach to the question of salvation, conversion, and the Christian life. We begin with the Reformation distinction between law and gospel.[37] We further distinguish between the ceremonial, judicial, and moral law. This is what the church has long called the "threefold division of the law" (*triplex divisio legis*).[38] The ceremonial or religious laws instituted under Moses were temporary and abrogated at the death of Christ. The moral law, however, is not temporary or Mosaic.[39] With the ancient, universal church and with the Reformation, we confess that the moral law is the abiding norm of the Christian life.

Roman Catholic critics charged the Reformation with fostering impiety and lawlessness (antinomianism) by confessing, preaching, and teaching that salvation (justification and sanctification) is by grace alone (*sola gratia*), through faith alone (*sola fide*). Both the Lutherans and the Reformed denied this charge. Both traditions confess the third use of the law.[40] In contrast to Rome, the Reformation churches confess that believers pursue the mortification of sin, to live to Christ, and consequent good works not in order to be justified but because we have been justified. We seek to live in obedience to God's holy law out of gratitude, in union with Christ.

So great is the necessity of sanctification and good works that, in *HC* 87, we confess, "No unchaste person, idolater, thief, covetous man, drunkard, slanderer, robber or the like shall inherit the kingdom of God" (1 Cor 6:9–10; see also Eph 5:5–6). As Ursinus writes, "good works are the fruit of our regeneration."[41] In *that* sense they may be said to be the *sine qua non,* but there is a *great* distinction needed: between "is," "because," and

37. See the discussion of law and gospel under *HC* 3.

38. Ross, *From the Finger of God*; Casselli, "Threefold Division," 175–207; Beza, *Clear and Simple Treatise*, 171; Beza, *Lex Dei*; Calvin, *Institutes* 4.20.15.

39. Ursinus, *Corpus doctrinae*, 505–12; Ursinus, *Commentary*, 490–92. See the discussion under *HC* 92.

40. Ursinus, *Corpus doctrinae*, 623–24; Ursinus, *Commentary*, 613–15. Ursinus responds to the antinomians in *Corpus doctrinae*, 624–28; Ursinus, *Commentary*, 615–18. The conversation on the use of the law between *nomologista*, *evangelista*, and *neophytus* in Fisher, *Marrow of Modern Divinity*, 317–37, is a useful introduction to the Reformed approach to the third (normative) use of the moral law and illustrates the clear distinction between Reformed orthodoxy, nomism, and antinomianism.

41. "Bona opera sint fructus nostrae regenerationis" (Ursinus, *Corpus doctrinae*, 479).

"through." What the Reformed churches confess is that it *is* the case that believers will be penitent, that is, they will recognize sin for what it is, confess it as sin, and repent of it, seek sanctification, and do good works.

Good works are the necessary, logical outcome of salvation. They are the fruit and evidence of new life and true faith (Matt 7:17–20; John 15:1–11; Col 1:10; Gal 5:22–23).[42] The good fruit that comes from new life, justification, and union with Christ never becomes the *ground* of our justification or salvation, nor does it ever become the instrument through which we are justified and saved. The ground of our justification and salvation is always the righteousness of Christ *for us,* and the instrument is never anything else but true faith in Christ.

In contrast to what is true of believers, there are those who profess faith in Christ who wish to be regarded as believers, whose profession of faith the church may have received as genuine. Matthew 6:2 calls such "hypocrites" (ὑποκριταὶ). Olevianus recognizes that there will be "hypocrites and despisers of grace" (*hypocritas et contemtores gratiae*) and "hypocrites and reprobates" who participate in the external administration of the covenant of grace.[43] They do not actually believe and therefore they are not actually penitent. More particularly, those whom the church has placed under discipline, who have demonstrated their unbelief by refusing to repent, are in grave danger and great jeopardy.[44] That someone has, during an affecting service, felt a wave of emotion, come forward, felt guilty, or even regretted the consequences of sins does not demonstrate that one is a believer. What demonstrates that one is a believer is true faith, a certain knowledge of Christ and the basics of the Christian faith, assent to their truth, and a personal, heartfelt trust in Christ and in his gospel. This true faith issues in fruit and evidence of it.[45]

In his *Smaller Catechism* (ca. 1561 or 1562), written in preparation for the drafting of the *HC*, Ursinus addresses these issues clearly.[46] He asks, "Can anyone who has been given true faith but does not good works be righteous before God? No. For only those who are led by the Spirit are

42. See the discussion under *HC* 86 of the necessity of fruit and evidence of salvation.

43. Olevianus, *De substantia*, 2.23, 47, 53, 61, 103; Clark, *Caspar Olevian*, 202–3.

44. See the discussion of the keys of the kingdom under *HC* 83–85.

45. See the discussion of the nature of true faith under *HC* 21.

46. Bierma et al., *Introduction*, 137–40.

the children of God. And it cannot happen that true gratitude to God not follow true faith."[47] He defines gratitude as "true conversion to God." By *conversio* he does not mean a shattering experience but a turning to God produced by the grace and Spirit of God.[48] Conversion is therefore "mortification of the old person and vivification of the new."[49] This is, of course, exactly what *HC* 88 says.

It is not that sinners cannot be saved. As Ursinus writes, there "remain in all saints, so long as they living on earth, many very serious sins, defects with which we are born, and perverse inclinations, as well as many sins of ignorance and weakness."[50] Rather, because God has given us new life and true faith, and through it union with Christ, "by virtue of their true conversion to God, they struggle against these sins their whole life, and therefore these sins are not imputed to them, their inchoate obedience is pleasing to God because of Christ."[51] Olevianus also writes of the believer's "inchoate obedience."[52] In this life, our faith remains "weak" (*infirmis*).[53] Both Calvin and Olevianus have a profound sense of human frailty in this life.[54] *HC* 87 is addressing those who sin impenitently. Christians may indeed commit the gross sins the catechism lists (from 1 Cor 6:9–10). What distinguishes the believer from the unbeliever is penitence, mortification, and vivification, which are the fruits of true faith.

This is why it is so important to distinguish between "is," "because," and "through." We are not saved *because* we are penitent or *through* being penitent or obedient. Christ's obedience and righteousness *alone* is the ground of salvation. Faith *alone* is the instrument of salvation, but believers *are* penitent. Repentance is the fruit of our new life and true faith. It is believers who repent. Unbelievers cannot repent because they lack new life and true faith. Thus, we should be on guard against the error that adds

47. Q. 72, in Bierma et al., *Introduction*, 155.

48. Reuter, *D. Zachariae Ursini*, 1:41. On the Reformed doctrine of conversion, see Clark, "Conversion."

49. Bierma et al., *Introduction*, 155.

50. Smaller Catechism 77, in Bierma et al., *Introduction*, 155

51. Smaller Catechism 77, in Bierma et al., *Introduction*, 155.

52. E.g., Olevianus, *Romanos Notae*, 6; Clark, *Caspar Olevianus*, 185–86. Our English word *inchoate* is derived from the Latin verb *incoho*, "to begin."

53. E.g., Olevianus, *Romanos Notae*, 374.

54. Clark, *Caspar Olevian*, 186.

obedience to faith (e.g., "faithfulness") as the instrument of salvation. This error denies the finished work of Christ, who alone satisfied the righteous law of God, who alone substituted for us on the cross, and who alone was raised for our justification.

Believers repent and are penitent, that is, they daily acknowledge the greatness of their sin generally and turn away from particular sins. Thus, when one believer comes to another believer to speak to him about a sin, a believer acknowledges his sin. A refusal to acknowledge sin, when it truly exists, is contumacy and an indicator of a serious spiritual problem.

The Reformed have always had to oppose both nomism and antinomianism. Ursinus repeats the historic Christian and Reformed view: "But the moral law, or Decalogue, has not been abrogated in as far as obedience to it is concerned."[55] Nevertheless, because it is deeply unhistorical, disconnected from the Scriptures, the Christian past, and the Reformation confessions and catechisms, American evangelicalism has long been influenced by antinomianism. Thus, the biblical and Reformed approach to repentance and faith may be a shock to the system. That someone has walked the aisle or prayed the prayer means little if it is not accompanied by evidence of true faith. Chief among those evidences is not perfection but penitence. It is to this sort of faith that James refers when he complains that some Christians profess faith but show no evidence of their faith (Jas 2:14). A mere profession of faith is not true faith and cannot save since it is not true faith. It is not, as Rome says, that our good works make faith what it is (*fides formata caritate*) or that we must augment our faith with good works (that is moralism), but it is the case that living trees produce fruit.[56]

The *doctrine* of the Christian life is remarkably simple. There are two parts: death and life. The *practice* of the Christian life, however, is quite another thing. The practice of the Christian life, the living out of our life in Christ, by grace alone, through faith alone, in union with Christ, is so difficult, so incomplete, so littered with failure that the apostle Paul nearly despaired of it. Remember that, as he comes to Romans 7, he has already preached about our guilt under sin and the law. He has already

55. Ursinus, *Commentary*, 496; Ursinus, *Corpus doctrinae*, 508.

56. *BC* 24, in United Reformed Churches in North America, *Liturgical Forms and Prayers*, 178–79; see the discussion under *HC* 61.

proclaimed the riches of God's free grace to sinners in Christ, received through faith alone. Paul has nowhere given us any good reason to think, as Pelagius suggests, that he is thinking of someone else, nor is there any good reason to think, as Arminius suggests, that he is now, in chapter 7, putting on a persona.[57] Rather, chapter 3 leads to chapter 4, which leads to chapters 5, 6, 7, and 8. Chapters 6–8 are a unit. In chapter 6 Paul follows his explanation of the gospel of free justification through faith alone with his doctrine of our identity and union with Christ and the Christian life of dying to sin (illustrated by baptism). In chapter 7 he faces honestly, even bluntly, the *experience* of the Christian life. The problem, he writes, is not the law, which is "good." It was not the law but the deadly chemistry of my sin and the law (Rom 7:13). The great problem lies not with the law, which is "spiritual," but with me. "I," writes Paul the believer, "am of the flesh, sold under sin" (Rom 7:14). It is a great paradox. "For I do not understand my own actions. For I do not do what I want, but I do the very thing I hate" (v. 15 ESV). Again (v. 16), the problem lies not with God's holy law but with me. There remains within me a principle, even though God has graciously granted to me new life, even though he has granted to me the gift of faith, and even though I am united to Christ. That principle is the sin that "dwells within me" (v. 17). As a consequence, the Christian experiences a conflicted reality. When we sin, "it is no longer I who do it" (v. 17) but that foreign principle, sin.

Non-Christians cannot say this because it is not true of them. In the unregenerate, sin is not a foreign principle. It not something else in them. When non-Christians sin, it is they who are doing it. There is no competition within them. There is only one principle at work, not two.

As Christians, however, we recognize that nothing good lives in our flesh, our sinful nature (Rom 7:18). By grace, as a believer, granted the principle of new life, "I have the desire to do what is right, but" because I live still live in this life, because I am not yet glorified, I too often lack "the ability to carry it out" (v. 18 ESV). It is not that I do not want to do good. I do but, in reality, "the evil that I do not want to do, I keep doing" (Rom 7:19). Because God has given me new life, I realize that, when I sin, when I act contrary to my new nature, it is not I "but sin that dwells

57. De Bruyn, *Pelagius's Commentary*, 105; Arminius, *Works*, 2:491.

within me" (Rom 7:20) that is doing it. There is a law at work in me, "that when I want to do right" (Rom 7:21), evil is right there. As a new creature in Christ, declared righteous only for the sake of Christ's righteousness imputed, "I delight in the law of God, in my inner being" (Rom 7:22 ESV), but too often there is within me a war waging (Rom 7:23). This war, like all wars, is terrible. It is exhausting. It is discouraging. It makes one cry, "Wretched man that I am! Who will deliver me from this body of death?" (Rom 7:24 ESV). Nevertheless, quite unexpectedly, the very fact of the struggle is encouraging. With Paul I say, "Thanks be to God through Jesus Christ our Lord! So then, I myself serve the law of God with my mind, but with my flesh I serve the law of sin" (v. 25 ESV). In the unbeliever, there is no struggle between the new life and the new man in which I serve God's holy law out of gratitude, and the old law of sin and death that still resides within me.

We find the greatest encouragement in the gospel. The first word of the gospel is: "There is therefore now no condemnation for those who are in Christ Jesus" (Rom 8:1 ESV). The second benefit of the gospel is that "the law of the Spirit of life has set you free in Christ Jesus from the law of sin and death. For God has done what the law, weakened by the flesh, could not do. By sending his own Son in the likeness of sinful flesh and for sin, he condemned sin in the flesh, in order that the righteous requirement of the law might be fulfilled in us, who walk not according to the flesh but according to the Spirit" (Rom 8:2–4 ESV).

Christ's fulfillment of the covenant of works in my place, his death as my substitute, the grace of new life, and "the law of the Spirit of life" has set us free from the law of sin and death. Since we are in the covenant of grace, we are free to resist sin and to obey our Savior out of gratitude. The principle of new life has triumphed over the old principle of sin and death. God the Son incarnate has set free believers from the tyranny of sin and death—not that they do not struggle mightily with it, and not so that, in this life, they never sin, but so that even though they sin they will not ultimately be defeated by sin and death. Christ has definitively conquered sin and death for us, and now he is at work in us gradually, graciously conforming us to himself. That is why we "walk not according to the flesh" but now, in Christ, we walk according to the Holy Spirit.

Question 88

In how many things does true repentance or conversion consist?

Question 89

What is the mortification of the old man?

Question 90

What is the vivification of the new man?

Question 91

What are good works?

Lord's Day 33

QUESTION 88

In how many things does true repentance or conversion consist?

In two things: the mortification of the old man and the vivification of the new.[1]

There are two parts to the Christian life: mortification, the putting to death of the old man, and vivification, the making alive of the new. This teaching is quite clear and simple, but, as we see in Paul's discussion of it in Romans 7:7–25, it is far from easy. Indeed, sometimes it seems to be impossible (Rom 7:24). Of course, it is not impossible because with God nothing is impossible (Luke 18:27).

In order to think about the Christian life clearly, biblically, and confessionally, we need to understand that we are not speaking about our standing before God but how we live in light of that declaration, in light of God's free, sovereign, gracious salvation, in union with Christ. We are asking about the *consequences* of free salvation and the gospel, not the conditions in order to receive them. By his righteousness and obedience, Christ has already fulfilled what our theologians call the *antecedent* condition for our salvation.

This is why the catechism asks about the nature of true repentance or true conversion.[2] Since the Second Great Awakening of the nineteenth century, American Christians have tended to talk about a conversion experience. In that context, Christians might speak of responding to an altar call or something of that sort. When the Reformed speak about conversion, however, we are speaking not of a single decisive event but rather of the daily dying to sin and living to Christ. Paul describes the Christian life in terms of a baptism, an identification with Christ's death:

1. "In wie viel Stücken stehet die wahrhaftige Busse oder Bekehrung des Menschen? In zwei Stücken: in Absterbung des alten, und Auferstehung des neuen Menschen" (Schaff, *Creeds of Christendom*, 3:339). "Quibus partibus constat conversio hominis ad Deum? Mortificatione veteris, et vivificatione novi hominis" (Niemeyer, *Collectio Confessionum*, 450).

2. It is important not to confuse the catechism's definition of conversion with the revivalist understanding of conversion. On this see Clark, "Conversion."

> We were buried therefore with him by baptism into death, in order that, just as Christ was raised from the dead by the glory of the Father, we too might walk in newness of life.
>
> For if we have been united with him in a death like his, we shall certainly be united with him in a resurrection like his. We know that our old self was crucified with him in order that the body of sin might be brought to nothing, so that we would no longer be enslaved to sin. (Rom 6:4–6 ESV)

He is not saying that every baptized person is necessarily, *ex opere* united to Christ, any more than he means to say that circumcision necessarily united Esau to Christ. Just as in Colossians 2:11–12, so too in Romans 6 Paul uses baptism as an illustration of death to explain what has happened to believers.[3] In baptism they have been identified with Christ's death. By grace alone, through faith alone, the Spirit has united us to Christ. Thus, united to Christ, we have died with Christ. There has been a decisive break with sin, which continues to be worked out in us personally.[4] Believers have been saved for a purpose, and Paul explains that purpose clearly: in order that "we might walk in newness of life" (Rom 6:4). The old man (what we were) has been crucified. The law offered life to us under the covenant of works (Rom 2:13; 7:10). When we fell, the law continued to demand perfect obedience, and through it we learned the greatness of our sin and misery (Rom 7:7). In Christ, however, under the covenant of grace, we have died to the law and thus to the reigning power of sin (Rom 6:14; Gal 2:19). As a consequence we are no longer enslaved to sin. As Paul makes clear in chapter 7, there remains in the Christian life a mighty struggle, but God has won a decisive victory for us, and despite our experience, we believe that purpose is being gradually realized in us by God's grace.[5]

Olevianus follows Paul closely in his discussion of the Christian life.[6] He affirms both the reality of our ongoing sin *and* our free justification in

3. The federal vision theology teaches that baptism confers all the benefits of Christ provisionally. This is a serious error that has been rejected by several orthodox Reformed communions (see Clark, "Baptism and the Benefits").

4. Murray, *Redemption Accomplished and Applied*, 177–86.

5. See the discussion of Rom 6–8 under *HC* 87.

6. Clark, "Reception of Paul," 297–318; Olevianus, *Romanos Notae*, 265–316.

Christ. The latter is all the more important because our "sanctification or renovation to the image of God, in this life, is imperfect."[7] We only sustain the test of divine judgment by faith, which apprehends Christ and his "imputed obedience," the ground of justification, which is perfect and superior to the righteousness of the law.[8]

Nevertheless, the "Holy Spirit is effective in us through the gospel."[9] It is the Spirit who "inserts us into Christ by creating in us faith, by which we receive Christ offered [in the gospel]," and with him his eternal righteousness imputed to us.[10] From this flows the two parts of the Christian life. It is impossible to separate Christ and the Spirit of sanctification, "who renews us to repentance, which consists of the mortification of the old man and the vivification of the new, which is always the whole of salvation."[11]

QUESTION 89

What is the mortification of the old man?

Heartfelt sorrow for sin, causing us to hate and turn from it always more and more.[12]

Residents of the late modern West generally do not like to think about or discuss death. Ask your tablemates at lunch today what they think

7. "Cùm autem sanctificatio seu renovatio ad Dei imaginem in hac vita sit imperfecta" (Olevianus, *De substantia*, 2.16).

8. "Ita ut examen iudicii divini sive rigorem Legis non sustineat, quamvis à Christo fide apprehenso veniat, tamen in rationem iustitiae coram Deo non venit, sed sola imputata obedientia Christi, quae est perfecta, imò omni iustitia Legis superior: ideoque ea vestiti intrepidè coram Deo consistimus. Rom. 5. 2. Cor. 5" (Olevianus, *De substantia*, 2.16).

9. "Per Evangelium enim in nobis efficax est Spiritus Sanctus" (Olevianus, *De Substantia*, 2.16).

10. "Qui Christo nos inserit creando in nobis fidem, qua Christum oblatum recipimus cum iustitia aeterna, quam nobis imputat Dan. 9. Philipp. 3" (Olevianus, *De Substantia*, 2.16).

11. "Cum Spiritu sanctificationis, qui nunquam à Christo separari potest, quo nos renovat ad resipiscentiam, quae constat mortificatione veteris et vivificatione novi hominis, quaeque tota semper salutaris est. Rom. 6. v. 5. 6" (Olevianus, *De Substantia*, 2.16).

12. "Was ist die Absterbung des alten Menschen? Sich die Sünde von Herzen lassen leid sein, und dieselbe je länger je mehr hassen und fliehen" (Schaff, *Creeds of Christendom*, 3:339). "Quid est mortificatio veteris hominis? Vere et ex animo dolere, quod peccatis tuis Deum offenderis, eaque magis ac magis odisse et fugere" (Niemeyer, *Collectio Confessionum*, 450).

about death. How do they hope to die? What happens after death? Where do they want to be buried? Few things will—pardon the pun—kill a conversation more quickly than raising the matter of death. Our reluctance to discuss death or even to think about it is remarkable because, unless Christ returns first, every single one of us will go through it. It is a truly universal fact of human experience. We are naturally reluctant to discuss it because we know intuitively that it is wrong, that it is not natural—no matter what the New Age gurus and others may tell us. If death is so wonderful and beautiful, why are we wired with a fight-or-flight impulse? Why do we struggle mightily in the water when we think we may be drowning? The most calm, rational person you know turns into a crazed animal when drowning. I know this because as a lifeguard I was trained to disable a drowning person so I could drag him to shore. Our fight-or-flight impulse, the rapid pulse, the shot of adrenaline, the tunnel vision, and all the other natural, instinctive features of our fight to survive are not the products of nurture. They are the products of a fallen nature. This is because God did not create us to die. God created us to live in communion with him forever. Our rebellion destroyed that relationship and brought death into the world.

Still, our aversion to thinking about death in the late modern West seems to be even stronger now than it once was. Four or five decades ago, death came more quickly for most of us than it does today. In rural communities, people were more likely to die at home. Funerals were conducted differently—for example, it was expected that there would be an open casket. Indeed, the space we today call the "living room" was once called the "parlor," and one of the major functions of the parlor was to host a visitation of the deceased. Today we gather in funeral homes for that purpose. In short, in a more agrarian society, death was nearer. In more urban and suburban societies, death seems remote. We tend to die in hospitals or in nursing homes, and death itself is more alien.

In Colossians 2:11–12 and Romans 6:3–4, when the apostle Paul uses death to explain the first major aspect of the Christian life, he assumes that his hearers and readers will be more personally familiar with death than we are today. The same is true of the period in which the catechism was written. Calvin died at age fifty-five. Ursinus, the primary author of the catechism, died at age forty-nine. Olevianus, a contributor to the catechism, died at the same age. The plague was a regular feature of sixteenth-century life. In the mid–fourteenth century, Europe's population was reduced by millions in just a few years as the plague swept through.[13] One observer said that bodies were stacked in the street like lasagna.[14] There were no antibiotics. The practice of medicine in the period was crude and often harmful. Anesthetics as we know them did not exist.

In order to understand the Reformed doctrine of the Christian life, we must try to dislocate ourselves from our late modern experience and try to sympathize with the world in which Scripture was written and in the world which the catechism was written. Scripture unabashedly uses death as a metaphor for the Christian life. After all, we Christians believe in and follow the God-Man, who saved us by living for us and by dying for us, and he died one of the most shameful, horrible deaths imaginable then or now. People today object to capital punishment on the grounds that it is cruel because the anesthetic drugs do not work quickly enough. There were no effective anesthetics for the crucified. It was meant to be a brutal, humiliating death.

The apostle says, "Do you not know that all of us who have been baptized into Christ Jesus were baptized into his death? We were buried therefore with him by baptism into death" (Rom 6:3–4 ESV). If we substitute "identified" for "baptized," we get his meaning. Christians have been identified with Christ's death just as all the Israelites were identified with Moses as they crossed the Red Sea (1 Cor 10:2). This is our new identity. This is how Paul continues to explain the Christian life:

> For if we have been united with him in a death like his, we shall certainly be united with him in a resurrection like his. We know that our old self was crucified with him in order that the body of sin might be brought to nothing, so that we would no longer be enslaved to sin. For one who has died has been set free from sin. Now if we have died with Christ, we believe that we will also live with him. We know that Christ, being raised from the dead, will

13. See, e.g., Kelly, *Great Mortality*, for an introduction.

14. Kelly, *Great Mortality*, xiii.

never die again; death no longer has dominion over him. For the death he died he died to sin, once for all, but the life he lives he lives to God. So you also must consider yourselves dead to sin and alive to God in Christ Jesus. (Rom 6:5–11 ESV)

All baptized Christians have been outwardly identified with Christ's death. Those who, by God's sovereign grace, by the mysterious work of the Holy Spirit, have received new life have also received true faith, and through that faith alone, by the Spirit, are united to the risen Christ. This is what Paul means by "united with him." The old man, the old principle, the first Adam, has been crucified. A fundamental change has been made. In the ancient world, death was often the only escape from bondage. This is what Paul is thinking as he describes our liberation from the bondage and dominion of sin. Having been united, by grace alone, through faith alone, to Christ, having therefore died with him and having been raised with him, we are free. It is not that we no longer sin, but we are no longer trapped in slavery. We are free.

As the liberated, we are penitent for our sin and seek to mortify it. According to the catechism, repentance *is* sanctification and conversion. Modern evangelicals tend to think in triumphalist or perfectionist categories, but when the catechism thinks of sanctification, the first thing of which it thinks is not sinlessness but an honest recognition of our sinfulness and an honest, heartfelt repudiation of our sinfulness and our particular sins.

It is necessary for the Christian to be converted, that is, to be daily mortifying sin and being made alive in the new man. It is necessary as a consequence of the grace we have received.[15] In his *Larger Catechism*, Ursinus calls "true conversion" (as defined above) "the fruit of faith to which God's covenant of grace obligates us and by which true faith is recognized."[16] He writes, "Wherefore the conversion of man, in this life, is necessary so that without this necessary conversion, after this life no one reaches eternal life."[17] This is a good example of the distinction between

15. See the discussion of the consequent necessity of sanctification under *HC* 87.

16. *Larger Catechism*, 142, in Bierma et al., *Introduction*, 189.

17. "Conversio hominis in hac vita adeo est necessaria, ut sine Necessaria nemo salutem aeternam post hanc vitam consequatur, secundu-dicta: Nisi quis renatus fuerit ex aqua & spiritu, non potest

"is," "through," and "because." We are not saved through our conversion, that is, it does not replace faith as the instrument of salvation, nor does conversion does not become the ground of our salvation. It is the case, however, that those have been saved by grace, who have received new life and true faith, will mortify sin and be made alive in the new man. Those who refuse seek to mortify sin and to be made alive lack the principle of new life and the grace of true faith: "Unless one is born of water and the Spirit, he cannot enter the kingdom of God" (John 3:5).

In place of the Roman Catholic sacrament of penance, the Reformed use as synonyms *regeneration, renovation, repentance, conversion,* and *penance.*[18] *Repentance* (*respiscentia*) is a favorite term, which Theodore Beza uses in his Latin translation of the New Testament. For example, in Acts 2:38, where the Vulgate uses *agite poenitentia* ("do penance"), Beza uses *resipiscite* ("repent"), which, as Ursinus explains, signifies "to become wise after having done a thing; so μετανοια is from μετανοεω, which means to become wise after having committed something wrong; to change the mind, and to alter the purpose."[19] This way of characterizing conversion, he argues, is superior to *penance* (*poenitentia*), which refers mainly to sorrow (*dolorem*) after sin, penance also "is more obscure" and describes only part of what is in view.[20] "Conversion to God is the change of a corrupt mind and will excited in the elect by the Holy Spirit, through the preaching of the law and the gospel, which is followed by zeal for good works and conformity of life to all the commandments of God."[21]

To be sure, conversion generally and mortification specifically are not mere mechanical processes. In the Christian, sorrow (*dolor, leid sein*) for sin is genuine, and is essential to repentance, conversion, and

---

ingred-regnum caelorum" (Ursinus, *Corpus doctrinae*, 480).

18. Regenerationem, renuovationem, resipiscentiam, conversionem, poenitentiam (Ursinus, *Corpus doctrinae*, 481. NB: in the 1634 edition, the page is marked 482 when it should read 481). See CCC §980.

19. Ursinus, *Commentary*, 469; Beza, *Novum Domini*, loc. cit.

20. Ursinus, *Commentary*, 469; Ursinus, *Corpus doctrinae*, 482.

21. "Conversio ad Deum est mutatio mentis & voluntatis prauae in bonam, à Spiritu sancto per praedicationem legis et evangeii electis excitata, quam consequitur studium bonorum operum et vitae conformatio ad omnia DEI mandata" (Ursinus, *Corpus doctrinae*, 482).

mortification. It is "from the heart" (*von Herzen*) or from the center of our being (*ex animo*). Our English word *heart* is etymologically related to the German noun *Herz*, and we communicate well enough with our English word, but the noun *animus*, used in the Latin text of the catechism, is more ambiguous. It can refer to the soul, the very animating spirit within humans, as well as to the intellect. It is comprehensive of everything that we are distinct from our bodies.

Ursinus explains that we speak of *mortification* since the dead can no longer perform the actions proper to the life they once lived. So it is with us. Since we have died to the covenant of works and to sin, we no longer live to sin or for sin.[22] This is not the say that mortification is easy. It is not (Gal 5:17). Paul calls mortification the "crucifixion of the flesh" for good reason (Gal 5:24).[23] Ursinus notes that we speak specifically of the "mortification of the old man" because "it is not the substance of man but sin, but sin in man which is destroyed."[24] This is an important point that we have not always kept in view. The Reformed are neither hermetics nor gnostics. We affirm the essential goodness of creation per se even as we recognize the effects of the fall. Grace does not destroy human nature but renews it.[25]

The mortification of sin is the beginning of sanctification. As we saw under *HC* 88, this teaching is not complicated, but neither is it easy. Death is never easy, if only because it always entails loss. The truth is, to the degree we are Adam's children, we like sin. It is pleasurable for a while to think evil, vindictive, murderous, or lustful thoughts. It is momentarily satisfying to gratify sinful desires, but only for a while. In that way sin is like drug abuse. The first hit from an illegal narcotic may be thrilling, but take a look at a longtime drug abuser and try to believe that it is still fun or glamorous. After a while, drug abuse becomes just another job: satisfy the habit. So it is with familiar sins.

We, who are united to Christ, are called to recognize sin for what it is, to call it what it is: sin. This is a good reason to eschew therapeutic

22. Ursinus, *Commentary*, 470.

23. Ursinus, *Commentary*, 471.

24. Ursinus, *Commentary*, 471.

25. See the discussion of nature and grace under *HC* 66.

language. We are dysfunctional, but the root of dysfunction is sin. We all have medical, psychological, and emotional issues, and they are real and should be addressed properly, but the root of it all is sin. Redescribing sin as something else ultimately leads to despair. When we face our sins for what they are, there is hope because grace is for sinners. This is why it is so important not to fall into the Roman Catholic error of describing grace as a medicine. It is not. Grace is God's free favor toward us in Christ. It is grace that sets us free. It is grace that delivers us from bondage. It is grace that gives us hope when we are in the midst of the existential, daily struggle against temptation and sin. This is why Paul writes:

> So then, brothers, we are debtors, not to the flesh, to live according to the flesh. For if you live according to the flesh you will die, but if by the Spirit you put to death the deeds of the body, you will live. For all who are led by the Spirit of God are sons of God. For you did not receive the spirit of slavery to fall back into fear, but you have received the Spirit of adoption as sons, by whom we cry, "Abba! Father!" The Spirit himself bears witness with our spirit that we are children of God, and if children, then heirs—heirs of God and fellow heirs with Christ, provided we suffer with him in order that we may also be glorified with him. (Rom 8:12–17 ESV)

We will consider the making alive of the new man under *HC* 90, but know that the beginning of living is death. Because we have died with Christ, we are not debtors to sin. Because we are free, because the Spirit indwells us, by God's free favor, we can put to death "the deeds of the body," that is, sin (Rom 8:13). We are led by the Spirit. We are not slaves but sons. We have full and free access to the Father. These are not conditions that we must fulfill in order to be accepted and saved. These are truths that we must trust and appropriate for ourselves as we are tempted.

Death is unpleasant, but, in contrast to nihilists of our age, it is not the end. It is the beginning of life. Christ was raised, but in order to be raised for our justification, he had first to die for our justification. So it is with us. We will be raised, but we must first die to sin daily. We must learn to regard it as God does and to regard ourselves as God does. Only then are we able to "turn from it more and more," and turn from it we must.

QUESTION 90

What is the vivification of the new man?

Heartfelt joy in God through Christ, causing us to take delight in living according to the will of God in all good works.[26]

When the *HC* was written, the word *regeneration* was used in two senses at the same time. Sometimes it meant the spiritual awakening from death to life sovereignly and freely wrought by the Holy Spirit, which is the way we tend to use it most of the time today. It also, and perhaps more frequently, referred to progressive sanctification, the gradual, gracious work of the Spirit in us bringing us to conformity to Christ. The same writers who gave us the catechism regularly spoke of sanctification as "regeneration" and "renewal" in the image of Christ. Olevianus writes that Christ "regenerates from eternal death through faith in Him."[27] That expression would be incoherent with everything else he writes about order of salvation (*ordo salutis*) if we were to take it to refer to being awakened from spiritual death to spiritual life. It makes perfect sense, however, when we understand him to be speaking of the Christian's progressive sanctification. In that instance "regenerates" signifies "to sanctify." Like Calvin, he and Ursinus also spoke of regeneration the way the Synod of Dort did against the Remonstrants, that is, of the initial awakening from death to life wrought by the Holy Spirit, through the preaching of the law and the gospel.[28] Thus, he writes that believers are but partly regenerated. For

26. "Was ist die Auferstehung des neuen Menschen? Herzliche Freude in Gott durch Christum, und Lust und Liebe haben, nach dem Willen Gottes in allen guten Werken zu leben" (Schaff, *Creeds of Christendom*, 3:339). "Quid est vivificatio novi hominis? Vera laetitia in Deo per Christum, et serium ac promptum studium instituendi vitam ex voluntate Dei, omniaque bona opera exercendi" (Niemeyer, *Collectio Confessionum*, 451).

27. Olevian, *Firm Foundation*, 96.

28. Olevian, *Firm Foundation*, 108, 96. See Clark, *Caspar Olevian*, 184–85 with n11. "The means or instrumental causes of conversion are the law—the gospel, and again, the doctrine of the law after

Olevianus, the Spirit-flesh dichotomy of Romans 7 means that part of the soul remains unregenerate (*non regentita*).[29] Indeed, we are not wholly sanctified or renewed or regenerated in that sense.

This way of speaking about the gradual renewing of the Christian is the background to the catechism's discussion of the second aspect of sanctification: vivification, or the making alive of the new man. In older English usage, for example, in the Nicene-Constantinopolitan Creed (381), we used to speak of Christ judging the "quick and the dead," that is, the living and the dead. In medical terms the expression "quickening" has sometimes been used to describe the fetal development. So, having been initially and decisively quickened, renewed, or regenerated, we are now, by grace alone, through faith alone, being renewed and sanctified into the image of Christ.[30] The Spirit who gave us life initially and decisively continues, by virtue of our union and communion with Christ, to work in us, through the use of ordinary means—attending to the preaching of the gospel, the use of the sacraments, and prayer—to bring us into conformity to Christ and especially, under this heading, to make us alive more and more.[31]

What does that mean? As *HC* 90 says, a person who being made alive is increasingly taking delight in living according to God's moral will revealed in his holy law. Before the Spirit gave us new life, we did not have such an orientation or disposition. So, he has graciously changed our stance, and more fundamentally has delivered us from death into life.

To press the point a bit, a corpse takes delight in nothing. It simply decays. Spiritually, before God made us alive, we were inanimate, dead. We had no interest in Christ or in his moral will. Now, by *sola gratia*, since God has made us alive, we do. That is a marvel. Now, united to Christ

---

that of the gospel. For the preaching of the law goes before, preparing and leading us to a knowledge of the gospel: 'for by the law is the knowledge of sin.' (Rom. 3:20.) Hence, there can be no sorrow for sin without the law. After the sinner has once been led to a knowledge of sin, then the preaching of the gospel follows, encouraging contrite hearts by the assurance of the mercy of God through Christ" (Ursinus, *Commentary*, 472).

29. This material is taken from Clark, *Caspar Olevian*, 196–97. See Olevianus, *De substantia*, 2.19.

30. Ursinus writes, "The Holy Spirit, or God himself, is the chief efficient cause of our conversion. Hence, it is that the saints pray that God would convert them, and that repentance is frequently called in the Scriptures the gift of God" (Ursinus, *Commentary*, 472).

31. E.g., Clark, *Caspar Olevian*, 191–209; Ursinus, *Commentary*, 473–74, *contra* Pelagius.

by the grace and Spirit of Christ, through faith, we have a new stance, a new disposition toward Christ and his moral will for us because we have new life. It is imperative that we not reverse that order. We are not sanctified, and we are certainly not justified or saved, because we have a new disposition. That is Roman Catholicism. We have a new disposition and we are developing new habits of godliness *because* God has made us alive, because we are no longer spiritually dead to Christ, his gospel, and his law.

One of the fruits and evidences of this new principle granted to us and worked in us by God's sovereign grace is delight in what is good, true, right, and holy. Our English translations follow the German text (*Herzliche Freude*) by using "heartfelt joy." The Latin text says "true joy." Paul, speaking as a Christian, says, "For I delight [συνήδομαι] in the law of God, in my inner being" (Rom 7:22 ESV). The verb that Paul uses only occurs once in the New Testament and not at all in the LXX, but its root is related to the word that is often translated "pleasures" or "passions" in the New Testament, and it refers to strong desires or feelings. In other words, using related terms from other contexts to help us interpret Paul's language, it seems a strong term describing a persistent state and not a passing emotional experience. In Psalms 1:2 and 39:9, the LXX translates the Hebrew word for "delight" (חֵפֶץ) with the noun (θέλημα) that is frequently used in the New Testament for the moral will of God, for example,

- "Your will be done" (Matt 6:10)
- "but the one who does the will of my Father" (Matt 7:21)
- "whoever does the will of my Father"(Matt 12:50)
- "My food is to do the will of him who sent me" (John 1:13)

In other words, the concepts of delighting in the Lord and the objective, revealed moral will of God are inextricably bound together. The Christian is a "new creation" (2 Cor 5:17; Gal 6:15) wrought by the Spirit, through the word, who delights in what pleases God. We know what that is through his law and gospel. Thus, as citizens in the kingdom of God, we realize daily and gradually that it "is not a matter of eating and drinking but of righteousness and peace and joy in the Holy Spirit" (Rom 14:17 ESV). Because we have been crucified with Christ, he now lives in us, "and the life I now live in the flesh I live by faith in the Son of God, who loved me and gave himself for me" (Gal 2:20 ESV). As new creatures, we love Christ's new commandment: "that you love one another: just as I have loved you, you also are to love one another" (John 13:34 ESV; cf. 1 John 2:7). Since we have been released from the condemnation of the law, we "serve in the new way of the Spirit and not in the old way of the written code" (Rom 7:6 ESV). We are no longer bound to the 613 Mosaic commandments[32] because in the new covenant (Jer 31:31–33) the Spirit is writing God's law not on tablets of stone but on tablets of flesh (Eph 2:15). We have a "new self, created after the likeness of God in true righteousness and holiness" (Eph 4:24 ESV; cf. Col 3:10).

Ursinus identifies three marks of vivification: "1. A knowledge of the mercy of God, and an application of it in Christ. 2. Joy and delight arising from the fact that God is reconciled to us through Christ, and that obedience is begun in us and shall be perfected. 3. An ardent desire to perform new obedience, or to sin no more, but to render gratitude to God during our whole life, and to retain his love, which desire is itself new obedience."[33] The second benefit of the covenant of grace is progressive sanctification, and it has two parts: mortification and vivification. Sanctification means all our faculties are being made alive. It is "the work of God's free grace, whereby we are renewed in the whole man after the image of God, and are enabled more and more to die unto sin, and live unto righteousness" (WSC 35).[34] By the Spirit we are enabled because all our faculties are being renewed, made alive. This is great news to which we must return again and again, even as we struggle with sin. Despite our sin, we are being renewed. Let the Evil One say and do as he will. He cannot put Jesus back in the tomb, and he cannot put us back under condemnation. The law convicts us and guides us, but it no longer condemns us who died with Christ, who have been raised with him, and who are being vivified by the same power that raised Jesus from the dead.

32. The rabbis counted 613 Mosaic laws.

33. Ursinus, *Commentary*, 471; Ursinus, *Corpus doctrinae*, 483–84.

34. Westminster Assembly, *Humble Advice of the Assembly*, 10.

QUESTION 91

What are good works?

Those only which proceed from true faith, and are done according to the law of God, unto his glory; and not such as rest on our own opinion or the commandments of men.[35]

The source or fountain of good works is true faith. Ursinus explains, "Both parts of conversion flow from faith."[36] By using this expression, the catechism deliberately takes us back to *HC* 21, where true faith is defined, and to *HC* 60, which are among the several places where the catechism says that true faith is the sole instrument (*sola fide*) of justification and salvation. True faith is also the instrument of union and communion with Christ, and it is thus the headwaters of the believer's new, Spirit-wrought life in Christ. In other words, true faith is essential to good works. Any work that does not proceed from true faith is no good work at all. Whatever does not proceed from faith is sin (Rom 14:23). Here we disagree sharply with Rome, which teaches that people can and must prepare for grace. At Trent Rome declared: "If anyone says that the sinner is justified by faith alone, meaning that nothing else is required to cooperate in order to obtain the grace of justification, and that it is not in any way necessary that he be prepared disposed by the action of his own will, let him be anathema."[37]

According to Rome, one is able to prepare oneself for grace and cooperate with grace. Rome confesses that "through the observance of the commandments of God and of the Church" faith is "co-operating with good

35. "Welches sind aber gute Werke? Allein die aus wahrem Glauben nach dem Gesetz Gottes ihm zu Ehren geschehen, und nicht die auf unser Gutdünken oder Menschen-Satzung gegründet sind" (Schaff, *Creeds of Christendom*, 3:339–40). "Quae sunt bona opera? Tantum ea, quae ex vera fide, secundum legem Dei fiunt, et ad eius solius gloriam referuntur: non ea autem quae a nobis opinione recti conficta, aut ab hominibus tradita sunt" (Niemeyer, *Collectio Confessionum*, 451).

36. "Utraque conversionis pars manat ex fide" (Ursinus, *Corpus doctrinae*, 484). On the definition of "conversion," see the discussion under *HC* 88–90. On faith as an instrument of conversion, see Ursinus, *Commentary*, 472–73.

37. Trent, session 6, canon 9 (Schroeder, *Canons and Decrees*, 43).

works" toward the "increase" in justice (righteousness) toward eventual justification.[38]

> For since Christ Jesus Himself, as the head into the members and the vine into the branches, continually infuses strength into those justified, which strength always precedes, accompanies and follows their good works, and without which they could not in any manner be pleasing and meritorious before God, we must believe that nothing further is wanting to those justified to prevent them from being considered to have, by those very works which have been done in God, fully satisfied the divine law according to the state of this life and to have truly merited eternal life, to be obtained in its [due] time, provided they depart [this life] in grace.[39]

For Rome, acceptance with God is the product of medicine infused into the sinner through the sacraments and our free cooperation with that grace.[40] By grace, according to Rome, we are said to be infused also with "virtue" (power), and it is this infusion and our union with Christ that makes our good works "pleasing and meritorious" before God. In short, for Rome, the answer to *HC* 91, "What are good works?" is not "those only which proceed from true faith" but rather those that are the product of divinely infused grace and virtue, and our free cooperation with the same.

We must see the contrast intended by the catechism. We begin with *sola fide* and nothing else. Apart from the new life that the Spirit sovereignly and freely gives, and the gift of faith, which accompanies new life (the catechism does not recognize the existence of regenerate persons who do not yet have true faith), we are incapable of good works as defined by the catechism. We have always understood that unbelievers are capable of doing *civil, common,* or *secular* good. The primary authors and editors of the catechism, like the other Reformed theologians of the period, were well read in the classics and intelligent about the marvelous cultural

38. Trent, session 6, chapter 10 (Schroeder, *Canons and Decrees*, 36).

39. Trent, session 6, chapter 16 (Schroeder, *Canons and Decrees*, 41).

40. *Contra* the medieval and Roman notion of grace as medicine, see Ursinus, *Commentary*, 415, and this work under *HC* 61. On the Roman Catholic sacramental system, see the discussion under *HC* 66, 68.

achievements by unbelievers. The implied distinction here is between the *sacred* and *secular*.

Good works do not commend us to God, but they do flow necessarily from true faith, and they have as their goal the glory of God.[41] This aspect of good works also distinguishes them from common, secular, or civil works. To be sure, a great building or painting does necessarily testify at least indirectly to the Creator, but the catechism has in view here good works in relation to our standing before God. A great painting or building adds nothing to one's standing before God. Believers do good works to testify to the free grace they have received in Christ and to glorify the Savior, their Father, and the Spirit who made them and gave him them life. It is a mark of Christians that they want to glorify the God who created them, sustains them, and redeemed them.

Therefore, the intent of good works does matter, but not unto justification. The Roman Catholics argued that a good work might be credited with merit if one had the proper intent. They were forced into this sophistry by confusing justification with sanctification. The Reformation theologians and churches, by properly distinguishing and ordering justification and sanctification, made it possible again to think about and value intent correctly. We will pay attention to intent as we think about the marks of a good work.

Good works are essential to the Christian life. They are the fruit and evidence of our free justification (*sola fide*) and our free salvation (*sola gratia*) in Christ alone to the glory of God alone (*soli Deo gloria*). We can no more do without them than the orange tree can do without fruit. If it is the Triune God alone who has saved us, and that is true, and if it is true that the Triune God has raised us from spiritual death to spiritual life, granted us faith, union with Christ, and all his benefits (and that is all true), then all the glory must go to him. By nature, after the fall, we were like the Israelites with our backs to the Red Sea and a the great army coming down upon us. God the Son has conquered Pharaoh, as it were, for us. By his Spirit, operating through his word and sacraments, he is at work in us, conforming us to his own image. All we have is nothing except

41. See the discussion of the chief end of humanity under *HC* 86.

what God has given us. Whatever good has been done in us or through us, it only reflects his glory.

When the framers of the catechism faced the question of good works, the chief problem before them was the imposition of laws, traditions, and practices that were neither clearly taught in Scripture nor a good and necessary consequence from Scripture. Ursinus specifically mentions worship: "No creature has the right to institute the worship of God."[42] Gradually, through the late patristic and medieval periods, Christians found themselves burdened with a bewildering array of obligations in the church calendar (e.g., saints' days and days of obligation), alleged sacramental obligations (e.g., penance), various acts of piety (e.g., prescribed prayers), and even financial obligations (e.g., indulgences). Ursinus, echoing the Reformed consensus, denounces all this as "will-worship," which, along with "every fiction concerning good intentions in worship," is excluded by the principle that righteousness is what God has revealed in his word.[43]

In response to all these unbiblical and sometimes ungodly burdens on the Christian conscience, in worship and in the Christian life, the Reformation boldly reasserted the clarity, the uniqueness, and final authority of holy Scripture (*sola Scriptura*). A good work is that which comes "from faith," is commanded by God, and is directed "principally to the honor and glory of God."[44]

In our age, even though those in the Roman Catholic Church and in some sects remain trapped in a system of manmade obligations, perhaps the more pressing challenge is subjectivism, the denial of an objective truth or, in this case, a fixed, objective standard for ethics and morality. Professing Christians regularly talk about the Christian moral life with no reference to God's holy law, as if there were no revealed fixed standard. They express this in a variety of ways. Sometimes people flatly reject the abiding validity of the moral law as summarized in the Ten

---

42. "Nulla enim creatura habet ius instituendi cultum Dei" (Ursinus, *Corpus doctrinae*, 489).

43. "Excluditur hac conditione omnis ἐθελοθρησκεία, et commentum de bona intentione" (Ursinus, *Corpus doctrinae*, 490). Ursinus's language here and under *HC* 96–98 would be quite familiar to the theologians seated at the Westminster Assembly, since many of them had studied Ursinus's *Corpus doctrinae*. See Clark and Beeke, "Ursinus, Oxford and the Westminster Divines," 2:1–32.

44. Ursinus, *Commentary*, 477–78; Ursinus, *Corpus doctrinae*, 490–91.

Commandments, or as summarized by our Lord in Matthew 22:37–40, or as summarized in the moral teaching of the New Testament Epistles. Such a denial of God's moral law is called antinomianism.[45] This is an old error that has been with us in various forms throughout the history of the church. There were gnostic and Marcionite groups in the second century that thought that they were too spiritual to obey God's moral law. The same sort of attitude existed in the Middle Ages among the Albigensians and arose again in the sixteenth century in the wake of the Reformation. The antinomians worried that teaching the abiding validity of God's moral law would lead believers back to the Roman Catholic doctrine of justification with God through works. The magisterial Protestant theologians and churches, with one voice, all rejected antinomianism as contrary to the teaching of Holy Scripture.[46] Antinomianism arose again in the seventeenth century, particularly in England, in the context of the English Civil War and partly in response to nomism.[47] Again, the Reformed churches rejected both neonomianism (acceptance with God through grace and works or law keeping) *and* antinomianism in favor of free acceptance with God and salvation by grace alone (*sola gratia*), through faith alone (*sola fide*), in Christ alone. They affirmed sanctification (and obedience to God's law) in union and communion with Christ as the natural, necessary consequence of free justification and salvation.

In the modern period, particularly in the context of American revivalism and especially after the Second Great Awakening in the nineteenth century and under the influence of various forms of dispensationalism and new covenant theology, it has become widely held that the Decalogue is not for today or no longer binds the Christian as the norm of the Christian life.[48] These traditions tend to have a weak understanding of the relation between creation (nature) and grace (salvation and renewal). Typically Christians from these traditions see God's moral law as peculiar to the Mosaic epoch in redemptive history and neglect the its grounding in God's

45. See the discussion of antinomianism under *HC* 86.

46. E.g., *Formula of Concord* VI, in Kolb and Wengert, *Book of Concord*, 502–3.

47. Como, *Blown by the Spirit*.

48. E.g., Chafer, *Grace*; Ryrie, *Dispensationalism Today*; Hodges, *Gospel under Siege*; Wells and Zaspel, *New Covenant Theology*; Reisinger, *New Covenant Theology and Prophecy*.

nature and revelation in creation, that is, in natural law.[49] With the fathers and the medieval church, the Reformed churches distinguish between the temporary Mosaic legislation (e.g., the ceremonial and judicial laws) and the permanent moral law that was repeated in but not unique to the Mosaic epoch.[50]

Apart from overt antinomianism, there are varieties of practical antinomianism in which professing Christians do not even bother to articulate a rationale for ignoring God's moral law. They simply proceed as if there were no revealed moral law. So far divorced are they from historic Christianity, so influenced are they by the subjectivist spirit of our late modern age, and so apparently unaware of basic biblical teaching are they that some professing Christians simply assume we must have been left to our own devices to decide right from wrong. Some Christians appeal to the leading of the Spirit and other such things to justify all manner of behavior. Each of these is a subspecies of subjectivism, wherein the subject (the person having the experience) becomes the norm. It is a denial of the objectively revealed moral will of God.

The Reformed churches confess that God revealed his moral law in the beginning, in creation, and that it continues to be revealed in nature and is written in the conscience of every image-bearer who has ever lived. In that way it is universal and natural. This is Paul's teaching in Romans 1:18 and 2:14. The law revealed in nature is, in the new covenant, written on the heart of every believer as though on tablets of flesh: "I will put my law within them, and I will write it on their hearts" (Jer 31:33; see Ezek 11:19; 36:26; 2 Cor 3:3).

Here it seems important to see how the catechism provides an objective, divinely revealed, clear basis for the determining what is a good work. Not everything that we imagine qualifies as a good work. In the end, Rome and the subjectivists end up in the same place: both substitute human authority (experience or claims to an unwritten tradition) in place of God's sufficient word.

This goes to the matter of Christian liberty. Where God's word does not speak explicitly or implicitly, there is liberty. One may think, for

49. See the discussion of natural law under *HC* 92.

50. See the discussion of the threefold division of the law under *HC* 87.

example, that circumcision is a good practice. Another may not. The New Testament is clear that the practice of circumcision no longer has any religious or spiritual significance. Its practice is a matter of liberty. The apostle Paul repeatedly asserts the liberty of the Christian to eat meat offered to idols, so long as it is not part of a religious meal. In Romans 14 he writes:

> As for the one who is weak in faith, welcome him, but not to quarrel over opinions. One person believes he may eat anything, while the weak person eats only vegetables. Let not the one who eats despise the one who abstains, and let not the one who abstains pass judgment on the one who eats, for God has welcomed him. Who are you to pass judgment on the servant of another? It is before his own master that he stands or falls. And he will be upheld, for the Lord is able to make him stand.
>
> One person esteems one day as better than another, while another esteems all days alike. Each one should be fully convinced in his own mind. (Rom 14:1–5)

God says that, in the new covenant, all foods are clean (Acts 10:15; 11:9). The old Mosaic ceremonial laws and distinctions have been fulfilled. Nevertheless, there were some who were raised in the old system who, quite understandably, struggled with the transition from the old covenant to the new. If one wants to keep the old calendar, that is one's choice, but one may not impose it on another. Christ has broken down the dividing wall (Eph 2:14). The Jerusalem Synod (Acts 15:6–21) rejected the imposition of the old ceremonial laws and restrictions on gentile Christians.

The objectively and clearly revealed moral law as the baseline for Christian ethics is essential to Christian living and Christian liberty. James calls it "the law of liberty" (Jas 1:25) because it frees us from the tyranny of human opinion. It does not answer every question, and it does not intend or claim to answer every question, but it is an essential starting place. What must Christians do in response to God's grace and in union with Christ? Love God with all our faculties and our neighbor as ourselves (Matt 22:37–40). What does that look like? The law gives us the outline:

1. We worship the one true, Triune God.
2. We worship the Triune God the way he commands.
3. We revere his name.
4. We keep the Christian Sabbath/Lord's Day in rest and worship.
5. We obey divinely instituted authorities.
6. We seek our neighbor's welfare.
7. We keep ourselves sexually pure.
8. We respect our neighbor's property.
9. We tell the truth.
10. We receive gratefully only what God has given us.

There are necessarily other facets of the Christian life—for example, wisdom, but wisdom loves God's law, begins with it, and seeks to understand, apply, and obey it. The Triune God has not left us to guess what he expects of us:

> He has told you, O man, what is good;
> and what does the Lord require of you
> but to do justice, and to love kindness,
> and to walk humbly with your God? (Mic 6:8 ESV).

God has spoken. We are not the measure of all things. Our experience is not final. Our intuitions and feelings must give way to objective revealed truth. Imagined continuing revelation is just illusory and a potential source of bondage. No Christian is bound to what another Christians claims to have heard from God. Together we are bound to God's clear, objective, sufficient word so that no one, not even the church, can impose on us what God himself has not imposed.

Further, as Ursinus reminds us, we are able to do good works only by virtue of the grace and work of the Holy Spirit within us.[51] "Without the

---

51. Ursinus, *Corpus doctrinae*, 492; Ursinus, *Commentary*, 479–80.

grace and continual direction of the Holy Spirit, even the most holy persons on earth can do nothing but sin, as is evident from the examples of David, Peter, and others. Yea, without regeneration, no part of any work that is good in the sight of God, can ever be begun, inasmuch as we are all by nature evil and dead in sin."[52]

Ursinus and Olevianus agree that even our "best works," however, in this life "are all imperfect and defiled by sin" (*HC* 62). Our works, even though we are regenerated, are tainted because we still "do many things which are evil" and "sins in themselves," because we "omit doing many good things" that we ought to do, and because our good works are not "so perfectly good and pure as the law requires; for they are always marred with defects, and polluted with sins."[53]

> Believers' obedience and good works are still sullied with the stains of the flesh and are imperfect; much that is sinful still clings to their good works. Thus if their works were presented before the judgment seat of God, they would of necessity be liable to the sentence that God has already pronounced in His Word, "Cursed is everyone who does not continue in all things which are written in the book of the law, to do them" (Gal. 3[:13]).[54]

By the grace of God, however, we do not seek to present ourselves to God on the basis of our good works or through our good works. We trust in Christ's work for us and seek to do good works out of gratitude, for our neighbor's good, and for God's glory.

52. Ursinus, *Commentary*, 480.

53. Ursinus, *Commentary*, 481; Ursinus, *Corpus doctrinae*, 493–94.

54. Olevian, *Firm Foundation*, 115–16.

QUESTION 92
What is the Law of God?

QUESTION 93
How are these commandments divided?

QUESTION 94
What does God require in the first commandment?

QUESTION 95
What is idolatry?

Lord's Day 34

Question 92

What is the Law of God?

God spoke all these words, saying:

First Commandment

I am the Lord your God, who has brought you out of the land of Egypt, out of the house of bondage, you shall have no other gods before me.

Second Commandment

You shall not make for yourself any graven image, or any likeness of anything that is in heaven above, or that is in the earth beneath, or that is in the water under the earth: you shall not bow down yourself to them, nor serve them: for I the Lord your God am a jealous God, visiting the iniquity of the fathers upon the children unto the third and fourth generation of them that hate me; and showing mercy unto thousands of them that love me, and keep my commandments.

Third Commandment

You shall not take the name of the Lord your God in vain; for the Lord will not hold him guiltless who takes His name in vain.

Fourth Commandment

Remember the sabbath day, to keep it holy. Six days shall you labor, and do all your work: but the seventh day is the sabbath of the Lord your God: in it you shall not do any work, thou, nor your son, nor your daughter, your manservant, nor your maidservant, nor your cattle, nor your stranger that is within your gates: for in six days the Lord made heaven and earth, the sea, and all that in them is, and rested the seventh day: wherefore the Lord blessed the sabbath day, and hallowed it.

Fifth Commandment

Honor your father and your mother that your days may be long upon the land which the Lord your God gives you.

Sixth Commandment

You shall not murder.

Seventh Commandment

You shall not commit adultery.

Eighth Commandment

You shall not steal.

Ninth Commandment
You shall not bear false witness against your neighbor.
Tenth Commandment
You shall not covet your neighbor's house, you shall not covet your neighbor's wife, nor his manservant, nor his maidservant, nor his ox, nor his donkey, nor anything that is your neighbor's.

APPENDIX TO QUESTION 92

Because it is impractical to include the German and Latin texts of *HC* 92 in a footnote, they are appended here in succession:

FRAGE 92

Wie lautet das Gesetz des Herrn?
Gott redet alle diese Worte:
Das Erste Gebot
Ich bin der Herr, dein Gott, der Ich dich aus Aegyptenland, aus dem Diensthause, geführet habe. Du sollst keine anderen Götter vor Mir haben.
Das Andere Gebot
Du sollst dir kein Vildniss, noch irgend ein Gleichniss machen, weder dess, das oben im Himmel, noch dess, das unten auf Erden, oder dess, das im Wasser unter der Erde ist; du sollst sie nicht anbeten, noch ihnen dienen. Denn Ich, der Herr, dein Gott, bin ein starker, eifriger Gott, der die Missethat der Väter heimsucht an den Kindern bis in's dritte und vierte Glied, derer, die Mich hassen, und thue Barmherzigkeit an vielen Tausenden, die Mich lieben und Meine Gebote halten.
Das Dritte Gebot
Du sollst den Namen des Herrn, deines Gottes, nicht missbrauchen, denn der Herr wird den nicht ungestraft lassen, der seinen Namen missbraucht.
Das Vierte Gebot
Gedenke des Sabbathtages, dass du ihn heiligest. Sechs Tage sollst du arbeiten, und alle deine Werke thun: aber am siebenten Tage ist der Sabbath des Herrn, deines Gottes; da sollst du keine Arbeit thun,

noch dein Sohn, noch deine Tochter, noch dein Knecht, noch deine Magd, noch dein Vieh, noch der Fremdling, der in deinen Thoren ist; denn in sechs Tagen hat der Herr Himmel und Erde gemacht, und das Meer, und alles, was darinnen ist, und ruhete am siebenten Tage: darum segnete der Herr den Sabbathtag, und heiligte ihn.

Das Fünfte Gebot

Du sollst deinen Vater und deine Mutter ehren, auf dass du lange lebest im Lande, das dir der Herr, dein Gott giebt.

Das Sechste Gebot

Du sollst nicht tödten

Das Siebente Gebot

Du sollst nicht ehebrechen.

Das Achte Gebot

Du sollst nicht stehlen

Das Neunte Gebot

Du sollst kein falsch Zeugniss reden wider deinen Nächsten.

Das Zehnte Gebot

Lass dich nicht gelüsten deines Nächsten Hauses; lass dich nicht gelüsten deines Nächsten Weibes, noch seines Knechts, noch seiner Magd, noch seines Ochsens, noch seines Esels, noch alles, was dein Nächster hat.[1]

92[2]

Quae est Lex Dei?

Loquutus est Deus omnia verba haec:

Primum Praeceptum

Ego sum Dominus Deus tuus, qui eduxi te ex Aegypto, domo servitutis. Non habebis Deos alienos in conspectu meo.

Secundum.

Ne sculpas tibi simulacrum, nec ullam imaginem effingas eorum, quae aut supra sunt in coelo, aut infra in terra, aut in aquis sub terra:

1. Schaff, *Creeds of Christendom*, 3:340–42.

2. This presentation, with the exception of the biblical prooftexts, reproduces the text as it appears in Palatinate Church, *Catechesis religionis christianae*, 38–41. Cf. Niemeyer, *Collectio Confessionum*, 451–52.

neque incurves te illis, neque colas ea. Ego enim sum Dominus, Deus tuus, fortis, Zelotes, vindicans peccata patrum in filiis, idque in tertia et quarta progenie eorum qui oderunt me: et misericordia utens in millesimam eorum, qui diligunt me, et observant praecepta mea.

Tertium.

Ne usurpes nomen Domini Dei tui temere. Neque enim Dominus dimittet eum impunitum, qui nomen eius vane usurpaverit.

Quartum.

Memento ut diem Sabbathi sanctifices. Sex diebus operaberis, et facies omne opus tuum: At septimo die Sabbathum erit Domino Deo tuo. Non facies ullum opus, nec tu, nec filius tuus, nec filia tua, nec servus tuus, nec ancilla tua, nec iumentum tuum, nec advena, qui est intra portas tuas. Nam sex diebus fecit Deus coelum, terram, mare, et quaecunque in iis sunt, et requeivit die septimo, ideoque benedixit dici Sabbathi, et sanctificavit eum.

Quintum.

Honora Patrem tuum et matrem tuam, ut diu vivas in terra, quam tibi Dominus Deus tuus daturus est.

Sextum.

Non occides.

Septimum.

Non committes adulterium.

Octavum.

Non furaberis.

Nonum.

Non dices contra proximum tuum falsum testimonium.

Decimum.

Non concupisces domum proximi tui, nec concupisces uxorem proximi tui, nec servum eius, nec ancillam, nec bovem, nec asinum, nec quicquam eorum, quae sunt proximi tui.

God's word teaches us to have the highest, most reverent view of God's law generally. The psalmist declares, "Oh how I love your law! It is my meditation all the day" (Ps 119:97 ESV). To be sure, in Psalm 119 the noun תּוֹרָה probably has a broader sense than just the moral law; nevertheless, the Scriptures repeatedly teach the same attitude toward to moral law. After all, God's moral law is a subset of the broader category. When Psalm 40:8 says, "I delight to do your will, O my God; your law is within my heart" (ESV), the psalmist is surely delighting in God's moral law. Notice how God's "will" (i.e., that of which God approves) and his "law" (*Torah*) are a delight. Tragically, Adam, whom God created with the ability to obey God's law, in righteousness and true holiness, in order that he might know God, love him, and enter into a state of blessedness with him, freely and mysteriously chose to disobey God's law.[3] That lawlessness was the original sin (1 John 3:4). In that sin all humanity was plunged into moral darkness and corruption (Rom 5:12–21). As the *New England Primer* had it, "In Adam's fall, we sinned all."[4] Paul and Augustine nod in agreement. Israel was tasked with obeying God's law, and according to the prophets she did not: "But they did not obey your voice or walk in your law. They did nothing of all you commanded them to do" (Jer 32:23 ESV).

THREEFOLD DIVISION OF THE LAW

After discussing the law in general, the very next topic to which Ursinus turns in his exposition of this question is the traditional Christian threefold distinction in the biblical law.[5] With the ancient and medieval church, the Lutheran and Reformed theologians embraced this distinction and used it consistently in their explanation of the continuity and discontinuity between Moses (the old covenant) and Christ (the new covenant). The moral law is grounded in the divine nature and thus always has abiding validity. God has always obligated us to love him with all our faculties and our neighbor as ourselves. Further, the same law that God gave to Adam before the fall was repeated at Sinai and by the prophets.[6] Just as God offered eternal blessedness to Adam under the "covenant established

3. See the discussion under *HC* 6.

4. *New England Primer*, n.p.

5. Ursinus, *Commentary*, 490–92; Ursinus, *Corpus doctrinae*, 503–5. See the discussion of the threefold division of the law under *HC* 87.

6. Ursinus, *Corpus doctrinae*, 503; Ursinus, *Commentary*, 490–91.

in creation," God offered "the favor of God and eternal life" "to all those who render perfect obedience."[7]

The ceremonial and judicial laws are categorically distinct from the moral law. They were instituted under Moses and were intentionally temporary, "binding the Jewish nation until the coming of the Messiah."[8] They were "signs, symbols, types, and shadows of spiritual things to be fulfilled in the New Testament."[9] The judicial laws were "for the establishment and preservation of the Jewish commonwealth" and in force until the coming of the Messiah.[10] They served to distinguish the Jewish national people from the other nations and as types of the kingdom of Christ.[11]

The ceremonial and judicial laws were abrogated and expired with the coming of Christ.[12] Daniel prophesied this abrogation (Dan 9:27). As Hebrews 7:12 says, "When there is a change in the priesthood, there is a change in the law." Christ is a Melchizedekian priest (Ps 110:4; Heb 7:11–18). With the incarnation, death, resurrection, and ascension of Christ, the entire Mosaic system was made "obsolete" (πεπαλαίωκεν; Heb 8:13). Ursinus appeals to the decree of the Jerusalem Synod (Acts 15:28–29).[13]

THEONOMY

The Reformed writers in the sixteenth century were aware of a scheme proposed by Andreas Bodenstein von Karlstadt (1486–1541) whereby the Old Testament Jewish law would be used for civil law.[14] We know this

7. Ursinus, *Commentary*, 491. See *BC* 14, which speaks of the "commandment of life" given before the fall. The phrase "covenant established in creation" is from the *Larger Catechism*, 135, in Bierma et al., *Introduction*, 188. On Ursinus's doctrine of the covenant of nature, Lyle Bierma argues the covenant of nature appeared in the 1562 *Summa theologiae*, but there was an "abrupt change" in Ursinus's thinking and the doctrine receded in his later writings. See Bierma, "Law and Grace," 99–103, 109–10. Todd Smedley disagrees and argues for an extensive and continuing use of the covenant of nature in Ursinus's theology ("Covenant Theology of Zacharias Ursinus," 196–230).

8. Ursinus, *Commentary*, 491.

9. Ursinus, *Commentary*, 491; Ursinus, *Corpus doctrinae*, 504.

10. Ursinus, *Commentary*, 491.

11. Ursinus, *Commentary*, 491.

12. Ursinus, *Commentary*, 492–93; Ursinus, *Corpus doctrinae*, 505; Westminster Assembly, *Humble Advice of the Assembly*, 33.

13. Ursinus, *Commentary*, 493.

14. *Apology of the Augsburg Confession* 16.3–6, in Kolb and Wengert, *Book of Concord*, 231.

program as *theonomy*.[15] Calvin rejects this notion categorically.[16] Ursinus addresses this proposal at length and rejects it.[17] "The ordinary and correct answer to this question is, that the ceremonial and judicial law, as given by Moses, has been abrogated in as far as it relates to obedience; and that the moral law has also been abrogated as it respects the curse, but not as it respects obedience."[18] With the advent of Christ, neither the ceremonial nor the judicial laws as such have any authority over the Christian conscience. To the objection that the government God instituted in Israel must be the best government, Ursinus replies that the argument is fallacious because it takes as absolute what was true only "in a certain respect."[19] The Mosaic judicial laws were best "for that time, that country, and nation."[20] Like the rest of the orthodox Reformed in the sixteenth and seventeenth centuries, Ursinus was so opposed to theonomy that he allowed that the Mosaic judicial laws may be observed so long as a nation did so "without attaching to it the idea of necessity."[21] They could be enforced insofar as they agreed with nature and reason, not because they came from Moses.[22] The *BC* and WCF capture the doctrine of the Reformed churches regarding the judicial laws. In *BC* 25 we confess:

> We believe that the ceremonies and symbols of the law have ended with the coming of Christ, and that all foreshadowings have come to an end, so that the use of them ought to be abolished among Christians. Yet the truth and substance of these things remain for us in Jesus Christ, in whom they have been fulfilled. Nevertheless, we continue to use the witnesses drawn from the law and prophets

---

15. E.g., Bahnsen, *Theonomy in Christian Ethics*.

16. Calvin, *Institutes* 4.20.14; see the 1536 *Institutes* 6.48.

17. Ursinus, *Commentary*, 492–95; Ursinus, *Corpus doctrinae*, 505–7.

18. Ursinus, *Commentary*, 492.

19. Ursinus, *Commentary*, 495.

20. Ursinus, *Commentary*, 495.

21. Ursinus, *Commentary*, 495.

22. E.g., Polanus, *Substance of the Christian Religion*, 100–102; Junius, *Mosaic Polity*, 60; Rollock, *Lectures upon the Passion*, 87–88; Wollebius, *Compendium*, 1.16.6; Witisus, *Economy*, 2.411; Turretin, *Institutes of Elenctic Theology*, 11.26.2–10; Gillespie, *Wholesome Severity Reconciled*, 6–7; Dickson, *Truth's Victory over Error*, 144–45.

> to confirm us in the gospel and to regulate our lives with full integrity for the glory of God, according to his will.[23]

Like Ursinus, the Reformed churches address the ceremonial and judicial laws together. They were *both* shadows and types. *Both* have ended, and the use of them is to be abolished "among Christians." The Westminster divines are even more pointed in their rejection of theonomy: "To [the people of Israel] also, as a body politic, he gave sundry judicial laws, which expired together with the State of that people; not obliging any other now, further than the general equity thereof may require."[24]

THE ABIDING VALIDITY OF THE MORAL LAW

In Exodus 34:27 Scripture says that Yahweh spoke directly to Moses to say, "Write these words, for in accordance with these words I have made a covenant with you and with Israel" (ESV). Thus, whatever follows was an essential part of the national covenant with Israel. In verse 28 we read that Moses "wrote on the tablets the words of the covenant, the ten words" (עֲשֶׂרֶת הַדְּבָרִים). Of course, "ten words" does not mean that there were literally only ten words on the tablets. Here *word* means "revelations" or "disclosures" or "sayings," or better, "commandments." From this we should infer that the moral law is God's word. The moral law did not appear *de novo* at Sinai. God's law was a restatement to Israel, in typological clothing, of the law he first delivered in the garden.

The moral law has existed, in God, from all eternity. It is a reflection and revelation of his nature and character. Second, the law was revealed in creation.[25] WLC 92 reflects the Reformed consensus:

> What did God at first reveal unto man as the rule of his obedience?
> The rule of obedience revealed to Adam in the estate of innocence, and to all mankind in him, besides a special command

23. United Reformed Churches in North America, *Liturgical Forms and Prayers*, 180.

24. WCF 19.4, in Westminster Assembly, *Humble Advice of the Assembly*, 33. The Reformed understood general equity to mean natural law. The theonomists typically reject natural law as a category and thus redefine it. For the Reformed consensus, see Perkins, *Works*, 8:16–17; Wollebius, *Compendium*, 1.16.6; Ussher, *Body of Divinity*, 204; Rutherford, *Free Disputation*, 288–89; Rutherford, *Divine Right of Church-Government*, 493–94; Troxel and Wallace, "Men in Combat," 307–18.

25. Olevianus, *Exposition*, 12–13; Olevianus, *Romanos*, 34, 65; Ursinus, *Commentary*, 36, 148, 492.

not to eat of the fruit of the tree knowledge of good and evil, was the moral law.[26]

The moral law was woven into the fabric of things. The Decalogue as we have it in Exodus 20:3–17 and Deuteronomy 5:7–21 is the Israelite expression of the abiding moral law. The Israelite national covenant expired with the death of Christ. Its redemptive-historical purpose was to point to Christ as the righteous covenant keeper (Gal 3:23; 4:31; Rom 7:1–6).

In the modern period, however, among evangelicals and especially under the influence of the various types of dispensationalism, the accent has fallen on discontinuity, leading many to ignore the old threefold distinction as irrelevant, as if everything that happened in redemptive history is passé or useful only for character studies.[27]

Another reason modern evangelicals tend to think this way is the loss of nature as a category of thought. The fathers, medievals, and Reformers all used two great categories by which to understand the world: nature (or creation) and redemption (or grace). To be sure, they understood and related those categories differently, but they all used the categories. Because the Reformers had the category "nature," they had a way of thinking about the way the world was originally ordered, the way things were intended to be. They also had a way of understanding God's moral law. They knew that God's law was grounded in his nature (more about that later) and that law was expressed in creation or in nature. They spoke without embarrassment of God's natural law. In the modern period, particularly after the colorful and influential Swiss theologian Karl Barth (1886–1968), the category of natural law came under suspicion among his many followers and among those evangelicals he influenced.[28] *Contra* Barth and others, the Protestants had a virtually universal consensus that the natural law was substantially identical to the Decalogue.[29]

Without the idea that God's moral law is revealed in creation, in nature, a part of the fabric of human existence, it is more difficult to think about a moral law that is fixed in the consciences of all people, in all times.

26. Westminster Assembly, *Humble Advice of the Assembly*, 25.

27. See the discussion of antinomianism under *HC* 91.

28. Barth and Brunner, *Natural Theology*; Clark, "Calvin and the *Lex Naturalis*," 1–22; Grabill, *Rediscovering the Natural Law*; VanDrunen, *Natural Law*.

29. Clark, *Caspar Olevian*, 167n135; Clark, "Calvin and the *Lex naturalis*," 8–12.

Nevertheless, the great tradition of the church had very good reason to speak as it did on this point. The apostle Paul teaches explicitly that God has revealed his law in nature and impressed it on the human conscience: "For what can be known about God is plain to them, because God has shown it to them. For his invisible attributes, namely, his eternal power and divine nature, have been clearly perceived, ever since the creation of the world, in the things that have been made. So they are without excuse" (Rom 1:19–20 ESV).

God has revealed himself and his moral law in creation. That knowledge is universal. It is not, however, as Paul makes clear, a *saving* knowledge. Indeed, after the fall, the natural knowledge of God is a condemning knowledge, but it is a true knowledge. Further, Paul says, by nature all humans not only know God but also know his moral law: "For when Gentiles, who do not have the law, by nature [φύσει] do what the law requires, they are a law to themselves, even though they do not have the law. They show that the work of the law is written on their hearts, while their conscience also bears witness, and their conflicting thoughts accuse or even excuse them on that day when, according to my gospel, God judges the secrets of men by Christ Jesus" (Rom 2:14–16 ESV).

The work of the law is written (ἔργον τοῦ νόμου) on the hearts (ἐν ταῖς καρδίαις) of every human. The law known by nature is the same in substance as the moral law revealed to Adam and given to Israel at Sinai. Thus, the moral law is perpetual and universal. Ursinus and Olevianus articulate this very understanding repeatedly. For example, Olevianus explains that all were guilty *before* the law was given at Sinai because the substance of the law was already in force in the legal covenant made with Adam before the fall. His doctrine of natural law is thus bound up with his federal theology of the first Adam and the last Adam, Christ.[30] For Olevianus, the testimony of our natural obligation to God is "partly in the law of nature, inscribed in minds and partly written in the law on the two tablets."[31] For Ursinus, the moral law "agrees in every respect with

30. Clark, *Caspar Olevian*, 165–68. E.g., *Romanos Notae*, 27, 57, 58, 97, 272, 195, 200, 288; *Galatas Notae*, 68; *Philippenses et Colossene Notaes*, 42; *De substantia*, 1.1.2, 7–9; 1.2.1; 1.5.31.

31. "Huius naturalis obligationis testimonium Deus extare voluit partim in lege naturae inscripta mentibus, partim in lege scripta in duabus tabulis" (Olevianus, *De substantia*, 2.5).

the Decalogue."[32] The moral law is known both from nature and from Scripture.[33] The Decalogue is the sum of the moral law taught in Scripture.

> *The natural and moral law* were the same in man before the fall, when his nature was pure and holy. Since the fall, however ... a considerable part of the natural law has become obscured and lost by reason of sin, so that there is only a small portion concerning the obedience which we owe to God still left in the human mind. It is for this reason that God repeated, and declared to the church the entire doctrine and true sense of his law, as contained in the Decalogue. The Decalogue is, therefore, the renewal and re-enforcing of the natural law, which is only a part of the Decalogue.[34]

For the framers of the catechism, to say that the law of God is the Decalogue meant that it was the moral law, given initially to Adam in creation, republished at Sinai, and summarized repeatedly in various ways throughout Scripture (e.g., Matt 22:37–40; cf. *HC* 4).

The evidence for the abiding validity of the natural and moral law is extensive. The apostle Paul quotes the fifth commandment in Ephesians 6:1–3 and applies it to New Testament Christians. First John 3:4 defines sin as "lawlessness" (ἀνομίαν). How can there be lawlessness without a law, and what other law is there than God's moral law? The "new commandment" (John 13:34; 15:12) of which Christ spoke is not absolutely new, as the apostle John explains (1 John 2:7–8; 2 John 5). We are to love one another as Christ loved us and gave himself for us. It is new *in the way it is articulated* and in the *circumstances* in which it is articulated—that is, in light of the fulfillment of the promise of a Redeemer—but the command to love one's neighbor is hardly new. Leviticus 19:18 says, "You shall love your neighbor as yourself: I am Yahweh." When Paul says, "Love is the fulfilling of the law" (Rom 13:10), he is articulating the substance of the moral law that has been in effect since creation. One finds partial summaries of the Ten Commandments scattered throughout the New Testament, for example, Romans 2:22–24; 1 Corinthians 6:9–10; and Galatians 5:19–20. In Matthew 15:3 our Lord Jesus appealed to the

32. Ursinus, *Commentary*, 492.

33. Ursinus, *Commentary*, 492.

34. Ursinus, *Commentary*, 492.

moral law as fixed and permanent over against the manmade traditions of the rabbis and Pharisees.

When we confess "the law of God," we refer specially to the moral law as we have received it from God in nature and in Scripture, in the history of redemption. In *HC* 19 we recognize that law was revealed under types and shadows, and thus in the new covenant Christ has fulfilled the types and shadows. Thus, Ursinus writes of the partial abrogation of the moral law.[35] This is why, though we honor the Christian Sabbath, we do not keep a Saturday Sabbath because the Saturday Sabbath belongs to the types and shadows. We recognize that the land promise attached to the fifth commandment is no longer in force. God no longer has a national people, but the substance of the moral law as expressed at Sinai is still in force.

The law is abrogated in another sense too. Those who, by grace alone, through faith alone, have received what Olevianus calls the substance of the covenant of grace are no longer under the law as a covenant of works. God has imputed Christ's merits to us. God has removed the curse of the law from those who are in Christ.[36] We are no longer under the law "as it respects constraint."[37] It is in this sense that Paul says we are no longer under law (a covenant of works) but under (a covenant of) grace (Rom 6:14).

The moral law has not been, nor can it be, abrogated as the moral norm of the Christian life.[38] This is the intended sense of our Lord's words in Matthew 5:17, "Do not think that I have come to abolish the Law or the Prophets; I have not come to abolish them but to fulfill them" (ESV).[39]

GOD'S LAW IS TRUE

Thus, God's moral law is not some mere convention, some arbitrary word from God that bears no relation to who and what he is. Of course, we do not and by nature cannot know God as he is in himself. The Triune God in himself is hidden from us (Ps 10:5; Isa 55:8–9; John 1:18; 14:8–11). Nevertheless, what God says to us about himself is true. Our Lord Jesus said, "Your word is truth" (John 17:17). There is a divinely ordained, stable

35. Ursinus, *Commentary*, 495–96; Ursinus, *Corpus doctrinae*, 505–7.

36. Ursinus, *Commentary*, 495.

37. Ursinus, *Commentary*, 495.

38. Ursinus, *Commentary*, 496.

39. See the discussion under *HC* 115 regarding the three uses of the law.

relationship between God's word, in this case his law, and who and what God is. His law is what he wants us to know of his character and attributes relative to his moral will for us.

Therefore, we should oppose the nominalism of our late modern age, which seeks to deconstruct all norms as arbitrary conventions. In the world as God ordered it, there are fixed truths. He has ordained language to communicate those truths and himself. His moral law is one of the chief places where God reveals himself. When the moral law says, "You shall have no other gods before me" and "You shall not take the name of the Yahweh your God in vain," it reflects God's holiness. God says of himself, "For the Lord your God is a consuming fire, a jealous God" (Deut 4:24; cf. Deut 9:3). Leviticus 11:44 reveals to us something of God's holiness: "For I am the LORD your God. Consecrate yourselves therefore, and be holy, for I am holy." God is the antithesis of that which is common. He is pure. He is clean. He is righteous. The Levitical laws (e.g., 10:10, "You are to distinguish between the holy and the common, and between the unclean and the clean" [ESV]) distinguishing between clean and unclean, even though illustrative of future realities, help us to understand the difference between a holy God and us, a fallen, unholy people. The God who redeemed Israel out of Egypt with plagues and through the Red Sea is the God who redeems us graciously and calls us to holiness and purity (Jas 4:8). According to James, being "double-minded" is the antithesis of purity toward God. The writer to the Hebrews sounds like an Old Testament prophet when he says, "For our God is a consuming fire" (Heb 12:29), but he was writing to New Testament believers about very real New Testament realities.

THE DISTINCTION BETWEEN LAW AND GOSPEL

We have already considered this distinction under *HC* 2–3, but it is worth pausing to address the distinction for four reasons: (1) the distinction between law and gospel is built into the structure of the catechism and thus essential to understanding it correctly, (2) the distinction was essential to the Reformation, (3) Ursinus devotes a section to it during his lecture on this question, and (4) in the modern period, there has been in some

Reformed circles a campaign against this basic Reformation distinction.[40] Thus, it needs to be reasserted clearly and vigorously.

In its nature the law of God demands "personal, perfect, and perpetual obedience."[41] The law, as Ursinus writes, "promises rewards to those who render perfect obedience."[42] The gospel "promises the same blessings on condition that we exercise faith in Christ, by which we embrace the obedience which another, even Christ has performed in our behalf. … The gospel teaches that we are justified freely by faith in Christ."[43] A new obedience is the necessary and natural *consequence* of our justification, but our new obedience is no part of our justification. The gospel offers life to sinners, but the law "works wrath" and is the ministry of death (2 Cor 3:7; Rom 4:15).[44] This is why it was perfectly right and faithful to Reformed theology, as John Murray (1898–1975) taught, to distinguish between the principle of law and the principle of gospel or grace: "The purity and integrity of the gospel stands or falls with the absoluteness of the antithesis between the function and potency of law, one the one hand, and the function and potency of grace, on the other."[45] It was to recognize the different nature of the two kinds of words in Scripture that Olevianus writes,

> For this reason the distinction between law and Gospel is retained. The law does not promise freely, but under the condition that you keep it completely. And if someone should transgress it once, the law or legal covenant does not have the promise of the remission of sins. On the other hand, the Gospel promises freely the remission of sins and life, not if we keep the law, but for the sake of the Son of God, through faith.[46]

40. E.g., Barth, *Community, State, and Church*; Lillback, *Binding of God*, 125. For a survey and response, see Clark, "Letter and Spirit," 331–64; Clark, "Law and Gospel." Ursinus writes, "Quid lex moralis ab Evangelio differat" (*Commentary*, 497–98; Ursinus, *Corpus doctrinae*, *Corpus*, 509–10).

41. WLC 20, in Westminster Assembly, *Humble Advice of the Assembly*, 4.

42. Ursinus, *Commentary*, 497.

43. Ursinus, *Commentary*, 497.

44. Ursinus, *Commentary*, 497; Ursinus, *Corpus doctrinae*, 510.

45. Murray, *Principles of Conduct*, 186.

46. "Ut retineatur discrimen legis et Evangelii. Lex non promittit gratis, sed sub conditione, si omnia feceris. Et si quis eam semel sit transgressus, non habet lex seu foedus legale promissionem remissionis peccatorum: Evangelium verò gratis promittit remissionem peccatorum, & vitam si non

For Olevianus, this distinction was fundamental to the Reformed reading of the Bible and Christian theology, piety, and practice. He learned it from Luther, of course, but Calvin reaffirmed it to him, and Calvin sometimes discusses it under the heading of law and gospel but more frequently under the heading of law and grace. Therefore he makes the same distinction as Luther and for the same reasons.[47]

THE THREE USES OF THE LAW

It seems useful to address this topic briefly here since this distinction developed early in the Reformation.[48] The three uses of the law are its civil use (*usus politicus sive civilis*), as the norm for public life and to restrain sin; the pedagogical use (*usus elenchticus sive paedogagicus*), whereby we learn the greatness of our sin and misery; and the normative use (*usus didacticus sive normativus*), or the third use of the law (*tertius usus legis*), whereby the law serves as the norm of the Christian life.[49] These uses are numbered differently by different writers. Sometimes the civil use is listed first, and sometimes the pedagogical use occurs first. Calvin treats the pedagogical use of the law as the first use, the civil use as the second, and then the normative use, which he calls the "principal" and the proper end of the law.[50] Ursinus distinguishes the uses of the law according to the fourfold state of humanity:

- Before the fall, the law had two uses: (1) "the entire and perfect conformity of man with God" and (2) "a consciousness of the divine favor, and certain hope of eternal life," by which

praestiterimus legem, propter Filium Dei, per fidem" (Olevianus, *Romanos Notae*, 148). See Clark, "Law and Gospel"; Clark, "Letter and Spirit," 331–64.

47. On Calvin's many debts to Luther, see Clark, "'Subtle Sacramentarian' or Son?," 35–60.

48. See the discussion under *HC* 115.

49. Muller, *Dictionary of Latin and Greek*, s.v. "usus legis." Among orthodox Christians, however, there has never been any doubt that the moral law (*lex moralis*) is a reflection of the divine nature and has abiding validity as the norm for the Christian life. This use of the law is but one of three identified by Luther and Melanchthon in the 1520s and 1530s, in controversy with the antinomians, and inherited by the framers of the catechism along with the rest of the Reformed theologians and churches. See Edwards, *Luther and the False Brethren*, 156–79; Wengert, *Law and Gospel*; Althaus, *Theology of Martin Luther*, 266–73; Silcock, "Introduction to 'The Antinomian Disputations,'" 22–25. Luther *formally* taught two uses of the law but *substantially* taught three uses of the law.

50. Calvin, *Institutes* 2.7.6–9, 10–11. "Tertius usus, qui et praecipuus est, et in proprium Legis finem proprius spectat" (Barth, *Joannis Calvini Opera Selecta*, 3:337.23–24; Calvin, *Institutes* 2.7.12).

the law "promises life to those who render a perfect obedience to its requirements. 'Which if a man do, he shall live in them.' (Lev. 18:5.)"[51]

- After the fall, among the unregenerate, the law has two functions: (1) the civil use, whereby the natural law and that spoken through "ministers and magistrates" restrains corruption "in the church and beyond it" (Rom 2:14); (2) it "accuses, convinces, and condemns all those who are not regenerated, because they are unrighteous before God, and subject to eternal condemnation."[52]

- In nature restored through Christ, among the regenerate, the law has "many uses": for example, the preservation of discipline because of the weakness of the flesh, a knowledge of sin, "the rule of divine worship and the Christian life" (*norma cultus divini et vitae Christianae*).[53]

- "In nature perfectly restored and glorified after this life," the law will continue to have a use even after the conclusion of the ministry of the church, since the elect will have a knowledge of the law, and full conformity to it will be accomplished in them.[54]

---

51. Ursinus, *Commentary*, 612–13. "Before the fall" translates "In natura integra" (Ursinus, *Corpus doctrinae*, 622).

52. Ursinus, *Commentary*, 613. "After the fall" translates "In natura corrupta" (Ursinus, *Corpus doctrinae*, 622). "In the church and beyond it" translates "in ecclesias et extra eam" (623).

53. Ursinus, *Corpus doctrinae*, 624. The phrase "norma cultus divini" is italicized in the original. "In nature restored through Christ" translates "In natura per Christum instaurata" (623).

54. Ursinus, *Corpus doctrinae*, 624; Ursinus, *Commentary*, 614.

QUESTION 93

How are these commandments divided?

Into two tables: the first of which teaches in four commandments, what duties we owe to God; the second, in six, what duties we owe to our neighbor.[55]

Historically, the commandments have been ordered differently.[56] Philo, Josephus, the Eastern Orthodox, and the Reformed number the commandments as we have them in *HC* 92.[57] The Syrian tradition, Augustine, Rome, and the Lutherans combine what we regard as the first and second commandments. In their numbering, what the Reformed regard as the third commandment becomes the second. They divide into two commandments what we regard as the tenth commandment.

PROLOGUE AND COMMANDMENTS

The orthodox Jewish tradition regards the prologue as part of the first commandment. Calvin, Ursinus, and the Westminster divines, however, distinguish between the preface to the commandments and the commandments themselves, between the gospel prologue and the commandments as the norm of the Christian life. The words of Exodus 20:1–2 are different in character from verses 3–17. Verse 2 is a declaration of the good news of free salvation by grace alone: "I am Yahweh your God, who brought you out of the land of Egypt, out of the house of slavery." That was good news for sinners who grumbled against Moses. The Ten Commandments proper begin in Exodus 20:3. Yahweh kept the promise he made to Abraham "to be God to you and to your children after you" (Gen 17:7). In Exodus 6:7 he repeats the essence of that promise: "I will take you to be my people, and I will be your God, and you shall know that I am Yahweh your God, who has brought you out from under the burdens of the Egyptians." In

55. "Wie werden diese Gebote getheilet? In zwei Tafeln: deren die erste in vier Geboten lehret, wie wir uns gegen Gott sollen halten; die andere in sechs Geboten, was wir unserm Nächsten schuldig sind" (Schaff, *Creeds of Christendom*, 3:342). "Quomodo dividuntur haec praecepta? In duas tabulas, quarum prior quatuor praeceptis tradit, quo pacto nos erga Deum geramus: Posterior sex praeceptis, quae officia proximo debeamus" (Niemeyer, *Collectio Confessionum*, 452).

56. See the chart in Baker, "Ten Commandments, Two Tablets," 7.

57. Baker, "Ten Commandments, Two Tablets," 7. See Ursinus, *Commentary*, 500.

Exodus 20:2 he announces that he is who he said he is and did what he promised to do. The God of Abraham, Isaac, and Jacob makes and keeps gracious promises, and he has kept covenant of grace with his church. He has delivered his church from bondage.

Verse 3, however, is not a declaration of good news. It is a commandment. In traditional Protestant terms, the law comes at Sinai not in its pedagogical use but in its normative use, that is, the third use of the law (*tertius usus legis*).[58] The effect is to say, "In light of all that I have graciously, freely done for you, here is what I expect as a consequence." We were not saved because we met a condition. We were saved by grace alone, through faith alone (and even that faith is a gift; Eph 2:8–10). The obligations we gratefully take up under the third use of the law are consequent obligations. We seek to love God with all our faculties and our neighbor as ourselves because God first loved us.

This distinction between the gospel of Exodus 20:2 and the law that begins in verse 3 is as old as the Reformation. Calvin treats Exodus 20:2 and parallel passages, for example, Leviticus 19:3, this way:

> *I am the Lord your God.* In these first four passages he treats of the same points which we have observed in the preface to the Law; for he reasons partly from God's authority, that the law should be reverently obeyed, because the Creator of heaven and earth justly claims supreme dominion; and, partly, he sets before them the blessing of redemption, that they may willingly submit themselves to His law, from whom they have obtained their safety. For, whenever God calls Himself Jehovah, it should suggest His majesty, before which all ought to be humbled; whilst redemption should of itself produce voluntary submission.[59]

Calvin follows Luther's fundamental distinction between law and gospel as two categories or two kinds of divine speech. Ursinus follows Calvin here. "The first commandment is in two parts: commandment and preface. The words of the preface are, 'I am Yahweh your God, who led you out of the land of Egypt, the house of bondage.' This preface pertains

58. See the discussion of the third use of the law under *HC* 86, 115.

59. Calvin, *Commentaries on the Four Last Books*, 1.343.

to the whole decalogue."[60] The Westminster divines express this distinction explicitly in the Larger Catechism.[61]

The preface to the commandments is one thing, the commandments another. The gospel has consequences, but those consequences do not turn the gospel into law, nor do they turn the law into good news for sinners with respect to our standing with God. Otherwise the order followed by the Eastern Orthodox and the Reformed churches agrees with the orthodox Jewish order.

TWO TABLES

There is an inherent order in the commandments or the Ten Words. The first four commandments speak directly to our relationship with God, our duty to love the Triune God with all our faculties, and the second six speak to our duty to love our neighbor as ourself. The church has traditionally referred to this distinction when speaking of the "two tables" of the law.[62] This order is reflected in *HC* 93. Our Lord Jesus gave us this outline in Matthew 22:37–40: "And he said to him, 'You shall love the Lord your God with all your heart and with all your soul and with all your mind. This is the great and first commandment. And a second is like it: You shall love your neighbor as yourself. On these two commandments depend all the Law and the Prophets'" (ESV).

The first three commandments are explicitly, undoubtedly focused on our duty to the Lord. The fourth commandment, as we shall see, functions as a sort of logical turning point in the Decalogue since its first aspect is toward God but its second aspect certainly has one's neighbor in view. Like the rest of the commandments, the fifth commandment is focused on neighbor.

There is some benefit in getting the order of the commandments right. Ursinus observes that it helps generally to understand the structure of the Decalogue in order to "understand the sense and scope of the whole law"

60. "PRIMI PRAECEPTI sunt duae partes: Praeceptum: Praeceptum et praefatio. Praefationis verba sunt: *Ego sum Iehova Deus tuus, qui eduxi te è terra Aegypti, domo servitutis*. Praefatio haec pertinet ad totum decalogum"(Ursinus, *Corpus doctrinae*, 518); Ursinus, *Commentary*, 507.

61. WLC 101, in Westminster Assembly, *Humble Advice to the Assembly*, 28.

62. Ursinus, *Commentary*, 498.

as well as the "perfection of obedience" required by it.[63] Further, Ursinus says, we prioritize the first table over the second (Acts 5:29).[64]

It is worth paying attention to this issue because in some numberings the second commandment becomes truncated. Further, it makes little sense of the commandments to divide the tenth commandment.

Ursinus makes a valuable observation that the Decalogue is organized according to what is commanded and forbidden "in the mediate and immediate worship of God."[65] "Generally in the Decalogue, the worship of God is commanded."[66] Whatever is contrary to God's law is forbidden. The worship of God is either immediate, that is, when we are performing good works toward God directly or mediately, when we are doing good works toward our neighbor.[67] The immediate touches the worship of God internally, in the heart, as required by the first commandment and externally, as normed by the second commandment.[68] The immediate, external, private worship of God is normed by the third commandment, and the immediate, external public worship of God "consists in the sanctification of the sabbath and is delivered to us in the fourth commandment."[69]

Finally, we should note that there are two aspects to every commandment: a positive injunction, something that is to be done, and a prohibition, something that is forbidden.

QUESTION 94

What does God require in the first commandment?

That on peril of my soul's salvation, I avoid and flee all idolatry, sorcery, enchantments, invocation of saints or of other creatures;

63. "Ut sententiam et scopum toius legis et perfectionem obedientiae melius intelligamus" (Ursinus, *Corpus doctrinae*, 511).

64. "Regulam vulgatam observemus, praecepta secundae tabulae cedere praeceptis primae in eodem genere cultus" (Ursinus, *Corpus doctrinae*, 511); Ursinus, *Commentary*, 498.

65. "Dividitur decalogus secundum materiam subiectam, seu secundum res, quae iubentur aut prohibentur in decalogo, in tum Dei immediatum et mediatum" (Ursinus, *Corpus doctrinae*, 513).

66. "Generaliter in decalogo praecipitur cultus Dei" (Ursinus, *Corpus doctrinae*, 513).

67. Ursinus, *Corpus doctrinae*, 513; Ursinus, *Commentary*, 500.

68. Ursinus, *Commentary*, 500–501.

69. "Publicus consistit in sanctificatione sabbathi, et traditur in quarto praecepto" (Ursinus, *Corpus doctrinae*, 513).

and that I rightly acknowledge the only true God, trust in him alone, with all humility and patience expect all good from Him only, and love, fear and honor him with my whole heart; so as rather to renounce all creatures than to do the least thing against his will.[70]

When Yahweh Elohim said to Adam, "You may eat from any tree in the garden except the tree of the knowledge of good and evil" (Gen 2:16–17), he was saying, in effect, "You are my prophet, priest, and king, but you must respect me as Lord and God over all." The Lord placed a boundary beyond which Adam, as Yahweh's servant, was not to go.[71] He articulated in one command the two tables of the moral law. He was to love God with all his faculties by believing his word and by obeying him. By obeying the "commandment of life," as *BC* 7 has it, he was also to love his neighbor, Eve, by defending the garden, preserving its sanctity, and by defeating the Evil One.[72] Johannes Cocceius (1603–1669) explains,

> The covenant of works requires the obedience of *all* the precepts, so that to have sinned in one of them incurs the guilt of them all (James 2:10), because of course in the transgression of the smallest precept of whatever kind is profanation and contempt of Him who gave the whole law (ibid., v. 11). ... Surely all the precepts are connected to one another by a certain necessity. For we are not

70. "Was fordert der Herr im ersten Gebot? Dass ich, bei Verlierung meiner Seelen Heil und Seligkeit, alle Abgötterei, Zauberei, abergläubische Segen, Anrufung der Heiligen oder anderer Creaturen, meiden und fliehen soll, und den einigen wahren Gott recht erkennen, ihm allein vertrauen, in aller Demuth und Geduld, von ihm allein alles Gute gewarten, und ihn von ganzem Herzen lieben, fürchten, und ehren; also, dass ich ehe alle Creaturen übergebe, denn in dem Geringsten wider seinen Willen thue" (Schaff, *Creeds of Christendom*, 3:342). "Quid postulat Deus in primo praecepto? Ut, quam mihi chara est salus animae meae, tam studiose vitem et fugiam omnem idololatriam, magiam, incautationem, superstitionem, invocationem sanctorum, aut caeterarum creaturarum: unicum autem et verum Deum recte agnoscam, ipsi soli fidam, summa humilitate, ac patientia me illi subiiciam, ab eo solo omnia bona exspectem; denique intimo cordis affectu ipsum amem, reverear, venerer, adeo ut omnibus potius creaturis renunciem, quam ut vel minimum contra eius voluntatem committam" (Niemeyer, *Collectio Confessionum*, 453).

71. Witsius capitalizes on this same general approach in *Economy of the Covenants*, 1.80–91. See Wollebius, "Compendium," 64–66; Heidegger, *Concise Marrow of Christian Theology*, 9.13 (pp. 64–65).

72. United Reformed Churches in North America, *Liturgical Forms and Prayers*, 167; Kline, *Kingdom Prologue*, 85–89.

able to love God if we hate our neighbor, nor are we able to love our neighbor if we hate God.[73]

Adam chose to dishonor his Lord, to break the law, and to break the covenant of works. He placed a god ahead of Yahweh Elohim, his Creator, his Lord, and the sovereign God who spoke all things into being, who created Adam in his image out of the dust of the earth. It was Yahweh Elohim who breathed life into Adam. Truly it was in God that Adam lived, and moved, and had his being (Acts 17:28). Nevertheless, mysteriously, tragically, Adam chose to listen to the serpent and to lies rather than to believe and obey the truth. When he chose death over life, when he aspired to know as God knows, in that moment he became an idolater.

It is against this background, and years of idolatry prior to Abraham, and Egyptian paganism and idolatry, and Canaanite idolatry, that we must understand the first commandment, which says: "You shalt have no other gods before me." The Hebrew text says literally, "You shall not have any other *elohim* before my face."[74] "Elohim" is the generic word for God in the Hebrew Bible. When Genesis 1:1 says, "In the beginning God created the heavens and the earth," the word for "God" is "*Elohim*." There is perhaps a play on words here. We know that God is one. The most fundamental confession in the Hebrew Scriptures is Deuteronomy 6:4, "Hear O Israel, Yahweh our God, Yahweh is one." The irony here is that the intent of the word in Exodus 2:3 is clearly plural. The nations around the Israelites were idolaters and polytheists. Yahweh, the God who is, who said to Moses, "I am what I am" (Exod 3:14), is completely intolerant of any other gods. He calls them all idols, that is, gods we have made in our own image. That is the reverse of reality. God made us in his image (Gen 1:26), but as corrupt sinners, we turn reality on its head and pretend that we are God and that we get to determine reality.

This is the language we use in a Christian marriage ceremony. We renounce all others. We pledge ourselves completely to the God of Abraham, Isaac, and Jacob, the God and Father of our Lord Jesus Christ, the Triune God: Father, Son, and Holy Spirit. We seek no others. As Christians we give up trying to manipulate God through sorcery,

73. Cocceius, *Doctrine of the Covenant*, 2.18 (pp. 31–32).

74. לֹא יִהְיֶה־לְךָ אֱלֹהִים אֲחֵרִים עַל־פָּנָיַ (Exod 20:3).

superstition, praying to saints and even to the Virgin Mary. With the psalmist we say: "Whom have I in heaven but you? And there is nothing on earth that I desire besides you" (Ps 73:25 ESV). Idolatry is the opposite of complete trust in and submission to Christ.[75] The commandment itself rests on the categorical distinction, i.e., the distinction between the Creator and the creature.[76] Ursinus says the first commandment "describes and distinguishes God the lawgiver from all creatures, law givers, and false gods."[77] The God to whom we owe obedience first and foremost is the God who is (Exod 3:14), who spoke into nothing to make all that is (Gen 1:3). Because he is *Yahweh Elohim* who sovereignly creates and redeems, he has authority to institute laws and to demand our reverent, joyful, grateful submission and obedience.[78]

The essence of the command is that the only God worthy of our worship (both immediate and mediate)[79] is the self-existent God, who redeems helpless sinners *sola gratia, sola fide*. As a consequence of the grace we have received in Christ and as part of the process of sanctification (mortification and vivification), in union with Christ, the commandment requires certain virtues and prohibits certain vices.[80] It calls us to the formation of (1) knowledge of God, (2) faith, (3) hope, (4) love of God, (5) fear of God, (6) humility, and (7) patience.[81]

1. *Knowledge of God*. We cannot love what or whom we do not know. Calvin was right to say that "the right order of teaching" requires that we begin with God rather than with ourselves.[82] A true knowledge of God begins with God as he as revealed himself, as he as accommodated himself.[83] The vice, the corruption of the virtues that ought to belong to

75. See the discussion under *HC* 95.

76. Clark, *Recovering the Reformed Confession*, 124–51 (esp. 145).

77. "Describit et discernit Deum legis latorem ab ominibus creaturis, legum latoribus et fictitiis numinibus" (Ursinus, *Corpus doctrinae*, 518); Ursinus, *Commentary*, 507.

78. Ursinus, *Corpus doctrinae*, 518; Ursinus, *Commentary*, 507.

79. Ursinus, *Corpus doctrinae*, 519. On this distinction see the discussion under *HC* 93.

80. See the discussion of mortification and vivification under *HC* 88–90. Ursinus's plain use of virtue ethics contradicts the claim that the Reformation meant an abandonment of virtue in Christian ethics. See Ballor, "Reconciling Virtues and the Decalogue," 47–61; Sytsma, "John Calvin and Virtue Ethics," 519–56.

81. Ursinus, *Corpus doctrinae*, 519–20; Ursinus, *Commentary*, 508.

82. Calvin, *Institutes* 1.1.3.

83. Clark, *Recovering the Reformed Confession*, 140–44.

Christians,[84] here is the ignorance of God. When God redeems us, he gives us a desire to know the God who created and redeemed us. The first commandment compels us to seek to have a right understanding of God, insofar as it is possible, from Scripture and in light of the ecumenical creeds and Reformed confessions.

The traditional Reformed piety, which opposed superstition, the use of magic, and the like, is correct.[85] Magic (not sleight of hand or illusions) is the attempt to circumvent God's control of the world. It is paganism. There might have been a time when it seemed harmless to play at things that bordered the impious (e.g., horoscopes). Now, however, in a post-Christian culture, it seems imperative to avoid any hint of superstition. William Perkins (1558–1602) opposed superstition and magic mightily as being born of self-love and discontent and grounded in a covenant with the devil.[86] When we ask beings or powers other than God for our daily needs, we have done as he wrote. The same might be said of any attempt to gain secret knowledge or insight about the future through any sort of divination, the interpretation of signs, and the like.[87]

2. *Faith. Faith* is knowledge, assent, and trust.[88] Its antithesis is unbelief. Magic, superstition, and divination are manifestations of unbelief. Unbelief is the rejection of what God has said (Gen 3:1). All Christians occasionally struggle with doubt, but unbelief is skepticism. It locates authority within oneself rather than in God. Faith says, "Lord, I believe, help my unbelief"(Mark 9:24).

3. *Hope. Hope* has assurance because it trusts the God who is and in his word. Ursinus helpfully distinguishes between faith as embracing

---

84. Our English word *vice* is derived from the Latin *vitium*, "corruption," and still means that.

85. Ursinus, *Commentary*, 509; Ursinus, *Corpus doctrinae*, 520–21.

86. Perkins, *Works*, 9:311–12, 324–28. There was a great deal of concern in the period about witches and witchcraft, leading to witch hunts, trials, and even capital punishment for convicted witches, which Perkins supported, even though he was critical of sloppy judicial procedure regarding witches, and no witches were executed during Perkins's career. See Lee, "'Righteous before God,'" 24; Schaefer, *Spiritual Brotherhood*, 25; Patterson, *William Perkins*, 153–54. Not all the Reformed in England favored the execution of witches, however. See McGinnis, "'Subtiltie' Exposed," 665–86; Monter, *Witchcraft in France*.

87. Ursinus, *Commentary*, 510; Ursinus, *Corpus doctrinae*, 521.

88. See the discussion under *HC* 21.

the present benefits of God and hope as embracing the future benefits.[89] Despair is the antithesis of hope. In certain important respects, the late modern West is a culture of despair with the attending symptoms.[90] Despair is to grieve as those who have no hope (1 Thess 4:13). It is to reject the sufficiency of Christ and the reality of his resurrection, eternal life, and the grace of God.[91]

4. *Love. Love* for God acknowledges him to be what he says he is, what he has revealed himself to be: our Creator and redeemer. Love regards God as the highest good, the one we seek, know, and serve above all. We know instinctively and from experience what love is, but Scripture tells us: "In this is love, not that we have loved God but that he loved us and sent his Son to be the propitiation for our sins" (1 John 4:10 ESV). Love is giving oneself over to another. Christ gave himself over to death for us. We love him because he first loved us (1 John 4:19). Love leads to a desire to be with God and to be like him.[92]

The corruption of love is hatred. It seems almost unworthy to speak much of hatred for God. We know that instinctively since we are all, by nature, after the fall, haters of God (Rom 1:30), which manifests itself in idolatry and all manner of wickedness. It is born of contempt for God. It despises God. The unregenerate mind is at war with God (Rom 7:7). It prefers self above all even though it may make a pretense of love for God. The chief example of this is, of course, Judas.

5. *Fear of God.* This is an unfamiliar concept in the late modern world.[93] Ursinus, however, helps us by distinguishing between two kinds of fear: *servile* and *filial.* This distinction is essential to Christian piety. Believers do not have a *servile* fear of God. They ought to have a *filial* fear of God. The difference is between the covenants of works and grace. Everyone under the covenant of works, after the fall, can only have a servile fear of God. Those for whom Christ has fulfilled the covenant of works are, *sola*

89. "Oritur autem spes ex fide: quia certus de praesentia Dei erga se voluntate, certus est etiam de futura" (Ursinus, *Corpus doctrinae*, 523).

90. Chief among them is the rising suicide rate. Centers for Disease Control and Prevention, "Suicide Rising across the US."

91. Ursinus, *Commentary*, 512.

92. Ursinus, *Commentary*, 512.

93. Ursinus, *Corpus doctrinae*, 524–26.

gratia, in a covenant of grace, in which Christ has extinguished the wrath of God for us, in which the Spirit is graciously and gradually conforming us to the image of Christ, and in which we look forward with joy and not dread to Christ's return and the coming vindication.[94] Ursinus explains the difference:

> Servile fear, such as the slave has for his master, which consists in fleeing punishment without faith and without a desire and purpose of changing the life, being accompanied with despair, flight and separation from God—such a servile fear differs greatly from that which is filial. 1. Filial fear arises from confidence and love to God; that which is servile arises from a knowledge and conviction of sin, and from a sense of the judgment and displeasure of God. 2. Filial fear does not turn away from God, but hates sin above every thing else, and fears to offend God: servile fear is a flight and hatred, not of sin, but of punishment and of the divine judgment, and so of God himself. 3. Filial fear is connected with the certainty of salvation and of eternal life: servile fear is a fear and expectation of eternal condemnation and rejection of God, and is great in proportion to the doubt and despair which it entertains of the grace and mercy of God. This is the fear of devils and wicked men, and is the commencement of eternal death, which the ungodly experience already in this life. "I heard thy voice in the garden and I was afraid." "The devils believe and tremble." (Gen. 3:10. James 2:19).[95]

Servile fear arises from fear of judgment. Filial fear arises from God's grace and love. In that sense, filial fear is a reverent respect. Servile fear is a dread nearer to hatred than love. Pious respect for God draws us closer to him, and servile fear drives us away. Filial fear is a work of God's grace in our hearts. It reinforces and rests on God's gracious promises to us in Christ.[96] As God's adopted sons, in Christ, we "persevere diligently in the use" of the means of grace, expecting the Spirit to encourage us.[97]

---

94. See the discussion of this topic under *HC* 52.

95. Ursinus, *Commentary*, 514.

96. On this distinction See Canons of Dort 1.15–16.

97. Canons of Dort 1.16, in United Reformed Churches in North America, *Liturgical Forms and Prayers*, 263.

Under this head, contumacy, the stubborn refusal to submit to divinely instituted authority, is the vice to be avoided. Those who do not fear God shake their fist at him. Experienced pastors and elders would tell us that it is one of the vices with which they are most often confronted in the church as people defy all attempts, however gentle and gracious, at correction and discipline.

6. *Humility*. "Humility or ταπεινοφροσύνη is the recognition that the good works that are in us and done through us are not from any worth or faculty of ours."[98] Humility is the recognition that all goods, including good works, come from God. It is subjection to God and counting others more significant than oneself (Phil 2:3). This is not false modesty but rather a recognition of things as they are. It is not an *affect* (an experience) as much as a *habitus* or disposition.

Its opposite, of course, is pride (*superbia*) or arrogance.[99] It regards one's gifts as one's own invention. It does not fear or honor God. It is not subject to God. It does not yield to others. It is, as Ursinus writes, "to admire oneself and gifts" as if they were self-generated. Thus, Scripture calls pride an "abomination" to God (1 Pet 5:5; Prov 16:5).

7. *Patience. Patience* "arises from the knowledge of divine wisdom, providence, righteousness, and goodness."[100] Out of this source, patience submits to God's law in the knowledge of his virtues. It trusts his omniscience and good will toward his people, in Christ. Impatience, then, in this sense, is sin because it is unbelief in the divine virtues. It trusts one's own experience and one's interpretation of that experience over God's self-disclosure in Christ and in his word.

98. "HUMILITAS seu ταπεινοφροσύνη, est agnoscere, quod bona omnia, quae in nobis sunt and per nos fiiunt non ex dignitate aut facultate aliqua nostra, sed ex gratuita Dei bonitate existant" (Ursinus, *Corpus doctrinae*, 526).

99. Ursinus, *Corpus doctrinae*, 526.

100. "Patientia est ex agnitione divinae sapientiae, providentiae, iustitiae, et bonitatis" (Ursinus, *Corpus doctrinae*, 527).

QUESTION 95

What is idolatry?

Idolatry is to conceive or have something else on which to place our trust in place of, or besides the one true God who has revealed Himself in his Word.[101]

Our English word *idolatry* is transliterated from a Greek noun (εἰδωλολατρία) for "image worship" (Gal 5:20; 1 Pet 4:3). Calvin famously wrote of fallen humanity, "Man's nature, so to speak, is a perpetual factory of idols."[102] After the fall, by nature, idolatry is our default mode. It is the worship of the creature rather than the Creator (Rom 1:25). Anytime we put anything in the place of God, that is idolatry. The history of redemption and the history of the secular world is replete with examples of idolatry. Perhaps the most notorious case is that recorded in Exodus 32 wherein, while Moses was on the mountain, the Israelites made a golden calf (Exod 32:8), worshiped it, and attributed to it their salvation. The Israelites, of course, were surrounded by idol-worshiping nations, and too often they too became idolaters (Ps 78:58) like their neighbors.

It is easy to tell the difference between idols and God. All idols are creatures of our making, whether we make them by hand, heart, or imagination. All idols are subject to destruction and lead to destruction (Hos 8:4). Of course, we confess with the apostle Paul that "an idol has no real existence" (1 Cor 8:4). Whether we fabricate them with our hands, in our minds, or in our hearts, idols change. They come and go. When they disappoint us, we dispose of them and make another—hoping for a better outcome.

God, however, is unmade. He was in the beginning (Gen 1:1; John 1:1). We cannot change or kill him. He simply is (Exod 3:14).[103] This is why Christians do not speak about "my Christ," as if there are as

101. "Was ist Abgötterei? An Statt des einigen wahren Gottes, der sich in seinem Wort hat offenbaret, oder neben demselben, etwas anderes dichten oder haben, darauf der Mensch sein Vertrauen setzt" (Schaff, *Creeds of Christendom*, 3:342). "Quid est idololatria? Est loco unius Dei, aut praeter unum illum et verum Deum, qui se in suo verbo patefecit, aliud quippiam fingere aut habere, in quo spem reponas" (Niemeyer, *Collectio Confessionum*, 453).

102. Calvin, *Institutes* 1.11.8.

103. See the discussion under *HC* 26.

many Christs as there are believers, nor do they say, "My God would not do that." God is not the creation of the human imagination, and he is not a human projection. The language of the third step of Alcoholics Anonymous, "Made a decision to turn our will and our lives over to the care of God *as we understood Him,*" is the quintessence of idolatry.[104] It was turning their lives over to "God as we understood him" that caused the Israelites to make a golden calf (Exod 32:4). It was turning their lives over to "God as we understood him" that caused the Israelites to make golden calves at Bethel and Dan (1 Kgs 12:28–30). Scripture is stoutly and consistently opposed to thinking of, worshiping, or even speaking of God "as we understand him."

The first commandment also forbids Roman Catholic corruptions of Christian piety. The invoking of saints, for example, Luther's plea when he was in the lightning storm, "St. Anne help me! I will become a monk,"[105] or the invocation of the Blessed Virgin, is forbidden by the first commandment.[106] There is "one mediator between God and men, the man Christ Jesus" (1 Tim 2:5 ESV). There is no *mediatrix*. There are no other mediators. To invoke another mediator or an ostensible *mediatrix* is idolatry.[107]

Our *BC* (26) makes two excellent points in this regard:

> And who will be heard more readily than God's own dearly beloved Son? So then, sheer unbelief has led to the practice of dishonoring the saints, instead of honoring them. That was something the saints never did nor asked for, but which in keeping with their duty, as appears from their writings, they consistently refused. We should not plead here that we are unworthy—for it is not a question of offering our prayers on the basis of our own dignity but only on

104. Bill W., *Twelve Steps and Twelve Traditions*, 34; emphasis original; Bill W., *Alcoholics Anonymous*, 48.

105. Roper, *Martin Luther*, 33–34.

106. The Roman Catholic Ave Maria (Hail Mary): "Hail Mary, the Lord is with thee, Blessed are thou among women and blessed is the fruit of thy womb; Holy Mary, Mother of God, pray for us sinners, now and at the hour of our death" (*CCC* §2676–77). See the discussion of the invocation of saints under *HC* 30. The Virgin Mary is truly blessed, and the fruit of her womb is blessed, but just because she is glorified does not mean that she is omniscient, nor does it make her omnipresent.

107. Ursinus also discussed the invocation of saints under the third commandment (*Commentary*, 542–48).

the basis of the excellence and dignity of Jesus Christ, whose righteousness is ours by faith.[108]

Part of the popular appeal of the cult of the saints has been the notion that we need a mediator (or mediatrix) beside the Son because we think, for example, that the Son will be more willing to hear his mother than us, or that God will be more willing to hear saints than us. Paul also had to persuade his readers that Jesus is the only Mediator. "For there is one God, and there is one mediator between God and men, the man Christ Jesus, who gave himself as a ransom for all, which is the testimony given at the proper time" (1 Tim 2:5–6 ESV). It was Jesus, not Moses, who died for us and who was raised for us. He is the "mediator of a new covenant" (Heb 9:15; 12:24). Further, neither the blessed Virgin nor any of the martyrs ever thought, after their death, that they should become an object of prayer or an intercessor. The confession is quite right to remind us that such things dishonor them and their memory. In Christ we have the best possible Mediator.

Popular superstition is idolatry. Athletic superstitions are forms of idolatry. God cannot be manipulated any by stupid superstition we practice. The first commandment means that every palm reader is a liar, and anyone who visits a palm reader is a fool and an idolater. Seeking to know what God has not revealed (e.g., "God's secret will") is "soothsaying."[109] How often do we do that under the pretense of piety?

Either one knows the God who is, who was in Christ reconciling the world to himself (2 Cor 5:19), or one does not. If one does not like the God who is, then one is an idolater and needs to repent because the God who is comes in judgment.

The good news is that Jesus came to save idolaters—and we are all idolaters by nature and inclination. As sinners we tend to love our things, our friends, our family, our job, our social image and status more than God. Each of those loves is a violation of the first commandment: "You shall have no other gods." By his unconditional favor, earned for us by Christ, God receives us idolaters, changes our hearts and minds, and replaces idolatry with true faith in Christ the Son, God the Father, by the Spirit and leads us to worship the true God truly.

108. United Reformed Churches in North America, *Liturgical Forms and Prayers*, 181.

109. See the discussion under *HC* 94.

QUESTIONS 96

What does God require in the second Commandment?

QUESTION 97

May we not make any image at all?

QUESTION 98

But may not pictures be tolerated in churches as books for the people?

Lord's Day 35

QUESTIONS 96–98

What does God require in the second Commandment?
That we in no way make any image of God, nor worship him in any other way than he has commanded us in His Word.[1]

May we not make any image at all?
God may not and cannot be imaged in any way; as for creatures, though they may indeed be imaged, yet God forbids the making or keeping any likeness of them, either to worship them, or to serve God by them.[2]

But may not pictures be tolerated in churches as books for the people?
No, for we should not be wiser than God, who will not have His people taught by dumb idols, but by the lively preaching of his word.[3]

Because the three questions of Lord's Day 35 are so closely connected, the commentary will address them as a unit.

Few topics are more incendiary in the church than that of the public worship of God, yet no topic is more important to the Christian theology, piety, and practice than public worship. This is a recipe for a crisis, which is where we find ourselves in the modern period. Each week Christians

1. "Was will Gott im andern Gebot? Dass wir Gott in keinem Wege verbilden, noch auf irgend eine andere Weise, denn Er in seinem Wort befohlen hat, verehren sollen" (Schaff, *Creeds of Christendom*, 3:343). "Quid postulat secundum Praeceptum? Ne Deum ulla imagine aut figura exprimamus, neve ulla alia ratione eum colamus quam qua se in suo verbo coli praecepit" (Niemeyer, *Collectio Confessionum*, 453).

2. "Soll man denn gar kein Bildniss machen? Gott kann und soll keineswegs abgebildet werden; die Creaturen aber, ob sie schon mögen abgebildet werden, so verbietet doch Gott derselben Bildniss zu machen und zu haben, dass man sie verehre, oder ihm damit diene" (Schaff, *Creeds of Christendom*, 3:343). "An nullae ergo prorsus fingendae sunt imagines aut simulacra? Deus nec ulla ratione effingi debet, nec potest: creaturas autem, etsi exprimere quidem licet: vetat tamen Deus, earum imagines fingi, aut haberi, quo vel ipsas, vel Deum per ipsas colamus, aut honoremus" (Niemeyer, *Collectio Confessionum*, 453).

3. "Mögen aber nicht die Bilder als der Laien Bücher in den Kirchen geduldet werden? Nein: denn wir sollen nicht weiser sein denn Gott, welcher seine Christenheit nicht durch stumme Götzen, sondern durch die lebendige Predigt seines Worts will unterwiesen haben" (Schaff, *Creeds of Christendom*, 3:343). "An autem in templis imagines tolerari non possunt, quae pro libris sint imperitae multitudini? Minime: neque enim decet nos sapientiores esse Deo, qui suam Ecclesiam non mutis simulacris, sed viva praedicatione verbi sui vult erudiri" (Nimeyer, *Collectio Confessionum*, 454).

gather for public worship twice each Lord's Day (or they should). Thus, we gather 104 times each year. We become intimately familiar with forms of worship, songs, tunes, creedal statements, and practices that have become woven into the fabric of our lives and our memories. When we hear a familiar tune, memories may come flooding back. The experience becomes very personal.

Nevertheless, as important as our experience is and as much a part of the fabric of our lives as our favorite things about public worship may be, God's law is still the norm for public worship. We must be prepared to measure even beloved practices and songs by God's law. The first commandment speaks to whom we worship. The second commandment speaks to how we worship the true God:

> You shall not make for yourself a carved image, or any likeness of anything that is in heaven above, or that is in the earth beneath, or that is in the water under the earth. You shall not bow down to them or serve them, for I the LORD your God am a jealous God, visiting the iniquity of the fathers on the children to the third and the fourth generation of those who hate me, but showing steadfast love to thousands of those who love me and keep my commandments. (Exod 20:4–6 ESV)

SCRIPTURE AND THEOLOGY

In *HC* 96 the Reformed churches confess a particular interpretation of the second commandment, which they share with the church of the first seven centuries and which all the Reformed churches in the sixteenth and seventeenth centuries accepted universally.

John 1:18 says, "No one has ever seen God; the only God, who is at the Father's side, he has made him known" (ESV). The apostle John says in 1 John 4:12, "No one has ever seen God." No human being has ever seen God immediately. This is the clear teaching of Jesus himself:

> Jesus said to him, "I am the way, and the truth, and the life. No one comes to the Father except through me. If you had known me, you would have known my Father also. From now on you do know him and have seen him."

> Philip said to him, "Lord, show us the Father, and it is enough for us." Jesus said to him, "Have I been with you so long, and you still do not know me, Philip? Whoever has seen me has seen the Father. How can you say, 'Show us the Father'?" (John 14:6–9 ESV)

The apostle Paul teaches the same thing:

> I charge you in the presence of God, who gives life to all things, and of Christ Jesus, who in his testimony before Pontius Pilate made the good confession, to keep the commandment unstained and free from reproach until the appearing of our Lord Jesus Christ, which he will display at the proper time—he who is the blessed and only Sovereign, the King of kings and Lord of lords, who alone has immortality, who dwells in unapproachable light, whom no one has ever seen or can see. To him be honor and eternal dominion. Amen. (1 Tim 6:13–16 ESV)

Apart from the incarnation of God the Son, no mere mortal has ever seen God. Because God is necessarily invisible, because none of us has ever seen him as he is in himself, any picture we might make of him is necessarily and merely the product of our imagination. It is a fabrication made up of created things. Making God in our own image is the definition of idolatry.[4]

Again, Scripture is very clear about this: "Being then God's offspring, we ought not to think that the divine being is like gold or silver or stone, an image formed by the art and imagination of man" (Acts 17:29 ESV). Elijah mocked the prophets of Baal for their stupidity, for praying to inanimate objects: "And they took the bull that was given them, and they prepared it and called upon the name of Baal from morning until noon, saying, 'O Baal, answer us!' But there was no voice, and no one answered. And they limped around the altar that they had made. And at noon Elijah mocked them, saying, 'Cry aloud, for he is a god. Either he is musing, or he is relieving himself, or he is on a journey, or perhaps he is asleep and must be awakened'" (1 Kgs 18:26–27 ESV). Medieval churches frequently depicted God the Father, God the Son, and God the Holy Spirit, even

4. See the discussion under *HC* 95.

though the ancient Christian church did not. The church does sometimes fall into corruption.

Rome defends the depiction of the persons of the Trinity on the basis of the distinction between adoration (δουλεία) and worship (λατρεία).[5] The Reformed churches reject that distinction because it has no biblical foundation and no practical difference. Wilhelmus à Brakel (1635–1711) articulates the Reformed consensus:

> As far as the popish distinction is concerned, we maintain that this distinction of words is but a vain fabrication, which is neither to be found among the Greek writers nor in God's Word. Yes, if one were to consider these words etymologically, *douleia* would be a much higher level of service than *latreia,* for *douleia* is a service which serfs render to their masters, and *latreia* is a service which a hired servant renders for wages. Scripture knows of no such distinction. Not only must God be served with *latreia,* but also with *douleia*. Consider only the following passages: "Serving (δουλεύων, *douleuon*) the Lord with all humility of mind" (Acts 20:19); "... serving (δουλεύοντες, *douleuontes*) the Lord" (Rom. 12:11). The word *latreia* signifies both the rendering of service to creatures as well as to God: "God ... gave them up to worship (λατρεύειν, *latreuein*) the host of heaven" (Acts 7:42); "... and worshiped and served (ἐλάτρευσαν, *elatreusan*) the creature more than the Creator" (Rom. 1:25). Yes, Scripture considers it idolatry to serve with *douleia* those who are not very God: "Ye did service (ἐδουλεύσατε, *edouleusate*) unto them which by nature are no gods" (Gal. 4:8).[6]

Ursinus writes against this distinction at length. He quotes Augustine's saying, regarding the "cult of the dead," that the saints "are to be honored as examples to imitate, not worshiped as objects of a religious cult." [7] The "distinction," Ursinus writes, "which they make between the worship of adoration and veneration is of no force, inasmuch as these are not different forms of worship, but one and the same; neither do they belong to the

5. See the discussion of the distinction between δουλεία and λατρεία under *HC* 80.

6. À Brakel, *Christian's Reasonable Service*, 3.92.

7. Ursinus, *Commentary*, 542–43; Augustine, *True Religion*, 55, 108. NB: The word *cult* is derived from the Latin noun *cultus* and, as used in this context, refers to religious worship.

saints, or to any creature, but to God alone, because he knows and hears in all places and at all times the thoughts, the groans and desires of those who call upon him, and relieves their necessities."[8]

IMAGES OF CHRIST

The question becomes a little bit more difficult when we think about depictions of Jesus, God the Son incarnate. All the commandments are challenging for us sinners, but this one seems to be particularly challenging because we live in a visual age. The assumption seems to be that if we cannot see a thing, then it must not be real.

Further, many Christians have grown up with images of Christ. Indeed, it is not unusual to see otherwise faithful Reformed congregations with large, stained-glass representations of Christ. Films about Christ, once controversial, are now regarded as commonplace. The 1959 film *Ben-Hur* portrayed only Christ's hands. It was not until 1961 that a film attempted to portray Christ's face. It was controversial then, but today it is unremarkable.

The argument in favor of images of Christ is this: God the Son took on humanity; therefore we may portray his humanity in paintings, statues, on stage, and in film. Further, the argument goes, if we say that we may not portray Christ, then we are in danger of denying his true humanity. The problem with this argument is that the reverse is true.[9] It is when we attempt to depict Jesus's humanity that we deny it. In 1692, Thomas Watson asked, "Quest. 1. If it be not lawful to make the image of God the Father, yet may we not make an image of Christ, who took upon him the nature of man?" He answered the question this way: "Resp. No. Epiphanius seeing an image of Christ hanging in a church, broke it in pieces; 'tis Christ's Godhead, united to his manhood, that makes him to be Christ; therefore to picture his manhood, when we cannot picture his Godhead, is a sin, because we make him to be but half Christ; we separate what God hath joined, we leave out that which is the chief thing,

8. Ursinus, *Commentary*, 543.

9. For more on these issues see VanDrunen, "Pictures of Jesus," 214–27; VanDrunen, "Iconoclasm, Incarnation and Eschatology," 130–147; Perkins, "Images of Christ," 201–15; Hyde, *In Living Color*.

which makes him to be Christ."[10] Heinrich Bullinger, in the *Second Helvetic Confession* (chap. 4), writes that God the Son did not become incarnate to make work for carvers and artisans.[11] Calvin agrees. In his 1559 *Institutes* he writes:

> God, indeed, from time to time showed the presence of his divine majesty by definite signs, so that he might be said to be looked upon face to face. But all the signs that he ever gave forth aptly conformed to his plan of teaching and at the same time clearly told men of his incomprehensible essence. For clouds and smoke and flame [Deut 4:11], although they were symbols of heavenly glory, restrained the minds of all, like a bridle placed on them, from attempting to penetrate too deeply. Therefore Moses, to whom, nevertheless, God revealed himself more intimately than to the others [Exod 33:11], did not succeed by prayers in beholding that face; but he received the answer that man is not able to bear such great brightness [Exod 33:20]. The Holy Spirit appeared under the likeness of a dove [Matt 3:16]. Since, however, he vanished at once, who does not see that by one moment's symbol the faithful were admonished to believe the Spirit to be invisible in order that, content with his power and grace, they might seek no outward representation for themselves? For the fact that God from time to time appeared in the form of a man was the prelude to his future revelation in Christ. Therefore the Jews were absolutely forbidden so to abuse this pretext as to set up for themselves a symbol of deity in human form.[12]

As a matter of history, there are no images of Christ from the first century or from anyone who ever saw Jesus.[13] Further, Jesus authorized no representations of his humanity. The apostles authorized no icons of

---

10. Watson, *Body of Practical Divinity* (1692), 280 (spelling modernized); Epiphanius of Salamis, *Panarion* 1.105. On the validity of Epiphanius's rejection of images of Christ, see Carpenter, "Answering Eastern Orthodox Apologists," 431–32.

11. "Tametsi enim Christus humanam assumpserit naturam, non ideo tamen assumpsit, ut typum praeferret statuarijs atque pictoribus" (Müller, *Die Bekenntnisschriften*, 174.9–10); Dennison, *Reformed Confessions*, 2:815–16.

12. Calvin, *Institutes* 1.11.3.

13. Were there icons of Christ from the first or even the second century, the debate would obviously be rather different.

Jesus. Hippolytus of Rome (ca. AD 170–236) warned that the followers of the second-century gnostic leader Carpocrates made "counterfeit images of Christ, alleging that these were in existence at the time (during which our Lord was on earth, and that they were fashioned) by Pilate."[14] In the early third century Origen wrote that the Christians permitted no icons of Christ.[15] Ironically, it was the gnostics who tended to venerate images of Christ, not the orthodox fathers.[16] Lactantius (ca. 250–ca. 325) denounces the use of images as contrary to religion: "Wherefore it is undoubted that there is no religion wherever there is an image. For if religion consists of divine things, and there is nothing divine except in heavenly things; it follows that images are without religion, because there can be nothing heavenly in that which is made from the earth."[17] By definition, he argues, an icon is an imitation and thus necessarily false.

Images of Christ were flatly forbidden at the regional Synod of Elvira (ca. AD 309).[18] The church refused to sanction images through the fifth century.[19] Icons of Christ were not widely permitted until the violent iconoclasm controversy was resolved in favor of icons in the late eighth century at the Second Council of Nicaea (AD 787). The secular and ecclesiastical fighting continued until the middle of the ninth century, when those who

14. Hippolytus of Rome, *Refutation of All Heresies* 7.20 (*ANF* 5:114).

15. "But whether Orpheus, Parmenides, Empedocles, or even Homer himself, and Hesiod, are the persons whom he means by 'inspired poets,' let any one show how those who follow their guidance walk in a better way, or lead a more excellent life, than those who, being taught in the school of Jesus Christ, have rejected all images and statues, and even all Jewish superstition, that they may look upward through the Word of God to the one God, who is the Father of the Word" (Origen, *Against Celsus* [*ANF* 6:627]).

16. "They also possess images, some of them painted, and others formed from different kinds of material; while they maintain that a likeness of Christ was made by Pilate at that time when Jesus lived among them. They crown these images, and set them up along with the images of the philosophers of the world; that is to say, with the images of Pythagoras, and Plato, and Aristotle, and the rest. They have also other modes of honouring these images, after the same manner of the Gentiles" (Irenaeus, *Against Heresies* 1.25.6 [*ANF* 1:351]). "Evidently many gnostics also fostered a cult of images, even owning statues of gods such as those found among the archeological remains of mystery cults" (Rudolph, *Gnosis*, 225–26).

17. Lactantius, *Divine Institutes* 2.19 (*ANF* 7:68).

18. Canon 36: "Ne picturae in ecclesia fiant" (Hefele, *History of the Councils*, 1:151).

19. Eastern Orthodox claims to the contrary, the evidence from the house-church in Dura Europos, Syria (ca. AD 235), regarding ecclesiastical approval or use of icons of Christ is ambiguous at best (Carpenter, "Answering Eastern Orthodox Apologists," 424–25).

held the most ancient, ecumenical Christian view (the iconoclasts) were finally defeated politically.[20]

The iconoclast arguments were not defeated *theologically*. From February to August 754, a council of 338 bishops met at Constantinople.[21] They produced a *Definition*, which anticipates the arguments the Reformed would make eight centuries later. They rightly observe that the iconodules were contradicting the consensus of the ancient church.[22] They rightly note that depictions of God the Son incarnate *divide* the two natures in the same way Nestorius was accused of doing.[23] The argument that says, "we represent only the flesh of Christ which we have seen and handled" is a "Nestorian error. For it should be considered that that flesh was also the flesh of God the Word, without any separation, perfectly assumed by the divine nature and made wholly divine."[24] The Reformed repeated nearly verbatim their second major argument: God has already instituted images of Christ, but the iconodules ignore them in favor of their own inventions: "The only admissible figure of the humanity of Christ, however, is bread and wine in the holy Supper. This and no other form, this and no other type, has he chosen to represent his incarnation."[25] No sixteenth-century Reformed writer was as pointed against images of the blessed Virgin as the iconoclasts in AD 754: "But we will also consider what may be said against these in particular. Christianity has rejected the whole of heathenism, and so not merely heathen sacrifices, but also the heathen worship of images. The Saints live on eternally with God, although they have died. If anyone thinks to call them back again to life by a dead art, discovered by the heathen, he makes himself guilty of blasphemy."[26]

As the Reformed did in the sixteenth century, the bishops appeal to the plain sense of the second commandment and pronounced anathemas on whomever "in future dares to make such a thing, or to venerate it, or set it up in a church, or in a private house, or possesses it in secret,

20. Kleinbauer, "Icon."

21. Hefele, *History of the Councils*, 5:307–15. NB: Hefele is quite hostile to the iconoclasts.

22. Schaff and Wace, *Epitome of the Definition* (*NPNF* 2/14:543); Perkins, "Image of Christ," 14.

23. Schaff and Wace, *Epitome of the Definition* (*NPNF* 2/14:543).

24. Schaff and Wace, *Epitome of the Definition* (*NPNF* 2/14:544).

25. Schaff and Wace, *Epitome of the Definition* (*NPNF* 2/14:544).

26. Schaff and Wace, *Epitome of the Definition* (*NPNF* 2/14:544).

shall, if bishop, presbyter, or deacon, be deposed; if monk or layman, be anathematised, and become liable to be tried by the secular laws as an adversary of God and an enemy of the doctrines handed down by the Fathers."[27] They pronounce anathema on anyone "who ventures to represent the divine image (χαρακτήρ) of the Word after the Incarnation."[28]

Thus, on this point, the Reformed represented the consensus of the church before the iconodule victory. The position of the *HC* on images is ancient and not a Reformed invention. We agree that images of God the Father, God the Son, and of God the Holy Spirit (even doves) are forbidden. The teaching of the catechism represents the near-universal Reformed consensus.[29] The Reformed churches and confessions are united on this. The Reformed theologians of the Reformation and orthodox periods were united against images. The Hungarian Reformed Churches rejected the use of images, calling them "marks and occasions of idolatry."[30] Even Luther, who took a different position on the application of (what we number as) the second commandment from the Reformed, condemned their use in the early 1520s and expected that people would give them up as they matured in the faith. Heiko Oberman explains:

> With regard to Luther's judgment on images, we are not in the dark. In his report to his confidant Nikolaus Hausmann on the situation he found in Wittenberg, he was unambiguous: "*Damno imagines*." The elimination of images, however, should be brought about by means of a consensus grounded in the faith. As far as the intended action goes, Luther's posture in 1522 appears no different from the position Erasmus had counseled six years earlier—images should be tolerated until they can be removed *sine tumultu*. On March 17, having just arrived from the Wartburg, he summarized his strategy

27. Schaff and Wace, *Epitome of the Definition* (*NPNF* 2/14:544).

28. Schaff and Wace, *Epitome of the Definition* (*NPNF* 2/14:544).

29. If we include the Thirty Nine Articles of the Church of England under this heading, we find perhaps some variation by omission. Article 22, under purgatory, condemns the "Romish Doctrine concerning Purgatory, Pardons, Worshipping, and Adoration, as well of Images as of Reliques" (Church of England, *Book of Common Prayer*, 702).

30. The Debrecen Synod (1567), art. 16, in Dennison, *Reformed Confessions*, 3:111.

on images this way: "They would fall of themselves if people were taught and knew that before God symbols are nothing."[31]

As it turned out, Luther's expectation was naive. Calvin notes that, were we to look for opportunities to make images, we need not wait for the incarnation. If they were nevertheless forbidden then, so they remain forbidden now, in light of the incarnation:

> God, indeed, from time to time showed the presence of his divine majesty by definite signs, so that he might be said to be looked upon face to face. But all the signs that he ever gave forth aptly conformed to his plan of teaching and at the same time clearly told men of his incomprehensible essence. For clouds and smoke and flame [Deut 4:11], although they were symbols of heavenly glory, restrained the minds of all, like a bridle placed on them, from attempting to penetrate too deeply. Therefore Moses, to whom, nevertheless, God revealed himself more intimately than to the others [Exod 33:11], did not succeed by prayers in beholding that face; but he received the answer that man is not able to bear such great brightness [Exod 33:20]. The Holy Spirit appeared under the likeness of a dove [Matt 3:16]. Since, however, he vanished at once, who does not see that by one moment's symbol the faithful were admonished to believe the Spirit to be invisible in order that, content with his power and grace, they might seek no outward representation for themselves? For the fact that God from time to time appeared in the form of a man was the prelude to his future revelation in Christ. Therefore the Jews were absolutely forbidden so to abuse this pretext as to set up for themselves a symbol of deity in human form.[32]

"Pretext" is a significant word in this context. In their nature, images of the Triune persons tend to blur the distinction between the Creator and the creature, and this is done on the pretext of the incarnation.

Calvin's Second Genevan Catechism (1545) rejects not only the making of any kind of picture or sculpture by which to represent the deity but

31. Oberman, *Two Reformations*, 89.

32. Calvin, *Institutes* 1.11.3.

also making them for instructional purposes or for their use in worship.[33] The language of WSC 51 is virtually identical to that of the *HC*.[34] WLC 109 pointedly condemns "the making of any representation of God, of all or any of the three persons, either inwardly in our mind, or outwardly in any kind of image or likeness of any creature whatsoever."

One of the great concerns of the catechism is to preserve the distinction between the Creator and the creature. Pedagogically, this distinction is reinforced by the absence of images. God is so transcendent, so qualitatively different from us, so holy, that he cannot be imaged or represented. The very attempt to represent him in an icon is, in that very act, whether intended or not, an attempt to blur the line between God the Creator and the creature. Thus, the catechism affirms that *creatures* may be imaged, in part, because they can be represented, even as the Creator cannot and may not be imaged.

So far we have been addressing the *religious* or *sacred* use of images. *HC* 97, however, implicitly distinguishes between the *sacred* use of images and the *secular*. The Reformed do not oppose images of creatures for secular uses. The Reformed have always appreciated beauty and fine art. In their realism, the Dutch Renaissance painters, whatever their personal confessional orthodoxy, manifested the Reformed appreciation of creation and of the Creator who designed, created, and sustains all things. We reject the use of images for *sacred* purposes, but not for *secular* or common purposes. This distinction is on analogy with Paul's in 1 Corinthians 8 and 10. In chapter 8 he establishes that, so long as our eating of meat offered to idols does not cause a weaker brother to stumble, we are free. This is because the pagan gods do not actually exist, and there is a secular use even of food that the butcher has offered to his pagan gods. In 1 Corinthians 10:19–22, however, Paul places another limit on our freedom. We are not free to participate in a pagan *religious* meal. By analogy, images of creation are a matter of Christian liberty up to the point that they are put to a religious use.

33. Dennison, *Reformed Confessions*, 1:487.

34. Westminster Assembly, *Humble Advice of the Assembly*, 32–33.

THE RULE OF WORSHIP[35]

Because worship is such an intensely personal matter, because the habits of worship become so ingrained into our lives and identities, it is easy for us to think that if we like something, God must approve of it, especially when it is done as part of worship. This is why there is a second aspect to the teaching of the catechism under Lord's Day 35: the rule of worship (*regula cultus*), as Calvin puts it.[36] We express this rule in these words: "nor worship him in any other way than he has commanded" (*HC* 96). In *BC* 7 we confess, "For the whole manner of divine worship which God demands of us has been written" in Scripture.[37] Ursinus explains it thus:

> It must be commanded by God. No creature has the right to institute the worship of God. ... By this condition is excluded all ἐθελοθρησκεία (will-worship),[38] and the fiction of good intention, when men do evil that good might come, or when they invent works, which they impose upon the worship of God, which, indeed, are not evil *per se*, but which are not commanded by God. It is not sufficient for the worship of God that a work is not evil or not forbidden but it must commanded by God, according to the sayings: "Obedience is better than sacrifice" and "Walk in my commandments." "In vain do they worship me with the commandments of men." (1 Sam. 15:22. Ez. 20:19. Matt. 15:9.).[39]

---

35. Ursinus uses the expression "norma cultus divini" (*Corpus doctrinae*, 624).

36. "Porro, universalis est regula, quae purum Dei cultum a vitioso discernit: ne comminiscamur ipsi quod nobis visum fuerit, sed quid praescribat is, qui solus iubendi potestatem habet, spectemus." *Supplex exhortatio ad invictissimum caesarem carolum quintum*, in Calvin, *Opera quae supersunt omnia*, 6:453–534. See the English translation in Calvin, *Necessity of Reforming*, 6–7. See Clark, *Recovering the Reformed Confession*, 228–30; Clark, "Calvin's Principle of Worship," 247–69. Perhaps the definitive defense of the regulative principle is Gillespie, *Dispute against the English Popish Ceremonies*; Ames, *Fresh Suit against Human Ceremonies*.

37. "Nam quum illic omnis divine cultus ratio, quem Deus a nobis exigit, fuissime descripta sit, nulli hominum, ne Apostolis quidem, fas est aliter docere, quam iampridem in sacris Literis edocti sumus" (Müller, *Die Bekenntnisschriften*, 234). The Latin text as authorized by the Synod of Dort makes clear that the context here is not general service but divine worship (Clark, *Recovering the Reformed Confession*, 231–44).

38. This is an allusion to Col 2:23.

39. "Ut sit mandatum à Deo. Nulla enim creatura habet ius instiuendi cultum Dei...Excluditur hac conditione omnis ἐθελοθρησκεία, et commentum de bona intentione, cum homines mala faciunt, ut eveniant bona, vel ipsi confingunt opera, quae Deo pro cultu obtrudunt, non quidem per se mala sed, tamen non praecepta à Deo. Nam ad cultum Dei non sufficit, aliquod opus non esse malum, vel non prohibitum, sed oportet esse à Deo praeceptum, secundum dicta: '*Obedientia melior est sacrifciis.*

Ursinus spent several years immersed in the Lutheran academic and church cultures. He knew the Lutheran principle and pointedly contrasts the Reformed principle with it. As he explains Lord's Day 35, the Reformed understanding of Scripture rejects good intentions. A practice, however beneficial it is supposed to be, may not be imposed on public worship unless it is commanded by God.

Thus, the Reformed distinguish between the *elements* of worship and the *circumstances* of worship. Ursinus distinguishes between those ceremonies God himself instituted, for example, the preaching of the word and sacraments, and those ceremonies the church instituted. The former "can only be changed by God himself."[40] The latter are "the various circumstances" connected to worship.[41] Ursinus articulates the classical Reformed understanding of circumstances as distinct from elements. They "include the determinations of circumstances necessary or useful for the maintenance of the moral precepts of the first table; of which kind are the time, the place, the form and order of sermons, prayers, reading in the church, fasts, the manner of proceeding in the election of ministers, in collecting and distributing alms, and things of a similar nature, concerning which God has given no particular command."[42] An element of worship is an administration of the word (e.g., read, preached, or made visible in the sacraments) or a response to the word (in prayer or song). These are essential to worship and solely determined by the word of God because it is alone sufficient and normative for worship (*sola Scriptura*). A circumstance is determined by *nature*.[43] The congregation must meet at an agreed time and place. They must use a shared language. These are circumstances, and

---

Inpraeceptis meis ambulatbitis. Frustra me colunt mandatis hominum'" (Ursinus, *Corpus doctrinae*, 399–490). See Ursinus, *Commentary*, 477; Calvin, *Institutes* 4.10.24.

40. Ursinus, *Commentary*, 574; e.g., Calvin, *Institutes* 4.10.23.

41. Ursinus, *Commentary*, 574.

42. Ursinus, *Commentary*, 521.

43. "Whatever is of circumstance in the manner of its performance, not capable of especial determination, as emerging or arising only occasionally, upon the doing of that which is appointed at this or that time, in this or that place, and the like, is left unto the rule of moral prudence, in whose observation their order doth consist. But the superaddition of ceremonies necessarily belonging neither to the institutions of worship nor unto those circumstances whose disposal falls under the rule of moral prudence, neither doth nor can add any thing unto the due order of gospel worship; so that they are altogether needless and useless in the worship of God" (Owen, *Works*, 15:469–70).

they are morally *adiaphora*.[44] Whenever circumstances are made essential or religious, they are to be rejected.[45]

As a matter of history, when the catechism was drafted and adopted in the Palatinate and beyond, the Reformed churches mainly sang God's word (mostly Psalms), and they did so without instrumental accompaniment.[46] Deborah Rahn Clemens writes, "Like many other Reformed communities, Frederick III banned the use of organ music."[47] The organ returned briefly during the reign of Frederick's gnesio-Lutheran son, Ludwig VI (1539–1583), who succeeded his Reformed father from 1576–1583, but was banned again when the Palatinate returned to Reformed control. The organ did not return to Holy Spirit Church until 1655.[48]

In rejecting the use of musical instruments, the Reformed churches recovered the apostolic and universal ancient Christian practice.[49] Indeed, any "attempt to speak about 'musicians' in emerging Christianity is an exercise in anachronism."[50] "It was perhaps as late as the tenth century when the organ was played as part of the service."[51] Even then instruments were largely unknown in public worship in the West until the fifteenth

---

44. We should resist the modern trend that seeks to expand the definition of circumstances as a justification for good intentions or pragmatic decisions.

45. Clark, *Recovering the Reformed Confession*, 230; Ursinus, *Commentary*, 574.

46. Good, *Origin of the Reformed Church*, 147–48. The early Christians followed the practice of the synagogue in eschewing musical instruments in worship. See Clark, *Recovering the Reformed Confession*, 244–46; Vitringa, *Synagogue and the Church*, 200–207; Dugmore, *Influence of the Synagogue*; Price, *Old Light on New Worship*, 67–116; Smith, *Music in Ancient Judaism*, 116. I am grateful to Noah Frens for calling my attention to this passage. See Girardeau, *Instrumental Music*, 85–98; Folely, *Foundations*, 68, 80–82; Music, *Instruments in Church*, 19–33, 43; Ferguson, *A Cappella Music*, 63–76.

47. Clemens, "Foundations of German Reformed Worship," 227.

48. Clemens, "Foundations of German Reformed Worship," 228. We may doubt her supposition as to why Frederick removed the organ (i.e., for practical rather than theological reasons). She cites only Poppen, "Das Erste Kürpfalzer Gesangbuch," but offers no primary-source evidence. Frederick followed the Calvinist pattern on most matters, e.g., *fractio panis*, the removal of ornaments from the churches, and the institution of a church order modeled on the Genevan church order. On Frederick's Calvinist influences, see Clark, *Caspar Olevian*, 22–28. On the controversy between the Genevans and the Zürichers over the Palatinate church order, see Gunnoe, *Thomas Erastus and the Palatinate*, 163–209.

49. Clark, *Recovering the Reformed Confession*, 244–57.

50. Folely, *Foundations*, 68. For the patristic approach to Ps 150 et al., see McKinnon, *Music in Early Christian Literature*, 18–23, 28–170.

51. Ferguson, *A Cappella Music*, 96. It was believed in the late sixteenth century (e.g., Nassau Confession, 1578, in Dennison, *Reformed Confessions*, 3:515) that Pope Vitellian permitted the first organ (in Spain) in the late seventh century. Music (*Instruments*, 34) dates the introduction of the first organ in the Western church to AD 757.

century.[52] The churches in the East did not adopt them. Everett Ferguson writes, "The great majority of Orthodox and other Eastern churches still do not use an instrument in worship."[53] Thus, when the Reformed rejected the use of instruments in public worship as a return to types and shadows, they were rejecting a relative novelty in the life of the church. They were not rejecting the ancient practice of the church. Further, they were making the same arguments against the use of instruments as the early church made, for the same reasons.[54] Chrysostom's approach to Psalm 150 was typical:

> [God] allowed those instruments, then, for this reason: because of their weakness, and because he wanted to temper them in love and harmony, to raise their understanding through enjoyment of what accrues to their benefit, and to lead them to great zeal through enticement of this sort. For knowing their thoughtlessness, laziness, and carelessness, God wished to arouse them by this stratagem, blending the sweetness of melody in with the effort of paying attention.[55]

Calvin echoes the fathers repeatedly throughout his body of work. For example, in his commentary on Psalm 33:2 he argues:

> For even now, if believers choose to cheer themselves with musical instruments, they should, I think, make it their object not to dissever their cheerfulness from the praises of God. But when they frequent their sacred assemblies, musical instruments in celebrating the praises of God would be no more suitable than the burning of incense, the lighting up of lamps, and the restoration of the other shadows of the law. The Papists, therefore, have foolishly borrowed this, as well as many other things, from the Jews.[56]

52. *ODCC*, s.v. "organs." The use of instruments in the Mass was so unfamiliar to Thomas in the mid- to late thirteenth century that, in *ST* 2a2ae 91.2, he simply restates the patristic arguments (e.g., repl. obj. 4) against the use of musical instruments in public worship.

53. Ferguson, *A Cappella Music*, 96.

54. On the patristic condemnation of the use of musical instruments in Christian worship, see Ferguson, *A Cappella Music*, 88–95.

55. Chrysostom, *In Psalmum CL*, trans. McKinnon, *Music in Early Christian Literature*, 83.

56. Calvin, *Commentary on the Book of Psalms*, 1.538–39.

He repeats this approach in his commentary on Psalm 149:2; 150:3. The note on Psalm 150:3 in the 1559 Geneva Bible explains, "He maketh mention of those instruments which by God's commandment were appointed in the old Law, but under Christ the use thereof is abolished."[57]

These convictions were universal among the Reformed in the sixteenth and seventeenth centuries. The Hungarian Reformed Church confessed their rejection of the use of instruments in 1562 and again in 1567.[58] In 1574, the Provincial Synod of Churches of Holland and Zeeland demanded that the playing of organs in worship be discontinued.[59] The 1578 National Synod of Dort also called for the removal of organs from the churches.[60] In the same year, the Reformed Church in Nassau-Dillenburg also confessed their rejection of the use of instruments in worship.[61] In 1644, the Westminster Assembly ordered the destruction of the organ in "Paul's and Westminster."[62]

In the modern period the principle articulated by the *HC*, the *BC*, Calvin, and Ursinus has come to be known as the regulative principle of worship, as distinct from the normative principle.[63] The latter holds that we may do in public worship whatever is not forbidden by Scripture. It is the principle of the Lutherans, Anglicans, and most evangelicals.

In public worship the Reformed did not ask, "May we do it?" but "What has God commanded?" These are two distinct questions. This is the Reformed application of the *sola Scriptura* principle, in light of the second commandment, to public worship. Ursinus is alluding to *sola Scriptura* when he invokes the sufficiency of Scripture. If there is anything for which Scripture is sufficient, it is the governance of public worship. We see it implied rather clearly in Scripture:

> You shall surely destroy all the places where the nations whom you shall dispossess served their gods, on the high mountains and on

57. *Bible and Holy Scriptures Conteyned.*

58. Dennison, *Reformed Confessions*, 2:565–66; 3:11.

59. De Ridder, "Church Orders," 159.

60. De Ridder, "Church Orders," 220.

61. Dennison, *Reformed Confessions*, 3:515.

62. Letter of 18 February 1644 in Baillie, *Letters and Journals*, 1:421. The reference to "Paul's" probably refers to the Old Cathedral, which burned in the Great Fire of 1666. *ODCC*, s.v. "St Paul's Cathedral, London."

63. Clark, *Recovering the Reformed Confession*, 231–44.

> the hills and under every green tree. You shall tear down their altars and dash in pieces their pillars and burn their Asherim with fire. You shall chop down the carved images of their gods and destroy their name out of that place. You shall not worship the LORD your God in that way. But you shall seek the place that the LORD your God will choose out of all your tribes to put his name and make his habitation there. There you shall go, and there you shall bring your burnt offerings and your sacrifices, your tithes and the contribution that you present, your vow offerings, your freewill offerings, and the firstborn of your herd and of your flock. (Deut 12:2–6 ESV)

Not only did Yahweh demand that we worship him alone, but he reserved for himself the right to determine where and how he was to be worshiped. "You shall not worship Yahweh your God in that way" is an explicit articulation of the rule of worship. Hebrews 12:28 specifically teaches that the God of the Old Testament is the God of the New: "Let us offer to God acceptable worship, with reverence and awe" (ESV). This is the language of the Old Testament. In the rule of worship, the Reformed have recovered and preserved the apostolic and ancient Christian teaching about how we are to worship God.

ON THE TEACHING OF THE FAITH

Just as we have struggled to preserve the principle of worship in the modern period, so too the Reformed churches have often defaulted to approaches to catechesis, that is, Christian education, that are foreign to our theology, piety, and practice. This is symbolized by the presence of images of Christ in our Christian education materials.

Gregory I (ca. AD 540–604), writing to an iconclastic Bishop Serenus, argues: "If nothing else, should not even this thought have restrained thee, so as not to despise other brethren, supposing thyself only to be holy and wise? For to adore a picture is one thing, but to learn through the story of a picture what is to be adored is another. For what writing presents to readers, this a picture presents to the unlearned who behold, since in it even the ignorant see what they ought to follow; in it the illiterate read."[64] The catechism reduces his argument to one line, "books for the people," and rejects it. Before Gregory, however, Sixtus III (fl. AD 432–440) instituted

64. Gregory the Great, *Selected Epistles* (*NPNF* 2/13:53).

mosaics of the Holy Trinity in a church in Rome.[65] The arguments of John of Damascus (ca. AD 660–750) carried the day until the Reformation.[66] He admits to "worshipping and honouring" images (ostensibly) of the "Savior, and that of our Lady, and those too, of the rest of the saints and servants of Christ."[67] His first argument is that humans are image-bearers and therefore it is wrong to eschew other images as well. When we honor images, we are honoring the prototype.[68] He also invokes the divine institution of images under Moses. He argues that images can be abused just as sacrifices can be, but that does not invalidate sacrifices per se. As already indicated above, his chief argument is still in use today: God the Son became incarnate, thereby giving warrant to images. His final appeal is to the alleged unwritten tradition of the church.

The Damascene's argument rests on an unproven assumption: that there is an unwritten apostolic tradition to which one may appeal to justify images. His argument has clay feet. The claims by the Damascene and Rome notwithstanding,[69] there is no empirical evidence of an *authoritative*, unwritten tradition of the sort claimed by the Damascene. One of the very earliest reflections on the tradition of the apostles comes to us from the Fragments of Papias, drawn from Eusebius and other sources, and dated to circa AD 120. Papias was a leading pastor in Asia Minor. Irenaeus reports that, like Polycarp, he knew the apostle John.[70] He wrote a five-volume work, *Exposition of the Sayings of the Lord*, of which we have only fragments now. Among them, the question of an unwritten tradition is significant. In 3.11 we read, "The same writer has recorded other accounts as having come to him from unwritten tradition [παραδόσεως ἀγράφου], certain strange [ξενας] parables of the Lord and teachings of his and some other statements of a more mythical [μυθικωτερα] character."[71] As Michael Holmes observes, Papias wrote many things that raise more questions than they answer, but we need not guess what these unwritten

65. Didron, *Christian Iconography*, 1:3.

66. Damascene, *Exact Exposition* (*NPNF* 2/9b:88).

67. Damascene, *Exact Exposition* (*NPNF* 2/9b:88).

68. He cites Basil, *De spiritu sancto* 18.

69. On Rome's claims, see *CCC* §76–78, 82.

70. Holmes, *Apostolic Fathers*, 722; Eusebius of Caesarea, *Church History* (*NPNF* 2/1:170).

71. Holmes, *Apostolic Fathers*, 738–39.

traditions were. There is a list among the fragments. They include claims about a future earthly kingdom of Christ of ten thousand years (3.12), which Eusebius (or another editor) dismisses as a misunderstanding of the apostles' teaching (3.12b–13): "I suppose he got these ideas through a misunderstanding of the apostolic accounts, not perceiving that the things said by them were spoken mystically in figures."[72] Eusebius indicates what sort of sayings these were, and they were *descriptive* or narratives more than *prescriptive* texts. Papias himself (3.14) was aware that there were existed "other accounts of the words of the Lord." He gives them no authority, nor does he accord authority to the "traditions of the elder John" (3.14) or even identify him. In short, in the Fragments of Papias we have record of the existence of unwritten traditions and even sayings of our Lord, but they are given no clear authority. Certainly they do not compete with, nor are they regarded as superior to, Scripture. In at least one instance, they are dismissed as confused and contrary to Scripture.

The anonymous treatise to a certain Diognetus (ca. AD 150) clarifies what the early church typically said about the traditions of the apostles of the second century. It was written by a highly intelligent and articulate teacher. In *Ad Diognetum* 11.2 the author addresses specifically the question of an "apostolic tradition" (ἀποστόλων παράδοσις; 11:7). In 11.6 he writes, "Whereupon the fear of the law [φόβος νόμου] is sung, and the grace of the prophets is recognized, and the faith of the gospels is established, and the tradition of the apostles [ἀποστόλων παράδοσις] is preserved, and the joy of the Church exults." Our author recognized four sections of Holy Scripture: the Mosaic law, the Old Testament Prophets, the New Testament Gospels, and the apostolic Epistles. The phrase "tradition of the apostles" was a synonym for the Epistles. Everything here is written and public. None of it is unwritten or secret.

Irenaeus, in *Against Heresies* 3.4.2, writes, "To which course many nations of those barbarians who believe in Christ do assent, having salvation written in their hearts by the Spirit, without paper or ink, and, carefully preserving the ancient tradition, believing in one God, the Creator of heaven and earth, and all things therein."[73] The tradition to

72. Eusebius, *Ecclesiastical History* 3.39.11–12 (*NPNF* 2/1:172).

73. *ANF* 1:417.

which Irenaeus refers was the *rule of faith* (*regula fidei*), which did exist, in substance, fifty years before Irenaeus and eventually became what we know as the Apostles' Creed. This is no secret, unwritten dominical or apostolic tradition.

The first serious claim regarding an unwritten apostolic authority that the church is entitled to invoke against heretics was made by Basil the Great (ca. AD 330–379). In *On the Holy Spirit* 66 he writes: "Of the beliefs and practices whether generally accepted or publicly enjoined which are preserved in the Church some we possess derived from written teaching; others we have received delivered to us 'in a mystery' by the tradition of the apostles; and both of these in relation to true religion have the same force."[74]

Basil records a litany of practices that he takes as obviously sound and unquestionable, including making the sign of the cross, turning eastward at prayer, the prayer of invocation in the administration of the Supper, the blessing of baptismal water, the use of anointing oil in baptism, threefold baptism, and the renunciation of Satan and angels at baptism. He freely admits that neither any "apostle or the Gospel has recorded" these things, but they are "of great importance to the validity of the ministry, and these we derive from unwritten teaching." The authority for these practices he argues is "silent" and "mystical." It comes from nothing other than "unpublished and secret teaching which our fathers guarded in a silence out of the reach of curious meddling and inquisitive investigation." He continues in this vein for the rest of chapter 66 and the beginning of chapter 67, and it is, on its face, without force. We find Basil making up an unwritten tradition out of whole cloth in order to justify his preferences and practices.

The rest of the Damascene's arguments are easily dispatched. It simply does not follow that because humans are divine image-bearers that therefore humans are warranted to form images of God. The unstated middle premise of his argument, that we may imitate God in this way, is false. It assumes what it must prove, that we are authorized to make such images. The second commandment obviously forbids them; thus, the rest of his case hinges on the incarnation as a basis for images, and that has already been answered. His argument that by making images we honor

74. *NPNF* 2/8:40–41.

the prototype is the argument from good intention, which we reject on the basis of the rule of worship. His argument from the Old Testament sacrifices assumes what it cannot prove, that God has instituted images of himself for religious use.

Thus, the catechism's reply is exactly right: we should not be wiser than God, whose revealed will is specific and clear. He wills that his people be taught by the living (*viva*) preaching of the word of God. God has attached no promises to icons and images. He *has* attached promises to the preached word.[75] Icons are not an ordained means of grace. The preaching of the word and the holy sacraments are. Indeed, it is not as if Christ has not given to us visible signs and seals. Holy baptism and the Lord's Supper are visible representations of the gospel, but they do not purport to be images of the Father, Son, or Holy Spirit. Not only should we not seek to be wiser than God, but we should be satisfied with what he has given us.

Historically, there was a correlation between a decline in catechesis (instruction) in the church and the rise of images. The early church catechized new members sometimes for as long as three years. In the late medieval period, as the number and use of images of God proliferated, catechesis fell into neglect. One of the first things that Lutheran and Reformed churches did in the 1520s and following was to reinstitute a vigorous catechetical program, in which children in the congregation were expected to memorize the catechism. In the Reformed churches this was typically accompanied by a removal of images. The Ecclesiastical Ordinances, in Geneva, of 1541 require that children make profession of faith and be tested by the Consistory.[76]

The same is true in the modern period. In the Reformation, as the Reformed churches cleansed themselves of images of God, they also developed a rigorous catechetical program for the children and adults of the congregation. There was Bible study, catechism instruction (typically done by the minister), and chiefly catechism sermons held in the afternoon as part of the second worship service on the Christian Sabbath.[77]

---

75. See the discussion under *HC* 65.

76. Clark, *Recovering the Reformed Confession*, 161.

77. Clark, *Recovering the Reformed Confession*, 293–342; Clark, "Classical Christian Catechesis."

Ursinus is surely right to point us to Exodus 12:26–27, "And when your children say to you, 'What do you mean by this service?' you shall say, 'It is the sacrifice of the LORD's Passover, for he passed over the houses of the people of Israel in Egypt, when he struck the Egyptians but spared our houses'" (ESV). This is a simple but clear illustration of catechesis, that is, instruction by question and answer.[78] Ursinus notes a similar pattern in Exodus 13:8–10, when Moses instructed parents to rehearse to their children the history of salvation. Ursinus also appeals to the example of Timothy, who was "acquainted with the sacred writings" as a child (2 Tim 3:15), and to the early Christian historian Socrates (ca. AD 380–450), who reported the words of Eusebius of Caesarea, at Nicaea, "'Our form of catechising ... is in accordance with the mode which we have received from the Bishops who have preceded us, and according as we were taught when we laid the foundation of faith and were baptized, and according as we have learned from the Scriptures,' etc."[79]

In the modern period generally and especially since World War II, it seems evident that catechetical standards have slipped considerably in the Reformed churches. Children are rarely able to recite the catechism from memory, and we may rightly wonder how many enter adulthood well instructed in the faith. Since the Lord has ordained the hearing of the word read, preached, and taught, which we have summarized in the catechism, confessed in the *BC*, and defended in the Canons of Dort, and since he has ordained prayer and the sacraments as instruments of Christian growth, let us give ourselves to them in confidence that the Lord will use them to bring our covenant children to receive all the benefits of the covenant of grace.

78. Ursinus, *Commentary*, 12.

79. "Nostra, inquit, formula ad hunc modum se habet, sicut ab episcopis, qui nos antegressi sunt, accepimus: sicut cum fidei fundamenta iecimus, cumque baptizati sumus, audivimus: sicut à divinis scripturis didicimus, etc" (Ursinus, *Corpus doctrinae*, 12), paraphrasing Socrates, as presented in Christopherson and Curterius, *Historiae Ecclesiasticae Scriptores Graeci*, 400. See Socrates Scholasticus, *Ecclesiastical History* (*NPNF* 2/2:10). The early Christian historian Socrates is not to be confused with the Greek philosopher of the same name who lived ca. 469–399 BC.

Question 99

What is required in the third Commandment?

Question 100

Is the profaning of God's name, by swearing and cursing, so grievous a sin, that His wrath is kindled against those also who do not help as much as they can to hinder and forbid the same?

Lord's Day 36

Questions 99–100[1]

What is required in the third Commandment?

That we must not by cursing, or by false swearing, nor yet by unnecessary oaths, profane or abuse the name of God; nor even by our silence and connivance be partakers of these horrible sins in others; and in sum, that we use the holy name of God in no other way than with fear and reverence, so that he may be rightly confessed and worshipped by us, and be glorified in all our words and works.[2]

Is the profaning of God's name, by swearing and cursing, so grievous a sin, that His wrath is kindled against those also who do not help as much as they can to hinder and forbid the same?

Yes truly, for no sin is greater and more provoking to God than the profaning of his name; wherefore he even commanded it to be punished with death.[3]

We live in a radically egalitarian age in which people routinely show disrespect to officials at all levels of government. The spirit of the

1. For this Lord's Day we follow Ursinus's pattern by considering the two questions together, since the first is the positive aspect of the command and the second is the prohibitive aspect.

2. "Was will das dritte Gebot? Dass wir nicht allein mit Fluchen, oder mit falschem Eid, sondern auch mit unnöthigem Schwören den Namen Gottes nicht lästern oder missbrauchen, noch uns mit unserm Stillschweigen und Zusehen, solcher schrecklichen Sünden theilhaftig machen; und in Summa, dass wir den heiligen Namen Gottes anders nicht, denn mit Furcht und Ehrerbietung gebrauchen, auf dass er von uns recht bekennet, angerufen, und in allen unsern Worten und Werken gepriesen werde" (Schaff, *Creeds of Christendom*, 3:343–44). "Quid sancit Deus tertio praecepto? Ut non solum execrando, aut peierando, verum etiam temere iurando, nomen Dei contumeliose, aut irreverenter ne usurpemus: neve tacendo aut connivendo, horrendis istis sceleribus communicemus: sed sacrosancto Dei nomine non nisi summa cum religione et veneratione utamur: ut vera et constanti confessione, invocatione, omnibus denique verbis et actionibus nostris ipse celebretur" (Niemeyer, *Collectio Confessionum*, 454).

3. "Ist denn mit Fluchen und Schwören Gottes Namen lästern so eine schwere Sünde, dass Gott auch über die zürnet, die, so viel an ihnen ist, dieselbe nicht helfen wehren und verbieten? Ja freilich: denn keine Sünde grösser ist, noch Gott heftiger erzürnet, denn Lästerung seines Namens: darum er sie auch mit dem Tode zu strafen befohlen hat" (Schaff, *Creeds of Christendom*, 3:344). "Estne igitur adeo grave peccatum iurando, aut dira imprecando, nomen Dei temerare, ut Deus etiam iis succenseat, qui quantum in se est, illud non prohibent aut impediunt? Certe gravissimum: Neque enim ullum est peccatum maius, aut quod Deum gravius offendat, quam sacri ipsius nominis contumelia. Quocirca etiam id scelus morte multari voluit" (Niemeyer, *Collectio Confessionum*, 454).

modern age is to make everything common or profane. Everything is fodder for comedy, and nothing is revered.

There are some things we must revere, and first among those is the name of God. The third commandment is that we revere the name of God and that we not abuse or falsely invoke the name of Yahweh Elohim (יְהוָה אֱלֹהֶיךָ; Exod 20:7). Here God identifies himself by his covenant name, the name by which he made himself known to Abram and on whose name Abram called (Gen 12:8; 13:4). Before the king of Sodom, Abram invoked his covenant to Yahweh (Gen 14:22). It was Yahweh whom Abram believed for justification by grace alone, through faith alone (Gen 15:6; Rom 4:3; Gal 3:6). God identified himself to Abram by his covenant name (Gen 15:7) when he said, "I am *Yahweh,* who brought you out of Ur of the Chaldees." It was in the name of Yahweh that God made his covenant with Abram (Gen 15:18). It was in the name of Yahweh that God instituted the sign of initiation into the visible covenant community under the types and shadows (Gen 17:1). Exodus 3:13–15 is crucial here. Moses asks *Elohim* (אֱלֹהִים) how to answer the question, "What is his name?" God first announces himself as the self-existent one: "I am that I am" (v. 14). The importance of this can hardly be overstated. The God who will redeem his church is not like the handmade gods of the pagan Egyptians. The God of Abraham, Isaac, and Jacob is the God who is. He is also the God who entered into a covenant of grace with Abraham. Verse 15 begins with "he," but the pronoun refers back to *Elohim* in verse 14. He says to Moses, "Say this to the people of Israel: '*Yahweh,* the *Elohim* of your fathers, the Elohim of Abraham, the Elohim of Isaac, and the Elohim of Jacob, has sent me to you.' This is my name forever, and thus I am to be remembered throughout all generations."[4]

That the abuse of God's holy name was a capital crime under the Mosaic law (Lev 24:16) tells us how God regards abuse of his name. It was called "blasphemy" (e.g., 1 Sam 2:22–25; 3:13; Neh 9:18; Rev 13:1–5). The catechism reminds us of this fact to drive home how much we, who know God in Christ, who have received new life by the Holy Spirit, should value the name of God. The correlate to the Old Testament judicial law is church discipline.

4. See Ursinus, *Commentary*, 536–37.

The first thing we need to say about the name of the Lord, *Yahweh Elohim*, is that it, like the Lord himself, is holy. It is unique. It is clean. It is pure. It is undefiled. It is set apart. It is not common or ordinary. Believers are obligated to treat that name accordingly. After all, our Lord himself taught us to pray, "Let your name be sanctified" (Luke 11:2). According to Scripture, God's name is who he is and who and what he is to us. There is the closest relationship between God's name and God. In fact, we do not really understand how close that relationship is. In late modern North America we tend to assume that names are arbitrary or sentimental. In Scripture, however, names are not generally arbitrary. *Esau* is a good example. It means "red and hairy," and he was named Esau because he was red and hairy (Gen 25:25). Our Savior was named Jesus, which means "*Yahweh* saves" because, as Matthew 1:21 says, "he shall save his people." So, the names God, Lord, Almighty, Yahweh, Jesus, Holy Spirit, and Father are all intimately related to who God is and what and who he is to us.

Yahweh Elohim is our covenant-making and covenant-keeping God. Behind that relationship is his immutability. The God who entered into covenant with Abraham, Isaac, and Jacob, the God who made covenant with Moses and Israel, is the God who just is. The gods of the nations are contingent. They are idols. The God of history and salvation just is.

Sometimes Scripture refers simply to God as "the name" (e.g., Lev 24:11; אֶת־הַשֵּׁם). Modern Hebrew reflects seeks to preserve the holiness of God's name by refusing to use it. It uses the biblical expression "*Ha Shem*" ("the name") for God. This is contrary to Scripture since God's word uses the names *Elohim, Yahweh* (assuming the vowel points), *El Shaddai*, and so on. The name *Jesus* is equally holy, and Scripture uses it many times.

Leviticus is the book of holiness, and in it Yahweh himself institutes ceremonies to point to Christ and to illustrate his holiness. Leviticus 19:12 illustrates this when it says, "You shall not swear by my name falsely, and so profane the name of your God: I am *Yahweh*." When we see the name LORD in small capital letters in the English Bible, that is the signal that the Hebrew text says *Yahweh*, God's covenant name.

This commandment is not an easy thing, particularly in a culture that seems to regard it as a duty to tarnish any sacred thing as soon as it is discovered. To begin to obey this commandment is to distinguish between that which is common, which we used to call *secular* (as distinct from *secularist*), and that which is holy, that which is pure. God's name belongs to another order. This is why we do not use God's holy name as a curse word. God's name is pure, but cursing is common and even dirty. The two things do not belong together. The government requires us to swear oaths and sometimes to invoke the name of God. We must do that carefully. Our Lord Jesus said, "Let what you say be simply 'Yes' or 'No'; anything more than this comes from evil" (Matt 5:37 ESV). James 5:12 says the same thing.[5]

Our catechism says that we should not stand by when others abuse God's holy name. This is a perhaps one of the more difficult applications of the law in the catechism since we live in a world in which the Lord's name is abused almost constantly. To further complicate things, we live in a post-Christian culture in which there is a lingering memory of Christianity where, unlike the ancient world, people regularly abuse the holy name of our Savior.

There are a few things to consider here. First, when God gave this commandment to Israel at Sinai, he gave it to her as Yahweh's national people. Under the old covenant law, blaspheming the name of God is a capital offense (Lev 24:16). After the cross, there are no national peoples of God. Now God's people are found among every tribe, tongue, and nation. Thus, we must understand that the threat embedded in the third commandment, "Yahweh will not hold him guiltless," applies to the visible church and not to any particular nation.

Second, when the catechism was written Christendom was a given. There was, until 1806, a Holy Roman Empire. The European and British states saw themselves as God's national peoples. Virtually everyone was regarded externally as a Christian; thus, when someone blasphemed and another corrected him, he was correcting another professing (at least nominal), baptized Christian. The last part of the answer reflects this context when it says, "so that He may be rightly confessed and worshipped by us, and be glorified in all our words and works." The "us" in that phrase "by us" refers to citizens of the Electoral Palatinate and members of the state church therein. The propriety of a state church was unquestioned.

5. See the discussion under Lord's Day 37 concerning oaths.

Third, we have no evidence that in the first century Christians went about correcting (and certainly not stoning) pagans who surrounded them. We see Paul's principle for relating to the predominantly pagan surrounding culture in 1 Corinthians 5:9–13. When he exhorted the Corinthian congregation not to associate with the sexually immoral, he clarified that he was not referring to the pagans, "since then you should have to go out of the world" (1 Cor 5:10). That, he assumes, is an impossibility. In verse 12 he adds, "For what is it to me to judge those outside [the church]?"[6] In verse 13 he concludes, "God judges those outside [the church]."[7] The pagans around them invoked constantly and superstitiously the gods of the pagan pantheons. Paul teased them about it in his speech in Athens at the Areopagus (Acts 17:22–31). When pagans use the word *god* loosely, they are not abusing the *covenant* name, *Yahweh*.

Certainly Christians ought not to abuse the name of God, and when we see professing Christians abusing the name of the Lord, we have a duty gently to correct them. Correcting post-Christian, pagan Westerners (or others who have no knowledge of the Christian faith) about the abuse of God's name requires wisdom and grace. It is perhaps an opportunity to instruct them and to give witness to the faith. Certainly we who believe, who profess the Christian faith, ought to be distinct from the pagans around us. Certainly Christians ought to demonstrate to the pagans around us that *we* regard the name of God as holy by the reverent way we use it (Rom 2:24).

For example, should we find ourselves standing in line somewhere, should we correct the person next to us who abuses the Lord's name? Opinions on this will differ, but it will help us to distinguish between what we expect of professing Christians and what we expect of unbelievers. The apostle Paul instructs Christians on when they are and are not free to eat meat offered to idols (1 Cor 8; 10:14–33), but he does not instruct the pagans. Those who believe it is wrong to eat meat offered to idols are free not to eat it, but those who believe it is permitted are free to eat. Perhaps this is a guide to responding to abuses of the Lord's name in the public square. If one is convicted that one should speak to unbelievers

---

6. *τί γάρ μοι τοὺς ἔξω κρίνειν;*
7. τοὺς δὲ ἔξω ὁ θεὸς κρινεῖ.

about their abuse of God's name, one way to approach them is to say something like this: "Dear friend, I understand that you do not believe the Christian faith, but I do, and I would be grateful if you would respect the Christian conviction that God's name is to be treated with reverence. In our understanding, it is a great sin to abuse his name." We may well imagine that such might be a first for that person.

Whatever the pagans do and however they use God's name, they will have to give account to God. Believers who have been saved from the wrath of God by the holy Son of God, who have been baptized in the name of the Father, the Son, and the Holy Spirit, however, ought to revere it out of gratitude and holy fear.

The underlying principle is to learn to distinguish what is sacred and what is common. As believers, as Christians, we are obligated to set aside the holy name of God, the covenant name of the Lord who saved us, who sent his only begotten Son, because that is his name. The name *Jesus* not only means "*Yahweh* saves," but his name *is Yahweh* (Acts 2:34). In the Hebrew text of Psalm 110, the text says, "*Yahweh* says to *Adonai*" (אדֹנִי), but when Peter quotes Psalm 110:1, as Luke records it in Acts 2:34, the same word for "Lord" is used to represent both Yahweh and El (*κύριος τῷ κυρίῳ μου*). The person of the Holy Trinity who spoke at Sinai, who gave his holy law, was God the Son. He is the revealer of God (John 1:1–3, 18; 14:9; 1 John 1:1–3; Heb 1:1–3; 12:18–29). He is the Word, and that Word became incarnate. So, when we or another believer or perhaps anyone else uses the holy name of Jesus carelessly or as a curse word, they are making common (profaning) the name of the Lord who thundered at Sinai and who saved us by becoming incarnate for his elect.

In our culture little is held sacred except perhaps our sovereign identity and our all-important feelings. God, however, is holy, and he demands that his name be treated with reverence, as something that is holy. As we contemplate how we ourselves have profaned God's beautiful name, we may be thankful that we have a Savior who so revered his Father's name that he never profaned it even once, and his perfect obedience is imputed to all who believe as if we had never violated the third commandment. The Holy Spirit who sustained him through his trials and who raised him from the dead is at work in us helping us to learn to pray "Hallowed be your name" in true faith.

To that end, Ursinus identifies seven virtues to be fostered by Christians under the third commandment:

1. *Teaching the true doctrine.*[8] This is part of the positive aspect of the commandment. Just as we are not to abuse the Lord's name, positively, we are to teach Christian truth in his church and in Christian families. Ursinus mentions specifically the duty to instruct covenant children in the Christian faith.[9] One sin of omission here is "refraining from conversation respecting God and divine things."[10] Another sin is corrupting divine truth.

2. *Praising and glorifying God.*[11] When the psalmists praise God, they praise his name and his attributes. For example, Psalm 8:1 says, "How majestic is your name in all the earth!" The psalmist praises God's works (e.g., the heavens, 8:3; humanity, 8:4–8; and his saving work, 9:1–11). The vices of the contempt of God, blasphemy, and the cursing of God are forbidden.[12] By "cursing," Ursinus refers to *execration* and *imprecation.*[13] These are *maledictory* oaths against our neighbor when we ask of God "wicked things" against our neighbor with whom we are at odds.[14] In such a case, writes Ursinus, we are seeking to make God the executioner of our private revenge. We should be careful, then, how we invoke the imprecatory language of the Psalms especially in regards to evil in this world. It is one thing to pray the imprecatory psalms while we leave to God who are the enemies to be destroyed. It is another to think that we know precisely who God's enemies are.

3. *Confessing the truth about God.*[15] The virtue here is to confess the truth about God on general principles on the basis of what we know from Scripture.[16] We confess what we know about his revealed will. The vice is to deny the truth or refuse to say what we know to be true "for fear of hatred or the cross or reproach."[17] This is particularly relevant in a

8. Ursinus, *Commentary*, 537–38.
9. Ursinus, *Commentary*, 538.
10. Ursinus, *Commentary*, 538.
11. Ursinus, *Commentary*, 538–39.
12. Ursinus, *Commentary*, 538.
13. "Exsecratio seu imprecatio omnis" (Ursinus, *Corpus doctrinae*, 550).
14. Ursinus, *Commentary*, 538.
15. Ursinus, *Commentary*, 539–40.
16. Ursinus, *Commentary*, 539.
17. Ursinus, *Commentary*, 539.

post-Christian culture. The apostle Peter exhorts believers in Asia Minor to be ready to give an account for the hope that lies within them with just this situation in view (1 Pet 3:15).

Apostates, that is, those who have learned and perhaps even confessed the faith but who go on to deny it, also fall under this heading and condemnation. They violate the third commandment. Apostates throw away whatever they knew about the truth "with the determined counsel and desire of the heart to oppose God," which desire is accompanied with "no grief or sorrow for having rejected the truth" (1 John 2:19).[18] "If this happens after the truth has once been acknowledged certainly, it becomes the sin against the Holy Spirit, for which there is not forgiveness in this life nor in the life to come."[19] Another vice here is to conceal the truth "where the glory of God and salvation of our neighbor require a confession of it."[20] This is particularly true when our silence creates the impression that certain errors are true. The parents of the man who was born blind had opportunity to give a simple testimony to the saving grace of Christ, but they refused (John 9:20–23).[21]

Remarkably, it is also possible to speak in defense of the truth in an untimely way.[22] This happens when we speak at a time or in a way that gives opponents of Christ an opportunity to revile him or to stir up opponents of Christ against his church. In such cases one speaks "without advancing the glory of God and the salvation of anyone, and without any necessity demanding a confession of the truth and the time and under the circumstances in which it was made."[23] This is giving to dogs what is holy and casting pearls before pigs (Matt 7:6). Distinguishing between when to speak and when to remain silent is a matter of wisdom.

4. *Gratitude.*[24] This is confessing the benefits we have received freely from God (Col 3:17).[25] Ingratitude is the vice that refuses to give thanks

---

18. Ursinus, *Commentary*, 539.

19. "Et si fiat post veritatem, certo agnitam, est peccatum in Spiritum sanctum, ex quo nulli resipiscunt, ideo non remittitur, neque in hoc, neque in futuro seculo" (Ursinus, *Corpus doctrinae*, 550).

20. Ursinus, *Commentary*, 539.

21. See Clark, "Encouraging Lay Witnessing," 247–61.

22. Ursinus, *Commentary*, 540.

23. Ursinus, *Commentary*, 540.

24. Ursinus, *Commentary*, 540–41.

25. Ursinus, *Commentary*, 540.

to God for his gifts and benefits. We are ungrateful when we are not sufficiently grateful for the gifts and graces of God or when we neglect them and do not use them to his glory (Matt 25:26–27).[26]

5. *Zeal for God's glory.*[27] The law of God calls us to be zealous for God's name and glory. This is an early and authentic Reformation imperative: *soli Deo gloria* ("to God alone be the glory").[28] That humanity's chief end is to glorify God and enjoy him forever was Reformed teaching well before the Westminster Assembly.[29] Phineas's zeal for the glory of the Lord is instructive (Num 25:1–13).[30] The church had begun, to use the language of Scripture, "to whore with the daughters of Moab" (Num 25:1). The people began to violate the first commandment, bowing down to the Moabite idols. One man was particularly brazen, and Phineas was so incensed, so full of holy zeal, that he executed the judgment of the Lord on them immediately. To be sure, we are not under the Mosaic covenant, and the proper analogy for the new covenant church would be church discipline (rather than capital punishment), but the point stands.

Its opposite is, as Ursinus notes, "timidity or want of firmness," which "consists in not being afflicted with grief on account of reproach cast upon God, and so not caring for the divine glory, and in not having or showing any desire in word and deed to prevent this reproach."[31] This is a particular duty among the covenant people who are marked by the name of Yahweh. This is what Phineas did and what we ought to do. We are baptized into the name of the Father, the Son, and the Holy Spirit and as such ought to honor the Lord's name.

We should note well, however, as Ursinus does, that there is such a thing as "false zeal," which is a zeal for God "but not according to knowledge" (Rom 10:2–3).[32] As with defending the faith, when to defend the

26. Ursinus, *Commentary*, 541.

27. Ursinus, *Commentary*, 541.

28. "Soli deo gloria" is an early and authentic, if somewhat neglected, Reformation slogan. E.g., it was appended to a 1520 edition of Luther's 1519 *Meditation on Christ's Passion* (*WA* 2:142; *LW* 42:14). It occurs in in Bullinger, *In priorem d. Pauli ad Corinthios epistolam*, 72; in Junius, *Animadversiones in roberti bellarmini*, 21. See VanDrunen, *God's Glory Alone*.

29. See the discussion under *HC* 86.

30. Ursinus, *Commentary*, 541.

31. Ursinus, *Commentary*, 541.

32. Ursinus, *Commentary*, 541.

honor of God and when to remain silent is a matter of wisdom. Proverbs 26:4 and 26:5 are *both* God's word. Sometimes the honor of God requires us to answer a fool, and sometimes it requires us to remain silent since to answer would insult the divine honor. In this we should be sure that it is the honor of God's name (and not our own) that is in view.

6. *Calling upon the Lord.*[33] Prayer honors God's name.[34] We are commanded to call upon his name to glorify God, to sanctify his name, and to ask provision for our needs.[35] Scripture exhorts us to "call upon the name of the Lord" (Ps 105:1). William Tyndale and other sixteenth- and seventeenth-century translators translated the future passive of the verb "to give" (δοθήσεται) in Matthew 7:7 as "shall be given."[36] This is a statement of policy rather than an intent (e.g., "will give," as in the ESV and others). The vice here is to neglect calling on the name of the Lord and to refuse to ask him for our needs, which tends to dishonor his name. Calling on false gods—for example, the gods of the pagans and sects, or the god of Islam—is obviously a violation of the first commandment. It violates the third commandment when Christians seek to syncretize or synthesize Christianity with a non-Christian religion. Formalism and lip service, going through the motions, also dishonors God's name.[37] We should not be surprised when the pagans "heap up empty phrases" (Matt 6:7), but it dishonors God when Christians do it. The Reformed rejected the Pentecostal excesses of the Anabaptists in the sixteenth century, and so we should in our age.[38]

7. *Lawful or religious swearing.*[39] We will discuss this issue at length under Lord's Day 37. Suffice it to say here that Christians may swear solemn oaths before the civil magistrate (e.g., in court) and in the church (e.g., in church membership) reverently in obedience to the third commandment. What is forbidden is *false* swearing, dissembling, and lying under oath. Vain, useless, careless oaths are also forbidden. Christians

33. Ursinus, *Commentary*, 541–42.

34. See the discussion of prayer in general under Lord's Day 45.

35. Ursinus, *Commentary*, 541.

36. Daniell, *Tyndale's New Testament*, 29; *New Testament: A Facsimile.*

37. Ursinus, *Commentary*, 542.

38. See the discussion under *HC* 53.

39. Ursinus, *Commentary*, 548–49.

have no business taking oaths in casual conversation. The rejection of oaths altogether is an Anabaptist error. Obviously, swearing, even in jest, by idols or false gods, is forbidden. Oaths taken in the commission of a crime or to ungodly ends are also sin.[40] We ought to bear in mind our Lord's command and ought to heed it in our day:

> Again you have heard that it was said to those of old, "You shall not swear falsely, but shall perform to the Lord what you have sworn." But I say to you, Do not take an oath at all, either by heaven, for it is the throne of God, or by the earth, for it is his footstool, or by Jerusalem, for it is the city of the great King. And do not take an oath by your head, for you cannot make one hair white or black. Let what you say be simply "Yes" or "No"; anything more than this comes from evil. (Matt 5:33–37 ESV)

The apostle James summarizes this command thus: "Let your 'yes' be yes, and your 'no' be no, so that you may not fall under condemnation" (Jas 5:12 ESV).

40. Ursinus, *Commentary*, 548–49.

Question 101

But may we swear reverently by the Name of God?

Question 102

May we swear by the saints or by any other creatures?

Lord's Day 37

QUESTIONS 101–2

But may we swear reverently by the Name of God?
Yes, when the magistrate requires it, or when it may be needful otherwise, to maintain and promote fidelity and truth to the glory of God and our neighbor's good; for such an oath is grounded in God's Word, and therefore was rightly used by the saints in the Old and New Testament.[1]

May we swear by the saints or by any other creatures?
No, for a lawful oath is a calling upon God, that he, as the only searcher of hearts, may bear witness to the truth, and punish me if I swear falsely; which honor is due to no creature.[2]

On the basis of our Lord's words in Matthew 5:33–37 and on the basis of James 5:12, the Anabaptists in the 1520s rejected the use of oaths. The 1527 Schleitheim Confession fairly represents Anabaptist opinion:

> Seventh. We are agreed as follows concerning the oath. The oath is a confirmation among those who are quarreling or making promises. In the Law it is commanded to be performed in God's Name, but only in truth, not falsely. Christ, who teaches the perfection of the Law, prohibits all swearing to His [followers], whether true or false,—neither by heaven, nor by the earth, nor by Jerusalem, nor

1. "Mag man aber auch gottselig bei dem Namen Gottes einen Eid schwören? Ja: wenn es die Obrigkeit von ihren Unterthanen oder sonst die Noth erfordert, Treue und Wahrheit zu Gottes Ehre und des Nächsten Heil dadurch zu erhalten und zu fördern. Denn solches Eidschwören ist in Gottes Wort gegründet, und derhalben von den Heiligen im alten und neuen Testament recht gebraucht worden" (Schaff, *Creeds of Christendom*, 3:344). "Potestne quis etiam pie per nomen Dei iurare? Postest, cum vel magistratus id exigit, vel alioqui necessitas, hoc pacto fidem firmari, et veritatem stabiliri postulat: quo et gloria Dei illustretur, et aliorum saluti consulatur. Nam eius generis iusiurandum, verbo Dei sancitur, ideoque etiam a sanctis in veteri et novo foedere, recte est usurpatum" (Niemeyer, *Collectio Confessionum*, 454).

2. "Mag man auch bei den Heiligen, oder andern Creaturen einen Eid schwören. Nein: denn ein rechtmässiger Eid ist eine Aurufung Gottes, dass Er, als der einige Herzenskündiger, der Wahrheit Zeugniss wolle geben, und mich strafen, so ich falsch schwöre, welche Ehre denn keiner Creatur gebühret" (Schaff, *Creeds of Christendom*, 3:344–45). "Estne licitum iurare per Sanctos autalias creaturas? Non: Nam legitimum iuramentum est invocatio Dei, qua petitur, ut is tanquam unicus cordium inspector, testimonium det veritati et iurantem puniat, si sciens fallat: Porro hic honos nulli creaturae convenit" (Niemeyer, *Collectio Confessionum*, 454–55).

by our head—and that for the reason which He shortly thereafter gives, For you are not able to make one hair white or black. So you see it is for this reason that all swearing is forbidden: we cannot fulfill that which we promise when we swear, for we cannot change [even] the very least thing on us.[3]

In Lord's Day 37 the catechism repudiates the Anabaptist view for reasons it makes explicit, but there are implicit reasons as well, which we will address below. First, however, let us define our terms. An oath "is the invocation of God, which asks him, as the only inspector of the heart, to give witness to the truth and punish the one swearing falsely."[4] Ursinus properly cites the apostle Paul himself as swearing just such an oath: "But I call God to witness against me—it was to spare you that I refrained from coming again to Corinth."[5] He swore an oath to the Roman and Philippian congregations as well: "For God is my witness" (Rom 1:9; Phil 1:8).

First, the Anabaptists concede that the Old Testament permits oaths. Deuteronomy 6:13 says, "It is Yahweh your God you shall fear. Him you shall serve and by his name you shall swear" (שׁבע). Deuteronomy 10:20: "You shall fear Yahweh your God. You shall serve him and hold fast to him, and by his name you shall swear."

Second, the Anabaptist position assumes such a high degree of discontinuity between the Mosaic covenant and the new covenant as to create a *substantial* discontinuity. This is a fundamental difference between the Anabaptist movements and traditional Christian theology, dating to the second and third centuries and continuing through the medieval and Reformation periods.

The Anabaptist relation of the old and new covenants borders on Marcionism. Such view of discontinuity is grounded not in Scripture but in an overrealized eschatology, which assumes that the new covenant is of such an eschatological character that it is substantially different from the administrations of the covenant of grace during the typological periods

3. Leith, *Creeds of the Churches*, 289; Calvin, *John Calvin*, 92–105; Balke, *Calvin and the Anabaptist Radicals*, 253–59.

4. "Iuramentum est invocatio Dei, qua petitur, ut is tanquam unicus cordium inspector, testimonium det veritati-et iurantem puniat, si sciens fallat" (Ursinus, *Corpus doctrinae*, 561); Ursinus, *Commentary*, 550.

5. On the significance of oaths in the ancient Near East and in Scripture, see Kline, *By Oath Consigned*.

(under Noah, Abraham, Moses, and David). This, in turn, rests in part on an incorrect interpretation of Jeremiah 31:31–34. We have to understand that language the way we understand prophetic language generally, that future conditions are characterized hyperbolically. Further, the contrast that Jeremiah actually makes, between the *Mosaic* covenant and the new covenant, is often overlooked. In other words, in Jeremiah 31:31–34 the new covenant is described as new *specifically relative to Moses*.

Nevertheless, we should face squarely the challenge presented to the historic Christian view, reflected in Lord's Day 37, by the teaching of our Lord and James.

> Again you have heard that it was said to those of old, "You shall not swear falsely, but shall perform to the Lord what you have sworn." But I say to you, Do not take an oath at all, either by heaven, for it is the throne of God, or by the earth, for it is his footstool, or by Jerusalem, for it is the city of the great King. And do not take an oath by your head, for you cannot make one hair white or black. Let what you say be simply "Yes" or "No"; anything more than this comes from evil. (Matt 5:33–37 ESV)

How do we interpret our Lord's words? In Matthew 5:30, just before his teaching on oaths, our Lord says, "And if your right hand causes you to sin, cut it off and throw it away. For it is better that you lose one of your members than that your whole body go into hell" (ESV). Were we to use the hermeneutic of the Anabaptists, it would seem impossible to avoid the conclusion that our Lord taught self-mutilation. That seems unlikely. In fact, our Lord was using a rhetorical technique known as *hyperbole* (ὑπερβολή), an intentionally exaggerated statement intended to call attention to a problem, to provoke further thought, but not to be taken literally. Both the call to dismemberment and the apparent prohibition against oaths are examples of hyperbole.

Calvin argues that Jesus was replying hyperbolically to certain Jewish practices whereby they swore vain oaths without appearing to do so. "The Jews had circuitous or indirect ways of swearing: and when they swore by heaven, or by earth, or by the altar, (Mat. 23:18) they reckoned it to be next to nothing; and, as one vice springs from another, they defended, under this pretence, any profanation of the name of God that was not openly avowed."[6] Under this interpretation, the injunction not to swear at all (ὅλως) is not intended to prohibit all oaths but specifically to address the invocation of heaven and earth *in lieu* of invoking God. By invoking heaven and earth as witnesses, they were implicitly invoking God (Heb 6:13–20). The answer, as Calvin writes, is honesty and simplicity of speech. "Fairness and honesty in our words are, therefore, demanded by Christ, that there may be no longer any occasion for an oath."[7] This is the effect of James's reflection on our Lord's teaching: "But above all, my brothers, do not swear, either by heaven or by earth or by any other oath, but let your 'yes' be yes and your 'no' be no, so that you may not fall under condemnation" (Jas 5:12 ESV).

Ursinus reminds us that Deuteronomy 10:20 commands us to swear, when appropriate, by God's name alone.[8] God alone is immutable (Mal 3:6; Heb 13:8). The writer to the Hebrew Christians affirms the continuing necessity and righteousness of swearing oaths by God: "For people swear by something greater than themselves, and in all their disputes an oath is final for confirmation" (Heb 6:16 ESV). When we do that we are imitating God, says Hebrews, who confirms his promises with an oath against himself: "So when God desired to show more convincingly to the heirs of the promise the unchangeable character of his purpose, he guaranteed it with an oath, so that by two unchangeable things, in which it is impossible for God to lie, we who have fled for refuge might have strong encouragement to hold fast to the hope set before us" (Heb 6:17–18 ESV).

In contrast to God, all creatures are immutable. The theological ground beneath the Reformed affirmation of reverent oaths is the distinction between the Creator and the creature. We reject oaths by the latter and affirm those by the former. Only God is omniscient, and therefore it is appropriate to swear an oath by his name.

The case of Ananias and Sapphira (Acts 5:1–11) serves as a warning to the church of the danger of lying, which is what happens when one swears falsely. When the pagans swear falsely in secular or civil matters, their punishment belongs to God, but it is especially grievous when

6. John Calvin, *Commentary on a Harmony*, 1:294.

7. Calvin, *Commentary on a Harmony*, 1:296.

8. Ursinus, *Commentary*, 550.

Christians, in religious matters, swear falsely. In this regard, one place where Christians swear properly by God's name is when we take membership vows. Those are sacred oaths. When Christians who have professed the faith stand before God and the congregation and swear an oath to be faithful in response to God's grace and then abandon the visible church, that is a violation of the third commandment (and the fifth too, but we will come to that later). When professing Christians break their membership vows, they have treated as common a promise made over the holy name of God. That is why church membership was so difficult to obtain in the ancient church. In view of the sacred oath that is sworn, we might do well to make it a little more difficult in our day.

When we invoke God, we are pledging to tell the truth. Implicit here is that the truth is, that we can find it, and that we can and must articulate it. As we will see under the exposition of *HC* 112, the churches categorically reject Pilate's skepticism (John 18:38). After all, our Lord himself is the truth. The apostle John contrasts Christ with Moses. Christ came "full of divine favor and truth" (John 1:14), in contrast to Moses, through whom the law was given, through whom a system of types and shadows was administered. Jesus is the promised reality (John 1:17–18). He is "the Truth" (John 14:6), and in Christ believers know the truth: "And you will know the truth, and the truth will set you free" (John 8:32). The Spirit witnesses to the truth (John 15:26). Christians worship in the Spirit and in the Truth (John 4:23–24).[9] God is sanctifying believers in his word, the truth (John 17:17).

The two senses of truth meet in Christ. The truth is what is and what God has said. We need not choose between them. Christian speech should be characterized by the truth. We should be known as people of the truth, who heartily and consistently speak the truth. So we should agree with Ursinus when he writes, "Only such oaths as are evidently not opposed to the Word of God, and which are made concerning things *true, certainly known, lawful, possible, weighty, necessary, useful,* and worthy of such and so great a confirmation or of such things as require a confirmation for the

9. On this interpretation of John 4, see Clark, *Recovering the Reformed Confession*, 272–77.

glory of God and the safety of our neighbor."[10] Unnecessary oaths are the opposite of these things.

One question that plagued Reformation-era Christians, which perhaps troubles us less because we are the recipients of their ministry on our behalf, is the validity of certain oaths. Not a few people entered into monasteries and took religious vows to a life of obedience to the rules of that order. When the Reformation came to a town and the monasteries were dissolved, some Christians found themselves in crisis. They had embraced the Reformation convictions of *sola Scriptura, sola gratia, sola fide,* and *solid Deo gloria,* but what of their vows? Calvin discusses this problem at some length.[11] He sets a threefold test for the validity of vows or oaths. We must determine "(1) who it is to whom the vow is made; (2) who we are who make the vow; (3) lastly, with what intention we make our vow."[12]

The monastic vows violate the first test, since it is God who determines how he will be worshiped (Col 2:23). Calvin calls will-worship "accursed."[13] Vows are necessarily limited by the person making them: "I mean nothing else here than that you are to temper your vows to that measure which God by his gift sets for you, lest if you try to go beyond what he allows, in claiming too much for yourself, you cast yourself headlong."[14] Thus it is willful and foolish for those who have not received the gift of celibacy to pledge a life of celibacy (e.g., in monastic life). It is sinful for a man to abandon his responsibilities to his family in order by leaving his family to poverty in order to go on a lifelong mission to the Amazon. Finally, regarding intention, Calvin classifies two types of vows or oaths: with regard to the past (e.g., vows of thankfulness or repentance) and with regard to the future.[15] In general, all "believers have one common vow which, made in baptism, we confirm and, so to speak, sanction by catechism and receiving the Lord's Supper. For the sacraments are like contracts by which the

10. Ursinus, *Commentary*, 554. Emphasis original.

11. Calvin, *Institutes* 4.18.8–21.

12. Calvin, *Institutes* 4.18.2.

13. Calvin, *Institutes* 4.18.2; Ursinus, *Commentary*, 551: "The moral worship of God is perpetual. A lawful oath forms a part of the moral worship, being one of the ways in which we call upon God. Therefore it is perpetual."

14. Calvin, *Institutes* 4.18.3

15. Calvin, *Institutes* 4.18.4–5.

Lord gives us his mercy and from it eternal life; and we in turn promise him obedience."[16] Our vow of obedience is a consequent obligation, a stipulation of the covenant of grace.[17] We promise grateful obedience *because* we have been saved by grace alone, through faith alone, in Christ alone.

We are not bound by what Calvin characterizes as "perverse vows," that is, monastic vows that were illegitimate from the start.[18] All "unlawful or improperly conceived vows, as they are of no value before God, should be invalid for us."[19] Truly Galatians 5:1 applies here: "For freedom Christ has set us free; stand firm therefore, and do not submit again to a yoke of slavery" (ESV). Monastic and all other rash, illegitimate vows and oaths are slavery. We might well apply the Reformation critique of monastic vows to membership oaths taken by those who join religious cults. All the vows taken by members of secret societies are *ipso facto* illegitimate and nonbinding (however violent the sanction might promise to be). We should also apply the Reformation critique to the proliferation of religious "sects in the world [that] today claim for themselves the name of 'the church'" but that lack the marks of the true church.[20] Vows made to such entities are invalid and cannot bind the conscience of the Christian.[21]

---

16. Calvin, *Institutes* 4.16.6.
17. Calvin, *Institutes* 4.18.6.
18. Calvin, *Institutes* 4.18.7.
19. Calvin, *Institutes* 4.18.20.
20. *BC* 29, in United Reformed Churches in North America, *Liturgical Forms and Prayers*, 185–87.
21. Ursinus, *Commentary*, 554–56. Perhaps the most foundational Reformation treatise on this is Luther's 1520 *Freedom of the Christian* (*LW* 31:333–76).

Question 103

What does God require in the fourth commandment?

Lord's Day 38

Question 103

What does God require in the fourth commandment?

In the first place, God wills that the ministry of the gospel and schools be maintained, and that I, especially on the day of rest, diligently attend church, to learn the Word of God, to use the holy sacraments, to call publicly upon the Lord, and to give Christian alms. In the second place, that all the days of my life I rest from my evil works, allow the Lord to work in me by his Spirit, and thus begin in this life the everlasting sabbath.[1]

According to the catechism, the Lord's Day is both a day of celebration (*Feiertag, dies festa*) *and* the Christian Sabbath, that is, a day of rest. Our English noun *Sabbath* is transliterated from the Hebrew noun שַׁבָּת. It is the day of rest and worship. The verb שָׁבַת means "to stop working or to take a holiday."[2] On the Christian Sabbath, we begin to experience something of the eternal Sabbath. If there ever was a time when Christians needed to stop their business, to rest, to worship, and to set aside time for the care of the poor in their midst, that time is now. At no time in its history has the church been so distracted, pulled in so many competing and contradictory directions, and so alienated from the creational and redemptive pattern as it is today.

That is a large claim, but we can confirm that it is reasonable with just a little knowledge of history. Prior to the industrial age, the world operated largely on an agrarian schedule. Farmers work hard, but the pace of life is typically a little slower in agrarian cultures than it is in urban and

1. "Was will Gott im vierten Gebot? Gott will erstlich, dass das Predigtamt und Schulen erhalten werden, und ich, sonderlich am Feiertag, zu der Gemeine Gottes fleissig komme, das Wort Gottes zu lernen, die heiligen Sacramente zu gebrauchen, den Herrn öffentlich anzurufen, und das christliche Almosen zu geben. Zum andern, dass ich alle Tage meines Lebens von meinen bösen Werken feire, den Herrn durch seinen Geist in mir wirken lasse, und also den ewigen Sabbath in diesem Leben anfange" (Schaff, *Creeds of Christendom*, 3:345). "Quid praecipit Deus in quarto praecepto? Primum, ut Ministerium Evangelii et Scholae conserventur: utque ego cum aliis, tum praecipue festis diebus, studiose coetus divinos frequentem, verbum Dei diligenter audiam, utar sacramentis, precibus publicis meas quoque preces adiungam, pro facultatibus aliquid conferam in pauperes. Deinde, ut in omni vita a pravis actionibus vacem, Domino concedens, ut per Spiritum sanctum in me suum opus faciat, atque ita sempiternum illud sabbathum in hac vita exordiar" (Niemeyer, *Collectio Confessionum*, 455).

2. Holladay, *Concise Hebrew and Aramaic Lexicon*, s.v. "שַׁבָּת" and "שָׁבַת"; Ursinus, *Commentary*, 561.

suburban cultures. An agrarian culture is more in sync with natural patterns. The rise of the industrial economy put a great strain on the creational pattern, and the postindustrial age might have offered some relief but for the natural inclination of fallen humans to fill time with everything but rest, worship, and ministry to the suffering in their midst.

Roughly contemporary with the rise of industrialization, evangelical theology, piety, and practice was undergoing a revolution. Whereas, in the sixteenth and seventeenth centuries, *evangelical* denoted "confessional Protestant" (Lutheran and Reformed), by the mid–nineteenth century *evangelical* came to denote one of the revivalist traditions.[3] Further, much of evangelical theology and piety was increasingly colored by a dispensational reading of Scripture that emphasized discontinuity between the various epochs of redemption and between the Old and New Testaments, as well as focusing strongly on eschatology. Much of the rest of nineteenth-century evangelical theology, piety, and practice was heavily affected by what Reformed folk should regard as an overrealized eschatology. A sound theology should account for both creation and redemption (nature and grace), but since the eighteenth century, evangelical theology has largely failed to do that.

A BRIEF DEFENSE OF THE CHRISTIAN SABBATH

In contrast to modern evangelical theology, confessional Reformed theology does not regard the fourth commandment as abrogated.[4]

A CREATIONAL PATTERN

That there is a Sabbath built into the creational pattern is evident in the second chapter in God's word (Gen 2:2): "And on the seventh day God finished his work that he had done, and he rested [יִּשְׁבֹּת] on the seventh day from all his work that he had done" (ESV). God worked, as it were,

3. Hatch, *Democratization of American Christianity*, 3–5; Turner, *Without God, without Creed*, 141; Clark, "'Magic and Noise,'" 87–91; Clark, *Recovering the Reformed Confession*, 212–20. Abraham (*Coming Great Revival*) argues this thesis persuasively. See Dayton, "Some Doubts," 245–51.

4. Clark, *Recovering the Reformed Confession*, 295–326. On the controversy between the Cocceians and the Voetians over the abrogation of the Christian Sabbath, see Carmichael, *Continental View*, 106–71; van Asselt, *Federal Theology*, 76.

for six mornings and evenings and rested, as it were, on the seventh. That God is said to have "worked" and "rested" is significant. The God who created the heavens did not become tired. Indeed, the verbs "to work" and "to rest" can only be applied to him figuratively.

This revelation came under Moses, but it refers to a time before the Mosaic covenant was instituted.[5] That the sovereign Lord, by whose powerful word all things came into being, rested on the seventh day was meant to be startling. It was meant to say that the pattern of working and resting is built into the nature of things. The six days are meant for labor and for the fulfilling of our vocation.[6] The Sabbath is set aside for worship, rest, and love of neighbor. Further, that a day was set aside as holy (קדשׁ) even *before the fall* is most significant. There was, as yet, no corruption in the garden. Everything was ritually and morally clean, and yet one day out of seven was consecrated, set aside for rest and worship, which means that God built this pattern of working and resting into the nature of things. We know this is the correct interpretation because the Lord himself revealed it in Exodus 20:11: "Because [כִּי] in six days Yahweh made heaven and earth, the sea, and all that is in them, and rested on the seventh day. Therefore Yahweh blessed the Sabbath day and made it holy." At Sinai, God explained that the Saturday Sabbath pattern being instituted under Moses in Israel was grounded in the prior and fundamental *creational* pattern.[7] The Decalogue was a restatement of the prior, more foundational, permanent creational law. All humans should observe the creational six-and-one pattern in the same way that all humans should observe the moral law concerning respecting authority, against sexual immorality, against theft, against lying, and against coveting. The Sabbath pattern is just as permanent, just as built into the nature of things, just as universal as they are.

---

5. Remarkably, in disputation 21, "On the Sabbath and the Lord's Day," in the *Synopsis Purioris Theologiae*, we read, "But it is not entirely clear when that day was established, or to whom it was commanded; that is, whether it was presented to mankind as a whole already from the beginning, even before the fall into sin (i.e., when the world was created) or whether in fact it was ordained late for the Jewish people, at the time when the law was given through Moses" (*Synopsis purioris* 21.13, in te Velde, van den Belt, and van Asselt, *Synopsis Purioris Theologiae*, 1.521).

6. Ursinus, *Corpus doctrinae*, 569.

7. It seems that Cocceius also denied that the Sabbath is grounded in creation (Carmichael, *Continental View*, 148–49).

When some Pharisees asked our Lord about marriage and divorce in heaven he said, "Because of your hardness of heart Moses allowed you to divorce your wives, but from the beginning it was not so" (Matt 19:8 ESV). He addressed the Sabbath in the same way. Our Lord confirmed this understanding when he refuted the Pharisees' corruption of the Sabbath by reminding them, "The Sabbath was made for man, not man for the Sabbath. So the Son of Man is Lord of the Sabbath" (Mark 2:27). When was the Sabbath made for man? In creation. There is a creational pattern, of which the Sabbath is a part. We should not expect the creational pattern to be revoked but renewed, as in the case of our Lord's teaching on marriage and the Sabbath. Our Lord normed the Mosaic law with creation. In other words, the creation pattern (nature) is logically prior to Moses. The creational patterns are permanent. The old, Mosaic concessions were temporary.

A GRACIOUS PATTERN

The Sabbath is grounded in the creational pattern, but the Sabbath pattern was *also* restated, in Deuteronomy 5:12–15, to a redeemed covenant people. This time it was grounded in redemption. Thus, Christians, who have been redeemed from the Egypt of sin by Christ the Passover Lamb, have a double reason to observe this six-and-one pattern. Deuteronomy 5:15 reminds us that we should remember that we too were slaves, and thus we should remember those who work for us. In the new covenant, the Christian Sabbath is inaugurated in the new creation, in the resurrection of Christ (2 Cor 5:16–17; Gal 6:15). The typological pattern is replaced with the new covenant reality. The typological pattern is replaced by a one-and-six pattern. The new creation was inaugurated in the resurrection, and each new week begins on the first day with worship, rest, and service.

In the sixteenth century, Ursinus defended this creational view of the Sabbath pattern against those whom he called "the Anabaptists." In his context, to defend the Sabbath's abiding validity from creation and under multiple administrations of the covenant of grace, Ursinus distinguished between the Sabbath as instituted *immediately* under Moses and the Christian Sabbath as instituted *mediately*, that is, by Christ, through the apostles. Thus, Ursinus explains: "Yet we must not suppose that we are restricted or tied down either to Saturday, Wednesday, or any other day. The apostolic church, to distinguish itself from the Jewish synagogue, chose, in the exercise of the liberty conferred upon it by Christ, the first day of the week in the place of the seventh, because on that day the resurrection of Christ took place, by which the internal and spiritual Sabbath is begun in us."[8] Although using language that has caused some to see a rejection among some Reformed (e.g., Calvin) that Christ instituted a particular day of the week as Christian Sabbath, the sixteenth-century context reveals a complex background that explains a greater unity.[9] For Ursinus, as for Calvin, the mediated institution of the Sabbath is a real institution, and it is connected to a definitive saving act in history: the bodily resurrection of Christ. Against the Anabaptists, Ursinus responds, "The distinction between days is not prohibited to Christians *simpliciter*, but with the opinion of worship or the necessity of observance."[10] His expression "opinion of necessity or worship" refers to what the Synod of Dort called "rigid observance," which was "prescribed particularly for the Jewish people," and his category of immediate divine imposition.[11]

In the wider background, the medieval church calendar as it had developed by the sixteenth century was complex, layered, and burdensome. The church began with the major liturgical seasons, Advent, Christmas, Lent, Easter, Ascension, Pentecost, Trinity. To that layer the church added days between the holidays (so-called ordinary days). The church later added saints' days. By the fourteenth century, every day of the year had a saint's day attached. The medieval church year and calendar, should a Christian attempt to keep it rigorously as Christians were meant to keep it, as a matter of obligation, was far more burdensome than the old Israelite religious calendar under Moses and David. Further, the Reformed also had to contend with a group of Judaizing "Seventh Day" Anabaptists, who held to the Saturday Sabbath.[12] Then there were the antinomians, who argued that the moral law was no longer in force. In contrast, Ursinus

8. Ursinus, *Commentary*, 563.

9. E.g., Calvin, *Institutes* 2.8.33–34. On Luther and Calvin's view of the Sabbath, see Clark, *Recovering the Reformed Confession*, 309–15.

10. "Prohibetur Christianis discrminen dierum non simplicter, sed cum opinione cultus vel necessitatis observatum" (Ursinus, *Corpus doctrinae*, 576).

11. Godfrey, *Saving the Reformation*, 239–40. The rules are given below.

12. Clark, *Recovering the Reformed Confession*, 309.

says, "But although the ceremonial Sabbath has been abolished in the New Testament, yet the moral still continues, and pertains to us as well as to others; for there is now just as much necessity for a certain time to be set apart in the Christian church for the preaching of God's word, and for the public administration of the sacraments, as there was formerly in the Jewish church."[13] He had a clear theological principle for his view of the Lord's Day.

Reformed theologians and churches had to work out their understanding of the Christian Sabbath against this complex background. We must remember also that Luther had inveighed against those who broke the Christian Sabbath.[14] Calvin's language in the *Institutes* must be read in light of his language in his biblical commentaries and in his sermons.[15] His students and successors did not understand him or the other early Reformed writers (e.g., Bullinger) as denying the six-and-one pattern or as denying the sacredness of the Christian Sabbath as a day of rest, worship, and alms. The Sabbatarians against whom Calvin complained were not Reformed adherents to the Christian Sabbath or Lord's Day.[16]

The predominant Reformed view was and is that Christ, by his resurrection, appointed Sunday as the Lord's Day and Christian Sabbath. Some have inferred from Paul's words in Romans 14:5—that one "person esteems one day as better than another, while another esteems all days alike" (ESV)—that Sunday does not officially have a particularly sacred role in the new covenant (other passages, e.g., Col 2:16, are sometimes also invoked).[17] For the Reformed, any sixteenth-century rhetoric that *seems* to suggest the same view must be read within the wider context of arguments against the Anabaptists and Roman church calendar. For us today, the specifically Mosaic ceremonies encompassing greater

13. Ursinus, *Commentary*, 563.

14. Clark, *Recovering the Reformed Confession*, 310.

15. Clark, *Recovering the Reformed Confession*, 309–15.

16. Thus, we should not be misled by F. L. Battles's anachronistic note to *Institutes* 2.8.32 (1:399n41), where he writes, "It is clear from this passage and from sec. 34 that for Calvin the Christian Sunday is not, as in the Westminster Confession XX.8, a simple continuation of the Jewish Sabbath" changed into the first day of the week.

17. Harrison Perkins engages this view in *Reformed Covenant Theology*, 38n76. For versions of this view, see Schreiner, "Good-Bye and Hello," 159–88; Carson, *From Sabbath to Lord's Day*. I am grateful to Harrison Perkins for his help with this section.

imposition of multiple feast days and festivals have gone away, but the obligation to worship God on the Lord's Day remains. In short, we are not under the types and shadows or the Jewish Sabbath laws, but those truths do not abrogate the Sabbath principle generally, nor the Christian Sabbath specifically.

SABBATH AND SABBATHS

Not infrequently the question arises about the relation between the weekly Sabbath and the "sabbaths" Paul mentions in Colossians 2:16–17, where Paul writes of "a feast, or new moons, or sabbaths."[18] It is sometimes assumed that Paul was referring here to the weekly Sabbath of Exodus 20 and Deuteronomy 5. When we consider all the evidence, however, the best conclusion is that Paul was not referring to the weekly Sabbath but to *monthly* features of the Israelite religious calendar.

The use of *feast* in this context is a clue to the Old Testament background of his expression. Specifically, the phrase "new moon and sabbaths" in Colossians 2:16 is not a reference to the weekly creational Sabbath. There were monthly feasts, new moons, and Sabbaths in the Israelite religious calendar, which were temporary and typological and not part of the creational pattern. Unlike the creational pattern, the monthly Israelite Sabbaths were never intended to be perpetual.

- "and whenever burnt offerings were offered to the LORD on Sabbaths, new moons, and feast days, according to the number required of them, regularly before the LORD" (1 Chr 23:31 ESV)
- "on the Sabbaths and the new moons and the appointed feasts of the LORD our God, as ordained forever for Israel" (2 Chr 2:4 ESV)
- "burnt offerings for the Sabbaths, the new moons, and the appointed feasts, as it is written in the Law of the LORD" (2 Chr 31:3 ESV)
- "for the showbread, the regular grain offering, the regular burnt offering, the Sabbaths, the new moons, the appointed

18. ἐν μέρει ἑορτῆς ἢ νεομηνίας ἢ σαββάτων (Col 2:16).

feasts, the holy things, and the sin offerings to make atonement for Israel, and for all the work of the house of our God" (Neh 10:33 ESV)

- "at the feasts, the new moons, and the Sabbaths, all the appointed feasts" (Ezek 45:17 ESV)
- "And I will put an end to all her mirth, her feasts, her new moons, her Sabbaths, and all her appointed feasts" (Hos 2:11 ESV)

In each instance, Colossians 2:16 uses the same nouns used in the LXX. Paul uses a form of the noun *Sabbath* that does not occur in the LXX. It occurs only once with the other key terms (*feasts, new moons*), which is decisive. When Paul writes "new moons and sabbaths," he is not referring to "the first of the Sabbath," which is usually translated "on the first day of the week."[19]

Because of the number of religions active in Colossae in the first century AD, it is difficult to know with certainty the exact opponents whom Paul was battling, but it is likely that they were Judaizers of some sort, who were devoted to angels and so on and who wanted to go back to the ceremonial law. They may well have synthesized their Judaism with some Greek ideas. At any rate, it is clear that when he invoked "shadow" (σκιὰ) in Colossians 2:17 to describe the monthly feast, new moons, and Sabbaths, Paul was not referring to the *creational* weekly Sabbath but to the ceremonial monthly "sabbaths and new moons" of the Israelite ritual calendar. The Colossians were in danger of being deluded by a philosophy that was attempting to lead them back to the types and shadows of the Israelite religious calendar.

EXPOSITION

There are two parts to the commandment: the commandment proper and its ground.[20] The commandment is the prohibition from servile labor and

19. Ἐν δὲ τῇ μιᾷ τῶν σαββάτων (Acts 1:7).

20. "Quarti praecpti duae sunt partes: *praeceptum et ratio praeceptii*" (Ursinus, *Corpus doctrinae*, 568; emphasis original).

to grant rest. The ground is the creational pattern.[21] There are two aspects to the commandment, that which is moral, that is, grounded in the divine nature and in creation and therefore perpetual, and that which is ceremonial.[22] The principle of rest and worship on one day of the week is "moral and perpetual," and the seventh-day Sabbath is ceremonial and temporary.[23] The essence of the commandment, rest and worship, is perpetual and moral not only because it is grounded in the divine nature and in the nature of creation but because its end is the "perpetual conservation of the public celebration of God in the church and the ecclesiastical ministry."[24]

The Jewish Sabbath was intentionally temporary and ceremonial. It was for the observance of "Mosaic worship."[25] It was a "sacrament, that is, a type of the sanctification of the church through the Messiah to come."[26] The Jewish Sabbath, that is, the seventh-day Sabbath, "was, together with the other ceremonies and types, fulfilled and abolished by the coming of the Messiah."[27]

The Synod of Dort adopted six rules for understanding the Christian Sabbath.[28]

Rules on the observation of the Sabbath, or the Lord's Day, with the agreement of the brothers from Zeeland the following concepts were explained and approved by Doctor Professors of Divinity.[29]

1. In the fourth commandment of the divine law, part is ceremonial, part is moral.

---

21. Ursinus, *Commentary*, 557; Ursinus, *Corpus doctrinae*, 568.

22. Ursinus, *Commentary*, 557; Ursinus, *Corpus doctrinae*, 568. On this distinction as applied to OT Sabbath legislation, see Junius, *Mosaic Polity*, 29–36, 71–85.

23. Ursinus, *Commentary*, 557; Ursinus, *Corpus doctrinae*, 568.

24. "*Finis* praecepti est publica Dei celebratio in ecclesia, et conservatio ministerii ecclesiastici perpetua" (Ursinus, *Corpus doctrinae*, 568).

25. Ursinus, *Commentary*, 557.

26. "Sacramentum, hoc est typum sanctificationis ecclesiae per Messiam venturum" (Ursinus, *Corpus doctrinae*, 568).

27. Ursinus, *Commentary*, 557–58.

28. The rules as presented here are translated by Godfrey in *Saving the Reformation*, 239–40, from the Latin text in Sinnema et al., *Acta Et Documenta*.

29. Session 164, May 17 p.m. This section is translated from Kuyper, *De Post-Acta of Nahandelingen*, 184–86.

2. The ceremonial was the rest of the seventh day after creation, and the rigid observance of that day peculiarly prescribed for the Jewish people.

3. [The] Moral truly is that certain and appointed day is fixed for the worship of God and so much rest as is necessary for the worship of God and for holy meditation on Him.

4. Since the abrogation of the Sabbath of the Jews, the day of the Lord must be solemnly sanctified by Christians.

5. This day has always been observed since the time of the Apostles by the ancient catholic church.

6. This day must be so consecrated to divine worship that on it one ceases from all servile works, except those of love and present necessity; and also from all such refreshing activities as impede the worship of God.[30]

These rules are eminently wise and sufficiently clear as to require only a little explanation. The "servile works" to which the synod refers is an established category among the Reformed. Ursinus explains and defines them thus:

> God does not prohibit the doing of works of all sorts but only such as are servile, i.e., impediments to the worship of God and the use of the ministry, which declaration is added elsewhere pronounced: "you shall do no ordinary work" etc. (Lev 23:25). Works indeed that are not an impediment to the use of Sabbath but rather works of the sort that glorify and confirm the worship of God, either the sacred ceremonies, love of neighbor and one's own life, or in some other way pertains to the necessity of another life, so that they are not able to be deferred, not only are they not prohibited on the Sabbath but most of all does the observance of the Sabbath require it.[31]

30. E.g., Wollebius, *Compendium*, 2.7.8.

31. "Opera vero, quae sabbati usum non impediunt, sed potius illustrant et confirmant, qualia sunt opera ad cultum Dei, sive ad caeremonias sacras, sive ad dilectionem proximi, et ad sive vel alienae vitae necesitatem sic pertinentia, ut in tempus liud reiici non possint, non modo sabbatho

The English word *servile* is a transliteration of the Latin adjective *servilis*.[32] It can denote menial labor, but in the context of Sabbath it signifies "work which is forbidden on the Sabbath and (according to some observances) on certain other days; typically understood as laborious or mechanical work, but sometimes including any kind of work that is carried out purely for personal gain."[33] That is the sense in which both Ursinus and the synod use it.[34]

THE PURPOSES OF THE CHRISTIAN SABBATH

The Christian faith has three parts: theology, piety, and practice. Theology is what we confess and teach the Scriptures to reveal. Piety is our relation to God. Practice is the outworking of those truths. The catechism addresses all three. Since we have laid out the framework of the Christian Sabbath, as grounded in both creation and redemption (nature and grace), let us consider the teaching of the catechism in particular as to the purposes of the Christian Sabbath:

1. THE MINISTRY OF THE GOSPEL

The Christian Sabbath (Lord's Day) is the one day in seven set aside for public worship and the official proclamation of the gospel and the administration of the keys of the kingdom. The egalitarian spirit of the age does not like to recognize special offices in the church, but the Reformed churches confess three such offices in the church: minister, elder, and deacon.[35] Paul uses the two different nouns to describe his office and that held by Tychicus and Epaphras: minister (λειτουργός, Rom 15:16; διάκονος, Eph 3:7; 6:21; Col 1:7; 4:7). He implicitly distinguishes Timothy from the elders and gives him distinct duties from the presbyters (2 Tim 4:1–4) so

non prohibet, sed maxime ad observationem eius requirit" (Ursinus, *Corpus doctrinae*, 569). Willard's translation (Ursinus, *Commentary*, 558–59) paraphrases this paragraph.

32. *OED*, s.v. "servile."

33. *OED*, s.v. "servile."

34. "And so what is forbidden is any work or business that we undertake: business that is servile, that involves machinery, that is laborious, that brings in a profit, work that is daily or ordinary. Both private and public work are included, that is, what we are used to perform either on our own or in public (Isaiah 58:3[,13])" (*Synopsis Purioris Theologiae*, 21.27, in te Velde, van den Belt, and van Asselt, *Synopsis Purioris Theologiae*, 1.529–31).

35. *BC* 30–31, in United Reformed Churches in North America, *Liturgical Forms and Prayers*, 187–88.

that he is fairly classed with the pastors rather than the elders. The New Testament distinctly describes the offices of elder (Acts 11:30; 14:23; 15:2, 4, 6, 22; 16:4; 20:17; 21:18; 22:5; 23:14; 24:4; 25:15; Titus 1:5; 1 Tim 4:14; 5:17, 19; 1 Pet 5:1) and deacon (Acts 6:1–6; Phil 1:1; 1 Tim 3:8, 10, 12). The administration of the gospel belongs to the office of minister (or pastor). The oversight of the ministry belongs to the elders, and to the deacons belongs the administration of the ministry of mercy in the congregation.

By the administration of the gospel, God is celebrated publicly, the "piety and faith of the elect is excited and fostered by public exercises," believers are mutually edified in the faith of the gospel, and they provoke one another to piety.[36] Agreement in doctrine and the worship of God is preserved. When we gather for worship, the church is made visible before the world and shown to be distinct from it.[37]

2. SCHOOLS MAINTAINED

When the catechism mentions schools, it alludes to the necessity of the education of ministers, which is essential to the ministry of the gospel. Ursinus explains, "The maintenance of schools may be embraced under this part of the honor which is due to the ministry; for unless the arts and sciences be taught, men can neither become properly qualified to teach, nor can the purity of doctrine be preserved and defended against the assaults of heretics."[38] That the maintenance of schools is mentioned in the catechism witnesses to the Reformed conviction that our ministers must be learned. This conviction is our inheritance from the broad Christian tradition. The Reformation churches struggled mightily to educate ministers so that they could read God's word in its original languages and preach the law and gospel faithfully.[39] The revivalist and Pietist traditions have tended to devalue an educated ministry, and the Reformed

36. Ursinus, *Corpus doctrinae*, 568. "Piety and faith of the elect is excited and fostered by public exercises" translates "pietas et fides electorum publicis exercitiis excitetur et foveatur."

37. Ursinus, *Corpus doctrinae*, 568.

38. Ursinus, *Commentary*, 570.

39. Apropos of Ursinus's concern for the official ministry of word and sacrament: "Moderation and allowance in bearing such infirmities and imperfections of ministers as do not greatly and evidently corrupt and impede the objects of the ministry, and injure the church by giving offence. 'Against an elder receive not an accusation, but before two or three witnesses' (1 Tim. 5:19)" (Ursinus, *Commentary*, 570).

churches have not always succeeded in resisting the siren song of pragmatism in this regard.

3. REST

By "rest" the catechism refers to a fundamental break with the work week. It means to stop our business, our commercial activity, and even organized sports. The point is not to bind the conscience but to remind us that the Lord's Day is distinct from the other six days. The guidance provided by the synod is most useful here. It may tend to infringe on Christian liberty to forbid "refreshing activities" *between* worship services, but it contradicts the intent of the fourth commandment to engage in work or sport that interferes with attendance at public worship and the means of grace, prayer, and charity toward one's neighbor in need.[40]

4. WORSHIP

Worship refers to the public assembly of God's people in stated services. Christ has granted to his church authority to call God's people together for public worship on the Christian Sabbath (Lord's Day). God's people ought to long to be together (*communio sanctorum*) to call on God's name. In worship the Lord speaks to his people through the word, and they respond to him with his word. It is a holy dialogue from which, barring extraordinary circumstances, a Christian ought not to be absent.

5. LEARNING GOD'S WORD

Christian education encompasses catechetical instruction in the congregation. This brief but pregnant reference to education witnesses to the Reformed conviction that not only must the ministry be educated but also the congregation. The fourth commandment "requires all those who are called to teach in the church, faithfully to deliver and expound sound doctrine, both publicly to those who assemble together for the purpose of receiving instruction and to everyone privately as occasion and necessity may admit and require."[41] The catechetical instruction of baptized

---

40. Ursinus writes of a "certain time set apart in the church for the preaching of the word and for the administration of the sacraments, or for the public worship of God, during which time there is a suspension or abstinence from all other works" (*Commentary*, 562).

41. Ursinus, *Commentary*, 567.

children prior to profession of faith and communion was thorough (e.g., they memorized the *HC*), and it was preached in catechism sermons in the afternoon.[42]

6. USING THE SACRAMENTS

We also gather to hear the announcement of the law and the gospel and to participate in the sacraments. In the word we are grounded again in objective, divinely revealed reality. We are reconnected to God's free grace earned for us by Christ and as revealed to us in Christ. According to *BC* 29, the pure administration of the sacraments is one of the three marks of the true church.[43]

7. PRAYER

One advantage of setting aside one day in seven is that we there is space and time for both private and public prayer, "in which we united our own confession, thanksgiving and prayer with the church; for God will not only be invoked by everyone privately, but also publicly by the whole church, for his own glory and our comfort."[44] The Christian Sabbath is the divinely ordained day set aside for corporate and private prayer. Communing with God, around his word together as congregations, as families at table, and privately is essential to Christian piety. Without setting aside time, the practice of prayer tends to wither and become infrequent.

8. WORKS OF MERCY

The Lord's Day is also a day for mercy. When our Lord healed the man with the withered hand on the Jewish Sabbath (Matt 12:9–14), when he declared, "The Sabbath was made for man, not man for the Sabbath" (Mark 2:27), and when he allowed the disciples to pluck grain on the Sabbath (Luke 6:1–5), he was restoring essential aspects of the Sabbath as God instituted it. The Sabbath was always *for humanity*, that is, for humanity's benefit. Even before the fall the Sabbath pointed Adam to the future

42. Clark, *Recovering the Reformed Confession*, 293–95.

43. United Reformed Churches in North America, *Liturgical Forms and Prayers*, 186; Ursinus, *Commentary*, 568. See the discussion under *HC* 65.

44. Ursinus, *Commentary*, 569.

state of blessed communion with God.[45] After the fall, the Sabbath continued to point us to everlasting communion with God, in the Mediator. It is also a time of healing and renewal. It is a time of feeding the hungry. The Son of Man *is* Lord of the Sabbath. Thus, the official ministry of mercy of the church is directed to the church, but certainly Christians in the capacity as believers and private persons are obligated to show mercy to all of God's image-bearers (humans) and to other creatures as well. The Christian Sabbath is a day for showing mercy to those in need in our congregations and beyond.[46] Mercy takes time, and the Sabbath is that time.

9. SANCTIFICATION

Our doctrine of sanctification is that it is the work of the Spirit within us, in light of the gospel that Christ is *for* us. It is gradual and never completed in this life.[47] Sanctification takes time, and the Lord's Day is time specifically set aside by God for worship, prayer, and acts of mercy. It leads to the use of the divinely ordained means of grace, which the Spirit uses tolead us into conformity to Christ. The Christian Sabbath is a day for contemplating the greatness of our sin and misery outside Christ and the wonder of God's grace to us in Christ. It is the divinely ordained day for giving ourselves over to being sanctified. We are daily seeking to die to sin and to be renewed in grace, but on the Lord's Day we are able to devote ourselves to it uniquely.

10. ANTICIPATING HEAVEN

Finally, the Christian Sabbath is a day for anticipating the new heavens and the new earth. Some, perhaps many, think that the new heavens and earth are principally a renewal of our cultural life, but the picture we get from Scripture is rather different, and our catechism leads to think of the new heavens and the new earth more in cultic (worship) terms than cultural terms. The first image we get of heaven, in Revelation 4:1–11, is decidedly religious, and it sets the pattern for the rest of the book. The church victorious and the angels are at worship, not at work. The Lord's

45. See the discussion under *HC* 6.

46. Ursinus, *Commentary*, 569.

47. See the discussion under *HC* 88–90.

Day is an anticipation of being before the face of the living God (*coram Deo*), which is the consummation of what was intended in the covenant of works: blessed communion with God. Sin ruined that, but grace is restoring us and preparing us for that communion, which Christ earned for his elect.

Question 104

What does God require in the fifth commandment?

Lord's Day 39

Question 104

What does God require in the fifth commandment?

That I show all honor, love and faithfulness to my father and mother, and to all in authority over me; submit myself with due obedience to all their good instruction and correction, and also bear patiently with their infirmities, since it is God's will to govern us by their hand.[1]

With the fifth commandment, we turn to the second table of the law.[2] Under the second table we think directly about our duties to our fellow image-bearers and secondarily about our duties to God.[3] Our Lord summarized the essence of the second table in one sentence: "You shall love your neighbor as yourself" (Lev 19:18; Matt 22:39). In the fall we broke the fifth commandment in the first instance by rebelling directly against God. God commanded Adam to submit to his revealed will and through that submission to show love to God and to his neighbor and to all for whom he was the federal head (Rom 5:12–21; 1 Cor 15:45). Since the fall humans have carried on Adam's ignominious tradition. Cain rebelled against worshiping God truly and, in a jealous rage, murdered his brother, who did worship God truly (Gen 4:1–8). The world that then was (2 Pet 3:6) became so rebellious against God that he wiped clean the slate, as it were, and started over.

Rebellion against God manifests itself in rebellion against divinely instituted human authorities, which has become a mark of the modern period. Since Jean-Jacques Rousseau, the post-Christian West has gradually rejected most established authorities and all social hierarchies.[4] It

1. "Was will Gott im fünsten Gebot? Dass ich meinem Vater und Mutter, und allen, die mir vorgesetzt sind, alle Ehre, Liebe und Treue beweisen, und mich aller guten Lehre und Strafe mit gebührlichem Gehorsam unterwerfen, und auch mit ihren Gebrechen Geduld haben soll, dieweil uns Gott durch ihre Hand regieren will" (Schaff, *Creeds of Christendom*, 3:345). "Quid nobis iniungit Deus in quinto praecepto? Ut parentibus, atque adeo omnibus qui nobis praesunt debitum honorem amorem et fidem praestemus, nosque ipsorum fidelibus praeceptis et castiga ionibus ea, qua par est, obedientia submittamus: Tum etiam, ut eorum vitia et mores nostra patientia toleremus, illud semper cogitantes, Deum nos illorum manu velle ducere ac regere" (Niemeyer, *Collectio Confessionum*, 455).

2. Ursinus, *Commentary*, 574.

3. Ursinus used the categories "mediate" and "immediate" (Ursinus, *Corpus doctrinae*, 584).

4. Trueman, *Rise and Triumph*, 105–28.

bristles against the assertion of even the most basic and lawful authority. In the fifth commandment, however, God asserts that he, as the supreme authority, has instituted lesser authorities, to whom we owe not mere grudging obedience but a "debt of honor, love, and faith" (*debitum honorem amorem et fidem*).[5] Among those to whom we owe fidelity are parents, civil authorities, and ecclesiastical authorities.

As with the other commandments, in the fifth commandment there are two parts: duties and prohibitions. Our duty to divinely instituted authorities is to submit and honor or to honor and submit. The prohibition is implied in the conditional promise, "that your days may be long." The commandment prohibits us from dishonoring and disobeying those whom God has placed in authority over us. There are, in the divine administration of the world, *superiors* and *inferiors*, not relative to inherent human dignity but relative to the office we occupy.[6]

Our parents are first among those to whom we owe obedience, but the list of authorities to whom we must submit does not end there. Indeed, Ursinus calls the fifth commandment "the foundation, cause, and bond of obedience to all the other commandments" in the second table.[7] In Scripture we see the fifth commandment reflected in the Old Testament judicial laws, for example,

> If a man has a stubborn and rebellious son who will not obey the voice of his father or the voice of his mother, and, though they discipline him, will not listen to them, then his father and his mother shall take hold of him and bring him out to the elders of his city at the gate of the place where he lives, and they shall say to the elders of his city, "This our son is stubborn and rebellious; he will not obey our voice; he is a glutton and a drunkard." Then all the men of the city shall stone him to death with stones. So you shall purge the evil from your midst, and all Israel shall hear, and fear. (Deut 21:18–21 ESV)

5. Niemeyer, *Collectio Confessionum*, 455.
6. Ursinus, *Corpus doctrinae*, 575.
7. Ursinus, *Commentary*, 575.

That legislation and such judicial punishments expired with the death of Christ.[8]

Nevertheless, Deuteronomy 21 illustrates the Lord's attitude toward disobedience to parents. That same principle is expressed in the New Testament. In Ephesians 6:1 Paul speaks directly to the fifth commandment: "Children, obey your parents in the Lord, for this is right." We have a divinely inspired application of the fifth commandment in Ephesians 6:2–4: "'Honor your father and mother' (this is the first commandment with a promise), 'that it may go well with you and that you may live long in the land.' Fathers, do not provoke your children to anger, but bring them up in the discipline and instruction of the Lord" (ESV).

Note how Paul interprets the fifth commandment by paraphrasing it. He quotes it but then changes the promise from "that your days may be long in the land Yahweh your God is giving you" to "that it may go well with you and that you may live long in the land." This is a clear indication of the nature of the progress of revelation and redemption from the old covenant to the new. There is now no national people of God, and there are no more national promises. There is no earthly promised land, and therefore the nature of the promise has changed from the typological land promise to the general equity of the fifth commandment. Believers are the Israel of God (Gal 6:16). We have no land promise since Christ is the land, the rest (Heb 4:8–13), and has broken down the dividing wall between Jew and gentile (Eph 2:14).

Paul turns what was a temporary promise to national Israel into a general principle for Christians. We obey those in authority over us in order that it may go generally well with us, namely that we will be able to live quiet, godly lives without interference from the authorities (1 Tim 2:2). This is the language of general axiom and not an absolute promise.

There are others to whom we must submit: "tutors and guardians of students," "schoolteachers, teachers and ministers of the church," "higher and lower civil authorities," and elders.[9] All these offices act "in the place of parents."[10]

8. See the discussion under *HC* 92.

9. "2. *Tutores* et curatores pupillorum. 3. *Praeceptores*, doctores, ministri ecclesiae. 4. *Magistratus* superiores et inferiores. 5. *Seniores*" (Ursinus, *Corpus doctrinae*, 585; italics original).

10. "Quia hos omnes Deus nobis dat parentum loco" (Ursinus, *Corpus doctrinae*, 585).

Paul also applies the fifth commandment to an administrative order within the family: "Wives, submit to your own husbands, as to the Lord. For the husband is the head of the wife even as Christ is the head of the church, his body, and is himself its Savior. Now as the church submits to Christ, so also wives should submit in everything to their husbands" (Eph 5:22–24 ESV). These are challenging words, of course, in a postfeminist world. They do not teach an order of being (ontology) among males and females, but they do reflect a divinely intended order. Peter teaches the same principle of complementary relations between husbands and wives:

> Likewise, wives, be subject to your own husbands, so that even if some do not obey the Word, they may be won without a word by the conduct of their wives, when they see your respectful and pure conduct. Do not let your adorning be external—the braiding of hair and the putting on of gold jewelry, or the clothing you wear—but let your adorning be the hidden person of the heart with the imperishable beauty of a gentle and quiet spirit, which in God's sight is very precious. For this is how the holy women who hoped in God used to adorn themselves, by submitting to their own husbands, as Sarah obeyed Abraham, calling him lord. And you are her children, if you do good and do not fear anything that is frightening. (1 Pet 3:1–6 ESV modified)

This is an area where Christians have an opportunity to be distinct from the prevailing culture *both* by respecting the creational order *and* by showing godly, biblical mutual support and love. This is what Paul says in Ephesians 5:

> Husbands, love your wives, as Christ loved the church and gave himself up for her, that he might sanctify her, having cleansed her by the washing of water with the word, so that he might present the church to himself in splendor, without spot or wrinkle or any such thing, that she might be holy and without blemish. In the same way husbands should love their wives as their own bodies. He who loves his wife loves himself. For no one ever hated his own flesh, but nourishes and cherishes it, just as Christ does the church, because we are members of his body. "Therefore a man

> shall leave his father and mother and hold fast to his wife, and the two shall become one flesh." This mystery is profound, and I am saying that it refers to Christ and the church. However, let each one of you love his wife as himself, and let the wife see that she respects her husband. (Eph 5:25–33 ESV)

Again Peter teaches the very same thing: "Likewise, husbands, live with your wives in an understanding way, showing honor to the woman as the weaker vessel, since they are heirs with you of the grace of life, so that your prayers may not be hindered" (1 Pet 3:7 ESV).

As Christians seek to reassert creational and biblical patterns of living in our late modern age, it is imperative that we do not overreact. We seek properly to insist that

- There is a creational, natural order.
- Creational order can be determined by looking carefully at creation.
- There are two sexes (male and female).
- The two sexes are distinct and complementary.

In an age when gender-neutral restrooms and speech codes penalize any recognition of biological differences between the sexes, we are better served by being careful about how we assert the differences between males and females. Further, the assumptions of the Victorian era lingered well into the 1950s and 1960s.[11] There was a time when Christians could assume a broader social sympathy with the idea of creational order, but that assumption is no longer tenable in the late modern West.

There are other implications of this commandment on which the New Testament reflects explicitly. For example, the apostle Paul speaks directly to the relationship between employers and employees.

> Bondservants, obey your earthly masters with fear and trembling, with a sincere heart, as you would Christ, not by the way of eye-service, as people-pleasers, but as bondservants of Christ,

11. Miller, *Beyond Authority and Submission*, 61–75.

> doing the will of God from the heart, rendering service with a good will as to the Lord and not to man, knowing that whatever good anyone does, this he will receive back from the Lord, whether he is a bondservant or is free. Masters, do the same to them, and stop your threatening, knowing that he who is both their Master and yours is in heaven, and that there is no partiality with him. (Eph 6:5–9 ESV)

We are not slaves, as some of the first-century Christians were, to whom Paul wrote in Ephesus, but those of us who work for others are not utterly free either. It does not take much imagination to see the parallels. Should one refuse to do what one's supervisor tells one to do, one will not likely be employed very long with that company. Even those who are self-employed will testify that they have plenty of masters to whom they must give account. Bosses and masters are not without accountability, since they too, according to Paul, will have to give account to their heavenly Master. The apostle Peter writes similar instructions, in virtually identical language, to the churches in Asia Minor (1 Pet 2:18–25).

A third sphere in which we must submit is in civil life. Again, the apostle Paul gave us an explicit application of the fifth commandment:

> Let every person be subject to the governing authorities. For there is no authority except from God, and those that exist have been instituted by God. Therefore whoever resists the authorities resists what God has appointed, and those who resist will incur judgment. For rulers are not a terror to good conduct, but to bad. Would you have no fear of the one who is in authority? Then do what is good, and you will receive his approval, for he is God's servant for your good. But if you do wrong, be afraid, for he does not bear the sword in vain. For he is the servant of God, an avenger who carries out God's wrath on the wrongdoer. Therefore one must be in subjection, not only to avoid God's wrath but also for the sake of conscience. For because of this you also pay taxes, for the authorities are ministers of God, attending to this very thing. Pay to all what is owed to them: taxes to whom taxes are owed, revenue to whom revenue is owed, respect to whom respect is owed, honor to whom honor is owed. (Rom 13:1–7 ESV)

And again in Titus 3: "Remind them to be submissive to rulers and authorities, to be obedient, to be ready for every good work, to speak evil of no one, to avoid quarreling, to be gentle, and to show perfect courtesy toward all people. For we ourselves were once foolish, disobedient, led astray, slaves to various passions and pleasures, passing our days in malice and envy, hated by others and hating one another" (Titus 3:1–3 ESV). The apostle Peter is also very clear about our obligation as Christians to the civil magistrate:

> Be subject for the Lord's sake to every human institution, whether it be to the emperor as supreme, or to governors as sent by him to punish those who do evil and to praise those who do good. For this is the will of God, that by doing good you should put to silence the ignorance of foolish people. Live as people who are free, not using your freedom as a cover-up for evil, but living as servants of God. Honor everyone. Love the brotherhood. Fear God. Honor the emperor. (1 Pet 2:13–17 ESV)

Paul and Peter were articulating what is known as "distributive justice," which is distinct from "universal justice," which superiors owe to inferiors and the latter to the former.[12] Under distributive justice, the magistrate has a responsibility to give to the righteous what is theirs. In theological terms we could call this a sort of covenant of works.[13] Nevertheless, it is a historical fact that the Caesars under whom the New Testament was written, whether Claudius, Nero, or Vespasian, could be quite cruel and often unjust. When Paul wrote to the church at Rome to submit to Caesar as God's minister (διάκονός; Rom 13:4), he was instructing believers to submit to a reprobate whom even the pagan Romans found disgusting. Nevertheless, God, in his sovereign providence, placed Nero and the other Caesars in power and called Christians to submit to them.

---

12. "Universal justice" translates "iustitia universalis" (Ursinus, *Corpus doctrinae*, 589). "Distributive justice" translates "iustitia particularis sive distributiva" (589; Ursinus, *Commentary*, 580).

13. Strict distributive justice should be tempered by *aequitas* (Ursinus, *Corpus doctrinae*, 591), the virtue, when there is probable cause "lessens the rigor of strict justice." See Calvin, *Calvin's Commentary on Seneca's De Clementia*.

The fifth commandment requires us to regard an *office*, not a *person*.[14] This is not an easy thing for sinners, and perhaps it is particularly difficult for Americans, for whom the rebellious impulse is particularly strong. The experience of the first-century Christians was not that of rebellion but of martyrdom at the hands of wicked rulers.[15]

In the Middle Ages, a theory of resistance to tyrannical or corrupt popes developed.[16] In the sixteenth century, Protestants elaborated on William of Ockham's theory of resistance to tyrants.[17] Calvin argues a conservative position, that lesser magistrates have a divinely given right or authority to keep tyrants in check.[18] In the face of war of the French crown against the Reformed, Theodore Beza and others argued that tyrants disqualify themselves from submission. Arguably, when the American colonies rebelled against the British crown, those elected representatives who led the rebellion against the British crown and Parliament were lesser magistrates. However beneficial a certain rebelliousness may have been or may be in civil life—since in a democratic republic one of the offices of the people is to act as a check against the unbridled exercise of authority—in the church rebellion is very destructive.

Christians are to be marked by a certain reverence for divinely ordained authorities. Paul submitted to wicked Nero. The apostle John was exiled by a wicked Caesar (Domitian). The early Christians were pursued and martyred by evil rulers. Our major defense was that we were no threat to the existing civil order but rather only sought to be left alone to worship and live quietly.[19] Of course, we do not live in a monarchy but in a republic, and we have duties as citizens of that republic. Our civil magistrates also have duties to their citizens, chief among which is to keep the peace and to seek justice according to the moral and natural

14. *Pace* Calvin, *Institutes* 4.20.28. We should be more careful than sixteenth-century authors typically were in drawing straight lines between the kings of Israel and postcanonical kings.

15. Calvin, *Institutes* 4.20.24, 26.

16. E.g., Tierney, *Ockham, the Conciliar Theory*; Ozment, *Age of Reform*, 157–64, 419–22.

17. E.g., Languet, *Vindiciae Contra Tyrannos*; Franklin, *Constitutionalism and Resistance*; Beza, *Concerning the Rights*; Althusius, *Politica*.

18. Calvin, *Institutes* 4.20.29.

19. E.g., *Ad Diognetum* 5:4–17; 7:3–9 in Holmes, *Apostolic Fathers*, 702–3, 706–7; Justin Martyr, *First Apology* 1–7, 11, 17 (*ANF* 1:163–66, 168).

law of God in the second table.[20] Justice requires that the civil magistrate "defend those who obey and coercing and punishing those who violate civil discipline."[21] It is the civil magistrate's duty to enact "positive laws" (*leges positivas*), which are applications of natural law that prescribe particular duties.[22] They are obligated to execute the laws they prescribe.[23]

Another sphere in which Christians must apply the fifth commandment is in the visible, institutional church. Indeed, after Christendom, the church has no coercive authority or power. Thus, modern Christians think themselves free to ignore her discipline. Nevertheless, despite all our natural resistance to authority and despite our suspicion of the church, the fact is that our Lord Jesus instituted the very visible church against which we so easily rebel. That the visible church has definite, delegated authority from the Christ is clear:

> Simon Peter replied, "You are the Christ, the Son of the living God." And Jesus answered him, "Blessed are you, Simon Bar-Jonah! For flesh and blood has not revealed this to you, but my Father who is in heaven. And I tell you, you are Peter, and on this rock I will build my church, and the gates of hell shall not prevail against it. I will give you the keys of the kingdom of heaven, and whatever you bind on earth shall be bound in heaven, and whatever you loose on earth shall be loosed in heaven." Then he strictly charged the disciples to tell no one that he was the Christ. (Matt 16:16–20 ESV)

To the apostles and the visible church, Christ gave the keys of the kingdom. Just two chapters later, our Lord explained in detail how he intended for those keys to be used. In Matthew 18:17–20 it is the visible church that is binding, loosing, and agreeing. Our Lord is speaking in terms borrowed from the Old Testament. The word for "church" (ἐκκλησίᾳ) is the very

20. Here we must dissent from Ursinus, who reflected the ancient assumption that the magistrate had a role in enforcing *both* tables of the Decalogue (e.g., Ursinus, *Commentary*, 578; Ursinus, *Corpus doctrinae*, 587). There is simply no warrant for such an assumption in the NT or in the early patristic authors.

21. "Defendendo servantes, coercendo ac puniendo violantes disciplinam" (Ursinus, *Corpus doctrinae*, 587).

22. Ursinus, *Corpus doctrinae*, 587; *OED*, s.v. "positive."

23. Ursinus, *Corpus doctrinae*, 588.

word the Greek translation of the Hebrew Scriptures uses to translate the Hebrew word (קָהָל) for covenant assembly.

It is against this background that we best interpret the exhortation by the writer to the Hebrews when he says: "Obey your leaders and submit to them, for they are keeping watch over your souls, as those who will have to give an account. Let them do this with joy and not with groaning, for that would be of no advantage to you" (Heb 13:17 ESV). The leaders to whom he refers are ecclesiastical, not secular. Paul wrote to the Thessalonian congregation about the reality of ecclesiastical authority: "If anyone does not obey what we say in this letter, take note of that person, and have nothing to do with him, that he may be ashamed" (2 Thess 3:14 ESV).

Nevertheless, there are limits on ecclesiastical authority. This visible church is bound first of all to God's word (*sola Scriptura*). The church is a servant of or minister of God's word. Therefore, it has no authority to command or act contrary to that word. Further, in Reformed and Presbyterian churches, there are church orders or constitutions that limit the authority of the visible church and its officers. When, however, the church, in its officers, is acting and teaching according to the word of God, within its ordained authority, believers have a duty before God to submit to it even when it is unpleasant.

The root of our struggle with submission in church, at work, and at home is resentment. That is why the catechism is so helpful. We are to bear with the infirmities of those who rule over us in the home, in civil government, at work, and even in the visible church. Those who rule over us are sinners. They are not perfect, and we may not expect them to be. In this sense we must learn to see them as Christ's servants for our good. The more we look at them as Christ's servants and the less we consider their persons, the easier it will be for us to submit to them.

QUESTION 105

What does God require in the sixth commandment?

QUESTION 106

Does this Commandment speak only of murder?

QUESTION 107

But is this all that is required, that we do not murder our neighbor?

Lord's Day 40

QUESTIONS 105–7

What does God require in the sixth commandment?
That I do not revile, hate, insult or kill my neighbor either in thought, word, or gesture, much less in deed, whether by myself or by another, but lay aside all desire of revenge; moreover, that I do not harm myself, nor willfully run into any danger. Wherefore also to restrain murder the magistrate is armed with the sword.[1]

Does this Commandment speak only of murder?
No, but in forbidding murder, God teaches us that he abhors its very root, namely: envy, hatred, anger, and desire of revenge; and that in his sight all these are hidden murder.[2]

But is this all that is required, that we do not murder our neighbor?
No, for in condemning envy, hatred, and anger, God requires us to love our neighbor as ourselves, to show patience, peace, meekness, mercy, and kindness toward him, and to prevent his hurt as much as possible; also to do good even unto our enemies.[3]

---

1. "Was will Gott im sechsten Gebot? Dass ich meinen Nächsten weder mit Gedanken, noch mit Worten oder Geberden, viel weniger mit der That, durch mich selbst oder Andere, schmähen, hassen, beleidigen oder tödten; sondern alle Rachgierigkeit ablegen, auch mich selbst nicht beschädigen, oder muthwillig in Gefahr begeben soll. Darum auch die Obrigkeit, dem Todtschlag zu wehren, das Schwert trägt" (Schaff, *Creeds of Christendom*, 3:346). "Quid Deus flugitat in sexto praecepto? Ut proximum neque cogitatione, neque verbis, neque gestibus, nedum factis, vel per me vel per alium, contumelia afficiam, aut oderim, aut laedam, aut occidam: Sed omnem vindictae cupiditatem abiiciam. Ad haec ne me ipsum laedam, aut sciens in aliquod periculum coniiciam. Quocirca etiam ne caedes fierent, Magistratum gladio armavit" (Niemeyer, *Collectio Confessionum*, 455).

2. "Redet doch diess Gebot allein vom Tödten. Es will uns aber Gott durch Verbietung des Todtschlags lehren, dass Er die Wurzel des Todtschlags, als Neid, Hass, Zorn, Rachgierigkeit, hasset, und dass solches alles vor ihm ein heimlicher Todtschlag sei (Schaff, *Creeds of Christendom*, 3:346). "Atqui hoc praeceptum solam caedem prohibere videtur? At caedem prohibendo, docet Deus, se radicem et originem caedis, iram scilicet, invidiam, odium, et vindictae cupiditatem odisse, atque ea omnia pro caede ducere" (Niemeyer, *Collectio Confessionum*, 456).

3. "Ist's aber damit genug, dass wir unsern Nächsten, wie gemeldet, nicht tödten? Nein: denu indem Gott Neid, Hass und Zorn verdammt, will Er von uns haben, dass wir unsern Nächsten lieben, als uns selbst, gegen ihn Geduld, Friede, Sanftmuth, Barmherzigkeit und Freundlichkeit erzeigen, seinen Schaden, so viel uns möglich, abwenden, und auch unsern Feinden Gutes thun" (Schaff, *Creeds of Christendom*, 3:346). "An vero id satis est, non neminem eo quo dictum est, modo, occidere? Non est satis: Dum enim Deus iram, invidiam, odium damnat, postulat, ut proximum aeque ac nos ipsos diligamus, et ut humanitate, lenitate, mansuetudine patientia, et misericordia erga eum

The preservation of life is at the center of Lord's Day 40. The correct application of the sixth commandment, however, requires us to be clear about exactly what is forbidden. Because some older English translations used the term *to kill* instead of *murder*, some have inferred that all killing is prohibited. Such an understanding, however, raises insuperable difficulties since God's word itself commands the taking of human life in some instances (e.g., Gen 9:6; Exod 21:12; Rom 13:4). The apostle Paul teaches us that the Lord Jesus, when he returns, will kill the lawless one "with the breath of his mouth" (2 Thess 2:8). The German text of the answer in *HC* 105 uses the generic verb *Tödten,* "to kill." The Latin text uses the same verb used by the Vulgate for the sixth commandment, *occido.* Both verbs can be used generically or specifically to refer to murder. Older English translations of the catechism translate the sixth commandment as "Thou shalt not kill."[4] That is how the Authorized Version (KJV) translated it in 1611.[5] In the pre-Reformation period, the Wycliffe Bible translated the commandment, "Thou schalt not sle."[6] The verb *sle* is Middle English for "slay." *Schalt* is a spelling variant of shall. In the early sixteenth century, Tyndale translated the sixth commandment as "Thou shalt not kyll."[7] The ASV (1901) followed the AV, as did the RSV in the mid-twentieth century. Since World War II, translations (e.g., NASB, NIV, ESV) have tended to use "murder" instead of "kill" in Exodus 20:13.

It is an interesting question why the translators of the AV used the verb *kill.* The Tyndale translation, from which the AV borrowed heavily, uses the word *murder* only twice. It uses *kill* much more frequently, even when the context referred to murder. The AV uses *kill* interchangeably with *murder* regularly. The verb *to murder* certainly existed, but it might not have been used as frequently as we use it now. The AV was also influenced by the Vulgate, which uses the verb *occido,* which may mean "to kill" or "to murder."[8]

---

utamur, quodque ei damno esse possit, quantum in nobis est, avertamus: Ad summam, ita animo affecti simus, ut ne inimicis quidem benefacere dubitemus" (Niemeyer, *Collectio Confessionum,* 456).

4. So the Tercentenary edition. See Schaff, *Creeds of Christendom,* 3:341.

5. *Holy Bible Conteyning.*

6. Wycliffe, *Holy Bible.*

7. Daniell, *Tyndale's Old Testament.*

8. *Biblia Vulgata.*

The Latin text of *HC* 106 clarifies the meaning by using the noun *caedis*, which refers specifically to murder. The context of Lord's Day 40 makes clear that is what is under discussion is not all killing generically, which in this context would make little sense. When the catechism was adopted, in the Palatinate, capital punishment was in place and practiced without controversy. When the state executes a capital sentence, it does so without envy, hatred, and so on. In other words, the catechism clearly has in view an *immoral* taking of another human life, and specifically those vices that give rise to murder.

God's natural, moral law, which reflects his nature and which he revealed to Adam in the garden, was expressed under Moses in the sixth commandment as "You shall not murder" (Exod 20:13). The verb (רצח) used in both Exodus 20:13 and Deuteronomy 5:17 has a variety of senses in Scripture. In Numbers 35:21, 25 it refers to someone guilty of manslaughter who had the right to flee to a city of refuge. It is used eleven times in Numbers 35 in that sense. In Deuteronomy 22:26 it is used of murder. The LXX uses φονεύω in all these cases, and that is the word Matthew 5:21 uses.

The sixth commandment is not an absolute prohibition against killing. The very same *Torah* that forbids manslaughter and murder also teaches that, in some cases, some people are to be put to death by the state (e.g., Gen 9:6; Exod 19:12; 21:12–17, 29; 31:14–15; Lev 24:17).

The protection of legally innocent human life is grounded in the reality that, even after the fall, humans are still image-bearers in the broad sense. Thus, Calvin writes, "The Lord has willed that we consider those two things which are naturally in man, and might lead us to seek his preservation: to reverence his image imprinted in man, and to embrace our own flesh in him."[9] We must distinguish two aspects of the image of God: general and special.[10] The special or spiritual aspect is, after the fall, destroyed and is only renewed by God's free grace alone (*sola gratia*), through faith alone (*sola fide*) in Christ alone, in union and communion with Christ. As a consequence of our salvation and justification, the Spirit is at work in believers renewing them in the image of Christ, which gracious process shall only be completed in glory (2 Cor 3:18; Col 3:10; Eph 4:24; 1 Cor

9. Calvin, *Institutes* 2.8.40.

10. See Ursinus, *Commentary*, 31–32.

15:49). Typically, the classical Reformed theologians speak of the image in the broader sense as having been defaced or obliterated, that is, painted over. It is present but marred.[11] In Genesis 9:6, the intent behind invoking the history of creation is to say that humans are still image-bearers.

In the Mosaic covenant, God not only commanded his people to drive out the Canaanites, as in Exodus 23:20–33, but sometimes sanctioned the large-scale taking of human life in military operations. Our Lord Jesus did not tell soldiers to quit their jobs, nor did he tell Pilate that he had no business punishing criminals. What Pilate and the other authorities did to Jesus was unjust because he was innocent and righteous, not because the authorities had no brief from God use capital punishment. There were, after all, a number of capital crimes in the Torah in which the taking of life was commanded as the punishment (e.g., Exod 19:12; 21:12–17, 29; 31:14–15).

The injunction against murder and the institution of capital punishment is grounded not in the temporary, typological, positive Mosaic judicial laws but in creation and in natural law.[12] That is why, even in the new covenant, the state is sanctioned to take life in the execution of justice. Thus Paul says in Romans 13:4 that the magistrate does not "bear the sword to no purpose."[13]

ABORTION

Like Calvin, Ursinus reminds us that the "end of this commandment is the preservant of the life and health of the body, and so of the safe of both of ourselves and of others."[14] The intent of the sixth commandment is that we hurt neither ourselves nor anyone else physically, or by speech, thought, or intent of the heart.[15] Nowhere is this commandment more frequently violated in our time than in the taking of legally innocent human life in the act of abortion. Since 1973 no fewer than fifty million human beings have lost their lives due to abortion. Since 1973 Americans have killed as many people as were killed during World War II. It is a widespread

11. E.g., "Postquam ergo in eo obliterata fuit caelestis imago" (Calvin, *Institutes* 2.1.5; Barth, *Joannis Calvini Opera Selecta*, 3:232.39–233.1).

12. See the discussion under *HC* 85, 104.

13. οὐ γὰρ εἰκῇ τὴν μάχαιραν φορεῖ.

14. Ursinus, *Commentary*, 583; Calvin, *Institutes* 2.8.40.

15. Ursinus, *Commentary*, 584.

practice. Genesis 1:27 says: "So God created man in his own image, in the image of God he created him; male and female he created them" (ESV). Adam and Eve were humans bearing the image of God from the moment they were created. When they conceived and gave birth to Cain and Abel, they gave conceived and gave birth to human beings. When the world was re-created after the flood, God specifically instituted protections for legally innocent human life.

> And God blessed Noah and his sons and said to them, "Be fruitful and multiply and fill the earth. The fear of you and the dread of you shall be upon every beast of the earth and upon every bird of the heavens, upon everything that creeps on the ground and all the fish of the sea. Into your hand they are delivered. Every moving thing that lives shall be food for you. And as I gave you the green plants, I give you everything. But you shall not eat flesh with its life, that is, its blood. And for your lifeblood I will require a reckoning: from every beast I will require it and from man. From his fellow man I will require a reckoning for the life of man.
>
> "Whoever sheds the blood of man,
> by man shall his blood be shed,
> for God made man in his own image." (Gen 9:1–6 ESV)

This legislation is creational in character. It is not part of the typological, temporary Mosaic judicial laws. Further, it clearly distinguishes between human and nonhuman life. We are free to kill and eat animals and plants because they are not human. Anyone who takes another human life unjustly has committed a capital crime. Genesis 9:6 links the image of God to human flesh and blood. Consider Psalm 139:14, which says that we are fearfully and wonderfully made, and that we were knit together in the womb. The psalmist assumes the humanity of what is knit together in the womb. John the Baptist leaped in his mother's womb (Luke 1:44). That is a human behavior.

Both pagans and Christians have forbidden abortion. According to J. Ryan Davidson: "The Middle Assyrian Laws, which date as far back as the early eleventh century BC, specifically addressed abortion." He adds: "Originally, the Roman republic legally allowed abortion. However, that stance may have changed around Cicero's time because the empire needed more citizens."[16] So the pagans both prohibited and permitted abortion.

In the Christian tradition the testimony has been fairly consistent. *Ad Diognetum* 5:6, from the middle of the second century, says of the Christians, "They marry like everyone else, and have children, but they do not throw away [ῥίπτω] their offspring."[17] The expression "throw away their offspring" is ambiguous. In the nineteenth century Alexander Roberts and James Donaldson translated it, "They do not destroy their offspring."[18] Some have taken it to refer to abortion; others, for example, Michael Holmes, take it to refer to leaving a child to die of exposure.[19] Even if it refers to the latter, it seems odd that this early Christian would oppose infanticide, the murder of infants postpartum, but permit it in utero. The noun (τὰ γεννώμενα) in *Ad Diognetum* is used in the fourth century AD, at the Synod of Ancyra (AD 314), to refer to the abortion of an infant conceived in prostitution.[20]

Even if *Ad Diognetum* is ambiguous, there is plenty of unambiguous testimony among the fathers. In *Didache* 2.1, best dated within the first quarter of the second century, abortion is described as a violation of God's law: "And the second commandment of the Teaching; You shall not commit murder, you shall not commit adultery, you shall not commit pederasty, you shall not commit fornication, you shall not steal, you shall not practice magic, you shall not practice witchcraft, you shall not murder a child by abortion nor kill that which is born."[21] The *Didache* clearly distinguishes between children who are unborn and children who are born, teaching that it is murder to kill a child at either point. Thus, the Christian

16. Davidson, "Abortion in Antiquity."

17. γαμοῦσιν ὡς πάντες, τεκνογονοῦσιν· ἀλλ' οὐ ῥίπτουσι τὰ γεννώμενα (Holmes, *Apostolic Fathers*, 702–3).

18. "Epistle of Mathetes to Diognetus" (*ANF* 1:26).

19. Holmes, *Apostolic Fathers*, "they do not expose their offspring."

20. Περὶ τῶν γυναικῶν τῶν ἐκπορνευουσῶν καὶ ἀναιρουσῶν τὰ γεννώμενα καὶ σπουδαζουσῶν φθόρια ποιεῖν ὁ μὲν πρότερος ὅρος μέχρις ἐξόδου ἐκώλυσεν, καὶ τούτῳ συντίθενται φιλανθρωπότερον δὲ τι εὑρόντες ὡρίσαμεν δεκαετῆ χρόνον κατὰ τοὺς βαθμοὺς τοὺς ὡρισμένους (*adde* πληρῶσαι). "Women who prostitute themselves, and who kill the children thus begotten, or who try to destroy them when in their wombs, are by ancient law excommunicated to the end of their lives. We, however, have softened their punishment, and condemned them to the various appointed degrees of penance for ten years" (Hefele, *History of the Councils*, 1:220).

21. οὐ φονεύσεις τέκνον ἐν φθορᾷ οὐδὲ γεννηθὲν (Holmes, *Apostolic Fathers*, 252).

view of humanity distinguished itself from the pagan Roman view. In the third century Tertullian, the father of Latin theology, wrote: "In our case, murder being once for all forbidden, we may not destroy even the *foetus* in the womb, while as yet the human being derives blood from other parts of the body for its sustenance. To hinder a birth is merely a speedier man-killing; nor does it matter whether you take away a life that is born, or destroy one that is coming to the birth."[22] Tertullian explicitly characterizes abortion as murder.

Athenagoras, a Christian apologist writing in the late second century, distinguishes between the behavior of the Christians and that of the pagans:

> And when we say that those women who use drugs to bring on abortion commit murder, and will have to give an account to God for the abortion, on what principle should we commit murder? For it does not belong to the same person to regard the very foetus in the womb as a created being, and therefore an object of God's care, and when it has passed into life, to kill it; and not to expose an infant, because those who expose them are chargeable with child-murder, and on the other hand, when it has been reared to destroy it. But we are in all things always alike and the same, submitting ourselves to reason, and not ruling over it.[23]

The consensus position of the fathers was reaffirmed in the early medieval church by the Council of Trullo (692) in Constantinople. Canon 91 says: "Those who give drugs for procuring abortion, and those who receive poisons to kill the foetus, are subjected to the penalty of murder."[24] The epitome of canon 91 elaborates on this moral teaching to the same effect but adds that abortion is a sin not only because it murders an infant human in utero, in the womb, but also because it jeopardizes the woman, whose life is also sacred.

The pastoral response to those women who have aborted their children is that to abort an infant in all but the most extreme medical circumstances,

22. Tertullian, *Apology* 9 (*ANF* 3:25).

23. Athenagoras, *Plea for the Christians* (*ANF* 2:147).

24. *NPNF* 2/14:404. Abortion in the ancient world was typically induced by the ingestion of drugs.

that is, to save the physical life of the mother, is sin, but it is not the unforgivable sin.[25] Men and women who have been involved in abortion in whatever way can be forgiven for the sake of Christ. Jesus forgives sinners. Acknowledge your sin, repent (turn away from it heartily), trust Christ for your righteousness, accept his forgiveness freely given. Remember, he forgave his murderers. He forgives all sinners who turn to him in true faith.

JUST WAR AND SELF-DEFENSE

As citizens in a twofold kingdom, Christians have both public and private duties.[26] The public defense of those who are legally innocent is among those public duties. The Christian who holds public office, for example, as a law enforcement officer or executive officer, acts on behalf of the community, state, or nation.[27] The Reformed churches are indebted here to Augustine's "just war theory."[28] There are relatively righteous causes even in a fallen world, even if that just cause is prosecuted imperfectly.[29] It was righteous to defend the free world against fascism in World War II. It was just to defend the free world against global communism in the Cold War. This is why Christians may serve on juries or as lawyers, judges, governors, or soldiers. In that public capacity, that is, when they act on behalf of the public, with the authority of just laws, they may do things that they may not do as private persons or citizens.

It is on similar grounds that the Augustinian tradition has defended the justice of self-defense. There can be little doubt that the Hebrew Scriptures teach a right to self-defense. Would Abel (Gen 4:8) have sinned had he defended himself against Cain? Was Abel morally obligated to allow Cain to murder him? It would seem not. After all, we have already learned from Genesis 1:26 that God created human beings in his image. Legally

25. Women whose lives are threatened in the course of the delivery of their infants retain the right of self-defense.

26. "Duplex esse in homine regimen" (Calvin, *Institutes* 3.15.15; Barth, *Joannis Calvini Opera Selecta*, 4:294.5).

27. Contra the Anabaptist Schleitheim Confession, art. 6, which forbids Christians to serve in the government (Leith, *Creeds of the Churches*, 288–89).

28. See, e.g., Augustine, *City of God* 4.15; 19.7; 19.15.1 (2:57–59; 6:149–51, 187–91).

29. "War is either a necessary defence against such as are guilty of robbery, cruelty or oppression; or it is a just punishment for wicked outrages, which is undertaken by the force of arms by the ordinary power" (Ursinus, *Commentary*, 587).

innocent human life is sacred to God. This is the basis for the postdiluvian legislation in Genesis 9:5–6. By analogy, the image of God in humanity is sufficient warrant for self-defense. Francis Turretin is helpful here:

> XV. Second, defensive homicide is not forbidden when anyone, for the purpose of defending his own life against a violent and unjust aggressor (keeping within the limits of lawful protection), kills another. To be considered as lawful protection, it is necessary: (1) that the aggressor unjustly assails and falls upon us; (2) that the defender be placed beyond all blame, while every other way of escaping morally by speaking or flying or yielding is shut against him; (3) that the defense be made during the very attack and not after it is over; (4) that nothing is done by him either under the impulse of anger or with the feeling and desire of revenge, but with the sole intention of defending himself.
>
> XVI. The reason is clear. Although it is not lawful to return like for like and to avenge oneself, still to repel force by force and to defend oneself belongs to natural and perpetual right (especially where the aggression is simply violent and destitute of all public authority) even unto the slaying of the aggressor (although not intended by itself, but inasmuch as we cannot otherwise defend our lives and free ourselves from his unjust oppression). Nor do civil laws alone approve this, as is evident from the Codex to the Cornelian law and to the Aquilian law: "All laws and all rights allow the repelling of force by force" (cf. Corpus Iuris Civilis, I: Digesta 48.8 ...). But God himself is found to have intimated this clearly in the law where a case of private defense is set forth from which a judgment can be formed concerning the practice of that law: "If a thief be found breaking up" (in the very act) "and be smitten that he die, there shall no blood be shed for him" (Ex. 22:2). If the sun be risen upon him, there shall be blood shed for him if doubtless the slayer could discover that he had come only for the purpose of stealing and not of killing.[30]

The passage to which Turretin appeals says, "If a thief is found breaking in and is struck so that he dies, there shall be no bloodguilt for him,

30. Turretin, *Institutes of Elenctic Theology*, 11.17.15–16 (2:115).

but if the sun has risen on him, there shall be bloodguilt for him" (Exod 22:2–3 ESV). Under the Mosaic judicial laws, if a homeowner finds a thief in his house in the middle of the night, and the homeowner kills the thief, the homeowner is innocent. Should the homeowner kill the thief during daylight, when the homeowner can see that the burglar is a thief and not attempting homicide, the homeowner is guilty. The principle, which did not expire with the Mosaic judicial laws, is that a person has a natural, creational right to self-defense. The natural right of self-defense, to which Turretin refers, is part of the creational pattern predating but persisting under Moses and under the new covenant.

This significant truth helps us to understand the New Testament teaching in regard to the sword and self-defense. The Anabaptists (and many modern evangelicals in their wake) had an overrealized eschatology, that is, they understood the new covenant era in redemptive history to be more eschatological or more heavenly than it really is. Thus, they rejected the natural right of self-defense.[31] With this background we have the categories we need to understand what the New Testament says about the sword, the civil magistrate, and the right of self-defense. The New Testament speaks of the sword both literally and metaphorically. Our Lord Jesus commanded his disciples to purchase literal swords:

> And he said to them, "When I sent you out with no moneybag or knapsack or sandals, did you lack anything?" They said, "Nothing." He said to them, "But now let the one who has a moneybag take it, and likewise a knapsack. And let the one who has no sword sell his cloak and buy one. For I tell you that this Scripture must be fulfilled in me: 'And he was numbered with the transgressors.' For what is written about me has its fulfillment." And they said, "Look, Lord, here are two swords." And he said to them, "It is enough." (Luke 22:35–38 ESV)

31. E.g., Schleitheim Confession, art. 6, in Leith, *Creeds of the Churches*, 288. Williams (*Radical Reformation*, 342–43) distinguishes three types of Anabaptist pacifism: (1) Erasmian prudential pacifism, which does not reject just wars in theory but held most to be avoidable; (2) "evangelical pacificism of coventicular separatism" of the sort we see in the Schleitheim; and (3) "provisional and interim pacifism," which anticipates a future bloody apocalyptic war in which they will be vindicated.

If swords were inherently evil, our Lord could not have commanded his disciples to buy them, and if they were never to be used, then the command to buy them is nonsensical. This passage alone seems to be overwhelming *prima facie* evidence against the pacifist rejection of the right of self-defense. Our Lord commanded his disciples to buy swords for no other reason than for self-defense. Even if the swords were for self-defense only against animals (sheer assumption), that is still a form of self-defense. They did not need swords for hunting—there were ways of hunting without swords (e.g., fishing and trapping). Any claim that the ownership and use of weapons for self-defense is unchristian must reckon with our Lord's own words.

The biblical evidence is more balanced. It is true that our Lord rebuked Peter for cutting off Malchus's ear (Matt 26:51–52; John 18:11), but it is also true that Peter owned a sword and that Jesus did not tell him to get rid of it. He told him to return it to its scabbard. This passage is paradigmatic for distinguishing self-defense from martyrdom. Jesus was not acting as a citizen of the temporal realm but as the King of kings, to whom his Father had given an everlasting spiritual kingdom. He was acting in his capacity as King of a kingdom that was not to be established by military force. He was acting in his capacity as Savior and Redeemer of those whom the Father gave to him from all eternity. This is the distinction between self-defense and martyrdom. Defending legally innocent and helpless victims from a murderer is just. In such a case, one is acting *in lieu* of the civil magistrate, with the authority of criminal law.

When a pagan magistrate arrests Christians and demands that we renounce Christ or face death, we must choose death, as we did in the first, second, and third centuries. We must obey God rather than people (Acts 5:29). Our Lord warned of coming persecutions: "So everyone who confesses me before men, I also will confess him before my Father who is in heaven, but whoever denies me before men, I also will deny before my Father who is in heaven" (Matt 10:32–33).

The first-generation Anabaptists, given their pacifism and their over-realized eschatology, concluded that Christians may not serve in civil government, but such a conclusion was and remains unwarranted. Erastus was "city treasurer" (ὁ οἰκονόμος τῆς πόλεως; Rom 16:23). He was clearly a Christian *and* a part of the civil government. Our Lord did not command the centurion to resign his commission as an Roman military officer (Luke 7:1–10). God used Cornelius the centurion (Acts 10:1–33), and he presumably participated in the outpouring of the Spirit recorded there.

If swords (and the purpose for which they are intended) are either inherently evil (a view that seems closer to gnosticism than to Christianity) or now forbidden to Christians, why then does the New Testament consistently employ the metaphor of the sword? If something is either inherently unjust (e.g., murder), it would not be a fitting metaphor for the Christian life. Were the sword wholly inappropriate for Christians, it could not adequately illustrate the shape of our Christian discipleship. Nonetheless, the sword is used as a metaphor for the Christian life and even for God's word (Heb 4:12). Our Lord himself said metaphorically that he came to bring a sword to divide one against the other (Matt 10:34). The apostle Paul uses martial imagery to describe the Christian life and struggle against sin:

> For we do not wrestle against flesh and blood, but against the rulers, against the authorities, against the cosmic powers over this present darkness, against the spiritual forces of evil in the heavenly places. Therefore take up the whole armor of God, that you may be able to withstand in the evil day, and having done all, to stand firm. Stand therefore, having fastened on the belt of truth, and having put on the breastplate of righteousness, and, as shoes for your feet, having put on the readiness given by the gospel of peace. In all circumstances take up the shield of faith, with which you can extinguish all the flaming darts of the evil one; and take the helmet of salvation, and the sword of the Spirit, which is the word of God, praying at all times in the Spirit, with all prayer and supplication. (Eph 6:12–18 ESV)

Notice to what end Paul employs this military imagery: spiritual warfare. Christians are not called to gear up and go to literal warfare to advance the kingdom of God or for spiritual purposes. Soldiers do not march under the banner of Christ. They march for the common good, as God's ministers in the civil, common sphere. Still, this imagery would hardly be appropriate for Christians were swords both unknown and forbidden to Christians in the new covenant.

Christian pacifism is misguided because it confuses two distinct spheres of God's sovereign rule over all things. It ignores the semi-eschatological condition under which Christians exist until the return of Christ. It confuses the sacred and the secular. Weapons are forbidden as a means for the institutional church to pursue her mission, which is spiritual. They are not forbidden to Christians, and they are not forbidden to the secular authorities. Paul says, "The weapons of our warfare are not of the flesh but have divine power to destroy strongholds" (2 Cor 10:4 ESV). In short, it is the result of a series of category mistakes that makes some unable to understand and synthesize what Scripture actually says about the Christian's role in civil life generally and in the new covenant specifically.

MURDER IN THE HEART

Finally, the heart of the issue is the human heart. Our Lord says,

> You have heard that it was said to those of old, "You shall not murder; and whoever murders will be liable to judgment." But I say to you that everyone who is angry with his brother will be liable to judgment; whoever insults his brother will be liable to the council; and whoever says, "You fool!" will be liable to the hell of fire. So if you are offering your gift at the altar and there remember that your brother has something against you, leave your gift there before the altar and go. First be reconciled to your brother, and then come and offer your gift. Come to terms quickly with your accuser while you are going with him to court, lest your accuser hand you over to the judge, and the judge to the guard, and you be put in prison. (Matt 5:21–25 ESV)

Our Lord, whose nature the law reflects, who gave the law to Adam and to Moses, pressed beneath the surface of the matter to get to the source of murder, which is the sort of unrighteous anger whereby one has already murdered one's neighbor in one's heart and mind. It is this sort of sinful anger that, when nurtured, grows up to become murder with the hands (Jas 1:14–15). "Therefore this law also forbids murder of the heart, and enjoins the inner intent to save a brother's life. The hand, indeed, gives birth to murder, but the mind when infected with anger and hatred conceives it. See whether you can be angry against your brother without burning with desire to hurt him. If you cannot be angry with him, then you cannot hate him, for hatred is nothing but sustained anger."[32] This same sort of anger is manifested in murderous language, ῥακά and "You fool" (μωρέ). The first is a transliteration of an Aramaic insult (רֵיקָא). "It expresses vexed disparagement which may be accompanied by displeasure, anger, or contempt, and which is usually addressed to a foolish, thoughtless, or presumptuous person. The insult was regarded as harmless: 'blockhead,' 'donkey.'"[33] Jesus uses the traditional Hebrew rhetorical device of parallelism to intensify the problem of murderous anger. If we call our neighbor a "blockhead," we are in danger of a temporal punishment under religio-civil authorities (the Sanhedrin). If, however, we say "Fool!" we are liable to the much greater jeopardy of eternal punishment.

Like almost everything else our Lord said, this saying is challenging since the word *fool* is relatively common in Scripture (e.g., Pss 14:1; 39:8; 49:10; 53:1; Prov 10 et passim). The entire book of Proverbs is a contrast between the wise son and the fool. We are enjoined repeatedly in Proverbs to regard as and to call certain kinds of persons fools. Our Lord himself, in his condemnation of the Pharisees (Matt 23:17), used the very same word as used in Matthew 5: "You blind fools!" (μωροὶ). The apostle Paul calls us, perhaps ironically, in 1 Corinthians 3:18 to become "fools" for the sake of the gospel.

Thus, we must pay attention to our Lord's intention rather than to the exact verbiage, lest we miss the point. Murder is rooted in the denial of the humanity of another person created in the image of God. When, in our hearts, we have denied the essential humanity of another, that is expressed in words such as "blockhead" and "fool" in the sense in which our Lord used them in Matthew 5:22.

According to James, murder also arises out of covetousness: "You desire and do not have, so you murder" (Jas 4:2 ESV). It would be truly remarkable if, in the congregation to which James wrote in the first half of the first century, there were literal cases of murder. Thus, it seems likely that James was speaking hyperbolically and metaphorically. Those

32. Calvin, *Institutes* 2.8.39.

33. Joachim Jeremias, "ῥακά," in Kittel and Friedrich, *Theological Dictionary of the New Testament*, 6:973–76.

Christians were murdering each other with their hearts and mouths, but the root of it was a refusal to accept God's providence and to be content.

The catechism mentions related impulses, for example, the desire for revenge. Cain's murder of Abel is characterized as "revenge" (Gen 4:24). Jealousy, envy, and hatred of one's neighbor are all forms of unbelief. What begins as simmering bitterness is kindled into more, leading to the literal taking of matters into one's own hands, the taking of life.

Christians must know their own hearts. They must know how desperately wicked their hearts are (Jer 17:9), and they must be realistic about that of which each of us is capable. With the help of God's grace and by the power of the Spirit, in virtue of our union with Christ, we need to mortify daily the root of murder in our hearts and to pursue its opposite, the seeking of the well-being of our neighbors. The true fulfilling of this commandment is not the mere absence of murder from our hands or even from our hearts, but real love toward our neighbor—notice that we are not talking about warm feelings but love. Those are two distinct things. Sometimes we may have warm feelings toward our neighbor, and sometimes we may not. Our feelings are beside the point. We are seeking to cultivate an attitude, a disposition, of patience, peace, meekness, mercy, and all kindness toward our neighbor.[34] We do so by seeking our neighbor's good rather than harm. We do this with our hands, our feet, our tongues, our keyboards, and our mobile devices. Our model is Christ. When he was reviled, he did not revile in return. When we are reviled, we bless (1 Pet 2:23; 1 Cor 4:12). That is the standard to which Christians, as private persons, are called.

34. See Ursinus, *Commentary*, 585–89, for an excellent discussion of the virtues to be fostered under this heading.

Question 108

What does the seventh Commandment teach us?

Question 109

Does God forbid nothing more in this commandment than adultery and such gross sins?

Lord's Day 41

QUESTIONS 108–9

What does the seventh Commandment teach us?
That all unchastity is accursed of God, and that we should therefore loathe it with our whole heart, and live chastely and modestly, whether in holy wedlock or in single life.[1]

Does God forbid nothing more in this commandment than adultery and such gross sins?
Since both our holy body and soul are temples of this Holy Spirit, it is his will that we keep both pure and holy. Therefore, he forbids all unchaste actions, gestures, words, thoughts, desires, and whatever may entice thereto.[2]

The seventh commandment forbids all sexual immorality (e.g., adultery) in thought, word, affection, and deed. It commands sexual chastity and those virtues that lead to chastity.[3] The commandment intends to preserve marriage as between a man and a woman.[4] That the word *chastity* is practically archaic says much about the state of the West, but chastity is a Christian virtue. Our English word *chastity* is medieval, derived from the Latin noun *castitas*. In English usage it signifies "purity from unlawful sexual intercourse."[5] Ursinus characterizes the virtue of

1. "Was will das siebente Gebot? Dass alle Unkeuschheit von Gott vermaledeiet sei, und dass wir darum ihr von Herzen seind sein, und keusch und züchtig leben sollen, es sei im heiligen Ehestand, oder ausserhalb desselben" (Schaff, *Creeds of Christendom*, 3:347). "Quae est sententia septimi praecepti? Deum omnem turpitudinem execrari: ideoque nos eam penitus odisse et detestari debere: contraque temperanter, modeste et caste, sive in sacro coniugio, sive in vita coelibe vivere oportere" (Niemeyer, *Collectio Confessionum*, 456).

2. "Verbietet Gott in diesem Gebot nichts mchr denn Ehebruch und dergleichen Schauden? Dieweil beide unser Leib und Seele ein Tempel des Heiligen Geistes sind: so will Er, dass wir sie beide sauber und heilig bewahren; verbietet derhalben alle unkeusche Thaten, Geberden, Worte, Gedanken, Lust, und was den Menschen dazu reizen mag" (Schaff, *Creeds of Christendom*, 3:347). "Nihilne amplius prohibet Deus hoc praecepto, quam adulterium, et id genus turpitudines? Cum corpus et animus noster templa sint Spiritus sancti, vult Deus ut utrunque pure sancteque possideamus. Idcoque facta, gestus, sermones, cogitationes, cupiditates foedas, et quicquid hominem ad ista allicit, id universum prohibet" (Niemeyer, *Collectio Confessionum*, 456).

3. Ursinus, *Commentary*, 590.

4. From the perspective of nature and grace, homosexual marriage is oxymoronic. On marriage, see Ursinus, *Commentary*, 592–95.

5. *OED*, s.v. "chastity."

chastity as a "virtue contributing to the purity of body and soul, agreeing with the will of God, and shunning all lusts prohibited by God, all unlawful intercourse and inordinate copulation."[6] Purity and chastity are the opposite of sexual immorality. Our sexual behavior and attitudes, our habits, are reflections of what we love, of where we find fulfillment. Proverbs portrays foolishness as a prostitute because like a prostitute, foolishness promises fun and satisfaction but actually gives bitterness and death.

As we seek to understand and apply the seventh commandment, we do so in an unchaste age. Indeed, we are in the midst of a sexual revolution that has been underway for a century, which is being institutionalized even in law—for example, the legalization of homosexual marriage (*Obergefell v. Hodges*). If we are to be faithful to Scripture and the catechism, we need to be reoriented to sexual chastity as God intends it.

SEXUAL IMMORALITY GENERALLY

The sexual revolution has been a cruel joke. In the 1960s the sexual revolutionaries promised free sex without any commitment. What we got instead were sexually transmitted diseases and alienation. That alienation is especially tragic since, as the apostle Paul reminds us, the conjugal union between a man and woman is an illustration of the wonderfully intimate relationship between Christ and his church (Eph 5:32). Sexual unchastity is about more than having sex with the wrong person; it is about corrupting a creational pattern and corrupting an analogy that is meant to point to a glorious spiritual mystery.

God's word is quite clear and even pointed about sexual immorality. Leviticus 18 illustrates how God views sexual immorality. For example, in Leviticus 18:20 God prohibits adultery and moves immediately in the next verse to warn against offering one's children to Molech, to a prohibition of male homosexuality, which verse 22 calls an "abomination" (תּוֹעֵבָה). It prohibits bestiality (vv. 18–23). All these things made Israel unclean.

6. Ursinus, *Commentary*, 590. Ursinus quotes a maxim, the source of which he does not identify: "God is chaste, and will be called upon by those who are of a chaste mind, and has regard to such prayers" (590). Philip Melanchthon uses a similar expression in a similar context in his 1543 edition of the *Common Places*: "And rulers must be urged and entreated to remember their duty under the command of God, to understand that God is chaste and righteous, and that they have been put in the position of divine service so that they may be the image of God, that they may be chaste and upright, and uphold chastity and righteousness among the people" (Melanchthon, *Loci Communes (1543)*, 259).

The punishment for these crimes was most grave. Those punishments have expired with the of the death of Christ, but God has not changed. Sexual immorality is still a sin. Bestiality and homosexuality are still an abomination. Our Lord Jesus forbids sexual immorality (e.g., Mark 7:21; πορνεία). The apostle Paul forbids sexual immorality (πορνεία) generally and in particular in 1 Corinthians 5:1–2, 9–13; 6:9, 13–20.

THE INTENTION OF SEXUAL CHASTITY

We must understand two essential aspects to sexual union: its creational pattern and its spiritual significance. It seems widely accepted now that everything is a construct, that is, an arbitrary rule that can be undone or deconstructed at will, but everything is not an arbitrary construct because the natural pattern is built into creation itself, ordained by God, and reflects his nature. We should follow the pattern set by our Lord, who, when challenged over the toleration of polygamy under Moses, appealed to the creational pattern as the norm: "But from the beginning it was not so" (Matt 19:8). As humans made in the image of God, God created us to reflect him and to live according to the order he established. This means that there is a *givenness* to human life, entailing that there are divinely established limits and norms built into the nature of things. The creational pattern established by God is monogamous sex between a man and woman within the bounds of marriage. Because there is a creational pattern, because God intended us to relate to one another a certain way, sexual infidelity is not only sin against God's holy moral law but also terribly damaging.

THE GRAVITY OF SEXUAL SIN

In the wake of the sexual revolution, it has become accepted wisdom in some quarters that sexual sin is no different from any other sin. In one sense that is true, since James 2:10 says that to break one commandment is to break them all. Nevertheless, Paul issues pointed warnings to the Corinthian congregation about the *special* dangers of sexual sin: "Flee from sexual immorality [πορνείαν]. Every other sin a person commits is outside the body, but the sexually immoral person sins against his own body. Or do you not know that your body is a temple of the Holy Spirit within you, whom you have from God? You are not your own, for you were bought with a price. So glorify God in your body" (1 Cor 6:18–20 ESV). Ursinus is correct to call sexual sin "most rude."[7]

Paul distinguishes between sexual immorality and "every other sin." Does this mean that sexual sin is worse than other sins? Not necessarily, but it does mean that sexual sin is distinct from others. It is not easy to say exactly how sexual sin affects us differently from other sins. After all, gluttony and drunkenness certainly affect the body, yet not in quite the same way. Perhaps the difference is this: sex is about the union of two persons. In sex, we give ourselves to one another. That union signifies "Christ and the church" (Eph 5:31–32; Gen 2:24; 1 Cor 6:16). For a Christian to commit sexual sin is not only to transgress the moral law but to defile a sign. In sexual immorality, then, we enter into a sort of false communion. That is different from overeating or theft. Sexual immorality leaves a mark on the soul in way that other sins do not.

Perhaps this uncertainty explains why people are so quick to defend and justify sexual sin in a way that they are not regarding other sins and vices. Our culture is quick to say that sexual sins are the result of a created disposition (and therefore good) even though there is virtually no evidence to support such a claim. In truth, after the fall, we do all have a natural inclination to sin. Idolatry, murder, and sexual immorality do all come naturally to all of us after the fall (Matt 5:19).

As Paul says, Christians, however, those who believe in the Lord Jesus Christ, who have been justified by grace alone (*sola gratia*), through faith alone (*sola fide*), have been "bought with a price" (1 Cor 6:20). Our Lord Jesus laid down his life for us. We are not our own (1 Cor 6:19). This is the first thing we learn in the catechism: "I am not my own but belong body and soul, life and death to my faithful Savior."

Remember, Christians seek to obey God's law, not as a cause or instrument of our free acceptance with God or our salvation, but out of gratitude, by grace alone, in union and communion with Christ. Thus Paul does not write, "Honor God with your bodies in order that you might be bought with a price." He writes the opposite: "Because you were bought with a price. Therefore, honor God with your bodies" (1 Cor 6:20). It is

7. *Crassissima* (Ursinus, *Corpus doctrinae*, 599).

in this light that we consider the seventh commandment: "You shall not commit adultery" (Exod 20:14).

DIVORCE

Ursinus writes that the "design of this commandment is ... the guarding of marriage, or keeping it holy."[8] The intimacy of the marriage union illustrates the relations between Christ and his church. The modern myth of painless divorce is self-justifying propaganda. There are two grounds for divorce. The first and unambiguous ground is that expressed by our Lord Jesus: "But I say to you that everyone who divorces his wife, except on the ground of sexual immorality, makes her commit adultery, and whoever marries a divorced woman commits adultery" (Matt 5:32 ESV). The second ground, given by Paul (1 Cor 7:12–16), makes a believing spouse guiltless (and free to remarry): "if the unbeliever leaves [χωρίζεται] let him leave" (1 Cor 7:15).[9]

When divorce happens on the grounds of sexual immorality, it recognizes the damage that has already been done to the marriage and to the people in the marriage. Sexual immorality is so terrible and damaging that it is grounds for dissolving a union, sanctioned by God, that illustrates the relationship between Christ and his church.

Whether called to single life or to marriage, Christians are to live chastely, that is, with our eyes fixed on Christ. At this point, the requirements of the seventh commandment overlap with those of the tenth. If married, we must be satisfied with the spouse God has given us. If single, we are to live sexually chaste lives, and our focus is to be on the Lord all the more since we do not have the responsibilities of a spouse and children.

PORNOGRAPHY

We live in a visual culture awash in readily available pornographic video and images, and not merely outside the church. It is a silent, unspoken cancer afflicting singles and marriages in congregations across the developed world. Chastity means that Christians must abstain from not only physical sexual immorality but *virtual* sexual immorality. We are not to

8. Ursinus, *Commentary*, 590; Ursinus, *Corpus doctrinae*, 599.

9. Murray, *Divorce*; Douma, *Ten Commandments*, 274–83.

be fantasizing or imagining sex with other people or watching sex or lusting after someone's body. Chastity means recognizing that we belong to Christ, that we have been bought with a price, and it means ordering our sexual affections accordingly even when no one else is about. Despite the illusion created by entertainment media, sexual immorality is not glamorous. It is sad, depressing, and lonely. It embitters those who produce it and destroys those who consume it. God designed men, by nature, when called to marriage, to give themselves to one woman. Women who are not gifted with singleness are intended to give themselves to one man. Sex is intended to be shrouded in trust and mutual commitment. Pornography turns that intimacy into a sad, miserable transaction that leaves all involved hating themselves and others.

HOMOSEXUALITY, INCEST, TRANSGENDER, AND QUEER SEXUALITY

There are two basic categories of analysis for understanding the nature of this question: nature and grace. Nature signifies "part of the creational fabric" or "reflective of the divine order in creation." The "queering" of human sexuality is a deliberate renunciation of the very idea of boundaries or nature.[10] It seeks to deconstruct the patterns that God has constructed, that is, the heterosexual creational pattern.[11]

The Reformed approach is antithetical to French philosopher Michel Foucault (1926–1984) and others. We begin with and affirm the goodness of creation. Ursinus categorizes this species of lust as "contrary to nature and from the devil." Certain sexual sins are contrary to nature per se and even nature after the fall.[12] We are to regard them as "heinous sins and abominable transgressions."[13]

10. Allen, "Queering the Academy," 681–84.

11. E.g., Foucault, *History of Sexuality*, vol. 1. For context, the reader should know that Foucault was homosexual and practiced the deconstructed sexual ethic he preached. He was "promiscuous and even reckless." He advocated pederasty and died of AIDS in 1987. See Johnson, "Michel Foucault." Posthumously, he was accused of sexually abusing boys during a stay in Tunisia. See Campbell, "French Philosopher Michel Foucault."

12. Ursinus, *Commentary*, 590; Ursinus, *Corpus doctrinae*, 599.

13. Ursinus, *Commentary*, 590; Ursinus, *Corpus doctrinae*, 599.

God created humanity in two sexes, male and female (Gen 1:27). Our Lord himself confirmed this understanding of the creational pattern. When the Pharisees approached our Lord to try to trap him in a question regarding divorce and remarriage, Jesus responded by measuring the temporary Mosaic laws against the permanent moral and natural law: "Have you not read that he who created them from the beginning made them male and female, and said, 'Therefore a man shall leave his father and his mother and hold fast to his wife, and the two shall become one flesh'? So they are no longer two but one flesh. What therefore God has joined together, let not man separate" (Matt 19:4–6 ESV). When the Pharisees tried to leverage the natural pattern with the temporary Mosaic law again, Jesus replied by again appealing to his intention in creation: "Because of your hardness of heart Moses allowed you to divorce your wives, but from the beginning it was not so" (v. 8 ESV).

That phrase, "from the beginning it was not so," is significant for our understanding of human sexuality. The norm for sexual relations was established and ordered before the fall. The rejection of the differences between the sexes, the adoption of a bisexual or transsexual or transgender identity, is contrary to the natural pattern. It is the product of the vitiating power of sin. Such identities are abnormal and contrary to nature. Paul makes this quite clear in Romans 1:26–27:

> For this reason God gave them up to dishonorable passions. For their women exchanged [μετήλλαξαν] natural relations for those that are contrary to nature [εἰς τὴν παρὰ φύσιν]; and the men likewise gave up natural [τὴν φυσικὴν χρῆσιν] relations with women and were consumed with passion for one another, men committing shameless acts with men and receiving in themselves the due penalty for their error. (ESV)

Paul was familiar with Greco-Roman homosexuality. It was openly displayed in the cities. He first addresses what we today called lesbian affection and sexual relationships in verse 26. He condemned such out of hand on the basis of the natural or created pattern.

Scripture also makes it clear that homosexuality and even same-sex attraction is sin. The rule of biblical interpretation Ursinus uses here seems especially relevant to this discussion: "From the appearance of one thing, all the cognates and the rest are understood."[14] In other words, the burden of proof rests with those who deny that same-sex attraction per se is sinful, which is not what is argued in the 1973 Report 42, adopted by the Christian Reformed Church.[15]

The catechism helps us here. The German text of the catechism has "Lust," the sense of which can run the gamut from joy to sinful sexual desire, which is what it denotes in English. The qualifier is "unchaste" (*unkeuschen*). The Latin text of the catechism helps us to know the original understanding of this language. It has *cupiditates foedas* or "unclean desires." The adjective *foedus* is quite strong. It signals "disgusting," "filthy." Beza's *Novum Testamentum*, which first appeared in 1559 and was used widely after the publication of the catechism, helps us here, as he uses *foedis affectibus* in Romans 1:26.[16] For Beza, the affections themselves are not merely "disordered" but morally repugnant. In other words, neither Beza (a major influence on the catechism) nor the catechism sequesters desire from action the way Report 42 does. We know this because Ursinus explains: "Where the cause is condemned, there the effect is also condemned; and where the effect is condemned, there the cause is condemned."[17]

The cause to which Ursinus refers is desire (*libido*).[18] As was typical of the premodern Christian world, Ursinus does not mention homosexuality explicitly but tacitly when he writes, "The lusts of which the apostle

---

14. "Ex una specie reliquae et cognatae intelliguntur" (Ursinus, *Corpus doctrinae*, 599); Ursinus, *Commentary*, 590.

15. Report 42, adopted in 1973 by the Christian Reformed Church in North America (*Acts of Synod*, 609–33), argues that same-sex attraction is not sinful but same-sex sexual behavior is. The report says, "From the perspective of Scripture and the general conclusion of modern research, homosexuality is a disordered condition and a handicap comparable to other abnormal physical and psychological conditions." It regards the behavior as "unnatural" but does not apply that category to homosexual desire: "It is an exchange of the natural use of sex for the unnatural. Homosexualism is the penalty for man's apostacy [*sic*] from the true worship of God resulting in the depravity of those who engage in it." In a puzzling passage, the report argues that, for the homosexual, given his orientation, same-sex attraction is "natural" and heterosexual attraction is "unnatural." The report concludes that a homosexual orientation may be immutable, and one of the ways in which the NT differs from the OT is that the NT makes a place for celibate (i.e., nonpracticing) homosexuals: "In Christ the unmarried, the heterosexual and homosexual are offered an alternative to the married state in the companionship provided by the redeemed community."

16. Beza, *Novum Domini*.

17. Ursinus, *Commentary*, 590.

18. Ursinus, *Corpus doctrinae*, 600.

Paul speaks in the first chapter of his Epistle to the Romans, are of this class, as the confounding of sexes." Such desires, he writes, should be punished by the civil magistrate.[19] Those who have come of age in the era of *Obergefell v. Hodges* may need to be reminded that homosexuality was a crime almost everywhere until very recently. We are in the midst of a radical sexual revolution.

Scripture does not lead us to think of same-sex attraction or desire as morally neutral in distinction from homosexual activity. In Romans 1:26–27 Paul is describing the consequences of the fall. The first of these is that God "gave up" (παρέδωκεν) unbelievers to "dishonorable passions" (πάθη ἀτιμίας). The first category that Paul invokes is a sinful desire. This clause alone would seem to be prima facie evidence against a hard distinction between same-sex desire or attraction and same-sex behavior.[20] The traditional Christian way to speak about such disordered desires is *concupiscence*.

In verse 27, Paul again invokes the category of "desire" (ὀρέξει) as part of his indictment of homosexuality. It is true that it is "inflamed" (ἐξεκαύθησαν), but are we really to think that, for Paul, desire to have same-sex relations is morally neutral and becomes sinful only when "inflamed"?

Paul condemns not only behavioral sins but also sins of the heart or sins of desire. In 1 Corinthians 6:9, he includes πόρνοι ("the sexually immoral") among those who are excluded from the kingdom of God. This is a broad category that includes desires.[21] Consider Ephesians 5:5 where Paul says, in part, "every sexually immoral person" (πᾶς πόρνος) shall not inherit the kingdom of God. That category occurs in a list of gross sins. Next is "impure" (ἀκάθαρτος), then "coveteous" (πλεονέκτης). Impurity entails sins of desire, which is also the essence of coveting. In other words, it is impossible to affirm Ephesians 5:5 and its parallels without including sinful sexual desire or attraction, including homosexual attraction. Third, our Lord said, "Whoever looks at a woman with the intention

19. Ursinus, *Commentary*, 591.

20. At our distance, it seems evident that Report 42 was driven more by 1960s science than Scripture and historic Reformed theology. It is striking how infrequently the word *sin* appears in Report 42. The word *repent* occurs twice, and the words *repentance* and *penitent* occur not at all. It is hard to imagine a report on homosexuality from 1857 or even 1927 speaking as Report 42 does.

21. This appears most clearly under the abstract noun, πορνεία, which includes a wide range of behaviors and dispositions (*BAGD*, s.v. "πορνεία").

of lusting after her has already committed adultery" (Matt 5:28). This speaks to sexual attraction. It is sin for a man to entertain sexual desire for a woman who is not his wife. It is sin for a someone to be sexually attracted to someone of the same sex. These desires, desire for sex outside marriage or same-sex attraction, are concupiscent and not consonant with our new life in Christ.

Christian opposition to homosexuality is not grounded in the Mosaic judicial laws, and thus, we do not seek to enforce the Mosaic judicial legislation in civil life after the expiration of the Mosaic administration of the covenant of grace. The judicial punishment of homosexuality, under Moses (Lev 20:13), however, is illustrative of how abhorrent homosexuality is to God. There is equally clear teaching on homosexuality in the New Testament. In fact, the judicial laws in the *Torah* were intentionally temporary and typological, and the Christian view is that Christ fulfilled them. The New Testament rejection of homosexuality is in natural law, which is reflective of the divine nature, and thus existed long before the institution of the Mosaic judicial laws and have universal application.

Some have claimed that the category of homosexual is a nineteenth-century construct that we must deconstruct.[22] To the contrary, the New Testament had not only a concept of homosexuality but a vocabulary to describe it. In 1 Corinthians 6:9 and 1 Timothy 1:10, Paul condemns the sexually immoral (πόρνοι), idolaters (εἰδωλολάτραι), adulterers (μοιχοὶ), the effeminate (μαλακοι), and homosexuals (ἀρσενοκοῖται). The standard definition is "a male who practices homosexuality, pederast, sodomite."[23] This is the way the word was understood in early Christian, postcanonical usage, though it occurs in the same sense in the Sibylline Oracles (sixth century BC) 2.73.[24]

Of course, we want to avoid the etymological fallacy (deducing the meaning of a word by adding up its letters or component parts) because it can lead to false conclusions, but in this case usage confirms what adding up the letters suggests: αρσην = "male" and κοιτης = "bed" or a euphemistic reference to sexual relations. I translate μαλακοι as "effeminate" because

22. E.g., Foucault, *History of Sexuality*, 1:43.

23. *BAGD*, s.v. "ἀρσενοκοίτης."

24. Moulton and Milligan, *Vocabulary of the Greek Testament*, s.v. "αρσενοκοιται."

of the way it is used in the LXX for the "soft parts" and is used elsewhere in the sense of "effeminate, of a catamite, a male who submits his body to unnatural lewdness (1 Cor 6:9)."[25] In brief, Paul rather graphically accounts for both the active and receptive roles in homosexual relations.

The second category of analysis by which to understand this issue is grace. Homosexuality and similar sins are incompatible with nature but *also* incompatible with the new life in Christ. Here 1 Corinthians 6:11 is clear: "Of such *were* some of you." Idolatry, drunkenness, sexual immorality, homosexuality characterized the lives of some Corinthian Christians before they received new life, but such patterns are not to characterize their lives *after* their profession of faith.

Paul is announcing God's judgment on several classes of sinful behaviors and warning those who commit them impenitently (without sorrow or struggle) that they must acknowledge their sin for what it is and turn to and put their trust in Jesus the Savior. Jesus was obedient and died for heterosexual and homosexual sinners, and offers free acceptance with God on the basis of faith (trust) in Jesus, the gracious Savior of helpless sinners.

Those tempted to gross sexual immorality know that sexual chastity and holiness are never easy, and are particularly difficult in an age when sin crouches at seemingly every door (Gen 4:7), but by God's grace it is possible to persevere, to grow in godliness, and to mortify sin—even persisting sexual temptations and sins. When we violate the seventh commandment, whether in thought, word, or deed, we should confess our sins to God, turn from them, and know that Jesus has nailed all our sins, even our sexual sins, to the cross. For Christ's sake, God forgives all our sins. The Evil One would like nothing more than for Christians to conclude (1) that their sexual sins make them irredeemable and (2) their sexual temptations are beyond the transforming grace of God. They are not.

SINGLENESS

In the Middle Ages, the church came to associate chastity most closely with monastic life. In reaction, perhaps, in the modern period there has been a tendency to devalue the chastity of singleness. Our older Reformed writers, however, appreciated God's call to singleness, regarding it as a

25. *BAGD*, s.v. "μαλακος."

virtue.[26] Thus, we should not overlook the value of the single life. Paul says that singleness is a good and valuable, and if one is single when one comes to faith and is able to remain in that state, one should: "To the unmarried and the widows I say that it is good for them to remain single, as I am" (1 Cor 7:8 ESV). Singles are not second-class citizens in the kingdom of God, even though sometimes we unintentionally make them to feel that way. Let singles rejoice in God's grace and gifts and use them to fulfill their vocations in the world and in the church.

26. "Castitas coelebs est virtus vitans omnes vagas libidines extra coniugium" (Ursinus, *Corpus doctrinae*, 590).

QUESTION 110

What does God forbid in the eighth commandment?

QUESTION 111

But what does God require of you in this commandment?

Lord's Day 42

QUESTIONS 110–11

What does God forbid in the eighth commandment?

God forbids not only such theft and robbery as are punished by this magistrate, but God views as theft also all wicked tricks and devices, whereby we seek to get our neighbor's goods, whether by force or by deceit, such as unjust weights, ells, measures, goods, coins usury, or by any means forbidden of God; also a covetousness and the misuse and waste of His gifts.[1]

But what does God require of you in this commandment?

That I further my neighbor's good where I can and may, deal with him as I would have others deal with me, and labor faithfully, so that I may be able to help the poor in their need.[2]

The purpose of the eighth commandment, Ursinus writes, is "the conservation of things or possessions, which God has freely given to each one for sustaining life."[3]

RECOGNIZING PROVIDENCE AND PROPERTY

One of the first things a child must learn is the distinction between *mine* and *yours*. Almost from the cradle, as the children of Adam, we seem to

1. "Was verbietet Gott im achten Gebot? Er verbietet nicht allein den Diebstahl und Räuberei, welche die Obrigkeit straft; sondern Gott nennet auch Diebstahl alle böse Stücke und Anschläge, damit wir unseres Nächsten Gut gedenken an uns zu bringen, es sei mit Gewalt oder Schein des Rechtes, als unrechtem Gewicht, Elle, Mass, Waare, Münze, Wucher, oder durch einiges Mittel, das von Gott verboten ist; dazu auch allen Geiz und unnütze Verschwendung seiner Gaben" (Schaff, *Creeds of Christendom*, 3:347). "Quid vetat Deus in octavo praecepto? Non solum ea furta et rapinas, quas magistratus punit: sed furti nomine comprehendit, quicquid est malarum artium et aucupiorum, quibus aliena captamus, et ad nos vi aut specie recti transferre studemus: qualia sunt, iniquum pondus, iniusta ulna, inaequalis mensura, fucosa merx, fallax, moneta, usura, aut alia quaevis ratio aut modus rem faciendi a Deo interdictus. His adde omnem avaritiam, et multiplicem divinorum donorum prfusionem et abusum" (Niemeyer, *Collectio Confessionum*, 456–57).

2. "Was gebietet dir aber Gott in diesem Gebot? Dass ich meines Nächsten Nutzen, wo ich kann und mag, fördere, gegen ihn also handele, wie ich wollte, dass man mit mir handelte, und treulich arbeite, auf dass ich dem Dürftigen in seiner Noth helfen möge" (Schaff, *Creeds of Christendom*, 3:348). "Quae sunt ea quae Deus hic iubet? Ut commoda et utilitates proximi, quantum possim, adiuvem et augeam: cum eo sic agam, ut mecum agi cuperem: sedulo et fideliter opus faciam, ut aliorum quoque egestati subvenire queam" (Neimeyer, *Collection Confessionum*, 457).

3. "*Finis praecepti* est conservatio rerum seu posessionum, quas Deus singlis elargitur ad vaeae sustentationem" (Ursinus, *Corpus doctrinae*, 605).

desire that which is not ours. In the fall we violated all of God's moral law in one act (Jas 2:10). As Ursinus suggested, behind all that we and our neighbors have is the providence of God.[4]

One aspect of the original sin is that we stole what did not belong to us. "So when the woman saw that the tree was good for food, and that it was a delight to the eyes, and that the tree was to be desired to make one wise, she took of its fruit and ate, and she also gave some to her husband who was with her, and he ate" (Gen 3:6 ESV). The woman saw, desired, took, and ate. That fruit did not belong to our first parents. It belonged to God. He had not authorized us to eat from the tree of the knowledge of good and evil. Satan promised that if we stole and ate we would be blessed. Theft did not bring the promised happiness. It brought death and shame.

When a child takes what does not belong to him, even the most permissive parent corrects him because we know instinctively that theft is wrong. Jean-Jacques Rousseau (1712–1778) derided fences as arbitrary, and Karl Marx (1818–1883) argued that property is a *bourgeois* privilege, but the truth is that, in the world as God has ordered it, there is a difference between what is ours and what has been entrusted to others.[5] The truth is that Rousseau was justifying his dissolute life, and Marx's work seethes with envy.[6]

The recognition of yours and mine is not arbitrary. It is grounded in God's order of creation. We know it by nature (Rom 2:14–15). People may theorize about giving away *other* people's belongings, but rarely do they legislate the redistribution of their *own* property. After the communist revolution in Russia, the proletariat (working classes) continued to live in misery, now under the party bosses.

Obviously, theft is as old as sin, and there are as many ways to steal as there are humans. Absalom stole the hearts of the men Israel away from King David (2 Sam 15:6). Scripture plainly forbids kidnapping and then selling into slavery those who have been kidnapped (Deut 24:7). Under Moses that was a capital offense. In recent years we have been made

4. See the discussion of *HC* 26–28.

5. Rousseau, *Discourse on the Origin*; Marx, *Capital*, 377–78; Karl Marx, *Communist Manifesto*, in *Capital*, 419–25.

6. On Rousseau, see Trueman, *Rise and Triumph*, 105–28. On Marx and envy, see Schlossberg, *Idols for Destruction*.

aware (again) of the crime of human trafficking. The older Reformed writers address this crime explicitly. In his commentary on the catechism, Gijsbertus Voetius (1589–1676) specifies four types of kidnapping:

1. Stealing children, who were robbed from their parents by Roman Catholics and brought to a monastery or enrolled in the Jesuit order.
2. Stealing in the form of slavery. People were sold into slavery, a widespread phenomenon in the East and West Indies.
3. Stealing children from their parents with the aim of using them as beggars. Such children, according to one report, were often mutilated and maimed so that they could arouse sympathy when they went around begging.
4. Stealing young girls. Against the will of her parents, a young man carried out his plans to marry a young girl.[7]

Moses legislated against kidnapping people into slavery because it is an ancient and widespread practice. God's people are not to do it, but they have. As Thomas Sowell observes, though the "Antebellum South produced a huge volume of apologetic literature trying to justify slavery on racist grounds, no such justification was considered necessary in vast reaches of the world and over vast expanses of time."[8] As J. Douma says, those who have been redeemed out of slavery (Exod 20:1) "should realize how serious stealing other people is."[9]

Theft is so commonplace that our Lord took it as a given that thieves break in and steal (Matt 6:19). He knew that the prophet Jeremiah spoke the truth when he said, "The heart is deceitful above all things, and it is exceedingly corrupt: who can know it?" (Jer 17:9 ASV). Surely people steal out of hunger, but our prisons are not full because people did not have enough food. Our first parents did not steal because they had been corrupted by their environment. Infants and children do not take the toys

7. Kuyper, *Voetius' Catechisatie*, 2:1053, as quoted in Douma, *Ten Commandments*, 287.
8. Sowell, *Thomas Sowell Reader*, 245–46.
9. Douma, *Ten Commandments*, 287.

of their playmates because they have been corrupted by materialism and greed. It is not what goes into a child but what comes out of his little heart that corrupts him (Matt 15:11).

Since the fall, theft has always been with us, but it has perhaps never been so easy. The development of the internet has created the impression that intellectual property should be free. Digital content is regularly stolen. Criminals still rob banks, and burglars still break into houses to steal.

Calvin writes:

> God will not neglect to judge as a thief anyone who has taken advantage of a simple man, or who as has sold him goods in an underhanded way, seeing that he has outwitted him through a fault of judgement. Anyone who also overcharges an illiterate person is equally a thief. Moreover, if an artisan makes a faulty good and the buyer cannot perceive the flaw, or especially if someone takes whatever he can and sells what unquestionably does not belong to him (justifying it on that basis) that he is dealing with a rich man who has a full purse, it is all the same. Therefore if a man engages in any of these practices—although he may be able to get away with it in the world's eyes—the judgement of God will nevertheless run its course.[10]

Electronic theft of various sorts is so much a part of daily life today that we might forget how God regards theft: "Or do you not know that the unrighteous will not inherit the kingdom of God? Do not be deceived: neither the sexually immoral, nor idolaters, nor adulterers, nor men who practice homosexuality, nor thieves, nor the greedy, nor drunkards, nor revilers, nor swindlers will inherit the kingdom of God" (1 Cor 6:9–10 ESV). Theft is classed with other gross sins: sexual immorality, idolatry, adultery, homosexuality, greed, drunkenness, reviling, and swindling.

Laziness is a cause of theft, whether in fraud (Mic 6:11), robbery, or something as seemingly innocuous as plagiarism. Why go to all the trouble of translating, analyzing, and explaining a passage of Scripture to a congregation when all one must do is to download a world-class sermon from a gifted and famous preacher? In the internet age we have seen

10. Calvin, *John Calvin's Sermons*, 188–89.

a dramatic rise in plagiarism among preachers and students. Preachers are losing their positions because of plagiarism, and teachers across the country are faced with a flood of plagiarized student essays. Consider tax evasion: few like to pay taxes, but our Lord and the apostles command us to pay our taxes (Luke 20:19–26; Rom 13:6–7). It is theft to report falsely so as to avoid paying what is owed.

Another cause of theft is what Paul calls "the love of money," which, he says, "is a root of all kinds of evils. It is through this craving that some have wandered away from the faith and pierced themselves with many pangs" (1 Tim 6:10 ESV). The love of money, the insatiable desire to have more and more, has caused some to abandon the faith. Here it is hard not to think that the apostle is reflecting on Judas, who "had the moneybag" (John 13:29), betrayed our Lord for "thirty pieces of silver" (Matt 27:3), hanged himself, and "burst open in the middle" (Acts 1:18).

Underneath those causes of theft is unbelief in God's goodness and dissatisfaction with his providence. Christians ought to be convinced that nothing comes about by chance, but everything comes from God's fatherly hand (Jer 5:24; Matt 5:45).[11] Behind our discontent with God's providence is idolatry, particularly the presumption that if were we sovereign that we would arrange things more satisfactorily. To which the unquestioned, almighty God says, "Where were you when I laid the foundation of the earth?" (Job 38:4 ESV).

The good news is that, in Christ, by grace alone, through faith alone, there is salvation for thieves (λῃσταί): "Then two thieves were crucified with him, one on the right and one on the left" (Matt 27:38). One of those thieves mocked Jesus, but the other recognized the greatness of his sin and misery and turned in faith to the Savior who justifies and saves thieves. There is also new life for thieves that does not include theft. Paul says, "And such *were* some of you" (1 Cor 6:11)

VOCATION AND WORK

The eighth commandment has a positive purpose: "Let the thief no longer steal, but rather let him labor, doing honest work with his own hands, so that he may have something to share with anyone in need"

11. See the discussion of *HC* 28.

(Eph 4:28 ESV). Instead of coveting and stealing, believers are charged to work and give.

Vocation is the antidote for the envy that fuels theft. Vocation is a biblical and Christian idea.[12] Whereas the medieval and Roman churches tended to locate vocation only in monasteries and in the call to ministry, the Reformation churches argued that every image-bearer has a vocation, that secular work is not inherently defiled or defiling.[13] Secular work is just as honorable as sacred work. We are called in Scripture to do our work to the glory of God and to the well-being of our neighbor.[14]

Each of us has a vocation, a divine calling, in God's world. Calvin characterizes our vocation as a divine assignment that the Lord has given to each of us.[15] We should each think of ourselves as a sentry, assigned to a post and to a duty so that we do not "heedlessly wander about throughout life."[16] "It is enough," he writes, "if we know that the Lord's Calling is in everything the beginning and foundation of well-doing."[17] Discovering one's calling gives a focus and a direction to one's life and service. If we are pursuing a calling, then we are not working merely to accumulate wealth. Under the doctrine of vocation, we work to serve God and our neighbor, thereby showing God's love to our neighbor and glorifying God with our work.

Our culture is narcissistic, but Christians are called to think of others first. Parents work to care for their children. We work so that we can contribute to the benevolent offering and thus relieve the suffering of brothers

12. We should distinguish the Reformation doctrine of vocation from its caricature by Max Weber (1864–1920) in *Protestantism and the Spirit of Capitalism*. Weber was neither a Reformation scholar nor a theologian, but he was a German sociologist who wrote with the sort of imperious authority that moderns find simultaneously attractive and intimidating. The Weber thesis has been discredited, but some are still taught that Calvinism produced all the excesses of the early industrial period as Calvin's heirs sought to prove their election by their industry. Compare the second Geneva Catechism on the eighth commandment, which contradicts Weber's caricature of Calvin and the Calvinists. See *Calvin's Catechism*, QQ. 204–7, in Dennison, *Reformed Confessions*, 1:494–95; Calvin's 1555 sermons on the eighth commandment, e.g., the one given on Wednesday, July 3, in *John Calvin's Sermons on the Ten Commandments*, 185–201.

13. Calvin, *Institutes* 3.10.6. E.g., Martin Luther, *On Councils and the Church* (*LW* 41:3–178); Wingren, *Luther on Vocation*.

14. See the discussion under *HC* 91.

15. Calvin, *Institutes* 3.10.6.

16. Calvin, *Institutes* 3.10.6.

17. Calvin, *Institutes* 3.10.6.

and sisters in the congregation.[18] We work hard and well to fulfill our vocation in this world and thus to bring glory to God by reflecting the image of God. We were created to be prophets, priests, and kings.[19] In Christ, we are being renewed in Christ's image. We provide services and goods at a fair market price (Paul did not give away his tents, and Joseph made a living as a craftsman), thereby serving our neighbor. We ought to fulfill our calling in this world, to be the very best butcher, baker, or candlestick maker we can be to God's glory.

Reflecting the modern turn, it has become commonplace to see political leaders extolling the virtues of unemployment and sounding quite like Marx regarding the virtues of leisure. That they now speak like Marx makes one think that there has been a fundamental cultural shift relative to work, and it is hard not to think that people no longer view work as inherently good and valuable.

Aspects of this turn are not entirely new. The sixteenth-century Anabaptists misunderstood Acts 2:44–45, "And all who believed were together and had all things in common. And they were selling their possessions and belongs and distributing the proceeds to all, as any had need" (ESV), as introducing compulsory communalism. Christians are no more compelled to communalism or communism than they are to rebuild the temple (Acts 2:46). Luke recorded a series of evidences of the Spirit's work in the early church. One of those evidences is that believers were so devoted to one another that they willingly sold their own property in order to meet the material needs of other believers during a famine.

In *BC* 36, the Reformed churches rejected the Anabaptist interpretation of Acts 2:44–45 (and practice): "And on this matter we denounce the Anabaptists, other anarchists, and in general all those who want to reject the authorities and civil officers and to subvert justice by introducing common ownership of goods and corrupting the moral order that God has established among human beings."[20]

In contrast to the modern ethos, in the Christian understanding of the world as God has ordered it, work is inherently good. God is, as it were,

18. Klooster, *Our Only Comfort*, 2.1017.

19. See the discussion under *HC* 6.

20. United Reformed Churches in North America, *Liturgical Forms and Prayers*, 197.

a worker. He is, after all, the Creator. He made us in his image. He gave us work to do in the garden even before the fall (Gen 2:15). Work is an important way in which we express our status as bearers of the divine image. It continued to be valuable after the fall, even if it became difficult and frustrating (Gen 3:17–19). When the apostle Paul learned that some believers in Thessalonica were quitting their jobs because they thought Jesus was coming immediately, he told them to get back to work, and that if anyone would not work, he should not eat (2 Thess 3:10).

As valuable as work is, rest is also essential, and Reformed Christians ought thus to treasure the Christian Sabbath.[21] Leisure and retirement are complex questions, but suffice it to say here that working oneself to death is not virtuous. It breaks the sixth commandment as we confess it. The pattern of work and rest is embedded in creation and is reflected in redemption. God made us to do more than work. God made us social creatures, and by grace he has saved us to commune and fellowship with the saints. As we age, we ought to strive to be useful to Christ's kingdom, but retirement from daily labor is honorable, and how we spend those years is a matter of Christian liberty.[22]

THE VIRTUES TO BE DEVELOPED

Ursinus considers seven virtues to be cultivated under this commandment:[23]

1. *Commutative justice.*[24] In arithmetic, quantities with commutative properties give the same result whatever their order. They are interchangeable.[25] In commerce, "commutative justice then consists in preserving an equality between merit and reward, wages and labor etc."[26] Ursinus alludes here to not only Aquinas and Aristotle but also to the distinction, in the *Institutes of Justinian* (AD 533), among those things that are naturally in

21. See the discussion under *HC* 103.

22. Contra Piper, *Rethinking Retirement.*

23. Ursinus, *Corpus doctrinae*, 605–9; Ursinus, *Commentary*, 596–99.

24. "Iustitia Commutativa" (Ursinus, *Corpus doctrinae*, 605). Ursinus here follows Thomas (*ST* 2a2ae 61.1), who in turn adapted Aristotle's distinction between commutative and distributive justice, which refers to dealings between persons in which there is an exchange in which "each of the contracting parties gives and receives an equivalent" (*OED*, s.v. "commutative"). Distributive justice is that which is "directed to the private individual" (*ST* 2a2ae 61.1, resp. dic.).

25. *OED*, s.v. "commutative."

26. Ursinus, *Commentary*, 596.

common to all (e.g., water, air, etc.), those things that are held in public trust (e.g., rivers, ports, etc.), those things that are possessed by no one, "things sacred, religious, and holy,"[27] and finally the largest share of things that are held privately.[28] "All contracts are included under commutative justice."[29]

2. *Contentment*.[30] The essence of contentment is being "satisfied and contented with our present possessions, which we have honestly acquired," such that we would rather endure poverty than to desire what does not belong to us or what is unnecessary.[31] God's word says, "But godliness with contentment [αὐτάρκεια] is great gain" (1 Tim 6:6 ESV). Contentment is a challenging notion for economies predicated less on production and saving and more on spending and consuming. Advertisers bombard us with messages urging us to consume and accumulate as rapidly as possible. This is avarice. Its opposite is the refusal to receive anything. Ursinus characterizes that as "inhumanity."[32]

3. *Fidelity*. Faithfulness is perhaps best understood by considering its opposite. Calvin writes, "Infidelity, then is the root of the defection" (of Adam and Eve).[33] He continues to explain that from infidelity "arose ambition and pride, to which is joined ingratitude."[34] Fidelity (faithfulness) is born of gratitude for God's mercy, grace, and providence. It is to have a care, first of all, for the things of others. In that regard, it is to discharge one's duty without reference to one's own interests. It is also to fulfill one's duties appropriate to one's calling, "so that we may have is necessary to sustain us and ours, and that we may have that with which to supply the wants of others, all of which is done with the design that we may glorify God thereby."[35]

---

27. Ursinus, *Commentary*, 596.

28. Ursinus was alluding to Justinian's *Institutes*. For a modern edition see Justinian, *Institutes of Justinian* 2.1 (pp. 35–45).

29. Ursinus, *Commentary*, 596.

30. Ursinus uses αὐτάρκεια in the second sense of being content with one's circumstances. Arndt et al., *Greek-English Lexicon*, s.v. "αὐτάρκεια." See 1 Tim 6:6.

31. Ursinus, *Commentary*, 597.

32. *Inhumanitas* (Ursinus, *Corpus doctrinae*, 607).

33. "Proinde infidelitas radix defectionis fuit" (Calvin, *Institutio* 2.14; Barth, *Joannis Calvini Opera Selecta*, 3:232.6).

34. "Hinc autem emersit ambitio, et superbia, quibus annexa fuit ingratitudo" (Barth, *Joannis Calvini Opera Selecta*, 3:232.6–7).

35. Ursinus, *Commentary*, 597.

4. *Liberality*. This is the virtue of generosity whereby the Christian seeks, out of what the Lord has entrusted to him, to give freely, with love, "for the sake of godliness and charity," without being compelled, to others.[36] The classical sense of *liberalitas* is apt here: "a way of thinking befitting a freeman; a noble, kind, or friendly disposition, noble spirit, kindness, affability."[37] Calvin explains in his commentary on Matthew 5:42: "Again, we see the rule which the Spirit lays down in another passage for liberality. Let us ... not ... think that they have discharged their duty when they have aided a few persons, but to study to be kind to all, and not to be weary of giving, so long as they have the means. ... We now see what it is, to have an open hand to petitioners. It is to be generously disposed to all who need our assistance, and who cannot return the favour."[38]

5. *Hospitality*. Hebrews 13:1–2 says, "Let brotherly love continue. Do not neglect to show hospitality to strangers, for thereby some have entertained angels unawares" (ESV). Reflecting on this passage, Ursinus defines hospitality as a "species of liberality" by which we host strangers and travelers and "especially those who have been banished on account of the profession of the gospel."[39] It is, according to Calvin, one of the ways that we love our neighbor as ourselves, by relieving their needs.[40]

6. *Parsimony*. We might be surprised to see *parsimony* listed as a virtue. In modern usage this noun has come to signify "excessive unwillingness to part with money or other material resources."[41] When Ursinus wrote, *parsimonia* signified frugality or thrift.[42] We ought to "guard against all unnecessary expense." Thus defined, it keeps liberality from becoming prodigality.

7. *Frugality*. Ursinus distinguishes *frugalitas* from *parsimonia* by restricting the former to proper disposition of household affairs.[43]

36. Ursinus, *Commentary*, 598.

37. Lewis and Short, *Latin Dictionary*, s.v. "Libertas."

38. Calvin, *Commentary on a Harmony*, 1.301–2.

39. Ursinus, *Commentary*, 598.

40. Calvin, *To the Romans*, 467–68.

41. *OED*, s.v. "parsimony," 2.

42. Ursinus, *Corpus doctrinae*, 608. See Lewis and Short, *Latin Dictionary*, s.v. "parsimonia."

43. Ursinus, *Corpus doctrinae*, 608; Ursinus, *Commentary*, 599.

Question 112

What does the ninth commandment require?

Lord's Day 43

QUESTION 112

What does the ninth commandment require?

That I bear false witness against no one, wrest no one's words, be no backbiter or slanderer, join in condemning no one unheard or rashly; but that on pain of God's heavy wrath, I avoid all lying and deceit as the very works of the devil; and that in matters of judgment and justice and in all other affairs I love, speak honestly and confess the truth; also in so far as I can, defend and promote my neighbor's good name.[1]

Ursinus writes, "The scope or the end of the ninth commandment is the sanction and continuation of the truth between men."[2] When the catechism was written, there was general agreement that the truth *is*, that it is objectively true and known to be such. It is not that there were never radical subjectivists in Christendom, but the skeptics were a minority. Today, the skeptics and the subjectivists control the culture-forming institutions (e.g., education, politics, art, commerce, and entertainment).

IN DEFENSE OF TRUTH

The truth is that which is and speech that accords with and reports what is. It is the opposite of a lie, which is "when anyone speaks or declares by outward signs differently from what he thinks, and from what the thing itself is. To lie is to go against one's own mind and knowledge."[3] In the garden the Evil One spoke the opposite of what he knew to be true. He

1. "Was will das neunte Gebot? Dass ich wider Niemand falsch Zeugniss gebe, Niemand seine Worte verkehre, kein Afterreder und Lästerer sei, Niemand unverhört und leichtlich verdammen helfe; sondern allerlei Lügen und Trügen, als eigene Werke des Teufels, bei schwerem Gottes-Zorn vermeide, in Gerichts- und allen andern Handlungen die Wahrheit liebe, aufrichtig sage und bekenne, auch meines Nächsten Ehre und Glimpf, nach meinem Vermögen, rette und fördere" (Schaff, *Creeds of Christendom*, 3:348). "Quid exigit nonum praeceptum? Ne adversus quempiam dicam falsum testimonium, nullius verba calumnier, nulli obtrectem, aut convicium faciam, neminem temere, vel indicta causa condemnem. Verum omnis generis mendacia, fraudes, ut opera Diaboli propria, nisi in me gravissimam iram Dei concitare velim, omni cura fugiam: In iudiciis caeterisque negotiis veritatem secter, et id quod res est libere et constanter profitear. Ad haec famam aliorum et existimationem, quantum queam, defendam et augeam" (Niemeyer, *Collectio Confessionum*, 457).

2. "Scopus seu finish noni praecepti est sanctio et conservatio veritatus inter homines" (Ursinus, *Corpus doctrinae*, 610).

3. Ursinus, *Commentary*, 601.

began by questioning the veracity of God's word: "Did God actually say, 'You shall not eat of any tree in the garden'?" (Gen 3:1 ESV). The woman collaborated with the Evil One by adding to the Lord's command, "Neither shall you touch it, lest you die" (3:3 ESV). Then the devil revealed his agenda by openly lying about God and his word: "For God knows that when you eat of it your eyes will be opened, and you will be like God, knowing good and evil" (Gen 3:5 ESV). That was not true. God was not protecting himself from competitors—that is the lie that the gnostics told in the second century. The lie was that truth differed from what God said, that reality was not what God said it was.

Until modernity, we generally recognized that there was an objective reality. Long before Moses, we recognized that God constituted objective reality and constituted us to recognize it. One of the great and tragic features of late modern life is the loss of objective reality. We regularly are given to believe that there are multiple versions of reality. To be sure, we do perceive reality differently, but not such that there is no such thing as a generally agreed objective reality. There are not six billion different ways to interpret a stop sign. Stop signs work more or less the same way the world over. Our experiences and perceptions are not so radically different from each other that there is no commonality or shared sense experience.

This is no mere academic concern. The ninth commandment says, "You shall not bear false witness against your neighbor" (Exod 20:16 ESV). If there is no such thing as objective reality, then there is no such thing as a "false witness." If, after all, there are as many realities as there are people, who is to say what is a "false witness"? Yet Scripture everywhere assumes and teaches that we may know objective truth and must speak that truth.

The apostle John writes,

> So Pilate entered his headquarters again and called Jesus and said to him, "Are you the King of the Jews?" Jesus answered, "Do you say this of your own accord, or did others say it to you about me?" Pilate answered, "Am I a Jew? Your own nation and the chief priests have delivered you over to me. What have you done?" Jesus answered, "My kingdom is not of this world. If my kingdom were

> of this world, my servants would have been fighting, that I might not be delivered over to the Jews. But my kingdom is not from the world." Then Pilate said to him, "So you are a king?" Jesus answered, "You say that I am a king. For this purpose I was born and for this purpose I have come into the world—to bear witness to the truth. Everyone who is of the truth listens to my voice." Pilate said to him, "What is truth?" (John 18:33–38 ESV)

Pilate's reply was as cynical as it was false, and it was false on two counts: First, there is truth. Ironically, Pilate promptly went out to the crowd and told them the truth, that he found no guilt in Jesus because Jesus was innocent and positively righteous. Not only had Jesus not transgressed the law, but he had fulfilled it perfectly every day and in every way.

Second, Jesus *is* the truth. Jesus said, "I am the way, the truth and the life. No one comes to the Father except through me" (John 14:6). Jesus is not *a* truth or merely *a* witness to the truth (you and I do that). Jesus *is* the truth. All humans are liars (Ps 116:11), but God is the truth and he tells the truth.

This dialogue with Pilate gives us an indicator of what truth is: that which is. Telling the truth is speech that reflects what is. Jesus was innocent, and Pilate told the truth. He said what was.

The Gospel of John testifies repeatedly to the reality that Jesus is the truth. He is the "true light" that comes into the dark world (1:9). He is the Word incarnate, full of grace and truth (1:14). He is the reality as distinct from the Mosaic types and shadows (1:17). He is the true bread from heaven (6:32). His flesh is true food, and his blood is true drink (6:55). He said that his testimony about the Father was true (8:14) and the Father was true (7:28). Believers know the truth, and the truth sets us free (8:32).

It is fashionable now to suggest that truth claims are really just constructs, conventions, things that people make up to control other people. That is simply wrong. The deconstructionist emperor has no clothes, and what is more, you and I can see that he is naked, and like the little boy in the story, we should speak up and say so. The deconstructionists write books which they expect us to interpret in the way that the author intends, telling us that we readers may make of the books of others whatever we will. That is nothing but literary vandalism.

Our Lord Jesus told us that when two witness agree, that is truth. "Yet even if I do judge, my judgment is true, for it is not I alone who judge, but I and the Father who sent me. In your Law it is written that the testimony of two people is true" (John 8:16–17 ESV). In order to explain the truth of his witness about himself, he appealed to the Old Testament law that said that every legal matter must be established by two or three witnesses. He was acting as one of the witnesses. The Father is the other. Jesus the truth was not a skeptic about our ability to know and tell the truth. He did not say that we know the truth in exactly the same way he knows it, but we do know and tell the truth.

Lying has become endemic in our culture. Newspaper writers plagiarize, and newscasters and politicians fabricate events regularly. Sometimes they even lie about their own biography. Lies and plagiarism are not isolated to journalists and politicians. Pedestrian preachers become suddenly eloquent as they present as their own sermons that they did not write.

WHAT IS PROHIBITED

Negatively, the ninth commandment forbids "bearing false witness" and "all other things which are closely allied to it."[4] Certainly this commandment applies most directly to the courtroom. There we are under a sacred obligation to say what we know to be the truth.[5] Our testimony is to represent, to the best of our knowledge, what really was. Obviously, that obligation does not end in the courtroom.

WHAT IS COMMANDED

Positively, the commandment requires us to tell the truth, to bear true witness, to tell the truth about and to our neighbor. In the internet age, everyone is our neighbor. It has never been easier to gossip than it is today. A text here, a social media post there, and a reputation is destroyed. The catechism even calls lying and deceit the "work of the Devil." The moral

4. Ursinus, *Commentary*, 600. Ursinus says that lying is the genus or the class and treats forms of lying as species of the same (*Corpus doctrinae*, 610).

5. See the discussion of *HC* 99.

law says, in effect, one shall not bear false witness about one's neighbor online. It means that Christians must not gossip. If one does not know something to be true from direct experience or from firsthand testimony, then a report may well be gossip. Even if one has firsthand knowledge of a thing, that knowledge is not a license to repeat a story. There are other considerations: Is it edifying? Does it hurt or help my neighbor? Is it wise? These are important questions as we seek to govern our tongues according to God's word (Jas 1:26; 3:1–12).

THE VIRTUES TO BE DEVELOPED AND VICES TO BE AVOIDED

Ursinus identifies eight virtues to be cultivated under the ninth commandment. We will consider a few of them briefly.

1. We strive to be true and to tell the truth. Ursinus calls this "veracity." It is a purpose of the will to one who "speaks and loves the truth," and who "has a desire to promote it for the glory of God and the salvation (*salutem*) of my neighbor."[6] Being both true *and* truthful begins with a "firm purpose or choice in the will ... to embrace true thoughts and opinions," and defend the truth as a matter of duty.[7] It is a determination to keep promises (e.g., contracts) and to avoid dissembling. Being true and truthful entails "boldness, which is a virtue by which we profess the truth fearlessly and willingly to as great an extent as required by the time, place, and necessity of the occasion."[8] The vices here to be avoided include lying, including fraud, deceit, dissembling, so-called white (or courtesy) lies, slandering, backbiting, and neglecting to discover and tell the truth.[9]

Traditionally, Christians have distinguished between *mendacious* lies, *jocular* lies, and *officious* lies.[10] The first is clearly forbidden and does not merit more discussion. As J. Douma notes, a tall tale, for example, the fable of Paul Bunyan, insofar as it does not intend to deceive, is not a lie.[11]

6. Ursinus, *Commentary*, 601, revised in light of Ursinus, *Corpus doctrinae*, 611.

7. Ursinus, *Commentary*, 601.

8. Ursinus, *Commentary*, 601.

9. Ursinus, *Commentary*, 601. Ursinus refers to white lies with *mendacia officiosa* (611).

10. Douma, *Ten Commandments*, 324–25.

11. Douma, *Ten Commandments*, 325.

Insofar as an *officious* lie is made out of politeness or to avoid conflict, it is forbidden.

There are some difficult cases, however, under this heading, for example, the lie of necessity as in the case of the Hebrew midwives (Exod 1:15–22) and Rahab (Josh 2). Ursinus's approach reflects the traditional position that, for example, the midwives and Rahab are not praised or blessed for lying but for their faith in rescuing God's people.[12] "Following in the footsteps of Augustine, the church has throughout her history rejected the lie of necessity almost universally."[13] Both Calvin and Ursinus condemn the women for lying.[14] We have often *assumed*, however, that the midwives were lying and that the Jewish mothers in that circumstance were not giving birth more quickly than normal.[15] We owe deference to tradition, but may we say *a priori* that the Lord did not work a redemptive miracle and that the Jewish midwives were not lying? John Murray writes, "We need not suppose that the midwives' reply to Pharaoh was altogether void of truth. There is good reason to believe that the Hebrew women often bore their children without the aid of the midwives."[16]

Nevertheless, assuming the traditional view, it seems difficult to separate the faith of the midwives from their lie to murderous authorities. Hebrews 11:31 says that we know that Rahab had faith *because* she gave the spies a "friendly welcome." Those spies were in the process of committing both an act of war *and* an act of deception. That friendly welcome included protecting the spies from those who sought to seize and kill them, and her lie was essential to that protection. James 2:25 says that Rahab's faith was evidenced (or vindicated; ἐδικαιώθη) by her works, which involved

12. Murray (*Principles of Conduct*, 138), writes, "It should not go unnoticed that the New Testament Scriptures which commend Rahab for her faith and works make allusion solely to the fact that she received spies and sent them out another way. … The approval of these actions does not logically … carry with it the approval of the specific untruth spoken to the king of Jericho."

13. Douma, *Ten Commandments*, 326.

14. Augustine takes this position, as does Aquinas and Peter Martyr. See Calvin, *Commentaries on the Four Last Books*, 1.34–35n3. In his 1554 dialogical explanation of the decalogue, Pierre Viret argues that even though figures in redemptive history lied, we should not, since God has not commanded it, and we should not be wiser than God (*Exposition of the Ten Commandments*, 2.379).

15. Regarding the midwives, Douma writes, "Clearly that was a falsehood" (*Ten Commandments*, 327), but he does not indicate how he knows that was a falsehood.

16. Murray, *Principles of Conduct*, 141.

receiving the spies, hiding them, and lying to the enemy to protect them.[17] It is true, as Murray notes, that neither James nor Hebrews mentions the lie, but assuming the traditional view, had the midwives and Rahab not lied, there would not have been stories to which Hebrews and James could appeal. In other words, it is difficult to distinguish the lie from her faithful acts.

David deceived Achish (1 Sam 21:13).[18] The book of Judges would be very different without the various acts of military deception (e.g., Ehud). We recognize the necessity of deceit in war. General Patton helped to win World War II in part by convincing the Axis powers, through the use of deception (e.g., rubber tanks and phony radio traffic), that he intended to invade France at Pas-de-Calais.[19] Pharaoh was attempting to commit genocide against the Israelites, and the Israelites were at war with the Canaanites. Perhaps the traditional view, in this instance, does not properly account for the categorical difference between war and peace? As Murray writes of the midwives, "It was not an obligation to tell Pharaoh the whole truth."[20] Reformation history illustrates how difficult it can be to be rigorously consistent here. For example, consider the Five Prisoners of Chambéry, Antoine Laborie, Jehan Vernou, Jean Trigalet, Bertrand Bataille, and G. Tauray, all Reformed pastors who were arrested in June 1555 and sentenced to death for the sake of the gospel.[21] On July 25, they wrote to the Company of Pastors recounting how, under interrogation, in an attempt to save the lives of believers, they denied any knowledge of secret Reformed worship services being conducted in the valley of Pragela (near Turin, Italy).[22] On August 1, 1555, they wrote to the Company of Pastors in Geneva, "Have we achieved anything by what we have done? Have we, by our misguided prudence, prevented what we feared from

---

17. ἐδικαιώθη is translated "vindicated" on the strength of Jas 2:14, where the issue is *not* the instrument of justification but the evidence of faith or the lack thereof. On this see *BC* 24. The point James is making in vv. 24–25 is the same as v. 14. The same verb, in the same form, almost certainly means "vindicated" in 1 Tim 3:16. Jesus was not declared righteous because of his resurrection. Rather, his resurrection demonstrated his righteousness.

18. Viret, *Exposition of the Ten Commandments*, 2.378.

19. Douma agrees with this point (*Ten Commandments*, 327).

20. Murray, *Principles of Conduct*, 141.

21. Hughes, *Christian Ethics*, 198.

22. Hughes, *Christian Ethics*, 198. See Bretschneider, *Corpus Reformatorum*, 43:694–97.

happening? Alas, no. For three or four days later, when we were still sorrowing over our fault, the news came that Satan was inflicting his fury on those whom we wished to preserve."[23] Calvin responded, "Your prudence in responding is truly from the Spirit of God and not from the cunning of the world."[24]

These are difficult cases, and it would be a mistake to use them to justify deception outside war, nor is there any justification for the Islamic doctrine of *Taqiyah,* wherein faithful Muslims are permitted to lie to infidels. Christians are not in a state of war with all pagans at all times. War and wartime deception is by definition exceptional.[25] In the same way, we should distinguish between military deception and lies we tell to avoid giving offense. The midwives and Rahab were looking out for the interests of others. When we tell lies of courtesy, we are usually looking out for ourselves.

2. *Candor*. In contemporary English usage *candor* denotes "freedom from reserve in one's statements," which is a little different from what Ursinus intended.[26] It is a virtue that "understands, in a proper light, things correctly and honestly spoken or done, and puts the most favorable construction upon such things as are doubtful, in as far as there are any just reasons for doing; and does not readily entertain suspicions, or indulge them, although there might be sufficient cause for doing so."[27] The vice here illuminates the virtue by contrast. Calumny finds fault with the innocent "where there is no reason for it" but also puts "the very worst construction upon" things said or written that are not worthy of suspicion. Since we live in the age of the "hermeneutic of suspicion," it behooves Christians to strive to believe all things (1 Cor 13:7).[28] As Ursinus writes, this is no

23. Hughes, *Register of the Company*, 312.

24. "Cependant avisez que vostre prudence à respondre soit vrayement de l'esprit de Dieu et non pas de l'astuce du monde" (Bretschneider, *Corpus Reformatorum*, 15:708). I am grateful to Chris Gordon for pointing me to this episode.

25. See the discussion under *HC* 105.

26. OED, s.v. "candour"; cf. Lewis and Short, *Latin Dictionary*, s.v. "candor," which literally refers to something brilliantly shining. Figuratively it refers to "purity, integrity, sincerity."

27. Ursinus, *Commentary*, 602.

28. See the discussion under *HC* 6.

license to "foolish credulity," that is, to give assent to something rashly or when there is "sufficient evidence" to the contrary.[29]

3. *Simplicity*. This is the opposite of *duplicity*. It is the truth spoken "clearly and without ambiguity."[30] The world rewards clever ambiguity, but simplicity is a virtue of one who "honestly and openly speaks and does what is true, right, and understood in arts and common life."[31] Calvin is helpful here. "Equally we must not call 'black' 'white' under the pretext that we are forbidden to offend anyone."[32] This is a salutary note when we are being pressured to regard words as mere conventions, lacking any connection to reality.

The Evil One is a liar and the father of lies (John 8:44). Christians ought to be relentlessly committed to the truth as God has revealed it in nature and in Scripture. Not only do we need to assert that there is truth in nature and grace, and not only must we tell the truth about God and our neighbor, but we need to tell the truth to our neighbor. We have bad news to tell to everyone: "All have sinned and fall short of the glory of God" (Rom 3:23). We have a great, precious, and objective truth to tell: Jesus is God the Son incarnate, and he came to earth to save sinners, "of whom I am first" (1 Tim 1:15). Let us tell it wisely, sincerely, and simply.

---

29. Ursinus, *Commentary*, 603. Emphasis original. See Calvin's explanation of this virtue in *Institutes* 2.8.48 and in Calvin, *Sermons on the Ten Commandments*, 204–6.

30. "Est perspicua veritatis sine ambagibus" (Ursinus, *Corpus doctrinae*, 613).

31. Ursinus, *Commentary*, 603.

32. Calvin, *Sermons on the Ten Commandments*, 211.

Question 113
What does the tenth commandment require?

Question 114
Can those who are converted to God keep these commandments perfectly?

Question 115
Why then does God so strictly enjoin the ten commandments upon us, since in this life no one can keep them?

Lord's Day 44

QUESTION 113

What does the tenth commandment require?

That not even the least inclination or thought against any commandment of God ever enter our heart, but that with our whole heart we continually hate all sin and take pleasure in all righteousness.[1]

In a world in which we are surrounded by death and corruption, it is most difficult to imagine what it must have been like to be without sin, but Scripture says (thus we confess) God created us "in righteousness and true holiness."[2] In the beginning we were not sinful. We did not have any moral, intellectual, psychological, or emotional corruption. We were not yet glorified, but we were not sinful. The Lord made a covenant with us in which we were offered glory on the condition that we obey him completely, that we pass a test by obeying the "commandment of life."[3] The remarkable thing is that we were completely prepared for this test and able to pass it. We had no latent disability, no inherent concupiscence, that is, "a corrupt inclination or an inordinate affect, desiring that which God prohibits."[4] The life and blessedness God offered us was to be glorious beyond imagination. Nevertheless, quite mysteriously, we freely chose something other than what God offered us. When the Evil One offered us equality with God, we had the freedom to choose contentment with God and his promises, but we did not. We freely chose to covet what did not belong to us.

The question of concupiscence is of the essence of this commandment. Indeed, Ursinus writes of "this commandment, which concerns

1. "Was will das zehute Gebot? Dass auch die geringste Lust oder Gedanken wider irgend ein Gebot Gottes in unser Herz nimmermehr kommen; sondern wir für und für von ganzem Herzen aller Sünde seind sein, und Lust zu aller Gerechtigkeit haben sollen" (Schaff, *Creeds of Christendom*, 3:348). "Quid prohibet decimum praeceptum? Ne vel minima cupiditate, aut cogitatione, adversus ullum Dei praeceptum corda nostra unquam solicitentur: sed ut perpetuo, et ex animo omne peccatum detestemur, contraque omni iustitia delectemur" (Niemeyer, *Collectio Confessionum*, 457).

2. See the discussion under *HC* 6.

3. *BC* 14 (United Reformed Churches in North America, *Liturgical Forms and Prayers*, 167). See the discussion under *HC* 7 concerning whether grace was necessary before the fall.

4. "Quae est inclinatio prava vel affectus inordinatus, appetens ea quae Deus prohibuit" (Ursinus, *Corpus doctrinae*, 616). See the discussion of concupiscence under *HC* 2, 6–7, 40, 109.

concupiscence."[5] Thus, to us sinners, the tenth word in God's moral law says: "You shall not covet your neighbor's house, you shall not covet your neighbor's wife, nor his manservant, nor his maidservant, nor his ox, nor his donkey, nor anything that is your neighbor's" (Exod 20:17).

The catechism treats the tenth commandment as a summary of the whole law. "The scope or end" of this commandment "is the rectitude of all the affections toward God and neighbor and his things and an internal obedience, which is to be included also in all the other commandments."[6] The moral law begins and ends with love. In the first commandment we are to love God with all our faculties. The last commandment diagnoses what we actually love since coveting is all about what we love, what we desire, and who we are.

Before the fall, we had the power, in our intellect, affections, and will, to do what the law commands. After the fall, our intellect, our affections, and our will are all bent, corrupted, darkened so that, apart from God's restraining mercies and his favor merited for believers by Christ, we not only lack the power to obey but even the desire.

We, in Adam, broke God's law. We chose to believe and obey a lie rather than to believe and obey God's truth. When the Lord came to inquire, Adam tried literally to cover up (Gen 3:7; *BC* 23). Why? Because he knew he was naked. How did he know that he was naked? Because he broke the "commandment of life," that is, the covenant of works. He made a false covenant with a false god and ate from the tree of the knowledge of good and evil.

The problem, of course, is never the law. God's word says, "What then shall we say? That the law is sin? By no means! Yet if it had not been for the law, I would not have known sin. For I would not have known what it is to covet if the law had not said, 'You shall not covet.' But sin, seizing an opportunity through the commandment, produced in me all kinds of covetousness. For apart from the law, sin lies dead" (Rom 7:7–8 ESV).

5. "Praeceptum de concupiscentia esse unum, non duo, manifestum est" (Ursinus, *Corpus doctrinae*, 615). Ursinus is returning to the question of the numbering of the commandments. See the discussion under *HC* 93.

6. "Scopus seu finis decimi praecepti est, affectuum omnium erga Deum et proximum et res eius, rectitudo, et obedientia interna, quae in omnibus etiam aliis praeceptis includenda" (Ursinus, *Corpus doctrinae*, 615).

When he wants to explain how the law teaches us the greatness of our sin and misery, Paul goes to the tenth commandment. Commit adultery, steal, lie, or murder, and likely as not someone else will find out. Coveting, however, is a sin that usually only God sees. It is the one with which we think we can get away, but sin it is. In Romans 13:9 Paul lists coveting with the rest of the second table of the moral law: "For the commandments, 'You shall not commit adultery, You shall not murder, You shall not steal, You shall not covet,' and any other commandment, are summed up in this word: 'You shall love your neighbor as yourself'" (ESV).

What is the root of covetousness? James says: "But each person is tempted when he is lured and enticed by his own desire. Then desire when it has conceived gives birth to sin, and sin when it is fully grown brings forth death. Do not be deceived, my beloved brothers. Every good gift and every perfect gift is from above, coming down from the Father of lights, with whom there is no variation or shadow due to change" (Jas 1:14–17 ESV). The root of covetousness is concupiscence. In *On Marriage and Concupiscence* (ca. AD 419), against the Pelagians, Augustine denies any "carnal concupiscence" before the fall.[7] Calvin writes, "Those who have said that original sin is 'concupiscence' have used an appropriate word, if only it be added—something that most will by no means concede—that whatever is in man, from the understanding to the will, from the soul even to the flesh, has been defiled and crammed with this concupiscence. Or, to put it more briefly, the whole man is of himself nothing but concupiscence."[8]

We must not think that we sinned originally or that we sin now because we are creatures. The fall is a great mystery, and we should not go blaming God or implying that the fault is in our finitude or createdness. After the fall, we were born with ungodly desires, with concupiscence. Ursinus reminds us that it was the Pelagians who taught that concupiscence was not sin.[9] Behind that error of the Pelagians (which, he reminds us, was

7. Augustine, *On Marriage and Concupiscence* 1.18 (*NPNF* 1/5:271).

8. Calvin, *Institutes* 2.1.8.

9. Ursinus, *Corpus doctrinae*, 616; Ursinus, *Commentary*, 606. We should not imagine that Pelagianism is only an ancient heresy. The neo-Augustinians in the fourteenth and fifteenth centuries charged the Franciscan theologians Ockham and Biel with Pelagianism. The Synod of Dort repeatedly charged Arminius and the Remonstrants with Pelagianism, and it persists in our day in a variety of ways, whether denying the effect of the fall on Adam's children, the doctrine of perfectionism,

condemned at the Council of Ephesus in AD 431) is the notion that concupiscence is the *propensity* to sin but not sin itself. The orthodox, however, say that corrupt and disordered inclinations, planning sin, and committing sin are all sin.[10]

James says that good gifts come from God (Jas 1:17), but sinful, evil desires come from our corrupt hearts (Jas 1:15). That is just what our Lord Jesus taught:

> And he called the people to him and said to them, "Hear and understand: it is not what goes into the mouth that defiles a person, but what comes out of the mouth; this defiles a person." Then the disciples came and said to him, "Do you know that the Pharisees were offended when they heard this saying?" He answered, "Every plant that my heavenly Father has not planted will be rooted up. ... Do you not see that whatever goes into the mouth passes into the stomach and is expelled? But what comes out of the mouth proceeds from the heart, and this defiles a person. For out of the heart come evil thoughts, murder, adultery, sexual immorality, theft, false witness, slander. These are what defile a person. But to eat with unwashed hands does not defile anyone." (Matt 15:10–13, 17–20 ESV)

When the tenth commandment says, "You shall not covet," it goes to the root of the fifth commandment: we desire to rule over authorities; to the sixth commandment: we desire to take life unjustly; to the seventh commandment: we desire to find sexual satisfaction outside the order God has established; to the eighth: we desire what God has not given, so we steal it; and to the ninth: we desire people to think what we want, not what is, so we lie and cover up. It is all rooted in covetousness. James says:

> What causes quarrels and what causes fights among you? Is it not this, that your passions are at war within you? You desire and do not have, so you murder. You covet and cannot obtain, so you fight and quarrel. You do not have, because you do not ask. You ask and

---

confusing nature and grace, or treating the prelapsarian and poslapsarian states as identical. In Christian ethics, we see the influence of Pelagianism in the case of those who, like the Pelagians, regard same-sex attraction as concupiscent but not sinful per se.

10. Ursinus, *Commentary*, 606; Ursinus, *Corpus doctrinae*, 616.

> do not receive, because you ask wrongly, to spend it on your passions. You adulterous people! Do you not know that friendship with the world is enmity with God? Therefore whoever wishes to be a friend of the world makes himself an enemy of God. (Jas 4:1–4 ESV)

We covet because we are corrupt. The only way out of the cycle of corruption is repentance, recognizing sin and our sinful nature, calling it what it is, turning from it in faith, and calling on the Savior in confidence. He is in the business of saving sinners. His Spirit is in the business of progressively, gradually sanctifying sinners.

The antithesis of coveting, of desiring what is not ours, is to rest in what God has given to us. Our Lord Jesus, the last Adam (1 Cor 15:45), did just that, "who, though he was in the form of God, did not count equality with God a thing to be grasped, but emptied himself, by taking the form of a servant, being born in the likeness of men" (Phil 2:6–7 ESV).

Adam, who was not in the "form of God," reached out his hand, as it were, to take what was not his. He was not content. He tried to fill himself. Jesus poured himself like a drink offering for us. He obeyed all the way to the cross. He took on himself our sin and bore our judgment and died our death that we might be freely accepted by God, only for the sake of Christ's righteousness imputed to us (*sola gratia*) and received through faith alone (*sola fide*).

Now, through faith in Christ, in union and communion with him, by grace alone, we are gradually learning contentment. Jeremiah Burroughs (1600–1646) defines contentment thus: "Contentment is an inward, quiet, gracious frame of spirit—the whole soul, judgment, thoughts, will, affections and all are satisfied and quiet."[11] This is the antithesis of our age. We are more like the Rolling Stones than we are like Jeremiah Burroughs. We try and we try, but we "can't get no satisfaction." It is because we look in the wrong places. The apostle Paul learned contentment under very difficult circumstances. "For the sake of Christ, then, I am content with weaknesses, insults, hardships, persecutions, and calamities. For when I am weak, then I am strong" (2 Cor 12:10 ESV). His circumstances were never going to provide contentment. He had to find it elsewhere. "Not that I am speaking of being in need, for I have learned in whatever situation

11. Burroughs, *Rare Jewel*, 11.

I am to be content. I know how to be brought low, and I know how to abound. In any and every circumstance, I have learned the secret of facing plenty and hunger, abundance and need. I can do all things through him who strengthens me" (Phil 4:11–13 ESV). The secret is that Christ is our contentment. We belong to him "with body and soul, both in life and in death." What is our only comfort, contentment, in life and death? Christ *for* me and Christ *in* me, that is, in our union with Christ.

Nevertheless, the Rolling Stones were on to something. Living in the prosperous West presents a real challenge in this regard. We are offered a near-constant barrage of products, each one promising happiness. Genuine capitalism is a good thing, but we have never before had so much and been so discontent. In contrast:

> But godliness with contentment is great gain, for we brought nothing into the world, and we cannot take anything out of the world. But if we have food and clothing, with these we will be content. But those who desire to be rich fall into temptation, into a snare, into many senseless and harmful desires that plunge people into ruin and destruction. For the love of money is a root of all kinds of evils. It is through this craving that some have wandered away from the faith and pierced themselves with many pangs. (1 Tim 6:6–10 ESV)

It is not easy for Adam's children to learn contentment. It begins with Christ. By grace, daily we die a bit more to the false promises of this world and learn to accept that Christ's promises are genuine, to rest in that, and to accept whatever circumstances he provides are enough for the moment. The apple is shiny and seems full of promise, but only Christ is true and full of life.

Question 114

Can those who are converted to God keep these commandments perfectly?

No, but even the holiest men, while in this life, have only a small beginning of this obedience; yet so, that with earnest purpose they begin to live not only according to some, but according to all the Commandments of God.[12]

We might wonder why the catechism asks this question. Scripture, history, and experience seem to tell us that, short of glory, no human reaches perfection in this life. The answer is suggested by Ursinus's exposition of *HC* 114, which turns to a four-point refutation of Pelagianism. That answer echoes the beginning of his exposition of this question: "Which question in order to be rightly understood, we must distinguish between the nature of man in integrity, in the fall, in turn in the restoration."[13] This is the Augustinian way of proceeding. With Augustine, against the Pelagians, we distinguish clearly human nature before the fall from human nature after the fall. It was a fundamental error of Pelagius to blur that distinction. The doctrine that humans can achieve perfection after the fall is *also* a distinctly Pelagian conviction. As Ursinus explains, "In the state of integrity, perfect, complete obedience to the entire law was possible for human nature according to all parts and degrees as it was for the angels. For man was created in the image of God in perfect sanctity and righteousness."[14] Here Ursinus is drawing on his earlier work on the prelapsarian covenant of works, as distinct from the postlapsarian covenant of grace.[15]

As mentioned under the previous question, this question-and-answer reminds us that Pelagianism is a recurring temptation even for the

---

12. "Können aber die, so zu Gott bekehret sind, solche Gebote vollkommen halten? Nein; sondern es haben auch die Allerheiligsten, so lange sie in diesem Leben sind, nur einen geringen Anfang dieses Gehorsams; doch also, dass sie mit ernstlichem Vorsatz, nicht allein nach etlichen, sondern nach allen Geboten Gottes anfangen zu leben" (Schaff, *Creeds of Christendom*, 3:349). "Possuntne autem illi, qui ad Deum conversi sunt, haec praecepta perfecte servare? Minime: Verum etiam sanctissimi quique, quamdiu vivunt, habent tantum exigua initia huius obedientiae: sic tamen, ut serio ac non simulato studio, non secundum aliqua tantum, sed secundum omnia Dei praecepta vivere incipiant" (Niemeyer, *Collectio Confessionum*, 457).

13. "Quae quaestio ut recte intelligatur, distinguenda est hominis natura integram, lapsam, rursus instaurationem" (Ursinus, *Corpus doctrinae*, 618).

14. "Natura integra possibilis erat integra totius legis obedientia secundum omnes partes et gradus, sicut angelis. Erat enim homo conditus ad imaginem Dei in perfecta sanctitate et iustitia" (Ursinus, *Corpus doctrinae*, 618).

15. See the discussion of this topic under *HC* 6.

Reformed. The Synod of Dort convicted Remonstrants of being Pelagians.[16] They were not satisfied with the confession of the Reformed churches: "These works, proceeding from the good root of faith, are good and acceptable to God, since they are all sanctified by his grace. Yet they do not count toward our justification—for by faith in Christ we are justified, even before we do good works. Otherwise they could not be good, any more than the fruit of a tree could be good if the tree is not good in the first place" (*BC* 24).[17] The Remonstrants are but one example illustrating the persistence of Pelagianism long after it was condemned at the Council of Ephesus (AD 431). In order for us to beware of moralism, we must know how it appears, in what shapes it comes, and what its features are. Otherwise we will be victimized by it again, and for that to happen would be both unnecessary and tragic.

It is urgent to grasp these issues as we consider *HC* 114. We have just finished working through the third use of God's holy moral law.[18] One temptation we sinners face, as we consider the law, is to put ourselves back under it as the ground or instrument of our standing before God or for our final salvation. Of course, this is not at all how Scripture presents the law to the Christian. Scripture presents it as the norm of the Christian life. This is why we distinguish between the first or pedagogical use, wherein the law teaches us the greatness of our sin and misery and drives us to Christ, and the third or normative use of the law. By nature, as sinners, we are utterly incapable of keeping the law for our standing with God or for our salvation. Were that the test then, we would all be justly condemned, because the law demands "perfect and personal" obedience.[19]

Calvin understood this. In 1547, replying to the (Roman) Council of Trent, he argues:

> I besides hold that it is without us, because we are righteous in Christ only. Let them produce evidence from Scripture, if they

16. Canons of Dort, refutation of errors 2.6; 3/4.2, 10; refutation of errors 3/4.7, 9; refutation of errors 5.2 (United Reformed Churches in North America, *Liturgical Forms and Prayers*, 270, 271, 273, 277, 278, 282); sentence pronounced on the Remonstrants in Schaff, *Creeds of Christendom*, 3:578–79.

17. United Reformed Churches in North America, *Liturgical Forms and Prayers*, 178.

18. This discussion and that under *HC* 115 assumes the threefold division of the law. See the discussion under *HC* 92.

19. WCF 7.2, in Westminster Assembly, *Humble Advice of the Assembly*, 15.

> have any, to convince us of their doctrine. I, while I have the whole Scripture supporting me, will now be satisfied with this one reason, viz., that when mention is made of the righteousness of works, the law and the gospel place it in the perfect obedience of the law; and as that nowhere appears, they leave us no alternative but to flee to Christ alone, that we may be regarded as righteous in him, not being so in ourselves. Will they produce to us one passage which declares that begun newness of life is approved by God as righteousness either in whole or in part? But if they are devoid of authority, why may we not be permitted to repudiate the figment of partial justification which they here obtrude?[20]

Moralists always imply or say that God is satisfied with our best efforts. They always seek to dull the cutting edge of the law as the Franciscans did in the fourteenth and fifteenth centuries by suggesting that, on the basis of congruent merit, God is prepared to accept our best efforts. In contrast, we confess the "perfect satisfaction, righteousness, and holiness of Christ" (*HC* 60).

Instead of lowering the bar of righteousness (from performance to intent), the biblical teaching is to confess that God's law always remains an expression of his unyielding righteousness. After all, Scripture says, "Cursed be anyone who does not confirm the words of this law by doing them" (Deut 27:26 ESV; cf. Gal 3:10). God does not change, and neither does his law, but in Christ our relation to the law has changed. Christ has satisfied the law *for us,* and as a consequence his Spirit is working in us, gradually, graciously conforming us to it. Nevertheless, even in Christ we remain fallen and imperfect.

Our sanctification cannot be the ground or instrument of our standing before God or even of our salvation because it is, in this life, never perfect. Traditionally, we have appealed to Romans 7:14–15: "For we know that the law is spiritual, but I am of the flesh, sold under sin. For I do not understand my own actions. For I do not do what I want, but I do the very thing I hate" (ESV). The traditional Augustinian and Reformed interpretation of this passage has been that it refers to Paul's struggle as a Christian. Believers know the law to be right and spiritual. They also

---

20. Calvin, *Tracts Relating to the Reformation,* 3.116.

know themselves to fall woefully short of what the law requires. In the very same epistle Paul explicitly juxtaposes law and grace as two distinct principles: "So too at the present time there is a remnant, chosen by grace. But if it is by grace, it is no longer on the basis of works; otherwise grace would no longer be grace" (Rom 11:5–6 ESV).

The law says, "Do and live" (Luke 10:28), but grace says: Christ has fulfilled the law for you, as your substitute. Believe and be saved. Moralists cannot have such a clear distinction. They quickly reach for a handful of mud to obscure the distinction and to make the one look like the other.

ACCORDING TO THE WHOLE MORAL LAW

Another temptation we face as we consider the moral law is antinomianism. Just as the Reformed churches reject legalism, so too we reject antinomianism, the denial of the abiding validity of the moral law as the norm of the Christian life. In modern American evangelical history, we might think first of the controversy over "free grace" within dispensational circles, in which the advocates of free grace denied the abiding validity of the moral law as summarized in the Ten Commandments.[21] There are other movements, for example, new covenant theology and progressive covenantalism, whose chief difference from Reformed theology's understanding of the moral law is most obviously seen regarding the abiding validity of the fourth commandment.[22] Although progressive covenantalism affirms (theologically) that God's character and moral law itself are immutable, they reject important hermeneutical principles that undergird classic Reformed theology's understanding of the fourth commandment as a creational institution with abiding validity for the new covenant believer. They understand keeping the Sabbath only in terms of "ceasing from our

21. Horton, *Christ the Lord*, surveys the issues and literature. Hodges, *Absolutely Free!*, is typical of the dispensational antinomian approach, and MacArthur, *Gospel according to Jesus*, is representative of the dispensational nomist reaction. Remarkably, MacArthur agrees with the antinomian position on the fourth commandment. See MacArthur, "Understanding the Sabbath."

22. E.g., Blomberg, "Sabbath as Fulfilled"; Carson, "Tripartite Division"; Naselli, "What Is a Biblical Theology." Wells and Zaspel, *New Covenant Theology*: "Previously we identified our view as a species of '*new covenant theology*,' yet given significant differences within *new covenant theology*, *progressive covenantalism* better described our overall viewpoint." See Gentry and Wellum, *Kingdom through Covenant*, 35; Glodo, "Dispensationalism," 538–39; Swain, "New Covenant Theologies."

works, placing our trust in Christ, and starting to live into what it means to be his new-covenant people."[23]

Our current discussions are nothing new. In earlier periods, Samuel Rutherford (1600–1661) opposed "familists" (a spiritual sect in the early to mid–sixteenth century that denied the visible church and its ministry), and defended Martin Luther from the charge of antinomianism.[24] Roughly contemporary with the debates in the British Isles about the time of the Westminster Assembly, there were, in the American colonies, heated theological and political debates over the "free grace" teaching of John Cotton (1585–1652) and Anne Hutchinson (1591–1643).[25] Of course, as already mentioned, Luther and Philip Melanchthon opposed Johannes Agricola (1494–1566) as an antinomian.[26] Indeed, the spirit of antinomianism goes back to the gnostics and the Valentinians, who, like many of the early Anabaptists, denied the reality of Christ's humanity and the reality of physical reality generally. The gnostics used to say, "Give to the flesh the things of the flesh and to the spirit the things of the spirit." To the degree such a spirit-matter dualism and the attitudes of Anabaptists came to influence American evangelicals in the nineteenth century, to the same degree they have been affected by antinomianism.

The fundamental error of all the antinomians—whether the second-century gnostics, Agricola in the early sixteenth century, Hutchinson in the seventeenth, or some in the modern "free grace" movement—is their ignorance of or rejection of creation as a category of thought and as a pattern for life. Further, many ostensible adherents to Reformed theology do not seem to grasp that the law did not first appear at Sinai, and they react to the antinomians by insisting on versions of continuity between Moses (the old covenant) and Christ as to blur the genuine distinction between them. In some cases this leads to theonomy or to virtual Roman Catholicism and to nomism (moralism), which teaches that believers are

23. Wellum, "3 Reasons." It is difficult to see how, from a Reformed perspective, Wellum's view is not antinomian. Como (*Blown by the Spirit*, 326–30) observes that some seventeenth-century antinomians kept the Christian Sabbath quite strictly, despite their theology. In this case, the view articulated by the progressive covenantalists could be characterized as worse than antinomian. I am grateful to Richard Lucas for his help in understanding the progressive covenantal view.

24. On the familists, see Como, *Blown by the Spirit*; Engelbrecht, *Friends of the Law*.

25. Schaefer, *Spiritual Brotherhood*, 264–28.

26. Wengert, *Law and Gospel*, 68.

still under the covenant of works and that our justification and salvation are conditioned on our personal obedience.[27] If the law is grounded in God's nature and if its substance was revealed first in creation as a perpetual pattern, then it does not begin with Moses or rest on Moses. Thus, even though Moses and the old covenant were temporary and even though the old covenant has expired, the moral law has not therefore expired.

In contrast to antinomianism, confessional Protestants affirm the abiding validity of moral law not as a covenant of works but as the moral and ethical standard for the Christian life. Confessional Protestants distinguish between the way believers are no longer under the law (for justification and salvation) and the way the law continues to function as the norm for the Christian life. Paul says in Romans 7:4 that we have died to the law as the way of salvation and justification. He does not say that the law no longer norms our life. Indeed, he says the exact opposite in verses 5–7. Believers, united to Christ by grace alone, through faith alone, by the Spirit, are no longer under the law for acceptance with God. In that sense we have been "released from the law" and are no longer under "the written code," but it is quite mistaken to conclude from those phrases that the law no longer norms our life. Paul appeals to the law as our norm repeatedly. The commandment that promised life to us under the covenant of works condemned us because we did not keep it (vv. 10–12). The law is good and spiritual (Rom 7:14), but, in Adam, we are sinful and slaves to sin. The law is good and holy: "For I delight in the law of God, in my inner being" (Rom 7:22 ESV). This is the confession and struggle of the believer.

We are not perfectionists because we do not minimize the effects and consequences of the fall. Neither do we minimize the righteousness and holiness demanded by God's law. We are not perfectionists because we do not imagine that we can obey God's law sufficiently for justification or salvation. Such a notion is a direct assault on the perfection and finished work of Christ for us who believe.[28]

The question is, since we have been saved, since we have been justified freely, how do we respond? Here the language of the catechism helps again: we strive "seriously" (*serio*) and not with a mere outward

27. See the discussion in the appendix to *HC* 92 regarding theonomy.

28. *BC* 22. See the discussion under *HC* 30.

zeal (*non simulatio studio*) to live not according to some but according to all of God's holy moral law. We do so by living in union and communion with Christ. We do so because God has redeemed us by his free grace, because he has freed us (Rom 6:15–19; 8:2) to serve him, in the Spirit, as living sacrifices (Rom 12:1–2), to manifest the marks of a Christian (Rom 12:9–21), to submit to divinely ordained authorities (Rom 13:1–7), to fulfill the moral law: "Owe no one anything, except to love each other, for the one who loves another has fulfilled the law. For the commandments, 'You shall not commit adultery, You shall not murder, You shall not steal, You shall not covet,' and any other commandment, are summed up in this word: 'You shall love your neighbor as yourself.' Love does no wrong to a neighbor; therefore love is the fulfilling of the law" (Rom 13:8–10 ESV). This is the substance of the Ten Words as the standard for the Christian life, to which redeemed sinners seek to conform their lives out of gratitude and in union with Christ.

Question 115

Why then does God so strictly enjoin the ten commandments upon us, since in this life no one can keep them?

First, that as long as we live we may learn more and more to know our sinful nature, and so the more earnestly seek forgiveness of sins and righteousness in Christ; secondly, that without ceasing we diligently ask God for the grace of the Holy Spirit, that we be renewed more and more after the image of God, until we attain the goal of perfection after this life.[29]

29. "Warum lässt uns denn Gott also scharf die zehn Gebote predigen, wenn sie in diesem Leben Niemand halten kann? Erstlich, auf dass wir unser ganzes Leben lang unsere sündliche Art je länger je mehr erkennen, und [so viel]1 desto begieriger Vergebung der Sünden und Gerechtigkeit in Christo suchen. Darnach, dass wir ohne Unterlass uns befleissigen, und Gott bitten um die Gnade des Heiligen Geistes, dass wir je länger je mehr zu dem Ebenbilde Gottes erneuert werden, bis wir das Ziel der Vollkommenheit nach diesem Leben erreichen" (Schaff, *Creeds of Christendom*, 3:349). "Cur igitur vult Deus legem suam adeo exacte et severe praedicari, eum nemo sit in hac vita, qui eam servare possit? Primum, ut in omni vita magnis magisque agnoscamus, quanta sit naturae nostrae ad pecandum propensio, tantoque avidius remissionem peccatorum, et iustitiam in Chrito

In the ancient world a teacher (a pedagogue) was neither a friend nor a therapist (Gal 3:19, 23–24). He was more a legal figure whose job it was to see that the student memorized his lessons properly. This is why Paul describes the law as a "tutor" (παιδαγωγός; Gal 3:24). By common law (still in effect today), the teacher acts *in loco parentis*, in place of one's parents. The traditional assumption was that sensible parents would discipline their children with corporal punishment. That is almost certainly the assumption behind Hebrews 12:7 when it says, "For what son is there whom his father does not discipline?" (ESV). It is clear from Holy Scripture that God is a judge and a Father, and his law is a reflection of his unbreakable, immutable righteousness.

As we saw under *HC* 114, even though believers are no longer under the moral law for justification and salvation, part of our ongoing restoration into the image of Christ (Eph 4:24; Col 3:10) is learning to delight in God's law (Ps 119:70, 97).[30] Nevertheless, as Paul recognizes in Romans 7, there remains a persistently difficult relationship between the justified, saved sinner and God's holy law.

The doctrine that the law always accuses (*lex semper accusat*) is not exclusively a Lutheran doctrine.[31] To be sure, this language is found the Lutheran confessions, and in that form one finds it principally in Lutheran writers, but one does find Reformed writers saying very similar things. To give but three examples, Martin Bucer (1491–1551) uses similar language in his commentary on Romans, as does Olevianus in his 1579 commentary on Romans and Peter Martyr Vermigli (1499–1562) in his 1551 commentary on 1 Corinthians.[32] Ursinus uses similar language of the law's function

---

expectamus: Deinde, ut hoc perpetuo agamus, illud semper meditemur, et pratiam Spiritus sancti a Patre imploremus, quo indies magis ac magis ad imaginem Dei renovemur, donec aliquando tandem, postquam ex hac vita decesserimus, propisitam nobis perfectionem laeti assequamur" (Niemeyer, *Collectio Confessionum*, 458).

30. This discussion assumes the traditional threefold division of the law. See the discussion under *HC* 92. Ursinus began his exposition of this question by tracing the distinction between the moral (e.g., the Ten Commandments), judicial, and ceremonial (religious) laws (Ursinus, *Corpus doctrinae*, 622; Ursinus, *Commentary*, 612).

31. E.g., *The Apology of the Augsburg Confession*, art. 4 (Kolb and Wengert, *Book of Concord*, 126.38).

32. Bucer, *Metaphrasis et enarratio*, 231; Olevianus, *Romanos Notae*, 93; Vermigli, *In selectissimam*, 477. Cf. Olevian, *Firm Foundation*, 110–12; Olevianus, *Exposition*, 104, where Olevianus discusses the accusations of our conscience and the devil, which are defeated by our justification.

to those not in a state of grace.[33] Perhaps most importantly, however, are Ursinus's comments on this question, where he listed seven uses of the law for the Christian.[34]

1. the conservation of discipline (*conservatio disciplina*)[35]
2. the knowledge of sin (*agnitio peccati*)
3. the rule of divine worship and the Christian life (*norma cultus divini et vitae Christianae*)[36]
4. the declaration of the law (*declaratio legis*)
5. the voice of the law (*vox legis*)
6. the admonition of us as the image of God (*est commonefactio de imagine Dei*)
7. the testimony to the future eternal life (*est testimoninm de futura vita aeterna*).

The catechism itself, however, begins with the second use: the knowledge of sin. The first reason that God "wills to have his law to have his law preached so severely and exactly" (as the Latin text of the catechism has it) is that we might know the greatness of our sin and misery. It is true, Ursinus concedes, that we think first of the pedagogical use of the law relative to *unbelievers,* but it pertains to *believers* too, even in the covenant of grace.[37] In this use, the law serves as a mirror (*speculum*) of our sins and drives us to humility, to Christ, and leads us to sanctification and to prayer for conformity to Christ.

This is the convicting and correcting (2 Tim 3:16) function of the law in the Christian life. For Ursinus (and Olevianus), the law remains the law, and we remain sinners. "If we say we have not sinned, we make him a liar"

33. "Lex enim accusat, convincit, et damnat omnes non renatos, quod sint iniusti coram Deo" (Ursinus, *Corpus doctrinae,* 623).

34. Ursinus, *Corpus doctrinae,* 623–24; Ursinus, *Commentary,* 613–14.

35. Ursinus, *Corpus doctrinae,* 623.

36. Ursinus, *Corpus doctrinae,* 624.

37. "Hic quoque usus etsi praecipue ad non renatos spectet: tamen ad renatos etiam pertinet" (Ursinus, *Corpus doctrinae,* 623).

(1 John 1:10). The legalist thinks that, now that we have grace, we have no need of the gospel or that the gospel is only to help us obey the law. The antinomian thinks that now that we have grace, we have no need of the law.[38] Both are wrong. The Reformation was a rejection of both nomism *and* antinomianism. Neither the nomist nor the antinomian understands the law or the gospel correctly. The gospel is that Christ obeyed in the place of, died for, was resurrected for, and intercedes for sinners. God justified us in order that we might be gradually, graciously sanctified, and that means being brought into conformity to Christ and to his holy law.

The law teaches us that we are never done with the gospel, that we cannot move on from the gospel, as though it were milk and obedience is meat (Heb 5:12–13). It teaches us to continue to seek the forgiveness of our sins for Christ's sake alone. It teaches us that we are not yet fully sanctified, indeed, that in the bright light of God's holy law, we have only a small beginning of sanctification (*HC* 114). This is why the catechism speaks of our seeking the forgiveness of sins more earnestly and our righteousness in Christ.

The last part of the answer anticipates the next section of the catechism. The law is a stimulus to prayer, and one of our first prayers is to acknowledge our ongoing struggle with our sin and our continuing need for sanctification. The law is God's objective measure of righteousness. Though we can never stand before God, either in justification or even in salvation, on the basis of or through our Spirit-wrought sanctity, that does not mean that we do not now seek the formation of actual, personal righteousness (Matt 5:6) within ourselves. We certainly do. Our personal righteousness is no part of our standing before God, but it is a necessary effect and a fruit and evidence of our justification and sanctification. It is the product of grace. The Reformed churches reject the idea that we are justified or even saved by the formation of a disposition (*habitus*), but, in Christ, we do seek now the formation of godly dispositions. Constant prayer is one of those dispositions and practices that is being formed in us. We have been forgiven, but we continue to seek forgiveness because we continue to sin.

38. See the excursus on antinomianism below.

Particularly, we pray for the gift of the Holy Spirit, who is actively, graciously, mysteriously working in us to conform us to Christ. The wonder is that he does so in part through prayer. One of the great lies of the Evil One is that Christians need not pray, or that prayer is not very important after justification, or that because of our sins, God no longer hears our prayers—as though we were again on a works footing with God. We go to the Father, in the name and righteousness of the Son, the Spirit helping us, to confess our sins, to say, as the Book of Common Prayer says, "There no health in us." Indeed, the General Confession of sin in the 1662 Book of Common Prayer is an excellent guide to confessing one's sins:

> ALMIGHTY and most merciful Father; We have erred, and strayed from thy ways like lost sheep. We have followed too much the devices and desires of our own hearts. We have offended against thy holy laws. We have left undone those things which we ought to have done; And we have done those things which we ought not to have done; And there is no health in us. But thou, O Lord, have mercy upon us, miserable offenders. Spare thou them, O God, who confess their faults. Restore thou them that are penitent; According to thy promises declared unto mankind in Christ Jesu our Lord. And grant, O most merciful Father, for his sake; That we may hereafter live a godly, righteous, and sober life, To the glory of thy holy Name. Amen.[39]

To those who have trusted Christ and confessed their sins comes this gospel promise, which we accept prayerfully and for which we give heartfelt thanks in prayer:

> ALMIGHTY God, the Father of our Lord Jesus Christ, who desireth not the death of a sinner, but rather that he may turn from his wickedness, and live; and hath given power, and commandment, to his Ministers, to declare and pronounce to his people, being penitent, the Absolution and Remission of their sins: He pardoneth and absolveth all them that truly repent, and unfeignedly believe his holy Gospel. Wherefore let us beseech him to grant us true

39. Church of England, *Book of Common Prayer*, 39.

> repentance, and his Holy Spirit, that those things may please him, which we do at this present; and that the rest of our life hereafter may be pure, and holy; so that at the last we may come to his eternal joy; through Jesus Christ our Lord.[40]

The Christian life is a penitent life. We shall never be done with sin in this life, but we are learning daily to die to sin and to live to Christ. That begins with the daily prayer for forgiveness of our sins.

The same Holy Spirit who gave us new life, who united us to Christ, who is actively at work in us, will also glorify us. As Geerhardus Vos wrote a century ago, glory is preeminently the realm of the Holy Spirit.[41] We are running, Paul says, with the Spirit's help, a race toward an imperishable prize (1 Cor 9:25). There is great effort involved in the struggle against sin and toward glory (Phil 3:12–14), but the Spirit enables the struggle. There is a place between "let go and let God" and "you are on your own."

God's holy law is spiritual and good. One day we will be spiritual and good too. Until that time, the law continues to illumine the dark places in our hearts, minds, and wills. Believers run to Christ our Savior for grace, forgiveness, renewal, and ultimately for glorification: total conformity to Christ, the firstborn from the dead (Rom 8:29; Col 1:15, 18).

EXCURSUS AGAINST THE ANTINOMIANS, LIBERTINES, AND SIMILAR FANATICS WHO DENY THAT THE DECALOGUE IS FOR TEACHING IN THE CHRISTIAN CHURCH

This an adaptation of the heading in Ursinus's *Corpus Doctrinae*, where he tackles the antinomians.[42] It tells us most of what we need to know about how he viewed the antinomians but we, no less than Ursinus, are troubled by antinomians in our time, and thus it will repay us to consider briefly his eleven points.

---

40. Church of England, *Book of Common Prayer*, 39–40.

41. E.g., Vos, *Pauline Eschatology*, 298.

42. "Agumenta, Antinomorum, Libertinorum, et similum fanaticorum, quod decalogus non sit docendus in ecclesia Christiana" (Ursinus, *Corpus doctrinae*, 624). The excursus appears in Ursinus, *Commentary*, 615–18.

First Timothy 1:8–11 says:

> Now we know that the law is good, if one uses it lawfully, understanding this, that the law is not laid down for the just but for the lawless and disobedient, for the ungodly and sinners, for the unholy and profane, for those who strike their fathers and mothers, for murderers, the sexually immoral, men who practice homosexuality, enslavers, liars, perjurers, and whatever else is contrary to sound doctrine, in accordance with the gospel of the glory of the blessed God with which I have been entrusted. (ESV)

Notice how Paul walks through the Ten Commandments and applies them to us. His regular use of the Decalogue (e.g., Rom 13:8–14; Eph 4:17–6:9) shows us that we may not say that the Ten Commandments are not for today, no longer in force as the standard of Christian ethics. Because God's law is grounded in God himself, because it is an appropriate reflection of his nature and character, it is justly the pattern of the Christian life. This is the pattern we see in Psalm 40. The needy sinner cries out to God for salvation (v. 1), which God graciously gives—it was he who caused us to see that we were blind and in danger, in a "pit of destruction" (v. 2)—and in response to God's free grace to us, in Christ, the believer says, "I delight to do your will, O my God; your law is within my heart" (v. 8 ESV).

It is vitally important for Christians to understand the distinction between the pedagogical use and the normative use of God's moral law. Failure to grasp and use this distinction leads either to nomism or to antinomianism, that is, denial of the third or normative use of the law. In the pedagogical use, the law is a taskmaster or a tutor (Gal 3:24), a harsh teacher with a ruler in hand with which to beat us sinners when we transgress. This use of the law is the expression of God's holy, relentless righteousness (justice), which must be satisfied either by ourselves or by another. In short, it is a covenant of works.[43]

---

43. "What does the divine law teach? It teaches the kind of covenant (*foedus*) that God established with mankind in creation (*in creatione*), how he managed in keeping it, and what God requires of him after establishing a new covenant of grace (*novum foedus gratiae*) with him—that is, what kind of person God created, for what purpose, into what state he has fallen, and how he ought to conduct his life after being reconciled to God" (Ursinus, Larger Catechism, 10, in Bierma et al., *Introduction*, 164; Ursinus, *Commentary*, 1.10); see Perkins, *Reformed Covenant Theology*, 50.

In its third use God's moral law guides our new life in Christ. It is not a covenant of works but a "perfect rule of righteousness."[44] The third thing a Christian must know is how he is "to be thankful to God for such redemption." The law norms our new life. This is why we confess that good works are "only those which proceed from truth faith, are performed according to the law of God, and to his glory" (*HC* 91). Louis Berkhof characterizes the third use this way: "The law is a rule of life for believers, reminding them of their duties and leading them in the way of life and salvation. This third use of the law is denied by the Antinomians."[45]

There is a way of life, that is, there is a way that believers live. There is a way of salvation, a path that believers walk toward eternal life, in the grace of Christ, in union with Christ. It is essential to distinguish between "is" and "through" or "because." The nomist wants to turn "is" into "through" or "because." We are not saved *through* our obedience. That is nomism. We are not saved *because* of our obedience. That is Pelagianism. Nevertheless, those to whom God has sovereignly given new life, and true faith and union with Christ, will seek to live, *sola gratia, sola fide* according to God's moral law.

Here Ursinus helps us. He addresses directly whether (*utrum*) good works (*bona opera*) are necessary (*necessaria*) to salvation (*ad salutem*) or whether they are "pernicious" (*perniciosa*) to it.[46] As mentioned in the first part of this essay, Ursinus was well aware of the controversies Melanchthon and the Protestants had experienced in the 1530s, 1540s, and 1550s over how to relate justification to sanctification, and sanctification to good works and salvation. George Major (1502–1574) proposed that they are "necessary" to retaining salvation, and Nicholas von Amsdorf (1483–1565) that they are "pernicious" or injurious to it.[47] Ursinus criticizes both ways of speaking as "ambiguous and scandalous," vague and liable to give offense. He was particularly unhappy with von Amsdorf's expression since it tends to diminish (*damnare*) trust (*fiduciam*) but also

44. Westminster Assembly, *Humble Advice of the Assembly*, 19.2 (p. 33).

45. Berkhof, *Systematic Theology*, 615.

46. Ursinus, *Corpus doctrinae*, 478.

47. Timothy Wengert argues that Major intended to say only that good works are necessary as a consequence of justification (*Dictionary of Luther*, s.v. "Major, George").

zeal for good works.[48] Major's thesis can be retained if it is understood properly.[49] "They are necessary unto salvation not as cause to effect or as merit to reward but as part of salvation itself, as antecedent to consequent or as means to an end."[50]

Later Reformed theologians described good works as constitutive of salvation. This reflects the "is" of good works. We are not saved *because* of good works. They never become the *ground* of salvation. We may be confident that "medium" does not mean "instrument," since Ursinus is elaborating on the expression "part of salvation itself" (*pars ipsius salutis*). He continues to explain the relationship of good works to salvation by analogy with justification. Good works are necessary to salvation as they are necessary "unto righteousness" (*ad iustitiam*) or "unto justification" (*ad iustificationem*) or "in those being justified" (*in iustificandis*), that is, as a consequence of justification (*quam consequens iustificationis*), since sanctification (*regeneratio*) is inseparably conjoined with justification.[51] This is Calvin's doctrine of the "twofold grace of God" (*duplex gratia Dei*) or Olevianus's "double benefit" (*duplex beneficium*). Justification gives rise to progressive sanctification, and sanctification produces good works as fruit and evidence of salvation.[52]

Ursinus is unwilling to say things about salvation (the broader concept) that he could not say about justification (the narrower concept). It is "ambiguous" (*ambigue*) to talk about the necessity of good works in justification since such a way of speaking may be understood to make good works prior or antecedent to justification (*ante iustificationem*), which way of speaking would overturn the material cause of the Reformation. He is unequivocally and irrevocably committed to justification *sola gratia, sola fide*. Neither is he willing to say that good works are a "cause of justification" (*causa iustificationis*).[53] Rather, he wants to follow Augustine:

48. Ursinus, *Corpus doctrinae*, 478.

49. Ursinus, *Corpus doctrinae*, 478. The marginal note in the 1616 edition of the *Corpus doctrinae* says, "the degree to which good works are necessary." See Pareus, *Corpus Doctrinae*.

50. "Quod sint necessaria ad salutem, non tanquam causa ad effectum, vel tanquam tum ad mercedem, sed tanquam pars ipsius salutis, vel tanqam antecedens ad consequens, vel tanquam medium, fine ad finem" (Ursinus, *Corpus doctrinae*, 478).

51. Ursinus, *Corpus doctrinae*, 478.

52. Venema, *Accepted and Renewed*; Clark, *Caspar Olevian*.

53. Ursinus, *Corpus doctrinae*, 479.

good works do not precede (*praecedunt*) being justified, but they follow the justified.[54]

Ursinus lists and responds to eleven antinomian objections to the abiding validity of the moral law for the Christian. The more significant are summarized here:

1. "That which cannot be kept is taught uselessly."[55] That we cannot keep it is no reason not to teach the moral law in the church. The problem is not with the law (Rom 7:12) but with us. The law has multiple functions simultaneously, and the objection ignores those functions (e.g., the civil use, the normative use, and the pedagogical use).

2. "Christ is not a legislator."[56] There is a sense in which this sentence is true but a sense in which it is false. Insofar as he is our Mediator, the principal office of which is to attain salvation, he is not a legislator, but insofar as he was the "cleanser" (*repurgator*) and renewer (*restaurator*) of the law, he is a legislator.[57]

3. "Christians are not ruled by the law but to the Spirit of regeneration."[58] Christians do not have a servile relation to the law, that is, we are not motivated by a fear of punishment. In that sense we are not under the law, but because we are free we are not under constraint. We obey the law freely, cheerfully, and gratefully as befits redeemed people.

4. "We are not under law, but under grace."[59] In the sense in which Paul intended these words in Romans 6:14, they are true. We are no longer under the covenant of works for justification and salvation. Christ has met the terms of the

54. Augustine, *Ennaratio in Psalmum* 110.3 (English 111.3); Augustine, "Expositions on the Book of Psalms" (*NPNF* 1/8:545).

55. "Quod non potest servari, inutiliter docetur" (Ursinus, *Corpus doctrinae*, 624).

56. "Christus non est Legislator" (Ursinus, *Corpus doctrinae*, 625).

57. Ursinus, *Corpus doctrinae*, 625.

58. "Christiani non reguntur lege, sed spiritu regenerationis" (Ursinus, *Corpus doctrinae*, 626).

59. "Non sumus amplius sub lege, sed sub gratia" (Ursinus, *Corpus doctrinae*, 626).

"commandment of life" for us. Nevertheless, the law continues to obligate us to grateful obedience not in order to be justified or saved but because we have been justified and saved by grace alone, through faith alone. We are, as Ursinus reminds us, no longer under the curse of the law. We are no longer under condemnation (Rom 8:1).

5. "The law is not necessary to salvation."[60] This is true in one sense and false in another. It is true that the law as instrument and ground is not necessary to salvation, but it is false to say that the law plays no role in norming our grateful, Spirit-wrought obedience in union with Christ. Ursinus writes, "Even though the doctrine of the law is not necessary in order that we might be saved through obedience to it, it is nevertheless necessary on account of other uses."[61] Those other uses are the seven that Ursinus listed earlier.

6. "We have all things in Christ ... therefore we should not go back from Christ to Moses."[62] This is perhaps the most frequently heard objection by contemporary antinomians, who identify the moral law utterly with Moses. This is a significant error. God first gave the moral law in creation *before* Moses. It is grounded in creation. We see this in Exodus 20:11, where the Decalogue itself appeals to the creational pattern. Paul says that the gentiles, who did not have the Mosaic law, did by nature what the law requires (Rom 2:14). Thus, this objection ignores Paul's doctrine of natural law. They do this because typically this form of antinomianism is found among those who generally lack the category of nature because, in their scheme, grace has destroyed nature or creation. The Reformed do not destroy nature but affirm it as a reality and a category of analysis.[63] This objection, as suggested earlier,

60. "Lex non est necessaria ad salutem" (Ursinus, *Corpus doctrinae*, 627).

61. "Etsi doctrina legis non est necessaria ut per eius obedientiam servemur; est tamen necessaria propter alios usus" (Ursinus, *Corpus doctrinae*, 627).

62. "Omnia habemus in Christo ... ergo non est retrogrediendum à Christo ad Mosen" (Ursinus, *Corpus doctrinae*, 627–28).

63. On nature and grace, see the discussion under *HC* 66.

also ignores the many appeals to and applications of the moral law in the New Testament. Our Lord himself restated and summarized the moral law in Matthew 22:37–40: "You shall love the Lord your God with all your heart and with all your soul and with all your mind. This is the great and first commandment. And a second is like it: You shall love your neighbor as yourself. On these two commandments depend all the Law and the Prophets" (ESV). When he said that he came not to destroy but to fulfill the law and the prophets (Matt 5:17), he meant it. Grace does not destroy the role of the law as the norm of the Christian life. This is why our Lord said that whoever teaches the moral law will be called great in the kingdom of heaven (Matt 5:19).

Question 116
Why is prayer necessary for Christians?

Question 117
What belongs to such prayer which is acceptable to God and which he will hear?

Question 118
What has God commanded us to ask him?

Question 119
What is the Lord's Prayer?

Lord's Day 45

QUESTION 116

Why is prayer necessary for Christians?

Because it is the chief part of thankfulness which God requires of us; and because God will give his grace and Holy Spirit only to those who earnestly and without ceasing beg them of him, and render thanks unto him for them.[1]

We begin our consideration of the Lord's Prayer and the last section of the catechism, which has been an extended consideration of the life of thankfulness, lived in grace and in union with Christ. Prayer, we say, is the chief part of thankfulness.[2] Thus, no act is more basic to the Christian life, to Christian worship, to piety, and to growth, and yet prayer is also uniquely and strangely difficult. Experience tells us that the struggle to pray is common to believers. We do not often hear people confess that, for weeks, they could not bring themselves to eat. Yet Christians say such things about prayer. Nevertheless, prayer is as basic to the Christian life as eating is to bodily life, and just as we need to be taught what food is good for us (and what is not), so too we need to learn what prayer is and is not.

Ursinus defines prayer thus: "Prayer consists in calling upon the true God, and arises from an acknowledgment and sense of our need, and from a desire of sharing in the divine kindness, in true conversion of heart and confidence in the promise of grace for the sake of Christ the mediator, asking at the hands of God such temporal and spiritual blessings as are necessary for us; or in giving thanks to God for the benefits received."[3] It is instructive that Ursinus begins with the *objective* truth: the object of prayer, the true God, is essential to prayer. There are also essential *subjective* qualities to prayer. It comes out of a genuine sense of need and a

1. "Warum ist den Christen das Gebet nöthig? Darum, weil es das vornehmste Stück der Dankbarkeit ist, welche Gott von uns fordert, und weil Gott seine Gnade und Heiligen Geist allein denen will geben, die ihu mit herzlichem Seufzen ohne Unterlass darum bitten, und ihm dafür danken" (Schaff, *Creeds of Christendom*, 3:350). "Quare Christianis necessaria est precatio? Quia praecipua pars est eius, quam Deus a nobis postulat, gratitudinis. Tum, quia illis tantum suam gratiam et Spiritum sanctum Deus largitur, qui veris gemitibus, continenter haec ab eo petunt, et pro iis ipsi gratias agunt" (Niemeyer, *Collectio Confessionum*, 458).

2. Calvin, *Institutes* 3.20.1–3.

3. Ursinus, *Commentary*, 619, revised in light of Ursinus, *Corpus doctrinae*, 628.

desire to benefit from God's kindness. It comes out of a true turning to God and true faith in Jesus.

The *genus* (class) of prayer is "invocation or adoration." There are two species of prayer, petition and thanksgiving.[4] To petition is to ask God for bodily and spiritual necessities. To give thanks is to acknowledge God and his gifts, and commit oneself to respond appropriately.[5] We also distinguish between public and private prayer. The latter, Ursinus explains, is that personal interaction with God that "a faithful soul has with God, asking, alone and apart from others, certain blessings for himself, or for others; or giving thanks for benefits received."[6] Calvin calls prayer a "conversation" (*colloquium*) with God.[7] "This form of prayer is not restricted to any particular words or places, for oftentimes the heart, when burdened and distressed, gives utterance to nothing more than sighs and groans."[8] The former is that done in church, together with the saints, and led by the minister.[9]

Prayer is necessary because it is an essential element of our sanctification, the gradual, gracious, Spirit-wrought work of conforming believers to the image of Christ. Just as we are learning daily what it means to die to sin and to live to Christ, so too we daily learn how imperfect and inconsistent our prayers are and what it means to pray as our Lord taught, in the Spirit, to the Father.

Prayer is the chief means, the principal instrument through which we express our gratitude to God for his favor merited for us by Christ and given freely to us, for his mercy so that we do not experience the consequences of sin generally and of our sins in particular, and for his general mercy and kindness to his creation and to his image-bearers. That the catechism assigns prayer to thankfulness reminds us again of where we are in the catechism, that we have confessed the greatness of

---

4. Ursinus, *Corpus doctrinae*, 628.

5. Ursinus, *Commentary*, 619.

6. Ursinus, *Commentary*, 620.

7. Calvin, *Institutes* 3.20.4; Barth, *Joannis Calvini Opera Selecta*, 4:300.7–8.

8. Ursinus, *Commentary*, 620.

9. Ursinus, *Commentary*, 620. He reckons that 1 Tim 2:8 refers to private prayers, but judging by the context, it seems rather than Paul is there envisioning public prayer, specifically prayer during the worship service.

our sin and misery, we have confessed the faith, we have been received into Christ's church, and that we gather weekly with the Christ-confessing covenant community (the visible church) to receive the ministry of word and sacrament.

When we say that God gives his favor and Holy Spirit only to those who ask, we are saying that God answers the prayers only of those who believe. It is believers who have received God's free grace in Christ. It is believers who have been saved. It is believers who have been justified. It is believers who are being gradually, graciously conformed to Christ (sanctification). It is believers who are thankful. Therefore it is believers who pray.

A thorough study of Scripture concerning prayer would require its own volume. In a sense, the history of redemption is the history of prayer. Almost as soon as the story of sin and redemption begins, we find a record of prayer. Genesis 4 begins and ends with worship. Abel brought an acceptable offering, and Cain did not. The latter's jealousy led him to murder. At the end of the chapter (v. 26), with the announcement of the birth of Seth, Scripture reports: "At that time people began to call upon the name of Yahweh." This seems like a reference to public worship, but it is interesting that worship is characterized by the act of calling on the name of the God of the covenant, Yahweh. Prayer begins with calling on the name of God. The Lord's Prayer begins by invoking the name of the Father. We often begin, "O Lord ..." Prayer is in the vocative mood.

Repeatedly in the history of Israel, the people sin, Moses prays for them and intercedes on their behalf with Yahweh, and he relents (e.g., Num 11:2; 21:7–8; Deut 9:26–29). The entire Psalter (Pss 1–150) is a collection of the prayers of God's people. Every sort of prayer one might pray is given to us in the Psalms. One thinks of Solomon's great prayer in 1 Kings 8:22–53 or of Daniel's confession of sin on behalf of the exiled covenant community in Daniel 9:4–19. Our Lord Jesus instructed his disciples (and us) frequently on the importance and nature of prayer. Believers are not to pray as the (Pharisaic) hypocrites did (Matt 6:5–7) by calling attention to ourselves, in order that our piety might be recognized by others, nor do we pray like pagans, who seek to impress the gods with verbal excess.

Those prayers are not the prayers of the grateful redeemed. Those are the prayers of those who are still seeking to impress. Believers know that they no longer have to impress others or God, that Jesus Christ, God the Son incarnate, is our high priest, mediator, and substitute. Believers know that they stand before God solely on the basis of Christ's righteousness imputed, by grace alone (*sola gratia*), that Christ and all his benefits are received through faith alone (*sola fide*).

This gets to one part of the Christian's struggle to pray faithfully. No one loves us more than Christ. No one has given more to us than our faithful God and Father. The Holy Spirit indwells us and prompts us to pray, yet we are tempted to change the footing of our prayer from the covenant of grace to the covenant of works. When we seek to relate to God, to call on his name, as if we were under works for acceptance (justification) and salvation (deliverance from the wrath to come) on the basis of our works (our performance), we must fail. We cannot be reminded too often that the starting point of prayer is a clear understanding that we are in a covenant of grace, that God, for Christ's sake, graciously hears and answers our prayers according to his mercy and wisdom.

For our part, our prayers are always corrupted by sinful thoughts, desires, and choices. Our prayers need to be progressively sanctified just as we need to be progressively sanctified. We go to the Father only on the basis of what Christ has done. We pray with the Spirit helping us. We pray as redeemed sinners. We do not pray as those who have met the terms of the law (the covenant of works) but as needy sinners received by grace. The needy cry out freely to God because they know their need and trust God's gracious promises. Those who approach God on another basis will necessarily struggle. Those who seek to hide from God their sins and need will struggle. Indeed, one great struggle of prayer is the struggle to be honest before God about who and what we are in ourselves.

Another aspect of the struggle of prayer is our struggle with sin. As believers, we continue to wrestle with sin (as Paul says in Rom 7), and to the degree we have yet to be sanctified, to that degree we are reluctant to humble ourselves before God and to acknowledge him as Lord and ourselves as needy sinners. Prayer is the chief way of dying to ourselves and living to Christ.

Here it is helpful to distinguish between the way that prayer is a means of grace and the way the word and sacraments are means of grace. The latter two are objective. They come to us from outside us (*extra nos*). The Christ and gospel they bring us to we receive *sola fide*. They are objective instruments. Prayer is our *response* to the gospel. It is the instrument through which we reply from the heart, with thanks, to God for all he has done. It is the first expression of the grateful, believing heart. There is another difference. The word and sacraments do not ebb and flow. They do not need to grow or to be sanctified. The word and sacraments are holy, and that does not change depending on our sanctity. Our prayers, by contrast, do need to be sanctified, and our Lord Jesus does that. He presents our prayers to the Father as our high priest (Heb 2:17, 3:1; 4:14–15; 5:1, 5, 10; 6:20; 7:1, 26–28; 8:1–3; 9:7, 11, 25; 13:11). Before the Father, they are as perfect as he is. In short, we pray as those who are in a covenant of grace because Christ has fulfilled for us the terms of the covenant of works.

Prayer is distinct from the word and the sacraments insofar as it is in prayer that we ask for what is promised in them. That is why we say that God gives his grace and Spirit only to those who ask for them and who give thanks for them. Not everyone who hears the gospel or who receives the sacraments (the objective means) receives what they signify. Only believers receive what they signify, and it is believers who pray for what is offered, for forgiveness, for righteousness, for sanctification, and for our daily necessities. Only believers give heartfelt thanks for what Christ has done for us and for what the Spirit is now doing in us, in union and communion with Christ. Thus, our prayer life can never be separated from our life in the communion of the saints and our due use of the other ordinary means of grace (the preaching of the gospel and the use of the sacraments) instituted by our Lord.

Prayer, then, calling on the name of the Lord, in faith, in confidence, in Christ, is the first act of the believer. It is the act of the grateful recipient of mercy and grace. It is the act of needy sinners. It is the act of one who is in the midst of a mighty struggle between what is to be and what presently is. It is the act of the believer, first corporately with God's people in joyful solemn assembly and also daily, quietly, in one's closet, as it were.

Question 117

What belongs to such prayer which is acceptable to God and which he will hear?

First, that with our whole heart we call only upon the one true God, who has revealed Himself to us in his Word, for all that He has commanded us to ask of him; secondly, that we thoroughly know our need and misery, so as to humble ourselves in the presence of his divine Majesty; thirdly, that we be firmly assured, that notwithstanding our unworthiness, he will, for the sake of Christ our Lord, certainly hear our prayer, as he has promised us in his Word.[10]

What are the qualities that mark Christian prayer? The first quality we confess is that prayer is calling to God "with our whole heart." Calvin writes of a "right and true contemplation of God."[11] True prayer comes from a believing heart. Contrary to the caricature that is often drawn of the Reformed, ours is a religion of the heart as much as it is a religion of the intellect. What distinguishes the Reformed confession from other traditions is that we do not set these two aspects of the soul against each other. Prayer can be and should be *both* rational *and* heartfelt.

The second quality is that it directed to the only God. Of course, to pray to another god is idolatry. It is misdirected, wicked, and accursed. This tells us that just as there is a *subjective* aspect to prayer (i.e., it is from the heart), there is an *objective* aspect: it is normed by God's word. Though we typically think of the rule of worship relative to *HC* 96–98,[12] God's

10. "Was gehört zu einem solchen Gebet, das Gott gefalle, und von ihm erhört werde? Erstlich, dass wir allein den einigen wahren Gott, der sich uns in seinem Wort hat geoffenbaret, um alles, das er uns zu bitten befohlen hat, von Herzen anrufen. Zum andern, dass wir unsere Noth und Elend recht gründlich erkennen, uns vor dem Angesicht seiner Majestät zu demüthigen. Zum dritten, dass wir diesen festen Grund haben, das Er unser Gebet, unangesehen, dass wir's unwürdig sind, doch um des Herrn Christi willen gewisslich wolle erhören, wie Er uns in seinem Wort verheissen hat" (Schaff, *Creeds of Christendom*, 3:350). "Quae ad eam precationem requiruntur, quae Deo placeat, qaueque ab ipso exaudiatur? Ut a solo vero Deo, qui se in verbo suo patefecit, omnia, quae a se peti iussit, vero cordis affectu petamus, et intimo nostrae indigentiae ac miseriae sensu, nos in conspectu divinae Maiestatis, supplices abiiciamus, huic firmo fundamento innitamur, nos a Deo, quanquam indignos, propter Christum tamen certo exaudiri, quemadmodum nobis in suo verbo promisit" (Niemeyer, *Collectio Confessionum*, 458).

11. Calvin, *Institutes* 3.20.4.

12. See the discussion of the rule of worship under *HC* 96.

word also regulates our prayers. We may pray to God, that is, respond to his grace, only in the ways that he has authorized.[13] Calvin explains, "We have noted another point: not to ask any more than God allows. For even though he bids us pour out our hearts before him [Ps. 62:8; cf. Ps. 145:19], he still does not indiscriminately slacken the reins to stupid and wicked emotions; and while he promises that he will act according to the will of the godly, his gentleness does not go so far that he yields to their willfulness."[14]

Our Lord consistently appealed to divinely revealed norms, to God's holy law. He said that he had not come to destroy the law but to fulfill it (Matt 5:17–20). He was not an antinomian. He did not teach that the moral law only existed for Israel but has now been abolished. He taught the opposite.[15] When he met the woman at the well, she questioned him about worship. She tried to throw dust in the air, as it were, suggesting that no one really knew how to worship God truly. Jesus replied: "You worship what you do not know; we worship what we know, for salvation is from the Jews. But the hour is coming, and is now here, when the true worshipers will worship the Father in spirit and truth, for the Father is seeking such people to worship him. God is spirit, and those who worship him must worship in spirit and truth" (John 4:22–24 ESV).[16]

According to Jesus, there are divinely revealed, objective norms by which God must be approached. Not everything that we want to do in worship or say in prayer is approved by God. Indeed, our confidence in prayer is that "if we ask anything according to his will he hears us" (1 John 5:14 ESV). Again, it is God's will, not ours, that is final. The truth is, as Paul says, "We do not know how to pray as we ought." Paul says, "The Spirit helps us in our weakness. For we do not know what to pray for as we ought, but the Spirit himself intercedes for us with groanings too deep for words" (Rom 8:26 ESV).

---

13. This rule is to be distinguished from the normative rule, which assumes that we do in worship or say in prayer whatever is not forbidden by God (Calvin, *Institutes* 3.20.5).

14. Calvin, *Institutes* 3.20.5.

15. Failure to observe the threefold distinction in the law (moral, judicial, ceremonial) leads to the mistaken notion that the moral law expired with the temporary Israelite laws. See the discussion under *HC* 87.

16. See the discussion of this passage in Clark, *Recovering the Reformed Confession*, 272–77, for a justification of the translation offered above.

True prayer is filled with Scripture—what is more appropriate to say to God than what he has already said to us?—and is controlled by Scripture. We are to ask what God has commanded we ask of him. When our prayers begin with Scripture, are filled with Scripture, and end with Scripture, we may be sure that what we are praying is what God would have us ask of him.

We pray not to the God of our imagination, God "as we understood him," as they say in Alcoholics Anonymous (steps 3, 11).[17] That is the essence of idolatry. We do not pray to false gods or to any other God than the Triune God who has revealed himself in Scripture, in Christ, as Father, Son, and Holy Spirit. There is no other God (Deut 6:4).

The same Scripture that reveals to us the Triune God also reveals to us the greatness of our sin and misery, our need.[18] After the fall God said to Adam (and to us): "Cursed is the ground because of you; in pain you shall eat of it all the days of your life" (Gen 3:17 ESV). True prayer is conditioned by the knowledge of our profound need and our unworthiness to come to him in our own capacity. This is why, however intimate prayer may be, we do not come before God casually. Believers are sinners (Rom 3:23) redeemed by Christ. As we shall see, we do come to God our Father, in Christ, but we come reverently and with appropriate "reverence and awe, for our God is a consuming fire" (Heb 12:28–29 ESV).

True prayer comes in true faith, in confidence grounded not in our personal performance but in Christ's obedience for us and in his gracious promises to us (Matt 21:22; Mark 6:22; John 14:13–14; 1 Pet 3:12; Jas 5:13–18) This is what it truly means to pray in the name of Christ.[19] When we say "in Christ's name" or "in Jesus's name," that is not a magic talisman or a secret code that requires God to hear our prayers. Rather, praying in Christ's name is something we do more than something we say. Calvin writes, "For as soon as God's dread majesty comes to mind, we cannot but tremble and be driven far away by the recognition of our own unworthiness, until Christ comes forward as intermediary, to change the throne of dreadful glory into the throne of grace. As the apostle also

17. Bill W., *Twelve Steps and Twelve Traditions*, 34, 96.

18. Calvin, *Institutes* 3.20.6.

19. Calvin, *Institutes* 3.20.17.

teaches how awe should dare with all confidence to appear, to receive mercy, and to find grace in timely help [Heb. 4:16]."[20]

Thus, in some traditions, prayers are concluded formally in Christ's name. In other Christian traditions, prayers are simply concluded with an amen. What matters, however, is that we are able to approach God our Father because Christ's righteousness has been imputed to us and because he is interceding for us (Rom 8:34) as our high priest (Heb 2:17; 3:1; 4:14–5:10; 7:1–12:2).[21]

True prayer is not an exercise in building self-esteem. Our confidence rests in Christ, the Word of God (John 1:1–3), and in God's promises to us in Christ. It takes comfort in Christ's high priestly work and knows the Spirit is at work in us helping us to make known those needs that we cannot articulate (Rom 8:26). In our age, conditioned as it is by Pentecostalism, our understanding of what Paul means is clarified by Calvin's explanation: "Therefore, in order to minister to this weakness, God gives us the Spirit as our teacher in prayer, to tell us what is right and temper our emotions. For, 'because we do not know how to pray as we ought, the Spirit comes to our help,' and 'intercedes for us with unspeakable groans' [Rom. 8:26]; not that he actually prays or groans but arouses in us assurance, desires, and sighs, to conceive which our natural powers would scarcely suffice."[22]

Question 118

What has God commanded us to ask him?

All things necessary for soul and body, which Christ our Lord included in the prayer that he himself taught us.[23]

20. Calvin, *Institutes* 3.20.17.

21. Calvin, *Institutes* 3.10.18–21.

22. Calvin, *Institutes* 3.20.5.

23. "Was hat uns Gott befohlen, von ihm zu bitten? Alle geistliche und leibliche Nothdurft, welche der Herr Christus begriffen hat in dem Gebet, das Er uns selbst gelehret" (Schaff, *Creeds of Christendom*, 3:350–51). "Quae sunt ea quae a se peti iubet? Omnia tum animae tum corpori necessaria, quae Dominus noster Iesus Christus ea precatione, quam nos ipse docuit, complexus est" (Niemeyer, *Collectio Confessionum*, 459).

According to Calvin, prayer is "properly confined to entreaties and supplications."[24] "Scripture," he writes, "with good reason enjoins us to use both constantly."[25] It is in view of the necessity of prayer that James writes as he does about prayer (Jas 5:13–18). If anyone is suffering, they should pray. The prayer of the righteous person has great power. This is a challenging word to autonomous modern Western people. America, at least traditionally, has been the home of rugged individualism, which was a very useful trait for pioneers and settlers who turned over ground for the first time, who built cities from nothing. Farms were some distance from each other. Before electricity and telephones, communication was very slow. So, if a plow broke, a farmer had to fix it by himself. I suppose some small farmers still work this way. In such a culture, asking for help, or at least doing so often, is seen as a sign of weakness. It means another man has to stop his work and come help you with yours.

In contrast to rugged individualism, prayer is a confession to another of our need and weakness. Perhaps this is one of the most difficult aspects of prayer. Here is where it is vital to distinguish between works and grace. In the covenant of works, one truly is on one's own. "Do your own work" was a regular refrain among my teachers. Looking at a schoolmate's exam is cheating, a violation of the covenant of works. Prayer, however, belongs to the covenant of grace, and in prayer God's covenant people turn to the God of the covenant, who said, "I am Yahweh, and I will bring you out from under the burdens of the Egyptians, and I will deliver you from slavery to them, and I will redeem you with an outstretched arm and with great acts of judgment. I will take you to be my people, and I will be your God, and you shall know that I am Yahweh your God, who has brought you out from under the burdens of the Egyptians" (Exod 6:6–7).

The God to whom we pray is *the* covenant-making and covenant-keeping God. However isolated we might be from others, whether on the farm or on the internet, we believers are not isolated from God. He keeps his covenant promise to be our God. Our part of the covenant of grace is to respond to his grace, in union with Christ, by making use of the means he has graciously provided. Even those means, the objective (preaching

24. Calvin, *Institutes* 3.20.28.

25. Calvin, *Institutes* 3.20.28.

and sacraments) and the subjective (prayer), are gifts, and when we do make use of them, it is by grace. Nevertheless, in union and communion with Christ we do make a free (uncoerced) choice to respond with thanks to that grace, in that grace. It is not as if, having begun the Christian life by grace, we finish by works: "Let me ask you only this: Did you receive the Spirit by works of the law or by hearing with faith? Are you so foolish? Having begun by the Spirit, are you now being perfected by the flesh?" (Gal 3:2–3 ESV).

So, prayer is part of the communion we have with our gracious Father, in Christ, with and by the Spirit. The same God who created and sustains us, who loved us so much that he sent his only begotten Son, delights to hear our prayers and to answer them.

Our understanding of prayer differs considerably from much of what is commonly accepted in contemporary evangelical circles. For example, we find nothing in Scripture that commands us, either by precept or example, to pray the way the "health and wealth" preachers teach. In contrast, we pray for "all things necessary for body and soul." A vehicle may be necessary, but a jet certainly is not. Health is a necessity (Jas 5:13–14). Rain is a necessity (Jas 5:17–18). Forgiveness is a necessity (Jas 5:15). We ask our heavenly Father for everything we need because "Every good gift and every perfect gift is from above, coming down from the Father of lights, with whom there is no variation or shadow due to change" (Jas 1:17 ESV). In prayer we trust our Father with all our anxieties (Matt 6:25–34; 1 Pet 5:7). God's word says, "Do not be anxious about anything, but in everything by prayer and supplication with thanksgiving let your requests be made known to God" (Phil 4:6 ESV). God cares for us more than we care for ourselves. He is trustworthy and capable of meeting all our physical and spiritual needs.

Question 119

What is the Lord's Prayer?

Our Father in heaven, hallowed be your name, your kingdom come, your will be done in earth, as it is in heaven. Give us this day our daily bread. And forgive us our debts, as we forgive our debtors, and lead us not into temptation, but deliver us from evil: for yours is the kingdom, and the power, and the glory for ever. Amen.[26]

Not only is our God willing and able to hear and to help, but he has given us a pattern by which to pray. There is a subset of evangelicals, some dispensationalists, who, because their confusion over the history of redemption, will not pray the Lord's Prayer because they do not believe it is for "the church age," as they say.[27] Such a view of the Lord's Prayer is not only starkly unbiblical (it represents a significant misunderstanding of the history of redemption and the kingdom of God, that it is both inaugurated and yet to be consummated), but it is also contrary to the universal practice of the Christian church for more than two millennia. The Reformed churches follow the ancient and ecumenical pattern of using the Lord's Prayer both in our public worship services and in our private devotions.

Our Lord was answering the disciples' request. He was teaching them how to pray. Instead of refusing to use the words and pattern our Lord intentionally gave us, we should receive them with thanks and use them. When the disciples asked Jesus to teach them how to pray (Luke 11:1–13; Matt 6:5–13), they were not asking for a prayer that applied only to them or that would not apply to us, and when our Lord gave them the prayer, he was answering their question. He was teaching them (and us) how to pray. The whole context of the prayer, particularly in Luke 11, makes this

---

26. "Wie lautet das Gebet des Herrn? Unser Vater, der du bist in den Himmeln:1 Geheiliget werde dein Name. Dein Reich komme. Dein Wille geschehe auf Erden, wie im Himmel. Unser täglich Brot gieb uns heute. Und vergieb uns unsere Schulden, wie auch wir vergeben unsern Schuldigern. Und führe uns nicht in Versuchung, sondern erlöse uns vom Bösen. Denn dein ist das Neich, und die Kraft, und die Herrlichkeit in Ewigkeit. Amen" (Schaff, *Creeds of Christendom*, 3:351). "Quae est illa precatio? Pater noster, qui es in coelis: Sanctifcetur nomen tuum: Veniat regnum tuum: Fiat voluntas tua, quemadmodum in coelo, sic etiam in terra: Panem nostrum quotidianum da nobis hodie: Et remitte nobis debita nostra, sicut et nos remittimus debitoribus nostris: Et ne nos inducas in tentantionem, sed libera nos a malo. Quia tuum est regnum, potentia, et gloria in secula, Amen" (Niemeyer, *Collectio Confessionum*, 459).

27. E.g., the note in the *Scofield Reference Bible* on Luke 11:1–4 says in part: "Used as a *form*, the Lord's prayer is, dispensationally, upon legal, not church ground; it is not a prayer in the name of Christ (cd. John xiv. 13, 14; xvi. 24); and it makes human forgiveness, as under the law it must, the condition of divine forgivness; an order which grace exactly reverses (cf. Eph. iv. 32)" (Scofield, *Holy Bible*). Witsius (*Dissertations on the Lord's Prayer*, 125) observed in his day that there were "some Christians to be found, who, from strange superstition, would rather have Christ's words wholly suppressed than employ them in expressing their own prayers to God."

quite clear to those who do not have an *a priori* notion of what the kingdom of God must be (an earthly Israelite kingdom) by which the words of Christ can be (unfairly) levered aside. We are those in Luke 11:5–13 who need to know that God is, in Christ, our friend, who, like a friend, will rise and give us whatever we need (Luke 11:8).

In answer to the question, from the opposite side, whether we are *restricted* to the words of the Lord's Prayer, Ursinus responds, "That Christ delivered this form, not that we should be restricted to these words, but that we might know what things we should ask of God, and how we should ask them. It is a general form respecting the manner, and the things which we should pray for."[28]

The structure of the Lord's Prayer is in three parts: (1) introduction (*exordium*), (2) petitions (*petitiones*), and (3) conclusion (*clausula*).[29] We consider these sections below.

Regarding the text of the Lord's Prayer, there are two variants to note. First, *HC* 119 includes the traditional doxology, "Yours is the kingdom and the power and the glory forever, Amen." This doxology, however, does not appear in the oldest manuscripts of Matthew 6:13.[30] It is drawn from 1 Chronicles 29:10–13. It appears first in later, Byzantine copies of the New Testament. A shorter version appears in *Didache* 8.2, which is probably best dated to the very early second century.[31] There is certainly nothing wrong with a biblical doxology, and it is perfectly appropriate to pray it, but knowing that it was a later addition helps to understand the variation in practice. Its omission is not a sign of theological or biblical infidelity.[32]

---

28. Ursinus, *Commentary*, 625.

29. Ursinus, *Corpus doctrinae*, 635.

30. Metzger, *Textual Commentary*, on Matt 6:13 (pp. 14–15). The doxology is absent from important witnesses to the Alexandrian text (א, B) and the Western text (D and Old Latin), and from important patristic commentaries on the Lord's Prayer (Tertullian, Origen, Cyprian). See Aland and Aland, *Text of the New Testament*, 306–7.

31. ὅτι σοῦ ἐστιν ἡ δύναμις καὶ ἡ δόξα εἰς τοὺς αἰῶνας (Holmes, *Apostolic Fathers*, 357).

32. Herman Witsius (1636–1708), in his commentary on the Lord's Prayer, was aware of some of the questions around the doxology. In the sixteenth century, Theodore Beza had addressed the question, and before him Erasmus. Witsius recognized that the doxology was not acknowledged by Tertullian, Cyprian, or Augustine (among others). He argued that it was (at the time) in the most ancient copies and appealed to Bellarmine, Stephanus, and Erasmus as authorities in support of the doxology. Our text base, however, has grown considerably since the sixteenth and seventeenth centuries, as has our knowledge of the transmission of the text. See Witsius, *Dissertations on the Lord's Prayer*, 370–73.

Second, Luke 11:4 says, "Forgive us our sins," whereas the parallel passage in Matthew 6:12 says "forgive us our debts."[33] There is, of course, no contradiction since Luke's text says, "as we forgive everyone who is indebted to us." Debt is a metaphor for sin. Further, many Christians have learned the Lord's Prayer, known to many by its Latin title *Pater noster* (our Father), from the widely used Roman Catholic form or from the *Book of Common Prayer* (1662), which says, "forgive us our trespasses, as we forgive those who trespass against us."

33. καὶ ἄφες ἡμῖν ⸀τὰς ἁμαρτίας⸁ ἡμῶν (Luke 11:4). καὶ ἄφες ἡμῖν ⸀τὰ ὀφειλήματα⸁ ἡμῶν (Matt 6:12).

Question 120

Why did Christ command us to address God thus: "Our Father?"

Question 121

Why is it added: "in heaven"?

Lord's Day 46

QUESTION 120

Why did Christ command us to address God thus: "Our Father?"

To awaken in us at the very beginning of our prayer that childlike reverence for and trust in God, which are to be the ground of our prayer, namely, that God has become our Father through Christ, and will much less deny us what we ask of him in faith than our parents refuse us earthly things.[1]

Less than a century ago, mass communication was radically different than it is today. Ours could easily be called the age of communication technology. Just as we have developed remarkably powerful ways to send messages to one another, our ability to communicate personally and directly seems to have diminished sharply. This is decline is important because prayer is a form of mostly verbal, personal communication between Christians and our God. Our word *communication* is a Latin word (*communicatio*) that means, in our time, "interpersonal contact, social interaction, association, intercourse."[2] Embedded in the word is idea of communion, a "the action of sharing or holding something in common with others."[3] The very notion of prayer, of addressing God directly in the name of Christ, assumes that we understand the importance of interpersonal communication and communion with God. Prayer is a form of direct personal address to the tripersonal God. It is not a dialogue in the usual sense of that word. Contrary to the charismatic and Pentecostal movements, we do not pray and wait for a verbal response. That not only denies the sufficiency of Holy Scripture for the Christian faith and life but

1. "Warum hat uns Christus befohlen, Gott also anzureden: Unser Vater? Dass Er gleich im Anfang unsers Gebets in uns erwecke die kindliche Furcht und Zuversicht gegen Gott, welche der Grund unseres Gebetes sein soll, nämlich, dass Gott unser Vater durch Christum worden sei, und wolle uns viel meniger versagen, warum wir ihn im Glauben bitten, denn unsere Väter uns irdische Dinge abschlagen" (Schaff, *Creeds of Christendom*, 3:351). "Cur praecpit Christus, ut ita Deum compellemus: *Pater noster*? Ut statim in ipso precationis exordio, convenientem Dei filiis reverentiam et fiduciam erga Deum in nobis excitet, quae nostrae precationis fundamentum esse debet: nimirum, Deum propter Christum nobis Patrem factum esse, et quae vera fide ab eo petimus, nobis multo minus negare, quam parentes nostri, nobis bona terrena denegant" (Niemeyer, *Collectio Confessionum*, 459).

2. *OED*, s.v. "communication." See Lewis and Short, *Latin Dictionary*, s.v. "communicatio."

3. *OED*, s.v. "communion."

leads to an unbiblical, sometimes paralyzing quest for direct, extracanonical special revelation. It is a dialogue insofar as God has revealed himself, his gospel, and his moral will to us in his word. We listen to his word read and read it. We see and receive the gospel made visible in the holy sacraments.[4] These are all true, reliable, canonical messages from God to us, his people. In prayer we are responding to his word by adoring him, confessing our sins, giving thanks, and making our petitions known.

Despite the appearance of intimacy, much of our electronic communication is not truly personal. Sending a text message is not the same thing as having a conversation with another person. Electronic transmission of information ("we will meet you at 7:00 p.m. at the restaurant") is impersonal. We know instinctively that it is morally wrong to end a relationship by text message.

Prayer is a quintessentially *personal* communication and communion because, in communion with God, we come to realize over and again our dependence on our Father and to make known our most basic and profound needs to him (Matt 6:25–34). Thus, the one to whom we are taught principally to pray is our heavenly Father.

Ursinus reminds us that God is our Father in two respects: nature (creation) and grace (redemption). Because of sin, left to nature, we would be under condemnation. In the covenant of grace, through faith alone, in Christ, God has become our Father, and we have become his adopted sons (Rom 8:15; Gal 4:5; Eph 1:5). Thus, the word *Father* reminds us of our status in Christ.[5]

There are four reasons we address God as father.

First, God wills it.[6]

Second, "that we may know and acknowledge him to be our Father, who for the sake of the Son of God our mediator, adopted us as his children, when we were his enemies."[7] This note is in contrast to the modernist tendency toward universalism, the universal, saving fatherhood of God.[8] In contrast, the biblical truth and the ecumenical Christian

4. Calvin, *Institutes* 4.14.3.

5. Ursinus, *Commentary*, 626–27. See the discussion of adoption under *HC* 33.

6. "Deus ergo à nobis vult invocari" (Ursinus, *Corpus doctrinae*, 636.)

7. Ursinus, *Commentary*, 627; Ursinus, *Corpus doctrinae*, 636. See John 20:17.

8. McClymond, *Devil's Redemption*.

conviction is that Christ is the only and eternally begotten Son of God. He alone is the "way, the truth, and the life" (John 14:6). God is our Father only for Christ's sake (Luke 6:36; 12:30, 32; John 8:19). When we say, "Our Father," we are implicitly acknowledging Christ as God's only Son and the only Savior.

Third, filial reverence and honor demands it. As a practical matter, in our informal age, it might be more important than ever for us stop and remember what it means to call God our Father. It is, as Ursinus notes, necessary to speak to God as our Father that "we may direct true prayer to God, who is the Father of our Lord Jesus Christ."[9]

Fourth, we address God as our Father because it begets in us, his adopted sons, confidence that, for Christ's sake alone, he hears our prayers. Our Lord said, "What father among you, if his son asks for a fish, will instead of a fish give him a serpent; or if he asks for an egg, will give him a scorpion? If you then, who are evil, know how to give good gifts to your children, how much more will the heavenly Father give the Holy Spirit to those who ask him!" (Luke 11:11–13 ESV). As adults, particularly, we need that "filial reverence and trust" in God to be awakened, since genuine communication and communion is grounded in trust. Where such confidence in the other party is lacking, genuine communication is impossible.[10]

Here we might also add, as Ursinus observes, that we speak in the first-person plural because "we do not pray alone." Rather, the "whole church" prays. It is true that we do pray at home, privately, but the first-person plural here reminds us that prayer is first a *corporate* act of the Christ-confessing covenant community.[11] Praying in the first-person plural admonishes us to "mutual love," which, he notes, is a "habitual quality," that is, something wrought within the Christian by the Holy Spirit as a part of sanctification.[12] Where there is no true neighbor-love, there is no true prayer, because where there is no neighbor-love, there is no true faith, and without true faith, there is no prayer.[13]

---

9. Ursinus, *Commentary*, 627; Ursinus, *Corpus doctrinae*, 636.

10. Ursinus, *Commentary*, 627; Ursinus, *Corpus doctrinae*, 636.

11. Ursinus, *Commentary*, 628; Ursinus, *Corpus doctrinae*, 637.

12. Ursinus, *Corpus doctrinae*, 637.

13. Ursinus, *Corpus doctrinae*, 637.

A couple of other questions arise under this head, which we should address briefly. Does it follow that, because the Lord's Prayer teaches us to address God as our Father, thereby we may not also invoke the Son or the Holy Spirit? Ursinus argues that such a conclusion does not follow because it ignores the sense in which we are address God as Father: "Again: the name of the Father, as the name of God, when it is opposed to creatures, must be understood essentially [*essentialiter*]; and where it is used in connection with the other persons of the Godhead, it must be understood personally. The name Father must, therefore, here be understood essentially."[14]

When Ursinus says *essentialiter,* he refers to the divine essence as distinct from the three divine persons. The contrast here is not between the divine persons (Father, Son, and Spirit) but between God and the creature. This same answer applies to the objection that because Christ is called our brother (e.g., Heb 2:11) that therefore he cannot be Father.[15] The Father, Son, and Spirit are consubstantial but personally distinct. When the divine essence is in view, relative to creatures, we use one mode of speech. When the relations between the persons are in view, we use the other.

Question 121

Why is it added: "in heaven"?

That we may have no earthly thought of the heavenly majesty of God, and from his almighty power expect all things necessary for body and soul.[16]

When our communication and communion with our heavenly Father breaks down, it is always our fault. The Father has not moved or changed. He us loves immutably in Christ. He still hears our prayers for

14. Ursinus, *Commentary,* 627; Ursinus, *Corpus doctrinae,* 636.

15. Ursinus, *Corpus doctrinae,* 637.

16. "Warum wird hinzugethan: Der du bist in den Himmeln? Auf dass wir von der himmlischen Majestät Gottes nichts Irdisches gedenken, und von seiner Allmächtigkeit alle Nothdurft Leibes und der Seele gewarten" (Schaff, *Creeds of Christendom,* 3:352). "Cur additur: *Quis es in coelis*? Ne de coelesti maestate Dei humile quippiam aut terrenum cogitemus: simul etiam, ut ab eius omnipotentia, quaecunque animo et corpori sunt necessari, expectemus" (Niemeyer, *Collectio Confessionum,* 459).

Christ's sake. He sustains us still. He is gracious still toward his Christian for Christ's sake. It is we who are mutable (changeable), who are unfaithful, whose faith waivers. Sometimes it is because we strangely forget that our Father is in heaven. There is a reason our Lord taught us to address "Our Father in heaven."

We sinful humans have always been tempted to confuse God with the creation. It is called pantheism (everything is God) or sometimes panentheism (everything is in God). In contrast, Scripture distinguishes sharply between the Creator and the creature (Rom 1:25). It does so at the very beginning of the story: "In the beginning God created the heavens and the earth" (Gen 1:1). There was when God was and we (and all creatures) were not. God spoke creation into being. He is immutable, infinite, and he is one (Mal 3:6; Deut 6:4). One of the earliest heresies faced by the ancient church, which reemerged in the late sixteenth century in Socinianism and again in recent decades in open theism, was called the anthropomorphite heresy.[17] The anthropomorphites refused to see that figurative speech in Scripture is just that. God does not actually, literally repent (Gen 6:6). He does not literally, actually have fingers (Exod 31:18; Ps 8:3), nor does he, in himself, have a hand (Isa 48:13) or eyes (Gen 6:8), and so on. These are all figures of speech, but the anthropomorphites, Mormons, and open theists think he does.[18]

The Lord's Prayer is also a good reminder that heaven is not some faraway, imaginary place about which to fantasize. Heaven is a reality. It is God's dwelling place.[19] Our Lord Jesus is still incarnate there. Whatever it is, it is not clouds and angels with harps. It is preeminently the place where things are as they ought to be, where they are utterly conformed to God's holiness and to his Holy Spirit.[20] Materialism tells us that we can only find help in this life, but the Christian faith teaches us to reject the closed, materialist view of the universe. It is not even as if God must break in, as it were. He is already here, operating constantly, immutably by his power and by his Spirit.[21] Yet, he is pictured for us as being in heaven so

---

17. See the discussion under *HC* 11.

18. Pinnock, *Most Moved Mover*, 34–35.

19. Ursinus, *Commentary*, 628–29.

20. Vos, "'True' and 'Truth.'" See also Vos, *Pauline Eschatology*, passim.

21. Ursinus, *Corpus doctrinae*, 638.

that we will remember his transcendence and his glory. One goes to a king in his palace, and so we go, as it were, to our Father in his heaven with the knowledge that our humanity is represented there by Jesus, our Mediator, and that our Father, our Great King, hears us for his sake (Heb 10:19–25).

Our heavenly Father has earned our trust, not only by creating and mercifully sustaining us but by freely saving his people, by giving us new life, faith, and through faith alone, all of his benefits. God has become our Father *sola gratia, sola fide*. Our Father has earned our trust by sending his only begotten Son (John 3:16). He has adopted us (Rom 8:15; Gal 4:5; Eph 1:5) and sealed our adoption with his Holy Spirit (2 Cor 1:22; Eph 1:13; 4:30). Our Lord urges us to "ask," to "seek," and to "knock" (Matt 7:7). Our Father is ready to hear us and ready to answer according to his purposes, our benefit, and his glory. If we do not ask, if we do not pray, if we do not unburden our hearts to our heavenly Father, it is because we do not believe. We should confess that too, and he will renew our hearts even as we ask it because his Spirit is gradually, graciously renewing us and replacing our unbelief with heartfelt, childlike trust.

Citizens of the developed, affluent, modern world may struggle more than Christians in other parts of the globe with the importance of heaven to biblical Christianity. There has been a steady drumbeat in the modern period to convince us of the centrality of earth to Christianity such that anyone who talks too much of heaven falls under a degree of suspicion. Nevertheless, our Lord teaches us to address our Father *in heaven* because that is the source of our help. "My help comes from Yahweh, who made heaven and earth" (Ps 121:2). He is, after all, Creator of "heaven and earth" (Gen 1:1). When Melchizedek blessed Abram (Gen 14:18), he characterized God as "possessor of heaven and earth." Yahweh is the "God of heaven" (Gen 24:7; cf. Neh 1:5; Ps 57:3; Jonah 1:9). The New Testament writers are unabashedly enthusiastic about heaven. Paul says that Christians have a "heavenly citizenship" (Phil 3:20). God has blessed us in Christ with "every spiritual blessing in the heavenly places" (Eph 3:10). In Christ, we have come not to Sinai but to "Mount Zion, the city of the living God, the heavenly Jerusalem" (Heb 12:22). We are fascinated with heaven because that is where Christ is (1 Pet 3:22), seated at the right hand of the Father.

We address our Father in heaven as a shorthand way of remembering the divine attributes, that he is immense, immutable, incorruptible, good, great, and rich toward us in Christ.[22] When we call on our heavenly Father, it moves us to confidence that just as he saved us, he will also hear our prayers—because he fills all things with himself, he is always near (Acts 17:27). It draws us away from this world, as important is it is, toward heaven "that the minds of all who worship him may be elevated and fixed on heavenly things."

22. Ursinus, *Commentary*, 629.

Question 122

What is the first petition?

Lord's Day 47

QUESTION 122

What is the first petition?

"Hallowed be your name," that is: Grant us first, rightly to know you, and to sanctify, magnify and praise you in all your works, in which your power, goodness, justice, mercy and truth shine forth; and further, that we so order our whole life, our thoughts, words, and deeds, that your name may not be blasphemed but honored and praised on our account.[1]

Our familiarity with the Lord's Prayer (Matt 6:9–13) might give us the impression that it is rudimentary. It is not. Right at the outset we face a challenge. The first challenge is the grammar and how to get it into English. It will be useful to our prayers to know a little grammar. The Greek verb used in Matthew and in Luke 11:2 (ἁγιάζω) is in the passive voice and the imperative mood. "Joey threw the ball" is in the active voice. Joey is acting upon the ball. "Joey was hit by the ball" is in the passive voice. Joey is being acted upon by the ball. The Gospel writers use the verb "to sanctify" in the passive voice to signal that something is being acted upon by someone or something else. The subject of the action is the name of the Lord. The verb is in the imperative mood. We use the indicative mood to signal a narrative. "Joey threw the ball" is in the indicative mood. Were Joey at second base, and should there be a play at home, the catcher might say, "Joey, throw the ball!" That is the imperative voice. The catcher is urging Joey to do something. The verb "to sanctify" is in the imperative. It is an urgent request. When we pray, "Holy be your name" or "Hallowed be thy name," as in the AV (1611), we are making an urgent request that something be done. We are not wishing

1. "Was ist die erste Bitte? Geheiliget werde dein Name; das ist: Gieb uns erstlich, dass wir dich recht erkennen, und dich in allen deinen Werken, in welchen leuchtet deine Allmächtigkeit, Weisheit, Güte, Gerechtigkeit, Barmherzigkeit und Wahrheit, heiligen, rühmen und preisen. Darnach auch, dass wir unser ganzes Leben, Gedauken, Worte und Werke dahin richten, dass dein Name um unsertwillen nicht gelästert, sondern geehret und gepriesen werde" (Schaff, *Creeds of Christendom*, 3:352). "Quae est prima petitio? *Sanctificetur nomen tuum*; hoc est: Da principio, ut te recte agnoscamus, et lucentem in omnibus operibus tuis omnipotentiam, sapientiam bonitatem, iustitiam misericordiam veritatem tuam veneremur, praedicemus et celebremus: Deinde, ut universam vitam nostram, cogitationes, sermones et actiones, eo semper dirigamus, ne sanctissimum nomen tuum propter nos contumelia afficatur, sed honore potius et laudibus illustretur" (Niemeyer, *Collectio Confessionum*, 459–60).

that something that is not presently so might be. There is another mood or two for that (the subjunctive or the optative). We are urging him who has the power to make it so.

The first petition of the Lord's Prayer is that God himself, who is holy, who is both transcendent and utterly morally pure and righteous, should act so that his name should come to be regarded as holy. The antithesis of holiness is corruption. We know when something is clean and good and as it ought to be. A white shirt with a ketchup stain is not right because it is not clean. It needs to be washed and probably bleached. To sanctify is to set apart, to acknowledge as distinct, pure, clean, and as set apart to the Lord. Here we are urging the Lord to act so that he himself is regarded as he is, "most holy and most pure, or essential holiness, uncreated, which is God himself."[2] To sanctify, in this sense, is to "to acknowledge, reverence and praise that which is already in itself holy."[3]

Remember, Scripture consistently uses God's name in place of God himself.[4] Herman Witsius says that the "name of God, however, does not strictly denote God, as he exists in himself, but as he reveals and makes himself known to rational creatures."[5]

In Genesis 4, we read that people began to call upon the name of Yahweh (Gen 4:26). We are not to take "the name" of Yahweh Elohim in vain (Exod 20:7). God's name is majestic (Ps 8:1, 9). When we praise God's name, we praise him. His name is who and what he is to us: our holy, gracious, covenant-making and covenant-keeping God.

Second, the first petition begins the second part of the Lord's Prayer.[6] In the first petition, as Calvin says, we turn away from ourselves:

> In the first three petitions we ought to lose sight of ourselves, and seek the glory of God: not that it is separated from our salvation, but that the majesty of God ought to be greatly preferred by us to every other object of solicitude. It is of unspeakable advantage to

2. "Ipsum Deum sanctissimum et purissimum, seu sanctitatem essentialem, increatam, quae est Deus ipse" (Ursinus, *Corpus doctrinae*, 640).

3. Ursinus, *Commentary*, 630.

4. Ursinus, *Commentary*, 630; Ursinus, *Corpus doctrinae*, 639.

5. Witsius, *Sacred Dissertations on the Apostles' Creed*, 188; Clark, *Recovering the Reformed Confession*, 119–45.

6. See the discussion under *HC* 119.

> us that God reigns, and that he receives the honour which is due to him: but no man has a sufficiently earnest desire to promote the glory of God, unless (so to speak) he forgets himself, and raises his mind to seek God's exalted greatness.[7]

It is not our name that is to be revered but God's. His name is holy. It is the Christian's deepest desire to see everyone recognize our Father for who and what he is, the Holy One, the God of creation and redemption, he who adopts his people out of sin, death, and judgment and into grace, life, and communion. Ursinus notes that this petition is placed first in the prayer because "it comprehends the end and design (*finis et scopus*) of all the rest, inasmuch as the glory of God should be the end of all our affairs, actions and prayers."[8]

Third, though God is the one whom we are asking to act, we do have a part. Implicit in our urgent request to the Father to sanctify his name is a plea that he might also sanctify us.[9] This is a prayer, as the language of the catechism itself implies, for our progressive sanctification or our progressive conformity to the image of Christ, which is the second aspect of what Calvin calls the "twofold grace of God" (*duplex gratia Dei*) and what Olevianus calls the "double benefit" (*duplex beneficium*) of the covenant of grace.[10] We sinners are justified *sola gratia, sola fide* in order that "sin should be extirpated daily from our nature."[11] Part of our prayer for the sanctification of God's name is that "he would regenerate us and make us more and more holy, so that in our whole life we may prevent his name from being blasphemed, and may magnify and declare it with honor and praise in every conceivable way."[12]

Our sanctification has a greater role in the setting apart of God's name than we may realize. This is something we could learn from the early Christian fathers. They spent proportionally more time on moral theology

7. Calvin, *Commentary on a Harmony*, 1.318.

8. Ursinus, *Commentary*, 629; Ursinus, *Corpus doctrinae*, 639.

9. Ursinus, *Commentary*, 630.

10. See the discussion under *HC* 70; Venema, *Accepted and Renewed*; Clark, *Caspar Olevian*, 181–209; Olevianus, *De substantia*, 1.1.2; 2.65, 69; Olevianus, *Exposition*, 11.

11. Olevianus, *Romanos Notae*, 206.

12. Ursinus, *Commentary*, 631. Ursinus is using *regnerate* as a synonym for *sanctify*. Calvin, Olevianus, et al. also used it this way in the period before the conflict with the Remonstrants (Clark, *Caspar Olevian*, 185n11).

and on what we call the doctrine of sanctification than we tend to do. To be sure, it can at times be wearying, but the more our surrounding culture begins to mirror the pagan Greco-Roman culture within which they served Christ, the more we are able to understand why they so emphasized sanctification. There was not a great lot they could do or even sought to do about the surrounding culture. With one possible third-century exception in Syria, until the early fourth century, Christians met in modified private homes. They did not have ostentatious buildings, and certainly they had little cultural influence. The time and place for their assemblies for worship were sometimes closely guarded secrets, all the more during times of persecution. One thing Christians could influence, however, was their piety and godliness. When the pagan critics did actually examine them, they did not find moral fault in them.[13] In his defense of the Christians, Justin Martyr urges pagans to investigate the Christians so that they and everyone else can see that the Christians are guilty of none of the crimes with which they were charged in popular rumors.[14] It would not take very long to discover the various scandals that have brought Christianity into disrepute in the last few decades. Ultimately, however, we pray that our heavenly Father might sanctify his name because it is a job only he can do.[15] We are urging him to work powerfully for his own glory first of all in us but also beyond us.

---

13. Wilken, *Christians as the Romans Saw Them*, 22, 72–73.

14. "But lest any one think that this is an unreasonable and reckless utterance, we demand that the charges against the Christians be investigated, and that, if these be substantiated, they be punished as they deserve" (Justin Martyr, *First Apology* 3 [*ANF* 1:163]).

15. "But we cannot of ourselves sanctify and hallow the name of God" (Ursinus, *Commentary*, 632).

Question 123

What is the second petition?

Lord's Day 48

QUESTION 123

What is the second petition?

"Your kingdom come," that is: so govern us by your word and Spirit, that we submit ourselves to you always more and more; preserve and increase your church; destroy the works of the devil, every power that exalts itself against you, and all wicked devices formed against your holy Word, until the fullness of your kingdom come, wherein you shall be all in all.[1]

In his *Exposition of the Apostles' Creed*, Olevianus begins with the kingdom of God:

> It is certain that there are two spiritual kingdoms, even in this world: the kingdom of darkness and the kingdom of light. Every person necessarily belongs to one or the other here in this life. ... The one is the kingdom of Christ, made up of all who repent, believe in Christ, and are baptized in His name. It also includes their children, unless, when they are grown, through unbelief they reject the benefit that is offered. But the other is the kingdom of Satan and darkness, made up of all who do not repent and do not believe in Christ.[2]

For Olevianus, as for Ursinus, to pray for the coming of the kingdom of God (or the kingdom of heaven, which they regarded as synonyms) was to pray for God's universal administration of the world through his

1. "Was ist die andere Bitte? Dein Reich komme; das ist: Regiere uns also durch dein Wort und Geist, dass wir uns dir je länger je mehr unterwerfen; erhalte und mehre deine Nirche, und zerstöre die Werke des Teusels und alle Gewalt, die sich wider dich erhebt, und alle bösen Rathschläge, die wider dein heiliges Wort erdacht werden, bis die Vollkommenheit deines Reichs herzukomme, darin du wirst Alles in Allen sein" (Schaff, *Creeds of Christendom*, 3:352–53). "Quae est secunda petitio? *Veniat regnum tuum*; hoc est: regas nos ita verbo et Spiritu tuo, ut nos tibi magis magisque subiiciamus. Conserva et auge Ecclesiam tuam, destrue opera Diaboli omnemque potentiam se adversus maiestatem tuam efferentem; irrita fac omnia consilia, quae contra verbum tuum eapiuntur, quoad plene tandem ac perfecte regnes, cum eris omnia in omnibus" (Niemeyer, *Collectio Confessionum*, 460).

2. Olevianus, *Exposition*, 9; see also xxii–xxiii.

general providence and specially through his administration of salvation through the visible, institutional church.[3]

Ursinus, Olevianus, and the catechism reflect the Reformed inaugurated (not consummated) eschatology.[4] When Christ came, he inaugurated his kingdom in a special way—it was certainly present in redemptive history in, with, and under the types and shadows. By speaking of an inaugurated eschatology, we account for our Lord's declaration, "The time is fulfilled, the Kingdom of God is at hand" (Mark 1:15). Judas was disappointed, along with others, because Jesus did not fulfill their expectations of a political, earthly dominion. Our Lord explained to Pilate, "My kingdom is not of this world. Were my kingdom were of this world, my servants would have been fighting, that I might not be delivered over to the Jews. But my kingdom is not from the world" (John 18:36 ESV).[5] Jesus's kingdom is not an earthly kingdom; it is not of this world, but it is certainly in the world. The kingdom is at hand (ἤγγικεν). Jesus was casting out demons because the kingdom had arrived (Matt 12:28). The time to repent and believe is now, because the kingdom is present (Luke 10:9, 11; 11:20). Nevertheless, the kingdom of God was not fully realized in history. It is semirealized. As citizens of the kingdom of God, we participate in spiritual, heavenly realities (Mark 10:15; Acts 14:22), but there is a future realization of the kingdom in fullness (Mark 9:47; 14:25; Luke 19:11; 1 Cor 6:9, 10). Christians are citizens of the heavenly kingdom (Phil 3:20).

This inaugurated eschatology is in contrast to those dispensationalists (e.g., the classic and modified) who reject the notion that, in his incarnation and ministry, our Lord Jesus inaugurated the kingdom of God.[6] It is also in contrast to those, not infrequently former dispensationalists, who run to the other extreme by adopting "full preterism" (or hyperpreterism),

---

3. Olevianus, *Exposition*, 10. Ursinus writes, "The special kingdom of God—that which he exercises in his church consists in sending the Son from the Father, from the very beginning of the world, that he might institute and preserve the ministry of the church, and accomplish his purposes by it—that he might gather a church from the whole human race by his word and Spirit—rule, preserve and defend it against all enemies—raise it from death, and at length, having cast all enemies into everlasting condemnation, adorn it with heavenly glory, that God may be all in all, and be praised eternally by the church" (*Corpus doctrinae*, 633; see also 644).

4. See the discussion under *HC* 57–58.

5. Ursinus, *Commentary*, 633; Ursinus, *Corpus doctrinae*, 644.

6. E.g., Pentecost, *Things to Come*, 446–66. Contrast that view with Blaising and Bock, *Progressive Dispensationalism*, 257–62. See the discussion under *HC* 50.

which holds that Jesus returned in AD 70.[7] This view is heresy against the catholic Christian faith, which confesses the future, bodily return of Christ in the seventh article of the Apostles' Creed.[8] It is akin to the error of Hymenaeus, Philetus, and Alexander, who were teaching people that the general resurrection had already happened (2 Tim 2:16–18; 1 Tim 1:20). Prior to the rise of dispensationalism and its attending reactions, the eschatological options tended to be less extreme. Historic premillennialism (chiliasm) was looking for an earthly, literal, millennial kingdom of Christ on the earth, but it was not utterly tied to the restoration of national Israel. Until the early twentieth century, we tended to speak of the alternative view, that Christ had inaugurated his kingdom and would consummate it at his return, as postmillennialism. From the early twentieth century forward, we distinguished between postmillennialism and amillennialism.

The older form of postmillennialism postponed the millennium to a future earthly glory age. In that it was very much like chiliasm (historic premillennialism) except that it did understand the millennium of Revelation 20:5 to be a figure of speech.[9] More recent versions of postmillennialism (e.g., that espoused by the reconstructionist and theonomic movements) tends to speak more like the amillennialists regarding the inauguration of the millennium beginning with the resurrection of Christ, *but* they speak like the older postmillennialists regarding a future earthly glory age before Christ returns.[10]

---

7. Mathison, *When Shall These Things.*

8. "Inde venturus est ad iudicandum vivos et mortuos" (Schaff, *Creeds of Christendom*, 2:45).

9. Richard Bauckham identifies two types of postmillennialism. The first he associates with Joachim of Fiore (ca. 1135–1202). It anticipates an "age of the Spirit," i.e., "a period of spiritual prosperity and peace for the church on earth, which was identified with the millennium of Rev. 20, though not primarily derived from that text." The second form he associates with Thomas Brightman (d. 1607), who taught "the millennium would come about through the Spirit-empowered preaching of the gospel, resulting in the conversion of the world and the world-wide spiritual reign of Christ through the gospel." This is quite close to what we most often see among the modern postmillennial movement. The theonomic reconstructionist movement looks forward to a coming social collapse, out of which will emerge a reconstructed Christian society in which the earth will be mostly converted before Christ's return. See Bauckham, "Millennium."

10. Hoekema, *Bible and the Future*, 177–80; Riddlebarger, *Case for Amillennialism*, 236–39; Venema, *Promise of the Future*, 341–54; Bavinck, *Reformed Dogmatics*, 4:674; Berkhof, *Systematic Theology*, 718; Berkhof, *History of Christian Doctrines*, 271–72; Strimple, "Amillennialism," 81–129.

The Lutheran and Reformed churches pointedly and forcefully rejected the doctrine of a future earthly golden age. The Lutherans denounced the "Jewish dream" of an earthly messianic kingdom.[11] The Swiss Reformed followed suit even more pointedly in the Second Helvetic Confession: "Moreover we condemn the Jewish dreams that before the day of judgment there shall be a golden world in the earth; and that the godly, shall possess the kingdoms of the world, their wicked enemies being trodden under foot. For the evangelical truth in Matthew 24 and 25, and Luke 21, and apostolic doctrine in the second epistle to the Thessalonians 2, and in the second epistle to the Timothy 3 and 4, are found to teach far otherwise."[12]

BC 37 says nothing about a golden age before the return of Christ. In it we confess, "When the time appointed by the Lord is come (which is unknown to all creatures) and the number of the elect is complete, our Lord Jesus will descend from heaven, bodily and visibly, as he ascended, with great glory and majesty, to declare himself the judge of the living and the dead. He will burn this old world, in fire and flame, in order to cleanse it."[13]

We should not dismiss as pessimistic the sixteenth-century Reformation consensus on eschatology. That assumes the correctness of the (Anabaptist) "golden age" eschatology, which must be demonstrated and which the churches have rejected. Certainly, the eschatological expectation of the principal author (Ursinus) and editors of the catechism was amillennial, that is, they rejected both a literal millennium and any idea of a future earthly golden age before Christ's return. Their reading of Scripture was forged in the fires of persecution for the gospel. They were not pessimistic about the ability of the Savior to call all of his elect to new life and to true faith.

What the postmillennialist critics of amillennialism call optimism we might better call, in the broad sense, Judaizing. That is the point the Lutherans and the Swiss Reformed were making when they denounced

11. *Apology of the Augsburg Confession*, art. 16, in Kolb and Wengert, *Book of Concord*, 232.7. See Augsburg Confession, art. 17.

12. Dennison, *Reformed Confessions*, 2:830. Chapter 11 of the Sandomierz Confession (1570) in Dennison, *Reformed Confessions*, 3:201.

13. *BC* 37, in United Reformed Churches in North America, *Liturgical Forms and Prayers*, 198. See Ursinus, *Commentary*, 635; Ursinus, *Corpus doctrinae*, 645.

glory-age thinking. For them such an eschatology required the confusion of Jewish eschatological expectations for a Christian eschatology.

It is not pessimistic to say that there will be no earthly glory age before Christ's return or an earthly millennial reign after Christ's return. It is difficult to see how the prerequisite to be optimistic is to affirm some sort of earthly golden age, whether literal (chiliastic/premillennial) or figurative (postmillennial). It is properly optimistic to hold, as the amillennialists do, that the sovereign Lord Jesus is saving every single one for whom he became incarnate, for whom he obeyed, for whom he died, for whom he was raised, and for whom he is interceding now at the right hand of the Father.

Psalm 2 describes the present reign of King Jesus:

> He who sits in the heavens laughs,
> The Lord scoffs at them.
> Then He will speak to them in His anger
> And terrify them in His fury, saying,
> "But as for Me, I have installed My King
> Upon Zion, My holy mountain." (Ps 2:4–6 NASB95)

Reformed amillennialism holds that no earthly power can stop the spread, through his divinely ordained means, of the kingdom of God (Matt 16:18). No civil ruler or cultural power can prevent the sovereign Holy Spirit from working powerfully through the gospel and sacraments, from conforming Christ's flock to Christ's image.

The first comfort of the martyrs has always been that Christ is reigning now, and in his sovereign, mysterious providence, he sometimes sends his children through great suffering. A second comfort, however, which we find richly reflected in Revelation, is that justice is coming. That is why French Reformed (Huguenot) martyrs sang Psalm 68 on the way to the gallows. "God shall arise and by his might, put all his enemies to flight." They knew that justice delayed was not justice denied. They knew that our ruling King Jesus would return in glory to consummate the defeat of his enemies that he inaugurated on the cross.[14] They knew that he sat in the heavens and laughed at his enemies, who will be crying at that last day.

---

14. *BC* 37.

He will cast them into the pit, and heaven will rejoice. The chiliasts and postmillennialists seek an earthly glory age, but all the attitude of the catechism is: wait, there will be a new heavens and a new earth. It will not be an earthly millennial glory age, but there will be a glorious consummation.

Regarding the chiliastic reading of Revelation 20, we should say that reading Revelation 20:5 selectively and literally ignores the apocalyptic genre in which Revelation was given, the sort of language being used (i.e., figurative and hyperbolic), and the setting, structure, and function of Revelation. The amillennial reading recognizes that our Lord Jesus gave Revelation to John, most likely in the early 90s AD.[15] The churches of Asia Minor were greatly troubled by the growing pressure they felt from Jewish synagogues on the one hand and from pagans on the other. There was not yet an organized, government-sponsored persecution of the church, but were it happening today, believers would probably use the word "persecution" to describe their experience. The emperor Domitian (AD 81–96), like his father Vespasian, thought the Christians were atheists because they denied the Greco-Roman pantheon. The period between AD 93 and 96 has sometimes been called the reign of terror. Flavius Clemens was martyred—even though some accounts deny that his death was a martyrdom.

The function of Revelation was to explain, in highly symbolic language, to the seven churches of Asia Minor and to us, what is the nature of the relations between Christ's present reign and our frequent suffering in this life until Christ's bodily return to consummate his kingdom. This is why amillennialists reject the notion that the reign described in Revelation 20 should be read literally. In order to read it this way, one must extract it from a highly figurative narrative. Figures of speech, analogies, and metaphors are all true, but they are true in the way they are intended. If we say, "It is raining cats and dogs," only a very small child runs to the window to look for actual cats and dogs falling from the clouds. Everyone else realizes that it is a figure of speech. When Revelation speaks of blood rising as high as horse's bridle for sixteen hundred stadia (approx. 150 miles), it is speaking in symbolic language (Rev 14:20).

Thus, how one understands the kingdom is very closely related to one's eschatology. Here we ought to be instructed by the language Olevianus

15. Hemer, *Letters to the Seven Churches*, 1–11; Beale, *Book of Revelation*, 4–20.

and Ursinus use. There is a general aspect of God's kingdom, but the Lord's Prayer is considering what Ursinus calls the "special" or saving aspect. It is to this aspect that Olevianus refers. The catechism, Ursinus, and Olevianus thought of that aspect or sphere of the kingdom relative to its institutional expression in the visible church. When we pray "your kingdom come," we are praying that God the Holy Spirit would work powerfully through the ordinary means of grace to bring all his elect to new life and true faith.[16]

When we pray for the kingdom to come, we are praying for something spiritual, not something ethereal. To say that the kingdom of God is *spiritual* is to say that it is of the Holy Spirit.[17] So, we are praying for the realization of God's reign in the earth to be accomplished by the power of the Holy Spirit. In this petition we are asking the Holy Spirit to bring all of the elect to new life and true faith. We are praying for the conversion of the lost. We are praying for the progress of the kingdom both in this antepenultimate time (between Christ's ascension and his return) and in its consummation at Christ's return.

The advance of the kingdom in this world is the work of the Holy Spirit through the word of God in the hearts, minds, and wills of believers. Thus, this petition is also a prayer that we, to whom the Spirit has graciously given new life and with it true faith and through faith union and communion with Christ, would be increasingly conformed to Christ. When we pray for sanctification, for mortification (putting to death the old man) and vivification (the making alive of the new), we are praying for the coming of the kingdom of God. The kingdom is God's. We are its grateful recipients.

The petition is corporate and specifically relative to the visible, institutional church. Though we might not be familiar with this way of understanding this petition, the older Reformed writers and the Reformed confessions tend to associate the visible manifestation of the kingdom of God with visible, institutional church. When *BC* 36 says "Kingdom of Christ" (*le royaume de Jésus-Christ*), it refers to the visible, institutional

16. Ursinus, *Commentary*, 633; Ursinus, *Corpus doctrinae*, 643–44.

17. Ursinus, *Commentary*, 633; Ursinus, *Corpus doctrinae*, 644.

church.[18] According to *HC* 82, it is the ministry of the visible church to make use of the keys of the kingdom. When one is excommunicated, one is excluded from the kingdom of Christ (*HC* 85). It is through the external call of the gospel that the Spirit brings the elect into the kingdom of God (Canons of Dort 3/4.10).[19] WCF 25.2 identifies the "visible church" with the "kingdom of the Lord Jesus Christ, the house and family of God."[20] The kingdom of God is indeed, as the WSC (102) says, "kingdom of grace."[21]

The manifestation of the kingdom in the visible church may not be impressive to the world, and indeed, judged by external appearances, it is not. In this, however, she is much like her head and Savior Jesus. He was not well regarded during his earthly ministry, and so he was crucified as a failure and disappointment. Our God, however, is in the business of great reversals. On the third day the tomb was empty. Not long after, he ascended to glory. The crucified Savior became the cornerstone of a building (the church) that neither the religious authorities nor secular authorities could have imagined (Eph 2:20; 1 Pet 2:6–7). Two thousand years later, the Spirit is using his church to bring his elect to faith all across the globe, despite the efforts of false religions, hostile cultures, and government persecutions to prevent it.

When we pray for the advent of the kingdom of God, we are praying that the Holy Spirit would use his appointed weapons, the word and church discipline, to conquer spiritual enemies.[22] Our Lord never promised a glorious millennium on the earth, but he is nevertheless crushing his enemies under his feet (1 Cor 15:27). Just as the cross was a paradoxical way to defeat his enemies, so too is the suffering of the church is a paradoxical, unexpected way to defeat the Evil One and his minions, but that is how he has promised to operate, through the foolishness of the gospel (1 Cor 1:21–25). There is a place between naturalism (which views the world as closed to spiritual forces) and hyperspiritualism (which sees demons around every corner). Christ is risen. He is ascended. He is ruling the nations with a rod of iron (Ps 2:9). He has crushed the serpent on the

18. Schaff, *Creeds of Christendom*, 3:432.

19. United Reformed Churches in North America, *Liturgical Forms and Prayers*, 272–73.

20. Bower, *Confession of Faith*, 316.

21. Westminster Assembly, *Humble Advice of the Assembly*, 21.

22. Ursinus, *Commentary*, 634; Ursinus, *Corpus doctrinae*, 644.

cross and is crushing him. The Evil One may afflict us (1 Pet 5:8), but he has no power over us. God has defeated him. No principality, no authority, no power can contest God (Rom 8:38; Eph 3:10; 6:12; Col 1:16; 2:15). He has defeated them all.

Our Lord Jesus announced the inauguration of his kingdom. By his Spirit, through the preaching of gospel, he is conquering his enemies and making them willing and grateful citizens of his kingdom.[23] His visible church is his embassy to the world. The sacraments are his signet ring, certifying the truth of his promises to those who believe. His kingdom has not yet been realized in its fullness, but it will be when he returns and is all in all (1 Cor 15:28). When he comes in royal glory, "every eye will see him, even those who pierced him, and all tribes of the earth will wail on account of him. Even so. Amen" (Rev 1:7 ESV).

---

23. Ursinus, *Commentary*, 635; Ursinus, *Corpus doctrinae*, 645.

Question 124

What is the third petition?

Lord's Day 49

QUESTION 124

What is the third petition?

"Your will be done in earth as it is in heaven," that is: grant that we and all people renounce our own will, and without gainsaying obey your will which alone is good; that so every one may fulfill his office and calling as willingly and faithfully as the angels do in heaven.[1]

One of the most striking moments in the Gospels is our Lord's prayer in Garden of Gethsemane (Matt 26:36–46; Mark 14:32–42; Luke 22:39–46). We are given compelling evidence in those moments of our Lord's true humanity. This is not the story the gnostics told. The Jesus character in the gnostic accounts only *appears* to be human. The gnostics and docetists were convinced that he could not actually be human, hence their docetic (from δοκέω, "to seem, appear") Christology. The Jesus of history, of the Gospel narratives, is true God and true man. In that prayer he genuinely struggled. That much is evident from his sorrow and grief (Matt 26:37), from his request that the disciples watch with him (v. 38), and from his prayer three times (v. 44) that the Father might permit "this cup" to pass from him (vv. 39, 42). This is the antithesis of much of the quasi-gnostic piety of Pietism and modern evangelicalism, which does not account for the genuine struggle that humans experience in prayer.[2] Our holy, righteous, sinless Lord Jesus, the God-Man, struggled greatly in prayer as the crucifixion approached.

1. "Was ist die dritte Bitte? Dein Wille geschehe auf Erden, wie im Himmel; das ist: Verleihe, dass wir und alle Menschen unserem eigenen Willen absagen, und deinem allein guten Willen, ohne alles Widersprechen, gehorchen; dass also Jedermann sein Amt und Beruf so willig und treulich ausrichte, wie die Engel im Himmel" (Schaff, *Creeds of Christendom*, 3:353). "Quae est tertia petitio? *Fiat voluntas tua, quemadmodum in coelo, sic etiam in terra*; hoc est: Da, ut nos et omnes homines, voluntati propriae renunciantes, tuae voluntati, quae sola est sancta, prompte et sine ulla murmure pareamus: atque ita singuli mandatum nobis munus fideliter et alacriter exequamur, quemadmodum faciunt Angeli in coelo" (Niemeyer, *Collectio Confessionum*, 460).

2. Clark, *Recovering the Reformed Confession*, 72–78. The contemporary Christian song, popularized by Doug Oldham (1930–2010), "I Just Came into His Presence" (1979), captures the quasi-gnostic character both of the Pietist approach to prayer and that of too much of modern evangelicalism.

Second, this passage is striking because of the impulse it generates in us to correct it. The narrative is meant to make us uncomfortable. It was one thing for the disciples to be sleepy and careless. It is another for us, who live in light of the cross, who know better now than the disciples did that night, to duck the implications of this text. The hard truth is that our Lord knew what was about to happen. It was not his arrest, as revolting as that scene was, about which he was praying. Neither was it his humiliation before the soldiers, nor his trials before the Jewish authorities and the Roman governor Pilate, that caused him pray thus. It was not even his carrying his own cross up Calvary that caused him to pray so. It was not his awful death about which he prayed. The cup to which he referred was his carrying of our sins into judgment, which the Noachian flood, the ritual holocaust of countless animals, countless circumcisions, the destruction of the Canaanites, the ten plagues in Egypt, and the destruction of Pharaoh's army in the Red Sea prefigured. All those anticipations were mere shadows of what was to be transacted at the top of this hill. It was not the physical suffering but the spiritual abandonment and the outpouring of righteous divine wrath about which he prayed.

The heroic thing was not the endurance of the physical torture but that he kept the covenant he made with his Father (John 17) from eternity. Knowing what was to come, he said to Peter, "Shall I not drink the cup that the Father has given me?" (John 18:11 ESV). Indeed, he willingly took the cup given to him by the Father, and he drank it in our place.

When we think of the third petition of the Lord's Prayer, we must do so only against the background of our Lord's own prayer. We pray this petition as those for whom the perfectly obedient suffering servant laid down his life. We do not pray this prayer in order to be accepted with God but because we have been accepted and we have been saved by what Christ has done for us, and because his Spirit, which he gave to us, has made us alive with him and united us to him through faith alone (*sola fide*). Because we are united to him, because his Spirit is at work in us, because he has adopted us as sons, he is enabling us to say, "Not my will but yours" to our heavenly Father.

We are asking that the Lord might "make it so and give that we might do your will, which alone is just and holy, and not ours, which is depraved, and that we might submit to you. Therefore we pray."[3] It is a prayer that we might deny ourselves and that we might be ready to "submit ourselves willingly to God in all things."[4] Insofar as this petition requires self-denial, it is perhaps the most countercultural thing we could possibly pray. We may live in the most narcissistic age in human history. In contrast, our Lord's food was to do his Father's will (John 4:34). Thus, the first aspect of our prayer, under this petition, is for the grace to renounce ourselves and our own interests and for the grace to give ourselves and our will over entirely to our Father's interests and will. According to Paul, the Holy Spirit is working in us, "training us to renounce ungodliness and worldly passions, and to live self-controlled, upright, and godly lives in the present age" (Titus 2:12 ESV).

We are also praying that we might fulfill our calling in this world.[5] The apostle Paul gives a general rule concerning what to do upon conversion. It is not that we should leave what we were doing before and go do something that someone else regards as spiritual, but rather "in whatever condition each was called, there let him remain with God" (1 Cor 7:24 ESV). This is the biblical and consequently the old Protestant and Reformed notion of vocation or calling. In the sixteenth and seventeenth centuries, our theologians and confessional documents said very little about a calling to effect change, let alone to transform society. Perhaps it was because Paul commands us to "aspire to live quietly, and to mind your own affairs" (1 Thess 4:11 ESV) or because he taught Christians "to do their work quietly and to earn their own living" (2 Thess 3:12 ESV). They knew that Paul taught us to pray "that we may lead a peaceful and quiet life, godly and dignified in every way" (1 Tim 2:2 ESV). There is much more explicit language in the New Testament about Christians living quietly amid the pagans than there is about Christians transforming the surrounding pagan culture. When Paul thinks of transformation, he thinks much less about the Roman Empire than he does about Christians: "Do not be conformed to this world, but be transformed by the renewal of

---

3. "Effice et da, ut nos homines faciamus voluntatem, non nostram, quae est prava, sed tuam, quae sola est iusta et sancta, tibique obtemperemus. Petimus igitur" (Ursinus, *Corpus doctrinae*, 647; Ursinus, *Commentary*, 637–38).

4. Ursinus, *Commentary*, 638. See the discussion of mortification under *HC* 88–89.

5. Ursinus, *Commentary*, 638. See the discussion of vocation under Lord's Day 42.

your mind, that by testing you may discern what is the will of God, what is good and acceptable and perfect" (Rom 12:2 ESV).

Might the transformation of Christians have consequences for the surrounding culture? Perhaps, but we cannot ignore Christian history between circa AD 33 and 313 (Edict of Milan). In that time Christians were alternately ignored, despised, then openly and violently persecuted. Two hundred and eighty years is a reasonable test period. The legalization of Christianity, followed by its imposition as the official religion of the empire, in 380 by Theodosius I, not only changed the status of Christianity legally but also changed the expectations of Christians regarding their relation to the broader culture.[6] We should not assume that the establishment of Christianity as the state religion is the normative mode of existence of Christianity in the period between the ascension of Christ and his glorious return.

In contrast to the expectations of some, the catechism is relatively subdued. It speaks of our office and our calling. When we pray, "Your will be done on earth as it is in heaven," it is a modest prayer that we might be enabled to do those things Paul exhorts. If we deliver milk, that we might do it well each day. If we cut hair or teach school, that we might do it as unto the Lord (Col 3:23).

Finally, Psalm 103:20 tells us that the angels, about whom we read relatively little in Scripture, are models of total devotion to the Lord's will.[7] When we pray that God's will might be done on earth as it is heaven, we are not praying to know what God knows (the categorical distinction), nor are we praying for secret knowledge about his will. Rather, we are praying for the grace to do what God has revealed to us. Our prayer is that the Holy Spirit would work "in us that which is pleasing" in our Father's "sight, through Jesus Christ" (Heb 13:21).

Like the petitions we have already considered, this too is a prayer for Spirit-wrought sanctification, that our union and communion with Christ

---

6. The imperial Edict of Thessalonica (sometimes also referred to as *Cunctos populos*) was promulgated on February 27, 380. A version of that decree was attached to the Second Helvetic Confession (1566), and the Latin text of the edict is published in Schaff, *Creeds of Christendom*, 3:235. An English translation of the edict is published in Ehler and Morrall, *Church and State*, 6–7. See the discussion under *HC* 85.

7. Ursinus, *Commentary*, 637; cf. 640.

might be more fully realized in this life, in anticipation of the life to come. It is not the prayer of overrealized eschatology. It is not a prayer that the kingdom might be realized fully in this life prior to Christ's return. That is a theology of glory, which the Reformed repudiate, for example, in the Second Helvetic Confession (chap. 11).[8]

Our Lord Jesus was in a covenant of works, for us, that we who believe might receive all the benefits of the covenant of grace: justification, sanctification, and glorification (salvation). As we pray, "Not my will but yours," may the Lord gradually realize in us conformity to the image of Christ.

8. See the discussion of this topic under *HC* 123.

Question 125

What is the fourth petition?

Lord's Day 50

QUESTION 125

What is the fourth petition?

"Give us this day our daily bread," that is: be pleased to provide for all our bodily needs, so that we may thereby acknowledge you to be the only fountain of all good, and that without your blessing neither our care and labor, nor your gifts can profit us; that we may therefore withdraw our trust from all creatures and place it alone in you.[1]

We are often tempted to set asking and trusting against each other, but, of course, this is a false choice. When a child asks his father for breakfast, he trusts that his father will provide. It does not occur to him to think, "If my father really loved me, I would not have to ask him for breakfast. He would just do it." We should take a lesson from a child. Psalm 104 celebrates the Lord's marvelous provision. Yahweh's trees, the cedars of Lebanon, are watered abundantly (v. 16). The Lord provides for a wide variety of creatures (from stork to rock badger; vv. 17–18). He makes the moon to shine at night and the sun in the day (v. 19). As part of God's perfect, all-wise providence, "Man goes out to his work and to his labor until the evening" (v. 23). All creatures look to God the Creator as their provider:

> These all look to you,
> to give them their food in due season.
> When you give it to them, they gather it up;
> when you open your hand, they are filled with good things.
> When you hide your face, they are dismayed;
> when you take away their breath, they die
> and return to their dust.

1. "Was ist die vierte Bitte? Gieb uns heute unser täglich Brot; das ist: Wollest uns mit aller leiblichen Nothdurft versorgen, auf dass wir dadurch erkennen, dass Du der einige Ursprung alles Guten bist, und dass ohne deinen Segen weder unsere Sorgen und Arbeit, noch deine Gaben uns gedeihen, und wir derhalben unser Vertrauen von allen Creaturen abziehen, und allein auf dich setzen" (Schaff, *Creeds of Christendom*, 3:353). "Quae est quarta petitio? *Panem nostrum quotidianum da nobis hodie*; hoc est, suppedita nobis omnia, quae sunt ad hanc vitam necessaria, ut per ea agnoscamus, te unicum fontem esse, ex quo omnia bona emanant, ac nisi tu bendicas, omnem nostram curam et indiustriam, atque adeo tua ipsius dona, nobis infelicia et noxia esse. Quapropter da, ut fiduciam nostram ob omnibus creaturis aversam, in te solo colloceamus" (Niemeyer, *Collectio Confessionum*, 460).

> When you send forth your Spirit, they are created,
> and you renew the face of the ground.
> (Ps 104:27–30 ESV)

Now, the animals to which the psalmist refers do not pray, but they, like us, are dependent on God. When he gives life, they live. When he withdraws his support, they (and we) die and return to the dust from which they were taken. We are image-bearers formed from the dust of the earth, animated by the Lord.

Unlike the other creatures, as image-bearers, we are made to be in communion with God the Father, in Christ the Son, through the Spirit. As his adopted sons (Rom 8:15; Eph 1:5), we are to ask him for all our needs. God is both the immutable Father of lights, from whom every good and perfect gift comes (Jas 1:17), and the God who hears our prayers. Too often we are more like the rock badger (Ps 104:18) than we are like adopted sons for Christ's sake. The psalmist, however, says: "Yahweh is near to all who call on him, to all who call on him in truth. He fulfills the desire of those who fear him; he also hears their cry and saves them" (Ps 145:18–19).

When we call out to God our Father to meet our needs, we call on him in faith, in trust and confidence, for Christ's sake, that he hears our prayers and is more willing to hear than we are to pray.[2] Sometimes we think that our material needs are beneath God's attention. Nothing could be further from the truth. It is a lie of the Evil One to think this way because our physical, material, bodily needs (note: we are talking about needs, not desires) are basic and persist. God commands us to bring our needs to him. If we stop looking to God, our needs are not going away. We will look to someone or something. That one or thing is necessarily an idol. To refuse to look to our heavenly Father for our needs is a quick route to idolatry.

This is one reason why our Lord taught us:

> Ask, and it will be given to you; seek, and you will find; knock, and it will be opened to you. For everyone who asks receives, and the one who seeks finds, and to the one who knocks it will be opened.

2. In paraphrasing Isa 37:21, Luther writes, "God is more quick to hear than we are to pray" (*LW* 16:320). Various forms of are widely used, and the language above occurs in some contemporary versions of the *Book of Common Prayer*. The earliest use this form I have found is in Garratt, *Our Father*, 13.

> Or which one of you, if his son asks him for bread, will give him a stone? Or if he asks for a fish, will give him a serpent? If you then, who are evil, know how to give good gifts to your children, how much more will your Father who is in heaven give good things to those who ask him! (Matt 7:7–11 ESV)[3]

Observe the imperatives: "ask" (αἰτεῖτε), "seek" (ζητεῖτε), "knock" (κρούετε). Our Lord did not juxtapose trusting with asking. Asking is an expression of trusting. We do not ask those whom we do not trust. Refusing to ask is an act of unbelief. Imagine that one does not trust a coworker. A lack of trust makes it difficult to confide in that coworker or to ask for help. One fears that coworker will betray a confidence or interpret a request for help as a sign of weakness. Asking is trusting.

We petition our heavenly Father because he has promised to hear and help us. "God has promised to give us all things necessary for our life, and has promised them in order that we might desire and pray for them, and that we might have a firm confidence that we shall obtain things necessary for us."[4] We ask that we might be "secure spiritually, not fleshly."[5] We ask him for our daily necessities for his glory, that we might praise him for his gracious provision.[6] When our needs are met, this edifies the church and encourages believers. It also brings us comfort, as our Father provides for us and thus reminds us of his care for us.[7]

To whom should we go but God (Ps 73:25)? Who else can meet our needs? The apostle Paul prosecuted the pagans at Mars Hill for their blindness in calling on gods who could neither hear nor speak to meet their needs. He remonstrated with them about the God who is, whom they knew by nature, whom they knew naturally and intuitively (though not savingly apart from God's special, sovereign, regenerating grace):

> The God who made the world and everything in it, being Lord of heaven and earth, does not live in temples made by man, nor is he served by human hands, as though he needed anything, since

3. Ursinus, *Commentary*, 642.
4. Ursinus, *Commentary*, 642; Ursinus, *Corpus doctrinae*, 652.
5. "Simus securi spiritualiter, non carnaliter" (Ursinus, *Corpus doctrinae*, 652).
6. Ursinus, *Commentary*, 642.
7. Ursinus, *Commentary*, 642.

> he himself gives to all mankind life and breath and everything. And he made from one man every nation of mankind to live on all the face of the earth, having determined allotted periods and the boundaries of their dwelling place, that they should seek God, in the hope that they might feel their way toward him and find him. Yet he is actually not far from each one of us, for
>
> "In him we live and move and have our being";
> as even some of your own poets have said,
> "For we are indeed his offspring." (Acts 17:24–28 ESV)

We know that Paul was referring to the universal, natural knowledge of God because he quotes not one but two pagan writers, one most likely Epimenides of Crete (sixth or seventh century BC), whom Paul also quotes in Titus 1:12 ("All Cretans are liars, evil beasts, and gluttons"). He also quoted a Greek poet from the fourth century BC. He takes these truths as self-evident to sane, rational people. In other words, these truths are so basic that one need not be regenerate to see them as true. To be sure, to appreciate them fully, as they should be appreciated, to believe them truly, one must be regenerated, but Paul was preaching the law to pagans from pagan writers.

That is how foolish it is to seek our daily well-being anywhere else or from anyone other than the God and Father of our Lord Jesus Christ. Friends tire and families disappoint. Only God is immutably faithful. Only he is omnipotent. Only he is omnipresent and immense. Only he is always nearby. Only in him do we live and move and have our being. Only he is capable of hearing our prayers, and only he never tires of hearing from us. Only he is able to help us.

We should notice that, in Psalm 104, one of the ways the Lord answers our prayers is work. We should not think that labor is outside the Lord's providence. Steady, gainful employment, through which we fulfill our vocation before the Lord and in the world, is one of the ways the Lord provides. We pray for work, and then, by God's grace, we go and do it as God gives us employment and enables us to do it.[8] Through that provision and process he answers our prayers. We are not praying for food,

8. See the discussion of providence under *HC* 26–28.

clothing, and other necessities to drop out of the sky. Sometimes the Lord does provide in unusual and marvelous ways, but that is why we distinguish between the ordinary and the extraordinary providence of God. We have no promise from God (whatever the health-and-wealth preachers may say) that he will cause necessities to drop out of the sky. We do have a promise that he will use means, and work is one of those means. Paul says, "If anyone is not willing to work, let him not eat" (2 Thess 3:10 ESV). It is unbelief to treat God like a cosmic slot machine or as if we had to manipulate him to get what we want. Like believing children, we trust him enough to ask for what we need, and, as believing adults, we make use of the means he provides in answer to godly prayers.

Ursinus's observation is useful that the petition for daily sustenance is sandwiched between "that we might both commence and end our prayers with petitions for spiritual blessings as being most important; and that the obtaining and receiving of temporal benefits might confirm in us more and more a confidence of obtaining spiritual blessings."[9]

Of course, we pray confidently when we petition God according to his moral will revealed in Scripture. "God has not determined in his Word what corporal goods he will give to us."[10] That is, there is no specific promise in the word that the Lord will give us *this* thing or *that*, but we have general promises that he will provide for our basic needs.

> Therefore I tell you, do not be anxious about your life, what you will eat or what you will drink, nor about your body, what you will put on. Is not life more than food, and the body more than clothing? Look at the birds of the air: they neither sow nor reap nor gather into barns, and yet your heavenly Father feeds them. Are you not of more value than they? And which of you by being anxious can add a single hour to his span of life? And why are you anxious about clothing? Consider the lilies of the field, how they grow: they neither toil nor spin, yet I tell you, even Solomon in all his glory was not arrayed like one of these. But if God so clothes the grass of the field, which today is alive and tomorrow is thrown into the oven,

9. Ursinus, *Commentary*, 641; Ursinus, *Corpus doctrinae*, 651.

10. "Non enim determinavit in verbo, quae bona corporalia nobis dare velit" (Ursinus, *Corpus doctrinae*, 653).

> will he not much more clothe you, O you of little faith? Therefore do not be anxious, saying, "What shall we eat?" or "What shall we drink?" or "What shall we wear?" For the Gentiles seek after all these things, and your heavenly Father knows that you need them all. But seek first the kingdom of God and his righteousness, and all these things will be added to you.
>
> Therefore do not be anxious about tomorrow, for tomorrow will be anxious for itself. Sufficient for the day is its own trouble. (Matt 6:25–34 ESV)

God remains free, and he has not specified in his word exactly which temporal blessings he will give because (1) we often pray ignorantly and do not ask for those things that are good for us, and (2) God gives us those things that are for our good. Every parent knows these things to be true, and they remain true for us throughout this life.[11]

11. Ursinus, *Commentary*, 643.

Question 126

What is the fifth petition?

Lord's Day 51

QUESTION 126

What is the fifth petition?

"And forgive us our debts as we forgive our debtors," that is: be pleased for the sake of Christ's blood, not to impute to us miserable sinners our manifold transgressions, nor the evil which still always cleaves to us; as we also find this witness of your grace in us, that it is our full purpose heartily to forgive our neighbor.[1]

One of the most persistent temptations Christians face is that of turning the covenant of grace into a covenant of works. As we pray, we must always be reminded that we who trust in Jesus Christ as our substitute and Mediator are not in a covenant of works but in a covenant of grace. Remember too that this exposition of the Lord's Prayer occurs in the third part of the catechism, in which the church confesses the *consequences* of the covenant of grace and not the *conditions* of the covenant of works. Prayer is an expression of gratitude, a means of grace, not a work that we perform to earn favor with God or to achieve salvation.

The colorful metaphor used by our Lord himself in the fifth petition, "debts" (ὀφειλήματα in Matt 6:12) or "owing" (ὀφείλοντι in Luke 11:4), drives home the point quite powerfully. As Ursinus writes, our sins are called debts "because they make us debtors to God both in respect to the obedience which we have failed to render, and also to the punishment we are bound to pay in consequence thereof."[2]

The metaphor of debt is fitting because borrowing and repaying money is a covenant of works. There was a time when debtors who could or would not repay a loan faced not only the obligation of repayment but

1. "Was ist die fünfte Bitte? Vergieb uns unsere Schulden, wie auch wir vergeben unseren Schuldigern; das ist: Wollest uns armen Sündern alle unsere Missethat, auch das Böse, so uns noch immerdar anhänget, um des Bluts Christi willen nicht zurechnen, wie auch wir diess Zeuguiss deiner Gnade in uns sinden, dass unser ganzer Vorsass ist, unserem Nächsten von Herzen zu verzeihen" (Schaff, *Creeds of Christendom*, 3:353–54). "Quae est quinta petitio? *Remitte nobis debita nostra, sicut et nos remittimus debitoribus nostris*; hoc est: nobis miserrimis peccatoribus, omnia peccata nostra, atque eam etiam pravitatem, quae in nobis etiamnum haeret, propter Christi sanguinem ne imputes: quemadmodum nos quoque hoc tuae gratiae tesimonium in cordibus nostris sentimus, quod firmiter nobis propositum habemus, omnibus, qui nos offenderunt, ex animo ignoscere" (Niemeyer, *Collectio Confessionum*, 460–61).

2. Ursinus, *Commentary*, 648–49; Ursinus, *Corpus doctrinae*, 658.

prison for failure to repay (Matt 18:27).[3] Even today, when a bank loans money, it expects to be repaid. If the borrower fails to pay the mortgage on a home, eventually a sheriff's deputy will appear at the house. The delinquent borrower will be evicted, and the house will be repossessed and sold to repay the mortgage. Pleading will change nothing. Banks are not in business to be merciful and gracious. It is a kind of covenant of works.

Christians, that is, those who have received true faith, however, are not in a covenant of works because Jesus Christ has fulfilled the covenant of works for them (Rom 5:12–21; John 19:30; Gal 3:13). We ask for and receive forgiveness of sins only "on account of Christ's satisfaction."[4] Those are gospel words: "for us" (1 John 3:16; Titus 2:14; 1 Thess 5:10; Eph 5:2; Rom 8:32–32). The Pelagian says, "I have done." The Roman Catholic and the Remonstrant say, "By grace (however defined) and my free cooperation with grace, I have done." The Reformed church confesses, "Christ has done it all for me."[5] Paul says: "Therefore, just as sin came into the world through one man, and death through sin, and so death spread to all men because all sinned. ... Therefore, as one trespass led to condemnation for all men, so one act of righteousness leads to justification and life for all men. For as by the one man's disobedience the many were made sinners, so by the one man's obedience the many will be made righteous" (Rom 5:12, 18–19 ESV).

God offered Adam eternal life, communion with him, and glory on the condition that he obey the moral law summarized by the "commandment of life," that is, the command not to eat of the tree of the knowledge of good and evil (Rom 7:10).[6] Adam disobeyed God's moral law and plunged himself and all humanity into corruption and death (Eph 2:1–4). As Paul says, sin brings death (Rom 6:23). When he says, "All have sinned and fall short of the glory of God" (Rom 3:23 ESV), he is thinking of Adam and of us in Adam. We need another federal head, another representative, a substitute. Jesus the Messiah is that substitute for all who believe.

---

3. Ursinus, *Commentary*, 649.

4. "Propter satisfactionem Christi" (Ursinus, *Corpus doctrinae*, 659).

5. See the discussion under *HC* 21, 56, 60, among others.

6. *"le commadement de vie"* (Schaff, *Creeds of Christendom*, 3:398); *BC* 14, in United Reformed Churches in North America, *Liturgical Forms and Prayers*, 167. See the discussion under *HC* 6.

As long as the principal remains unpaid and the interest on the debt continues to compound, the debtor's misery grows daily. Every debtor wishes that someone, somehow would come and help. If only the debt could be wiped out. For those who believe in Christ, God imputes our debts, our sins, to him. This is the teaching of our Lord himself (Luke 22:37). Our translators do not always help us because they use a variety of English words for the same Greek word (λογίζομαι), "to impute" or "to reckon." This is the language of accounting or banking, and this is why the debt metaphor is so apt. In the fall we all became debtors to God and to his justice. He must collect. Grace is that God the Son covenanted with the Father before all time (Ps 110; John 17) to come as our substitute to pay the debt we incurred but would not and could not pay.[7] That is beyond mercy—for example, forgiving the interest. That is grace. He paid the entire debt, principal and interest. This is why Scripture says in Genesis 15:6 and Romans 4:3, "Abraham believed God and it was imputed to him as righteousness." Paul goes on immediately in verse 4 to explain the difference between a covenant of works and a covenant of grace: In the covenant of works, "his wage is not credited to him as grace but what is owed." In a covenant of grace, "to the one who does not work but believes him who justifies the ungodly, his faith is imputed as righteousness" (Rom 4:5 ESV). Because Christ has fulfilled the covenant of works for us, in our place, as our substitute, believers are in a covenant of grace, not a covenant of works.

The Lord's Prayer in Luke says, "Forgive us our sins [ἁμαρτίας] for also we forgive everyone owing us." In Matthew 6 it says, "Forgive us our debts as we forgive our debtors." We may be tempted to turn that "as" into a cause or instrument of our forgiveness, as if, in the Lord's Prayer, we were placed on a legal, conditional, works footing before God, but that is not at all what our Lord is teaching here.[8] If the forgiveness we receive

7. VanDrunen and Clark, "Covenant before the Covenants," 167–96; Fesko, *Covenant of Redemption*; Fesko, *Trinity and the Covenant*.

8. Ursinus, *Commentary*, 650–51. Here we should dissent respectfully from part of Ursinus's response to the objection that if we do not forgive perfectly, we are not perfectly forgiven. His reply appeals to the sincerity of our forgiveness. It would be better to say that either one is a believer and therefore forgiving others or not. God's forgiveness of our sins is not conditioned on (as Ursinus himself writes) the degree of our forgiveness but by whether we are covered by the imputed righteousness of Christ. One who impenitently refuses to forgive others has demonstrated his unbelief

is proportional to the forgiveness we give, then we are all condemned because none of us has forgiven perfectly. Rather, we forgive because we have been forgiven. Ursinus explains,

> For the particle as, as used in this petition, does not signify the degree of forgiveness, or teach that the forgiveness which we extend to others is equal to that which God extends to us; but it signifies the kind of forgiveness, or the truth and sincerity of the forgiveness which we and God extend, that God will as truly forgive us as we certainly and truly forgive our neighbor from the heart; or to express it more briefly, we may say, that there is here not a comparison according to the degrees, but according to the truth and reality of the thing, so that the sense is, God so perfectly forgives us our sins as, we truly and certainly forgive our neighbor.[9]

As believers we are conscious of our sins, and as believers we continue to ask for forgiveness. We are not presumptuous. Even though our sins are forgiven for Christ's sake alone, because we continue to sin we must continually ask forgiveness for the sins we commit now and in the future because God wills that we do so.[10] We see this very thing in Psalm 51. David confesses his sin; he begs for forgiveness and for sanctification. He approaches God in prayer as a sinner. As such, he has no claim, in himself, on God. David knows his sin. He confesses it (vv. 2–4). He knows the source of his sin, that he was born corrupt (v. 5). He knows that he by nature is unrighteous, but God is by nature righteous (v. 6), and that only God can justify him and cleanse him (v. 7). God must hide his face, as it were, from David's sins. He needs his transgressions covered over and taken away. He needs to be washed. Failing God's grace, David must be "cast away" from God's face (v. 11). He has blood guilt. Left to himself, he is lost. He must be restored. Only then can he experience the joy of being in the presence of God.

This is the prayer of the tax collector (Luke 18:13), "God be merciful to me a sinner." Jesus says that the one who prays that prayer goes home

---

(Matt 6:15) and therefore is under condemnation for that reason. Ursinus himself writes as much (*Commentary*, 651).

9. Ursinus, *Commentary*, 650–51; Ursinus, *Corpus doctrinae*, 660.

10. Ursinus, *Commentary*, 650; Ursinus, *Corpus doctrinae*, 659. "nihil ominus vult" (660).

justified, not on the basis of the quality of his prayer, nor on the basis of anything done by him or wrought in him (WCF 11.1), but only for the sake of Christ's righteousness credited (imputed) to him and received through faith alone (*sola fide*).

Unbelievers do not pray this prayer. Unbelievers are dead in sin, and dead people do not pray. Those to whom God has freely given life come to see themselves for what, apart from grace, they are. Psalm 51 and Luke 18:13 reflect the prayers of believers. We still sin. We need forgiveness, which God grants freely for Christ's sake alone. Our forgiveness is not contingent on the perfection of our forgiveness of others, *but* we forgive others because God has forgiven us. That is why we forgive others seventy times seven (Matt 18:22). That is why we forgive and restore the penitent (2 Cor 2:7) so that he is not overcome "with excessive sorrow." It is as forgiven people that we forgive one another (Eph 4:32). Our Lord is teaching us just what Paul says in Colossians 3:13, "As the Lord has forgiven you, so you also must forgive" (ESV).

Here it seems appropriate to mention one of the blessings of the Reformation that we ought to recover in modern Reformed worship: the declaration of pardon (or the absolution) after the reading of the law and the confession of sin.[11] This is a ministerial (not priestly) act in which the minister declares to the congregation what is true, that as many as have confessed their sins and trusted Christ are accepted by God for Christ's sake and freely forgiven. God forgives sins, not the minister, but he declares that good news—God forgives sins!—to the congregation, in Christ's name and by his authority. It was the practice of the Reformed church in Strasbourg under Martin Bucer to include the absolution in the liturgy. Calvin pronounced the absolution while he served there, but he was prevented by the city council from pronouncing the absolution upon his return to Geneva in 1538. Deborah Clemens explains,

> Following the corporate confession, the absolution was clearly given. Although Calvin preferred to use an absolution it was not allowed in Geneva and therefore dropped out of the Calvinistic liturgies. The Dutch also did not use one. But Bucer fiercely believed

11. Clark, *Recovering the Reformed Confession*, 283–84; Clark, "Calvin's Principle of Worship," 263–65; Clemens, "Foundations of German Reformed Worship," 246–47; Hyde, "Lost Keys," 140–66.

> in the power of the absolution. Even though ministers are not vicars of Christ with uncontrolled power (a Protestant criticism of the use of the absolution in Rome) ordained clergy do represent the Church and speak the absolution on the strength of Christ's commission to the Apostles. Absolution readmitted the penitent to Communion and also fortified awareness of the ongoing process of sanctification in the people's lives.[12]

Lyle Bierma observes that Olevianus agreed with Bucer and defended the ministerial absolution in the liturgy because the authority of the proclamation belongs to the gospel, not to the minister.[13] Others, such as Johannes à Lasco (1499–1650), who led the Reformed Reformation in Friesland for decades, also preserved the absolution. In Heidelberg, after the confession of sin, the form read:

> Then shall the minister declare unto penitent believers the forgiveness of sins, and say unto the impenitent the judgment of God, and say:
>
> > Hearken now unto the comforting assurance of the grace of God, promised in the gospel to all that believe.
> >
> > Thus saith our Lord Jesus Christ: For God so loved the world, that he gave his only begotten Son, that whosoever believeth in him might not perish but have everlasting life.
> >
> > Unto as many of you therefore, beloved Brethren, as abhor yourselves and your sins, and believe that you are fully pardoned through the merits of Jesus Christ, and resolve daily more and more to abstain therefrom and to serve the Lord in true holiness and righteousness: I declare according to the command of God, that they are released in heaven from all their sins, (as he hath promised in his

12. Clemens, "Foundations of German Reformed Worship," 246. She cites Nichols, "Intent of the Calvinist Liturgy," 102; Hageman, "Liturgical Origins," 123; van de Poll, *Martin Bucer's Liturgical Ideas*, 115, regarding the Dutch Reformed liturgies. See Hyde, "Lost Keys," 151–52, who documents the Dutch resistance to absolution.

13. Bierma, "Lutheran-Reformed Polemics," 69; Clemens, "Foundations of German Reformed Worship," 246.

> Gospel) through the perfect satisfaction of the most holy passion and death of our Lord Jesus Christ.[14]

The declaration of pardon, however, was followed by what is known in the Anglican tradition as the commination or the declaration of judgment on the impenitent:

> But as there may be some among you, who continue to find pleasure in your sin and shame, or who persist in sin against their conscience, I declare unto such, by the command of God, that the wrath and judgment of God abides upon them, and that all their sins are retained in heaven, and final that they can never be delivered from eternal damnation, unless they repent.
>
> And inasmuch as we doubt not, but that our prayers are sanctified by the sufferings of Jesus Christ, and therefore acceptable to God, let us heartily call upon Him, and say: Our Father, etc.[15]

It is in keeping with the teaching, intention, and practice of the Palatinate church, when the catechism was drafted and adopted, that the minister declare God's pardon of believers and his judgment on unbelievers after the reading of the law and the confession of sin.[16]

Because Christ has met the terms of the covenant of works for us and because God has made a covenant of grace with us, in Christ, there is free acceptance with God and free salvation and free sanctification by the Spirit. As members of the covenant of grace, we ask for forgiveness of our sins with confidence, knowing that we are forgiven freely for Christ's sake. We pray with appropriate sorrow for sin (we are not presumptuous), and we beg him earnestly for the grace to continue to grow in conformity to Christ.

---

14. This form is from 1585, which was a republication of the 1563 liturgy, republished again in 1684. See Baird, *Presbyterian Liturgies*, 223, 228–29.

15. Baird, *Presbyterian Liturgies*, 229–30. Baird's translation of the 1585 liturgy is taken from Bomberger, "Old Palatinate Liturgy," 81–96. For a remarkably different account of absolution in the Palatinate liturgy, see Atherton, "Pursuit of Power," 25–48. The article omits any reference to the existence of the 1585 liturgy or the Reformed liturgical use of absolution in Strasbourg, Heidelberg, and Friesland.

16. In United Reformed Churches in North America, *Liturgical Forms and Prayers*, 100–101, there is a brief assurance of pardon included at the end of the prayer of confession and even (in Prayer of Confession—2) the prayer of confession from the 1662 Book of Common Prayer, but neither is as fulsome as that contained in the Heidelberg liturgy, nor is there a judgment on unbelief.

Question 127
What is the sixth petition?

Question 128
How do you close this prayer?

Question 129
What is the meaning of the word "Amen"?

Lord's Day 52

QUESTION 127

What is the sixth petition?

"And lead us not into temptation, but deliver us from evil," that is: since we are so weak in ourselves that we cannot stand a moment, and besides, our deadly enemies, the devil, the world and our own flesh, assail us without ceasing, be pleased to preserve and strengthen us by the power of your Holy Spirit, that we may make firm stand against them and not be overcome in this spiritual warfare, until finally complete victory is ours.[1]

Before we consider what temptation (*tentatio*) is and how we ought to respond, we must address some preliminary matters. The authors of the catechism understood the world rather differently than most do today. The discrepancy is particularly acute when we face the matter of spiritual evil in the world.

In the nineteenth century, Karl Marx (1818–1883) diagnosed our most basic problem in material terms. He prescribed an eschatological solution that was entirely material. He himself said that he had turned G. W. F. Hegel's (1770–1831) spiritual view of history and the future upside down by materializing it. He replaced Hegel's spiritual dialectic with a class struggle.[2] Marx was part of a broader movement that effectively sought to close the world around us.[3] The Enlightenment rationalists said that what the human intellect cannot understand comprehensively cannot be true. The Enlightenment empiricists said that what we cannot experience with our senses cannot be true. Though the Enlightenment movements

1. "Was ist die sechste Bitte? Und führe uns nicht in Versuchung, sondern erlöse uns vom Bösen; das ist: Dieweil wir aus uns selbst so schwach sind, dass wir nicht einen Augenblick bestehen können, und dazu unsere abgesagten Feinde, der Teufel, die Welt, und unser eigen Fleisch, nicht aufhören uns anzufechten: so wollest Du uns erhalten und stärken durch die Kraft deines Heiligen Gristes, auf dass wir ihnen mögen festen Widerstand thun, und in diesem geistlichen Streit nicht unterliegen, bis das wir endlich den Sieg vollkommen behalten" (Schaff, *Creeds of Christendom*, 3:354). "Quae est sexta petitio? Ne nos inducas in tentationem, sed libera nos a malo; hoc est: quoniam ipsi natura adeo debiles et infirmi summus, ut no momento quidem subsistere possimus: infensissimi autem hostes nostri, Satam, mundus, ac nostra ipsorum caro, nos continenter oppugnant: tu nos sustentes, et Spiritus tui robore firmes, ne in hoc Spirituali certamine succcumbamus, sed tantisper illis fortiter resistamus, donec integram tandem victoriam obtineamus" (Niemeyer, *Collectio Confessionum*, 461).

2. Trueman, *Rise and Triumph*, 163–92.

3. Taylor, *Secular Age*, 551–92.

pretended to transcend religion, these *a priori* claims about what can or cannot be and what can and cannot be known were essentially religious. Indeed, many of the leading Enlightenment figures were deists and unitarians. For them, as Philip W. Dyer once said, God had "gone to the corner for a beer and he never returned."[4] From this we see right away that the Enlightenment was not, as has frequently been claimed, the "triumph of reason over religion" but the substitution of one set of religious convictions for another. In the Enlightenment human autonomy ostensibly replaced God's sovereignty. Human reason and human sense experience replaced divine authority revealed in nature and Scripture, and mediated through the visible, institutional church. The Enlightenment was a religious revolution.

As a consequence of the Enlightenment or modernity, we began to think of the world and our existence as closed. Of course, the Enlightenment produced a mystical reaction (Hegel was not entirely wrong) in Romanticism, the quest for a certain quality of religious and emotional experience.[5] In their heads, Romantics were rationalists, but in their hearts they were mystics. This Romanticism was influential among nineteenth- and twentieth-century evangelicals, more than a few of whom are Pietists and mystics in their affections but rationalists in their intellects. The old, closed modernism has also given rise to late or what Zygmunt Bauman calls "liquid" modernity, which manifests itself in radical subjectivism.[6] This is the root of the notion of self-identity that contradicts nature, but nature can only be defied so long. A fellow can tell himself that, in his subjective reality, there is no gravity, but he will be hard pressed to convince gravity that it does not exist. For all their supposed reaction to modernity, like the Romantics before them, late moderns are still moderns. When push comes to shove, underneath postmodern garb beats the heart of a modern who lives in a closed world, but now the limits are set subjectively. Reality is what *she* experiences it to be, what *she* says it to be, but *she* knows that Jesus could not have been raised from the tomb. Self is still the measure of truth or what can be.

---

4. Dyer made this remark in class in the fall semester of 1979 at the University of Nebraska.

5. On the relations between Pietism, Romanticism, and the quest for illegitimate religious experience, see Clark, *Recovering the Reformed Confession*, 74–98.

6. Bauman, *Liquid Modernity*.

The point of this survey is to say that modernity has influenced Christians more than we realize. As a practical matter, we tend to live as if God did not exist. Remonstrant philosopher Hugo Grotius (1583–1645) writes, "And indeed, all we have now said would take place though we should even grant, what without the greatest Wickedness cannot be granted, that there is no God or that he takes no Care of human affairs."[7] Dietrich Bonhoeffer (1906–1945) cites Grotius and paraphrases him as writing *etsi Deus non daretur* ("even if God did not exist").[8] Bonhoeffer argues:

> And the only way to be honest is to recognize that we have to live in the world *etsi deus non daretur*. And this is just what we do see—before God! So our coming of age forces us to a true recognition of our situation *vis à vis* God. God is teaching us that we must live as men who can get along very well without him. The God who is with us is the God who forsakes us (Mark 15.34). The God who makes us live in this world without using him as a working hypothesis is the God before whom we are ever standing. Before God and with him we live without God. God allows himself to be edged out of the world and on to the cross.[9]

For Bonhoeffer, the results of the Enlightenment were unquestionable, and thus he was forced to articulate a dialectical version of Christianity and to adopt a "death of God" theology.[10] Others react to modernity by turning to a superstitious, Manichaean, hyperspiritual view of the world in which providence is replaced by demons. More on this below. Certainly the language of Grotius (whatever he meant by it exactly) and Bonhoeffer is not fitting for orthodox Christians. Obviously, we cannot avoid facing the problem posed by the Enlightenment (and the various suborthodox responses to it), but neither should we succumb to it. The modernist creed of human autonomy relative to God, human perfectibility, and so

---

7. Grotius, *Rights of War*, book 1, prolegomena, art. 11 (1:89). "Et haec quidem quae iam diximus, locum haberent etiamsi daremus, quod sine summo scelere dari nequit, non esse Deum, aut non curari ab eo negotia humana" (Grotius, *Hugonis grotii de iure*, prolegomena, 4–5 [unpaginated]).

8. Bonhoeffer, *Letters and Papers*, 218–19.

9. Bonhoeffer, *Letters and Papers*, 219.

10. Those who would remake Bonhoeffer into an American neoevangelical would do better to understand him in his own Enlightenment, neo-orthodox theological context.

on is not inevitable. The tomb is still empty. Christ still reigns. Though we do not sit in judgment over the Holy Scriptures, it is entirely reasonable to believe the reasonable testimonies concern the saving work of God recorded in Holy Scripture.

In response to the hyperspiritual reaction to the Enlightenment, in whatever form it may take, we should agree that Christians really do have spiritual enemies. The apostle Paul refers to them as "powers and principalities" (Rom 8:38; Eph 6:12; Col 1:16). He says: "For we do not wrestle against flesh and blood, but against the rulers, against the authorities, against the cosmic powers over this present darkness, against the spiritual forces of evil in the heavenly places" (Eph 6:12 ESV). The apostle Peter is not engaging in hyperbole when he writes: "Be sober-minded; be watchful. Your adversary the devil prowls around like a roaring lion, seeking someone to devour" (1 Pet 5:8 ESV).

Furthermore, we have an enemy within since, in Adam, we are dead in sins and trespasses (Eph 2:1–4; Rom 1–3). We are "dust" (Ps 103:14–16). The traditional Augustinian and Reformed view of Romans 7 says that Paul was speaking as a Christian when he wrote: "But I see in my members another law waging war against the law of my mind and making me captive to the law of sin that dwells in my members. Wretched man that I am! Who will deliver me from this body of death?" (Rom 7:23–24 ESV). There is a war within us. We are weak. We do sin. We are often wretched. God the Spirit is working within us, but the results of that work are not always quickly and easily perceptible. Scripture does not teach, and thus we do not confess, a theology of glory that looks for perfection in this life. We battle ourselves (the flesh, i.e., our sinful nature). "The spirit is willing but the flesh is weak" (Matt 26:41). Paul says, "For the desires of the flesh are against the Spirit, and the desires of the Spirit are against the flesh, for these are opposed to each other, to keep you from doing the things you want to do" (Gal 5:17 ESV). We struggle against "the world," that is, all those spiritual forces arrayed against Christ and his spiritual kingdom (Col 2:20).

We are on guard against the Evil One, but we are not paranoid. We are not afraid. As powerful as the Evil One may be, he is not as powerful as he would like us to think he is. He is not omnipresent, and further he is, as Luther taught us, defeated by "one little word": Jesus.[11] We should say to him as our Lord said to Peter, "Get behind me, Satan" (Mark 8:33). He has no authority over us. We have been bought with the most precious blood of Christ (1 Cor 7:23; 1 Pet 1:9). We have been declared righteous. We have been saved. We are being saved, and we will be saved by grace alone, through faith alone, in Christ alone (Eph 2:8–10). Grace defeats Satan. It is only when (were it possible) we put ourselves back under the covenant of works that we have anything to fear because then he has a case against us. Now, however, that we are righteous in Christ, he and his servants have nothing on us.

The antidote is a living, Holy Spirit–wrought connection to the true vine (John 15:5) by grace alone, through faith alone. We need to put on the "whole armor of God" (Eph 6:11, 13). That armor is God's word, his holy gospel, the instrument of faith, truth, and prayer:

> having fastened on the belt of truth, and having put on the breastplate of righteousness, and, as shoes for your feet, having put on the readiness given by the gospel of peace. In all circumstances take up the shield of faith, with which you can extinguish all the flaming darts of the evil one; and take the helmet of salvation, and the sword of the Spirit, which is the word of God, praying at all times in the Spirit, with all prayer and supplication. (Eph 6:14–18 ESV)

Christ's righteousness is ours, through faith alone, by imputation. As a consequence, he is also graciously, gradually making us righteous by the work of his Holy Spirit. By faith we trust Christ and his word to be true even though the world, the flesh, and the devil ask, "Has God said?" or assert, "God has not said." We know his lies when we read and hear them. In other words, we start with the objective realities—justification, salvation, truth—and we appropriate them through faith alone, by grace alone. We pray, "Lead us not into temptation but deliver us from evil (or the Evil One)" in the Spirit, in the truth as it is in Christ.

In this petition, we pray, "And bring [εἰσενέγκῃς] us not into temptation [πειρασμόν], but deliver us from evil" (or the Evil One). Ursinus

11. "A Mighty Fortress Is Our God," in Christian Reformed Church, *Psalter Hymnal: Centennial Edition*, 516.

helps us to distinguish the two types (*species*) of temptation.[12] "One species is from God and the other is from the devil."[13] We are using the word in two distinct senses simultaneously. When we speak of the first species, we are thinking about spiritual trials "of our faith, piety, repentance, and obedience," which occur when we face "oppositions and hinderances" to our deliverance (*salutis*), for example, "all evil, the devil, our sinful nature, desires, the world, afflictions, calamities, the cross [i.e., suffering for the faith] etc."[14] Through these things the Lord demonstrates the existence within us of "faith, patience, hope, and firmness."[15] The Lord led the patriarchs through these sorts of trials in order to sanctify them and to strengthen their faith.

The second type may not be predicated of God: "*the temptation of the devil* or that by which the devil and our flesh and the impious tempt us, by solicitation, to sinning and to sin itself." [16] Satan's temptation of our Lord in the wilderness would be an example of this sort of temptation (Matt 4:1–11). Satan tempts us to sin, but the Lord is incapable of being tempted or of tempting us to sin, and he tempts no one (Jas 1:13). God takes us through trials in order to sanctify us (Heb 2:10). The petition "Bring us not into temptation" is a prayer to be delivered from both classes of temptation (Matt 26:39).[17] "Temptations, therefore, insofar as they are tests, castigations, martyrdom, etc.,—God sends them. Insofar as they are evil and sin, God does not will them insofar as to will is to approve and effect them but he *permits* them."[18] We are in the midst of the mystery of divine sovereignty and the problem of evil. What we must do is to affirm what we know to be true, that God is sovereign and he may not be charged with being the author of sin. Within the scope of providence, humans

12. Ursinus, *Corpus doctrinae*, 662.

13. "Alia est Dei, alia diaboli" (Ursinus, *Corpus doctrinae*, 662).

14. "Per omnia mala diabolum, carnem, cupiditates, mundum, afflictiones, calamitates, crucem, etc." (Ursinus, *Corpus doctrinae*, 662). See the discussion of the problem of evil under *HC* 6.

15. "Ut nobis et aliis nostra fides, patientia, spes et constantia" (Ursinus, *Corpus doctrinae*, 662).

16. "*Tentatio diaboli* seu qua diabolus et caro nostra, atque etiam impii nos tentant, sollicitatio ad peccandum, quae et ipsa peccatum est" (Ursinus, *Corpus doctrinae*, 662–63).

17. Ursinus, *Commentary*, 654.

18. "Tentantiones igitur, inquantum sunt explorationes, castigationes, martyria, etc immittit eas Deus. Inquantum vero sunt malum et peccatum, Deus eas non vult, quatenus velle est approbere et efficere, sed permittit" (Ursinus, *Corpus doctrinae*, 663).

make free, uncoerced choices to sin and evil and are responsible to God for those choices. Thus, the we should follow Ursinus's language here.

God has accomplished the victory and has inaugurated its realization in us. We are not yet glorified, but we wait expectantly for Christ to return and to make all things what they will be. "Beloved, we are God's children now, and what we shall be has not yet appeared; but we know that when he appears we shall be like him, because we shall see him as he is" (1 John 3:2 ESV). So we pray this petition in confidence knowing that the very same Savior who obeyed in our place, who was crucified in our place, who sanctified the grave for us and then left it empty, will preserve us from all the fiery darts and lies about us.

The Enlightenment turn to a closed world was a lie. We do not live in a closed world. Our greatest threats and needs are not material. They are spiritual, and for them the rationalists and empiricists have no answer, but the gospel of the empty tomb and our ascended Savior most certainly does.

QUESTION 128

How do you close this prayer?

"For yours is the kingdom, and the power, and the glory, for ever," that is: all this we ask of you, because as our king, having power over all things, you are willing and able to give us all good; and that thereby not we, but your holy name may be glorified for ever.

We come to the doxology of the Lord's Prayer. The word *doxology* is composed of two Greek words (δόξᾰ + λογία), and the term was taken over into medieval Latin and thence into English in the mid–seventeenth century. The *Oxford English Dictionary* defines it as a "liturgical formula of praise to God."[19] Before the church took to writing doxologies, God himself gave us doxologies in his word. The 150 Psalms (or the Psalter) are composed of five books. At the end of each book there is a doxology (Pss 41; 72; 89; 106; 149–150).[20]

19. *OED*, s.v. "Doxology."

20. Reformed Presbyterian Church of North America, *Book of Psalms*, 576, s.v. "Doxologies."

The Lord's Prayer, as we typically recite it, ends with a doxology, a formula of praise to God. As previously noted, that doxology is not in the oldest biblical manuscripts of Matthew 6:9–13.[21] Bruce Metzger explains that "the ascription at the close of the Lord's prayer" occurs in late copies of the Gospels. A version of the doxology occurs in *Didache* 8.2, but, in the form in which we know it, the earliest text in which it occurs is from the fifth century.[22] Most of the texts in which it occurs are from the ninth century AD.

> The absence of any ascription in early and important representatives of the Alexandrian (א B), the Western (D and most of the Old Latin), and other (*f*) types of text, as well as early Patristic commentaries on the Lord's Prayer (those of Tertullian, Origen, Cyprian) suggests that an ascription usually in a threefold form, was composed (perhaps on the basis of 1 Chr 29:11–13) in order to adapt the Prayer for liturgical use in the early church. Still later scribes added "of the Father and of the Son and of the Holy Spirit."[23]

As Metzger suggests, when we say, "Yours is the kingdom and the power and the glory forever, Amen," we are using words drawn from 1 Chronicles 29:11–13: "Yours, O Lord, is the greatness and the power and the glory and the victory and the majesty, for all that is in the heavens and in the earth is yours. Yours is the kingdom, O Lord, and you are exalted as head above all. Both riches and honor come from you, and you rule over all. In your hand are power and might, and in your hand it is to make great and to give strength to all. And now we thank you, our God, and praise your glorious name" (ESV). It is perfectly appropriate to end our prayer with God's word, but we should not be alarmed if, in a worship service, a congregation should happen to pray the prayer as it is found in the oldest copies of Matthew 6.

In 1 Chronicles 29:10, King David, as he so often promised to do in the Psalms, begins by blessing Yahweh before the congregation. To the covenant God, Yahweh, belongs the glory, the power, and the victory over his enemies. He is head over all things. The kingdom belongs to him. He

21. See the discussion under *HC* 118–19.

22. Holmes, *Apostolic Fathers*, 357.

23. Metzger, *Textual Commentary*, 13–14.

has defeated his enemies. He lifts up to glory, and he casts down as he pleases. Ursinus paraphrases this part of the doxology thus: "Therefore, thou, O God, since thou art our king, more powerful than all enemies, having all things in thy power, both good and evil—evil, so that thou art able to restrain and repress them; good, so that there is no blessing so great that thou canst not give, if it be agreeable to our nature; since we are thy subjects, be present with us by thy power and save us, seeing thou hast a love for thy subjects and canst preserve and defend them."[24]

This doxology is quite fitting for Christians to pray. Yahweh has become incarnate ("and the Word became flesh," John 1:14). He kept his covenant that he made with Adam after the fall, to crush the head of the serpent. He kept his covenant he made with Noah, to deliver his people through the judgment flood. He kept his covenant with Abraham, to give him a heavenly city (Heb 11:10), sons without number, and to be his God and the God of his offspring. Paul explains, "For the Scripture says, 'Everyone who believes in him will not be put to shame.' For there is no distinction between Jew and Greek; for the same Lord is Lord of all, bestowing his riches on all who call on him. For 'everyone who calls on the name of the Lord will be saved'" (Rom 10:11–13 ESV).

Jesus the Lord was crucified. He was dead. He was buried, but he did not stay that way. He was raised on the third day. His tomb is empty. He has ascended and is seated at the right hand of the Father in glory. He is ruling all things by the word of his power (Heb 1:3). As a good king, he is looking after his people as a good shepherd tends to his sheep. "The Lord knows how to rescue the godly from trials, and to keep the unrighteous under punishment until the day of judgment" (2 Pet 2:9 ESV).

This was the confession of the apostolic church:

> He was manifested in the flesh,
> vindicated by the Spirit,
> seen by angels,
> proclaimed among the nations,
> believed on in the world,
> taken up in glory. (1 Tim 3:16 ESV)

24. Ursinus, *Commentary*, 657–58.

Through Christ, the Spirit helping us, we glorify the Father—we praise the one, holy, Triune God—for his gracious, sovereign salvation given freely, through faith alone to all his people, all those whom the Father gave to the Son in all eternity (John 17; Ps 110).[25] We praise him for his deliverance from the Evil One and for his kind providence and preservation of us in all times and places. Consider that, at the moment our Lord Jesus was arrested, virtually no one was willing to identify himself publicly with Jesus, not even Peter, who renounced Jesus three times (Matt 26:75). In the early second century and through the third century, pagan civil authorities tortured Christians. In the sixteenth century, Roman Catholic authorities arrested us, cut out our tongues (so we could no longer sing God's word), and set us on fire simply for acknowledging Christ alone as the head of his church. Despite all the fury of the Evil One, here we are yet. The Greco-Roman pantheon is recognized for what it was—foolish idolatry—but the crucified Messiah reigns. His *is* the kingdom, the power, and the glory forever.[26]

Question 129

What is the meaning of the word "Amen"?

Amen means: So shall it truly and surely be, for my prayer is much more certainly heard of God than I feel in my heart that I desire things of him.

There are a couple of expressions that we use in prayer almost without thinking. One of them is the word *amen*. This little term is more important than we might think. In at least one place in Scripture, it is used as a substitute for truth. God is described as the "God of Amen" (Isa 65:16), which is translated in the ESV as the "God of truth." It is used in the ratification of a covenant in Jeremiah 11:5:

> You shall say to them, "Thus says Yahweh, the God of Israel: Cursed be the man who does not hear the words of this covenant

25. See the excursus on the eternal generation of the Son under *HC* 33, 126.

26. Ursinus, *Commentary*, 657–58.

> that I commanded your fathers when I brought them out of the land of Egypt, from the iron furnace, saying, Listen to my voice, and do all that I command you. So shall you be my people, and I will be your God, that I may confirm the oath that I swore to your fathers, to give them a land flowing with milk and honey, as at this day." Then I answered, "Amen, Yahweh." (Jer 11:3–5)

"Amen" is more than a mere way to end a prayer. It is a confirmation of God's oath to his covenant people.

It is used this way in Revelation 22:20. We use it most frequently as an affirmation after the doxology attached to the Lord's Prayer. It is used this way in Psalm 72:19: "Blessed be his glorious name forever; may the whole earth be filled with his glory! Amen and Amen!" (ESV). Paul uses it at the end of his doxology in Romans 9:5. It is used as a liturgical response in 1 Corinthians 14:16.[27]

When we say "amen" at the end of our prayers, it is not merely a signal that we are done praying. It is a heartfelt affirmation of all that God has promised to us in the gospel, which we receive through faith alone (*sola fide*). To say the word *amen* is a confession of faith. When we say it in faith, we are affirming that God will do what he has promised.

When we say "amen" in faith, we are saying that God's objective promises are true despite my subjective experience and condition. Witsius writes:

> By this word we express our sincere acknowledgments of the kingdom, power, and glory of God; our earnest desire to obtain from God such valuable blessings; and our faith resting on the promises of God, "the confidence that we have in him that if we ask any thing according to his will, he heareth us." Luther, with his wonted liveliness of manner, wrote to Melanchthon in the following terms:—"I pray for you, I have prayed, and I will pray, and I have no doubt I shall be heard, for I feel the AMEN in my heart."[28]

It is fitting that the catechism comes to a close by emphasizing the objective reality of our justification and salvation by grace alone (*sola gratia*) and the subjective appropriation of that truth in our own hearts, since

27. This summary relies on Myers, *Eerdmans Bible Dictionary*, s.v. "Amen."

28. Witsius, *Sacred Dissertations on the Apostles' Creed*, 382.

that is where the catechism began. Our subjective comfort is grounded in the objective reality accomplished for us, which we receive through faith alone (*sola fide*). It is out of the reality that God has graciously saved us and is graciously sanctifying us as we live the Christian life.

Preface to the Heidelberg Catechism

We, Frederick, by the grace of God, Elector Palatine on the Rhine, Archcarver and Elector of the Holy Roman Empire, Duke in Bavaria, etc., present to all and each of our Superintendents, Pastors, Preachers, Officers of the Church, and Schoolmasters throughout our Electorate of the Rhenish Palatinate, our grace and greeting, and do enjoin you to hereby know:

Inasmuch as we acknowledge that we are bound by the admonition of the Divine word, and also by natural duty and relation, and, have finally determined to order and administer our office, calling, and government, not only for the promotion and maintenance of quiet and peaceable living, and for the support of an upright and virtuous walk and behavior among our subjects, but also and above all, constantly to admonish and lead them to devout knowledge and fear of the Almighty and His holy word of salvation as the only foundation of all virtue and obedience, and to spare no pains, so far as lies in us, with all sincerity to promote their temporal and eternal welfare, and to contribute to the defense and maintenance of the same.

And, although apprised on entering upon our government, how our dear cousins and predecessors, Counts Palatine, Electors, etc., of noble and blessed memory, have instituted and proposed diverse Christian and profitable measures and means for the furtherance of the glory of God and the upholding of civil discipline and order:

Notwithstanding, this purpose was not in every respect prosecuted with the appropriate zeal, and the expected and desired fruit did not accrue therefrom—we are now induced not only to renew the same, but also, as the exigencies of the times demand, to improve, reform, and further to establish them. Therefore we also have ascertained that by no means the least defect of our system is found in the fact that our blooming youth are disposed to be careless in respect to Christian doctrine, both in the schools and churches of our principality—some, indeed, being entirely without Christian instruction, others being unsystematically taught, without any established, certain, and clear catechism, but merely according to individual plan or judgment; from which, among other great defects, the consequence has ensued, that they have, in too many instances, grown up without the fear of God and the knowledge of His word, having enjoyed no profitable instruction, or otherwise have been perplexed with irrelevant and needless questions, and at times have been burdened with unsound doctrines.

And now, whereas both temporal and spiritual offices, government and family discipline, cannot otherwise be maintained—and in order that discipline and obedience to authority and other virtues may increase and be multiplied among subjects—it is essential that our youth be trained in early life, and above all, in the pure and consistent doctrine of the holy Gospel, and be well exercised in the proper and true knowledge of God.

Therefore, we have regarded it as a high obligation, and as the most important duty of our government, to give attention to this matter, to do away with this defect, and to introduce the needful improvements:

And accordingly, with the advice and cooperation of our entire theological faculty in this place, and of all Superintendents and distinguished servants of the Church, we have secured the preparation of a summary course of instruction or catechism of our Christian Religion, according to the word of God, in the German and Latin languages; in order that the youth in churches and schools may be piously instructed in such Christian doctrine and be thoroughly trained therein, but also that the Pastors and Schoolmasters themselves may be provided with a fixed form and model by which to regulate the instruction of youth, and not, at their option, adopt daily changes, or introduce erroneous doctrine:

We do herewith affectionately admonish and enjoin upon every one of you, that you do, for the honor of God and our subjects, and also for the sake of your own soul's profit and welfare, thankfully accept this proffered Catechism or course of instruction, and that you do diligently and faithfully represent and explain the same according to its true import, to the youth in our schools and churches, and also from the pulpit to the common people, that you teach, and act, and live in accordance with it, in the assured hope, that if our youth in early life are earnestly instructed and educated in the word of God, it will please Almighty God also to grant reformation of public and private morals, and temporal and eternal welfare. Desiring, as above said, that all this may be accomplished, we have made this provision.

Given at Heidelberg, Tuesday, the nineteenth of January, in the year 1563 after the birth of Christ, our dear Lord and Savior.[1]

1. Richards, *Heidelberg Catechism*, 3–11.

Bibliography

PRIMARY SOURCES

Abelard. *Commentary on the Epistle to the Romans*. Translated by Steven R. Cartwright. Washington, DC: Catholic University of America Press, 2011.

Alsted, J. H. "Locus Liii. De Morte Aeterna." In *Synopsis Theologiae Exhibens Oeconomiam Singulorum Locorum Communium Theologicorum*, 125–26. Hanau, 1627.

———. *Methodus Sacrosanctae Theologiae*. Hanover, 1614.

Althusius, Johannes. *Politica*. Translated by Frederick S. Carney. Indianapolis: Liberty Fund, 1995.

Alting, Hendrik. *Historia Ecclesiae Palatinae*. Amsterdam, 1644.

Ames, William. *A Fresh Suit against Human Ceremonies in God's Worship …* Rotterdam[?], 1633.

———. *A Sketch of the Christian's Catechism*. Translated by Todd Rester. Grand Rapids: Reformation Heritage Books, 2008.

Andreae, Jakob, and Théodore Beza. *Lutheranism vs. Calvinism*. St Louis: Concordia, 2017.

Aretius, Benedict. *A Short History of Valentinus Gentilis the Tritheist*. London, 1696.

———. *Valentini Gentilis Iusto Capitis Supplicio*. Geneva, 1567.

Arminius, James. *The Works of James Arminius: The London Edition*. Translated by James Nichols and William Nichols. Grand Rapids: Baker, 1996.

Augustine. *City of God*. Translated by William M. Green et al. Cambridge, MA: Harvard University Press, 1957.

———. *De fide et operibus*. In *Opera*. CSEL 41. Vienna: F. Tempsky, 1900.

———. *On Faith and Works*. Translated by Gregory J. Lombardo. Ancient Christian Writers 48. New York: Newman, 1988.

———. *Teaching Christianity*. Translated by Edmund Hill. Hyde Park, NY: New City, 1996.

———. *True Religion*. In *On Christian Belief*, edited by Boniface Ramsey, 15–103. Hyde Park, NY: New City, 2005.

Baillie, Robert. *Letters and Journals Written by the Deceased Mr Robert Baillie, Principal of the University of Glasgow*. Edinburgh, 1775.

Barth, Petrus, and Wilhelm Niesel, eds. *Joannis Calvini Opera Selecta*. Munich: Christian Kaiser, 1926.

Bastingius, Jerome. *An Exposition Or Commentarie Upon the Catechisme of Christian Religion Which is Taught in the Schooles and Churches Both of the Lowe Countryes, and of the Dominions of the Countie Palatine*. Cambridge, 1589.

Baxter, Richard. *Aphorisms of Justification*. London, 1649.

Bernard. *On Grace and Free Choice*. Translated by Bernard McGinn. Oxford: Cistercian Publications, 1988.

Beveridge, Henry, and Jules Bonnet, eds. *Selected Works of John Calvin: Tracts and Letters*. Grand Rapids: Baker, 1983.

Beza, Theodore. *The Christian Faith*. Translated by James Clark. Lewes, UK: Focus Christian Ministries Trust, 1992.

———. *A Clear and Simple Treatise on the Lord's Supper*. Translated by David C. Noe. Grand Rapids: Reformation Heritage Books, 2016.

———. *Concerning the Rights of Rulers over Their Subjects and the Duty of Subjects towards Their Rulers*. Translated by H. A. Murray. Capetown: H.A.U.M., 1956.

———. *Confessio Christianae Fidei*. Geneva, 1560.

———. *Confession de Foi du Chrétian*. Geneva, 1558.

———. *Confession de la Foi Chrestienne*. Geneva, 1559.

———. "A Defense of Justification through the Righteousness of Christ Alone Freely Imputed, Obtained by Living Faith." In *Justification by Faith Alone: Selected Writings from Theodore Beza, Amandus Polanus, Francis Turretin*, edited by R. Scott Clark and Casey Carmichael, 1–124. Grand Rapids: Reformation Heritage Books, 2023.

———. *Lex Dei, Moralis, Ceremonialis, et Politica, Ex Libris Mosis Excerpta, et in Certas Classes Distributa*. Geneva, 1577.

———. *A Little Book of Questions and Responses*. Translated by Kirk M. Summers. Allison Park, PA: Pickwick, 1986.

———, ed. *Novum Domini Nostri Iesus Christi Testamentum*. Basel, 1559.

———. *Questionum et Responsionum Christianarum Libellus*. Geneva, 1570.

The Bible and Holy Scriptures Conteyned in the Olde and Newe Testament. Translated According to the Ebrue and Greke, and Conferred With the Best Translations in Diuers Languges. With Moste Profitable Annotations Vpon All the Hard Places, and Other Things of Great Importance as May Appeare in the Epistle to the Reader. Geneva: Rouland Hall, 1560.

Biblia Vulgata. Stuttgart: Deutsche Bibelgesellschaft, 1969.

Birch, T. Bruce, ed. *The De Sacramento Altaris of William of Ockham: Latin Text and English Translation*. Burlington, IA: Lutheran Literary Board, 1930.

Bonaventure. *The Breviloquium*. Patterson, NJ: St. Anthony Guild, 1962.

———. *The Soul's Journey into God, the Tree of Life, the Life and St Francis*. Translated by Ewert Cousins. New York: Paulist, 1978.

———. *Tria opuscula seraphici doctoris s. bonaventurae: breviloquium, intinerarium mentis in deum*. Florence: College of S. Bonaventure, 1944.

Bonnet, Jules, ed. *Letters of John Calvin*. Edinburgh: T. Constable, 1855.

Boston, Thomas. *Human Nature in Its Fourfold State and a View of the Covenant of Grace*. Aberdeen: George and Robert King, 1850.

Bower, John R. *The Confession of Faith: A Critical Text and Introduction*. Grand Rapids: Reformation Heritage Books, 2020.

Brakel, Wilhelmus à. *The Christian's Reasonable Service*. Translated by Bartel Elshout. Grand Rapids: Reformation Heritage Books, 1994.

Bres, Guy de. *La Racine, Source, et Fondement de Anabaptistes Our Rebaptizes de Nostre Temps*. Pierre de Sandre, 1565.

———. *The Rise, Spring, and Foundation of the Anabaptists Or Rebaptized of Our Time*. Translated by Joshua Scottow. Cambridge, 1668.

Bretschneider, C. G., ed. *Corpus Reformatorum*. Halle: C. A. Schwetschke et Filium, 1834.

Bruyn, Theodore de, ed. *Pelagius's Commentary on St Paul's Epistle to the Romans: Translated with Introduction and Notes*. Oxford: Oxford University Press, 1993.

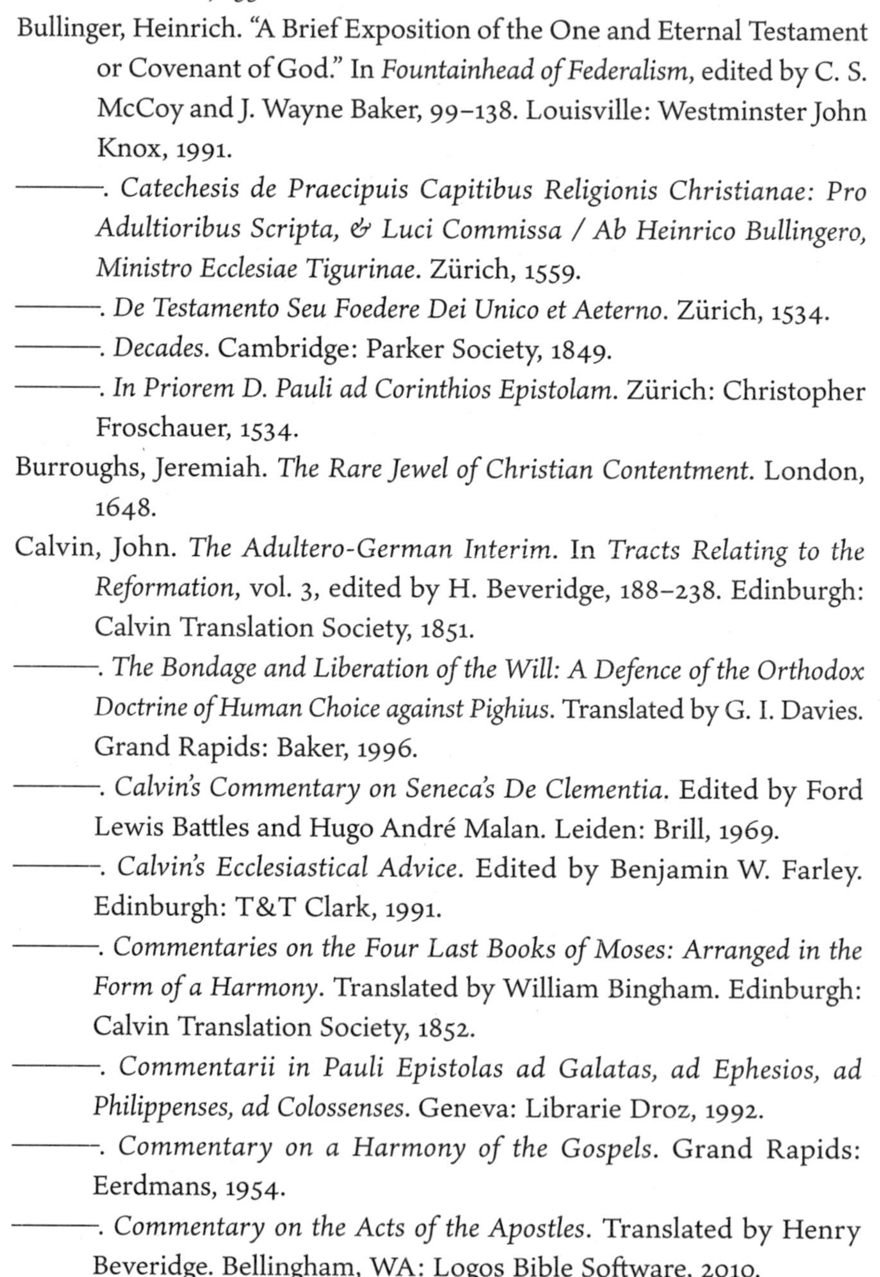

Bucer, Martin. *Catechismus Ecclesiae et Scholae Argentoratensis*. Strasbourg, 1544.

———. *Metaphrasis et Enarratio in Epist. D. Pauli Apostoli ad Romanos Etc.* Basel, 1536.

Bullinger, Heinrich. "A Brief Exposition of the One and Eternal Testament or Covenant of God." In *Fountainhead of Federalism*, edited by C. S. McCoy and J. Wayne Baker, 99–138. Louisville: Westminster John Knox, 1991.

———. *Catechesis de Praecipuis Capitibus Religionis Christianae: Pro Adultioribus Scripta, & Luci Commissa / Ab Heinrico Bullingero, Ministro Ecclesiae Tigurinae*. Zürich, 1559.

———. *De Testamento Seu Foedere Dei Unico et Aeterno*. Zürich, 1534.

———. *Decades*. Cambridge: Parker Society, 1849.

———. *In Priorem D. Pauli ad Corinthios Epistolam*. Zürich: Christopher Froschauer, 1534.

Burroughs, Jeremiah. *The Rare Jewel of Christian Contentment*. London, 1648.

Calvin, John. *The Adultero-German Interim*. In *Tracts Relating to the Reformation*, vol. 3, edited by H. Beveridge, 188–238. Edinburgh: Calvin Translation Society, 1851.

———. *The Bondage and Liberation of the Will: A Defence of the Orthodox Doctrine of Human Choice against Pighius*. Translated by G. I. Davies. Grand Rapids: Baker, 1996.

———. *Calvin's Commentary on Seneca's De Clementia*. Edited by Ford Lewis Battles and Hugo André Malan. Leiden: Brill, 1969.

———. *Calvin's Ecclesiastical Advice*. Edited by Benjamin W. Farley. Edinburgh: T&T Clark, 1991.

———. *Commentaries on the Four Last Books of Moses: Arranged in the Form of a Harmony*. Translated by William Bingham. Edinburgh: Calvin Translation Society, 1852.

———. *Commentarii in Pauli Epistolas ad Galatas, ad Ephesios, ad Philippenses, ad Colossenses*. Geneva: Librarie Droz, 1992.

———. *Commentary on a Harmony of the Gospels*. Grand Rapids: Eerdmans, 1954.

———. *Commentary on the Acts of the Apostles*. Translated by Henry Beveridge. Bellingham, WA: Logos Bible Software, 2010.

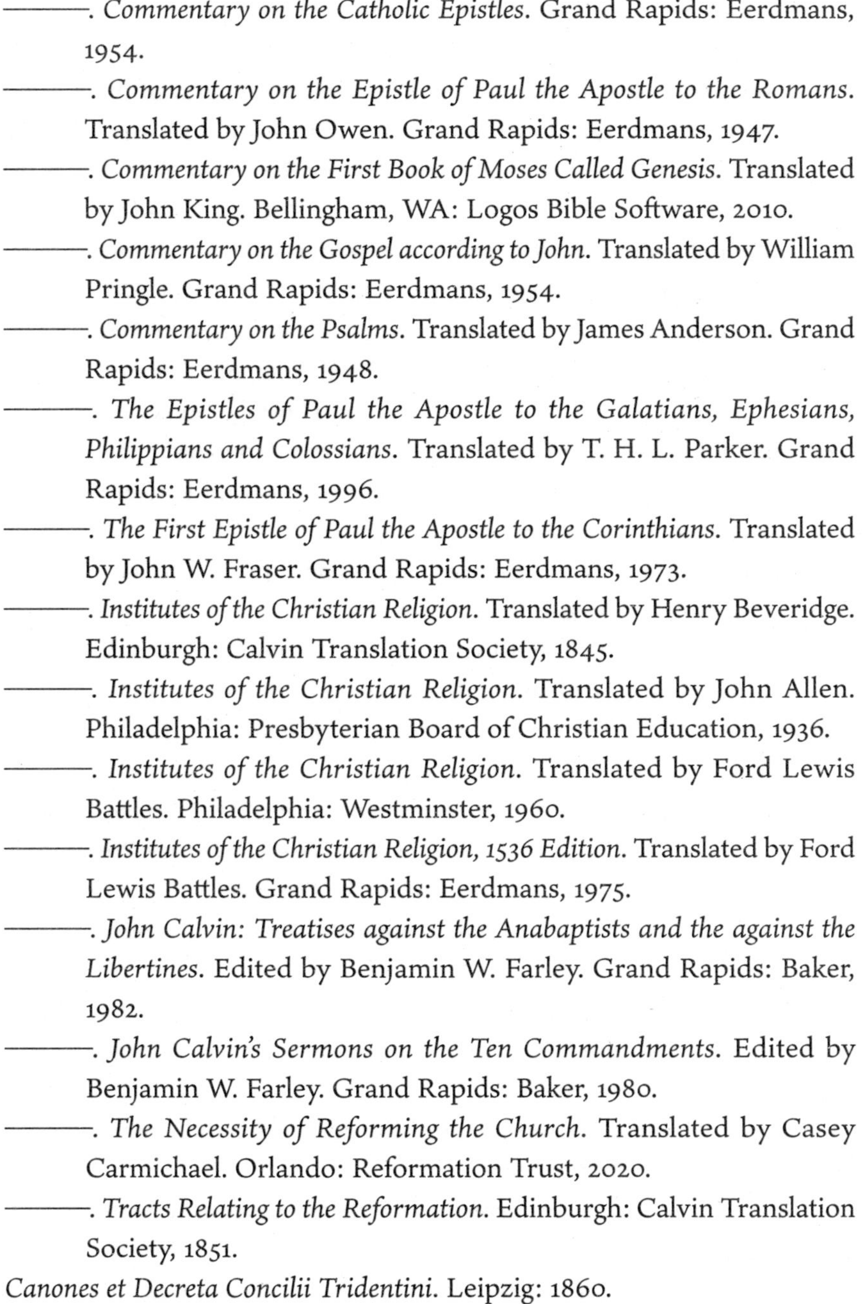

———. *Commentary on the Catholic Epistles*. Grand Rapids: Eerdmans, 1954.

———. *Commentary on the Epistle of Paul the Apostle to the Romans*. Translated by John Owen. Grand Rapids: Eerdmans, 1947.

———. *Commentary on the First Book of Moses Called Genesis*. Translated by John King. Bellingham, WA: Logos Bible Software, 2010.

———. *Commentary on the Gospel according to John*. Translated by William Pringle. Grand Rapids: Eerdmans, 1954.

———. *Commentary on the Psalms*. Translated by James Anderson. Grand Rapids: Eerdmans, 1948.

———. *The Epistles of Paul the Apostle to the Galatians, Ephesians, Philippians and Colossians*. Translated by T. H. L. Parker. Grand Rapids: Eerdmans, 1996.

———. *The First Epistle of Paul the Apostle to the Corinthians*. Translated by John W. Fraser. Grand Rapids: Eerdmans, 1973.

———. *Institutes of the Christian Religion*. Translated by Henry Beveridge. Edinburgh: Calvin Translation Society, 1845.

———. *Institutes of the Christian Religion*. Translated by John Allen. Philadelphia: Presbyterian Board of Christian Education, 1936.

———. *Institutes of the Christian Religion*. Translated by Ford Lewis Battles. Philadelphia: Westminster, 1960.

———. *Institutes of the Christian Religion, 1536 Edition*. Translated by Ford Lewis Battles. Grand Rapids: Eerdmans, 1975.

———. *John Calvin: Treatises against the Anabaptists and the against the Libertines*. Edited by Benjamin W. Farley. Grand Rapids: Baker, 1982.

———. *John Calvin's Sermons on the Ten Commandments*. Edited by Benjamin W. Farley. Grand Rapids: Baker, 1980.

———. *The Necessity of Reforming the Church*. Translated by Casey Carmichael. Orlando: Reformation Trust, 2020.

———. *Tracts Relating to the Reformation*. Edinburgh: Calvin Translation Society, 1851.

Canones et Decreta Concilii Tridentini. Leipzig: 1860.

Capito, Wolfgang. *Kinder Bericht Und Fragstuck Von Gemeynen Puncten Christlichs Glaubens*. Basel, 1527.

Cartwright, Thomas. *Christian Religion*. London, 1611.

———. *A Confutation of the Rhemists*. Leiden, 1618.

"Church Order Formulated in the National Synod Convened and Held by Order of the High and Mighty States General of the United Netherlands, at Dordrecht in the Years 1618 and 1619." In *The Church Orders of the Sixteenth Century Reformed Churches of the Netherlands Together with Their Social, Political, and Ecclesiastical Context*, edited by Richard R. DeRidder, 546–85. Grand Rapids: Calvin Theological Seminary, 1987.

Clark, R. Scott, and Casey Carmichael, eds. *Justification by Faith Alone: Selected Writings from Theodore Beza, Amandus Polanus, Francis Turretin*. Grand Rapids: Reformation Heritage Books, 2023.

Cocceius, Johannes. *The Doctrine of the Covenant and Testament of God*. Translated by Casey Carmichael. Grand Rapids: Reformation Heritage Books, 2016.

Cochrane, Arthur C. *The Reformed Confessions of the Sixteenth Century*. Philadelphia: Westminster, 1966.

Cyprianus. *Opera Omnia: Epistulae*. CSEL 3/2. Vienna: C. Geraldi Filium Bibliopolam Academiae, 1871.

Cyril of Jerusalem. *The Gospel according to St John*. Translated by P. E. Pusey. London: Rivingtons, 1874.

Daniell, David, ed. *Tyndale's New Testament: Translated from the Greek by William Tyndale in 1534*. New Haven: Yale University Press, 1989.

———, ed. *Tyndale's Old Testament Being the Pentateuch of 1530, Joshua to 2 Chronicles of 1537, and Jonah*. New Haven: Yale University Press, 1992.

Dennison, James T., ed. *Reformed Confessions of the 16th and 17th Centuries in English Translation*. Grand Rapids: Reformation Heritage Books, 2008.

Denzinger, Heinrich Joseph Dominik, ed. *Enchiridion Symbolorum*. Freibourg: Herder, 1960.

DeWitte, Petrus. *Catechizing upon the Heidelbergh Catechisme*. Amsterdam, 1664.

Dickson, David. *Truth's Victory over Error*. Edinburgh, 1684.

Ehler, Sidney Z., and John B. Morrall, eds. *Church and State through the Centuries: A Collection of Historic Documents with Commentaries*. London: Burns and Oates, 1954.

Elliott, J. K., ed. *The Apocryphal New Testament: A Collection of Apocryphal Christian Literature in English Translation*. Oxford: Oxford University Press, 1993.

Evans, Ernest, ed. *Tertullian's Homily on Baptism: The Text Edited with an Introduction, Translation, and Commentary*. London: SPCK, 1964.

Fairweather, E. R., ed. *A Scholastic Miscellany: Anselm to Ockham*. Philadelphia: Westminster, 1956.

Faulenbach, Heiner, and Judith Becker, eds. *Reformierte Bekenntnisschriften 1, 3*. Neukirchen: Neukirchner, 2007.

Fisher, Edward. *The Marrow of Modern Divinity*. Fearn, UK: Christian Focus, 2009.

Franklin, Julian H., ed. *Constitutionalism and Resistance in the Sixteenth Century: Three Treatises*. New York: Pegasus, 1969.

Frederick III. *A Christian Confession of the Late and Most Noble and Mightie Prince, Friederich of That Name the Third, Count Palatine by Rhein*. London: 1577.

———. *Kirchenordnung Wie Es Mit Der Christlichen Lehre, Heiligen Sacramentem, Under Ceremonium, Inn Des Durchleuchtigisten Hochgeboren Fürsten Und Herzen, Herrn Friedrich Pfalzgrauen Bei Rhein*. Heidelberg, 1563.

Gelasius of Cyzicus. *Συνταγμα Seu Commentarius Actorum Nicaeni Concilli*. Translated by Robert Balfour. Marseille: Frederick Morell, 1599.

German Reformed Church in the United States. *The Heidelberg Catechism in German, Latin and English with an Historical Introduction*. New York: Scribner, 1863.

Gibson, Jonathan, and Mark Earngey, eds. *Reformation Worship: Liturgies from the Past for the Present*. Greensboro, NC: New Growth, 2018.

Gillespie, George. *A Dispute against the English Popish Ceremonies*. 2nd ed. Edited by Christopher Coldwell. Dallas: Naphtali, 2013.

———. *Wholesome Severity Reconciled with Christian Liberty*. London, 1647.

Grotius, Hugo. *Hugonis Grotii De Iure Belli Ac Pacis Libri Tres*. Paris, 1625.

———. *The Rights of War and Peace*. Translated by Richard Tuck. Indianapolis: Liberty Fund, 2005.

Hall, Peter, ed. and trans. *The Harmony of Protestant Confessions*. London: J. F. Shaw, 1844.

Heidegger, J. H. *The Concise Marrow of Christian Theology*. Translated by Casey Carmichael. Grand Rapids: Reformation Heritage Books, 2019.

Hippolytus. Edited by John Behr. On the Apostolic Tradition. Crestwood, NY: St . Vladimir's Seminary Press, 2001.

Holmes, Michael W., ed. *The Apostolic Fathers: Greek Texts and English Translations*. Grand Rapids: Baker, 1999.

The Holy Bible Conteyning the Old Testament and the New ... by His Maiesties Specall Comandment. Appointed to be Read in Churches. London: Robert Barker, 1611.

Hughes, Philip Edgcumbe, ed. *The Register of the Company of Pastors of Geneva in the Time of Calvin*. Grand Rapids: Eerdmans, 1966.

Jud, Leo. *Catechismus. Christliche Klare Und Einfalte Ynleitung in Den Willenn Unnd in Die Gnad Gottes*. Zürich, 1534.

Junius, Franciscus. *Animadversiones in Roberti Bellarmini Controversiam Vii. Quae Est Quarta Secundi Tomi Disputationum Eius, De Ecclesia Triumphante, Sive De Gloria & Cultu Sanctorum*. Geneva, 1609.

———. *Defensio Catholicae Doctrinae De S. Trinitate Personarum in Unitate Essentiae Dei, Adversus Samosatenicos Errores*. Geneva, 1590.

———. *The Mosaic Polity*. Translated by Todd M. Rester. Grand Rapids: CLP Academic, 2015.

———. *A Treatise on True Theology with the Life of Franciscus Junius*. Translated by David Noe. Grand Rapids: Reformation Heritage Books, 2014.

Justinian. *The Institutes of Justinian*. Translated by J. B. Moyle. Oxford: Oxford University Press, 1883.

Kuyper, Abraham, ed. *Voetius' Catechisatie Over Den Heidelbergschen Catechismus*. Rotterdam: Gebroeders Huge, 1891.

Kuyper, H. H., ed. *De Post-Acta of Nahandelingen Van De Nationale Synode Van Dordrecht in 1618 En 1619 Gehouden Een Historische Studie*. Amsterdam: Hoeveker and Wormser, 1899.

Lang, August. *Der Heidelberger Katechismus Und Vier Verwandt Katechismen*. Leipzig: Deichert, 1907.

Languet, Hubert. *Vindiciae Contra Tyrannos, Or Concerning the Legitimate Power of a Prince over the People and of the People over a Prince*.

Translated by George Garnett. Cambridge: Cambridge University Press, 1994.

Lasko, Johannes à. *De Catechismus, Oft Kinderleere, Diemen Te Londen, in De Duydtsche Ghemeynte Was Ghebruykende*. Emden, 1557.

Leith, John H. *Creeds of the Churches: A Reader in Christian Doctrine from the Bible to the Present*. Louisville: John Knox, 1982.

Lombard, Peter. *The Sentences*. Toronto: Pontifical Institute of Mediaeval Studies, 2007.

———. *Sententiae in Iv Libris Distinctae*. Rome: Collegii S. Bonaventurae ad Claras Aquias Grottaferrata, 1971.

Luther, Martin. *Commentarius Secundus in Epistolam Ad Galatas*. Wittenberg, 1535.

———. "The Freedom of a Christian." *LW* 31:333–76.

———. *Parvus Catechismus Doctoris Martini Lutheri Latino Germanicus*. Erfurt, 1593.

Melanchthon, Philip. *Loci Communes (1543)*. Translated by J. A. O. Preus. St. Louis: Concordia, 1992.

Micron, Marten. *Der Kleyne Catechismus, Ost Kinder Leere Der Duychter Ghemeynte Van London*. London, 1561.

———. *Ein Kort Unterricht Voor Den Eentfoldegen Christen De Desz*. Emden, 1554.

———. *A Short and Faythful Instruction, Gathered Out of Holy Scripture Composed in Questions and Answeres, for the Edifyeng and Comfort of the Symple Christianes, Whych Intende Worthely to Receyue the Holy Supper of the Lorde*. Emden, 1559.

Müller, E. F. Karl, ed. *Die Bekenntnisschriften Der Reformierten Kirche in Authentischen Texten Mit Geschichtliher Einleitung Und Register*. Zurich: Theologische Buchhandlung, 1987.

Müntzer, Thomas. *Schriften Und Briefe*. Edited by Franz Günther. Güttersloh: Güttersloh Verlagshaus G. Mohn, 1968.

The New Testament: A Facsimile of the 1526 Edition. Translated by William Tyndale. London: British Library, 2008.

Niemeyer, H. A. *Collectio Confessionum in Ecclesiis Reformatis Publicatarum*. Leipzig: Julius Klinkhardt, 1840.

Olevianus, Caspar. *Brevis Admonitio De Re Eucharistica*. Herborn, 1587.

———. *De Inventione Dialecticae*. Geneva, 1583.

———. *De Substantia Foederis Gratuiti Inter Deum Et Electos*. Geneva, 1585.

———. *Expositio Symboli Apostolici*. Frankfurt, 1576.

———. *An Exposition of the Apostles' Creed*. Translated by Lyle D. Bierma. Grand Rapids: Reformation Heritage Books, 2009.

———. *A Firm Foundation. An Aid to Interpreting the Heidelberg Catechism*. Translated by Lyle D. Bierma. Grand Rapids: Baker, 1995.

———. *In Epistolam ... ad Romanos Notae*. Geneva, 1579.

———. *In Epistolam D. Pauli Apost. Ad Galatas Notae*. Geneva, 1578.

———. *In Epistolas D. Pauli Apostoli Ad Philippenses Et Colossenses Notae*. Geneva, 1580.

Origen. *Commentary on the Epistle to the Romans: Books 1–5*. Translated by Thomas P. Scheck. Washington, DC: Catholic University of America Press, 2001.

Orthodox Presbyterian Church. *The Confession of Faith and Catechisms*. Willow Grove, PA: Committee on Christian Education of the Orthodox Presbyterian Church, 2005.

Owen, John. *The Works of John Owen*. Translated by William H. Goold. New York: Robert Carter and Brothers, 1851.

Palatinate Church. *Catechesis Religionis Christianae, Quae Traditur in Ecclesiis Et Scholis Palatinatus*. Heidelberg: Michael Schirat, 1563.

Pareus, David, ed. *Corpus Doctrinae Christianae Ecclesiarum À Papatu Romano Reformatorum*. Geneva: Samuel Crespin, 1616.

———, ed. *Corpus Doctrinae Christianae Ecclesiarum À Papatu Romano Reformatorum Ex Ore Quondam Magni Theologi D. Zachariae Ursini in Explicationibus Catechetcis*. Hanover: Jacob Lasche, 1651.

Perkins, William. *Cases of Conscience*. London, 1606.

———. *The Works of William Perkins*. Grand Rapids: Reformation Heritage Books, 2014.

Plato. *The Republic*. Translated by Paul Shorey. Cambridge, MA: Harvard University Press, 1982.

Polanus, Amandus. *The Substance of the Christian Religion*. Translated by E. W. London, 1595.

Prosper. *Defense of St. Augustine*. Translated by P. de Letter. Westminster, MD: Newman, 1963.

The Qur'an. Oxford: Oxford University Press, 2004.

Reformed Church in the United States. *Heidelberg Catechism: 450th Anniversary Edition*. Reformed Church in the United States, 2013.

Reformed Presbyterian Church in North America. *The Book of Psalms for Worship*. Pittsburgh: Board of Education and Publication of the Reformed Presbyterian Church of North America, 2009.

Reid, J. K. S., ed. *Calvin: Theological Treatises*. London: Westminster, 1954.

Reuter, Q., ed. *D. Zachariae Ursini ... opera Theologica*. Heidelberg, 1612.

Ridder, Richard de, ed. *The Church Orders of the Sixteenth Century Reformed Churches of the Netherlands Together with Their Social, Political, and Ecclesiastical Context*. Grand Rapids: Calvin Theological Seminary, 1987.

Rohls, Jan. *Reformed Confessions: Theology from Zurich to Barmen*. Translated by John Hoffmeyer. Louisville: Westminster John Knox, 1998.

Rollock, Robert. *Lectures upon the Passion, Resurrection, and Ascension of Christ*. Edinburgh: Woodrow Society, 1844.

———. "A Treatise of God's Effectual Calling." In *Select Works of Robert Rollock*, edited by William M. Gunn, 129–273. Edinburgh: Woodrow Society, 1849.

Rutherford, Samuel. *The Divine Right of Church-Government and Excommunication ...* London, 1646.

———. *A Free Disputation against Pretended Liberty of Conscience*. London, 1649.

Schaff, Phillip, ed. *The Creeds of Christendom*. Grand Rapids: Baker, 1983.

Schaff, Philip, and Henry Wace, eds. *Epitome of the Definition of the Iconoclastic Conciliabulum*. New York: Charles Scribner and Sons, 1900.

Scharp, Johannes. *Cursus Theologicus*. Geneva, 1628.

Schmitt, F. S., ed. *S. Anselm Cantuariensis Archepiscopi Opera Omnia*. Edinburgh: Thomas Nelson and Sons, 1938.

Schroeder, H. J., ed. *Canons and Decrees of the Council of Trent*. Rockford, IL: Tan Books, 1978.

Thomas Aquinas. *Summa Theologiae: Latin Text and English Translation*. Cambridge: Blackfriars, 1964.

The Three Forms of Unity. Birmingham, AL: Solid Ground Christian Books, 2010.

Tuckney, Anthony. *Praelectiones Theologicae*. Amsterdam, 1679.

Turretin, Francis. *Institutes of Elenctic Theology*. Translated by George Musgrave Giger. Phillipsburg, NJ: P&R, 1992.

United Reformed Churches in North America. *Liturgical Forms and Prayers of the United Reformed Churches in North America Together with the Doctrinal Standards of the URCNA*. Wellendport, ON: United Reformed Churches in North America, 2018.

United States Catholic Conference. *Catechism of the Catholic Church*. Vatican: Libreria editrice, 1997.

Ursinus, Zacharias. *Commentary on the Heidelberg Catechism*. Translated by George W. Williard. Phillipsburg, NJ: P&R, 1985.

———. *Corpus Doctrinae Ecclesiarum a Papatu Romano Reformatarum*. Hanover, 1634.

———. "A Godly Meditation upon Death." In *Faith in the Time of Plague: Selected Writings from the Reformation and Post-Reformation*, edited by Todd M. Rester and Stephen M. Coleman, 247–70. Philadelphia: Westminster Seminary Press, 2021.

———. "*Summa Theologiae*." In *D. Zachariae Ursinui Opera Theologica*, vol. 1, 10–33. Frankfurt, 1612.

———. *The Summe of the Christian Religion*. Translated by Henry Parry. London, 1587; 1645.

Ussher, James. *A Body of Divinity*. London, 1658.

Van Mastricht, Petrus. *Theoretico-Practico Theologia*. Utrecht, 1699.

Vermigli, Peter Martyr. *In Selectissimam D. Pauli Apostoli Priorem Ad Corinthios Epistolam*. Zürich, 1551.

Viret, Pierre. *The Christian and the Magistrate: Roles, Responsibilities and Jurisdictions*. Translated by R. A. Sheats. Monticello, FL: Psalm 78 Ministries, 2015.

———. *Exposition of the Ten Commandments*. Translated by R. A. Sheats. Monticello, FL: Psalm 78 Ministries, 2020.

———. *Thou Shalt Not Kill: A Plea for Life*. Translated by R. A. Sheats. Monticello, FL: Psalm 78 Ministries, 2016.

Vitringa, Campegius. *The Synagogue and the Church*. Translated by Joshua L. Bernard. London: B. Fellowes, 1842.

Watson, Thomas. *A Body of Practical Divinity*. London, 1692.

Wesley, John. *A Plain Account of Christian Perfection*. New York: James & John Harper, 1821.

Westminster Assembly. *The Humble Advice of the Assembly of Divines sitting at Westminster Concerning a Shorter Catechism*. London, 1648.

———. *The Humble Advice of the Westminster Assembly of Divines sitting at Westminster Concerning a Confession of Faith*. London, 1647.

———. *The Westminster Standards*. Audubon, NJ: Old Paths, 1997.

Witsius, Herman. *Conciliatory or Irenical Animadversions on the Controversies Agitated in Britain*. Translated by Thomas Bell. Glasgow: W. Lang, 1807.

———. *Dissertations on the Lord's Prayer*. Translated by William Pringle. Escondido: den Dulk Christian Foundation, 1994.

———. *The Economy of the Covenants between God and Man Comprehending a Complete Body of Divinity*. Translated by William Crookshank. London: T. Tegg and Son, 1837.

———. *Hermanni Witsii Exercitationes Sacrae in Symbolum Quod Apostolorum Dicitur Et in Orationem Dominicam*. Amsterdam, 1697.

———. "On the Efficacy and Utility of Baptism in the Case of Elect Infants Whose Parents Are under the Covenant." *Mid-America Journal of Theology* 17 (2006): 121–90.

———. *Sacred Dissertations on the Apostles' Creed*. Edinburgh: A. Fullarton, 1823.

Wollebius, Johannes. "Compendium Theologiae Christianae." In *Reformed Dogmatics*, edited by John W. Beardslee, 29–262. New York: Oxford University Press, 1965.

Wycliffe, John. *The Holy Bible, Containing the Old and New Testaments, with the Apocryphal Books: Later Version*. Oxford: Oxford University Press, 1850.

Zell, Matthäus. *Frag Vnnd Antwort, Vff Die Artikel Des Christlichen Glaubens. Zu Einer Erklärung Der Selbigen, Für Die Kinder*. Zürich, 1535.

Zwingli, Huldreich. "Catabaptistarum Strophas Elenchus." In *Zwinglis Werke* 6:1–196. Münich: Kraus Reprint, 1981.

———. "An Exposition of the Faith." In *Zwingli and Bullinger*, edited by John Ballie and John T. McNeill, 254–62. Philadelphia: Westminster, 1953.

———. *Huldreich Zwinglis Sämtliche Werke*. Münich: Kraus Reprint, 1981.

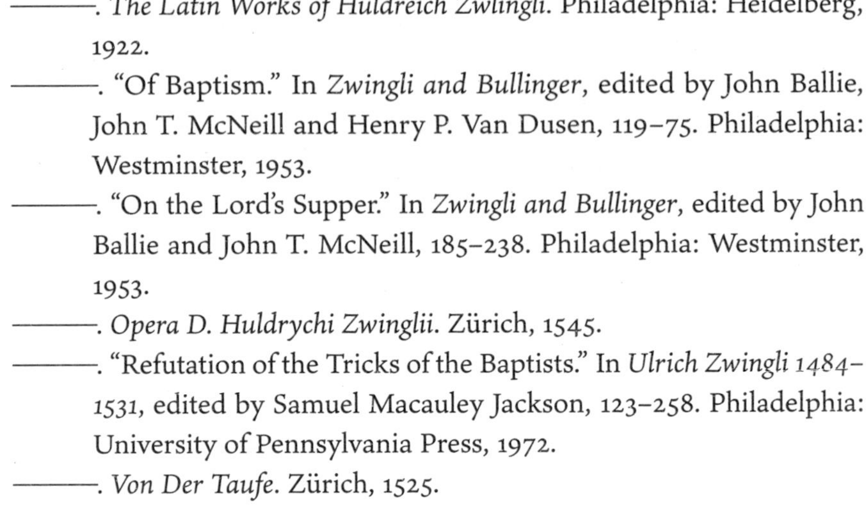

———. *The Latin Works of Huldreich Zwlingli.* Philadelphia: Heidelberg, 1922.

———. "Of Baptism." In *Zwingli and Bullinger*, edited by John Ballie, John T. McNeill and Henry P. Van Dusen, 119–75. Philadelphia: Westminster, 1953.

———. "On the Lord's Supper." In *Zwingli and Bullinger*, edited by John Ballie and John T. McNeill, 185–238. Philadelphia: Westminster, 1953.

———. *Opera D. Huldrychi Zwinglii.* Zürich, 1545.

———. "Refutation of the Tricks of the Baptists." In *Ulrich Zwingli 1484–1531*, edited by Samuel Macauley Jackson, 123–258. Philadelphia: University of Pennsylvania Press, 1972.

———. *Von Der Taufe.* Zürich, 1525.

SECONDARY LITERATURE

Abraham, William J. *The Coming Great Revival: Recovering the Full Evangelical Tradition.* San Francisco: Harper & Row, 1984.

Aland, Kurt. *Did the Early Church Baptize Infants?* Translated by G. R. Beasley-Murray. Philadelphia: Westminster, 1963.

Aland, Kurt, and Barbara Aland. *The Text of the New Testament.* Translated by Erroll F. Rhodes. Grand Rapids: Eerdmans, 1987.

Alexander, Amy K. "'Not by Stars or Skill': Providence in the Theology of Thomas Bradwardine," MA diss., Westminster Seminary California, 2012.

Allen, Louisa. "Queering the Academy: New Directions in LGBTQ Research in Higher Education." *Higher Education Research and Development* 34, no. 4 (2015): 681–84.

Allison, C. F. *The Rise of Moralism: The Proclamation of the Gospel from Hooker to Baxter.* London: SPCK, 1966.

Alpen, Heinrich Simon van. *The History and Literature of the Heidelberg Catechism and of Its Introduction into the Netherlands.* Translated by J. F. Berg. Philadelphia: William and Martien, 1863.

Althaus, Paul. *The Theology of Martin Luther.* Philadelphia: Fortress, 1966.

Armstrong, John, ed. *The Compromised Church.* Wheaton, IL: Crossway, 1998.

Arndt, William, et al. *A Greek-English Lexicon of the New Testament and Other Early Christian Literature*. Chicago: University of Chicago Press, 2000.

Asselt, Willem J. van. *The Federal Theology of Johannes Cocceius (1603–1669)*. Leiden: Brill, 2001.

———. *Introduction to Reformed Scholasticism*. Grand Rapids: Reformation Heritage Books, 2011.

Atherton, Ruth. "The Pursuit of Power: Death, Dying, and the Quest for Social Control in the Palatinate, 1547–1610." In *Dying, Death, Burial and Commemoration in Reformation Europe*, edited by Elizabeth C. Tingle and Jonathan Willis, 25–48. London: Routledge, 2015.

Aulén, Gustaf. *Christus Victor: An Historical Study of the Three Main Types of the Idea of Atonement*. New York: Macmillan, 1951.

Baalen, J. K. van. *The Heritage of the Fathers: A Commentary on the Heidelberg Catechism*. Grand Rapids: Eerdmans, 1948.

Bagchi, D. V. N. "Sic Et Non: Luther and Scholasticism." In *Protestant Scholasticism: Essays in Reassessment*, edited by Carl R. Trueman and R. Scott Clark, 3–15. Carlisle, UK: Paternoster, 1999.

Bahnsen, Greg L. *Theonomy in Christian Ethics*. Nutley, NJ: P&R, 1977.

Baird, Charles W. *The Presbyterian Liturgies: Historical Sketches*. Grand Rapids: Baker, 1960.

Baker, David. "Ten Commandments, Two Tablets: The Shape of the Decalogue." *Themelios* 30 (2005): 6–22.

Balke, Willem. *Calvin and the Anabaptist Radicals*. Translated by William Heynen. Grand Rapids: Eerdmans, 1981.

Ballor, Jordan J. "Reconciling Virtues and the Decalogue: Zacharias Ursinus (1534–1583) on the Ethical Teachings of the Heidelberg Catechism." *Journal of Christian Studies* 2, no. 1 (2023): 47–61.

Ballor, Jordan J., David S. Sytsma, and Jason Zuidema, eds. *Church and School in Early Modern Protestantism: Studies in Honor of Richard A. Muller on the Maturation of a Theological Tradition*. Leiden: Brill, 2013.

Barrett, Matthew. *Simply Trinity: The Unmanipulated Father, Son, and Spirit*. Grand Rapids: Baker, 2021.

Barrs, Arie. "Theory and Practice of Preaching on the Heidelberg Catechism." In *The Spirituality of the Heidelberg Catechism: Papers of the International Conference on the Heidelberg Catechism Held in Apeldoorn 2013*, edited by Arnold Huijgen, 232–56. Göttingen: Vandenhoeck & Ruprecht, 2015.

Barry, John D., et al., eds. *The Lexham Bible Dictionary*. Bellingham, WA: Lexham Press, 2016.

Barth, Karl. *Church Dogmatics*. Edinburgh: T&T Clark, 1936.

———. *Community, State, and Church: Three Essays*. Gloucester, MA: Peter Smith, 1968.

———. *The Heidelberg Catechism for Today*. London, 1964.

———. *The Theology of the Reformed Confessions*. Translated by D. L. Guder and J. L. Guder. Louisville: Westminster John Knox, 2002.

Barth, Karl, and Emil Brunner. *Natural Theology: Comprising "Nature and Grace."* Translated by P. Fraenkel. London: Centenary, 1946.

Bauckham, Richard. "Millennium." In *New Dictionary of Theology*, edited by Sinclair Ferguson and David F. Wright, 428–29. Leicester, UK: Inter-Varsity, 1988.

Bauer, Walter, William Arndt, Felix Wilbur Gingrich, and Frederick W. Danker. *A Greek-English Lexicon of the New Testament and Other Early Christian Literature*. Chicago: University of Chicago Press, 1979.

Bauman, Zygmunt. *Liquid Modernity*. Oxford: Polity, 2000.

Bavinck, Herman. *Reformed Dogmatics*. Grand Rapids: Baker Academic, 2003.

Beachy, Alvin J. *The Concept of Grace in the Radical Reformation*. Nieuwkoop: B. DeGraaf, 1977.

Beale, G. K. *The Book of Revelation: A Commentary on the Greek Text*. Grand Rapids: Eerdmans, 1999.

———. *A New Testament Biblical Theology: The Unfolding of the Old Testament in the New*. Grand Rapids: Baker Academic, 2011.

Beeke, Joel. "Faith and Assurance in the Heidelberg Catechism and Its Primary Composers: A Fresh Look at the Kendall Thesis." *Calvin Theological Journal* 27 (1992): 39–67.

Beeke, Joel, and Sinclair Ferguson. *Reformed Confessions Harmonized*. Grand Rapids: Baker, 1999.

Beeke, Jonathan. *Duplex Regnum Christi: Christ's Twofold Kingdom in Reformed Theology*. Leiden: Brill, 2020.

Beets, H. *Compendium Explained.* Grand Rapids: Eerdmans/Svensma, 1919.

Belcher, Richard P., Jr. *Prophet, Priest, and King: The Roles of Christ in the Bible and Our Roles Today*. Phillipsburg, NJ: P&R, 2016.

Benedict XVI. "General Audience." June 10, 2009. www.vatican.va/content/benedict-xvi/en/audiences/2009/documents/hf_ben-xvi_aud_20090610.html.

Bente, F. *Historical Introductions to the Symbolical Books of the Evangelical Lutheran Church*. St Louis: Concordia, 1922.

Berkhof, Louis. *The History of Christian Doctrines*. Grand Rapids: Eerdmans, 1937.

———. *Systematic Theology*. Grand Rapids: Eerdmans, 1938.

Bethune, G. W. *Guilt, Grace and Gratitude: Lectures on the Heidelberg Catechism*. Edinburgh: Banner of Truth, 2001.

Bierma, Lyle D. *The Doctrine of the Sacraments in the Heidelberg Catechism: Melanchthonian, Calvinist or Zwinglian?* Princeton, NJ: Princeton Theological Seminary Press, 1999.

———. "Law and Grace in Ursinus' Doctrine of the Natural Covenant." In *Protestant Scholasticism: Essays in Reassessment*, edited by Carl R. Trueman and R. Scott Clark, 96–110. Carlisle, UK: Paternoster, 1999.

———. "Lutheran-Reformed Polemics in the Late Reformation: Olevian's Proposal." In *Controversy and Conciliation: The Reformation and the Palatinate, 1559–1583*, edited by Derk Visser, 51–71. Allison Park, PA: Pickwick, 1986.

———. "Olevianus and the Authorship of the Heidelberg Catechism: Another Look." *Sixteenth Century Journal* 13 (1982): 17–27.

———. *The Theology of the Heidelberg Catechism: A Reformation Synthesis*. Louisville: Westminster John Knox, 2013.

———. "Ursinus and the Theological Landscape of the Heidelberg Catechism." In *The Spirituality of the Heidelberg Catechism: Papers of the International Conference on the Heidelberg Catechism Held in Apeldoorn 2013*, edited by Arnold Huijgen, 9–24. Göttingen: Vandenhoeck & Ruprecht, 2015.

———. "*Vester Grundt* and the Origins of the Heidelberg Catechism." In *Later Calvinism: International Perspectives*, edited by W. F. Graham, 289–310. Kirksville, MO: Sixteenth Century, 1994.

Bierma, Lyle D., Charles D. Gunnoe, Karin Y. Maag, and Paul W. Fields. *An Introduction to the Heidelberg Catechism: Sources, History, and Theology*. Grand Rapids: Baker, 2005.

Blaising, Craig A., and Darrell L. Bock. *Progressive Dispensationalism*. Wheaton, IL: Victor Books, 1993.

Blomberg, Craig. "The Sabbath as Fulfilled by Christ." In *Perspectives on the Sabbath*, edited by Christopher John Donato, 305–58. Nashville: B&H Academic, 2011.

Boer, Erik A. de. "Adoration or Idolatry? Heidelberg Catechism 80 in the Context of the Catechetical Teaching of Johannes Anastasius in the Palatinate." In *The Spirituality of the Heidelberg Catechism: Papers of the International Conference on the Heidelberg Catechism Held in Apeldoorn 2013*, edited by Arnold Huijgen, 129–47. Göttingen: Vandenhoeck & Ruprecht, 2015.

Bomberger, J. H. A. "The Old Palatinate Liturgy of 1563." *The Mercersburg Review* 2, no. 1 (1850): 81–96.

Bonhoeffer, Dietrich. *Letters and Papers from Prison*. Translated by Reginald H. Fuller. New York: Macmillan, 1953.

Bornkamm, Heinrich. *Luther in Mid-career: 1521–1530*. Translated by E. Theodore Bachmann. Philadelphia: Fortress, 1983.

Bray, Gerald Lewis. *Creeds, Councils, and Christ*. Downers Grove, IL: InterVarsity, 1984.

Bromiley, Geoffrey W., ed. *The International Standard Bible Encyclopedia*. Grand Rapids: Eerdmans, 1979.

———. Introduction to Huldrych Zwingli, "On Baptism." In *Zwingli and Bullinger*, edited by John Ballie et al., 13–40. Philadelphia: Westminster, 1953.

Bruggen, J. van. *Annotations on the Heidelberg Catechism*. Translated by A. H. Oosterhoff. Neerlandia, Canada: Inheritance, 1991.

Bruggink, Donald. *Guilt, Grace, and Gratitude: A Commentary on the Heidelberg Catechism Commemorating Its 400th Anniversary*. New York: Half Moon, 1963.

Burn, A. E. *An Introduction to the Creeds*. London: Methuen, 1899.

Campbell, Matthew. "French Philosopher Michel Foucault 'Abused Boys in Tunisia.'" *The Sunday Times*, March 28, 2021. www.thetimes.co.uk/article/french-philosopher-michel-foucault-abused-boys-in-tunisia-6t5sj7jvw.

Canadian Reformed Churches. *Book of Praise: Anglo-Genevan Psalter, Revised Edition*. Winnipeg, Manitoba: Premier Printing, 1984.

Carmichael, Casey B. *A Continental View: Johannes Cocceius' Federal Theology of the Sabbath*. Göttingen: Vandehoeck & Ruprecht, 2019.

Carpenter, John B. "Answering Eastern Orthodox Apologists Regarding Icons." *Themelios* 43, no. 3 (2018): 417–33.

Carson, Donald A. *Becoming Conversant with the Emerging Church: Understanding a Movement and Its Implications*. Grand Rapids: Zondervan, 2005.

———, ed. *From Sabbath to Lord's Day: A Biblical, Historical, and Theological Investigation*. Eugene, OR: Wipf & Stock, 1999.

———. "The Tripartite Division of the Law: A Review of Philip Ross, *The Finger of God*." In *From Creation to New Creation: Biblical Theology and Exegesis in Honor of G. K. Beale*, edited by Daniel M. Gurtner and Benjamin L. Gladd, 223–36. Peabody, MA: Hendrickson, 2013.

Casselli, Stephen J. "The Threefold Division of the Law in the Thought of Aquinas." *Westminster Theological Journal* 61 (1999): 175–207.

Centers for Disease Control and Prevention. "Suicide Rising across the US." November 27, 2018. archive.cdc.gov/#/details?url=https://www.cdc.gov/vitalsigns/suicide/index.html.

Chadwick, Owen. "The Making of a Reforming Prince: Frederick III, Elector Palatinate." In *Reformation, Conformity, and Dissent: Essays in Honour of Geoffrey Nuttall*, edited by R. B. Knox, 44–69. London: Epworth, 1977.

Chafer, Lewis Sperry. *Grace*. Chicago: Moody, 1922.

Chalke, Steve, and Alan Mann. *The Lost Message of Jesus*. Grand Rapids: Zondervan, 2004.

Champion, Justin A. I. "Deism." In *The Columbia History of Western Philosophy*, edited by Richard H. Popkin, 437–45. New York: MJF Books, 1999.

Christian Reformed Church. *Acts of Synod*. Kalamazoo, MI: Board of Publications of the Christian Reformed Church, 1973.

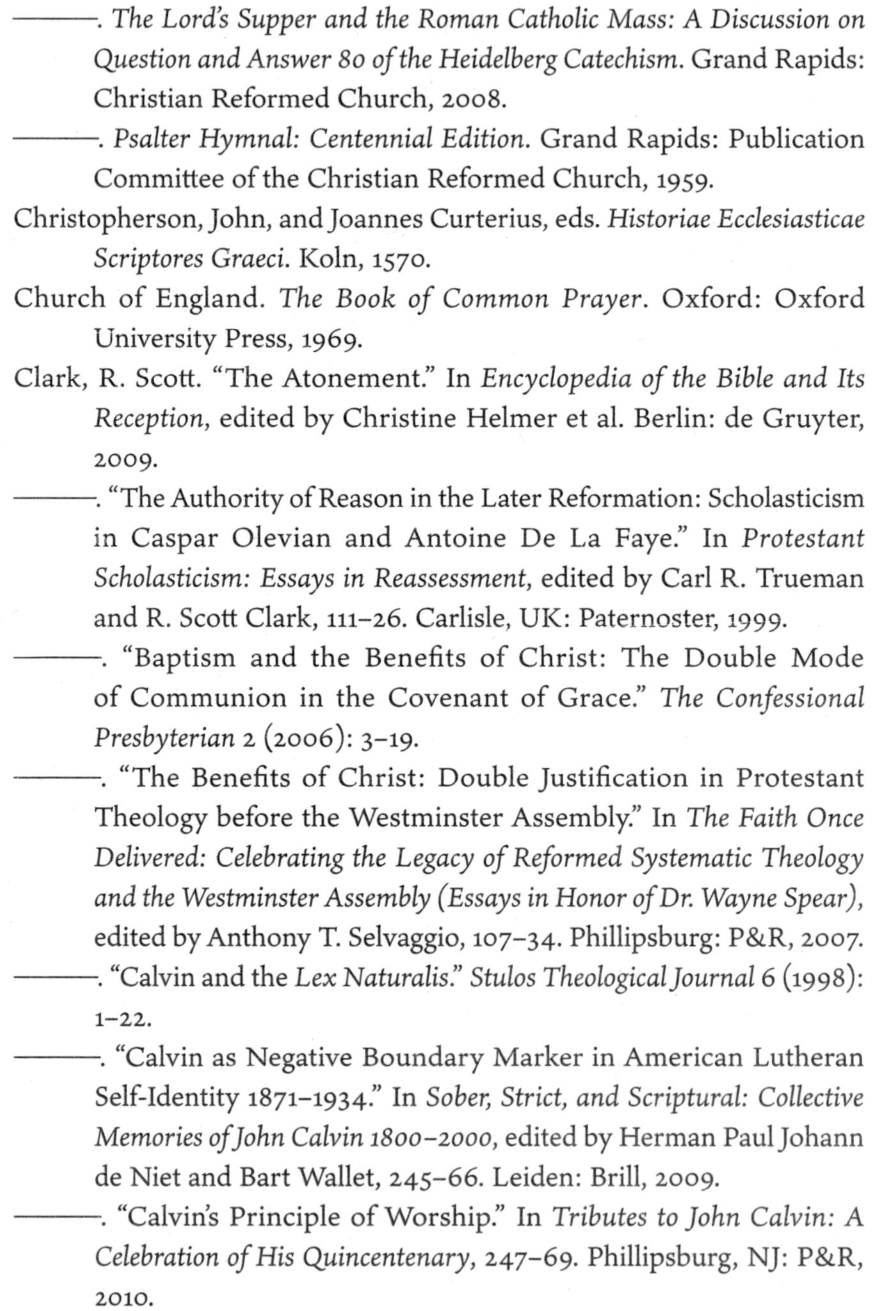

———. *Acts of Synod 1975*. Grand Rapids: Board of Publications of the Christian Reformed Church, 1975.

———. *The Lord's Supper and the Roman Catholic Mass: A Discussion on Question and Answer 80 of the Heidelberg Catechism*. Grand Rapids: Christian Reformed Church, 2008.

———. *Psalter Hymnal: Centennial Edition*. Grand Rapids: Publication Committee of the Christian Reformed Church, 1959.

Christopherson, John, and Joannes Curterius, eds. *Historiae Ecclesiasticae Scriptores Graeci*. Koln, 1570.

Church of England. *The Book of Common Prayer*. Oxford: Oxford University Press, 1969.

Clark, R. Scott. "The Atonement." In *Encyclopedia of the Bible and Its Reception*, edited by Christine Helmer et al. Berlin: de Gruyter, 2009.

———. "The Authority of Reason in the Later Reformation: Scholasticism in Caspar Olevian and Antoine De La Faye." In *Protestant Scholasticism: Essays in Reassessment*, edited by Carl R. Trueman and R. Scott Clark, 111–26. Carlisle, UK: Paternoster, 1999.

———. "Baptism and the Benefits of Christ: The Double Mode of Communion in the Covenant of Grace." *The Confessional Presbyterian* 2 (2006): 3–19.

———. "The Benefits of Christ: Double Justification in Protestant Theology before the Westminster Assembly." In *The Faith Once Delivered: Celebrating the Legacy of Reformed Systematic Theology and the Westminster Assembly (Essays in Honor of Dr. Wayne Spear)*, edited by Anthony T. Selvaggio, 107–34. Phillipsburg: P&R, 2007.

———. "Calvin and the *Lex Naturalis*." *Stulos Theological Journal* 6 (1998): 1–22.

———. "Calvin as Negative Boundary Marker in American Lutheran Self-Identity 1871–1934." In *Sober, Strict, and Scriptural: Collective Memories of John Calvin 1800–2000*, edited by Herman Paul Johann de Niet and Bart Wallet, 245–66. Leiden: Brill, 2009.

———. "Calvin's Principle of Worship." In *Tributes to John Calvin: A Celebration of His Quincentenary*, 247–69. Phillipsburg, NJ: P&R, 2010.

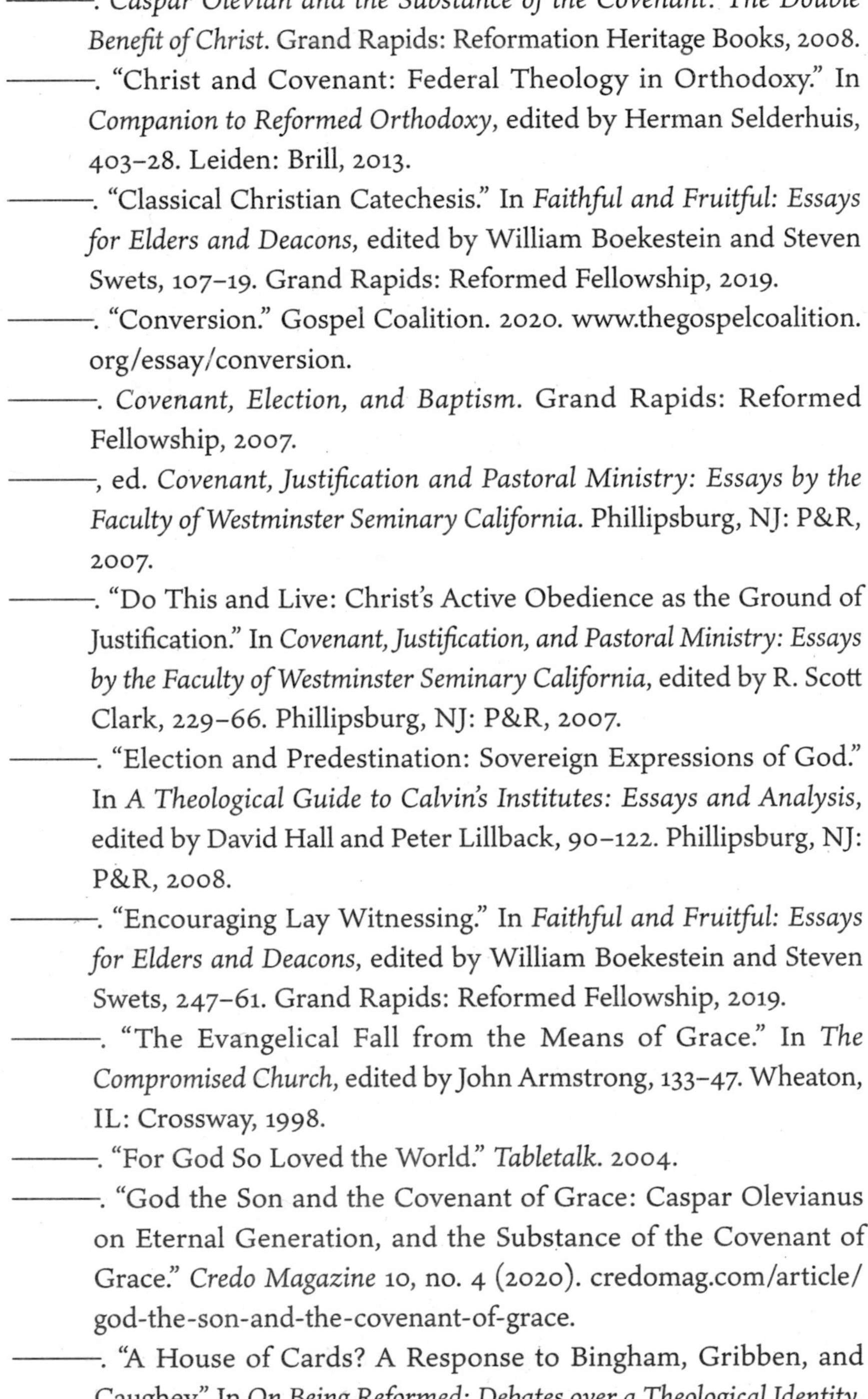

———. *Caspar Olevian and the Substance of the Covenant: The Double Benefit of Christ*. Grand Rapids: Reformation Heritage Books, 2008.

———. "Christ and Covenant: Federal Theology in Orthodoxy." In *Companion to Reformed Orthodoxy*, edited by Herman Selderhuis, 403–28. Leiden: Brill, 2013.

———. "Classical Christian Catechesis." In *Faithful and Fruitful: Essays for Elders and Deacons*, edited by William Boekestein and Steven Swets, 107–19. Grand Rapids: Reformed Fellowship, 2019.

———. "Conversion." Gospel Coalition. 2020. www.thegospelcoalition.org/essay/conversion.

———. *Covenant, Election, and Baptism*. Grand Rapids: Reformed Fellowship, 2007.

———, ed. *Covenant, Justification and Pastoral Ministry: Essays by the Faculty of Westminster Seminary California*. Phillipsburg, NJ: P&R, 2007.

———. "Do This and Live: Christ's Active Obedience as the Ground of Justification." In *Covenant, Justification, and Pastoral Ministry: Essays by the Faculty of Westminster Seminary California*, edited by R. Scott Clark, 229–66. Phillipsburg, NJ: P&R, 2007.

———. "Election and Predestination: Sovereign Expressions of God." In *A Theological Guide to Calvin's Institutes: Essays and Analysis*, edited by David Hall and Peter Lillback, 90–122. Phillipsburg, NJ: P&R, 2008.

———. "Encouraging Lay Witnessing." In *Faithful and Fruitful: Essays for Elders and Deacons*, edited by William Boekestein and Steven Swets, 247–61. Grand Rapids: Reformed Fellowship, 2019.

———. "The Evangelical Fall from the Means of Grace." In *The Compromised Church*, edited by John Armstrong, 133–47. Wheaton, IL: Crossway, 1998.

———. "For God So Loved the World." *Tabletalk*. 2004.

———. "God the Son and the Covenant of Grace: Caspar Olevianus on Eternal Generation, and the Substance of the Covenant of Grace." *Credo Magazine* 10, no. 4 (2020). credomag.com/article/god-the-son-and-the-covenant-of-grace.

———. "A House of Cards? A Response to Bingham, Gribben, and Caughey." In *On Being Reformed: Debates over a Theological Identity*,

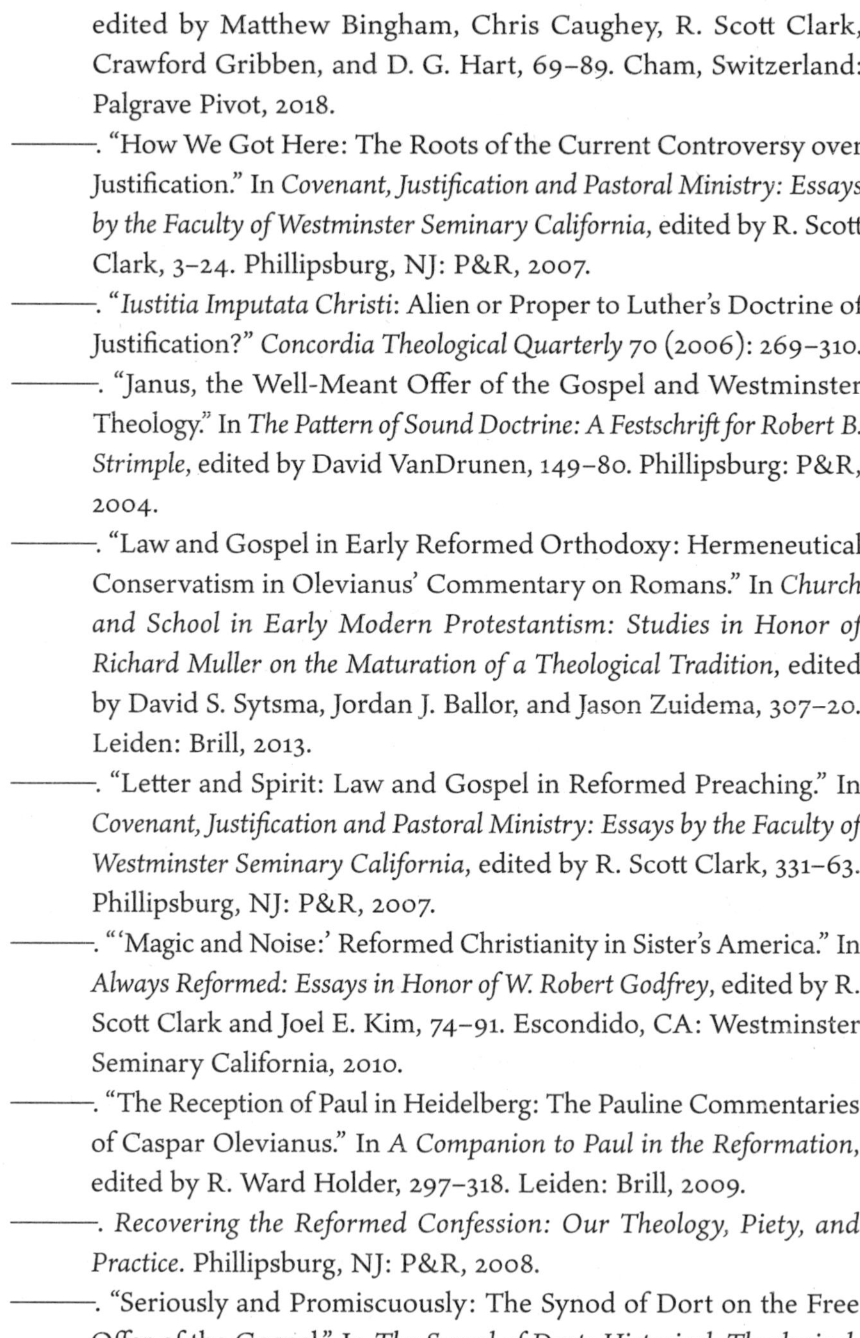

edited by Matthew Bingham, Chris Caughey, R. Scott Clark, Crawford Gribben, and D. G. Hart, 69–89. Cham, Switzerland: Palgrave Pivot, 2018.

———. "How We Got Here: The Roots of the Current Controversy over Justification." In *Covenant, Justification and Pastoral Ministry: Essays by the Faculty of Westminster Seminary California*, edited by R. Scott Clark, 3–24. Phillipsburg, NJ: P&R, 2007.

———. "*Iustitia Imputata Christi*: Alien or Proper to Luther's Doctrine of Justification?" *Concordia Theological Quarterly* 70 (2006): 269–310.

———. "Janus, the Well-Meant Offer of the Gospel and Westminster Theology." In *The Pattern of Sound Doctrine: A Festschrift for Robert B. Strimple*, edited by David VanDrunen, 149–80. Phillipsburg: P&R, 2004.

———. "Law and Gospel in Early Reformed Orthodoxy: Hermeneutical Conservatism in Olevianus' Commentary on Romans." In *Church and School in Early Modern Protestantism: Studies in Honor of Richard Muller on the Maturation of a Theological Tradition*, edited by David S. Sytsma, Jordan J. Ballor, and Jason Zuidema, 307–20. Leiden: Brill, 2013.

———. "Letter and Spirit: Law and Gospel in Reformed Preaching." In *Covenant, Justification and Pastoral Ministry: Essays by the Faculty of Westminster Seminary California*, edited by R. Scott Clark, 331–63. Phillipsburg, NJ: P&R, 2007.

———. "'Magic and Noise:' Reformed Christianity in Sister's America." In *Always Reformed: Essays in Honor of W. Robert Godfrey*, edited by R. Scott Clark and Joel E. Kim, 74–91. Escondido, CA: Westminster Seminary California, 2010.

———. "The Reception of Paul in Heidelberg: The Pauline Commentaries of Caspar Olevianus." In *A Companion to Paul in the Reformation*, edited by R. Ward Holder, 297–318. Leiden: Brill, 2009.

———. *Recovering the Reformed Confession: Our Theology, Piety, and Practice*. Phillipsburg, NJ: P&R, 2008.

———. "Seriously and Promiscuously: The Synod of Dort on the Free Offer of the Gospel." In *The Synod of Dort: Historical, Theological, and Experiential Perspectives*, edited by Joel R. Beeke and Martin I. Klauber, 89–104. Göttingen: Vandenhoeck & Ruprecht, 2020.

———. "'Subtle Sacramentarian' or Son? John Calvin's Relationship to Martin Luther." *Southern Baptist Journal of Theology* 24 (2018): 35–60.

———. "The Synod of Dort: Keeping Venom from the Lips." *Ordained Servant* 28 (2019): 9–29.

Clark, R. Scott, and Joel Beeke. "Ursinus, Oxford and the Westminster Divines." In *The Westminster Confession Into the 21st Century: Essays in Remembrance of the 350th Anniversary of the Publication of the Westminster Confession of Faith*, edited by Ligon Duncan, 2:1–32. Ross-Shire, UK: Mentor, 2003.

Clark, R. Scott, and Joel E. Kim, eds. *Always Reformed: Essays in Honor of W. Robert Godfrey*. Escondido, CA: Westminster Seminary California, 2010.

Clemens, Deborah Rahn. "Foundations of German Reformed Worship in the Sixteenth Century Palatinate." PhD diss., Drew University, 1995.

Clendenin, Daniel B. *Eastern Orthodox Christianity: A Western Perspective*. Grand Rapids: Baker Academic, 2003.

Coakley, Sarah. "Persons in the 'Social' Doctrine of the Trinity." In *The Trinity: An Inter-disciplinary Symposium on the Trinity*, edited by Stephen T. Davis et al., 123–44. Oxford: Oxford University Press, 1991.

Coleman, Stephen M., and Todd M. Rester, eds. *Faith in the Time of Plague: Selected Writings from the Reformation and Post-Reformation*. Philadelphia: Westminster, 2021.

Como, David R. *Blown by the Spirit: Puritanism and the Emergence of an Antinomian Underground in Pre-Civil-War England*. Stanford, CA: Stanford University Press, 2004.

Cross, F. L., et al. *The Oxford Dictionary of the Christian Church*. Oxford: Oxford University Press, 1997.

Cummins, Neil. "Lifespans of the European Elite, 800–1800." *The Journal of Economic History* 77, no. 2 (2017): 406–39.

Davidson, J. Ryan. "Abortion in Antiquity." In *Lexham Bible Dictionary*, edited by John D. Barry et al. Bellingham, WA: Lexham Press, 2016.

Davis, Thomas J. *This Is My Body: The Presence of Christ in Reformation Thought*. Grand Rapids: Baker Academic, 2008.

Dayton, Donald W. "Some Doubts about the Usefulness of the Category 'Evangelical.'" In *The Variety of American Evangelicalism*, edited by Donald W. Dayton and Robert K. Johnston, 245–51. Downers Grove, IL: InterVarsity, 1991.

DeJong, P. Y., ed. *Crisis in the Reformed Churches*. Grand Rapids: Reformed Fellowship, 1968.

Dellen, Idzerd van, and Martin Monsma. *The Church Order Commentary*. Grand Rapids: Zondervan, 1954.

DeYoung, Kevin. *The Good News We Almost Forgot: Rediscovering the Gospel in a 16th-Century Catechism*. Chicago: Moody, 2010.

Didron, Adolphe Napoleon. *Christian Iconography: The History of Christian Art in the Middle Ages*. Translated by E. J. Millington. New York: Frederick Ungar, 1965.

Douma, J. *The Ten Commandments: Manual for the Christian Life*. Translated by N. D. Kloosterman. Phillipsburg, NJ: P&R, 1996.

Drake, K. J. *The Flesh of the Word: The Extra Calvinisticum from Zwingli to Early Orthodoxy*. Oxford: Oxford University Press, 2021.

Dugmore, C. W. *The Influence of the Synagogue upon the Divine Office*. London: Oxford University Press, 1944.

Duguid, Iain. "Covenant Nomism and the Exile." In *Covenant, Justification, and Pastoral Ministry*, edited by R. Scott Clark, 61–88. Phillipsburg, NJ: P&R, 2007.

Edwards, David L., and John R. W. Stott. *Evangelical Essentials: A Liberal Evangelical Dialogue*. Downers Grove, IL: InterVarsity, 1988.

Edwards, Mark U. *Luther and the False Brethren*. Stanford: Stanford University Press, 1975.

Ellis, Brannon. *Calvin, Classical Trinitarianism, and the Aseity of the Son*. Oxford: Oxford University Press, 2012.

Embree, Warren C. "Ethics and Interpretation." PhD diss., University of Nebraska, 1991.

Engelbrecht, Edward. *Friends of the Law: Luther's Use of the Law for the Christian Life*. St Louis: Concordia, 2011.

Evans, Christopher Hodge. *The Kingdom Is Always but Coming: A Life of Walter Rauschenbusch*. Grand Rapids: Eerdmans, 2004.

Evans, William B. *Imputation and Impartation: Union with Christ in American Reformed Theology*. Eugene, OR: Wipf & Stock, 2008.

Fairbairn, Don. "Salvation as Theosis: The Teaching of Eastern Orthodoxy." *Themelios* 23, no. 3 (1998): 42–54.

Ferguson, Everett F. *A Cappella Music in the Public Worship of the Church*. Abilene, TX: Desert Willow, 2013.

———. *Baptism in the Early Church: History, Theology, and Liturgy in the First Five Centuries*. Grand Rapids: Eerdmans, 2009.

Ferguson, Sinclair. *The Whole Christ: Legalism, Antinomianism, and Gospel Assurance—Why the Marrow Controversy Still Matters*. Wheaton, IL: Crossway, 2016.

Fesko, J. V. *Beyond Calvin: Union with Christ and Justification in Early Modern Reformed Theology (1517–1700)*. Göttingen: Vandenhoeck & Ruprecht, 2012.

———. *The Covenant of Redemption: Origins, Development, and Reception*. Göttingen: Vandenhoeck & Ruprecht, 2016.

———. *Justification: Understanding the Classic Reformed Doctrine*. Phillipsburg, NJ: P&R, 2008.

———. "On the Antiquity of Biblical Theology." In *Resurrection and Eschatology: Theology in the Service of the Church: Essays in Honor of Richard B. Gaffin, Jr.*, edited by Lane G. Tipton and Jeffrey C. Waddington, 443–77. Phillipsburg, NJ: P&R, 2008.

———. The Theology of the Westminster Standards. Wheaton, IL: Crossway, 2014.

———. *The Trinity and the Covenant of Redemption*. Fearn, UK: Mentor, 2016.

Folely, Edward. *Foundations of Christian Music: The Music of Pre-Constantinian Christianity*. Collegeville, MN: Liturgical Press, 1996.

Foucault, Michel. *The History of Sexuality*. Vol. 1, *An Introduction*. Translated by Robert Hurley. New York: Pantheon Books, 1978.

Frame, John M. *The Doctrine of God*. Phillipsburg, NJ: P&R, 2002.

Gaebler, Ulrich. *Huldrych Zwingli: His Life and Work*. Translated by Ruth C. L. Gritsch. Edinburgh: T&T Clark, 1986.

Gaffin, Richard B., Jr. *By Faith Not by Sight: Paul and the Order of Salvation*. Phillipsburg, NJ: P&R, 2013.

———. *Resurrection and Redemption: A Study in Paul's Soteriology*. Phillipsburg, NJ: P&R, 1978.

Garcia, Mark. A. *Life in Christ: Union with Christ and Twofold Grace in Calvin's Theology*. Milton Keynes, UK: Paternoster, 2008.

Garratt, Samuel. *Our Father, or, Jesus Teaching to Pray*. London: Wertheim and MacIntosh, 1854.

Genke, Viktor, and Francis X. Gumerlock, eds. *Gottschalk and a Medieval Predestination Controversy: Texts Translated from the Latin*. Milwaukee: Marquette University Press, 2010.

Gentry, Peter J., and Stephen J. Wellum. *God's Kingdom through Covenants: A Concise Biblical Theology*. Wheaton, IL: Crossway, 2015.

———. *Kingdom through Covenant: A Biblical-Theological Understanding of the Covenants*. Wheaton, IL: Crossway, 2018.

Gifford, Edward Hamilton. "The Catechetical Lectures of S. Cyril: Introduction." *NPNF* 2/7, i–lviii.

Giles, Kevin. *The Eternal Generation of the Son: Maintaining Orthodoxy in Trinitarian Theology*. Downers Grove, IL: IVP Academic, 2012.

Girardeau, John L. *Instrumental Music in the Public Worship of the Church*. Richmond, VA: Whittet and Shepperson, 1888.

Glodo, Michael J. "Dispensationalism." In *Covenant Theology: Biblical, Theological, and Historical Perspectives*, edited by Guy Prentiss Waters, J. Nicholas Reid, and John R. Muether, 525–50. Wheaton, IL: Crossway, 2020.

Godfrey, W. Robert. "Faith Formed by Love or Faith Alone?" In *Covenant, Justification, and Pastoral Ministry: Essays by the Faculty of Westminster Seminary California*, edited by R. Scott Clark, 267–84. Phillipsburg, NJ: P&R, 2007.

———. *John Calvin: Pilgrim and Pastor*. Wheaton, IL: Crossway, 2009.

———. "John Hales' Good-Night to John Calvin." In *Protestant Scholasticism: Essays in Reassessment*, edited by R. Scott Clark and Carl R. Trueman, 165–80. Carlisle, UK: Paternoster, 1999.

———. *Saving the Reformation: The Pastoral Theology of the Canons of Dort*. Orlando: Reformation Trust, 2019.

———. "Tensions within International Calvinism: The Debate on the Atonement at the Synod of Dort, 1618–1619." PhD diss., Stanford University, 1974.

Goertz, Hans-Jürgen. *Thomas Müntzer: Apocalyptic Mystic and Revolutionary*. Translated by Jocelym Jaquiery. Edinburgh: T&T Clark, 1993.

Goldberg, Jonah. *Liberal Fascism*. New York: Doubleday, 2007.

Good, J. I. *The Heidelberg Catechism in Its Newest Light*. Philadelphia: Publication and Sunday School Board of the Reformed Church in the United States, 1914.

———. *The Origin of the Reformed Church in Germany*. Reading, PA: Daniel Miller, 1887.

Goodman, Felicitas D. "Phonetic Analysis of Glossolalia in Four Cultural Settings." *Journal for the Scientific Study of Religion* 8, no. 2 (1969): 227–39.

Gooszen, Maurits A. *De Heidelbergsche Catechismus: Textus Receptus Met Toelichtende Teksten: Bijdrage Tot De Kennis Van Zijne Wordingsgeschiedenis En Van Het Gereformeerd Protestantisme*. Leiden: Brill, 1890.

Gordon, Bruce. *Calvin*. New Haven: Yale University Press, 2009.

Grabill, Stephen. *Rediscovering the Natural Law in Reformed Theological Ethics*. Grand Rapids: Eerdmans, 2006.

Gribben, Crawford. *John Owen and English Puritanism: Experiences of Defeat*. Oxford: Oxford University Press, 2016.

Gritsch, Eric W. *Thomas Müntzer: A Tragedy of Errors*. Minneapolis: Fortress, 1989.

Grudem, Wayne A. *The Gift of Prophecy in the New Testament and Today*. Rev. ed. Westchester, IL: Crossway Books, 2000.

Gunnoe, Charles D., Jr. "Swiss Students and Faculty at the University of Heidelberg, 1518–1622." In *Church and School in Early Modern Protestantism: Studies in Honor of Richard A. Muller on the Maturation of a Theological Tradition*, edited by David S. Sytsma, Jordan J. Ballor, and Jason Zuidema, 255–69. Leiden: Brill, 2013.

———. *Thomas Erastus and the Palatinate: A Renaissance Physician in the Second Reformation*. Leiden: Brill, 2011.

Hageman, Howard. "The Liturgical Origins of the Reformed Churches." In *Heritage of John Calvin*, edited by John H. Bratt, 110–36. Grand Rapids: Eerdmans, 1973.

Haleem, M. A. S. Abdel, ed. *The Qur'an: English Translation and Parallel Arabic Text*. Oxford: Oxford University Press, 2010.

Hall, David W., ed. *The Practice of Confessional Subscription*. Oak Ridge, TN: Covenant Foundation, 2001.

Harbaugh, Henry. "Creed and Cultus." In *Tercentenary Monument in Commemoration of the Three Hundredth Anniversary of the Heidelberg Catechism*. Chambersburg, 1863.

Hart, D. G. *Defending the Faith: J. Gresham Machen and the Crisis of Conservative Protestantism*. Baltimore: Johns Hopkins University Press, 1994.

———. *The Lost Soul of American Protestantism*. Lanham: Rowman & Littlefield, 2002.

Hartley, J. E. "Pledge." In *The International Standard Bible Encyclopedia*, rev. ed., ed. Geoffrey W. Bromiley, 886. Grand Rapids: Eerdmans, 1979–1988.

Hatch, Nathan O. *The Democratization of American Christianity*. New Haven: Yale University Press, 1989.

Hefele, Charles Joseph. *A History of the Councils of the Church*. Translated by William R. Clark. Edinburgh: T&T Clark, 1871.

Heick, Otto W. "Consubstantiation in Luther's Theology." *Canadian Journal of Theology* 12, no. 1 (1966): 3–8.

Hemer, Colin J. *The Letters to the Seven Churches of Asia in Their Local Setting*. Sheffield: JSOT Press, 1986.

Hill, C. E. *Regnum Caelorum: Patterns of Future Hope in Early Christian Eschatology*. Oxford: Oxford University Press, 1990.

Hodge, A. A. *A Commentary on the Confession of Faith*. Philadelphia: Presbyterian Board of Publication and Sabbath-School Work, 1869.

Hodge, A. A., and B. B. Warfield. *Inspiration*. Philadelphia: Presbyterian Board of Publication, 1881.

Hodge, Charles. *Systematic Theology*. New York: Scribner, Armstrong, 1873.

Hodges, Zane C. Absolutely Free!: A Biblical Reply to Lordship Salvation. Dallas: Redencion Viva, 1989.

———. *The Gospel under Siege: A Study on Faith and Works*. Dallas: Redención Viva, 1981.

Hoekema, Anthony A. *The Bible and the Future*. Grand Rapids: Eerdmans, 1979.

———. *Saved by Grace*. Grand Rapids: Eerdmans, 1989.

Hoeksema, Herman. *The Triple Knowledge: An Exposition of the Heidelberg Catechism*. 3 vols. Grand Rapids: Reformed Free Publishing Association, 1972.

Holladay, William L. *A Concise Hebrew and Aramaic Lexicon of the Old Testament*. Grand Rapids: Eerdmans, 1971.

Holopainen, Toivo J. *Dialectical Theology in the Eleventh Century*. Leiden: Brill, 1996.

Holweg, Walter. *Neue Untersuchungen Zur Geschichte Des Heidelberger Katechismus*. Neukirchen: Neukirchener Verlag, 1961.

Horton, Michael S., ed. *Christ the Lord: The Reformation and Lordship Salvation*. Grand Rapids: Baker, 1993.

———. *The Christian Faith: A Systematic Theology for Pilgrims on the Way*. Grand Rapids: Zondervan, 2011.

———. *Justification*. 2 vols. New Studies in Dogmatics. Grand Rapids: Zondervan, 2018.

———. *Ordinary: Sustainable Faith in a Radical, Restless World*. Grand Rapids: Zondervan, 2014.

———. "Which Covenant Theology?" In *Covenant, Justification, and Pastoral Ministry*, edited by R. Scott Clark, 197–227. Phillipsburg, NJ: P&R, 2007.

Hughes, Philip Edgcumbe. *Christian Ethics in Secular Society*. Grand Rapids: Baker, 1983.

Huijgen, Arnold. "Practicing Gratitude: The Spirituality of Prayer in the Heidelberg Catechism." In *The Spirituality of the Heidelberg Catechism: Papers of the International Conference on the Heidelberg Catechism Held in Apeldoorn 2013*, edited by Arnold Huijgen, 206–24. Göttingen: Vandenhoeck & Ruprecht, 2015.

———, ed. *The Spirituality of the Heidelberg Catechism: Papers of the International Conference on the Heidelberg Catechism Held in Apeldoorn 2013*. Göttingen: Vandenhoeck & Ruprecht, 2015.

Hyde, Daniel R. "The Holy Spirit in the Heidelberg Catechism." *Mid-America Journal of Theology* 17 (2006): 211–37.

———. *In Defense of the Descent: A Response to Contemporary Critics.* Grand Rapids: Reformation Heritage Books, 2010.

———. *In Living Color: Images of Christ and the Means of Grace.* Grandville, MI: Reformed Fellowship, 2009.

———. "Lost Keys: The Absolution in Reformed Liturgy." *Calvin Theological Journal* 46 (2011): 140–66.

———. "The Principle and Practice of Preaching in the Heidelberg Catechism." *Puritan Reformed Journal* 1 (2009): 97–117.

———. *With Heart and Mouth: An Exposition of the Belgic Confession.* Grand Rapids: Reformed Fellowship, 2008.

International Theological Commission. "The Reciprocity between Faith and the Sacraments in the Sacramental Economy." 2020. www.vatican.va/roman_curia/congregations/cfaith/cti_documents/rc_cti_20200303_reciprocita-fede-sacramenti_en.html.

Janz, D. R. "To Hell (and Back) with Luther: The Dialectic of Anfechtung and Faith." *Seminary Ridge Review* 13 (2011): 41–55.

Jeremias, Joachim. *Infant Baptism in the First Four Centuries.* London: SCM Press, 1960.

Johnson, Daniel. "Michel Foucault: The Prophet of Pederasty." The Critic, 2021. thecritic.co.uk/issues/april-2021/michel-foucault-the-prophet-of-pederasty.

Johnson, Gary L. W., and Ronald N. Gleason. *Reforming or Conforming? Post-conservative Evangelicals and the Emerging Church.* Wheaton, IL: Crossway, 2008.

"A Joint Federal Vision Profession." 2007. rscottclark.org/a-joint-federal-vision-profession-2007.

Jones, Hywel R. "Justification by Faith Alone: No Christian Life without It." In *Covenant, Justification, and Pastoral Ministry: Essays by the Faculty of Westminster Seminary California*, edited by R. Scott Clark, 285–308. Philipsburg, NJ: P&R, 2007.

Jones, Mark. *Antinomianism: Reformed Theology's Unwelcome Guest?* Phillipsburg, NJ: P&R, 2013.

Jones, Norman. *Study Helps on the Heidelberg Catechism.* Reformed Church in the US, 1981.

Keister, Lane B. "Intinction: An Historical, Exegetical, and Systematic-Theological Examination." *Mid-America Journal of Theology* 29 (2018): 149–72.

Kelly, J. N. D. *Early Christian Doctrines*. London: Bloomsbury, 1977.

———. *Golden Mouth: The Story of John Chrysostom—Ascetic, Preacher, Bishop*. Ithaca, NY: Cornell University Press, 1995.

Kelly, John. *The Great Mortality: An Intimate History of the Black Death, the Most Devastating Plague of All Time*. New York: HarperCollins, 2005.

Kersten, G. H. *The Heidelberg Catechism*. Sioux Center, IA: Netherlands Reformed Book Publishing, 1992.

King, N. Q. *The Emperor Theodosius and the Establishment of Christianity*. Philadelphia: Westminster, 1960.

Kittel, Gerhard, Geoffrey W. Bromiley, and Gerhard Friedrich, eds. *Theological Dictionary of the New Testament*. Grand Rapids: Eerdmans, 1964.

Kleinbauer, W. E. "Icon." In *Encyclopedia of Early Christianity*, edited by Everett Ferguson, Michael P. McHugh, Frederick W. Norris, and David Scholar. New York: Routledge, 1990.

Kline, Meredith G. *By Oath Consigned: A Reinterpration of the Covenant Signs of Circumcision and Baptism*. Grand Rapids: Eerdmans, 1968.

———. *Kingdom Prologue: Genesis Foundations for a Covenantal Worldview*. Eugene, OR: Wipf & Stock, 2006.

Klooster, Fred H. "The Heidelberg Catechism: Origin and History." Unpublished syllabus, Calvin Theological Seminary, 1989.

———. *Our Only Comfort: A Comprehensive Commentary on the Heidelberg Catechism*. 2 vols. Grand Rapids: Faith Alive Christian Resources, 2001.

———. "The Primacy of Ursinus in the Composition of the Heidelberg Catechism." In *Controversy and Conciliation: The Reformation of the Palatinate 1559–83*, edited by Derk Visser, 51–72. Allison Park, PA: Pickwick, 1986.

Knight, George. *The Faithful Sayings in the Pastoral Letters*. Nutley, NJ: P&R, 1969.

Kolb, Robert. "Christus Victor." The Gospel Coalition, www.thegospelcoalition.org/essay/christus-victor.

———. "Georg Major as Controversialist: Polemics in the Late Reformation." *Church History* 45 (1976): 455–68.

———. *Nikolaus Von Amsdorf (1483–1565): Popular Polemics in the Preservation of Luther's Legacy*. Nieuwkoop: DeGraaf, 1978.

Kolb, Robert, and James A. Nestingen. *Sources and Contexts of the Book of Concord*. Minneapolis: Fortress, 2001.

Kolb, Robert, and Carl R. Trueman. *Between Wittenberg and Geneva: Lutheran and Reformed Theology in Conversation*. Grand Rapids: Baker Academic, 2017.

Kolb, Robert, and Timothy Wengert, eds. *The Book of Concord: The Confessions of the Evangelical Lutheran Church*. Minneapolis: Fortress, 2000.

Kruger, Michael J. *Christianity at the Crossroads: How the Second Century Shaped the Future of the Church*. Downers Grove, IL: InterVarsity, 2018.

Kuiper, Herman. *Calvin on Common Grace*. Goes: Oosterbaan and Le Cointre, 1928.

Kuyper, Abraham. "Calvinism and Confessional Revision." *The Presbyterian and Reformed Review* 2 (1891): 369–99.

Lee, Inwoo. "'Righteous before God': William Perkins' Defense of the Doctrine of Justification in Elizabethan England." PhD diss., Westminster Seminary California, 2020.

Leff, Gordon. *Bradwardine and the Pelagians: A Study of His De Causa Dei and Its Opponents*. Cambridge: Cambridge University Press, 2008.

Leftow, Brian. "Anti Social Trinitarianism." In *The Trinity: An Interdisciplinary Symposium on the Trinity*, edited by Stephen T. Davis et al., 203–50. Oxford: Oxford University Press, 1991.

LeGoff, Jacques. *The Birth of Purgatory*. Translated by Arthur Goldhammer. Chicago: University of Chicago Press, 1981.

Lehmann, Karl, ed. *Justification by Faith: Do the Sixteenth-Century Condemnations Still Apply?* New York: Continuum, 1997.

Letham, Robert. *Union with Christ: In Scripture, History, and Theology*. Phillipsburg, NJ: P&R, 2011.

Lewis, Charlton T., and Charles Short. *A Latin Dictionary*. Oxford: Oxford University Press, 1879.

Liddell, Henry George, Robert Scott, and Henry Stuart Jones. *A Greek-English Lexicon*. Oxford: Oxford University Press, 1996.

Lillback, Peter. *The Binding of God: Calvin's Role in the Development of Covenant Theology*. Grand Rapids: Baker, 2001.

Loetscher, Lefferts. *The Broadening Church: The Study of Theological Issues in the Presbyterian Church since 1869*. Philadelphia: University of Pennsylvania Press, 1954.

Lusk, Rich. "A Response to 'The Biblical Plan of Salvation.'" In *The Auburn Avenue Theology, Pros and Cons: Debating the Federal Vision*, edited by E. Calvin Beisner, 118–48. Ft. Lauderdale, FL: Knox Theological Seminary, 2004.

MacArthur, John F. *The Gospel according to Jesus: What Is Authentic Faith?* Rev. and exp. anniversary ed. Grand Rapids: Zondervan, 2008.

———. "Understanding the Sabbath." Grace to You, 2009. www.gty.org/library/sermons-library/90-379.

Machen, J. Gresham. *Christianity and Liberalism*. New York: Macmillan, 1923.

———. *The Virgin Birth of Christ*. New York: Harper & Brothers, 1930.

Macy, Gary. *The Banquet's Wisdom*. Ashland City, TN: OSL, 1992.

———. *Theologies of the Eucharist in the Early Scholastic Period: A Study of the Salvific Function of the Sacrament according to the Theologians c. 1080–c. 1220*. Oxford: Clarendon, 1984.

Mair, A. W., and G. R. Mair, eds. *Hymns and Epigrams. Lycophron: Alexandra. Aratus: Phaenomena*. Cambridge, MA: Harvard University Press, 1921.

Marshall, Walter. *The Gospel-Mystery of Sanctification*. New York: Southwick and Peluse, 1811.

Marthalier, Bernard L. *New Catholic Encyclopedia*. Washington, DC: Catholic University of America Press, 2003.

Martin, R. P. "Poetry in the NT." In *The International Standard Bible Encyclopedia*, rev. ed., ed. Geoffrey W. Bromiley, 899. Grand Rapids: Eerdmans, 1979–1988.

Marx, Karl. *Capital*. Translated by Samuel Moore. Chicago: William Benton/Encyclopaedia Britannica, 1952.

Matheson, Peter, ed. *The Collected Works of Thomas Müntzer*. Edinburgh: T&T Clark, 1988.

Mathison, Keith A., ed. *When Shall These Things Be? A Reformed Response to Hyper-Preterism*. Phillipsburg, NJ: P&R, 2004.

McClymond, Michael J. *The Devil's Redemption: A New History and Interpretation of Christian Universalism*. Grand Rapids: Baker Academic, 2018.

McCracken, George E., ed. *Early Medieval Theology*. London: SCM Press, 1957.

McGinnis, Andrew M. *The Son of God beyond the Flesh: A Historical and Theological Study of the Extra Calvinisticum*. New York: Bloomsbury, 2014.

McGinnis, Timothy Scott. "'Subtiltie' Exposed: Pastoral Perspectives on Witch Belief in the Thought of George Gifford." *The Sixteenth Century Journal* 33 (2002): 665–86.

McGuckin, John Anthony. *The Path of Christianity: The First Thousand Years*. Downers Grove, IL: InterVarsity, 2017.

McKay, David. "From Popery to Principle: Covenanters and the Kingship of Christ." In *The Faith Once Delivered: Essays in Honor of Wayne R. Spear*, edited by Anthony T. Selvaggio, 135–70. Phillipsburg, NJ: P&R, 2007.

McKinnon, James W. *Music in Early Christian Literature*. New York: Cambridge University Press, 1987.

Menninger, Karl A. *Whatever Became of Sin?* New York: Hawthorn Books, 1973.

Merkle, Benjamin R. *Defending the Trinity in the Reformed Palatinate*. Oxford: Oxford University Press, 2015.

Metzger, Bruce M. *A Textual Commentary on the Greek New Testament*. Stuttgart: Deutsche Bibelgesellschaft, 1994.

Miller, Rachel Green. *Beyond Authority and Submission: Women and Men in Marriage, Church, and Society*. Phillipsburg, NJ: P&R, 2019.

Milton, Anthony, ed. *The British Delegation and the Synod of Dort (1618–1619)*. Woodbridge, UK: Boydell, 2005.

———. "A Distorting Mirror: The Hales and Balcanquahall Letters and the Synod of Dordt." In *Revisiting the Synod of Dort (1618–1619)*, edited by Fred van Lieburg and Aza Goudriaan, 135–61. Leiden: Brill, 2011.

Monsma, Martin. *The New Revised Church Order Commentary*. Grand Rapids: Zondervan, 1967.

Monter, E. William. *Witchcraft in France and Switzerland: The Borderlands during the Reformation*. Ithaca, NY: Columbia University Press, 1976.

Morse, Wilbur Earl. *A History of Unitarianism: Socinianism and Its Antecedents*. Boston: Beacon, 1965.

Mortimer, Sarah. *Reason and Religion in the English Revolution: The Challenge of Socinianism*. Cambridge: Cambridge University Press, 2010.

Moulton, James Hope, and George Milligan. *The Vocabulary of the Greek Testament*. London, 1930.

Mouw, Richard. *Talking with Mormons: An Invitation to Evangelicals*. Grand Rapids: Eerdmans, 2012.

Mueller, Theodore. *Christian Dogmatics*. St. Louis: Concordia, 1934.

———. "A Linguistic Analysis of Glossolalia." *Concordia Theological Quarterly* 45 (1981): 186–91.

Mühling, Andreas. "Caspar Olevian Und Die Einführung Des Heidelberger Katechismus." In *The Spirituality of the Heidelberg Catechism: Papers of the International Conference on the Heidelberg Catechism Held in Apeldoorn 2013*, edited by Arnold Huijgen, 25–33. Göttingen: Vandenhoeck & Ruprecht, 2015.

Muller, Richard A. *After Calvin: Studies in the Development of a Theological Tradition*. Oxford: Oxford University Press, 2003.

———. *Calvin and the Reformed Tradition: On the Work of Christ and the Order of Salvation*. Grand Rapids: Baker Academic, 2012.

———. *Dictionary of Latin and Greek Theological Terms Drawn Principally from Protestant Scholastic Theology*. Grand Rapids: Baker, 1985.

———. "Incarnation, Immutability, and the Case for Classical Theism." *Westminster Theological Journal* 45 (1983): 22–40.

———. *Post-Reformation Reformed Dogmatics: The Rise and Development of Reformed Orthodoxy, ca. 1520 to ca. 1725*. Grand Rapids: Baker, 2003.

Murray, John. *Collected Writings*. Edinburgh: Banner of Truth, 1976.

———. *Divorce*. Philadelphia: Orthodox Presbyterian Church, 1953.

———. *Principles of Conduct*. Grand Rapids: Eerdmans, 1957.

———. *Redemption Accomplished and Applied*. Grand Rapids: Eerdmans, 1955.

Music, David W. *Instruments in Church: A Collection of Source Documents*. Lanham and London: The Scarecrow Press, 1998.

Myers, Allen C., ed. *The Eerdmans Bible Dictionary*. Grand Rapids: Eerdmans, 1987.

Naselli, Andrew David. "What Is a Biblical Theology of the Sabbath?" In *40 Questions about Biblical Theology*, edited by Andrew David Naselli, Jason S. DeRouchie, and Oren Martin, 257–66. Grand Rapids: Kregel Academic, 2020.

Nevin, John Williamson. *History and Genius of the Heidelberg Catechism*. Chambersburg: German Reformed Church, 1847.

The New England Primer. Boston: Edward Draper, 1777.

Niceta of Remesiana. "On the Benefit of Psalmody." In *Source Readings in Music History*, edited by Oliver Strunk and Leo Treitler, 128–31. New York: Norton, 1950.

Nichols, James H. "The Intent of the Calvinist Liturgy." In *The Heritage of John Calvin*, edited by John H. Bratt, 87–109. Grand Rapids: Eerdmans, 1973.

Nichols, Stephen J. "The Dispensational View of the Davidic Kingdom: A Response to Progressive Dispensationalism." *The Masters Seminary Journal* 7 (1996): 213–39.

Nicole, Roger. *Standing Forth: Collected Writings of Roger Nicole*. Fearn, UK: Mentor, 2002.

Niesel, Wilhelm. "The Witness of the Power of the Holy Spirit in the Heidelberg Catechism." PhD diss., 1963.

Nill, Michael. *Morality and Self-Interest in Protagoras Antiphon and Democritus*. Leiden: Brill, 1985.

Oberman, Heiko A. "Facientibus Quod in Se Est Deus Non Denegat Gratiam: Robert Holcot O.p. And the Beginnings of Luther's Theology." In *The Reformation in Medieval Perspective*, edited by Stephen Ozment, 119–41. Chicago: Quadrangle Books, 1971.

———. *Forerunners of the Reformation: The Shape of Late Medieval Thought*. New York: Holt, Rinehart, and Winston, 1966.

———. *The Harvest of Medieval Theology: Gabriel Biel and Late Medieval Nominalism*. Cambridge, MA: Harvard University Press, 1963.

———. *Luther: Man between God and the Devil.* Translated by Eileen Waliser-Schwarzbart. New Haven: Yale University Press, 1889.

———. *The Reformation: Roots and Ramifications.* London: T&T Clark, 2004.

———. *The Two Reformations: The Journey from the Last Days to the New World.* New Haven: Yale University Press, 2003.

———. "Wir Sein Pettler. Hoc Est Verum. Covenant and Grace in the Theology of the Middle Ages and Reformation." In *The Reformation: Roots and Ramifications*, 91–115. Grand Rapids: Eerdmans, 1994.

Old, Hughes Oliphant. *The Reading and Preaching of the Scriptures in the Worship of the Christian Church.* Grand Rapids: Eerdmans, 1998.

Osborne, Thomas. "Faith, Philosophy, and the Nominalist Background to Luther's Defense of the Real Presence." *Journal of the History of Ideas* 63, no. 1 (2002): 63–82.

Ozment, Steven E. *The Age of Reform: 1250–1550: An Intellectual and Religious History of Late Medieval and Reformation Europe.* New ed. New Haven: Yale University Press, 2020.

Parker, T. H. L. *Calvin's Preaching.* Louisville: Westminster John Knox, 1992.

———. *John Calvin: A Biography.* Philadelphia: Westminster, 1975.

Patterson, W. B. *William Perkins and the Making of a Protestant England.* Oxford: Oxford University Press, 2014.

Payne, Jon D., ed. *A Faith Worth Teaching: The Heidelberg Catechism's Enduring Heritage.* Grand Rapids: Reformation Heritage Books, 2013.

Pelikan, Jaroslav. *The Christian Tradition: A History of the Development of Doctrine.* Chicago: University of Chicago Press, 1971.

———. *Credo. Historical and Theological Guide to Creeds and Confessions of Faith in the Christian Tradition.* New Haven: Yale University Press, 2003.

Pelikan, Jaroslav, and Valerie R. Hotchkiss. *Creeds and Confessions of Faith in the Christian Tradition.* New Haven: Yale University Press, 2003.

Pentecost, J. Dwight. *Things to Come.* Grand Rapids: Zondervan, 1958.

Perkins, Harrison. "Images of Christ and the Vitals of the Reformed System." *Confessional Presbyterian* 14 (2018): 201–15.

———. "*Meritum Ex Pacto* in the Reformed Tradition: Covenantal Merit in Theological Polemics." *Mid-America Journal of Theology* 31 (2020): 57–87.

———. *Reformed Covenant Theology: A Systematic Introduction*. Bellingham, WA: Lexham Press, 2024.

———. *Righteous by Design: Covenantal Merit and Adam's Original Integrity*. Fearn, UK: Mentor, 2024.

Peterson, Robert A. *Hell on Trial: The Case for Eternal Punishment*. Phillipsburg, NJ: P&R, 1995.

Pettegree, Andrew. *Reformation and the Culture of Persuasion*. Cambridge: Cambridge University Press, 2005.

Pinnock, Clark. *Most Moved Mover: A Theology of God's Openness*. Grand Rapids: Baker Academic, 2001.

Piper, John. "For Freedom Christ Has Set Us Free." May 29, 1983. www.desiringgod.org/messages/for-freedom-christ-has-set-us-free.

———. "Foundational Passions. Session 1. Part 1." Accessed July 12, 2021.

———. *The Purifying Power of Living by Faith in Future Grace*. Sisters, OR: Multnomah, 1995.

———. *Rethinking Retirement: Finishing Life for the Glory of Christ*. Wheaton, IL: Crossway, 2009.

Plantinga, Cornelius. "The Threeness/Oneness Problem of the Trinity." *Calvin Theological Journal* 23 (1988): 37–53.

Poll, Gerrit Jan van de. *Martin Bucer's Liturgical Ideas: The Strasbourg Reformer and His Connection with the Liturgies of the Sixteenth Century*. Assen, Netherlands: Kominklijke van Gorcum, 1954.

Poppen, Hermann. "Das Erste Kürpfalzer Gesangbuch Und Seine Singweisen." In *Verofflentichungen Des Vereins Für Kirchengeschichte in Der Evangelischen Landeskirche Badens*, 21–125. Baden: M. Schauenburg, 1938.

Price, John. *Old Light on New Worship*. Avinger, TX: Simpson, 2007.

Purvis, Zachary. *Theology in the University in Nineteenth-Century Germany*. Oxford: Oxford University Press, 2016.

Rainbow, Jonathan. "Double Grace in John Calvin's View of the Relationship between Justification and Sanctification." *Ex Auditu* 5 (1989): 99–105.

———. *The Will of God and the Cross: An Historical and Theological Study of John Calvin's Doctrine of Limited Redemption*. Allison Park, PA: Pickwick, 1990.

Raitt, Jill. *The Colloquy of Montbéliard*. Oxford: Oxford University Press, 1993.

Reid, Lucy. *She Changes Everything: Seeking the Divine on a Feminist Path*. London: T&T Clark, 2006.

Reisinger, John G. *New Covenant Theology and Prophecy*. Frederick, MD: New Covenant Media, 2012.

Richards, George W. *The Heidelberg Catechism: Historical and Doctrinal Studies*. Philadelphia: Publication and Sunday School Board of the Reformed Church in the United States, 1913.

Riddlebarger, Kim. *A Case for Amillennialism: Understanding the End Times*. Grand Rapids: Baker, 2003.

Roper, Lyndal. *Martin Luther: Renegade and Prophet*. New York: Random House, 2016.

Ross, Philip. *From the Finger of God: The Biblical and Theological Basis for the Threefold Division of the Law*. Fearn, UK: Christian Focus, 2010.

Roukema, Riemer. "The Good Samaritan in Ancient Christianity." *Vigiliae Christianae* 58, no. 1 (2004): 56–74.

Rousseau, Jean-Jacques. *Discourse on the Origin of Inequality*. Translated by Franklin Philip. Oxford: Oxford University Press, 1994.

Rudolph, Kurt. *Gnosis: The Nature and History of Gnosticism*. Translated by P. W. Coxon et al. San Francisco: Harper & Row, 1987.

Ryrie, Charles C. *Dispensationalism Today*. Chicago: Moody, 1965.

Samarin, William J. "Sociolinguistic vs Neurophysiological Explanations for Glossolalia: Comment on Goodman's Paper." *Journal for the Scientific Study of Religion* 11 (1972): 293–96.

Sayers, Dorothy L. *Creed or Chaos*. New York: Harcourt Brace, 1949.

———. "The Lost Tools of Learning." In *A Matter of Eternity*, edited by Rosamond Kent Sprague, 107–36. Grand Rapids: Eerdmans, 1973.

Scaer, David P. "The Concept of *Anfechtung* in Luther's Thought." *Concordia Theological Quarterly* 47 (1983): 15–30.

———. "He Did Descend to Hell: In Defense of the Apostles' Creed." *Journal of the Evangelical Theological Society* 35, no. 1 (1992): 91–99.

Schaefer, Paul R. *The Spiritual Brotherhood: Cambridge Puritans and the Nature of Christian Piety*. Grand Rapids: Reformation Heritage Books, 2011.

Schaff, Philip. *History of the Christian Church*. New York: Charles Scribner's Sons, 1910.

Schlossberg, Herbert. *Idols for Destruction: Christian Faith and Its Confrontation with American Society*. Nashville: Thomas Nelson, 1983.

Schreiner, Thomas R. "Good-Bye and Hello: The Sabbath Command for New Covenant Believers." In *Progressive Covenantalism: Charting a Course between Dispensational and Covenant Theologies*, edited by Stephen J. Wellum and Brent E. Parker, 159–88. Nashville: B&H Academic, 2016.

Scofield, C. I., ed. *The Holy Bible Containing the Old and New Testaments: Authorized Version*. New York: Oxford University Press, 1909.

Scott-Baumann, Alison. *Ricoeur and the Hermeneutics of Suspicion*. London: Continuum, 2009.

Seeburg, R. *Textbook of the History of Doctrines*. Translated by Charles E. Hay. Philadelphia: Lutheran Publication Society, 1904.

Selvaggio, Anthony T., ed. *The Faith Once Delivered: Essays in Honor of Dr. Wayne R. Spear*. Phillipsburg, NJ: P&R, 2007.

Shaver, J. L. *The Polity of the Churches*. Chicago: Church Polity, 1947.

Sherwin-White, A. N. "Pilate, Pontius." In *The International Standard Bible Encyclopedia*, rev. ed., edited by Geoffrey W. Bromiley, 867. Grand Rapids: Eerdmans, 1979–1988.

Silcock, Jeffrey G. "Introduction to 'The Antinomian Disputations.'" *LW* 73:22–25.

Simpson, J. A., and E. S. C. Weiner, eds. *The Oxford English Dictionary*. Oxford: Clarendon, 1991.

Sinnema, Donald W. "The Second Service in the Early Dutch Reformed Tradition." *Calvin Theological Journal* 32 (1997): 298–333.

Sinnema, Donald, et al., eds. *Acta Et Documenta Synodi Nationalis Dordrechtanae (1618–1619)*. Göttingen: Vandenhoeck & Ruprecht, 2015.

Smedley, Todd. "The Covenant Theology of Zacharias Ursinus." PhD diss., University of Aberdeen, 2011.

Smith, John Arthur. *Music in Ancient Judaism and Early Christianity*. Farnham, UK: Ashgate, 2011.

Sowell, Thomas. *A Thomas Sowell Reader*. New York: Basic Books, 2011.

Spaan, Howard B. *Christian Reformed Church Government*. Grand Rapids: Kregel, 1968.

Spicq, Ceslas. *Theological Lexicon of the New Testament*. Peabody, MA: Hendrickson, 1994.

Spijker, Willem van't, ed. *The Church's Book of Comfort*. Grand Rapids: Reformation Heritage Books, 2009.

———. "The Theology of the Heidelberg Catechism." In *The Church's Book of Comfort*, edited by Willem van't Spijker, 89–128. Grand Rapids: Reformation Heritage Books, 2009.

Stanglin, Keith D., and Thomas H. McCall. *Jacob Arminius: Theologian of Grace*. Oxford: Oxford University Press, 2012.

Steinmetz, David C. *Luther in Context*. Grand Rapids: Baker Academic, 2002.

Stephens, W. P. *The Theology of Huldrych Zwingli*. Oxford: Oxford University Press, 1986.

Stonehouse, N. B. *J. Gresham Machen: A Biographical Memoir*. Grand Rapids: Eerdmans, 1954.

Stonehouse, N. B., and Paul Wooley, eds. *The Infallible Word*. Philadelphia: Westminster Theological Seminary, 1946.

Strimple, Robert B. "Amillennialism." In *Three Views on the Millennium and Beyond*, edited by Stanley N. Gundry and Darrell L. Bock, 81–129. Grand Rapids: Zondervan, 1999.

Stuart, W., and G. Hoeksema. *Church of the Christian Reformed Church as Adopted by the Synod of 1920*. Grand Rapids: Van Noord, 1921.

Swain, Scott R. "New Covenant Theologies." In *Covenant Theology: Biblical, Theological, and Historical Perspectives*, edited by Guy Prentiss Waters, J. Nicholas Reid, and John R. Muether, 551–69. Wheaton, IL: Crossway, 2020.

Symington, William. *Messiah the Prince: The Mediatorial Dominion of Jesus Christ*. Pittsburgh: Crown & Covenant, 2012.

Sytsma, David S. "John Calvin and Virtue Ethics: Augustinian and Aristotelian Themes." *Journal of Religious Ethics* 48 (2020): 519–66.

Taylor, Charles. *A Secular Age*. Cambridge, MA: Harvard University Press, 2007.

Thelemann, Otto. *An Aid to the Heidelberg Catechism*. Translated by M. Peters. Grand Rapids: Douma, 1959.

Tierney, Brian. *Ockham, the Conciliar Theory, and the Canonists*. Philadelphia: Fortress, 1971.

Tipton, Lane. "The Function of Perichoresis in the Divine Incomprehensibility." *Westminster Theological Journal* 64 (2002): 289–306.

Torrance, Thomas F., ed. *The School of Faith: The Catechisms of the Reformed Church*. London: James Clarke, 1959.

Toth, Peter. "New Questions on Old Answers: Towards a Critical Edition of the 'Answers to the Orthodox' of Pseudo-Justin." *Journal of Theological Studies* 65, no. 2 (2014): 550–99.

Troxel, Craig, and Peter J. Wallace. "Men in Combat over the Civil Law: 'General Equity' in WCF 19.4." *Westminster Theological Journal* 64 (2002): 307–18.

Trueman, Carl R. *The Rise and Triumph of the Modern Self: Cultural Amnesia, Expressive Individualism, and the Road to Sexual Revolution*. Wheaton, IL: Crossway, 2020.

———. "A Small Step toward Rationalism: The Impact of the Metaphysics of Tommaso Campanella on the Theology of Richard Baxter." In *Protestant Scholasticism: Essays in Reassessment*, edited by Carl R. Trueman and R. Scott Clark, 181–95. Carlisle, UK: Paternoster, 1999.

Trueman, Carl R., and R. Scott Clark, eds. *Protestant Scholasticism: Essays in Reassessment*. Carlisle, UK: Paternoster, 1999.

Turner, James. *Without God, without Creed: Origins of Unbelief in America*. Baltimore: Johns Hopkins University Press, 1985.

Van Dixhoorn, Chad. "Post-Reformation Trinitarian Perspectives." In *Retrieving Eternal Generation*, edited by Fred Sanders and Scott R. Swain, 180–207. Grand Rapids: Zondervan, 2017.

Van Til, Cornelius. *Common Grace*. Philadelphia: P&R, 1947.

———. *The Defense of the Faith*. Philadelphia: P&R, 1980.

———. *An Introduction to Systematic Theology*. Philadelphia: Westminster Theological Seminary, 1971.

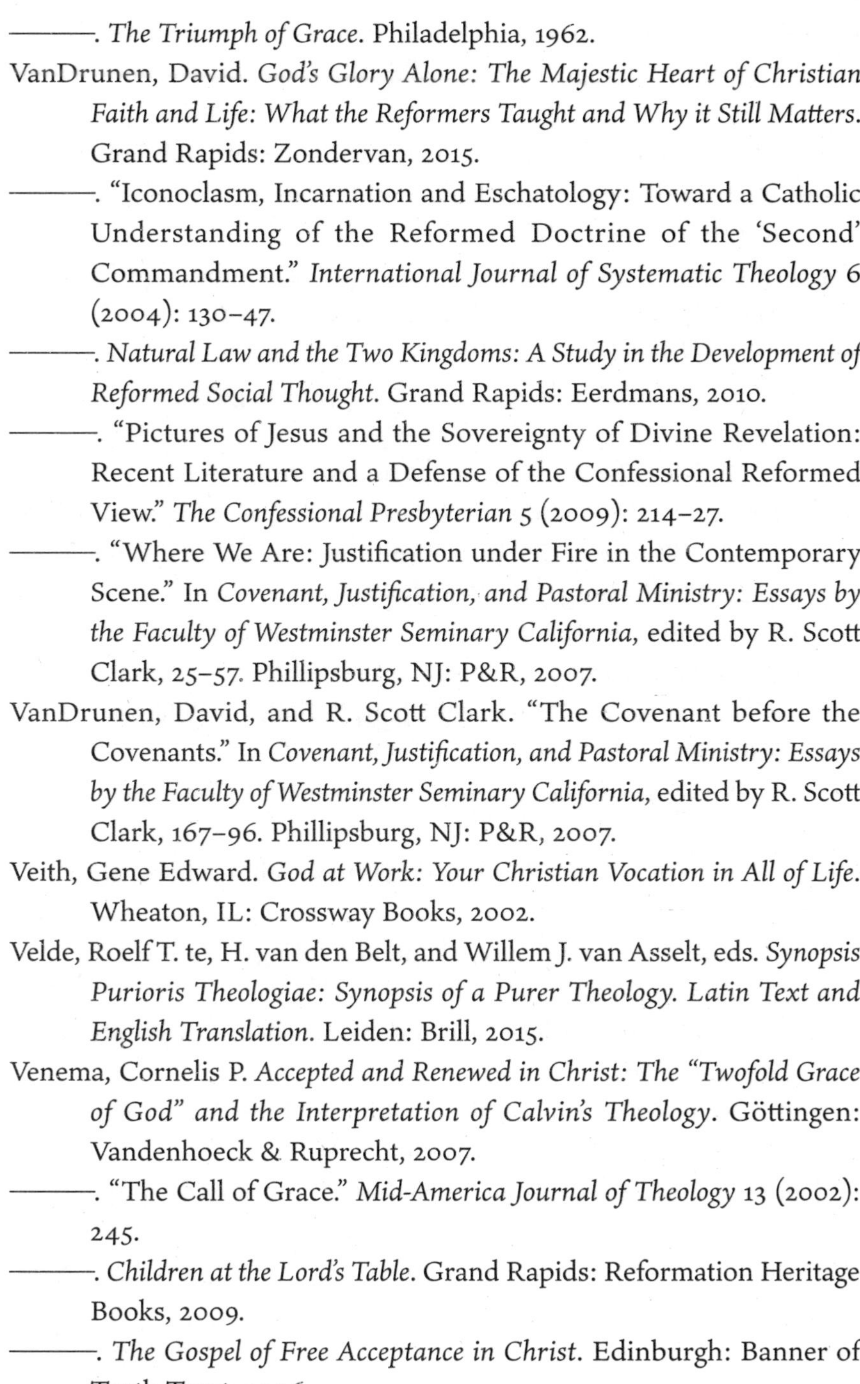

———. *The Triumph of Grace*. Philadelphia, 1962.

VanDrunen, David. *God's Glory Alone: The Majestic Heart of Christian Faith and Life: What the Reformers Taught and Why it Still Matters*. Grand Rapids: Zondervan, 2015.

———. "Iconoclasm, Incarnation and Eschatology: Toward a Catholic Understanding of the Reformed Doctrine of the 'Second' Commandment." *International Journal of Systematic Theology* 6 (2004): 130–47.

———. *Natural Law and the Two Kingdoms: A Study in the Development of Reformed Social Thought*. Grand Rapids: Eerdmans, 2010.

———. "Pictures of Jesus and the Sovereignty of Divine Revelation: Recent Literature and a Defense of the Confessional Reformed View." *The Confessional Presbyterian* 5 (2009): 214–27.

———. "Where We Are: Justification under Fire in the Contemporary Scene." In *Covenant, Justification, and Pastoral Ministry: Essays by the Faculty of Westminster Seminary California*, edited by R. Scott Clark, 25–57. Phillipsburg, NJ: P&R, 2007.

VanDrunen, David, and R. Scott Clark. "The Covenant before the Covenants." In *Covenant, Justification, and Pastoral Ministry: Essays by the Faculty of Westminster Seminary California*, edited by R. Scott Clark, 167–96. Phillipsburg, NJ: P&R, 2007.

Veith, Gene Edward. *God at Work: Your Christian Vocation in All of Life*. Wheaton, IL: Crossway Books, 2002.

Velde, Roelf T. te, H. van den Belt, and Willem J. van Asselt, eds. *Synopsis Purioris Theologiae: Synopsis of a Purer Theology. Latin Text and English Translation*. Leiden: Brill, 2015.

Venema, Cornelis P. *Accepted and Renewed in Christ: The "Twofold Grace of God" and the Interpretation of Calvin's Theology*. Göttingen: Vandenhoeck & Ruprecht, 2007.

———. "The Call of Grace." *Mid-America Journal of Theology* 13 (2002): 245.

———. *Children at the Lord's Table*. Grand Rapids: Reformation Heritage Books, 2009.

———. *The Gospel of Free Acceptance in Christ*. Edinburgh: Banner of Truth Trust, 2006.

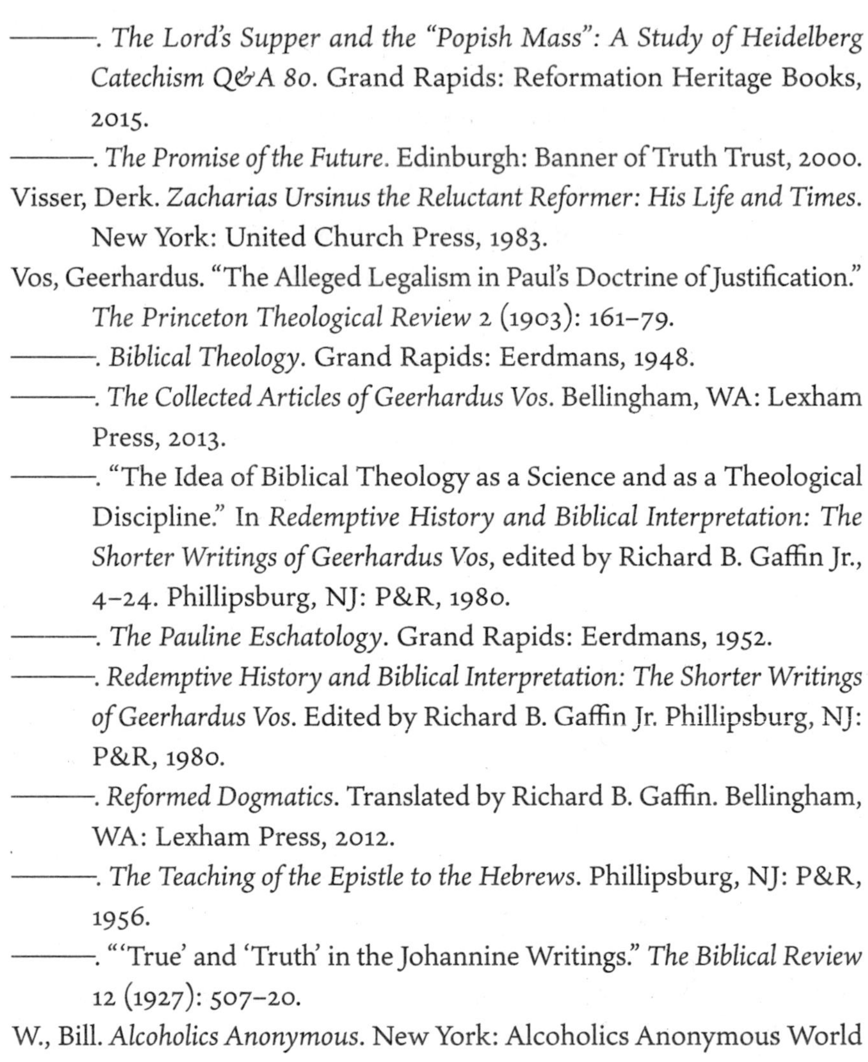

———. *The Lord's Supper and the "Popish Mass": A Study of Heidelberg Catechism Q&A 80*. Grand Rapids: Reformation Heritage Books, 2015.

———. *The Promise of the Future*. Edinburgh: Banner of Truth Trust, 2000.

Visser, Derk. *Zacharias Ursinus the Reluctant Reformer: His Life and Times*. New York: United Church Press, 1983.

Vos, Geerhardus. "The Alleged Legalism in Paul's Doctrine of Justification." *The Princeton Theological Review* 2 (1903): 161–79.

———. *Biblical Theology*. Grand Rapids: Eerdmans, 1948.

———. *The Collected Articles of Geerhardus Vos*. Bellingham, WA: Lexham Press, 2013.

———. "The Idea of Biblical Theology as a Science and as a Theological Discipline." In *Redemptive History and Biblical Interpretation: The Shorter Writings of Geerhardus Vos*, edited by Richard B. Gaffin Jr., 4–24. Phillipsburg, NJ: P&R, 1980.

———. *The Pauline Eschatology*. Grand Rapids: Eerdmans, 1952.

———. *Redemptive History and Biblical Interpretation: The Shorter Writings of Geerhardus Vos*. Edited by Richard B. Gaffin Jr. Phillipsburg, NJ: P&R, 1980.

———. *Reformed Dogmatics*. Translated by Richard B. Gaffin. Bellingham, WA: Lexham Press, 2012.

———. *The Teaching of the Epistle to the Hebrews*. Phillipsburg, NJ: P&R, 1956.

———. "'True' and 'Truth' in the Johannine Writings." *The Biblical Review* 12 (1927): 507–20.

W., Bill. *Alcoholics Anonymous*. New York: Alcoholics Anonymous World Services, 2001.

———. *Twelve Steps and Twelve Traditions*. New York: Alcoholics Anonymous World Services, 1953.

Walvoord, John F. *The Millennial Kingdom*. Grand Rapids: Zondervan, 1983.

Warfield, B. B. *Calvin and Calvinism*. New York: Oxford University Press, 1931.

———. *Revelation and Inspiration*. New York: Oxford University Press, 1927.

———. *Two Studies in the History of Doctrine: Augustine and the Pelagian Controversy: The Development of the Doctrine of Infant Salvation.* New York: Christian Literature, 1897.

———. *The Works of Benjamin B. Warfield.* New York: Oxford University Press, 1932.

Waters, Guy Prentiss. *The Federal Vision and Covenant Theology: A Comparative Analysis.* Phillipsburg, NJ: P&R, 2006.

———. *Justification and the New Perspectives on Paul: A Review and Response.* Philipsburg, NJ: P&R, 2004.

———. "The Theology of Norman Shepherd: A Study in Development, 1963–2006." In *The Hope Fulfilled: Essays in Honor of O. Palmer Robertson,* edited by Robert L. Penny, 207–31. Phillipsburg, NJ: P&R, 2008.

Waters, Guy P., and Ligon Duncan, eds. *Children and the Lord's Supper.* Fearn, UK: Mentor, 2011.

Weber, Max. *Protestantism and the Spirit of Capitalism.* Translated by Talcot Parsons. London: Allen & Unwin, 1930.

Wells, Tom, and Fred G. Zaspel. *New Covenant Theology: Description, Definition, Defense.* Frederick, MD: New Covenant Media, 2002.

Wellum, Stephen J. "3 Reasons Sunday Is Not the Christian Sabbath." The Gospel Coalition, 2020. www.thegospelcoalition.org/article/sunday-not-christian-sabbath.

Wengert, Timothy J., ed. *Dictionary of Luther and the Lutheran Traditions.* Grand Rapids: Baker Academic, 2017.

———. *Law and Gospel: Melanchthon's Debate with John Agricola of Eisleben over Poenitentia.* Grand Rapids: Baker, 1997.

Wenham, John William. *Easter Enigma.* Grand Rapids: Academie Books, 1984.

Wilken, Robert Louis. *The Christians as the Romans Saw Them.* New Haven: Yale University Press, 1984.

Williams, George Hunston. *The Radical Reformation.* Kirksville, MO: Sixteenth Century Journal, 1992.

———, ed. *Spiritual and Anabaptist Writers.* Library of Christian Classics 25. Philadelphia: Westminster Press, 1957.

Williamson, G. I. *The Heidelberg Catechism: A Study Guide.* Phillipsburg, NJ: P&R, 1993.

Willis, E. David. *Calvin's Catholic Christology: The Function of the So-Called Extra Calvinisticum in Calvin's Theology*. Leiden: Brill, 1966.

Wilson, James P. *Notes on Thomas Ridgley, a Body of Divinity*. Philadelphia, 1815.

Wingren, Gustaf. *Luther on Vocation*. Translated by Carl C. Rasmussen. Philadelphia: Muhlenberg, 1957.

Wolters, Albert M. *Creation Regained: Biblical Basics for a Reformational Worldview*. Grand Rapids: Eerdmans, 2005.

Woolsey, Andrew A. *Unity and Continuity in Covenantal Thought: A Study in the Reformed Tradition to the Westminster Assembly*. Grand Rapids: Reformation Heritage Books, 2012.

Wright, N. T. *Justification: God's Plan and Paul's Vision*. Downers Grove, IL: IVP Academic, 2009.

Zwierlein, Cornel. "The Palatinate and Western Europe, 1555 to 1563." In *Profil Und Wirkung Des Heidelberger Katechismus: Neue Forschungsbeiträge Anlässlich Des 450 jährigen Jubiläums = the Heidelberger Catechism: Origins, Characteristics, and Influences: Essays in Reappraisal on the Occasion of Its 450th Anniversary*, edited by Jan Sieverman and Christoph Strohm, 163–88. Gütersloh: Gütersloch Verlagshaus, 2015.

Subject & Author Index

Confessional Documents Index

Second Helvetic Confession

Westminster Confession of Faith

Westminster Larger Catechism

Westminster Shorter Catechism

SCRIPTURE INDEX

OLD TESTAMENT

Exodus

Leviticus

Numbers

Deuteronomy

NEW TESTAMENT

Mark

Luke

James

1 Peter

2 Peter

1 John

APOCRYPHA

1 Maccabees